CRIME, JUSTICE AND CORRECTION

McGRAW-HILL SERIES IN SOCIOLOGY

CRIME, JUSTICE AND CORRECTION

PAUL W. TAPPAN

*Professor of Sociology and Law
Chairman, Department of Sociology and
Anthropology of Washington Square College
New York University*

McGRAW-HILL BOOK COMPANY, INC.

New York   Toronto   London

1960

CRIME, JUSTICE AND CORRECTION

. V

THE MAPLE PRESS COMPANY, YORK, PA.

TO LINDA, DONNA, AND JAMES

PREFACE

The fundamental subject matter of criminology is included in this volume: the nature, prevalence, and causation of crime; the procedures and major problems in the administration of justice; and the methods of correctional treatment. Several features, however, distinguish it from other texts. Perhaps the most basic of these is the effort to achieve a fuller synthesis of the behavioral sciences and in doing so to avoid reliance upon any narrow and deterministic concept of the offender. In recent years the idea of developing "systematic" and broadly generalized theories of causation has become popular in some quarters. Loosely eclectic concepts of "multiple factor" causation have been criticized, but at the same time equally loose forms of cultural determinism have been proposed in their place. Often, in attempts to explain too much too simply, "integrated theories" have been stretched while the facts of criminality have been distorted in order to fit complex social realities into a doctrinal scheme. There appear to be at least four sound reasons to limit the emphasis on cultural influences in theoretical and applied criminology and to view such influences as only one phase, however important, in criminal etiology: (1) Noncultural phenomena are fundamental. Why, in an "exploitative" and criminogenic culture are not all individuals habitual criminals? The query in more realistic form: In a society where there is some balance of forces that, on the one hand, promote conformity, and on the other nonconformity, how should the criminality of a minority be explained? Rather clearly the divergence in behavior results from variabilities in individuals and in group relationships rather than merely in culture or subcultures. (2) As a practical matter, not all the phenomena relating to criminal behavior can be defined or measured equally well. Tools of empirical research can be and are applied with reasonable effectiveness to differentiate between criminals and noncriminals in their personal and social characteristics and in their interrelationships and in recent years to distinguish the qualities of criminals of different types. We lack comparably sound devices to determine those elements of culture that may be criminogenic or to measure their impact. Cultural evaluations in criminology are imprecise and often highly judgmental. (3) We lack both the means and the will planfully to alter the economic, social, and political context to which crime is commonly attributed. Even if more effective devices for measuring the content of culture are developed, they will presumably not produce deliberate social revolution to reduce crime. (4) In applied penology we do and apparently must rely in the main upon manipulation of individuals and their relationships to the going social system in order to produce increased conformity to law. We achieve a limited but apparently real measure of success in doing this through dealing with offenders rather than through evaluations of culture.

Social-cultural theories of crime causation have generally depreciated the significance of individual variability in physique, psychology, and experience. In this volume behavior is viewed as a product of all these influences. Crime is not a unitary phenomenon, however, and criminals cannot be well understood by lumping them together without regard to type. Criminology must look to the development of more sharply defined typologies of offenders, categories that display clusters of characteristics which both differentiate between criminals and distinguish them from noncriminals. Crime surely reflects cultural and subgroup influence, but for meaningful theory on the dynamics of criminal etiology we must look to the disparities of response to the cultural context by differing types of offenders. In this text the author starts with the concept of behavior as the consequence of differentiated response to environment and experience. He makes an effort to relate this concept not only to the causation of crime but to its correctional treatment. Further refinement of the theory requires additional empirical research.

Authorities in the United States have been generally slow to recognize the significance of law and jurisprudence for criminological theory. Criminologists here have ordinarily been sociologists with strong environmental predilection, less frequently psychiatrists and biologists of narrower orientations. Few have displayed much appreciation for the role of law in behavioral science. This volume attempts to remedy that defect in some measure, not only in its legal definition of crime and penal sanctions, but in the analyses of a number of problems that are partially legal in character. Such analyses involve extended attention to the administration of justice and to related constitutional and social problems. More detailed consideration is given to the police and juridical processes than has been traditional. Law and policy are analyzed as they relate to juvenile and young adult offenders, mental and emotional deviates, and habitual criminals. Special attention is given to the problem of sentencing, central as this is to public policy, to social control, and to individual treatment. Limitation on space makes it impossible to consider all phases of criminological inquiry, but the author has made an effort to fill some of the gaps that have commonly occurred elsewhere.

In acknowledging the sources of this text, the author is compelled to express his special indebtedness to his mentors of graduate school days. Twenty-five years ago he was introduced at the University of Wisconsin to a seminal environment of which this volume is to a large extent a product. John L. Gillin, dedicated teacher, innovative researcher, practical penologist, and zealous humanitarian, was primarily responsible for the author's career as criminologist. The lofty, capacious intellect of E. A. Ross offered to us who were his students a sociology broad in scope and deep in penetration. Kimball Young's greatest contribution has come, perhaps, through his rare grasp of the diverse and interrelated forces through which human personality is motivated. Such synthesis of behavioral theory as the author may achieve is grounded in Kimball Young's lucid formulation of an integrative social psychiatry. His generous friendship as teacher, dissertation advisor, and erstwhile colleague has given a cherished warmth to scholarship. Samuel Stouffer instilled a respect for scientific method, critical assessment, and empirical research, all of which are vital to criminology as they are to the social and behavioral sciences generally. Ralph Linton strengthened his students' disposition to comparative and analytical inquiry. It was at Wisconsin, too, that the author was first introduced to the study of law and found its fundamental relationship to the social and behavioral sciences.

In more recent years many persuasive influences have borne upon the author's orientation. These have come most frequently perhaps from his associates in the fields of correction and of law. James V. Bennett, Director of the Federal Bureau of Prisons, practical idealist, leader in contemporary penology, lawyer, colleague, and friend, has contributed to the author as to many others something of his vision as well as his realism. The author's tenure as Chairman of the United States Board of Parole provided associations at Bureau headquarters and with staff in all the Federal correctional and penal institutions. These associations served to increase the deep respect that he has always held for the personnel and policies of the Federal correctional system. In this text pictures and illustrative materials have been drawn from the Bureau files with its permission. Case studies of parole applicants interviewed by the author are disguised, of course, as to names, dates, and places. Among other correctional authorities, Richard A. McGee, Director of Corrections in California, Sanford Bates of New Jersey, and Russell Oswald of Wisconsin and New York have indirectly contributed much to this volume, as they have directly contributed to contemporary corrections in America.

For several years the author has enjoyed a close association with

Herbert Wechsler, professor of law at Columbia University and chief reporter on the Model Penal Code of the American Law Institute. As associate reporter on sentencing and treatment phases of the Code, the author has had the responsibility of examining problems in this field with a purpose of achieving more sound statutory policies for dealing with offenders. In approaching anew the varied and subtle problems involved, he has drawn heavily from Professor Wechsler's breadth and balance of intellect and from his keen critical judgments. The author's profound respect for the law as a democratic aspiration and his critical regard for mischiefs in some of its content and administration derive from too many sources to trace them here. Association with such jurists of wisdom and idealism as the late Chief Justice Arthur T. Vanderbilt of New Jersey, Justice Learned Hand of New York, and Justice John V. Barry of the Victoria Supreme Bench, supports his confident affirmation of faith in law as our best instrument to balance the conflicting interests of men.

The author is profoundly indebted to a number of his colleagues for the stimulation they have given to this work. Sheldon and Eleanor Glueck, most prolific and catholic criminologists of our time (and, indeed, perhaps of any time), have been a source of continuous inspiration to the author's relatively modest contributions to this field. Lucy J. Chamberlain, professor emeritus of sociology of New York University, has read and edited this manuscript most carefully and made many useful suggestions on content and style. Her encouragement and support over a period of fifteen years have been vital to this work. T. Conway Esselstyn, professor of criminology at San Jose State College, and Norval Morris, dean of law at the University of Adelaide, have reviewed portions of the manuscript at different stages and have given constructive counsel. They have had deeper influence upon the author's values and thinking, too. At various stages and in different forms others have played important parts in the development of these materials. Students and colleagues have provided much of the motivation.

The author also expresses here his gratitude to certain foundations, institutions, and agencies for assistance, direct and indirect, that they have given to the preparation of criminological materials that are used in this volume. Funds received from the Social Science Research Council for advanced interdisciplinary study, from the Fulbright program for lecturing and research in Australia, from the American Philosophical Society and New York University for studies in England and western Europe made possible the conduct of researches and the opportunity to become acquainted with the work and ideas of criminological authorities of many countries. On the national scene the author has had notable guidance and assistance in his work with the American Law Institute, the American Correctional Association, and the National Probation and Parole Association. Acknowledgment is made to Judge Herbert F. Goodrich and the American

Law Institute for the use of text and commentary materials from the Model Penal Code and to E. R. Cass of the American Correctional Association and to Will Turnbladh of the National Probation and Parole Association for their generous aid in the author's work.

Appreciation is given here to Mrs. A. B. Smith and Mrs. E. L. Bruns for their superb assistance in the preparation of manuscript. Appropriate acknowledgments are made in footnotes for material quoted at various places in the book.

Paul W. Tappan

CONTENTS

Part One

CRIME AND CAUSATION

Chapter 1

CRIME, THE CRIMINAL, AND CRIMINAL LAW

In an effort to understand the problems of crime and its treatment, our first task is to delineate the scope of the subject. On superficial thought this task might appear to be elementary. In fact, however, the issues involved are not easy, nor have they been resolved by any general agreement among criminologists. Indeed, in recent years there has been a growing disparity of views among authorities in the field as to who is the criminal and what the nature of crime. This confusion is unfortunate, for the whole subject of criminology depends upon a clear understanding of who should and who should not be included in the class of criminality. There are various practical difficulties involved in attempting to secure representative samples of criminals for purposes of research, but the most fundamental problem is that of determining the specific connotations of the criminal universe. Who does and who does not belong in this group? The present chapter is intended to explore this issue. It is a question that flares out into some of the most important issues in criminology: How large a social problem is here involved? What types of individuals should we and can we seek to influence by way of the police, courts, and correctional system? What types and what magnitude of services are needed to exercise this influence? These and lesser problems flow from the basic criteria defining crime and the criminal.

DIFFERING CONCEPTIONS OF CRIME

Definitions of crime differ largely because they are formulated by authorities of significantly different training and orientation. Many criminologists are not directly interested in the phenomenon of crime, per se, but only in its implications for personality or social deviations. Thus, for example, clinical specialists are inclined to consider crime as merely symptomatic of underlying behavioral disorders; they look to the etiological problem in the individual and perhaps to the treatment of such disorders as they may find. "Criminals" are submitted to their investigations, generally from the courts or prisons, and the psychiatrist, psychologist, or caseworker is not at all concerned with whether the individual is a represent-

3

4 CRIME AND CAUSATION

ative criminal or, perhaps, whether he is in fact a criminal at all, but is concerned with his peculiarities of adjustment or personality. For the most part there is little effort to clarify even the issue that *is* relevant to definition and, incidentally, to the treatment policy of the state: whether such deviations as may be discovered in the offender are directly or significantly related to his criminal acts and whether they should be dealt with, therefore, through correctional resources. This difference in approach to criminological problems accounts, at least in some measure, for the fact that clinicians commonly identify criminality with emotional illness and look upon clinical therapy as the solution to crime, a matter that will be discussed in greater detail at a later point.

Social scientists are inclined to view society and its problems broadly. The social processes, including social control, and the social pathologies, including crime, are generally looked upon in terms of group interaction and the impact of society and culture on the individual. Within the framework of general social science it is not surprising, though from the point of view of criminological investigation it is unfortunate, that crime has been equated by distinguished sociologists with antisocial behavior and by ethnologists with generic custom and taboo. Very commonly the result has been to confuse the basic political problems of policy in criminal and correctional legislation and the sociological problems of differentiation between significantly different types of social norms and of social regulation.

Proponents of social reform and social action, widely varied in their training and experience if not in emotional set, appear to be inclined to even more rudimentary approaches to social problems. A reformer may show a tendency to reach impatiently for solutions through that agency with which he himself happens to be associated. Such a tendency very commonly blurs both the nature of the problem to be solved and the sort of agencies and skills that are designed to deal with it. The ultimate effects attendant upon the reformer's efforts may be quite different from those he contemplated, either because the goals were not clearly formulated, or because the measures and facilities employed were not appropriate.

Crime and Conduct Norms

Several views that are held by various criminologists require particular mention.[1] Some authorities suggest that criminal categories set up by the

---

[1] For a general analysis of the problems of definition discussed here and their implications for the scope of criminological research, see George L. Wilber, "The Scientific Adequacy of Criminological Concepts," *Social Forces,* vol. 28, pp. 165–175, 1949; Jerome Michael and Mortimer J. Adler, *Crime, Law, and Social Science,* 1933; Clarence R. Jeffry, "The Structure of American Criminological Thinking," *J. Crim. L.,* vol. 46, pp. 658–673, 1956; Thorsten Sellin, *Culture Conflict and Crime,* 1938; and Tappan, "Who Is the Criminal?" *Am. Soc. Rev.,* vol. 12, pp. 96–103, 1947.

law do not meet the demands of scientists because they are of a "fortuitous nature" and do not "arise intrinsically from the nature of the subject matter" so that the content of criminology should be differently focused.[2] There is little consensus, however, as to what the province of criminology should be. Moreover, under the suggestions that have been put forward it would be even more difficult than under orthodox definitions to settle upon a universe of criminal deviates distinct from others in the population. One proposal has been that we should study all individuals who violate "conduct norms," apparently without reference to the particular types of norms involved or to the varying consequences of breach in different areas of conduct. One must agree wholeheartedly that it is desirable to investigate general conduct norms and their violation. The writer has suggested elsewhere that it would be worthwhile to segregate the various classes of such norms, to determine relationships between them, and to understand similarities and differences among the norms themselves, their sources, methods of imposition of control, and their consequences.[3] This area is part of the subject matter of "social control," a field of sociological inquiry that is still in a regrettably primitive state.[4] If more careful and empirical investigation were devoted to this broad subject, the results might well help to clarify phenomena in the field of criminal law violation.

Social control, however, is a different and larger field of inquiry than criminology, not a substitute for it, and it would be unfortunate indeed to confuse the philosophical mysticisms and the normative vagueness of the former with the relatively well-developed theory and factual information that have come from generations of criminological analysis. It would be

[2] See, for example, Thorsten Sellin, op. cit., pp. 21–22. Florian Znaniecki has offered this definition of crime and the framework of criminology, surely a ponderous and equivocal foundation for research: "Because a collective system has social validity in the eyes of each and all of those who share in it, because it is endowed with a special dignity which merely individual systems lack altogether, individual behavior which endangers a collective system and threatens to harm any of its elements appears quite different from an aggression against an individual (unless, of course, such an aggression hurts collective values as well as individual values). It is not only a harmful act, but an objectively evil act [sic !], a violation of social validity, an offense against the superior dignity of this collective system. . . . The best term to express the specific significance of such behavior is crime. We are aware that in using the word in this sense, we are giving it a much wider significance than it has in criminology. But we believe that it is desirable for criminology to put its investigations on a broader basis; for strictly speaking, it still lacks a proper theoretic basis. . . . Legal qualifications are not founded on the results of previous research and are not made for the purpose of future research; therefore they have no claim to be valid as scientific generalization—nor even as heuristic hypotheses." Florian Znaniecki, "Social Research in Criminology," Soc. and Soc. Res., vol. 12, p. 207, 1928. (Reprinted by permission.)

[3] Tappan, op. cit., pp. 101–102.

[4] See, however, the sophisticated analysis of Richard T. LaPiere, A Theory of Social Control, 1954, for a real advance over what has come before in this field.

useful to know more of the psychological and social influences associated with nonconformity to different types of norms. Experience thus far indicates that we may learn more by investigating specific types of breach of particular and specialized standards than by making a broadly "ethological" study of nonconformity. We may learn more by attempting to determine why some individuals take human life deliberately or negligently, why some take property by force and others by subterfuge, why some find erotic gratification from children and others from men or by forcible coercion of the female than we shall learn in seeking some universal formula to account for any and all behavior that violates social interests. We should like to know how such nonconformity differs in cause and effect from, for example, the behavior of the faddist, the Communist in a democracy, the atheist in a religious culture, the boor in a socially sophisticated setting. Findings within the field of criminology itself show clearly that there are significant differences in nonconformists. It is equally clear that these differences are widely varied in their relation to the security of society and to political policies of prevention, control, and treatment. The point made here is that, however valuable may be the larger study of social control of widely assorted deviations, the narrower inquiry into behavior that violates the norms established by the criminal law is *sui generis;* while not unrelated to other classes of deviations, such conduct has been deemed by the state to be especially significant to the protection of important personal and property interests. For the most part, minimum levels of essential conformity are here involved.

Crime as Antisocial Behavior

A somewhat different and more prevalent view has been that crime should be defined simply as antisocial behavior. This notion has been attractive in part because of our feeling that crimes *should be* antisocial conduct and that antisocial conduct should be criminal. Unfortunately this position is overly simple, for conceptions of what is antisocial vary greatly among reformers and moralists. It is highly desirable that there be real consensus on the dangerousness of the conduct involved and the appropriateness of applying criminal sanctions for purposes of control; it is not reasonable officially to penalize conduct that is quite commonly approved or that is not in fact injurious to important social interests. Beyond this, criminal conduct should be of the sort that can be effectively deterred or treated through correctional measures, and many forms of undesirable behavior are too subtle or devious to be mended by the blunt tools of criminal law. Problems that are essentially psychiatric or moral, for example, and that are without criminal implication cannot well be resolved by correctional techniques in the usual case. Conceptions of what is antisocial vary in time, place, and intensity. Where there is wide disagreement as to policy, the legislature generally will not act; but if it does, as experience has very clearly shown, law is often nullified in practice by lack of sufficient public or official support. This has been the experience with the prohibition amendment, with sexual psychopath laws, with habitual criminal statutes, and with innumerable pieces of minor legislation. But, quite aside from the question of what *should be* made criminal from the viewpoint of ideal policy formulations, crime is in fact what the state through its legislature and courts says it is.

White-collar Crime

A special class of cases that illustrates very well both the problem of definition and of legal policy is that of so-called "white-collar crime." Much attention has been devoted to such "crime" in recent years, and properly so, for peculiarly difficult problems of public policy as well as causation and treatment are involved in this area.[5] However, there is possibly less consistency involved in analyses of white-collar "criminality" than there is in any other category of crime. The white-collar criminologists represent one particular group among those who contend that the criminologist should study antisocial behavior rather than criminal law violation as such. Some of them contend that the convict classes are merely our petty criminals, the few whose depradations have been on a small scale, who have blundered into difficulties with the police and courts through their ignorance and stupidity.[6] The important criminals, those who do irreparable damage with impunity, deftly evade the machinery of justice, it is maintained, either by remaining technically within the law, or by exer-

[5] See, for example, Edwin H. Sutherland, "White Collar Criminality," *Am. Soc. Rev.*, vol. 5, pp. 1–12, 1940; "Is 'White-collar Crime' Crime?" *Am. Soc. Rev.*, vol. 10, pp. 132–139, 1945; "Crime of Corporations," in Cohen, Lindesmith, and Schuessler (eds.), *The Sutherltnd Papers*, pp. 78–99, 1956; *White Collar Crime*, 1949; Marshall B. Clinard, "Criminological Theories of Violations of Wartime Regulations," *Am. Soc. Rev.*, vol. 11, pp. 258–270, 1946; *The Black Market*, 1952; Frank E. Hartung, "White-collar Offenses in the Wholesale Meat Industry in Detroit," *Am. J. Soc.*, vol. 56, pp. 25–35, 1950. See also, Walton Hamilton and Irene Till, "Antitrust in Action," *TNEC Monograph No. 16*, 1941, reprinted in part in Kenneth Culp Davis, *Cases on Administrative Law*, 1951, pp. 37–48. The author wishes to make it clear here, since there has been some misconstruction of his view in literature on the subject, that he believes white-collar crime, properly and precisely defined, to be not only a legitimate but an important phase of criminological inquiry. He deplores the loosely normative connotations that have been attached to the concept by some of Sutherland's interpreters, and he believes that they have resulted in some confusion so far as needed empirical research in this area is concerned.

[6] See, in particular, Harry Elmer Barnes and Negley K. Teeters, *New Horizons in Criminology*, 1943, 3d ed. 1959. This popular text is responsible in considerable measure for accentuating the moral evaluative approach to white-collar crime as well as for spreading the notion that convicted criminals are merely the stupid and ineffectual offenders who happen to get caught.

cising their intelligence, financial prowess, or political connections. In seeking definitions of white-collar crime, one finds a rather remarkable diversity, but characteristically the definitions are loose and sometimes doctrinaire.

When the late Professor Sutherland launched the concept, it was applied to those individuals of upper socioeconomic status who violate the criminal law in the ordinary course of their business activities.[7] This usage accords with legal ideas of crime and points moreover to the difficult problems of enforcement in the field of business crimes. Popularization of the concept by other criminologists, however, has led to loose and slanted usage. It has been suggested that one may determine the existence of such crime "in casual conversation with a representative of an occupation by asking him, 'What crooked practices are found in your occupation?' " Confusion increases as we are informed by another proponent of this concept that "There are various phases of white-collar criminality that touch the lives of the common man almost daily. The large majority of them are operating within the letter and spirit of the law . . . In short, greed, not need, lies at the basis of white-collar crime."[8] In his later papers, Sutherland defined crime as a "legal description of an act as socially injurious and legal provision of penalty for the act."[9] Thus, while he continued to adhere to a legal conception of criminality, he apparently considered the connotation of his term too narrow if confined to violations of the criminal code; by a slight modification of definition he included conduct violative of any law, civil or criminal, when it is "socially injurious."

Concerning this development of imprecise and slanted definitions, the writer has said elsewhere:[10]

In the light of these definitions, the normative issue is pointed. Who should be considered the white-collar criminal? Is it the merchant who, out of greed, business acumen, or competitive motivations, breaches a trust with his consumer by "puffing his wares" beyond their merits, by pricing them beyond their value, or by ordinary advertising? Is it he who breaks trust with his employees in order to keep wages down, refusing to permit labor to organize or to bargain collectively, and who is found guilty by a labor relations board of an unfair labor practice? May it be the white-collar worker who breaches trust with his employers by inefficient performance at work, by sympathetic strike or secondary boycott? Or is it the merchandiser who violates ethics by under-cutting the prices of his fellow merchants? In general these acts do not violate the criminal law. All in some manner breach a trust for motives which a criminologist may or may not disapprove for one reason or another. All are within the framework of the norms of ordinary business practice. One seeks in vain

---

[7] Sutherland, "Crime and Business," *The Annals*, vol. 217, p. 112, 1941.
[8] Barnes and Teeters, *op. cit.,* pp. 42–43.
[9] Sutherland, "Is 'White-collar Crime' Crime?" *op. cit.,* p. 132.
[10] Tappan, *op. cit.,* pp. 99 f. (Reprinted by permission.)

for criteria to determine this white-collar criminality. It is the conduct of one who wears a white collar and who indulges in occupational behavior to which some particular criminologist takes exception. It may easily be a term of propaganda. For purposes of empirical research or objective description, what is it?

Whether criminology aspires one day to become a science or a repository of reasonably accurate descriptive information, it cannot tolerate a nomenclature of such loose and variable usage. A special hazard exists in the employment of the term "white-collar criminal" in that it invites individual systems of private values to run riot in the area of economic ethics where gross variation exists among criminologists as well as others. The rebel may enjoy a veritable orgy of delight in damning as criminal almost anyone he pleases. One imagines that some experts would thus consign to the criminal classes any successful capitalistic business man. The reactionary or conservative, complacently viewing the occupational practices of the business world, might find all in perfect order in this best of all possible economic worlds. The result may be fine indoctrination or catharsis achieved through blustering broadsides against the "existing system." It is not criminology. It is not social science. The terms "unfair," "infringement," "discrimination," "injury to society," and so on, employed by the white-collar criminologists cannot, taken alone, differentiate criminal and noncriminal. Until refined to mean certain specific actions, they are merely epithets.

Vague, omnibus concepts defining crime are a blight upon either a legal system or a system of sociology that strives to be objective. They allow judge, administrator, or conceivably sociologist, in an undirected, freely operating discretion, to attribute the status "criminal" to any individual or class which he conceives nefarious. This can accomplish no desirable objective, either politically or sociologically.

Unfortunately, norms of proper behavior in the economic fields of production, distribution, and advertising have been difficult to develop, partly because the commercial revolution took place so rapidly. Drawing lines between efficient and practical competitive behavior by the sharp but skilled and honest businessman, on the one hand, and the criminal practices of the dishonest and overpowerful, on the other, has proved extremely difficult. Interpretations and enforcement of the modern laws directed against various forms of white-collar crime have revealed the complex and controversial character of such policy, in part but not entirely by any means, because of the wealth and power of many of those who are brought to trial. The excessive tolerance that has developed for a loose economic and political morality is also at fault to a great extent. Unlike most forms of crime, white-collar depradations commonly have a diffused impact upon many in the society but little direct or obvious injury to single individuals. Moreover, and this is a peculiarly subtle problem, much of the white-collar conduct disapproved by some criminologists does have economic value. Often the policy question is one of balancing gain and loss from the behavior involved. Finally it should be noted that our court and correctional systems have little to offer in the way of effective treatment, training, or even of deterrence in the handling of individuals of the sort here involved.

Our definitions of crime cannot be rooted in epithets, in minority value judgments or prejudice, or in loose abstractions. Within a system of justice under law, crime must be defined quite precisely and in accordance with the explicit formulations of the legislature. Such crime will not include all behavior that is antisocial, for reasons that we have noted, nor even all conduct that should be made criminal.

THE ELEMENTS OF CRIME

Loose conceptions concerning the connotations of crime, the criminal, and criminology have tended in some measure to limit the reasonableness of our ideas about the purposes of law, police, courts, and correctional measures. As a matter of reality, however, the varied speculations as to what the subject matter of criminology should be have had little significant influence upon empirical research in the field. Offenders convicted by the courts of criminal law violations are a distinct and accessible group, unlike other less precisely defined categories of deviates. Criminological investigation has been directed traditionally, and still is today, to these convicted offenders. It is submitted that, while the research leaves something to be desired from the point of view of the samples of criminals studied, it focuses properly upon individuals whose acts are specifically criminal, as defined by statute and legal controls, rather than upon violations of conduct norms, antisocial behavior, or psychiatric aberrations.

What then is the legal definition of crime as it has been employed in practice, not only in our courts of law, but in criminology as well? *Crime is an intentional act or omission in violation of criminal law (statutory and case law), committed without defense or justification, and sanctioned by the state as a felony or misdemeanor.* This simple definition requires some elaboration, for its terms have special technical import. Its elements will be considered below seriatim:

The Concurrence of Act and Intent. It is a basic principle of the Anglo-American system as well as most other systems of justice that neither an act alone nor an intent alone is sufficient to constitute a crime; the two must concur to establish criminal responsibility, for it would be futile and dangerous for the state to attempt to punish individuals merely for a subjective state of mind, so difficult to determine with certainty, or for conduct engaged in by mistake. "Act" is interpreted, however, to include a failure to act where there is a positive duty, as in the criminal negligence of a parent or physician.[11] American law has not gone so far as that of

---

[11] For an extended treatment of the theory underlying criminal omissions, see Jerome Hall, *General Principles of Criminal Law,* 1947, chap. 9.

some other countries in establishing such duty lest criminality be imputed for nonfeasance in cases where many honest and reasonable men would hesitate to act.

"Intent," or *mens rea,* has been rather broadly interpreted so as to apply to behavior that is rooted in socially dangerous mental states.[12] Thus, while in a narrow sense intent implies a specific purpose to do what the actor has in fact done, it has been held enough to constitute a culpable *mens rea* where the offender intended to do some other wrong than the one he accomplished (as where A shoots intending to hit B but in fact injures C or, failing quite miserably, hits no one, but may be held, nonetheless, for the *attempt* implicit in his action and state of mind). Where the offender had no specific purpose but was criminally negligent he may be held responsible for the injury that flowed naturally from his conduct.[13] The offender is held responsible for all the wrong that might reasonably be expected to result from his acts. The standard for such criminal negligence depends upon the degree of care that a reasonable person should exercise under the circumstances, but often it depends also upon the utility of the act, if any, in relation to its dangerousness. Thus, while in a real sense it is perilous folly to drive an automobile at all in modern city streets, and the more so if they are slippery, and while vehicular homicides are the common and inevitable consequence, there is wide tolerance for such activity. There is general acceptance also—perhaps too much so—of the incidental casualties left in his wake as the police officer attempts to halt the fleeing felony suspect. The state will have little consideration, on the other hand, for the oaf who shoots into the air for the mere pleasure of it and thereby causes injury—however little "intended" in any real sense— or for the one who kills while driving recklessly. Thus, intent may sometimes be imputed where none exists because the defendant should have seen the danger he created or, in other instances, it may be transferred from the act intended to the one performed.

While it is in derogation of common-law principles, an absolute standard of liability has come to be attached to some types of conduct, so that the individual may be found criminal though the facts may clearly negate

[12] See *ibid.,* chaps. 5–10.

[13] The traditional language applied in the cases to the mental states accompanying violations of law so as to create criminal liability, such as "gross," "wanton," or "culpable" negligence or "recklessness," is imprecise and commonly tautological. The Model Penal Code proposes in Section 2.02 that culpability should be based on proof that the person acted "purposely, knowingly, recklessly, or negligently," as the law may require for the particular offense. Each of these gradations of *mens rea* is defined in rather specific terms. For example, a person acts "negligently" with respect to a material element of an offense "when he should be aware of a substantial and unjustifiable risk that the material element exists or will result from his conduct." Mere negligence, however, is not a sufficient basis on which to predicate culpability under the Code unless the substantive crime is so defined that it specifically attaches liability in such a case.

intent or even negligence.[14] The purpose here is to put men on notice of the need for special care to inform themselves of the facts so as to be protected against the hazard of violation. This standard may decrease the frequency of violations and it certainly facilitates prosecution, but it is a dangerous principle to employ when penal sanctions are involved.

Violation of the Criminal Law. There are important differences between the criminal and the noncriminal, or civil, law, differences that have come to be clouded somewhat both in certain modern legislation and in some sociologists' analyses of crime, as we have seen. The result is quite unfortunate from the point of view of social policy. The primary function of criminal law is to protect society against the infringement of important rights of person and property. The interest is focused primarily upon group rather than individual protection, and the sanctions employed through penal law are designed to deter potential criminals, so far as possible, from violating the social rules and to repress or incapacitate the actual offender from persistence in such a course. The civil law of torts, contracts, property, and so on, is directed, on the contrary, to the protection of the rights of individuals rather than the mass. The measures employed are generally damages, designed to restore the vicitim to his *status quo ante,* so far as possible. But since an award of money often will not resolve a threatened or actual loss, civil courts may employ such other measures as requiring the specific performance of a contract, restitution for an injury, or an injunction against continued violations.

It is clear at once that the same act may constitute both a crime against the state and a violation of an individual's private interests. There is considerable overlapping between criminal and tortious conduct, as in assault or fraud. The similarity between the two is increased by the fact that the consequences to the offender may appear superficially the same when a criminal court imposes a fine and a civil court assesses damages. They are different, however, in that the damages are designed to restore the victim, whereas the fine is intended to penalize and deter the socially undesirable conduct.[15] Where there is a right of civil action, there is no double jeop-

---

[14] Strict liability, not requiring even a showing of negligence, has come to be applied by a rather wide range of special regulatory legislation. This includes phases of the pure food and drug laws, giving false weight, liquor laws (as to age or content of beverages), polluting streams, owning a house used for prostitution, possessing lottery slips or narcotics, selling margarine, misleading advertising, and other offenses. The Model Penal Code would not permit any term of imprisonment to be applied in any case where liability was absolute.

[15] The English authorities, Stephen and Professor Kenny, have observed that crimes and torts are not mutually exclusive, that "criminal wrongs and civil wrongs . . . are often one and the same act as viewed from different standpoints, the difference being not one of nature but one of relation." Kenny, *Outlines of Criminal Law,* 1936, p. 22. In his analysis of the differences between crime and tort, Hall observes that in the case of crime there is always a "social harm" created, though there may be no injury necessarily to an individual or any damage of any sort (for

ardy in a civil and a criminal trial of the same issue and the courts' findings may be the same or different. The criminal court, however, properly requires a higher standard of proof to find the defendant a criminal and to impose sanctions of the penal law. An odium attaches to the criminal status and its penalty that is not present where a civil court mediates a controversy between two or more individuals or firms. By and large the man accused of wrong would prefer to pay heavy damages to the victim rather than a light fine to the state.[16] Indeed, too often his reputation is more seriously damaged by the publicity of a criminal trial, regardless of its outcome, than it would have been by a civil assessment of damages.

The tools of the criminal law are blunt, however necessary and utilitarian they may be. It is poor policy promiscuously to enact penal legislation for conduct in which the social threat is innocuous or imaginary or where the infliction of penalties cannot protect the public interest; and criminal laws should define quite sharply the wrong that is intended to be prohibited.[17] This is the reason for our rule of "justice under law," that conduct must be specifically prohibited by statute in order to attach to it the shame of crime. A loose substantive law of crimes is an abomination

---

example, in cases of sedition, attempts to commit suicide, and possessory offenses). Hall believes that a fundamental distinguishing characteristic of crime is moral culpability in the actor that justifies the application of punitive sanctions. In the case of tort, on the other hand, there may be and generally is no guilty intent or culpability; most torts involve only negligence or strict liability. Characteristically, however, compensable harm is done to the individual or his interests. Where any culpable or intentional wrongdoing was involved, Hall suggests, this is not in itself significant in a tort action except as a means by which economic damage may be inflicted upon an individual. He observes, as an exception to other torts, however, certain classes where an individual's rights may be invaded without specific injury to him (e.g., trespass, nuisance, infringement of trademarks) or where he need not prove actual damage (e.g., false imprisonment, libel, some forms of slander, criminal conversation, and malicious prosecution). In such cases the tort law may be a more drastic and effective agency than penal law but its effect is to vindicate the rights of the individual. See Hall, op. cit., chap. 7.

[16] See, in this connection, Frank E. Hartung, "Common and Discrete Values," *J. Soc. Psych.* vol. 38, pp. 3–23, 1953, in which he found quite consistently in a series of samples greater disapproval of criminal than of civil defendants. This bears, of course, on the discussion below of white-collar crime and, in particular, the lumping of civil actions with criminal under a common label.

[17] Observe, in contrast, the principle of crimes by analogy that prevail in some countries. The Russian Penal Code of 1926 defined crime in these terms: "A crime is any socially dangerous act or omission which threatens the foundation of the Soviet political structure and that system of law which has been established by the Workers' and Peasants' Government for the period of transition to a Communist structure." (II–6.) "In cases where the Criminal Code makes no direct reference to particular forms of crime, punishment or other measures of social protection are applied in accordance with those Articles of the Criminal Code which deal with crimes most closely approximating, in gravity, and in kind, to the crimes actually committed." (II–10.) Penal Code of the RSFSR, 1934.

within the democratic framework of justice, though such laws have been enacted here from time to time. The terms of many statutes dealing with disorderly conduct, vagrancy, wayward minors, juvenile delinquency, and conspiracy illustrate this undesirable imprecision. Contemporary hearings on "loyalty" and "security" display a similar lack of sufficiently definite standards, and while these are not criminal adjudications, they have a similar effect upon the accused.

Administrative Justice

A special problem involving this imprecision of criminal law has developed as a phase of modern efforts to extend controls widely in areas of politicoeconomic behavior. Governmental authorities are strongly tempted, when they seek to establish new policy, to employ what may be deemed vigorous control measures that will assure effective instrumentation of a program, even if the sanctions they set may be harsh or inappropriate. As administrative agencies of government designed to achieve special objectives have proliferated, there has been considerable—probably quite excessive—reliance upon the use of criminal court actions and sanctions to coerce conformity. In some legislation, antitrust laws, for example, this has involved a triple threat of criminal sanctions (usually a fine going to the state), of civil sanctions (damages going to the victim), or of administrative measures (cease and desist orders, etc.), according to the choice of the authorities charged with administration of the policy. There are no clear criteria, for the most part, to determine which set of sanctions should be employed, so that policy in the choice may depend on the judiciousness of the administrators, sometimes on their crusading zeal, their conception of fairness, or their response to the pressures of political or business influence.[18] The provision in a number of laws for "punitive

---

[18] In 1938, an American Bar Association Committee asserted: "Administration, with its ideal and function of getting things done, has, and from its ideal will have, a tendency to act from one side. An administrative agency is not unlikely to have been set up to get things done in the interest of one side which controls or has the favor of the executive for the time being." *A.B.A. Rep.,* vol. 63, pp. 331, 342, 1938. In one case in which orders of the National Labor Relations Board were held unenforceable because of the bias of the examiner the court found him "guilty of threatening, badgering, and arguing with the witnesses, making statements during the hearing contradictory to the true facts, cutting short cross-examination, and acting more in the role of a prosecutor than impartial examiner." *NLRB v. Washington Dehydrated Food Co.,* 118 F.2d 980 (9th Cir. 1941), cited in Davis, *op. cit.,* p. 458.

An equally serious aspect of civil, as against criminal, adjudication is involved in the combination of functions that are entrusted to a single, commonly very powerful agency. This was the subject of adverse comment in *Minority Report,* Attorney General's Committee on Administrative Procedure, 1941, pp. 203–204: "Moreover, the consolidation of functions has done more than enable a single agency to act successfully as legislator, investigator, prosecutor, jury, judge, and

damages" in civil suits and the empowering of civil courts or administrative agencies to adjudicate that defendants have committed a "misdemeanor" are two further developments that have tended to blur the distinction between criminal and civil law in certain areas of administrative government.

Criminal procedure, as will be noted in fuller detail at a later point, is designed quite properly to avoid convictions either where substantive policy is not clear-cut or where the evidence is insubstantial. This policy in our system of justice has a dual aspect: on the one hand, it avoids imputing an injurious stigma to individuals whose conduct is not distinctively offensive to the community, and on the other, the stigma of conviction facilitates effective control where the conduct is truly dangerous. There is another side to this picture. Naturally, if the criminal law is employed promiscuously and without discrimination from assorted other legal and administrative measures, the effect is inevitably, to reduce the effectuality of and respect for criminal sanctions. This appears a sufficient reason to decry the trend toward an increasingly undiscriminating employment of this branch of the law, and to repudiate the suggestion that criminal law should be applied more extensively in the areas of ordinary economic relationships. It appears that through the misdemeanor convictions of corporations and business executives for violations of governmental policies we have already come dangerously close to losing both the stigma and

---

appellate tribunal. Agencies are empowered to act in several of these capacities at a single stage of proceedings. As investigator, an administrative agency, after making its own rules and regulations, may often summon witnesses and examine them in secret—a privilege otherwise accorded only to grand juries and denied to such important public officers as the Attorney General and the officials of the Department of Justice. It may, under some statutes, "visit" or inspect premises without a warrant—a power accorded no other public agency except a judge or a jury, and then only after a case has been instituted and the parties apprised of the charges against them. It may threaten the imposition of penalties if the demands for information are not met—a power otherwise accorded only to judges, and then only after valid subpoenas have issued. It may threaten to impose regulations—¹ a power otherwise accorded only to Congress. It may threaten to prosecute and to judge—a power otherwise divided between the Department of Justice and the courts. It may threaten to withhold benefits—a prerogative otherwise accorded only to Congress. Though this is not the normal course of administration, the exercise of such power is restrained only by human forbearance." *Ibid.,* p. 462.

See, also, Arthur T. Vanderbilt, "The Place of the Administrative Tribunal in Our Legal System," *A.B.A.J.,* vol. 24, p. 267, 1938: "I am not suggesting that administrative agencies be abolished or that they be deprived of their powers of adjudication. Nor am I suggesting that administrative officials should always be lawyers. I do submit, however, that when our administrative agencies act as judges they should have the attributes, the working conditions and the professional environment of judges—the safeguards that centuries of experience have demonstrated to be essential to the maintenance and administration of what Blackstone called common justice. . . ."

the control that criminal law should establish. While this is in itself less important, the result is also seriously to blur the distinctions between civil and criminal law that on very sound grounds have been established in our legal tradition.[19]

In light of the inadequate legal standards, it is not surprising, perhaps, that some sociologists interested in white-collar crime have quite uncritically grouped together as crimes the adjudications of criminal and civil courts and administrative bodies in their studies of violations of antitrust statutes, the National Labor Relations Law, O.P.A. legislation, wage and hour laws, black-marketing operations, and Federal Trade Commission orders, quite without reference to procedures of adjudication, level of proof required, or the sanctions permitted in connection with different types of legal action.[20] The result, however, has been to extend the con-

---

[19] The case cited below in the press illustrates the lack of sufficiently well-defined legal standards for the prosecution of antitrust cases, where the selection of the method to pursue is in the hands of the Attorney General. His decision in this case was sound, but it was *his* decision, rather than one of uniform and continuing policy.

CRIMINAL SUIT INQUIRY

INTO TV ENDED BY U.S.

The Federal Government has abandoned an anti-trust investigation by a New York grand jury into the radio and television manufacturing industry in so far as criminal action is concerned, James B. McGranery, Attorney General, announced today. He said that the evidence accumulated to date did not justify any criminal action.

Documents and data would be studied, however, for a determination if a civil anti-trust suit was warranted, he added.

The material subpoenaed for the grand jury, Mr. McGranery stated, "suggests that removal of whatever restraints exist in the industry should more properly be the subject of civil litigation than of criminal prosecution." The study of the documents, to date, he added, *"has not disclosed the use of force, strong arm tactics or activities of a similar nature." New York Times,* Jan. 20, 1953.

[20] Professor Sutherland offered a rationalization for this in these terms: "The criminologists have made use of case histories and statistics of juvenile delinquents in constructing theories of criminal behavior. This justifies the inclusion of agencies other than the criminal court which deal with white-collar offenses." "White-collar Criminality," in Cohen, Lindesmith, and Schuessler, *op. cit.,* p. 53. There is no good reason why criminologists should not study the action of administrative agencies. There is every reason, however, to avoid confusing the tribunals as to cases handled, procedures employed, status implications, and results achieved. In 1948, Professor Sutherland reviewed his study of decisions against seventy large corporations involving restraints of trade, misrepresentation in advertising, infringement of patents, copyrights, and trademarks, rebates, unfair labor practices, financial fraud, violations of war regulations, and a small miscellaneous group of other laws. He held that 98 per cent of the corporations were criminal recidivists and that 90 per cent were "habitual criminals." He found 980 adverse decisions in all, 425 of which were made by civil or equity courts. See "Crime of Corporations," *op., cit.,* pp. 80–81. These are interesting data so far as the behavior of corporations is concerned. If they had been employed for the purpose, the materials might well

fusion among criminologists concerning distinctions between crime, anti-social behavior, and ordinary business practice. In the author's view, a *conviction in a criminal court* under one of these statutes creates a criminal status, whether or not the law is sound in so providing. The wisdom of such law as a matter of governmental policy ought, of course, like other criminal laws, to be carefully considered. Clearly, on the other hand, the *administrative* decision by a governmental agency—commonly allowing no effective due process in hearing or appeal—should not and does not create a criminal status. To class such individuals with other criminals in criminological research investigations serves only to confuse a subject matter that is already sufficiently complicated.

These comments are not intended to deny the significance of commercial criminality, with its specialized problems of social policy, enforcement, evidentiary proof, and treatment measures. Such matters have large importance today, in part because we need to distinguish between different types of real criminality and of correctional methods that may be used effectively in treatment. The subject matter of criminology will profit more, however, from making an objective analysis of what is and is not crime, what should and should not be made criminal, and what measures

---

reveal something about the nature and changes in Federal practices in controlling business enterprise. The extent to which there is any sound and definitive standard to determine when a criminal court adjudication rather than civil measures should be employed is of special interest to criminology. In its present form the material merely attests the confusion that exists in adjudicative procedures and the application of the criminal law in corporate practice.

Compare the analysis of enforcement under the Sherman Act, in which Hamilton and Till observed: "In five decades the number of criminal actions has run to 252, yet in only 24 did the trial court impose penal sentences. But even so poor a showing on paper exaggerates the reality. Eleven of the cases involved trade unions; 96 out of the 102 defendants involved served sentences which ran from a few months to 2 years. Two of the suits, strictly speaking are not anti-trust cases, but concern the activities of alleged German spies during the World War. The Sherman Act served, for want of a better, as the instrument for incarcerating 8 suspects in jail. Only the 11 cases which remain are really in point; they alone involve violations of the Sherman Act by business men. In 10, actually racketeering practices—threats, intimidations, holdups, personal violence—entered as a significant element in insuring conviction. Thus out of the whole number, a single suit proclaims that along with the racketeer and the trade union official, the respectable man of business goes to jail for restraint of trade. In Trenton Potteries, sentences were pronounced upon 8 individuals, but were suspended by the trial court and the terms were never served. . . . It is obvious that as a sanction the prison sentence has virtually been a dead letter. . . . The average fine imposed upon the individual is small. The 97 cases in which fines were imposed involve some 1,500 individuals and corporations. As an average, this runs to about $2,000 per defendant. . . . The sums expended in defending a suit are vastly in excess of the legal penalties that may be imposed. In the Madison Oil case the court, after trial of the defendants, assessed $65,000 in fines. Estimates of the legal expense of the defendants vary from $2,000,-000 to $2,500,000. . . . " "Antitrust in Action," *op. cit.,* p. 43.

may be usefully applied for the deterrence and treatment of the wrong-doer than from indiscriminately lumping as "criminals" individuals whose conduct has differed significantly or whose hearings and adjudications were quite unlike. The "watering down" of the meaning of crime in a system of law and of the subject matter of criminology in social science seriously disserves our objectives to understand and control undesirable behavior. In this writer's opinion white-collar crime should be defined, like any other crime, in terms of violations of the criminal law. Moreover, it appears that the utility of the concept is unreasonably limited when such crime is defined in terms of "violations committed by *businessmen* in the ordinary course of business activities." There appears no sound reason to distinguish and focus upon such conduct as more devious or dangerous than the varied occupational offenses committed by other types of white-collar groups: professionals, labor leaders, administrators, advertisers, and others. If there is justification for separate analysis of businessmen's crimes, it is necessary to show how and why such criminality and its as-sociated problems differs from or exceeds other occupational criminality by those who are clad in white collars. Thus far the term has lent itself more to criticism of business enterprise than to an objective and discrimi-nating analysis of a specialized criminological problem.

Defenses and Justification. An act otherwise criminal may not result in liability in certain circumstances. Several exculpatory factors are provided in most legal codes, including infancy, insanity, the defense of oneself or one's close relatives, coercion, necessity, and the prevention of crime. In general any of these may be submitted in evidence at trial under a plea of not guilty. The inclusiveness of such defenses varies considerably in dif-ferent jurisdictions, however, for example, as in the age level and type of crime involved where a child is charged, in the mental capacity of the insane person, the particular circumstances involved in the defense of person or property, and so on. The matters of infancy and insanity will be discussed in later chapters.

Treatment Sanctions. There are several matters of significance here. In the first place, only those sanctions may be employed that are specifically provided by penal law for the crimes involved. Punitive limits are thereby established. While other penalties or controls may ensue from criminal conviction, the deprivation of civil rights, such as loss of licenses, of the right to practice one's profession, of one's job or reputation, these are not a part of the court's sentence as such.[21] A number of states have enacted legislation in recent years to remove certain of these disabilities, either after the completion of sentence or upon proof of reformation, or to avoid criminal conviction in the first instance.[22]

---

[21] See Tappan, "The Legal Rights of Prisoners," *The Annals,* vol. 293, pp. 99–112, 1954; "Loss and Restoration of Civil Rights of Offenders," *N.P.P.A. Yearbook,* pp. 66–107, 1952; and Chapter 15 in this text.

[22] See Chapter 14.

Felony or Misdemeanor. As we have noted above, the sanctions imposed upon the criminal are defined by statute. More particularly, they are divided in most jurisdictions into the two classes, felony and misdemeanor, according to the seriousness of the crime involved. There is considerable overlapping between these categories, crimes that are misdemeanors in some states being felonies in others, and vice versa. They differ generally, however, in that felonies are the more serious offenses, including murder and manslaughter, burglary, robbery, rape, kidnapping, grand larceny, and other acts that are seriously injurious or dangerous.[23] Felonies are generally punishable by imprisonment in a state institution, usually a prison, for a period of one year or more up to life.[24] Felonies may also be sanctioned by the death penalty for the most serious types, or by fines, suspended sentence, or probation, as the statutes may provide. Misdemeanors are punishable generally by imprisonment for less than a year, ordinarily under a definite term, in a local or county institution, usually a jail. Alternatively, the courts may apply a fine, probation, or suspended sentence in accordance with statute.

A number of jurisdictions have established a third class of violations in their criminal codes, offenses which by special provision are less than crimes. These are characteristically infractions of relatively small social or moral consequence, such as disorderly conduct, vagrancy, violation of municipal ordinances, and intoxication. Such acts in other jurisdictions are included among the misdemeanors. It is sound policy to distinguish between these lesser violations and criminal acts, thereby avoiding the unnecessary attribution of criminal status to individuals who offer little or no real threat to the safety of the community. The offenses involved very commonly represent what are in fact social welfare, medical, and psychiatric problems, and they ideally should be handled to a large extent by noncorrectional resources, if they are available. Certainly there is little

---

[23] The traditional felonies as well as some crimes now classified as misdemeanors have been known as crimes *mala in se* because they have been deemed inherently evil. An act *malum prohibitum,* wrong merely because the state has condemned it, is enacted to mediate between conflicting social interests and may lack any intrinsic moral reprehensibility. Under this theory *malum prohibitum* would apply to many misdemeanors. Many people criticize the classification of crimes into the felony and misdemeanor categories on the ground that there is no meaningful dividing line between the two and that, very commonly, conduct that in one state would be a felony is a misdemeanor elsewhere and vice versa. Absurdities appear frequently where a crime is divided into grades, part of which are felonies, part misdemeanors. The felonious criminal is often allowed to plead to a misdemeanor in such a case. There are two sound general reasons for retaining the traditional common-law classification. Some kind of gradation of crimes according to degree of seriousness is desirable and perhaps inevitable in dealing with crimes. From a practical point of view, it would be most difficult or impossible completely to revolutionize our systems of courts and of correctional facilities, which are organized in nearly every state on the basis of the distinction between felonies and misdemeanors.

[24] See Chapter 15 for a discussion of the forms of prison sentencing.

sound reason to treat them as crimes, with all the attendant disadvantages to effective treatment that are implied by strong social opprobrium and by the often defective correctional facilities available for handling the minor offender. Lacking other facilities, the same sorts of correctional measures are applied as those that are used for misdemeanors, though jail confinement is employed in a somewhat smaller proportion of cases and for shorter periods of time.

This analysis of the nature of crime has been extended because, as was originally noted, the definition is basic to conceptions of causation, court action, and correctional treatment. It has involved, too, some brief consideration of related matters of policy and differentiation of conduct for purposes of social control. In summary it is suggested that researches on crime, as distinguished from other types of deviant behavior, should deal solely with acts that are prohibited by the criminal law and treated under the penal law.

THE CRIMINAL

This brings us to the problem of defining "the criminal," a matter which involves difficulties of its own. It should be clear at the start that to understand and treat the criminal we require as sharp a delineation as possible of those who are criminals. This involves other and, in some respects, more difficult issues than defining crime itself. It is easy enough to describe the criminal, as the dictionaries do, as "one who commits a crime, especially one who is discovered and convicted," but this leaves a host of problems to be resolved. In an abstract sense the criminal is one who has committed a crime, as defined in the pages above, whether or not he is discovered, convicted, or treated as a criminal. It would be desirable to learn the distinguishing characteristics of a representative sample of criminals so defined, but it would be quite impossible to do so. Obviously this abstractly defined population differs to a significant extent from those violators who are discovered by the police, those who are convicted by the courts, and those who are treated through correctional measures.[25]

It should be observed that those who are arrested for crimes are not necessarily guilty. Many of them, indeed, are acquitted and some, but not all, of those acquitted are innocent. On the other hand, among those found guilty by the courts, some unknown percentage is innocent. Erroneous convictions are less common—and properly so—in our system of justice than failures to arrest or to convict the guilty. These difficulties accentuate the problem of distinguishing between known and actual criminals.

Among the practical problems involved in criminological research, one of the most difficult is the selection of samples as representative as pos-

[25] Problems involved in the discovery and conviction of criminal suspects are discussed in Chapters 11 and 12.

sible of either criminals in general or a particular class of criminals. It is not easy to secure a group that can be studied in a systematic way over a period of time. The problem of selection of samples will be discussed in Chapter 3.

In summary of the comments above, one may say that for purposes of criminological research the term "criminal" requires more explicit formulation so that one may know what part of the criminal population is being analyzed. These are, perhaps, the most obvious categories:

1. Generally, "the criminal" is one who violates the criminal law, whether or not he is discovered or convicted. While such usage is conceptually accurate, its value for empirical research is seriously limited by the impossibility of securing a representative sample of such criminals.

2. The criminal suspect is one who is arrested or charged with crime, though he may or may not be in fact a criminal. The widely quoted statistics of the FBI are based for the most part on this category and on arrests for "crimes known to the police." The latter group has been referred to as the most useful for index purposes because it is the most complete group available. It should be reiterated, however, that not all of such cases, by any means, are criminals in fact.

3. Defendants are those tried in criminal courts about whom statistics are available in court data. As will be observed in a later chapter, many of these cases are discharged or acquitted at some stage in the proceedings, and the purpose of trial is to determine whether the accused is in fact criminal.

4. Criminals convicted and sentenced are the most accurately selected sample of offenders that our procedures of policing and trial can provide among the total universe of individuals who are criminal. As compared to the category described in (1) above, this is a small and distorted sample. On the other hand, it is a peculiarly important group because it consists of individuals who, in most cases, have committed the crimes for which they were convicted. They have been exposed to the pressures of disapproval by their associates and the general public; to the humiliations of arrest, trial, and conviction; and to the influences of the correctional sanctions imposed by the court. For these reasons it is a distinct group of special significance to the community and to the criminologist. It should be noted specifically that the experiences leading up to and following upon conviction, particularly in the first exposure of the offender, have tremendous impact upon the criminal. Indeed, these may have greater significance for his future conduct and attitude than did the commission of the criminal act itself. It is an unfortunate by-product of a system of criminal control, essential as it is, that its effect may be to confirm in criminality some individuals who would not have continued to offend had they not been discovered in the first violation.

5. Distinction among criminals must be made not only in relation to the comparative seriousness of their criminal histories, but also in relation to the differential impact upon them of the forms of treatment, or correctional measures, to which they have been exposed.

6. Finally, there is the discharged criminal who has undergone correctional sanctions of one or several sorts, who should be differentiated from the other

classes in terms of the completion of treatment. A serious difficulty should be noted here. The officially discharged offender does not, upon his return to freedom, escape from serious consequences of his conviction. He has a criminal record, affecting his future civil rights, his amenability to the habitual criminal laws, and his susceptibility to arrest and detention. Sometimes more significant than these, his relationships with friends, relatives, potential employers, and the general community are adversely affected, making his adjustments to responsibility difficult. This is the reason for the recent concern in a few jurisdictions to develop "rehabilitation statutes" to relieve the offender from the persisting restrictions that hamper his living. While his legal status may be improved thereby, it has proved impossible thus far to affect the general community response to the ex-convict. This is a vital problem for public education by the criminologist rather than a matter for statutory resolution.

The criminologists' generalizations about the offender ought to reveal quite explicitly which among these conceptions of the criminal is being employed at any particular time and how it is relevant to the conclusions that are drawn. Where the term is being used quite loosely to include those whose alleged offenses have not been proved in a criminal court, this should be made clear. Furthermore, the practice should be avoided of including within the meaning of criminality any conduct that has not been made criminal. Deterioration to an epithetical terminology will serve no useful purpose in criminology.

The Dynamic Conservatism of the Criminal Law

Crime is, as we have emphasized, a matter of legal definition. It differs in time and place in accordance with the variations in standards that the laws may have established. Crime is, therefore, variable, relative, and dynamic rather than absolute or permanent in its quality. This variability is one reason why some authorities have suggested that crime as defined by law is not a sociological entity, derived from the nature of a sociological subject matter. It should be noted, however, that all forms of normative control are relative and variable in some measure. Custom, fashion, morality, and tradition each derives from the culture and society in which it is found. Law differs from these other norms, to be sure, but not by any means in an independence from the people or the values of the society where it is found. Legal norms, more than others, are the product of reflection and rational deliberations by legislatures and courts. They are the result of real efforts to fit social rules to the needs of a people. Law is in fact more conservative than some other forms of control and there has been frequent criticism of "lags" in legal standards. Such slowness to change is generally characteristic of well-established rules of social policy, however, for it is essential to social stability that the basic "rules of the game" be definite and fixed rather than too easily responsive to ephemeral changes in the social climate of opinion.

In the Anglo-American system of criminal justice two principles stand out as standards of conservatism that are considered, nevertheless, to be essential to a fair system of law. One is the doctrine of justice according to law, *nullum crimen sine lege,* meaning that there is no crime without a law that quite specifically prohibits the behavior involved.[26] While in a sense this means, as some scholars have stressed, that laws create crimes, this is a superficial fact, as will be noted more fully in our discussion of the content of the law. To put it simply here, criminal law is the consequence of careful consideration and consensus as to the need for a rule to ensure some regularity of conduct and to protect a significant social interest. The rule may not be perfect or permanent—usually it is neither. Generally, however, it is quite stable; it resolves conflicting interests and values; it provides a standard to solicit some uniformity of behavior.

It is commonly said that the citizen is presumed to know the law. More accurately phrased, within a system of justice according to law, the individual must be held responsible for violations whether or not he knows the specific provisions of the statutes and of court decisions. In fairness, however, the rules must be both reasonably stable and clear as guides to conformity. This principle, pertaining to statutory law in the main, is strengthened further by the common-law rule of precedent that guides court decisions, the doctrine of stare decisis (*stare decisis et non quietas movere*): to let the weight of decisions stand and not to disturb settled things. This doctrine, too, while it has been subject to criticism for its conservative influence, accords essentially with our common sense of justice. The rules of the game should not be radically altered after the stakes are down. This is the more true because the significant rules of criminal law are bulwarked by penal sanctions of a largely afflictive character. The state may not condemn and punish the man whose conduct has not been quite specifically prohibited. Nor may the court go far in interpreting the facts or in applying the law to alter the rule itself. Criminal and penal laws are strictly constructed in order to avoid injustice.

It is apparent that laws sometimes need to be changed either because they were wrong at the start or because conditions have so changed that a new standard of conduct is desirable. Sometimes the gap between what is and what should be the law runs deep and long. Such is the common complaint of reformers, quite frequently used as a rationalization for defining the scope of criminology in terms of antisocial behavior rather than law violations. It should be observed, however, that quite aside from the need for some stability in the law, as noted above, large-scale changes in criminal and penal law are not to be undertaken lightly. Where protection of social interests, of individual freedom, and of the offender himself are

---

[26] The coordinate principle, *nulla poena sine lege* (prohibiting the employment of a sanction in the absence of a penal law), is taken further to imply that penal statutes should be strictly construed. See Hall, *op. cit.,* chap. 2. Also see Chapter 15 of this text on criminal sanctions.

involved, the creation and punishment of a new crime or the elimination of an old one is a highly responsible task.[27] The fairness of a rule proposed and the feasibility of its enforcement are crucial. Until there has been thoughtful consideration and agreement on a superior alternative, there is reason for a presumption in favor of an existing legal rule. This should retard neither critical analysis of the inadequacies in existing law nor the search for better rules. But it puts upon the innovator a positive duty to perform much more than the simple task of criticism: he must give substantial proof of the superiority of his specific preferences. There has been a great deal of critical attack upon the content of the criminal law, but most of the criticisms fall short of providing realistic and satisfactory alternatives upon which reasonable men could agree and which the state could hope to enforce.

We have suggested that law is relative and dynamic in character. When the need for change becomes sufficiently clear and agreement on a feasible rule can be achieved, new laws are created. This is a political-legislative process, for the most part, rather than a judicial one, under our system of law. Courts are required to apply statutes which they disapprove and in doing so they sometimes call upon the legislature, in their opinions, for change in law. Courts sometimes play a more affirmative role than this in the law-making process, however. Some "strong" judges have quite deliberately and obviously changed the content of the law—though they rarely do so to any radical extent in the criminal field.[28] Some modify the

---

[27] In his *Paradoxes of Legal Science,* 1928, Benjamin Cardozo points to the complexity of functions that the law must serve and to the need for a balancing of conflicting interests. He makes it clear that the tasks of legal formulation and decision making require a judicious equilibrium: "The reconciliation of the irreconcilable, the merger of antitheses, the synthesis of opposites, these are the great problems of the law. . . . We have the claims of stability to be harmonized with those of progress. We are to reconcile liberty with equality, and both of them with order. The property rights of the individual we are to respect, yet we are not to press them to the point at which they threaten the welfare or the security of the many. We must preserve to justice its universal quality, and yet leave to it the capacity to be individual and particular. The precedent or the statute, though harsh, is to be obeyed, yet obeyed also, at the sacrifice not seldom of the written word, are to be the meliorating precepts of equity and conscience. Events are to be traced to causes, yet since causes are infinite in number, there must be a process of selection by which the cause to be assigned as operative will vary with the end in view. Is this dreamland or reality?" Pp. 4–5.

[28] The view of the judge as being merely a machine applying the written word is not realistic, though ideally his task is performed objectively and impersonally. Cardozo has put it well: "I have spoken of the forces of which judges avowedly avail to shape the form and content of their judgements. Even these forces are seldom fully in consciousness. They lie so near the surface, however, that their existence and influence are not likely to be disclaimed. But the subject is not exhausted with the recognition of their power. Deep below consciousness are other forces, the likes and the dislikes, the predilections and the prejudices, the complex

rules to a less significant extent, intentionally or inadvertently, inaugurating a new line of precedent. Judicial modifications of the law are made easily and commonly, however, by differentiating the facts in the immediate case from those in other cases which have been adjudicated under an interpretation that this court disapproves. Thus the judge can, in effect, establish a new rule, a new line of precedent.

THE CRIMINAL LAW

We propose in the remainder of this chapter to summarize the elements that enter into the criminal law in action. Popular notions of law center on statutes and, as has been noted, formal enactments are an important part of legal norms, particularly as they dramatize innovations in the rule of law. The "law in books" is not, by any means, however, the equivalent of "law in action" and, moreover, both these phases of law—the formal and the dynamic—are products of a combination of factors.[29] Legislative enactments constitute, in a very real sense, the ultimate focalization of influences that are themselves essential ingredients in the emergence of written

---

of instincts and emotions and habits and convictions, which make the man, whether he be litigant or judge. . . . The great tides and currents which engulf the rest of men, do not turn aside in their course, and pass the judges by. We like to figure to ourselves the processes of justice as coldly objective and impersonal. The law, conceived of as a real existence, dwelling apart and alone, speaks, through the voices of priests and ministers, the words which they have no choice except to utter. This is an ideal of objective truth toward which every system of jurisprudence tends. It is an ideal of which great publicists and judges have spoken as of something possible to attain. 'The judges of the nation,' says Montesquieu, 'are only the mouths that pronounce the words of the law, inanimate beings, who can moderate neither its forces nor its rigor.' See Marshall, in *Osborne v. Bank of the United States,* 9 Wheat. 738, 866. The judicial department 'has no will in any case. . . . Judicial power is never exercised for the purpose of giving effect to the will of the judge; always for the purpose of giving effect to the will of the legislature; or in other words, to the will of the law.' It has a lofty sound; it is well and finely said; but it can never be more than partly true." *The Nature of the Judicial Process,* 1921, pp. 167–169.

[29] For effective expositions of the doctrines of legal realism, which focus upon "what courts do in fact," to use his phrase, see Jerome Frank, *Courts on Trial,* 1949; *Law and the Modern Mind,* 1936; and "What Courts Do in Fact," *Ill. L. Rev.,* vol. 26, p. 645, 1932. Roscoe Pound has made the point that there is danger in the realistic position, taken at its extreme, in that "from assuming that we do not in practice attain a high degree of objectivity, or indeed any at all, it leads to an idea that we need not try to attain it and ought not to try to attain it because the attempt would be only pretence. . . . It is true that the personality of a judge will affect his interpretation and application of a legal precept to some degree. But he has been trained in the tradition of the law, as have his fellow judges also. From judges steeped in that tradition we may expect to get, and experience shows that we do get, substantially the same technique of reading and interpreting a precept and of applying it." *Justice According to Law,* 1951, pp. 36–37.

law. An important limiting factor is that of constitutional provisions which establish standards and prohibitions both on what may be included in the substantive law and on the procedures that may be employed in securing criminal convictions. Among these are such provisions as the rules against *ex post facto* laws, class legislation, cruel and unusual punishments, the requirement of due process, and other standards and procedures that are a part of our legal system. Such requirements operate not only to abrogate enactments that contravene constitutional policy but, more often, to prevent the enactment of statutes whose constitutionality is seriously in doubt. Legislative drafting is ordinarily performed with constitutional issues closely in mind.

Public Opinion

Public opinion plays a significant role in determining the effect of the law in action. Legislation is commonly the product of a recognized public need or demand. Thus we have observed in recent years effective clamor for special laws against offenses involved in illicit drugs, sex, gambling, racketeering, and communistic activities. Not infrequently, civil laws and sometimes criminal legislation are put forward through the pressure of limited, special interest groups, such as churches, trade associations, organized labor, professional societies, censorship groups, or ethnic minorities. Occasionally such legislation is enacted even where there is no wide consensus as to its desirability or, indeed, though preponderant opinion is hostile to it. However, where public opinion does not support the law, characteristically it is nullified either through repeal, as in the Eighteenth Amendment, or through failure of enforcement, as in our Blue Laws.

Public opinion is not an ideal criterion for good or effective legislation because it may be too emotionally charged by propaganda, prejudice, or the excessive stimulation of some unusual crisis. Thus, the contemporary sex psychopath and habitual criminal legislation, for example, has been badly devised and poorly implemented. Community opinion sometimes changes rapidly, too, so that laws enacted during an apparent crisis may be inappropriate both to public needs and changing sentiments. This has proved to be true of some of our loyalty and security laws that were hastily adopted. It is a fortunate, and conservative, aspect of the law that legislation is generally a rather slow, rational, and compromising process in which alternatives and consequences are considered. It responds quite slowly to the popular temper. It is less empirical than the administrative edicts of a totalitarian system, and while often its delays may not only frustrate the reformer but, indeed, may too long postpone needed action, its errors are fewer and less disastrous. It is slower "to get rolling" but is more likely, we believe, to roll in the right direction.

A very significant aspect of the influence of public opinion in a democracy is that, since many divergent, often conflicting interests are represented, the need that is apparent or peculiar to some groups may disserve the wants of others. A large part of the criticism directed against the law results from the impatience of the critics whose values are not fully or quickly implemented. This may well be true, for example, in the area of white-collar "crimes" that have not been prohibited by the law. In a democracy that falls short of perfection, those with power and privilege may exert strong influence on legislation, sometimes preventing or delaying the establishment of policies appropriate to the needs of the majority. It is also true, on the other hand, that political and industrial democracy tends in large measure to protect the common weal and improve the lot of the majority, generally at the expense of the social elite. In conclusion one may say, relative to the role of public opinion, that it is a limiting and directing factor, both in legislation and in administration. However, there are many opinions of different publics and these are sometimes quite temporary phases of popular belief and of minority interests. Such opinion is unlikely to secure the passage or enforcement of legislation, particularly in the field of crime. The influence of the church over censorship and vice legislation is an outstanding exception.

Custom

Among the components of law, custom is one important ingredient. Sometimes customs are enacted into law. Often in the application of a fact situation to a legal rule, existing custom is consulted to determine the reasonableness of the defendant's behavior or whether, for example, the accused has been negligent. Custom, as traditionalized group behavior, is an important control over conduct in all human society. It has the support of public opinion and sanctions of group disapproval, which vary with the significance attached to the particular behavior. Some anthropologists, taking a broad view of social control in preliterate societies, have equated law with custom and taboo.[30] This is a confusing simplification of the matter. In the first place, a greater part of custom is too unimportant to group welfare to become crystallized into law. More important than this, however, is the fact that as certain customs deemed sufficiently vital to the

[30] William Seagle provides an effective analysis of the role of custom in the law and of the distinction between law and custom. See *The Quest for Law*, 1941, pp. 10 ff. He observes that "To fail to distinguish law and custom is to confuse the normative with the existential. . . . Primitive 'law' is customary law par excellence. Its only sanction lies in habit. With advances in political organization, however, customary law begins to break down rapidly, or rather its recognition begins to depend upon the sanctions of the political government. The 'customs' are thus rapidly translated into 'law' and thus enter upon a new existence." Compare Bronislaw Malinowski, *Crime and Custom in Savage Society*, 1936, and "A New Instrument for the Study of Law—Especially Primitive," *Yale L. J.*, vol. 51, p. 1237, 1944.

group are formulated into legal rules in cultures that have developed juridical controls, these norms take on a special character quite distinct from primitive customs in nonlegal society. They are more precise and technical. Procedures of formal proof are established, whether well or poorly designed to discover the facts. Sanctions are generally more sharply defined and more specifically allocated to offenses. Once these rules are established, group disapproval attaches not only to the breach of the norm but to the status of "criminal" itself. It is true, however, that as society becomes organized and as community and neighborhood relationships become secondary or anonymous and a large body of law accumulates, *both* the primary controls of public opinion and the formal law become less effective. Broad social-cultural changes are responsible for the increasing ineffectuality of social control. It is not that either law or public opinion are intrinsically weak devices for control but that any sort of social control becomes more difficult to exert.

Prelegal custom and law are similar in much the same sense that religion, magic, and medicine are similar. The latter has evolved in part from the former in each case, but with such transformations in the process that the product bears little resemblance to its source. The end result has a character of its own and produces distinct and different consequences both to the offender and to the community in the form of firmer and more diversified controls, professional specializations, distinct attitudes toward crime, and various other peculiarities. Moreover, while some customs are crystallized into laws and are thereby strengthened and perpetuated as customs, laws may also have the effect of establishing customs directly or indirectly. Thus, for example, civil rights legislation has begun to establish new patterns in the relationships of employers and personnel in hotels, restaurants, and other public places to minority group members. The wages and hours laws have had widely ramified implications for employer and employee behavior. Desegregation law is changing race relations and associated attitudes. Custom influences and is influenced by the law.

Morality

The morality of a people is an especially important ingredient of custom, that part of custom that is considered peculiarly essential to group welfare and to the highest values of the society. Mores exert highly significant influence upon the law but differ from law as a form of social control in important respects.[31] Many moral standards that are of the highest moment

---

[31] Seagle draws a major distinction between law and morals on the basis of the politicality of legal control and the relative fluidity of morals: " . . . law is a mode of regulating conduct by means of sanctions imposed by politically organized society. Law is 'normative'; that is, it prescribes rather than describes. But it not only indicates the range of allowable conduct; it is imperative in form and content. This imperative character is possessed by virtue of its sanctions,

to the group are not amenable to legal enactment or enforcement. There are several reasons for this. Most important, perhaps, the purposes of law and morality, while they overlap and reinforce each other, are not identical by any means. Supported by religion, morality strives toward the ideal, suggesting standards for man's reach that may be well beyond his grasp. It promises rewards and penalties that, as Professor Ross noted, are both unlimited in extent and quite inexpensive, though they relate to the distant and unknown future. It also establishes basic taboos, but both the commands and the prohibitions of morality are, for the most part, general and relatively vague rather than technically precise. Their enforcement is not standardized by established or formal methods of procedure and adjudication. Sanctions to ensure conformity, while they carry a heavy emotional freight, may be quite vague and tenuous, particularly under conditions of modern living.

As compared to morality, law is designed to ensure a sharper system of

---

which are threats of consequences in case of disobedience. Yet it is neither the imperative nor the normative aspects of law that give it its unique character. It is the fact that the sanction is applied exclusively by organized political government. This is what distinguishes law from religion, morals, and customs." *Op. cit.,* p. 7.

"Divergence of law and morality may be based on the fact that moral sentiments are not sufficiently well mobilized, or they may be changing. The law aims at least at some degree of definiteness and certainty, while moral values are fluid and shifting. It may perhaps be ventured that at least in secular societies the moral claims which are most likely to secure recognition are those which are coupled with an economic interest. But there must also be taken into consideration the fact that legal machinery is too cumbersome to justify efforts to give legal sanction to highly delicate moral values. The struggle against the liquor evil in the United States may be remembered as a recent case in point." *Ibid.,* p. 9.

Roscoe Pound in *Social Control through Law* suggests the major practical limitations precluding the successful achievement through law of everything that we should like as a matter of social ideals and ethical considerations:

"1. The difficulties involved in ascertainment of the facts to which legal precepts are to be applied. . . . All these devices to which we resort in order to prevent perjury do not enable us to act with assurance on the testimony of witnesses on which we must mainly rely for giving us the facts.

2. The intangibleness of many duties which morally are of great moment but defy legal enforcement.

3. Subtlety in the modes of seriously infringing important interests which the law would be glad to secure effectively if it might, as in the fields of domestic relations, rights of privacy.

4. The inapplicability of the legal machinery of rule and remedy to many phases of human conduct, to many important human relations, and to some serious wrongs (the duty, for example, of the husband and wife to live together, of the child to obey his parents).

5. The necessity of appealing to individuals to set the law in motion—which puts a special burden on legal administration of justice under Anglo-American democracy, for our policy depends on individual initiative to secure legal redress and enforce legal rules pretty largely." Pp. 54–62.

See also Cardozo, *The Paradoxes of Legal Science,* pp. 15–17.

control. It aims to be practicable and enforceable rather than ideal, to be technically definitive so as to make clearly evident what conduct is prohibited, to provide well-institutionalized and formal procedures of discovery and adjudication, and to apply specific and salutary sanctions for breach. Ultimately its design is to protect the public rather than to assure the salvation of souls. The latter is irrelevant to the function of the state as such. While the law must attempt to formulate and apply norms that will assure a minimum of good citizenship, it cannot seek the ideal of saintliness. That higher standard it is the function of the home and church to achieve by methods that make more intimate appeal to conscience and affection than the state can do.

It is not to be imagined, however, that the criminal law and mores are entirely distinct in operation. They are interdependent and mutually supportive to a large degree. Indeed the law depends, perhaps more heavily than it knows, upon conformity to the mores as a support to the standards of the state. It has been said that where the mores are adequate the laws are unnecessary, and if the mores are inadequate law is ineffective. This contention contains some truth as well as a large ingredient of error. The thoroughly "good man," who is motivated sufficiently to a high plane of personal conduct because of religious and family conditioning, requires the added and more immediate threat of stigma and punishment for crime little or not at all.[32] It may be cynical to believe that such individuals are rare in the twentieth century. Certain it is, however, that many persons require a combination of the undercurrent sense of moral guilt and the risk to social and occupational status, together with the more intense, often paramount fear that is stirred by the threatened sanctions of the state in order to assure their conformity. Many such individuals who "cross the line" and are discovered and convicted, thereby lose the deterrent influence of moral, social, and legal control, so that crime becomes thereafter an easy pattern of life. There are many individuals who are quite unaffected by moral considerations, who have little prestige or security to lose, but who will nevertheless conform much or all the time to the minimum standards of the criminal law primarily because it is dangerous to their comfort and security not to do so. Crime may pay in the single instance, but crimes do not, and the ordinary person knows that the ultimate risk is too great to justify the gamble. Even the repeating offender is deterred in greater or lesser measure in his criminal behavior, often indeed by his moral scruples and by the low status that attaches to certain specific criminal offenses.

Morality supports crime control therefore, but is itself bulwarked by the criminal law both through the educative influence of official prohibi-

---

[32] See O. W. Holmes, Jr., "The Path of the Law," *Harv. L. Rev.,* vol. 10, p. 457, 1897, for a discussion of the "bad man" who is concerned not with the platitudes of morality but with the disagreeable consequences that may attend the violation of law.

tions and the threatened risks for discovered violations. The relative effectuality of mores, public opinion, and law in deterring misconduct is undeterminable, but violation of the basic rules of the group invites penalties from each of these areas of control. The threat to the violator by the state and its legal sanctions is the strongest control, since criminal penalties threaten his moral and community status as well as his liberty. This is even more true as our society becomes increasingly urbanized and secularized. The effectiveness of pressures from the church, neighbors, and the community of friends is seriously diminished, and state controls are increasingly important. The path of wisdom as well as righteousness is clearly directed by the imminent presence of the cop, the court, and the correctional institution. With help from other social institutions, to be sure, but to an extent that many authorities are unwilling to recognize, the state keeps men "in line" today, and if its foreboding sanctions were removed or greatly diluted, one might reasonably anticipate the disaster of a vastly intensified struggle of man against his fellows.

Religious Influences

Before leaving the subject of morality and religious control, it should be noted further here that the content of the criminal law and the emotional support to its enforcement have come to a very large extent from the church. Among the numerous influences that have played a significant role in the origins and early implementation of the law and during virile periods in its later development, the church has made a prominent imprint upon criminal jurisprudence and upon correctional measures, too. The writer has summarized the historical role of religion and morality in criminal law elsewhere in these terms:[33]

Throughout human history religion has played a compelling role in relation to the criminal law. Among primitives the religious element is paramount, for fear of the supernatural has led the superstitious to a slavish obedience to the norms that are believed to be sanctioned by the tribal gods. Among preliterates the leaders have been priests as well as law givers, characteristically as a single function where tribal rules have been conceived to be no more than divine will. Even as law came to be institutionally differentiated from religion, the state continued to support group customs that bore also a supernatural sanction. Quite aptly it has been said, "Ancient law was a religion, a sacred text, and justice a collection of rites." Among the Greeks and Romans worship of the sacred hearth-fire and of heroes in the family line, sacrificial rites, and other religious duties were a central part of their familistic systems of law. Pontiffs of the church were learned in the law and, indeed, were for a considerable time the only jurisconsults of Rome. Matters of morality, family relations, wills, and property were considered an exclusively religious concern in early Roman history. And with the development of secularization in the law, "natural law"

[33] From the author's article on "Criminal Law" in *Collier's Encyclopedia*, 1959. (Reprinted by permission.)

doctrine perpetuated the authority of religious ideas through the thesis that there were eternal and immutable laws proceeding from the gods with which the civil governance of man must be in harmony: judges only seek to discover the inevitable and ordained will of the deities. Similar theories have had a remarkable vitality even to the present day in asserting a paramount law of God or of nature to be sought by earthly judges in their administration of justice.

An especially significant religious source in the evolution of criminal law may be traced through the old Mosaic law of the Hebrews. Here was established the basic and persistent philosophy of retribution for injury. In this tribal theocracy, revenge was supported through the solidarity of the family in the blood feud which called upon the kin of the victim to retaliate for the wrong. The rule of *Lex Talionis*, "An eye for an eye, and a tooth for a tooth," familiar in Babylonian as in later Hebraic law, was designed to limit the expression of familistic vengeance. The visiting of the sins of the father upon the children was a part of the Divine justice in the early law that gave way in an ethical revolution by the time of Ezekial to the establishment of the principle of individual responsibility.

The Christians were in conflict with the law and the state religion during the period of greatest Roman legal development. Out of opposition to the pagans and their judicial oaths the Church forbade its members to litigate in the courts. They built a powerful hierarchy of bishops, archbishops, and patriarchs to whose authority they looked in secular as well as spiritual matters. The sanctions of excommunication and partial exclusion, penance, scourging, pilgrimages, etc., were at first somewhat ineffective because the "law of penance" lacked both a system of criminal procedure and any real precision in its norms of forbidden conduct. After Christianity became the official religion of the State under Constantine, the Church came to enjoy larger legal powers, since the excommunicate might be prosecuted as well as a heretic. Moreover, there developed in the Church a definite system of criminal law, a special procedure more effective than the confessional, and distinct courts. Ecclesiastical pressure succeeded in conferring jurisdiction upon the church courts over the clergy in criminal cases. With the cooperation of civil authorities, unfree persons might be punished without limitation by the Church, and the State recognized Church jurisdiction over "delicta mixta" by omitting to prosecute crimes that had already been punished by the Church. Generally the laity preferred the milder ecclesiastical criminal justice in which the penalties were chiefly "poenae medicinales" intended by moral reformation to remedy the faults of the guilty. For those heretics who were weak in the faith, however, the Church could demand and secure from the State the most extreme penalties. Others, under the corrupting system of indulgences that developed, might purchase the forgiveness of their sins. A further power accrued to the Church through the "benefit of clergy" under the liberalized interpretation of which any literate might escape the secular courts into ecclesiastical jurisdiction. As a result of all this, the power of the canonical courts over criminal acts extended rapidly to include sex offences, marital relationships, and even many secular crimes as well as noncriminal matters of legitimacy, wills, contracts, and other property interests.

During the medieval period in England there was a repeated effort by crown and parliament to limit the benefit of clergy. After the reign of Henry VIII, statutes were passed "without benefit of clergy" and with the Protestant Reformation the ecclesiastical courts disappeared for a time but were reestablished in 1660. Successive acts of Parliament restricted their jurisdiction, however, and the common law courts employed writs of prohibition to restrain their action, so that by the beginning of the nineteenth century the canonical courts had lost their jurisdiction save for purely ecclesiastical matters and matrimonial and testamentary actions. Finally, in 1857, these powers too were transferred to secular courts. By this time, however, the authority which had accrued to church law during the long medieval phase of decadence in the Roman law, when no other coherent body of effective regulation existed, had established a persistent tradition of Mosaic retribution, religious moralism, and police measures greatly exceeding the appropriate limits of state interference.

Administrative Aspects

Commonly we consider legal norms only in terms of the substantive rules, even if we view them with deeper perspective than mere formal statutes. From the point of view of the law in action, however, the implementation is sometimes more important than the rule. It is not our purpose here to analyze in detail the role and operation of the functionaries of justice. These matters are discussed in later chapters. It must be noted, however, that whether enacted law will be applied, how generally it will be enforced, and the interpretation that will be attached to it depend very fundamentally not only on the constitution, custom, mores, and public opinion but also—reflecting these influences in part, of course—on the efficiency and the attitudes of police, prosecution, judges, and jurors. These agencies can and sometimes do nullify or distort the formal rule. They tend to do so particularly under the sway of public sentiments, which may be intense or indifferent, but individual biases, too, sometimes exert a quite excessive influence. The ultimate test of what the law is, as the "legal realists" have emphasized, is determined by the decision of the court and the facts of the particular case. This is itself affected largely by the actions of police and prosecution in bringing the defendant in and presenting evidence against him, by the immediate temper of the community and the more customary attitude toward the offense involved, and to a very considerable extent by the objective and judicious quality of the judge. It is probable that the state of the judge's digestion—so commonly used by contemporary realists as an explanation of the judicial process—has minute significance for the content or the administration of the law.

CONCLUSION

In this chapter it has been submitted that law is a unique form of social control, differing from but related to less formal types of regulation in its norms, enforcement procedures, and sanctions. Like most social norms, the law is relative and variable, but it is more stable and conservative than other forms of control are. Under conditions of modern society, as mores and public opinion have become decreasingly effective means of control, law has become relatively more and more important as a means to establish the minimal level of conformity required for social cohesion and community protection.

Crime causation will be discussed in later chapters. It may be noted here, however, that, since criminal norms are defined by and vary with a complex of social-cultural phenonema, one should not anticipate that different types of criminal conduct would reflect some single factor or set of factors, whether of a biological, psychological, or social variety. While there may be certain variables commonly recurring in relation to criminality, neither the single crime nor crimes in general can be considered to be rooted in a single causal explanation. Causes vary widely, as do crimes themselves.

Chapter 2

THE PREVALENCE AND DISTRIBUTION
OF CRIME

In Chapter 1 we concluded that crime is a matter of legal definition. Its occurrence is determined by legal adjudication. However antisocial particular conduct may be deemed, it is not "crime" in any meaningful sense unless and until it has been proscribed by the substantive criminal law. It may cease to be criminal if such law is changed. Under this definition, obviously, distinction may be drawn between (1) crimes, (2) acts that under some standard of normation should be made criminal, and (3) conduct that may be socially undesirable but that cannot be controlled reasonably and effectively by the criminal and penal law. No objective and accurate measurement can be made of the prevalence of behavior that falls in either of the two latter categories. The securing of data on crime, defined as conduct that is legally prohibited and officially adjudicated as such, presents difficult problems. It is possible to secure sufficiently accurate information, however, to make reasonably sound judgments on the prevalence and trends of criminal conduct and on the facilities required to cope with it.

CRIMES KNOWN TO THE POLICE

The most complete data available relate to crimes known to the police. The police make formal reports on these offenses as a result of complaints, observation, or information from which it can reasonably be concluded that a statutory violation has occurred. Such data leave something to be desired for a number of reasons. Often victims are at fault and fail to report. Some types of crimes, such as sex offenses, assaults, confidence and extortion rackets, are under reported by victims who wish to avoid publicity or reprisal. Many petty thefts and burglaries are not reported either because the victim is unaware of his loss or because he prefers to sustain a loss rather than suffer inconvenience with little hope of restitution. In many cases the victim of crime will not complain if the offender is a relative or close acquaintance. On the other hand, official complaints are made in some instances where in fact no crime has occurred. Reports of rape, incest, and sodomy are particularly unreliable. In other types of cases, too, complainants report erroneously that they have suffered a loss for any of a variety of reasons.

Inaccurate data on known crimes must also be attributed in part to the police. The reporting and recording practices of local departments and sheriffs have become more uniform over the past generation, largely through the persuasive influence of the Federal Bureau of Investigation in carrying out its mandate to collect national statistics.[1] Many policing agencies, however, do an inadequate statistical job because of lack of specialized attention to this task.[2] The efficiency of the police in discovering crimes is related to the adequacy of personnel and their enforcement policies. The latter varies from time to time, particularly in such areas of vice as gambling, prostitution, pornography, and the like, so that police reports may reflect temporary crusades of vigorous enforcement. Too, the police may be aware of certain crimes but may have some motive to avoid reporting them. This is because their efficiency is sometimes evaluated by the amount of disparity revealed in official reports on known crimes and crimes cleared by arrest. Police want, so far as possible, to secure arrest clearance on crimes they have reported.[3] In part because of the relatively inaccurate reporting on minor crimes, the FBI has in the past secured and

[1] By congressional order, the Federal Bureau of Investigation has acted as a clearing house for national police statistics since 1930. Until 1958 the Bureau published *Uniform Crime Reports* twice annually. The number of cooperating police agencies has increased regularly through the years, from 400 in 1930 to 6,808 in 1957. During the latter year, data were received from 3,857 urban police departments, 2,666 sheriffs, 14 state police departments, 259 law enforcement agencies in rural township and villages, and 12 police agencies outside the forty-eight states. These police agencies represented over 90 per cent of the urban population and about 68 per cent of the rural.

In accordance with the recommendations of a Consultant Committee on Uniform Crime Reporting in 1958, the Federal Bureau of Investigation has changed its reporting system in a number of important respects. Beginning in 1959, *Uniform Crime Reports* will be published only once each year, while quarterly the FBI will publish preliminary crime figures showing trends and numbers of major crimes reported in cities with populations over 100,000. Furthermore, the Bureau will exclude hereafter from its reporting of major crimes, negligent manslaughters (mainly traffic deaths), larcenies under $50, and statutory (nonforcible) rape, all of which are referred to in the text below. Consequently, data relating to 1958 and subsequent years will not be comparable to the earlier figures published by the Bureau. The data provided in this chapter are, in the main, for the year 1957, published in 1958, with comparisons to other years. Some of the data are drawn from the bulletin published in 1959.

[2] The FBI recognizes the variability in the completeness and correctness of the data they publish and, while the Bureau has found the reports received increasingly accurate, they print this caveat each year:

"In publishing the data sent in by chiefs of police in different cities, the FBI does not vouch for their accuracy. They are given out as current information which may throw some light on problems of crime and criminal-law enforcement."

[3] Thus, in New York City, for example, known crimes were collected on a precinct level until 1950 and the volume of offenses was grossly under reported until that time. Between 1949 and 1952, the FBI stated that since complete data were

recorded data from local departments relative to crimes known to the police only in connection with certain classes of major felonies listed in the tables below. On the other hand, the Federal agency publishes data on crimes cleared by arrest for all types of offense (with the exception of ordinary traffic violations). These reports provide limited information on the age, sex, and race of apprehended offenders. This material will be considered later in the chapter.

As suggested above, the FBI projects estimates on the major crimes each year for the entire country. The estimates for 1958 are presented in Table 1 below. An increase of 9.3 per cent over the previous year

Table 1. Estimated Number of Major Crimes in the United States, 1957–1958

Crime index classification	Estimated number of offenses		Change	
	1957	1958	Number	Per cent
Total...............	1,422,285	1,553,922	+131,637	+9.3
Murder..................	8,027	8,182	+155	+1.9
Forcible rape.............	12,886	14,561	+1,675	+13.0
Robbery..................	66,843	75,347	+8,504	+12.7
Aggravated assault.........	110,672	113,530	+2,858	+2.6
Burglary..................	603,707	679,787	+76,080	+12.6
Larceny over $50..........	354,972	391,550	+36,578	+10.3
Auto theft................	265,178	270,965	+5,787	+2.2

SOURCE: *Uniform Crime Reports,* 1958, p. 1.

brought the total number of major crimes to more than 1.5 million. It will be apparent at once from the data that property crimes (larceny, auto theft, burglary, and robbery) constitute the greatest police problem so far as numbers are concerned. The personal crimes, while much smaller in volume, are serious for their violence and have been increasing in frequency.

It should be observed that the major felonies on which information is provided in a new Crime Index, employed by the FBI for the first time in the publication of 1958 data (Table 1), differ somewhat from the classification of eight "Part I" felonies that have been reported in prior years. Manslaughter by negligence and statutory rape (where the victim is under the age of consent) have been omitted under the revised reporting scheme. Only thefts exceeding $50 in value of property stolen are included in the new index. A wide variety of behavior is covered by "aggravated assault," which includes assault with intent to kill and assaults by shooting,

---

not reported by New York City, the figures submitted by that city were not tabulated. A new police commissioner, Thomas Murphy, put the collection of statistics on a centralized basis after he came into office in 1950. As a consequence there was an apparent jump between 1948 and 1952 from 2,726 to 42,491 burglaries and from 7,713 to 70,949 thefts, as well as large increases in other felonies.

cutting, stabbing, maiming, poisoning, scalding, or by the use of acids. Robbery includes strong-arm robbery, stickups, armed robbery, assault to rob, and attempts to rob. Burglary includes housebreaking, safecracking, or any unlawful entry to commit a felony or a theft, and attempts to commit such acts. Auto theft covers both commercialized theft and "joy-riding." Tables below that are drawn from earlier issues of the Uniform Crime Reports show a larger volume of major crime than does the index now employed and the data are not comparable to those of 1958.

Urban Crime Rates and Trends

Table 2 presents urban crime rate data that reveal trends since 1941. The rates were computed on the basis of the number of crimes of each type committed per 100,000 inhabitants in the general population, thus

Table 2. Urban Crime Trends
(Offenses known to the police, January to December, inclusive, for selected years;
rates per 100,000 inhabitants in cities of all sizes)

Offense	1941	1945	1949	1953	1957
Murder, nonnegligent manslaughter.....	5.48	5.49	5.76	4.8	5.1
Manslaughter by negligence...........	4.54	4.39	3.32	3.6	3.5
Rape..............................	9.18	11.54	12.49	11.7	15.1
Robbery...........................	49.4	54.3	64.7	64.0	64.3
Aggravated assault.................	48.4	59.8	82.6	84.6	90.2
Burglary—breaking or entering........	332.0	359.3	419.1	409.9	502.9
Larceny—theft.....................	944.0	889.9	1023.4	988.1	1317.8
Auto theft........................	188.5	241.5	165.5	194.8	254.7

SOURCE: *Uniform Crime Reports,* Annual Bulletins, 1941, 1945, 1949, 1953, and 1957.

taking into account to some extent changes in size of population. The rates of the 1940s, however, are all based upon the 1940 census and those of the 1950s on the 1950 census, so that the rates of the latter part of each decade are inflated.[4] The years used in this and subsequent comparable tables in this chapter were selected to show, at reasonably brief class intervals, conditions in the major crime classifications as they existed in the prewar, peak-of-war, postwar, and more recent years. These rates reveal relatively little change during the period from 1941 to 1950, with the exception of small declines in manslaughter and car theft. Population changes are not revealed. In fact, if the data were adjusted to the increases that occurred in the general population, we would see that murder,

[4] In some jurisdictions, California being the best example, there was a startling drop in the published crime rates from 1949 to 1951. For example, burglary rates dropped from 756.8 to 523.5 and larceny rates from 2,122.2 to 1,669.4. This reflected the change in computation from a 1940 census base to 1950, a decade during which the California population increased 50 per cent. Since 1953, the FBI has noted the increase in population in its annual bulletins.

robbery, theft, and burglary remained relatively constant while rape and aggravated assault increased somewhat. The FBI analysis shows that during the decade of the forties crime increased only 11.8 per cent while the population increased 16.8 per cent.[5] Crimes against property decreased 5.7 per cent during that period, while crimes against the person increased

Table 3. City Crime Trends, 1937–1957
(Offenses known to the police in 353 cities with over 25,000 inhabitants; total population 42,719,693 based on 1950 decennial census)

Year	Total	Murder, non-negligent manslaughter	Manslaughter by negligence	Rape	Robbery	Aggravated assault	Burglary—breaking or entering	Larceny—theft	Auto theft
1937	605,447	2,479	1,978	3,047	26,696	19,841	137,757	325,974	87,675
1938	613,062	2,133	1,428	2,967	27,836	18,765	138,939	346,178	74,816
1939	637,514	2,223	1,229	3,235	26,347	19,063	145,208	369,442	70,767
1940	661,988	2,208	1,469	3,207	25,269	20,312	146,361	391,812	71,350
1941	661,132	2,295	1,852	3,513	24,212	20,736	138,043	393,615	76,866
1942	619,165	2,278	1,698	3,903	22,903	22,914	123,642	372,664	69,163
1943	604,554	2,030	1,428	4,349	22,636	22,126	127,368	342,337	82,280
1944	621,925	2,141	1,424	4,592	22,301	25,698	132,768	346,060	86,941
1945	702,720	2,361	1,723	3,042	27,671	28,026	156,835	375,488	105,574
1946	745,282	2,629	1,724	5,225	31,028	30,228	171,029	405,829	97,590
1947	708,014	2,535	1,481	5,268	29,395	31,004	164,709	396,798	76,824
1948	704,410	2,533	1,450	4,987	27,850	31,014	163,965	402,543	70,068
1949	734,925	2,332	1,308	5,137	29,693	32,144	173,312	422,583	68,416
1950	736,721	2,370	1,544	4,994	25,909	32,350	170,708	425,325	73,521
1951	779,458	2,302	1,557	5,306	26,086	31,884	169,209	457,977	85,137
1952	809,267	2,471	1,688	5,302	28,644	36,136	181,216	460,921	92,889
1953	845,208	2,439	1,599	5,449	31,813	38,064	191,339	476,771	97,734
1954	876,275	2,352	1,573	5,339	34,139	37,976	206,426	497,201	91,269
1955	884,682	2,410	1,643	5,910	30,675	38,785	202,660	505,011	97,588
1956	1,003,641	2,502	1,766	6,502	31,471	39,439	218,248	586,969	116,744
1957	1,096,337	2,533	1,722	6,752	34,641	39,833	247,845	632,215	130,796

SOURCE: *Uniform Crime Reports,* Annual Bulletin, 1957, Table 27.

29.5 per cent, mainly because of increases in the assault rate. Some part of the apparent increases may be accounted for by efforts of the FBI during this decade to obtain more complete figures on "cutting" fights in many local communities where these had not previously been handled as serious offenses. Table 3 shows that during the war years there was an

[5] *Uniform Crime Reports,* Annual Bulletin, 1955, p. 82.

Table 4. City Crime Rates,
(Offenses known to the police

Population group	Criminal homicide	
	Murder, nonnegligent manslaughter	Manslaughter by negligence
Total, Groups I–VI 3,276 cities; total population, 98,317,123:		
Number of offenses known.............................	4,380	2,794
Rate per 100,000...................................	4.5	2.8
Group I 45 cities over 250,000; population, 38,517,456:		
Number of offenses known.............................	2,428	1,482
Rate per 100,000...................................	6.3	3.8
5 cities over 1,000,000; population, 17,909,957:		
Number of offenses known.............................	1,022	463
Rate per 100,000...................................	5.7	2.6
8 cities, 750,000 to 1,000,000; population, 6,766,964:		
Number of offenses known.............................	533	256
Rate per 100,000...................................	7.9	3.8
9 cities, 500,000 to 750,000; population, 5,311,311:		
Number of offenses known.............................	321	316
Rate per 100,000...................................	6.0	5.9
23 cities, 250,000 to 500,000; population, 8,529,224:		
Number of offenses known.............................	552	447
Rate per 100,000...................................	6.5	5.2
Group II 85 cities, 100,000 to 250,000; population, 12,653,265:		
Number of offenses known.............................	662	471
Rate per 100,000...................................	5.2	3.7
Group III 173 cities, 50,000 to 100,000; population, 11,809,981:		
Number of offenses known.............................	420	338
Rate per 100,000...................................	3.6	2.9
Group IV 361 cities, 25,000 to 50,000; population, 12,603,836:		
Number of offenses known.............................	353	239
Rate per 100,000...................................	2.8	1.9
Group V 820 cities, 10,000 to 25,000; population, 12,934,621:		
Number of offenses known.............................	278	138
Rate per 100,000...................................	2.1	1.1
Group VI 1,792 cities under 10,000; population, 9,797,964:		
Number of offenses known.............................	239	126
Rate per 100,000...................................	2.4	1.3

SOURCE: *Uniform Crime Reports*, 1958, Table 8.

1958, by Population Groups
and rate per 100,000 inhabitants)

Forcible rape	Robbery	Aggravated assault	Burglary—breaking or entering	Larceny—theft		Auto theft
				$50 and over	Under $50	
8,266 8.4	60,356 61.4	78,957 80.3	471,007 479.1	295,659 300.7	909,808 925.4	215,070 218.8
5,349 13.9	43,282 112.4	50,677 131.6	230,022 597.2	155,978 405.0	339,368 881.1	120,937 314.0
3,078 17.2	23,688 132.3	28,411 158.6	105,171 587.2	87,962 491.1	117,628 656.8	44,949 251.0
807 11.9	7,607 112.4	10,914 161.3	38,564 569.9	20,978 310.0	75,963 1,122.6	28,444 420.3
494 9.3	4,482 84.4	3,665 69.0	30,107 566.8	14,681 276.4	47,790 899.8	19,176 361.0
970 11.4	7,505 88.0	7,687 90.1	56,180 658.7	32,357 379.4	97,987 1,148.8	28,368 332.6
856 6.8	6,543 51.7	10,085 79.7	72,459 572.7	40,076 316.7	150,322 1,188.0	32,732 258.7
669 5.7	4,173 35.3	7,090 60.0	53,783 455.4	35,484 300.5	118,445 1,002.9	22,291 188.7
506 4.0	2,739 21.7	4,297 34.1	47,137 374.0	29,639 235.2	124,087 984.5	17,570 139.4
492 3.8	2,238 17.3	4,219 32.6	41,765 322.9	21,860 169.0	116,292 899.1	13,893 107.4
394 4.0	1,381 14.1	2,589 26.4	25,841 263.7	12,622 128.8	61,294 625.6	7,647 78.0

actual decline in total felonies reported, with appreciable drops in robbery, burglary, and theft. This will be discussed later in an analysis of the relationship of age to crime.

The rates since 1950 reveal marked increases over those of the 1940s in burglary and theft. The rates for murder and manslaughter remained relatively stationary throughout the period, while rates for rape and assult, especially the latter, increased considerably. The *Annual Crime Reports* of 1956 painted a gloomy picture, indicating that for every 100 urban crimes just before World War II we then had 162. The increase may be accounted for in some part by the continuing improvement in crime reporting. Too, the consciousness of crime as a serious social problem has grown in recent years, undoubtedly resulting in greater police activity. The fact remains that we can account for an ostensible increase of more than 30 per cent in major crimes between 1950 and 1959 only on the basis of actual increases both in numbers and rates. Larceny and burglary have made up a great part of the recent increment in the total of felonious crimes.

Crime by Population Groups

The greatest part of the increase in crime rates over the past two decades may be traced to two phenomena: urbanization and the growing delinquency of young people. The first of these will be discussed here, the latter under the analysis of arrest rates. Table 4 breaks down the 1957 crime rates for major offenses by population groups. There are several points of interest in the data. The popular conception is that high crime rates are characteristic of large cities and that there is a tendency for crime rates to increase or decrease according to population size. Nevertheless the figures appear to show that more of the serious crimes are committed in cities with populations from 100,000 to 250,000 than in cities over 1,000,000 and that cities with populations from 750,000 to 1,000,000 have higher crime rates generally than do the largest metropolises. These differences may be accounted for in some measure by the different ways of discovering and reporting crimes. It is also interesting to note that, except for burglary and the larcenous offenses, crime rates are apparently higher in the rural areas than in small cities.[6] More significant, in terms of differential crime rates, is the fact that since 1944, when the FBI started providing trend data on rural crimes, the rates reported from rural areas have increased more rapidly than the urban rates. The rate of increase has been approximately twice as great during nine of the fourteen years. It seems reasonable to infer from these data as well as from other trends in rural society that the process of cultural urbanization of rural areas has been accompanied by a rather rapid criminalization of the hinterland. Increases in the "city crimes" of burglary and larceny have

[6] In 1957 the rural reporting area covered a total population of over 40 million.

been especially marked in some of these years. Country areas have far to go, however, to achieve the rates that prevail in the large cities.

Seasonal Variations

The *Uniform Crime Reports* reveal monthly and seasonal variations in rates for each of the major felonies. The patterns are quite consistent

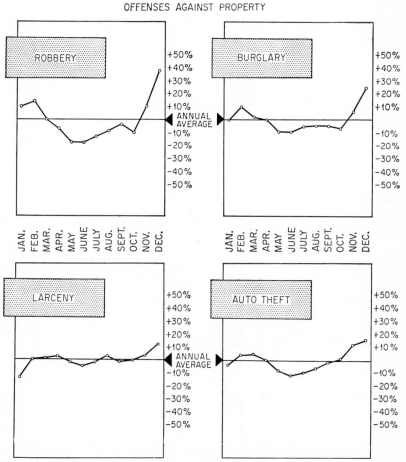

OFFENSES AGAINST PROPERTY

FIGURE 1. Monthly variations, offenses against property. (*Uniform Crime Reports, Annual Bulletin, 1957, Fig. 13.*)

from year to year. Marked deviations in the pattern that sometimes occur, however, suggest the influence of other than seasonal factors. Characteristic seasonal variations are found in the 1957 crime data, illustrated in Figures 1 and 2. It will be observed that, in general, crimes against the person are at their height during the summer months, while crimes against property show opposite seasonal trends, being highest during the cooler period of the year. Certain of the crimes, notably robbery, burglary, rape, and aggravated assault, display more marked and consistent relationship to seasonal factors than do the others.

Murder, assault, and rape are warm-weather crimes, their peaks occurring characteristically between July and September. The long, warm

OFFENSES AGAINST THE PERSON

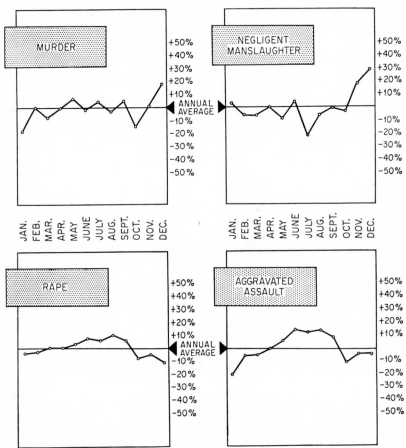

FIGURE 2. Monthly variations, offenses against the person. (*Uniform Crime Reports, Annual Bulletin, 1957, Fig. 12.*)

days of the third quarter of the year encourage more social contacts of men and greater opportunity, therefore, for crimes of personal aggression. Perhaps climatic factors have significant influence upon temper and emotions, as some climatologists have maintained. Quite commonly murder and assault show an upswing in December and in some years (e.g., 1951, 1955, 1956, 1957, 1958) the high for murder occurs during that month. In contrast to other crimes against the person, negligent manslaughter is lowest during the summer months and rises usually to a high peak in November and December. This category is composed very largely of traffic deaths, so that it appears quite natural that it should be most prevalent during the time of year when early darkness and road conditions make driving most hazardous. Strangely, however, there is a sharp decline in such fatalities during January.

The low points for robbery, burglary, and auto theft occur regularly during the summer months, between May and September, reaching their height in the season from December to February. Sometimes auto theft is low after the start of the year. The range in the seasonal variation is often very marked in robbery. Larceny displays the least well-defined pattern of seasonal variation among the major crimes. Generally it runs from a low point at the start of the year, gradually increasing until it reaches its peak in the late fall. More than the other classes of crime, however, larceny is a conglomerate of offenses differing considerably in character. The FBI has found over some years that purse snatching, shoplifting, and thefts from cars are most frequent during October to March, while bicycle thefts are lowest during this period. Pocket picking reaches a peak at the end of the year but is low at the beginning of the year. The theft of auto accessories is highest in the early months of the year and lowest in December.[7] One may reasonably hypothesize that the prevalence of the property crimes in the winter months is related both to the opportunities that this season provides for predatory crimes and to the more acute material needs for food and shelter.

State and Regional Variations

Table 5 reveals that crime rates vary by sections of the country as well as by degree of urbanization. The two are undoubtedly interrelated in some measure, but state and regional variations appear to reflect other influences as well, such as the age, sex, and racial structure of the population, economic activities and standards, and climatic and other factors.[8] States and regions differ considerably in their cultural content and this is reflected in very considerable measure in varying crime rates. Indeed, the range of variation in crime rates from one region to another is wider than any range of variation we have observed between the population groups of varying size. The differences between the extremes in individual states is

[7] *Uniform Crime Reports,* Annual Bulletin, 1953, p. 85.

[8] The FBI lists the following as factors that may effect the amount of crime in a community: "The composition of the population with reference particularly to age, sex, and race; the economic status and activities of the population; climate; educational, recreational, and religious facilities; the number of police employees per unit of population; the standards governing appointments to the police force; the policies of the prosecuting officials and the courts; the attitude of the public toward law-enforcement problems; the degree of efficiency of the local law-enforcement agency."

Table 5. City Crime Rates, 1957, by Geographic Divisions and States
(Offenses known per 100,000 inhabitants; population based on 1950 decennial census)

Division and state	Murder, nonnegligent manslaughter	Robbery	Aggravated assault	Burglary— breaking or entering	Larceny —theft	Auto theft
United States.....	5.1	64.3	90.2	502.9	1,317.8	254.7
New England..........	1.4	19.5	21.9	329.6	849.3	222.6
Connecticut........	2.1	19.2	39.4	370.7	804.3	173.3
Maine............	1.2	9.1	12.4	225.7	1,034.1	126.7
Massachusetts.......	1.3	22.9	18.2	318.7	817.0	263.6
New Hampshire....	0.4	2.8	2.8	181.3	658.7	80.9
Rhode Island.......	1.2	14.8	25.2	451.3	1,127.1	200.8
Vermont..........	0.9	2.8	.....	138.9	678.7	96.7
Middle Atlantic........	3.1	49.9	83.4	389.4	818.7	178.2
New Jersey........	2.7	49.1	63.9	467.9	855.4	230.2
New York........	3.2	45.9	96.1	381.4	874.7	167.1
Pennsylvania......	3.1	57.9	70.6	358.2	688.7	170.7
East North Central.......	4.7	82.3	70.7	392.5	1,221.5	204.3
Illinois.............	6.0	123.6	78.1	343.7	746.1	133.4
Indiana............	3.9	49.8	50.7	486.5	1,496.1	291.9
Michigan..........	4.1	95.1	132.9	534.6	1,735.4	292.2
Ohio..............	4.9	60.4	39.7	375.3	1,263.6	205.3
Wisconsin..........	1.7	10.6	18.3	190.1	1,281.1	152.5
West North Central......	3.6	59.6	53.9	435.6	1,381.5	214.0
Iowa..............	1.2	15.0	9.0	342.0	1,278.6	115.8
Kansas............	4.1	39.5	59.3	500.5	1,682.4	139.8
Minnesota.........	1.0	38.7	8.8	402.7	1,251.9	188.0
Missouri...........	7.3	126.5	123.1	572.1	1,487.5	334.7
Nebraska..........	2.7	17.6	30.5	247.9	1,153.7	197.4
North Dakota.......	....	11.0	8.4	209.8	1,502.2	190.4
South Dakota.......	1.7	6.6	0.6	184.4	1,067.2	71.5
South Atlantic*.........	10.2	61.4	197.7	613.7	1,484.2	273.7
Delaware.........	8.4	56.2	27.4	607.3	1,694.8	252.3
Florida............	11.6	87.5	113.6	1,093.9	2,198.5	303.4
Georgia...........	13.9	44.5	137.0	590.4	1,366.4	257.3
Maryland..........	8.1	75.3	216.2	394.7	1,158.2	445.5
North Carolina......	12.3	28.7	354.7	487.2	1,266.1	186.8
South Carolina......	9.1	32.8	104.6	613.5	1,612.4	195.9
Virginia...........	9.2	63.5	203.6	642.6	1,731.1	292.7
West Virginia......	3.7	33.3	60.4	269.0	713.4	126.4
East South Central.......	12.6	42.6	113.8	549.2	1,037.6	280.0
Alabama..........	16.2	36.6	125.2	518.7	975.9	209.1
Kentucky..........	8.6	70.2	124.5	642.7	1,267.9	520.1
Mississippi.........	12.9	20.6	103.9	365.9	851.6	107.6
Tennessee..........	12.2	36.9	99.8	584.9	1,002.7	240.6

Table 5. City Crime Rates, 1957, by Geographic Divisions and States (Continued)

Division and state	Murder, nonnegligent manslaughter	Robbery	Aggravated assault	Burglary—breaking or entering	Larceny —theft	Auto theft
West South Central......	9.2	51.2	102.7	690.0	1,658.1	334.6
Arkansas...........	7.6	33.3	131.6	453.9	1,111.6	133.4
Louisiana.........	9.6	78.3	94.5	539.9	1,171.7	507.2
Oklahoma........	3.6	34.5	40.0	644.1	1,773.3	251.5
Texas.............	10.6	49.0	116.4	769.0	1,830.5	324.4
Mountain.............	4.7	76.4	55.4	704.8	2,488.9	403.3
Arizona..........	13.9	114.6	182.5	1,152.7	3,935.0	811.3
Colorado.........	3.9	120.7	47.7	813.7	2,076.4	416.4
Idaho............	3.7	18.8	14.7	405.3	2,284.4	154.2
Montana..........	2.6	29.2	25.8	335.3	2,221.9	261.4
Nevada...........	7.5	142.0	67.3	1,107.9	3,674.8	483.9
New Mexico.......	7.0	49.0	66.2	920.4	3,426.1	685.1
Utah.............	1.1	52.8	34.5	524.3	2,149.5	222.1
Wyoming..........	2.9	43.7	21.8	371.3	1,536.9	170.4
Pacific...............	4.2	115.0	118.6	895.0	2,468.1	482.1
California.........	4.5	130.7	144.3	976.4	2,561.5	523.1
Oregon...........	3.6	53.9	34.2	536.3	1,976.4	261.6
Washington........	2.9	60.7	19.8	637.6	2,219.0	375.0

* Includes the District of Columbia.

SOURCE: *Uniform Crime Reports,* Annual Bulletin, 1957, Table 31.

even greater. There are, moreover, large differences between states in the several regions, so that while there is some measure of homogeneity in the crime rates of certain regions, such as New England, the Middle Atlantic, the East South Central, and the Mountain states, state-to-state variations appear to be of greater significance.

One notable aspect of regional differences in crime rates lies in the relationship between types of crime and climatic conditions, a relationship that appears to be generally similar to the one existing between season and crime. Rates for aggressive crimes against the person, murder, nonnegligent manslaughter, and assault, are greatest in the southern sections of the country. Homicide has occurred most frequently for a number of years in the East South Central states, with especially high rates in Alabama and Tennessee. Georgia, however, has had the highest rate in the country for several years. Aggravated assault has occurred most frequently, in proportion to the population, in the South Atlantic states, especially in North Carolina. On the other hand, the rates have been low for the aggressive crimes in the northern regions of the country, especially in New England. All crime rates have tended to be low in Maine, Vermont, and New Hampshire during the period that the FBI made its reports.

Property crimes, too, have been surprisingly low in rate, though high in volume, in the populous New England and Middle Atlantic states. Robbery, burglary, and car theft have been most prevalent in the Pacific states. The high rates of these crimes in California suggests the influence of the rapid changes that have gone on in that state, both in urbanization and population increases. The rates may also reflect the fact that California provides the most accurate and complete crime statistics in the United States. It should be observed, however, that while the robbery rate has been very high in California, that of Nevada has exceeded it. Similarly, while the California burglary rate has exceeded the national average by nearly 100 per cent, the rates in Nevada, Florida, and Arizona, have been considerably higher. The California car theft rate was surpassed by Arizona and New Mexico. Ordinary larceny, in its various forms, was highest in rate in the Mountain states in 1957. Arizona and Nevada have had higher larceny rates than California in recent years. National crime figures would have been more than twice as high if the rates observed in these states had prevailed generally.

CRIMES CLEARED BY ARREST

Arrest data are more reliable in some respects than are records on crimes known to the police. Theoretically all arrests result in formal bookings that are easy to tabulate for summary reports. In fact, arrest practices vary in different jurisdictions, as we shall observe in Chapter 11. In some cities a considerable number of individuals who, from the point of view of legal definition, have been arrested are not booked by the police on any formal charge and may be released, therefore, without official record of the transaction. Since 1953, however, the FBI has endeavored to secure information on all cases held by the police, even where persons are released without a court appearance and where juveniles are charged merely with delinquency.[9] This has undoubtedly improved the accuracy of reporting. The arrest data provide information regarding age, sex, race, and, until 1952, prior criminal record. The Bureau has secured and published such data not only in relation to major crimes, which we have discussed above, but to a supplementary group of lesser offenses that include all other law violations except minor traffic offenses. These appear in Table 6. Significant differences should be noted, however, between arrest data and the figures on crimes known to the police, which we have discussed above. The two types of information are not fully comparable. On the one hand, a single crime known to the police may result in some instances in a number of arrests and, on the other, the arrest of a single individual may clear a number of crimes that he has committed. Where juvenile and youth gang activities are involved, arrests on suspicion may mount when there is no

[9] *Uniform Crime Reports,* Annual Bulletin, 1954, p. 108.

crime known to the police. Similarly, ex-convicts, parolees, and other suspicious characters may be rounded up in considerable numbers without adequate legal justification. In some jurisdictions these pickups are recorded in the official data; elsewhere they are not. It should be observed that arrests for petty offenses, such as intoxication, disorderly conduct, and vagrancy, which constitute so large a part of all arrests, are poor indexes of crime and that reporting practices in these areas are still very defective. Statistics on arrest for minor offenses reveal more about police practices than about the volume of crime.

Juvenile Delinquency

Juvenile delinquency statistics are less complete and less reliable than statistics on crimes for a variety of reasons. Police data are of little value because there is a wide variation in local practices in dealing with juveniles and because a substantial proportion of delinquency petitions are initiated by parents and agencies other than the police.[10] It has been estimated by the U.S. Children's Bureau that about 1.7 million juveniles, roughly 5 per cent of all children in the ages between 10 and 17, come to the attention of the police for misbehavior each year.[11] Approximately three-quarters of these cases are handled directly by the police without referral to courts, and presumably many, if not most, of such cases are not delinquent in any significant sense.[12] Data on arrest by age groups, as reported in *Uniform Crime Reports* for 1958, are given in Table 6. Only about 10 per cent of all the persons arrested were under the age of 17. The data on arrests are heavily weighted by minor offenses, however, which are more characteristic of the mature in age. The areas of specialization in juvenile and youthful offences appear in Tables 6 and 7. They are burglary, larceny, and car theft, typically youthful and urban offenses. On the other hand, it will be observed that young people commit only a small proportion of the aggressive and dangerous crimes, such as homicide, rape, and assault. Few are arrested for drunkenness or the other vices, such as gambling and narcotics. With so much public concern about the involvement of the young in the use and sale of drugs, the latter point is of some special interest. In 1957 only ninety individuals under the age of 17 were arrested in the reporting area for narcotic violations.

Court data also provide a poor index of the volume and nature of juvenile misconduct, in part because delinquency is so vaguely defined in law and in the policy and practice of children's courts. Statistics collected by the Children's Bureau for 1945 revealed that 41 per cent of boys' cases

[10] In 1945, 71 per cent of juvenile court cases were referred by the police. Among girls, however, only 52 per cent were so referred. *Social Statistics,* U.S. Children's Bureau, 1945, p. 11.

[11] I. Richard Perlman, "Delinquency Prevention: The Size of the Problem," *The Annals,* vol. 332, p. 3, March, 1959.

[12] *Social Statistics, loc. cit.*

Table 6. Arrests by Age Groups, 1958; 1,586 Cities over 2,500, Total Population 52,329,497

Offense charged	Total	Age Under 15	15	16	17	18	19	20	21	22
Total...................................	2,340,004	106,892	52,776	62,240	62,307	63,109	58,424	54,267	58,762	55,691
Criminal homicide:										
(a) Murder and nonnegligent manslaughter.....	2,303	17	19	44	50	57	59	71	70	74
(b) Manslaughter by negligence........	1,166	12	7	29	30	45	46	33	34	49
Robbery...........................	14,968	980	637	836	962	1,080	1,060	941	864	744
Aggravated assault..................	25,824	670	393	599	678	767	732	760	819	847
Other assaults.....................	82,454	2,050	1,153	1,556	1,762	2,299	2,358	2,400	2,810	2,989
Burglary—breaking or entering.........	61,045	13,768	5,765	6,023	4,904	3,923	2,985	2,341	2,135	1,807
Larceny—theft......................	118,325	28,584	9,988	10,576	8,241	6,468	4,647	3,547	3,008	2,784
Auto theft.........................	30,240	5,018	5,666	5,368	3,334	2,053	1,491	1,052	795	665
Embezzlement and fraud..............	19,489	186	75	76	140	274	352	426	495	601
Stolen property; buying, receiving, etc....	5,504	685	287	370	358	303	286	221	202	193
Forgery and counterfeiting............	11,317	121	128	235	283	375	396	412	467	506
Forcible rape.......................	3,680	108	123	214	237	297	289	241	213	204
Prostitution and commercialized vice.....	17,482	27	25	46	97	261	483	492	790	946
Other sex offenses (includes statutory rape).	24,517	1,618	867	923	859	861	852	846	901	966
Narcotic drug laws..................	9,863	43	44	106	183	290	347	434	446	480
Weapons; carrying, possessing, etc.....	18,611	726	640	849	857	886	838	726	812	790
Offenses against family and children....	23,701	101	36	59	95	422	513	573	780	877
Liquor laws........................	52,707	711	1,337	2,955	4,491	4,544	4,174	3,353	1,099	964
Driving while intoxicated.............	102,219	11	18	186	403	857	1,274	1,685	2,446	2,648
Disorderly conduct..................	281,997	9,158	4,923	6,368	7,316	10,614	10,019	9,455	10,572	9,803
Drunkenness.......................	908,957	655	998	2,240	3,855	6,652	7,812	8,855	12,855	13,174
Vagrancy..........................	88,351	765	675	1,409	1,739	2,752	2,382	1,979	2,219	1,942
Gambling..........................	61,546	94	107	129	245	481	611	779	1,115	1,202
Suspicion..........................	96,740	3,659	2,770	4,131	7,019	7,099	5,720	4,798	4,735	4,119
All other offenses...................	276,998	37,115	16,095	16,913	14,169	9,439	8,698	7,847	8,080	7,317

50

Table 6. Arrests by Age Groups, 1958; 1,586 Cities over 2,500, Total Population 52,329,497 (Continued)

Offense charged	Total	Age								
		23	24	25–29	30–34	35–39	40–44	45–49	50 and over	Not known
Total	2,340,004	54,576	55,610	260,117	279,461	275,803	239,538	211,998	387,049	384
Criminal homicide:										
(a) Murder and nonnegligent manslaughter	2,303	68	64	369	363	291	231	158	297	1
(b) Manslaughter by negligence	1,166	42	31	189	165	145	95	62	152	
Robbery	14,968	696	629	2,403	1,537	796	389	197	215	2
Aggravated assault	25,824	867	884	4,259	3,878	3,390	2,283	1,676	2,322	
Other assaults	82,454	2,966	3,200	14,616	13,423	10,782	7,236	4,792	6,054	8
Burglary—breaking or entering	61,045	1,680	1,435	5,452	3,710	2,203	1,307	787	814	6
Larceny—theft	118,325	2,350	2,225	9,003	7,500	5,735	4,233	3,312	6,094	30
Auto theft	30,240	495	656	1,485	1,018	638	341	184	193	12
Embezzlement and fraud	19,489	643	656	3,545	3,884	3,085	2,051	1,380	1,620	
Stolen property; buying, receiving, etc.	5,504	149	141	609	518	411	289	219	263	
Forgery and counterfeiting	11,317	483	434	2,068	1,988	1,442	843	506	630	
Forcible rape	3,680	180	143	536	351	239	124	85	96	
Prostitution and commercialized vice	17,482	940	997	3,892	2,939	2,142	1,342	933	1,128	2
Other sex offenses (includes statutory rape)	24,517	855	816	3,696	3,001	2,484	1,729	1,161	2,078	4
Narcotic drug laws	9,863	525	561	2,595	1,776	892	445	312	384	
Weapons; carrying, possessing, etc.	18,611	712	658	2,784	2,217	1,832	1,155	896	1,233	2
Offenses against family and children	23,701	963	926	4,953	4,599	3,556	2,361	1,384	1,501	2
Liquor laws	52,707	928	981	4,180	4,502	4,591	4,059	3,620	6,216	2
Driving while intoxicated	102,219	2,651	2,865	13,795	15,490	15,613	13,900	11,298	17,077	
Disorderly conduct	281,997	8,924	8,884	40,295	38,443	33,103	25,111	19,331	29,649	29
Drunkenness	908,957	13,616	14,693	80,088	110,696	131,874	129,001	125,630	246,014	249
Vagrancy	88,351	1,909	1,890	8,250	9,550	10,295	9,912	9,484	21,182	7
Gambling	61,546	1,349	1,419	8,018	9,686	9,204	7,849	6,767	12,485	6
Suspicion	96,740	3,574	3,538	13,450	10,298	7,297	5,068	3,847	5,597	11
All other offenses	276,998	7,011	7,108	29,587	27,929	23,763	18,184	13,977	23,755	11

SOURCE: *Uniform Crime Reports*, 1958, Table 17.

51

and 79 per cent of girls' were brought before the courts for such minor misconduct as carelessness or mischief, truancy, running away, ungovernability, and petty sex offenses.[12a] There are no more recent national data on the reasons for referral. A large proportion of children's cases, 52 per cent in 1956, are handled unofficially, without a determination of the fact of delinquency.[13] How many of these were truly delinquent is a conjectural matter. While it appears that many children who are taken to court have not been involved in serious offenses, there is a very large incidence of delinquency that does not come to the attention of the courts. Public and

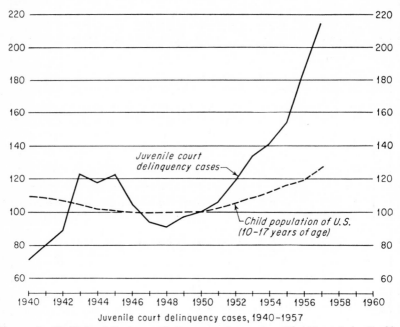

Juvenile court delinquency cases, 1940–1957

FIGURE 3. (*I. Richard Perlman, Delinquency Prevention: The Size of the Problem, The Annals, vol. 322, p. 3, March, 1959.*)

private social agencies deal with more children guilty of minor breaches of law than do the courts.[14] Research evidence indicates, moreover, that many cases of delinquency, including serious violations, are undetected.[15]

[12a] *Ibid.*

[13] *Juvenile Court Statistics,* 1956, p. 3.

[14] A Children's Bureau study of delinquents in five public agencies in the District of Columbia concluded that only 43 per cent of delinquent children dealt with by those agencies were known to the juvenile court. The agencies had dealt with 98 per cent of the cases of running away, 95 per cent of truancy, 76 per cent of sex offenses, 46 per cent of ungovernability, 23 per cent of carelessness or mischief, 21 per cent of assault and injury to the person, and 20 per cent of stealing. Edward E. Schwartz, "A Community Experiment in the Measurement of Delinquency," *Nat. Prob. Assoc. Yearbook,* pp. 157–182, 1945.

[15] See Austin L. Porterfield, *Youth in Trouble,* 1946, pp. 37–51; Fred J. Murphy,

In spite of their limitations, juvenile court statistics provide the most useful information available on the extent and trend of delinquency.[16] Since the Children's Bureau has been collecting such data for more than thirty years, there is some uniformity in reporting by the courts. On the basis of a national sample of more than five hundred reporting courts, the Bureau concludes that over 600,000 cases of delinquency were referred to children's courts in 1957, involving an estimated ½ million different children, or about 2.3 per cent of all individuals between the ages of 10 and 17.[17] The size of the problem may be judged somewhat more realistically, however, by the total frequency of cases that will become involved in court delinquency during the 8-year age span. The Bureau's Chief of Juvenile Delinquency Statistics estimates on the basis of 1957 rates that this will amount to about 12 per cent for both sexes and 20 per cent for boys alone.[18]

The official data indicates a steep upward trend in juvenile delinquency cases since 1950. The volume of cases more than doubled during the period from 1948 to 1958, while the child population increased a little more than 20 per cent. Since it is predicted that the age group from 10 to 17 will increase by nearly 50 per cent between 1954 and 1965, it is reasonable to believe that children's courts may handle a million or more alleged delinquents annually by the latter date if present trends of conduct and court policy continue. The chart shown on the facing page indicates the trend since 1940.[19]

Youth and Crime

Tables 6 and 7 show that young adults aged 18 and over are more often involved than juveniles in assault, robbery, rape, and homicide and that they are less frequently involved in burglary, larceny, and car theft. In fact, individuals in the age range from 18 to 25 are more frequently arrested than persons of any other age, and they contribute disproportionately to the more serious felonies. There have been significant changes in the arrest rates of young adults, however, during the years that the FBI has tabulated

Mary M. Shirley, and Helen L. Witmer, "The Incidence of Hidden Delinquency," *Am. J. Orthopsychiat.*, vol. 16, pp. 686–696, 1946; James F. Short, Jr., "A Report of the Incidence of Criminal Behavior, Arrests, and Convictions in Selected Groups," *Proc. Pacific Sociol. Soc.*, pp. 110–119, 1954; James S. Wallertstein and Clement J. Wyle, "Our Law-abiding Law-breakers," *Prob.*, vol. 25, pp. 107–112, March-April, 1947.

[16] See Perlman, "Reporting Juvenile Delinquency," *N.P.P.A.*, vol. 3, pp. 242–249, July, 1957.

[17] Perlman, "Delinquency Prevention: The Size of the Problem," *loc. cit.*

[18] *Ibid.*

[19] During the period 1940–1951, police arrest data displayed a very closely similar trend. Since 1951 the revision of fingerprint record procedure of the FBI has made its data incomparable to the preceding period.

Table 7. Percentage of arrests of persons under 18, 18–21,

Offense	1941				1945			
	Under 18	18–21	21–25	Total arrests	Under 18	18–21	21–25	Total arrests
Homicide...........	2.9	10.1	16.3	6,628	6.0	8.6	13.7	5,381
Aggravated assault....	2.7	9.3	15.4	37,826	3.9	8.6	14.8	43,006
Robbery............	8.5	24.5	23.0	12,165	12.8	22.4	23.4	14,795
Rape...............	6.6	21.2	20.7	5,930	11.8	18.3	18.1	6,702
Burglary............	22.1	24.5	16.5	30,037	29.5	20.3	15.6	29,303
Larceny............	13.8	19.5	15.8	58,396	16.3	17.2	16.1	50,560
Auto theft.........	26.9	30.7	17.9	14,057	33.2	27.9	19.2	17,789
Arrests, all offenses...	5.9	11.7	13.9	630,568	9.1	11.9	14.6	543,852

data on the subject. During the period prior to World War II, the age of most frequent arrest in the United States was 20 or higher. In 1939–1941, 19 was the modal age of arrest and in 1942 and 1943 it dropped to 18. Arrests were most frequent at 17 in 1944–1945 but the modal age rose to 21 in 1946, and during the ensuing years it has remained at that level or higher for the most part. In 1958, however, the ages of most frequent arrest were 18, 17, 16, and 21, in that order. These changes reflect war influences in part, for juvenile arrests accelerated during the period from 1942 to 1945, while arrests in the age group from 18 to 21 dropped somewhat during the period when this age group was drafted into the services. Juvenile arrests were below the prewar level after 1946 for a brief interval, while arrests of offenders between 18 and 20 and between 21 and 25 increased sharply for a time.

In Table 7 above we have computed data from the FBI reports that show the percentages of arrests for major felonies for each of certain youthful age groups in several selected years. These data do not reveal changes in rates from year to year, as such, for the FBI figures are based upon a different reporting base for successive years.[20] Moreover, as the *Uniform Crime Reports* point out, their age, sex, and race statistics since 1952 have been more complete than statistics previously gathered. Recent data have been based on special arrest forms rather than on fingerprint arrest cards.[21] This means that the figures since that date are more accurate, especially in relation to offenders under 18 years of age who, as noted above, have been under represented in official statistics. How appreciably this has affected the completeness of reporting on major felonies,

[20] Total arrest figures for the offense categories are given for these years, however, so that the arrest data may be computed for each age from the percentage figures to discover the actual arrests reported.

[21] *Uniform Crime Reports,* Annual Bulletin, 1953, p. 108.

and 21–25 and totals of arrests, for selected years and crimes

1949				1953				1957			
Under 18	18–21	21–25	Total arrests	Under 18	18–21	21–25	Total arrests	Under 18	18–21	21–25	Total arrests
3.3	8.6	16.4	6,436	4.0	8.7	13.9	3,390	6.3	8.8	11.9	3,245
1.7	8.4	17.2	58,870	6.0	7.3	13.2	21,114	9.0	7.9	13.3	23,266
6.0	20.1	27.4	21,623	18.0	18.4	20.6	11,786	26.4	18.3	19.6	11,820
6.8	23.6	24.2	9,449	16.2	21.6	18.2	4,023	19.5	24 6	20.9	4,780
16.2	22.0	21.3	45,892	49.3	13.9	11.7	36,879	54.8	13.2	10.2	51,398
8.7	16.9	19.2	67,647	40.1	11.1	9.9	68,195	51.3	11.1	8.0	102,476
18.1	25.7	23.2	19,119	53.6	16.2	11.2	20,391	67.6	13.0	7.5	29,121
4.2	10.6	16.4	792,029	8.4	6.3	10.2	1,791,160	12.3	7.0	9.7	2,068,677

SOURCE: *Uniform Crime Reports, Annual Bulletins,* 1941, 1945, 1949, 1953, 1957.

it is impossible to say. It may well be that the apparently very large increases in the proportion of certain crimes shown to have been committed
by juvenile offenders exaggerate the actual changes. It is possible that during the period prior to 1952 youngsters under 18 were responsible for a
considerably larger proportion of the property crimes than the data then
revealed. Certainly ostensible changes in crime trends may actually reflect
altered police practices of investigation, arrest, and reporting. In any event
it appears from the table that arrests of youths under 18 have constituted
not only a very large but, since 1949, a rapidly increasing part of arrests
throughout the country for all major types of crime, especially for assault,
burglary, theft, and car theft. The increases have been particularly marked
in the age groups of 16 and below. On the other hand, in the age group
from 18 to 21 the proportion of felony arrests, after dropping during the
war years and rising for a brief time thereafter, has continued to decline
since 1948. Except for the violent crimes, the decline in the proportion of
arrests in this age group was substantial between 1949 and 1958, particularly for crimes of burglary and car theft.[22] The proportion of arrests in
the age group from 21 to 25 decreased during the war period, regained and
passed its prewar level in 1946, but has declined even more rapidly than
the 18- to 21-year group since 1947, especially in the theft categories. Some
generalization may be made about the proportionate distribution of arrests.
It appears that the percentage of arrests of youths under 18 for property
crimes, though the trend was interrupted by a postwar decline, has in-

[22] The FBI summary tables providing information on young offenders cast the
data in classes showing all arrests under 18, under 21, and under 25, thus pointing
up the very large proportion and number of crimes committed within the total age
ranges. Since the figures may be misleading concerning the part played by those
between 18 and 21 and those between 21 and 25, Table 7 was formulated to show
rates specifically within each age range.

creased greatly as compared to other age groups over the past two decades, while the proportion of arrests of men between 18 and 25 has declined markedly. While the facts cannot be determined precisely from the Federal data, it appears that these changes are characteristic of the actual arrests for these ages as well as for the proportion of arrests. This suggests that criminality matures and declines at an earlier age than was true a generation ago and that there is somewhat less cause for alarm about the crime rates, as such, of the youthful offender aged 18 and over than has sometimes been believed. On the other hand, youths from 18 to 21 had the highest arrests of all age groups for robbery and rape, 18 being the modal age, and men from 21 to 25 showed the highest rates for homicide and assault, the modal age in the latter group being 24. Their crimes are more dangerous, if less numerous, than those of the younger offenders.

Sex Differences in Arrest Rates

Since 1946 women have accounted for 10 to 11 per cent of all arrests reported to the FBI. In 1958 their proportion was 10.6. This represents a significantly higher percentage of all arrests than was characteristic in the 1930s, when arrests of women constituted about 7 per cent of the total. War influence may easily be discerned again in the sex ratios displayed in the crime rates from 1942 to 1946. During the former year the proportion of female arrests was similar to that during the 1950s. In 1942 and 1943, however, the number of female arrests rose sharply, especially among girls below the age of 21,[23] while male arrests declined. In 1945 and 1946, male arrests increased considerably, while a marked decline occurred in female arrests during the latter year.

Although women have come to contribute in excess of 10 per cent to the total arrests in the United States, this figure is somewhat misleading; out of 248,439 arrests of females in 1958, major felonies were charged in only 9.9 per cent of these cases. Theft alone represented 6.8 per cent and aggravated assault 1.6 per cent of the total. In declining order of frequency, women were charged with drunkenness, disorderly conduct, larceny, prostitution, minor assault, liquor law violations, and vagrancy. These offenses constitute two-thirds or more of the offenses of women in recent years. Among men, too, major felonies account for little more than 10 per cent of arrests, but they much exceed their proportionate share of all arrests in the crimes of robbery, aggravated assault, burglary, car theft,

---

[23] The arrest rates for females during the period 1937–1946 is given in *Uniform Crime Reports,* Annual Bulletin, 1946, p. 123, where the data are broken down into age groups. These are the totals for all age groups:

1937	1938	1939	1940	1941	1942	1943	1944	1945	1946
35,976	37,780	43,818	51,950	57,799	70,353	79,122	83,600	84,144	68,742

and rape. In diminishing frequency, their arrests are for drunkenness (38.8 per cent of all their arrests, concentrated in the age range from 35 to 45), disorderly conduct, larceny, driving while drunk, assault, vagrancy, and burglary.

During the war years the FBI published data showing comparative ages of males and females, indicating at that time that the most frequent age of arrest of women was usually from one to three years higher than that of men. Subsequent reports have not published data on this subject.

Race Differences in Arrest Rates

The FBI provides a general breakdown of arrest data according to major racial categories. The material is not intrinsically informative concerning the relationship between race and criminality. In 1958, 67.6 per cent of those arrested in the United States were white, 29.7 per cent Negro, and 2.7 per cent of other races. This may be compared with figures estimated by the Bureau of the Census indicating that 89.3 per cent of the population in 1954 was white and 10.7 per cent nonwhite. The minority racial groups other than the Negro comprise approximately 0.5 per cent of the total population. The disproportionate prevalence of arrests is apparent in the minorities other than oriental. In recent years white arrests have varied, generally constituting from 67 to 74 per cent of the total number of arrests, while Negro and Indian minorities have exceeded the expectancy from 2½ to 3 times.

Until 1941, the *Uniform Crime Reports* provided rates for the number of arrests of Negroes, native whites, and foreign-born whites per 100,000 of each group over 15 years of age in the general population. Population figures were based on the 1930 census. These data indicated an especially disproportionate excess of arrests of Negroes for homicide, robbery, assault, larceny, illegal possession of weapons, violation of liquor laws, disorderly conduct, and "suspicion."[24] Their rates were lower than rates of the white race in forgery and counterfeiting and in driving while intoxicated. While the rates varied somewhat through the 1930s, the differences were very similar through the decade. Unfortunately, information of this sort has not been provided in recent years. In any event, of course, such data require interpretation, not only in terms of differential pressures toward criminal behavior, but in variations in law enforcement as well.

Prior Arrest Record

Until a few years ago, the *Uniform Crime Reports* provided information annually on the number of arrestees during the year who had prior fingerprint records on file. The practice was discontinued in 1952. It may be

[24] *Uniform Crime Reports,* Annual Bulletin, 1940, p. 225. For assault the Negro rate is about seventeen times that of the white rate. See Chapter 8.

noted, however, for comparison with other data given in this volume, that 60.2 per cent of those arrested in 1951 had prior arrest records, varying from 61.9 per cent of the males to 45.5 per cent of the females. Among persons who committed major crimes, prior arrests were lowest for sex offenses, homicide, rape, and arson; 41.4 per cent, 44.8 per cent, 46.7 per cent, and 48.2 per cent, respectively.[25] At the other extreme, rates of prior arrest, next to vagrancy and drunkenness, were highest in the categories of violation of narcotic laws, forgery and counterfeiting, embezzlement and fraud, robbery, and burglary; 70.7 per cent, 70.0 per cent, 64.8 per cent, 64.7 per cent, and 58.8 per cent, respectively. At the age of 20, 46.2 per cent of the males had had prior arrest records. Other reports of the 1940s indicated a very similar relationship of offense to prior record. It would be useful to have available continuing and accurate records, not only in relation to the proportion of cases with prior arrests, but also in relation to those with prior convictions. At this time, however, information of this sort can be secured only in connection with offenders who are now in prison.

RECIDIVISM

Recidivism rates may be defined in terms of the percentage of persons convicted of crimes who are subsequently reconvicted.[26] To secure accurate information on such rates would require follow-up after conviction of representative samples of offenders in all categories of sentencing. Distinction should be made between juvenile delinquents, minor offenders, and felons. From such data useful inferences could be drawn, not only concerning the seriousness of the problem of recidivism, per se, but also concerning the effectiveness of treatment and prevention. Unfortunately, we lack the kind of information that is needed for entirely satisfactory analysis of the problem, but there are suggestive data from which tentative conclusions may be inferred. Some statistics are available on the frequency of prior arrests and also on the recidivism of probationers, prisoners, and parolees. Differing judgments on the seriousness of the problem of criminal repetition have been drawn from the data. Commonly, these have exag-

[25] Note that the relatively low rates of recidivism, as indicated by the FBI reports for such crimes as sex offenses, homicide, rape, and arson, is in conflict with much popular thinking in the field. These offenders are generally not recidivistic "fiends."

[26] Commonly recidivism rates are computed on the basis of the reimprisonment of offenders who have previously been committed to prison. Since this involves primarily the more serious felons, the data inflate considerably the actual problem of criminal repetition. In some countries recidivism is defined as a matter of law in terms of repetition of crime before the lapse of a specified period of time. This is a reasonable way to measure the criminalism of offenders and the efficacy of treatment. On the problem of recidivism generally, see *N.P.P.A.J.*, vol. 4, July, 1958.

gerated the frequency of failure. The lack of well-developed state and national statistics makes it extremely difficult to appraise the effectiveness of the measures we employ to deter crime and to reform offenders.

As suggested by the arrest data we have presented, the ostensibly high rates of rearrest reflect, to a great extent, police practice in cases of vagrancy and drunkenness[27] and, to a lesser extent, ordinary larceny and breaking and entering, offenses of high frequency but relatively small social importance. Among major felonies, only robbery reveals a frequency of prior arrests as high as 60 per cent, and the percentage is less than 50 for major crimes against the person. The rates undoubtedly reflect to a degree the common practice among police of picking up men who are known to have prior records, especially in communities where criminal registration statutes are in operation.[28] Furthermore, as we shall indicate in Chapter 13, in less than 50 per cent of the cases of arrests for major crimes is there sufficient evidence to justify a conviction and, among those convicted, less than 50 per cent are committed to prison. The FBI arrest data offers an exaggerated base for inference about the frequency of repeated convictions for serious crimes.

Probation Failures

National *Criminal Judicial Statistics,* the publication of which was ended in 1946, did not provide information on the frequency of offenders with prior criminal records. Therefore, we lack information on reconviction rates that might provide some basis for appraising the effectiveness of the courts' various sanctions. Furthermore, data on the failure rates of offenders other than those committed to prison are few and unreliable. Some jurisdictions have reported on probation experience, however. Their evidence indicates both that probationers have had prior criminal records less frequently than other offenders and that they are less often convicted for subsequent crimes. It is probable that for the whole country fewer than one-third, and possibly less than one-quarter, of probation cases are revoked. Only a minority of these failures involve the commission of a felony. Considering that probationers are held to a higher standard of behavior than are ordinary citizens and are sometimes imprisoned on quite trivial grounds, we may infer that probation constitutes successful treatment for a great majority of probationers. The fact that probation is

---

[27] Drunkenness and vagrancy display the highest of all rearrest rates, 71.0 and 73.0 per cent, respectively.

[28] Questionnaires directed to interstate compact administrators in 1958 elicited the information that local felon registration laws are in operation in fifteen states, including California, New Jersey, New York, Ohio, and Pennsylvania, where there are large cities and numerous crimes. See W. Keith Wilson, William McPhee, and LeGrand Magleby, "Criminal Registration Laws," *N.P.P.A.J.,* vol. 4, p. 273, July, 1958.

used in over 30 per cent of felony cases in the United States, with a relatively small proportion of failures, suggests that the total problem of criminal recidivism is not so great as has commonly been believed.[29]

There are no official figures on the reconviction rates of offenders who are fined or on those whose sentences are suspended. It is reasonable to believe, however, that criminals whose cases are disposed of in either of these ways would not have high rates of repetition as compared with prisoners or probationers.

Prisoner Recidivism

Data on prior criminal history are often drawn from maximum-security prison populations and it is largely for this reason that the frequently published recidivist figures appear high. The fact is that these institutions contain in increasing proportion the detritus from our courts: the most serious and aggressive, impenitent, conniving, immature, and irresponsible of our criminals. Maximum-security prisons receive the offenders who have failed under other forms of correctional effort. It is not surprising that a considerable proportion of these convicts are subsequently reconvicted.

National figures on the prior commitment records of prisoners were available through 1946.[30] In that year, 51.1 per cent of the prisoners released had previously experienced incarceration, 30.9 per cent in prison and 20.2 per cent in a jail or a juvenile institution only. Of the entire group, 12.9 per cent had had two or more prior prison commitments. The proportion of cases under first commitment varied widely, from 8.4 per cent in Kentucky to 86.3 per cent in Virginia. Federal prison statistics indicate an increase in recidivism rates since 1946. In that year, 44.1 per cent of Federal prisoners had experienced prior commitments (18.4 per cent in jail or juvenile institutions), while in the fiscal year ending June 30, 1957, 65.5 per cent had previously been incarcerated.[31] The increase reflects in some measure both the increased use of probation for the better cases and the growth in the number of Federal crimes. During the period from 1946 to 1957, the proportion of recidivists among prisoners in Wisconsin apparently declined from 63.2 per cent to 49.9 per cent.[32] There has been little follow-up research to discover what proportion of prisoners are returned to prison, but there are data on parolees that will be presented below.

Prisoner recidivism rates should vary with the character and program of

---

[29] For a fuller discussion of probation failure rates, see Chapter 19.

[30] Even at that time, the data obtained did not include prior convictions where the prisoner had been sentenced to probation, fine, or suspended sentence. See *Prisoners in State and Federal Prisons and Reformatories*, 1946, pp. 94–95.

[31] *Ibid.*, and *Federal Prisons*, 1957, chart 7.

[32] John W. Mannering "Significant Characteristics of Recidivists," *N.P.P.A.J.*, vol. 4, pp. 211–218, July, 1958.

the institution involved. There is little information available on medium- or minimum-security prisons to disclose what the variations are, but the figures at hand confirm the hypothesis. The medium-security Wallkill Prison in New York State, for example, has found that of a group of 2,980 prisoners released in the years between 1932 and 1946, 2.6 per cent were recommitted for new crimes and 19.1 per cent for technical violations of parole.[33] As is the case with probation and with superior institutional facilities, high success rates reflect the care in selection of offenders rather than the excellence of program alone.[34] Wallkill chooses from the population of the other institutions of the state those prisoners who are considered good risks for limited custody. Among the prisoners in the sample referred to, only 29 per cent had had prior criminal convictions, but not all of these had been committed to prison. Moreover, Wallkill had retransferred 12.7 per cent of its prisoners to other institutions on the ground that they were unfit for the program there.

Parole Revocations

More comprehensive state data are available on parole revocation and reimprisonment rates than on other forms of recidivism. This is in part because parole ordinarily requires supervision of offenders for extended periods, and information relating to success and failure is therefore relatively easy to secure. Failure rates of parolees are discussed in Chapter 23. In three populous jurisdictions where crime rates are high (New Jersey, New York, and California), 40.5, 44.9, and 45.5 per cent of parolees, respectively, were recommitted for violations during a span of a few years after release. Comparable data are not available in most states, but it is reasonable to believe that in many the rates would be lower. Many of the failures are the result of technical violations rather than new crimes. Considering that a majority of parolees have had prior criminal convictions, that many have previously been incarcerated, and that as prisoners they have been exposed to criminogenic as well as corrective influences, it is not strange that about one-fourth of them are returned to prison for the commission of new felonies. There is reason to believe that the rate of recidivism in this group, as well as among offenders generally, is related to such variables as the age of the offender, his prior criminal history, and the nature of his immediate crime. These factors may be more important than the nature of the correctional experience, itself, in determining which offenders will recidivate.

[33] Wallkill Prison, Status of Release as of Dec. 31, 1946, compiled by service unit. (Photostated.)

[34] The significance of the selective process by which the quality of an institutional population may be determined is also well illustrated in the comparative study of the Highfields experimental facility in New Jersey and the Annandale Reformatory there. See H. Ashley Weeks, *Youthful Offenders at Highfields,* 1958 (discussed in Chapter 18 of this text).

Age and Recidivism

Research studies have made it quite clear that the age of first delinquency and arrest is correlated with subsequent criminal history. The Glueck study, *Five Hundred Criminal Careers,* in which they followed the history of 500 reformatory inmates for a period of ten years after discharge, revealed failure rates graded from 73.8 per cent for individuals whose first delinquency occurred before the age of 11 down to 44.5 per cent for those who were 17 or more at the time of their first offense.[35] The Gluecks reached a similar conclusion on the basis of another sample of 1,000 juvenile delinquents whom they studied over a period of fifteen years.[36] In both studies they observed that there was a significant decline in offenses committed as the individual matured.[37] Recidivism rates shown in these studies are higher than those found elsewhere partly because of the broad definition of failures that the Gluecks have used.[38]

Studies of prisoners in three Federal institutions display a similar decline in the number of prisoners with prior records according to age of first arrest.[39] Thus at the Atlanta Penitentiary, 29.3 per cent of those who had first been apprehended for an offense before the age of 15 were recidivists, whereas only 5.6 per cent were repeaters among those who had not been arrested before the age of 40. At the Chillicothe Reformatory comparable failure rates ranged from 11.6 per cent to zero. More recently, Mannheim and Wilkins found in a study of Borstal boys in England that youths who had been first convicted before the age of 12 were considerably more recidivous (65 per cent) than those whose first convictions occurred after the age of 21 (46 per cent).[40] Thorsten Sellin summarizes several studies from penal registries in Austria that confirm the existence in these countries of a similar pattern of recidivism. The probability of reconviction varies inversely with the age of first conviction.[41] These studies point up two other

[35] Sheldon Glueck and Eleanor Glueck, *Five Hundred Criminal Careers,* 1930; *Later Criminal Careers,* 1937; *Criminal Careers in Retrospect,* 1943.

[36] *One Thousand Juvenile Delinquents,* 1934; *Juvenile Delinquents Grown Up,* 1940.

[37] The Gluecks found during the fifteen-year time span covered by their investigation of reformatory inmates that 32.3 per cent persisted in crime throughout the period while 33.5 per cent reformed entirely, 5 per cent relapsed briefly and then again became noncriminal, and 28.9 per cent became minor offenders. *Criminal Careers in Retrospect,* p. 121.

[38] Failures were defined to include arrests, violations of the conditions of probation or parole, known offenses that might have resulted in arrest, conduct reports in correctional institutions, and official reports during military service. Sheldon Glueck and Eleanor Glueck, *op. cit.,* pp. 149–150.

[39] *Attorney General's Survey of Release Procedures,* vol. 4, chap. 11 and appendix A.

[40] Hermann Mannheim and Leslie T. Wilkins, *Prediction Methods in Relation to Borstal Training,* 1955, p. 65.

[41] "Recidivism and Maturation," *N.P.P.A.J.,* vol. 4, pp. 241–252, July, 1958.

matters of significance: (1) the younger the individual is at the time of his sentence, the shorter is the interval between his first and subsequent crimes; and (2) the probability of reconviction is directly related to the number of prior convictions.

The studies of the English Borstal populations further confirm the relationship between recidivism and age. Youths aged 16 to 23 are committed to any of eight open-type or five "closed" Borstals.[42] Mannheim and Wilkins made an intensive follow-up study of 720 of those boys who had been sentenced between 1937 and 1950. Sixty-eight per cent of the boys had been convicted of some prior offense before the age of 16 and fifty per cent had had a prior institutional experience.[43] The researchers found that 52.6 per cent of the boys were subsequently reconvicted, 24.0 per cent once only and 28.6 per cent twice or more.

A truer impression of the recidivism of juveniles could be gained from following up samples of children's court delinquents than from the data that are more commonly available. Such material, some of which has been summarized above, is based upon the prior offense histories of adult offenders and, to a lesser extent, the subsequent criminality of incarcerated juveniles or adolescents. Patently, neither provides an accurate index of the recidivism of delinquents.

Despite the high recidivism rates displayed by young offenders who are committed to correctional institutions, most of them have abandoned crime within a few years. Relatively few of those who are convicted for the first time after they have reached maturity offend again. If this were not so, there would be a gradually increasing ratio of arrests in each successive age range rather than the marked decline that is observed to occur. Larceny, car theft, and burglary, offenses that together make up more than 90 per cent of major felonies, are preeminently youthful and repetitive crimes. After the age of 25, there is a rapid falling off in the numbers of individuals who commit these offenses.

IMPROVED CRIME STATISTICS

In this chapter we have observed major reasons for the inadequacy of our crime statistics. One authority has said that the statistics in the United States are the poorest of any major country in the Western world. It must be recognized, however, that much of the problem lies in the fact that we have a large and complicated variety of police, court, and correctional

[42] A report of the prison commissioners in 1952 noted that among 8,190 boys who had been released from these institutions, 59 per cent of those discharged from open-type institutions has not been reconvicted, while only 39 per cent of those released from the closed institutions were not convicted again. See *Report of the Commissioners of Prisons for the Year 1952,* London, referred to in Mannheim and Wilkins, *op. cit.,* p. 110.

[43] Mannheim and Wilkins, *op cit.,* p. 79.

systems, that the states themselves differ considerably in social and cultural characteristics as well as in their laws, and that we have a heterogeneous as well as a large population. Moreover, the interstate character of much contemporary crime and the migratory habits of our criminals increase the difficulties under a Federal system of securing comparable data from different jurisdictions and satisfactory information concerning the recidivism of convicted offenders. These are problems that cannot be easily overcome in the effort to improve criminal statistics. Other major Western countries have a much easier task in securing uniform national data on crime.

The compilation of crime statistics is a relatively recent development, having begun in France in the 1820s. The preparation of national statistics in the United States was a very late development of the 1930s, as we have noted. While there is some difference of opinion about the degree of accuracy of the data currently obtained by the FBI, it is clear that reporting has improved a great deal in its coverage and completeness. The Bureau has been successful in developing more uniform reporting in recent years. So far as major felonies are concerned, useful comparisons can be made from year to year and from state to state. Significant changes in rates and trends can be traced in part, at least, to their sources. Thus it is possible to draw inferences concerning the adequacy of police resources in a state or city, the relation of policing to prosecution, and the possible need for more effective police measures in relation to certain crimes and during particular months and seasons. Age and recidivist data are useful as they focus upon the need for more effective preventive measures at certain points in the sweep of crime.

It would be highly desirable to secure widespread enactment of a uniform criminal statistics act. There has been organized effort in this direction for twenty years, supported by the National Conference of Commissioners on Uniform State Laws and the American Bar Association. Professor Sellin redrafted an act for this purpose in the 1940s. His draft provided for the establishment of a state criminal statistics bureau to be directed by a trained statistician with appropriate powers to develop an effective system of reporting and recording. The bill itself has made very little headway thus far. Published state reports are few and inadequate, except for those from California, New York, and a few other states. As we have suggested, however, there is some ground for optimism based on the increasing cooperation that has developed between local communities and the FBI in their efforts to bring about more uniform methods of reporting and collecting statistics. At the time of writing there is a movement toward greater refinement of criminal statistics, a development that is highly desirable.

Chapter 3

CAUSATION

More research has been devoted to the problem of the causation of crime than to any other phase of criminological inquiry. This has undoubtedly reflected in part our pervasive curiosity to discover why man behaves and misbehaves in the ways that he does. In modern times, particularly, there has been the additional and very practical desire to probe the causes of crime in order to prevent and control its occurrence more effectively. Because of the contemporary doctrine that "behavior is caused" and the emphasis upon "treating the causes" to resolve criminality, the discovery of the etiology of crime has appeared to be crucial. Our knowledge of cause has been steadily increasing, but the study and interpretation of the dynamics of behavior, criminal or otherwise, presents numerous and serious difficulties, noted in the pages below. It is the purpose of this chapter to consider the meaning of causation, to look in a preliminary way at the methods employed in causation research, and to appraise the trends of such research.

CAUSATION AND CRIMINALITY

To illustrate at the start the problems involved in ascribing cause to criminal behavior, let us consider the case of a murderer whom the author interviewed at a parole hearing in 1954. We must look to the influences that may have been related to the act that he committed and to their possible implications for his future.

James Hubert was sentenced in 1943 to a term of life imprisonment for the crime of murder, committed when he was 20 years old. His sentence was subsequently reduced to thirty years.

Hubert spent the first few years of his life as an unwanted child in a defective family situation. During his infancy, when a worker from a social agency was called to his home by irate neighbors, his mother threatened to use James as a weapon to strike the visitor. Both of the parents were alcoholics who frequently engaged in violent brawls. Before James was born, his father was sent to jail for kicking his pregnant wife in the stomach. James has vivid memories of the brutal beatings he received at the hands of his father. Frequently he ran away from home and was always soundly thrashed upon his return. He reports that his father dallied with a succession of women and that when he was 5 he observed his father's sexual intercourse with two of these women. The parents separated when James was 8 years old, and his mother died soon afterward from alcoholism.

After he was discarded by his parents, James was placed with an aunt in a stable home in the Bronx where he was given more care and affection than he had previously received. In later years he has maintained close ties with this relative. James continued to experience considerable difficulty, however, both at school and in the neighborhood. From the age of 10 he was almost continuously under the supervision of the children's court for truanting, pilfering, and breaking into stores. In 1937, at the age of 15, he violated probation by burglarizing the home of a neighbor and was remanded to Bellevue Hospital for observation. At that time Dr. Doshay reported: "This boy is handicapped by his poor intelligence, by an ugly appearance because of his jutting teeth, and a speech impediment, all of which deprive him of companionship with normal boys of his own age. . . . He does not reveal any psychopathic trends in his make-up, and it is not believed that he would harm others because intrinsically he seems to be a rather mild mannered and good natured boy." At that time James tested as a dull child, with an IQ of 80, but the court committed him to Letchworth Village where he was held with mentally defective children until 1941. In the opinion of an examiner at the Village, James was a psychopath.

James had no employment history of any consequence before he entered the Army in 1942. He had been in the armed forces for fourteen months and in Italy two months when he was arrested for the murder of a 10-year-old girl. He said that he had been walking down a ravine and that she followed him. He called her and gave her some candy. She said, "Americano no good," upon which he "got excited" and hit her across the face with his fist; she fell down and began to bleed from the mouth and to yell. He says that he became "scared and nervous" and began kicking her about the head until she became quiet. He admits that he knew what he was doing, but says that he couldn't seem to stop.

At the time of his commitment to an army disciplinary facility, Hubert was diagnosed as a "constitutional psychopathic personality" with emotional instability and inadequate personality, associated with borderline intelligence. His IQ test at that time was rated 89. In 1944 Hubert was transferred to Atlanta Penitentiary where he was found to display schizoid personality trends, insecurity, and a "retiring personality." He was not considered deviant to any serious degree, however. He tested at 91 on the U.S. Public Health Service mental test and 97 on the Army Alpha, within the normal range of intelligence. Upon subsequent transfer to another penitentiary in 1945 and again in the institutional reports of 1947, 1948, and 1949, the prison authorities described him as a psychopath, though some of his reports indicated that "his insight and judgment appear to be fair." In 1954 a prison psychiatrist devoted a thoughtful reconsideration to Hubert's history and described the excellent adjustment that he had displayed during his prison commitment. He observed, too, that the subject's army record, as reported by his captain, had been good until the time of his crime. He concluded that "there definitely is not a condition of psychopathic personality existing, but rather we are dealing with a mature, well-adjusted individual who has good insight and good goals established." The chaplain described him then as "quiet, self-possessed, kind and considerate." His record displays a general spirit of cooperation and diligence in his work.

The case of James Hubert reveals better than many others the difficulties in drawing conclusions about the causes of a crime and in making predictions as to the future. Should we attach some significance here to the subject's constitutional state, inferring a pathological diathesis either from the alcoholic history of his parents or from the diagnosis of constitutional psychopathy that was made after his conviction? Or should fault be attributed instead to other physical peculiarities, his appearance and poor intelligence, in particular. These qualities certainly had their effect upon his inadequate personality. Presumably, his relative lack of critical intelligence had some consequence for his apparent failure of self-control at a time of considerable emotional stress.

Hubert twice witnessed the "primal scene" as a child and experienced repeated brutality at his father's hands. These facts invite theoretical speculation in the analytic tradition. Did this father's conduct produce a castration complex and deep feelings of inadequacy in his son? Had Hubert in fact attempted to bribe his victim to sexual intercourse and, frustrated by his impotence, vented a neurotic compulsive rage upon her? Or was it guilt feelings that made him quiet her, as so many anxious rapists before him have done to their victims in this all too effective and permanent way? It has been shown that murder is often related to brutality in the offender's experience with his father. Was this crime, for Hubert, a retaliation upon the father by a means not unlike that his father had often used on members of the female sex?

Was Hubert truly a psychopath, in the social psychological sense of that term, without implication of constitutional influence? Unloved by his mother and lacking a father image with which to identify as an ego ideal, he appears to have been fertile soil for the development of the conscienceless psychopathic structure of personality. If he was a psychopath at the time of his crime, what influence had this upon his mind, emotions, and behavior? Could the fact that he was psychopathic account for an unprovoked murder of an unknown child?

Should a diagnostician place emphasis, perhaps, upon Hubert's social history? As an unloved child in a grossly incompatible home, his father a "jail bird," his "family of orientation" shattered during his childhood, he was reared in a primary group that was seriously damaging. He displayed a pattern of delinquency from an early age and lived in a neighborhood where law violations were not uncommon. Juvenile court, probation, and an extended institutional experience were a part of his formative juvenile and adolescent experience. It appears that he was unaccepted and a failure even as a delinquent. His crucial crime of manhood was the epitome of senselessness and failure.

What quantum of significance should one attach to any of the variables that are known about James Hubert or to the unique conglomeration of them all? What more should we know about him before a fair appraisal might be made? These are the basic and obvious questions of causation. There are also important problems of prognosis, since Hubert must be released from prison sooner or later. Has he matured sufficiently so that, even if he was once properly designated a "psychopath," he has since ceased to be? Or, as an inadequate and somewhat defective person, has he developed over a ten-year period to such a level of competence and stability that he should no longer be feared? He has some ties in the community and a good prison record. Within a protected environment he displays fair insight and judgment. Is this sufficient to carry him through in the community where he must face serious responsibilities unaided? These are issues that must be faced by the diagnostician who would understand this offender and by the correctional authorities who must take responsibility for decisions on release.

It is clear that the causal interpretation that one would be inclined to attach to this crime would reflect the orientation of his training and thinking as well as the kind and amount of knowledge that he might discover about the case. Whether one looks for near or distant "causes," for intangible psychic or for more tangible social or physical relationships, or for a single or multiple explanation depends upon his training and experience. The viewpoints that behaviorial scientists and, in particular, criminologists of differing backgrounds bring to their interpretations of crime reflect differences in approach. There has been thus far, unfortunately, little harmonization of their divergent views.[1]

Is Causation Proximate or Essential?

A somewhat similar problem is faced both by law and criminology in the effort to assess cause. Where should one affix responsibility for an event? A chief difference in these two fields, however, lies in the fact that the law must attempt to charge some individual with culpability, whether in a civil action where damages must be assessed to the victim or in a criminal action where the responsible parties must be punished. For these purposes the courts can overlook many of the factors that may have played an important role in determining the result; usually their task is to determine whether there is a clear and sufficient reason to attach responsibility to a particular individual or individuals. In criminology the effort is, on the contrary, to seek the physical, psychic, social, and cultural motivations that result in a prohibited action. In both areas, however, it is necessary to determine whether certain individuals or influences have affected

[1] There is some tendency, particularly among certain sociological criminologists, to integrate varying causal orientations while continuing for the most part to stress the impact of the group rather than individual factors. See Chapters 7 and 8.

to a significant extent the particular event involved. The ultimate question, therefore, is: What extent of influence is required in order to attach causal significance? The subordinate, but often equally difficult, question is: How can the degree of influence that is exerted by any particular factor or combination of factors be established?

In the law, either of two standards has generally been employed in determining liability. One of these is the standard of *proximate cause,* which raises the question of whether the particular event, on the basis of which responsibility has been imputed to a party, is close enough in the "chain of causation" or the sequence of influences to justify attaching liability. This establishes no clear standard for responsibility, obviously, but imposes upon the court the duty of working out, through the flow of case law, precedents establishing the *proximity* of influence on which future decisions will be predicated. This sort of criterion, if applied in the domain of criminological theory, would exclude from significant causal relationship those predisposing influences of character and early social experience to which psychiatric and casework criminologists have attached primary significance.

The other major conception employed in the law for the determination of liability is the necessary cause, the *cause but for which the particular result would not have occurred:* the *sine qua non.* As a general principle, civil liability or criminal responsibility cannot be imputed unless the defendant's act was causal in this sense. Like proximate cause, this standard is somewhat tenuous and elastic. There are cases, of course, in which the conclusion is quite clear; for example, where the death of the victim would not have occurred when it did but for the blow inflicted by the defendant, or where the activity of the offender was essential to, though perhaps only a part of, the consummated crime. On the other hand, there are instances where the essentiality of the role of the accused is quite equivocal. If he had not sold the weapon to the assailant, the sugar and hops to the bootlegger, or had not advised the pregnant female of the abortionist's services, would they have engaged in the illicit activity? Different courts take conflicting positions on these issues and the resulting precedents come to control future decisions in the particular jurisdictions involved. The result may be satisfactory as a means of serving public policy. The decisions are not too difficult to reach, particularly under the doctrine of *sine qua non.* Where the legislature desires to extend liability beyond that established by the courts, it may do so by specific enactments.

Cause is a more difficult matter in the behavioral sciences. The significance of an influence cannot be determined by fiat or by some standard of public policy: either an influence is important or it is not. Loose inference is not a satisfactory basis for evaluating the significance of a factor in the history of an offender. For this reason in part etiological investigations that postulate cause in intangible and unmeasured psychic or social

factors, without standards of comparison to normality, evaluate unsatisfactorily the impact of a particular influence on a subsequently occurring
crime. It is too easy to infer a posteriori from the sequence of events in a
single case that the prior factor has been a significant influence upon the
subsequent crime. Indeed, doctrinaire theory may postulate such influence.
From the point of view of logic, this *post hoc, ergo propter hoc* reasoning
can produce neither certainty that there is any influence at all nor, if there
is, any fair appraisal of the nature and significance of that influence. The
discovery of a common sequence is a basis only for more intensive exploration of the existence and extent of a relationship.

Statistical study of a sample of offenders, if it is sufficiently refined, may
reveal the frequency and statistical significance of a relationship, as, for
example, between a particular narrowly defined type of behavior and a
factor that is found to be associated with it. Again, however, this does not
reveal the nature of the relationship but merely its prevalence. Increasingly
precise correlations of statistical relationship, careful etiological inquiry
into similar behavioral situations, and the intuitions derived from experience in dealing with the particular problem all help to reveal how and
why two phenomena (viz., delinquency and the broken home) are associated. However, because of the complexity of phenomena involved in
human conduct, the result remains in some degree tentative. In the study
of causation one can hope for little more than increasingly precise evaluations of the significance of influences upon conduct as a result of research
and experience. Such informed appraisals must give way in the face of new
or refined observations. In estimating causal significance there is special
danger in assuming that a close temporal relationship between factors indicates cause. The high frequency of a statistical correlation is apt to be
more important, though it points chiefly to a need for exploring the nature
and reasons for the relationship rather than to direct causal significance.
Refined correlations and intercorrelations bring increasingly close approxi-
mations to causal significance.

The Behavioral Gestalt and Holistic Theory

Opposed to the idea that one factor alone or a few in combination may
produce behavior is the idea that the act is a part of a total context in
which all of the infinity of variables in the particular case are involved.
The variables include the individual with his physiological-constitutional
base, his total personality and experience, his particular physiological and
emotional-intellectual-temperamental state at the time of the act, and the
situation complex to which he is responding, not only the objective circumstances themselves, but also the apperceptive reactions that he brings to
them. Such an approach to crime contrasts with traditional conceptions of
cause; it is even broader than the ordinary ideas of multiple causation.
This view of the vast causal configuration is realistic in the sense that it

conforms, apparently, to the nature of personality and the dynamics of conduct. It is a useful doctrine conceptually, moreover, because it denies the validity of common simplistic and static ideas about "the factors" causing crime. For purposes of evaluating the potency of particular influences, however, this holistic approach to causation, taken alone, leaves the investigator wholly at a loss. The idea that crime is an item uniquely associated with an infinitely complicated and interrelated flow of influences offers no focus for appraising the significance of particular or associated items. The act is *sui generis,* and so is the combination of circumstances that produced it.

In striving for a science of understanding and skills to influence behavior, it is essential to combine what is unique but similar and, so far as possible, to derive principles that relate to uniformities in the behavior of these similar phenomena. It is dangerous to assume similarity between circumstances that are quite different and to infer general principles too broadly from slight similarities and from inadequate evidence. One particular hazard, to which we have alluded, is that a static conception of society and personality may lead the investigator to assume that a particular event or condition will have the same meaning in quite different contexts. Nonetheless, the classification and generalization of principles should go on, but with increasing precision of analysis. Many of the oversimplifications and loose generalizations of criminology have already been abandoned as the tools of inquiry are sharpened and as interpretation becomes more critical. Future investigations should speed the testing of hypotheses and the refinement of our information.

We may conclude from the comments above that cause means simply a more or less direct and meaningful relationship in which one factor or event tends sensibly to produce another. Cause as an abstract concept does not imply any specific degree or kind of relationship but only a power of one variable to produce the particular consequence involved. Hence a cause may be very slight or very important in its effect. Moreover, it appears, the cause that is very important in one case or context may be very slight in another. Causes operate not in isolation but in related interplay, so that a factor has no constant significance in different cases. The influence, for example, of the broken home, of incompatible family relationships, of parental rejection, of inconsistent disciplining, of neurotic anxiety, of psychopathic trends, and so on, may have very different significance in varied contexts because such influences are associated with diverse other variables that both take meaning from and give meaning to the particular cause involved.

Samples of Criminals

In addition to the issue of "cause" itself, numerous obstacles have beset criminologists in their effort to discover the causes of crime. One central difficulty, the defining of crime, has been discussed in an earlier chapter. There has been little clarity or consensus on what crime itself is and, if anything, confusion on the point has increased in this generation at the same time that procedures have become more refined in the effort to delineate causal influences more sharply. In practice criminologists have used the convicted offender as representative of criminals, even though they have considered that definition improper or inadequate.

It may be noted further that the employment of any one group of offenders, whether it is an imprisoned or some other specialized population, does not provide a representative sample of either those who commit or those who are convicted of crimes. The selective processes determining the treatment that courts apply to criminals presumably result in a quite different, though overlapping, range of criminal, social, and psychological types among the groups that are submitted to different forms of correction. Thus, a study of the more serious, older, more socially deprived, and more defective criminals that are committed to prisons should result in a significantly more pathological view of criminals than should a study of probationers or of criminals fined or remanded to jails. The nonrepresentative character of the populations studied has come to be fairly generally recognized so that, while it remains a difficult, if not insuperable, problem to secure better cross sections of offenders, the scholar is aware today that generalizations derived from particular studies reflect in some considerable part the peculiarities of the groups selected for research. Similarities and differences are found in comparing the observations derived from different criminal populations.

Issue may be raised concerning the sorts of research data that we possess and the implications of these data for the etiology of adult criminality. Most intensive sociological research studies have been based upon juvenile or adolescent delinquents in institutions rather than upon criminals. Writings on the adult offender generally proceed on the implicit assumption that the causes of delinquency and crime are the same or, to put it differently, that the criminal is the delinquent grown up and unreformed. Undoubtedly this is true in a measure, but only in limited measure. Juvenile delinquents and adult criminals do differ in ways and to degrees that research has not yet fully clarified. Many delinquents reflect primarily youthful instability and, with the growth of some maturity, cease to commit offenses. Some express through their delinquencies other transient influences of the early years.

One study of five samples of Detroit juveniles who had been found delinquent between 1920 and 1940 investigated the subsequent arrest history of each group during a period of five years after the individuals had attained the age of 17.[2] On the average, 30.6 per cent of the juveniles

[2] H. Warren Dunham and Mary E. Knauer, "The Juvenile Court in Its Relationship to Adult Criminality," *Social Forces*, vol. 32, pp. 290–297, March, 1954.

were subsequently registered with the police for adult arrests. Over the years the proportion of juveniles apprehended as adults varied only to a small extent. Whereas 46 per cent of those children who had been before juvenile court more than once were later arrested as adults, this was true for only 24 per cent of those who had committed only one offense. The data on arrests are almost certainly incomplete, but they point to the conclusion that a great majority of juvenile delinquents, in particular those who have not been incarcerated, do not become adult offenders. It also appears, as we have indicated in Chapter 2, that most adult offenders who have not been committed to reformatory or prison do not have prior delinquency records.[3]

It is apparent from both research data and case-history materials that many criminals are, in a sense, unregenerated juvenile delinquents or adolescent offenders. But they are not merely matured delinquents; their criminality must reflect to some extent their peculiarities as adults and these peculiarities must certainly be different from those of "reformed" offenders. Moreover, it is clear that many law violators do not get started until they are adults and, while their behavior assuredly proceeds in part from earlier developments in character, their conduct also arises out of specifically adult personality and experience. It is erroneous to conceive the criminal's capacity for crime as fully developed by the "predisposing influences" of infancy or childhood, awaiting fulfillment through "precipitating circumstances" of a later age. Character continues to evolve in response to the continuum of experience and it reflects the varying influences that operate at different levels of maturity.

Statistical Researches on Crime Causation

The paragraphs above refer to the difficulty of securing representative samples of the criminal population when the researcher seeks to discover the prevalence of particular causal influences in criminality. It is necessary to consider the nature of statistical research into causation in somewhat greater detail, for this has constituted the great bulk of criminological research thus far.

In the usual pattern of research the criminologist selects a sample of somewhere between 100 and 1,000 juvenile or adult offenders from a correctional institution. He then proceeds to determine the frequency with which certain traits or factors appear in this group. Less costly and time-consuming studies are based largely or entirely on paper records, such information as might be available tabulated therein to secure a descriptive picture of the group. In the more ambitious studies, however, the investigators determine the factors that they believe are important and directly study the offenders to discover the prevalence of these factors. Particularly in earlier years, these researches were designed to get at merely a few quite

[3] See section on "Recidivism" in Chapter 2.

general and simple matters, such as the intelligence level, employment, marital status, recreational habits, educational background, church affiliation, and the like. Dr. William Healy, in his famous study *The Individual Delinquent,* published in 1915, secured information of a rather general character on "mental peculiarities," heredity, physical conditions, and environmental factors. Cyril Burt's study in England, *Juvenile Delinquency,* similarly identified broad psychological and social factors.

More recently, investigators have sought to learn much more about the population and, in particular, to secure more subtle and refined points of information concerning the psychological and social circumstances of offenders. Thus, for example, Sheldon and Eleanor Glueck, in their most recent research, *Unraveling Juvenile Delinquency,* employed a large staff of authorities over an eight-year period and secured information on 402 factors, including 149 items of social data, 55 on physique, 30 relating to medical condition, 56 on psychological conditions, 57 Rorschach items, and 55 from psychiatric examination. This study constitutes the most inclusive body of information that has been procured thus far on a delinquent population. However, the investigator secures information only on what he is looking for in his sample of criminals, not on all that is there or necessarily on what is most important in them; this is an unfortunate limitation of the statistical studies. Indeed, for convenience and simplicity in the tabulating of data, the researcher is wont to focus upon material or measurable items, and it is quite likely that these items are least important as compared with some of the intangibles of personality and their interrelationships.

Former studies were essentially descriptive in that they investigated only an offender population, though the researchers commonly drew contrasting inferences to nondelinquents on the basis of their general impressions. In recent years, however, it has been the practice in more careful research to select a control group of nonoffenders; researchers study members of this nonoffender group to determine the prevalence of the same factors observed in the offender group. This practice has permitted more objective and accurate appraisal of the relative frequency of the variables' occurrence and, hence, the significance of the variables in relation to criminality. Some of the studies have reflected a careful job of selecting the controls to match the offenders in certain respects. Healy and Gillin both used siblings to discover why one member of the family commits offenses and others do not. Other studies selected control groups that were partially similar in age and neighborhood. In their research referred to above, the Gluecks painstakingly selected 500 controls and matched them by pairs with 500 training school delinquents according to age, ethnic background, intelligence, and submarginal neighborhood of residence. This study also tested the significance of the difference between the prevalence of the traits observed in the two samples, thus sharply delineating those qualities that significantly differentiated the two groups.[4] In this research the Gluecks sought to observe and emphasized in their findings the interrelationship of the physical, psychological, and social variables that produced delinquency.

As a result of these researches a considerable number of characteristics deemed to differentiate offenders from nonoffenders have been segregated; these qualities will be noted in later chapters. This information is valuable as a matter of description and of differentiation between delinquents generally and nondelinquents. As a basis of understanding causation, however, this information has a number of limitations. The greatest difficulty, perhaps, is intrinsic to the statistical technique: factors are handled as though they were independent and static entities. These factors are traits caught at a particular cross section in time, for the most part, though there may be some effort, as in the Glueck investigation, to discover social data pertaining to earlier periods in the offenders' lives. Psychiatric and psychological diagnostic data, in particular, may give distorted impressions of cause, because at the time of observation the individuals have gone through experiences subsequent to their offenses that may have had a profound effect upon their responses. Beyond this temporal problem, moreover, there is a perhaps even greater difficulty: the offenders are generally dealt with as though they were merely masses of autonomous traits that can be summed for purposes of deducing causal factors. In reality the significance of a variable depends in large measure upon the other qualities with which it is associated in the individual, when and how these qualities interact rather than merely what they are. The static conception of causation is quite misleading, therefore, in relation to the dynamic nature of personality and behavior. It is certain that significant differences exist in the relationship between traits, as they are customarily surveyed in a static cross section of an imprisoned population. Statistical measurements provide quite limited insight into behavioral sequences and criminal etiology. These measurements are useful mainly, perhaps, in pointing out the areas that need more intensive and discriminating investigation.

Another important problem is involved in the causal analysis of groups of criminals. Put in simplest terms, this is the problem of lumping, of studying criminals as though they were all of a single and distinct order separable from and contrasted with a singular order of noncriminals. Our most ambitious, large-scale researches on criminals, some measuring numerous "criminogenic" factors with considerable nicety of detail, have studied mass offender groups that were thoroughly heterogeneous in their criminality. With increasing modern effort to make more exact and meaningful comparisons rather than mere descriptions of criminals, the careful investigations have come to select, often with great painstaking effort, matching control groups of noncriminals and to compare the offenders with

---

[4] Sheldon Glueck and Eleanor Glueck, *Unraveling Juvenile Delinquency,* 1950, pp. 75 ff. See Chapters 8 and 17 below.

these control groups in order to discover the statistically significant differences existing between criminals and noncriminals.

Various problems are involved in the employment of this sort of statistical research on criminals and controls as a basis for inferring causes. Some of these difficulties will be considered elsewhere in this work. There can be little question, however, that there is some utility in discovering significant differences between properly selected groups, thereby securing suggestive leads for further probing into the relevance and interrelationship of the factors in criminal histories. The traditional researches referred to above, however, have not been directed to appropriately distinguished groups. The criminal populations studied have included as a single, unique category, "criminal," such diverse types as murderers, burglars, robbers, thieves, rapists, embezzlers, arsonists, sodomists, carnal abusers, income tax violators, bigamists, fornicators, and various other types of offenders. The researchers have sought to discover within this lumping of diverse men the prevalence of social and psychological qualities that set them off from another mass of noncriminal men. The absurdity of this approach would seem to be clear, though apparently it has not been. It perhaps reflects the age-long inclination to view offenders as a phenomenon uniform and distinct from noncriminals. This form of bimodal oversimplification has retarded behavioral science in its more general phases.

Surely it must be apparent today that the contrasts are great between offenders against property and those who offend against the person.[5] The differences are even more striking between such classes as murderers and embezzlers, homosexuals and professional thieves, income tax violators and robbers. Common sense and ordinary observation of criminals lead one to believe that there is greater difference between these criminal categories than there is between members of the category and the average noncriminal. It is highly probable, for example, that offenders convicted of embezzlement, theft, income tax violation, and bigamy resemble more closely the noncriminal than they do rapists, kidnappers, and robbers. To measure and average off, as the criminological researches generally do, such factors as the family status, employment history, educational background, religious affiliation, or personality structures of divergent criminal types is utter nonsense statistically and criminologically: the result minimizes the significance of some differences and exaggerates the significance of others; in any event, it confuses the differences and the similarities between particular types of criminals and noncriminals.

What we need to know, far more than the differences between "criminals" generically and noncriminals, is what significant differences there may be between thieves and noncriminals, rapists and noncriminals, burglars and noncriminals, etc. Our statistical researches have attempted to

[5] Material in subsequent chapters will point to some of the differences between different types of offenders.

discover the least useful sort of distinction. It is possible that, in measuring the traits in a cross section of the prison population, the differences observed in comparison to noncriminals reflect much more such matters as conviction and sentencing variations, the relative influence of different sentence lengths and the effects of the imprisonment experience itself than they reflect actual differences between criminals and noncriminals. Certainly differences that exist in relation to particular classes of criminals are largely cancelled out by the process of lumping together those criminals who are quite different.

Individual Case Methods of Research

For the most part, psychiatric and other case researches into crime causation have not attempted to measure differences between criminals and noncriminals as the statistical-sociological studies have done.[6] The psychiatrists have generally approached the causation problem by intensively studying individual cases to discover the emotional deviations and the dynamics of delinquency as delinquency has developed through the psychosexual history of the individual. Consequently, such investigations have tended far more to point up variations in criminal etiology in the individual offender, postulating influence upon criminality from the offender's personality structure and the sequence of events deemed to have affected his emotional responses. This approach has avoided the statistical and sociological hazards of lumping various types of criminals together in the effort to discover correlations between criminality and specific variables.

On the other hand, the individualized approach has failed to establish standards of psychiatric or social normality and of noncriminality, so that one cannot determine from these studies what differences or what degrees of variation distinguish the delinquent from the nonoffender. Where etiological significance is imputed to a neurotic trait, a psychopathic trend, or some emotional deviation, it is generally impossible to determine to what extent, if at all, this quality in the offender can be distinguished from the qualities in other individuals who do not commit crimes. It is quite possible, as a consequence, that the interpretation of a clinician may impute significance to a trait or experience that has no real importance for the crime.

[6] A detailed account is not given here of the variety of genetic or historical methods that have been employed in studying criminals. Aside from the case histories developed by social workers and psychiatrists, life history documents, commonly autobiographical, have been used to a limited extent. See, for example, the volumes by Clifford Shaw, *The Natural History of a Delinquent Career,* 1931; *The Jack Roller,* 1930; *Brothers in Crime,* 1938; and the numerous autobiographical studies written by former criminals. The participant observer technique, in which the researcher participates in the group living of offenders, has also been employed and, as compared with extraneous observation, it provides particularly valuable insight into the attitudes of individuals as well as the dynamics of the group.

On the other hand, an event that has had little motivating significance in a nonoffender and, perhaps, in some offenders may prove in the instance of a particular criminal to exert a very considerable impact because of its relationship to other factors in his social-emotional history.[7]

Individual case research gives valuable insight into the ways in which the association of circumstances and events may produce criminal behavior. This sort of genetic and dynamic interrelationship of variables, focusing on *how* factors are associated in the criminal's history rather than on merely *what* factors are involved, provides a depth perspective that is lacking in the cross-sectional studies of the statistician. At the same time it does not, of course, offer satisfying information about either the strength of a particular influence or its prevalence in criminal histories. Moreover, such dynamic etiological investigation is particularly susceptible to subjective and parochial interpretations in accordance with the peculiarities of the investigator's training and experience. The importance that the investigator attaches to what he observes may reflect himself as much, or more than, the data he observes. He may find dynamisms (e.g., the primal scene, penis envy) that other authorities do not.[8] It is particularly difficult to appraise or confirm psychic intangibles. Such limitations withal, it is clear that these studies are valuable and that they provide considerable information about the patterns of personality and the behavioral sequences that lead to different types of crimes. It is hoped that they may also come to reveal more about the significant differentia that lead some emotionally or socially deviated individuals to law violations and not others. More fruitful results should flow, too, from the coordinated efforts of different types of behavioral specialists, psychiatrists, caseworkers, sociologists, social psychologists, and others, as they attempt to synthesize their various orientations and insights in the search for causes.

Continuing investigations of a statistical nature should also be valuable in the search for the qualities in the criminal and the circumstances that distinguish him from those who conform to legal standards. As we have suggested, in any attempt to discern what differentiates particular types of criminals from the law-obedient, there is a fundamental need to turn our attention from the genus criminal to the widely varied species of criminality. To be sure, this in itself promises to be a complicated task. There is fairly convincing evidence that the same general forms of motivations that lead certain individuals to one form of offense may lead others to a quite

---

[7] It is clear that where a trait is important in the etiology of certain crimes because of its dynamic relationship to other influences rather than because of its intrinsic importance it would be found nonsignificant in a statistical study of a mass of offenders.

[8] The different schools of psychiatry and psychology, for example, have produced varied and sometimes conflicting doctrines regarding etiology. This is discussed in the chapters on psychological factors in crime.

different crime. Thus, for example, the erotic frustrations and distortion that may be expressed quite directly in an act of rape or, on a subtler level, in seduction can be manifested more deviously by the symbolic act of burglary, wherein the "breaking and entering" serves a very similar physiological and psychic purpose. In the more refined study of the etiologies of different forms of crime, one may find congruous motives for certain of the ostensibly quite different criminal acts. Per contra, one may be sure to discover different patterns of influence in the emergence of the same crimes. Thus, for example, while some burglaries are undoubtedly partially erotic in psychic origin, it would seem that the great majority are not. Even so apparently direct an expression of physical drive as rape may reflect quite different elements of eroticism, aggression, psychopathic deviation, and ego status. If statutory rape (a consensual act with a female under the age of consent) were studied, it might be very difficult indeed to discover significant elements of difference between those who have committed such acts and the average young male in the population.

One may expect to find some overlapping, then, in the causes of different crimes and some differences in the causes of the same crime. Beyond this, it is probably true that there is some measure of significant difference between nonconformists who violate criminal laws and those individuals who rigorously conform, though as we have noted above, the variations between categories of criminals largely level off these differences. All this suggests the need for greater refinement in the study of the dynamics of criminality; refinement is needed in each of the different forms of crime, however, rather than in either the statistical study of criminals en masse, where they are all deemed to be similar, or strictly individualized case researches, where they are all assumed to be different. Neither lumping nor thorough individuation can produce the knowledge of uniformities and differences on the basis of which our understanding of cause, prevention, and treatment can be developed systematically. In this volume some effort is made in the analysis of crimes and their causes to point up differences between various classes of criminality. Unfortunately, the dearth of the sort of research data on the basis of which one would desire to make appropriate comparisons limits the comprehensiveness of this material. Aside from the research of John L. Gillin, which was directed to a comparison between offenders against person and property among inmates at the Wisconsin Waupun Prison, little effort has been made to distinguish the quality of different classes of criminals. The dynamics of sexual crimes have been investigated in recent years mainly through psychiatric studies; but the study of other forms of criminality has been, for the most part, quite limited and superficial. Any treatment of the causation of different crimes inevitably reflects these limitations of the data.

The Development of Theories concerning Crime Causation

During the major part of human history violation of law and mores has been explained quite simply on the basis of sinfulness or "evil will." Some men freely chose to do wrong. Not until the eighteenth century do we find some substantial evidence that man recognized external as well as internal forces through which he was induced to crime, exemptions for nonresponsibility, or reduced capacity to conform. Since that time and particularly during the present century, under the impact of the biological, social, and behavioral sciences, awareness of the complexity of forces by which behavior is guided or determined has grown rapidly. Monistic and particularistic explanations have persisted, but criminologists have come generally to recognize the "multiple causation" of crime.[9] Among sociologists this has generally implied a focus upon the multiplicity of social and cultural factors with which crime has appeared to be correlated; among psychiatrists and psychologists it has meant either a sequence of dynamic incidents in the development of character structure or the concatenation of personality variables disposing the individual to crime.

There is a strong disposition among authorities today to attempt to formulate more or less systematic theories of causation that may be taken to explain criminality; these theories are ordinarily formulated in terms of the discipline to which the authority subscribes. This is exemplified among the more popular writings by the "differential association" theory[10] of the late Professor Sutherland and by the delinquency area hypothesis of the late Clifford Shaw;[11] these formulations have more recently been drawn into a theory of delinquent "subcultures."[12] Some authorities have preferred to interpret individual pathological behavior as a reflection of social disorganization or of cultural conflict.[13] Others have emphasized the role of criminality as one of the modes by which some individuals in an anomic society seek success as measured by material rewards; this is a matter of fitting defective means to culturally approved ends.[14] Those of psychological orientation, on the other hand, have more commonly conceived motivation in terms of personality deviations and sometimes, more specifically, in terms of instinctual hypotheses and ego dynamics that are deemed to produce inappropriate responses to reality.[15] For the most part, so far as they have

[9] As we shall observe in subsequent chapters, these include economic, climatic, hereditary, endocrinological, ethnological, and psychoanalytic determinisms. They are, in general, more sophisticated than the simplifications of another day, but they attempt to explain the complexities of human behavior in terms of a single or badly oversimplified explanation.

[10] See p. 108.

[11] See pp. 205–207.

[12] See pp. 181–183.

[13] See pp. 174–181.

[14] See pp. 170–174.

[15] See pp. 141–145.

purported to explain crime generally, the effect of these theories has been to perpetuate the limited and parochial doctrines of the separate disciplines. Some authorities have employed more eclectic and interdisciplinary approaches to criminal behavior, in so far as the available data permit.[16] The result lacks the simplicity of the more systematic expositions that have found appeal among the various "schools" of criminology.

In so far as crime is explored through a multiple disciplinary orientation, it comes to be viewed as the product of complex and interrelated forces. This would appear to be the most fruitful approach to crime in a basic text in the field. Only through drawing upon the research from physiology and biochemistry, psychology and psychiatry, sociology and ethnology, and their related disciplines can we come to a more complete and accurate understanding of criminal behavior. A systematizing of theory is desirable in so far as we can incorporate therein the diversified data that come from the behavioral fields, but by excluding or distorting facts to preserve uncomplicated theory we do disservice both to criminology and to the discipline on which such theory is founded. Neither crime nor its treatment can be rendered simple by formulary dogma.

In the chapters that follow, rather detailed consideration will be given to findings and theories relating to criminal behavior. For convenience of description and interpretation, these findings are classified into physical, psychological, and social factors. It should be emphasized, however, that from the point of view of human behavior the separation is artificial and misleading. Mind and personality are inextricably linked with heredity and constitution. Response to the social-cultural environment is related both directly and indirectly to the mind and body. It is true, as the sociologists stress, that man does not live in a vacuum. It is equally true, however, as the physical and behavioral sciences make fully clear, that the individual's biochemical and psychological composition determines the meaning of environmental forces.

Criminal etiology will be considered in this work as part of the phenomenon of uniformity and variation of behavior in human society. This may be viewed in terms of biopsychological and cultural regularities, on the one hand, and of differences in biological equipment and in the environment, on the other. Kluckhohn and Murray have put the relationship rather neatly in terms of field theory: *"There is the organism moving*

[16] See Sheldon Glueck and Eleanor Glueck, *Unraveling Juvenile Delinquency,* 1950. The author of this text has made some effort in this direction; see, in particular, Tappan, *Juvenile Delinquency,* 1949, and "Sociological Motivations of Delinquency," *Am. J. Psychiat.,* vol. 108, pp. 680–685, 1952. Glaser suggests that " 'integrative' theories, which evoke a complex image to unite data underlying diverse monistic theories, are more useful than 'pluralistic' theories, which preserve diverse images." It is undoubtedly true that we need the further development of theory by which criminological data may be drawn together from its varied sources. Also it is true that such theory should not do violence to the data.

through a field which is structured both by culture and by the physical and social world in a relatively uniform manner, but which is subject to endless variation within the general patterning due to the organism's constitutionally-determined peculiarities of reaction and to the occurrence of special situations."[17] The uniformities of culture and the similarities in man's biopsychological organization and function result in a very considerable uniformity of conduct. Constitutionally established individual differences, operating within a cultural context that permits wide variation, result in some fairly substantial disparities in behavior from one person to another. Man tends to exaggerate the prevalence and significance of differences while overlooking the uniformities. These deviations are commonly looked upon as strange and pathological phenomena, but it is clear that from a sociopsychological point of view crime as well as other deviated behavior is an exceptional but quite "normal" consequence of individualized response to an elastic cultural framework.

[17] Kluckhohn and Murray, "Personality Formation: The Determinants," in Clyde Kluckhohn, Henry A. Murray, and David M. Schneider, *Personality in Nature, Society, and Culture,* 1953, p. 65. (Italics not in the original.)

Chapter 4

PHYSICAL, CONSTITUTIONAL, AND HEREDITARY FACTORS

One of the recurrent controversies in the field of criminology concerns the role of biological factors in criminal etiology. This is, of course, a part of the broader question of the relation between such factors and human personality. Most criminologists in the United States have given very little attention to this problem, except in a negative and critical way. This is in large part because of the strongly environmentalist orientation of the sociological criminologists and because of the preoccupation of the dynamic psychiatrists with their postulated processes of psychogenesis. As one psychiatrist has stated the matter, "Positivistic ideologies have . . . produced a tendency to underestimate or even to ignore the necessity of appraising constitutional and hereditary aspects of psychiatry. It is hardly an exaggeration to state that these factors are actually taboo in general psychiatric discussions. . . ."[1] The sociologists have contented themselves, for the most part, with showing that crime is not inherited, that biology does not determine criminality, and that biological researches in

[1] F. A. Freyhan, "Psychiatric Realities, An Analysis of Autistic Trends in Psychiatric Thinking," *J. Nervous Mental Disease,* vol. 106, no. 4, October, 1947. Freyhan quotes a pertinent comment of the distinguished psychiatrist Nolan D. C. Lewis: "Many psychiatrists still show no tendency to distinguish between the problems of mechanism and of psychic content, or of fundamental etiology and psychogenesis. These workers are so exclusively concerned with the determinants of the psychic content that it is apparently impossible for them to see below the anecdotal level." Nolan D. C. Lewis, *A Short History of Psychiatric Achievement, New York,* 1941.

William H. Sheldon also noted the psychoanalysts' aversion to recognizing constitutional influences on behavior and temperament: "The psychoanalytic approach is called by psychoanalysts a dynamic one, and the literature of this group has appropriated the term psychodynamics to refer to the process by which the patient got the way he is. This process is nearly always reviewed in such a way as to place virtually the entire burden of causation on those factors with which the psychoanalysts have elected to concern themselves. They have selected their causative factors in such a way as to overemphasize grossly certain external agencies for which neither the patient nor his heredity can be blamed, and to underemphasize grossly not only the rest of the environmental story but the whole of the story of constitutional and temperamental differences." William H. Sheldon, Emil M. Hartl, and Eugene McDermott, *Varieties of Delinquent Youth,* 1949, p. 866.

criminology often do not support the conclusions of the investigators. While criminology has come to recognize a multiplicity of causal influences and has on the whole become modestly eclectic in its search for these influences, most often it has repelled the suggestion that man's body is something more than an instrument of the psyche or a repository of social and cultural influences. Part of the difficulty lies in the fact that much still remains to be learned about the relationships of body, mind, and behavior. But, unfortunately, there is little inclination, among criminologists in particular, to discover these relationships.[2] The somewhat naïve and exaggerated views expressed on criminal biology during the nineteenth century may be responsible in some measure for the pendular swing of contemporary criminological positivism in its repudiation of the body.[3] Moreover, there appears to be a repugnant reaction to the idea that man's body sets limits to his development. Patently, these are not sound reasons for avoiding a search for the facts. Indeed, as Dr. Myerson has suggested, we may well be complicating our problems by this avoidance: "It is obvious that if there is a constitutional basis to a good deal of the ills of mankind, mere cure of the individual case only pushes the problem of diseases on to the next generation in increasing measure."[4] Some of the evidence relating to physical factors and crime will be reviewed in this chapter and an interpretation of the data will be suggested.

EARLY THEORIES

Scholarly interest in the relation of physique to personality runs far back in history. Indeed, some of the basic conceptions about this relationship that have been put forward in recent years are strikingly similar to views expressed well before the birth of Christ. Hippocrates, living between 460 and 370 B.C., was the first of the philosophers to recognize and describe two major body types: the short, thick *habitus phthisicus,* sometimes known today as the pyknic type, and the long, thin *habitus apolletticus.* He tried to show relationships between these physical types and various diseases, much as some modern scientists have attempted to do,

[2] Kimball Young points out the increasing recognition of the interrelationships of constitutional and psychological factors in the study of personality and mental disease: "The data at hand indicate in a very clear way that the bodily and mental processes are fundamentally unified and must be discussed together if we are to get an adequate naturalistic view of human thought and behavior." *Personality and Social Adjustment,* 1940, pp. 741–742.

[3] "Phases of psychiatric thinking have been compared to a swinging pendulum. At present the pendulum appears to have swung to the extreme pole of panenvironmentalism. . . . Insight is necessary in order to avoid the note of intolerance which creeps into discussions as soon as dynamic concepts are critically approached." Freyhan, *op. cit.*

[4] Abraham Myerson, "Some Trends of Psychiatry," *Am. J. Psychiat.,* vol. 102, p. 571, 1946.

though with greater precision of technique, of course. Aristotle (384–322 B.C.) found an association between the shape of the body and mental characteristics. In his *Physiognomica,* he wrote that "there was never an animal with the form of one kind and the mental character of another: the soul and the body appropriate to mankind always go together, and this shows that a specific body always involves a specific mental character." In the seventeenth century "anthropometria" was first developed by Elzholzius as a technique of actual measurement rather than one of mere description of the body and physiognomy for purposes of classification. Two centuries later "morphometry" came to be widely used with detailed statistical measurements of the body. Phrenology also developed, largely under the influence of Gall (1757–1828), as an attempt to correlate temperamental and emotional responses to external configurations of the head. As early as 1797 Halle divided morphological structure into three categories quite similar to those employed in modern times by Kretschmer and Sheldon: the abdominal, the muscular, and the thoracic-cephalic.

Lombrosian Theory and Its Sequel

The most significant impetus to modern morphological theory in criminology and research came from Cesare Lombroso (1835–1909),[5] the father of the Positive or Italian School of Criminology, though other European scholars had pointed to an apparent relationship of criminality and cranial measurements more than a generation before his time. A physician, Lombroso was considerably influenced by Darwin and the theory of natural selection. With other Italians of his period, he sought "atavistic" characteristics in the criminal population, the "stigmata of degeneration" that he believed characterized both the criminal and the savage. He taught that the "born criminal" could easily be distinguished from the noncriminal by various anomalies of structure, mainly anomalies of the skull, including "sclerosis, asymmetry, retreating forehead, exaggeration of the frontal sinuses and of teeth, asymmetries of the face, and above all the middle occipital fossa of males, the fusion of the atlas and the anomalies of the occipital opening." He did not have measurement norms for the noncriminal population for purposes of comparison, however, and his prominent student Enrico Ferri observed that 63 per cent of the sample of soldiers studied displayed similar "stigmata of degeneration."[6] Lombroso countered with the proposition that such anomalies reveal a biological disposition that may be brought into expression by environmental influences and that it was primarily the influence of physical primitivity, rather than the environment, out of which criminality develops.

Lombroso has sometimes been considered the founder of "scientific criminology" because of his physiological study of individual offenders.

[5] Cesare Lombroso, *Crime, Its Causes and Remedies,* 1911.
[6] Enrico Ferri, *Criminal Sociology,* 1917.

In recent years this view has been strongly criticized by certain American criminologists on the ground that earlier studies in France on geographic and social influences on crime were no less scientific.[7] In any event Lombroso established a quasiscientific foundation for the still very strong emphasis on criminal biology among Europeans and for the recurrent interest in this subject of a limited number of Americans. More than this, he together with Ferri, Garofalo, and others of his time stimulated the study of the individual criminal and investigations into social and psychological forces in crime, relatively new orientations that have had tremendous influence on modern criminological theory and research. The emphasis of the Italian school on social, economic, and cultural as well as biological factors in causing crime has proved a powerful force in the development of the deterministic view that crime is caused by forces beyond man's voluntary control. In a sense, the research and theory of the Italian School were a broadside attack upon the prior conceptions of free will and of punishment as a just retribution for the criminal's choice to engage in morally reprehensible behavior.

A few years after the death of Lombroso, Charles Goring conducted a very complete study of anatomical characteristics of some 3,000 criminals in England and compared them to the characteristics of a noncriminal control group.[8] He divided the offenders into crime categories and then classified them on the basis of thirty-seven anthropometric measurements, comparing each group with the averages for the entire group. Goring found no important differences either between the different groups of prisoners or between the prisoners and the controls. He concluded that "there is no such thing as an anthropological type of criminal" but "it appears to be an equally indisputable fact that there is a physical, mental, and moral type of normal person who tends to be convicted of crime." Goring observed that prison inmates were physically inferior, on the whole, to persons of the same age in the general population. While those convicted of violence to the person were stronger than the average noncriminal, most offenders against property—thieves, burglars, etc.—were below normal in height and weight. He believed, however, that social-cultural influences as they influenced the individual were of primary significance; the physically inferior are more often imprisoned because their occupations and competitive struggle may lead them to crime and because they are more likely to be convicted.

Among contemporary scholars in the United States, the late E. A. Hooton, a physical anthropologist at Harvard, has supported the Lombrosian theory of biological primitivity, with relatively little modification.[9]

---

[7] Alfred Lindesmith and Yale Levin, "The Lombrosian Myth in Criminology," *Am. J. Sociol.*, vol. 42, pp. 653–671, 1937.

[8] Charles Goring, *The English Convict: A Statistical Study*, 1913.

[9] E. A. Hooton, *The American Criminal, An Anthropological Study*, 1939; *Crime and the Man*, 1939.

His view is epitomized in this conclusion: "Whatever the crime may be, it ordinarily arises from a deteriorated organism. . . . You may say that this is tantamount to a declaration that the primary cause of crime is biological inferiority—and that is exactly what I mean."

The following interpretations from Hooton's work reveal similarities to Lombroso's conceptions:

Criminals as a group represent an aggregate of sociologically and biologically inferior individuals. . . . Marked deficiency in gross bodily dimensions and in head and face diameters are unequivocal assertions of undergrowth and poor physical development.

Low foreheads, high perched nasal roots, nasal bridges and tips varying to extremes of breadth and narrowness, excesses of nasal deflection, compressed faces and narrow jaws fit well into the general picture of constitutional inferiority. The very small ears with submedium roll of helix, prominent antihelix and frequent Darwin's point hint at degeneracy.

. . . smaller size, inferior weight and poorer body build, his smaller head, straighter hair, absolutely shorter and relatively broader face, with prominent but short and often snubbed nose, narrow jaws, small and relatively broad ears.

There can be no doubt of the inferior status of the criminal both in physical and in sociological characteristics. The poorer and weaker specimens tend to be selected for antisocial careers and for ultimate incarceration. The dregs of every population mixed and pure are poured into the prison sink.

Criminals are organically inferior. Crime is the resultant of the impact of environment upon low grade organisms. . . . It follows that the elimination of crime can be effected only by the extirpation of the physically, mentally and morally unfit or by their complete segregation in a socially asceptic environment.

Hooton concluded that criminals should be segregated in some unpopulated area where they should be left to reproduce and develop their own social organization. Strangely, in light of his evaluation of biological causation, he suggested that after a time they might come to achieve successful ends:

Either the United States Government, or possibly the various State governments, should expropriate some very considerable tract of desirable land and establish a reservation for permanent occupation by paroled delinquents. Such a reservation should have its frontiers closed under the supervision of State or Federal officers. . . . Emigrants from prison into such a reservation should be kept there permanently. I am rather inclined to believe that in a generation or two some of these penal reservations might develop into such prosperous and progressive areas that the inhabitants would be unwilling to receive more colonists from the jails. If natural selection were allowed to operate in such a society, it might work out its own salvation. It would, however, be quite essential to keep out extraneous politicians, criminologists and uplifters.

Hooton took physical measurements of a sample of 4,212 native white prisoners from correctional institutions in Massachusetts, primarily, and of a minority from eight other states. He compared these with measurements of 313 civilians from Massachusetts and Tennessee. One biologist has criticized the research for its "extreme biological bias" in interpretation, for its failure to use an adequate and comparable control group, for its assumption of causal relationship from correlations observed, even where such correlations were very slight, and for its inferring of organic inferiority from differentials that in fact appear to show biological superiority to the noncriminals.[10] This criticism expresses the general view among criminologists of the significance of Hooton's research:[11]

Indeed, on rereading Hooton's conclusions and surveying his data, one is struck by the complete lack of connection between them. In his conclusions he insists on the organic inferiority of offenders. And yet, his observations showed only few, slight and unimportant differences between offenders and civilians and, in general, surprising agreement. Professor Hooton professed to believe in biological inferiority when he began his study. He continued to believe in biological inferiority when he was finished. For the learned anthropologist, having once adopted a theory, was apparently unwilling to be dissuaded by mere facts, even though the facts were the product of his own efforts.

MODERN CRIMINAL BIOLOGY

The research and theory of William H. Sheldon and, before him, that of Ernest Kretschmer are much more significant for an understanding of personality, generally, and of the role of biological factors in crime, in particular. Criminologists have given these authorities far less attention than their material warrants, largely because of the antibiological orientation that we have previously noted.

Prior to Kretschmer some effort had been made not only to distinguish body types, as we have suggested above, but to classify types of psychosis and personality. To a large extent Kraepelin was responsible for linking the dual classes of schizophrenia and manic-depressive psychoses with the lesser mental manifestations, schizoid and cyclic personality patterns, in the normal population.[12] Kretschmer developed a more elaborate classification of body types than had previously been employed.[13] (1) the *asthenic,* characterized by a slender frame, narrow shoulders, long thin arms, long thin chest and stomach, angular face; (2) the *athletic,* with strong development of muscles and skeleton, broad shoulders, thick chest, tapering trunk, narrow pelvis, shapely tapering legs, a firm face with prominent jaw and short nose; (3) the *pyknic,* marked by rounded figure

[10] M. F. Ashley Montagu, "The Biologist Looks at Crime," *The Annals,* vol. 217, pp. 50–51, September, 1941. See also Richard M. Snodgrasse, "Crime and the Constitution Human," *J. Crim. L.,* vol. 42, pp. 19–29, 1951.

[11] James S. Wallerstein and Clement J. Wyle, "Biological Inferiority as a Cause for Delinquency," *Nervous Child,* vol. 6, pp. 467–472, 1947.

[12] E. Kraepelin, *Manic-depressive Insanity and Paranoia,* 1921.

[13] E. Kretschmer, *Physique and Character,* 1925.

with deep chest and obese abdomen, soft limbs, rounded shoulders; (4) the *dysplastic,* characterized by asymmetry of organs; and (5) mixed types. Kretschmer furthermore associated these body types with the psychiatric and personality classifications that Kraepelin and Bleuler had worked out. He found that pyknics generally were cyclic personality types or manic-depressive, if psychotic. The asthenic and athletic morphologies he found associated with introversion and schizophrenia.

Other scholars have attempted to verify the Kretschmer findings concerning the relation of body type to personality. The study of a group of criminals incarcerated at Joliet, Illinois,[14] confirmed to a very large extent his observations on mental hospital patients in Germany. Mohr and Gundlach, in this latter inquiry, found the same relationship between the three major body types and personality trends, but they believed that there existed a rather continuous progression of physical characteristics from one body type to another and that there were similar gradations of personality patterns. Other studies have tended to support Kretschmer's findings of a direct relationship between body types and temperament, though the clustering of physical traits has been questioned, suggesting that mixed and graded classes are characteristic rather than a preponderantly trimodal distribution.[15]

[14] George J. Mohr and R. H. Gundlach, "The Relation between Physique and Performance," *J. Exp. Psychol.,* vol. 10, pp. 117–157, 1927. The investigators found *asthenic* and *athletic* types more often convicted of burglary, robbery, and larceny, while *pyknics* were more often imprisoned for fraud, violence, and sex offenses. Another investigation performed with a small sample of college students reached the conclusion that the concept of physical-mental types could not be supported by the evidence. However, the performance tests that were employed have been criticized as inappropriate for drawing definite inferences about type categories. See Klineberg, Asch, and Block, "An Experimental Study of Constitutional Types," *Genetic Psychol. Monogr.,* vol. 16, pp. 145–221, 1934.

[15] Sheldon, who has built very largely and elaborately on the Kretschmer identification of physique and temperament, has suggested that the latter has made four major contributions to the "constitutional outlook":

"1. He had revived the typology concept in what had previously been its most highly developed form, had rewritten and sharpened it, had made it convincingly readable. Moreover he had done this during a period when the tide of academic and sophisticated thought had been running hard against him.

"2. He had been the first to introduce the idea of dysplasia, and this represented a long stride in psychology for it leads naturally to the notion of mixture of components instead of types, hence to quantification and to a conception of continuous multidimensional distributions.

"3. He had extended the type concept beyond morphology to include temperament. His classic descriptions of cycloid and schizoid 'temperamental types' had already become literature in the English translation as well as in the original German.

"4. He had demonstrated a statistical relationship between physical structure and temperamental function. I believe that to him belongs the credit for being the first to achieve this extremely important step in modern psychology." Sheldon, Hartl, and McDermott, *op. cit.,* pp. 55–56. (Reprinted by permission.)

SHELDON'S SOMATOTYPES AND DELINQUENCY

Dr. William H. Sheldon, who is professionally trained both as a psychologist and a psychiatrist, has made what is undoubtedly the most significant modern contribution to research and theory relating to the role of biology in human personality and criminal behavior. He contributes uniquely to the wedding of biology with psychology and psychiatry. Perhaps this fact together with the climate of our time has limited his audience to a serious extent. The comprehensiveness of the investigations he has pursued is tremendously impressive; his research is published thus far in three volumes, *The Varieties of Human Physique, Varieties of Temperament,* and *Varieties of Delinquent Youth.* Each is a long work and leads into the succeeding volume. Also, his usage of the technical language of biology, psychiatry, and social science does not encourage the amateur criminologist. Among those who make the effort to study his materials, many are repelled by the broad sociophilosophical judgments that are interpolated somewhat facetiously through his texts, interpretations that often do not follow very clearly from the data. Others are halted by the novelty of the terminology that he has constructed in the exposition of his thesis. His definition of delinquency, for example, is obtuse.

From Sheldon's point of view the human body is a composite of three major components, each of which is present in some measure in all individuals. Rather than a classification of distinct types of physique, however, he observes—as have some of the critics of Kretschmer—that there are gradations and combinations of the physical characteristics. Sheldon has associated the morphological structure of the individual with temperamental and other personality responses, emphasizing the continuum rather than a narrow typology of such relationships. In his inquiries he has studied the body in five regions: (1) head, face, neck; (2) arms, shoulder, hands; (3) thoracic trunk; (4) abdominal trunk; (5) thigh, calf, and feet. The sum total of these regional assessments gives an average for the body. Nude photographs are taken, left, lateral, front, and back. Sheldon's is the most objective technique of morphological measurement to date and is in the process of being further perfected to note the influence of age, sex, and race factors.

For each individual studied Sheldon develops a "somatotype," a quantification of the primary components determining the morphological structure of an individual. In practice the somatotype is a series of three numerals, each expressing the approximate strength of one of the three primary components in a physique. The first numeral always refers to endomorphy, the second to mesomorphy, the third to ectomorphy.

Sheldon defines these physical components, with much greater detail, in the following terms:

Endomorphy, or the first component: Relative predominance in the bodily economy of structure associated with digestion and assimilation. Relatively great development of the digestive viscera. . . . Endomorphy means relative predominance of the vegetative system, with a consequent tendency to put on fat easily. Note that this is similar to Kretschmer's pyknic type.

Mesomorphy, or the second component: Relative predominance of the mesodermally derived tissues, which are chiefly bone, muscle, and connective tissue. . . . Mesomorphs tend toward massive strength and muscular development. . . . Endomorphs get roly-poly, globular, and pendulous. Mesomorphs just swell up in their generally athletic mold. This is analogous to the athletic type of Kretschmer.

Ectomorphy, or the third component: Relative predominance of the skin and its appendages, which include the nervous system. In the ectomorph there is relatively little bodily mass and relatively great surface area— therefore greater sensory exposure to the outside world. . . . Morphologically, ectomorphy means flatness and fragility throughout the body, with a comparatively high height-weight index. This is similar to the asthenic type.

Sheldon employs mathematical symbols graded from 1 to 7 to indicate the intensity of each of the components in the individual. Thus a subject with a somatotype of 5-4-2 would be most strongly endomorphic but with a considerable mesomorphic component and a small ectomorphic element in his structure. He would be termed a mesomorphic endomorph.

Three temperamental patterns are said to correspond with the three physical components described above. They are:

Viscerotonia:[16] relaxation, conviviality, and gluttony for food, company, and affection or social support (oral types).

Somatotonia: assertiveness, physical adventurousness, energetic, love of domination and power, courage, aggressiveness (urethral types).

Cerebretonia: restraint, love of privacy, overintensity, apprehensiveness, secretiveness, emotional restraint, hypersensitivity (anal types).

Sheldon found, as had Kretschmer, not only that body forms related to psychiatric disorders and temperamental patterns but that a full range of psychological qualities corresponded to physical characteristics, as noted in the diagram from his text on psychiatric variables. He observed, moreover, that at the "morphological poles" of pure or nearly pure endomorphy, mesomorphy, or ectomorphy (such as 7-1-1, 1-7-1, 1-1-7) psychiatric diagnosis becomes extremely difficult, the individual characteristically displaying mixed psychiatric characteristics.[17]

---

[16] Sheldon uses the suffix "-otic" to refer to abnormal or pathological overmanifestation and "-penic" to refer to lack of or abnormally low degree of a component.

[17] Sheldon illustrates the point: "Similarly the extreme mesomorphs, 2-7-1's, 1-7-1's, 1-6-2's, and so on perplex the psychiatrists. These mesomorphs get labeled both manic and paranoid, rarely hebephrenic (although not infrequently 'catatonic,'

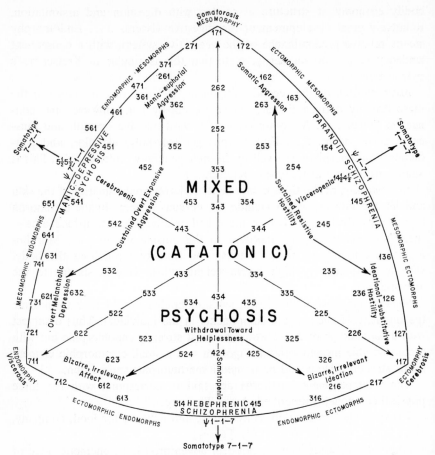

FIGURE 4. Diagram for the psychotic reaction patterns. (*Sheldon, Hartl, and Mc-Dermott, Varieties of Delinquent Youth, Fig. 5, p. 59. Reprinted by permission.*)

As a result of his observations, Sheldon has formulated a set of "psychiatric poles" that lie, as noted in the accompanying diagram, midway between the morphological poles. It will be observed that manic-

which seems to be a wastebasket category). One 2-7-1 in the first series I studied at Worcester had been diagnosed as a manic-depressive psychotic five times and paranoid schizophrenic six times—ten changes of diagnosis alternating between two diagnoses. He seemed to be balanced right in the middle, between those two diagnostic typologies, and I think that in fact he was so balanced. His biological position was almost perfectly centered between the two psychiatric poles." *Op. cit.,* pp. 56–57.

Among 343 possible combinations of somatotype components, Sheldon found only 76 in actual practice and these were distributed in characteristic clusters as revealed in the diagram on delinquents. Presumably, had the sample been larger, there might have been a somewhat wider range.

depressive psychosis is found in those combining mesomorphic and endo-morphic qualities, paranoid schizophrenia in the combined ectomorph and mesomorph, and hebephrenic schizophrenia in the mixed ectomorph and endomorph.[18] The diagram shows his observations as a distribution of emotional, intellectual, and behavioral qualities as they relate to the somatotypes.

The Varieties of Delinquent Youth is based upon Sheldon's study of a sample of 200 delinquent youths in a private treatment institution, the Hayden Goodwill Inn (HGI), in Boston. As in his previous investigations, he somatotyped these cases from photographs and studied their person-alities. He also explored their social and criminal histories. It was believed that about half of the sample became delinquent because of insufficiencies, mental and medical, and because of psychopathic personality. Among the remainder Sheldon found what he believed to be significant relation-ships between their delinquency and their somatotypes, more particularly (1) those lacking in a normal cerebrotonic component (the cerebropenics), (2) those deficient in the viscerotonic element (the visceropenics), and (3) the somatopenics. In his study, Sheldon states:[19]

In the delinquency of (our sample) there seemed to be three components of sufficiently general manifestation to raise the question as to whether they may not be primary to all delinquency, and each component has its own heroic overtone. First there was Dionysian delinquency, which appears to stem from pathological lack of the cerebrotonic component, or from a disproportionate predominance of the tensions arising from soma and gut. The religious outlook which has been rightly or wrongly associated with the late stages of the Roman civilization is a good example of Dionysian delinquency. The religion of the Freudian psychoanalysts is a revival of the same thing. Both are expressivistic, antidisciplinary religions. The outlook of the average American businessman is, in the middle of the twentieth century, essentially Dionysian. The boys (in this group) were predominantly Dionysian in their manifest patterns of ex-pression.

Second, there is a paranoid delinquency, stemming apparently from patho-logical lack or disengagement of the viscerotonic component; thus from dis-proportionate predominance and bad integrations of tensions from the soma and forebrain. Lack of viscerotonic participation in a personality is lack of sweet reasonableness, of a sense of fair play, and of the capacity for give and take. When paranoia is wedded to ambitious power ruthless hate and cunning are at play wherever power can reach. For our time Hitler will doubtless stand

---

[18] Sheldon expresses the opinion that these psychoses are not distinct and uniform clinical entities, as one might infer from traditional psychiatry. He suggests con-stitutional and temperamental deviations from case to case, inferrable from the variations in somatotypes and psychiatric indices: "Young psychiatrists are taught to classify disease, but psychiatric disease is clearly an event in a continuum and psychiatric patients, like other people, are expressing components of personality which appear to vary along multidimensional axes." *Ibid.,* p. 409.

[19] *Ibid.,* pp. 860–862. (Reprinted by permission.)

as the symbol of paranoid delinquency, with the Prussian ruling caste drawn up behind him in arrogant array. . . .

Third, there is hebephrenic delinquency, stemming from pathological lack or disengagement of the somatotonic component (and thus, at least before general deterioration sets in, with disproportionate predominance and bad integrations of tensions from the viscera and forebrain). All three delinquencies express ways of failure of the humor balance. We dwell on a promontory that seems to slope off to the northwest, to the northeast, and to the south. At the top is strength in all the primary components of temperament—affective strength, conative strength, cognitive strength. Integration of all three components is health and humor. Failure in any direction is disaster.

From the charting of the delinquents one can see that a disproportionately large number were cerebropenics in temperament and mesomorphic-endomorphic in somatotype. From these data they appear to be a most significant delinquent type. Sheldon describes them as "Dionysian," by which he refers to the exuberant, extraversive, noninhibited, and predatory qualities that characterize this range of body forms.[20] Constitutionally and temperamentally they are at the opposite extreme from the mass of hospitalized schizophrenics.

Sheldon suggests that the predatory quality observed so commonly among the delinquents may be a normal consequence of their morphological structure and its associated temperamental characteristics:[21]

[20] Sheldon said, "Perhaps the persistently criminal boy is expressing not so much a 'psychogenic resentment against the mother' as a Dionysian reaction which is almost as much a product of his constitutional design as the way he walks . . . the level of persistent effort at predation reached by the HGI boys who present primary criminality could probably not have been maintained without a strong temperamental predisposition toward predation." *Ibid.,* p. 830.

[21] *Ibid.,* pp. 827–828. (Reprinted by permission.) A variety of criticisms has been directed at the Sheldon research. While generally approving, Hooton has noted that Sheldon devoted insufficient attention to factors of race, sex, and age as they affect physique. Meredith has criticized the ambiguities and indefiniteness of statement and the confusion of findings and theory in some of the Sheldon research. Howard V. Meredith, "Comments on 'Varieties of Human Physique,'" *Child Develop.,* vol. 11, pp. 301–309, 1940. Other researchers have found it difficult to apply the somatotyping technique as described by Sheldon because of the lack of sufficient standardization and the variation in individual standards of decision on classification. See Leopold Bellak and Robert R. Holt, "Somatotypes in Relation to Dementia Praecox," *Am. J. Psychiat.,* vol. 104, pp. 713–724, 1948, and J. T. Shaplin, "Personal Equation in Somatotyping," cited by Adelaide K. Bullen and Harriet L. Hardy, *Am. J. Anthropol.,* n.s., vol. 4, p. 39, 1942, cited in Snodgrasse, *loc. cit.* As Snodgrasse observes, the somatotyping technique has been employed by others in their researches on the relationship between physique and skills and personality traits. See, in particular, Sheldon Glueck and Eleanor Glueck, *Unraveling Juvenile Delinquency,* 1950, chap. 15, and Carl C. Seltzer, F. L. Wells, and E. B. McTernan, "A Relationship between Sheldonian Somatotype and Psychotype," *J. Personality,* vol. 6, pp. 431–436, 1948.

I have lived among quite a number of different groups of people, floc-
culating as they have along numerous cleavage lines, and some of the groups
have seemed to enjoy life after their own fashion. But I have a somewhat unhappy suspicion that no group of them all has been fundamentally happier
than the first two platoons of the HGI series. Those boys were on the whole

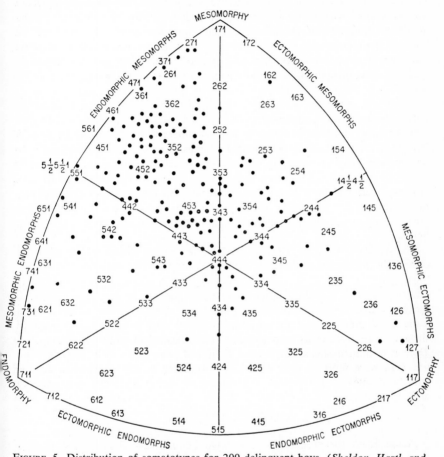

FIGURE 5. Distribution of somatotypes for 200 delinquent boys. (*Sheldon, Hartl, and
McDermott, Varieties of Delinquent Youth, Fig. 20, p. 729. Reprinted
by permission.*)

having a good time. . . . The youngsters must be judged against their own
standards and criteria, if they are to be judged at all. They were doing pretty
well at finding a way of life that served their own purposes, and they had fun,
probably more fun than average or ordinary people have. They were more
interesting than ordinary people are. If they were to be compared, individual
for individual, with the social work profession that with manifest bewilderment
was trying to ride herd on them, I think that the boys had the better of it. . . .
The comparatively brighter and more competent ones among the first two

platoons, and more noticeably among all the platoons of the second company, presented another quality along with the Dionysian buoyancy, or perhaps it is but another aspect of the buoyancy. This is the quality of unabashed or unashamed predation. In the minds of most of the youngsters who looked on themselves as "takers" (rather than as workers or servants of society or whatnot) there was no doubt as to what life was for. "The world is my oyster. I should worry," was the favorite rejoinder of No. 126 to every frontal or flank attack on his position. He was Dionysian by temperament and predatory in outlook. To him predation was the normal outlook on life and he was no more ashamed of being predatory than is a marsh harrier. Now quite an important question, for anybody who would understand delinquency, would be this: Is predation a normal outlook for the human species? Is it the normal way of life *for some members* of the species? Are some men and women so endowed, morphologically and temperamentally, that it is quite normal for them to seek to prey upon others and to seek to live off others without "contributing" as it is normal for some of the rest of us weaklings to seek to live as workers, public servants, research scientists, prostitutes, preachers, and so on? Our society is organized on the premise that the question is superfluous, that an affirmative answer is self-evident. I do not mean that you will find public protocols recognizing the predatory element in any current attempt at a social *apologia,* any more than you will find public recognition of the sexual element in a Methodist hymn.

The youngsters at the HGI seemed to be more realistically aware of the essentially predatory philosophy underlying the social structure than were those who had been—and still were—attempting to reeducate those youngsters away from such a philosophy. I many times had the feeling, in talking with the boys, that I was in a false position. I felt sometimes like an envoy of a *dishonestly* predatory enterprise sent to decoy and to trap into a kind of slavery those free spirits who had thus far managed to elude the snare. . . . They saw human society in a truer light and were more truly engaged with life than were most of their elders who were professedly engaged in dealing with "delinquency" but in fact were concerned mainly with their own security and righteousness.

OTHER STUDIES

Aside from the researches that have been noted above, most studies of criminals either have neglected the influence of physical factors or have found few significant differences. Such studies have suffered from the lack of norms or control groups for comparison. Both Goring, in England, and Healy and Bronner, in the United States, have observed the incidence of physical deviations among offenders. The latter found that nearly three-fourths of a sample of female delinquents were overdeveloped, while over half of the boys in a group of 2,000 juvenile recidivists were below normal. Healy and Bronner inferred that physical ailments had been a major factor in causing delinquency in only 4 per cent of their cases but had been a minor factor in 23.3 per cent. In his study of 1,000 juvenile delinquents, William Healy found well-marked "stigmata" in 133 cases, mainly anomalies of the external ear, palate, and jaws and the shape of the head.[22] He concluded, however, that if the cases of mental abnormality were taken out of this series the proportion of cases with such peculiarities would be little if any larger than the proportion found in the general population. He points to the common relationship between physical defects and mental, nutritional, and environmental deficiencies as being the more significant correlation.

In their most recent investigation Sheldon and Eleanor Glueck found little difference between their delinquent sample and their controls in general health and physical condition.[23] However, they found, in accordance with Sheldon's observations and in using the somatotype system that he developed, that their delinquents unlike the controls were predominantly of the mesomorphic constitutional type, solid, muscular, with broad shoulders and tapering waists. Delinquents were somewhat stronger than nondelinquents in the endomorphic components and weaker than nondelinquents in the ectomorphic. The Gluecks found evidence of a lag in physical development until about the fourteenth year, at which time the delinquents tended to spurt forward to superiority over the nondelinquent controls with whom they were compared. Bodily disproportions and variations within the sample were less common among the delinquents. Strong masculine physical components were found much more commonly among the delinquents, too.

In 1956 the Gluecks offered a more intensive analysis of the interrelationships between body types and selected traits and sociocultural factors that had been studied initially in *Unraveling Juvenile Delinquency*. More particularly, they sought to discover what traits and factors exert a statistically significant differential influence on the delinquency of different body types. They concluded[24] that:

(1) The basic morphologic differentiation of the physique types is accompanied by differences in the incidence among them of certain traits, some of which are actually associated with delinquency, others potentially so. (2) Differences in the physical and temperamental structure of body types bring about some variation in their response to environmental pressures. (3) Differences in the incidence of certain traits among the physique types, as well as divergences in their reactions to the environment, are reflected in certain differences in the etiology of delinquency among the body types.

The observation of a greater association of destructive-sadistic trends and of emotional instability with the delinquency of mesomorphs than with that of ectomorphs[25] illustrates their specific findings. They also found

---

[22] William Healy, *The Individual Delinquent*, 1915, p. 146.

[23] Sheldon Glueck and Eleanor Glueck, *op. cit.*, chaps. 14, 15.

[24] Sheldon Glueck and Eleanor Glueck, *Physique and Delinquency*, 1956, p. 249.

[25] *Ibid.* See pp. 149 ff. for an analysis of the sixty-seven traits that were studied in relation to four major body types.

among sociocultural factors a number that exerted a varied influence on the delinquency of different body types.[26] Thus, for example, influences that had an especially unfavorable impact upon ectomorphs included emotional disturbance in the father, the gainful employment of the mother, the broken home, low conduct standards of the family, incompatibility of the parents, a lack of family cohesiveness, careless supervision by the mother and her lack of attachment to the boy, and unsuitable discipline by the father. It appears that, while in general individuals of mesomorphic build are more prone to delinquency, the "sensitive ectomorph" may be adversely affected to a greater extent by a considerable variety of social variables. On the other hand, a lack of family group recreation and meagre recreational facilities in the home appeared to have been more damaging to mesomorphs.

BIOCHEMISTRY AND CRIME

Endocrinology is an infant science and much remains to be discovered concerning the influence of the ductless glands and the hormones they secrete upon man. From the evidence already at hand, however, it is very clear that the endocrines may profoundly affect the constitution and the behavior of the individual. Abnormal structure or functioning of the glands sometimes results in extreme deviations in mentality, emotionality, and other aspects of personality. It appears that the hormones affect feelings, emotions, and behavior through their influence upon all organs of the body in general and upon the brain and nervous system in particular. Podolsky suggests that thyroxin, parathyrin, adrenalin, and cortin, as well as the estrogens and androgens—all glandular secretions—greatly influence conduct through their effects on the brain.[27] He refers to a study[28] conducted some years ago by several psychiatrists at Sing Sing to discover any relationship that might exist between criminal behavior and biochemical composition:

It was found that in cases of robbery and burglary the prisoners usually lacked pituitrin and parathyrin in their bodily chemistry. In criminal actions involving grand larceny there was a lack of parathyrin and pituitrin, but there was an increase in thyroxin and thymus hormones. In petty larceny there was a lack of parathyrin and pituitrin but an increase in thymus secretion. Murderers usually had a decrease in the amount of parathyrin, but there was an abnormal increase in thymus, adrenalin, and thyroxin.

Further studies revealed that in fraud there was an increase in thyroxin but a decrease in pituitrin and parathyrin. In forgery there was too much thyroxin

[26] *Ibid.* The relation of sociocultural factors and somatotypes is summarized on pp. 208–209.

[27] Edward Podolsky, "The Chemical Brew of Criminal Behavior," *J. Crim. L.,* vol. 45, pp. 675–679, 1955.

[28] *Ibid.,* p. 678. (Reprinted by permission.)

and thymus and too little parathyrin. Rapists were found to have an over-whelming supply of thyroxin and estrogens and too little pituitrin. Those prisoners who had been sentenced for assault and battery were found to have too much adrenalin, too much thyroxin and too little pituitrin and the estrogens. When the blood of the Sing Sing inmates was analyzed it was found that the great majority of them had an excessive amount of nonprotein nitrogen in the blood; their blood sugar level was too low, their uric acid and cholesterol levels were always above normal.

Podolsky observes that biochemical evaluation of criminal personality is still in its infancy. Certainly we do not yet know what etiological significance should be attached to such findings. The findings suggest interesting possibilities for future improvements in our understanding of the offender and in our treatment measures.

Berman, one of the prominent students of endocrinology, has suggested that there are various endocrine types of personality in which one or another of the hormones may dominate the pattern of the individual's behavior:[29] (1) the uninhibited, irresponsible, and criminalistic *thymocentric;* (2) the *thyroid* types, displaying either the traits of cretinous insufficiency or of impulsive and energetic hyperthyroidism; (3) the *adrenal* types, either the vigorous and persevering hyperadrenals or the irritable and dull adrenal insufficients; (4) the *pituitary* types, either hypermasculine or feminine in features and disposition; (5) the restless, unsatisfied *parathyroid* types; and (6) the inadequately masculine *gonadocentric* personalities.[30] Berman indicated that these types generally occur in mixtures rather than in a pure form. It is generally thought that Berman has exaggerated the role of the glands in personality; his theory of types has not been subjected to empirical investigation, but his material highlights the significant role of the endocrines in numerous personality disturbances.

The particularistic determinism that weakens Berman's analysis of the role of the glands in personality and behavior is considerably surpassed in a later volume devoted to the influence of the glands on crime. Schlapp maintained that "the glandular theory of crime accounts for all the discrepancies, errors, oversights, and inadequacies of the earlier explanations."[31] In his view most criminality and mental deficiency arises from bodily disorders: " . . . most crimes come about through disturbances of the ductless glands in the criminal and through mental defects caused by endocrine troubles in the criminal's mother. . . . Criminal actions are in

---

[29] L. Berman, *The Glands Regulating Personality,* 1922.

[30] Compare this with Sheldon's observation concerning the influence of the masculinity component: "It is apparently from the gynandromorphic groups that most of the 'peeping' and sexually exhibitionistic males are recruited. These appear to be men in whom the sexual drive is so intense and imperative, and the threshold of excitement so low, that the impulse detonates by combustion induced at long range." Sheldon, Hartl, and McDermott, *op. cit.,* p. 256.

[31] M. Schlapp and E. H. Smith, *The New Criminology,* 1928, p. 72.

reality reactions caused by the disturbed internal chemistry of the body."[32] Schlapp conceded some significance to environmental influences, but believed that in the main these influences produced unbalance or malfunctioning of the endocrines and, when occurring in the gestant mother, resulted in defective offspring.[33]

Schlapp illustrates the role of the endocrine in crime by a case of kleptomania, from which we quote his concluding comments:[34]

A few months later Lilly found herself in New York with an hour to kill before train time. She was drawn to another store and tried to resist the impulse, being both conscious of the danger and somewhat frightened by her recent experience. But she went against her own judgment and in spite of fears. In other words, the inhibitory power was in abeyance, owing to the irritation of the cells in certain neuron groups of a disordered chemical fluid. Once more she was attracted by some objects hardly worth stealing—stockings. She admired them, was seized with the same kind of nervous attack and tried to make off with a few pairs. She was again caught and this time was held for the court, with the result that she was referred to the clinic for examination.

She was, as might have been expected, in a state of exaggerated emotionalism, revealed high blood pressure, variable pulse, disturbed metabolism and other symptoms of chemical abnormality. These latter were not so marked as might have been expected and this fact seemed to argue a disease in some of the glands whose condition is not revealed by the tests now available and in use. . . . She was given sedative and various gland substances (sic!). . . . In a few weeks she was greatly changed for the better. A position in a suburban private school was found for her where the attending physician watched her continued gland medication. Today, after the elapse of six years, she is in good physical condition, her nervousness has subsided, she has had no recurrence of the kleptomanic attacks and she has been teaching school and attending to her small flock of children steadily and with marked patience and ability. She may be said to have made a permanent recovery.

Obviously the diagnostician's evaluation of an endocrinological pathology in this case is quite unsatisfactorily vague. Descriptions of the phenomenon are adequate but the etiological analyses are not. This case, like many others, however, raises the question of whether biological and, very likely, specifically endocrinological pathologies may not be at the root of certain neurotic disturbances that the dynamic psychiatrists have generally assumed to be purely psychogenic. We need to learn much more about the specific consequences of glandular and other biological functioning for personality and behavior. This calls for extended research. As the biologist Montagu has said in criticism of the studies that have been performed thus far: "Writing now as a student of scientific method, I should venture the opinion that not one of the reports on the alleged relationship between

---

[32] *Ibid.*, p. 28.
[33] *Ibid.*, p. 135.
[34] *Ibid.*, p. 218. (Reprinted by permission.)

glandular dysfunctions and criminality has been carried out in a scientific manner, and that all such reports are glaring examples of the fallacy of *false cause*." Again he says: "The fact is that as far as the endocrine system and its relation to personality and behavior are concerned, we are still almost completely in a world of the unknown, and that to resort to that system for an explanation of criminality is merely to attempt to explain the known by the unknown."[35] This criticism is excessive, for a good deal is known about the effects of certain endocrine dysfunctions on personality and, moreover, analysis of crime causation is today very largely a matter of explaining the known by what is only very partially known.

Hypoglycemia and Calcium Deficiency

Hypoglycemia is a condition produced by a low level of glucose in the blood, which is caused by excessive utilization of sugar or by interference with the formation of sugar in the liver. It has been recognized for some years that the amount of sugar present in the blood has an important bearing upon man's social behavior. Marked agressiveness, excitement, impairment of will power and moral perception, irritability, negativism, and a strengthening of sexual drives have been attributed to the hypoglycemic state. One authority has compiled a list of reported crimes that were committed during a state of spontaneous hypoglycemia. These included disorderly conduct, assault and battery, attempted suicide and homicide, cruelty against children and spouse, various sexual perversions and aggressions, false fire alarms, drunkenness, embezzlement, petty larceny, willful destruction of property, arson, slander, and violation of traffic regulations.[36]

Podolsky cites an English case[37] in which the relationship between a crime and hypoglycemia was shown quite clearly, resulting in discharge of the defendant:

A twenty year old man, living alone with his mother, stabbed her to death with a kitchen knife, inflicting many wounds on her body. In the five days preceding the murder he had worked hard and had had but irregular meals. Also, there had been some quarreling with his mother over money. On the morning of the day of the murder he struck her, a very unusual act for which he apologized. He ate poorly on that day. He had his last carbohydrate meal at noon. Between 9 and 10:30 P.M. he drank four pints of mild ale. At 11 P.M. there was again a quarrel with his mother over money and she pushed him out of her room. At this moment he suddenly felt thirsty, went to the kitchen to get a bottle opener, saw a knife, and then "something came over" him: "I was like a homicidal maniac." He stabbed his mother to death, then realized what he had done, wiped the knife for fingerprints, washed and dressed, and left the house. There is a gap in his memory for seven hours following the crime. The next day, he gave himself to the police and made a full statement.

---

[35] Montagu, *op. cit.*, pp. 55–56.

[36] Podolsky, *op. cit.*, p. 675.

[37] *Ibid.*, pp. 676–677. (Reprinted by permission.)

After the patient's arrest, his family physician notified the defense that two years prior to the crime a sugar tolerance curve had shown a tendency to hypoglycemia. Hiss and Sargent performed a number of tests which showed that the prisoner was definitely suffering from hypoglycemia. They expressed the opinion that his blood at the time of the crime must have been below 100 mgm. and that his brain at that time was functioning abnormally; and that his judgment was impaired at the time. The verdict was: "Guilty but insane."

Lack of calcium also appears to be associated with crime as a result of the emotional instability that characterizes the victims of calcium starvation. Such individuals often display violent tempers, tending to scream and strike out. "He throws things about and attacks his aggressor without any sense of judgment arising to inhibit these rapid changes. One such person, during an interval of extreme calcium deprivation, threw his sister out of the window because of some disparaging remark she had made. Another shot at a group of schoolmates with a gun that was handy at the moment."[38] Individuals with such calcium deficiencies display characteristic bodily features and biochemical conditions. It is quite reasonable to believe that the relationships between body form and temperament that have been observed by Kretschmer, Sheldon, and others may reflect biochemical abnormalities.

THE ROLE OF HEREDITY

The influence of heredity is a subject of ever recurrent interest relating to human personality and conduct. The strong environmentalistic bias among authorities on behavior today together with the reaction against some of the biologists' overly simplistic determinism have led, as we have suggested, to the criminologists' failure to explore the hereditary and constitutional influences with critical discrimination. Much of the problem in this regard lies in the fact that no clear distinctions can be drawn between the influences of heredity and of environmental conditioning upon the personality characteristics of the individual. There can no longer be any serious doubt that the genes play a tremendously important part in establishing at conception the basic potentialities and trends of the organism. Difficulty of interpretation arises from the fact that significant environmental influences, chemical, thermal, and others, affect the fetus during the gestation period and that a highly complex social-cultural milieu affects the organism after birth. As traits appear or change during the various phases of maturation, it is quite impossible to determine the relative role played by the individual's heredity and by the environmental influences to which he has been exposed. This is obviously true of well-developed trait complexes and, more particularly, of personality characteristics in

---

[38] *Ibid.,* p. 677.

which societal pressures exercise highly persuasive and persistent but variable influences. As Montagu has stated:[39]

There is every reason to believe that the genetically determined nervous morphological differential is, in any human population, as variable as any of its physical characters. But once this has been granted, it must be said that there is equally good reason to believe—and this is the important point—that the observable differences in the behavior between different individuals is to a far larger extent determined by cultural factors than by the total number of biological factors which operate from within the individual. Chief among these biological factors is the microscopic structure of the nervous system itself, and it cannot here be too often emphasized that that very structure is itself, to the most important extent, structurally and physiologically, organized by the action, from birth to maturity, of cultural influences. It is principally to this unique capacity that the species Homo sapiens owes most of those qualities which are implied in the term "human being."

Montagu places a degree of emphasis here upon cultural factors in personality differentiation that is somewhat unusual for a biologist. It should be observed, however, that the individual's heredity and his physiological organization impose restrictions upon the extent of development in particular directions that can occur through environmental conditioning. Although man characteristically does not realize his capacities to any very full extent, the biological limitations may nevertheless exert a very important restrictive influence on the individual's development. It is often said that man inherits potentialities or predispositions, expressions that are not precisely accurate, since technically one inherits only genes through which traits may evolve. As a practical matter, however, abilities and disabilities arising from heredity do enhance as well as limit particular lines of development in the individual, and these may be extremely important. In a complex society where formal education is emphasized, for example, the inherent capacity for the development of specific intellectual abilities is obviously very significant. Channels of occupational choice and the limits of possible proficiency in one's skills are automatically limited at conception. The fact that the ranges of developmental possibility are wide in a highly differentiated society, even where there are hereditary handicaps, does not belie the fundamentally nondemocratic restrictions initially imposed by nature. Moreover, original limitations and capacities tend to be exaggerated by social-cultural influence that bring out and encourage in some the expression of traits that are highly prized in a particular society and age and that proportionately penalize the lack of others. Aside from the matter of particular abilities and disabilities, in which the important role of heredity is very clear, one may well infer from the data on physique and temperament that, probably as a result of glandular function, hereditary influences on constitutional structure, play

---

[39] Montagu, *op. cit.*, p. 49. (Reprinted by permission.)

a suasive part in influencing the personality type and, through it, the potential range of social roles of the individual. To put it simply, while heredity does not *determine* the abilities, personality, or roles of the individual, it appears that heredity does both establish limits and, within the framework of the particular society, facilitate or inhibit development in these areas. Therefore heredity is important, though in indirect ways, in the development of delinquency and crime.

Neither crime itself nor criminality is inherited, of course. Crime, as we have seen, is a cultural phenomenon, determined by social-legal definition and highly variable in time and place. It appears clear that a criminological predisposition as such is not heritable, though a considerable amount of research that has been conducted from time to time has sought to prove such inheritance. Montagu summarizes several German and American studies of identical twins and fraternal twins, in which one or both members were criminal. Such studies have generally concluded that the greater frequency of concordance (both being criminal) in identical twins than in two-egg twins implied an inheritance of criminality.[40] The data are shown in this table:

Table 8. Criminal Behavior of Twins

Author	One-egg twins		Two-egg twins	
	Concordant	Discordant	Concordant	Discordant
Lange (1929)	10	3	2	15
Legras (1932)	4	0	0	5
Kranz (1936)	20	12	23	20
Stumpff (1936)	11	7	7	12
Rosanoff (1934)	25	12	5	23
Total	70	34	37	75
Per cent	67.3	32.7	33.0	67.0

SOURCE: Montagu, "The Biologist Looks at Crime," *The Annals,* vol. 217, p. 53, September, 1941.

The fact is that the greater similarity in the behavioral history of the identical twins can be accounted for, at least in part, by the fact of their closer companionship and identification, the greater probability of both encountering influences leading to crime if one does. While such studies do not specifically prove hereditary influence, this typical rejoinder of the environmentalists does not disprove such influence, either. The question is unresolved by the research data.

A number of studies have been made of family lines distinguished by hereditary taints, notably those of the Jukes, the Kallikaks, and the Nams. Such studies do not show, of course, that all of the pecularities that appear in the family line are hereditary. However, it appears quite obvious that

[40] *ibid.,* p. 53.

the numerous social problems occurring in such families are the product in part of hereditary defects and of the deficient environments in which such individuals have lived.[41]

Professor Sheldon points to the excessive reproduction of the parents of the sample of 200 delinquents whom he studied: " . . . 941 known offspring, plus an indeterminate number not reported in records available to us." As he points out with some irony, this is greatly in excess of the production of female university graduates of comparable age during the same period. The diseugenic consequences have serious import, not only for criminality, but for innumerable other problems.[42]

SEX CRIMES AND PHYSICAL FACTORS

The relationship of constitutional and physical factors to criminality is more apparent in the case of sexual crimes than in other forms of law violation. Since the major *initial* motive to sexual behavior is biological, it is quite clear that the individual's hormonal secretions affect the strength of the drive in a very basic way. This is not to say that the strength of the individual's need is exclusively determined by his endocrines, for personal and cultural factors profoundly affect his psychic requirements for erotic activity; but the frequency and forcefulness of the sexual potential and the individual's total sexual output are defined by the gonads in the male.[43] Within the limitations of the individual's biological potentiality there is a wide range of possibilities in the extent to which

[41] See Estabrook, *The Jukes in 1915,* 1916.

[42] Sheldon, Hartl, McDermott, *op. cit.,* pp. 837–838.

[43] Kinsey found that, while 77.7 per cent of the males in the population engage in some form of sexual outlet between 1.0 and 6.5 times per week, the remainder fall into extreme ranges down to zero and up to more than 29. See Kinsey, Pomeroy, and Martin, *Sexual Behavior in the Human Male,* 1948. Variation is even wider in the female. No definite norms have been established to define an excessive, inadequate, or ordinary degree of sexual drive, but the variations have been expressed generally in terms of fairly obvious extremes: the hyperversion of those with excessively strong drive, and the hypoversion of those whose impulses are abnormally weak. It should be noted that, while biologically or statistically either of these conditions is abnormal, it is the hypersexual about whom the community is ordinarily the most concerned. This reflects popular misinformation, for in fact psychosexual deviations are more characteristic among the undersexed, who for that very reason have more for which to compensate. Castration anxiety, varying degrees of impotence, frigidity, fears of infertility, feelings of inadequacy relative to the opposite sex—these quite often mark the psychological responses of the hyposexual. A lack of apparent or normally channelled sexual drive may be caused, of course, either by endocrinological-physiological deficiencies or by psychological blockings. In either case, the feelings and fears may be dangerous from a social point of view, for the individual is wont to feel the need for proving his virility. Otto Rank has maintained that the neurotic murderer is always one who attests his manhood by taking life. Whether or not this thesis be correct, it is certainly true that rapes, sadistic physical aggressions, pedophilia, and murder are sometimes expressive of the individual's underlying impotence.

gonadal activity may be stimulated by personal and social influences and in the direction that the drive may assume, these factors being based upon the conditioning experiences of the individual. Nevertheless, just as intellectual capacity may limit and, in some measure, direct personal growth, so the strength of the organic sexual drive has real meaning in the individual's erotic and personality history. It determines how much repression or sublimation the community expects of him, for example. Our criminal courts accord no attention to individual differences in the strength of the sexual urge. It is somewhat ironic that they treat a sexual deficient, a man of ordinary drive, and another with powerful gonadal pressures in the same way if convicted of a sexual crime, though each represents a rather different problem from the other.

Homosexuality

Homosexuality is one of the most common sexual aberrations; according to Kinsey, it is found in fairly persistent form in some 30 per cent of the population and as an exclusive and permanent pattern of behavior in 4 per cent.[44] This paraphilia has been the subject of a great amount of dispute among the experts concerning both its etiology and prognosis for cure. Homosexuality was long considered to be entirely a constitutional phenomenon, rooted in the physiological feminism of the male and masculinism in the female. Krafft-Ebing, Hirschfeld, Bauer, Weil, and many others have taken this view. Various scholars are currently doing considerable research on the endocrine balance of the homosexual, predicated on the hypothesis of a constitutional foundation. Some workers, including Clifford Wright, Abraham Myerson, and Rudolph Neustadt, have found an imbalance in the androgen-estrogen ratio in the homosexual and consider the estrogenic excess to be associated with the deviated sexuality.[45] Others have found such physiological correlates of homosexuality as disordered basal metabolism, abnormalities of the central nervous system, hypoglycemic states, etc.

Franz J. Kallman has been working with identical and fraternal twins to discover possible genetic relationships in homosexuality and believes that his material shows quite conclusively that there are important hereditary and constitutional foundations for true homosexuality in the male.[46]

[44] Kinsey's research indicates that only approximately 50 per cent of all males have neither overt nor psychic experience in homosexuality after adolescence. Some 30 per cent have at least incidental homosexual experiences over a period of three years or more between the ages of 16 and 55. Ten per cent are more or less exclusively homosexual for at least three years, and 4 per cent are exclusively so throughout their lives. Kinsey, Pomeroy, and Martin, *Sexual Behavior in the Human Male*, 1948, p. 392.

[45] See A. Myerson and R. Neustadt, "Symposium on Social Psychiatry, Bisexuality and Male Homosexuality: Their Biologic and Medical Aspects, *Clinics*, vol. 1, p. 942, 1942.

[46] F. J. Kallman, "Twin Studies in Relation to Adjustive Problems in Man," *Trans. N.Y. Acad. Sci.*, May, 1951.

Sandor Ferenczi has taken the view that there are two main homosexual classes. "The subject homosexual" is a true invert with feminism that is based upon a constitutional predisposition, reinforced by a defective environment. He is attracted by strongly masculine males and is characterized by the feminine qualities of narcissism, passivity, and intuitiveness. Ferenczi holds that such individuals are not obsessed by guilt feelings or inner conflicts. "The object homosexual," on the other hand, is an obsessional neurotic, basically male, but with conditioning experiences that have turned his interests toward young males.[47]

Perhaps the soundest nonparochial view of the etiology of sexuality is provided by Dr. George W. Henry in a study "without personal bias or theoretical assumptions" of homosexuals in the courts of New York City. He concludes that these sex variants remain at an immature level of sexual development because of constitutional deficiencies, the influences of family patterns of sexual adjustment, and lack of opportunities for psychosexual development.[48] Dr. Henry maintains, moreover, that constitutional deficiencies in the homosexual may be structural, physiological, and psychological, the structural ones being least evident and the psychological ones most easily demonstrable. As he points out, the relative contribution of heredity and environment is an academic question that cannot be precisely determined, but whatever may have been contributed by the germ plasm is nurtured in the family situation.

One homosexual in Dr. Henry's sample combined transvestism with his passive, generally effeminate trends. Of poor intelligence and dwarf physique, this homosexual was weak and girlish in appearance. He was excessively dependent upon his mother, whom he assisted habitually in housework. As a sickly and fearful child he slept with her quite commonly. He witnessed parental intercouse while very young and had an early experience of masturbation by his brother. He admired strong, tall, well-built men and became an easy prey to aggressive males. In the development of his homosexual pattern he adopted feminine attire as well as the use of cosmetics and came to operate a house for male prostitution.[49]

THE SIGNIFICANCE OF BIOLOGICAL FACTORS

Montagu appears to take the extreme position that biology is quite unrelated to criminality, suggesting in effect that crime is biologically normal and that therefore there is no relationship between criminal behavior and biological structure:[50]

[47] Sandor Ferenczi, *Sex in Psychoanalysis*, 1922, chap. 12.
[48] George W. Henry, *Sex Variants, A Study of Homosexual Patterns*, 1948, p. 1023.
[49] *Ibid.*, pp. 15–16.
[50] Montagu, *op. cit.*, pp. 46–47. (Reprinted by permission.)

From the standpoint of the mechanistic biologist, criminal behavior is a form of behavior which, like most others, serves the purposes of the organism, but which has been arbitrarily delimited by a social group and termed "criminal." The biologist may fully recognize that the behavior which a particular society terms "criminal" may have important social consequences for the group, but since these consequences are not likely to produce either a temporary or a permanent change in the biological character of the group, such consequences are no concern of his. The "criminal" behavior which is socially recognized still remains behavior which, from his standpoint, cannot be differentiated from any other *normal* behavior of the organism.

I emphasize *normal* here, because I wish to draw attention to the fact that criminal behavior is, from the biological standpoint, as normal as any other form of behavior. . . .

Many students of crime tend rather to approach the study of criminal behavior as if such behavior were in itself abnormal, as if there were something intrinsically "wrong" with the organism exhibiting this "wrong" behavior. The persistent and practically serious error committed here is, quite unjustifiably, to translate a judgment of social value into one of biological value. Much of the thinking and writing about crime, in America as in Europe, is vitiated by this serious error. It is this error which has to a very large extent been responsible for the belief that there exists some relation between criminal behavior and the biological structure of the organism.

To the author it appears that the reasoning here represents a flight from an unjustified biological determinism to an equally unjustifiable repudiation of physical influences on criminality. Certainly neither the fact that crime is culturally defined nor the fact that it is biologically and socially normal in an etiological sense should be taken to mean that specific forms of criminal conduct are unrelated to the physical condition or to the hereditary traits of the offender. Rather, the nature of crime and its etiology suggest that there is no uniform hereditary or biological taint or peculiarity out of which crimes generally arise. Of this we are very sure. We are equally sure that, whatever may be the role of physiological influences in the particular criminal instance, social and cultural factors are to a very large extent responsible for the behavior itself as well as the group's interpretation of it. Physical and hereditary influences are nonetheless causally related to personality and behavior. And in so far as criminal acts proceed from peculiarities of personality, disposing the individual toward particular lines of conduct, it is reasonable to impute to biology both the foundations out of which such personality variables develop and, *pro tanto,* a role in the criminal behavior that ensues. The significance of such biological influences for crime varies greatly both with the extent of its impact upon personality and with the nature of the relationship between the personality traits and criminal behavior. These matters cannot, as we have suggested, be measured exactly, because of the intimate association of sociocultural with physical factors in man's body, psyche, and behavior. It appears evident, however, that organic pathologies and deviations of many mental deficients, for example, and of seniles, epileptics, cretins, paretics, and encephalitics, are primarily responsible for their peculiarities of behavior, including sometimes crime.

There is mounting evidence that constitutional factors play a determinative role in the occurrence of some personality deviations that in the past have been attributed wholly to dynamic elements in life experience. Thus, for example, "functional psychoses" appear increasingly to have an organic, probably a chemical, foundation. We find that chemical and electroencephalographic tests discover such disorders and that biochemical therapies treat them. Current research indicating a metabolic disturbance in alcoholics suggests that this form of addiction may be rooted in a specific endocrinological pathology. There are important and still unanswered questions concerning the role of heredity and constitutional factors in cases of psychopathic personality, emotional instability, certain temperamental traits, and other personality variables that are found more often among criminals than in the general population. It appears more than possible that a generation hence much that is treated among psychological and social factors in criminogenesis will come to be included among the constitutional influences upon crime. We should anticipate a greater appreciation of biopsychological and biosocial influences in behavior.

It should be observed further that it is not always deficiency that is associated with criminality. The superior intelligence of the fraud and the con man, the physical strength and agility of the "cat burglar," the winsome charms of the call girl, and the mechanical skills of the car thief are all conditions (though not determinants, of course) of the crimes involved just as surely as are the subnormalities associated with other offenses, such as vagrancy, many sex crimes, and petty theft. Conversely, approved behavior is not a necessary consequence of a healthy body. As one wag has said, "A lot of good behavior is due to poor health." That some sorts of physical superiority may serve as well as deficiency in facilitating certain forms of law violation is nicely illustrated in the case of Daisy Smith. Her physical charms and intelligence were distinct assets in her field. It is possible, though not clear from the evidence, that her offenses may have been influenced by an unfortunate childhood experience and the failure of her marriage.

Daisy was orphaned as a young child by the death of her father. The mother soon remarried but the stepfather also died while the prisoner was still quite young. She, together with a large family of sisters and brothers, had little parental supervision, being left largely to their own devices while the mother was absent from the home. At the age of 13 Daisy was raped by a visitor at her home and acquired gonorrhea as a result of the attack. Except for this event, her social history during the formative years is quite unremarkable. Her occupational history has been generally quite stable. At the age of 18 she became a checkroom attendant and, after working at this for four years, operated a power machine in the manufacture of women's clothing for nearly ten years. In 1941 she married a surgeon, but her marital relationship was an unhappy one and she secured a divorce from him in 1946, without issue from the marriage. The following year Daisy was sentenced to thirty days in the workhouse in Chicago for keeping a disorderly house. On arrests involving the same offense she was discharged in 1951 and 1952. She admitted having engaged in prostitution quite regularly since her divorce, asserting that more customers were referred to her than she could handle, so that she had interested other girls in going to work for her. She operated a small gift shop in a downtown hotel as a front for the call-girl business. Some of the girls were referred to her as an accommodation by friends from other cities with whom Daisy had become acquainted.

Daisy has established an excellent institutional record during her imprisonment. She is securing training in laboratory work and asserts her intention to continue in such work if she can after release. In light of her age and the recent difficulties she has encountered, together with the fact that she is capable of earning a fair if less remunerative livelihood in other ways, it is unlikely that Daisy will return to her former employment.

Constitutional factors, especially deficiencies, often appear to be associated with delinquency because of the barrier they raise to the offender's working out of normal social adjustments. It is also true, of course, that the vast majority of people in poor mental or physical health are not law violators. The major difficulty in this class of cases appears to lie in the compensatory reactions of the offender to his peculiarity, his feelings of inferiority, and reactive aggression. In other instances, defect may reduce the individual's capacity to compete occupationally as well as socially. Generally the severity of an abnormality is of itself less important than the strength of the person's subjective response to it. Antisocial behavior is, of course, only one among the various possible types of reaction that the offender may display. In the course of research in the Girls Term Court in New York City, which is a morals court for female adolescents, the author observed a pathetic illustration of the effects of a constitutional factor on a girl's delinquent history.[51]

Sixteen-year-old Jane displayed a long history of recalcitrance and sex offenses that resulted to a very large extent from her physical condition. An illegitimate, unwanted child, her mother had attempted to produce an abortion during the latter part of her pregnancy by jumping from a moving automobile. A premature delivery was the result and the infant was so badly injured as to require the removal of both legs at the hips. A greater part of her life was spent in a succession of institutional commitments as a neglected and delinquent child. Because of her unattractive appearance and disposition, her delinquencies, and the amount of care she required, foster-home placement was not

[51] Tappan, *Delinquent Girls in Court,* 1947.

a successful solution. The extended series of institutional confinements failed to provide her the warmth, affection, and security she badly needed, and her reactive aggressions served only to make her even less loved among her associates and supervisors. She was provided with artificial limbs by which she was able to move about adequately, but the legs never fitted properly and her feelings of inadequacy were to a great extent a result of her role as the "legless" girl in the institutions where she had been placed. When she was fourteen, she was tried in boarding-home placement where she might have more freedom. It was then that her sex delinquencies started, a clear expression of her emotional deprivations, of her desire to be a normal girl and to make up for some of the fun that she had missed. At the time she was seen, Jane suffered from badly developed infections, both syphilis and gonorrhea, and from gangrene as a result of friction and lack of proper care of her limbs. She was committed by the court to a reformatory for delinquent girls where it is most unlikely that she will receive any of the help that she has needed and failed to find.

Chapter 5

PSYCHOPATHOLOGY AND CRIMES AGAINST THE PERSON

The etiological approaches to crime are varied. For the most part, the views of differing specialists have been parochial rather than integrative or eclectic. Studies are avowedly "sociocultural," "clinical," "dynamic," "biological," etc.[1] The result is inevitably a fragmented picture of the offender. Each specialized approach tends to exaggerate some classes of influence and interpretation and to neglect others. One may be led alternatively to see the criminal as a victim of social or economic circumstances, the product of cultural conditioning, a psychopathological deviate, a member of an anthropometric class, a personality type deficient in superego organization, a mechanism conditioned to antisocial behavior, or in any of a wide variety of other quite limited contexts. As criminology matures there is a gradually increasing recognition not only of the multiple causation of crime but also of the need to assimilate the findings and the methodologies that have contributed to the field. The bias of special disciplines is remarkably persistent, however.

Perhaps nowhere are the difficulty and the consequent losses to the substance of criminology better represented than in the material that comes, on the one hand, from the sociologists and, on the other, from those who follow one or another of various individualized "clinical" approaches: the dynamic psychiatrists, the psychobiologists, and the neuropsychiatrists. Conflicting ideas in relation to causation, prevention, and treatment of crime reflect differences in the perceptions and interpretations of authorities in these fields. This is especially to be deprecated in that so large a part of the contributions to criminological theory and correctional practice have come from the assorted and thus far quite unassimilated behavioral sciences.

In discussing the problem of the varying orientations in his general field,[2] Dr. Thomas Meyers, a practicing psychiatrist experienced in forensic psychiatry, observes the great differences between approaches of the

[1] For illustrations of efforts to develop systematic theories, see Chapters 3 and 7.
[2] See Thomas J. Meyers, "The Riddle of Legal Insanity," *J. Crim. L.*, vol. 44, pp. 330 ff., 1953.

following specialists: (1) The *organicists,* who view mental illness and its treatment in terms of anatomy, physiology, and pathology, make up the largest single group. He notes that the more extreme organicists, the "hard-shell" variety composed mainly of neurosurgeons, neurologists, and neuro-physiologists, "tend to wave aside conjectural symbolisms and refuse to accept dynamisms as explanatory of behavior." (2) The *psychoanalysts* are "much smaller numerically, but obviously more vociferous . . . generally a very positive group (who) give the impression that they have the answers" and who differ widely both ideologically and philosophically from the organicists, mainly in interpreting behavior in terms of complicated intrapsychic dynamisms. These interpretations are based largely on hypothecated processes of psychosexual development, early distortions of which are believed to lead to maladjustment. Diagnosis and therapy involve deep probing or analysis to discover these roots of deviation. As Meyers notes, there are wide variations in this dynamic or psychoanalytic school, including mainly the "Orthodox Freudians," "Neo-Freudians," followers of Carl Jung, Alfred Adler, Wilhelm Reich, Theodore Reik, Otto Rank, W. Stekel, and various others who have elaborated or departed more or less from the theories of "the masters." Considering the wide disparities among the experts in this area, Meyers' comment that "many analysts are impatient and a little intolerant of others who do not hold the same views as they" is interesting. (3) The *psychobiologists,* who are for the most part the most pragmatic, are the least dogmatic among the psychiatric authorities. They are physicians trained to the theory and clinical practices of both psychology and psychiatry and are generally eclectic in their interpretations and practice. Though their approach is largely dynamic, "they regard their patients as psychobiological units and not as psychic projections." Meyers considers that the followers of Adolf Meyer, Harry Stack Sullivan, the Menninger Clinic, and graduates of the Washington School of Psychiatry represent these more broadly oriented psychobiologists. Each group varies from the other in emphasis.[3]

PSYCHOLOGICAL DEVIATION

One of the interesting and controversial aspects of criminological theory concerns the relationship of crime to psychological deviation. Are criminals "mentally ill" generally or rarely? Where the offender suffers from a mental disease or disorder, must it be looked upon as a contributing cause or as *the* effective cause of his criminality? What bearing should the presence of psychological deviation have upon his criminal status? Should he be held fully or partially responsible? Whether held criminal by a court or

[3] Variation is as great among the psychologists as among the psychiatrists. Both display wide areas of disagreement concerning the facts of psychic life and their interpretation. See Calvin S. Hall and Gardner Lindzey, *Theories of Personality,* 1957.

not, should he be treated differently from other offenders? Criminologists, psychiatrists, and lawyers have pondered deeply on these and other related questions. They have arrived thus far at little agreement, though some of the difficult problems involved have been clarified in a measure. Certain of these questions will be considered here; others will be discussed in later chapters dealing with the treatment of the deviate in courts and institutions.

Part of the difficulty involved in the relationship of crime and psychological aberration is definitional and semantic and part of it is diagnostic. What is psychopathology? Mental disorder or disease? Psychological deviation? It is often difficult to draw the line between sickness and health. Deviation is a relative term; statistically it relates to the frequency with which particular characteristics occur in a population. If a trait is distributed generally, it must be considered normal in this statistical sense. The idea of a "sick society" or the idea of the individual as the product of a pathological culture is, therefore, a contradiction of terms. It is also apparent that normality and deviation vary with time and place according to prevailing circumstances. There can be little doubt, for example, that under conditions of contemporary living in the United States it is inevitable, universal, and *normal*—our family, economic, and political organizations being what they are—that men should suffer some measure of psychological discomfort.[4] Mental conflict, neurotic traits, and psychopathic trends prevail very generally in our society.[5] It appears to the writer that those authorities who consider that criminals are mentally or emotionally ill must find similar qualities spread through the noncriminal population. "Illness" becomes meaningless for purposes of distinguishing criminals from others and providing treatment that is differentiated to meet their needs.

The conception of normality that is based upon disease or disorder is rather different from the statistical conception. With the development of modern biology and chemistry, disease can often be diagnosed through the presence of pathogenic germs or through the fairly exact measurement of symptoms manifesting illness. Criteria for medical diagnosis of many diseases are quite well standardized and definitive. This is largely true for organic psychoses, as it is true for other forms of organic disease. Con-

---

[4] Robert Merton has said, " . . . specialized areas of vice and crime constitute a 'normal' response to a situation where the cultural emphasis upon pecuniary success has been absorbed, but where there is little access to conventional and legitimate means for becoming successful. . . . " *Social Theory and Social Structure,* 1957, p. 145. See Chapter 7 below for an analysis of Merton's theory.

[5] Whether the ratio of psychologically sick to well is 1 to 10, 1 to 5, or 1 to 1 in the community has been a matter of speculation among the authorities. Their varying estimates have related, of course, to the breadth of their definitions of illness and more generally to their psychiatric orientation. See the discussion below in the text relating to the prevalence of deviations.

siderably more difficult problems are raised, however, where "functional" disorders are involved, purportedly without organic cause, though the physical symptoms of some functional disorders are quite clear-cut. Where the functional deviations are psychological, the difficulties are especially great, for here the criteria and measurements of disorder are not so sharply drawn. The difficulty of diagnosis is increased by the fact that the disorders are not uniform, at least as presently conceived. Patients with similar diagnoses may differ considerably from each other; the single patient may display differing symptomatology at different times. Experts in psychiatry themselves vary considerably in their skills, in the orientation of their training, and consequently in their diagnoses.

"The amorphous character of contemporary psychiatry," as Dr. Guttmacher has described it, leads to considerable difficulty in attaining any consensus among the authorities concerning the entities of disease or disorder. They do not communicate with any uniformity to lawyers or other laymen on the essential issues involved in the diagnosis and the treatment of either the psychological deviate or the criminal. This problem has become more acute with the burgeoning of dynamic psychiatries and with their impact upon criminological thought. Traditional diagnostic and neurological psychiatry, with its emphasis upon the classification of mental disease and disorder, has attained considerable consensus on the pathological syndromes. In contrast, the followers of analytic psychiatry have been primarily preoccupied with uncovering the roots and tracing the dynamic etiology of emotional disorder, having relatively little concern for diagnosis as such, and having considerable distrust of homogeneous classifications of aberration. Their emphasis is upon the unique quality of personality. The dynamically oriented psychiatrist or caseworker tends to believe that the individual who suffers emotional discomfort should be probed to discover the sources of this discomfort.

Causal Relations between Deviation and Crime

Some of the problems involved in causational analysis have been discussed in an earlier chapter and need not be repeated here. The issue is complex and particularly important in the immediate context because the causal relation between mental disorder and crime determines in the particular case whether the individual should be considered criminal or not responsible and whether he should be handled as a medical or as a correctional problem. It is easy to argue in a holistic approach to personality that any deviation, whether it is a psychosis, a severe character defect, or some minor peculiarity, influences the individual's behavior generally. The argument is quite unpersuasive, however, concerning the specific significance of a psychological trait in the occurrence of a criminal act. It is obvious, for example, that hypochondriacal complaints, prison psychosis, and the Ganser syndrome, commonly found among criminals, have ordinarily had no special bearing on the crimes committed. Mental and emotional conflicts of some offenders may be quite dissociated from their crimes. It is reasonable to believe too that one who suffers from a manic-depressive psychosis or from paranoia may commit acts that are not a product of the psychosis in any realistic sense. The greater the personality disturbance and the more pervasive its influence upon his psychological processes, the more probable it is that that condition has been influential either in directly motivating abnormal behavior (criminal or otherwise) or in so reducing his critical capacity, his self-control, or his emotional balance that he could not easily inhibit his impulses or otherwise conform to required standards. However, a psychological deviation may differ in form and intensity from one individual to another and from one time to another in the same individual. Deviation may have differing degrees of influence upon an individual's thinking, feelings, and behavior. So it is that particular conduct, whether criminal or otherwise, may be influenced little, much, or perhaps not at all by a psychological trait. The relationship, especially the degree of association, is highly important to criminological theory and policy in interpretation of the causes of a crime, in the related matter of responsibility or accountability for the crime, and in the form and content of correctional treatment that may be employed most effectively to modify behavior. Unfortunately there is no measuring device to gauge the influence of a psychological deviation in producing a criminal act. One can only draw inferences a posteriori; an easy identification of crime and emotional disorder may mislead one to conclude both that there is a direct causal relationship and that treatment of the disorder will remedy the criminality.[6]

One further though lesser difficulty relating to the emotional disturbances of offenders should be noted. Diagnostic observations on criminals are made at times when the deviations discovered may reflect supervening influences that have provoked disorder after the criminal act. Offenders studied during or after trial quite naturally display apprehensive and aggressive responses occasioned by discovery and by the danger of conviction. Those observed during imprisonment reveal the consequences of incarceration. Depression, reactive aggression, and deterioration are very common. Furthermore, one is likely to discover disturbances where drugs are used for diagnostic purposes, but such deviations are often of recent origin or of temporary character. Therefore, where research reveals a certain prevalence of psychological disorders in a criminal sample, this cannot be taken to mean that such disorders played a significant criminogenetic role in all or necessarily even in a majority of such cases. It is not surprising that psychological deviations appear to prevail to a greater extent

---

[6] For more detailed statements of this view by the author, see Tappan, "Sociological Motivations of Delinquency," *Am. J. Psychiat.,* vol. 108, pp. 680–685, 1952, and "Concepts and Cross Purposes," *Focus,* vol. 31, pp. 65–69, 1952.

among criminals than among nonoffenders. The circumstances under which criminals live and the experiences that they undergo may well account for much of the higher incidence of aberration found to exist among them. However, a great majority of psychotics, psychoneurotics, psychopaths, and other psychological deviates do not commit crimes. The problems of criminality and of psychopathy are, for the most part, distinctly different.

Where psychopathologies are associated with criminality, it is quite clear that personal rather than property crimes are ordinarily involved. Sexual offenses, assault, and homicide are associated with mental and emotional disorders with relatively high frequency. Furthermore, when individuals who display some form of aberration commit offenses against property these offenses commonly mask a purpose to assault the person.[7]

The Prevalence of Psychiatric Deviations

Bearing in mind the cautions noted above in regard to findings on the incidence of psychological aberrations among criminals, let us consider the evidence relating to the frequency of such deviations. As one might anticipate, in the light of discrepant psychiatric views of diagnosis, there is tremendously wide variation among the research observations. Thus, at one extreme, a vast majority of delinquents or criminals may be found abnormal. At the Pontiac Reformatory in Illinois, 99.5 per cent of incoming inmates were diagnosed as psychiatric deviates during the period 1919–1929; most of these inmates were considered "psychopathic."[8] A number of authorities have taken the view that *all* offenders are emotionally ill, though some authorities would except the "accidental" or "circumstantial" criminal.[9]

In this connection it should be noted that the early studies more generally discovered that high proportions of offenders were mentally deficient and psychopathic than has been characteristic in recent investigations.[10] This undoubtedly reflects, among other things, the changes in testing and criteria that have taken place. A summary of studies conducted by the National Committee for Mental Hygiene, published in 1931, showed gross variation in the extent of psychiatric deviation that had been diagnosed in correctional institutions in different states.[11] Most of the variation

[7] For legal procedures employed in dealing with the mentally disordered, see Chapter 14.

[8] These figures were given by Professor Sutherland in *Principles of Criminology,* 1947, p. 103.

[9] See, for example, writings of David Abrahamsen and Robert Lindner. Compare Manfred Guttmacher, *Psychiatry and the Law,* 1952, pp. 24–25.

[10] See Bernard Glueck, "Concerning Prisoners," *Ment. Hyg.,* vol. 2, pp. 1–42, 1918; *First Annual Report,* Psychiatric Clinic, Sing Sing Prison, National Commission for Mental Hygiene, 1917; Victor V. Anderson, "Mental Disease and Delinquency," *Ment. Hyg.,* vol. 3, pp. 177–198, 1919.

[11] *Report on the Causes of Crime,* vol. 1, National Commission on Law Observance and Enforcement, 1931, pp. 50 ff.

can be attributed to differences among the diagnostic authorities rather than the prisoners.

A large-scale study was made of the incidence of mental deviations among criminals at the psychiatric clinic of the General Sessions Court in New York City. Bromberg and Thompson, reporting on diagnostic observations of nearly ten thousand felons in that court between 1932 and 1935, found that 1.5 per cent were psychotic, 6.9 per cent psychoneurotic, 6.9 per cent psychopathic, and 2.4 per cent feeble-minded.[12] Among the remainder, however, they found evidence of aggressiveness, emotional instability, suggestibility, immaturity, and other personality deficiencies in a large proportion of cases. Subsequent data on a total of over five thousand offenders from 1940 and 1948 gave essentially similar results.[13] So far as major disorders are concerned, the observations of Dr. Winfred Overholser on more than five thousand felons studied under the Briggs law in Massachusetts over a period of fourteen years revealed that some 15 per cent were abnormal, though only a minority of these were psychotic.[14] Similarly but more recently, at the Elmira Reception Center in New York the staff believed that close to 15 per cent of the young adult offenders were in need of rather intensive psychiatric therapy.[15] Looking at the problem from a different viewpoint, some inquiry has been made into the frequency of criminality among psychotic patients. H. W. Dunham has compared the number of male offenders who were found to be insane at the time of trial and who were committed to the Illinois Security Hospital with the number of psychotics committed to psychopathic hospitals in that state during the same period; the proportion was 1.7 per cent.[16] Another study in Michigan inquired into the history of psychotic patients at a state hospital there, discovering that 21.1 per cent had had criminal records but that 10 per cent of the total group had committed their offenses before onset of the psychosis occurred.[17] The data on psychological abnormality with all their limitations reveal quite clearly that few psychotics are crim-

---

[12] See W. Bromberg and C. B. Thompson, "The Relation of Psychoses, Mental Defect, and Personality to Crime," *J. Crim. L.*, vol. 28, pp. 70–89, 1937.

[13] See W. Bromberg, "Personality Factors in Crime," in *Crimes of Violence*, University of Colorado Press, 1950; *Crime and the Mind: An Outline of Psychiatric Criminology*, 1948.

[14] Winfred Overholser, "The Briggs Law of Massachusetts," *J. Crim. L.*, vol. 25, p. 859, 1935, and "The History and Operation of the Briggs Law of Massachusetts," *Law and Contemp. Probs.*, vol. 2, p. 436, 1935.

[15] Glenn Kendall, Superintendent of the Elmira Reception Center, Report of a special study.

[16] See H. W. Dunham, "Social Psychiatry," *Am. Soc. Rev.*, vol. 13, p. 183, 1948, and "The Schizophrene and Criminal Behavior," *Am. Soc. Rev.*, vol. 4, p. 352, 1939.

[17] M. H. Erickson, "Criminality in a Group of Male Psychiatric Patients," *Ment. Hyg.*, vol. 22, p. 459, 1938.

inal and that a vast majority of criminals are not psychotic. Figures on psychoneurosis and psychopathic personality are too variable, as are the concepts themselves, to offer much insight into the prevalence of these disorders among criminals. The data from the General Sessions clinic are suggestive.

It appears that about 5 per cent of the population becomes sufficiently incapacitated by mental disorders to require commitment to hospitals.[18] We cannot judge the frequency of such deviations among offenders at the time that their criminal acts were committed or about how often these abnormalities, when they were present, have been a major cause of the crimes involved.[19]

This chapter deals with the major psychopathologies in their relation to crime; these include the psychoses, functional and organic, the psychoneuroses, and psychopathic personality. An increasing number of authorities, among both criminologists and psychoanalytic psychiatrists, would extend the concept of mental illness to include a variety of lesser personality deviations that are more commonly found among offenders. Yet these deviations appear to be significantly different in character and in their implication for crime. Such personality variants will be considered in the ensuing chapter.

PSYCHOSES AND CRIME

Functional Psychoses

It is beyond the scope of this volume to provide any detailed analysis of psychopathology. However, it is important for the student to under-

---

[18] In 1938 Landis and Page estimated that one out of every twenty persons will eventually be admitted to and will spend a part of his life in a mental hospital and that one out of ten will be incapacitated by mental disease but will not be committed to a hospital. *Modern Society and Mental Disease,* 1938, p. 25. Similar conjectures, based in part on hospital and army data, have been made by other authorities. See *Report No. 1956,* American Public Health Association. In 1955 the average daily mental hospital census in the United States was 740,295 patients. See Howard A. Rusk, in *New York Times,* Apr. 28, 1957. In 1954 Richard Weil, Jr., president of the National Association for Mental Health, reported that 2,500,000 individuals were being treated in hospitals, clinics, or offices for some form of mental disorder. He believed that 5 million others who went to general hospitals for physical ailments were suffering from mental or emotional disturbance. See *New York Times,* Oct. 25, 1954. In New York and other states more than 25 per cent of the state operating budget is devoted to caring for the mentally ill. In 1954 the National Mental Health Committee estimated that the total national cost of mental illness was $2,867,877,000. *New York Times,* Jan. 15, 1956.

[19] It is relevant to observe, too, that offenders who were not psychotic at the time of their offenses, though sometimes in a borderline state, may crack under the strain of trial, sentence, or incarceration. See Guttmacher and Weihofen, *Psychiatry and the Law,* 1952, pp. 42, 438, and Bromberg, *Crime and the Mind,* 1948, p. 26.

stand the apparent relationships between criminality and some of the more commonly prevailing forms of psychological abnormality. The remainder of this chapter is devoted, therefore, to a consideration of the major aberrations associated with crime and to some of the processes that psychiatrists consider of special significance in the occurrence of criminality. Certain of the major psychoses that are found among criminals will first be considered.[20] These psychoses may be divided into two major categories, the functional and the organic. In the former there are no known physiological causes of the disorders, though they may have somatic consequences. While functional psychoses are considered, particularly by dynamic psychiatrists, to result from a strictly psychological etiology, many authorities believe that some if not all of these psychoses are caused at least in part by physical factors.[21]

[20] Even the terms "psychosis" and "mental illness" are ill-defined in the psychiatric and psychological literature, in part because they are matters of degree of disorder or impairment. Commonly the legal concept of "insanity," which refers to commitability, is confused with psychosis. Differentiation between the psychoses and neuroses is not clearly drawn, so that a patient may be diagnosed as one or the other by different psychiatrists. The following is more adequate as a general definition than most of the efforts in the literature:

"The psychoses are those forms of mental illness in which the most profound disturbance of the personality occurs. The degree of disturbance varies within wide limits, and is dependent upon the type of psychosis and its degree of severity. The personality changes which characterize the more severe psychotic illnesses result in changes in the patient's behaviour, which affect his relations with his external environment, and it is this disturbed relationship between the patient and external reality which is the chief distinguishing feature between well marked psychotic illness and the milder forms of mental illness, the neuroses and the psychoses, in which the patient's relations with his environment are only very slightly disturbed." Angus MacNiven, "Psychoses and Criminal Responsibility," in L. Radzinowicz and J. W. C. Turner (eds.), *Mental Abnormality and Crime*, p. 8. (Reprinted by permission.)

Landis and Page observe that "There are such marked differences between the interests, emotions, and desires of the psychotic and normal person that his reaction is withdrawal from or denial of much of reality as seen by his associates." *Op. cit.,* p. 10. The Freudian literature in general emphasizes the overpowering of the conscious and a turning away from reality as a consequence of the strength of the repressed unconscious. See Freud, *New Introductory Lectures on Psychoanalysis,* chap. 1. Henry W. Brosin finds that these features distinguish psychoses from psychoneuroses: damage to the ego functions, especially in relating to reality and lack of integration of the ego; search for infantile pleasures, narcissistic, autoerotic, and symbolic; delusional and hallucinatory symptoms; more open expression of emotions and projection rather than repression; reduction of anxiety and guilt manifestations; gross flight or massive withdrawal under stress rather than symptom formation. See "Contributions of Psychoanalysis to the Study of the Psychoses," in Franz Alexander and Helen Ross (eds.), *Dynamic Psychiatry,* 1952, p. 298.

[21] Biochemical research supports the belief that these psychoses have a physical foundation. From this research it has become apparent that the body chemistry of the schizophrenic differs from that of the normal individual and that patients of this type respond to pharmacotherapy. See Chapter 18.

Schizophrenia, sometimes known by the older term dementia praecox, is the most common form of psychosis both in the general population and among criminals.[22] It is also one of the most difficult to treat because the deviate is psychologically inaccessible to therapeutic efforts. The schizophrene is characterized generally by lack of normal integration of his intellectual, emotional, and volitional processes. However, the disorder takes such varied forms that some psychiatrists believe it should be considered a series of distinct pathological types.[23] Schizophrenia is commonly classified into four main types, though mixtures of these are not uncommon. (1) The simple form is characterized by both mental and physical seclusiveness and inertia, a deep "mental apathy" that is chronic, usually punctuated with delusional or hallucinatory episodes. Such individuals rarely become involved in serious crime, though they may be found quite occasionally among vagrants and prostitutes. (2) The hebephrenic generally reveals a rapid regression during adolescence into an elaborate fantasy world and a disregard of social reality and of his personal hygienic requirements. His delusions are ordinarily of a grandiose character and these occasionally though quite rarely lead to criminality, including murder. (3) Catatonic disorders display a variety of symptoms, reflecting for the most part volitional blocks or deficiencies. Its most familiar guise is *cerea flexibilitas* or waxy flexibility characterized by physical immobility; the patient moves not by his own volition but only when manipulated. The individual with such disorders may go through phases of automatism and hypersuggestibility, stereotyped movements and speech. Catatonics often suffer a series of similar and more prolonged attacks, ultimately

[22] Schizophrenics have made up 47 per cent of the patients in mental hospitals in the United States (57 per cent in New York State in 1954), though they constitute only about 25 per cent of the admissions. The persistence of the illness accounts for this disparity; schizophrenic patients have been hospitalized on the average for thirteen years and many have remained for life. The picture has become more optimistic in these cases.

[23] Describing schizophrenia in general terms, Dr. Guttmacher has said: "Several workers have suggested that we might more accurately speak of the schizophrenias or the schizophrenic-reaction types than of schizophrenia, since such diverse clinical entities come under this head. The outstanding features of these disorders are the bizarre thought content and the odd behavior of the patient, his apparent alienation from the world of reality, an apathetic flattening of mood which may at intervals be punctuated by apparently inappropriate periods of great intensity, the presence of delusions (false beliefs), illusions (false interpretations of stimuli), and hallucinations (perception of external stimuli not present). To these are added the patient's lack of awareness and understanding of his illness and a serious disruption in his social relationship to other individuals. If the disease progresses there is behavioral deterioration thought by many to be due to structural changes in the brain. However, the observed instances in which this process seems to be reversible and absence of consistent post-mortem changes has led others to view this deterioration as a result of a functional blocking." Guttmacher and Weihofen, *op. cit.,* p. 73. (Reprinted by permission.)

succumbing to chronic disorder. As one should expect in light of the nature of the pathology, they are not frequently criminal but may attempt suicide or aggressions against others, ordinarily in the early phases of the disorder. (4) Paranoid schizophrenia is the most dangerous form of the schizophrenic disorders; it is manifested characteristically by delusions of persecution and grandeur and by hallucinations. Ordinarily it develops progressively over a period of years. Paranoids have committed the most serious crimes, chiefly in the form of attacks upon their imagined persecutors. Every court is plagued by at least a few paranoid litigants who are attempting to establish their supposed rights or to defend themselves against imagined harrassment.

Much research and attention has been directed to the etiology of schizophrenia as well as to treatment methods, as we have observed in the general discussion of functional psychoses. It is clear that schizophrenia occurs usually in schizoid personalities who are characterized by excessive introversion, seclusiveness and detachment, sensitivity, radicalism, or suspiciousness. In some instances a basis for the break from reality may be inferred; sometimes the onset appears to be related to disease or emotionally freighted problems that the individual has been unable to face. Kretschmer, Sheldon, and his followers have held that certain physical types are inclined to schizophrenia, the slender "asthenic" or ectomorphic body build and the muscular "athletic" types.[24] Adolph Meyer has attributed the disorder to the individual's maladaptation to his environment. Other analysts believe that schizophrenia results from emotional deprivations during the first year of life. The older literature placed major emphasis upon pathological heredity. Many cases, such as the following, appear to show a pathogenic diathesis together with an unfavorable family situation and a defective social history:

At the age of 17 Robert Douane was committed to the Springfield Medical Center on a three-year term for a car theft; he and a 14-year-old codefendant committed the theft. Douane has been a delinquent since 1947 when he was 11 years old. In that year his mother was committed to a mental hospital in Chicago as "insane." Robert's sister is also psychotic. His father, a brutal and unstable alcoholic, has rejected his son completely, often having subjected him to cruel beatings during his childhood. The boy was committed to the Indiana Hoosier School in 1947 for habitual truancy from school and petty thievery. He ran away from the parental school, too, and was soon involved in a series of larcenies in Chicago. This resulted in his commitment to the Illinois Boys Training School from which he was paroled in 1950. Robert entered the Army at that time but was soon medically discharged with a diagnosis of schizophrenia, simple type. He lived a nomadic life then for some months, stealing cars and traveling to the West Coast. He was picked up in a stolen vehicle in Washington and was found at trial to be insane. They made a diagnosis of catatonic schizophrenia at the Eastern State Hospital where he was confined

[24] See Chapter 4, especially pp. 91–93.

with the criminally insane. He managed to escape from there by bending and crawling through the bars of his cell.

When Douane was arrested on his present charge he admitted to the agents of the FBI under questioning that he had stolen more than twenty cars in and around Chicago, stripping them to sell parts to junk dealers. He also admitted that he had been involved in numerous burglaries, robberies, and thefts in Chicago and other cities. His depredations were ordinarily committed in the company of groups of young men with whom he had hung around. Upon admission to Springfield, Douane was diagnosed as a simple schizophrene, though he was considered to be mentally competent. He is currently classified as a chronic neuropsychiatric patient of borderline intelligence (IQ, 75) and with numerous sociopathic traits. In addition to the nomadic, restless trends described, his social history indicates that he has had no lasting personal relationships, has displayed no interest in women, and has never worked anywhere for more than a week or two. He drinks excessively and engages in homosexual activities both during his imprisonment experiences and in the community. In parole interview he is affable but displays marked facial grimaces and behaves in a generally silly fashion. At this time it appears unlikely that he will work out an adequate adjustment in society.

Paranoia is a psychosis that at once is extremely dangerous to the community and quite commonly evades official attention unless and until it is too late. Pure paranoia must be distinguished from paranoid personality and paranoid schizophrenia. Each has in common the characteristics of suspiciousness, feelings of persecution, and exaggerated ego sensitivity. The paranoid personality without psychosis is a very common phenomenon, especially among schizoid types—individuals who are harassed by fears, doubts, suspicions, and a sense of unappreciated importance. Because of their excessive and sometimes partially imaginary responses to the wrongs that others perpetrate upon them, these people are difficult. When they are more than normally aggressive or antisocial, they are dangerous. The paranoid schizophrenics, whom we have already discussed, may be distinguished from the paranoiacs in that the former characteristically display some fragmentation of personality and loss of contact with reality, poor reasoning, deterioration of intellectual activity, and variation in delusional content. The paranoid schizophrenic's delusions are not well systematized. Except in terms of the course of the disorders it is commonly difficult to distinguish between other paranoid psychoses and pure paranoia.

Pure paranoia is quite rare, at least in our mental hospitals and prisons. According to most authorities, they make up not more than 1 or 2 per cent of the psychotic population, though without a doubt many remain undiscovered.[25] Pure paranoia may be distinguished by the fact that logical reasoning is maintained, "a formally correct superstructure on a false foundation, accepted as true and maintained in the face of contrary

[25] See, for example, Landis and Page, *op. cit.*, p. 17.

evidence." Contact with reality is preserved and the individual may make fairly adequate social adjustments for years, concealing the delusional system that constitutes the major characteristic of the disorder. It is generally a disorder of middle life but may have its onset in the twenties. In the pure paranoiac the delusions of persecution and grandeur are well systematized and coherent, generally expanding slowly and with little change in the basic content. Ordinarily the paranoiac is submissive to authority. This together with his normal and often superior intelligence results in failure either to hospitalize or imprison most paranoiacs. Nevertheless, because paranoiacs take their delusions very seriously, they represent a considerable danger to the public. They are potential murderers and assaulters but may adequately repress their inclinations to attack imagined persecutors. It is generally believed that the paranoiac remains almost wholly unsusceptible to treatment in spite of his intelligence and continuing contact with reality. Mental states ranging from paranoid to paranoiac may be found with some frequency among professional people.

Considerable mystery surrounds the etiology of paranoia and of other functional psychoses. The condition develops in paranoid personalities, but the reasons why some paranoids develop delusional systems and others do not is not clear. Psychoanalysts have suggested that the paranoiac is a homosexual personality and that his responses result from projection, reversal, and transference.[26] They find a close if not universal relationship between psychic homosexuality, paranoia, and alcoholism.[27] A recent study of fifty-two murderers, thirty-two of whose victims were relatives, conducted at the Spring Grove State Hospital in Maryland, supports this theory.[28] The reporters found quite routinely that victim-wives had been "long-suffering and overburdened by having to do more than their share of looking after the family." In the progressive marital attrition that preceded the attack, they had retreated increasingly into a masochistic role and frigidity. Making their own behavior irreproachable, superficially observed at least, they caused their husbands to become more and more

[26] "The theory is that the repression of the unwelcome belief that a person is especially attracted to persons of the same sex is, in cases of paranoia, unsuccessful; and this repugnant complex tends to assert itself in delusional disguise as the chief symptom of paranoia. The mechanism involves the unconscious premise on the part of, say, a male: 'I love the man'; this repugnant idea becomes 'I do not love him'; and by the interposition of the mechanism of projection, it becomes 'he hates me' (i.e., he does not love me). Similarly these mechanisms are used to explain not only persecutory delusions, but delusions of grandeur, religion, love, jealousy, etc." Bernard Glueck, *Mental Disorder and the Criminal Law*," 1925, p. 364, ftn.

[27] Angus MacNiven, *op. cit.*, p. 27. See also W. Muncie, *Psychobiology and Psychiatry*, 1948, p. 365.

[28] A. A. Kurland, J. Morgenstern, and C. Sheets, "A Comparative Study of Wife Murderers," *J. Soc. Therapy*, vol. 1, no. 2, pp. 7–16, 1955. The researchers also employed in this study a group of women who had been injured or threatened by their husbands but who survived.

tormented by an increasing accumulation of unconscious guilt, which appeared to be "one of the most destructive forces in the priming of the ultimate explosion." The husbands were demanding, antagonistic, and quarrelsome. They displayed "a strong homosexual conflict, suggesting the passive, unconsciously homosexual male who projected this attitude in his wife. When he finally reacted to a wave of overwhelming hostility, he murdered his wife rather than attack the suspected lover of his wife." Eleven of the twelve husbands displayed paranoid reactions, six of these associated with schizophrenia. Seven were alcoholic. A progressive sado-masochistic relationship was found in some of the cases, stimulated on the husband's side by increasing anxiety in relation to his unemployment and financial worries, his personal inadequacies, and his irascible temper.

Manic-depressive psychoses, sometimes described as cyclic or circular disorders, are characterized by phases of manic and/or depressive attacks that last anywhere from a few days to several months or, rarely, years, with varying intervals between such attacks.[29] During these attacks perception is usually insufficient and judgment is severely impaired. In the more severe phases of the disorder, illusions are common and hallucinations fairly frequent. Delusions are of changeable character, sometimes grandiose, occasionally persecutory. Generally orientation and memory are little affected, though amnesia for the attack itself is common. During manic phases the patient experiences extreme elation (euphoria), psychomotor excitement, and flight of ideas. In depression he displays inattention, anxiety, fixed ideas, psychomotor retardation. The disorder may occur in mixed states, e.g., agitated depressions or maniacal stupors; in some instances it is expressed in a recurrent succession of similar states, maniacal or melancholic, rather than in alternation or circular phases. The cycles are much like the mood variations of normal people but are exaggerated to a more or less extreme extent.

Involutional melancholia, which usually occurs after the age of 40, is sometimes considered a mixed form of manic-depressive psychosis, characterized by agitation and depression together with delusions of sin and self-reference and often extreme anxiety. Its origin is commonly associated with the menopause in women.

The manic-depressive psychoses usually have their beginning in youth and occur more often in families that have displayed histories of mental pathology.[30] They are more prevalent among women than men. Unusual emotional stresses may play a part in the onset. Some authorities believe

[29] Clifford Beers, in his book *A Mind That Found Itself,* 1924, offered an autobiographical account of a manic-depressive history that is one of the milestones in the literature.

[30] In 1954, 5.6 per cent of the patients in New York State mental hospitals were diagnosed as involutional melancholia, 3.9 per cent as manic-depressives. The Bureau of the Census report in 1935 indicated that throughout the country only 2 per cent were hospitalized for the former, 12 per cent for the latter.

that these patients should be divided into two groups: those who have inherited a severe constitutional taint, and those who are precipitated into the disorder by external conditions that they cannot face rationally. Jeliffe and White suggest that the psychosis represents a compromise and a defense to psychic conflict,[31] an extraverted means of coping with reality as contrasted with the malignant introversion of schizophrenia.

Manic phases of psychosis are sometimes associated with aggressive crimes, disorderly conduct and assault in particular. Melancholia is more often linked with suicide or attacks upon members of the family. Prognosis is quite favorable for this psychosis. Recovery from the single attack is characteristic, though the probability of recurrence is always considerable.

John L. Gillin, in his study of prisoners at Waupun in Wisconsin, describes one of the offenders committed there for incest who suffered from depressive states that, together with other factors in his social history, appear to have been responsible for his offense:[32]

. . . I-7, a second-generation German laborer thirty-five years old, has an I.Q. of 90. He was sent to prison for sexual relations with his ten-year-old stepdaughter. He had never been arrested previously.

He is the eighth of ten children, of whom the four oldest died in infancy. His father, a farmer in good circumstances, died when he was seventeen. The family was a close-knit one having few contacts outside the Roman Catholic Church, of which they were staunch members. An older sister became a nun, and the prisoner himself was educated for the priesthood.

Several members of his family had been deranged. An aunt was known to be queer, almost a monomaniac on the subject of religion, and an insane uncle committed suicide. Three of the mother's sibs became insane.

A taste for solitude manifested itself even during the childhood of the prisoner, when he shunned play in order to practise the violin or read. As a young man he refused to attend parties, and with the years he became constantly more seclusive. Throughout childhood and adolescence his interest was in religious activities.

Shortly after his father's death he had a nervous breakdown, after which he continued to suffer from recurrent spells of melancholia. He had gonorrhea at the time of his entrance into prison. At the age of twenty-one he was dismissed, because of his mental state, from the college that was preparing him for the priesthood. This frustration of his ambition probably impaired his rather precarious balance. Returning home, he ran his mother's farm until he was drafted. The Army discharged him with a medical certificate after keeping him in a mental ward for some time. He then began to work in a paper mill

[31] "Manic-Depressive Psychoses," in Gardner Murphy (ed.), *An Outline of Abnormal Psychology,* 1929, pp. 127–128.

[32] Reprinted with permission of the copyright owners, the Regents of the University of Wisconsin, from John L. Gillin, *The Wisconsin Prisoner,* the University of Wisconsin Press, Madison, Wis., 1946, pp. 109–110.

in northern Wisconsin, but did not succeed in holding this nor any other job for long. He moved frequently from city to city until his arrest in 1927.

After his discharge from college, which impaired his social status as well as his nervous balance, he married a woman of ill repute with an illegitimate daughter. She proved a poor housekeeper and absolutely undependable. Thus his marriage supplied no stabilizing influence. Ten children were born of the union.

The Catholic chaplain of the prison reports that his mood fluctuates greatly; at times he is troubled by religious scrupulosity, at others he reacts violently against the church. His relations with his wife and children had been equally changeable. There is no question but that a family history of mental disorder and emotional instability go far to explain the conduct of this prisoner.

Organic Psychoses and Psychoneuroses

General paresis, or dementia paralytica, is a disease of middle and old age, characterized by progressive mental and physical deterioration leading to paralysis and death within a few years.[33] It appears that syphilitic infection of the central nervous system is the primary cause, though only a small proportion of syphilitics develop this disease. Paresis is marked by clouding of consciousness, disorientation, amnesia, impairment of judgment, both apathy and irritability, and sometimes hallucinations and delusions of grandeur. Both the defective judgment of the individual and the common sexual hyperesthesia during the early course of the disease may lead to criminal acts.

Senile psychoses may take any of several different forms, chiefly senile dementia, senile delusional insanity, and cerebral arteriosclerosis.[34] They are characterized by retrogressive amnesia running back from the present to the past, defective judgment, irritability and egotism, and in some cases delusions, hallucinations, and disorientation.[35] In senile dementia exaggerated sexual excitement is often associated with impotence, pro-

---

[33] Only 1.1 per cent of the first admissions of New York State mental hospital patients were in this category, 3.3 per cent of the total resident population in 1954.

[34] Senile psychoses represent a large proportion of intake in state hospitals. New York State reported in 1954 that 23.5 per cent of first admissions suffered from senile psychosis and that 15.7 per cent displayed psychosis with cerebral arteriosclerosis (separately listed in the statistics). The resident population included 5.6 per cent of the former and a similar proportion of the latter.

[35] Bernard Glueck has described the progressive organic deterioration that occurs in psychotics in these terms: "As the disorder progresses, with its gradual destruction of the nervous tissue, there is a deterioration of mental processes in the inverse order of their acquirement; that is, the earliest symptoms of the disease consist of the destruction of the higher sentiments and mental integrations which were acquired last, and when these, and the controlling power, are destroyed, the primitive forces have practically free play. The instincts of acquisitiveness, hunger, and sex, especially, are very active, the patients perhaps collecting all sorts of useless objects, as in childhood, or taking whatever they desire, eating ravenously, or committing indecent acts and sex offenses." Bernard Glueck, *op. cit.,* p. 330.

ducing indecent and criminal acts in some cases. Sometimes they become involved in acts of carnal abuse with small children, sometimes in bestiality. The latter is illustrated by one of the sex offenders that Gillin studied at Waupun.[36] The offense in this instance, as in many others where sexual relations with animals are involved, is associated with inferior intelligence and frustration:

. . . S-6, a man of sixty-four divorced; was the youngest of eight children of native-born parents, an unskilled laborer, and a Methodist. His I.Q. is 72.

In his background are several arrests for drunkenness, supporting the diagnosis of chronic alcoholism made by prison authorities. He was convicted of sodomy with a female goat.

The community and family background were very demoralized. When he was eight years old, he lost his parents and was sent to an orphanage, where he remained for about a year and was then sent to live with foster parents on a farm in another county. The foster father was very cruel to the boy and beat him unmercifully; the foster mother protected him and he remembers her with much affection. He finally ran away, and when he was thirteen was placed in the home of his sister. His school work had of course been much interrupted, and he finally stopped at the age of thirteen, when he had reached the third reader.

Thus his childhood was a poverty-stricken one—financially, recreationally, and socially. He enjoyed few of the established relationships that do so much to stabilize a personality. He was a docile, high-grade imbecile, and so much of a homebody that as a young man he was known as "Grandpa."

He had worked for a number of firms as a common laborer. His wages were always low, but he was an industrious worker whenever he could get a job. Before his commitment he had been out of work for about four years, and at the time of his arrest was an inmate of a county poorhouse.

He had his first sexual experience at the age of twenty-one and until his unhappy marriage four years later was promiscuous. His wife, abetted by her mother, was unfaithful to him. The couple continued to live together for about twenty years, however, though they separated several times. They had a large family, several of whom died in infancy. Most of the others became charges upon the public.

With such a background this aging man, denied normal relationships and probably affected by senile deterioration, which is sometimes accompanied by strong sexual desires, saw no way to satisfy them except through bestiality, an infantile method of sexual expression not infrequent among men suffering from senility. His low I.Q. probably helped to set a lifelong pattern of social irregularity. He had never developed self-control nor established a socially approved pattern of behavior.

Epileptic Disorders. So-called "epilepsy" is manifested in such a variety of forms that today persons generally believe it represents differing pathological conditions that have traditionally been grouped together. Epilepsy is commonly divided into several classes: *grand mal,* in which a fit of

[36] Gillin, *op. cit.,* pp. 100–101. (Reprinted by permission.)

unconsciousness and gross tonic contractions of the muscles are characteristic; *petit mal,* a mild and incomplete form of attack involving only momentary loss of consciousness; Jacksonian epilepsy, in which there is a localized motor disturbance resulting from a cortical lesion; and various "epileptic equivalents," in which different symptoms are expressed. Serious criminality appears to be most often associated with certain of these equivalents, particularly states of epileptic furor or excitement in which impulsiveness and brutality may be expressed, epileptic delirium wherein violence and destructiveness are common, and epileptic automatism or psychic epilepsy in which the individual may commit apparently conscious impulsive acts that he has forgotten quite completely when he recovers from the attack. The disease is characterized by a reduction of emotional control, stubbornness and irascibility, sexual excitement, egoism, apathy alternating with irritability, and impulsiveness. Persistence of the disorder commonly leads to progressive dementia, amnesia, impairment of judgment, and delusional systems.

The onset of epilepsy is usually during youth; it is sometimes apparently precipitated by disease, excessive fatigue, alcoholism, or a toxic element. However, in the family line of a very high proportion of the afflicted, some form of defective heredity exists, so that in some cases the disorder is considered to be associated with inherited physiological deficiencies. Epileptic attacks may result from brain tumors or abscesses, cases in which surgery is indicated to terminate the disorder. Other patients who display symptoms that are ostensibly epileptic are in fact hysterics. Such cases can be distinguished from "true or essential epilepsy" on the basis of electroencephalographic examination, which displays a quite distinctive pattern in the case of the latter. The hysteric requires treatment for the neurosis involved. In the majority of cases of epilepsy, however, whatever brain pathology causes the attacks is not known and treatment is symptomatic rather than curative.[37] Phenobarbital is employed for infrequent *grand mal* seizures, dilantin for more frequent attacks or for the psychic equivalents of epilepsy, and tridione for minor attacks or *petit mal.* While in the recent past epilepsy has been considered highly resistant to treatment, the drug therapies have proved quite successful in controlling the symptoms and their associated psychological and physical consequences.

During states of altered consciousness, the epileptic will commit acts of indecency, breaches of the peace, or crimes of violence varying from petty assaults to rape or murder. Epileptics will also commit crimes during states of clear consciousness. Dr. MacNiven illustrates the abnormal and criminal behavior of a young epileptic in the English courts who was charged wth rape:[38]

[37] See Philip Polatin and Ellen C. Philtine, *How Psychiatry Helps,* 1951, pp. 221–226.

[38] Angus MacNiven, *op. cit.,* p. 49. (Reprinted by permission.)

His history showed that he developed symptoms of epilepsy when he was 8 years of age, and he was under treatment for a year in an epileptic colony.

He had a fairly good scholastic record, but during his latter years at school his conduct was undisciplined and he neglected his work. As he grew up his behavior became more and more abnormal. In his home he was irritable and quarrelsome. If his whims were not humoured he would fly into a violent temper, in which he abused his mother and swore. This form of behaviour was in marked contrast to his attitude to his mother at other times, when he was most affectionate and considerate to her. He spent money recklessly. His behaviour in business showed lack of judgment and shrewdness. He was described by his father as vain and boastful. He was very untruthful. He sometimes related stories of successful business deals, which often turned out to be grossly exaggerated or quite untrue.

In prison, while waiting trial, the accused was irritable and quarrelsome. His mood alternated between states of despair in which he gave in to maudlin weeping, threw himself to the ground and threatened to commit suicide, and states of violent rage in which he uttered ferocious threats against the warders. While he was in prison he was observed to take epileptic fits.

When he was examined he was found to be clear in his mind. There was no gross impairment of his intellect or his memory. He looked somewhat drowsy and he talked in a slow, monotonous voice. Once or twice during the interview he seemed to become slightly confused for a few moments. At these times there would be a pause in his conversation and the patient explained that during these attacks he experienced an acute sense of mental fatigue and an inability to recollect events in their proper sequence. At times during the interview he became slightly emotional, but on the whole, his behaviour was not grossly abnormal. He was able to give a clear and connected narrative of the events which occurred on the day when the crime was committed and he was able to say how the offense occurred.

When the case came into court a plea of insanity in bar of trial was put forward. The plea was sustained and the patient was sentenced to be detained during His Majesty's Pleasure.

Psychoneuroses and Neuroses. Today these two terms are generally used interchangeably, as they are in this text. Freudian literature, however, has made a division, largely discarded at the present time, between "true neuroses," neurasthenia and anxiety neurosis, which were believed to be rooted in immediate sexual frustrations, and the "psychoneuroses," hysteria and the obsessional neuroses, which were deemed to flow from pathogenic repressions of sexuality in childhood, particularly from the Oedipus complex.[39] Today, even in the literature of analytic psychiatry, the neuroses are considered to be quite wide, loose, and overlapping categories. The etiologies of neuroses are also interpreted in a wide

[39] The section below on ego psychology provides a brief treatment in accordance with current analytic theory on the dynamic roots of psychoneuroses and psychopathic personality. See also Otto Fenichel, *The Psychoanalytic Theory of Neurosis,* 1945, and, for a brief treatment, R. D. Gillespie, "Psychoneurosis and Criminal Behaviour," in Radzinowicz and Turner (eds.), *op. cit.,* pp. 72 ff.

variety of ways. Standard works on psychopathology submit for the most part the classes of neurotic disorder briefly described below, with minor variations. It should be noted, however, that neurosis is a relative concept. Some degree of neurotic disorder is found almost universally in the population, undoubtedly a consequence of the circumstances of complexity and conflict in which man lives from his earliest years. In the average individual neurotic traits are not so severe and disturbing that they interfere seriously with his efficiency. Indeed, neuroses are commonly distinguished from psychoses on the ground, among others, that they are "part reactions," involving only phases of the individual's personality. Ordinarily neuroses are not criminogenic, they do not affect judgment or intellectual capacity, and they do not involve the more dramatic symptoms that characterize psychotic syndromes, such as delusions, hallucinations, dementia, or fragmentation of personality. In more extreme cases of neurotic disorder, however, the affective and volitional phases of personality may be seriously distorted, producing serious disturbances in patients' psychological and behavioral life. Neurosis in its most serious manifestations shades into psychotic disorders, so that there is often disagreement among diagnosticians about whether a patient suffers merely from a psychoneurosis or whether he is actually psychotic. The former may precede the latter. A vast majority of neurotics are not so disabled that they require hospitalization. They are found frequently, of course, in jail and in prison populations, but in many cases there is no reason to believe that the neurotic disorders were responsible for the criminal activity.[40]

The opinion has been expressed above that neuroses are not in the ordinary case criminogenic. This is not to deny that many offenders display neurotic traits but to emphasize that most neurotics are not criminal and to question the nature of the relationship between crime and neurosis when they occur in the same individual. Dr. Guttmacher has observed that it is difficult to estimate the incidence of neurotic criminality because offenders rarely undergo adequate psychiatric examination. He suggests that if thorough diagnostic studies were made the figures on neurotic criminality might run as high as 10 per cent.[41] Without regard to the frequency involved, it appears that compulsive neurosis is sometimes ex-

---

[40] Psychoanalytic literature has devoted considerable emphasis to the "neurotic criminal" and, in particular, to the "criminal out of a sense of guilt." This apparently reflects to a large extent the traditional Freudian emphasis upon psychoneuroses and the analysts' preoccupation with neurotic patients. Analysts have had little success and displayed relatively little interest in dealing with psychotics, psychopathic personalities, and criminals. For discussions of the neurotic criminal, see F. Alexander and H. Staub, *The Criminal, the Judge and the Public*, 1931, and Ives Hendrick, *Facts and Theories of Psychoanalysis*, 1939, p. 72.

[41] Guttmacher and Weihofen, *op. cit.*, p. 395. But query how far the neuroses that might be discovered should be identified with the criminality itself? Guttmacher's view is that the search for punishment is very rare as a motive to crime. *Op. cit.*,

pressed in unlawful outlets, ordinarily in crimes against the person. These constitute a small proportion of all crimes, as we have seen. Such criminality will be discussed below under *psychasthenia*. Much less commonly, the neurotic offender may be a "criminal out of the sense of guilt," seeking punishment in order to alleviate the feelings of guilt. This has been interpreted as resulting from an unresolved Oedipal attachment to the mother together with strong hostility toward the father, accompanied by deep anxiety that can be overcome only by suffering. The unconscious masochistic search for suffering may become channeled in crime and the guilt feelings may be mitigated through punishment. The assumption is that the punishment merely feeds the need temporarily and that, as it recurs, the neurotic must offend again.

Obsessive-compulsive and *impulse neuroses* are sometimes classed as obsessional neuroses or as psychasthenia. Abnormal fears, anxiety, and compulsive behavior are typical of these disorders.[42] Feelings of inadequacy, depersonalization, and nervous tics are also very common. The psychological symptoms are generally considered to represent symbols to the individual of feelings and thoughts that he cannot tolerate in their direct form. He may very actively resist the symptomatic behavior, too, and is sometimes aware of its irrational character but is impelled by unconscious motives to act out his difficulty or to suffer miserably in his fears. Freud considered that obsessions constituted a "transformed reproach" or overcompensation for a sexual act experienced in childhood. P. Janet, who first described psychasthenia as a distinct disorder, believed that it resulted from a lowering of psychological tension resulting in an inadequate perception of reality and fears of the unknown.

Many compulsive or impulsive acts are socially innocuous, though they may be painful to the neurotic and may reduce his efficiency and stability. Certain compulsions are extremely dangerous, however, and others produce recurrent criminality.[43] Thus pyromania, the compulsive setting of fires, and homicidal compulsions are obviously dangerous motives to

---

p. 395. Abrahamsen, on the other hand, like a number of other analysts, believes that it is common. David Abrahamsen, *Crime and the Human Mind*, 1944, p. 32. Also see Reich, "The Need for Punishment and the Death Instinct," *Int. J. Psychoanal.*, vol. 17, p. 257, 1931.

[42] Distinction is sometimes drawn between compulsive neurosis in which the acts are painful to the subject and impulse neurosis wherein the subject derives some positive pleasure from the behavior, even though he may resist it. Otto Fenichel, *The Psychoanalytic Theory of Neurosis*, Norton, 1945.

[43] In these cases the criminal act may be viewed as a psychoneurotic symptom. Some authorities distinguish between such psychological "symptoms" and "crime," which is deemed to be the direct expression of antisocial impulses. See Gillespie, *op. cit.*, p. 82. The distinction is patently oversimplified in the sense that in any case, presumably, law violations are symptomatic of the diverse influences out of which they are produced.

criminality. Kleptomania (compulsive stealing) and dipsomania (compulsive drinking) are more common but less serious disorders. Though the symbolic relationship is generally less clear, it appears that some cases of burglary and car theft are also compulsive and substitutive acts, displacing more direct expression of the sexual impulse. A number of forms of pathological impulse clearly reveal in the behavior itself the close relationship that often exists between psychasthenias and repressed sexual drives or memories. Typical are the paraphilias: pedophilia, zoophilia, gerontophilia and necrophilia (erotic cathexis upon young children, animals, aged, and dead bodies, respectively), exhibitionism, voyeurism, transvestism, fetishism, frotteurism, homosexuality, and other somewhat rarer phenomena. These disorders assume special importance under the criminal law in those jurisdictions where "irresistible impulse" constitutes a defense. They are a particularly difficult problem from the point of view of public policy and psychiatric interpretation; unquestionably the impulses involved are sometimes strong, exaggerated perhaps in those individuals who are incapable of normal heterosexual behavior, but like other sexual impulses, they vary in intensity between different individuals and at different times. As a matter of fact the evidence indicates quite clearly that these deviates are most often psychosexually hypoverted rather than oversexed, commonly attempting to attest their manliness in ways that are easier or more acceptable to them than normal coitus. A conclusion that an impulse is "irresistible" can rest only on the evidence that it has not been resisted. It makes little more sense to relieve the homosexual, pedophile, kleptomaniac, or burglar of criminal accountability than it does to relieve other offenders whose behavior is induced by psychological-social drives and who fail to find legitimate behavioral outlets.

Dr. Manfred Guttmacher cites an instance of arson from among his cases at the Supreme Bench in Baltimore that illustrates the translation of the sexual impulse into a form of behavior that we do not ordinarily consider erotic. The deep conflict experienced by this pyromaniac in the expression of his compulsive drive is quite typical of the neurotic. This offender had set fires resulting in more than a million dollars' worth of damage during a four-year period. On each occasion the compulsive act was preceded by intense feelings of guilt and anxiety: "At such times he would feel weak, break out in a cold sweat and become very tremulous. He often became nauseated and sometimes vomited. He felt miraculously better the moment he gave way to his urge and struck the match." After the fire had been lit, the oestrus would recede and he could return home to a peaceful sleep. This man had been made fire warden of the shop in which he worked because he had been found so prompt to discover fires.[44]

[44] See Guttmacher and Weihofen, *op. cit.*, pp. 57–60, and Guttmacher, *Sex Offenses*, 1951, pp. 40–41.

The compulsive character of neurotic crime may also be illustrated by instances of murder that have been associated with sexual deviation; the history of William Heirens exemplifies this type of crime.[45] Heirens began during childhood to employ female underclothing as a fetish, experiencing orgasm as a result at an early age. Later the act of breaking through windows to obtain feminine garments (technically burglary, under the law) brought him keen excitement. By the age of 17 he had committed twenty-five burglaries, one robbery, an assault to murder, a kidnapping, and three murders. The psychiatrists who studied this offender have described the neurotic, compulsive drives that impelled him to crime. In Heirens' own words: "I would just put my head on the table, then the headache would get too strong and I thought if I could just get out it would help. . . . When I got these urges I would take out plans and draw how to get into certain places. I would burn up the plans; sometimes they helped. . . . On one occasion, I took off my clothes and thought if I did that I would not be able to get out. I would get ready for bed. I resisted for about two hours. I tore sheets out of place and went into a sweat. . . . I went out and burglarized that night."

The words Heirens wrote with lipstick on the wall of a room where he had just murdered one of his victims dramatically expresses the neurotic nature of his motivation: "For Heaven's sake catch me before I kill more. . . . I cannot control myself." As Lucy Freeman, the journalist authority on mental health, has pointed out in her study of William Heirens' background, this 17-year-old college student was unlike one's conception of a berserk killer; he was a gentle, attractive youth of middle-class religious parents without prior family history of crime or psychosis. He was found to be sane, pleaded guilty at trial, and is now serving a life sentence in Illinois. In some jurisdictions he might have been found not guilty by reason of "irresistible impulse."

The substitutive character of neurotic criminal behavior is illustrated more clearly in kleptomania than in most other forms of compulsive crime. Such acts are committed both by the male and by the female. They have a higher incidence in women than do most of the paraphilias, which except for varying degrees of masochism are relatively rare in that sex. Quite commonly the pleasure thief displays his erotic need by thefts of objects that are obviously genital symbols. In a case before the Iowa Supreme Court the 18-year-old defendant, a bright and industrious high school student leading some of his classes, stole a schoolbook valued at 75 cents. The evidence in this case on the part of defendant was all directed to his mental condition. It was shown that three of his brothers or sisters were idiotic, that he had become addicted to compulsive self-abuse, that his behavior at times was peculiar, and that he had an in-

[45] See Kennedy, Hoffman, and Haines, "A Study of William Heirens," *Am. J. Psychiat.*, vol. 104, p. 113, 1947, and Lucy Freeman, *Before I Kill More*, 1955, p. 309.

ordinate desire for possessing articles of personal property with no regard to any special value they might have and for many of which he could have no use. A list of the property found in his possession is set out in the record. Many of the articles were stolen by him. It is too lengthy to give *in extenso*. The following enumeration should convey an idea of the character of the accumulation: " . . . 14 silverine watches, 2 old brass watches, 2 old clocks, 25 razors, 21 pairs of cuff buttons, 15 watch chains, 6 pistols, 7 combs, 34 jackknives, 9 bicycle wrenches, 4 padlocks, 7 pairs of clippers, 3 bicycle saddles, 1 box of old keys, 4 pairs of scissors, 5 pocket mirrors, 6 mouth organs, rulers, guns, belts, calipers, oil cans, washers, punches, pulleys, spoons, penholders, ramrods, violin strings, etc."[46]

It is rather clear from the evidence here that the defendant's thefts were inspired by the neurotic compulsion to appropriate symbols of genitalia and that some of the objects stolen might be interpreted as an expression of his castration anxiety. In a minority of jurisdictions such compulsive theft is not punishable when the court concludes that it was based upon "irresistible impulse," an exception to the more commonly prevailing limitations on insanity as a defense to crime. In most states the neurotic behavior does not exempt one from responsibility or punishment.[47]

The specifically and obviously sexual paraphilias, such as exhibitionism, voyeurism, and frotteurism, display the distorted erotic elements in the neurotic personality more obviously than do any of the offenses illustrated above. Since such substitutive forms of sexuality are commonly repugnant to the individual, however, they too are often disguised in some measure. This was true in the instance of a frotteur studied by Dr. David Abraham-

---

[46] *State v. McCullough,* 114 Iowa 532. See also *State v. Riddle,* 245 Mo. 451.

According to Fabian L. Rouke, 87 per cent of shoplifters steal because of some emotional difficulty and fewer than 10 per cent steal as a means of livelihood. He suggests that less than 3 per cent steal property for their own use. In working with a considerable number of shoplifters referred to him for therapy, Rouke has concluded that they fall into four major categories. The first of these, which has been emphasized most by the analysts, is theft as a symbolic sexual gratification. He cites the instance of a married woman who on several occasions had stolen articles from a store as a means of relief from tension, having rejected strong sexual impulses toward men other than her husband. The value of the articles stolen appeared to have varied with the intensity of the desire. A second group had stolen as a means of satisfying an unconscious need for humiliation and punishment. Among these Dr. Rouke found a woman who had fallen in love with another man while her husband was in the service and who ultimately divorced her husband. Her guilt feelings led to theft as a means of being caught, humiliated, and punished. A third group stole to secure acceptance and status, through attractive dress, for example. Finally, some were attempting to revenge themselves against their parents by bringing disgrace to them. This is often associated with seriously damaged parent-child relationships. *J. Soc. Therapy,* vol. 1, p. 95, April, 1955.

[47] See Chapter 14.

sen at Sing Sing, who simulated robbery as a cover for his sexual act of touching the victim.[48]

Hysterias are most commonly expressed in the form of conversion states, ostensible organic disorders for which there is no apparent physical basis in the patient's constitution. They often take the form of anesthesias, paralyses (loss of sight or vision, for example), spasms or tics, and tremors. Many people believe that the so-called "psychosomatic disorders," such as migraine, colitis, gastric ulcers, frigidity or eroticism, and other pathologies, are hysterical in origin. Hysteria may also occur in various forms of disturbance of consciousness, such as dissociation, somnambulism, amnesia, fugues, and unconscious acts. In Freudian theory hysteria, like psychasthenia, results from libidinal repression. In hysteria, however, the affect of the repressed conflict is converted into a physical symptom instead of being expressed through impulse or fear.[49]

For the most part hysterics are not much of a problem for the criminal law. Dr. Guttmacher suggests, however, that there is a significant group of criminals closely akin etiologically to them. In this group are offenders who may manage moderately well under ordinary conditions but who become overwhelmed by the stress of unusual circumstances. Their crimes may be committed rather automatically in a dissociated state of confused consciousness. He suggests that these individuals possess ego strength sufficient to ordinary requirements of adjustment but that they are incapable of rational action under great stress. Our recent experience with soldiers under fire, some of whom developed temporary hysterical symptoms, others who sought escape in amnesia or illness, exposed the role of emotional stress in neurosis more clearly than prior studies had done.

Neurasthenia and Anxiety Neurosis. Neither of these disorders is very important criminologically, though both are found often enough in prison populations, apparently because of the psychological strains of confinement. Neurasthenia is displayed in excessive feelings of fatigue, distractible attention, hypochondria and irritability, and various peculiar subjective sensations. Anxiety neuroses are similar to neurasthenia for the most part but, as the term suggests, are marked especially by anxiety or such "equivalents" of anxiety as cardiac, vasomotor, and respiratory disturbances, trembling, stammering, vertigo, and diarrhea. Freud attributed neurasthenia to sexual excesses and anxiety neurosis to inadequate sexual gratification. Other authorities have suggested that glandular deficiencies

---

[48] *Governor's Report on the Study of 102 Sex Offenders of Sing Sing Prison*, New York State, March, 1950.

[49] Guttmacher points out that, while the symptoms developed by the hysteric seem injurious to his happiness and welfare, they unconsciously exercise a significant function in his adjustment: "the soldier's hysterical blindness keeps him out of battle, the woman's vomiting distresses her errant husband, or the frustrated maiden-lady's anxiety symptoms atone for, and help keep from consciousness, unacceptable sexual feelings." Guttmacher and Weihofen, *op. cit.*, pp. 28–29.

or disturbances may be associated with these and other neurotic states. Guttmacher finds that neurasthenia occurs most frequently in individuals of inadequate personality. The "criminal out of a sense of guilt" may be interpreted as a variety of anxiety neurotic.

Psychopathic Personality

The psychopathic personality is considerably more important for crime causation than either psychosis or neurosis. It is particularly prevalent among youthful offenders and habitual criminals. Contemporary dynamic psychiatrists have given more attention to this disorder in their interpretations of criminality than they have given to any other type of aberration. Yet it is a particularly elusive and frustrating concept in its present-day usage. Differently oriented experts rarely agree on either the nature or the etiology of this condition. In a large part because of this lack of consensus, the American Psychiatric Association has abandoned the term as a diagnostic category, though psychiatrists continue to employ the term. In recent years, however, the concept of psychopathic personality has been brought into sex crime statutes in a considerable number of states and into defective delinquency laws in a few.[50]

Some psychiatrists define the psychopathic state by exclusion, as a condition of psychological abnormality in which there is neither psychosis nor psychoneurosis but in which there are chronic abnormal responses to the environment. Various writers have concluded that it is a condition permitting no uniform definition at all. Some authorities have maintained that the psychopathic traits are present in a large segment of the population, that in the usual life history they prove to be innocuous or even advantageous determinants of success, and that the deviant condition is one of degree rather than one of kind.

A substantial body of medical opinion has conceived the psychopathic traits as biological and hereditary; the terms "constitutional psychopath" and "constitutional psychopathic inferiority" imply this etiology. Others have maintained as vigorously that the state is environmentally conditioned; these authorities would define the disorder in terms of the pathological home situations of neglect and emotional deprivation from which the psychological reaction patterns are thought to have arisen. Some of the latter prefer the term "sociopathic personality."

Psychiatry has delineated a pure type of psychopathic personality that is quite precisely defined and identifiable. This condition may be deemed

---

[50] See Chapter 14. In other writings the author discusses in some detail psychopathic personality in relation to crime and, in particular, the legislation recently developed. See *The Habitual Sex Offender,* Report to the New Jersey Legislature, February, 1950, and L. Radzinowicz (ed.), *Sexual Offences,* 1957. Some of the material below is adapted from these.

to include the following characteristics in a more or less marked degree. Note that these are all closely interrelated qualities of character:

1. A lack of conscience, or "superego," and hence an absence of ordinary guilt feelings about one's derelictions.

2. Deficient attachment to or affection for others, a failure to respond to the ordinary motivations founded in respect or regard for one's fellows, and therefore a disposition to ruthlessness and exploitation.

3. Excessive aggression directed outward against the environment rather than inward in repression of selfish drives.

4. An infantile level of response, seeking immediate satisfactions, often in primitive forms of behavior, sexual and otherwise.[51]

Perhaps it is apparent from the nature of the disorder that psychopathic personality characteristics should occur, as they do, with some frequency in the criminal population. The egocentric, asocial character structure may facilitate criminality where the individual does not appreciate the advantage of at least a minimal conformity in his own self-interest. The point that deserves some emphasis, however, is that psychopathic personality is not synonymous with antisocial personality or behavior. Most psychopaths do not commit crimes; most antisocial criminals are not psychopaths. Antisocial attitudes and conduct may result from any of a variety of conditioning influences. Data from some correctional systems showing a very high rate of psychopaths reveal a badly oversimplified practice of equating criminality with psychopathy; thus the latter term ceases to have any significance as a diagnostic entity.

One of the parole applicants whom the author interviewed illustrates particularly well the common characteristics of the psychopathic personality and the sort of childhood situation out of which these peculiarities develop:

Earnest Jones, now 41 years of age, is the illegitimate son of a promiscuous mother and an unknown father. Comparatively little is known about his social history other than his involvements with the law, in part because of his patho-

[51] Many persons who display psychopathic traits, at least on superficial observation, do not seem to have been affected by the typical influences that are believed to cause psychopathy. This suggests that they are not "true psychopaths." Further evidence supports such a conclusion. Some analytic psychiatrists have observed that many of such cases, when subjected to more careful scrutiny, reveal underlying characteristics of other pathologies rather than psychopathic personality and that many are in fact neurotics, some prepsychotics, others emotionally unbalanced, a few epileptoid, etc. Consequently such authorities have come to believe that the prevalence of real psychopathic personality is considerably smaller than has ordinarily been believed and that some of the traits ascribed to this disorder may often represent a protective veneer concealing the basic motives to deviation. Compare Hulsey Cason, "Psychopath and the Psychopathic," *J. Crim. Psychopathol.*, vol. 4, no. 3, p. 522, January, 1943; Cason Hulsey and M. J. Pescor, "A Statistical Study of 500 Psychopathic Prisoners," *Public Health Reports*, vol. 61, pp. 557–574, April, 1946; and Hulsey Cason, "The Symptoms of the Psychopath," *Public Health Reports*, vol. 61, p. 1833, December, 1946.

logical mendacity and the difficulty of checking the veracity of his claims. It appears that he was reared by foster parents during his early years, after being abandoned by his mother, and that later he was cared for by a woman of considerable wealth. Beyond this, the facts are much confused by the fantastic tales that he has told.

At the age of 10 Jones was committed to the Bureau of Juvenile Research in Columbus, Ohio, for accepting money under false pretenses. There they found him to be a highly intelligent but psychologically unhealthy individual. They reported that "The boy has enough intelligence and ambition to become a very brilliant man if he is given the proper direction and education . . . (but) he has a pseudo-mature attitude toward things which we think is very unhealthy. He attempts in every way to act like and compete with adults and consequently has very little use for boys and girls." At this time the boy displayed enuresis, especially at times when he was questioned about his family, a matter about which he was always extremely sensitive.

Again, at the age of 13, Jones was taken to children's court, this time in New York, on suspicion of having taken money from the pocket of an actor who had befriended him. He was committed to a juvenile training school on this occasion and was then transferred to a rehabilitative farm program where, he maintains, the superintendent insisted on performing degenerate sexual practices upon him.

In 1930, when he was 17, Jones was arrested in Gainesville, Florida, for passing a worthless check. He was adjudged insane and committed to a state hospital there where he was diagnosed as a constitutional psychopatic inferior. At the hospital he told authorities that he had been subject to severe attacks of nervousness since 1927 because of overstudy, having matriculated at Oxford University in Edinburgh, England (*sic*), and having studied prelaw for a time at the University of Wisconsin. Jones was released on this occasion after two and a half months to his wealthy foster mother. He returned to school and completed the first year of high school which ended his formal education. The record indicates that he became much disturbed at school when women of the parent-teacher association objected to his taking part in a school play because he was illegitimate. The principal reminded him of his past and took him out of the play. At this time he ran away and maintained himself for a time by begging and cashing fictitious checks.

Back in Ohio in 1932 Jones pretended to be an officer of the American Legion and collected a considerable sum of money in an imaginary campaign. Again he was declared insane and committed to the Massilon Hospital where he was diagnosed as a psychopathic personality with psychosis but was discharged as improved after nine months. It appears that he spent much of the ensuing five years searching around the country in an attempt to discover who his true mother and father were.

In 1935 in Kansas City Jones encountered a woman who claimed to know his antecedents. He said that she informed him that he was "just a plain bastard" and gave him the whole story of his background. He found his birth certificate in the official records in that city. He claims that thereafter he "went to a whore house in Kansas City and the girls there took care of me for about six weeks." From there Jones went on to San Francisco where he met a man, Dan Jones, who had a considerable effect upon him. This man was a fugitive from justice in Mexico. He was a homosexual and a drifter with a record for passing bad checks. He had worked for a time as a journalist and in a carnival. Apparently his own feats of mendacity were considerable and the two were of congenial temperament. He established a fatherly sort of relation with Earnest and the latter adopted his name, Jones, and pretended to be his nephew in order to secure relief in California.

The ensuing years have been marked by quite continuous difficulties with the authorities. Jones was arrested for vagrancy in San Francisco in 1937 and for forgery in Los Angeles in 1940. In 1941 he was committed to Rikers Island in New York on an indefinite sentence for petit larceny. He was charged with impersonating a naval officer in New York in 1942 and a Federal agent in Chicago in 1943, the latter charge resulting in his committment to the Federal Penitentiary at Terre Haute for a year. At this time the medical diagnosis described him as a psychopathic personality with alcoholism and pathological mendacity but superior intelligence. Almost directly after release from the Indiana institution, Jones was convicted of impersonation in Pittsburgh and was sentenced to another year. In 1946 he did a year at the Cook County Jail for operating a con game and was returned to Rikers as a parole violator in 1947. Shortly after his discharge from the institution in New York City, he was again sentenced to a Federal institution, this time for impersonating a government agent. He was held to the maximum of his term but his conditional release was revoked soon after discharge for transporting stolen property interstate to Chicago. In 1950 he was again committed to Federal prison on a bad check charge, this time for three years, and was paroled in 1953 only to be returned as a violator in 1954 for impersonation and bad checks.

In spite of his record of repeated criminality, Jones continues to make a favorable impression on everyone he meets. In 1946 he was trustee in the warden's office in Chicago. The latter describes him: "He is a crackerjack. I could not have had a better man in my office. He is simply a swell fellow on the inside. I liked him so much that I went the limit for him. I even gave him $50 out of my own pocket the last day that he was in jail. That was three years ago and all I ever received back from him was three cards, with no return address. But that's all right. . . . I can't say too much for him." Another jail warden has said of him: " . . . a high-class fellow, who I think deserves a break and for whom I want to do something. I have not looked up his past record, but I am not interested in that. I am interested in what the man is now. . . . " It would be difficult to find higher commendation for an habitual criminal. The record attests the superb effectiveness of this psychopathic con man, his consummate skill in selling authorities on the idea of his penitence for wrongs into which he "had been led," and his determination to stay out of trouble in the future.

During this period Jones is known to have used at least twenty-six aliases, such as Colonel, Earl, Doctor, and other titles of eminence. He claimed to be of royal blood, reared by a Scottish earl, and to hold advanced educational degrees from Oxford and Cambridge. He has told of traveling in the Orient with his father, a retired British General, "about ninety times." He says that he has worked as a scenario writer at $750 per week, that he was married to a woman with an income of $4,200 per month, that he has been disinherited by a wealthy father who had come into an estate of $800,000. He also asserts that he has held a professorship in a London college at 1,500 pounds a year. All of this has been told at different times with an embroidery elaborated according to the varying gullibility of his audiences but always with much earnestness and sincerity on his part.

Jones is a classic example of the psychopathic personality, apparently developed largely through his defective family situation and slanted by his traumatic response to illegitimacy. His career of impersonation appears to be a reflection of his inordinate preoccupation with his parentage and an effort not only to conceal his identity but to prove his superior origins. His intelligence and attractiveness have served him well, as is so commonly the case among psychopaths, in the egoistic exploitation of others and in the concealment of his remorseless disregard for them.

Ego Psychology: A Theory of the Etiology of Psychopathic Personality and Neurosis

As has been noted above, there are various theories concerning the etiology of neurotic and psychopathic disorders. It is quite probable that the pattern of psychogenesis varies considerably, at least in different forms of neurotic disorders. Dynamic psychologists have suggested what they believe are two quite typical and contrasting modes of personality development out of which psychopathic personality, on the one hand, and neurotic personality, on the other, characteristically develop. These patterns emerge out of what is generally termed a "dynamic ego psychology," relating to the differential development of the id-ego-superego structure of the individual. The non-Freudian may raise some question about the mystical and formally structuralized conceptions that the Freudians employ in explaining their theory of ego psychology and the related Oedipal situation. It appears, however, that neither the mystical-instinctual explanations nor the somewhat animistic descriptions of psychic components are essential to an understanding of the processes involved. These explanations may be interpreted in terms more credible to the behaviorist or to the social psychologist. The dynamic analysis referred to appears to make a good deal of sense when one attempts to understand personality responses. Certainly the psychoanalysts find that the mechanisms vary frequently among their patients, though the inferences they draw from their findings are far from uniform. A brief summary of the theory of ego psychology is presented below.

The infant is thought to be dominated by his "id impulses," which are defined as instinctive asocial drives.[52] His behavior is marked by the

[52] Sigmund Freud, in his work *An Outline of Psychoanalysis*, 1933, chap. 1, defined the id as "the oldest of the mental provinces or agencies. . . . It contains everything that is inherited, that is present at birth, that is fixed in the constitution—above all, therefore, the instincts, which originate in the somatic organization and which find their first mental expression in the id in forms unknown to us."

"pleasure principle" in that he seeks the immediate satisfaction of his erotic and other biological wants. The "ego" emerges with the individual's capacity to distinguish between himself and other objects.[53] As the social psychologist G. H. Mead has put it in nonpsychiatric terms, "the individual becomes an object to himself in experience" and it appears to be through this conception of oneself that the ego develops into a critical faculty of self-censorship and control as the person relates himself to his universe. Training in the family, the process of learning to delay and limit one's satisfactions, establishes the nucleus of the "superego."[54] Superego development occurs mainly, however, in the resolution of the Oedipus complex, as the child learns to control his demands in terms of the authority represented by the father and through identification with him. The introjection of social and parental taboos and prescriptions contributes further growth to the superego, as it comes to represent the standards and ideals of both home and community.[55] It is thus that the "reality principle" develops; the person learns to respond to social authority in abnegation of the pleasure principle.

[53] "Ego" is defined as part of man's "psychical organization which is interpolated between his sensory stimuli and perception of his bodily needs on the one hand, and his motor activity on the other; and which mediates between them with a certain purpose." Freud, *The Question of Lay Analysis,* 1936, chap. 2.

[54] Freudian emphasis has been primarily on the role of the father in the formation of the son's superego: "The fear of the father, the wish to be loved by him, and the tendency to take him as a model, thus represent the main springs in the process of identification as far as its inhibitory effect is concerned; an effect actually wished by the son. This identification produces an inner psychic agency . . . the Super-Ego." Alexander and Staub, *op. cit.,* p. 44.

[55] This enlarged conception of the superego, which recognizes the role of agencies outside the home and at ages of greater maturity, represents a growth beyond original Freudian doctrine. It is thus expressed in one of the standard works: "During the course of development, figures of authority, capable of rewarding and punishing—the father, the mother, father- and mother-surrogates, God, admired exemplars, priests and teachers, magistrates and policeman—associated with a heterogeneous system of moral principles, laws, and conventions, become incorporated in the personality as a distinguishable establishment which is termed 'superego.' Depending on the ideology that has been inculcated as part of the socialization process, the superego can represent one or usually several of the following: 'voice of God,' the 'eternal laws of conduct,' the 'right,' 'moral truth,' the 'commandments of society,' the 'good of the whole,' the 'will of the majority,' or merely 'cultural conventions.' But once the superego has been accepted with an emotional attitude compounded of fear, respect, and love, the individual becomes a true carrier of the moral culture of his society, who inhibits many of his delinquent impulses, not so much out of fear of external retributions as out of dread of superego disapproval, the secret pains of guilt and remorse. This, at least, is the picture in the Judaic-Christian world. In some cultures, 'shame' (the fear of being discovered in nonconformity by others) appears more powerful than 'guilt' (self-punishment) in inducing inhibition." Murray and Kluckhohn, "Outline of a Conception of Personality," in Kluckhohn, Murray, and Schneider, *op. cit.,* 1953, p. 44. (Reprinted by permission.)

An adequate inhibition of the id impulses requires consistency and affection in the disciplining of the child. The child's learning to give up what he wants has been described as a process of psychic bribery in which the mother's love and its threatened withdrawal, by way of an apparent or partial rejection, induce him to deny his immediate wants in order to gain approval. Lacking the reward of maternal love, there is no motive for self-denial. Moreover, for the development of an adequate and integrated superego, the child requires a model in the father with which he may identify rather fully his ego ideal.

The psychopathic personality is commonly defined in terms of the id-dominated character, lacking normal superego development. Without mother love and frequently without a father, he does not learn to identify or sympathize with others; instead he exploits them if he can. The psychopath lacks the guilt feelings and anxiety expressed by the normal person as a result of defiance or misconduct in the face of parental disapproval; he is without remorse or neurotic conflict. The psychopath works out his antisocial drives directly without inhibition or guilt. In erotic behavior, as in character development generally, the psychopath is immature, commonly displaying "polymorphus-perverse" enjoyments without ordinary refinements of choice.

This idealized picture of the psychopath occurs very rarely in the pure form described, but many criminal offenders display some measure of psychopathic traits. Indeed, most of us occasionally expose psychopathic qualities as a result of persisting traits of infantilism, feelings of parental rejection, and hostility toward authority. A majority of men, however, manage to repress their antisocial impulses toward crime most of the time. The criminal in his inadequate deference to social authority is often in reality defying the father and expressing his infantile and aggressive demands upon a hostile world.

It is believed that the neurotic personality structure develops through a contrasting sequence of social-emotional relationships.[56] Here the child does learn to identify with parental figures; indeed, he does so too

---

[56] Murray and Kluckhohn summarize the variants that may emerge from differing composition in the development of the ego: "The socially deviant forms of personality may arise as a result of various dynamisms and their interactions. The study of concrete cases shows that the processes are often excessively complex. But let us first state the matter over simply. If, as a result of special combinations of factors operating in the life of one individual, the primary biological impulses remain unchecked, such an individual will be variously known as 'anti-social,' 'criminal,' or 'id-dominated.' If, on the other hand, an individual emerges from his socialization with his impulse life unusually inhibited and with an exaggerated need for and dependency upon the approval of others, this type of person may be designated as 'neurotic,' 'conscience-ridden,' or 'superego-minded.' But if, as a result of a more fortunate admixture and integration of both biological and cultural demands, an individual emerges who represents a balanced type, we speak of him as 'normal,' 'rational,' or 'ego-controlled.'" *Ibid.*, p. 133. (Reprinted by permission.)

strongly. The parents are characteristically severe, neurotic, and demanding personalities, exploiting the dependence of their child. Consequently the child develops an over-rigid superego; he is fearful and anxious to conform to the excessive requirements imposed upon him. Real or imagined failure is accompanied by strong feelings of guilt and even more rigid repression. Unlike the psychopath, who expresses overeasily his id drives, the neurotic denies and inhibits them. Such drives may then be translated into assorted substitutive outlets, fears, compulsions, and efforts to dissolve the feelings of guilt.

The psychiatrist Richard L. Jenkins has constructed a diagrammatic representation of types of poorly socialized personality structures that

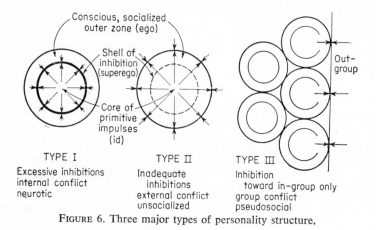

FIGURE 6. Three major types of personality structure.

he has observed in child guidance clinics.[57] These personality structures include the neurotic and psychopathic (unsocialized) patterns and a pseudosocial and delinquent-oriented socialization. The diagrams may aid in visualizing the processes involved. Type I pictures the overrepressive superego observed in compulsive and anxiety-ridden personalities. Type II displays the lack of adequate inhibition found in the psychopath or in the child with behavior disorders who "acts out" his problems. Type III, the "pseudosocial" personality, has been socialized but in relation to deviant in-group norms. It is the class described by Alexander as the "normal criminal" and by Sutherland in terms of "differential association" typified in members of delinquent gangs.

[57] R. L. Jenkins and Lester Hewitt, "Types of Personality Structure Encountered in Child Guidance Clinics," *Am. J. Orthopsychiat.*, vol. 14, pp. 84–94, 1944, and R. L. Jenkins, "A Psychiatric View of Personality Structure in Children," *Nat. Prob. Assoc. Yearbook*, 1943, pp. 199–218. (Figure reprinted by permission.)

Chapter 6

PERSONALITY DEVIATIONS AND CRIME

A variety of psychopathologies related to criminal behavior were summarily considered in the last chapter. These diseases and disorders, while they occur rather infrequently in the criminal population, assume some special importance because individuals so afflicted more often commit crimes against the person and commit their violations with relatively more persistence when they are criminal. The criminal law recognizes these aberrations indirectly because of their apparent bearing on crime and responsibility. The present chapter deals with a variety of personality deviations that are not typically included in the nosologies of mental disorder, although they sometimes occur in association with the major psychopathologies or with crime. The discussion includes mental deficiency, various minor psychological disturbances, alcoholism, and narcotic addiction. On the whole, these abnormalities reflect environmental influences and social definitions rather than merely individual morbidity. They are found more often among offenders against property. By and large, they are not dealt with in mental hospitals and do not receive any special consideration, ordinarily, under the rules of the criminal law.

MENTAL DEFICIENCY

Before considering the nature of mental deficiency and its influence on crime, distinctions should be drawn between this psychological condition and others that have already been considered, particularly because "defect" and "insanity" are commonly confused at law. Feeble-mindedness is the consequence of the failure of the mind to develop; it is a generalized incomplete or arrested intellectual capacity, a *subnormality*. If the deficiency is sufficiently great, the individual is incapable of contracting or suing without the benefit of a guardian under the civil law. If he is unable to understand the nature of the proceedings or to defend himself, he may not be subject to prosecution at the criminal law. Though prosecuted, he has a defense under the insanity provisions of the law if he was unable, to put it most simply, to distinguish right from wrong. Psychosis, on the other hand, is an *abnormality* of mental functioning based upon disease or disorder. In certain psychoses, as has been pointed out, the pathology may result in deterioration of mental capacity as well as delusions, hallucinations, and other symptoms peculiar to particular disorders. At law, the tests for capacity and defense are similar under the rules concerning insanity in the various jurisdictions.[1] From psychological and social points of view, however, feeble-mindedness and psychosis are distinctly different. One very important difference is that, while mental defect affects intellectual or rational powers primarily, psychoses generally involve distortions in the emotional and volitional spheres and may influence only certain phases of thinking or believing. Controversy over the rules on insanity as a defense relates in large part to this contrast, since these rules exculpate the individual from responsibility only where he has lacked capacity to understand, whether such incapacity has resulted from psychosis or from feeble-mindedness.

Mental deficiency is divided into three levels of severity: idiocy, with a mental age below 3 years; imbecility, where mental age may range between 3 and 7 years, inclusive; and moronity, with a mental age from 8 to 11 or 12 years. Each of these classes is sometimes graded further into low, middle, or high. Mental deficiency is further classified according to clinical and etiological types. The first of these is the endogenous or hereditary, in which the defect is transmitted through a subnormal endowment in the genes. At one time many people believed that this category represented 90 per cent or more of the deficients, but today it is generally considered to include somewhere between one-third and one-half. The other class is the exogenous, nonhereditary or pathological group of deviates whose deficiencies result from organic causes. In these cases the deficiency is said to be secondary, i.e., secondary to some pathology of the nervous tissue. Among the main pathologies involved are thyroid deficiency (cretinism), an accumulation of cerebrospinal fluid within the ventricles of the brain (hydrocephalus), small and underdeveloped skull (microcephalus), inflammation of the brain (encephalitis), hemorrhagic lesions of the brain at birth (Little's disease) or serious injury to the brain after birth, syphilitic infection of the brain centers, and Mongolian idiocy. There are a few other less common neuropathological disorders. It is generally believed that at least one-third of the mental defectives are a product of these nonhereditary pathologies. Upwards of one-third of all mental defectives are of an undetermined and sometimes mixed etiology. Cases involving pathological embryonic development are often, though improperly, included among the hereditary defectives.

Intelligence is distributed on a normal, bell-shaped curve through the population. Hence, there are relatively very few idiots, about four times as many imbeciles, and sixteen times as many morons. There are considerably larger groups, of course, of individuals of "normal" mentality

[1] See Chapter 14.

who are "dull" and "dull-normal." It is commonly difficult to distinguish between high-grade morons and the dull in individual cases, even when they are tested. Different maturity levels are employed as bases for computing intelligence tests by different scoring scales. Variability in test performance is common because of changes in environment, stimulation, physical condition, and other influences. Hence, the lines are arbitrary and not clearly drawn. Moreover, many of those classed as dull have greater social, emotional, and behavioral problems than do the general run of defectives, largely because their perceptions and critical faculties are more refined. Indeed, one psychiatrist who has devoted considerable attention to the adjustment of defectives finds that at the higher levels the chief problems arise from attempting to compensate adequately for feelings of inferiority that are based upon actual inadequacy.[2]

At one time many people believed that mental deficiency was very common among offenders and that it represented a major influence in crime causation.[3] Such thinking has been discarded almost entirely today as psychological tests have improved and the testing itself has been performed more carefully under standardized conditions. Later investigations have shown that the prevalence of mental deficiency among delinquents and criminals does not greatly exceed that in the general population. One study puts the ratio at 1.2 to 1.[4] Another authority suggests that one-third of juvenile delinquents are defectives, approximately 15 per cent of youthful and young adult offenders, and about 8 or 10 per cent of adult criminals.[5] This may be compared with the rate of from 1 to 3 per cent in the general population. Some excess should be expected in any event because defectives are more easily apprehended and convicted than are normal or superior individuals and because those who are deficient are more likely to be committed to correctional institutions. Moreover, in terms of the testing situation, it would seem that incarcerated offenders have less motivation than do others to perform at the level of their capacities. The official data indicate not only that defectives are a small minority among offenders but also that their prison disciplinary records, their parole violation rates, and their recidivism are very similar to those of offenders

[2] See Florence Powdermaker, "Social Adjustment of the Feeble-minded," *The Annals,* vol. 149, pp. 59–69, 1930.

[3] In 1931 Edwin H. Sutherland reviewed some 350 reports of studies made of the intelligence of criminals and delinquents and found that the proportion diagnosed as defective declined from over 50 per cent during the period 1910–1914 to 20 per cent in 1925–1928. The differences were attributed to methods used by the testers and changes in test scoring. See "Mental Deficiency and Crime," in Kimball Young (ed.), *Social Attitudes,* 1931, chap. 15.

[4] See L. D. Zeleny, "Feebleminded and Criminal Conduct," *Am. J. Soc.,* vol. 38, pp. 564–578, 1933.

[5] Edgar A. Doll, "Mental Deficiency," in *Encyclopedia of Criminology,* Philosophical Library, 1949, p. 230; Masland, Sarason, and Gladwin, *Mental Subnormality,* 1958.

with normal intelligence. It is surprising, if anything, that the disparities are not greater than they appear to be. In any event it is clear that in some instances deficient intelligence does have an important bearing upon criminality. In the criminal population as a whole, however, it is a small factor as compared with other criminogenic influences.

The relationship between feeble-mindedness and crime is largely occasioned by the unfavorable competitive position of these individuals and by their difficulties in working out adequate compensations for their deficiencies. Defectives, for the most part, are not more aggressively antisocial than persons of normal intelligence. They are handicapped, however, in their social, educational, and occupational adjustments. Repeated experiences of failure in school, in the community, and on the job involve a progressive attrition in which some defectives succumb to the temptation of achieving through minor crimes what they cannot achieve legitimately. They lack the foresight, the capacity for inhibition, and the critical judgment that might dissuade one of normal intelligence from following his impulse. They are sometimes persuaded to delinquency by more able companions because they are naïve and easily led. Generally, however, unless there are other, more dangerous and antisocial elements of personality present, the mentally deficient do not commit seriously aggressive crimes. Such additional characteristics are not ordinarily the consequence of feeble-mindedness.

The Gluecks, in their *Unraveling Juvenile Delinquency,* provide some special insight into the relationship of test performance and delinquency.[6] In selecting their samples, the Gluecks matched the controls with the delinquents for general intelligence so that no inferences could be drawn as to relative intelligence of the delinquent and the nondelinquent; particular attention was given, however, to comparing the qualities of intelligence in the two groups. The Gluecks found that the offenders performed more poorly at the verbal level, especially in vocabulary, information, and comprehension. Offenders varied more than did the nondelinquents in different parts of the verbal test. Rorschach testing showed further that they displayed poorer powers of observation and less common sense, a less methodical approach to problems, and a greater amount of unrealistic thinking.

A considerable number of the candidates that the author has interviewed for parole were of borderline or defective intelligence. Characteristically their histories revealed the complication of an inadequate family situation or deleterious associations, commonly both. Their offenses reflect limited intellectual ability in the usual instance. Such offenders having defective intelligence are illustrated briefly in the cases below:

John Dickley was one of thirteen children brought up in a rural section of Maryland completely without social or educational advantages. His parents,

---

[6] *Unraveling Juvenile Delinquency,* pp. 198 ff.

who bore poor repute in the area, separated in 1949 when John was 14 years old. The father was a heavy drinker, neither willing nor able to support his family, so that the children were raised for the most part in foster homes. On a series of occasions John ran away from his home placements, occasionally living with an uncle. His record of delinquency began in 1945, when at the age of 11 he was taken to juvenile court for destroying property. The following year he was committed to a Maryland training school for persistent delinquency, including vandalism, car theft, and breaking and entering a service station. He escaped from there on one occasion but was returned after being apprehended in another stolen car. He was arrested nine times during the period 1945–1953. John has never had any steady employment, though he worked briefly as an unskilled laborer in a factory on one occasion. In 1951 he was rejected for the draft because of poor test performance. Early in 1953 he traveled around the country with Ringling Brothers Circus. It was during that year that he was apprehended with a codefendant stealing mail from a mail box in a private home; he admitted that they had committed similar offenses together several times. At the Federal reformatory John was found to have an IQ of 72 and appeared to be both slow and dull-witted. He lacks any plan for his future.

Robert Wills comes from a desperately defective family and community situation. His father is serving time at the Ohio Penitentiary as a parole violator after a first release; he was convicted for stabbing with intent to kill. Robert's mother, a thoroughly inadequate parent and a slovenly housekeeper, had divorced the father and married again. A sister was an imbecile and another sibling was the product of an act of rape, which the mother maintains was intended for Robert's older sister. Since 1943, when he was 8 years old, this youth has been in trouble for destruction of property, theft of mail, breaking and entering, stealing, attempted robbery, and disorderly conduct. He was given probation and returned to probation for most of these offenses, but he was sentenced to training school in 1948 for truancy and again in 1952 for "tampering with a car." In 1953 he was sentenced to Chillicothe for car theft. There he was found to be of dull intelligence, complicated by emotional disturbances manifested in persistent enuresis and severe phobias.

MENTAL AND EMOTIONAL CONFLICTS, INSTABILITY, DISTURBANCES, AND OTHER PSYCHOLOGICAL FACTORS

Materials from clinics working with delinquent and problem children and research data derived from the psychological study of young offenders have commonly emphasized the importance of mental and emotional factors in producing delinquency. In their study *New Light on Delinquency and Its Treatment,* Healy and Bronner found that among 143 cases of delinquents studied intensively by clinical teams 91 per cent suffered from major emotional disturbances as contrasted with only 13 per cent of their nondelinquent controls.[7]

[7] These "major emotional disturbances" included feelings of frustration (forty-five

In one of his earlier works, Healy focused attention on the relationship between mental conflicts and delinquency, suggesting that the repression of emotionally toned memories of experience may result in their displacement into any of varied forms of misconduct.[8] He found conflicts arising from sex experiences, forbidden sex knowledge, parentage, and related matters. While Healy recognized that the etiology of the misconduct observed was similar to that involved in the formation of neuroses, he believed that "the pathway from mental conflict to misconduct is straighter than are the steps between mental conflict and nervous disorders." Emotional conflicts are common among youths generally and are significantly more common, it appears, among delinquents. Yet, even with the special focus upon such conflict in Healy's early work, he found that only a rather small percentage of delinquencies resulted from this etiology.[9] Emotional conflicts are more frequently resolved in other ways. It is fair to conclude that in specific instances of delinquency there may be a rather direct relationship between the misconduct and highly affective experiences that have been repressed (e.g., a sexual initiation or observation of a sexual act, a sudden discovery that one is adopted or that one's parent is a criminal). Such cases appear to be fairly infrequent.

The Glueck research provides useful insight into the significance of personality and temperament in the offender. In comparing delinquents with nondelinquents, interpretation from Rorschach protocols led to the conclusions that delinquents were to a significantly greater extent socially assertive, defiant, ambivalent to authority, resentful of others, hostile, suspicious, destructive-sadistic, impulsive, vivacious, and extroversive.[10] To a lesser extent than the nondelinquents they were submissive to authority, fearful of failure and defeat, cooperative with and dependent upon others, conventional, masochistic, or self-controlled. Psychiatric interviews, conducted independently of the Rorschach testing, led to conclusions regarding the temperament of the youths studied that tended both to confirm and to extend the psychological test conclusions. The delinquents were more dynamic and energetic, aggressive, adventurous, suggestible, stubborn, impatient, acquisitive, materialistic, self-centered, tense (as a result of emotional relationships with the family or with companions), in con-

---

cases), rejection (fifty-three cases), inadequacy (sixty-two cases), emotional disturbances about the family (forty-three cases), and sibling rivalry or jealousy (forty-three cases). However, there were only nineteen cases of "deep-set internal emotional conflicts" and eleven of an unconscious sense of guilt and need of punishment that one might consider semipathological. See *New Light on Delinquency and Its Treatment*, p. 49. It should be noted, furthermore, that since these were cases in child guidance clinics they might be expected to display emotional conflicts more frequently.

[8] Healy, *Mental Conflicts and Misconduct*, 1917.

[9] Seventy-four such cases were found in one sample of a thousand.

[10] See *Unraveling Juvenile Delinquency*, chap. 18.

flict about inferiority feelings, and extroversive in expressing their tensions.[11] They displayed less capacity "to operate on a fairly efficient level," less emotional stability, and less capacity for self-criticism, conventionality, conscientiousness in achieving goals, realism in facing situations, or practicality. However, the delinquents were found to be less frequently neurotic than were the members of the control group.[12]

Statistically significant differences between delinquents and nondelinquents were observed in the prevalence of the traits noted above. It should be remarked, however, that for the most part only a minority of either the delinquents or nondelinquents displayed any one of the qualities noted; the occurrence of the traits in the two groups overlapped considerably. This may be illustrated by the prevalence of certain qualities that one might ordinarily imagine are correlated with delinquency.

Table 9. Qualities of Temperament and Delinquency

Trait	Delinquents		Nondelinquents		Difference
	Number	Per cent	Number	Per cent	Per cent
Aggressive..........................	75	15.1	25	5.0	10.1
Extroverted in action...............	282	56.7	142	28.5	28.2
Emotionally stable.................	90	18.1	249	49.0	−31.8
Neurotic..........................	122	24.6	177	35.8	−11.2
Suggestible........................	297	59.8	131	26.3	33.5
Conventional......................	123	24.7	242	48.5	23.8
Egocentric........................	68	13.7	11	2.2	11.5
Conflict of boy and father..........	114	22.8	26	5.2	17.6
Inferiority feelings.................	126	33.2	94	18.4	14.8
Emotional conflicts................	339	74.8	163	37.6	37.2

SOURCE: Adapted from materials in Glueck, *Unraveling Juvenile Delinquency*, chap. 19.

The Glueck data appear to show that conflict situations in the home are a fertile source of misconduct. They found that the affectional relation between the youth and each of his parents and the parents' disciplinary practices had a particularly high value for predicting delinquency in their samples.[13] Conflict with the father was much more common among offenders than among nonoffenders. The significance of the family situation for delinquency is discussed in greater detail in the chapter on social factors. Here it should be noted that the problem is not exclusively socio-

[11] *Ibid.*, chap. 19.
[12] The psychiatrist found "marked neuroticism" in 3.2 per cent of the delinquents and 5.1 per cent of the nondelinquents, mild neuroticism in 16.3 per cent of the delinquents and 23.2 per cent of the nondelinquents. This confirms the impression that delinquents are not typically frustrated or neurotic individuals.
[13] *Ibid.*, chap. 11 and p. 261.

logical. The personalities of the offender and his parents are involved as are the sociopsychological situation of attitudes and relationships as well as the social-cultural elements in the family and community.

The role of inferiority feelings in relation to delinquency is, like emotional conflicts, somewhat inconclusive. Adlerian analysts, a small minority among psychiatric criminologists, emphasize very strongly the sense of inadequacy in human maladjustments. They find that these inadequacy feelings are universal but differentially compensated, so that some individuals may be aided to achievement while others are doomed to failure through the ways in which they handle these feelings. However prevalent the sense of inferiority may be, it is apparent that it does not necessarily produce delinquency. Where it is found among delinquents, a causal relationship does not necessarily exist. There can be no real doubt, however, that delinquencies are sometimes compensatory. In such instances the behavior must be interpreted in the light of the total personality, the individual's potentialities and inclinations, rather than in terms of the inadequacy feelings alone.

The relationships of both emotional instability and suggestibility to delinquency appear in the table adapted from the Glueck data. As in other matters of temperament and personality, the influence of these qualities is largely indirect. Most individuals who display them do not become offenders, but the traits do involve some more or less serious limitation of self-control or inhibition. Consequently it may be assumed that emotional instability and suggestibility facilitate the expression of antisocial and aggressive impulses. In this connection it should be noted further that delinquents reveal a strong disposition to extraversive action.[14] They work through their problems outwardly rather than by inhibition or internalization. It appears that the nondelinquent may more frequently meet his social and emotional difficulties subjectively through fantasy, repression, internal compensations, or a retreat from reality. From the viewpoint of mental hygiene the results, of course, are not always healthy, but these methods of solving problems avoid the aggressions that may involve the extrovert in legal difficulties. This helps us to understand why delinquents less frequently manifest neurotic traits than do nondelinquents; on the average they are more often rid of their problems through externalizing them. Such individuals, as the author has suggested elsewhere, need stronger guilt feelings and firmer inhibition in the interest of public protection. The result will be less emotionally satisfying to them, in general.

In the case study below, taken from the author's files, the specific etiological significance of the offender's personality organization is not entirely clear; it appears, however, that the combination of his subjective traits to-

---

[14] This observation conforms with Dr. William Sheldon's interpretation of his somatotypes of delinquents where, however, he describes them in terms of "Dionysian buoyancy" and "unabashed predation." See Chapter 4.

gether with the deficiencies of his home were responsible for the difficulties in which he became involved.

Frank Newton was 21 years of age when he started serving a five-year sentence in a Federal correctional institution for theft and interstate transportation of stolen cars. He is a young man of excellent general intelligence, testing at an IQ of 115 at the time of his admission to prison, but he is an emotionally insecure personality lacking in warm personal attachments. He has spent most of the past ten years in correctional institutions. Treatment personnel at the prison believe that his excursions into crime do not reflect a real purpose to follow an antisocial way of life, as much as they reflect insecurity, passivity, and instability, his lack of goals and too spontaneous response to suggestion or temptation. It appears that mental conflicts generated by the discovery that he was an adopted child may have played an important role in the beginning of his delinquencies.

Newton knew nothing of his real parents, having been reared entirely by an adoptive mother. His home situation provided him little care or supervision, for his adoptive father died when he was 3 years old and the woman whom he believed to be his mother had to work outside the home. Newton first learned that he was adopted in 1945, when he was 15 years of age. It was shortly thereafter that he was arrested for the first time, on a charge of breaking and entering. This resulted in his commitment to a Kentucky reform school where he remained for one year. Only a few months after his release he was picked up for car theft and returned to the reformatory where he was retained until 1949 both on the theft charge and as a parole violator. After release he was employed for some three weeks by a pipe line company with which he traveled to Texas. He then broke into a café and stole $300. He was arrested quickly, the money still in his possession, and was committed to the Huntsville State Prison for two years. Upon discharge from this institution Newton worked for a few months in a Fort Worth café where he met the two codefendants who induced him to go with them in a stolen car. They went first to Kentucky where he visited his mother and then proceeded to Ohio. He and his associates stole two other cars en route.

During his Federal imprisonment Newton has made an excellent adjustment, displaying a considerably increased maturity and stability. He has done particularly good work in the educational department of the institution, earning meritorious good time because of his sincere and persistent efforts. He has no desire upon release to live again with his foster mother. Family and community ties are entirely lacking. However, while at the Federal correctional institution he has been befriended by a local Brotherhood of Saint Andrew and he plans after release to work for a member of this organization, a reputable businessman who has become attached to Newton and who has promised to take him into his home. This young man has had a constructive experience during his present commitment and has attained a considerable measure of maturity. He does not appear to be a seriously antisocial personality in spite of his offense history. Moreover, he has a positive community situation before him upon parole release. It appears that he has a better-than-average chance of making good.

In 1950, shortly before the appearance of the Glueck research, Karl F. Schuessler and Donald R. Cressey conducted a critical survey of 113 studies that had been made during the previous twenty-five years in testing the personality characteristics of offenders.[15] As a result of their inquiry they found that 42 per cent of the studies showed personality differentiations in favor of the noncriminals while the remainder were indeterminate in their conclusions. Schuessler and Cressey criticized the tests employed, the nonrepresentative character of the samples, the inadequate control groups, the a priori hypotheses, and the interpretations attached to the data gathered. Their survey makes it quite clear that the personality testing of offenders has given us only very equivocal data. One cannot thus far generalize on criminals or delinquents as a class on the basis of the studies. Indeed, it appears quite dubious that this can be done in the future. It should prove more fruitful to investigate the personality manifestations of specific categories of offenders, defined as precisely as possible, and to compare the manifestations of these offenders with those of carefully matched control groups. The Glueck material is more suggestive than earlier researches, but its significance is limited by the nature of the sample, which consisted of repetitive institutionalized youthful offenders from the Boston area. More personality testing and psychiatric investigation must be done under controlled conditions before we can arrive at very sound conclusions on the role of personality factors in criminal behavior. Too little clarification has come thus far from the generalized theories of the sociological criminologists, from the dynamic conceptions of the analysts, and from the testing tools and techniques employed by the psychologists.

ALCOHOLISM

The use of intoxicating liquors is dealt with here separate from other psychological and physical disorders because there is no consensus concerning the psychobiological foundations of the urge to drink and because some of the current researches indicate that the causes may vary considerably among different individuals. There is a general awareness of the importance of alcoholism as the nation's fourth greatest health problem, and an increasing amount of attention has been given to excessive drinking in recent years in the effort to uncover the motivations, effects, and useful treatment methodologies. There is much disagreement about these matters, however, at the time of writing. Even less is known about the relation of drinking to crime than is known about the problem of alcoholism generally, but it has been assumed for many years that there is an important correlation between the two.

Estimates of the prevalence of drinking and excessive drinking in the

[15] "Personality Characteristics of Criminals," *Am. J. Soc.,* vol. 55, pp. 476–484, 1950.

United States have varied widely during the 1950s. It has been said that 70 million Americans drink at least occasionally and that there are 4 million heavy drinkers and 1 million chronic alcoholics.[16] The economic loss directly attributable to alcoholism has been estimated at more than a billion dollars each year. This includes some 35 million dollars believed to go to hospital care of alcoholics, 25 million dollars for local jail maintenance of such persons, and 188 million dollars for the cost of crimes committed by offenders under the influence of liquor. In New York City there is an estimated number of between 200,000 and 300,000 chronic alcoholics, costing private and public agencies 200 million dollars annually, including 50 million in lost wages and 13 million in home relief (nearly 10 per cent of the city's relief costs).[17] Eighty-five per cent of the male alcoholics are between 35 and 55 years of age. On the average, their life span is believed to be reduced by twelve years.

Theories of the causation and appropriate treatment of alcoholism vary considerably. The prevailing view among authorities is that alcoholism constitutes a psychiatric abnormality symptomatic of underlying personality illness or disorder that requires psychotherapy. Seliger has classified alcoholics and the personality motivations that he found among them:[18]

[16] This was the report in April of 1952 of Dr. Robert V. Seliger, chief psychiatrist of the Neuropsychiatric Institute in Baltimore to the National Committee on Alcoholic Hygiene. At that time there were over 90 million individuals 20 years of age or over in the population. Seliger, "Psychiatric Orientation of the Alcoholic Criminal," *J. Am. Med. Assoc.*, vol. 129, pp. 421 ff., 1945. Some authorities have estimated that one out of every fifteen or sixteen who drink become alcoholic, while the Yale Center of Alcoholic Studies has put the figure at 6 per cent. The number of "pathological alcoholics" has also been set by different authorities at 3 million (in 1948) and at 5 million (in 1955). Estimates concerning the proportion of alcoholics who are women have varied from one-seventh to one-half, with the observation as to the latter that the female alcoholic is shielded from discovery and treatment. There is some agreement, in any event, that the number and proportion of female alcoholics is on the increase. The varying data appear to reflect the difficulty of securing reliable reports and differences of opinion as to what constitutes alcoholism. It is ordinarily defined merely as an inability to control the impulse to drink.

Alcoholic psychoses, which may result from addiction, are characterized by gradual mental and physical deterioration. Progressive amnesia, defective judgment, irritability, hallucinations, and sometimes delusions are found in this type of psychosis. Commonly there is also sexual excitability together with impotence. Korsakoff's syndrome or psychosis is a polyneuritis characterized by loss of memory (retrograde amnesia) that is caused by prolonged alcoholic consumption together with severe deficiency of food intake. More than 18,000 alcoholic psychotics are committed to hospitals annually.

[17] An estimate of the Committee on Alcoholism of the Welfare and Health Council of New York City. See *New York Times*, Dec. 1, 1952.

[18] Seliger, "Psychiatric Orientation of the Alcoholic Criminal," *op. cit.* (Reprinted by permission.) See also Seliger, "A Psychiatrist Looks at the Causes of Alcoholism," *J. Ind. Med.*, April, 1948, revised and reprinted, 1949. Narrower explanations have been put forward by Sandor Ferenczi, who held that sexual maladjustments, particularly homosexuality, were the basic cause (see Ferenczi and Otto Rank, *The*

The dynamics of personality motivation which may be found in any of these groups are summarized as self pampering tendencies illustrated by a refusal to tolerate at all any unpleasant state of mind; a drive for self expression without the resolve to take the practical steps to attain it; a more than usual craving for excitement and pleasure of the senses; a habit of sidestepping duties and obligations leading to the habit of substituting the rosy anesthesia of alcoholic day dreams; a definite insistent need for the feeling of self confidence, self importance, calm and poise that some temporarily obtain from alcohol.

It is also our conviction that alcoholism is evidence of latent or overt homosexuality as medically defined, or of self destructive tendencies and deep lying anxieties, hostilities and tensions stretching far back to infantile formation of attitudes, sentiments and interpersonal relationships in which identification and imitation play a decisive role. Contrary to popular opinion, science has no proof that alcoholism is hereditary, although some individuals with an alcoholic ancestry may have lowered resistance or be more sensitive to alcohol. Social inheritance involving the identification and imitation mechanisms would seem to be the basic factors, not heredity as such.

On the basis of his own studies and others, Seliger concludes that in any full description of the varieties of alcoholics one finds virtually all of the personality types exhibited by mankind. "Nevertheless," he asserts, "it always represents the psychobiological reaction of an individual personality to life and life situations, plus habit formation with respect to emotional reactions and the use of alcohol."

The Yale Center of Alcoholic Studies has observed that "There is much writing but almost no disciplined knowledge" concerning the relationship between criminality and alcoholism but expressed the belief that, in part through the employment of the Alcometer (devised at the Laboratory of Applied Physiology of which the Center is a unit), it would be possible to discover the number of arrested offenders who had been drinking, how much alcohol was present in their systems at the time, and the significance of alcohol in different types of criminal behavior.[19] Robert V. Seliger, too, has indicated that the evidence thus far is insufficient for definitive conclusion on whether alcohol inhibits or releases aggressive drives and damaging activities against society,[20] though its effect is certainly to relax

---

Development of Psychoanalysis, 1925); Oskar Diethelm, who has emphasized the psychological need of those who suffer feelings of depression and inadequacy (Diethelm, *Treatment in Psychiatry,* 1936); James Wall, who has stressed mother attachment, lack of ambition, and homosexuality (Wall, "A Study of Alcoholism in Men," *Am. J. Psychiat.,* vol. 93, May, 1956); Curtis Prout, who consistently found an "ego-discrepancy" in a sample of alcoholics, "a discrepancy between what he was and what he would like to be" (*New York Times,* Feb. 24, 1957); and others. See also Nolan D. C. Lewis, "Personality Factors in Alcoholic Addiction," *Quart. J. Studies Alc.,* vol. 1, pp. 21 ff., 1940.

[19] See also, in relation to testing for alcohol and legal aspects of the problem, Glenn C. Forrester, *Chemical Tests for Alcohol in Traffic Law Enforcement,* 1950.

[20] Seliger, "Psychiatric Orientation of the Alcoholic Criminal," *loc. cit.*

judgment and control. A beginning has been made toward more systematic research than was possible a few years ago, but we do not yet know to what extent alcohol is criminogenic.

Perhaps the most informative study available thus far comes from Columbus, Ohio, where the urine of 882 persons arrested during or immediately after the commission of a felony during a two-year period was analyzed to determine alcohol concentration.[21] It was found that 64 per cent of the felons were under the influence of alcohol to an extent sufficient to reduce their inhibitions (0.10 per cent or more of urine alcohol being taken as enough to accomplish that result). Crimes of physical violence were most frequently associated with intoxication: eleven displayed such a concentration of alcohol for every one who was sober in crimes of cutting and stabbing; eight to one, in the carrying of concealed weapons; ten to one, in nonfelonious assaults; and four to one, in shootings and murders. While crimes involving the illegal appropriation of property were much less frequently related to drinking, two to one among those apprehended for robbery, burglary, larceny, and car theft were under the influence of alcohol.[22] The author of the report points out that, since not all offenders are apprehended during or shortly after they commit crimes, the data secured may be somewhat misleading; but it appears that only through such a study as this can one determine with fair accuracy how many *among those apprehended early* have been drinking and have consumed enough to be affected by it.

Dr. Ralph Banay has estimated that 25 per cent of the total number of offenders he studied at Sing Sing revealed a close or direct causal relationship between their crimes and alcoholism.[23] A number of institutional tallies have indicated that as many as 60 per cent of felony prisoners and up to 80 per cent of jail and county penitentiary inmates are alcoholics or heavy drinkers.[24] In a very large part of the latter group, arrests resulted from the intoxicated condition of the prisoners, convictions being based on disorderly conduct or vagrancy; these arrests were often made with insufficient evidence to support legitimate convictions on such charges.[25]

[21] Lloyd M. Shupe, "Alcohol and Crime," *J. Crim. L.*, vol. 44, pp. 661–665, 1954.

[22] It is interesting to observe, as compared with the other classes, that 55 per cent of the rapists and 57 per cent of those arrested for felonious assault were not intoxicated, most of them showing no alcohol. See also Seliger, "Alcohol and Crime," *J. Crim. L.*, vol. 44, pp. 438–442, 1953, where he reviews two small studies that have been made.

[23] Study cited in Seliger, *ibid.*, p. 439.

[24] See Paul R. Brown, "The Problem Drinker and the Jail," *Quart. J. of Studies Alc.*, vol. 16, pp. 474–483, 1955.

[25] Chief Magistrate Murtagh of New York City has taken the position that there is "no moral basis" for making public intoxication a violation of law, that the arrests and convictions that do occur are actually unsupported by the present laws,

None of the studies referred to define what is meant by "alcoholism"; for the most part they use the term loosely, so that it is difficult to know how prevalent addiction is in the criminal population. Except for Banay's estimate, there has been little or no attempt to determine the proportion of cases in which drinking had a significant etiological relationship to crimes committed. Patently, information is especially desirable on this point from a criminological point of view. Institutional and court personnel very commonly make broad generalizations attributing crimes to drinking, but it is fairly clear that in a majority of cases drinking is parallel to rather than the cause of criminality; in any case both crime and alcoholism may well reflect inadequacies of personality. It is notable that in the population at large at least 70 per cent of the population aged 20 and over drink occasionally and that 4 per cent or more are heavy drinkers. Comparable statistics on the prison and court populations would be desirable as well as more precise inquiry into the nature of the relationship between drinking and the offenses committed. Lacking this, we can draw no reliable inferences concerning the possibility that depriving the offender of liquor will affect his criminal behavior. Probation and parole conditions that prohibit drinking to all offenders under supervision are based on moralistic conjecture for the most part, at least so far as non-alcoholic felons are concerned. On the other hand, deteriorated alcoholics almost inevitably persist in their drinking and repetitive jail commitments so long as they do not receive treatment.[26] If endocrinological and other biochemical research fulfills its apparent promise in this respect, the prospect for the future appears somewhat brighter. Until some curative therapy can be provided for alcoholics on an outpatient clinic basis, it appears that indefinite commitments up to a year or two in state misdemeanant farms is more effective in bringing their drinking under control

---

and that alcoholism should be handled as a medical problem by the public health authorities and by civil commitment rather than by criminal courts. For an excellent article on abuse of vagrancy legislation, especially in dealing with alcoholics, see Caleb Foote, "Vagrancy Type Law and Its Administration," *U. Pa. L. Rev.,* vol. 104, pp. 603 ff., 1956.

[26] The problem is illustrated in caricature by various specific cases: The 63-year-old offender in Schenectady has recently completed service of his 198th jail term for public intoxication. He has spent a total of 4,047 days in jail, more than eleven years. A 51-year-old Seattle alcoholic has been arrested 223 times for drunkenness in twenty-five years and has spent nearly half of that period in jail on short sentences. *Seattle Times,* Oct. 17, 1946, cited in Caleb Foote, *ibid.,* ftn. 167. Foote quotes from a Philadelphia House of Correction report that 40 per cent of the 5,166 inmates committed to that jail in a recent year had had prior commitments there, 6.3 per cent of them more than ten times, 1.4 per cent more than thirty. *Loc. cit.* It is significant to note, however, that in a sample of vagrancy or habitual drunkenness cases only 13 per cent had prior records for offenses of other sorts and these involved, in the main, only minor criminality. For material relating to treatment, see Chapter 18.

and in improving their health than are the terms in local jails that have been the traditional means of briefly "drying them out." When such drinking has not been accompanied by serious offenses, legal provision should be made for civil rather than criminal commitment.

The author has interviewed hundreds of prisoners who have been habituated to heavy drinking; many fared well while in prison, perhaps because their anxieties were calmed in the protected environment, but many repeatedly encounter difficulties when faced with freedom and responsibility in the community. The following is a fairly typical illustration:

Richard Dobbs, 55 years of age, is serving a two-year sentence for probation violation in a Federal prison as a result of issuing bad checks. He is a habitual criminal and an excellent prisoner. Dobbs has been arrested seventy-one times since 1916 for various crimes, including burglary, larceny, assault with a deadly weapon, attempted murder, liquor law violations, car theft, robbery, grand larceny, forgery, false pretenses, and intoxication. He has been imprisoned thirty-eight times, for periods in excess of one year on eight of these occasions.

The prisoner has a high average intelligence and a tenth-grade education. He attends Catholic services regularly at the prison. He displays a responsive attitude toward his officers and the institution program and is earning meritorious good time for his excellent work performance as orderly in the machine shop. His work is characterized in these terms: "On this assignment he is doing an outstanding job in the cleanliness of these shops, and is without exception the best orderly ever assigned here from the standpoint of keeping everything spic and span: for instance he will immediately clean up oil or grease that gets spilled on the floor, never waiting until it gets tracked all over the place which could cause someone to slip and fall. These shops were never kept so clean as they are at the present time. . . . His cooperation is very good and his attitude toward both inmates and officers is excellent." He is never reported for disciplinary problems.

Dobbs has had work experience in various unskilled occupations, as a bartender, truck driver, cook, and soldier, but has had no extended periods of employment except during his incarceration. His major difficulty is chronic alcoholism, together with a lack of any goals for personal achievement. He has been married but was divorced because of his periodic drinking bouts and lack of responsibility. He has no plans for the future.

NARCOTIC USE AND ADDICTION

Man's desire to employ substances that provide a pleasurable, stimulating, or narcotic effect upon the central nervous system has been expressed universally and in ancient as well as modern civilizations. Such drugs as tobacco, caffeine, alcohol, the tranquilizers, and benzedrine are very widely employed as a relatively harmless means of enjoyment. Habituation is common. Drugs with more extreme effects have also been commonly used in many societies: opium and its derivatives from the poppy seed in China, India, and elsewhere; mescaline from the cactus peyote among certain Indian tribes; betel chewing in India and Polynesia; Indian hemp (hashish or marijuana) in Africa, Asia, and Mexico; coca chewing and cocaine in South America; the intoxicating pepper (kava-kava) in the South Sea Islands; and intoxicating toadstools in Mexico and Siberia. These and other narcotics are used to produce euphoria, sedation, erotic fantasies or hallucinations, feelings of strength, anaesthesia, analgesia, aphrodisia, excitement, and allied states.[27] The separation of morphine from opium in 1803, of heroin from opium in 1898, and the perfection of the hypodermic needle for subcutaneous injections in 1855 gave an impetus to the use of the alkaloid depressants and led to the consequent development of drug addiction. Subsequently numerous pharmaceutical derivates and compounds of opium and morphine have been developed, including in addition to heroin and codeine such commonly used narcotics as dilaudid, laudanon, eucadol, dicodid, acedicon, and genomorphine. The experimentation with the more recent drugs has aimed at so altering the opiate's chemical composition as to eliminate such secondary effects as euphoria while retaining the analgesic property for purposes of medication. The experimentation has not been entirely successful, however, and these habit-forming substances have recruited many addicts.

Medicine containing opiates was widely distributed in the United States without prescription and at low cost during the eighteenth and nineteenth centuries; by the beginning of the present century addiction is said to have become very common here. Estimates of the prevalence of usage and addiction to narcotics are highly unreliable. This is in part because the vice is hidden and in part because of differences of opinion as to what constitutes addiction.[28] During periods of heightened concern about the distribution of drugs, when official investigations are made and policing activities stepped up, the number of users disclosed may be increased very rapidly, giving the impression of a contagion that may be largely or wholly fictitious. Estimates of the number of addicts in the United States at the turn of the century ranged from 100,000 to a million.[29] In 1919 one newspaper suggested that there were 5 million addicts; this inflated figure undoubtedly reflects the anxiety associated with the increase in the

[27] See Erich Hesse, *Narcotics and Drug Addiction*, 1946, for a description of the varieties of narcotics and the distribution of their use.

[28] David W. Maurer and Victor H. Vogel, *Narcotics and Narcotic Addiction*, 1954, pp. 6–7.

[29] The question relates to how far one must be habituated and dependent before he is "hooked." There is a further issue as to what constitutes an addictive drug. Marijuana (reefers), so widely used in many cities since the fad developed in the late 1940s, is classed with the narcotics in Federal and many state penal laws and they are lumped together in arrest and conviction data; but from a medical point of view there is a significant difference, since the former is not an addictive narcotic, i.e., it does not develop a physiological dependence. The nature of addiction is discussed in the text below.

use of narcotics that occurs in postwar periods. Dr. Howard Rusk's estimate that in 1914 there were 150,000 to 200,000 addicts throughout the nation is probably as reasonable as any, though his figures, too, are conjectural.[30] According to an authority of the Federal Bureau of Narcotics, there were 100,000 "known addicts" in 1929 and 35,000 in 1956, but the Bureau believed that in fact there were probably 300,000 in the former year and 60,000 in the latter.[31] In spite of the hysteria that marked public and official reaction to the problem during the early 1950s, it appears fairly clear that the volume of drug addiction has dropped very significantly in the past twenty-five years, especially in consideration of the fact that since 1930 the total population has increased more than 50 million. Drug use and addiction have been concentrated mainly in large cities, especially New York, Chicago, Washington, and a few others.

A more serious aspect of the contemporary narcotics problem has been the development of the drug habit among young people in metropolitan areas, though the extent of their use of drugs has probably been exaggerated. In 1953 the executive director of the Welfare and Health Council in New York City publicized an estimate of a council committee reporting that in 1952 there were at least 3,300 addicts under 21 years of age in the city and probably two or three times that number.[32] The police

[30] See *New York Times,* May 20, 1952.

[31] Reports of Commissioner Harry J. Anslinger and James C. Ryan, supervisor, *San Francisco Chronicle,* June 27, 1956; *New York Herald Tribune,* June 26, 1955. The 60,000 figure was arrived at by a study committee appointed by President Eisenhower in 1954. Data of quite a different sort have been published annually in the *Uniform Crime Reports,* but they provide a poor index of changes in the volume of narcotics use or addiction and not very good evidence of variations in arrests in recent years. Prior to 1952 the data relating to narcotics arrests were based on fingerprint cards submitted by local communities. They offer some testimonial to the increase in police activity in narcotics cases. Non-Federal arrests reported ranged from 3,370 in 1933 and 2,327 in 1934 to 2,629 in 1940, 1,935 in 1945, 6,546 in 1949, 8,539 in 1950, and 13,030 in 1951. Beginning in 1952 the system of reporting was changed to provide more accurate data based on annual reports from cooperating police departments. The number of reporting cities has varied considerably in subsequent years, so that data on arrests are not directly comparable from year to year. Arrests for narcotics violations, however, have remained a quite uniform proportion of the total reporting population and of all criminal arrests reported. Arrests for narcotics violations have constituted from 0.3 to 0.4 per cent of all arrests reported. The publicity given to increased arrests in 1950 and 1951 in some cities stimulated exaggerated concern. Thus, New York reported a 43.7 per cent gain in narcotics arrests in 1951 over 1950; there were 3,302 arrests in the later year for narcotics violations. This probably reflected in some fair part the expansion of the narcotics squad of the New York City Police Department from 27 to 41 and then to 100 members. Arrests for possession of narcotics increased greatly, especially among youths. There were sixteen times more narcotics arrests of teen-agers in New York in 1950 than in 1946; but there had been only thirty-three such arrests in the former year.

[32] *New York Times,* May 27, 1953. Lieutenant Bazlom of the narcotics squad estimated that there were 6,000 teen-age addicts in the city. *New York Times,* June 15, 1951.

arrested 544 youths under 20 on narcotics charges during 1952. Only thirty narcotics users were identified among the 300,000 high school students in that year.[33] Various authorities have indicated that 13 per cent of the nation's narcotic addicts are youths. *Uniform Crime Report* data somewhat confirm this figure, showing in 1952, 1955, and 1956 that approximately 13 per cent of those arrested on narcotics charges were below the age of 21.[34] The Federal Committee on Narcotics observed, however, that 87.6 per cent of these young addicts were over the age of 18.[35] Data on cases involving marijuana and addictive drugs and data on possession, sales, and addiction in a technical sense have not been broken down, but there is some indication that many of the younger offenders use only marijuana and that among those who have used heroin a large proportion have not become addicted before discovery.[36]

The nature and effects of addiction will now be considered and then the sorts of individuals who tend to become habituated. Addiction is a state of periodic or chronic intoxication produced by repeated consumption of a natural or synthetic narcotic. It is characterized in the main by an overpowering compulsion to take the drug, by a tendency to increase dosage as a result of the tolerance that develops, and by a dependence upon the drug's effect that may be both psychological and physical.[37] The dependence is related to the desire to avoid painful withdrawal symptoms.[38] The development of habituation and dependence, though the physico-psychological mechanisms are unknown, is a process in which the user first relieves physical or emotional discomfort or, in many instances, seeks a euphoric thrill by employing a relatively small amount of an opiate.

[33] *Ibid.*, April 30, 1952. In the previous year there were 154 "known cases."

[34] In 1951, however, 18.7 per cent of narcotic arrests reported were of youths under 21 and 3.7 were of youths under 18. This was at the peak of the drive against juvenile drug addiction.

[35] *New York Times*, Feb. 6, 1956. In 1956 there were 292 arrests of youths under 18 reported to the FBI in a total reporting population of 41,219,052, which included the major metropolitan centers.

[36] Authorities in the field have observed that a large proportion of the young offenders committed for treatment have been using the drug for only a short time and respond favorably to therapy.

[37] See, *inter alia*, Harry J. Anslinger and William F. Tompkins, *The Traffic in Narcotics*, 1953; Orin R. Yost, *The Bane of Drug Addiction*, 1954; Maurer and Vogel, *op. cit.*; Citizen's Advisory Committee to the Attorney General on Crime Prevention, *Narcotic Addiction*, California, 1954; V. H. Vogel, H. Isbell, and K. W. Chapman, "Present Status of Narcotic Addiction," *J. Am. Med. Assoc.*, vol. 138, pp. 1019–1026, 1948.

[38] Withdrawal is characterized by chills, vomiting, diarrhea, yawning, sneezing, irritability, and hot flashes. Commonly muscular twitching, headaches, confusion, tantrums, and delirium are observed. The patient may attempt suicide to secure relief. The symptoms may be largely alleviated by gradual reduction of the drug, but in many jails the inmates receive the "cold turkey" treatment of complete abstinence.

After becoming adjusted to the effects of the drug, he requires a larger dosage to secure escape or to feel normal. In time, with an altered bodily equilibrium, he may need a quantity that would promptly kill the ordinary, nonaddicted adult in order to remain in bearable physical and mental condition. With a lowering of the drug level in the blood and tissue, the abstinence syndrome sets in and the addict must seek relief. Often a beginning is made, especially among youngsters in search of "kicks," by smoking marijuana, sometimes by taking benzedrine ("goof balls"), or occasionally by drinking alcohol. With the persuasion of an addict-pusher, the narcotic-prone personality may be led to try heroin, the most popular of the euphoric opiates; once he is "hooked," for a greater and quicker pleasure he follows a regular habit of "mainlining" with hypodermic injections (the needle and spoon) into his veins. Mainlining will cost him daily from $10 to $100, depending on the market and the size of his habit. A voluntary "kicking of the habit," it is generally agreed, is then virtually impossible, although the addict may welcome commitment for gradual reduction on morphine, methadon, or chlorpromazine so that he can start again with greater satisfaction on smaller intake.

Some inquiry has been made into the sort of individuals who become addicted. No typical addict personality has emerged, but it has been remarked in a general way that emotionally immature, dependent personalities, quite similar to alcoholics, are commonly found among users. Literature on the subject describes four general categories of addicts: (1) the "medical" or "accidental" group that has become habituated through extended use in the treatment of a physical illness,[39] (2) psychoneurotic types who seek to relieve their anxieties or to remove imaginary ills, (3) "psychopaths" or persons suffering from character disorders who seek release of their unconscious aggressive drives and hostility against society, and (4) psychotic types. In the latter it is commonly difficult to determine, except during periods of withdrawal, whether they are in fact psychotic or, if they are, whether the condition is a consequence of the psychosis.[40] This classification provides little differentiation from the criminal population generally. However, it has been reported on the basis of a study at the Federal Narcotic Hospital at Lexington not only that addicts display family

[39] See R. H. Felix, "An Appraisal of the Personality Types of the Addict," *Am. J. Psychiat.*, vol. 100, 1954, and Vogel, Isbel, and Chapman, *loc. cit.* Dr. J. DeWitt Fox of Detroit has estimated that narcotic addiction is 100 times more common among physicians than it is in the population generally. He suggests that emotional problems together with the pressure of work and the easy availability of the drugs account for this. Others have noted the prevalence of addiction among physicians and nurses.

[40] Vogel and Isbell, "Medical Aspects of Addiction to Analgesic Drugs," *Bull. Narcotics, U.N. Dep. Social Affairs*, vol. 4, 1950. The authors maintain in Vogel, Isbell, and Chapman, *op. cit.*, that the psychopathic category contains the largest group of addicts, but this may be a matter of the broad definition of the category.

background circumstances productive of serious adjustment difficulties but that addicts are a more difficult problem than offenders generally because the opiates are adaptively valuable: addiction represents a satisfying though malignant way of coping with emotional difficulties.

One of the author's students has added more specialized information by comparing a sample of thirty-two drug-using juveniles with a control group of similar size at the New York State Training School for Boys.[41] He found that to a significantly greater extent the drug users came from families in which they had been indulged by their mothers and felt hostility toward their fathers. The drug users came from a more limited geographic area, especially from Harlem. They lived in neighborhoods where narcotic usage was more prevalent and obtained their drugs in few sections of the city. They were older than nondrug users at the time of commitment and, while they displayed similar school and behavioral problems, they had more often committed their offenses alone and had less often run away from home than had members of the control group. The drug users displayed dependency and isolation as typical personality features.

Efforts to develop effective treatment methods for narcotic addiction have met thus far with very little success, even as compared with alcoholism and the deteriorative psychoses. This is very clearly indicated in the recidivist statistics in the *Uniform Crime Reports,* where 71 to 75 per cent of narcotics violators are shown to have had prior fingerprint records.[42] For the most part, discovered users are over the age of 18. Once started, they tend to persist in using drugs. There is an unwillingness among the addicted to recognize that their use of narcotics is a problem;

---

[41] Reviewed by the author in Simon Kleinman, "Narcotic Usage by Juveniles," *J. Pub. Admin.,* vol. 2, no. 1, pp. 17–33, 1956. See also Alan S. Meyer (ed.), "Social and Psychological Factors in Opiate Addiction," Review of research findings, 1952; Donald L. Gerard and Conan Kornetsky, "A Preliminary Report on Adolescent Opiate Addiction," paper presented at the American Ortho-psychiatric Meeting, Feb. 25, 1953; and Robert L. McFarland and William A. Hall, "A Survey of One Hundred Suspected Drug Addicts," *J. Crim. L.,* vol. 44, pp. 308–320, 1953. In the latter the authors carried on in connection with the municipal courts of Chicago an investigation into a sample of cases referred to the psychiatric staff at the House of Correction. No control group was used, so that the significance of the findings is not apparent. McFarland and Hall found that 62 of the 100 patients were either "immature with asocial or amoral trends" (forty cases) or "pathological personalities" (twelve cases). These patients displayed little anxiety in relation to their behavior, little in the way of interests, hobbies, or activities, and little desire for treatment. Only five cases were diagnosed as psychoneurotic, five as mentally deficient, and four as psychotic or near psychotic. Psychiatric treatment was deemed feasible in only thirteen cases and a good prognosis was found in less than 10 per cent of the cases. The average age of the patients was 23.9 years, with a range of from 17 to 49 years.

[42] The recidivist data were provided only until 1952 when the FBI system of reporting changed.

the mask to their emotional difficulties provided by the drug is too strong to abandon willingly or permanently.

Narcotics and Crime

The relationship between the use of narcotics and criminality has been considerably misunderstood; badly distorted or quite extraordinary tales of offenses committed by addicts have helped to exaggerate this misunderstanding.[43] Addicts are *not* a problem criminologically because the use of narcotics disposes them to commit criminal acts. Generally they are passive and asocial rather than antisocial individuals. They are disinclined to aggression except as this may be required to secure their supply. Narcotics probably inhibit what aggressive drives they do experience. They display little erotic interest, either heterosexual of homosexual, and therefore are not "sex fiends" as they are sometimes portrayed.[44] Kolb has remarked that "morphine changes the potential murderer into a mere thief." McFarland and Hall find that addicts are rarely psychoneurotics and that they do not generally suffer from feelings of guilt.[45] Moreover, while young apprehended offenders are commonly from the slums and many have participated in gang activity, they tend to leave the gang when they become addicted.[46] The user does not need the gang. Neither the youthful gang nor the professional mob wants users in its membership. Older addicts who have received their occupational training before starting the use of drugs are less often discovered and prosecuted; they are the "hidden addicts." Many can carry on in business or professions without serious inconvenience. Some authorities believe that these constitute a large proportion of drug users.

In so far as addiction constitutes a serious criminological problem, it is largely an indirect one. It is true that legislation today makes possession and use an offense in itself, but where the laws still permit, sentencing of the user is humane and he is generally viewed by authorities as a victim rather than as a dangerous criminal. In a more significant sense, then, the addict of lower socioeconomic class is criminal primarily because illicit narcotics are costly and because he can secure his daily requirements only

---

[43] Commissioner Anslinger, for example, spends twelve pages attempting to prove that addicts are fiends. He goes back to 1937 to find the case of a man who committed two rape murders, disemboweled himself, and then walked twelve miles before dropping dead. The physician who signed the death certificate indicated that he must have used narcotics to have stood the pain.

[44] See McFarland and Hall, *op. cit.,* p. 314.

[45] McFarland and Hall made this observation: "Frequently the impression was obtained that drug use was an ego-syntonic act, i.e., that no internal anxiety was engendered in the patient by the drug habit." *Ibid.*

[46] From a report of the Committee on Public Health Relations of the New York Academy of Medicine, reviewed in the *New York Times,* June 15, 1953.

by committing crimes that will pay for them. In the male this generally means persistent thefts, though burglary and robbery, particularly of drugstores, and forgery, either of prescriptions or checks, are not uncommon. A good many addicts engage in the sale of narcotics to others because it is more profitable and because it assures them easy access to their own supply. This is a more dangerous criminal activity. Through the influence of the young addict-pusher, other youths may be drawn into the use of drugs. This results in one of the difficult problems of policy in dealing with the narcotic traffic: how to deal with the youngster who has been "hooked," who is not especially disposed toward serious criminality, but who in effect is the "carrier" of a dangerous malady. Under prevailing legislation such individuals become subject to very long prison terms or to the death penalty. In the female, theft or prostitution is the common consequence of addiction, depending upon age, social position, and other factors. Occasionally, though not very often, the addict experiencing withdrawal symptoms will commit an assault or homicide if he is balked in his effort to secure relief. For the most part, however, drug users are amenable to police control once they have been apprehended, both because of their personality structures and because they are dependent upon the drug. The hidden addict, like the hidden alcoholic, who can afford to meet his requirement is a problem only to his family, if he has any, and in his employment, but not to public authorities.

The more serious criminal aspect of the narcotics problem lies in the organized local, interstate, and international distribution carried on by professional criminals. Federal enforcement agents properly concentrate on this group, but in the absence of effective measures of controlling opium production there is little chance of halting so lucrative a traffic.

As we have observed, the social history and personality of drug addicts, like those of other offenders, vary considerably. There is perhaps a somewhat greater uniformity, however, in the nature of the addicts' family relationships and in their failures to work out a constructive adjustment. The following description is taken from the institutional psychiatric report of one such individual:

Subject, a white male, American born 8-15-36 was sentenced to a three-year reformatory sentence. He has a mental age of 16 plus and intelligence quotient of 107+ described by the psychologist as being of "better than average intelligence but with score ranging from borderline to distinctly superior."

A confirmed drug user who is completely resistive to any change in the habit, admits freely that he continued to use drugs after having been introduced to them because he liked the feeling, and regardless of the consequences feels that he will again very likely return to drugs. He has reconciled himself to what he calls the inevitable. He very frankly states that he has had a good deal of dealing with psychiatrists and that what he has gone through at the interview is nothing new to him, and inasmuch as he has failed in the past;

"I don't think it will be worth my while to see a psychiatrist because I will only be resistive and give him a hard time."

This inmate's difficulties have always revolved around drugs. He was briefly examined in 1952 at Bellevue Hospital, and though we presently have no report from that institution, it is obvious that nothing of any import was discovered inasmuch as he was released shortly after admission. He was also at the Riverside Hospital and made three escapes from there. He was classified at that hospital as a neurotic character disorder with anxiety and hysterical features, and it was felt he was in need of individual psychotherapy. When first observed it was felt that he could profit from individual psychotherapy, though he is a type who when first seen can dissemble superficially exceedingly well. It was pointed out in the report that he projected hostility, verbalized freely but could not discuss his own conflicts. Towards the end it was finally decided that he was too resistive for therapy and he was discharged as having received the maximum hospital benefits, and there was nothing further that could be done. Here inmate admitted resentment and resistiveness to any treatment concerning drugs. He briefly gave history of himself, stating that he reached the second term of vocational high school at the age of sixteen, having been transferred from a parochial school. Admitted frankly that he never lived up to his full potentials, was satisfied to just get by. Admits he never worked after leaving school for he just didn't care to do so. At home he revealed himself as always unhappy and there was a great deal of sibling rivalry. Of his three sisters and one brother, he had this to say; "I don't like them. I had nothing to say to them and they had nothing to say to me." As for his mother, he added, "she was nervous, irritable, and had a nervous breakdown for a week and a half." When it was pointed out that he had not mentioned his father, he had this to say, "There is nothing to talk about. He goes to work, comes home, goes to bed, he goes to work in the morning comes home, goes to bed, the same routine." He tells this in a matter-of-fact calm voice, but one senses under the calmness is a deep abiding resentment.

SUMMARY: The general impression is gained that we are dealing with a youth who felt unloved, unappreciated, unwanted, and in his defense detached himself from members of his family. Unable to assert himself he grew up feeling defenseless, hence he needed external support to sustain his weak ego. Under drugs he found the support he needed. It is clear inmate is extremely resistive and reluctant to give up the support that sustains him. Removing the drugs from this emotional cripple is like removing a crutch from a physical cripple. Without it he cannot function or navigate. He would have to be completely revamped from the bottom up, but he would still be too resistive to the intensive and deep psychotherapy that would be so necessary, for before we can build up we have to break down and he cannot stand the pressure of having his defense broken down. He is classified as a sociopathic individual with drug addiction and with a deep neurotic core.

CONCLUSION

It would be unwise to depreciate the significance of psychological influences in delinquency and crime. Mental factors in crime are recognized in the law itself; mens rea is required before an act will constitute a crime, and provision for defenses and mitigations based on psychological states is gradually expanding. Certainly the criminologist must see every criminal act partially as being an expression of the offender's subjective condition and response patterns. The real difficulty relating to the role of psychological factors and crime lies largely in the interpretation of (1) what influence particular psychological states and processes play in causing criminality and how these relate to other nonpsychological factors and (2) what treatment inferences should be derived from psychological diagnostic findings. A strictly clinical orientation to criminality tends to overlook the significance of social, cultural, and biological influences on conduct. Obviously human behavior involves something more than subjective and individualized elements. It is a response *to* something: to tradition, laws, values, the home, school, church, group associations, etc. Knowledge and experience are an internalization of external realities, affected greatly of course by the biopsychological peculiarities of the individual and by his apperceptive mass. But the latter are themselves a part of and inseparable from the environment in which his personality has formed. It should be clear, therefore, that the individual's tendencies to react are partially a product of his outer world and of his prior experiences with that world. Moreover, the way that he will act in the future depends not only upon his personality dispositions but also upon the opportunities and the evocative stimulations that confront him and that, as they become a part of his experience, influence the patterns of his subsequent responses.

If one is reared in a slum family and rejected by his parents, if he feels inferior because of real or imagined defects, if he is a suggestible extrovert and adopts the values of an antisocial gang in his neighborhood, and if his parents lack the power or the will to redirect him, his thieveries with his group and his later burglaries on his own are not surprising. The pattern is common. One cannot, however, assign a particular quantum of significance to the diverse psychological influences or to the social determinants involved. They make up an interrelated whole. Perhaps this offender will be found, upon diagnostic study, to be neurotic, psychopathic, or psychotic. Or deeper analysis under hypnosis, amytol, or pentothal may stir up devious motives that do not fit neatly into the classical nomenclature of psychopathology. The dynamics of his delinquency still lie in a complex of biological, psychological, and social variables. It is unjustifiably parochial to see him merely as a psychological deviate or as merely a product of his environment.

Chapter 7

SOCIAL-CULTURAL THEORY

Crime is a social and cultural problem as well as an individual phenomenon. Neither crime nor the offender can be interpreted soundly without reference to the mores and the law, the agencies of social control and redirection, and the ethos in which social differentiation and individual deviation occur. In this chapter certain of the broader aspects of the society and culture with which crime appears to be associated and some of the sociological theories that have been put forward to explain the phenomenon of crime will be considered.

It should be observed in advance that, while these theories help to clarify the social motivations and processes that bear on crime and while they are attractive in their comprehensive simplicity, taken alone they may be misleading. Some criminological hypotheses suggest that individuals respond uniformly and mechanically to the social-cultural setting. Few take into account the role of individual variability while they exaggerate the extent of group uniformities. Commonly it appears that the proponent of a theoretical system considers that his particular hypothesis is adequate to the exclusion of other differing conceptions. This kind of analysis has discouraged the effort to integrate theory and has reinforced the traditional environmentalists' hostility to the postulates and researches of other behavioral disciplines. For the most part, the broad social and cultural explanations of crime are derived from abstract conceptualization rather than from empirical evidence. By their very nature the scope and limitations of the more inclusive hypotheses cannot well be tested.

Criminological theorists have come to criticize, and quite properly so, the chaotic eclecticism implicit in a loosely defined theory of the "multiple causation" of crime, which is supported merely by trait descriptions of offenders. Nevertheless, it is largely through the refinement of researches into differentiated characteristics and responses of criminals that progress will continue in criminology and correctional practice. The paramount need is for integrative research and integrative theory, through which criminality may be understood in its diversity as well as in its uniformity. This integration should come in part through the collaboration of the behavioral sciences and in part through increasingly precise knowledge about the dynamics of crime in particular classes of offenders. The major theories that provide some insight into the broad social-cultural processes that affect law violation will be considered below. Attention was previously given to the role of physical and psychological motivations. The apparent influence of more specific social factors related to crime will be discussed in Chapter 8 and some of the differences that appear to exist between major categories of offenders, in Chapter 9. This organization of material lies within the general context of the field theory referred to in Chapter 3.

CRIMINOGENIC ASPECTS OF THE SOCIAL ORDER

It is perhaps not too much to say that in a real sense crime is systemic in the contemporary American social-cultural pattern. This is not to suggest that we live in a "criminal culture" or in a "sick society"; these recently popular conceptions reflect an astigmatic focus upon the pathological by-products of a system. Nevertheless, as compared with other times and other people, our society is in some part criminogenic. This view may be affirmed and will be supported here by reference to several phases of our social-cultural context: (1) the goals we seek and the means by which we strive to attain them; (2) certain aspects of our general social-cultural complex and, in particular, the regulatory measures by which control is exerted over individual conduct; and (3) the transmission of anti-social norms within the system.

Goals and Means

Much of the crime in modern society is a means of avoiding frustration, on the one hand, and a reactive expression to the experience of frustration, on the other. The frustration itself may be partially interpreted within a framework of means and ends. Veblen's emphasis a generation ago upon the keenly competitive struggle for wealth has been elaborated by Merton in terms of materialistic goals that are deemed appropriate for all but that are available through legitimate means only to a few.[1] The desire for wealth and for the prestige and power that are associated with wealth as objects to be gained "without regard to initial lot or station in life" is sometimes conceived as a near-universal drive in contemporary society. The author submits, however, that this is a decreasingly accurate generalization in the midtwentieth century, as the fixity of socioeconomic lines

[1] See Robert K. Merton, *Social Theory and Social Structure,* 1957, p. 166–176, and the discussion below. Merton refers to a paper by Herbert H. Hyman, "The Value Systems of Different Classes," in R. Bendix and S. M. Lipset (eds.), *Class, Status and Power,* 1953, pp. 426–442, where Hyman observes considerable class variation in the extent to which success goals are internalized. *Op. cit.,* pp. 170–176. It appears that there is wide variation within and between social classes in the levels of aspiration, the limitations upon opportunity, and the personalities of aspirants. Simple generalization about the production of deviance seems unwarranted.

has come to be more generally accepted by the lower and lower-middle classes.[2] A majority of persons at these levels—and they constitute, of course, the great mass in the community—are realistic enough to accept, though not without some frustration, the futility of struggling for either fortune or fame. They lack the zest to fight against the limitations of a class organization that they conceive, at least so far as they are concerned, to be closed. Furthermore, the disparity in "life styles" has diminished in our age. Under the leveling influence of a welfare-oriented state, of a powerful trade unionism with its strong mass identification, and of a large and growing civil service, the "common man" has come ostensibly to accept the doctrine that he *is* common and that he should not attempt to be otherwise. As an anonymous unit, without separate aspiration, he silently approves the bargain struck by his collective and is temporarily content (until his group bargains again) with his acquisitions, the time-payment cottage, car, television, and children, so much like those of his equally anonymous neighbor. The flattening of class differentiations and the growing acceptance thereof promises, whatever its many other implications may be, to reduce the level of economic frustration felt by a large part of the population, the growing lower-middle class. Quite possibly, though empirical research has not yet provided real clarification, crime as well as other manifestations of discontent will become less common in this group.

The desire to achieve the traditional open-class goals of wealth and power appears, therefore, to characterize a diminishing though still significant part of the population, mainly individuals of middle-middle and upper-middle class, with a few others from below who see or imagine

[2] It should be observed, in this regard, that from the viewpoint of simple and generalized theory the law-obedience of noncriminals may be interpreted in terms of the absence of opportunity and motivation to engage in criminal activity. Conformist behavior must often reflect in some measure the lack of favorable occasion for satisfying deviance. This point has been made by Richard A. Cloward in "Illegitimate Means, Anomie, and Deviant Behavior," *Am. Soc. Rev.,* vol. 24, pp. 164–177, April, 1959. In the same issue Merton observes the value of Cloward's analysis in correcting an "unwitting and, it appears, untrue assumption" by pointing to the "socially patterned differences of access to *learning how* to perform particular kinds of deviant roles and of access to *opportunity for* carrying them out." *Ibid.,* p. 188.

Vance Packard has commented in detail upon the growing fixity of class levels since 1940 and upon the tendency of many people to accept the restrictions on upward mobility. Packard divides the "Diploma Elite" into (1) "The Real Upper Class" and (2) "The Semi-upper Class." "The Supporting Classes" he breaks down into (3) "The Limited-success Class," (4) "The Working Class," and (5) "The Real Lower Class." He finds that tension and strain are greatly increased among those who attempt to move into a higher status level because of the increasing class rigidity. All of us tend to consort with our own class, he finds, because we are more comfortable there and because varied pressures keep us there. *The Status Seekers: An Exploration of Class Behavior in America and the Hidden Barriers That Affect You, Your Community, Your Future,* 1959.

some opportunity for gain through their abilities and heroic effort. For those who enter the contest the personal attrition is intense. Most of the competitors must fail in some measure to achieve what they have dared to hope for. Not only the inherently incompetent but many who are able find, if they suffer much damage through their experiences, that they cannot for very long face and cope with the eroding competition. Some of these persons display deep scars from the struggle. Emotional and physical disorders are a mark of the ambitious. Along with neurosis, alcoholism, depression, and suicide, the unexpected crimes of the middle class occur occasionally among those who try for success and fail. Others develop some mechanism of self-protection. Choosing the role of the disenchanted and the indifferent, they attempt to avoid the struggle and decide to settle, if they can, for some level of relative security, incorporating at least the "necessities of life." But they find, if they identify themselves with the traditional system of economic and social evaluation, that the imperatives expand continuously. One is pressed to meet and then to surpass if possible the level of one's fellows. There is temptation to violate the rules of the game, loosely drawn as they are.

As we have suggested, persons of "proper" rearing who strive for the traditional goals of success may commit pecuniary crimes. A majority of offenders, however, lack the complacence and the attitude of acquiescent conformity that prevails among white-collar and blue-collar workers in the community. They also lack the ambitions and the opportunities of the starch-collar businessman or professional. They want material things but they look neither for acclaim nor ordinarily for wealth, and they make little pretence of following the rules of competitive acquisition. These persons appropriate what they can within a system that offers them little reward for legitimate undertaking. This happens most frequently, of course, in deprived socioeconomic groups. When lack of ordinary opportunity is mixed with weakness of personality, of talent, or of moral values, with carelessness, limited foresight, greed, or special pressing circumstance, the inadequate are led to take what they cannot or will not earn. This they do not to survive but to secure what they see others about them enjoy. The self-image of these individuals and the norms that in some measure they share facilitate the commission of crime.

There is another criminogenic element among the goals to which modern man aspires. He not only wants material things as such but pleasures too. Hedonism characterizes our age as much as materialism does. In general men search for enjoyment, not as a by-product of more constructive pursuit, but as an end in itself, one that may be reached most readily through sensual titillation; and this is best when the stimulation is sophisticated and commercial. Here there is not only a monetary nexus but some motive, too, to commit offenses against the person and against public morality. It may be noted that in the acquisition of goods and in the pursuit of pleasure attainment rarely produces the continuing satisfaction that is desired; there is frustration and repetitive effort both in the search and in the consummation. Thus our materialistic and hedonistic social goals involve a considerable amount of competition, frustration, and failure as well as a good deal of ingenuity and creativity. Large-scale crimes, continuous embezzlement, bank robbery, and vice rackets, for example, are likely to occur among those who aspire to high rewards without the exercise of legitimate talents or effort. The more frequent petty crimes express the limited ambitions and impulsive temptations of members of the lower class who, in general, have never dared to hope for great accomplishment or social recognition.

It has been suggested that the success and pleasure goals in our social system naturally entail some criminality. But crime derives more obviously from the means men use than from the ends they seek in social life. The problem here lies in the fact that the approved paths through which men may implement their wants have been less clearly prescribed than have the legitimate ends and, in part for that reason, these paths are not closely scrutinized. Some modes of attainment, to be sure, have been long and well defined by tradition; rewards are readily accorded the limited aristocracy of special talents that are channeled in proper ways. The leader of men, the imaginative entrepreneur, and the specialized professional are quickly acclaimed. Universally respectable avenues to high achievement are few, however, and difficult of access. There are other less clearly marked routes to material gain that accommodate a more rapidly moving, if less respectable, traffic. The law-obedient and morally conservative majority shun these dubious short cuts, but impatient, incompetent, or unregulated individuals are attracted to them. There is little curiosity about the way they have traveled and, should they attain a successful end, they may find some acclaim for their cleverness in getting through. Short of success, they may still enjoy the fruits of illegal enterprise, if they are fortunate, or they may spend a little time in prison, if they are not. Crime does pay in the short run for those who have little status or self-respect to lose, and offenders are afflicted with a short-run view. A variety of rationalizations facilitate their violations: the big shots, too, are thieves but on a greater scale; only suckers work; a fast buck will buy as much. And it is true, of course, that the coin of the ruthless businessman, the persuasive charlatan, the unscrupulous politician, the amiable gambler, the professional thief, or the anxious embezzler is as freely negotiable as any other in the market place. Who is to attach distinctions of individual worth?

Theoretical analyses of means and ends in producing criminality have emphasized for the most part the fact that certain individuals have limited opportunity to achieve success through legitimate channels; what has been said in the preceding paragraph may be interpreted in such terms. This conception may be misleading in its simplicity, however. The truth is that for every individual a diversity of choices exists in the opportunity structure of our society to implement the ends he seeks through either criminal or noncriminal activity; to be sure, the diversity of these choices is sometimes quite limited. The choice of means as well as ends varies from individual to individual in relation to his talents, training, personality, values, class, and residence. His selection among available means, which is a nonrational process for the most part, flows from his total life experience.

The opportunity to secure required experience and to achieve the goals of success through professional or organized crime is probably no greater than the opportunity for achievement through legitimate means. Those who fail in respectable pursuits do not ordinarily become successful in crime. It appears very likely that many of those who prosper in the underworld could have done as well through lawful enterprise. The author does not mean to deny that choice is influenced by the range of opportunities available to the individual to engage in specific forms of noncriminal or, indeed, of criminal behavior. The limiting effect of the opportunity structure is obvious. It is true, furthermore, that in neighborhoods characterized by high rates of crime the prevalent attitudes toward authority and legitimacy may often lead to preference for a criminal career. Nevertheless, it is apparent that, even among the grossly underprivileged, crime does not arise simply out of a closure of legitimate opportunities. The law violations in which any man engages must be interpreted on the basis of the complex configuration of biopsychological and social variables with which this section of the text is concerned.

The General Social-Cultural Context

Aside from goals and means, there are other aspects of contemporary culture that contribute to the prevalence of criminal and otherwise deviant behavior. One quite obvious and basic aspect includes the rapid and disjointed social changes of our age. Whether or not these changes are intrinsically desirable, they are a source of considerable difficulty, for man is required to adjust continuously anew to a rapidly revised cultural context: minimum wages, price supports, and the power of labor and government; universal military training, international responsibility, and the iron curtain; thermonuclear energy, ballistic missiles, and modern rocketry; the conquest of space and time. An infinite number of changes, many of them carrying huge impact, occur in the span of but a few years. While man is moderately adjustable in a physical sense, his mental habits and emotional responses display considerable fixity. We experience demands for rapid adaptation at the expense of personal integration and of emotional security. Some of the changes we experience hold a greater threat to life and social order than any we have known before; some revolutionize the patterns of labor and of leisure; and some are quite beyond the limits of ordinary comprehension or reasonable adjustment. Former habit and tradition offer little guide to the man whose world changes every decade. Neither he nor his schools can provide more than a shifting foundation and an obsolescent structure for his children. Deviant behavior is not strange in a revolutionary environment.

Our urban society and the depersonalization of human relationships are also related to crime. Both are associated with the development of industrialization, population growth, and urbanization during the twentieth century. With the decline of a rural social organization we lost much of the stabilizing influence of primary associations, the family, the neighborhood, grange, and work associations. These were all durably linked in the old tradition. We became uprooted and mobile, our time and interests being dedicated largely to the secondary levels of factory, store, labor union, political club, and auditoria of amusement. Kimball Young suggests that the shift to secondary groups has progressed to what may be called a "mass society," characterized by very considerable individuation and depersonalization, where the foci of integration are few and relatively weak. This shift has involved heavy psychic and social costs. It has meant diminished personal stability and attenuated as well as specialized relationships between men. The human attributes of sympathy, loyalty, and personal responsibility atrophy through disuse. The social cementation runs exceedingly thin. The consequence of these changes is personal anonymity and loss of the old regulatory processes of the neighborhood. One is not his brother's keeper.

This brings us to the central problem of social norms, a matter related quite directly to the question of means and goals discussed above. In a dynamic and loosely integrated society where material and hedonic ends are sought, the normative control of behavior becomes increasingly difficult.

In his volume *The Lonely Crowd: A Study of the Changing American Character,* David Riesman suggests in a detailed analysis that we have nearly completed the transition from a phase in which tradition determined social character to one in which "Inner-Direction" establishes the life pattern, a condition where tradition still helps in the selection of goals and general principles of action but where the individual is expected to find the paths to such goals largely on his own.[3] Riesman finds that over the past generation we have developed toward a phase of "Other-Direction" in which there are no fixed goals and wherein direction is sought through one's fellows. He notes the anxiety that results from this highly mobile adjustment process, from the continuous search for approval, and from

[3] David Riesman, Nathan Glazer, and Reuel Denney, *The Lonely Crowd, A Study of the Changing American Character,* 1953, pp. 23–30.

the difficulty of functioning as semiautonomous personalities. This trend away from social and personal integration is undoubtedly a major problem of our society. It spells particular difficulty for regularizing behavior and for controlling the deviant.

The social isolation in mass society, characterized by lack of adequate social norms and controls, has sometimes been called "anomie."[4] Merton and others have ascribed much of the crime and other forms of deviance that prevail in our society to the spread of anomic patterns. The theory is that those individuals who lack effective opportunity to achieve desired social rewards through methods approved by our traditional instrumental values may pursue a normless course to achieve similar rewards. They are encouraged to do so both by the anonymity and the easy mobility of urban living and by the increasing anomie of their associates. Merton says, "A mounting frequency of deviant but 'successful' behavior [as defined by the achievement of material goals] tends to lessen and, as an extreme potentiality, to eliminate the legitimacy of the institutional norms for others in the system. . . . In this way, anomie and mounting rates of deviant behavior can be conceived as interacting in a process of social and cultural dynamics, with cumulatively disruptive consequences for the normative structure unless counteracting mechanisms of control are called into play."[5]

It is dangerous to exaggerate the normless character of our culture; the deficiencies are relative. Some standards of our society are quite firmly fixed. The value attached to human life and personal liberties is probably no less strong than it was in the last century. Moreover, new norms have crystallized in our era. The sense of moral and social responsibility, for example, has expanded quite rapidly, if only partially, to encompass wider circles—from neighborhood and community to state, regional, national, and international realms. Even among those groups in the community

[4] See Richard T. LaPiere, *A Theory of Social Control,* 1954, pp. 326 ff., where he concludes that anomie is not an unnatural state of affairs and that it is not peculiar to our society or to our times. He questions that modern people experience a greater degree of anomie than do members of primitive, peasant, and other premodern forms of society. Scott Greer and Ella Kube maintain that a vast majority of contemporary city dwellers are not socially isolated, are seldom anomic, and are rarely lost. "Urbanism and Social Structure; A Los Angeles Study," cited in Dorothy L. Meier and Wendell Bell, "Anomia and Differential Access to the Achievement of Life Goals," *Am. Soc. Rev.,* vol. 24, p. 201, April, 1959.

[5] Merton, *op. cit.,* p. 180. See also Albert J. Cohen, *Delinquent Boys—The Culture of the Gang,* 1955, where he finds that anomie accounts for law violation primarily in the professional criminality of adults and in the property delinquency among older and semiprofessional juvenile thieves but does not believe that it explains "nonutilitarian" forms of delinquency that are commonly observed. Merton suggests, however, even as to the latter, that "the acute pressures created by the discrepancy between culturally induced goals and socially structured opportunities" may account for delinquent and other deviant behavior that is neither utilitarian nor rationally calculated.

where traditional values control behavior much less effectively than in the past, the prevailing condition may be described more aptly in terms of transition and displacement of norms than in terms of normlessness as such. In using the concept of anomie, there is some risk of falling into the tautology of equating crime and normlessness. Crime may be defined as a form of or a product of anomie without advancing significantly our understanding of what is involved.

Merton's analysis is useful, however, in directing attention to the weakening of some of our traditional values and to the difficulty of crystallizing new ones. A variety of interrelated elements in our society and culture, taken together, have resulted in a decline in both the precision and the effectiveness of social norms. These elements include, as we have seen, the nature of our social goals, the imprecision of the means prescribed for achieving them, the fungible character of material goods—especially money—the depersonalization and anonymity of mass society, the decline in the cohesiveness and the functional services of the family, and the relative ineffectuality of the control system. Man is left to chart and pursue his separate course with limited guidance either from the past or from his contemporaries. The weakening of mores and tradition accounts not only for the decline of informal social control but, *pro tanto,* for the loss of major supports to the system of legal norms and of correctional efforts. Attention is next directed to this problem of social and legal control.

Law and Social Control

One phase of the social-cultural context that has special relevance to the incidence of crime is the normative system by which behavior is regulated. The mores, constituting the basic and general rules of society, are evolved to protect the peace, order, and solidarity of the group. In the traditional society these standards, deeply embedded in the social institutions, are instrumented largely by the group's approbation of conformity and disapproval of deviation. The family, church, and neighborhood provide the child with an early, affective conditioning to the norms and strengthen the norms through persistent reaffirmation. In a relatively stable and uncomplicated society the group may enforce its will very effectively by ostracism and other measures of primary-group constraint. The rules are few and firm, uniformly supported by the elders. Roles and status are clearly fixed and there is little motive to discontent or striving. Religion plays a central if not the predominating role in community life. Emotional needs are well satisfied, offering little occasion for insecurity. Channels for the expression of the basic drives are too well established and accepted for group members to rebel or seek new outlets. While not everyone is perfectly fulfilled, self-realization is not a primary goal in the traditional society. There is little individual or cultural progress, but there is equally little crime and he who does offend is handled effectively, though without the sophistications of modern penology. In this sort of society social problems or individual pathology rarely threaten the security of the group. The difficulties that may arise usually come through innovations from outside, though exceptional and extreme biopsychological deviates may raise occasional problems in the group.

In the developed society, with its greater complication of personal and property relationships, custom alone is insufficient to assure the uniformities of conduct that are required and law emerges as a specialized means of control. Informal norms and sanctions remain important, certainly, in part because they constitute a source and a support of the law.[6] Rights and duties must be defined more precisely, however, for adequate regulation; expert personnel and procedures are required to discover the cunning violator; and breach must be penalized more sharply and precisely. Where unofficial controls break down, the authority of the state must intervene to protect and to punish. Thus criminal law and its correctional instruments become the ultimate regulators, though their effectiveness, like that of the mores, is circumscribed by public opinion and by the community reaction to constituted authority and to those who offend. The criminal must look forward not only to the deprivations officially imposed but to a degraded parade before the hostile eyes of his fellows.

As a result of the social and cultural shifts that have occurred in modern society, the traditional informal regulatory mechanisms have become relatively inffectual. These circumstances make official control more difficult. With the weakening of family, neighborhood, and community ties and with man's easy mobility and his superficial attachments, the potential offender is more ready to challenge authority. He can hope to evade discovery and may believe that, even if his delinquency is uncovered, he will not suffer greatly, for there can be little anguish when the emotional investment is small. Since police cannot be everywhere at once, the enforcement of public policy becomes increasingly difficult. The state must still rely on mores and interpersonal relations, attenuated as they are, and on increasingly vigilant policing to maintain order. Fortunately, this combination of official and informal controls together with their associated sanc-

---

[6] Albert J. Reiss, Jr., in "Delinquency as the Failure of Personal and Social Controls," *Am. Soc. Rev.,* vol. 16, p. 196, 1951, identifies law violation as a product of ineffectual controls: "Delinquency results when there is a relative absence of internalized norms and rules governing behavior in conformity with the norms of the social system to which legal penalties are attached, a breakdown in previously established controls, and/or a relative absence of or conflict in social rules or techniques for enforcing such behavior in the social groups or institutions of which the person is a member." Parsons has remarked that "Institutionally established behavior and reaction patterns undoubtedly have, among others, this latent function, that they provide the right stimuli to other persons to prevent them from embarking on too widely deviant trends of behavior." Since these controls are imperfect, "secondary" defences against deviance must be employed. Talcott Parsons in *Essays in Sociological Theory,* rev., 1954.

tions prove sufficient to constrain a majority of men most of the time in those areas of conduct where vital social interests are involved. In this regard, the point deserves some emphasis that the efficacy of official and informal social control is measured both by the conduct of those who avoid crime altogether and by the preponderantly conformist behavior of those who occasionally violate the law. The surprising thing, considering the developments of our century, is not the gradual increase in the prevalence of crime but is the fact that crime rates have not increased more steeply.

The Diffusion of Deviant Norms

The decline in the firmness of traditional norms and in the effectiveness of social control constitutes only a part of the normative constellation in contemporary society. Another important phenomenon is the spread of antisocial attitudes among some members of the community. The organization of these norms has been described as a "criminal subculture." This analogic term can be misleading if it is taken to suggest a structured and homogeneous social organization having a set of uniform cultural patterns distinct from those prevailing in the community at large. There is no separate and coherent "culture" here in any ethnologically meaningful sense. However, values and attitudes hostile to constituted authority do prevail in some families, especially in deprived areas of the city. The rebelliousness of these families is strengthened by the repressive efforts exerted by the conventional majority. A great part of what is taken to constitute a criminal subculture, however, is in fact merely a complex of ethnic and class-linked peculiarities of speech, manners, education, and tastes that are characteristic of the isolated ghetto. The dominant community often attaches an exaggerated and distorted significance to these deviations. Among the impoverished and segregated minorities one may find financial irresponsibility, as defined by people of higher class, and an assortment of modest vices, including drunkenness, meretricious matings, desertion, and petty assault. By and large, however, members of the lower class conform so far as they can to the imperatives of the middle class. A few rebel and, as a central aspect of their rebellion, express attitudes that deviate in part from the dominant mores, thus setting themselves apart from others. At the extreme, these attitudes are hardened and criminal. Rebellion occurs particularly in delinquency areas and among organized criminals. It may be observed, for example, in connection with urban vice organization and with patterns of bootlegging and feuding in isolated rural areas. Even here, the condition is not one of normlessness or of norms that are entirely different from those of others.

The norms of the antisocial vary considerably, as do those of noncriminals in today's society, but in general they reflect in caricature certain phases of the dominant culture; for example, the hostility to organized and repressive authority and the democratic view that one person or class should be as privileged as another. The former is expressed in a mixed fear and contempt for law, police, courts, and correctional agencies; the latter, in a search for devious unorthodox ways to acquire material things and sensory pleasures when traditionally approved channels are conceived to be either closed to them or too difficult to follow. Such rebels may adopt unorthodox attitudes and practices in their dealings with property and the person. Racketeering, theft, burglary, jack rolling, mugging, robbery, rape, and homicide become in some quarters accepted modes of appropriation and attack upon the established order. Those who find the traditional rules of the game intolerable may improvise to suit their convenience and pleasure. Deprived individuals who have not adopted the traditional mores or the norms prevailing in the middle class and who do not identify themselves with their victims may deviate without great discomfort. They may identify with, share, and transmit antisocial attitudes and practices that in varying forms and degrees prevail in their in-group.

Some fruitful criminological theories deal with the processes by which antisocial norms are spread. Collectively, these theories shed considerable light upon the diffusion of criminal patterns. The late Professor Sutherland's hypothesis of "differential association" focuses upon certain sociopsychological phases of the problem. He believed that criminal attitudes are transmitted by a preponderance of associations with individuals and values hostile to authority instead of with those representing conformity to and respect for law.[7] The major deficiency of this proposition lies in its failure to reveal why some individuals who are much exposed to evil ways accept and transmit them while others do not. Glaser proposes some refinement of the theory in suggesting that the process may be termed more accurately "differential identification."[8] Delinquency and crime are not contagious through contact; what the individual brings to his associations largely determines his response to them. Biological and psychological as well as experiential phenomena affect the individual's identification with norms and with the carriers of norms. Furthermore, reference group theory

[7] This theory is predicated on the assumption that "A person becomes delinquent because of an excess of definitions favorable to violation of law." E. H. Sutherland and Donald R. Cressey, *Principles of Criminology,* 1955, p. 78. Sutherland observed further that association with criminal and noncriminal patterns varies in "frequency, duration, priority, and intensity." The theory has been criticized for its mechanistic explanation of criminal behavior and for its inadequate allowance for personality factors. See also Albert Cohen, Alfred Lindesmith, and Karl Schuessler (eds.), *The Sutherland Papers,* 1956, part 1, and Donald R. Cressey, "Application and Verification of the Differential Association Theory," *J. Crim. L.,* vol. 43, pp. 43–52, 1952. Compare Walter C. Reckless, Simon Dinitz, and Ellen Murray, "Self Concept as an Insulator against Delinquency," *Am. Soc. Rev.,* vol. 21, pp. 744–747, 1956.

[8] Daniel Glaser, "Criminality Theory and Behavioral Images," *Am. J. Soc.,* vol. 56, pp. 433–445, 1956.

suggests that motivation of behavior may come not only from contact with and the expectancies of the individual's membership groups but from connection with other groups as well to which the individual may be oriented, even if his direct contacts with them are minimal.[9] It is not reasonable to believe, however, that in the ordinary case distant reference relations have an impact like that of primary and close secondary groups.

The recent research of Sheldon and Eleanor Glueck has renewed emphasis upon the special importance of the family and its patterns in influencing the behavior of the child. It is not the community or neighborhood mores alone that determine how the individual will believe and behave, but it is to a very large extent the patterns that the parents have drawn from their experience and that they transmit to their offspring. Those families that are most hard pressed by the society tend to cluster together in underprivileged areas of the city and to identify themselves as an in-group struggling against an inimical world. It is apparent, however, that even in the heart of "delinquency areas" a majority of parents cling to the fundamental mores and discourage the deviation of their progeny. While some children may stray for a time under the powerful influence of their contemporaries, they tend to adhere to patterns that they have grown up with in the home. On the one hand, this implies a pressure to lawful behavior; it also means, however, that in families where vice and crime prevail the young are influenced in unlawful directions. And where the family is not well integrated, where the children are rejected and disciplinary practices are poor, or where immigrant parents are in conflict with their young, there is greater danger of delinquency even if the parents are not themselves offenders. It is in this soil that the criminal superego grows. The social influences that are involved will be discussed in greater detail in the next chapter.

Criminal Subcultures and the Gang

Albert Cohen has attempted to define the mechanisms by which a criminal subculture is developed and transmitted in gangs. Cohen conceives a subculture as the values and habits of the gang that are differentiated from the predominant middle-class mores.[10] He holds that socially

[9] See Merton, *op. cit.,* chaps. 8–10, and Daniel Glaser, "The Sociological Approach to Crime and Correction," *Law and Contemp. Probs.,* vol. 23, pp. 690–692, 1958.

[10] Cohen, *op. cit.* See also Alison Davis and Robert J. Havighurst, "Social Class and Color Differences in Child-rearing," in Kluckhohn, Murray, and Schneider, *Personality in Nature, Society, and Culture.* More generally on gang organization, structure, and conflict, see Frederic M. Thrasher, *The Gang,* 1936; Furfey, *The Gang Age,* 1928; and Lewis Yablonsky, *A Field Study of Delinquent Gang Organization Behavior with Special Emphasis on Gang Warfare,* unpublished doctoral dissertation, New York University, 1957. For an analysis of effort to modify gang behavior and attitudes through trained area workers, see Crawford, Malamud, and Dumpson, *Working with Teen-age Gangs,* 1950.

deprived children of working-class homes internalize middle-class values and expectancies but become frustrated and ambivalent because they are unable to achieve success within the middle-class status system. The result, he believes, is a "reaction-formation"; the young people repudiate orthodox norms and establish a subculture that is composed of "nonutilitarian, malicious, and negativistic" values. This reaction constitutes "an attack on the middle class where their [the gang members'] egos are most vulnerable" and "expresses contempt for a way of life by making its opposite a criterion of status." Such individuals gain approval within their group by defiance of ordinary conventions and by loyalty to the subcultural code. Efforts of the dominant class to enforce its will upon those who subscribe to the gang culture only provoke further hostility and reinforce the gang members' identification with their minority and its norms.

This explanation of the persistence and intensification of conflict is useful. However, the author questions the validity of the hypothesis that working-class members generally crave success as it was once defined in the "American Dream" or that they turn to crime in order to succeed. Characteristically, the working-class ideology looks to modest in-plant mobility rather than to interclass movement. The author doubts that delinquent norms derive from a reaction-formation of the sort that Cohen suggests. Few working-class children experience such ambivalence toward the middle-class as to produce this emotional mechanism. Cohen admits the speculative character of the assumptions involved. In any event, it appears that the origin of gang attitudes is more complex than the theory suggests and that shared norms and gang behavior are something less than a "subculture."[11]

Gangs have become prevalent in many of our large cities. They offer a distinct status system, close personal relationships, and a protection to the in-group in relation to other gangs and to the repressions threatened by the larger conventional community. Acts of defiance, pugnacious rivalry, vandalism, theft, burglary, and assault are means of expressing contemptuous disregard of authority. Since the situations out of which gangs develop are somewhat uniform, it is understandable that different gangs display some similarity. It has long been apparent, however, that gangs also differ very

[11] A critical analysis of Cohen's monograph argues that "first, Cohen does not present adequate support for his formulation of 'the working-class boy's problem,' second, his description of the working-class boy's ambivalence toward the middle-class system does not warrant the use of the reaction-formation concept, and, third, his description of the delinquent subculture, the 'facts' to which his theory is addressed, is open to question." John I. Kitsuse and David C. Dietrick, "Delinquent Boys: A Critique," *Am. Soc. Rev.*, vol. 24, p. 213, April, 1959. They suggest that the motivations for participating in gangs are varied and that gang members' rejection of the standards of "respectable" society are a response to the formal negative sanctions, rejection, and limitation of access to prestigeful status imposed by the community. *Ibid.*, pp. 214–215.

considerably. Thrasher's work on the gang, first published in 1927, provided convincing evidence of this difference. What has not been made sufficiently clear is that gangs are amorphous, rather loosely organized associations with a changing and partially peripheral membership; Lewis Yablonsky has called them "near-groups." They display the antisocial manifestations of crowd behavior, some of which were remarked by LeBon in 1922: emotional excesses, mutual stimulation to aggression, a sense of anonymity, and a false assurance that they can defy the law with impunity. Unlike the ordinary crowd, however, the gang may recurrently engage in mass actions because it has at least a temporary core of leadership, a propinquity of residence, and some sharing of problems. This does not mean, however, that the mob behavior that occurs in gang rumbles is a culture pattern or that gang members individually are either normless or entirely homogeneous in their norms. Gang members not only vary from one to another but to a large extent they participate in and conform to the dominant cultural patterns. They are not wholly different from or completely at war with society. Contemporary efforts to deal more effectively with gangs are based in some part on recognition that the individuals involved are only somewhat different in orientation from youths with middle-class values and that they may be moved toward fuller acceptance and participation in the larger community.

Furthermore, it appears that so far as criminality and delinquency represent lower-class norms and behavioral patterns this is not simply a matter of gang association and activity. Though they represent a somewhat specialized phenomenon, gangs may be considered both a reflection of and an influence upon the standards of many others who live in deprived areas of the city. In economically and emotionally submarginal homes, whether or not gang membership is involved, equivalent attitudes, similar norms, and comparable, though not necessarily group-organized, antisocial behavior prevail. Here, too, there is animosity toward some phases of the dominant community and particularly toward oppressive forces of authority. Whether or not antisocial norms will prevail in particular families, however, depends very largely, as the Gluecks have indicated, upon the "under-the-roof" patterns of the particular home, upon its reference groups, and upon the controls that are exerted through the family line. There is much variation from family to family in these respects.

TOTALITARIAN WAR

Among the broad social-cultural phenomena of modern civilization, none carries a more devastating impact than war. Its ramifications are felt throughout the social system, not only during the period of conflict, but for years thereafter.

It is not an easy matter to weigh the influence of world war on crime or to estimate its relative significance against other less catastrophic factors in the society that have a more direct and continuing impact on many families. The figures on juvenile delinquency before and during World War II in the United States and in other countries revealed a considerable rise in juvenile delinquency, especially among females. Children's Bureau statistics showed that delinquency cases increased 60 per cent between the years 1938 and 1944; broken down the statistics showed an increase of 54 per cent for boys and 88 per cent for girls.[12] Cyril Burt has written that in England male juvenile delinquency increased 60 per cent and female delinquency 20 per cent, the increases occurring especially in evacuation areas and where air raids were most intense.[13] Other data from World War II and World War I reveal increases in delinquency. Juvenile convictions increased during the period 1914–1918 as much as 69 per cent in England, 63 per cent in Germany, and 52 per cent in Austria.[14] It appears that the increases occurred primarily in larcenous delinquencies while offenses against the person declined, with significant drops in the number of attacks on the person and in sex offenses shown in the figures of several countries.[15] Both English and American data reveal increased delinquency in lower age groups, particularly those under 14.[16]

In part the increases in official delinquency statistics are merely a continuation of trends of increase that had developed before the war. Some part of the change may well reflect the more vigorous policing and prosecution of children during a period when curfews became common; because of the publicity that was given to the problem, youngsters were expected to be delinquent. There is no real doubt, however, that much of the apparent increase was real. Burt attributed the high prevalence of delinquency to the breakup of homes through evacuation, absence of many fathers in the services, life in air-raid shelters, black-outs, decreased opportunities for normal education and recreational activities, the generally increased atmosphere of violence and destructiveness, and the lack of ordinary self-restraints. Disruptions of life patterns were less extreme in the United States but the increases in delinquency have been generally attributed to very similar sorts of influence: the breaking up of homes, geographical mobility in the population, lessening of supervision and con-

---

[12] *Juvenile Court Statistics,* U.S. Children's Bureau, 1946.

[13] Burt, "Delinquency in Peace and War," *Health Ed. J.,* vol. 1, pp. 165–172, 1943.

[14] Edwin H. Sutherland, "Crime," in William V. Ogburn (ed.), *American Society in Wartime,* 1943, p. 188.

[15] *Ibid.,* p. 189.

[16] The psychiatrist Ralph S. Banay suggested that increases were occurring in crimes of violence and sex in the United States as a consequence of emotional conflicts and tensions along with the relaxation of restrictions. See "Emotional Factors in Wartime Delinquency," *Prob.,* vol. 21, pp. 103–108, 1943. For material relating to England in wartime, see also George Godwin, "War and Juvenile Delinquency," *Cont. Rev.,* no. 910, pp. 251–255, 1941.

trol over children, increased employment of the young, increase in numbers of working mothers, and wartime conditions fostering aggressive behavior. The author has expressed his views of the motives involved elsewhere:[17]

There is little doubt that a dominant pressure toward unadjustment in the lives of most people during the war came from the breaking up of families, with all the emotional excruciations which that frequently implied. It was a matter of special importance for the young whose security was shattered in many cases by the absence, brief or extended, of the father from the home: in England it was observed that children suffered more in fears and insecurities from the disruption of their family lives than they did from actual air raids. Although for the most part children in the United States were not exposed to domestic changes as radical as those implied by urban evacuations in England, influences of a similar nature were revealed symptomatically in the emotional states and conduct problems of children and adolescents. The fruits of wartime childhood insecurities will be reaped for many years, in the personalities of those who reacted sensitively to the emotional disorganizing of the family. Less important, but undoubtedly of some significance, were the effects of a lack of adequate supervision, control, and guidance during years when parents were often too busily engaged in the war effort to give to their children the attention that is necessary for the healthy development of character and conduct. Those youngsters especially whose mothers were engaged in war production were too often left without regulation, affection, or care for many hours each week. There were reports particularly from boom towns and defense areas of children locked in trailers until their parents should return from work and other "door-key" children left to wander about the streets unguided. For many this meant only boredom: they were a "lost generation," unneeded and unwanted—too young for jobs or for war service. Many youths, not yet stabilized in character, who were subjected at once both to the emotionally disorganizing experiences of war and of adolescent maturation, expressed a poorly controlled emancipation and rebellion in their delinquencies. Others, slightly older, found work, money, and excitement easy to secure; many who were inexperienced in earning and spending money were led into trouble by the pleasures it could buy.

The disruptions of war are believed to produce a general deterioration of standards and controls, even among those whose personal and moral values have been stabilized. The old gods are no longer worshipped. The young child may not even have discovered any deity of his own to be abandoned. In addition, release of intense and explosive emotions, hate and aggression, is facilitated in the climate of war. Combative feelings are less carefully repressed or redirected, particularly among those who are too young to have learned control, and with frustrations commonly intensified hostile reactive behavior is widespread. Again, the young adolescent who was denied any adequate catharsis in work or war was particularly prone to express his fear, hate, and rage in violation of social norms. One common outlet was in gangs, which blossomed verdantly for several years. To a large extent these gangs chan-

[17] *Juvenile Delinquency*, pp. 155–157.

nelized belligerence in antisocial directions: gang wars were prevalent and homicidal, with ingeniously fabricated lethal weapons widely possessed and too often used. Youths aped their older brothers at the front, often with disastrous effect.

It has been noted that female offenses increased at an unprecedented rate during the war, both in sex violations and in crimes less orthodox among girls. The devil-may-care atmosphere of war years seems to have crumbled the moral codes of many, under the eager and easy pressure of boys who demanded an emulation of their own sacrifices: "Tomorrow we die." It is probably true too that cumulated passions find quick and temporarily satisfying catharsis in sexual behavior, unimpeded by customary standards.

It is apparent that war has a varying influence upon different groups in the population. There is substantial evidence that crime increases during wartime among women as well as among juveniles, particularly in theft. The evidence is conflicting as to sex offenses and personal assault; other countries indicate some reduction of these crimes. Such offenses are related, of course, to the availability of virile and contentious males in the population. Official statistics reveal a decline in the volume of adult male criminality during the war, both here and abroad. This is due primarily, of course, to the induction into the armed services of a very large proportion of those males from 17 to 24 who make up the most criminal age group in ordinary times. It is not wholly clear whether there is an actual decrease in the amount of crime committed by these young males. Sutherland has stated that during World War I in England the number of men convicted in civilian and military courts was lower than the number of criminals convicted during the average prewar year. The author's experience reveals that lenience was frequently shown young men already in the service or about to go in. However, it is very likely that under the rigorous, ordinarily well-supervised circumstances of military life, so comparable in some respects to prison routine, opportunities and impulses to commit crime are reduced. It is worth noting further that rates for minor crimes and offenses declined the most and that the violation of special war laws regarding price-fixing, the black market, and fraud accounted for a very considerable amount of the crimes that were committed.

In a critical commentary on the prevailing theories concerning wartime influences on crime, Sutherland observes that these theories are unproved, though the factors that they have suggested may play some role:[18]

The preceding criticisms of the theories of criminal behavior in wartime do not mean that the factors of contagion of violence, satiation of the need for violence, the diminishing role of the future, and national feeling have no effect on behavior. The criticisms mean rather that the respects in which these factors play a part have not been defined, the relations of these factors to one

---

[18] Sutherland, *op. cit.*, pp. 187, 199.

another have not been determined, and the factors have not been organized into a system of thought.

Finally, it is certain that war exercises some influence over postwar crime trends. Crime waves have been reported after the Civil War and the two World Wars in the United States and after major foreign wars. Crime appears to have increased after modern war particularly in the theft category. Female crime rates have also increased. The data are somewhat difficult to interpret, however, because increases may be interpreted partly in terms of the continuation of upward prewar trends. Increases have been explained by such factors as the development of unemployment with a closing down of war industries, the tendency to find criminal substitutes for war excitement, and lowered standards of morality accompanying the celebration of war's end. Presumably, when postwar dislocations are relatively small in the economic and family fields, the impact of war influences on the crime rates are not so great. It is clear, nevertheless, that years of war are disorganizing, particularly to impressionable youngsters, and that this disorganization plays a persisting role in the later emotional-social adjustments of those who have been quite harmfully affected. Many who come out of the highly regulated, totalitarian experience of military life are ill-prepared to assume ordinary responsibilities in the community. This is true even of some who have had exemplary military records.

Chapter 8

SOCIAL FACTORS IN CRIME

The last chapter dealt with certain broad social-cultural forces that influence the incidence of crime. The social factors that the author now proposes to consider have a more intimate and immediate impact upon the offender. There is individual variation in man's selective adaptation to culture, but idiosyncrasies of personality and behavior appear to flow more directly from specific influences in the family, neighborhood, and economy. It is to these more particularized factors that sociological criminologists have given their primary attention, ordinarily through studies of the comparative incidence of social characteristics among offenders and non-offenders.

THE FAMILY

There have been two major revolutionary transitions in world economic history that have entailed dramatic changes in the nature of the family. The first of these goes back some ten thousand years; at that time the skill in domesticating plants and animals resulted in a social organization characterized by a highly stable family system. Throughout subsequent ages a patriarchal pattern of family control has prevailed for the most part. This era was marked by quite consistent and well-integrated norms of family, religion, and social life. There was little resistance to traditional control as mediated through the head of the household and no great need for criminal law and public control. In the economy of agriculture and animal husbandry the family was a producing as well as a consuming unit; wives and children were large assets, cherished in part for their obvious utility. Moreover, the family performed all the major functions essential to the individual's life satisfactions. Education, religious and moral inculcation, recreation, and maintenance were essential phases of family living. In this context, deviation and psychological distress were uncommon.

The second great transition was initiated about two hundred years ago with the industrial revolution, a system of factory production and, later, of corporate enterprise. With its emphasis upon invention, mechanical change, speed, a monetary nexus, competition, and materialism, industrialization has entailed tremendous changes in the Western world, in the

social system generally, and in the family in particular. Most striking, perhaps, has been the defunctionalizing of the modern family as secondary
specialized agencies have taken over the occupational, educational, religious, recreational, political, and social control tasks previously performed in the home. As a consequence the solidarity and functional utility
of the family has been tremendously reduced. An inordinate emphasis
upon romanticism and happiness as the main motives to marriage has
resulted. Disillusionment is the virtually inevitable consequence of such
romantic idealism.

The atomizing of the productive system together with the intense competition for monetary rewards and the development of gross disparities in
income and wealth have also produced frustrations that are expressed
most acutely in the domestic arena. Wives and children become an economic liability unless they produce what they consume. The consequences
have been drastic. The birth rate has dropped and parents, particularly
fathers, spend relatively very little time with their children.[1] As the father's
attention becomes increasingly absorbed by his job, he loses authority in
the home. In so far as traditional family responsibilities are performed at
all, the tasks fall largely to the wife and mother and as a result, according
to some sociologists, a sort of maternal or matriarchal family has developed. At the same time, an increasing number of women, motivated by the
desire to help attain the materialistic and competitive goals of the family
group, have found opportunities in occupations that take them away from
their traditional roles of caring for their homes and children. It is not
strange, perhaps, that these developments, together with the influence of
fads in child psychology that for a time deplored restraint and stressed
permissiveness in rearing the young, have led parents to become fearful,
subservient, and rejective during the "century of the child." Children themselves are confused by the divisive pull of loyalties to parents, peers,
school, church, state, and other reference groups.

While it is not a perfect index, the rates of marital dissolution reflect the
changing character of the family. It has been estimated that divorces and
annulments increased well over 500 per cent during the period between
1890 and 1950. By the latter year, one divorce decree was granted for approximately every four marriages celebrated, and 44 per cent of these
were granted to couples with children. However, as later discussion will
show, broken homes are only part of the broader problem of the discord
in families that have too little to hold them together. Brought up in a

---

[1] In 1910 the average family in the United States was one of about five children
and nearly half of these families had five or more. At present there is a trend toward
earlier marriage and an increasing number of couples are having three or four
children as compared with a generation ago. See Clyde V. Kiser, "Is the Large
Family Coming Back?" *Child Study Assoc. Publ.,* 1958, and Paul C. Glick, *The
American Family.* 1959.

culture that emphasizes material satisfactions and hedonistic pleasures as well as the individual's right to personal freedom and self-expression, disillusioned men find that marriage does not provide an effortless ecstasy or a perfect self-fulfillment. Adults whose conduct in childhood was not subjected to responsible parental controls are not apt to be successful in controlling intelligently the behavior of their own children. It appears that delinquency is a normal phase of this familial-social context.

_ The home has been described as the cradle of the personality. The child's early experiences within the family group exert a profound and lasting influence on his later behavior. Here his character and attitudes are formed. The quality of his associations within the family group greatly affects his conduct in relation to other groups, as his experience expands to include them. The role played by the parental family is expressed in W. Lloyd Warner's concept of the "family of orientation" and in Robert Merton's description of the family as a "major transmission belt for the diffusion of cultural standards to the oncoming generation." Merton perceptively observes the relationship of this process to deviance. The specific content of what the family transmits is limited by the social stratum and by the groups with which the parents find themselves involved. The norms that a child incorporates need not have been made explicit by parental commands and exhortations. Indeed, values that a child derives from observing his parents' day-to-day behavior may be in conflict with the verbalizations of his parents. Thus it happens that some parents advise their offspring to obey the law but actually through their conduct persuade him to delinquency. It has been very generally recognized that the parental family plays a significant role in the etiology of juvenile delinquency. Relatively little attention, however, has been devoted to the subject of how relevant the adult's marital status and experience are to criminal behavior. It has been shown that a pair's ability to establish stable marital and parental relationships is greatly influenced by the patterns of adjustment that existed in the orientation of their respective families. In marriage and in parenthood they must work out their own peculiar patterns of adaptation; this commonly requires substantial changes in each member's modes of behavior. Some individuals avoid marriage or parenthood because of the apparent threat to their individualities. Some others who enter marriage may fail repeatedly. In any case the individual's experience in this regard vitally influences his subsequent life adjustment, his goals and ambitions, his mental and physical health, and his strength and weaknesses. We shall see that there is a relationship between marital condition and criminal behavior.

The Broken Home

While no one today seriously questions the importance of the family in relation to delinquency, interesting issues have been raised in recent years concerning whether law violation is causally related to the broken home, as such, or whether it is related only to the deeper faults in family relationships. In the early days of the juvenile court, authorities, impressed by the fact that from 40 to 50 per cent of delinquent children came from broken homes, were led to believe that this was the most important single factor producing delinquency.[2] A few years later students of the problem attempted to estimate the proportion of broken homes in the general population as a basis of comparison with delinquents and concluded that broken homes were nearly twice as frequent among delinquents.[3] Thereafter, Shaw and McKay attempted a more refined analysis of the problem by drawing a comparison population from the public schools in the same areas of Chicago that their delinquency samples were drawn from. They then adjusted the school population data for age and ethnic composition and found that 36.1 per cent of the adjusted sample, compared with 42.5 per cent of the delinquents, had come from broken homes. Shaw and McKay concluded that broken homes were not an important factor in causing delinquency.[4] Later studies have cast some doubt on the validity

[2] See Ernest Shideler, "Family Distintegration and the Delinquent Boy in the United States," *J. Crim. L.,* vol. 8, pp. 709–732, 1918, for a survey of early studies of broken homes and delinquency. Breckenridge and Abbott, in *The Delinquent Child and the Home,* 1912, reported that 34 per cent of delinquents were from broken homes. John Slawson, in *The Delinquent Boy,* 1926, found that 45 per cent in New York State correctional institutions were from broken homes. The Glueck study, *One Thousand Juvenile Delinquents,* 1934, found a similar percentage among cases going through the Boston Juvenile Court. The U.S. Children's Bureau reported in *Juvenile Court Statistics* that about 30 per cent of boys and 50 per cent of girls in children's courts during the latter 1920s and early 1930s came from broken homes.

[3] A number of the early studies attempted a crude control comparison by estimating the proportion of broken homes in the general population from census data and contrasting this with their figures on court or institutionalized delinquents. See Shideler, *op. cit.;* E. Bushong, "Family Estrangement and Juvenile Delinquency," *Social Forces,* vol. 5, pp. 79–83, 1926; M. G. Caldwell, "Home Conditions of Institutional Delinquent Boys in Wisconsin," *Social Forces,* vol. 8, pp. 390–397, 1930; S. B. Crosby, "A Study of Alameda County Delinquent Boys," *J. Juv. Res.,* vol. 13, pp. 220–230, 1929.
    Slawson's study, *op. cit.,* comparing delinquents with boys in three public schools of New York City, concluded that more than twice as many delinquents came from broken homes. In England, Cyril Burt also compared delinquents with public school children concerning "defective family relationships" and found a similar contrast in percentages. Comparing a population of Pennsylvania training school girls with girls in continuation school in Philadelphia, Mabel Elliott found a proportion of 52 to 22 per cent from broken homes. Elliott, *Correctional Education and the Delinquent Girl,* 1929.

[4] See *Report on the Causes of Crime,* National Commission on Law Observance and Enforcement, vol. 2, no. 13, 1931, especially pp. 264–280, and Shaw and McKay, "Are Broken Homes a Causative Factor in Delinquency?" *Social Forces,* vol. 10, pp. 514–524, 1932. At about the same time, Margaret Hodgkiss, studying a group of delinquent girls, found that 67 per cent of them were from broken homes, as

of this research. None of these studies however, has indicated so great a difference in the rate of broken homes among delinquents as the difference suggested by the earlier, unrefined investigations.[5] The lack of national population data on the family status of children has made rate comparisons generally unreliable.

One of the most comprehensive studies, conducted by Thomas B. Monahan in Philadelphia, involved 44,448 delinquents (24,811 of these being first offenders) appearing in the municipal court during the period 1949–1954.[6] Correlating their family status with color, sex, and recidivism, Monahan found a continuous decline in the percentage of juvenile offenders living with their own parents, running from white, male first offenders to Negro female recidivists.[7] According to the 1950 census for Philadelphia, only 7 per cent of the white children and 33 per cent of the nonwhite children under 18 years of age were not in husband-wife families. The data indicate that the breaking up of the home is differentially related to delinquency, affecting girls and Negroes most damagingly. The Gluecks have indicated that the type of break is also important. In their samples delinquency was correlated most frequently with early abandonment by unmarried parents, desertion, temporary separation, or prolonged absence because of incarceration of a parent. Among the nondelinquent controls, the first break in the family had occurred most frequently as the

compared with 45 per cent in a control group matched on age and nationality. See "The Influence of Broken Homes and Working Mothers," *Smith Coll. Studies Soc. Work,* vol. 3, pp. 259–274, 1933. The differential may well be explained by the greater inclination of courts to find girls whose homes have been broken delinquent. It is clear, too, that courts are more inclined to commit juveniles, especially girls, who come from broken homes.

[5] Maud A. Merrill, *Problems of Child Delinquency,* 1947. See also H. Ashley Weeks and M. G. Smith, "Juvenile Delinquency and Broken Homes in Spokane, Washington," *Social Forces,* vol. 18, pp. 48–55, 1939, and M. P. Wittman and A. V. Huffman, "A Comparative Study of Developmental, Adjustment, and Personality Characteristics of Psychotic, Psychoneurotic, Delinquent, and Normally Adjusted Teen Aged Youths," *J. Genet. Psych.,* vol. 66, pp. 167–182, 1945.

[6] Thomas P. Monahan, "Family Status and the Delinquent Child: A Reappraisal and Some New Findings," *Social Forces,* vol. 35, pp. 250–259, 1957. These findings included all the cases referred to juvenile court, whether or not they were held for a hearing. Hence, the sample was more complete than previous samples consisting entirely of institutionalized or adjudicated offenders.

[7] The percentages were: white male first offenders, 72.4; white male recidivists, 58.6; white female first offenders, 48.4; Negro male first offenders, 47.2; Negro male recidivists, 37.8; white female recidivists, 31.4; Negro female first offenders, 27.3; Negro female recidivists, 19.8. Monahan also observed that the percentage of all cases in the recidivist class among white boys increased from 32, where both parents were married and living together, to 38, where the father was dead and the boy living with his mother, to 42, where both parents were dead, to 46, where the parents were living apart, to 49, where the parents were divorced, to 55, where the boy was living with his unmarried mother. The same general pattern prevailed for both sex and color groups. *Ibid.,* p. 257.

result of divorce or separation, death of a parent, and prolonged absence because of illness.[8]

factors producing broken homes also produce criminals [handwritten annotation]

Inadequate Families

Despite the evidence of a relationship between delinquency and the broken home, it may well be that the association between the two can be accounted for largely or entirely on the basis of defective family relationships and baneful influences in the neighborhood preceding the breach. A number of authorities have expressed the view that this is the case.[9] The Gluecks, in the study referred to above, observed a very close relationship between delinquency and the affection and discipline received in the home. Parents of delinquents were found most frequently to be mentally retarded, emotionally disturbed, alcoholic, criminalistic, dependent, irresponsible, and ailing in health. Other studies arriving at similar conclusions show that delinquency is associated with parental crime, vice, alcoholism, mental disability, incompatibility, and with the attitudes and behavior of the parent toward the child.[10] These factors are undoubtedly important in producing both delinquency and broken homes.

Comparing training school and uncommitted high school delinquents

[8] Sheldon Glueck and Eleanor Glueck, *Unraveling Juvenile Delinquency,* 1950, pp. 88, 122.

[9] Monahan concluded his study with this comment: "All in all, the stability and continuity of family life stands out as a most important factor in the development of the child. It would seem, therefore, that the place of the home in the genesis of normal or delinquent patterns of behavior should receive greater practical recognition. The relationship is so strong that, if ways could be found to do it, a strengthening and preserving of family life, among the groups which need it most, could probably accomplish more in the amelioration and prevention of delinquency and other problems than any other single program yet devised." *Op. cit.,* p. 258. *Cf.* Gordon H. Barker, "Family Factors in the Ecology of Juvenile Delinquency," *J. Crim. L.,* vol. 30, pp. 681–691, 1940.

[10] The Gluecks found that physical punishment was the method of discipline favored by more than half of the mothers and by two-thirds of the fathers of their sample of delinquents as compared with one-third of the parents of nondelinquents. Few of the parents of the delinquents were inclined to reason with their sons. *Unraveling Juvenile Delinquency,* pp. 130–133. See also Cyril Burt, *op. cit.,* where he found "defective family discipline" among 79.5 per cent of his delinquents and among only 11.5 per cent of his control group; Sheldon Glueck and Eleanor Glueck, *Five Hundred Criminal Careers,* 1930, p. 119. Relative to other defects in the family, see *Unraveling Juvenile Delinquency,* table IX-6, p. 98; table IX-10, p. 101. Significant correlations were found especially with the occurrence of unfavorable traits in the mothers' families and, as the Gluecks observe, the mother assumes major responsibility in the early phases of child-rearing in our society. See also Harry Manuel Shulman, "The Family and Juvenile Delinquency," *The Annals,* vol. 261, pp. 21–32, January 1949; William Healy, in *The Individual Delinquent,* 1915, pp. 130–134, found that defective family situations were a major cause of delinquency in 19 per cent of a thousand cases he studied and a minor factor in 23 per cent, lack of parental control being a most common feature; Barker, *op. cit.;* and F. Ivan Nye, *Family Relationships and Delinquent Behavior,* 1958, Part III.

with a control group of nondelinquents, F. Ivan Nye found that broken homes were far more common among the committed offenders (48.1 per cent) than among the more serious high school delinquents (23.6 per cent), ostensibly because of differential treatment of children from broken homes.[11] He found a small but significant difference in delinquent behavior between youths from broken and unbroken homes; this he believed was the result of the loss of direct control in families with a single parent and of youths' confusion in those families where there was a stepparent. On the other hand, Nye found less delinquent behavior in broken than in unhappy unbroken homes. The happiness factor was much more closely related to delinquency than was formal family status.[12] His data also indicated that where homes were broken the individual's age at the time of the breach was unrelated to delinquency.[13]

° It is quite apparent that, where the home is not intact, economic problems are often increased.*The child may also be deprived of affection that he had previously experienced and of the guidance and example that should come from two parents.°Divorce or desertion may aggravate the child's immediate problems through the public disapproval that attaches to his family status and through the resulting damage to his self-image. All this suggests that, in some instances at least, the parents' efforts at reconciliation to prevent a formal rupture may be advantageous. On the other hand, where inadequate and rejective parents are seriously damaging the child, he may be better off as the result of their separation. It is certain that the break in marital ties has widely varying significance for children from different family constellations and that the personalities of the children involved affect their responses to this experience.

The case below illustrates the influence of a broken and inadequate family background. It is quite characteristic of the delinquency pattern often found in defective homes.

John Dickley, who is 19 years old, is serving eighteen months for thieving mail from the letter box of a private home. Together with a codefendant he had been stealing letters in order to find currency for several months before they were apprehended. John was first in trouble in 1945, at he age of 11, when he was taken to children's court for vandalism and destroying property. This involved breaking into a school building where he and two other children did extensive damage. The following year he was committed to the state training school in Maryland for persistent delinquency, charged with vandalism, car theft, and breaking and entering a service station. On one occasion he escaped from there and got into further trouble by stealing another car. In all, he was arrested nine times in the years 1945–1953.

Dickley was one of thirteen children reared without any of the normal advantages of training in a rural section of Maryland. The parents were known as ne'er-do-wells. The father was a heavy drinker, unwilling to support his

[11] Nye, *op. cit.,* p. 44.
[12] *Ibid.,* p. 51.
[13] *Ibid.,* p. 47.

family and of dubious capacity to do so. He deserted the mother in 1944 when John was 10. The children were raised in various foster homes. John never was able to get along in his placements and ran away a number of times, occasionally living with a disreputable uncle. He never attended school regularly and worked for only short periods of time, his five months as a factory laborer being the longest period of employment on the record. In early 1953, shortly before becoming involved in the immediate crime, he had joined Ringling Brothers' Circus and traveled around the country for a time but found the work too arduous. He had no army experience, having been rejected on the basis of written tests that indicated an IQ of 72. In interview he appears slow and dull-witted. He is completely without plans for the future and has no family to return to.

It is quite apparent, as has been suggested, that family influences go well beyond the problems of incompatibility and breach. Where relationships in the home are poor, the youth may develop reference groups elsewhere for his identification, perhaps with peers who are delinquent. The location of the home within the ecological structure of the community, more especially where it places the child in an area of high delinquency, may increase the opportunity for damaging associations in the neighborhood. Neglect and unconcern in the training of the child may ill prepare him to meet the deviant pressures of the community. Sometimes family members, either a parent or siblings, play a more active role in introducing the individual to delinquency. This happens where the value system of the home, its habits and attitudes, is antisocial and where the child learns contempt for law and authority there. The impact is stronger still where he is actually introduced to delinquent activities, whether through observing the criminality of his relatives or through outright initiation into illegal behavior patterns. The latter is very well illustrated in Clifford Shaw's *Brothers in Crime,* where a series of siblings were introduced, at successively earlier ages, to begging, thievery, and burglary. A similar pattern, running from parent to child in an incomplete family, is illustrated briefly here:

Edith May was first committed to the Alderson Reformatory for Women in 1937 for using the mails to defraud. She was then 17 years old. While there, she gave birth to her first daughter, Jane, and in the ensuing years she has borne four other children, though she has never been married. In 1950, Edith was again committed to Alderson, while Jane, then 13, was placed on probation for the same offense. They worked together in ordering various items from mail order companies, which they then sold without having paid for them. Edith scores 55 on IQ tests. At parole interview she had no plans whatever for the future except to live with her mother, a mental defective who also had a criminal record. The mother was caring for Edith's five children with relief funds provided by a welfare department.

While the studies reveal relationships between juvenile delinquency and family pathologies, they do not show how long the latter may continue to influence the behavior of the delinquent. It is reasonable to believe that young offenders who come from disorganized homes will continue to violate the law because the family situation specifically affects his adjustment in early years and because individuals that are once convicted will often repeat. On the other hand, the Gluecks have found in a fifteen-year follow-up study of 500 offenders that the fact that prisoners came from broken homes had no effect upon either adjustment in the correctional institution or subsequent parole success.[14] Indeed they found that successful probationers had more often come from broken homes than had unsuccessful probationers. Monachesi, studying juvenile and adult probationers, observed that, while the failure rate on probation of orphaned juveniles was higher than average, adult probationers succeeded more frequently when a parent was dead than when the family was intact.[15] Mannheim, in his study of Borstal boys in England, found that those who had come from broken homes succeeded as frequently after discharge as did those who did not come from broken homes.[16]

° A large number of adult criminals come from ostensibly good and intact homes, and it appears that, at least among those whose first offenses occur during the adult years, the broken or otherwise defective parental home may not be correlated significantly with criminality. Among criminals with prior delinquency records, any relationship that exists probably decreases as other social and psychological influences come to play a greater part.

The Criminal's Marital Status

The adult offender's own marital experience undoubtedly has an important relationship to his crimes. Only a limited amount of raw data is available on the marital status of criminals, and most of this relates to incarcerated offenders.[17] It is difficult to draw inferences from the figures, however, because marital status is related to offense and age of commitment to prison. Many prisoners have had too little time and opportunity before their imprisonment to marry or, if married, to divorce or separate.[18] Thus, the relatively high proportion of single males who are

[14] Sheldon Glueck and Eleanor Glueck, *Criminal Careers in Retrospect,* 1943, p. 209.

[15] Elio D. Monachesi, *Prediction Factors in Probation,* 1932.

[16] Hermann Mannheim and Leslie T. Wilkins, *Prediction Methods in Relation to Borstal Training,* 1955, p. 87.

[17] See *Prisoners in State and Federal Institutions,* National Prisoner Statistics, 1950, tables 4, 23, and 24, for the most recent available data on prisoners' marital status. More detailed information on marital status relating to offense was provided in *Prisoners in State and Federal Prisons and Reformatories,* 1946, table 35, and prior years.

[18] See Von Hentig, *Crime: Causes and Conditions,* 1947, pp. 269 ff., for a good analysis of the reasons why data relating to family status may be quite misleading as a basis for interpreting cause of crime.

convicted of burglary and car theft and, to a lesser extent, of ordinary larceny and robbery probably reflects the predominant youthfulness of offenders of these types rather than an indisposition to marital life. Those convicted of liquor law violations, embezzlement and fraud, commercialized vice, and nonsupport are generally older and most frequently married. National statistics broken down into age categories reveal that the marital status of the prison population is very closely related to age and it is probably this rather than the nature of the crime, with the exception of nonsupport and some types of sex offenses, that determines the marital condition of the inmate. Unfortunately there are no national court statistics on the marital status of convicted offenders generally, but it is certain that those who live with a wife are less frequently imprisoned and probably less frequently convicted than those who are single, separated, or divorced.

In their follow-up study of reformatory inmates, the Gluecks observed that at the end of a fifteen-year period almost half of the offenders were married and living with their wives, two-thirds of them in compatible relationships.[19] There had been a steady increase over the years in the proportion of inmates whose conjugal relationships were good. Approximately two-thirds of those married had assumed their marital responsibilities seriously. Three-quarters had become fathers and of these 63 per cent had displayed sincere affection for their children.[20] The Gluecks do not indicate the relationship of marital status to the avoidance of further offenses, but presumably it was positive. Monachesi's study of adult probationers revealed that those who were married succeeded much more frequently than those who were single, separated, divorced, or widowed.[21]

While empirical evidence on the question is unsatisfactory, it is apparent that stable and satisfying marriages tend to prevent or reduce criminality and in many instances they may be largely responsible for terminating criminal careers. Marriage has a greater impact on attitudes, emotions, self-esteem, and regard for others than do most life experiences and associations. Even a pretty poor creature can be measurably socialized and fulfilled if mate and progeny meet his personal needs fairly well. Mature criminals experience guilt and "take hold of themselves" in response to the needs and attitudes of their families, even when community, state, and church mean little to them.

Conversely, where the individual cannot find an acceptable mate or cannot attain compatibility in marriage the chances of his criminality are enhanced. Many prisoners have found their marriages intolerable or for a variety of reasons have avoided marriage entirely. It would be wrong, however, to assume that a prescription of marriage would remedy their problem. An individual can make no more of marriage than his capacity

[19] Sheldon Glueck and Eleanor Glueck, *op. cit.,* chap. 4.
[20] *Loc. cit.*
[21] *Op. cit.*

and experience permit. Moreover, an adverse experience in the parental family relationship diminishes appreciably the possibility of successful marriage, so that in many instances both the childhood and the adult experiences may dispose the individual toward defective personal relationships. The difficulties involved here and their resolution, if that is possible, lie in the individual and his developmental history, not in the act of marriage.

In the case below the individual coming from a pathological family situation was himself unable to work out a satisfying marital relationship in spite of his strong need for affection:

Jack Martin, 32 years of age, is serving eighteen months for car theft at a Federal prison. He has previously served two penitentiary terms, one for car theft in 1948 and another for burglary and theft in 1951. His official record shows some twenty arrests for larceny, car theft, burglary, rape, and obtaining goods under false pretenses. He has been arrested in eight different states and served time in four.

Martin was the third of sixteen children, nine of whom died before attaining maturity. His parents were well-known characters to the police, with long records for drunkenness and lewd and lascivious cohabitation. The mother had served three terms in state and county penal institutions and has lived promiscuously with several men in her home. The father was considered to be "absolutely no good"; he deserted his family from time to time and "never contributed to their support." Six of the surviving children were committed to the state industrial school in 1926 because of neglect. At the age of 9 Jack was committed for stealing and attempted homosexuality. He ran away from there frequently as he had from a succession of foster homes in which he had previously been placed. While he was in this training school his parents were both killed in an auto accident. Subsequently Martin was committed to a reformatory in Rhode Island as a result of his attempted homosexual relations with small boys. He made a good adjustment there, strangely enough, and after release he worked on a farm for several years and made a valiant effort to establish a home for his younger brothers and sisters. While engaged in farm work, Martin suffered a "nervous breakdown" and was committed to a state hospital from which he escaped on numerous occasions. After one of these escapes, he enlisted in the Army but later was given a medical discharge.

In 1944 Martin was married for the first time, but his wife soon left him, and shortly thereafter he was sentenced for the first time to prison for stealing a car. He was transferred to a mental hospital, however, and escaped from there after less than two years. Thereafter he wandered extensively around the country, working at odd jobs in a number of eastern and southern states, occasionally getting into trouble with the law. In 1948 he married again but this venture, too, failed and his wife divorced him in 1950. Again he followed his pattern of escaping from stress and "took to the road."

During his Federal imprisonment Martin has been a neat and polite individual, well liked by other inmates. His work has been reliable and his conduct excellent. The institution's psychiatric report notes his masochistic impulses and his sense of his own complete worthlessness. He suffers from chronic tension. He hopes to become a hospital orderly after release.

It would appear that Martin's difficulties lie to a great extent in his compelling need to find love objects and in his inability to hold them. There is no indication that he is a compulsive homosexual. The aggressive impulses that he has are turned inward. His history of nomadic crimes may well reflect his flights from failure and his search for acceptance. Certainly his feelings of unworthiness, confirmed by his continuing failures, may be traced to childhood experiences in the parental family.

Delinquency in "Good Families"

From time to time query is raised about delinquents from good homes, but little objective attention has been given to the problem thus far. Undoubtedly in "good" as in "poor" homes the dynamics of criminality vary widely. The former are less often characterized by specifically criminalistic attitudes and habits. There can be no doubt, however, that pathogenic influences that may result in crime occur in many ostensibly "good" homes. Many parents set highly materialistic standards for the family and expect too much from their children. Subtle emotional rejection of the offspring is also prevalent in an age when children represent both a financial liability and a large intrusion on the time and energies of parents. Commonly the treatment of the young has been extremely "permissive," not only as a consequence of the popular dogma of child rearing, but because it temporarily simplifies the task. Control and standard setting have become unpopular and it is very clear that the thoroughly undisciplined child does not automatically learn to accept authority when he attains mature age.

More difficult to appraise but probably of no less importance is the matter of parental ethics in the state of our present culture. Many reputable citizens steer courses close to the line of immorality and law violation in their business and personal activities and, occasionally, cross over if they believe they can do so with impunity. They reveal little sense of personal responsibility and little respect for law that would inhibit their activities, though they depend upon law for their protection against others. Through their experience with parental discipline and by inference from their parents' activities, children learn that the evil is in getting caught.

The author has already commented on the significance of such social-cultural influences as the decline in the ascendancy of primary groups, the depersonalization of human relationships, the deterioration of firm traditional norms, and the struggle for status as measured by material acquisitions. These factors affect individuals of all socioeconomic levels, and many children from middle- and upper-class homes lack the capacity or the will to work through their wants in legally approved ways. On an individual level, deficient intelligence, inadequate personality, strong aggression or hostility, a rejection of authority or an attitude of superiority to the law, emotional imbalance, an inclination to take indiscreet risks, and the incapacity of the unloved to identify with the welfare of others are qualities that may lead, within the framework of our society, to transgression of the official standards. The case of Charles Hundley in the next chapter illustrates the criminality of a well-endowed youth from a "good family." (See p. 226.)

In general, the individual of higher family status has more to lose through discovery and official action, so that he has a greater motive to conform. He is also more likely to escape conviction and punishment. Nevertheless, the official data show that the prestige bearers of the community do succumb to crime. Their offenses are more often of a subtle, commercial, or sophisticated character, tending in the total picture to reflect class values and higher levels of intelligence and skill.[22] Such crime may well represent a greater hazard in our society than the ordinary run of crime, for it reveals the breaking down of standards even among those who have more than average power, prestige, and ability. The revealed weakness of governmental, professional, and business leaders not only displays a dangerous decay at the higher levels of honor and repute but also provides an effective example and an easy rationalization for depredations among the masses of men.

Minority Groups and Crime

Statistics on conviction and imprisonment of members of immigrant and minority groups need interpretation. The major problem here appears to lie not in biological peculiarities and probably not in differences in the temperaments of nationality groups but, on the one hand, in the social-cultural pattern of the particular group and, on the other, in the difficulties that the "marginal man" experiences in working out adjustments to the way of life in America. These problems are found particularly among the offspring of foreign-born parents. Though the immigrant himself generally retains a sufficient integrity of personality and the sort of values and atti-

[22] Harry M. Shulman in "The Family and Juvenile Delinquency," *loc. cit.,* draws a number of inferences relating to class structure and crime. *Inter alia,* he suggests that "Aside from occupational opportunities, it may be pointed out that the personality structure involved in successful fraud is wholly consistent with middle-class education and training, depending not on a single successful attack or raid, as in the case of assault or theft, but on a more carefully controlled aggression involving knowledge and application of a wide range of technical skills and patience and fortitude in planning and carrying out extensive frauds as nearly within the letter of the law as technical skill will permit. This suggests that the middle-class child who in later life resorts to crime does so in the light of earlier experience which has taught him that the social order has few loopholes and many restrictions; whereas the poor child resorts to types of crime which suggest that earlier experience has taught him that the social order has many loopholes and few restrictions."

tudes conducive to normal adjustment, his children are often harassed by the cultural and personal conflicts of the marginal man, torn between the American mores and those of the parental culture. The first and second generations born in this country often experience an uncomfortable feeling that they are different from their more Americanized contemporaries. This feeling is intensified because of their lower standards of living, their competitive handicaps, and the deteriorated homes in which they live. Their delinquencies may be an expression of their desire to break away from parental authoritarianism, which appears to them to be excessive as compared with that exercised by American parents. Sometimes the misconduct is a symptom of maladjustment and rebellion in relation to the home, the school, or the neighborhood situation.[23]

Clifford Shaw, who has suggested that neighborhood and community influences may be responsible for the law violations found in minority nationality groups, made the following comments concerning the nationality migrations within the city of Chicago:[24]

At the beginning of the present century these areas of highest rates of delinquents, which are for the most part areas of first immigrant settlement, were occupied by the older immigrant groups, such as the Germans, Irish, and Scandinavians. Since that time, these nationalities have been succeeded by the newer immigrant groups, such as the Polish and the Italians. This change which took place both in the areas adjacent to the central business district and to the large industrial developments, did not bring about any appreciable change in the relative rates of delinquents in these areas. . . . When the German, Irish and other immigrant groups lived in the areas of high rates of delinquents they constituted a large proportion of the population in the juvenile court. As they moved out of these areas of high rates into areas of second and third immigrant settlements their children disappeared from the juvenile court at a rate far greater than the decrease in these nationalities in the total population of the city. They were supplanted in the juvenile court population by the Italians, Polish, Negroes, and other groups, all of whom moved into these areas of high rates of delinquents.

It should be observed that the phenomena involved here are more complex than the ecological movement of minority groups. Changes in delinquency rates may reflect various influences of Americanization, improvement of socioeconomic status, and selective determination of the families that move according to their ambitions and achievements.

Racial Groups and Crime

Negro minority groups present problems that are more complex and more persistent than those found in other ethnic minorities. The immigrant becomes acculturated and assimilated after a time, but the Negro has re-

[23] Tappan, *Juvenile Delinquency,* pp. 140–141.
[24] *Report on the Causes of Crime,* National Commission on Law Observance and Enforcement, vol. 2, no. 13, pp. 388–389, 1931.

mained largely unintegrated and apart. This difference is epitomized in their crimes. While Negroes make up approximately 10 per cent of the population, they account for about 30 per cent of all arrests in the United States and 60 per cent of arrests for urban crimes involving force or threat of force (murder, manslaughter, rape, robbery, and aggravated assault). It is often alleged that police are more inclined to arrest colored than white persons on suspicion, but a legitimate complaint is also made that police are less than diligent in dealing with crimes committed by Negroes against members of their own race. Probably police statistics inflate little, if at all, the comparative rates of Negro crime.

The criminality of Negroes is sometimes attributed to their migration from the South, with resulting difficulties in adjustment to a differing social-cultural system. However, it has been found that their crimes of violence are as disproportionately frequent in the South. The claim that poor housing explains the differential is equally unsatisfactory, for in such cities as Los Angeles and San Francisco the houses of Negroes are comparatively decent while their crime rates run high. Better housing and urban renewal are desirable in themselves, but experience has shown that the mere improvement of dwellings does not change the character and conduct of people. One authority has observed that "slum dwellers who move into brand-new public-housing projects often turn them into new slums as verminous and crime-ridden as the tenements they left behind."

High Negro crime rates can be traced primarily to the caste system that has segregated this race in ghettos, located very commonly in the most underprivileged areas of the city. There a large proportion of the Negroes cannot work out any real stability in family, work, or community life; consequently, their standards of morality and responsibility are low. A slave tradition and the persisting barriers of a rigid caste organization have isolated the great majority of Negroes socially and have deprived them of opportunity and ambition. Inevitably many of them lack both self-regard and respect for others. Upon this race converge those multiple influences of personality, family and neighborhood disorganization, economic privation, and asocial norms that are so generally associated with delinquency and crime without regard to race. But the Negro's difficulty is exacerbated by an identifying pigmentation that facilitates his segregation in a closed class and attracts the stereotyped rationalizations concerning his inferiority that serve to keep him inferior. So long as he remains socially segregated and deprived, it appears, he will continue to be more criminal than the dominant white.

It should be observed that there is a class system within the race itself, based on color, income, and occupational differentials. The small minority constituting a "brown middle class," to use Franklin Frazier's term, has been a relatively stable and conservative white-collar and professional group, aspiring to emulate, within the limitations imposed by their segregation, the standards and ways of life of the white middle class. Members of this group live outside the areas of high delinquency and avoid conflict with the law. It is among the "black proletariat" who live in the most disorganized sections of the city that rates of delinquency and crime are high. Their offenses reflect to a considerable degree the disorganization in their individual and family lives.

NEIGHBORHOOD AND COMMUNITY INFLUENCES

It is futile to try to assess the relative potency of the family and the neighborhood in affecting delinquency, though this has been the subject of some theoretical controversy.[25] Influences that apparently emanate from the family are colored by the surroundings of the home, the extent and quality of services available in the locality, and the kinds of associations to which family members have access. Evidence shows that, as families move from areas of high delinquency to those of low delinquency, the rates of law violation remain about the same as before in both areas, ostensibly indicating that it is more the neighborhood than the family situation that determines misconduct. But it is apparent that neighborhood influences are selectively filtered through the home and that either adverse or healthy circumstances may be counteracted in very considerable measure by the family. Any effort to distinguish strictly between the impact of the two inevitably leads to some confusion, because the selective processes by which residence is determined tend to attract to delinquency areas many families that are prone to delinquency. Here one finds the unemployed, the transients, large families with low living standards, minority group members, and people suffering from physical and other deviations. Yet specific families will not necessarily succumb to their problems. Both in the neighborhood and in individual families there are elements sufficiently strong to bring about conformity to the law.

The concept of neighborhood needs clarification. Functionally the neighborhood is not a force in itself but is merely a geographical area within which associations occur and self- and other images develop. The important thing is that different neighborhoods provide stimulus to and opportunities for different associations and identifications. Some uniformities of attitudes, values, and habits tend to develop in the locality, norms that are likely to be reinforced by common ethnic and socioeconomic factors among the residents. In the main, however, the dominant culture prevails, even in submarginal areas. A neighborhood is "delinquent" in only a very loosely descriptive sense.

[25] On neighborhood and community influences generally, see Sheldon and Eleanor Glueck, *Unraveling Juvenile Delinquency*, 1950, chap. 13; Shaw and McKay, *Juvenile Delinquency and Urban Areas*, 1942; and Henry D. McKay, "The Neighborhood and Child Conduct," *The Annals*, vol. 261, pp. 32–42, 1949.

The role of community influences may be observed in the activities and values of socially and geographically isolated people. The prisoner discussed below, while he is a rare specimen, illustrates the extreme peculiarity that may be manifested among contemporary insular folk:

Laurence Butts is a character from Leslie County, Kentucky, a rural, mountainous area famous for its bootlegging, feuds, and crime. He is 37 years of age, serving his first prison sentence, a term of two years for possession of three gallons of illicit whiskey. His record shows eight arrests since 1936 for rape, child desertion and bigamy, willful murder, operating a still, shooting into an occupied dwelling, carrying a deadly weapon, selling liquor to minors, and possession of liquor on which tax had not been paid. Most of these charges were dismissed, though Butts had been on probation on one prior occasion and had paid fines twice for liquor violations. The official record appears not to reflect at all fully the extent of his criminal and antisocial activities, however.

The Butts family is notorious in part for its long history of feuding with the Long tribe. Laurence's father was shot to death in 1946 by Rufus and Harold Long when the latter discovered him near their home. A few months later Laurence and his younger brother Caleb shot and killed both Rufus and Harold. Laurence displayed some pride in this accomplishment during his parole interview with the writer. He did not consider it strange that the case was dismissed, since "justice was done" by the retaliatory murders. In 1951 Laurence was indicted for shooting into an occupied dwelling and in the following year was indicted again for shooting a total of sixty-one times into the home of a well-known and dissolute prostitute. She failed to appear against him, however, and the charges were dropped. The man's successful encounters with legal authorities are attributed to his repeated perjury, coercion, and sharp practices. In 1953 Butts was shot through the middle finger of his left hand and through his left thigh at his bootlegging joint by another resident of the county who had "bad blood" with the Butts family. According to the county sheriff "there was more peace on Middle Fork River" during Laurence's recuperation than there had been in many months. No criminal action was taken.

The five children of the Butts family were brought up on their father's subsistence farm. They had little significant supervision and did not attend school with any regularity. Laurence tests at an IQ of 70 and is capable of fourth-grade performance. He himself has five acknowledged children from several of the six wives whom he has married and is said to have several illegitimate offspring. He is known as a ladies' man. His first marriage was a "shot-gun wedding" to a girl with whom he and a son of the Long family had been living jointly. His present wife enjoys a good reputation among her neighbors "since becoming a member of the church" but admits that she is "deathly afraid of her husband." Butts claims to have worked occasionally at farming, logging, saw-milling, and in the mines. Local authorities say, however, that he has spent most of his time operating gambling and bootlegging joints and moving from one place to another throughout the county when raids were threatened.

Oddly enough, both the sentencing judge and the United States attorney recommended parole for this offender. In any event he will soon return to

enliven Leslie County and on different occasions, perhaps, to both increase and reduce its population.

The Ecology of Delinquency and Crime

Clifford Shaw and his followers have developed, more than have others,
the ecological approach to delinquency investigation. They have popular-

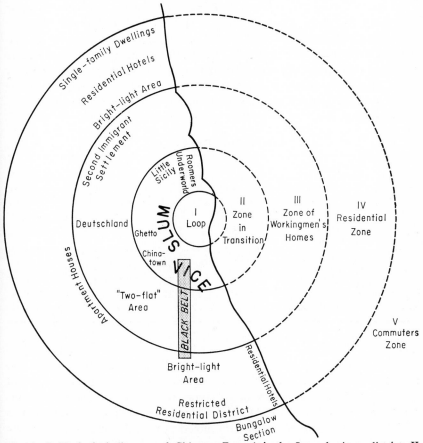

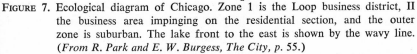

FIGURE 7. Ecological diagram of Chicago. Zone 1 is the Loop business district, II
the business area impinging on the residential section, and the outer
zone is suburban. The lake front to the east is shown by the wavy line.
(*From R. Park and E. W. Burgess, The City, p. 55.*)

ized the idea of "delinquency areas," sometimes termed "interstitial" or
"transitional" areas by other researchers. Shaw, McKay, and others have
pointed out the existence of graded zones of deterioration and delinquency
in many American cities where outward from the city center decreasing
rates of delinquency, crime, recidivism, and other forms of social pathol-

ogy may be found.[26] The groundwork for much of their analysis was laid in Park and Burgess' ecological research in Chicago and in some earlier studies investigating urban delinquency rates. Park and Burgess, in their volume *The City,* picture Chicago as divided into five concentric zones, each characterized by its peculiarities of residence, socioeconomic level, functions, and social influences. In simplified form their data on delinquency are correlated with this chart, shown on page 205.

In a 1942 publication, Shaw and McKay showed the relationship between the ecological zones of Chicago and a series of pathological traits including delinquency and crime rates, illustrating very clearly the declining morbidity from the loop area out to the commuters' zone.[27] It should be noted that, while the rates shown for adult criminals are considerably lower than those shown for delinquents and Boys' Court cases (covering males in the ages of 17 to 20), the amount of difference from zone to zone is comparable.

Table 10. Social Data by Zones

Community problems	Zones				
	I	II	III	IV	V
Rates of delinquents, 1927–1933	9.8	6.7	4.5	2.5	1.8
Rates of truants, 1927–1933	4.4	3.1	1.7	1.0	0.7
Boys' court rates, 1938	6.3	5.9	3.9	2.6	1.6
Rates of infant mortality, 1928–1933	86.7	67.5	54.7	45.9	41.3
Rates of tuberculosis, 1931–1937	33.5	25.0	18.4	12.5	9.2
Rates of mental disorder, 1922–1934	32.0	18.8	13.2	10.1	8.4
Rates of adult criminals, 1920	2.2	1.6	0.8	0.6	0.4

Shaw and McKay worked out in detail the rates for delinquency and each of the other indices of deterioration on the basis of square-mile areas in which the frequency of the variable was determined in relation to the population of each area. Table 10 shows the distribution of delinquents during the period 1927–1933. The Chicago research also revealed high correlations between the social data, noted in the table above, and certain community characteristics, including population mobility, median rentals, families on relief, families owning their homes, and minority-group residence, the rates in each category usually following quite closely the delinquency area zones. In the volume *Juvenile Delinquency and Urban Areas,* research by a number of scholars shows somewhat comparable data on twenty-one other cities in various parts of the country. Where such data were available, these studies displayed consistently the same general pattern of declining rates of adult criminality from the city centers outward as

[26] See Shaw and McKay, *op. cit.,* chap. 6.
[27] *Ibid.,* table 51, p. 158.

was revealed by the statistics on juvenile delinquency in the Chicago ecologists' studies.

It is obvious from the ecological research that, as Shaw asserted a generation ago, "the greatest concentrations of delinquents occur in the areas of marked social disorganization." He described the process briefly thus:[28]

In the process of city growth, the neighborhood organization, cultural institutions and social standards in practically all of the areas adjacent to the central business district and the major industrial centers are subject to rapid change and disorganization. The gradual invasion of these areas by industry and commerce, the continuous movement of the older residents out of the area and the influx of newer groups, the confusion of many divergent cultural standards, the economic insecurity of the families, all combine to render difficult the development of a stable and efficient neighborhood organization for the education and control of the child and the suppression of lawlessness.

Again it should be emphasized that the family living in a delinquency area acts as a selective filter of these influences and that certain families have the strength within themselves to remain stable and law abiding while continuing to live in such areas. Some families avoid such neighborhoods and others move out of them as soon as it is economically feasible to do so.

RECREATION

In the past leisure-time activities were associated almost entirely with the home and neighborhood. With the growth of urbanization and industrialization, however, commercial recreation has occupied an increasingly important role in the lives of both children and adults, particularly in urban centers. A number of studies have shown that a high proportion of delinquents spend their time in unguided pursuits or in unconstructive recreational activities. The Gluecks have found that their delinquents, more often than their nondelinquent controls, enjoyed exciting recreations,

---

[28] *Report on the Causes of Crime,* vol. 2, p. 387. It should be noted that Shaw's research and the ecological approach in general have had some criticism. Maurice R. Davie has indicated that the pattern of delinquency rates observed in Chicago and elsewhere do not exist in New Haven, Cleveland, and certain other cities. See "The Pattern of Urban Growth," in Murdock (ed.), *Studies in the Science of Society,* 1937. Professor Sophia Robison has attacked the entire principle of ecological research, particularly what she considers the establishment of arbitrary geographical limits of delinquency areas and the unreliable data on delinquency rates employed in such studies. See *Can Delinquency Be Measured?* 1936. While there are undoubtedly limitations to the validity of the ecological researches that have been done, as there are limitations in other phases of criminological investigation, it cannot well be doubted that this approach has proved its value both in extending our understanding of some of the processes involved in the development of delinquency and in establishing programs of prevention and treatment.

such as stealing rides, roaming the steets after dark, sneaking into movies, running away from home, gambling, drinking, setting fires, and engaging in destructive mischief. They were more inclined than the nondelinquents to play on street corners, in vacant lots, in railroad yards, and in places of commercial recreation. They engaged less frequently in recreation at home or on playgrounds.[29] This study, like others before it, indicated that delinquents are inclined to excessive movie attendance.[30] Such findings are interesting, but they raise rather than resolve questions concerning the relationship of these activities to delinquency.

Some leisure-time activities are themselves classified as delinquent behavior. The more seriously mischievous conduct of boy gangs is of this sort. To the boy engaged in illegal adventure his delinquency *is* recreation, with the added spice of special risk. It is noteworthy that among juvenile delinquents violations are committed most frequently in groups of two or more and that their rash escapades are designed "for the fun of it" rather than for profit or "out of malice." This is true at least of their early law violations.[31] The Gluecks found that delinquents chummed with other delinquents in 98.4 per cent of the cases studied, whereas only 7.4 per cent of the nondelinquents had delinquent associates as close friends.[32] Several studies have shown that delinquents are more gregarious than nondelinquents. They are sometimes led by their associations into situations where the risk of delinquency is increased. The inclination to show off, the stimulation of the gang, and the sense of impunity that the group gives lead almost inevitably to occasional activities that are illegal. In neighborhoods where the tradition of delinquency has been established, acts of vandalism, theft, and assault may be common and willful.

Furthermore, the studies have shown that delinquents are more outgoing and expressive than nondelinquents. While the latter may be content with reading, conventional games, and other leisure behavior of a more passive sort, the delinquents are inclined to work out their drives in overt activities.[33] It is not uncommon to find them running away from home. They display more interest in athletics, greater skill in sports, and according to some studies they join more clubs than do nondelinquents.[34] The

---

[29] *Unraveling Juvenile Delinquency,* pp. 160–161.

[30] See, for example, H. Blumer and P. M. Hauser, *Movies, Delinquency and Crime,* 1933, p. 198; William Healy and Augusta Bronner, *New Light on Delinquency and Its Treatment,* 1936, pp. 74–78 (but compare Healy, *The Individual Delinquent,* 1915, chap. 9); and Frederic M. Thrasher, *The Gang,* 1936, p. 113.

[31] The transition from delinquency for fun to delinquency for profit is nicely illustrated in Clifford Shaw's studies, especially *Brothers in Crime* and *The Jack Roller.*

[32] *Unraveling Juvenile Delinquency,* p. 164.

[33] *Ibid.,* chap. 13.

[34] For a consideration of the idea that athletic activities have great virtue in the prevention or treatment of delinquency, see Chapter 18.

extroverted and gregarious youngster, whether engaged for a time in group games or pursuing adventure with his fellows, is a significantly greater delinquency risk than is the placid and introspective boy who finds his quiet pleasures at home. In a mental hygiene sense, the former may be better adjusted than the latter in that he works out his problems overtly and experiences little anxiety about his misdeeds. However, the community has difficulty in controlling the extroverted and gregarious youth because of his personality type, associations, and opportunities to become involved in trouble.

In a study of probation failures in a juvenile and an adult sample, Monachesi found in 1932 that juveniles who commit their delinquencies in association with others, especially if there are five or more companions, get into trouble again less often than do youngsters who commit their offenses alone.[35] This seems to indicate that, while group delinquency is common, it is less apt to result in recidivism than law violations committed by the youngster alone. This conclusion is consistent with what we know about group behavior among the young. The individuals would avoid much of this conduct if they were not led on and stimulated by their fellows. In contrast it should be noted that, according to some studies, adult offenders are more inclined to recidivate if they have engaged in crimes along with two or more associates.[36] This may well reflect the professional criminality and gang activities that tend to be repetitive in many criminals. Monachesi also found that where the specific offenses appeared to have resulted from the influence of associates juveniles less often failed on probation, while the rate of failure among adult probationers was high. It appears fairly clear that criminal association is more serious than delinquent companionship as a factor in law violations. Monachesi's study brought out the adverse relationship between repeated offenses and such leisure activities as drinking and "immoral parties" and the frequenting of pool halls and "joints," observed in both the juvenile and the adult samples. Recidivism was particularly high among adults involved in such recreation. Failure rates were relatively low in both groups, however, where commercialized amusements were the chief forms of leisure activity.

Movies, comic books, cheap novels, radio, and television have been fine scapegoats for those seeking an easy explanation of delinquency and a simple method of cure. There has been much controversy over the extent of their influence, if any, on law violation. Dr. Frederic Wertham and some popular reformers have inveighed most vehemently against one or more of these recreational media,[37] but it has been the consensus among thoughtful behavioral scientists that they have little or no real significance

---

[35] Monachesi, *loc. cit.*

[36] *Ibid.* See also Lloyd Ohlin, *Selection for Parole*, p. 52. Some of the other parole prediction studies, however, have failed to confirm this relationship.

[37] See Wertham, *The Show of Violence*, 1949.

for delinquency.[38] In their worst forms they undoubtedly exercise poor influence on taste and interests, but it is questionable whether any child prone to delinquency requires either the incitement or the illustration that he may find in these media. Perhaps as strong a case can be made in their favor, so far as delinquency is concerned, in that they serve as partial vicarious outlets for impulses and desires that the community wishes to control.

Most of the population is exposed more or less frequently, through recreational and other media, to visual stimuli that are not approved by the puritans of the community. It is possible that mental defectives, the emotionally unstable, psychopathic personalities, and other pathological individuals are abnormally responsive to such influences. It has not been shown that they lead normal individuals to delinquency or crime. Surely it cannot be maintained that forms of recreation should be reduced to a level of total innocuousness in order to meet the needs of the personality deviates in the community. Balance and wisdom are required to develop proper controls over leisure-time activities. Censors rarely possess the needed qualities. In recent years appellate courts have displayed increasingly sophisticated judgment in these matters.[39]

THE ECONOMY

There is much controversy concerning the significance of economic factors in relation to delinquency and crime. From a Marxian point of view crime as well as many other social ills proceeds from the malignancy of a capitalistic industrial order. The Dutch criminologist W. A. Bonger similarly believed that "the part played by economic conditions in criminality is preponderant, even decisive." He attributed fault mainly to the pressures and abuses of the capitalistic system: child labor, long hours of work, economic insecurity, the ignorance of the poor, and bad housing.[40] In the research of recent years, many studies have pointed to a relationship between criminality and the economic circumstances of poverty, unemployment, poor homes, and poor neighborhoods. Other investigations, however, have concluded that economic conditions as such have been of minor importance as compared with other social influences and psycho-

[38] Former criminal court judge Charles F. Murphy, who was appointed to direct censorship for the Comics Magazine Association of America and who engaged in wiping out horror comics, asserted at the time of his appointment that he had never had an offender before him whose delinquency he thought should be attributed to the influence of comics. *New York Times,* Sept. 27, 1954.

[39] See Walter Gellhorn, *Freedom and Restraint,* and Morris L. Ernst and Alexander Lindey, *The Censor Marches On,* 1939.

[40] William A. Bonger, *Criminality and Economic Conditions,* translated by Horton, 1916.

logical factors.[41] On the surface the evidence appears to be conflicting. It is certain that the relationship is not as simple and unilateral as is sometimes believed.

In studies where criminality is attributed to economic influence, including especially poverty or unemployment, the usage of these terms is commonly quite loose ad the interpretation even looser. It makes little sense, for example, to find the cause of crime in unemployment or lack of income where offenders have chosen not to work at a legitimate occupation. While the official census tracts do not include professional thievery or burglary among the occupations engaged in by the population, listing individuals who engage in such crafts as "unemployed" is misleading at best.

[41] Representative of the negative findings on a causal relationship, the following may be cited: In his study of a thousand juvenile delinquents, William Healy found economic circumstances a major cause of their problem in only 0.5 per cent of the cases and a minor cause in only 7.1 per cent. *The Individual Delinquent*, 1915, chap. 8. In another study with Augusta Bronner, in which they divided their delinquent sample into economic categories, they found 5 per cent in a state of destitution, 22 per cent in poverty, 35 per cent in normal socioeconomic status, 34 per cent in comfort, and 4 per cent in luxury. Thus 73 per cent came from homes that were normal or better in economic condition. *Delinquents and Criminals*, 1926, p. 121. Cyril Burt, a British authority on delinquency, concluded from his researches in London that poverty alone does not cause crime. In his evaluation of another study in Liverpool he maintained that the emphasis placed on poverty, unemployment, and overcrowded homes was unwarranted by the data. *The Young Delinquent*, 1933, pp. 68–69. Burt did find that a majority of his sample of London delinquents were living in either poor or very poor homes but did not believe that the relationship to delinquency was rooted in economic factors. From her studies of the relationship of the business cycle to various social conditions Dorothy Swain Thomas concluded that the correlation was negative; data from New York City courts in the years 1870–1920 showed a coefficient of −0.35. Similarly, correlating British criminal statistics with a composite index reflecting the business cycle, she found a coefficient of −0.25 with all indictable crimes. *Social Aspects of the Business Cycle*, 1925. A more recent study in Los Angeles concluded that delinquency rose during prosperity and decreased during depressions. David Bogen, "Juvenile Delinquency and Economic Trends," *Am. Soc. Rev.*, vol. 9, pp. 174–184, 1944. In a comparable investigation in Philadelphia, studying relationships with the business cycle over a twenty-three-year period, J. O. Reinemann concluded delinquency is highest during extreme prosperity, though he found that the rates were also high during depression. "Juvenile Delinquency in Philadelphia and Economic Trends," *Temp. L. Q.*, vol. 20, April, 1947. Delinquency was low during "normal" economic conditions. Vernon Jones studied Massachusetts crime statistics during the twelve-year period 1920–1931 and observed an inverse relationship between employment and arrests for crimes against property. Juvenile delinquency did not increase during the depression years 1930–1931. "Relation of Economics Depression to Delinquency, Crime and Drunkenness in Massachusetts," *J. Soc. Psych.*, vol. 3, pp. 259–282, 1932. Helen Witmer, after follow-up investigations on problem children from thirteen clinics in different parts of the country, concluded that the emotional setup of the home far exceeded economic conditions in determining children's adjustments. "The Later Social Adjustment of Problem Children," *Smith Coll. Studies Soc. Work*, vol. 6, pp. 1–98, 1935.

"Poverty," "unemployment," and "need" are sometimes interpreted very loosely in research analyses.[42]

Another consideration suggests very strongly that there is no simple and direct relationship between financial need and crime generally. The quite common and ostensibly not unreasonable hypothesis that criminality results from economic insecurity and poverty is challenged by the prevalence and, indeed, the growth of property offenses under circumstances of increasing security and comfort. The high standards of living that have prevailed in the United States over a long period, as compared with other countries where crime rates are lower, is a familiar observation. It has been argued in the past, however, that gross disparities in wealth and income with many living in poverty and unemployment have intensified the rebellion of the "have-nots" and have led to crime. It is difficult to defend this position today in the light of the following developments over the past generation in the United States: the large-scale provisions for social security of the worker and his family, the full recognition of and the great power vested in labor organization with its job protections and retirement provisions, the usually prevailing condition of full employment, the expansion of medical and health insurance, the continuing drift into a middle-class society, and the ever closer approximation to "cradle-to-grave" security. These developments have not resulted in a reduction of crime. In fact there appears to have been an increase in the rate as well as in the volume of property offenses. This increase suggests that factors other than poverty, unemployment, need, or exploitation are involved in motivating individuals to crime. The author does not mean to deny that economic factors play some role in crime but suggests that the simplicity of view that has often been propounded is quite unsatisfactory.

The fact that the vast majority of individuals whose economic and employment circumstances are relatively poor do not commit crime indicates

[42] A recent study of the influence of probation on a group of offenders based its causal analysis on a series of five needs, "need" being defined as a "basic or primary motivation, wish, or want of an individual," and included among these the "need for a standard of living." The investigator believed that this need accounted for offenses in 35 per cent of his cases and that "of those who stole, three-fifths were impelled by economic need." It is fascinating, then, to discover those who are classed in this category, including those who had "disobeyed constituted authority . . . for economic reasons . . . many had bought untaxed liquor because it was cheaper." Others "failed to comply with various regulations because they did not care to spend the money or take the time." Members of another group, "whose method was the sale of proscribed goods or services, were almost wholly motivated by economic needs." It is submitted that any such interpretations of crime causation as these are of little value. Equally dubious are the investigator's conclusions that probation had been most helpful to adjustment in the economic area; improvement in financial status should have occurred during the period covered by the study (1937–1948), quite aside from the role that probation played in the lives of the offenders. Jay Rumney and Joseph P. Murphy, *Probation and Social Adjustment*, 1952, pp. 147, 244–245.

that crime is not a necessary consequence of impoverishment. On the other hand, the fact that a vast majority of those who are convicted in our courts and of those who recidivate come from the lower economic levels implies the existence of important relationships, and these relationships cannot be accounted for merely by the observation that the well-to-do more often escape discovery and conviction. Fault may be attributed to the economic and social system itself, as many writers like to do, or to individuals' greed, their lack of social responsibilities, or simply their inability to secure what they want. Settling upon an agreeable scapegoat, whether it is the society or the individual, solves no problems.

The significant point is that some individuals cannot readily achieve their wants legitimately or otherwise, and these individuals may seize what they cannot or will not earn. Few get into trouble for taking crusts of bread or for finding shelter from the elements. It is among the least competent in natural ability or training that competition is most difficult and criminality most frequent. In addition to their lack of special skills or education for a trade, these offenders generally display other associated difficulties, such as deficient sense of responsibility, lack of normal appreciation of rights of property, strong hostility or aggression, inadequate personality patterns, or unusual environmental stress. Moreover, the economically underprivileged also lack for the most part normal opportunities for maintaining good physical health, for enjoying the better forms of leisure-time activity and associations, and for securing many of the community services that they need. As has been noted, the delinquency area is characterized both by submarginal economic circumstances and by numerous forms of social and personal disorganization that may encourage crime. Robert Hunt's history is typical of many property offenders:

Robert Hunt, who is now 23 years of age, was sentenced to two years for car theft. He comes from a deplorable family background, an underprivileged home where he suffered from malnutrition and neglect. Robert lived with his parents, a married sister, and three other siblings in a four-room shanty in a blighted area of Atlanta, Georgia, which they rented for $27.50 a month. His parents were both employed as textile workers.

This offender has had no significant work history, having held unskilled jobs for only two very short periods. He was committed to the state training school in 1942 for staying away from home at night and for taking money from other children by force. He was held until 1945 and soon got into trouble again, being sent to work camp for two years in 1946 for car theft. In 1948 he was committed again for stealing four bicycles. He escaped during this sentence and was returned to the camp. In 1949 Hunt was committed to prison camp for car theft and in 1950 received a three- to four-year term for stealing another car. He was released in 1952 and committed under the Dyer Act in 1953. Hunt has spent over half his life thus far in correctional institutions. He gets along well now in a penitentiary; the reports are excellent for his work and behavior. He is prison-wise and unreformed.

Not all property offenders by any means are deficient in abilities or training. Many of normal and superior competence commit embezzlement, fraud, robbery, and other crimes. It appears that their offenses must generally be accounted for in terms other than inability to compete. In some instances these offenders have not had the strength to resist opportunity and temptation. Many of them, in haste to attain material rewards, lack the perseverance, the stability, or the conscience to achieve what they can by slow and legitimate means. Moreover, there is a greater tolerance, not only among themselves, but among officials, of the subtler and more complicated offenses they commit than of ordinary theft or burglary, for example, and there is a greater likelihood of "getting away with it."

Finally, it should be observed that there are relationships between particular types of crime and occupation as well as class. Certain occupations offer greater opportunity and temptation to crime than others. Thus, embezzlement is found very commonly among cashiers and other thefts among clerks and truckers who have access to goods or money. Domestics may easily be exploited sexually or financially and may do some exploiting themselves. The soldier may be led by his experiences in the Armed Forces to crimes of violence and passion. Poorly paid, single girls in cities may be drawn gradually into commercial prostitution. Doctors, dentists, and lawyers who are occasionally paid in cash may "forget" sizeable segments of their incomes. Trustees may fraudulently convert assets to their own use. Submarginal farmers take to bootlegging liquor. Casual inspection of prison records reveals the frequency of these relationships. An occupation does not directly cause criminality, of course, but whether a vulnerable person will succumb depends in considerable part upon his opportunities rather than upon his motives alone.

Chapter 9

PROPERTY OFFENDERS: TYPOLOGIES

Criminals are characterized by their diversity, both psychologically and sociologically. Yet, different as they are, they resemble closely and overlap the noncriminal population in their characteristics and in their range of variation. The criminologist may be misled in conceiving them as a single and separate species. There is not *a* criminal type of personality and there is not *a* criminal subculture. Researches that have been designed to distinguish the frequency of occurrence of specific traits in heterogeneous samples of offenders and of noncriminals cancel significant differences between offender types and conceal similarities between some classes of criminals and of noncriminals. Such studies may also produce a distorted conception of the way in which such variables are interrelated in the dynamic determination of delinquency. This is not to deny the utility of statistical studies or of some of the hypotheses that have been developed relating to divergent norms but to emphasize the need for critical interpretation of the data.

For lack of space the author does not attempt in this volume to delineate in any detail the differences between offender types. Aside from a study by John L. Gillin at Waupun Prison in Wisconsin, little research thus far supports such an analysis.[1] It may be worthwhile, however, to suggest a simple typology of property offenders that will point to some differences among them.

A CLASSIFICATION OF PROPERTY OFFENDERS

Crimes against the person are for the most part nonhabitual. They do not constitute a way of life. They are committed by criminal "amateurs," very often as a consequence of circumstantial factors or unusual pressures. Often amateurs' crimes are outbursts of passion, aggression, or pathological distortions of the sexual impulse. They comprise only a small percentage of the prison population. Property offenders are very different in a number of respects. They reflect a more diverse etiology. While a few

[1] *The Wisconsin Prisoner*, 1946. In a work not yet published Julian Roebuck has empirically derived a typology of felons.

215

suffer from severe abberations, a vast majority come within a normal range of psychiatric deviation. Crimes of property offenders derive from social, economic, and cultural circumstances and weaknesses of character rather than from extreme pathology. There are, however, significant differences in classes of personality and social history as they relate to different types of property crime. Furthermore, these offenders can be classified somewhat more sharply into levels of operation than can offenders against the person. The author believes the following divisions may have some utility for purposes of analysis. The major classes are the *simple* and the *professional*.

Simple criminality appears in two forms, *circumstantial* and *amateur*. The *circumstantial* offender is led to commit a single or rare crime as the result of the pressure of unusual circumstances that are beyond his power, at the time, to resist. He may be weak or the deviation pressures may be very strong. He may come from the "best" or from the "worst" of homes. He may be socially successful, though more commonly he is a failure. Such individuals are conformists, adequately socialized under normal conditions, and are nonrecidivous. The gregarious ones have often been influenced by a companion or gang, especially in crimes involving theft, burglary, and possession of narcotics. Others have more often been led into trouble by a crisis, a temporary emotional state, or an impulse. This is commonly found to be true in crimes of embezzlement, arson, and solitary theft. Offenders in this group make up a large part of probation cases and show high rates of success under probation supervision. Ordinarily offenders of this type constitute 20 per cent or more of a prison population. The "jolt" of a conviction is generally enough to keep the circumstantial offender out of further trouble.

The *amateur* criminal, as we use the term here, engages in crimes with little display of skill or intelligence. He lacks the advantages, also, of criminal organization. He may be a habitual or an occasional offender. Usually he has emerged from faulty home and community circumstances with character defects that make him easy prey to temptation. His orientation is nonconformist and antisocial, as in the professional criminal, but characteristically he lacks either the talent or the training to make it pay. A minority of able amateurs become professionals through their contacts and training and some assume minor roles in criminal organizations. Most of them, however, are incompetent amateurs. Amateur criminals make up over 50 per cent of the prison population and a rather considerable proportion of probationers. They fail at both crime and reformation. Imprisoned thieves, burglars, and "heisters" are generally amateurs. In maturity, many of them quit crime, having learned from repeated failure that life "on the outside" is simpler and less frustrating, even though it involves work. These are, for the most part, "the reformed." Some are long in learning the risks they run and the relative advantages of freedom. Others cannot make the grade for sustained periods of time and recurrently succumb to the temporarily easier way.

The professional property offender is either *solitary* or *organized*. The *solitary* professional criminal works alone in a craft that does not depend upon a "mob" for its success. The solitary professional is usually well endowed in ability, sometimes with a special manual or social skill that partially determines the form of his specialization. He is often more or less highly egocentric, ambitious, and self-taught in his specialty.[2] His attitudes are antisocial, though he ordinarily has elaborated rationalizations to exculpate himself, either by identifying the acceptable citizens' behavior and attitudes with his own, or by justifying his rejection of the ways of ordinary men. He may have come from ostensibly favorable community circumstances but has most commonly experienced conflicts and frustrating circumstances in home and neighborhood that have led to his aggressive, antisocial orientation. This type of criminal represents a quite small percentage of all criminals and an even smaller proportion of those in prison, generally not more than 5 or 10 per cent. Offenders in this group usually pursue their occupation quite steadily and with a relatively high degree of success. If they are realistic, they expect to suffer the periods of imprisonment entailed in the risks of their occupations. They work for higher stakes than does the simple criminal, and they ordinarily receive longer terms that are proportionate to the seriousness of their crimes. "Rehabilitation" in the traditional sense is uncommon in this group, for their antisocial attitudes are rarely changed. However, they may abandon their criminal occupations for some other more socially acceptable business if and when they have achieved a material success sufficient to make the risk of imprisonment appear unjustified. Prior experience of incarceration may hasten this rational rather than conversional decision. Ordinarily such offenders are criminally persistent so long as they must ply their crafts to live at the standard they desire and, perhaps, to lay away a stake for the future. Solitary professional criminals are most often forgers, burglars, robbers, or thieves of some specialized kind.

"White-collar crime," as the author uses this term, is a special type of solitary professional criminality. It involves real violations of the criminal law, systematically or repeatedly committed by business, professional, and clerical workers incidental to their occupations.[3] These individuals differ from others in their class. Their attitudes are more conventional and their

---

[2] Whatever may be said for the merits of the differential association theory as it applies to many offenders, it surely cannot be argued successfully that the robber, burglar, and ordinary thief must be associated with or trained by others of his kind.

[3] The position taken here is that conduct of the white-collar class that is merely unprincipled, exploitative, antisocial, reprehensible, or otherwise provocative is not crime unless it is also violative of the criminal law. Deviating further from common usage of the term, it will be observed, we include in this class individuals occupied in professional, clerical, or skilled work as well as businessmen.

violations are more subtle, often coming close to the line of legality. Because of the sophisticated nature of their offenses and because of the comparatively high status they enjoy in the community, these offenders are less frequently prosecuted and convicted than others. Moreover, because their offenses are apt to be considered relatively minor and the offenders regarded as "good people," their sentences are generally lenient when they are convicted. Representatives of this group are those who commit frauds, embezzlements, income tax violations, and fee-splitting delinquencies and some of those who engage in illegal sale of contraband and criminally prohibited restraints of trade.

The *organized* professionals, while not an exclusively modern phenomenon, represent the peak of criminal development. In proportion to their numbers these offenders are more difficult to control than any other group. Proficient, organized in outfits with strong codes designed for self-preservation, with habits of mutual aid that are common to "persecuted" minority groups, and protected by arrangements for fixing cases,[4] the organized professionals can in a high proportion of cases evade arrest, prosecution, conviction, or prison sentence. Cases where "the fix" has failed and where "small fry" have been sacrificed make up a very small percentage of any prison population.

Organized professionals are specialists in any of numerous criminal crafts that depend more or less upon coordination of group effort: confidence rackets, pocket picking, shoplifting, bank robbery, various forms of sneak-thievery, narcotics distribution, auto theft, and such vice rackets as gambling and prostitution. They are usually selected from the cream of the able amateurs or from legitimate occupations, i.e., those who have the skills, personal qualities, and contacts that are needed for effective coordination. Chic Conwell makes the point that a person can become a professional in the specialized rackets only if he is trained by professionals.[5]

The criminal gang can tolerate a membership of different levels of ability so long as the members conform to the rules. Thus, while its leader-

---

[4] See Edwin H. Sutherland (annot.), *The Professional Thief*, 1937, where Chic Conwell (the "professional thief") remarks upon the "fix": "In order to send a thief to the penitentiary, it is necessary to have the cooperation of the victim, witnesses, police, bailiffs, clerks, grand jury, jury, prosecutor, judges, and perhaps others. A weak link in this chain can practically always be found, and any of the links can be broken if you have pressure enough." P. 83.

[5] Conwell said, "It is ridiculous to imagine an amateur deciding to become a pickpocket, con man, pennyweighter (jewelry thief), or shake man (extortioner) without professional guidance. He knows nothing of the racket, its technique or operations, and he can't learn these things out of books. . . . The members of the profession generally started their occupational life in legitimate employment, although some of them entered other illegal operations before becoming professional thieves. Few of them came from the amateur thieves who are reared in the slums, for these youngsters seldom have the social abilities or front required of professional thieves." *Ibid.*, p. 21.

ship is dependent upon superior skills and organizational ability, the larger syndicates contain offenders of varying skill and background. Aside from the leaders, they are generally less able than solitary professionals, but the advantages of organization compensate for some limitations of ability. The lower echelons among the criminals cannot easily escape into respectability. The pressures of the mob are great. However, Conwell observes that professional thieves have retired into detective agencies, cab companies, cigar stores, hotels, farming, manufacturing, and the movies. Those who leave the group are usually the elite in the well-organized and persistent mobs. Like solitary professionals they may achieve wealth and independence sufficient to "go legitimate." However, the organized professional criminal is perhaps the least reformable of all criminals. He has been too long conditioned to crime and criminal attitudes and is too thoroughly controlled by his associates.

A simple functional classification such as the one presented above does not include all criminals, of course. Nor are the classes entirely distinct. Transition from one class to another occurs with some frequency. It is believed, however, that these categories make up the greater part of offenders against property. As was noted, there is an additional but relatively small group of property offenders whose crimes appear to a large extent to be related to serious psychiatric deviations. It should be emphasized further that no attempt is made in this classification to establish a series of simple causal hypotheses. Within these various levels of criminality, physical, psychological, and social influences play their varying, interdependent roles.

Theft

Except for circumstantial offenders, minor thieves of limited intelligence or ability are highly recidivous because they will not earn a modest living in other ways and because they lack the professional help to arrange "a fix," as organized criminals may do in some cases. Often they seem not to profit from experience, as is illustrated by the cases cited below:

POLICE RECORD TRAPS INDIGNANT THIEF . . . police records show fifty-one arrests and thirty-nine convictions of various offenses over the last thirty years . . . starting with a pickpocket charge in 1914 and including many jostling and minor theft convictions.[6]

"CRYING TILLIE" IN AGAIN. Notorious Pickpocket Held for Hearing after 19th Arrest. "Crying Tillie," who is 45 years old, has been arrested nineteen times in the last thirty-two years. The report said that she came from a respectable family and had a husband who can support her comfortably. In court she simply said: "It gives me a thrill."[7]

PAROLED CAR THIEF UP TO OLD TRICKS. 42-year-old has had an

---

[6] *New York Times,* Nov. 9, 1944. On shoplifting, see p. 135.

[7] *Ibid.,* Aug. 6, 1945.

insatiable desire to take automobiles that do not belong to him. On seven occasions before his first imprisonment he stole cars and was charged with grand larceny and was fortunate when these charges were lessened. This saved him from the effect of the Baumes Law until 1942 when he finally received the mandatory term.[8]

As we have suggested, organized thieves and con men are a very different breed from the simple thief. Professor Sutherland observed that organized thieves possess a complex of abilities and skills like other professionals, skills employed in the planning and execution of their crimes, in disposing of stolen goods, in fixing cases if they are apprehended and go to court, and in controlling other situations that may arise in the course of their occupation.[9] To be effective, con men require sharp wits, verbal persuasiveness, smoothness in their business relationships, keen judgment of character, and rapid adaptability. They maintain occupational and social distance from amateurs who lack these abilities and from those engaged in the "heavy rackets" (robbery, burglary, kidnapping) who rely on force or merely on manual dexterity for success in their crimes. Sutherland suggested that the qualities noted above were characteristic of the professional thief; it appears, however, that he was generalizing too largely from materials (particularly those of Chic Conwell) on the confidence rackets and that his analysis is applicable to only a very limited extent to other types of specialists, such as organized car or mail thieves, pickpockets, or shoplifters. The con man is an aristocrat among larcenous criminals, but few rise to this level. As Lemert has pointed out, aspirations to advancement and success are found among thieves just as they are found among other ambitious persons in our society. The mature thief who is a "solitary grifter" without technique or associates is a failure both as a citizen and as a criminal.[10]

[8] *Ibid.,* Jan. 5, 1951.

[9] In connection with the volume referred to Sutherland provides a detailed bibliography that includes numerous items written by former convicts. See pp. 247–252 in *The Professional Thief.* See also David Maurer, *The Big Con,* 1940, and W. T. Brannon, *Yellow Kid Weil,* 1948. Maurer expresses the opinion that the three big-con games, the wire, the rag, and the payoff, have produced more illicit gain for the operators and for the law than all other forms of professional crime, except prohibition law violations, during the period that they have been in operation, p. 17.

Edwin M. Schur in "Sociological Analysis of Confidence Swindling," *J. Crim. L.,* vol. 48, pp. 296–305, 1957, makes the point that fraud offenders are rarely uncovered, even more rarely prosecuted, and very lightly punished, so that the extent and seriousness of the problem, while believed to be very large, are not measurable. The "fundamental dishonesty of the victim," emphasized by Hans von Hentig, is one of the significant reasons why the operators of con games are rarely prosecuted. See *The Criminal and His Victim,* 1948, p. 384.

[10] Lemert describes the upward reach of the larcenous offender: "Vertical social mobility functions for criminal persons as well as for non-criminal, with criminals being 'on the make' in their status framework as well as others. Young thieves may begin their careers stealing automobile tires, pass from that to, say, jack-rolling

Because the methods employed by the big con and the organization required for this type of crime are so interesting, too little attention has been given to "con" types of personality that work in isolation rather than with a mob. These independent "con" types work sometimes with a considerable measure of success in spite of the lack of group support or of "the fix." There are many such "cons" in our prisons whose personalities are apparently similar to those who work the big con but who choose to work alone. Characteristically, they are personable, glib, exploitative individuals. They fit the stereotype of the psychopath and commonly are facile if not pathological liars.

Embezzlement

This crime is a specialized form of theft in which the offender occupies a position of financial trust that he violates by fraudulently converting money or property to his own use. A white-collar criminal, he is generally a solitary amateur. Embezzlers are a considerably superior group intellectually and are a more mature group in age than other classes of offenders. They are drawn to a great extent from among managers of businesses and clerical workers rather than from professional or laboring classes. Their types of employment are related to the opportunity and the skills required for embezzlement. More of them are married than other types of offenders. For the most part the embezzlers are relatively "substantial" citizens, approximating the norms of success in our society. Their values and attitudes probably differ little from those of successful businessmen who avoid trouble with the law.[11]

---

drunks, and from there they may move into 'heavy rackets.' Professional skill, large earnings, and ability to escape imprisonment serve as the criteria for advancement and acceptability into the higher ranking criminal occupations. Many aspirants never get beyond the lower rungs of the criminal-status ladder. Others get as far as the heavy rackets but never rise to elite status of grifter or to that of the criminal's criminal, the con man." Edwin M. Lemert, *Social Pathology*, 1951, p. 323. (Quoted by permission.)

[11] This appears to be true, too, of tax evaders and violators of antitrust laws. That they are not considered "ordinary criminals" is reflected in the mitigated sentences that they very commonly receive.

The United States Fidelity and Guaranty Company, in a study of 1,001 of them, has pictured the embezzler thus: "Your typical embezzler belongs in the white collar class. He is thirty-six years old. He is married. He has a wife and two children. He is not psychopathic or of feeble mind, nor does he live in a neighborhood where crime is widespread. His upbringing has been good. He is not the lowest paid person in his employer's organization, nor is he the highest. His friends and very often his wife imagine that his salary is $300.00 a month or more, but it is nearer $175.00 a month. He has a high school education. He lives comfortably. He has a medium priced car. His traveling has been confined to occasional week-ends and a two-week vacation in the summer. He is a good mixer. He participates in social and community affairs. He enjoys a good time. He likes a drink, but he rarely takes it during

In a great majority of cases embezzlers feel that they are temporarily borrowing the money they take. They do not conceive of themselves in the role of thief. They have been led to their violations of trust by a variety of pressures: spendthrift habits, a nagging or invalid wife, an ambitious family or ailing children, infatuation with a paramour, gambling losses, excessive drinking, or an unexpected emergency. They usually operate alone without accessories and in many cases, starting with a small peculation, they persist for years without being discovered. More often they commit suicide than abscond. Frequently the victims are sympathetic with these offenders, sensing perhaps their own similarities of weakness and of social status, and urge brief sentences and early paroles.[12] The writer has seen a fair number of these men in prison and finds that typically, as compared with other criminals, they have strong, sometimes abject, compunction for their crime. They are unhappy and depressed but constructively occupied prisoners. Few have retained any of the funds they have taken, but they are generally willing to make such restitution as they can.

Donald R. Cressey has studied a sample of 133 embezzlers as the basis for his exposition of a thesis on the etiology of this crime.[13] He has summarized his concluding hypothesis in these terms: "Trusted persons become trust violators when they conceive of themselves as having a financial problem which is non-shareable, are aware that this problem can be secretly resolved by violation of the position of financial trust, and are able to apply to their own conduct in that situation verbalizations which enable them to adjust their conceptions of themselves as trusted persons with their conceptions of themselves as users of the entrusted funds or property."[14] Cressey holds that when all of these variables are present, em-

---

business hours. He lives in every state in the Union, in every province of Canada, in large cities, in small cities. He is employed in every type of business. He is competent and smart. He has held his position for five and a half years. His employer regards him favorably and he has *honestly* earned the position of trust to which he has attained. In short, so far as his past record is concerned, he is a regular fellow, a normal individual with a better than average business reputation and future." *1001 Embezzlers; A Study of Defalcations in Business,* United States Fidelity and Guaranty Company, Baltimore, 1943, pp. 5–6.

[12] One is impressed by the striking disparities in treatment accorded embezzlers in sentencing; this phenomenon undoubtedly reflects the confusion of the courts when confronted by the defalcations, often very substantial, of ostensibly stalwart citizens. Thus, within a period of a few months in a recent year in the New York area, a civic leader in New Jersey was sentenced to ten to fourteen years on an embezzlement amounting to $459,689; a broker in Manhattan was given a suspended sentence after defalcations of more than $225,000; and a bank teller in Brooklyn received 2½ years for taking $48,224. Among nineteen former students at a metropolitan University who had been systematically thieving in its bookstore for a period of two years, two leaders received reformatory terms up to five years, two were given six-month jail terms, and fifteen received suspended sentences.

[13] *Other People's Money,* 1953.

[14] *Ibid.,* p. 191.

bezzlement occurs but in the absence of any one of them there will be no violation of trust. It is clear that the elements of opportunity and secrecy are essential to this crime and that the offenders engage in self-justifications for their conduct. Possibly the rationalizations of embezzlers are more exculpating than those of other law violators, for they do not identify themselves with criminals. Rationalizations are common among offenders generally, however. It appears, furthermore, that these rationalizations are developed or elaborated after the crime has been committed and especially after sentence. The hypothesis of a "non-shareable problem" is not entirely convincing to the writer, perhaps because whether or not a problem can be shared is a relative question.

Two embezzlers whom the author has interviewed illustrate rather well the varying motivations connected with this crime. These cases suggest the subtlety of distinctions sometimes drawn between need, wants, greed, and business acumen:

James Ross, a 62-year-old Italian American, is serving a four-year term at Lewisburg for embezzling $81,000 from a national bank. He had been employed there for a total of thirty-eight years and had been made cashier a few years prior to his thefts. For several years he took funds illegally, coercing other employees of the institution to cover up his defalcations, including the auditor, teller, and a bookkeeper. Ross' embezzlements were committed for purposes of investment. He was unusually successful in this respect and from time to time he replaced funds that he had taken. At the time of his conviction he returned all that remained of his "debt" to the bank as well as $16,000 in interest on his "borrowings" and admitted that in addition he had made a net profit of at least $35,000. He now has assets valued at $250,000. The bank considered the restitution with interest very fair and its president urged his parole. Other "distinguished citizens," including the county treasurer, the chief of police, the district attorney, and the mayor of the city, supported his application for early release. They pointed to his excellent reputation as a businessman in the community and maintained that he had "paid his debt" to society. Apparently, since Ross was astute in his financial transactions, no one objected to his retaining the profits of his criminal enterprise.

Edward Cott, a prisoner at Lewisburg Penitentiary, is 59 years of age, serving a term for bank embezzlement. For thirty-five years he had worked in the bank of a small community in Pennsylvania where he had been head teller for some time prior to his arrest. His reputation as a citizen and father was unsullied and he had never been in any sort of difficulty with the law. During the 1940s Cott earned a weekly salary of $43, an amount he found insufficient to meet his living expenses, and over a period of ten years he embezzled a total of $20,550. There were no collaborators in his crime. He succeeded in putting two sons through college and maintained his family in genteel poverty. After the discovery of his defalcation, Cott made such limited restitution as he could by selling the home in which he had a small equity and by borrowing from relatives. Because of the damage done to his reputation he plans to move to another community after release from prison.

Forgery

Forgers are an older group than burglars, robbers, and ordinary thieves; they also appear to be more intelligent than thieves, burglars, and arsonists. They are younger and less intelligent than embezzlers. The marital status of forgers reveals that a relatively high porportion are widowed and divorced in comparison with all other types of property offenders. Only 29.6 per cent of Gillin's sample had intact marriages as compared with 77.0 per cent of the embezzlers.

Forgers have an unusually high rate of recidivism as compared with other types of criminals, 70 per cent or more having prior arrest records. Some scholars believe that this indicates deep emotional disturbance. So far as one can judge from Gillin's material, however, they are not for the most part an emotionally deviated group.[15] He suggests that the relative infrequency with which forgery is prosecuted, the light sentences that are commonly administered, and the example of others who commit the offense and get away with it may better account for their recidivism. Beyond this it should be noted that forgery is an offense of "low visibility" and that it is a nonaggressive crime in which the victim may be partially culpable through his own negligence. In these respects it is rather similar to embezzlement, which may account for the ease with which offenders rationalize the commission of the crime. For the forger, however, it is much simpler to repeat the crime after he has once been apprehended than is the case with the embezzler who is commonly denied access to employment in positions of trust after he has once been discovered. The writer believes that the simplicity of forgery as a nonaggressive solution to financial problems and the ease of rationalizing the act may well explain the frequent repetition of this offense.

Edwin Lemert reports on 1,023 forgery cases whose records he has studied and on 29 forgers whom he interviewed.[16] He used this sample as a basis for the development of a theory of "naïve check forgery," by which he refers to inexperienced forgers without previous relationships with delinquents and criminals and without criminal record of other types. He states his hypothesis thus: " . . . naïve check forgery arises at a critical point in a process of social isolation, out of certain types of social

---

[15] In the author's experience, forgers and con men more often display psychopathic traits of personality together with high intelligence, but there appears to be little evidence of neurosis. According to a study made by T. Conway Esselstyn of a group of forgers in San Mateo County, California, these offenders appear to be immature, unstable, and unreliable. As in Gillin's group they were older, on the average, than other offenders, and in a high proportion of cases they had been married and either divorced or separated. See "Report on a Preliminary Study of Thirty-four False Check Writers," San Jose State College, June, 1957. (Mimeographed.)

[16] "An Isolation and Closure Theory of Naïve Check Forgery," *J. Crim. L.,* vol. 44, pp. 296–308, 1953.

situations, and is made possible by the closure or constriction of behavior alternatives subjectively held as available to the forger." He found, as did Gillin, that his forgers were older than other criminals and were of higher intelligence and longer education, that they displayed inordinately high rates of family instability, and that they were often skilled or craft workers. He noted further that they often come from well-to-do families in which their siblings have achieved some success. They rarely have had prior histories of delinquency. Lemert suggests that forgers are generally men of personal attractiveness, persuasive and ingratiating, who display an element of impulsiveness in their behavior. They appear to have normal attitudes and habits of law observance.

Lemert inferred from his case materials that forgery was a culmination of a process of social isolation, often initiated by traumatic marital disruptions, by alienation from the parental family, or by other influences such as physical handicaps or minority group affiliations. Commonly these factors lead to excessive drinking, occupational failures, promiscuous behavior, and other symptoms of personal isolation and demoralization. Lemert found more specifically conducive to forgery, however, the individual's progressive involvement in activities (e.g., a spree of carousing or gambling) that made the possession of money imperative and that built a sense of crisis: " . . . many of the type situations more specifically leading to forgeries—gambling, borrowing and 'kiting' to meet debts and business obligations, desertion and escaping authorities, and being the *bon vivant* tended to be dialectical, self-enclosed systems of behavior in the sense that the initial behaviors called for 'more of the same.' "[17]

Lemert suggests that the selection of forgery as the means of solving a problem is based upon the offender's lack of skills or opportunity to "close on" most other forms of crime and upon the attractiveness of a crime with such low social visibility. He found, furthermore, that in most instances the forger was obsessed with a sense of urgency at the time of his crime and had suffered a reduction of his ordinary inhibitions. In some instances there appeared to be a strong element of aggression present, occasionally against a particular person, or a need to punish someone.

The author has observed that habitual check forgers are immature and impulsive personalities, displaying long histories of social and economic unadaptability, often moving from city to city, leaving "cold checks" behind as they travel. It is dubious that, as Lemert believes, the forger cannot find some other criminal technique such as theft or burglary to satisfy his financial want, but the forger's choice may well be based upon his impulsive, immediate demand, the ease of committing the offense, and the fact that it is a more genteel crime. The case of Charles Hundley caricatures the solitary professional forger to some extent:

[17] *Ibid.*, p. 304.

Hundley was committed to Leavenworth Penitentiary in 1951 at the age of 28. He came from a good professional home where he was the only son and from which he received more than the ordinary advantages of comfortable living. Hundley had very superior intelligence, with an IQ of 145, and was an attractive young man in appearance, though he gave an impression of some personal weakness. This prison psychiatric reports on this man describe him as a chronic and severe antisocial personality, nomadic and unadjusted to any occupation, impulsive and uninhibited by temperament. He has no work history of any consequence.

The first official reports of Hundley date back to 1942, though it should be noted that throughout his history his parents have intervened to protect him from local authorities when he has gotten into trouble and it is quite probable that his delinquencies go back to childhood. He stole a car in 1942 but was released by the court in New York upon his promise to enter the Marines. Later in the same year he was arrested in the District of Columbia for passing bad checks but was put on probation to continue service with the Marines. He was medically discharged from the service early in 1944 on a diagnosis of psychopathic personality. Shortly thereafter he was sentenced to jail in California for forgery and a few weeks after release on parole was picked up in Pennsylvania on a similar charge. He was returned to California on a sentence to a road camp from which he escaped in the middle of 1945. In less than sixty days he was committed to the Ohio Penitentiary for cashing worthless checks in that state. From there he was released to return to California in early 1947 to serve a term at San Quentin for escape and forgery. Within six months of his release he was arrested in Florida for forgery and embezzlement. On this occasion he pleaded his mental condition as a defense to the charges and was allowed probation on his promise to undergo a prefrontal lobotomy. In spite of this drastic surgery he was convicted again for forgery within a year, this time in Massachusetts, and was sentenced to prison. Three days after his parole he was charged with grand larceny for issuing worthless checks in New York City but was given a suspended sentence. It was only a few months after this that he received his Federal prison sentence for forging checks, a term of four years. In spite of his record he was permitted to go out on parole after two years, partly because of the strong pleas of his mother, who stated that psychiatric treatment had been arranged for him. At this time he owed over eighteen years to prisons in various states for violation of parole had they wished to assert jurisdiction. He will serve no more time in prison, having died quite unexpectedly in early 1954 at the age of 31.

Robbery

The "heavy rackets," in which force or violence is used to appropriate property, especially robbery, is obviously a very different crime from embezzlement, forgery, or ordinary larceny. It implies some measure of courage, a readiness to confront and dominate the victim, and a spurning of subterfuge and of the easy rationalizations under which the embezzler or the forger is wont to take cover. The "heavy rackets" criminal's antisocial orientation is frank, direct, and deliberate. Ordinarily he starts as an amateur and may become either a solitary or an organized professional. Neither robbery itself nor its perpetrators are uniform phenomena, however. The range of behavior and skills involved is considerable, running from the ordinary "mugging" and "heist" in the street or home through hijacking and bank robbery. In his study Gillin secured some measure of the differences by separating those who had been convicted of assault and robbery from those who had been committed for bank robbery. The former group contained a rather large percentage of individuals with low intelligence scores similar to his sample of burglars. Interestingly, however, 11.9 per cent of the group were above average in IQ. This represents a larger percentage than is generally found among forgers, burglars, thieves, and arsonists. Very likely this percentage reflects the considerable disparity in intelligence in the robbery class. Ordinary robbers also display less uniformity in their occupational backgrounds than do other types of offenders. Many have been unskilled laborers but a surprising proportion have been professional, business, or clerical workers.

It appears that the nonprofessional "stick up," like the petty thief, is a person of limited intelligence and skills. Often he comes from a poor home and an underprivileged area where antisocial attitudes have been bred, though in some cases his crime is an act of desperation in a crisis situation. Some courage is required, though rather little, with gun in hand. The ordinary, unskilled robber is more likely to use force to commit his crime than is the professional. Also he more commonly engages in a variety of unspecialized crimes, according to his opportunity or convenience. Unless he is unusually able he does not advance to more skilled or professional forms of crime. Undoubtedly in some instances the act of robbery is a paraphiliac device to express virility, as some psychiatrists have maintained, but there is no evidence that this is a frequent motive.

Bank robbers represent a quite different group from the ordinary run of robbery cases. More often they are organized professionals. Gillin's data reveal some of the differences. Bank robbers are a considerably more intelligent group than other property offenders, embezzlers alone being superior to them. They show a distinct concentration in the 25- to 30-year age range in his sample; it is a group of mature vigor. More bank robbers have been businessmen and clerical workers and fewer have been laborers than was so among those convicted of assault and robbery. The two groups are very similar, however, as to marital status, a high proportion being single as compared with embezzlers and forgers. Gillin believed that a large number of them were emotionally maladjusted, having feelings of inferiority and a desire for recognition. He found that crisis situations precipitated the crime in many cases, generally because of domestic difficulties or loss of employment.

J. Edgar Hoover reports important recent changes occurring in the area of bank robbery. In the period from 1950 to 1955 the number of such crimes increased threefold (from 100 in 1950 to 307 in 1954). Whereas in the past such robberies have been the work of "highly organized and seasoned veterans" who planned to take only the apparently vulnerable banks, today the lone robber and the amateur have entered the field increasingly, often with little planning of their job and with much less discrimination as to the victim institutions. This represents a serious problem, but it should be observed that unarmed and unorganized offenders, embezzling employees, are five times more numerous today than are professional robbers.[18] One insurance manager has indicated that claims reports for merchandise and cash stolen by employees rose more than 50 per cent between 1947 and 1951, amounting to at least a billion dollars in the latter years. A director of the Federal Deposit Insurance Corporation found that 120 of the 416 bank failures occurring between 1933 and 1951 were caused by the defalcations and frauds perpetrated by trusted employees. Professional robberies are much rarer, smaller, and less injurious to the community.

Willie Sutton, "the most successful of modern bank robbers," illustrates particularly well a number of features commonly found in the professional criminal of this type. Born in 1900, he was brought up in a tough neighborhood in Brooklyn, where he hung out as a youth at One-Arm Quigg's Poolroom. He was known then as a natty, quiet, and smooth personality. Two explanations have been offered for the beginning of his long history of crime: one that he fell in with a mob of safe crackers after running away in 1921 to evade arrest as a murder suspect, the other that he was badly beaten by the police in 1923 upon his return to New York and that he turned to crime in resentment. Sutton was first committed to prison in 1926 for an attempt to open a safe, and shortly after release he committed his first daring robbery— the $130,000 daylight holdup of a jewelry store, which he had entered by posing as a messenger. This disguise, together with others, such as bank guard, Western Union messenger, and window cleaner, earned him the alias, "Willie the Actor." He was committed to Sing Sing for thirty years on this robbery conviction but sawed his way out of an "escape-proof" cell there after serving only two years. It was at this time that he turned to bank robbery. He was next sent to a Pennsylvania prison in 1933 on a fifty-year term for this crime. He escaped in 1947, wearing a guard's uniform.

Sutton was not captured again until 1952, when he was sentenced to thirty years at Attica Prison in New York for robbery, this to be added to terms for escape and other crimes totaling over 100 years. While at Attica he has written an autobiography in which he estimates that he had secured a total loot of some 2 million dollars from a score of robberies. Sutton's technique, sometimes copied by other bank robbers, was to select his banks carefully and to get to know the employees and their schedules and habits well. He would hold up the first employee arriving in the morning and admit others at gunpoint as they arrived, escaping before the bank opened for business.

[18] See H. N. Oliphant, "Amateurs in the World of Crime," *Readers Digest*, January, 1952, p. 83.

Sutton is an intellectual criminal, always urbane and polite, a dabbler in philosophy and Freudianism, who appears to have conceived of himself as a "gentleman adventurer, in many respects a Robin Hood." He boasted that he had never employed violence on anyone and that he stole only from "those who could afford it," often telling bank officials: "The insurance will cover this." His daring but careful and well-planned bank robberies appear to have been a very satisfying expression of his strong narcissism. At the same time he demonstrated that he was an expert in a craft in which the rewards for success could be considerable. His skill and intelligence withal, he has spent twenty-three of the last twenty-nine years in prison and most of the remainder in hiding out from the police. Presumably his bank robberies are ended unless he is able to escape again. In spite of his experiences, one cannot help being skeptical of the sincerity in his recent moral admonitions to the young that "crime does not pay." It is not difficult to predict what his future career preference would be if he were free to choose.[19]

Intelligence and a quick wit are essential to the professional bank robber, more essential perhaps than in any of the other property crimes except the confidence rackets. Self-control and subtlety are required in threatening force but avoiding its application and in calming victims to prevent alarm or outcry. In some cases the author has seen, courage, combined with a defective ego, has assumed megalomaniacal proportions. Like other professional property criminals, bank robbers are a migratory breed, ordinarily without strong personal or family attachments. However, they generally work with other experts either on a single job or on a series of jobs to learn the techniques from their fellows.

Burglary

Next to larceny, burglary is the most common property crime. Furthermore, burglars are quite similar to thieves in a number of respects, so that these two classes provide the basic leaven of the ordinary penal institution. Gillin found that burglars as a class were somewhat more intelligent than thieves but were less competent than embezzlers, forgers, and robbers. In the samples studied, burglars were slightly older than thieves, property offenders generally, and murderers, though national statistics show that burglary, to an even greater extent than larceny, is a crime of youth. Sixty-three per cent of the individuals arrested for burglary are under the age of 21. Three-quarters of the burglars in Gillin's sample were either single or divorced (60 and 15 per cent, respectively). More of them had been unskilled laborers than was true of any other group of property offenders. In this respect they resembled sex offenders. Gillin found that many of his burglars were emotionally disturbed as a result of either a conflict in family loyalties or a conflict in cultures, particularly the former.

[19] See articles on Sutton in the *New York Times,* Mar. 21, 1952; May 3, 1952; Apr. 7, 1955.

Failures in ordinary competition, the demoralizing influence of associates, and economic need were found in many cases. Gillin suggests that need was not usually a basic cause of their difficulties, however.

In the author's experience burglars are for the most part unspecialized and their crimes are simple. A great proportion of them are amateurs. They lack the subtlety of professional thieves, the opportunity of embezzlers, and the courage of robbers. It is true, of course, that some youths who start their criminal careers with theft and burglary possess the necessary ambition and cunning to progress to the elite forms of property crimes or to become highly proficient in a particular form of burglary (e.g., safe-cracking or hotel prowling). The run-of-the-mill burglar displays little versatility or craftsmanship. The specialist, however, may become very expert. Large police departments have special squads of detectives, safe and loft, pickpocket, racket, etc., assigned to the apprehension of such specialized criminals. These detectives are familiar with the professionals' fields of operation, their *modi operandi,* their fences, and other contacts.

A curious perversion of intellect and skill is encountered occasionally in the expert burglar, well illustrated in the case of a California professor of sociology, an occasional lecturer in criminology. This man had systematically looted many homes in exclusive neighborhoods near the university where he had taught for five years. His mentors considered him an unusually brilliant as well as a highly attractive young man. He had moved forward rapidly in his professions, both legitimate and illegitimate. This scholar has said that his youth was a difficult period. He had lived in a delinquency neighborhood of Los Angeles and had later worked his way through college. This is not unusual, however, for ambitious and able youths who achieve success. In attempting an explanation of his criminal behavior, the professor said after his arrest: "It apparently was because of some deep-seated impulse in me and a deficiency in my make-up that I just can't trace. . . . I can only say that as a result of my confused and misguided emotional frame of mind I was led to these things by neurotic invalidism." Loose rationalizations are easy for the intellectual, but it appears at any rate that he had been an emotionally unstable and egoistic personality. He had twice been married and divorced, his first wife describing him as violent, belligerent, and given to mad rages. A few days after his first wife secured a divorce, he was remarried to a wealthy and socially prominent woman. Even before this, however, he had become emotionally involved with a very attractive divorcee with whom he continued to cohabit near the campus before and after his second divorce. It was this woman who, after violent quarrels, was responsible for his arrest. She submitted a confession of his numerous burglaries that she had obtained from him. He said that she had coerced him into writing the confession "so she would have a hold on me and feel more certain of my affections" and alleged that she "turned him in" because of his refusal to marry her.[20]

Organized Vice

Attention has been given above primarily to the major felonious property crimes, simple and professional. Some consideration should also be given to another form of professional crime that is highly important in our society, organized vice.[21] This is important not so much because of the individual offenses, which are commonly misdemeanors, but because of the problems associated with the syndication of such crime. These problems will be considered below. Unfortunately, research data are lacking on the nature of the offenders involved.

The work of the Kefauver Committee, following upon the Attorney General's Conference on Interstate Crime and upon the investigations of several state and local bodies, floodlighted in 1950 and 1951 some of the problems of crime and the administration of justice in the United States.[22] Ostensibly the basic accomplishment of the committee was to explore the liaison between organized crime, politics, and business interests, operating on an interstate level. The committee made an excellent preliminary exploration into this "unholy alliance." However, the proofs of political corruption, racketeering associated with commerce, and the criminal exploitation of vice were not new by any means. Over the past half century there has been a succession of probes and exposés on a local, state, and federal level. Since the muckraking efforts of fifty years ago, by Lincoln Steffens, Ida Tarbell, and others, and the more recent Attorney General's national inquiries into our system of justice, grand juries and state and local commissions have made numerous investigations into particular problems of organized crime and vice, police practice, court operation, political corruption, and shady practices in public life.

Although, as noted above, the organization of crime and its insinuation into positions of political and economic power is not novel, the Kefauver inquiries uncovered several significant developments. They revealed more

[20] See *San Francisco Chronicle*, Nov. 10, 1951; *New York Sunday News*, Dec. 9, 1951. Similarly curious were the more recent burglaries admitted by a psychiatrist serving the Children's Court in New York City and by one of the author's former students, a probation officer in California.

[21] In 1950 the author did a study for the Commission on Organized Crime of the American Bar Association on the problem of organized crime and legal measures to meet that problem. Material in this section is drawn in part from his report to the commission. See Tappan, "Habitual Offender Laws and Sentencing Practices in Relation to Organized Crime," in Morris Ploscowe (ed.), *Organized Crime and Law Enforcement*, 1952.

[22] See Estes Kefauver, *Crime in America*, 1951, and Reports of the Special Committee to Investigate Organized Crime in Interstate Commerce.

clearly than ever before that the nation-wide integration of crime was a linking of regional interests into "syndicates." The inference was drawn, from inconclusive evidence, however, that there have been two major groups—the Capone gang in Chicago and the Costello-Adonis gang in New York—with Lucky Luciano acting as mediator of conflicting interests between the two. Because of the *ad hoc* organization of some of the criminal activities, the careful concealment of the chain of command, the undercover operations, and the lack of records or other tangible evidence of financial activities, it has been impossible thus far to do much more than guess about the structuring of these gangs and their methods of operation. It appears clear in any event that there have been important but informal and fluctuating links between the "mobs" in the chief urban crime centers. There is evidence of interlocking leadership, contractual agreements, the fixing of territories of monopolistic power, fairly definite hierarchies of authority, exchange of personnel, etc. More disquieting, however, is the strength of the bonds that link the mobsters with the police and politicians, including mayors and governors, and with legitimate business, especially some of the wire services, criminal lawyers, and philanthrophy.

The Changing Pattern of Organized Crime

Recent investigations have somewhat clarified the links between organized vice and the past history of crime. The rich profit to be made from the commercialization of vice has provided a lure to professional criminals. The public itself, ready and eager to be exploited, has offered an unlimited consumer market for gambling, liquor, sex, and narcotics. From time immemorial, the state has tried to repress one or another of these commodities but has succeeded thereby only in increasing their desirability to the public and their profitability to the criminal. In recent years, however, the problem has become more acute and extensive than ever before.

A primary factor in precipitating the organization of vice was the enactment of prohibition laws, offering as they did the motive and opportunity for large-scale commerce in the contraband. Rumrunning, highjacking, and the speak-easy provided the impetus to organization. These enterprises promised wealth and power at a moderate risk to those who would compete for the "take." The occupational hazards came mainly from competitors rather than from the law. Successful bootlegging operations demanded strong organization and leadership on both an interstate and extranational level. They also required the perfection of techniques of force, persuasion, influence, and bribery, reaching from the lowest to some of the highest places in law enforcement, politics, and business. Some experience in organization and procedures had already been developed through the traffic in prostitution and gambling in preprohibition days. Indeed, the history of New Orleans, Chicago, and other cities reveals the alliance of large-scale gambling enterprise with politics, philanthropy, business, and corrupt police, extending well back into the nineteenth century. Long experience in the development of practices and structure was carried over, in part, and came to full fruition in the more profitable business of the Volstead era. The end of prohibition created a vacuum. The illicit appetite for gambling was a natural to supersede legalized liquor as an outlet for the peculiar talents of the mobsters.

Extortion, rackets, commercialized murder, strike breaking, the corruption of labor unions, drug peddling, and other crimes offered further scope for the versatility of the strong-arm boys and their bosses. The nation saw two decades of the struggles for supremacy between the gang leaders, during which time unsolved murder, mayhem, and property destruction were standard evidences of official inefficiency, indifference, and too often plain corruption. It has been estimated that racketeering now costs the nation some 15 billion dollars annually and, according to Harry Gross, the gamblers' payoff to corrupt police in New York City alone has run to well over a million a year.[23]

To a great extent the success of the mobsters must be attributed to public apathy and to attitudes actually hospitable to gangsterism. Stronger than our bent for puritanism, censorship, or the policing of unorthodox behavior is our insistence on personal freedom. Our social morality has been marked by a strange hypocrisy. We sadly shake our heads at the revelation of evil and enact an abundance of legislation against it, but we close our eyes to its prevalence and avoid vigorous enforcement of the law. There has thus developed a tradition of covert tolerance for the vices, a kind of moral atrophy. Steadfastly we refuse to legalize vice—legalization might be taken to imply "approval of evil"—and then vigorously to regulate and control it. Finally, we do not enforce our rigid prohibitions.[24] We prefer, while openly parading our virtues, both to prohibit and to practice our vices. This has inevitably provided an ideal situation for undercover exploitation through criminal alliances that are specialized in providing the prohibited pleasures at a price. Corruption of law enforcement and political agencies has been a necessary prerequisite to the success of such enterprises. This has not been too difficult because the prevailing moral hypocrisy is as apparent to the agencies of law enforcement as it is to the criminal.

In regard to this development a nice distinction has been drawn between the bootlegger of yesterday and the gambler of today and "ordinary

[23] See *New York Times*, May 19, 1951; June 21, 1952; Sept. 7, 1952.

[24] We have had sporadic experiments with legalized gambling. Today ordinary gambling is legal, of course, in Nevada, and many forms, such as the race track, slot machine, chance board, and wheels, are legal in other states. There is controversy concerning the relative effectiveness of complete prohibition as against controlled gambling. See the issue on gambling, *The Annals*, vol. 269, May, 1950, in which some of the problems and controversies appear.

criminals." The former are "like the rest of us," offering a service that the public wants. It is easy enough for the well-tailored, ostensibly respectable entrepreneur in vice and for the politician or the police official, as well, to rationalize his role in these activities. The money to be made is "easy." There is little real public support for the law. Indeed, respected citizens at all levels of social and economic status participate in criminal activities. The problem lies mainly in our hypocritical allegiance to opposed values. Formally, we disapprove of "sin," especially for others, but unofficially and privately we insist on having such pleasures as we may find in a free and individualistic society. It is this combination of repression and license and of puritanism and hedonism in our culture that facilitates the corruption associated with the vice traffic.

The involvement of political parties, public officials, and businessmen with underworld characters, though it has developed on a large scale in many cities, has remained fairly well concealed most of the time. Occasionally, by means of grand jury and commission investigations, some evidence has appeared of the extent of this insidious growth. When the results have not been suppressed, the public has been provoked to display its capacity for moral indignation, limited by a feeling of helplessness and apathy. At no time have the people evidenced any very profound or persistent agitation. Instead the response has been one of impotence and resignation in the face of powers that are apparently immune to public control.

Part Two

THE ADMINISTRATION OF JUSTICE

Chapter 10

OBJECTIVES OF SENTENCING AND CORRECTION

In times past, particularly among European criminologists, considerable thought has been devoted to the philosophical premises underlying penal law and to consequent inferences concerning appropriate correctional methods. There has been relatively little of this retrospective and introspective emphasis in modern American criminology. Attention has been given instead to experimentation in treatment methods and, to some extent, to empirical research into the causation of crime and the effects of correctional techniques. By and large, the penal law and its administration have proceeded on the basis of inherited and concealed assumptions concerning purpose and methods. This is unfortunate in the sense that it results in an instrumentation of justice that is characterized by confused purposes and conflicting methodologies.

Systems of justice and correction are largely developed through accretion. New ideas and approaches are introduced from time to time and are tacked onto the preexisting structure, little or no effort being made to relate the new to the old or to eliminate the incompatible elements in the evolving system of methods and ends. The total objective remains for the most part inexplicit and confused. The forces of formalization and institutionalization further promote the confusion. As something new is introduced into the system—whether it is, for example, the addition of indeterminate sentences to preexisting good-time laws, rehabilitative parole to punitive prison terms, or the recidivists' security detention to the ordinary criminals' imprisonment "at hard labor"—the innovation is superimposed upon the accumulated base, but the assimilation of elements is very incomplete. The incompatibles remain unreconciled but manage to persist, and thus the measures of law and correction are marked by paradox and inconsistency. The impact of particular devices is weakened or nullified and the loss, unfortunately, may be of methods that are useful as well as of those that are harmful. The going system works but usually in ways that are unintended toward goals that are neither simple nor precise. Moreover, testing the efficacy of a particular penal law or correctional device is peculiarly difficult because it becomes so inextricably mixed with policy

237

and measures that differ both normatively and temporally. Even remote vestiges of penal practice tend to endure, and it may be impossible as a result to discriminate between what is obsolete, what is essential, and what is desirable in modern correction. The criteria are undefined.

It is proposed here to consider the objectives of the administration of justice and of correctional treatment. It is clear that this consideration raises some of the central issues of criminology. We need goals that are quite clearly formulated and generally agreed upon in order that our procedures may be designed to serve them as effectively as possible. In so far as there is confusion of purpose, the ultimate achievement of social control in the community's interest—a sufficiently difficult task in any event—must be still harder to accomplish. Unfortunately, from the point of view of maximum efficiency in the achievement of goals, it appears that there should be no single or simple objective of justice and correction. Compromises are required by which to harmonize differing and partially incompatible ends. Moreover, to increase the difficulties somewhat further, it is not to be supposed that the same specific objectives apply to every type of offender. Such matters as age, prior social and criminal history, psychiatric or medical condition, and the nature of the offense involved should modify considerably the immediate aims as well as the methods of court action and correctional treatment. As a result, the functions of determining guilt and sentence and of applying correctional measures require a careful weighing of the social and individual interests that are involved in the particular instance in order to maximize the attainment of community protection and individual rights.[1] In effect, the problem is similar to that of democratic government generally; it is the extremely difficult one of harmonizing values and interests to the ultimate social good and of avoiding restraints upon individuals or groups that are unnecessary.

Underlying Motives of Treatment Decisions

Preliminary to considering the objectives that a correctional system may be designed to serve and the methods that may be employed to attain those objectives, it should be noted that underlying motives that are usually inexplicit and often unintended impede the search for reasonable goals. Highly subjective, emotional, irrational, and often unconscious elements are involved in the formulation and instrumentation of sanctions, in particular such affective responses as fear, anger, hate, jealousy, vin-

[1] Dean Roscoe Pound has observed that "the end of law is the adjustment or harmonizing of conflicting or overlapping desires and claims, so as to give effect to as much as possible with the least sacrifice. It is the same as the end of all social control. The legal order is but that part of social control which is achieved through the activity of politically ordered society." Pound distinguishes the variety of social interests protected by law: the general security, the security of social interests (e.g., domestic, religious, political, economic), the general morals, the conservation of social resources, the general progress, and the individual life (e.g., free self-assertion, individual opportunity). See *Criminal Justice in America*, 1930, pp. 3–11, 57–58.

dictiveness, sentimentality, and indulgence. These subjective motives may often be detected upon critical observation in "crisis legislation" that is designed to deal in *ad hoc* fashion with a particular apparently pressing problem, such as narcotic use and sale, sex offenses, kidnapping, gambling, disloyalty, recidivism, juvenile delinquency, etc.

Moreover, in their implementation of the law the concealed motivations of courts and treatment agencies often are not open to scrutiny or remedy. Emotional drives may move the judge or jury, the warden, the classification committee, the parole board, and treatment officers either for or against the individual offender or the type of offense for which he was convicted. Many an authority has been "conned" by an engaging psychopath; many have despised the sex deviate or favored the embezzler. Not uncommonly the feelings of the policy implementor are similar to those which provoked the legislation. However, as Kinsey has shown in relation to the sex offender specifically, the legislator, the judge, the prison guard, and the probation or parole officer may feel quite differently about the way a particular type of criminal should be treated. Preferences and prejudices may be linked with class, age, sex, race or religion, and innumerable other factors. Often the subjective motives of the legislator will differ from those of the judge and from those of treatment agents; the dispositions and treatment personnel experience personal contact and specific factual situations whereas members of the legislature deliberate rationally and impersonally. The point is that those whose function it is to determine the fate of the criminal may disguise and rationalize very easily the emotional motivations of legislation and of its administration; the underlying irrational elements are difficult to discern or eradicate.

While these nonobjective responses may occasionally serve desirable social ends—perhaps, for example, in sympathetic sentiments toward the child delinquent or in fear of the assaultative criminal—by and large the emotional reactions are a poor guide to sound action in the treatment of the offender. The most common response to the criminal, that of anger and fear, tends to provoke similar hostile responses on his part that increase the difficulties of attempting to provide effective treatment or community protection for him. It is true that the emotional climate prevailing in the community and among its representatives who are charged with handling criminals must inevitably set limits to both the rational objectives and the methods that may be employed at any particular time. It is important to recognize, however, that the visceral responses of treatment authorities tend to mislead both policy and action; they exaggerate or nullify the more reasoned purposes of the state. Quite possibly the passions and prejudices of those who handle the criminal do more to deflect correctional efforts than any other type of influence. It is particularly important, therefore, for those who make policy and for those who implement it to search the motives for their actions and to test those motives against the ultimate goals that they would seek.

PRIMARY OBJECTIVES OF SENTENCING AND CORRECTION

The author has suggested that there is a difference between emotional motives underlying correction and the more objective, rational, and purposive or goal-directed types of actuation. The purpose of controlling and regulating behavior in accordance with certain personal and property interests that the state would protect is implicit in all criminal laws. The protection of society is generally held to be the main ultimate object of criminal and penal law. This goal is too general, however, to inform authorities at all concretely of appropriate methods. Indeed, it is far too easy to rationalize inapposite correctional techniques and to disguise emotional responses in terms of social protection. This broad design of protecting society may be used to justify almost any prohibition and penalty that the state may wish to establish. And there is no way to test effectively the success of sanctions in accomplishing this goal. It has been traditional to assume that the most oppressive sanctions will provide the most complete protection; this assumption is rooted in part in the intense counteraggressions of society against those who defy the rules. Contemporary penal law continues to reflect these strong punitive responses, rationalized in terms of the community's welfare. However, the combined forces of modern humanitarianism, rationalism, and criminological positivism have been redirecting our efforts away from excessive and gratuitous severity of punishment for crime and toward individualized treatment designed to rehabilitate the particular offender.

Unfortunately, the discovery that harshness of punishment does not protect the community and the fact that there is a seeming polarity between the method of retaliatory brutality against criminals en masse and the ideal of clinical treatment of the individual offender has led some criminologists to a highly inaccurate assumption. The conclusion has become common, even among estimable thinkers, that we must either punish crime retributively or correct the individual offender by therapeutic and, implicitly, nonpunitive methods.[2] Many authorities hold, with some reason, that punishing crime retributively has proved a failure in provoking the criminal to his own revenge, but they maintain, therefore, that the only

---

[2] A contemporary report following a state correctional survey epitomized this simple sort of dichotomous analysis: "To sum up, then, the criminal law and its administration in the United States are in a state of transition. At the moment they are trying to serve two irreconcilable masters—retributive punishment and treatment for rehabilitation. Treatment is concerned with what a man is and may be helped to become, rather than with his record, offense, or length of sentence . . . the concept of treatment is a newcomer in the prison world and procedures to effect treatment are an afterthought. . . . Punishment is interested only in what an offender has done. Treatment has to know why he offends. . . . As to purpose, spirit, and personnel, we have pointed out that retributive punishment has long dominated the thinking and program of our prisons and of the administration of the criminal law generally."

sound alternative is, eschewing punishment, to espouse a wholly clinical and positivistic approach to the offender. The error here, it appears, is not in finding social retribution as such a failure and is not in emphasizing a need for rehabilitative treatment of the criminal; instead the error lies in concluding too simply that these are the sole alternatives and that a single purposing of correction is feasible.

Let us now consider the rationale for correctional policy in larger perspective. It appears that there are five main ends that justice and correction may seek and that for many offenders several of these play a role. A major difficulty in policy formulation is to determine in relation to a particular criminal which objectives should control and by what methods such objectives may best be implemented. The major goals are *retribution, deterrence, incapacitation, individual intimidation,* and *reformation.* No one of these, it will be argued here, can be adopted to the exclusion of the others if the purpose is to protect society fully. On the other hand, the reasonableness and feasibility of a particular objective may vary considerably from one type of offender to another. This differential purposiveness will be discussed in more detail as we consider each of the objects of treatment policy.

Retribution

Retribution or social retaliation, though persistently criticized by modern advocates of a progressive penology, continues to be a major ingredient of our penal law and of our correctional system. Through the history of civilization it appears to have been the most widely prevalent and continuously persistent correctional motive, though it has taken numerous forms. The retaliatory response of the victim and of the community to the criminal's offense is a prepotent force with which any system of justice and correction must reckon. However much progressive and academic penology may attack retribution as being ethically indefensible, it remains and probably will continue to be the normal and near-universal response to atrocious crime.[3] Law and custom have lent firm support to the primitive psychological reaction of the victim and the community. More than this, various philosophical doctrines have been advanced to justify retributive punishment for crime. The rationale rests mainly on the doctrine of free

---

[3] One of the few vocal advocates of retributive punishment among contemporary scholars is Professor Jerome Hall. See his *Principles of Criminal Law,* 1947, especially pp. 157–169, 526–539. The principle of retribution was formulated in the *lex talionis,* the Mosaic doctrine expressed in *Deuteronomy,* 19:21: "Thine eye shall not pity, but life shall go for life, eye for eye, tooth for tooth, hand for hand, foot for foot." Renewed impetus was given to the retributive doctrine in the last century by the systematic exposition of free-will and punitive theory by Kant and Hegel. *Gibbons v. Gibbons,* 197 Misc. 962, 94 N.Y.S. 2d 9, 14 (1949), reaffirms the purpose of retributive punishment: "to make one suffer for what wrong he has done." Compare Henry Weihofen, *The Urge to Punish,* 1956.

will and moral guilt: the assumption that man is at least partially free to choose between alternatives of behavior and that his deliberate wrongdoing should be requited by penalties. This ideology is rooted very deeply in Judeo-Christian religion and in much of the philosophies that have affected Western thinking. It will be discussed in some detail below.

Few modern criminologists approve of the principle of retributive punishment and many during the past two generations have devoted their major persuasive efforts to replacing social revenge by reformation as *the* purpose of criminal law and correction. However, some have noted that an impartial administration of retributive penalties by the state does satisfy the public sense of justice and may help to neutralize, though at the expense of the hapless criminal, the sadistic and aggressive impulses in the community. In the public mind the man who rapes, kidnaps, murders, or steals "deserves" to be punished with severity, without regard to whether that treatment will make him better or worse or whether it will deter him or others from crime. The unfortunate consequences of this moral vengeance are believed to outweigh the limited good it may entail. As a practical matter, however, it appears likely that the effects of a retributive legal and moral tradition will persist for a long time, though mixed increasingly with other purposes of correctional treatment.[4]

It may be noted that in the fixing of retributive punishment the assessment of moral guilt will generally result in most severe penalties for those who have violated the taboos that are highly cherished in the community. Consequently, the murderer and the rapist, for example, would receive the harshest punishments and he who merely attempts the crime should be as severely handled. A very nice problem is raised about certain types of offenders where the moral standards and emotional responses are in transition: What are the just deserts of the homosexual? The exhibitionist? The embezzler? White-collar criminals generally?

Appropriate Goals of Sentencing and Correction

Much that has been written in recent years notwithstanding, punishment may be inflicted by the state with objectives that are neither moralistic nor emotional. In fact, there are two very important objectives of punishment that society cannot afford to neglect. These objectives are obvious enough but are too commonly ignored in the comments of positivistic criminologists. No single fact should be clearer to the criminologist than the necessity of preventing the dangerous criminal from repeating his offenses by

[4] Elsewhere the author has remarked: " . . . the doctrine of moral responsibility has been woven so tight into the fabric of the criminal and penal law that it can be reworked only very slowly, and then only for the most part by an embroidery at the edge that is ill patterned to the cloth. Ideas of partial responsibility, of irresistible impulses, psychopathic personality, and other extenuating circumstances have come to mitigate the full rigors of a retributive justice, but the ancient rationale persists as the essential design." *Contemporary Correction*, 1951, p. 7.

coercive repressive measures, even if these measures increase the difficulty in effecting his reformation. The *incapacitation* and *intimidation* of the repetitive delinquent, sometimes termed "individual prevention," is essential. The community cannot await the possible reformation of criminals living under conditions of freedom while they continue to inflict injury upon vital social interests. More controversial but certainly no less important is the need for *deterrence*, "general prevention," of potential criminals who may be dissuaded from crime by the threat and the administration of penalties. These repressive objectives, while they may be considered unfortunate limitations upon society's reformative efforts with the criminal, are no less essential ingredients in any sound and sane system of sanctions.[5] The place of each of these broad purposes in penology will be considered in a little more detail. As will be noted, they contribute to the confusion in correctional policy in that they imply somewhat different approaches to the offender.

General Prevention: Deterrence

The strongest competitor, thus far, to the principle of retribution for criminal guilt is the doctrine of deterrence, promulgated by the Classical school of criminology. The Classical movement started as a result of revulsion against the excesses that were practiced under the wide discretion of the pre-Classical judges to mete out individualized, retributive punishments. In the views of Bentham (1748–1832), Beccaria (1738–1794), Romilly (1757–1818), and others of their time, the objective of punishment should be to deter offenders and the severity of penalties should be no greater than necessary to prevent the occurrence of crime. Bentham's hedonistic calculus, proposing to determine the measure of pain in punishment required to overbalance the promised pleasure of a criminal act, presented a problem of accounting as difficult perhaps as that entailed in measuring moral guilt, but the emphasis upon minimizing the infliction of gratuitous suffering was, from a humanitarian point of view, a useful con-

---

[5] In *People v. Gowasky*, 219 App. Div. 19, 24, 25, 219 N.Y.S. 373 (1st Dep't. 1926), *aff'd.* 244 N.Y. 451, 155 N.E. 737 (1927), the court in upholding the constitutionality of the Baumes Law said: "suspension of judgment during good behavior works for the rescue and reformation of the individual who has been led to embark upon a criminal career, but the laws enacted for the reformation of the criminal should be administered with caution and circumspection to the end that the deterrent effect of the punishment meted out be not lost"; and that "the proper office of a penal statute is for the suppression of crime. Penalties are not provided as punishment for the individual who has gone wrong. Their imposition is alone justified for the effect the punishment may have upon the convict in preventing him from continuance in crime and in teaching him that 'the way of the transgressor is hard.' But the still greater effect to be attained is the deterrent effect the sentence may have upon those who may be inclined to follow the criminal course upon which the convict has embarked." Quoted in Orvill C. Snyder, "The New York Penal Law and Theories of Punishment," *Brooklyn L. Rev.,* vol. 21, no. 1, p. 17.

tribution to changing penal policy. Moreover, the methods and goals of deterrence implied a shift from a moral-metaphysical to a pragmatic basis of sanctions. A system based upon such a policy would apply sentences and treatment according to a definite and uniform scheme; though the penalties might be in some measure arbitrary, this would avoid the impossible task of determining the quantum of moral guilt and applying punishment apposite to the imponderables therein involved.

In the evolution of law, particularly of penal law, while new philosophies and measures are added, little is wholly lost. As in other phases of cultural change, there is a selective adaptation that blends the old with the new, with modifications of both. Certainly the moral-religious leaven of retribution and vengeance have exerted a persisting influence on modern penology, however much they have been deprecated by most criminologists of the twentieth century. With the spread of Classical doctrine, however, deterrence became for a time a very generally accepted rationale for criminal sanctions. The view prevailed that penalties are more just as well as more humane if they are definite, ascertainable, uniform, and applied without vindictive emotion. Moreover, the purpose of deterring crime has clearly been a more practical task, quite appropriate to the secular function of the state, than the older effort of political authorities to read the mind and measure the wrath of God. The growth of the deterrent doctrine represented a highly significant step, therefore, in distinguishing sacred and secular institutions and their functions, in establishing a standard of equality of treatment as a criterion of justice, and in pointing the state's objective to the prevention of crime rather than to the mere punishment of wrongdoing. Retributive and vengeful punishment, as distinguished from deterrent justice, has persisted largely in relation to forms of crimes and vice that have a strong moral pull at the emotions and in the behavior of those judges, correctional workers, and police who enjoy a large component of moral indignation. The offenses involved, whether or not they should be criminal in terms of the feasibility of effective political control, are characterized by the widest variability, and often the least effectuality, in enforcement, adjudication, and sentencing. This is the case particularly in times when the moral issues involved lack the support of uniformity and consensus of opinion and when doubts are widely held about the desirability of official action in the judicial-correctional field to control or remedy these problems.

As in the case of retribution, deterrence has come to be derogated in some quarters, particularly among those who subscribe to a positivistic criminology or "the new penology." The tenets of a clinical and individualized philosophy of treatment may be so interpreted that they condemn punishment in any form and, indeed, have been used by some authorities to suggest that all punishment is retributive and that the criminal law and its penalties do not deter. Since this issue is one of vital importance and, in the author's view, deterrence is a basic if not the primary function of the state's sanctions, these questions of deterrence and punishment must be considered in more detail here.

As an argument for the abolition of the deterrent doctrine, it is often maintained that neither the threat nor application of penalties does prevent crime. This position reflects the simplistic notion, too commonly prevailing in matters of social action, that nothing has been achieved merely because not everything is accomplished that we should like. It is sometimes said that high crime rates prove that sanctions do not deter or that penalties actually invite the crimes of men who seek punishment to dissolve their feelings of guilt. With tiresome frequency the illustration is cited of the pickpockets who actively plied their trade in the shadow of the gallows from which their fellow knaves were strung. These assertions have a superficial relevance but they do not dispose of the issue by any means.

Persons with a will to believe in the efficacy of an exclusively individualistic and positivistic correctional system often quote the words of Warden Kirchwey. His patent oversimplifications of man's behavioral motivations should be noted, for this sort of loose thinking and naïve criminological idealism pervert the ends of correction:[6]

[6] See George F. Kirchwey, "Crime and Punishment," *J. Crim. L.,* vol. 1, pp. 718–734, 1911. A good deal of contemporary writing on the purposes of penology reflects this same sort of complete rejection of deterrence and, quite commonly, of punishment for any purpose. Ordinarily such statements, whether they are made by sociologists or psychologists, are absolute, dogmatic, and highly oversimplified. They display considerable confusion concerning the issues involved. The following statements are fairly typical: "It is plain that, however futile it may be, social revenge is the only honest, straightforward, and logical justification for punishing criminals. The claim of deterrence is belied by both history and logic. History shows that severe punishments have never reduced criminality to any marked degree. It is obvious to anyone familiar with the activities of criminals that the argument for deterrence cannot be logically squared with the doctrine of the free moral agent, upon which the whole notion of punishment is based. If a man is free to decide as to his conduct, and is not affected by his experiences, he cannot be deterred from crime by the administration of any punishment, however severe." Harry E. Barnes and Negley K. Teeters, *New Horizons in Criminology,* 1951, p. 338. "The belief that punishment protects society from crime by deterring would-be law breakers will not stand up before our new understanding of human behavior." John Ellingston, *Protecting Our Children from Criminal Careers,* 1948, p. 43. Compare the comment of the eminent British forensic psychiatrist, Sir Norwood East: "In the present context *deterrence* may be regarded as the effect upon potential criminals of the legal treatment of actual criminals. Unfortunately we lack the means of assessing its importance. But it is not merely an intuitive speculation, and its practical value cannot be denied. Merciers' statement still deserves consideration: 'If punishment is to deter from crime, it need not be severe, but it must be enough to render the crime unprofitable. It need be no more than this, but it must be certain, and it must be speedy.' " *Society and the Criminal,* 1951, p. 265. The Norwegian educator Johs Andenaes, in a highly perceptive article on deterrence, quotes the British authority Sir James Fitzjames Stephen: "Some men, probably, abstain from murder because

It [punishment] cannot deter the mentally defective, they cannot appreciate their danger. It cannot deter the insane, their minds are too distorted to reason. It cannot deter the anti-social, they are at war with society and the danger but gives pleasing zest to the contest. It cannot deter the thoughtful and deliberate, for they have no intention of getting caught. Nor can it deter the impulsive, for impulse is always quicker than reason. Whom then will it deter? Why just you and me—those of us who have high standards and much personal pride, and who are law-abiding anyway.

It should be unnecessary here to analyze the partial truth and the large margin of fallacy in each of the assertions contained in this attack upon deterrence. In effect it says by implication, as do the majority of strictures against a deterrent correctional policy, that men are not moved by fear of the physical and psychological discomfitures threatened by the penal law. The error here lies in some part in the failure to recognize that the impact of significant deterrent influences in human motivation (and this is true as well, of course, of impelling or evocative influences) is largely unconscious and emotional, drawing upon deep-rooted fears and aspirations.

It is true, certainly, that the Classical doctrine of deterrence appears crudely oversimple in the light of modern conceptions of human behavior. In terms of reasonable goals for today it proposed to accomplish both too much and too little. This doctrine of deterrence was substantially more sound, however, than the position taken by those who deny any preventive effect to criminal sanctions. It is maintained here that the penal law and its application do in fact deter; indeed, with the declining efficacy of other forms of social control, it must be relied upon increasingly to maintain standards of behavior that are essential to the survival and security of the community. A complete failure of legal prevention cannot be inferred from the serious crimes committed by a small per cent of the population any more than can its success by the law obedience of the great preponderance of men.[7] The matter is not so simple.

---

they fear that if they committed murder they would be hanged. Hundreds of thousands abstain from it because they regard it with horror. One great reason why they regard it with horror is that murderers are hanged with the hearty approbation of all reasonable men." "General Prevention—Illusion or Reality." *J. Crim. L.* vol. 43, no. 2, p. 189, July-August, 1952. See also Edwin H. Sutherland and Donald R. Cressey, *Principles of Criminology,* 1955, pp. 288–290; E. A. Ross, *Social Control,* 1916, p. 125; Tappan, *Contemporary Correction,* chap. 1; Henry M. Hart, Jr., "The Aims of the Criminal Law," *Law and Contemp. Probs.,* vol. 23, pp. 401–442, summer, 1958.

[7] Professor Andenaes has observed that, as compared with the enormous amount of data that has been amassed on the characteristics of offenders, we know very little about the psychology of obedience to law: " . . . discussion often gives way to cock-sure general statements like 'I believe (or I do not believe) in general prevention.' Much has been written about general prevention; much talented effort has been spent in exploring its operation and importance. But the empirical data are still

One difficulty with the Classical theory was its implication that prevention occurred merely through repression by fear. Deterrence may be and, indeed, it commonly is defined in this limited sense. It appears in any event that group intimidation is the foundation of deterrence. General prevention is also served, however, by the educative-moralizing function of the law in strengthening the public's moral code. This involves the introjection of conscious and unconscious controls against violations. In some countries, notably the Scandinavian, considerable stress is placed upon this moralizing task of the penal law. Furthermore, the criminal and penal law, in providing standards of conduct and penalties, stimulates the habit of law-abiding conduct: it aids in the conditioning of accepted norms. Professor Andenaes suggests that the achievement of inhibition and habit formation are more important preventives to crime than the conscious fear of punishment itself.[8] We would define deterrence as the term is generally used here today as "the preventive effect which actual or threatened punishment of offenders has upon potential offenders."[9]

Not all individuals are equally deterred by the threat of the possible application of a particular penalty. Some types of crimes are not so well subject to repressive control as others. Those offenses against the person that involve a strong emotional element can less easily be constrained through the imposition of rational sanctions because the offender does not contemplate the consequences of his explosive acts.[10] The rare masochist or "criminal out of a sense of guilt" may seek punishment, as the Freudians have so often reiterated. Some hardened criminals do intend to avoid apprehension and may succeed. Certain types of individuals are challenged by threats and others are compelled to crime though they are aware of the consequences. All the pathological exceptions that may be enumerated, however—and they constitute in sum only a small minority of the population—do not refute the basic elements of ordinary human motivation. *Man*

---

lacking. If any attempt has been made to include it at all, it has usually—as in this paper—occurred by the use of chance observations, plus ordinary psychological theories. I believe we can make some progress in this way. But we shall not have firm ground to stand on before a systematic investigation is made into the effect of penal law and its enforcement on the citizen's behavior, and into the interrelation between the legal system and the other factors which govern behavior." *Op. cit.,* p. 197. (Quoted by permission.)

[8] *Ibid.,* pp. 179–180.

[9] John C. Ball, "The Deterrence Concept in Criminology and Law," *J. Crim. L.,* vol. 46, no. 3, p. 347, September-October, 1955.

[10] It is easy to exaggerate the role of unconquerable impulse in crime, however. Andenaes makes a pertinent observation in regard to rape: "That rape, on the other hand [as contrasted with incest], is a crime not alien to the normal human personality, can be verified in times of war and occupation. In an occupation army where discipline in this matter is lax, the incidence of rape is commonly high. If discipline is strict, on the other hand, as with the German army of occupation in Norway during the war, the crime hardly ever occurs." *Op. cit.,* p. 189.

is attracted by pleasure and repelled by pain. His habits are developed, in fair part at least, by the search for the one and the avoidance of the other.

It cannot well be doubted that the deterrent efficacy of penal law varies widely with individuals, their social class, age, life, experiences, intelligence, moral training, and other factors.[11] For some men who have never been in trouble with the law, the possible loss of repute through discovery in a crime is a sufficient restraint even if the likelihood of apprehension and prosecution is small and whether or not discovery would result in penal incarceration. Some individuals who have experienced strong moral training in their early years would feel too great a discomfort in defying moral or legal norms to undertake a crime, quite aside from specific pains and penalties in the law. Even among the insane and mentally defective a great majority conform to the law through their training and fear of consequences. While it is true that some men who have "done time" for a crime have *relatively* little to lose in the way of reputation and self-respect if they are convicted again, the probability that they will again suffer the frustrations of penal confinement if they persist in criminal behavior appears to be an effective intimidation to many.[12] In a real sense they have "learned a lesson" the hard way. The percentage of persistent and non-deterrable criminals in the population is small. On the other hand, with the conspicuous confusion of values that marks our age, surely equivocal and conflicting personal moralities characterize a very large proportion of the population.[13] This mass of men requires and responds in varying measure to the minatory controls of penal law, though perhaps less out

[11] John C. Ball has pointed to the need for objective empirical research on deterrence, relating deterrence to appropriate variables with which it is associated. He suggests that the following are significant: (1) the social structure and value system under consideration, (2) the particular population in question, (3) the type of law being upheld, (4) the form and magnitude of the prescribed penalty, (5) the certainty of apprehension and punishment, and (6) the individual's knowledge of the law as well as the prescribed punishment, and his definition of the situation in relation to these factors. *Op. cit.,* pp. 347–355.

[12] The matter of individual prevention through the intimidation of the offender is discussed in greater detail below.

[13] Andenaes comments on the limitations of moral inhibitions in controlling behavior: "Strong moral and social inhibitions against the criminal act appear alongside regard for the penal code. Now the question is: are not these moral and social inhibitions enough in themselves to keep most people from committing thefts, frauds, and so on? And then: will these moral and social inhibitions retain their strength if the risk of punishment is removed . . . ? The question here is not whether you or I would remain law-abiding even if there were no 'switch behind the back.' The question is whether there is not a fairly large group on the moral borderline who might go wrong, and whether they might not in turn draw others with them. What we are concerned with is, of course, a long-term process, where the full effect of a weakening in the judicial reaction to crime will not be felt before the passage of a generation or more . . . . Likewise we must not overlook the fact that the social reaction is connected in many ways to the judicial. This means not

of a fear of prison itself than fear of the accompanying loss of status in the community.

The law has itself recognized in some measure the variations in deterrability. Children or insane and feeble-minded adults who cannot understand or reason sufficiently are exempt from specifically criminal penalties. In some jurisdiction certain compulsive neurotics are spared under the rules of insanity as a defense. Similarly, somnambulism, coercion, hypnotic suggestion, and extremes of intoxication have been held to negate criminal guilt. It may well be, as is indicated in another chapter, that the defenses based upon psychological deviations should be extended further when appropriate standards can be constructed, but under present practice in the administration of justice the effort is made, so far as presently available criteria permit, to apply standards exempting from sanctions those who cannot be expected to understand and adapt to the official norms. Moreover, under the rather wide discretion permitted in modern sentencing practice, the state endeavors to apply its penalties most vigorously to those who clearly can but will not conform and with relative lenience to those whose violations are in some measure adventitious or negligent and to those who display penitence and are not deeply corrupted.

It is not to be supposed, therefore, that all men can or will be constrained by penal sanctions. And among those who do obey the law, this conformity cannot be attributed entirely to threatened official penalties. As we have noted, mores and tradition inculcated in the home, school, and church are powerful molders of behavior and attitudes. To a considerable extent they overlap and reinforce the legal standards.[14] In the nature of things the influence of the unofficial and official controls is not severable when the rule governing behavior is the same. It is absurd, however, to suggest that "where the mores are adequate, the law is unnecessary," for in this sense the mores are never wholly adequate: they do not have identical coverage with the law and the mere threat of disapproval or ostracism

---

simply that general behavior with regard to a category of acts is affected by the law's attitude toward them but also that it would be much easier to keep one's secret and thus avoid all social reprobation, if one did not have to consider the risk of their being brought to public notice through criminal prosecution." *Op. cit.,* p. 186. (Quoted by permission.)

The prevailing moral confusion among some of the intellectual elite as well as in the general public was well demonstrated in the television quiz scandals of 1959 and 1960. The fact that a large number of sophisticated individuals perjured themselves revealed an apparent contempt for law as well as morality.

[14] " . . . it seems likely that laws which reinforce existing mores are apt to be more effective than those which prohibit behavior not regulated by group sentiment. . . . Conversely, the fact that a considerable number of persons violate a general preventive measure is not in itself sufficient evidence to demonstrate its failure as a deterrent force. For it may well be that abolishment of the measure would result in general violation of the law." Ball, *op. cit.,* p. 350.

is insufficient to deter some men.[15] The further contention that "where the mores are inadequate, the law is ineffective" is similarly a seductive half-truth, and it is a more dangerous one in its disillusioning and inaccurate implications. Where the mores are inadequate, the impelling force of the criminal law must be the stronger to protect substantial rights and interests in the community. It appears, indeed, that this weakening of informal controls has characterized the situation in which we live; with the secularization of a mass society and with the decline of primary controls, standards must be set and enforced by the law or they will not be established at all. The task becomes more difficult as the state loses much of the supporting strength of familial and neighborhood controls, but it is a counsel of despair to maintain that in consequence we must descend to chaos. As Justice Holmes has very well maintained, there do exist "bad men of the law" who are not sufficiently guided by moral ideals and who require the stronger threats of deprivation that the state may apply. Indeed there are many men today who, if they had only to fear their primary group associates without a fixing of criminal status, would soon make off with their neighbors' property and wives.

Penalties designed to deter crime should be gauged so far as possible to the degree of social danger that is represented by the type of crime and by the repetition of crime. Maximum penalties must be sufficiently high to threaten a potentially severe punishment. From the point of view of deterrent objectives such highly dangerous crimes as murder, rape, and other brutal aggressions require heavy maximum penalties. On the other hand, it appears that minor sexual deviations and personal vices—however morally atrocious they may be to Christendom—offer little threat to the community and either should not be made criminal or, if they are, should require relatively small deterrent penalties.[16] It is particularly in this area

[15] In this regard see William Seagle, *The Quest for Law,* 1941, chap. 1. Sumner's analysis of the relationship between mores and law has given rise to considerable oversimplification and confusion in sociology in relation to the processes of social control and, in particular, the effectiveness of the mores.

[16] J. Michael and H. Wechsler, in *Criminal Law and Its Administration,* 1940, suggests that "the determination of the kinds of behavior to be made criminal involves three major problems: (1) What sorts of conduct is it both desirable and possible to deter; (2) what sorts indicate that persons who behave in those ways are dangerously likely to engage in socially undesirable behavior in the future; (3) will the attempt to prevent particular kinds of undesirable behavior by the criminal law do less good, as measured by the success of such efforts, than harm, as measured by their other harmful results." P. 11. Roscoe Pound has pointed out that "No legal machinery of which we have any knowledge is equal to doing everything which we might like to achieve through social control by law. Some duties which morally are of the highest moment are too intangible for legal enforcement. . . . Likewise, many cases involve serious and undoubted wrongs to individuals and yet may be too small for the ponderous and expensive machinery of prosecution." *Criminal Justice in America,* 1930, p. 62.

where criteria of morality and of social danger lead to differing conclusions that emotional-retributive impulses will most commonly differ from objective-deterrent needs of the community. Our legislatures and courts react intensely against certain morally offensive but socially rather innocuous behavior; this reaction is clear evidence of persisting retributive responses where deterrence is no great problem. One is led to the irresistible conclusion that the establishment of one-day-to-life sentences for sexual psychopaths has been based more upon retributive than either deterrent or rehabilitative purposiveness. Certainly these statutes have not provided curative treatment measures.[17] It is important for the legislature, court, and correctional agency to explore its purpose in order to avoid unnecessary excesses of punishment.

It appears that the certainty of discovery and punishment is a more significant element in general prevention than the severity of penalties. Our penal law loses deterrent effect because of the frequency with which offenders escape discovery, arrest, or conviction. This is illustrated by the ineffectuality in our experience of laws that have lacked vigorous public enforcement, e.g., prostitution, fornication, adultery, gambling, and other vice legislation.[18] Andenaes offers striking proof of the significance of policing for some types of crime:[19]

> In Denmark the Germans arrested the entire Danish police force in September 1944. During the rest of the occupation the policing was done by an improvised and unarmed watch corps, which was all but ineffectual except when the criminal was caught red-handed. . . . While in the whole of 1939 only ten cases of robbery were reported in Copenhagen, the figure by 1943 had risen to ten a month, as a result of wartime conditions. After the action against the police the figure quickly rose to over 100 a month and continued to rise. Theft insurance benefits quickly rose ten-fold and more. The fact that punishment was greatly increased for criminals who were caught and brought before the court could not prevent this. Crimes like embezzlement and fraud,

---

[17] See Tappan, *The Habitual Sex Offender,* Report to the New Jersey Legislature, 1950; "Sex Offender Laws and Their Administration," *Fed. Prob.,* vol. 14, no. 3, pp. 32–37.

[18] Failure of enforcement may indicate that the legislation itself is undesirable because it is not in accord with public and official attitudes or because it is unenforceable. On the other hand failure may simply reveal the need for more effective policing and prosecution. As is noted elsewhere, some types of crime (theft, for example), because of their low visibility or wide prevalence, cannot be controlled very effectively.

Referring to Norwegian experience in the enforced registration of bank accounts and securities in 1945, Professor Andenaes observes that on the basis of the registration it appeared that almost everyone evaded taxes who could do so without risk; this is a striking confirmation of the importance of policing for general prevention. He observes: "If there were such policing as to produce a risk of 25 per cent in making false tax declarations, tax evasion on a grand scale would be practically eliminated." *Op. cit.,* p. 185.

[19] *Ibid.* p. 187.

where the perpetrator is generally known, do not seem to have increased notably.

Some further loss in the deterrent efficacy of the law is occasioned by the increasing use of minor sanctions in place of imprisonment and by failure to prosecute offenders.[20] This has occurred on a considerable scale in our mitigative measures for dealing with young offenders, even in some jurisdictions to the age of 20 and higher. The question is raised of how far we can safely go to serve the ends of rehabilitation in our lenience with the young adult. Attorney General Aulie of Norway has pointed to a similar problem in that country. Lecturing before the Association of Norwegian Criminologists in 1947, he commented upon the gang activities of young offenders:[21]

We know from experience that when members of the gang are released after questioning pending the winding up of investigation, the young people almost invariably flock back together, usually with the idea of planning new escapades. They regard the intervention of the police as a temporary inconvenience, of negligible importance. They count on prosecution being waived for those with clean records, or at worst their being given suspended sentences. And they have reasons to believe that a dozen or so new thefts on top of those already counted against them will not make much difference if they are discovered.

The losses to deterrence observed above must be balanced against the ameliorative thrust of a system of justice and correction in which the protection and, wherever possible, the reformation of the individual are stressed. Unfortunately, our experts too often argue either for greater mitigations covering wider areas in the name of rehabilitation or for more severity of punishment in the interest of prevention, without solid effort on either side to balance the objectives or to weigh the consequences.

Unfortunately, little meaningful empirical research has been directed toward discovering the effectiveness of punishment in achieving either deterrent or other ends.[22] Norval Morris of Australia has investigated the relationship between length of prison confinement and duration of time before reconviction in a study of confirmed recidivists; he found no significant correlation between "time in" and "time out."[23] This may be taken,

[20] The point is illustrated by this newspaper account: "A Detroit mother was jailed today for five to fourteen years for embezzling $19,000, some of which she had used to further her daughter's hopes of a Hollywood career. Mrs. B. H. was scolded by Recorder's Judge for 'openly boasting you would get probation.' He sent her to the Detroit House of Correction. The daughter, 19 years old, is currently in a Hollywood television show."

[21] Quoted by Andenaes, *op. cit.,* p. 195. He comments, "If this observation is correct, it shows with all desirable clarity that the humanizing of penal practice must be kept within certain limits if it is not to lead to an undermining of respect for law and authority." *Op. cit.,* p. 195.

[22] See Ball, *loc. cit.*

[23] *The Habitual Criminal,* 1951, pp 368–370.

at least tentatively, to indicate that among long-term repeaters the duration of their imprisonment is not correlated with the length of their conformity as measured by time of reconviction. This study provides a refreshing departure from the traditional value judgments that are encountered in literature relating to deterrence. Within the purposes of that research, however, it could tell us nothing about general deterrence and little about individual prevention in the criminal population.

The Death Penalty and Deterrence

A considerable amount of material has been published both in the United States and abroad on capital punishment. This has confused the general issue relating to deterrence, unfortunately. Moreover, the available data are not very helpful. It has been customary to compare the homicide rates in states employing the death penalty with those where life imprisonment only is used.[24] Homicide rates are considerably higher in the former. The same observation has been made in European countries.[25] Moreover, the shift from one mode of punishment to the other by legislative changes both here and abroad has apparently had no significant effect in itself on homicide rates. Hence, it has been generally concluded that the death penalty has little or no greater effect than life imprisonment as a deterrent.[26] This may well be true. Several observations should be made, however, on the data employed and their significance:

1. The capital punishment issue provides little or no enlightment on the more general problem of the feasibility of general and individual prevention of crime. The question relating to the death penalty is whether the existence of such legislation is more of a deterrent to murder (or other capital crimes) than is life imprisonment.

2. To secure anything like a definitive answer to the narrow question of relative deterrence would require the holding constant of a number of related variables, and this has not been done.[27]

3. Murder is one of the poorest crimes by which to test deterrence; it is universally recognized that this offense is most frequently an emotional and impulsive crime, rarely subject to control by reason or by fear of consequences. Often the victim is closely associated with the offender. Commonly the crime is committed by psychological deviates or under the pressure of unusual circumstances.

[24] See Karl F. Schuessler, "The Deterrent Influence of the Death Penalty," *The Annals,* vol. 284, pp. 54–63, November, 1952. See also Edwin H. Sutherland, "Murder and the Death Penalty," *J. Crim. L.,* vol. 15, pp. 522–529, 1925, and George B. Vold, "Can the Death Penalty Prevent Crime?" *Prison J.* pp. 3–8, October, 1932.

[25] Thorsten Sellin, Memorandum on Capital Punishment, prepared for the British Royal Commission on Capital Punishment, 1951; *The Death Penalty,* American Law Institute, 1959.

[26] Schuessler, *op. cit.,* p. 56.

[27] Schuessler, *loc. cit.*

4. States that do not use capital punishment (Michigan, Wisconsin, Minnesota, Maine, Rhode Island, North Dakota) and foreign countries (Scandinavian and the Netherlands) are jurisdictions where the problem of crime in general and of murder in particular has been relatively small. On the other hand, Southern states that are characterized by crimes of violence against the person and populous states with high general offense rates have retained the penalty. The differences in homicide rates appear to reflect differentials in age, social class, ethnic background, community size, and season rather than death penalty legislation. Generalizations about the role of the death penalty have confused cause and effect.

5. The statistics ordinarily employed to bulwark the arguments on capital punishment leave much to be desired. Homicide rates drawn from the U.S. Census Bureau include justifiable and excusable homicides and some of those from the *Uniform Crime Reports* combine murder with nonnegligent manslaughter. *National Prisoner Statistics* does not differentiate degrees of murder. Thus we lack information on the number of crimes prosecuted to which capital penalties might be applicable. Such homicide data as we have are ordinarily applied quite crudely in comparing states (or sometimes adjacent states) that provide the death penalty to those that do not rather than to the frequency with which that penalty is actually applied. In a closer analysis of the data, however, Schuessler has recently found "a slight tendency for the homicide rate to diminish as the probability of execution increases."[28]

6. It is quite apparent that juries are less willing to convict and prosecutors more ready to take a lesser plea in states where capital punishment is used. It is clear that the death penalty is rarely applied in cases where it is applicable. (In 1950, 1,556 prisoners were received in state and Federal correctional institutions for murder and 82 prisoners were executed.[29]) Thus, it does not fulfill one important condition of effective deterrence: a high degree of certainty of application. The very general nullification of the intent of the law reduces the efficacy of the death penalty as an instrument of general prevention.

7. There are other considerations relevant to the controversy over the death penalty that seem more important than the question of the relative deterrent value of that sanction:

   a. In the light of the well-authenticated errors that occur in murder convictions of the innocent and the infliction of the supreme penalty, should the death penalty be condemned by reason of its irrevocability?

   b. Is deliberate homicide by the state itself ethically justifiable in a nation where a high premium is put on human life?

   c. Can other equally effective and less drastic measures be employed to prevent the occurrence of murder?

   d. Is the obvious superiority of the death penalty as an incapacitative measure a sufficient justification for its employment?

   e. Should the very large saving made possible by capital punishment, where it is applied, weigh heavily in its favor as against the great costliness of life imprisonment?

[28] Schuessler, *op. cit.*, p. 28.

[29] *Prisoners in State and Federal Institutions,* 1950, National Prisoner Statistics, 1954, tables 7, 8, and 44.

f. Is the death penalty, shorn today of its former more savage accompaniments, truly more cruel or less justifiable ethically than life imprisonment?

It may be clear that a resolution of the complex of problems noted above must be made in the last analysis on the basis of ethical and emotional reactions rather than on the basis of definitive empirical evidence. The trend over the past generation has been in the right direction (as conceived within the ethical scruples of the author) of gradually diminishing employment of the death penalty. Only one state today makes that sanction mandatory for murder. The trend appears to be toward further curtailment. Would its retention on the statute books be justified for its educational-moralizing value as the ultimate penalty if it were rarely to be exercised, and then exercised only when the offender appeared to be a continuing threat to the lives of others?

Individual Prevention: Incapacitation, Intimidation, and Reformation

Perhaps the incapacitative function of punishment has received little attention in the literature in part because the necessity for it is so obvious. Measures of quarantine are surely necessary in correction to prevent the repetition of crimes by dangerous offenders. In some of the states traditional penology has provided more than generously for this function in the form of maximum-security institutions and sentences that, as compared with other nations, are excessively long. England and various other countries have specifically recognized the need for incapacitative treatment by employing a "dual-track system," under which recidivists spend an initial term in punitive prison confinement; this term is followed by a period of theoretically nonpunitive "preventive detention," when their privileges as prisoners are considerably increased and when, theoretically, they are not being punished. While nothing closely analogous to this rather artificial distinction in treatment may be found in the United States, in nearly all states our recidivist laws provide for extended confinement and, in a number of jurisdictions, for life terms for the third or fourth felony offender.[30] Moreover, even for the single offense, statutes ordinarily provide sufficient range so that our courts may sentence according to the apparent requirements in the individual case.

Compared with criminal dispositions based upon retributive or upon deterrent motives, where the seriousness of the crime is the main consideration, the objective of incapacitating the criminal requires sentencing based more largely upon an assessment of his dangerousness as an individual. In the usual instance there will be some fairly close relationship between the assumed threat of the particular offender and the nature of the

---

[30] See Tappan, "Habitual Offender Laws and Sentencing Practices in Relation to Organized Crime," in Ploscowe (ed.), *Organized Crime and Law Enforcement,* 1952, pp. 113–177, and Chapter 16 below.

crime that he has committed.[31] There is often a considerable difference, however. In the case of homicide, for example, it has been shown that, while so serious a crime may appear to require long deterrent sentences, it is the sort of offense that commonly occurs as a consequence of extreme provocation or unusual circumstances. Correctional authorities have often remarked that the murderer is usually a person who would not commit another crime even if he were to go free; he does not need an incapacitative sentence. Low rates of recidivism for sex crimes also appear to indicate that prolonged incapacitative sentences are not required for most sex offenders, except for compulsive-neurotic types who engage in dangerous assaults.[32] On the other hand, in the case of many relatively minor offenses, such as vagrancy, prostitution, drunkenness, shoplifting, etc., our statistics and case records reveal a high probability of repetition. Many offenders are in and out of jails under short sentences literally scores of times. Their law violations occasion little injury but considerable nuisance to the community. The minor repetitive offender presents a considerable policy problem to the administration of justice and of correction. As will be noted elsewhere, many of these individuals ought not to be handled as criminals at all but as problems of social welfare.

Professor Andenaes observes that ordinarily there is no great conflict between general and individual prevention, especially when measures of individual intimidation go farther than punishment designed along general preventive lines, but that some problem may be raised when lenience is indicated in individual cases:[33]

But neither here should there be any real danger, so long as the milder special treatment does not become such a commonplace that the potential criminal can count on it and behave accordingly. Both the deterrent and the moralizing sides of general prevention are based primarily on the *average* reaction to certain offenses. Waiving of prosecution and the use of suspended sentence are so widely practiced that the conflict here has become acute.

It should be noted in relation to incapacitation that the prevention of repeated crime where imprisonment is indicated requires not only a sufficiently prolonged institutional custody but the partial and gradually diminishing constraint of parole regulation upon discharge from prison.

---

[31] In a study of fifteen research reports on prediction in parole and recidivism, the author found that the nature of the offense involved was believed to be significant in thirteen, that one did not investigate the relationship, and one found it to be an unreliable index. Quite aside from the risk of repetition itself, however, the offender who commits a serious crime may commit another of the same or similar sort. Even if the probability of repeating is smaller, the threat to the public may be greater.

[32] See Tappan, "Some Myths about the Sex Offender," *Fed. Prob.*, vol. 19, pp. 7–12, 1955, and data published in *Uniform Crime Reports.*

[33] Andenaes, *op. cit.*, pp. 195–196. (Quoted by permission.)

The requirement for a rigorous adherence to a set of rules under close supervision during the transition to full liberty in the community is an incapacitative device as well as a rehabilitative one. It is needed particularly for those offenders who are in danger of repeating. Unfortunately, our methods of discharge from prison have operated in such a way that those individuals who are the greatest threat to security are excluded from parole and are set loose upon the community without any supervision or restraint. While these dangerous individuals are justifiably detained in prison for a longer time, the lack of regulatory control after discharge is a serious weakness in current correctional practice.[34]

Intimidation of the Offender

Individual prevention requires not only that offenders be constrained against committing crime during the period of correction but that treatment measures be designed to persuade them against returning to a criminal way of life after their discharge. Presumably, sanctions that are sufficiently deterrent and incapacitative to provide protection to the community should be adequate to discourage recidivism in the usual case. Yet it appears that a very high percentage—in some states 60 per cent—of imprisoned offenders have had prior criminal records, and this is generally taken to mean that our correctional treatment is neither intimidative nor reformative.[35] There is some justification for this view, at least so far as prisoners are concerned, though the pessimistic conclusion is somewhat too simple. As the author shows elsewhere, offenders sentenced to prison constitute only a minor proportion of convicted criminals.[36] With the increasing employment of probation, by and large the more dangerous and repetitive offenders, the failures of the system, are sentenced to prison. Such figures as are available on probation and parole violation rates indicate that a high proportion survive the period of supervision.[37] Recent research also indicates that most of these offenders stay out of trouble for a period of years thereafter.[38]

[34] See Chapter 23, "Parole," and *Model Penal Code,* American Law Institute, Draft No. 5, art. 305.

[35] The Bureau of the Census reported on the prior commitments of offenders released from state and Federal prisons until 1946 when the practice was discontinued. In that year 53.9 per cent of the state prisoners had previously been committed one or more times (20.9 per cent of these to jail or a juvenile institution) and 44.1 per cent of the Federal prisoners had had prior commitments. See *Prisoners in State and Federal Prisons and Reformatories,* 1946, p. 94.

[36] *Criminal Judicial Statistics,* no longer published, noted that over 30 per cent received probation or suspended sentence in 1945 among twenty-five reporting states. See table 4 in that publication.

[37] See discussion of success and failure in the appropriate chapters on probation and parole.

[38] See, in particular, Ralph England, "A Study of Postprobation Recidivism," *Fed. Prob.,* vol. 19, no. 3, pp. 10–16, September, 1955.

FBI data on arrests have also been used to indicate the failure of our correctional measures.[39] Considered in the most favorable light, it must be concluded that our criminal sanctions are less effective in intimidating the former offender, at least until he has reached some maturity of age, than they are in deterring crime generally and in incapacitating criminals during the period of treatment.[40]

Special mention should be made here of the influence of habitual criminal legislation in controlling recidivism. As the author has observed elsewhere,[41] these laws have proved quite ineffectual in their general impact, mainly because the courts have displayed a great reluctance to apply life sentences established by such statutes. It appears quite clear that the recidivist laws have no real significance for the general deterrence of non-offenders: they are not threatened by them. In practice, moreover, such legislation provides limited incapacitative protection because of the infrequency of their application. On the other hand, many repetitive criminals have expressed their fear of being convicted as habitual offenders and have demonstrated it by quitting crime.

Before turning from the matter of individual prevention, a further comment should be made about the semantic problem involved in contrasting this goal of treatment with rehabilitation, as though they were incompatibly opposed. In fact "rehabilitative treatment" is not a parochially limited province of some single or small group of clinical specialists or techniques, as it is too often conceived. Rehabilitation and persuasive or intimidative measures are not distinct. Many people and varied methods, both positive and negative in impact, exert influence toward change in the offender; discovery, conviction, and sentence are among these influences. It is submitted that a major component of rehabilitation—of change toward conformity—is a normally fearful facing of the reality that crime involves unpleasant consequences. Effective measures of prevention, though they may be afflictive, can also be rehabilitative in a very real sense.

[39] See the discussion in Chapter 2 above.

[40] Yet, as Andenaes suggests, recidivism rates might be greater in the absence of the penalties that are employed: "We have figures on recidivism to tell how large a proportion of ex-convicts commit new crimes. Yet, even aside from the significant error that comes from the fact that figures on recidivism only cover cases where the ex-convict is *caught* committing a new crime, the figures can tell us nothing of *how great the recidivism would have been if there had been no punishment, or a different punishment.* . . . On the whole we can say that recidivism statistics are no more useful in measuring the individual-preventive effect of punishment than the ordinary crime statistics are useful in measuring its general-preventive effect. Both in an evaluation of individual prevention and of general prevention we can resort only to judgment based on psychology, practical experience and common sense." *Op. cit.,* p. 181 (italics not in original). (Quoted by permission.)

[41] See ftn. 30 above.

Rehabilitation

The development of emphasis upon individualized rehabilitation has had great impact upon modern law and correctional administration. The contribution of the Italian school of criminology represented in one sense a reaction against the mechanical and equalitarian character of Classical theory and the laws that it developed. Lombroso (1836–1909), though he is best known and most criticized for his doctrine of biological atavism as a cause of crime, made a tremendous contribution by giving his attention to the individual criminal and empirical research.[42] He was perhaps the major initiator of the trend to individualization in criminology. His contemporaries, Ferri (1856–1928) and Garofalo (1852–1934), differed considerably in their emphasis, pointing attention to the significance of social and economic factors in creating the conditions out of which crime develops.[43] Their thinking combined with that of Lombroso, however, to focus attention upon the complicated causation of crime and to entrench in criminology the deterministic conception that criminal behavior results from environmental circumstances and from conditions in the individual over which he has no control rather than from the sinfulness of offenders. From its attention to the individual and to differentially effective group influences, the Italian school concluded that offenders and their backgrounds should be studied with a view to differing treatment according to the personality and social needs of the individual. From these sources the followers of positivistic criminology have come to hold, either explicitly or implicitly, that man is not "responsible" for his behavior and therefore does not "deserve" punitive treatment.[44]

In order to explain the motivation of individual and group behavior in the twentieth century, psychiatric, psychological, and sociological theories have developed quite rapidly; consequently, several fresh lines of thought have both speeded and slanted positivistic criminology. These lines of thought have represented in part a pendular swing in complete reversal of former doctrine. The indiscriminate rejection of past experience has been unfortunate. The growth of behavioral sciences has brought some recognition that crime, like all human behavior, is complex in its motivations and is not easily redirected. With the prominence of Freudian theory, this new way of thinking has focused upon the significance of deep emotional and unconscious processes in influencing conduct. Sociological analysis has emphasized both the role of culture and the influence of institutions and groups, particularly primary associations, in affecting personality and behavior. The trend has been to stress corporate responsibility

[42] C. Lombroso, *Crime, Its Causes and Remedies,* 1911.
[43] See E. Ferri, *Criminal Sociology,* 1917, and R. Garofalo, Criminology, 1914.
[44] See discussion of free will and determinism below.

(the determinative influence of culture and the group) or psychiatric deviation (including relatively minor influences of emotional stress and volitional inadequacy) in inducing crime.

Much like the utopian constructs of other philosophers, the positivistic criminologists describe ideal and irreproachable goals of prevention, treatment, and cure. Also, as in other philosophical systems, there is little inclination to compromise with foreign purposes or methods. Clinical criminology in its more extreme form offers a beautiful and simple promised land, lying somewhere off in the future, where inert tradition-bound legislators and correctional authorities can be induced to abandon their punitive schemes. They will then employ properly trained clinical personnel, establish a permissive "treatment atmosphere," and allow the experts to proceed with individualized therapy. These experts will know that all offenders are "sick persons" requiring social and psychiatric diagnosis followed by treatment according to the causative pattern.

From the viewpoint of a less idealistic or ambitious objective of reformation, the effort in the correctional process is to treat the offender as effectively as possible within the limitations of the deterrent and incapacitative requirements of a realistic penology. The assessment of the offender's treatment needs is defined by his amenability to corrective handling and the feasibility of providing the needed treatment. This implies an individualized consideration, of course, just as incapacitation does. Also, like incapacitation, the duration of treatment would commonly relate in some measure at least to the seriousness of the problems which motivated the crime. However, in many instances the offender's crime may be of a minor character but his rehabilitation may require long-term treatment; perhaps no effective treatment modality is known, treatment personnel are not accessible, or the costs promise to be excessive in proportion to the danger threatened by the criminal. For example, in the instances of exhibitionists, peepers, consensual homosexuals, schizoid vagrants, compulsive petty thieves, disorderly alcoholics, or antisocial "psychopaths," it would generally be agreed that successful treatment is impossible in any appreciable number of cases or that it would be excessively prolonged and expensive. On the other hand, in most cases of "murder under stress," embezzlement, income tax violation, and statutory rape, while the crime itself is generally considered serious, no rehabilitative treatment is actually required to remedy personality or social defects. The individual is "well adjusted" except for such damage to his self-esteem and interpersonal relations as may result from his discovery and conviction.

In recent years the emphasis in rehabilitative treatment of the offender has been mainly upon the employment of casework and clinical measures designed first to discover the source of the individual's problems and then to provide therapeutic assistance to alleviate his difficulties and to enable him to cope more adequately with reality. Correctional casework in probation and parole and, to a lesser extent, in the institutional setting has been the primary focus of attention, although there has been an increasing stress upon individual and group psychotherapy designed to resolve the offender's emotional troubles. The offender is commonly looked upon as a disturbed person whose conduct deviations reflect his psychic and social difficulties and it is imagined that a resolution of these difficulties will produce appropriate adjustment. There are certain rather serious limitations to reformative treatment, however.[45] One limitation is that we are relatively ignorant not only of the specific causes of crime but, more particularly, of effective therapeutic measures to deal with them. Without the development of much more economical methods of clinical treatment, there is no prospect of probing and treating the deep underlying problems of criminals in any significant proportion of cases. These matters are discussed further in Chapters 17 and 18.

OTHER DETERMINANTS IN SENTENCING AND CORRECTION

The several objectives noted in the pages above define and often either limit or extend the correctional treatment to be applied to the criminal. Beyond these objectives certain other limiting factors should circumscribe both the extent and the nature of sanctions that may reasonably be employed. Among these limiting factors are certain basic *concepts of justice and humanity.* Constitutional provisions against cruel and unusual punishments reflect the deep antipathy in our culture toward brutal types of penalties. Few appeals or writs are taken in our courts against the sentences that are imposed or the treatment methods that are employed, but a few cases have held sentences to be unduly long in relation to the offense. Moreover, for the most part, the penal provisions of the statutes in the several states look to the limiting or the extension of the sentence in proportion to the seriousness of the crime. However, as illustrated in recent sexual-psychopath legislation and in some of the recidivist laws, for example, neither constitutional provisions nor humane sentiments provide very real protection against prolonged or permanent incarceration for minor offenses. It is the sense of humanity and justice in our legislatures and courts that provides the greater safeguard, and experience has shown that where legislation has gone too far in the length of sentence established for a particular offense the courts will generally nullify the law in practice. Even this sense of juridical proportion is no complete protection, however, and advocates of individualized, clinical correction have launched formidable assaults against a system that would limit treatment by the seriousness of the crime or the dangerousness of the criminal. In spite of this, the premise has remained fairly well intact that treatment duration should be

[45] Tappan, "Concepts and Cross Purposes," *Focus,* vol. 31, no. 3, pp. 66–67, May, 1952.

gauged at least roughly to the offense; this is the chief argument, perhaps, for retaining the distinction between felonies and misdemeanors.[46]

Certain practical considerations also affect the sanctions that may be employed by the penal law and the correctional system. The limitations on rehabilitative treatment appear at present to be particularly difficult. The greatest single problem, perhaps, is our persisting ignorance both of the causes of crime and of effective treatment modalities. As has been shown in preceding chapters, there is an abundance of theories concerning the etiology of crime. Cerebration relating to correctional treatment has not been so prolific. Indeed, aside from such general formulae as the need to apply treatment according to the causes of crime in the individual case, the several fields of specialization have expressed a largely pessimistic judgment of the potential efficacy of correctional efforts. Even the clinical criminologists take a dim view of the possibilities of treating many types of criminals effectively.

It would be absurd to suggest that we must wait to attempt rehabilitative treatment until we have arrived at full knowledge of the dynamics of crime and therapy. We must employ such knowledge and theories as we possess and must work empirically toward the improvement of our information and our tools. Nevertheless, in so far as our correctional hypotheses are conjectural, it is only just and reasonable that the power of treatment authorities over the life and freedom of the criminal should be limited by the measure of the offender's threat to the community.

Beyond the limitations of knowledge in the behavioral sciences, one of our gravest difficulties in the field of correction rests in the lack of available trained treatment personnel. Competent specialists in psychiatry, psychology, sociology, and casework are relatively few and expensive. Thus far we have employed only a token force of therapists in correction. Attention has gone for the most part to rather crude diagnostic functions, mainly the segregation of the insane and the mental defectives and, in some jurisdictions, the psychopaths. Psychiatric and psychological treatment have been minimal and casework guidance for the most part has been superficial. Even if funds were available for the purpose, as they are in a few places, it would not be possible to secure the amount and kind of talent considered necessary for effective correctional therapy. In many places positions are open in court clinics, diagnostic centers, and correctional institutions for psychiatrists, clinical psychologists, and trained caseworkers who cannot be found.[47] The low salaries generally provided for

---

[46] As will be observed in the chapter on sentencing, however, considerations both of incapacitation and reform point to the need for sentences of indefinite length so that release may be determined between a minimum and maximum on the basis of individual and social considerations.

[47] According to the Federal Bureau of Prisons, in 1950 in the 157 state and Federal correctional institutions in the United States (excluding Georgia), serving a population of 161,938, there were 23 psychiatrists, 67 psychologists, and 257

these specialists in the correctional system is, of course, an important part of the problem of short supply.

A further difficulty must be faced: authorities who have been invested with important powers under the traditional systems of sentencing and treatment are reluctant to relinquish their control in favor of some new scheme of correctional methodology. Many competent officials, including judges, probation personnel, institutional officers, parole boards, and supervisors, have performed quite ably under present procedures. Proposals for any radical reshuffling of power in the dispositions and treatment processes must take into account the quite natural opposition of those officials whose authority would be divested. This should not constitute a major barrier to change if it is clear that a new distribution of powers will improve sentencing and correction. On the other hand, it is too easy to produce on paper an ideal theoretical construct that in its actual implementation may fall short of the performance attained by an already well-established pattern of powers and functions.[48] The uncritical faith of some administrators in absolute administrative discretion deceives criminologists, more often perhaps than other visionaries, when reform is considered.

Finally, certain additional practical handicaps to establishing a rational policy of sentencing and treatment must be noted that arise out of inefficiencies in administration. It is common knowledge that a very large proportion of crimes committed do not result in conviction and sentence, mainly because the culprit is not discovered or the evidence is too weak to convict him. Under the circumstances of law violation and enforcement in the modern community it is inevitable that criminals will evade justice in a substantial number of cases. On the other hand, it is unlikely that the repetitive offender will escape penalties indefinitely. The effect, however, of the high mortality rate in criminal justice is to dilute very markedly both the deterrent and the incapacitative functions of the penal law. The idea that "if you are smart you can get away with anything" has become a prevalent notion among criminals. It extends too far, as well, into the

---

social workers employed. See *Prisoners in State and Federal Institutions*, 1951, table 42. It has been held that in order to provide more than merely custodial care in mental hospitals one psychiatrist is required for every 30 acute patients and one for every 200 chronic patients. See Guttmacher and Weihofen, *Psychiatry and the Law*, 1952, p. 313. Among the 7,500 psychiatrists in the United States, however, there are only 3,000 certified by the American Board of Psychiatry and Neurology, fewer than 900 who are practicing psychoanalysts, and little over 400 with membership in the American Psychoanalytic Association. *Ibid.*, p. 7. All this has obvious implications for the soundness of the view that prisons should be made into psychiatric treatment facilities and that probation and parole should be processes of psychotherapy, quite aside from the question of whether such goals would be intrinsically desirable on the basis of the problems involved.

[48] For a discussion of the Authority or "treatment tribunal" idea, see Chapter 16.

penumbra of potential offenders, reducing their fear and respect for law. When the convicted offender is a repeater, the limited efficiency of justice suggests a need to employ sufficiently long sentences for adequate protection of the community.

To quite similar effect is another practice that prevails in the administration of justice, the process of bargaining for pleas in our criminal courts whereby the criminal is permitted to take a reduced charge in return for pleading guilty. The obvious consequence of this practice is to convict and sentence offenders for something less, often substantially less, than the crimes for which they have been charged. Here again the consequence is somewhat reduced deterrence and incapacitation of the criminal. In so far as statutes may provide a sufficiently wide range of penalties so that the offender with a bad record may be retained in prison for a prolonged period, the unfavorable effects of bargaining may be reduced somewhat. However, one of the largest loopholes in our habitual criminal statutes results from the readiness of the courts to take a misdemeanor plea from the three-time-loser as a reward for his cooperation. No rational system of penal sanctions can be more effective than its administration.

The development and significance of certain elements in correctional policy, elements that have persisted in varying degrees in contemporary practice, have been considered above. Reference has been made to determinism and the doctrine of free choice. These theories have profound meaning for sentencing and correctional treatment; their implication will now be considered.

The Free Will versus Determinism Controversy

Certainly one very important reason for the controversy that has raged about free will and determinism lies in a failure to define or to agree upon the meaning of the terms. This failure in turn reflects in part the changing connotation and the arbitrary interpretation sometimes attached to these terms. The thorough-going determinist is inclined to conceive free will in terms of complete freedom of choice and total indeterminism while the moralist sees determinism as a thoroughly mechanistic interpretation of behavior and, sometimes, as a doctrine of predetermination. In fact, the concept of free will has increasingly absorbed the proposition that there is, as Father Coogan has put it, *"much determinism* in nature."[49] Dr. Abraham Wolf, philosopher at the University of London, has said, "No one

[49] Reverend John E. Coogan, "Free Will and the Academic Criminologist," *Fed. Prob.,* vol. 20, no. 2, p. 54, 1956. Father Coogan has repeatedly criticized academic criminology for its failure to accept the doctrine of free will. In addition to this article, see "A Rejoinder to the Strictures of the Determinist," *ibid.,* October-December, 1944; "The Myth Mind in an Engineer's World," *ibid.,* March, 1952; "Secularism Alien to Our Covenant Nation," *ibid.,* September, 1952. Replies by those who were criticized for their deterministic views are contained in the journals of June and September, 1952.

means by free will that any man is free to make any choice at any time. Obviously there could only be freedom within limits. A man's choice is limited by his heredity, by the conditioning to which he has been subjected, by social pressures, by his opportunities, by the means at his disposal."[50] The advocates of the free-will position maintain, however, as William P. Montague has put it, that "freedom at each present moment, to modify and supplement our past by a spontaneous effort not predetermined by that past, is both morally essential and physically real. . . . Each present moment has for its prerogative the thing we call free will."[51]

The determinist would ask the meaning of "spontaneous effort" and the implication of "predetermination by the past." A thorough-going determinist's position would be that behavior is caused by forces within and without over which man has no independent control. He would not, however, hold the position imputed to him by William McDougall that conduct is "the issue of conditions that existed and determined it in every detail long before" birth or that "it would be foolish . . . to take pains to choose the better course and to make efforts to realize it."[52] He would not even maintain that there is no element of indeterminacy in man's behavior, since the determinants of conduct may be evenly balanced. Moreover, in the light of the increasing evidence of irregularity and indeterminacy in nuclear activity, the determinist might well agree that there is similarly a certain play of irregularity in mental phenomena that are based upon an unpredictable action of synaptic connections. Few determinists would hold that complete prediction would be possible if they had full knowledge of the past and present elements leading to behavior and the way these elements were interrelated; the determinist would hold, however, that a high degree of predictive accuracy should theoretically be possible given such a hypothetical (and obviously forever impossible) situation.

The significant thing for us, however, is the fact that the implications of free will and determinism for criminology and penology do not relate to a limited measure of indeterminacy or of freedom but to the moral-philosophical postulates that are associated with these doctrines.[53] Through-

---

[50] *Encyclopaedia Britannica*, 1950 ed., vol. 9, pp. 748 f., quoted in Coogan, "Free Will and the Academic Criminologist," *op. cit.*, p. 49.

[51] "Free Will and Fate," *The Personalist*, vol. 24, no. 2, April, 1943, quoted in *ibid.*, pp. 50–51.

[52] *Introduction to Social Psychology*, 1926, pp. 240 f., quoted in *ibid.*, p. 53.

[53] Andenaes makes this point very well: "From the point of view of moral philosophy it makes little difference if—in a way corresponding to that in nuclear physics—allowance is made for a certain play of irregularity. What is decisive from the point of view of moral philosophy is not the question of strict regularity or not, but the contrast with the other trend of thought, the indeterministic, with its inherent conceptions of free choice, moral responsibility, and personal guilt. As we realize, this moral-philosophical Indeterminism is in its nature quite

out most of recorded history it has been assumed that criminals and sinners break the rules because they are weak or bad. Philosophy and religion have held that man possesses the power to make independent choices, that when he deliberately does wrong he is morally culpable in proportion to that wrong and should be punished in accordance with the measure of his moral guilt. There has been some diversity of views historically concerning whether such punishment should be predicated upon the need for expiation or atonement, upon retribution or a vindictive revenge. It has gradually been assumed to be in accordance with natural justice, evidenced in the inherent inclination of both the victim and group, that the wrongdoer should be considered morally responsible for his fault and punished therefor. While the doctrine of free will as a rationale for punishment has been considerably modified through the development of Classical and Italian criminological theories, its continuing effect may still be observed both in the content of some of the criminal law and in the approach of the courts, particularly where moral-religious issues are involved, as has already been noted. Many judges refer from time to time to the extent of the particular offender's freedom of choice and moral culpability or the punishment that he "deserves." Indeed, for the most part the legal principles of defense and mitigation have been based historically upon the presumed degree of the culprit's free and rational choice.

The Classical school adopted the position that punishment should be administered for practical reasons, to prevent crime and to protect public interests through deterrence, rather than gratuitously or for moral reasons; this position shifted the philosophical base of official sanctions. The development was in accordance with the secularization of political society, focusing the attention of state authorities upon the security of social interests rather than upon the punishment of religio-moral delinquency. This implied a difference in purpose; it also implied that many forms of conduct, however much they might be deprecated from a religious or moral point of view, should not be treated as criminal, either because they are of no concern to the state or because the limitations of official justice and correction are such that they cannot reach and constrain the behavior. The result has been an increased institutional specialization in which some matters of conduct are clearly the exclusive concern of the church and the deity and others are the exclusive province of the state. There remains, however, a considerable area of concurrent functions involving both sacred and temporal considerations; it has often proved quite difficult to determine what matters of morality and vice should and what should not be of

---

different from the Indeterminism of which we speak in nuclear physics. Neither strict regularity nor the assumption of a certain measure of irregularity can provide any support for conceptions of guilt and responsibility." Johs Andenaes, "Determinism and Criminal Law," *J. Crim. L.*, vol. 47, no. 4, p. 407, November-December, 1956. (Quoted by permission.)

official concern to the legislatures and courts. This has been illustrated in the handling of such questions as fornication, adultery, illegitimacy, juvenile delinquency, and sexual deviation.

Departure from the doctrine of free will has been stimulated far more by the emphasis of the Italian school upon biological and social causation and by the subsequent rapid developments in the behavioral sciences. Many authorities in the social, psychological, and biological sciences have concluded that man's *behavior is caused* and that one can discover to a very large extent, at least, why he behaves and misbehaves in the ways he does. While it is impossible to determine with accuracy the forces in the individual that motivate conduct, this difficulty is traced to ignorance and chance rather than to the operation in the individual of an independent free will that cannot be understood or controlled. Moreover, it is generally believed that enough of the important things can be discovered about many persons to control, redirect, and sometimes even to predict their conduct. These are in fact the goals of applied behavioral science. Such goals rest upon the belief that behavior is so determined and determinable that by careful and thorough diagnosis and by perceptive reconditioning treatment the individual may be led to change his responses. Under this hypothesis, what has been generally termed "the will" and the emotions as well as the intellect are still recognized as factors in the motivation and inhibition of behavior, but they are themselves conceived to be end products of the forces—biological, psychological, and sociocultural—that form the personality and its behavioral tendencies. From a completely deterministic viewpoint, since there is no free choice, there is no moral guilt in the traditional religious sense, and therefore punishment as a gratuitous infliction is not justified. On the other hand, measures that the individual apprehends as punishment or methods that are painful to him may be usefully applied to restrain or redirect behavior in accordance with either his own needs or those of the group. Thus punitive as well as clinical techniques are permissible in efforts at control and redirection of the deviate. Though he is not considered "responsible," the offender may be held accountable.

Modified Determinism

Many people who are interested in treatment of the criminal adopt some form of modified deterministic view of human conduct. It is difficult wholly to abandon the idea of conscious free choice. Egocentric esteem and man's interpretation of his introspections foster the belief that there is some independent identity of selfness out of which autonomous judgments and choices are made and that somehow one merits praise or blame in terms of these choices and their consequences.[54] However, the impact of

[51] Introspective "evidence" that free will exists is emphasized, among others, by W. H. Werkmeister: "The determinists . . . must show how it is possible for man

modern behavioral psychologies has been great enough to convince the strongest skeptic and moralist of the large extent to which experience, individual physical variability, and a variety of social influences affect conduct. While the effects are particularly obvious in more extreme deviates, even in the hypothetically average, "reasonable" individual the marks of cultural influence and of variation in body, mind, and experience can scarcely be ignored.

Probably a majority of philosophers, many behavioral scientists, and virtually all moralists today hold the position that, while conduct is obviously—in light of modern research and understanding of individual and social behavior—determined to a very large extent by internal and extraneous forces beyond the person's control, there nevertheless remains some province for free and independent choice and that the individual is to this extent "master of his fate." The existence of such an independent entity of function is, like the deterministic doctrine, a matter of faith or opinion and is not susceptible to empirical proof. While it has sometimes been maintained that there is evidence through intuition and introspection of free choice, dynamic psychiatry has made it quite clear that man is not aware of a great part of the emotional and unconscious elements that motivate and inhibit his responses. The mere fact that men are sometimes subject to processes of extended ratiocination, to conflict and hesitation in the resolution of action, and to rationalization in their explanations of conduct is no proof in itself that choice is either free or determined. Similarly, the fact that impelling and restraining forces at the point of action may be equally balanced, so that the result (even if all were known and understood) could not be predicted, indicates merely that in some instances aleatory factors determine behavior.

It is clear that a social scientist today must accept the principle that behavior is very largely directed by man's heredity, constitution and organism, life experiences and pressures, and cultural compulsives and that he can be controlled to a large extent by the manipulation of such influences. If this is not so, the investigations and theories in the behavioral fields are futile and we should abandon study of behavior. The point of greatest relevance for criminology, however, is that *whatever extent of free choice and, therefore, of personal culpability may exist in human behavior is not determinable by man.* Whether the same amount is apportioned to all men—fools, knaves, and geniuses, sick and well—cannot be discovered empirically. Whether free choice is equally accessible to the individual at

---

to be thoroughly and completely determined and yet to feel free. Merely to say that our feeling of freedom is an illusion is no explanation. . . . Our feeling of freedom, our feeling of authorship and responsibility, and our sense of guilt—intertwined though they are—are unmistakable facts of first-person experience; and that is the reason for accepting them as evidence." *A Philosophy of Science,* 1940, pp. 434f., quoted in Coogan, *loc. cit.,* p. 51.

different times and in relation to different classes of conduct is also beyond human demonstration. This means that men are in no position to measure the quantum of free choice or of moral responsibility and guilt to equate a proper retributive punishment. Such an effort is particularly inappropriate to the capacity of political authorities whose duty it is to enact legislation, police conduct, prosecute crime, judge criminals, and punish convicts. The task of measuring and administering punishments for moral wrong is sacred and metaphysical, a proper function of the deity but not of state officials. Secular authority, on the other hand, can and must attempt to restrain and deter offenders, to eliminate so far as possible pathological social influences that may promote criminality, and to rehabilitate individual offenders where it can. To reiterate, its purpose, however, is not to condemn badness per se or to save souls; its purpose is to protect the community.

Determinism and Treatment

It is submitted, in brief summation, that only a deterministic (or, if the reader prefers, only a partially free-will) view of criminal behavior makes sense in terms of contemporary understanding of human behavior and its motivation. What does this imply in terms of treatment of the criminal and the functions of the criminal court? Some implications of our premise are clear at once: the disutility and the inappropriateness of retributive punishment, the folly of perpetuating *legal* doctrines that impute either a free volition or a largely rational motivation to man's conduct, and the folly of attempting to measure moral guilt. The individual's attitudes and conduct reflect his organism and particularly his emotional impulses, the mold of his culture with the powerful impress of tradition, mores, and public opinion as they enforce the current ethos, and the total of his life experiences, particularly those in the family and in congeniality group settings. A reality-directed system of justice and correction must take fully into account this nature of man and his motivations.

If the view taken here is accepted, it follows that criminal behavior, being the product of complex influences, may be modified through an understanding of the individual offender and through efforts at preventive and rehabilitative treatment; this modification should be directed toward changing antisocial attitudes and habits where possible and toward repressing their expression when they cannot be changed sufficiently. This does not mean that with our present knowledge, limited diagnostic tools, and treatment facilities we can hope to understand the offender completely or treat him always effectively. Our ignorance and the poverty of our resources are serious when one considers the growing violence of crime and the difficulty of the task of controlling criminal behavior. However, it would seem that our knowledge is extensive enough to discover more effective methods of correction and control.

Criminal "Guilt" and Correctional Treatment

It has been maintained above that moral guilt is irrelevant and retributive punishment unjustified in the political setting. Nevertheless, guilt of crime and of injury to social interest are, of course, real. Moreover, punishment may be warranted to the extent that it can deter crime, establish standards of conduct, and redirect the criminal. While determinism may assume that there is little or no real responsibility for behavior in a moral sense, the state must in self-protection hold the individual *accountable* for the injuries he inflicts. Indeed, from the point of view of criminal treatment or crime prevention, the correctional worker must attempt to enlarge the sense of responsibility in the offender, to increase his feelings of guilt, and to convince him thoroughly that violation of the rules produces painful consequences. These treatment efforts may require moral and religious suasion as techniques for more effective control. The worst approach the worker can take toward the ordinary offender is to absolve him of guilt, to instruct him that he is not responsible for his errors, and to convey to him the view that he is an unfortunate creature of circumstance. The apparent inconsistencies here in relation to guilt and punishment arise mainly from the limitations of our language and from the historically rooted difficulties of discriminating between the roles of religion and government in dealing with sin and crime. The unfortunate consequence of the confusions is that, while some secular authorities would reach for the mantle of God to weigh the sin and the atonement of the criminal, others are equally unrealistic in proposing to abandon constraining sanctions and to apply instead clinical therapy to every offender.

The problem of criminal guilt involves some confusion both in language and philosophy, as we have seen. Part of the difficulty arises from the emotional and traditional connotations of this term, part out of the fact that it is employed in quite different senses by variously orientated specialists.[55] The following are particularly important usages:

1. Guilt as a finding of *fact* by a court that the defendant committed certain alleged acts in violation of the criminal law.

2. Guilt as a *moral* concept of the offender's willful dereliction, evidenced by a wrongful act and an evil intent.

3. Guilt in a *social* sense of the individual's violation of some interest that society needs to protect.

4. Guilt in a *psychological* sense, referring to the feelings of the individual who suffers compunction because of his infraction of social rules or because of a deep and often unconscious neurotic guilt, rooted sometimes in faulty psychosexual development.

Employed by retributive penology, guilt refers to the moral offensiveness of the actor, requiring punitive expiation. The author has suggested that in

[55] See Edmond N. Cahn (ed.), "Criminal Guilt," in *Social Meaning of Legal Concepts*, vol. 2, 1950.

modern penology punitive expiation should have no place, because its effect on both the offender and society is more damaging than it is useful. The moral connotations are removed in a deterrent penology. The important consideration lies in the violation of a social interest and the correlative need to protect the group by incapacitating the individual, thus warning others against similar violations. In a positivistic penology, too, guilt as a moral conception does not exist. The violation of a significant social interest does not imply a subjective turpitude or "responsibility" on the part of the actor, since the offender's behavior is a natural product of conditioning circumstances that he is not free to control. It is at this point that a special difficulty arises for the positivistic criminologist.

Psychiatric criminology has focused some special interest and attention upon the "sense of guilt" that may be found among criminals and non-criminals. This feeling is often rooted in the early psychosexual history of the individual and is commonly related to deviated drives, homosexual or otherwise. Such deeply rooted feelings of guilt function frequently on an unconscious level, causing a variety of forms of adaptive behavior, criminal and otherwise, including a search for punishment to alleviate the guilt feelings. Unlike these deep and unconscious responses are the feelings of guilt experienced by the "normal person" who feels remorse for the wrong that he has done, a sentiment that is a natural outcome of socialization, of identification and sympathy with others. While it is undesirable for an individual to be obsessed with intense neurotic guilt, the normal sense of guilt and "healthy anxiety" following antisocial behavior are important and desirable deterrents to crime. Indeed, the development of "the superego" is said to depend upon the anxieties and guilt sensations resulting from disapproved drives or behavior.

On the one hand there is the deterministic premise that the offender, though his crime has been established, is not "guilty" in a moralistic sense and, on the other, there is the realization that the offender must be made to feel "guilt" in order to counterbalance the strength of his antisocial impulses. While the correctional worker does not hold the offender responsible in a moral sense, he must be made to feel and to accept responsibility. The difficulty involved here is more a matter of semantics than of hypocrisy, but there is a notable difference between the *attitude* that the worker must feel toward the offender and the content of his *method* in attempting to stimulate feelings of guilt.

The Balance and Coordination of Objectives

The major goals of justice and correction have been considered above in a historical and philosophical perspective. The effective instrumentation of public policy depends, however, upon the balance and harmonization of objectives in the actual administration of sanctions. Unfortunately, neither the law makers nor the courts have given enough attention to questions of relative emphasis and to questions of compromise and variation. It has been more common and easier, certainly, to postulate a single goal and to suggest that a choice must be made between simple alternatives. In part because of the persisting controversies about ends and means, there has been little effort in the past to develop criteria for sentencing or correctional treatment.[56] The development of such criteria is very much needed. The author will not attempt a formulation of this sort, but it may be useful to posit certain hypotheses about the objectives and measures of justice in summarizing major views that have been expressed in this chapter:

1. The state should not attempt to establish criminal norms that are unnecessary or unenforceable by ordinary and reasonable methods of administration.

2. Penal provisions should not be so severe or so mild that they will tend either, on the one hand, to result in nullification for their harshness or, on the other, to invite the disrespect of criminals and of the general public for their lenience.

3. Crimes that pose serious threat or inflict serious danger upon the community, especially in the case of repetitive offenders, should generally be penalized more heavily in order to deter such conduct so far as possible and to incapacitate and intimidate offenders who are disposed to commit such crimes. The seriousness of the crime is the clearest indication of the public's need for protection and of the offender's need for control. The circumstances of the crime and the apparent attitude of the offender are important considerations, however, that may persuade toward mitigation or aggravation of the sanction.

4. Where the risk to the community is small, there is no justification either for inflicting extended imprisonment or regulation upon the individual or for requiring costly, long-extended treatment by correctional agencies. The minor offender should receive light criminal sanctions.

5. Rehabilitative treatment measures, applied in accordance with the apparent needs and deficiencies of offenders, may serve to redirect their attitudes and behavior to prevent further crimes. Correctional sanctions should not, however, be applied to individuals who have not been found guilty of crime, nor should they be disproportionate to the harm that the individual has done. In the interest of justice and humanity, therapy should not be much more onerous than is necessary for incapacitation, deterrence, and the intimidation of the offender.

6. Young individuals whose criminal histories are brief and whose psychiatric or social deviations are minor and susceptible to known treatment methods are most amenable to treatment emphasis. Ordinarily these individuals may be handled by methods that are not specifically punitive without serious weakening of the deterrent goals of the law. Usually they do not require extended incapacitation. Where effective correctional treatment can be provided early in the course of the offender's antisocial development, it is usually easier, more economical, and more effective.

[56] The *Model Penal Code* of the American Law Institute has formulated criteria for certain of the sentencing and correctional procedures. See, for example, S. 305.13 and 7.01–7.05. Also the N.P.P.A. has prepared a volume, *Guides for Sentencing*, 1957, designed to aid judges in the sentencing process.

Chapter 11

THE POLICE AND CRIME DETECTION

August Vollmer, former famous chief of police of Berkeley, California, has observed:[1]

The citizen expects police officers to have the wisdom of Solomon, the courage of David, the strength of Samson, the patience of Job, the leadership of Moses, the kindness of the Good Samaritan, the strategical training of Alexander, the faith of Daniel, the diplomacy of Lincoln, the tolerance of the Carpenter of Nazareth, and, finally, an intimate knowledge of every branch of the natural, biological, and social sciences. If he had all these, he might be a good policeman!

Policing as a specialized phase of the administration of justice is a modern phenomenon; it was developed to cope with the increase in property crime that accompanied the growth of cities. The night watch system, set up in London in 1680, was a forerunner of the police. Hutchinson states that men employed under this system "went about the streets at night periodically bawling out the condition of the weather, the hour, and the fact that all was well. This was in order that people might sleep peacefully. They were far more unpopular than the burglars, who at least had the decency to keep quiet."[2] Long before this, however, the task of keeping order had been assigned to constables and justices of the peace in England. The latter combined administrative and judicial functions, which were originally provided for under the laws of Edward I in the thirteenth century. When a felony or breach of the peace was committed the justices of the peace were empowered by common law to arrest the offender or to require others to do so "to prevent the riotous consequences of a tumultuous assembly." The duties of the constable also seem to have been

[1] Quoted in Read Bain, "The Policeman on the Beat," *Sci. Monthly*, vol. 48, p. 5, 1939.
[2] Robert H. Hutchinson, "The Lesson of Scotland Yard," *Harpers*, 1936, vol. 173, p. 320. For the development and policies of the English police, see also Jerome Hall, "Police and Law in a Democratic Society," *Ind. L. J.*, vol. 28, pp. 133–178, 1953; Patrick Pringle, *Hue and Cry, the Story of the Bow Street Runners*, 1950.

first fully defined during the reign of Edward I by the Statute of West-minster. *High constables* were appointed under this statute to keep the kings's peace in the hundred.[3] *Petty constables* were subordinate officers charged with keeping the peace within their village, town, or tithing.

Neither the constabulary nor the watch and ward system of preserving the peace proved adequate as the population expanded. Attention was drawn repeatedly during the latter part of the eighteenth century to the need for a system of crime prevention. As a result of the investigations by Sir Robert Peel, as reported in 1828, the famous Metropolitan Police Act was passed, creating in the following year the first thousand "real police," with both day and night duty. The public reaction was immediately hostile to the "Peelers" or "Lobsters," as they were called. Resistance persisted during the following decades as the system was expanded. Through wise leadership, the police were trained to avoid the use of force and to be co-operative and courteous. As a result their relations with the public steadily improved. The "Bobbies" have come to be respected even by the criminal. In accordance with deep British convictions about the administration of justice, the police do not carry guns and do not employ stool pigeons or informers. The traditions of fair play and of responsible public service have established a policing system in England that may well be envied in the United States as well as in other nations. The recent decline in the traditional British respect for the police as the result of several scandals in 1959 has emphasized anew the ambivalent public attitudes toward police authority in a democracy.

The night watch and constabulary systems were borrowed by the American colonies and it was not until the early part of the nineteenth century that police systems were established in some of our cities. Led by Peter Stuyvesant, the Dutch City Fathers established the "Rattle Watch" in 1658 to preserve law and order in Nieu Amsterdam. The "Rattle Watch" called the hours and sounded their rattles from nine o'clock in the evening until dawn, in accordance with British traditional practice. Boston established a night watch system as early as 1636. This practice persisted with little change until 1844, with no police protection during the day, except such as might be provided by military guard. In 1844 a municipal police force was established in New York City; this force was composed of full-time officers and was the first coordinated day and night force. Other urban areas soon followed the New York example. Official uniforms were adopted after the Civil War. At that time a multiplicity of policing agencies with overlapping jurisdiction and responsibilities had developed. Problems of social control have grown since that time and the tendency has been to proliferate new agencies to meet specific needs rather than to con-solidate or to improve the efficiency of the existing organization. As a result, an increasingly complex and uncoordinated development of policing

[3] This consisted of roughly one hundred free families or ten tithings.

units has occurred; this development has unfortunate consequences at all levels of government.

POLICE ORGANIZATION

In analyzing the complexity of present-day police services in the United States, Bruce Smith has observed that there are at least five strata conforming roughly to major levels of government.[4] There are (1) sheriffs and deputy sheriffs in over 3,000 counties, together with county police forces that have duplicated or displaced the sheriffs; (2) police in 15,000 villages, boroughs, and incorporated towns; (3) state forces in each of the states; (4) Federal police agencies, especially those attached to the Justice, Treasury, and Post Office departments; and (5) police of nearly 4,000 cities, approximately 20,000 townships, and an unknown number of magisterial and county districts. The organization of rural, state, Federal, and urban police departments will be considered briefly below. Special attention will be given to administrative organization in the urban departments. The remainder of the chapter relates to problems in modern police operations.

Contemporary Rural Police

Our rural and village policing has traditionally been based upon the use of sheriffs and constables whose functions were drawn largely from ancient Anglo-Saxon practice.[5] Throughout the country today sheriffs, usually chosen by popular election for short terms, exercise peace powers under the county system of government. Their duties are varied, generally including service of civil writs and custody of the county jail as well as keeping the peace. The role of the sheriff has been glamorized by the legends of his frontier prototype who was an active law enforcement officer and perhaps, sometimes, an effective one. Today the use of sheriffs has proved to be an ineffectual, inefficient, and often abusive method of policing. There are a number of explanations for this situation. Ordinarily there are few qualifications for the office and turnover is rapid. Removal from office by impeachment "for cause" is difficult. Many sheriffs continue in their former occupations, developing little specialized skill in law enforcement. While they are often on salary, they rely heavily on fees received for the performance of their official acts. They have commonly exploited this system, reaping profits especially from the feeding of prisoners. In some urban and metropolitan areas sheriffs have derived fantastic incomes from their office and they are sometimes the best paid administrative officers of the county. Studies in a number of states have indicated,

---

[4] Bruce Smith, *Police Systems in the United States,* 1940, p. 24; see also O. W. Wilson, "Progress in Police Administration," *J. Crim. L.,* vol. 42, p. 141, 1951.

[5] On rural policing see Smith, *op. cit.,* chap. 3; Raymond Moley, *The Missouri Crime Survey;* and Smith, *Rural Crime Control.*

furthermore, that the law enforcement functions of the sheriff have considerably declined.[6] In general he does not take seriously his statutory policing duties, though in some places sheriffs' deputies devote a part of their time to law enforcement. Usually they do not cooperate effectively with state or urban agencies, partly because they lack the skill to do so. At times when they do attempt police work on particular cases, they hope for political advantage. The sheriff is an anachronism in modern law enforcement, retained largely because the county is inclined to cling to powers and functions that this level of government cannot properly perform. Often, however, sheriffs are the only policing power in rural areas. In cities they are nonessential and unduly expensive.

The office of constable, which in England has involved duties relating to the militia, tax collection, highway supervision, and maintenance of the peace, gradually lost its early powers and prestige and was ultimately discontinued in 1856. By then the constable had become a well-established figure on the American scene. Although the importance of the office has diminished, it continues to be a feature of our rural and village society. As a rule the constabulary is even less effectual than the sheriff's office in police work. The constable is commonly charged by law with multiple functions in addition to keeping the peace and serving civil writs. He is rarely a full-time officer and is almost never trained or experienced in police work. For this reason and because constables usually receive no pay other than fees for special services, they contribute little to law enforcement. In villages, the constable or marshal is a counterpart of the rural constable, although he sometimes performs traffic duty. The constable is more of an anachronism than is the sheriff in contemporary law enforcement. In many towns and villages, especially in the East, the constabulary system has been replaced by full-time, more specialized police forces. Nevertheless, there remain today more distinct police agencies associated with the constabulary than with any other type of police organization.

In addition to sheriffs and constables, the policing of rural and village areas is performed by a variety of county police forces, including highway patrol forces, special county police units, parkway police, and prosecutor's aides. Increasingly these, along with the state police, are displacing the sheriff-constable systems in law enforcement activities outside our cities.

With the development of new and diversified types of police units, the tendency has been for the old forms to persist alongside the new. Consequently, in some areas police jurisdiction overlaps considerably while other areas lack minimal protection. The tradition of local autonomy leads

---

[6] There is wide variation, however, in the extent to which the rural sheriff participates in law enforcement. See T. C. Esselstyn, "The Social Role of a County Sheriff," *J. Crim. L.*, vol. 44, p. 177, 1953; *Crime and Its Control in the Hinterland*, unpublished doctoral dissertation, New York University, 1952. Esselstyn indicates that in one part of the county where his study focused the sheriff's arrest rate was 1373.6 per 100,000 whereas in other parts of the county the rate was 448.4.

to inefficient performance. Bruce Smith found that in the region surrounding Cincinnati there was a total of 147 independent and overlapping police agencies in 6 counties that included 51 townships, 13 magisterial districts, 12 cities, and 65 villages. Metropolitan Chicago embraces 350 police forces, municipal, county, and state. In the area surrounding Boston there are 40 different policing agencies.[7] In police regions removed from metropolitan areas, however, where no specialized service is available, the people must rely on the inadequate services of sheriffs and constables. The low rates of crime reported for rural areas may to some extent be explained by the fact that adequate personnel for the detection of crime are not available there.

State Police

Most state police departments developed during the past 100 years largely in response to the patent inadequacy of local policing by constables and sheriffs over whom the governor had no control.[8] Among the problems that led to establishment of state police systems were failures of the local authorities to regulate vice, to control labor disturbances, to patrol the highways, and to enforce the law in rural areas. In emergencies a number of governors used the state militia as a temporary expedient; this proved inadequate, however.

The state police have provided an increasing number of services to local police since the turn of the century; in a number of jurisdictions these services include state systems of criminal identification, crime laboratory services, compilation of criminal statistics, police training programs, and communications services, such as radio and teletype. As state police agencies have developed, they have not displaced local authorities in function, even when they have been assigned similar duties. Hence, there has been a considerable amount of overlapping and conflict in jurisdictional powers. The tradition of local autonomy has hampered effort to establish some measure of state control over local police departments. The high mobility of criminals in recent years has become an increasingly serious problem for the states, calling for interstate coordination in dealing with offenders. Interstate compacts that facilitate extradition and fresh pursuit across state lines as well as reciprocal cooperation in the supervision of probationers and parolees are important developments that have recently taken place in a majority of states.

Federal Police

Today there are nine Federal police agencies, five of which are located in the Treasury Department. Their activities are for the most part poorly

---

[7] See Smith, *Police Systems in the United States,* pp. 119–120.

[8] The establishment of the Texas Rangers in 1835 began the development of state police systems.

coordinated. The Federal Bureau of Investigation of the Department of Justice is the best known of the Federal agencies.[9] It has played a significant role in the recruitment and training of competent and well-educated personnel. Since 1924, when J. Edgar Hoover assumed administration of the Bureau, it has established procedures that have generally been considered both efficient and fair. The growth of the Bureau and of the other Federal police agencies is a reflection of the expanded scope of Federal criminal law relating to interstate criminal activities. In contrast to other countries, the United States as a Federal system of government has avoided the development of a national police force. Hoover has vigorously opposed and avoided involving his agency in matters that are strictly the responsibility of state and local police. On the other hand, where crimes are involved that are matters of both Federal and state jurisdiction, there has been an increasing coordination between the FBI and other police agencies.

Urban Police

In place of centralized police administration, we rely in the main upon largely uncoordinated local law enforcement through city, county, township, and rural agencies. Among these, city police are the most numerous and important. According to information furnished the FBI and published in *Uniform Crime Reports,* there were 174,973 full-time police department employees in 3,769 cities on April 30, 1957.[10] For the nation as a whole, there were 2.0 police officers per 1,000 inhabitants, but the average ranged from 1.5 in communities with a population of less than 10,000 to 2.5 in cities over 250,000. The highest ratio occurred in the large cities of New England (3.8 per thousand) and the lowest in villages of New England and of the West South Central region (1.2 per thousand). It is believed that the higher the ratio of police to inhabitants, the better are the chances of preventing crime. However, quantity is certainly not the only thing involved. The quality, training, distribution, and administration of the force are important factors in efficiency.

Administrative Organization of Urban Police Departments

The structuring of the administrative organization of police departments in American cities varies widely.[11] Some of the larger municipalities have reorganized their departments numerous times within a span of fifty years, often without apparent improvement in over-all performance. The effectiveness of the police seems to depend more largely upon the capacities of the head, the competence and reliability of his subordinates, and the quality

---

[9] See, *inter alia,* Don Whitehead, *The F.B.I. Story,* 1957, and *Annual Reports,* Federal Bureau of Investigation.

[10] *Uniform Crime Reports,* Semiannual Bulletin, 1957, p. 24.

[11] See O. W. Wilson, *Police Administration,* 1950, especially Chaps. 2 and 3, and Bruce Smith, *op. cit.*

of the force itself than upon the particular form of administrative structure. Nevertheless, efficient operation may either be facilitated or thwarted by the way in which a department is organized. Good organization will not in itself assure competence, but effective performance is impossible without an adequate administrative system. There is no single ideal form of structure either for police departments or for other large government agencies. Police systems vary greatly in geographical jurisdiction, in numerical strength, and in powers and responsibilities. Other agencies also vary from one city or state to another. Nevertheless, certain basic principles of public administration are applicable to systems that may vary in detail. Some of the principles that have come to be recognized in the policing field, where effective leadership and command are paramount, are applicable also to the field of correctional administration.

A major problem that must be worked out in an administrative system is the relationship between the span of control and the length of the chain of command. A wide span of direct control by the administrator over numerous minor subordinates, may place excessive physical and psychological demands upon the chief. In a small department this is necessary but in larger departments too many decisions concerning matters of petty detail and routine operation are demanded of the chief.

Executive efficiency and specialization may be increased by reducing the span of control through establishing intermediate levels of supervisory officials and by delegating command to these subordinates. This is an essential step in any large organization.[12] While this simplifies control and permits the chief to focus his attention upon creative direction, problems of weakened leadership may develop as a result of inadequate liaison through the chain of command.[13] Any organization must compromise between the advantages of a broad span with personal leadership of the executive and a long chain of command that permits the executive to devote his time to matters of policy. As Wilson has pointed out, the optimum height and width of a pyramid of command is determined by circumstances

[12] Delegating power to too many subordinates increases the difficulty of command by requiring too large a span of control. "Leading commentators on the theory of organization place the limits of this span of control at six subordinates, though in some cases police forces have extended it to eight, without loss of directive power." Bruce Smith, *The Baltimore Police Survey,* Institute of Public Administration, 1941, p. 69.

[13] Wilson observes: "The extra level of authority interposed between him and the level of execution . . . lessens his personal participation in police operations, impedes somewhat the easy and rapid flow of information up and down the channels of control, lessens the ability of the leader personally to control operations, and may diminish the effectiveness of his personality and add to the department red tape. Lengthening the chain of command is not, therefore, an unmixed good. Each added level of authority removes the chief by one or more intermediary from actual operations and consequently from the opportunity personally to direct, coordinate, and control the efforts of the force." *Op. cit.,* p. 42.

peculiar to the individual organization, such as "time available for administrative tasks, the competence and reliability of subordinates, and the ability of the head to delegate authority." Sometimes the disadvantages implicit in establishing several deputies between the administrator and his functional division heads are avoided by using a single assistant chief as executive officer. This imposes large responsibility on such an assistant and requires his thorough understanding of the policy of the chief.

Regardless of the type of pyramid adopted it is vitally important that the police system be effectively coordinated to assure clear delegation of authority and responsibility at all levels and consistent control of personnel at all times. Control, in turn, requires continuous inspection to discover whether the task is being properly performed, what results are being achieved, and what changes in policy and practice may be needed to increase effective performance.

Traditionally the administrative head of the police departments is appointed by the mayor and may be removed at his pleasure. The administrator of a municipality must place responsibility upon his police chief and must have confidence in him. This may justify the method of appointing the police chief. Sometimes the result has been to subject the police system to the influence of machine politics, however. To avoid this some cities have placed police administration under the control of city councils, independent administrative boards, or commissions of public safety. In other cities the executive head of the police is chosen by popular election. August Vollmer held the view that the chief should be selected under civil service with permanent tenure, subject to removal only for cause. The writer agrees that the police system as a whole should operate under an effective merit system but questions the advisability of selecting the chief police administrator under rigid civil service rules. It may be desirable to establish minimum standards for the chief police officer, but ideally the mayor should be free to select the best person he can find. The chief of police, in turn, should be free to appoint his assistant executive officer, in whom he must have complete confidence. It appears that these two positions, whether in police or correctional administration, should be exempt from the ordinary systems of civil service appointment and from residence requirements.

FUNCTIONS AND POWERS OF THE POLICE

While the police have been assigned many tasks in modern cities, some only distantly related to their basic purpose, essentially the police have one major function to which all others must be subordinated. This is the function of enforcing the criminal law by detecting violations and, in so far as is possible by just methods, by discovering those who reasonably appear to be guilty so that their innocence or guilt may be determined by judicial agencies. Subordinate to this task and less clearly defined is their responsibility of protecting the public through preventive activities of various sorts, such as street and highway patrol.

Professor Wilson describes fifteen major functions that must be performed in the modern urban police department; where the organization is large enough, each function requires some specialization in personnel and administrative structure. They are (1) patrol, (2) traffic, (3) detective, (4) vice, (5) juvenile, (6) records and communication, (7) laboratory, (8) jail operation, (9) maintenance, (10) planning, (11) inspection, (12) budgets and accounts, (13) personnel, (14) public relations, and (15) intelligence. The first five functions are direct field operations, to which ordinarily about two-thirds of a large urban police force is assigned. In considering the functions of the police, a question may be raised concerning the extent to which they should engage in such activities as the prevention of attempted crime, the arrest of "suspicious persons," the establishment of curfews, the imposition of censorship, and other repressive activities short of arrest. Difficulty in crime control arises from the fact that efforts directed at efficiency in the prevention and control of crime may not only protect potential victims but may also threaten innocent persons who chance to come under suspicion. It is apparent that maximum efficiency in the prevention of crime could be attained only by extensive invasion of the privacy and freedom of all citizens. By adopting the enforcement and control that we associate with totalitarian police policy, perhaps more crimes could be solved and more prevented than under our system. On the other hand, a rigorous deference to rights of privacy, insistence upon a fair degree of certainty as a basis of police action, in short, a firm adherence to traditional conceptions of due process must inevitably limit the effectiveness of the police in making arrests and in getting convictions. The rules and standards that guide police action will now be discussed.

How much success do we wish the police to achieve, as measured by crimes prevented, offenses cleared by arrest, and the conviction of suspected persons? How much are we willing to give up to attain a high level of effectiveness, as measured in these terms? Conditions of living in modern mass society, with its anonymity and rapid mobility, with its opportunities for the commission of property crimes that remain undiscovered, and with its opportunities for quick and thorough concealment, limit the success attainable by traditional methods of investigation and detection. The public and the press, unfortunately, are inclined to overlook the inherent handicaps that limit the efficacy of police work. They clamor for greater efficiency in bringing criminals to book. This pressure and the emphasis within the police department on getting results cause the relaxing of due process standards that are designed to prevent injustice. The officer, confronted in his daily work by practical problems and often by dangers to his personal security, is apt to be guided by expediency rather than by the rule of law. The latter may appear quite irrelevant or unrealistic to the police-man in hot pursuit of a suspect who may be armed. To catch his prey, to secure promotion or a citation, and to improve his record is of greater concern to him than "technical" rules. Any knowledge of the law that he may have is more apt to be used as a means of rationalizing or justifying his action than as a guide to his conduct.

In the words of one authority on police methods: "The law of arrest by peace officers illustrates the discrepancy between law in books and law in action. . . . A great majority of arrests by police officers are illegal in their inception, continuance, or termination. This illegality is hardly the fault of the police for they cannot fulfill both their duty to obey the law and their duty to protect the community."[14] This quotation reveals a serious problem. Are we to tolerate and justify, as these comments appear to do, illegal activities of the police in the interest of more effective crime repression? The answer is clear: If it can be shown that the rules are too restrictive, they surely should be changed. But where policing agencies deliberately violate both civil and criminal laws to accomplish their goals, an intolerable situation exists. To permit police to establish their own rules administratively, as they now do to a great extent, will not solve the problem. Legal policy should be revised and police action should be in accord with measures that the legislature considers reasonable and just.

The rights and interests of the entire populace are too much at stake to abandon to the discretion of police administration the task of formulat-ing the methods by which law is enforced and the public protected. For the same reason, when police violate the laws, the investigation and disciplining of their conduct cannot safely be entrusted to the police de-partment itself, with its common disposition to conceal and condone abuses. Public interests cannot safely be subordinated to the morale of policing agencies whose fierce *esprit de corps* may be integrated around their own illegal practices. It is a fundamental task of the criminal law, therefore, not only to provide standards for police practice that are reasonable and just but also to apply effective sanctions for the maintenance of such standards to assure that they are more than paper rules. The major rules relating to police practice, the deviations from such rules, and the implications of administrative practice for policy will be considered below.

The Law of Arrest

The law of arrest represents a basic area of official policy, of course. While there is some variation in different jurisdictions, many states have adopted the rules of arrest that prevail in New York. A police officer may arrest without a warrant for a felony when he has *reasonable cause* to believe that a felony has been committed and that the person arrested has com-

[14] Sam Bass Warner, "Investigating the Law of Arrest," *A.B.H.S.*, vol. 26, p. 151, 1940.

mitted it.[15] Prior to amendatory legislation of 1958, the police in New York could not effect a valid arrest for a felony without a warrant unless the crime had actually been committed. For a misdemeanor he may arrest only when the act was committed *in his presence,*[16] except for certain traffic crimes, such as leaving the scene of an accident or driving while intoxicated coupled with an accident. The private citizen may also arrest for any crime committed in his presence. He may arrest a felon when the crime has *in fact* been committed and when the suspect has *in fact* committed that crime. He acts at his peril and may be sued for false arrest if the accused did not commit the felony. These rules mean that to support a valid arrest by a police officer there must at least be a charge of a specific crime and real foundation for suspecting the arrestee of that crime.

These rules have been criticized for putting too heavy a burden on the police. The rule concerning arrest for misdemeanors, at least, appears too conservative, considering modern conditions of law enforcement. The policy recommended by the American Law Institute in the Uniform Arrest Act (Section 6) would be more appropriate today. It would empower the police to arrest for a misdemeanor, though the criminal act was not committed in the officer's presence, if he had reason to believe that the suspect would not be apprehended unless he were taken immediately. In the case of felonies, too, the New York rule is sound, making arrest lawful when the officer has no more than reasonable cause to believe that a crime has been committed as well as reasonable cause to believe that the suspect committed it. The law of arrest should be sufficiently liberal to permit the apprehension of individuals whose guilt of crime seems clear. Because of the greater seriousness of these crimes, the rules applying to felonies must be somewhat more liberal than those applying to misdemeanors.

Police practice in many if not all large cities departs considerably from these rules. Arrests "on suspicion" where there is no specific charge, arrests without booking, and roundups of suspicious characters or individuals with prior arrest records are very common. Such arrests are illegal. Often men are charged with disorderly conduct, vagrancy, or conspiracy, as a means of holding them when there is no legitimate basis for arrest. Quotations from statements of New York City officials illustrate the attitudes of administrators toward these illegal practices.

Addressing a graduating class of the police academy, F. H. LaGuardia said:[17]

[15] *N.Y. Code Crim. Proc.,* secs. 177 and 179. In general, on arrests without a warrent, see Tresolini, Taylor, and Burnett, "Arrest without Warrant: Extent and Implications," *J. Crim. L.,* vol. 46, p. 187, 1955, and Roy Moreland, "Some Trends in the Law of Arrest," *Minn. L. Rev.* vol. 39, p. 479, 1955.

[16] *Ibid.,* sec. 177.

[17] *New York Times,* Apr. 19, 1939.

Some of these tinhorns and vagrants have political influence with some politicians. Don't be afraid of them. You've got them on the run. You will not be censured or transferred for picking up these vagrants in tailor-made, up-to-the-minute fashion clothes. When you pick up any of these tailored punks and you have a suspicion that they'll flash a roll, you may take them to the Health Department for a physical examination. [This device permits holding the individual for forty-eight hours.]

2416 CITY ARRESTS FOR NOISE AREN'T QUITE ALL A HULLA-BALOO. "Generally the arrests under that classification are for gambling," a police officer said. Then he added: "We couldn't make the gambling charge stick, probably, so we booked 'em for making unnecessary noise."[18]

Chief Inspector John J. O'Connell ordered policemen throughout the city in a drive "to arrest all professional criminals and all potential criminals found awaiting opportunities to commit crime."[19]

POLICE START DRIVE ON NIGHT PROWLERS. Out of scores questioned they have held eleven men unable to identify themselves. . . . The raiders started out soon after midnight and worked until 4 A.M. The policemen were operating under order of the Commissioner to harry all places where it was suspected that criminals might gather.[20]

FORECASTS 1,000 WILL BE TAKEN IN POLICE ROUND-UP. Police Commissioner's prediction in the drive against vagrants, idle ex-convicts, and street corner hoodlums.[21]

145 OF 704 TAKEN IN "HOODLUM" DRIVE GUILTY. Civic group condemns mass arrest here.[22]

NINTH DRIVE BAGS 135 AS UNDESIRABLES. Last week-end a total of 405 persons were arrested.[23]

POLICE CONTINUE CRIME ROUND-UP. Total of 243 arrested since Friday. Many are freed by week-end courts. Majority of arrests were for disorderly conduct or vagrancy. Courts turning those arrested back into the streets almost as fast as they were picked up.[24]

It will be observed that high police and governmental officials have conspired in these arrest practices. In such drives those who suffer are most commonly individuals who cannot afford to protest, those who do not know their rights, members of minority groups, inebriates, homosexuals, unemployed men, and some who have prior arrest records. Moreover, as in other forms of police activity, it is difficult to make effective protest about methods that the police themselves have employed. In the rare cases where individuals have succeeded in securing a court hearing in the matter, the criminal courts have usually supported the police actions and the civil courts, when allowing damages, have set them at a nominal figure. Under

[18] *World Telegram and Sun*, May 27, 1944.
[19] *New York Times*, Dec. 2, 1945.
[20] *Ibid.*, Jan. 21, 1946.
[21] *New York Post*, Oct. 28, 1950.
[22] *New York Times*, Nov. 4, 1950.
[23] *New York Post*, May 8, 1955.
[24] *New York Times*, June 16, 1957.

present structure and practice, therefore, the sanctions are almost completely ineffective in assuring legal police arrests.

Use of Force

The use of force in effecting arrests raises issues that are related to the
right of arrest itself. The pertinent legal rules in New York and many
other jurisdictions are these: in the case of felonies the officer may use all
necessary means to effect arrest if the accused flees or forcibly resists after
notice of the arrest, but he may inflict serious bodily injury or death only
when it is reasonably necessary to do so in self-defense, to overcome
resistance, or to halt a fleeing felon.[25] The officer may not use force to
seriously endanger the life of a misdemeanant to prevent his crime or to
prevent escape. Under revised legislation in New York in 1958, however,
he may do so if the circumstances are such that one would have reasonable
cause for believing that the committed crime was a felony. The officer
may use such force as is necessary in self-defense against either the misdemeanant or the felon or to overcome resistance (which itself is made
a felony by statute in some jurisdictions).[26] Concerning self-defense the law
permits the officer and the private citizen the same right to use force. In
practice the police take advantage of this right to a degree that would not
be tolerated from the civilian. The police are always armed and are generally believed by the courts when they assert that a suspect threatened
violence. Considering the hazards of police work, some tolerance here is
inevitable and desirable; illustrations below indicate, however, that force
sometimes exceeds the bounds of reason. Similarly, in "overcoming resistance" police often resort to unnecessary brutality. Moreover, while
compulsion is legal only when the arrest is valid, the ordinary citizen
is usually helpless at the time. The officer may not have given the suspect
notice that he is being placed under arrest. Indeed, there may be no valid
basis of arrest, yet the officer may and often does subsequently testify
that an arrest was made for some offense, such as disorderly conduct,
vagrancy, breach of the peace, or intoxication. He may indicate further
that the suspect offered resistance and that it was necessary, therefore, to
maim him. It is generally difficult or impossible for the victim of a police
assault to prove that there was no ground for an arrest, that the officer did
not place him under arrest, that he did not offer resistance, or that the
force employed was unreasonable. He may suffer not only a concussion on
the spot but a felony conviction later. From a practical standpoint, therefore, it is exceedingly dangerous for the citizen to stand on his legal rights,
either to resist an unlawful arrest, or to protest interrogation or detention
when there has been no valid arrest.

[25] See *Handley v. State,* 96 Ala. 48 (1891); *Loveless v. Hardy,* 79 So. 37 (Ala.,
1918); *N.Y. Code Crim. Proc.,* sec. 174.

[26] *New York Penal Law,* sec. 1055.

The rule that the police may not use violence merely to arrest a misdemeanant is sensible, for misdemeanants are not dangerous enough to justify infliction of serious injury. It appears, however, that allowing the officer to take the life of the fleeing felon "when reasonably necessary" to prevent his escape is dangerously liberal, encouraging official slaughter of suspects who, if they are guilty of felonies at all, have commonly committed only property crimes.[27] Perhaps police power to employ the revolver should be granted where it is clear that the suspect has committed homicide or is himself armed and will escape if he is not shot. It appears that aside from this situation, the right to use force should be limited to self-defense and overcoming violent resistance. Under the broad discretion now allowed, it is too easy for the police to rationalize the use of homicidal force where there is not in fact a basis for arrest, where the offense involved is only a misdemeanor, where it would have been possible to apprehend the suspect without shooting him, and where the suspect has merely fled in fright. Too often when the police do shoot, the result is lethal, thus avoiding the need to prove either the officer's justification or the suspect's guilt. Too often innocent bystanders are injured. The arming and violence of our criminals must be attributed in some fair part to the promiscuous employment of force by our police and to their philosophy of "exterminating rats," as contrasted with the relatively humane operation of authorities in England and some other countries. Unfortunately, conflict between "cops" and criminals has sunk to a level difficult if not impossible to mitigate by reversing the processes of conflict.

The seriousness of these problems is illustrated by brief quotations and headlines from New York papers:

F. H. LaGuardia to 217 police rookies, 203 of them war veterans: "Any time you walk into a situation in which firearms are being used in the commission of a crime, *be quick on the trigger.* You've got a nightstick. You've got a gun. They're not meant to be ornamental. When you know there's a crime being committed and there's a criminal in the place, go in with your gun in your hand. *Go in shooting.*"[28]

BRONX BOY OF 12 SHOT BY PATROLMAN. Fled from an Apartment House that He Was Suspected of Attempting to Enter.[29] *PATROLMAN KILLS YOUTH.* 16-year-old shot when running away from auto accident.[30] *COP'S SHOT HITS BYSTANDER.* Patrolman nabs two young (age 14) auto thieves.[31] *POLICEMAN KILLS BOY AS BURGLARY SUSPECT.*[32] *BOY, 14, SHOT*

[27] See Tappan, "Official Homicide," *Forum,* vol. 106, pp. 398–404, 1946. There is variation and ambiguity in the law of the states concerning extent of the privilege to take life. Some jurisdictions require either that the victim be shown to have committed a felony or, elsewhere, that a felony had been committed by someone.

[28] *New York Times,* Dec. 2, 1945.

[29] *Ibid.,* Feb. 6, 1945.

[30] *Ibid.,* Feb. 8, 1946.

[31] *New York Post,* Nov. 9, 1945.

[32] *New York Times,* Aug. 21, 1946.

IN HEAD FLEEING FROM POLICE. The culmination of his joy ride in a stolen automobile.[33] *MAN, 32, MISTAKEN FOR BURGLAR, SHOT.* Felled by patrolman's bullet after he resents queries in Rockaway Park.[34] *POLICE KILL YOUTH IN "PROWLER" HUNT.* Victim walking dog in yard, father says—two officers call shooting justified.[35] *SHOT AS PEEPER; IN GRAVE CONDITION.* A 30-year-old Brooklyn student shot and captured as a Peeping Tom after a 10-block chase.[36] *COP SHOOTS SUSPECT BUT IT'S WRONG MAN.* Had mistaken his car for one wanted in a holdup.[37] *POLICEMAN SHOOTS BOY 14.* Youth's Companion Seized as Pair, Acting Suspiciously, Flee.[38] *PROWLER SHOT BY POLICE.* British Sailor dies of bullet wound in Hoboken.[39] *BRONX YOUTH, 17, IS SHOT FLEEING COP.* Patrolman surprised him and three companions playing blackjack and fired two shots to halt their flight. Men are being held on disorderly conduct charges.[40] *CIVILIAN IS SHOT AIDING POLICEMAN.* Man trying to help in capture of purse thief hit by bullet from policeman's pistol.[41] *SHOT COSTS CITY $270,000.* Man shot by patrolman's bullet during street disturbance. Officer fired a warning shot and then emptied his revolver into a group while making an arrest.[42] *OFF-DUTY PATROLMAN CHASES BROOKLYN THIEF, FIRES TWICE.[43] MOTHER OF BOY COPS KILLED ASKS A QUESTION.* 16-year-old Irving Lefkin shot by police when running from a suspected burglary.[44] *BOY, 15, IS KILLED BY A POLICE SHOT.* Lad is hit by probationary patrolman while fleeing from street vandalism. His three associates booked on charges of malicious mischief.[45] *EAST HARLEM GROUP RAPS "PUNISHMENT BY BULLET."* George Martinez, 16, alleged to have run when approached for questioning about rape of two teen-aged girls. . . . Victims have declared that George was in no way involved in the attack.[46]

Police Interrogation and the Third Degree

Upon arrest the suspect is entitled to be brought before a magistrate "without unreasonable delay" to determine whether reasonable grounds exist to hold him for trial. The law makes no provision, for the most part, about functions of police during the interval prior to arraignment, except negatively to prohibit excessive or illegal detention and the coercion of confessions or other involuntary self-incrimination. In fact, however, dur-

[33] *Ibid., June* 21, 1946.
[34] *Ibid.,* Dec. 25, 1948.
[35] *Ibid.,* Sept. 28, 1948.
[36] *World Telegram and Sun,* Feb. 3, 1951.
[37] *New York Post,* Jan. 24, 1952.
[38] *New York Times,* Mar. 13, 1953.
[39] *Ibid.,* Apr. 2, 1953.
[40] *Ibid.,* undated.
[41] *New York Times,* Feb. 20, 1952.
[42] *Ibid.,* May 26, 1953.
[43] *Ibid.,* Feb. 28, 1954.
[44] *New York Post,* Jan. 27, 1955.
[45] *New York Times,* Feb. 14, 1955.
[46] *New York Post,* Nov. 3, 1955.

ing this interim inquisitional procedures of fundamental significance occur, partly because arrests are commonly made on insubstantial grounds. In other cases, individuals are questioned extensively without the formality of an arrest because the police hope to secure a basis for booking.[47] Even where there is evidence to support an arrest, police and prosecution are disposed to exploit the confusion of the suspect before he has had an opportunity to "make up a story" and to secure any evidence they can to assure his conviction, either by extracting a guilty plea, or by building a strong case for the trial. Illegal practices of detention, abusive interrogation, and search are very common, for it is thus that administrative authorities make an ostensibly good "record" and achieve personal and political advantage.

Detention may be unlawful because the suspect has not been arrested and is held involuntarily for questioning, because he is held incommunicado (without opportunity to secure the help of counsel), or because it is excessively prolonged. The expedience of postponing the booking of the suspect until the authorities have enough of a case to hold him reduces the danger of court rebuke for any of these practices. In any event, evidence secured through these illegal procedures is generally admissible and often serves at trial to convict the defendant. The right of the individual to sue or prosecute the police is consistently a poor remedy, so that the unlawful practices "pay off" in terms of results and are pursued with impunity.[48]

[47] For a discussion of the methods of inquiry before trial in the United States and in civil law countries, see Chapter 12.

[48] The central issue in cases of excessive and illegal detention is whether any confession or admission that results is inadmissible by reason of involuntary self-incrimination. Ordinarily it has been held that illegal detention taken alone is not enough to require exclusion of such confessions. In *McNabb v. United States,* 318 U.S. 332 (1943), the court held that incriminating statements should not have been admitted where defendants had been held incommunicado for fourteen hours without production before a magistrate, had been subjected for two days to constant questioning by a series of officers, and had been denied access to counsel. Similarly in *Haley v. State,* 332 U.S. 596 (1948), a 15-year-old murder suspect was interrogated for 4½ hours and then held incommunicado for three days. *Upshaw v. United States,* 335 U.S. 410 (1949), went further in holding that illegal detention (for thirty hours in this case) in itself was sufficient to constitute coercion and to justify exclusion of a confession secured thereby. On the other hand, in *State v. Cooper,* 10 N.J. 532 (1952), the New Jersey Supreme Court held that illegal detention does not alone require exclusion but that careful scrutiny was required to determine whether coercion had been employed. See also *People v. Perez,* 300 N.Y. 208 (1949). Justice Douglas in a dissenting opinion in *United States v. Carignan,* 342 U.S. 36 (1951), commented on the "disreputable practice which has honeycombed the municipal police system in this country" of detaining and arraigning a man on one charge, commonly a minor one, and using his detention as a "vehicle of investigation" to secure a confession for some other crime. Fred Inbau in a note on "Legal Pitfalls to Avoid in Criminal Interrogations," *J. Crim. L.,* vol. 40, p. 211, 1949, pointed to the need to employ specially selected and trained personnel for the task of interrogation and concluded that such person-

The worst abuses at this stage lie not in the illegal detention itself but in the coercion of confessions and admissions. Batteries of skilled interrogators often induce confessions through intensive and prolonged questioning. In accordance with the amount of resistance of the victim, methods employed to induce cooperation include promises of lenience, threats of physical injury, blinding lights, denial of tobacco, water, food, and sleep.[49] Where suspects are more stubborn or their inquisitors more brutal, various forms of violence may be employed, beatings with the fist or rubber hose being most common, perhaps. Other more esoteric and effective measures are used, however, such as the water cure, probing the teeth with dull dentist's drills, kicking and squeezing the testicles, repeatedly striking the adam's apple, and pounding with soft objects (e.g., sand or oranges in

---

nel need to avoid *continuous* lengthy interrogation and *relay* questioning if convictions based upon confession are to be sustained by the United States Supreme Court. Concerning the views on admissibility shared by three of the justices, he suggests, "the interrogator's situation must be classed as a rather hopeless one, for he obviously cannot conduct an effective interrogation in the presence of the accused person's counsel, friends or relatives; nor is it ordinarily feasible to conduct a satisfactory interrogation after the arrested person has been promptly arraigned."

In 1957 it was held in the case of *Mallory v. United States*, 354 U.S. 449, that any confession must be excluded in a Federal trial if it is made while the arrested person is held in police custody in violation of Rule 5(*a*) of the Federal Rules of Criminal Procedure. Rule 5(*a*) requires production before a United States commissioner without unnecessary delay. In the Mallory case there had been a 7½ hour delay and this was held excessive, perhaps because it occurred at a time when a commissioner was available for arraignment. Since that case some Federal judges have excluded confessions secured in less than an hour after arrest on the theory that the Mallory case does not permit the police to detain an arrested person for any length of time to interrogate him for the purpose of securing a confession. In 1958 the Subcommittee on Improvements in the Federal Criminal Code of the Senate Committee on the Judiciary proposed that hearings should be held with a view to the development of clarifying legislation on the meaning of Rule 5(*a*). See also Chapter 12, ftn. 8.

[49] For case materials and discussion of the problem of the third degree, consult *Report on Lawlessness in Law Enforcement*, National Commission on Law Observance and Enforcement, 1931; Ernest J. Hopkins, *Our Lawless Police*, 1931; E. H. Lavine, *The Third Degree*, 1930; Albert Deutsch, *The Trouble with Cops*, 1954; Bader, "Coerced Confessions and the Due Process Clause," *Brooklyn L. Rev.*, vol. 15, p. 51, 1948; Note, *Dickinson L. Rev.*, vol. 54, p. 223, 1950; and Paulsen, "The Fourteenth Amendment and the Third Degree," *Stanford L. Rev.*, vol. 6, p. 411, 1954. Several convictions have recently been reversed where it appeared that confessions had been obtained by brutality or coercion. See *New York Times*, May 2, 1956; Jan. 14, 1957, for cases of Fikes, Leyra. In 1956 the *New York Post* noted that "During a five year period ending last year, the City of New York was faced with claims totaling $22,383,721.25 filed by New Yorkers, mainly Negroes—who charged that they had been subjected to police brutality in Our Town. . . . Today, 224 of these 349 damage actions are still pending, with 186 of them already before the courts. $38,131.79 already paid to complainants in 17 cases, officials estimate that the others will cost the city nearly a half million dollars." Deputy Commissioner Arm said today: "In the old days, a complainant would be chased out of a police station or his complaint would be pigeonholed."

cloth bags). In general the police prefer not to leave lacerations, contusions, broken bones, or other obvious manifestations of brutality that would give color to the suspect's later allegations of forced confession. Their assertions that the defendant fell down stairs or otherwise injured himself invite small credence in the courts.

The insidious growth of the habit of brutality among police officers has been discussed by James F. Johnson, a former state trooper, Secret Service agent, security officer, and private investigator:[50]

> I have noted a fearful thing; when a new member comes into the department whose natural instincts are opposed to brutality, finally takes the first step and employs the third degree and gets a confession, from then on he thinks it's the only way to handle prisoners. He becomes a subscriber to planned brutality. [The first beating, according to Mr. Johnson, is prompted by "association and example" of older members of the force or even superiors who rough up prisoners] . . . The average citizen who says, "it served the bum right" forgets the officer who resorts to brutality doesn't always confine his activities to the guilty. . . . If a cop gets into the habit of beating up bums he'll soon be beating up everyone who crosses his path. It is a deadly narcotic-type habit.

The seriousness of the problem of brutality and the use of the third degree and official reactions to such conduct may be clearly inferred from some of the press accounts. It will be observed that a succession of police commissioners have displayed considerable tolerance of abuses:

HOGAN TO HELP BEATEN VET. . . . H. charged that he was attacked by an unidentified plainclothesman in a back room of the West 135th Street Precinct and that he suffered a fractured cheek bone after being struck with a nightstick and a blackjack, and kicked several times in the abdomen. Later, H. said, a second plainclothesman warned him to keep quiet about the beating.[51]

COMMISSIONER VALENTINE, irked at a prisoner in the police line-up: "He's the best-dressed man in this room. . . . *Don't be afraid to muss 'em up. Blood should be smeared all over that velvet collar.*" Response of LaGuardia: "That's the way I like to hear you talk, Lew. Muss 'em up if necessary."[52]

"TOUGH" POLICY DUE FOR HARLEM TODAY. Fristensky. . . . will step into his new post today, ready to implement Mayor O'Dwyer's and Police Commissioner Arthur W. Wallander's "get tough" policy.[53]

5TH CASE CHARGES POLICE BRUTALITY (the fifth in eleven days). High police officials implied that the men involved were probably only carrying out Police Commissioner Arthur W. Wallander's directive to *"be kind to good people and rough with bums and criminals."* [Emphasis added.][54]

[50] *World Telegram and Sun,* Mar. 10, 1953.
[51] *P.M.,* July 3, 1945.
[52] *Time,* Sept. 17, 1945.
[53] *New York Times,* Dec. 13, 1946.
[54] *Ibid.,* Oct. 20, 1947 [italics added]; See also *Time,* Oct. 20, 1947: "Cops started punching the wrong people and the people started yelling"; *New York Times,* Oct. 11, 1947: "The police head, as he had done on Thursday, emphasized

YOUTH IS ACQUITTED AFTER POLICE "BEATING." Tierney Indicted On Beating Charge. At the station house, C. testified, Patrolman Tierney accused him of being a Communist. Then, he said, when no money was found in his wallet, the policeman cursed him and hit him across the ear, assertedly breaking his eardrum. C. said he appealed to policemen in another room for help, but his plea was ignored.[55]

POLICE PROTECTION. Police Commissioner Murphy says "police brutality" is a scare-phrase invented by newspapers. He says he will provide top criminal lawyers—free of charge—to defend accused cops. . . . Within the past two months Supreme Court juries have ordered New York City to pay $160,000 to three Negro victims of random police attack; one of the victims, awarded $58,500, is a hopeless cripple as a result of the beatings. But to date not a single policeman has been suspended or molested for these incidents.[56]

MONAGHAN URGES POLICE TO BE "ROUGH ON RATS!" An admonition to be "rough on rats" and maintain continuous warfare against the narcotics peddlers, gamblers and racketeers whom he thus characterized was issued to top officials of the Police Department yesterday.[57]

CITY WON'T ACT ON PLAN TO END COP BRUTALITY. Although reported cases of police brutality doubled in 1951 and resulted in damage suits against the City estimated at $3,000,000, the Police Department has rejected appeals for special police training in human relations and for a pilot project to improve community relations. 80 brutality cases investigated in 1951 were

---

that it was the policy of the department to 'get tough with bums' but to keep hands off decent citizens"; *Ibid.*, Sept. 13, 1947: "In Jail At The Time, Cleared of Theft. Prisoner beaten by the police to elicit a confession, magistrate is told. Mr. Schmier told the court the police had hung Randazzo by his hands and flogged him with a rubber hose until he confessed . . . pointing out bruises on Randazzo's face, arms, and legs. . . . We of the Legal Aid Society are confronted with situations like this time and again. Many an innocent man is in prison as a result of admissions to the police."

[55] *Ibid.*, Jan. 19, Jan. 31, 1951; see also *Daily News,* Jan. 5, 1951: "2d Beating Laid to Cop Under Official Probe."

[56] *New Yark Post,* Mar. 15, 1951.

[57] *New York Times,* Sept. 18, 1951. See also *Ibid.*, Sept. 21, Sept. 24, 1951: "*Sitter Case Youth Charges a Beating.* Baring back before court, he accuses police— magistrate orders medical report. When Magistrate Nunez asked the youth, charged with rape, why he was crying, he explained that he had been kicked and beaten by the police four times during the night in the West Sixty-eighth Street Station. . . . He told the jurist he had been beaten with a rubber hose, blackjacks, and a steel weight he believed to be the parking light of an automobile. . . . Detective Ryan denied striking C. at any time. . . . He added, however, that C. had fallen down a flight of stairs and twisted his ankle in coming into the courtroom. Magistrate Nunez declared: 'It has been stated that the third degree is employed as a matter of course in many states and has become a recognized step in the process that begins with arrests and ends in acquittal or conviction. This is one of the problems that have confronted the courts. Even though it may seem expedient to the authorities in order to apprehend the guilty, whether a man goes free or not is a small matter compared with the maintenance of principles which still safeguard a person accused of crime.' At this point, Assistant District Attorney Seidler protested, asserted that what the magistrate had said 'on the record' was 'an outrage.' "

summarized at meeting of New York Civil Liberties Union and the Community Church.[58]

P.O. CLERK ASKS CITY FOR 100 G IN COP BEATING. Was released without being booked on any charge.[59]

POLICE BRUTALITY CHARGED. Legal Aid Attorney says many of society's defendants were hurt. Of 8,300 defendants represented last year in Felony Court by the Legal Aid Society, one-third showed signs of physical injury, ranging from scratches to broken jaws. . . . Some line officers of the Police Department "think it's all right to use brutal methods in making an arrest or, which happens most often, when they question a defendant in the police station."[60]

As various authorities have noted, the secrecy of police interrogation proceedings together with the effectiveness of coercion and intimidation, commonly having the tacit consent of judicial and political officials, makes it extremely difficult for the victim of police brutality to secure redress. In the nature of things it is generally impossible for the suspect to prove that his confession has been involuntary or that he has been beaten; the suspect rarely has witnesses in his behalf and he fears retaliation. Only in most flagrant cases, therefore, is the sadistic or drunken officer disciplined or the victim protected. Experience in New York City in 1953 indicated very clearly that, with the cards already well stacked against victims of official assault, their lot can be made worse by removing in effect the deterrent influence of Federal civil rights legislation.[61]

[58] *New York Post,* Jan. 31, 1952.

[59] *New York Times,* Feb. 27, 1953, and see *World Telegram and Sun,* Feb. 25, 1953: *"Magistrates Accused of Hushing Brutality.* Councilman Brown charged 'what amounts to a conspiracy between the Magistrates' Courts and the police, from the precinct level up.' He cited the experience of E. W. Jacko, chairman of the legal redress committee of the N.Y. NAACP, who said magistrates often try to induce complainants to drop charges against police. 'Moreover,' Mr. Brown stated, 'the whole burden of collecting evidence, lining up the witnesses and getting them to court is put on the civilian. In the meantime, the police often try to talk the witnesses and even the complainants from appearing and pressing charges. . . . The citizen has all the breaks against him. The FBI is the only agency to turn to in cases of gross injustice by policemen. It is not handicapped by close contact with brother officers. The whole point is lost if the Police Department, as Commissioner Monaghan wants, lines up cases and witnesses and hands them, warmed-over, to the FBI.' "

[60] *New York Times,* Mar. 5, 1953.

[61] See Chapter 13, ftn. 26. The *New York Times,* Mar. 1, 1953, reported that the FBI investigates each year about 200 complaints of police brutality in the United States but that there are few prosecutions. "One reason is that most of the brutality charges grow out of incidents that take place in precinct stations and there are seldom any disinterested witnesses around a police station." At House Judiciary subcommittee hearings it was revealed that Commissioner Monaghan had on four occasions refused the FBI permission to interrogate policemen charged with beating Negroes in August of 1952. New York City police authorities reached an agreement that they should be allowed to make investigations of alleged brutality and report to the Attorney General before any interrogation by the FBI should be permitted. These investigations commonly involved months of delay that effectively excluded

As a consequence of the publicity that attended the revelation of promiscuous brutality inflicted in particular upon minority group members, the New York City Police Department changed its disciplinary policy, requiring early departmental trials without awaiting the results of civil actions in the courts and a Civilian Complaint Board was set up to deal promptly with complaints.[62] A few weeks later a plan was announced to strengthen the police training in minority group relationships through an in-service program.[63] Since 1953, during the police administrations of Commissioner Adams and Commissioner Kennedy, there has been little evidence of the brutality that was officially supported a few years ago and there has been a firm emphasis upon legality in police operations. At the same time, it is interesting to observe that under a revised system of police reporting the rate of clearance by arrests of crimes known to the police has greatly increased. Under Commissioner Kennedy the police have been disciplined more firmly than they have been for many years; this has occasioned disturbance in some quarters within the department. It is clear, however, that they have done a more effective job, not only in discovering criminals, but also in avoiding persecutory practices.[64]

Search and Seizure

The general rule on search and seizure appears simple enough, but in practice complicated issues have been raised concerning the methods that may be employed in police investigations and the sanctions by which proper procedures may be guaranteed. The chief questions are (1) What constitutes a legal search? (2) What may be the scope of such search? (3) What seized property may be admitted in evidence? Under the Fourth

---

any significant Federal protection through the statute. New York police authorities maintained that they were the "target of communistic and other radical groups" and the New York Post was accused of bolstering "the street corner punks and the gutter hoodlums . . . vermin [they had] encouraged to talk back to police officers." See the *New York Times*, Feb. 28, 1953; Mar. 2, Mar. 3, 1953. When Attorney General Brownell abrogated the memorandum of his predecessor, over fifteen complaints of violations were made on a single day and referred to the FBI for investigation. New York City paid more than $200,000 for damages on verdicts based on police brutality during 1951–1952. See *New York Times*, Feb. 19, 1953.

[62] *World Telegram and Sun*, Apr. 30, 1953, and *New York Times*, May 23, 1953.

[63] *New York Times*, Mar. 12, 1953; May 19, 1953.

[64] Evidence of ostensible improvement in police efficiency in New York was shown by considerable changes in the rate of crimes cleared by arrest between 1952 and 1957. The defective system of reporting was radically revised in 1953 and in that year the rate of felony clearance was 23.5 per cent. It went to 36.5 in 1954 under Commissioner Adams' administration and to 57.4 per cent in 1956 under Commissioner Kennedy. *New York Times*, Feb. 4, 1955; June 3, 1957. Evidence of increased discipline was shown by the considerable number of ousters of police officers during 1955 and 1956 after a long period of administrative tolerance of offenses committed by the police. See *New York Times*, Dec. 15, 1956, indicating a total of fifty-six discharges up to that time under the new commissioner.

Amendment, the Federal law is that search may be made under a warrant on the showing of probable cause and a description of the place or persons to be searched and the things to be seized.[65] Search and seizure may also be made in connection with a valid arrest.[66] The scope of the search that may be made is limited, but the case law has not clearly defined its legitimate extent and the view of the Supreme Court has shifted.[67] Where evidence is gained through illegal search and seizure by Federal officers, it is not admissible, according to case law laid down in 1914 and incorporated

[65] In general, articles seized under a warrant should be only those described in the warrant, though officers may seize visible instruments of crime at the scene. *Marron v. United States,* 275 U.S. 192 (1927). A warrant cannot be general but must be for a limited category of articles, such as contraband and stolen goods. *Gouled v. United States,* 255 U.S. 298 (1921). See Fraenkel, "Recent Developments in the Federal Law of Searches and Seizures," *Iowa L. Rev.,* vol. 33, p. 472, 1948.

[66] In *Trupiano v. United States,* 334 U.S. 699 (1948), conviction of the defendant was reversed by a divided court where Federal officers had made a lawful arrest and then, without a warrant, had seized an illegal still, equipment, and contraband property. It was held that the officers had had time and sufficient information to secure a warrant. However, in 1950 in *United States v. Rabinowitz,* 338 U.S. 886, where Federal officers had searched the defendant's office and discovered altered stamps, the search was held lawful as an incident of arrest although they could have secured a warrant. Similarly in *Brinegar v. United States,* 338 U.S. 160 (1949), where officers had pursued a suspected bootlegger and searched his car, the Supreme Court upheld a conviction based upon the seizure. This conviction was made on the ground that it is not practicable to secure a warrant to search a moving vehicle. In *Johnson v. United States,* 333 U.S. 581 (1948), where Federal officers had smelled opium coming from a room, they obtained entrance and placed Johnson under arrest, searching her room, where they found opium and a warm smoking apparatus. Conviction was reversed on the ground that arrest could not be justified by the search and at the same time the search be justified by the arrest: the validity of a search must be tested by the authority of the officer at the beginning of the transaction.

[67] In general authorities may not use an arrest as a basis for conducting a "fishing expedition." In *United States v. Willis,* 85 F. Supp. 745 (S.D. Cal. 1949), and in *Rochin v. California,* 342 U.S. 165 (1952), it was held that where authorities pumped the stomachs of defendants whom they suspected of having swallowed narcotics to avoid arrest the search was unreasonable and conviction should be reversed. In *Harris v. United States,* 331 U.S. 145 (1947), however, where the FBI had arrested a defendant under a valid warrant of arrest for cashing a forged check and then had searched his entire apartment for about five hours without success to find checks for evidence, a conviction was upheld based upon their discovery instead of classification cards and registration certificates. Four members of the court vigorously dissented on the grounds of the extent of the search and the seizure of contraband unrelated to the crime on which the arrest was based. In *Agnello v. United States,* 269 U.S. 20 (1925), the Supreme Court stated: "The right without a search warrant contemporaneously to search persons lawfully arrested while committing crime and to search the place where the arrest is made in order to find and seize things connected with the crime as its fruits or as the means by which it was committed as well as weapons and other things to effect an escape from custody is not to be doubted." How far such searches may be carried is not clear, but it appears that search connected with arrest may go further than search based on a warrant.

in the *Federal Rules of Criminal Procedure*.[68] Since the Fourth Amendment is applicable only to Federal agencies, however, evidence illegally seized by private individuals or by state law enforcement officers working independently is not excluded in Federal trials; thus the protection of the exclusionary rule has been considerably diluted.[69]

All of the state constitutions make provision comparable to that of the Fourth Amendment against unreasonable search and seizure. The issue of exclusion was raised in *Wolf v. Colorado,* 338 U.S. 25 (1949), where local officers had seized the personal medical records of a physician without a warrant and secured a conviction for abortion. The United States Supreme Court held that the Fourteenth Amendment does not forbid the admission of evidence in state courts secured through unreasonable search and seizure.[70] Hence, in accordance with the rules of evidence in the particular jurisdiction, the tainted seizure may be admissible.

Thirty states admit evidence illegally procured, as do the nations of the British Commonwealth generally, and provide protection against illegal invasion of personal and property rights merely through an action for damages against those who are responsible, if they are discovered. While the policy of admission or exclusion is a matter of rules of evidence that is not determined by the constitutional provision, it should be noted that the result of allowing such evidence to support the state's case is virtually to nullify the constitutional guarantee. The power to sue state officers for

[68] See *Weeks v. United States,* 232 U.S. 383 (1914), and Rule 41(*e*). In *Walder v. United States,* 347 U.S. 62 (1954), however, a limitation was established on the Federal rule when it was held that the government should have been allowed to impeach the denial of the defendant's testimony that he had never sold or possessed heroin by testimony that heroin had been found in his home, even though it had been discovered in an illegal search.

[69] See *Weeks v. United States,* 232 U.S. 383 (1914). The courts will not sanction apparent collusion between Federal officers and those who make illegal search, but such collusion is difficult to discover. Consult Note, "Judicial Control of Illegal Search and Seizure," *Yale L. J.,* vol. 58, p. 144, 1948; and 50 ALR2d 531, 1956.

[70] In the leading New York case, *People v. Defore,* 242 N.Y. 13 (1926), Judge Cardozo, in holding such evidence admissible, said: "We are confirmed in this conclusion when we reflect how far-reaching in its effect upon society the new consequences would be. The pettiest peace officer would have it in his power, through overzeal or indiscretion, to confer immunity upon an offender for crimes the most flagitious." Speaking against the New York rule United States Senator Robert F. Wagner said in 1938, "I profoundly believe that a search and seizure guarantee which does not carry with it the exclusion of evidence obtained by its violation is an empty gesture; it is an amendment which will be wholly ineffective in protecting the constitutional privacy which we seek to confer. If I may borrow a phrase of Justice Cardozo's which has not been quoted before, it speaks the word of promise to the ear and it breaks it to the hope. . . . To guarantee civil rights in theory and permit constituted authority to deny them in practice, no matter how justifiable the ends may be or may seem, is to imperil the very foundation on which our Democracy rests." In 1955 California adopted the exclusionary rule. *People v. Cahan,* 282 P. 2d 905, and see Note, *J. Crim. L.,* vol. 46, p. 430, 1955.

their illegal acts has proved to be a completely ineffectual sanction in the United States, so that the invasion of privacy is officially invited and very widely prevalent.[71] Criminal investigation is made easy and quick when the police can invade premises that have come under some suspicion and can seek evidence that may be used for a prosecution. There is little motive for officials who are guided more by their yen for "results" than for abstract principles of justice to secure a warrant, even if there are sufficient grounds to issue one; likewise once they have obtained a warrant there is little motive for officials to stay within its limiting provisions concerning what may be searched or seized. In an evasive deference to the law officials may most easily search without a warrant and, if contraband is found, *then* secure a warrant to support their seizure.

The free admission of evidence illegally obtained not only damages civil rights but the attitudes of the public, particularly among minority groups whose liberties are most frequently invaded. These damaging results have become very clear in New York City where for a number of years the police displayed a superb disregard for constitutional rights. One former justice told an investigating committee of the Bar Association there that in his term on the bench he had found that the police regarded warrants as "completely irrelevant." Justice Oliver, in reversing a prostitution conviction, said that the state constitutional rule against unlawful search and seizure "might as well be written by a sky-writer in a storm at night, for all it is worth." Justice Oliver wrote:[72]

Though persons have the right to resist unlawful invasion by police, as a practical matter when three or four police giants, armed with guns, break into a home, the prudent citizen, allergic to plastic surgery, gives up this constitutional right very rapidly. . . . The police do not bother about getting warrants. They know the rules of evidence so they laugh at the constitution, but the Court of Appeals laid down a plan for safeguarding the civil liberties of the people. It provided for sanctions so that the rule of evidence would not repeal and destroy the constitution. . . . The rule of evidence subordinates the courts to the lawlessness of the police. We are supposed to ratify the boldest and most lawless type of rough-house the police engage in.

Wiretapping

The Fourth Amendment came into force in 1791, a century before wiretapping was invented. In the leading case, *Olmstead v. United States,* 277 U.S. 438, 48 Sup. Ct. 564, it was held that wiretapping did not violate that amendment, though in his dissent Justice Taft noted that "Discovery

---

[71] On the considerable frequency of unlawful searches, see *Report of the President's Committee on Civil Rights,* 1947; "Judicial Control of Illegal Search and Seizure," *Yale L. J.,* vol. 58, p. 144, 1948; and Reynard, "Freedom from Unreasonable Search and Seizure," *Ind. L. J.,* vol. 25, p. 259, 1950.

[72] *New York Times,* July 10, 1951.

and invention have made it possible for the Government, by means far more effective than the rack, to obtain disclosure in court of what is whispered in the closet." Brandeis in his dissent commented trenchantly upon the dangers to a decent administration of justice of tolerating official illegality in measures of law enforcement:

Decency, security and liberty alike demand that government officials shall be subjected to the same rules of conduct that are commands to the citizen. In a government of laws, existence of the government will be imperilled if it fails to observe the law scrupulously. Our Government is the potent, the omnipresent teacher. For good or for ill, it teaches the whole people by its example. Crime is contagious. If the Government becomes a law-breaker, it breeds contempt for law; it invites every man to become a law unto himself; it invites anarchy. To declare that in the administration of the criminal law the end justified the means—to declare that the Government may commit crimes in order to secure the conviction of a private criminal—would bring terrible retribution. Against that pernicious doctrine this Court should resolutely set its face.

The strong criticism of this decision led in 1934 to the outlawing of wiretapping in the Federal jurisdiction by Section 605 of the Federal Communications Act, providing a fine up to $10,000 and imprisonment up to two years for violations.[73] In the Nardone case of 1937[74] it was held that transcripts and recordings of interstate messages could not be admitted

[73] Section 605 of the Federal Communications Act of 1934, drawn from a provision of the prior Federal Radio Act, provides: " . . . no person not being authorized by the sender shall intercept any communication and divulge or publish the existence, contents, substance, puport, effect, or meaning of such intrcepted communication to any person . . . and no person having received such intercepted communication . . . shall . . . use the same or any information therein contained for his own benefit or the benefit of another not entitled thereto. . . . " 47 U.S.C. sec. 605 (1948).

It has been said that this legislation making wiretapping a misdemeanor would, if strictly interpreted and enforced, end interception in state as well as Federal practice. There has been conflicting opinion, however, on the proper interpretation of the statute. Since the late 1940s some Federal agencies have adopted the view that the legislation does not purport to prohibit or penalize interception as such but only interception *and* divulging. This interpretation permits the investigating agency to develop leads through wiretapping, though with some danger of reversal. Furthermore, state and local agencies in a number of jurisdictions have held that the interdiction of Section 605 against any "person" is not applicable to them. Wiretapping is specifically permitted by constitution or statute in some jurisdictions (see discussion of New York below). Federal authorities have not prosecuted state officers for violation of the Federal statute. It appears unlikely that they will do so both as a matter of comity and because Federal agencies, too, employ interception. It is possible, however, that the Benanti decision of December, 1957, may have some influence on local as well as Federal practice. See text and footnote 80 below. Also consult Note, "Congressional Wiretapping Policy Overdue," *Stan. L. Rev.,* vol. 2, p. 744, 1950.

[74] *Nardone v. United States,* 302 U.S. 379 (1937).

into evidence and in *Weiss v. United States* (1939),[75] the interdiction was held to pertain to intrastate as well as interstate communications. A second Nardone case,[76] in 1939, precluded the use of evidence that was not itself an intercepted communication but that had been obtained as a result of an intercepted communication: the government must prove independent origin of its subsequent evidence. However, the Supreme Court has found that using a detectaphone to overhear a man talking into a phone in the next room was not a violation of the amendment.[77] The Court has also upheld the conviction of defendants who had confessed to crime on the basis of the content of wiretap recordings that the authorities revealed to them, holding that, as in the case of unlawful searches and seizures, only one whose rights have actually been infringed may have the protection of the exclusionary rule.[78] In this case none of the defendants had been parties to the intercepted conversations. The general rule applicable to searches and seizures, permitting a state under its rules of evidence to admit evidence illegally seized, has been applied specifically to information secured through unlawful wiretaps in the case of *Schwartz v. Texas* in 1952.[79] The Supreme Court has held in the Benanti case in 1957 that where state officers have turned information gained through wiretapping over to Federal authorities the latter may not use this in evidence in a Federal court.[80]

The Federal rule on unlawful searches and the practices of the FBI

[75] 308 U.S. 321 (1939).

[76] *Nardone v. United States,* 308 U.S. 338 (1939). However, this decision requires that the defendant, in any case where he protests, show not only the wiretapping but that a substantial part of the government's case against him was "a fruit of the poisonous tree," leaving it then to the prosecution to convince the trial court that its proof had an independent origin. The burden upon the defendant is a heavy one.

[77] *Goldman v. United States,* 316 U.S. 129 (1942). The Supreme Court has also held in the Rathburn case that where the police listened in on a telephone extension this did not constitute interception within the meaning of Section 605. *New York Times,* Dec. 10, 1957.

[78] *Goldstein v. United States,* 316 U.S. 114 (1942).

[79] 344 U.S. 199 (1952).

[80] In this case the New York police, acting with a warrant properly secured under New York law to intercept information concerning a state violation of the narcotic laws, discovered instead a quantity of alcohol lacking Federal tax stamps and a Federal conviction resulted. Although Federal officers took no part in the interception, Chief Justice Warren in his unanimous opinion for the court held that "the statute (Section 605) was violated if not earlier at least upon the disclosure to the jury of the existence of the intercepted communication. . . . " The court further held that Section 605 was intended by the Congress to apply to state as well as Federal practice, in effect disapproving the contention that the state may legalize interception and divulgence. *New York Times,* Dec. 10, 1957. There was dictum in this case that analogy to application of the Fourth Amendment was inappropriate because of the absolute prohibition of Section 605. *Weeks v. United States,* 232 U.S. 383 (1914). Query whether the much criticized policy of the Weeks case will be changed.

under that law have been very widely respected for a combining of justice and efficiency. Therefore it was something of a shock to many to be informed that in the Coplon case more than eighty tappers had "swarmed all over the wires" to secure evidence of espionage and that government agents had rifled private mail, had arrested the defendant on insufficient grounds without a warrant, and had destroyed both the evidence of the wiretapping and all the administrative records dealing with it in the New York office.[81] In response to public protests against this conduct Attorney General McGrath asserted that the Justice Department and the FBI had condoned "limited" use of wiretapping under Attorneys General Jackson, Clark, and Biddle.[82] Since two of these officials have since become justices of the Supreme Court, it is not difficult to imagine that such practice will continue. Attorney General Brownell submitted a bill to both houses of Congress in 1953 to legalize the use of evidence obtained by wiretapping in Federal criminal cases involving "national security or defense," providing no penalty for unauthorized tapping. In support of his bill the Attorney General said: "It is quite unrealistic and thoroughly unreasonable that though evidence is obtained showing a clear violation of the law against subversion the hands of the prosecuting officers are tied and their efforts to maintain the security of the nation are thwarted."[83]

Telephone tapping in New York began as early as 1895. Until 1916 it appears to have been employed by municipal police and Federal agents mainly to uncover drug peddlers, murderers, kidnappers, and other serious felons. Starting in 1917 the lines of aliens were intercepted on a vast scale. During Prohibition telephone tapping came to be used very widely not only to apprehend

---

[81] See comments of J. L. Fly, former chairman of the Federal Communications Commission, *New York Times*, Jan. 17, 1950.

[82] *New York Times*, Jan. 9, 1950. It appears that before 1924 tapping was freely practiced by the Federal agencies but was banned as "unethical tactics" in that year by Attorney General Stone. The government returned to its use in 1931 but Attorney General Jackson in 1940 imposed a firm prohibition on interception as a violation of law. J. Edgar Hoover condemned the practice at that time as "archaic and inefficient . . . a definite barrier in the development of ethical, scientific, and sound investigative technique." During the 1940s, however, the Bureau again employed interception and in 1949 Hoover indicated that tapping was employed "in a very limited type of cases with the express approval in each instance of the Attorney General. . . . " Clark and McGrath publicly admitted the practice in 1949 and 1950. When the storm of disapproval descended on the basis of the revelations of authorities' conduct in the Coplon case, Hoover indicated on Jan. 15, 1950, that only 170 taps were in existence on that day. In 1954 he was quoted as saying that FBI wiretaps had at no time exceeded 200 and that they were used only for such serious crimes as espionage, subversion, sabotage, and kidnapping. See Helfeld, "A Study of the Justice Department Policies on Wire Tapping," *Law. Guild Rev.*, vol. 9, p. 744, 1949; Note, *Harv. L. Rev.* vol. 53, p. 863, 1940; Comment by Hoover, *Yale L. J.*, vol. 58, p. 401, 1949; *New York Times*, Apr. 6, 1950; and Feb. 27, 1955; and *Washington (D.C.) Evening Star*, May 11, 1954.

[83] *New York Times*, May 9, 1953.

bootleggers but more generally in the investigation of petty vice. It appears that at this time wiretapping came increasingly to be used in divorce cases, blackmailing, and various rackets.[84] It was not until 1938, after the first Nardone decision, that the state constitution was revised to authorize tapping under court order. The Code of Criminal Procedure permits such orders to be issued on application of a district attorney, state attorney general, or a police officer above the rank of sergeant and the order is good for six months at a time.[85] Criminal penalties are provided for unauthorized tapping, but in 1955 there had been only one successful prosecution. The law does not make it an offense for a man without an official order to put a device on his own phone "to protect his business interests or the sanctity of his home."

Information concerning the prevalence of wiretapping is very difficult to secure. Testimony of some interest was brought before the Celler Committee[86] in 1953, however, and reports were made to the newspapers in 1955 because of the widespread concern that had been generated about the practice. The police commissioner of New York City reported that the police tapped 1,081 wires in 1954.[87] The district attorney's offices indicated that they secured "about 170 court orders a year."[88] It appears that approximately half of the lines tapped are public or semipublic phones, however, so that a very large number of users may be intercepted under a single order in the course of the life of the order. The police commissioner reported that 395 arrests resulted from the 1,081 taps, 327 of these for morals charges, including bookmaking and prostitution, and 68 for other offenses.[89] He did not provide information concerning convictions resulting from the arrests. It is impossible, of course, to determine how widespread illegal tapping has become, though devices may be used to detect interception on a user's line. It has been estimated that there are far more unauthorized than authorized tappings in New York City.[90] While New York has the questionable distinction of being the greatest center for legal and illegal telephone interception, it has been suggested that, per capita, tapping is even more common in Washington, D.C.[91]

[84] See *New York Times,* Feb. 2, 1955; The wiretap menace relates to the development of a specialist group in the field, rich rewards being involved in blackmailing, securing divorce evidence, and unscrupulous practices of businessmen and labor leaders.

[85] *Ibid.,* Feb. 25, 1955.

[86] *Wiretapping for National Security, Hearings before Subcommittee No. 3 of the House Committee on the Judiciary,* 83d Cong., 1st Sess. See Note, "Analysis of the Law and Practice under New York Constitutional and Statutory Provisions," *N.Y.U.L. Rev.,* vol. 31, p. 197, 1956, for an excellent review of practice in New York and the work of the Celler Committee.

[87] *New York Times,* Mar. 9, 1955.

[88] *Ibid.,* Feb. 25, 1955.

[89] *Ibid.,* Mar. 9, 1955.

[90] *Ibid.,* Feb. 27, 1955. The feature writer reported here: "A former law enforcement officer told this writer a few days ago: 'Detectives use wiretaps on maybe half of all the important police cases in New York, and many use wiretaps as a routine thing to pick up leads on bookmaking, prostitution and other crimes without bothering to get court orders or even to let their captains know they're tapping.' " One authority in the field of crime detection estimated that for every authorized wiretap "there are four more illegal wiretaps, either by the police or by private investigators."

[91] *Ibid.,* Feb. 27, 1955.

In recent years, as questions of national defense and security have been stressed, it has become increasingly common for proponents to recommend the use of wiretapping for purposes of criminal investigation in jurisdictions where it is now prohibited. A distinguished professor of criminal law, in commenting on the wiretap cases, doubts that the method is either unethical or unreasonable "in view of the fact that its purpose was solely to discover the identity of enemies of society. . . ."[92] This comment from a noted district attorney in New York City expresses the general view of prosecutors: "Is there anything so sacrosanct about a telephone conversation that a man can plot murder by phone and then his conversation cannot be used as evidence?" These superficial evaluations avoid the central point that opening the door to wiretaps as a means of law enforcement involves its abuse in minor as well as major cases; and indeed it appears from experience that abuse is much more frequent in minor cases.[93] Wiretapping involves invasion of the privacy of innocent as well as guilty individuals and, when promiscuously practiced, as it has been in New York City and elsewhere, it may be used for purposes of blackmail, political and business intrigue, and other despicable ends.[94] The goal of exterminating the enemies of society may be used to rationalize *any* measure of law enforcement, however illegal or uncivilized, that may be employed. Thus officials have attempted to justify third degree brutalities, illegal detention, shooting of suspects, unlawful seizures, and official trespass as well as wiretapping; the entire gamut of police state methods may be sanctioned. Justice Douglas of the Supreme Court Bench, speaking in 1953 of the "practices and procedures that impinge heavily upon the liberties of the citizens" and calling for a lawyers' crusade to revive official respect for the dignity of the individual, asserted that "we have built in this country a vast network of wiretappers and informers." It appears very clear, as in other phases of the means-ends controversy, that contemptible means contaminate benign objectives.

Entrapment and Informers

Entrapment is another technique occasionally employed in law enforcement that has been widely condemned. In entrapment the police initiate and instigate crime in order to make an arrest. As in the case of other illegal measures, entrapment is used most commonly in the areas of vice, particularly in the policing of prostitution, homosexuality, bootlegging, and

[92] John B. Waite, *Criminal Law and Its Enforcement*, 1947, p. 562.

[93] Robert M. Daru, chief counsel of a criminal bar inquiry in New York City, concluded that from 75 to 90 per cent of the authorized taps in the city were in cases of prostitution and bookmaking. *New York Times*, Dec. 12, 1948.

[94] Special Sessions Judge Frank Oliver has commented, "A man's home is not his castle in New York. It is just an uncovered garbage can for the police to pick over." Assistant District Attorney Julius Helfand, in connection with the presentment of a Kings County grand jury condemning "loose, irregular and careless" methods employed by the police department in wiretapping, charged that information was used by members of the department as a "club to blackmail and shake down bookmakers." See *New York Times*, Dec. 28, 1950. A City Hall figure informed a *Times* reporter that "It's pretty generally known that almost every wire at City Hall has a tap on it right now." *Ibid.*, Sept. 30, 1948.

narcotics. Where an act is performed that the defendant would not have engaged in had it not been for the persuasion of police officers, the officers are the procuring cause and the accused has a legitimate defense. Subtle questions are involved, however, in determining whether officers have gone too far in providing opportunity or in the instigation of an offense and in determining whether the defendant acted upon his own volition. The courts have expressed a considerable tolerance for artifice, deception, and stratagem in the apprehension of criminals but have drawn the line against the conduct of officers who "incite to and create crime for the sole purpose of prosecuting and punishing it."[95] The courts have said that it is contrary to public policy and law "to punish a man for the commission of an offense of the like of which he had never been guilty, either in thought or in deed, and evidently never would have been guilty of it if the officers of the law had not inspired, incited, persuaded, and lured him to attempt to commit it."[96] The courts have very commonly permitted the government to show in rebutting a defense of entrapment that the police had reasonable cause to believe the defendant was a person disposed to commit the offense, and the proof has usually involved an effort to show that the defendant had a bad reputation or had previously been convicted. This means, of course, that men with prior criminal records are particularly subject to entrapment and to conviction in spite of the official misconduct.[97]

The common use of quota systems in police vice-squad work encourages practices of instigation and entrapment. Too frequently, police blackmail is employed, the officer seducing his victims to crime and then promising immunity for a consideration.[98] The Seabury investigation in New York City in 1932 revealed a number of such instances.[99] The present chief magistrate of New York City has expressed the opinion that vice-squad work "inevitably corrupts the men engaged in it."

[95] *Sorrells v. United States,* 287 U.S. 435 (1932).

[96] *Ibid.*

[97] Thus in the case cited the court said, " . . . if the defendant seeks acquittal by reason of entrapment he cannot complain of an appropriate and searching inquiry into his own conduct and predisposition as bearing upon that issue. If in consequence he suffers a disadvantage, he has brought it upon himself by reason of the nature of the defense." In a concurring opinion Mr. Justice Roberts disapproved this contention, noting that the result would be to condone and render innocuous the conduct of officials where poor reputation could be shown and to permit conviction on the basis of the defendant's former acts or reputation.

[98] Albert Deutsch, *The Trouble with Cops,* 1954, pp. 85–87, and Morris Plowcowe, *Sex and the Law,* 1951, pp. 250–254. Deutsch quotes one vice-squad head as telling him: "I don't care how my men catch them, so long as they catch the right ones. You can't afford to be completely scrupulous. Rats must be trapped." P. 86. See also *New York Post,* Apr. 14, 1955, and *New York Times,* July 20, 1955, for indictments of members of the New York City Police Narcotics Squad and their conviction for inducing offenders to sell narcotics and share profits with them.

[99] Final Report of Samuel Seabury, Referee; In the Matter of the Investigation of the Magistrates' Courts.

Police work has traditionally relied rather heavily upon the use of informants, stool pigeons, or spies.[100] Very commonly these are petty criminals such as prostitutes, pimps, addicts, thieves, bookmakers, and more recently, in the Federal system, former Communists who are offered immunity in return for information that they may supply the authorities. Frequently they are paid either on a regular basis or in return for specific tips.[101] Deutsch describes the anomalous relationship that often develops between minions of the law and members of the underworld, especially the protection that is given to reliable "stoolies."[102]

It is the opinion of most police executives that abandonment of the informer system would be greatly damaging if not catastrophic.[103] J. Edgar Hoover has publicized its value by proclaiming that 2,700 arrests in a year's time had stemmed from secret information passed on to the Bureau.[104] While some authorities certainly recognize the ethical paradoxes associated with the system, in general they believe, as Professor Perkins has put it, that "most of the cases presented to them for solution can be best solved through the information which they receive from their contacts and through their knowledge of criminals and their *modus operandi,* hence their efforts are mainly directed toward making the contacts with those who can supply the police with information regarding the perpetrators of crime."[105] It is to this major reliance that Hoover attributes the failure of

[100] See generally Richard C. Donnelly, "Judicial Control of Informants, Spies, Stool Pigeons, and Agents Provocateurs," *Yale L. J.,* November, 1951.

[101] Deutsch reports that the Los Angeles Police Department has an $85,000 annual informer fund and that the Washington, D.C., department has $35,000. *Op. cit.,* pp. 96, 102. In 1955 the U.S. Justice Department reported that $43,000 had been paid to informants over a period of twenty-one months and that one ex-Communist had received $16,000. *New York Times,* Aug. 24, 1955. In 1946 defense counsel introduced a record indicating that the Kings County Prosecutor's Office had paid $9,712 to three convicts serving long sentences in Sing Sing in the course of preparing its case against Malinski for the slaying of a police officer. *New York Times,* June 20, 1946; June 26, 1946; July 9, 1946.

[102] Deutsch, *op. cit.,* p. 98.

[103] This was one conclusion from a questionnaire circulated among thirty-one police departments in 1953. See article by Donnelly, *loc. cit.* The authorities considered that paid informers were more useful than private citizens in furnishing information, for the most part.

[104] *New York Times,* July 29, 1957. This allegation was associated with his argument that the confidentiality of the FBI files should be preserved in order that information would continue to be forthcoming. How many of the tips received by the Bureau came from professional or paid informants, however, is not known. See ftn. 101.

[105] Rollin M. Perkins, *Elements of Police Science,* 1942, p. 39. See also O. W. Wilson, *Police Administration,* 1950, pp. 191–192, where in discussing the work of the vice division he recommends that, "Vice investigations should not be conducted by detectives charged with the investigation of crimes against persons and property because underworld characters engaged in vice operations are often valuable information sources to detectives investigating crimes. . . . Detectives

American detectives to "place much weight upon the application of scientific principles to the solution of the crimes which they are called upon to investigate." The argument is one of expedience compounded with a traditional disinclination to turn to newer and sounder though sometimes slower methods of investigation.

The problems involved in reliance upon criminal informers run deeper than does the anomaly of the alliance between the police and criminals. One of these is the condonation of crimes committed by stool pigeons, and sometimes the offenses in which they are involved are more serious than those they report to the police. In some instances stool pigeons may secure confidences from the authorities in the course of the relationship to provide information to fellow criminals that is even more valuable than the knowledge that they pass on to the police. Furthermore, as police authorities recognize, the information received from informers is commonly undependable; the "stoolie" can be trusted neither by the police nor by his criminal allies, and he can live only by deceiving them both. Some informers, particularly narcotic addicts, are commonly used to "set up" peddlers for arrest. Not infrequently, it appears, they have entrapped pharmacists, nurses, and acquaintances to procure drugs for them in order to secure release from criminal charges or to avoid police harassment. One of the worst illustrations of informant practice is the effort of narcotic agents to secure the "cooperation" of parolees through urging them to return to their former associations (in itself a violation of parole, of course) in order to provide information and secure arrest of peddlers and users.[106]

A specialized aspect of the informer problem relates to the fact that the information supplied is confidential. Policing and prosecutory authorities maintain that neither the sources nor the content of the reports they receive should be divulged, lest the sources of information should dry up and reprisals be taken against cooperative informants. Courts and congressional committees have generally followed this principle in derogation of the doctrine that a defendant should be fully informed of the charges against him and allowed to confront his accusers. The use of the "faceless informer" has been attacked, in particular, in political cases and the Justice Department has been charged with obtaining convictions by "purchased testimony" from "kept" witnesses who are coached to interpret liberal doctrines in such a way that it brings them within areas proscribed by the

---

should not be required to prevent the illegal operations of persons from whom they must seek information useful in their investigations."

[106] Juveniles, too, have been used to discover sex perverts and narcotic peddlers in some jurisdictions. Deputy Police Chief Lutz of the Moral Squad in Washington, D.C., was quoted in the *Washington Star*, May 13, 1954, as believing that "juvenile decoys could be used effectively for the purpose" and "if some youngster has been exposed to such a thing and wants to help us catch the person who did it that's fine," but that it was difficult to secure parents' permission. See *Sherman v. United States,* 356 U.S. 369 (1958).

Smith Act.[107] The FBI has argued that the sanctity of their files must be preserved, while the courts require that the accused be informed of accusations that have led to prosecution. In 1957 the Supreme Court held in the case of Albert Rovario, charged with a narcotics violation, that the government had no right to withhold an informer's identity where such knowledge would be relevant and helpful to the accused in preparing his defense.[108] In other cases in 1957 the Court has held that the trial court must decide what information from FBI informants must be revealed to the accused so that he may prepare a proper defense.

Bribery and Graft

More publicity has been given in recent years to the bribery and graft involved in gambling operations than to any of the other forms of police illegalities. Investigations and publicity of this condition preceded but were considerably increased by the Kefauver Senate investigation into organized crime. Indeed, for a period of over ten years there was virtually continuous investigation of the police tie-in with gambling in New York City; this together with a succession of police reorganizations and shake-ups appear to have had limited effect upon either gambling or its protection by the police. This investigation reached its peak in the Harry Gross trial and the police departmental trials that ensued, as will be noted below, but the main effect may well have been to make both the gambling and the protection more surreptitious for a brief time.

A beginning of the contemporary exposures dates from the special grand jury investigation in 1942 under Assistant Attorney General John Harlan Amen when ties between the police and gamblers were brought out. In the period between 1943 and 1945 Police Commissioners Valentine and Wallander made numerous shifts in the detective force in Brooklyn, Harlem, and the East Side where investigations by Amen and later by the City Investigation Commissioner Yavner revealed "laxity in suppressing gambling."[109] In 1946 the Broadway columnist Ed Sullivan, of the Daily News, broke a story that detectives were receiving from $1,700 to $3,000 per bookmaker per month from gamblers in different parts of the city. This precipitated Mayor O'Dwyer's decision to conduct an investigation through Investigation Commissioner Murtagh, and he ordered the police to "clean up the city."[110] Commissioner Wallander ordered 300 plainclothesmen into uniform, replacing them with "new blood," and reassigned nearly all of the inspectors in the department as a means of stopping bribery. Again in December of 1946 and in January and August of 1947 Wallander made extensive shifts and demotions, including

[107] *New York Times*, Jan. 8, 1956.

[108] *Ibid.*, Mar. 26, 1957; July 29, 1957.

[109] *New York Times*, Mar. 31, 1944; Jan. 17, 1945; and *New York Post*, Oct. 10, 1945.

[110] *New York Times*, Mar. 20, 1946; June 4, 1946; and Aug. 25, 1946; *New York Post*, June 5, 1946.

at least seventy officers above the rank of sergeant. This action was undertaken partly because of grand jury investigations of police graft.[111]

In December of 1949 the Brooklyn Eagle ran a series of articles on police protection of bookmakers that again stimulated concern in City Hall. Sweeping shifts in the department occurred then under Commissioner O'Brien in 1950 when, in January, he transferred many of the police captains, every inspector in the uniformed divisions, and all but one deputy inspector.[112] This was the most extensive shake-up since those under Commissioner Enright in the 1920s and under Wallander in 1946. In September of 1950 Harry Gross was arrested as the result of a two-year grand jury investigation under District Attorney Miles, an inquiry that O'Dwyer termed a "witch hunt,"[113] This investigation led to the disclosure of a 20-million-dollar-a-year gambling syndicate in Brooklyn, from which the police were alleged to receive a take of a million dollar's a year. Gross's refusal to testify when trial was begun, prevented criminal actions against the police, but the investigation resulted in the resignation of Commissioner O'Brien and his chiefs. When Commissioner Thomas Murphy came in he sent 336 plainclothesmen back into uniform, to be replaced by "untainted rookies."[114] In subsequent departmental trials at which Gross did testify, he identified 162 men on the force to whom he said he had paid graft. Gross had indicated previously that he could name 300 crooked cops who "took ice" from him. Of those identified, 110 either resigned or retired from the force, a few committed suicide, a number were dismissed after departmental trials, seven were convicted of perjury, and a few went to jail for short terms for contempt; but there were no convictions for graft. Murtagh, then chief magistrate of New York City, was put under arrest upon McDonald's accusation that he had "willfully and unlawfully" neglected to report to O'Dwyer his discovery of payoffs, stand-in arrests, collusion among policemen to establish arrest records, inefficiency among the higher echelon of the department, and corruption all along the line.[115] Commissioner Monaghan replaced Murphy after the latter's accession to the Federal bench.

In spite of criminal and departmental trials, there was continued evidence of links between the police and gamblers. In February of 1953 District Attorney McDonald showed movies taken by his investigators picturing bookies in continued operation in Brooklyn.[116] Monaghan, who had shifted sixty-nine detectives in December of 1952, dismissed or shifted some fifty additional detectives, captains, and other members of the force in February and March. Four officers were found guilty at departmental trials, three of these four were fined ten days' pay![117] He also established a special headquarters squad which made raids and arrests of bookies in Brooklyn whom the local division had apparently been unable to discover.

[111] *New York Times,* June 4, 1946; Dec. 12, Dec. 18, 1946; Jan. 20, 1947; Aug. 5, Aug. 11, 1947.

[112] *New York Post,* Jan. 9, 1950.

[113] *New York Times,* Sept. 24, 1950.

[114] *Ibid.,* Sept. 30, 1950.

[115] *Ibid.,* May 19, 1951; June 21, 1952; and Sept. 7, 1952.

[116] *Ibid.,* Feb. 15, 1953.

[117] *Ibid.,* Jan. 1, 1953; Feb. 23, 1953; Mar. 10, 1953; and Apr. 25, 1953.

The gambling persists and undoubtedly the payoffs to the authorities persist too. Max Lerner's comments on such practices in the New York Post offer a fair picture of the situation: "From the standpoint of the cops, big and small, the motive is fairly clear. The payments were part of a going system, and a weak and pliant man finds it easier to ride along with any system than to buck it. There was no crime, as they saw it, in letting the bookie spots operate, and certainly no harm in sharing the take. The only loser was the law itself, which was made contemptible by the contempt the lawless cops felt for it."[118] Over the past ten years the "system" has been bent somewhat but it has not been broken.[119] It is a pattern that has become common in our large cities, and in most of these cities there has been no such effort to root out the bribery and corruption as there has been in Brooklyn.[120]

Investigations of Police Practices in New York

In the pages above some of the common abuses in police practice have been analyzed. Unfortunately, because of the secretive character of their inquisitions, there is little general awareness of the nature and extent of the wrongs done in the name of law enforcement. From time to time the cumulative effect of brutality, oppression, perjury, and other illegal methods of police action stir the public conscience and the measures that have come to be widely tolerated are reappraised. Attempts are made, at least for a time, to reestablish the rule of law. Thus in New York investigations have been conducted at least once each generation over the past century to discover and root out these official perversions of power. Infamous practices have been discovered successively by inquiries in 1844 and 1873, by the Lexow investigation in 1894, by the *Page Report* of 1910 , by the Seabury Commission in 1932, and by the Bruce Smith Survey of 1952. The result has been generally some measure of police reorganization, a partial restoration of order, some reduction perhaps of official excesses, but a rather quick return to the familiar methods of doing business. The materials of these inquiries have laid the foundation for a growing tower of fear,

[118] *New York Post,* May 8, 1952.

[119] Not long after the revelation of gambling payoffs to the police, a highly organized traffic-ticket racket was revealed in New York City in late 1954, involving close to one hundred policemen. *New York Times,* Feb. 2, 1955. A vice ring in the Fifteenth Division resulted in the transfer of seven officers and sixteen plainclothesmen. *Ibid.,* Aug. 23, 1955. See Deutsch, *op. cit.,* chap. 1, for an account of the extent of police scandals in the early 1950s.

[120] See *New York Times,* July 29, 1949, for indictment of ex-chief and other policemen in Los Angeles for bookmaking, bribery, and harlotry; *ibid.,* May 9, 1950, for Chicago Crime Commission charge that police were taking monthly bribes to permit prostitution and clipping in the honky-tonks on the North Side; *ibid.,* May 3, 1952, for the ousting of twelve Philadelphia police for graft; *ibid.,* June 30, 1952, for graft and police protection in Washington, D.C.; and *ibid.,* Apr. 25, 1952, for indictment of fourteen officials in Bergen County, New Jersey, for failure to enforce the gambling laws. The publicity during this period reflected the awakening that occurred as a consequence of the Kefauver investigation into organized crime.

suspicion, disrespect, and in some quarters contempt for the minions of justice.

It is clear, of course, that not all police employ brutal methods of arrest or interrogation; few are trigger-happy; a small percentage take bribes or exact tribute; only a part offer exaggerated, distorted, or perjurious testimony to secure convictions as a deliberate practice; and only a fraction employ the various illegal methods of investigation to secure evidence. Nevertheless, when it is considered that a great proportion of the police are on traffic and other innocuous assignments where there is little or no opportunity for such malpractices and when it is observed that a considerable group of plainclothesmen and higher police officials become directly involved in or tolerate these official crimes, the magnitude of the total problem can be viewed only as profoundly serious. Moreover, the evidence indicates that there has been little sustained effort to control it. Indeed, the methods of disciplining police misconduct that are ordinarily employed appear to be intrinsically futile.

Bruce Smith, internationally recognized authority on police methods, in his 1952 study of the New York City Police Department, analyzed in some detail the ineffectuality of departmental trials in maintaining discipline.[121] He found there what he described as "a creeping paralysis of the arm of discipline." The following are excerpts from the report of his committee:

Back in 1928 the charges on which the policemen were accorded a departmental trial totaled well over 5,000 in number. The intervening years witnessed an almost uninterrupted decline in such rough indices of disciplinary action, with the level dropping to only some 600 charges by 1950. Court convictions of police show a slow decline over the years, but dismissals from the service have gone down by 90 per cent. Examination of the end results of departmental trials raises serious doubt concerning the efficacy of this arm of police control in securing good discipline from a considerable segment of the force.

The entire summary record of departmental trials and the penalties therein imposed, for the 20 years from 1931 to 1950 inclusive, has been subjected to close review. Selected here are the records of 583 individuals who were brought to administrative trial. They represent all of the major cases heard throughout the 20 year period, plus others with lengthy disciplinary records. [Few of these offenders were disciplined. In only 8 per cent was there a penalty greater than a fine of three days' pay.]

. . . But the extraordinary fact is that individual members of the force may be charged repeatedly with absences from duty, improper patrol and an occasional lapse into intoxication while on duty, without suffering more than a reprimand or the forfeiture of one to five days' pay.

. . . One of these was found guilty on 15 separate occasions, involving offenses that ranged from absence from post to loitering in bars or with a female, but with penalties that averaged only 1½ days of suspension for each

[121] *Report on the New York City Police Department,* Institute of Public Administration, 1953.

proved offense. After 12 years of such thoroughly unsatisfactory service, this patrolman was promoted to sergeant. . . . In two instances, patrolmen who were adjudged by the trial commissioner to have committed perjury in court each suffered suspension for only five days.

. . . Assaults with firearms, with intoxication as an aggravating element, feature the record of 51 policemen. Here the bite of penalties imposed is much sharper, though only about one-fourth of the men involved were dismissed. One was allowed to resign, and another was later promoted. Even there the lagging approach to such problems is indicated by the record of an intoxicated policeman who shot a civilian and received a 20 day fine. During the next six years he was tried on 18 separate occasions for absence from duty. When he came up for the 20th time, a somewhat tardy impatience by the trial commissioner caused his dismissal for being intoxicated and unfit for duty. Another patrolman in the course of but three and one-half years committed no less than four gun assaults while intoxicated.

. . . A rather large category comprises 120 patrolmen who have lengthy disciplinary records that include one or more offenses involving use of firearms, but without the aggravating element of intoxication. These embrace both deliberate assaults and accidental discharge. One of them was brought ϧ administrative trial 17 times in 12 years, was adjudged guilty 12 times but was fined a total of only nine days' pay.

During the regime of Commissioner Kennedy, disciplinary practices have been tightened up very considerably.

Quality of the Police Force

A considerable part of the problem involved in the performance of police departments lies in the quality of the officers as determined by their selection, training, supervision, and compensation. As has been noted previously, we demand much of the force—more, indeed, than they can possibly deliver—because our demands are neither consistent nor compatible. Read Bain has stated the problem in these terms:[122]

Under present conditions, the police have an almost impossible assignment. The marvel is not that they do their job so badly, but that they do it as well as they do. Poorly selected, ignorant, unintelligent, poorly trained, poorly equipped, poorly paid, poorly led, overworked, the butt of public mirth and condemnation, harassed by crooked politicians, they see a large percentage of the criminals they catch freed by shyster "criminal" lawyers, politician-judges, an antiquated, complicated and inefficient judicial system or by unscientific parole boards. They are called upon to enforce a thousand silly laws passed by socially ignorant legislators; they are blamed for the failure of the church, the home and the school to rear normal, socially adjusted children; they have to make people drive 40 miles an hour while the state builds roads and permits manufacturers to build cars that call for 80 miles an hour—and the police are blamed for the resulting deaths and injuries; they are called upon to club strikers, to enforce blanket labor-dispute injunc-

[122] Read Bain, *op. cit.,* pp. 4–5. (Reprinted by permission.)

tions and to interfere with freedom of speech; they are ordered to stop people from gambling, swearing, spitting, smoking, drinking and even from making love. If they are stupid and short tempered and unreasonable, there are plenty of so-called good citizens who are worse.

Good police work requires trained intelligence, sound physical condition, and a high level of character. Studies made of the intelligence and educational level of the police have provided a rather uniformly uncomplimentary picture of their mentality. Summarizing some of these materials in 1939, Bain found that at least 75 per cent of the policemen in the United States were mentally unfit for their work according to the rather modest standard of an Army Alpha score of 120. "About 25 per cent of the policemen in Los Angeles, Minneapolis, Kansas City and Cleveland get A and B ratings [scores from 135 to 212 and 105 to 134 respectively], while 91 per cent of California *freshmen* are in this category. The freshmen had 60 per cent A-men while the four cities in order had 9, 7, 5 and 4 per cent A-men [in their police departments]."[123] There is little evidence in the literature showing the physical condition of policemen, though it is known that in many communities the average age of men on the force is much too high, considering the heavy demands of the work, and that where retirement provisions are poor an excessive number of aging or unhealthy officers must be kept on light-duty assignments. Recent revelations concerning the conduct of police officers throughout the nation provide a rather uniformly somber picture of their character and habits.

Bruce Smith, in his investigation in New York City, noting that intelligence and aptitude tests were held in low esteem in the Civil Service Commission there and in many parts of the police department, recommended the use of improved test batteries to weed out the intellectually incompetent. He suggested that an excellent method to improve selection in a simple way would be to insist upon graduation from high school or an equivalency test as a basis for qualification, rather than merely using the present written examinations that "are little concerned with native intelligence, aptitude for police work or ability to learn."[124]

As to physical condition, Smith found that medical examinations conducted by the municipal Civil Service Commission in New York were

---

[123] *Ibid.*, p. 3. O. W. Wilson observes, however, that improved selection and personality evaluation have improved the quality of the police considerably over the past twenty years. "Progress in Police Administration," *J. Crim. L.*, vol. 42, p. 141, 1951.

[124] In spite of the criticisms made in the Smith Report on selection of officers for the force in New York and a finding of a grand jury in 1954 that recruiting was inefficient (*New York Times*, Apr. 30, 1954), standards of selection appear to have improved little if at all. This may be attributed in part to wages and to the dearth of good applicants. In late 1955 the Civil Service Commission found it necessary to regrade examinations with much greater lenience in order to pass a sufficient number of men. *Ibid.*, Dec. 28, 1955.

superficial (the average time for each candidate being forty-five seconds) and that men were accepted who were handicapped by "foot injuries, flat feet, overweight by as much as 70 pounds, leg wounds, missing fingers or injured hands, defective hearing, and mental disorders. Through negligence and conniving both the present and future value of each complement of recruits is heavily discounted at the outset." Similarly, concerning the investigations of character, Smith found that "On the critical issue of character investigation, the commission's record is a sorry one. Undue reliance is placed upon form letter inquiries. Unfavorable replies are not followed up. Criminal records of wide variety, paternity proceedings and other objectionable features are waived by the commission in three-fourths of the cases in which they arise." The results of poor character selection appear elsewhere in this chapter as evidence of corruption in the department. There are many other illustrative instances of the consequences of defective moral fiber in police work.[125]

Police Training

It is commonly recognized that in-service training programs are an important phase in the development of sound and effective police work. Most

[125] The following excerpts illustrate publicity attending police corruption in recent years:

"*Ex-Capt. Workman Gets 2½ to 5 Years.* Leibowitz Excoriates Police Grafter for Hour in Meting Out Maximum Sentence. Perjurer's take was $5,000 a month—citizens made 50 complaints in 5 years." *New York Times,* Apr. 18, 1952.

"*$20 'Shake-down' Laid to Detectives.* Pair accused by the owner of tavern in which sailor says he lost $700—they spurned his offer of $10 to 'forget' a sailor's complaint that he had lost the money there." *Ibid.,* June 11, 1952.

"*Two Patrolmen Indicted.* Suspended Queens Men Accused in Morals Shakedown. (Both had previously been cited for good police work.)" *Ibid.,* July 10, 1952.

"*Ex-Dective Gets 2½ Years in Jail.* Plotter of $20,000 shakedown excoriated by judge for violating 'sacred trust.' Was mastermind in an attempted $20,000 shakedown through a framed marijuana arrest." *Ibid.,* Dec. 22, 1952.

"*The Dope Scandal.* Two members of Police Narcotics Squad indicted for perjury on testimony they had been selling drugs." *New York Post,* Apr. 14, 1955.

"*9 Police, 21 Others Named in Vice Case.* Charge involving two 15-year-old runaway girls." *New York Times,* Aug. 23, 1955.

"*Nassau Policeman Seized as Burglar.* Son of retired burglary squad detective, said to have admitted four other burglaries." *Ibid.,* Oct. 25, 1955.

"*Ex-Policeman, 31, Seized as Robber.* Described as 'the mastermind of a band of criminals.' Ousted after nine years of service during which he won four commendations." *Ibid.,* Mar. 29, 1957.

The illustrations above reflect, at least in part, poor selection for police work, though certainly a more common problem than ordinary criminality among officers is what one psychiatrist has referred to as "little dictator complexes." The late Dr. Douglas M. Kelley, of the University of California at Berkeley, has suggested that 25 per cent of police officers are unfit in personality for their jobs and that every officer should be given psychiatric tests before appointment to root out the "Fuehrers" who "delight in pushing people around." *Ibid.,* Sept. 24, 1952.

large city and state policing agencies have training programs today and some provide very good specialized training. Los Angeles, Berkeley, Cincinnati, New York, and a few other cities have been praised for strong and diversified training, with increasing emphasis upon criminological subjects of causation and treatment. In recent years a growing number of public and private agencies and universities have been offering programs that have looked toward professionalization of the field. Outstanding among these are the National Police Academy and the FBI regional training programs, the Northwestern University Traffic Institute, the Delinquency Control Institute at the University of Southern California, and specialized police training programs at a number of universities.

Bruce Smith found in 1953 that training of the police in New York at the Police Academy had deteriorated seriously in recent years. Seasoned graduates, some of them in the highest ranks of the department, indicated that attending the recruit school was "just a waste of time." In such areas as human relations, criminology, and crime detection methods the training has been distinctly weak. Together with poor recruitment, the inadequate training of recruits and higher officers must be blamed for some of the inadequacies of "New York's Finest." When Police Commissioner Kennedy became chief of the department, he said that New York "probably has the worst police training facilities of any city in the Western world." He urged the construction of a new academy and encouraged the development of a police training program on an unprecedented scale both at the present academy and at the College of the City of New York. At the time of writing several hundred officers are studying for a degree of associate in applied science and others are studying for advanced degrees.

It should be emphasized that there is another and far more affirmative side to the picture of police selection and training. In a considerable number of urban departments today a new tradition has been or is being established. The emphasis in these departments is upon securing men of fine intelligence, education, and physical condition, providing salaries and promotional and retirement opportunities that are attractive to men of high calibre, and giving them training both in specialized skills and in human relations. There are at least twenty universities that now offer advanced programs of police training in various parts of the country, especially on the West Coast.[126] More and more commonly we find officers with college, graduate, and law school degrees on metropolitan forces, pushing successfully for the professionalization of police work and assuming leadership in

---

[126] See Donal MacNamara, "Higher Police Training at the University Level," *J. Crim. L.*, vol. 40, 1950. In-service training programs for police officers have been provided for over twenty years in such cities as Berkeley, Chicago, Cincinnati, Indianapolis, Louisville, San Francisco, and New York and in the National FBI Academy. See also *The University Teaching of Social Sciences: Criminology,* Unesco, 1957.

their departments. In many cities these officers face great obstacles in the inertia of deeply rooted conservative practice. Yet the scene is shifting rapidly in important cities throughout the country. Such outstanding leaders as the late August Vollmer in California, "the nation's greatest cop," J. Edgar Hoover with his leadership in the Federal system, and Bruce Smith and Commissioner Kennedy in New York have done much in promoting idealism and high standards of skill and honesty. These men bring fresh hope for effective performance in what, in terms of our ambivalent demands upon law enforcement activity, is one of the most difficult among our occupational specializations.

SCIENTIFIC CRIME DETECTION METHODS

Laboratory methods of crime detection can serve several useful and interrelated purposes.[127] They provide the investigator with information that may be used to carry forward his inquiry into the facts on the basis of which the commission of a crime or the identity of the culprit may be ascertained. Data thus derived may provide prosecution with evidence to present to the court in support of its case; this evidence is commonly substantial, if not conclusive. Such methods can not only make criminal investigation more speedy and efficient in many cases but, incidentally, should serve to reduce police reliance upon illegal and otherwise dubious procedures, such as coercion, illegal searches, excessive detention, entrapment, and the use of informers. Unfortunately, despite the rapid strides of modern science and of methods that are specifically appropriate to police investigation, police departments in the United States, even in large urban centers, have been slow to establish and have been even slower to exploit the resources for detection and identification.[128] There is a strong feeling among the "old-timers" and at the higher administrative levels (men at higher levels attain their positions through seniority pretty largely rather than through sophistication) that "nothing can take the place of the 'old and tested' police measures," which implies generally eliciting tips from

[127] For detailed information relating to criminalistics the student should consult O'Hara and Osterburg, *An Introduction to Criminalistics,* 1949 (an excellent volume); Maurice A. Fitzgerald, *Handbook of Criminal Investigation,* 1951; Söderman and O'Connell, *Modern Criminal Investigation,* 1945; and Rollin M. Perkins, *Elements of Police Science,* 1942.

[128] Authorities who should know have estimated that only a few thousand dollars are spent each year for significant research in criminalistics. Rather elementary courses in scientific crime detection methods are offered in a very few universities. There are relatively few police laboratories in existence, these being located in large urban centers. There are only three or four laboratory field units in existence. No standards or qualifications have been established for experts in the field: garage attendants and barbers have served as criminalisticians in some of our eastern states. No professional organization has been established for police laboratory workers.

informants, rounding up suspicious characters, and prolonged and persuasive interrogation. The "college boy's methods" may be all right, in their place, to convince a jury where it is tough to get the proof, after the men who really do the work have "cracked" the case in the backroom, but there is no use confusing science and police work, so it is felt. This means that, except in the rare case, usually involving a murder charge or in such exceptional instances as forgery, paternity, drunkenness, or drug addiction, where physical evidence is very obviously useful if not essential, there is little inclination to call upon "the experts." Even in these areas the employment of physical evidence is slow to develop. This appears to be the result more of administrative distrust and ignorance among the police than of the courts' excessive hesitancy to accept scientific evidence until it has come to be generally recognized as valid. The customary and often very long delay in the courts' recognition of objective evidence is largely a product of the failure of the police and prosecution to provide and test such evidence.

The measures of scientific crime detection are too numerous and technical to consider here in any detail. It may be worthwhile, however, to comment briefly on some of the particularly significant techniques that are now in use and their value for police work.

Bertillon Identification. Apparently it was the Belgian statistician Quételet who first observed, around 1840, that no two human beings have exactly the same dimensions. Founded upon this truism and the prevailing interest in physical anthropological measurements, the Parisian police clerk Alphonse Bertillon developed a new method of classifying criminal according to bodily measurements and in 1882 became director of the newly established Bureau of Identification. Under his system physical measurements were made in three major categories—over-all bodily size, measurements of the head, and measurements of the limbs. These categories were divided into eleven subclassifications, which were further divided and subdivided, making a total of 65 divisions and 65,610 subclassifications. As Söderman and O'Connell point out, the system had its limitations: "It was limited to adults, and there was often a marked difference in the measurements of a person who had been measured for a second time in the same department. A table of measurement allowances was introduced, but serious mistakes still could not be avoided. Persons having the same anthropometrical measurements as others already registered occasionally were arrested.[129] Anthropometrical description has come to be displaced largely by fingerprint descriptions during the twentieth century. A few criminal-biologists in western Europe are doing research on anthropometry but there is little interest in the subject in the United States.

Dactyloscopy. The science of fingerprint detection is based on the premises that there are no two identical fingerprints and that fingerprints are not changeable. Both of these assumptions are somewhat misleading, as a matter or fact, as are many of the popular assumptions about scientific crime detec-

---

[129] Söderman and O'Connell, *op. cit.,* p. 43.

tion. In fingerprint, as in all types of criminal investigation, one never finds complete identity of specimens. It is characteristic in physical science as in social science, though to a far less degree, to find similarity rather than uniformity. Inferences of identity are based upon degrees of probable error rather than upon complete certitude.

Fingerprints result from impressions on a surface where ridges of the fingers leave a deposit of perspiration composed of 98 per cent water with traces of a number of salts. The latent fingerprint is made visible usually by powdering with a fine brush, duster, or atomizer and the powdered print is ordinarily photographed for the records. Any of a number of powders may be used according to the nature of the material being examined. For such surfaces as paper, cloth, glass, and some woods and metals, any of various chemical methods of developing latent prints may be used, including such reagents as silver nitrate, iodine fumes, dyestuffs, hydrofluoric acid, and others. While fingerprints are relatively immutable, the fact remains that one never secures "perfect" print impressions, so that identification depends upon the probability of identity when there is a high degree of similarity. Moreover, while criminals have found no way to remove their prints permanently and completely, even by acid or fire, the print is modified by scars over a period of time. Sometimes, in fact, these marks are more useful than the native print itself in making identifications, but they may also make exact comparisons difficult or impossible. The relative individuality and indestructability of fingerprints are the basis for the employment of fingerprint systems as a primary means of identification in civilized countries.[130] A modified version of the Sir Edward Henry system, employed in the United States, is based upon a classification into four major categories of prints according to the patterns of arches, loops, and composite whorls; subclassifications are based upon the number of ridges from the center or core of the pattern, the "inner terminus," to the "outer terminus," or delta, formed by the bifurcation of a ridge or through the wide separation of two ridges that have run parallel.

Ballistics. As the term is popularly used, ballistics refers to firearm investigation in which projectiles used in crimes are studied to identify the type of weapon and the particular weapon from which such projectiles were fired.[131] Small arms today are made with rifled bores; in the process of manufacture helical grooves are cut into the inside of gun barrels in order to spin the bullet when it leaves the muzzle of the gun and give it greater accuracy, speed,

[130] O'Hara and Osterberg comment, "The fingerprint occupies a position of paramount importance in circumstantial evidence. There are many reasons for this: the simplicity with which fingerprints may be obtained; their conclusiveness in establishing identity; the immutable character of the fingerprint during life; and the existence of the common filing system." *Op. cit.,* p. 77. In 1958 the FBI reported filing its 150 millionth set of fingerprints; 32,775,532 of these were in criminal files.

[131] A ballistics bureau in the New York City Police Department was first established in 1918. At that time ballistics was not a recognized scientific specialization. Today New York handles between 3,500 and 4,000 ballistics cases each year. A Scotland Yard visitor in New York has recently made the interesting comparative observation that "In London, if we get as many as ten a year, we think it too blooming many."

and distance. The markings caused by these lands of the barrel and by the microscopic ridges worn by the use and other pecularities individualize both the weapon and correspondingly the bullets that are fired from it, making possible the identification of the firearm from which a projectile was fired. A bullet recovered from the scene of a crime may be studied to determine the make and model of the weapon from which it was fired and, as arms of this

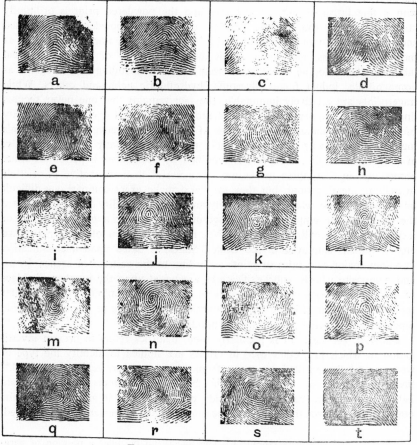

FIGURE 8. Types of fingerprints.

type are found, the expert can compare the evidence bullet with test shots fired from the weapons submitted. This is done with comparison microscopes that are especially designed for the analysis of firearms evidence. The similar markings can be shown to the jury in photomicrographs.

Photography. It has come to be generally recognized that photography is a valuable, and probably the most widely used, aid in the detection of crime and the perpetuation of evidence. Among other things it may be used to preserve the crime scene for use in further investigation and for later presentation of evidence;[132] to identify suspects, premises, and materials; and to present accurate copies of records, documents, handwriting specimens, and other types of evidence. It is used in conjunction with fingerprinting, ballistics, moulage, spectroscopy, and other crime detection techniques. There are other specialized forms of photography useful in detection: microphotography of very small objects, infrared photography to discover objects that are obscure to visible light, and ultraviolet photography for revealing differences in chemical composition (commonly useful in document examination) that cannot be seen by the naked eye.

Casting Methods. Like photography, casting is used to preserve the appearance of evidence, but it is more subject to errors because of pecularities of the materials employed. For that reason photographs of traces are generally taken before casting is done. The casting may be valuable to secure reproduction of marks that might disappear or be modified in time, for example, tire tracks, marks left by burglars' tools, footprints, and similar markings.[133] Sometimes casts of tooth indentations, scars, or human heads may be particularly useful for purposes of identification. Various materials may be used in casting, including plaster of paris, plasticine, wax, plestelina, and different forms of powdered agar composition. Plaster of paris is generally employed as an economical and simple basis of most routine work in this phase of criminalistics. The *moulage* method has become a characteristic technique in recent laboratory procedures. This involves the making first of a negative and then a positive cast; sometimes a third material is used to reenforce the brittle cast.

Microscopic, Chemical, and Blood Analysis. Each of these methods of analysis constitutes a significant phase of laboratory detection technique today. Crime detection has borrowed the techniques of chemistry, physics, biology, and the other physical sciences in so far as they are applicable to the problems of criminal investigation. The microscopic analysis examines materials too fine for the human eye, chemical investigations determine the presence and amount of materials that may be thus identified in test samples, and serology analyzes blood evidence for the identification (or exclusion) of suspected victims or perpetrators of crime. Generally human blood may be distinguished from animal bloods; the blood type can be analyzed from a stain; and the presence or absence of disease strains can be determined. Thus, blood chemistry may be very valuable in some cases in the elimination and in the discovery of important factual data.

In *People v. Wallage*,[134] where the charge was homicide, an expert chemist

[132] It is also true, unfortunately, that photography, more than most other scientific measures of criminal investigation, can be used to distort and to mislead the jury. It is, however, an invaluable method for preparing, preserving, and presenting evidence.

[133] A recent case illustrates the value of casting in burglary cases. An unusual footprint showing deformity was found outside a burglarized home; this led to the identification of the offender who had a foot deformity and to his confession of twenty-nine burglaries. *New York Times*, Dec. 30, 1952. A "cat burglar" was identified in 1949 on the basis of a moulage that had been prepared of hand and foot impressions found on the ledges outside hotel rooms that he had burglarized. He admitted at least sixty hotel burglaries when apprehended. *Ibid.*, July 15, 1949.

[134] 363 Ill. 30 (1930).

testified that a small quantity of paint was found on the shirt of the deceased that was found to be similar in color and composition to a sample from the fender of the defendant's car. Near a dented section of the fender he had found a series of fine parallel scratches, thirty-one to an inch under the microscope. When examination of the cloth weave of the deceased's shirt revealed thirty-one raised threads per inch, it was the expert's conclusion that the faint markings on the fender were made by the violent contact of a piece of woven cloth such as that found in the shirt worn by the decedent. The appellate court held that this evidence was properly admitted.

Spectrochemical Analysis. This process represents a specialized and increasingly important branch of investigative technique in the examination of minute traces. The spectrograph is an optical apparatus that produces a strip of light lines of different colors according to the chemical elements present in the trace. Luminous gas produced by the burning of the element produces the light waves seen in the spectroscope. Thus where material containing many elements is burned, the presence of each element can be detected in the spectrum and the constituents of the substance can be determined exactly. A spectrographic examination of minute clue materials may be compared to similar matter at the scene of a crime to determine identity of the substances. As O'Hara and Osterburg observe, "A flake of paint on the end of a jimmy, metal filings of a hacksaw blade, abrasive material on a crankcase, plaster or dirt on a hose, a fragment of glass, and the many other clue materials with which the police scientists deal can often be unmistakably 'fingerprinted' in this manner."[135] O'Hara informs the author that there is a virtually unlimited variety of uses to which spectrochemical analysis may be put in the future development of crime detection.

Lie Detection. The use of lie detection represents one of the most interesting and professionally most controversial areas of investigative technique. It holds some potential promise for ultimately revolutionizing crime detection itself and, in consequence, the entire process of criminal justice. At the least, as it has proved already, it can be an invaluable aid in some cases in securing admissions and evidence that could not otherwise be procured so easily, quickly, and humanely. Lie detection is based upon the fundamental principle that the effort required to lie results in a variety of physical symptoms, notably heightened blood pressure, rapid breathing, sweating, and increased pulse rate, and that these manifestations can be observed, measured, and interpreted under carefully controlled conditions. Critics of this method have maintained that the instruments used do not test "lying" as such but that they measure the emotional responses of the subject. In fact, it *is* emotional reactions that are measured, but they appear to be typical fear responses that are associated with lying and that can be differentiated by the expert from other emotional reactions that also display clinical symptoms.

Lie detection of various sorts is old and widespread historically, though it has made very slow progress in modern courts. Widely varied juristic methods have been noted in numerous cultures where the psychophysical basis of testing, though crude, has been nonetheless real. Some of the methods of the ordeal in continental and English history illustrate this. The relation

[135] O'Hara and Osterburg, *op. cit.,* p. 573.

of salivation to deception may be noted in the old Chinese practice of giving the accused dry rice to chew and the Bengalese practice of placing a hot iron on the tongue of the accused. Incidents have been noted in Plutarch's *Lives* and the *Gesta Romanorum* where an accelerated pulse was taken as evidence of the infidelity of a wife. The modern history of lie detection traces back to work performed by Lombroso in 1895. From a number of experiments he had conducted with criminals Lombroso sought to show the relationship of blood pressure and pulse changes to their deception under questioning. A generation later William Moulton Marston, working under Professor Muensterberg at Harvard, developed a test of deception based on blood pressure changes and, at about the same time, Vittorio Benussi published a report of his research on changes in respiration as a symptom of deception. It was John A. Larson who brought together some of this earlier work and in 1921 announced the completion of a cardiopneumopsychogram instrument to record simultaneously blood pressure, pulse, and respiration rates during questioning. An improved recording instrument was devised by Leonarde Keeler a few years later, known as the Keeler Polygraph, which measured galvanic reflexes as well as the pulse, blood pressure, and respiratory movements. Variations of these machines have been employed by different authorities in succeeding years. In the 1930s the Pathometer was developed at Fordham University, an instrument differing from the others. It is a psychogalvanometer, a machine that measures the resistance of the body to minute electric current, recording the involuntary electrical changes that occur at the surface of the skin (on the palms of each hand).[136]

Keeler describes briefly the ordinary examination procedure employed in lie detection:[137] In order that the effect of the existing environment, the present emotional state, and the physical condition of the subject may be determined, a polygraph recording is made for some minutes during which no questions are asked. Whatever the existing physiological and emotional conditions might be, the resulting polygraph curves indicate the "norm" for the period of the test. After this "norm" has been established, two or three irrelevant questions are asked, then questions pertaining to the crime, intermingled with irrelevant questions. Each question must be worded briefly and call for a "yes" or "no" answer. The examiner's mode of asking questions must be uniform as to rate, volume, and inflection of speech all through the test.

Various authorities writing on the validity of the detection techniques have estimated accuracy in from 85 to 99 per cent of the cases, assuming honest and competent examiners. Inbau, a leading authority in the field, has indicated on the basis of thousands of polygrams made by the Chicago Scientific Crime Detection Laboratory that in 15 to 20 per cent of the cases the results are too indefinite to justify a determination and that in another 5 per cent the results

---

[136] Other lie detection methods have been employed such as drugs, particularly sodium amytol, pentothal, and scopolamine, so-called truth serums that are designed to produce a narcosynthesis in which the inhibitions of speech are decreased; hypnotic suggestion; association tests, measuring hesitation and deviations of response; eye reactions; and neuromuscular movements. Loevinger has noted some fourteen different types of methods. See "Jurimetrics," *Minn. L. R.,* vol. 33, pp. 455 ff.

[137] Keeler, "Debunking the Lie Detector," *J. Crim. L.,* vol. 25, p. 156, 1934.

were erroneous.[138] Other experts have held that the percentage in both of these categories is smaller than Inbau found in Chicago, however.[139] Errors are more commonly made in failing to detect deception than in finding that the subject lies when actually he does not. This is fortunate, for a great advantage in the use of such detection is in the elimination of innocent suspects.

Lie detection evidence has not fared well, thus far, in the courts. A survey[140] in 1953 has noted some sixteen appellate court decisions dealing with the admissibility of such evidence. *Frye v. United States,*[141] decided in 1923, is the first reported decision dealing with the question. In this murder prosecution evidence from a blood pressure deception test was offered to show the innocence of the defendant and the Court of Appeals for the District of Columbia held that it had properly been excluded. (Some time after Frye was convicted a confession was made by the actually guilty person.) The subsequent decisions have quite consistently followed this precedent on the ground there stated that such results have "not yet gained such standing and scientific

---

[138] The major types of cases in which the lie detector technique appears to be unreliable, as noted by Inbau and others, are those in which the subject (1) suffers from some form of mental abnormality, such as feeble-mindedness, psychosis, psychoneurosis, or emotional instability; (2) has such physiological abnormalities as an excessively high or low blood pressure, a disease of the heart, or a respiratory disorder; (3) experiences unusually strong emotional tension as a result of fears or guilt feelings (that need not be related to the immediate crime at issue); (4) is unresponsive because of lack of fear, extended rationalizations, prolonged prior interrogation, etc.; and (5) has unobserved muscular movements that may produce misleading blood pressure indications. Special difficulty is found with morons, some psychoneurotics, psychopaths, and emotionally unresponsive persons. It should also be noted that it is the *conscious* lie that produces the revealing symptoms; where the subject believes that the truth is different than it is, his responses may mislead the interrogator. See Inbau and Reid, *Lie Detection and Criminal Interrogation,* 1953; W. M. Marston, *The Lie Detector Test,* 1938; Burack, "A Critical Analysis of the Theory, Method and Limitations of the 'Lie Detector,'" *J. Crim. L.,* vol. 46, p. 414, 1955.

[139] In 1952 Dr. Edward E. Cureton, of the department of psychology of the University of Tennessee, submitted questionnaires to 1,700 persons presumed to have informed opinions on the detection of deception. In replies he found 11 per cent who expressed no opinion on the validity of the tests and 3 per cent who considered that the polygraph has low validity as a deception indicator. The technique was considered to be "highly valid" by 63 per cent of the psychologists who replied; 65 per cent of the observers and experimenters; 74 per cent of the observers, experimenters, and examiners; 83 per cent of the examiners; and 87 per cent of the nonpsychologists. The tests were considered to possess "moderate to high validity" by 93 per cent of the psychologists; 97 per cent of the nonpsychologists; 91 per cent of the observers and experimenters; 95 per cent of observers, experimenters, and examiners; and 98 per cent of the examiners. Very few of the remainder considered that the tests were invalid, but a substantial proportion expressed no opinion. See E. E. Cureton, 'A Consensus as to Validity of Polygraphic Procedures,' in "The Polygraphic Truth Test, a Symposium," *Tenn. L. R.,* vol. 22, pp. 18–33, 1953 (reprint).

[140] William Wicker, 'The Polygraphic Truth Test and the Law of Evidence,' in "The Polygraphic Truth Test," *op. cit.,* pp. 1–18.

[141] 293 F. 1013 (D.C. 1923).

recognition among physiological and psychological authorities as would justify the courts in admitting expert testimony deduced from the discovery, development, and experiments thus far made." However, in one California appellate case[142] both parties agreed to take a polygraph test and the results were submitted in evidence over the objection of the party as to whom the results were unfavorable. In a New York lower court case in 1938[143] the results of a Pathometer test were allowed by a judge who considered that if the courts are to admit expert opinion relating to handwriting, psychiatric diagnosis, and other such matters they should also allow lie detection evidence. Some appellate decisions have suggested that if a proper foundation had been laid, showing the validity of such tests and the competence of the expert, the evidence might have been allowed;[144] but there has been virtually no support of lie detection in the case records thus far. However, lie detector tests have been admitted as evidence in unappealed and therefore unreported cases in a number of states, including New York, Indiana, Wisconsin, Illinois, Ohio, California, Michigan, and Washington.[145]

To the present time the greatest utility of the lie detection technique has been outside the court. Police departments and other investigating agencies are using such methods in cities throughout the country with a great deal of success. Reports from police departments using polygraphs have shown in a high proportion of cases, where the tests have shown that a suspect was lying about his guilt, that the suspect subsequently confesses upon observing the results of his tests. Confessions have been obtained, according to authorities, in from 50 to 85 per cent of the cases in which the test records have shown deception.[146] Nine police departments, reporting on the results of examining over 7,000 suspects, found that an average of 64 per cent of those whose responses indicated guilt confessed to the crimes involved.[147] Often where the suspect may not be ready to confess and where his test results could not be admitted into evidence, the tests lead nevertheless to highly useful information that may be employed in further police investigation. These cases, cited to the author by a police authority who has done considerable work with the Pathometer, are in point:

---

[142] *People v. Houser,* 85 Cal. App. 2d 686 (1948).

[143] *People v. Kenny,* 167 Misc. 51 (N.Y. Queens Co. Ct. 1938).

[144] *Boeche v. State,* 151 Neb. 368 (1949); *People v. Forte,* 279 N.Y. 204 (1938).

[145] Wicker, *op. cit.,* p. 5. A case of some special interest occurred in Kings County in 1943, *People v. Goldman,* where the defendant was convicted on conflicting testimony of sodomy and assault. The presentence investigation, among other relevant matters, revealed the good reputation of the defendant and the loose moral standards of the complainant female. The defendant was permitted to take a Pathometer test before sentence that indicated that no act of sodomy had occurred, upon which Judge Leibowitz set aside the conviction. At subsequent trial for assault, of which the defendant was convicted, Judge Taylor in the same court refused to admit lie detection evidence.

[146] See Inbau, "Scientific Evidence in Criminal Cases: II. Methods of Deception," *J. Crim. L.,* vol. 24, p. 1147, 1934.

[147] Paul V. Trovillo, 'Scientific Proof of Credibility,' in "The Polygraphic Truth Test," *op. cit.,* p. 48.

This case involved a fugitive in a murder case. Unable to trace the suspect, the police interrogated his wife, who vehemently denied any knowledge of his whereabouts. When a tap on her phone, a mail cover, and surveillance of her home failed to produce any results, she was asked if she would take a lie detector test and she assented. Asked first if she knew where her husband was, her negative answer was determined to be a lie. The next question was, "Is your husband in Maine?" "No." "Is he in New Hampshire?" "No." When the questioner reached Connecticut a lie reaction followed the "No." States were left for cities, and a query about Bridgeport sent the needle soaring. By the time a map of Bridgeport had been secured and questions started running through the north and south streets, the woman would no longer answer. She didn't, however, get up and cast off the electrodes and her reactions came through without verbal responses. The method was followed to the point where the fugitive husband's street address was determined. A telephone call to the police ensured the man's detention until he was called for.

In a Maine paper mill a million dollar paper machine was sabotaged by someone who threw rivets between its enormous rollers. The Pathometer was sent for, to be given to all employees who had had opportunity to accomplish the deed; further sabotage was feared. The plant foreman named three suspects, saying he was sure the investigation would not need to go beyond them. These three and several others were cleared by tests. The first record taken on the foreman himself showed guilt reactions; he became suddenly too sick for further tests. He is still sick. The plant has had no more sabotage, but management uncomfortably remembers having fired several employees in the past on accusations of one sort or another by the foreman who had been in the plant for twenty years.

The cashier of a shipping concern had been caught in an embezzlement and had confessed and returned $14,000; this was all that he had left, he said, of $40,000 he had stolen. The rest he claimed to have lost on the horses. A Pathometer test showed him to be lying. He hadn't lost the rest of the money but had cached it. Properly constructed interrogation revealed the hiding place and full recovery resulted.

A man suspected his wife of cheating while away at a summer hotel. Nothing could pacify him except that she take a lie detector test. If she "passed," then everything would be all right and they would live happily forever after. She took the test and was proved faithful. After a little thought, however, she sued her husband for a separation.

In addition to official criminal investigation, lie detection has come to be used widely in the fields of business and industry and, to some extent, in government. Polygraph tests have become standard procedure in a great many banks, stores, industrial plants, and other organizations throughout the country. Lloyd's of London and some bonding organizations here reduce the premium on fidelity bonds to banks that administer such tests to their employees. Preemployment and periodic examinations are conducted by some defense industries and govermental organizations where security is involved, including branches of the military service.[148] For such uses the percentage of cases in which definitive results cannot be secured is even smaller than the figures reported on its use in criminal investigation. An official of one large detective agency has estimated that the technique has made possible the successful solution of 99 per cent of the cases in which discovery was otherwise impossible.

In the light of such evidences of the utility of lie detection methods, why have our courts been so slow to adopt it? What is the desirable policy for the future? It is easy enough to attribute the present situation to the conservatism of our courts, but the courts have come to accept the evidence of such fields as psychiatry, handwriting analyses, and coroner's examinations where the data are of a considerably more equivocal character. The view that the courts should wait until lie detection evidence is infallible is scarcely tenable, for none of the evidence received in our criminal courts is of such a nature. Indeed, at the present time deception can be detected with greater accuracy by polygraphic examination than by any other known method of investigation. Nor is there any serious problem of involuntary self-incrimination.[149] It is palpably absurd to assume, as Marston did, that lie detection would lead to the end of crime because criminals would discover that they could not deceive authorities. Yet it is entirely reasonable to believe that at some future time many errors of justice that arise out of perjury may be avoided and that brutal physical and psychological coercion may be discarded because they are neither as reliable nor as just as is lie detection.

Inbau has summarized certain major difficulties that stand in the way of admitting lie detection evidence. One is the probability that a party would produce only those test results that were favorable to himself and that his opponent would not be able either to examine him under the lie detector or to cross-examine him if he refused to take the stand. This sort of problem is

[148] Concerning noncriminal interrogation and testing, Trovillo points out the wider purpose to discover the intent of the subject as to future behavior. It is important, for example, in testing employment applicants in banks and other business establishments to know not only what the subject has done but what he may contemplate doing in the future. *Op. cit.*, p. 41.

[149] Though the question has been raised quite frequently, there can be no very serious problem of coercion in polygraphic examinations, for the testing depends upon the cooperation of the subject. This means that not all suspects can be tested, of course, but that where they are the issue of involuntary self-incrimination is not a serious one. Trovillo says, "Evidence obtained from unwilling persons is apt to be so distorted by gross body movement that no one could interpret the charts. I know of not a single case in which force or intimidation has been used to secure consent." This appears not to be a serious limitation on the number to whom the test may be applied. "The fears that status will be lost if one refuses to take the test bear down upon every criminal suspect, to say nothing of the employee who searches his heart for a 'reasonable' excuse for not taking the test. For example, in a group of eleven hundred criminal suspects brought for polygraphic examination to the Chicago Police Scientific Crime Detection Laboratory, most of whom were suspected of felonies, only four persistently refused to take the polygraph tests—and of these four, three were later electrocuted for murder!" Paul V. Trovillo, 'Scientific Proof of Credibility,' in "The Polygraphic Truth Test," *op. cit.*, p. 35.

encountered, however, in any case where the parties have discretion as to the evidence, expert or otherwise, that they will submit. This problem can be met either by having tests made and submitted upon the order of the court or by stipulation of both the parties in advance of the testing. A more serious problem is posed by the allegations that lie detection is not yet adequately standardized as to instruments employed, the manner of conducting tests, the qualification of examiners, and interpretation of the records. Since effective testing techniques and instruments have come to be fairly well standardized, the outstanding difficulty is that of assuring that the "expert" is truly qualified to administer and interpret testing. This is a real problem and no less so because a similar problem is encountered in the fields of psychological and psychiatric evidence where the standards of expertness are also underdeveloped. Trovillo indicated in 1953 that approximately 100 police departments were using the tests, 55 personnel consultants and 183 examiners in nine states. To set oneself up as an expert and to employ the polygraph equipment, one does not need to have undergone any special training and experience, formal or otherwise, or to have secured any sort of license; consequently this field attracts the charlatan. Until qualifications and standards have been set, it appears that it would be undesirable to have lie detection evidence freely admitted in our courts; neither judge nor jury is in a position to interpret such evidence properly or to evaluate the competence of the ordinary practitioner. On this point Wicker has said:[150]

> The validity of polygraphic interrogation as a means of detecting deception cannot be assessed apart from the background, training, experience and integrity of the examiner. The examiner's ability in judging human nature, his understanding of the mechanical aspects of his equipment and of some of the principles of physiology and psychology, his experience in the art of interrogation and his integrity, are all significant factors in evaluating his diagnosis of a polygram. An untrained, inexperienced examiner is about as incapable of detecting deception with a polygraph as a layman is to diagnose a heart condition with a stethoscope or a cardiograph, but the interpretations of polygrams by examiners who are honest, competent and well trained have a high degree of accuracy as to the truth or falsity of the answers to crucial questions.

Elsewhere in this text the author notes the large difficulty in trial justice that lies in our necessary reliance upon crude court judgments of the reliability and credibility of witnesses according to their manner, features, voice, and consistency. A problem of equal if not greater seriousness exists in those cases where convictions occur on plea without a trial, cases in which the plea is often secured by administrative measures of coercion or persuasion or by a bargain that serves poorly the ends of justice. It is not unreasonable to believe that lie detection, properly standardized and interpreted, may come to relieve the inaccuracies and injustices that are implicit in present procedures. While such evidence should not be taken as conclusive, it should come to stand with other evidence bearing on the credibility and knowledge of witnesses. Experience thus far indicates, moreover, that its use, combined with proper interrogation, will result in valid confessions and admissions that are, even now, submissible

[150] William Wicker, *op. cit.*, p. 2.

in evidence. In many cases it will mean the elimination of innocent suspects as well as a more efficient determination of the guilty.

Expert Testimony

One of the serious problems relating to scientific evidence and its presentation in court is rooted in procedures under our adversary system of justice. Expert opinion testimony has fallen into poor repute, largely because under the practice in most states each side selects and pays its experts. They seek testimony favorable to their case rather than the highest measure of competence and impartiality from their witnesses. The consequent "battle of the experts" is often more confusing than informative to the jury.

Constructive proposals have been made to remedy some of the difficulties associated with the prevailing procedures. The Model Expert Testimony Act,[151] which has now been adopted in several states, provides that each side shall pay one-half of the fee of a court-selected expert, thus divorcing the witness from the source of his compensation. In the alternative, the parties may agree upon an expert whom the court would then appoint. Both would have access to the expert's report before trial. Under a system such as this, strong argument could be advanced for making lie detection testimony admissible in our courts.

[151] See the Model Code of Evidence, Rules 400–410, 1942, and the Federal Rules of Criminal Procedure, Rule 28, 1946, for provisions similar to those in the Model Expert Testimony Act.

Chapter 12

JUDICIAL PROCEDURES

In this chapter the author will consider the judicial procedures that are employed in the administration of justice in the United States. At the end of the chapter the court organization through which offenders are processed will be described summarily.

COMMON AND CIVIL LAW

Two major divisions of criminal law and procedure are generally distinguished in the Western world today: the common-law system derived in large part from Germanic origins and matured in England, and the civil-law form which derived from Roman law and reached its peak in France. A detailed study of the two would provide fascinating illustrations of the sociocultural evolution of legal institutions and of the diffusion and differentiation of control methods. Extended analysis is not possible here, but it may be useful to consider and compare the characteristics of these systems; the similarities and differences that appear have some special relevance to a critical view of trial and pretrial procedures in the prevailing administration of justice in the United States.

It may be noted first that certain characteristics are commonly deemed to distinguish the two systems. In particular the civil-law pattern is thought of in terms of an inquisitorial system of criminal justice. It is based upon detailed codifications of the law and relies upon the texts of outstanding legal scholars as a basis of judicial reasoning and decision. The common-law method, on the other hand, emphasizes the accusatorial system of trial and relies upon the "common law," both as a source of the basic law and as a process by which the law is continuously developed. Both of these systems have proceeded historically from trial forms that were accusatory and, while they diverged extensively in procedure and philosophy for a time, they have come to resemble each other more and more closely, especially during the past century and a half. As a consequence, the patterns in the administration of justice today, while they are marked by various differences in details, are best characterized as mixed systems in which the resemblances are great in their major procedures and premises. The two systems have faced essentially similar problems and, in some considerable

326

part through borrowing and adaptation, have arrived at similar methods. Thus, the major legal orders today employ both an inquisitional and an accusatorial phase of procedure. Extensive codifications have developed in common-law countries. Also in these countries legal literature, such as restatements of the law and commission reports, has assumed a growing importance, though legal texts still do not possess the authority that they are accorded in civil-law nations. Legal precedent, basic to the common-law process, plays an important role, too, in countries of the civil law, though it is not so essential in the latter.[1]

Concerning the virtues of a combined system, the American criminologist Morris Plowcowe has said:[2]

> French criminal procedure owes its character to the inquisitorial procedure of the *ancien régime* and to the English accusatorial system introduced by the Revolution. Its development from these two sources throws into high relief the fundamental problem of all modern criminal procedures, the problem of how to facilitate an effective repression of crime and at the same time protect individual liberties. In Europe, the solution offered by the present French code had great influence from the time of its adoption in 1808. It was taken as a model by legislators of other countries who were similarly beset by the demands of their governments for a stronger prosecution of crime and by the insistence of their liberal leaders that the rights of individuals be respected.

In the *Spirit of the Common Law,* Roscoe Pound has commented on developments in French and Anglo-American procedure as a consequence of which they have become more similar. He remarks specifically on the problems associated with pretrial procedures in the United States:[3]

> Perhaps no institution of the modern world shows such vitality and tenacity as our Anglo-American legal tradition which we call the common law. Although it is essentially a mode of judicial and juristic thinking, a mode of treating legal problems rather than a fixed body of definite rules, it succeeds everywhere in molding rules, whatever their origin, into accord with its principles and in maintaining those principles in the face of formidable attempts to overthrow or to supersede them. In the United States it survives the huge mass of legislation that is placed annually upon our statute books and gives to it form and consistency.

[1] A. Esmein says, in *A History of Continental Criminal Procedure,* 1913, p. 3: "Three fundamental types of procedure are, in effect, distinguishable—the *accusatory* type, the *inquisitorial* type, and the *mixed* type. The criminal law of almost every nation has begun with the accusatory procedure, and has changed to the inquisitorial procedure. An evolution in an opposite direction, however, is now apparent; everywhere there is a tendency to restore the essential safeguards of the accusatory system, *publicity,* and *confrontation.*"

[2] "Development in French Procedure," *J. Crim. L.,* vol. 23, pp. 372 ff., 1932. (Reprinted by permission.)

[3] Roscoe Pound, *Spirit of the Common Law,* pp. 1–2, 19 ff. (Reprinted by permission.) See also his *Criminal Justice in America,* 1930, and *Justice According to Law,* 1951.

It is a curious fact that during the last century opposite tendencies have been working and continue to work in French procedure on one hand and English and American procedure on the other. In France the tendency has been to ameliorate the severities of the law, to surround the accused with great safeguards at the expense of the prosecuting power. In England and the United States there is a strong tendency to strengthen the hand of the state at the expense of the accused, by a process of elimination of the technical rules that covered the accused as with a coat of mail. Recently the old inquisitorial procedure has shown its head in American in the so-called "Third Degree." Whether this is sporadic and will remain extra-legal or will find recognition remains to be seen. It has already reached sufficient magnitude to call forth legislation. So far this legislation has been against it, and in the extra-legal way in which it is practiced it is, undoubtedly, vicious. But it may well be that, protected as the criminal is in Anglo-American jurisprudence from the time of arrest to final judgment, surrounded as he is not only with all the presumptions and technicalities of the old English procedure, but also by the added constitutional safeguard of State and Federal constitutions, we may yet find it necessary to adopt something corresponding to the examination of the French *juge d'instruction;* in some States we have already followed France and practically abolished the grand jury.

PRETRIAL PROCEDURES IN THE UNITED STATES

The major phases of pretrial and trial procedure that are employed in the administration of our criminal justice today will now be discussed. The authorities have devoted critical attention to the criminal jury trial. However, a great majority of criminal cases do not go to trial. Pretrial procedures are in fact significantly more important in determining what happens to suspected criminals. The following important procedures will be considered: arrest and interrogation, preliminary hearing, indictment or information, other pretrial procedures, trial, and appeal. Because sentencing has come to be so important a phase of the administration of justice it will be considered at length in an ensuing chapter. It should be observed that the procedures to be discussed are commonly elided. In practice, sentencing often follows rapidly upon interrogation, the filing of an information, and the taking of a guilty plea.[4]

[4] There are numerous studies and evaluations of the administration of criminal justice in the United States and of specialized aspects of our system. Some of the latter will be referred to in the footnotes of this and the two ensuing chapters. Among the general works the student should consult: Sheldon Glueck, *Crime and Justice,* 1936; Arthur T. Vanderbilt, *Minimum Standards of Judicial Administration,* 1949; Clarence N. Callendar, *American Courts: Their Organization and Procedure,* 1927; Fred Rodell, *Woe unto You, Lawyers!* 1940; Percival Jackson, *Look at the Law,* 1940; Max Radin, *The Law and Mr. Smith,* 1938; John B. Waite, *Criminal Law in Action,* 1934. Two of the useful recent volumes are referred to repeatedly in the notes below: Lester B. Orfield, *Criminal Procedure from Arrest to Appeal,* 1947, and Ernst W. Puttkammer, *Administration of Criminal Law,* 1953.

Arrest, Complaint, and Preparation to Prosecute

A majority of criminal actions, particularly those involving more serious crimes, are initiated by police arrest without a warrant, ordinarily within a short time after the commission of the crime. The role of the police and problems connected with arrest are considered in Chapter 11. It is only noted here that arrest is the most important method of apprising the suspect that he is charged with the commission of a crime. This charge is based upon police opinion that there is reasonable ground to believe that he has committed the offense of which he is accused. Alternatively, custody of the suspect may be secured under a warrant of arrest, issued by the filing of a complaint under oath, together with an affirmation showing that a crime has been committed and that there is probable cause to suspect the accused. Suspects may also be brought before a court under a summons, though generally only for minor offenses and misdemeanors. A summons may be issued rather than a warrant if the magistrate has power to try the case summarily or if he has reason to believe that the defendant will appear in answer to the summons.

Frequently complaint is made against unnecessary and disgraceful arrest. It appears highly desirable that a summons be used more commonly as a substitute for arrest either with or without a warrant. Provision is made for some liberalization in the employment of the summons under such model codes as the Uniform Arrest Act (Section 9), the American Law Institute Code (Section 12), and the Federal Rules of Criminal Procedure (Rule 4a). Considerable inconvenience results from the fact that it is necessary in most jurisdictions to secure issuance of summonses as well as warrants from a judge or clerk of court. Frequently this means that either no arrest will be made or that the charge will be dropped by the officer.

A complaint, generally required to be in writing, is prerequisite to preliminary examination by a magistrate. Where custody was secured by a warrant, the complaint upon which the warrant was issued is sufficient, but where arrest was made without a warrant, a complaint that sets out the nature of the offense and the identity of the offender must be drawn prior to the hearing. In most states it is sufficient that the complaint is based upon information and belief rather than knowledge. The original complaint is commonly made by a private complainant, the victim, the prosecuting attorney superseding him as soon as a formal complaint has been issued. In many instances the police provide the information on which the complaint is drawn.

Concerning interrogation of the suspect by police and prosecutor, which has become so important an element of investigation prior to court action, the laws of procedure are largely and strangely silent. Provision is generally made for the early production of the accused before a magistrate for a judicial inquiry, and in theory our system of procedure avoids the inquisition that characterizes continental practice. The privilege against compulsory self-incrimination as well as the inadequate talents of the lay magistracy in the United States are major barriers to the sort of preliminary inquiry that is conducted by the *juge d'instruction* in France. As a result, between the assumption of custody by the police and the production of the suspect before a court, there is theoretically only such brief hiatus as is required to record his arrest and to take him before a magistrate. Thus he is protected presumably from the abuses that may occur in the secrecy of private judicial inquisition that civil-law countries employ. In fact, however, as was indicated in Chapter 11, the investigation conducted by the police and prosecution before trial is a kind of extralegal inquisition by which the state may be able to establish its case against the suspect.

The importance of this phase of the inquiry is attested by the fact that, according to official statistics, a large percentage of persons arrested for crime, who are entitled, therefore, to be produced before a magistrate, are released without being charged. Studies of large samples of arrests in different jurisdictions have indicated that somewhere between 44 and 48 per cent of those arrested have been released without being charged before a magistrate.[5] It is clear that many persons accused and detained should not have been placed under arrest. In order to avoid illegal arrest and detention, the authorities frequently hold suspects as material witnesses. Occasionally this detention is very prolonged.[6]

The prevailing practices of police and prosecution partially explain the weakened role of the preliminary and grand jury hearings; at these hearings the prosecutor merely brings out what he has been able to discover in secret process. Police and prosecution practices also account largely for the very high proportion of criminal cases that are settled on pleas of guilty to a lesser charge; the prosecutor has usually secured such pleas through interrogations conducted by his office with the aid of the police. Abuses that sometimes occur have prompted a number of authorities to recommend that a system of judicial inquisition similar to that employed on the Continent should be adopted here, thus ensuring the establishment of rules and protections to guide the processes of interrogation and charge. Thus the original inquiry into guilt might become primarily a function of the magistrate, guided by established principles of justice and humanity to the suspect. Failing this, it has been proposed that a recording of the police interrogation, with or without a filming of the process, should be required as evidence that the procedure has been fair and without coercion.

[5] See Sheldon Glueck, *Crime and Justice,* 1936, p. 82, and Lester B. Orfield, *Criminal Procedure from Arrest to Appeal,* 1947, p. 35.

[6] Ernst W. Puttkammer, *Administration of Criminal Law,* 1953, pp. 66–67. In "Pity the Poor Witness," Mitchell Dawson cites the case of a material witness in a vehicular homicide case who could not make bail and was retained in jail 110 days while the driver was let out on bond and ultimately, after conviction, was sentenced to 60 days. *Esquire,* March, 1946.

Usually these suggestions have met with intense opposition both from police and prosecutor's offices.[7]

It may well be argued that the police require greater freedom of some sorts in making arrests and in securing evidence than the law provides and that the prosecution should be allowed more time to interrogate and to gather evidence. The fundamental fact is, however, that under a system that strives toward justice under law, policy and practice should be guided firmly by the law and not by expedience or by the erratic whims of administrative conscience. It has been recommended that state laws should be changed to permit the police to detain any suspect for a period of two hours without being required to show cause and to frisk where there may be no basis for arrest.

Preliminary Hearing, Commitment, and Bail of the Accused

In conformity with the theoretical conceptions of an accusatory rather than an inquisitional system of justice, our law provides in most jurisdictions that the police shall produce the arrested party for a preliminary hearing without unreasonable delay.[8] Since an arrest occurs at the time that a person is taken into custody under a charge, this is taken generally to mean that the arrestee shall be brought before a magistrate within a twenty-four hour period.[9] Some cases have held that shorter periods are too long. The rule concerning unreasonable delay is often evaded by not recording an arrest officially until the authorities are satisfied that they can "make a charge stick." Moreover, even if it is shown that detention has

---

[7] Noting that there is no panacea to cure the problems involved in criminal investigation, Puttkammer discusses various proposals for achieving improvements. *Op. cit.,* pp. 78–79.

[8] "The Uniform Arrest Act, Section 11, reaffirms the existing rule that a person arrested must be brought before a magistrate 'without unreasonable delay' and provides that the delay shall not exceed certain periods. Section 2 provides that a suspect may be detained before arrest for a period not exceeding two hours. Section 11 provides that the period between arrest and bringing before a magistrate shall not exceed twenty-four hours except in two cases. The words 'if possible' are inserted because in several large western states it is physically impossible during the winter to get a prisoner to a magistrate within twenty-four hours of arrest. The second exception allows a person arrested to be held for a period not to exceed forty-eight hours in excess of the twenty-four hour period, if a judge so orders after good cause shown. The requirements of convincing a judge that good cause exists for postponing should speed up police investigation and reduce long periods of detention. The provisions would seem constitutional as being reasonable." Lester B. Orfield, *Criminal Procedure from Arrest to Appeal,* New York University Press, New York, 1947, pp. 38–39. (Reprinted by permission.) A study conducted by the Illinois Division of the American Civil Liberties Union in 1959 concluded that 20,000 defendants were held by Chicago police for at least 17 hours before they were booked; 2,000 were illegally detained for two days or more; and 350 were held three days or longer without being charged.

[9] See Chapter 11, especially ftn. 48.

been unreasonably prolonged, this alone does not constitute adequate grounds on which to discharge or acquit the suspect.[10] While the accused may be entitled to action against those who have detained him, this is no real protection either against the illegally prolonged custody or against abuses that may occur during that period. Hence, violation of the offender's right is actually invited where such violation may result in a confession, admissions, or the securing of additional evidence.

The purpose of a preliminary investigation is to discover whether the state has sufficient evidence to make out a prima-facie case to justify holding the accused for trial. A prima-facie case is one in which there is enough evidence to convict unless that evidence is contravened by testimony of the defendant and his witnesses. Though there is a difference in technical detail, reasonable grounds to support a legal arrest would ordinarily be sufficient to constitute a prima-facie case. It is significant to observe, therefore, that offenders who are charged by the police and who are brought before a magistrate are very frequently released after a hearing. Crime surveys have shown that discharges of felony cases at preliminary hearings have amounted to as much as 58 per cent in New York City, 55 per cent in Cincinnati, and 49 per cent in Chicago, while the total of felony discharges was only 17 per cent in Milwaukee and St. Louis.[11] This suggests either that the police have made unjustified arrests or that the magistrates have released suspects too freely in spite of evidence that is sufficient to justify the magistrates' retaining them for trial. Undoubtedly both of these errors occur, the former under the loose arrest practices that prevail in many communities, the latter where police magistrates are laymen, sometimes merely incompetent, sometimes venal. Crude data relating to the discharge of suspects by magistrates' courts in particular jurisdictions do not furnish a valid basis for inferring that suspects are being discharged too often where evidence supports their trial.

While the preliminary hearing is a statutory rather than a constitutional right, it is widely recognized in common-law countries. Judge Dickinson of the Federal district court in Pennsylvania has said: "One threatened with the charge of the commission of a crime has two rights. One is, of course, the right to a fair and impartial trial upon which the question of his guilt is determined; the other is the no less valuable right that he shall not be even called upon to answer to a criminal charge until some duly constituted tribunal has passed upon the preliminary question of whether he ought to be brought to trial."[12] The preservation of the right to a prelimi-

---

[10] *People v. Baxter*, 178 Misc. 625, 36 S. 2d 1020 (1942), and *People v. Mummiani*, 258 N.Y. 394, 180 N.E. 94 (1932).

[11] Raymond Moley, *Politics and Criminal Prosecution*, 1929, p. 28.

[12] *United States v. Fitzgerald*, 29 F. 2d 573 (1928). The purposes of the preliminary hearing have been very well summarized in a Wisconsin case in these terms: "The object or purpose of the preliminary investigation is to prevent hasty, malicious, improvident and oppressive prosecutions, to protect the person charged from

nary hearing appears to this writer to be important, if not indeed vital, because it requires the state to show in a public hearing that it has evidence that justifies bringing the case to trial and because it permits the defendant to rebut such evidence, avoiding the financial and psychic costs of trial where there is no need for it. Prosecutors have come to consider the preliminary hearing a perfunctory matter, however, and have maintained that it offers an undue advantage to the defendant in requiring the state to reveal its hand. In fact, the preliminary hearing does not commonly educe fresh information on the case—as the judicial inquiry is designed to do on the Continent—largely because the "inquisition" here has already occurred before the accused is produced before the magistrate. Preliminary hearings are commonly criticized for these reasons.

In general today where prosecution is by indictment the suspect has no right to a preliminary hearing, though some jurisdictions provide for it in certain cases. As prosecution by information[13] rather than by indictment has become increasingly common, it has generally been required that a hearing be provided before the information is filed unless the accused waives the right. A number of jurisdictions have abandoned the hearing, however, even where procedure by information is the practice.[14] Suspects may, in most jurisdictions, waive preliminary hearing where they are entitled to it and they often do so when they know that the state's case is strong enough to hold them for trial and particularly when the prosecution has agreed that a plea will be taken.

It appears that in the compromise between accusational and inquisitorial process that has developed in the United States' procedures of police-prosecution interrogation and magistrates' preliminary hearings, the interrogation has become an excessively significant administrative measure and the hearings less important than they should be. The preliminary

---

open and public accusations of crime, to avoid both for the defendant and the public the expense of a public trial, and to save the defendant from the humiliation and anxiety involved in a public prosecution, and to discover whether or not there are substantial grounds upon which a prosecution may be based." *Thies v. State,* 178 Wis. 98, 103 (1922).

Jerome Hall has commented, "A majority of all felony cases which appear in the courts are disposed of on preliminary hearings by magistrates. . . . As a consequence, the police magistrate and the prosecuting attorney loom up as by far the most important officials in our system with reference to the disposition of the greatest number of cases." *Theft, Law and Society,* 1935, p. 113.

[13] "A criminal information is an accusation or a complaint exhibited against a person for some criminal offense. It differs principally from an indictment in this, that an indictment is found upon the oath of twelve men and an information is only the allegation of the officer who exhibits it. 4 Bl. Comm. 308." *Cyclopedic Law Dictionary,* p. 573. See ftn. 21 below.

[14] Professor Orfield notes seven states that have dispensed with the requirement of a preliminary hearing: Connecticut, Florida, Indiana, Iowa, Louisiana, Vermont, and Washington.

hearing does serve important functions for the state and for the accused in avoiding unnecessary trials, but it does less than it should, in the writer's opinion, in the way of interrogation to elicit the information that is now secured by extralegal administrative methods. Dean Wigmore has recommended a practice that appears both useful and desirable from the point of view of improving justice "to provide a means of speedy confession which shall be less susceptible to abuses, while still taking advantage of the inherent psychological situation." To this end Wigmore would " . . . let every accused person be required to be taken before a magistrate, or the district attorney, promptly upon arrest, for private examination; let the magistrate warn him of his right to keep silence; and then let his statement be taken in the presence of an official stenographer, if he is willing to make one."[15] Suggestions of this sort have been rejected by the bench as well as by the prosecution. Members of the bench base their objections on the defendant's rights against self-incrimination, the incapacity of magistrates to conduct a full and proper interrogation, and the possible abuses that might come from the magistrate's abandoning his impartiality for a prosecutor's role.

North Carolina is apparently the only jurisdiction in which the effort is made fully to examine the defendant before a magistrate. There he is entitled to counsel; the examination is not taken in the presence of other witnesses and it is not taken under oath. The defendant is informed of the charge against him, that he need not answer, and that his refusal so to do shall not later be used against him. A right to counsel at preliminary hearing is provided by statute in some states and in some others the Federal constitutional provision for counsel is interpreted to apply to this as well as to later stages of procedure. In a number of states, however, no such right is provided. In England the right to counsel at the examination was established by the act of 1848 and in France it was established for the judicial inquiry in 1897. The right is an important one, for the unsophisticated suspect who lacks counsel may too easily be led to confusion and contradictions by a skilled prosecutor. At trial the prosecutor may show contradictory material in the record to confound the defendant and his counsel at a time when he *is* represented. Moreover, it is important to the tactics of the defense, as it is to the prosecution, to decide whether the revelation of particular matters should be made at the hearing or postponed until trial. This requires the guidance of counsel.

On the basis of the preliminary hearing, the accused may either be discharged or held to answer. In some states, but not in all, he may be held for an offense that is different technically or materially from that described in the complaint; in such a case the magistrate has received evidence at the hearing of such other offense. Where the hearing fails to show probable cause to hold the defendant for trial, he is entitled to release. Where cause is shown, the defendant may be admitted to bail or

[15] Wigmore, *Evidence*, 1940, pp. 319–320, quoted in Orfield, *op. cit.*, p. 70.

formally committed to jail to await action by the trial court. In most jurisdictions the prosecutor enjoys the power to delay filing an information and to delay bringing the accused to trial. At his discretion the prosecutor may "nol-pros" (refuse to prosecute) the case in a majority of states, releasing the accused from bail or jail. The American Law Institute Code of Criminal Procedure and other proposals have sought to curtail or to remove the prosecutor's power in this determinative area, but in general whether or not a case will be taken to trial remains his decision. Moreover, in some jurisdictions, though the defendant has been discharged upon a preliminary hearing, the prosecutor may take the case for hearing on the same complaint before another magistrate and in some states he may take the defendant before a grand jury notwithstanding such discharge.

Bail may be granted to a defendant at any or all of several stages of procedure: after arrest pending preliminary hearing, after binding over by the magistrate for grand jury action (or trial, where prosecution is by information), after indictment, after trial, and again pending appeal. Most commonly in the United States today the bail is a promise by a surety to pay a particular sum of money if the bailee does not appear as required. In the alternative, however, cash bail may be deposited or property may be pledged in the amount set by the court. The purpose of bail is simply to assure the presence of the defendant (and, in the case of material witnesses, their presence) at hearing, trial, and subsequent procedures. Bail is commonly considered a right of the defendant and a protection to his freedom and reputation. The state also has an interest in granting bail, thus to avoid the expense of jail maintenance and the possibility of supporting the accused's family.[16] In a great majority of states today all defendants are granted the right to bail at least before conviction, except in the case of capital offenses "where the proof is evident or the presumption great." A few jurisdictions leave the matter completely to the discretion of the courts.

From the viewpoint of defendants' interests there are numerous faults in present bail practices in the United States. One fault is that bail is often set too high in cases where the individual could be trusted to appear for trial. The situation is aggravated by the commonly excessive charges exacted by professional bondsmen.[17] The large volume of business in magistrates'

---

[16] Professor Orfield observes that approximately half of the commitments to jails in the United States are of persons awaiting trial and that when bail is furnished its cost often impoverishes the families involved. *Op. cit.*, p. 131.

[17] In 1948 a Kings County grand jury found six indictments, totaling ninety-two counts against professional bondsmen and runners. According to its presentment, "The evidence indicates that exorbitant fees are exacted for offenses of a petty nature, and in many instances, fees for legal services are left with the professional bail bondsmen or their runners, which strongly leads to the inference that fee-splitting is present." The State Department of Insurance, the licensing agency for bondsmen, was accused of "laxity, indifference and partiality" in supervision of bondsmen activity. *New York Times,* Mar. 19, 1948.

courts results in mechanical procedures of setting bail under which the defendant's character, record, and financial circumstances may be given little or no attention at all. Thus a great number of innocent persons are confined to jail each year, sometimes for prolonged periods, because they are unable to raise what is in fact excessive bail.[18] The interests of the accused are also injured where he is detained for an extended period through delays in the prosecution of cases or where the state is slow to indict or to try cases. Hardship, though of a less serious character, is undergone by those who are submitted to bail and whose cases are long deferred before trial because of the congested court calendars and the practice of trying jail cases before bail cases. Finally, the fact that the accused must go through bail procedure in some jurisdictions as many as five to seven times creates unnecessary difficulties.

There are also serious errors in bail practice from the point of view of the state's interest in securing the defendant's presence at trial. One of these is the practice of shopping for bail, through which defendants who are refused bail by one judge may seek to have it set by another. In those jurisdictions where bail is a vested right rather than a matter of discretion for the court, it is an unfortunate consequence that defendants are bailable though their criminal histories are serious and though they may have previously absconded while on bail. Another difficulty is that of "straw bail," which involves the acceptance of surety for very large amounts of bail bonds from bondsmen who have but small equity in the property they pledge.[19] Beyond this, where the bondsman is responsible and the bail collectible, courts frequently have failed to levy against the property. Naturally where foreefitures are not exacted, bail comes to have little value for assuring the appearance of defendants or material witnesses. Thus "jumping of bail" becomes common.

The American Law Institute Code of Criminal Procedure proposes remedies for a number of problems involved in bail practice. The Code provides that bail should be granted only as a matter of discretion rather than as a matter of right in cases where the defendant is charged with murder, treason, arson, robbery, burglary, rape, kidnapping, or any offense

---

[18] In illustration of the seriousness of this matter, Orfield notes that, according to an investigation of the New York Law Society, prior to the establishment of the Adolescent Courts in New York City, " . . . in the year ending June 30, 1939, 78 per cent of all defendants between the ages of sixteen and twenty-one, charged with felonies and serious misdemeanors in the boroughs of Manhattan, Brooklyn, and Queens in New York City, were committed to detention prisons because they were unable to post bail required for their release. Yet 1,431 or 64 per cent of these defendants ultimately were discharged, acquitted, given suspended sentences, or placed on probation." *Op. cit.,* p. 106. The writer has observed numerous cases, some of them in the adolescent courts, where bail for the young has been deliberately set high enough to assure that the youth could not meet it. Many prosecutors take a dim view of the youthful offender when they recommend a figure for bail.

[19] See Beeley, *The Bail System in Chicago,* 1927, and Orfield, *op. cit.,* pp. 119–126.

against the person likely to result in death. The Code also provides that where bail has been denied by one court no tribunal of equal or inferior jurisdiction may admit to bail unless an affidavit is filed to show new evidence that is material to the defense. Upon any application for bail, the defendant must make an affidavit concerning any prior application for bail. It provides that where any official accepts bail knowing that it is insufficient or knowing that the surety does not possess proper qualifications he is guilty of a misdemeanor. The Code recommends that the surety must be worth the amount specified in his undertaking, that he must show in an affidavit that he has the qualifications and means to cover his commitment, and that the undertaking shall be a lien on the real property noted in the affidavit. Furthermore, the bondsman must reveal what consideration or security he has received from the defendant for his undertaking. The Code also sets up a simplified procedure for the collection of bail, providing that where the bailee fails to appear the court shall make a record thereof and shall declare the bail forfeited unless a satisfactory explanation is received within ten days. It is the duty of the prosecutor in such cases to file a copy of this order with an appropriate official of the county who shall enter judgment against the surety and levy execution against the property. Finally registration is required of all professional bondsmen.[20]

Methods of Indictment and Information

According to the laws of the particular jurisdiction, the accused in a criminal case may be brought to trial either by indictment of a grand jury or by information of the prosecutor.[21] Historically the English grand jury

---

[20] For a recent and thorough study of bail practices in Philadelphia, see Caleb Foote, James Markle, and Edward Woolley, "Compelling Appearance in Court: Administration of Bail in Philadelphia," Pamphlet Series, No. 1, Institute of Legal Research, University of Pennsylvania, 1954.

[21] The information serves much the same function as an indictment but is prepared by the prosecutor without submission to a grand jury and is less lengthy and technical than the traditional form of indictments. However, the information must allege the offense with sufficient fullness and accuracy. It may be formulated simply in the terms of the statute. Today indictments too have generally been simplified and in New York and in a few other jurisdictions (notably California and Massachusetts) a short form of indictment may be employed that merely sets out the nature of the crime alleged, with a right in the defendant to demand a bill of particulars to inform him of the detailed acts that the state intends to prove in relation to his crime. This is essentially the recommendation made in the A.L.I. Code of Criminal Procedure. It has been considerably criticized on the ground that little is gained by setting up a system of two pleadings of which one is optional with the defendant. The accused is entitled to be informed in the accusation of the acts that are alleged against him and of the issues that are to be tried. See Orfield, op. cit., pp. 227–247. The Federal Rules of Criminal Procedure require that the "indictment or information shall be a plain, concise, and definite statement of the essential facts constituting the offense charged." It requires, moreover, that the accusation provide the citation of each statute, rule, or other provision of law that the defendant is alleged to have violated.

system goes back to 1166; it was an importation by Henry II from practices in Normandy that were rooted in the inquest. During the thirteenth and part of the fourteenth centuries members of the petit jury were part of the grand jury; when the two juries separated the distinct function of the grand jury became that of determining from the state's evidence whether there was ground for trial. In 1933 the grand jury system was virtually abolished in England, mainly it appears for reasons of economy. Under present procedure there, any person may charge an indictable offense (without grand jury action) either where a magistrate has already committed the case for trial or where a judge of the High Court has consented. France introduced the grand jury as part of its revolutionary reforms in 1791 to remedy the abuses of the judicial inquisition but abandoned it again in 1808 in the new code of procedure.

In the United States, while the Fifth Amendment established the grand jury indictment procedure for prosecutions of felony in the Federal courts, the Fourteenth Amendment has been held not to require indictment. A number of states do provide in their constitutions for grand jury indictment, but ten states specifically provide that the legislature may modify or abandon the procedure and in a number of states it is at the prosecutor's discretion whether to proceed by indictment or information. Moreover, where the accused has a constitutional right to the indictment by grand jury as a condition to his trial, it is generally held that he may waive this right and may proceed on the basis of an information filed by the prosecutor. Where grand juries are employed, they have two different functions: one is that of determining on the basis of the written accusations and the evidence brought forward by the prosecutor against the accused whether there is probable cause to hold him to trial and, upon that decision, finding a "true bill" or, if the evidence is insufficient, "no true bill." The jury also may act as an investigating or inquisitorial body with broad powers to determine what crimes have been committed in the jurisdiction, thus originating cases that had not previously been submitted to arrest and preliminary hearing.[22] These are usually cases that can most effectively be investigated in secret proceedings or where policing and prosecuting authorities have failed to act. In some jurisdictions a preliminary hearing is required prior to grand jury indictment but in most jurisdictions there is no such requirement. In some states it is customary to have both indictment and the preliminary hearing; this practice has been criticized on the ground that one procedure duplicates the other functionally in determining that there is probable cause to hold for trial. Since it lies within the power of the prosecutor to bring the accused before the grand jury even if he has been discharged by a magistrate or to charge a more serious crime before

---

[22] A very small percentage of criminal cases are initiated by grand juries in this way, but see pp. 305–307 above for illustration of the value of such inquisition in vice cases. Also see ftn. 25.

the jury, it has been maintained that where indictment procedure is used the preliminary hearing is unnecessary. The virtue of retaining the preliminary hearing in such cases rests primarily in the requirement imposed by law: that the defendant be produced before the magistrate within a brief time of his arrest and that he be there charged and confronted with evidence justifying his detention.

Grand juries in the United States range in size from five to twenty-three. (There were from twelve to twenty-three members in the English grand juries.) They are selected in different jurisdictions either by lot from such sources as tax rolls or voting registration lists or through a more discriminating selection by officials, such as jury commissioners or boards of supervisors. Generally grand and petit juries are selected from the same jury lists. Compared with petit juries, there is relatively little deliberate or standardized exclusion from grand juries on the basis of education, property ownership, prejudice, or otherwise. Unlike the common law, the American Law Institute Code and the Federal Rules of Criminal Procedure provide for challenge of grand jurors, though not peremptory challenges such as may be made in the selection of a trial jury. Rules in the various jurisdictions vary on when and how the accused may object either to irregularities in the selection or to action of the grand jury. Generally, where he has not had opportunity to object before a bill is drawn, the accused may object by a motion to quash the indictment or by a plea in abatement. The Model Code of Criminal Procedure of the A.L.I. provides that a motion may be made to quash an indictment on any of the following grounds:

1. That there was ground for challenge to the panel or to an individual grand juror and that the defendant had not been held to answer at a preliminary hearing at the time the grand jurors were sworn.
2. That a person other than a grand juror was present while the grand jurors were deliberating or voting and that there is reasonable cause to believe that the defendant was in fact prejudiced thereby.
3. That the requisite number of grand jurors did not concur in finding the indictment.
4. That the grand jury had no authority to inquire into the offense charged.

In general, under present practice, the accused is not entitled to the same protections against unreasonable grand jury actions that he is entitled to at trial, since the indictment is merely an accusation rather than a conviction, though it does create hardships and injury to the suspect. As an ex parte inquisition, the grand jury procedure involves a hearing only of the state's evidence, not of the accused's or of his witnesses'. Moreover, while the evidence received is supposed to be relevant and competent, indictments that are based in part upon illegal evidence (sometimes including illegal searches and seizures and involuntary self-incrimination) will nevertheless be sustained if there is some competent evidence to establish probable cause. Practice varies on whether a transcript or report should be made on the grand jury proceedings and whether there should be access to such records to show irregularity of procedure. The grand jury action is a thoroughly secret procedure, like the French judicial inquisition, so that at least until its indictment has been made public neither the jurors, witnesses, nor prosecutor may reveal any of its actions. Only one witness may be present at a time and no other persons are permitted to be present. After a true bill has been found, however, disclosure of its procedure or the evidence received may be made at the discretion of the court in some jurisdictions. Inspection of the transcript of its hearing may be made in a few jurisdictions, notably in New York. Since the issue of double jeopardy is not involved in an indictment, the general rule is that a case may be re-submitted for consideration by a grand jury where it has failed to indict, though this may be limited by a requirement that there be new evidence or, as provided by the A.L.I. Code, that there be an order from the trial court permitting such resubmission.

As compared with the "mortality rate" in preliminary hearings, a rela-tively small proportion of cases submitted to grand juries are eliminated by its action. Criminal justice surveys in the 1920s revealed a range of from 2 to 30 per cent of cases discharged by failure to indict, with an average of 18.5 per cent.[23] The Cleveland survey attributed these failures to the insufficient diligence of prosecutors in preparing their cases for sub-mission. This is a narrow view, however, for in fact the proportion of cases deserving elimination at this stage is determined by practices of the police and magistrates at preliminary hearings, where such hearings are used. The prosecutor may determine on his own in most jurisdictions that there is not sufficient evidence to seek indictment or, even after an indict-ment, to bring to trial. It is understandable, however, that a diligent and prudent prosecutor may prefer to seek a grand jury's determination rather than to exercise his own discretion to exclude borderline or dubious cases. Failures to indict in such instances do not reflect unfavorably either on the prosecutor or on the grand jury, though they may indicate the need for more limited and discreet arrest practices and for more professionalized adjudication at preliminary hearings.

Much has been written about the grand jury, pro and con. It has been urged that the grand jury has lost its early feudal function of protecting the accused from official despotism. The preliminary hearing, with its public character and with the opportunity for the defendant to be heard, provides better protection than does the secret jury session from which the defendant is excluded. Excessive delay in procedure inconveniences witnesses who must come before both a magistrate and a grand jury when one finding of probable cause should be sufficient.[24] The futility of the

---

[23] *Report on Prosecution,* National Commission on Law Observance and Enforce-ment, 1931, p. 207.

[24] See Orfield, *op. cit.,* pp. 183–184. Criminal justice surveys have revealed very

indictment process has also been argued on the ground that, whereas at the start the grand jury served significant policing and prosecuting roles, in the absence of such functionaries, today it has come to be dominated by the prosecutor who can, in effect, direct its action while escaping responsibility for its decisions. Finally, while there has been more general approval of the inquisitional than of the indictment function of the grand jury, the inquisitional process too has been attacked for conducting unreasonable fishing expeditions into crime and for engaging in insolent and irrelevant questioning of witnesses. The inquisitional process includes the power to require that a witness testify and that he produce records. This power may be abused in the case of an individual whom the grand jury plans to indict: requiring testimony and production of records deprives the individual of his privilege against self-incrimination.

Despite these defects, it has been contended that the grand jury should be retained with the information procedure as an alternative so that the defendant may choose between indictment and information. The grand jury has powers of subpoena and contempt citation that the prosecutor lacks, so that documents and testimony may be secured in the record during an early phase of the investigation without the necessity of showing probable cause at once, as the prosecutor must do to secure the binding over of a defendant by the magistrate. These powers together with the private and secret character of the inquiry make the grand jury investigation a more effective source of information to support criminal actions than our noninquisitive type of preliminary hearing can be. Properly employed, therefore, the grand jury may tend to diminish the resort of police and prosecution to coercion and illegal detention as a means of securing information from suspects and witnesses. Use of the grand jury may also help in some measure to reduce the hypertrophied functions of prosecution with their resultant threat to a sound administration of justice. Power in the hands of prosecutors to proceed by information, after a preliminary hearing, leaves it almost entirely to the discretion of this administrator to initiate actions and to procure the evidence upon which suspects may be taken to trial. This frequently lengthy and largely secret phase of administrative inquiry is not easily guided or limited by legal standards. In the light of the above discussion, there may be greater necessity to retain the grand jury in this country than there was in England, with its professionalized and nonpolitical prosecutors.

---

long delays between preliminary hearing and grand jury action in some states, particularly in areas of low population where a jury may not be sitting for some time. However, even where a prosecutor's information may be used rather than an indictment, delay may be occasioned in waiting for a term of court. As a solution to this problem, North Dakota has provided that where a defendant has been held on preliminary hearing and determines to plead guilty he may so plead before any district judge of the county involved, to be sentenced there without waiting for a term of court. In other jurisdictions the accused may avoid delay by waiving indictment

It appears desirable to permit the defendant to waive indictment. The trends toward making indictments simpler in form and doing away with the defendant's right to contest the indictment for technical inaccuracies are certainly steps in the right direction. Rules of amendment by the court should be liberalized and an excessively strict construction of indictments should be abandoned. More competent jurors should be selected in order to secure effective action. On the whole, however, it appears clear that the grand jury system should be improved rather than discarded and that it should continue to be used as an investigative[25] body and, unless and until the preliminary hearing is made more effective, also as an indictive body. It has been noted that both the preliminary hearing and grand jury indictment procedures have been criticized and that the abolition of either one or the other has been recommended. Some critics believe that both should be abandoned, giving the entire task of accusation and preparation for trial to the police and the prosecution. It is true that both the preliminary hearing and the grand jury indictment need to be improved. It would be very desirable to have a fully professionalized magistracy in all jurisdictions. Moreover, in part because the procedure by information is very commonly used in place of indictment, the preliminary hearing should be made a more effective tool of justice, the magistrate playing an active role in interrogating witnesses and in getting the facts on record early. Abandonment of the hearing and indictment procedures would not be a satisfactory solution to the problem.

The Prosecutor

An important part of the difficulty involved in the prosecution of crime lies in the inconsistent definitions of the prosecutor's role that prevail. Ideally, within the framework of a system of democratic justice, his task should be to secure the binding over and trial of those suspects against whom a prima-facie case can be made out through legal methods of detention and interrogation. It is part of his duty, too, to recommend the discharge of those against whom the legally obtained evidence is insuf-

[25] Orfield suggests that grand jury investigations are valuable in a number of situations: "It is well suited to investigate riots and public disorders of a like nature, corruption in office, certain extensive conspiracies, and cases with religious and racial aspects which ought to be conducted in a manner beyond suspicion of prejudice. Occasionally the proper protection of the complaining party is best achieved by basing the prosecution on a grand jury indictment rather than on his personal complaint. He will thus be better protected from reprisals and from suits for malicious prosecution. The prosecuting attorney is enabled to obtain the statements of witnesses on record. Unwilling witnesses may finally testify to avoid repeated subpoenas and appearances before the grand jury. He is enabled to obtain possession of documents by bringing them before the grand jury under a *subpoena duces tecum*. Finally, in cases of unusual difficulty, he is enabled to obtain the views of a representative group of substantial citizens before filing an accusation." *Op. cit.*, pp. 187–188. (Reprinted by permission. Footnotes in the original are omitted.)

ficient. On the other hand, the prosecutor and the police are under steady pressure from the public and the press to assure that known crimes are cleared by arrest, that evidence or confessions are secured, and that convictions result. When the emphasis is on getting results, little attention is paid to *how* these ends are achieved or to whether it is possible in individual cases to achieve them at all by methods that are legal and just. (However, where secret abuse is so blatant as to invite concern, public and press become intensely—though briefly—incensed at official turpitude.) Added to the public clamor, and partially a result of it, is the prosecutor's own conception of his task. He measures success mainly in terms of "results," defined by arrests and convictions, rather than by the subtler test of whether the evidence available through proper means establishes probable cause. The consequence is the curious but prevalent notion that the prosecutor's success is measured by the closeness of his approximation to a 100 per cent conviction rate. Since ambitious prosecutors in the United States are generally more interested in prestige and political preferment than abstract ideals of justice, they strive to rate in the high 90s. This sort of publicity is quite typical:

COURT CONVICTIONS NEAR 98% IN YEAR[26]
KEOGH OFFICE WON 96% OF CASES[27]
LOST FOUR OF 263 TRIALS[28]
U.S. Attorney in Brooklyn Won 98.6 P of '52 Criminal Cases
97.9% CONVICTIONS IN
U.S. COURT HERE[29]

One might attempt to justify the state attorney's emphasis on convictions on the ground that at his discretion those who are innocent may be discharged after questioning, at preliminary hearing, by failure to indict, by nolle prosequi, or by discharge before completion of trial. This would be a shallow interpretation of the prosecutor's function. To be sure, the prosecutor has these powers and exercises them often. Probably he does so much too frequently, in fact, in trying to retain mainly those cases on which he can secure convictions. *But it is the function of the trial court, not of the prosecutor, to determine whether the accused is guilty.* If police and prosecution have evidence establishing a prima-facie case, it should go to the trial court. Often the defendant may be able to rebut such evidence, sufficiently at any rate to raise a reasonable doubt. It is not the task of the prosecutor under the adversary system to uncover all the evidence on both sides, nor does he do so. When he does encounter sufficient evidence to indicate clearly enough the suspect's innocence, the suspect should be discharged, no matter how strong a case the state may

[26] *New York Times,* Mar. 14, 1946.
[27] *Ibid.,* Jan. 9, 1947.
[28] *Ibid.,* May 11, 1953.
[29] *Ibid.,* Jan. 19, 1958.

have built. However, where arrest and interrogation are conducted legally, it naturally follows that innocent persons will sometimes be arrested for probable cause, bound over by the state after preliminary hearing, but acquitted either because they can show their innocence or because their guilt cannot be proved beyond a reasonable doubt.

The issue here is not one of the prosecutor's fallibility, as is commonly assumed. It is not his duty to win judicial contests or to convict all defendants; it is his duty to present evidence tending to show guilt that is legally available and not to conceal evidence of innocence. The present emphasis on getting convictions is responsible for an excess of official misconduct. The execessively high proportion of cases where suspects are brought to confess or to plead guilt[30] and the proportion of cases where suspects are found guilty with or without a trial indicate the wrongs committed. Also, it is fair to infer that in many cases suspects are discharged because the prosecutor fears he cannot convict and that, even more frequently, suspects are persuaded to plead to some lesser offense in order to avoid prosecution. The man with a prior record of arrest or conviction, the one against whom the circumstantial evidence is fairly strong, the unsophisticated person, or the one who lacks the means to employ good counsel is placed in an extremely vulnerable position when he must choose between a "bargain" plea and the risks of a felony trial at the hands of a skilled prosecutor. If he cannot secure effective counsel during interrogation and at preliminary hearing, his vindication is often impossible, whether he is guilty or not. The prosecutor's discretion and his sense of justice may prove a feeble reliance in the case of friendless suspects.

Other Pretrial Procedures

After indictment or information the next formal procedure is that of arraignment in the trial court. This is a reading of the charge against the suspect with a demand upon him that he plead thereto. It is a right that may generally be waived by the defendant except in capital cases. In misdemeanor charges it is not required that the defendant be present, though he may be and generally is. The right to counsel at arraignment is recognized as important to the accused so that he may be guided in formulating a plea. In a majority of states the prosecution is required to provide the defendant with a list of witnesses that the state intends to call; in some states the prosecution must indicate the substance of the witnesses' proposed testimony. In some states the trial list of jurors is also furnished. As Orfield has pointed out, this information may be important to the accused

[30] It appears that on the average about 85 per cent of the cases convicted are on pleas, most of them for lesser offenses than those originally charged. Powerful inducements are required to secure such general "cooperation" toward the prosecutor's goals. As the result of the steady growth of this sort of administrative adjudication, the judge and trial court have come to play a declining role in the administration of justice.

in preparing his defense and may be important to the state in securing an expeditious settlement of controversies.[31]

The plea of the defendant after arraignment may, in accordance largely with common-law precedent, be one of several sorts. Where there is a defect in the indictment, he may plead in abatement or file a demurrer or a statutory motion to quash the accusation. Under modern liberalized rules of pleading, a motion to quash or dismiss the indictment must be made early, either at the time of arraignment or before trial commences, and may be used to raise such issues as the court's jurisdiction of the case, former acquittal or conviction, pardon, a statute of limitations, misjoinder of defendants or of offenses,[32] or misnomer of the defendant. Today more than one plea may be raised at once rather than in succession, as at common law, and the defendant may plead over and plead not guilty if his motion to quash is overruled, whereas formerly one could not plead inconsistently. In fact pleas such as these are rather rarely raised and they are even more rarely successful. Where such motions are not filed or where they are overruled the defendant then pleads guilty or not guilty. In the Federal jurisdiction and in some of the states, at the discretion of the court, the accused may plead *nolo contendere,* which is not an admission of guilt but an indication of readiness to accept conviction and sentence rather than go to trial. The defendant may plead guilty either to the offense charged or, with the approval of the court and the prosecutor, to some lesser offense. The result is to take the case from the jury and it remains only to sentence the offender. Orfield has suggested a number of justifications for the very common practice of taking pleas to lesser crimes:[33]

The common criticism has ascribed the waivers [of felony] to political and corrupt influences. On the other hand, it has been pointed out (1) that crimes have greatly increased in numbers, (2) that the courts are unable to care for the increased volume of cases, (3) that there is a heavy burden upon the public by way of jury and witness duties, and (4) that persons are reluctant to admit criminal liability since it carries the stigma of moral delinquency. There are other even more deep-seated causes. Officials may regard the law as too severe in any case. More frequently, mitigating circumstances provided by the facts or the reputation of the defendant lead officials to conclude that it is preferable

[31] Orfield, *op. cit.,* p. 279.

[32] A special problem of trial justice frequently involves a misjoinder of offenses or of defendants where they are brought before the court under a common indictment or information and may be tried together. The interest in efficiency and speed point toward joint trials but the effect may be prejudicial to defendants where, for example, evidence against one is inadmissible against another and, if allowed, may affect him adversely, where the pleas or defenses of the defendants differ, or where a law applies to some but not to others. The trend in the United States has been to adopt the common-law rule leaving severance of parties and defendants to the discretion of the court and to permit the court to consolidate indictment and trial in proper cases. The A.L.I. Code provides for severance but not for consolidation.

[33] Orfield, *op. cit.,* pp. 299–300. (Reprinted by permission.)

to inflict a lesser penalty than that fixed by the statute for the crime actually committed. In the third place, the case for the state may be weak for reasons beyond the control of the prosecuting attorney, such as want of thorough investigation by the police and lack of necessary witnesses. Finally, the ambition to establish a record for numerous convictions for use in future election campaigns plays a significant part. Discretion there must be, and possibly it can be exercised more deliberately by the prosecuting attorney than by the jury which was formerly the chief repository of such powers.

It is clear, at any rate, that one can find abundant rationalizations in support of the technique by which the state avoids trying most of those who are accused of crime. It is possible, though unlikely, that to require that the prosecutor file a statement of his reason for accepting each plea would better regulate the employment of his discretion. In a large number of jurisdictions the plea of guilty or *nolo contendere* may be withdrawn with the approval of the court and a not guilty plea may be submitted, at least before sentence, and in some jurisdictions even after sentence.

Where criminal cases go to trial they do so on the basis of a plea of not guilty. Under such a plea generally the defendant may raise such issues as self-defense, alibi, insanity or intoxication, or a statute of limitations. Generally he is not required to give notice in advance of the specific affirmative defenses that he intends to raise at trial, so that the prosecutor may be ignorant of the proposed line of defense. It has been proposed by the Wickersham Commission and other bodies that, since the defendant may generally have access to at least a part of the state's case through the preliminary hearing and inspection of the grand jury minutes, he should be required to give notice of affirmative defenses. The defendant must plead former jeopardy specially in most states; in fourteen he must give notice before trial if he intends to show an alibi; in eight a proposed defense of insanity must be raised by special plea.

Among the major reforms proposed in criminal procedure recommendations have been made for broadening pretrial procedures to simplify and sharpen the issues to be tried, as is done in civil procedure. Advocates of such change stress that trial should not be a game to test the skills of advocates but should be a more objective search for the truth. Orfield summarizes the position:[34]

The prosecution must be accorded the same advantage within constitutional limits as is the defendant, with respect to antecedent notice. The right of the defendant involves such steps as securing a copy of the indictment or information, together with the names of the witnesses upon whose testimony it was found, the jury panel, bills of particulars, a copy of the grand jury minutes when necessary, a list of witnesses to be called against him, and inspection and copy of the documents and objects in the prosecution's hands on a showing that such inspection seems reasonably necessary for the preparation of the

[34] *Ibid.*, p. 321. (Reprinted by permission.)

defense. The complementary right of the government involves notice of the names of the witnesses upon whom the defendant will rely, and through them advance notice of his defenses; and inspection of the evidence which he will introduce, so far as the Constitution permits. For both sides there should also be further provision for the taking of depositions, and their use upon trial, and more extensive use of the pre-trial conference.

A minority of jurisdictions in the United States allow prosecutors to take depositions of witnesses to assure that evidence will be available at trial and the new Federal Rules allow such depositions under a number of circumstances. The Federal Rules also allow the defendant a limited right to discover and inspect documents and materials in the hands of the prosecution at the discretion of the court. The previous rule permitted inspection, but it was a right usually denied. The statutes of only one state, Iowa, specifically allow the courts to compel the production of documents for the defendant's inspection; the privilege has been both granted and denied in the cases elsewhere. The Federal Rules provide for the use of subpoena to compel witnesses to attend criminal trials for the defense as well as for the government, and some state constitutions, as well as the Federal, provide for compulsory process. Most state codes and many treatises on criminal jurisprudence are silent on the subject. By and large there is little indication of any real trend toward the development of pretrial procedures to make the trial of criminal issues more simple and efficient; this development has occurred in civil cases, however.

TRIAL BY JURY

Where the defendant has been bound over at preliminary hearing and either an indictment or information has held him to trial, he may and in a majority of cases he does plead guilty.[35] In such instances, it remains only for him to be sentenced. If he pleads not guilty, however, a formal trial of the issue concerning the defendant's guilt follows. The procedure of the trial itself has become rather uniformly established on the model of that developed in England during the eighteenth and nineteenth centuries. The major elements of trial are considered briefly below.

The Petit Jury

Except in the case of minor offenses triable summarily by a magistrate and, in some states, other crimes that had not been defined prior to the adoption of the constitution, defendants are guaranteed the right of trial by jury. Prospective jurors, *veniremen,* are drawn from a list established from time to time in accordance with statutory requirements, usually prescribing that to qualify men must be citizens over 21 years of age, resident

---

[35] It is the general rule, however, that a defendant may not plead guilty to a murder indictment.

in the county, free from serious infirmities, and without criminal record. Either state or defense may object to the entire panel or array of veniremen on the ground that they have been drawn improperly in violation of the judiciary or procedural law.[36] Individual jurors may also be challenged in *voir dire* examination either for cause, on the ground that the summoned juror is disqualified generally or for bias, or peremptorily, without assignment of specific cause. Where challenge is for cause the judge must rule on its validity but any veniremen challenged peremptorily must be dismissed. The number of peremptory challenges allowed varies in different jurisdictions, twenty commonly being allowed where a capital crime is charged, fewer for other felonies. Ordinarily disqualifications are waived if they are not challenged. In a few jurisdictions examination of the panel is conducted entirely by the court instead of by the counsel, thereby obviating considerable delay and expense. Under the Federal Rules of Criminal Procedure [Rule 24(*a*)] the court may permit counsel for the defendant and the government attorney to conduct the examination or, in the alternative, do so itself.[37]

The right to jury trial may be waived by the defendant in more than half the states and in the Federal courts, though the right to waive is commonly restricted either on the basis of the seriousness of the crime involved or by requiring the consent of the court and the prosecutor.[38] In some cases, trials to the court have become more common than jury trials, partly because defendants expect both greater objectivity and more speedy trial from the bench than from lay jurors. The defendant may also waive the right to trial before the twelve jurors ordinarily required in a criminal jury trial through a stipulation either before or during trial. As trials have required an increasing length of time, there is danger that a juror will be incapacitated; it has become more common practice to impanel one or more alternate jurors to hear testimony and, in the case of the loss of a juror, to participate in the verdict. The A.L.I. Code provides for the use

[36] The Fourteenth Amendment requires that the jury be drawn impartially from a cross section of the community, avoiding the systematic and intentional exclusion of any qualified group of individuals. In the case of *Fay v. New York,* 332 U.S. 261, 67 S. Ct. 1613 (1947), however, a majority of the court upheld the use of the "blue ribbon" jury in New York City. Figures drawn by the state judicial council have revealed that convictions were returned by special juries in 83 per cent of homicide cases as against 43 per cent by ordinary juries. The blue ribbon jury is made up largely of professional, proprietary, and clerical people and has few of the service workers and laborers who may be found on most juries. Abolition of such juries has been proposed many times. See *New York Times,* Jan. 24, 1946; Feb. 25, 1952; and Feb. 15, 1956.

[37] The Institute Code, Section 275, provides for examination of the jurors by the court.

[38] Until 1930 it was the prevailing rule that the defendant could not waive jury trial. Appellate decisions that year in the Federal and Illinois courts led to adoption of a rule permitting waiver in over half the states.

of one or two alternate jurors and the Federal Rules allow as many as four.

A number of criticisms have been made of the way jury systems operate. One difficulty is the excessive length of time required for the impanelling of a jury when the *voir dire* is conducted by the parties, sometimes running into many days. Another is the quality of the jurors who are selected. Through exemptions and the excusing of individuals, men of superior training and intelligence ordinarily escape service. It is particularly difficult to find unbiased jurors both because of the method of selection and because of the trial by press that occurs in this country in important cases. In most jurisdictions judges are prohibited from commenting on the evidence; this increases the difficulty of their task and the probability of error. It is an unfortunate limitation on the judge's powers. In those jurisdictions where the jury is made arbiter of the law as well as of the facts and in other jurisdictions where the jury is charged with determining sentence, the jury is particularly unsuited to perform its tasks effectively. Peculiar difficulties of a psychological character confront the jury in its effort to arrive at truth. These difficulties, which call for the best possible skill in appraising and weighing evidence,[39] will be noted in the next chapter.

In spite of the criticisms that are commonly directed at the jury, experienced jurists very generally favor its retention. As opposed to judicial determination of facts, Dean Wigmore has noted the jury's special merits in reducing popular distrust of official justice, in producing a fair flexibility in legal rules, in educating the citizenry in the administration of justice, and in providing a balance of temperaments and views in arriving at a verdict. The major problems entailed in using the jury, instead of judicial determination of fact, could be resolved if the court would play the major

[39] The late Judge Jerome Frank, a vigorous critic of the jury system, has alleged that "not one verdict in 100 would stand if the court knew what went on with the jury." *New York Times,* July 19, 1950. In 1954 a survey was made of jurors who had served in federal district courts in six western states. Of 620 jurors who replied to a questionnaire, 87 jurors indicated that pressure to arrive at a quick decision prevented them from giving as much thought as they wanted to the merits of a case, 59 said they would have rendered an opposite verdict a week later, 258 acknowledged that they were confused by the judge's instruction, and 112 admitted reading about cases before or during a trial. *Rocky Mountain News,* Aug. 18, 1954. The jury system has also been criticized because of the time and money that it costs. It was reported in 1952 that New York City paid over a million dollars in juror fees and expenses in a single year. Records of the Consolidated Edison Company revealed that jury service during that year had cost the company 11,775 man-days, valued at over $200,000, not including executive personnel.

An experimental jury investigation has been conducted as part of the Law and Behavioral Science Project of the Law School at the University of Chicago. It has revealed, *inter alia,* the influence of social status and sex roles in jury deliberations. See Fred L. Strodtbeck et al., "Social Status in Jury Deliberations," *Am. Soc. Rev.,* vol. 22, pp. 713–720, December, 1957, and "Sex Role Differentiation in Jury Deliberations," *Sociometry,* vol. 19, pp. 3–12, March, 1956.

role in selecting jurors and if the court could assist the jury by commenting on the evidence.[40]

Opening of the Case and the Submission of Evidence

The usual practice is for the prosecutor to open the case to the jury with a statement of what he proposes to prove and then to offer evidence supporting the indictment. The defense counsel may cross-examine the state's witnesses. After the state has concluded, the defense may at its option outline what will be presented in defense. Defense counsel then submits the evidence in support of the defendant's case, his witnesses also being subject to cross-examination. Since a common ground of reversal on appeal is error in court rulings on the admissibility of evidence, the attorneys are diligent in protesting the evidence submitted and in taking exceptions. The court as well as the parties may interrogate witnesses or may call them on its own and interrogate them; in practice, however, the court rarely does so, largely because of the danger on an appeal of reversal for possible prejudice.

The order of trial related above has been modified under the code in New York, which provides for the opening of the defense after the prosecutor's original address to the jury but before any evidence has been submitted. Under either procedure the defendant may but need not testify in his own behalf. Failure to testify creates no presumption of guilt in legal theory. If the defendant does testify, he is subject like any other witness to cross-examination and the state may bring out a prior criminal record or other circumstances to refute his credibility. This hazard raises a major tactical problem for defense counsel when his client has previously been in difficulty for, while in theory the defendant may not be convicted on the basis of his former record, in fact jurors may too easily infer present guilt from past misconduct.

When the evidence in chief is in, each of the parties is offered opportunity to rebut the testimony submitted by the other. The court may allow either side, upon a showing of good cause, to reopen its case at any time before the verdict to offer additional evidence on the original case. It is customary for the defense to petition the court for acquittal on the ground that the state has failed to make out a prima-facie case. The court may find the defendant is innocent as a matter of law (on the theory that the jury could not reasonably find to the contrary) and may direct a verdict of acquittal, though generally decision is reserved on the matter.

Argument to the Jury

Unless the case is submitted to the jury by either or both sides without argument, defense counsel makes the first summation[41] and the state, since

---

[40] See Orfield, *op. cit.,* pp. 410–412.

[41] Minnesota is the only exception to this rule on the order of argument. See George Dession, *Criminal Law, Administration and Public Order,* p. 987.

it has the burden of proof, has the privilege of closing. There is considerable emphasis upon fine forensic oratory here and a wide latitude of argumentation is tolerated, though mistrials and reversals have not been uncommon as a consequence of excesses. Fair argument does not allow the attorneys to make statements of fact unsupported in the trial evidence, to appeal to prejudice, to use abusive or inflammatory language, or to conduct prolonged and confusing discussion of the law. Reasonable time must be allowed for argument, relative to the circumstances and complexity of the case. The judge has wide discretion in determining whether any statement of counsel constitutes misconduct. In many cases considerable impropriety has been allowed, especially if it has apparently been unintentional, if there has been a retraction, or if both sides have engaged in improper argument. As a general rule prosecution is not allowed to comment on a failure of the defendant to testify, but if the defendant did take the stand, the prosecutor may attack his credibility on the basis of his prior history.[42]

Charge to the Jury

After argument by counsel it is the duty of the judge to instruct the jury in all matters of substantive law that are necessary to the determination of the relevant facts of the case. In its conclusions concerning the facts, the jury is the sole arbiter of the weight and sufficiency of evidence, including the credibility of witnesses. An appellate court cannot later review the jury's findings of fact, though it may find that the jury clearly failed to follow the instructions of the trial judge, thus making it a matter of law rather than of fact alone. This might occur, for example, where a fact had been admitted at trial and has been included in the judge's charge. In most states the judge must instruct the jury that the defendant is presumed to be innocent, that his presumption can be overcome only by proof

---

[42] In the case of *State v. Baker,* 53 A.2d 53 (1947), Justice Jeffords of the Supreme Court of Vermont in a minority opinion pointed to the fallacy in the view that comment on the evidence is not unfairly prejudicial to the defendant: "The majority here take the position that if one is innocent he has nothing to fear in taking the stand. In *State v. Cleaves* from Maine, quoted from extensively in the majority opinion, it is said that the embarrassment of the prisoner, if embarrassed, is the result of his own previous misconduct, not of the law. I do not agree with either the position taken by the majority or the statement in the Cleaves case. In this latter case it is assumed that every respondent who is embarrassed by the predicament in which he is placed by the right of the jury to draw inferences against him if he fails to take the stand is a guilty person. This is not at all necessarily so. An innocent person may well be so embarrassed. He may be innocent of the crime charged but have a criminal record which will be paraded before the jury if he takes the stand. He may be innocent but easily confused by cross-examination and made thereby to appear guilty. His looks or personality may indicate guilt though he be innocent. Other examples might be given to illustrate that the innocent as well as the guilty are affected adversely by the statute in question to the derogation of their constitutional rights."

of his guilt beyond reasonable doubt,[43] and that they must not consider the punishment in determining guilt. In a minority of states and the Federal jurisdiction, as at common law, the judge is permitted to comment to the jury on the evidence and the credibility of witnesses as well as to inform them of the provisions of law, but a diminishing majority of states hold this improper by constitution, statute, or case decision. Only six states allow the court to comment on a defendant's failure to testify, the majority position reflecting the view that such comment constitutes an unfair coercion upon him.

At the close of the evidence, ordinarily, the parties may file written requests for instructions to be submitted to the jury; the adverse parties are provided with copies. The judge must inform counsel of his proposed actions on such requests prior to their arguments to the jury. Counsel objections to matters included or excluded from the judge's charge must be made before the jury retires to consider its verdict and these objections are argued out of the hearing of the jury. Since most appellate reversals are based upon erroneous or misleading charges by the court, counsel will exercise considerable effort to submit a large number of instructions favorable to its case and of such a nature that a refusal so to charge may be added as a grounds for appeal. To avoid reversals, judges tend to formalize their instructions on the basis of precedents that the higher courts have approved. In about one-half of the states the instructions to the jury must be in writing and in these states reversals for error are especially common. The appellate court may find, however, that the jury was not misled by nonprejudicial errors.

In the unusual case, where the evidence is so clear that the jury could not reasonably find the defendant guilty, the court may direct a verdict of acquittal, thereby holding the defendant innocent as a matter of law. A guilty verdict, however, may not be directed.

Jury Deliberation and Verdict

Following the judge's charge the jury ordinarily retires to deliberate, though it may arrive at a finding in open court. It is the jury's task to apply the law as instructed by the court to the facts as they may determine them to be. If necessary the jury may return to court to ask for further instruction and, if the parties consent, the judge may instruct them, but only orally and in open court. The jury must arrive either at a unanimous[44]

[43] Chief Justice Shaw of Massachusetts has given a generally approved definition of reasonable doubt in *Commonwealth v. Webster,* 5 Cush. 295 (1850): "such a doubt as would cause a prudent and reasonable man to act or to pause or to hesitate to act in the determination of any of the affairs of life of the highest importance to himself."

[44] The A.L.I. Code provides for the requirement of a unanimous verdict only in capital cases, for a five-sixths majority in other felonies, and for two-thirds in mis-

verdict of conviction or acquittal or at a conclusion that they cannot agree (a "hung jury"). In the latter case the defendant may be tried again. Because much time and cost are ordinarily involved, it is preferable that a decision be reached and the court may indicate to the jury the desirability of arriving at agreement. The court may not coerce the jury, however, and must exercise considerable caution in urging agreement. Where the crime charged consists of different degrees, the jury may find the defendant not guilty under the indictment but guilty of a lesser degree of the crime, of an included crime, or in some states, of an attempt.[45] In any case where the court believes that a conviction (but not an acquittal) was based upon the jurors' misunderstanding of the law the court may give further instruction and direct them to reconsider. When a verdict has been reached, it must be given in open court and, if a felony is involved, in the presence of the defendant. Upon rendering the verdict at the request of any party or upon the court's own motion, the jury may be polled and if there is not unanimous concurrence the jurors may be directed to reconsider or they may be discharged and the defendant tried again. If, however, the defendant is found to be not guilty, he cannot thereafter be tried for the same offense. If he is found guilty, the court may set aside the verdict where it is apparently defective, ambiguous, or unresponsive to the indictment and, in some jurisdictions, if it is impeached by jurors' affidavits showing that it was reached improperly. In such cases the defendant may be tried again. In several states and in the Federal courts the judge may go further to overrule a jury conviction and find the defendant innocent *non obstante veredicto.* Such a judgment is a full acquittal and the defendant may not be retried.

Judgment and Sentence

Following the verdict of the jury and any motions that may be made after verdict, the court pronounces judgment and sentence. It is the majority view that the judgment of the court must be in accordance with the jury's verdict, so that the judge lacks power to reduce the verdict to a lesser degree, though he might have directed a verdict or overruled a conviction. In urban courts, particularly, there is generally a postponement after judgment for probation investigation to supplement the court's information about the offender and to guide his sentencing. The complex issues involved in sentencing are discussed in ensuing chapters.

---

demeanors. The rule requiring unanimity has been criticized very frequently on the ground that the single, stubborn holdout juror exercises too much power and causes a costly mistrial.

[45] In several jurisdictions provision is made for special verdicts to be rendered by the jury, that is, a finding of specific facts from which the court then must derive the conclusion of law. Also in some states the jury is allowed to recommend leniency in sentencing or, in capital cases, that life imprisonment be employed instead.

ACTIONS FOLLOWING TRIAL

Motions after Verdict

Where a defendant has been found guilty, defendant's counsel may within a period of time ordinarily limited by statute move in arrest of judgment on the basis of defects appearing in the record or may move for a new trial on the basis of some unfairness to the defendant that does not appear on the face of the record.[46] The motion in arrest is commonly based upon the court's lack of jurisdiction, the insufficiency of the indictment or information, a verdict that is uncertain in meaning, or other substantial defects. The motion for a new trial is commonly used where unfair or unlawful methods were employed in securing the conviction or where there is newly discovered evidence that was not obtainable at the time of trial. The use of such motions is less time consuming and costly than appeal procedure. Some states, however, hold that if an appeal is taken the lower court is divested of power to vacate judgment.

In general there can be no new trial of an acquitted defendant. It has been held no deprivation of his privilege against double jeopardy, however, to bring him to trial again if it can be shown that the court lacked jurisdiction, that the indictment was seriously defective or void, or that the verdict resulted from the defendant's misconduct, fraud, or collusion.

When a court grants a new trial, the latter is conducted as if there had been no prior action and the former verdict may not be used or referred to. There is conflict as to whether the defendant may be convicted on counts of which he was previously acquitted or of a higher degree of crime, however. Surveys have revealed that, in practice, motions for new trial are very commonly allowed by the trial courts and they result in a substantial proportion of cases in the setting aside of convictions. This appears to reflect an effort to undo obvious errors at the original trial or in the jury's verdict. In at least fourteen states the defendant may appeal from an order denying new trial and in eleven states the prosecution may appeal from an order granting such retrial.[47]

The writ of error coram nobis is another device to correct injustice through further action by the trial court. The writ has been used in a variety of cases where errors of fact affecting the proceedings, unknown to the defendant at the time of trial and not in issue at the trial, are alleged. Such errors of fact include the death of a party, infancy of the defendant where no guardian ad litem had been appointed, insanity at the time of trial, and the inducement of a plea or confession by fear, violence, or ignorance.[48] It has been recommended that coram nobis be extended in

---

[46] See Puttkammer, *op. cit.,* pp. 209–213.

[47] See Orfield, *op. cit.,* pp. 510–513.

[48] Coram nobis is not available where the defendant has been found not guilty,

scope since, where the time allowable to move for a new trial or appeal has elapsed, the innocent defendant may have no other remedy. The appellate courts have held, however, that it should not be used as a substitute for ordinary appeal procedures. In some jurisdictions other forms of postconviction hearings have been established to provide a remedy where the defendant maintains he has been deprived of due process and where no other motion for relief is available.

Postconviction Remedies

Appeal may be taken by the defense from a conviction or from an order denying a motion to vacate a judgment of conviction within a time limited by statute.[49] Appeals are generally based upon allegedly erroneous rulings of the court on the admissibility of particular evidence offered at the trial or on the judge's instructions to the jury. Appeals may be based, however, as limited by statutory provisions, upon the jurisdiction of the court over the case, the venue,[50] or other errors. Error substantially prejudicial to the defendant must be shown. The higher court may reverse the conviction and order release of the defendant, reverse and remand for a new trial, affirm but with modifications, or simply affirm.

States have generally provided that the trial court may stay the imposition of sentence pending an appeal where it believes that there is good ground for such an appeal. Only if a stay is granted does the defendant have a right to be present at the appellate proceedings. In some jurisdictions appeals are allowed from the sentence of the court.

In a number of jurisdictions statutes have come to provide a limited and widely varying right of appeal to the state.[51] The A.L.I. Code of Criminal Procedure would provide very broadly for such a right. The Code of Criminal Procedure in New York allows state appeals where the trial court has granted a motion to arrest or vacate judgment or to grant a new trial, where it has ordered the dismissal of an indictment, and in

---

though he was committed as insane and sought release. *State v. Fisher,* 92 N.E. 2d 543 (Ind. 1950). The writ is commonly used by prisoners when the time for taking an appeal has lapsed or where an appeal has been decided against the defendant. Such efforts are usually unsuccessful. It has been held, however, in *United States v. Morgan,* 74 Sup. Ct. 247 (1954), that a state prisoner may attack a prior Federal conviction on which he has already served sentence by coram nobis, thus securing reduction of state sentence.

[49] There is no Federal constitutional right of appeal for state prisoners but the Federal courts will protect against state denial of due process where redress cannot be had in the state courts.

[50] Venue refers to the place, ordinarily the county, where the offense is alleged to have occurred and the act must be proved to have occurred in that jurisdiction. Place of trial may be changed, within the discretion of the court, to avoid injustice from mob influence, prejudice, etc.

[51] The arguments for giving the prosecutor a right to appeal are set down in Justin Miller, "Appeals by the State in Criminal Cases," *Yale L. J.,* vol. 36, pp. 486ff., 1927.

other cases where a verdict of not guilty has not been rendered. In Connecticut the prosecutor's right of appeal is almost coextensive with that of the defense.

A convicted state prisoner whose trial has not met the requirements of due process under the Fourteenth Amendment is entitled to redress in Federal as well as state courts. On the principle of comity, however, the state appellate courts are given the first opportunity to determine the constitutional issue and the prisoner must first appeal to the highest state court in order to secure review by the United States Supreme Court. Interpretation of the Fourteenth Amendment has greatly extended the requirements of due process in state criminal cases over the past thirty years. Leading cases where Federal remedy has been provided have included the denial of effective counsel in a capital case (the Scottsboro cases), exclusion of Negroes from grand and petit juries, and state use of coerced confessions and perjured testimony.[52] Aside from due process questions, Federal judicial power to take appeals from the state courts is rooted both in the right to determine the validity of state enactments that are alleged to be violative of the Federal Constitution or of state powers under the Constitution and in the right to test the validity of such state enactments under the constitution of the state itself. Appellate remedy must first be sought in courts of the state, but appeal may then be taken to the Federal Supreme Court where a constitutional issue is involved.

Article I of the Federal Constitution and similar provisions in most state constitutions establish the privilege of habeas corpus. The most famous writ in the law, habeas corpus is a means of removing illegal restraints upon personal liberty. The writ requires that the authority detaining a person bring him before the court that issued it to test the legality of the custody. Inquiry may then be made whether the court or office had jurisdiction to issue the process under which he is detained and whether he is restrained under due process of law. A person in state custody, if he first exhausts his state remedies, including habeas corpus, coram nobis, or writ of error, and if he elicits a denial of certiorari from the United States Supreme Court, may seek relief from a United States district court as a matter of due process. Since the case of *Johnson v. Zerbst,* 304 U.S. 458, 58 Sup. Ct. 1019 (1938), in which the United States Supreme Court held that the petitioner who had been convicted without aid of counsel was entitled to a determination of whether he had competently waived the right, "an avalanche of applications" have come from Federal prisoners based upon denial of the right to counsel. Collateral attack by way of habeas corpus upon state convictions has been sanctioned by the United States Supreme Court in a large variety of cases: con-

---

[52] See Earl Pollock, "Post-trial Remedies," *J. Crim. L.,* vol. 42, pp. 636–650, 1952; Boskey and Pickering, "Federal Restrictions on State Criminal Procedure," *U. Chi. L. Rev.,* vol. 13, pp. 266ff., 1946; and generally Walter F. Dodd, *Cases and Materials on Constitutional Law,* 1950, pp. 7–12.

viction under an alleged unconstitutional statute, lack of an indictment on an infamous crime, mob domination of trial, double jeopardy, compulsory self-incrimination, denial of counsel, lack of territorial jurisdiction, a prosecutor's knowing use of perjured testimony, inducing a plea of guilty by misrepresentation or coercion, suppression of testimony favorable to the defendant, and deprivation of trial by jury. The Supreme Court has held, however, that habeas corpus may not be used as a substitute for appeal. This has raised difficult problems for prisoners in some jurisdictions where they have been unable to assert an effective right of appeal under state procedures and have been denied habeas corpus.[53]

ORGANIZATION OF THE COURTS

It may be clear from what has already been said that a variety of courts are required to deal with criminal as well as with civil matters. A basic structure including courts for preliminary hearing, trial, and appeal is patently required. Unfortunately, however, the organization of courts has commonly developed without plan or reason into an awkward and inefficient complex of tribunals that are difficult and uneconomical to administer. Nowhere, perhaps, is this better illustrated than in New York where there is an outmoded system of at least eighteen kinds of courts, each having its own fixed jurisdiction and its own complement of judges, each largely autonomous in administration. In 1955 a Subcommittee on Modernization and Simplification of the Court Structure to the Temporary Commission on the Courts of New York State (the Tweed Commission) submitted a report recommending a marked simplification of the system that would reduce the variety of courts to five.[54] The report engendered considerable controversy among judges and justices of the peace and in the legislature and various modifications and alternatives were proposed.

Inferior Courts

A system of municipal "inferior courts" or courts of inferior jurisdiction is required universally to perform three basic functions in administering justice.[55] In some cities inferior courts are known as police or magistrates'

[53] See Pollock, *loc. cit.;* Stuart, "Corrective Processes for Unlawful Imprisonment," *Brooklyn L. Rev.,* vol. 15, p. 271, 1949; and Gottlieb, "Limitations of Collateral and Direct Attacks upon Prior Convictions," *Syracuse L. Rev.,* vol. 1, p. 121, 1949. As a consequence of the recognition of the inadequacy of state remedies in some jurisdictions it has been held that the prisoner may be excused from the requirement of exhaustion of such remedies before seeking Federal relief either by appeal or habeas corpus. See *Ex Parte Hawk,* 321 U.S. 114 (1944), and *Jennings v. Illinois,* 72 S. Ct. 123 (1951).

[54] The proposals of the subcommittee were set out in the *New York Times* for June 21, 1955. See also Arthur T. Vanderbilt, *Improving the Administration of Justice,* 1957, especially, pp. 18–20, on the need to simplify court organization.

[55] See Raymond Moley, *Tribunes of the People,* 1932, and *Our Criminal Courts,* 1930.

courts and in rural areas they are generally known as justice of the peace courts. They are presided over by magistrates, justices of the peace, or police justices, very often laymen; in recognition of the importance of the functions they perform and the ultimate economy of having these tasks done well, the trend has been to employ legally trained judges for this work in larger cities. In some places judges of the courts of ordinary criminal trial jurisdicton sit as magistrates and the higher criminal court judges possess the power to do so generally. In England the police courts have had jurisdiction over certain civil matters but in the United States their powers in the cities are ordinarily limited to the criminal functions noted below. However, justices of the peace commonly enjoy minor jurisdiction in civil cases as defined by statute.

Inferior courts generally have power to try certain misdemeanor cases as defined by state law or municipal ordinance. In some jurisdictions, such as New York, where certain minor violations are defined by law as "offenses less than crime" rather than as misdemeanors, these violations constitute the chief area of trial jurisdiction, though inferior courts may have some jurisdiction also over less serious misdemeanor cases. "Summary proceedings" are employed in magistrates' or police courts, somewhat informally and without jury, generally without a prosecutor, and in a majority of cases without defense attorneys. Characteristically, therefore, the magistrate must perform the functions of interrogator and advisor of state and defense witnesses, of judge in applying the rules of evidence, and of jury in weighing the evidence and arriving at a verdict. Since the magistrate generally has power to sentence to jail or penitentiary terms up to a year and sometimes to three years and to assess fines of considerable size, where several violations may be involved, his trial function is one of extreme importance. It is through the inferior court that the ordinary citizen derives his conception of justice as it applies to the run-of-the-mill offender. Unfortunately, the results often fall short of ideal because of the character of the magistrates, the volume of business they must conduct, and the disorder in their courts. Appeals may be taken from convictions in the inferior court to an appellate court. In New York such appeals are taken to an appellate part of the county courts, except that in New York City such appeals go to the appellate part of the Court of Special Sessions.

The second major function of the magistrates' courts is that of hearing preliminarily all cases of persons accused of crime, either felony or misdemeanor, except where such preliminary hearing has been waived by the defendant. As we have noted, this is a "sieving" procedure to determine whether the state has a prima-facie case that justifies taking it to trial. Where the court finds that there is a prima-facie case, it holds the defendant to answer for trial in a higher court or for grand jury action.

The magistrate's court is also empowered to set bail within limitations provided by statute when it holds the defendant to answer. Typically this power is restricted. Thus, in New York, only justices of the higher trial courts may admit to bail where the defendant is charged with a crime punishable by death, one where a probably fatal injury has been inflicted, or where, after having previously been convicted of a felony or twice convicted of certain misdemeanors, he is charged with possessing a weapon, burglars' tools, buying or receiving stolen property, unlawful entry, prison escape, pocket picking, or possession or distribution of narcotics.

Trial Courts

Courts of trial for felonies and for misdemeanors receive cases that have been indicted by the grand jury after being held over by the inferior court or cases against whom a prosecutor's information has been lodged. Ordinarily these are county courts and in some jurisdictions they are so titled; elsewhere they may be known as district courts or superior courts and by other titles. Sometimes they are state courts. Very commonly they have some civil as well as criminal jurisdiction. In New York State the county courts generally have jurisdiction over both felony and misdemeanor cases. In New York City, however, a Court of Special Sessions, with three judges sitting en banc without a jury, has jurisdiction over misdemeanor cases. In that state the Supreme Court also has power to try felonies and misdemeanors as well as civil cases. In practice the court does not generally exercise jurisdiction in misdemeanor cases; in felony cases it exercises jurisdiction only where the criminal calendar of the county courts warrants it.

As has been noted in the discussion of criminal trial, these courts provide trial by jury except where the jury is waived. In the latter case the judge determines the issues of fact as well as the issues of law, whereas under jury trial the jury determines the facts after instructions by the court concerning the applicable law.

Appellate Courts

Appellate courts review cases removed by appeal or error from lower courts. Characteristically in the state as in the Federal jurisdiction there are two levels of appeal.[56] Thus in New York appeal may be taken from the criminal trial courts to one of four appellate divisions of the Supreme Court and final appeal is to the Court of Appeals. Appellate courts hear both civil and criminal appeals. In many jurisdictions the highest appellate court is known as the supreme court. The nature of appeal has been previously discussed.

[56] For a criticism of multiple appeals, see Sunderland, "Intermediate Appellate Courts," *Am. L. School Rev.*, vol. 6, p. 693, 1929, quoted in Maynard E. Pirsig, *Cases and Materials on Judicial Administration,* 1946, pp. 536–543.

Chapter 13

JUSTICE AND EFFICIENCY

In this chapter the author proposes to look at the system of justice in terms of the results it achieves. Attention will be given first to such statistical evidence as is available concerning what has sometimes been called the "mortality rate" in criminal justice. We shall then observe, on the one side, the forms of special protection that have been erected by constitution and statute to protect the citizen from injustices and, on the other, the danger of convicting the innocent in spite of the measures that are employed.

THE "MORTALITY RATE" IN CRIMINAL JUSTICE

Many criminologists have recurrently criticized the allegedly excessive rates of discharge of accused persons at the several stages of criminal procedure. Figures on the release of suspects have often been interpreted to indicate failures of criminal justice, resulting from the inefficiency or corruption of the various agencies involved. The matter cannot be disposed of in this fashion, however. Factors that influence discharge practices are complicated and so are the policy issues involved. Unfortunately there is no way of establishing any firm standard by which the practices of the several agencies or the results they attain can be evaluated. Sometimes the public is inclined to believe that when crimes occur arrests should be made, that those arrested should be held to trial and convicted on the charges that were laid against them, and that they should be sentenced for those crimes. It comes as something of a shock to many when they discover that for the crimes known to the police relatively few are ultimately convicted, even fewer for the crimes that were originally alleged against them, and that it is the rare felon who goes to prison for his crime.

Consideration has been given to procedures employed by police and prosecutory agencies in prior chapters and these will not be reviewed in detail here. The data that are derived from the employment of these procedures and the implications of such data will be discussed in this section. It should be observed that there are important gaps and potentially misleading differences between the figures furnished by the police and those supplied by prosecution. Confusion results in part from a lack of adequate statistical information about the consequences that flow from the several procedures intervening between arrest and trial. Among suspects, some are released after interrogation, a considerable number are discharged after preliminary hearing, others are freed because grand juries fail to indict, a few profit from prosecutors' decisions not to bring them to trial, many take pleas to lesser charges, and only a relatively few go to prison. The limited data available on these stages of procedure display certain apparent discrepancies that reflect the effort of reporting agencies to provide a favorable view of their efficiency. The police sometimes under report the numbers of known crimes and of suspects released without a hearing in order that their published rates of clearance by arrest may be high. The prosecutor's office customarily reports those cases that plead guilty, constituting approximately 85 per cent of persons convicted, along with those that are held *after* the magistrate, grand jury, and prosecution have decided that they should go on trial. In calculating conviction rates, they may also eliminate those cases that prosecutors have decided during trial and before submission to the jury should be discharged. The result is an ostensibly very high "success rate" in prosecution. On the other hand, when data on crimes known to the police are compared with the outcome of trial and sentence, the "mortality rate" may appear excessive.

The procedures that the author has referred to are not uniformly established by law or practice. No criteria exist for what may constitute reasonable drop-out rates at the several stages and none can easily be determined because of the close interdependence between them. The machinery is human, and the professional capacity and personal inclination of the officials involved vary widely. It is apparent that if authorities sought by all means to discover and convict the guilty a great many innocent as well as guilty persons would suffer. A police state with illegal arrests and detention, unlawful searches and seizures, coerced confessions, entrapment, widespread use of police informants and spies, and improper methods of prosecution could result. The theoretical ideals of our system of criminal justice look to a full protection of the innocent from harassment and of the guilty as well as the innocent from unfair measures of coercion designed to elicit the proof of guilt. However, public, official, and journalistic pressures often lead to the employment of abusive methods. The result is a compromise in which the exercise of administrative discretion varies considerably. During some periods and in some communities, official lawlessness and persecution become widely rampant.

Statistics on Procedural Outcome

Table 11 is designed to show what may be called the "mortality rate in criminal justice" for the major felonies that were reported by the FBI in its 1958 bulletin. The table is based upon the number of crimes known

Table 11. Offenses Known to the Police, Cleared by Arrest, Persons Charged (Held for Prosecution), Found Guilty, and Sentenced, 1958, Number per 100 Known Offenses*

Offenses	Murder, nonnegligent manslaughter	Manslaughter by negligence	Forcible rape	Robbery	Aggravated assault	Burglary—breaking or entering	Larceny—theft	Auto theft	Total
Number known to police............	3,870	2,574	7,622	56,207	72,460	427,457	272,805	196,784	1,867,287
Disposition (per 100).............	100.0	100.0	100.0	100.0	100.0	100.0	100.0	100.0	100.0
Cleared by arrest............	93.5	89.8	73.0	42.7	78.9	29.7	20.2	26.9	26.4
Persons charged............	94.0	76.7	78.9	42.2	66.7	21.3	15.0	23.0	20.6
Convictions................	55.9	23.4	36.0	25.7	27.9	14.4	10.6	14.7	13.8
Convictions as percentage of persons charged...........	59.5	30.5	45.6	60.8	41.8	67.8	71.0	64.0	66.9

* Computed and adapted from *Uniform Crime Reports*, 1958, tables 5, 12, 14.

to the police, taken as 100, and reveals the proportion of such cases that result in arrest, charge, and conviction.[1] If the sentences applied in that year were similar to those published in *Criminal Judicial Statistics* for the early 1940s, approximately 5.5 of the 13.8 persons convicted were sentenced to prison or reformatory, 4.5 were sentenced to probation, 2.9 were committed to a jail or workhouse, and .9 received other dispositions. Such a drop-out rate as this suggests surely reduces to a very great extent the deterrent efficacy of the penal law. A study of the data will help to clarify some of the reasons why relatively few felonies result in prison sentences.

Several matters should be noted concerning the percentages shown in the table for the various procedural phases. First, as previously suggested, the offenses known to the police do not actually include all the crimes of which the police may be aware but, in so far as their reporting of the statistics may be accurate, only those that have been officially recorded. Moreover, the total of offenses known is undoubtedly a rather small percentage of the crimes actually committed.[2] This is the case particularly in instances of theft, assault, and rape. In some categories offenses actually committed may well be ten times greater than the offenses known to the police.

In relation to crimes cleared by arrest, and persons charged in court, it is clear that a very high percentage of the crimes against the person result in arrest and preliminary hearing. In contrast, the property crimes result in a relatively low proportion of arrests, particularly for ordinary larceny and auto theft. This is as one should anticipate, because most commonly there is no witness to the crime and the property may be difficult or impossible to trace. As a practical matter, the entire time of the police force could be consumed in pursuing evidence of theft without attaining the level of effectiveness that is characteristic in crimes against the person. It should be noted too that in relation to persons charged some individuals are accused of several of the offenses known and, in other cases, one of the known offenses may result in the charge of several persons. This affects to some extent the significance of the percentages shown in the table. It should be observed, further, that in the figures given on convictions several of the procedural stages (hearing, indictment or information, decision to prosecute, pleas, and trial) have not been broken down. Unfortunately, current data on these several phases are not available in official reports.

---

[1] Percentage figures on crimes cleared by arrest were based on statistics from 1,994 cities with a total population of 77,469,233, while those relating to convictions were based on statistics from 198 cities with a total population of 38,007,281.

[2] See Roscoe Pound, *Criminal Justice in America*, 1929, pp. 22 ff., on difficulties in law enforcement arising out of urbanization and see pp. 73 f. and 177 f. on the commonly adverse reactions of some courts to police evidence.

Figures on the number of crimes reported by the police are provided in the above table to indicate the actual volume of cases in each of the major crime categories. These figures reveal the reason why, in spite of relatively high rates of arrest and conviction for crimes against the person, the over-all percentages of arrest and conviction are low. The great majority of felonies fall into the classes of larceny, auto theft, and burglary and the arrest rates are low compared with other crimes. It is largely because of the difficulty in handling these crimes, so prevalent in our society, that the total conviction rate is as low as 13.8 per cent of known crimes. Apparently it would require a much larger and more efficient police force to raise that percentage very appreciably. On the average, however, nearly 70 per cent of those who are charged with major felonies and over 50 per cent of those arrested are convicted.

According to the FBI data it would appear that nearly 90 per cent of those convicted are found guilty of the offenses charged against them at the trial court. Figures from criminal justice surveys suggest, however, that nearly three-fourths of offenders are convicted for lesser crimes than those charged at arrest or at preliminary hearing. It is common practice for police to charge the gravest possible crimes at the time of arrest and for the prosecutor to do so at preliminary hearing in order to establish a ceiling that may be lowered in a process of bargaining.

Significance of the Statistics

To interpret arrest and judicial statistics with any accuracy several considerations must be taken into account. One is the variation in police practices in different jurisdictions. "Easy arrests" on slight suspicion normally should lead to a relatively high rate of elimination of suspects. Under varying state statutes which deal with the powers of police and the divergent administrative policies of police departments, there are large differences in the frequency with which innocent persons are brought to preliminary hearing. The tendency in metropolitan and large urban centers to arrest on slight justification may well account in part for the higher rates of acquittal commonly found in these cities. The difficulties of detection and apprehension of law violators in the metropolis is also reflected in court processing. Where urban conditions make it difficult to procure convincing evidence, the percentage of convictions should be lower. Another relevant factor is the relation between the courts and the police. A "cooperative" bench may hold or convict promiscuously on police testimony. In some courts, however, the evidence brought in by the police is very closely scrutinized. The "tightness of case" that the police or prosecutor considers necessary to bring defendants into court is based, in part, on the degree of hostility or cooperation usually encountered by them in the courts of the particular jurisdiction.

Another significant matter is the character of the courts of preliminary hearing in the particular jurisdiction. Trained, well-paid magistrates who hold long-term tenure are more efficient than lay magistrates and justices of the peace. The lay bench tends in its "rough and ready justice" to hold a larger proportion of cases to trial. Where dismissals at preliminary hearing are few, discharge rates tend to be higher at the levels of the grand jury or the trial court. The not uncommon inference that a low rate of discharge by these inferior courts is an indication of their effective administration of justice is quite unwarranted. The rate should depend largely on the policies that are employed by the police and by the prosecution in the particular jurisdiction. Performance data on criminal justice should normally reflect the influence of each level of procedure upon the next. No single phase can be assessed without reference to the others. When information concerning any stage is lacking, it is difficult or impossible to appraise the efficiency that prevails in other phases of the administration of justice.[3]

The role of the prosecuting attorney is a fundamental one in the processing of defendants. Yet, as in the case of the police, since much of the prosecutor's work is unofficial, extralegal, and administrative, it is difficult to make a fair judgment of the means, methods, objectives, and accomplishments of his office.[4] There is wide variation in the frequency with which prosecutors will exercise discretion to discharge defendants who refuse to plead guilty. In some jurisdictions only a very small percentage of cases are brought to trial, the majority being settled by plea or discharge. This may well indicate the zeal of the prosecutor and his desire to cut down the very large volume of business that confronts the criminal courts in major cities. The result is quick, easy, cheap, and "successful" prosecution. Elsewhere the finding of guilt is more frequently based on trials rather than on bargaining procedures. It is apparent that the way in which discretion is exercised by prosecutors greatly influences the results achieved at the several levels that are involved in the administration of justice.

The methods and accuracy of reporting court data may vary sufficiently to account for some of the apparent differences in rates of discharge and convictions from one jurisdiction to another. The way in which information is recorded may also lead to differing interpretations. Thus, for example, the high conviction rates commonly reported by prosecution appear to

[3] An ambitious research project has been undertaken by the American Bar Foundation on the administration of criminal justice in the United States; if continued, this project should provide a very considerable amount of data on the several phases of procedure that are discussed here. See *The Administration of Criminal Justice in the United States, Plan for Survey,* American Bar Foundation, 1955.

[4] See *Report on Prosecution,* National Commission on Law Observance and Enforcement, 1931; Raymond Moley, *Politics and Criminal Prosecution,* 1929; W. F. Willoughby, *Principles of Judicial Administration,* 1929; John B. Waite, *Criminal Law in Action,* 1934; and Arthur Train, *From the District Attorney's Office,* 1939.

be in marked contrast to the police data on the prosecution of arrests that result in conviction. The lumping of guilty pleas with jury convictions and the lumping of convictions for the offense charged with convictions for lesser degrees may convey a misleading impression of the consequences of criminal prosecution. Similarly the data relating to dispositions (suspended sentences along with commitments and dismissals with acquittals) provide a blurred picture of the "mortality rate" in criminal justice.

The Compromises of Justice

What we must seek is an optimum standard of justice that necessarily will make some compromise between the goal of efficiency and the protection of the innocent. The limitations of human powers of detection, apprehension, submission of evidence, and determination of guilt make it impossible always to allocate criminal responsibility accurately. This means that many offenders must be unapprehended and that many who are arrested should be discharged. Since it is usually impossible to determine guilt with absolute certainty, some innocent defendants inevitably will be convicted in the effort to protect society. The safeguards thrown around suspects by the law are properly designed to keep this group at a minimum. The punishment of nonoffenders is ultimately more costly than the occasional release of guilty defendants whose violations have not been clearly shown. Therefore, a high discharge rate may point to a large measure of care and accuracy in court processing. In contrast, an extremely high rate of arrest, of holding to trial, and of verdicts of guilt would tend to indicate common injustice through conviction of the innocent.

Requirements for speed and efficiency lead to further compromise with the ideals of justice. The existing state of public opinion influences the care that officials exercise in performing their duties. Public, pecuniary, and personnel limitations are obstacles to the attainment of justice. In any event, defendants must be dealt with rapidly enough so that the machinery of justice will not be clogged. Undue delay itself produces injustice. And defendants must be dealt with rapidly enough to meet reasonable demands for economy. Hence, some degree of failure in our courts is virtually inevitable.

Rights and Privileges Guaranteed the Accused

As has been seen, only a minority of crimes result in conviction. This is largely because of the failure of the police to discover and prosecutors to convict persons who have committed crimes against property. Any considerable increase in the effectiveness of police and prosecution would appear to require abandonment of important protections that have been devised to guard suspects against abusive methods of investigation and trial. The constitutional and statutory guarantees that are designed to provide such protection will now be discussed. Some of these guarantees have previously been considered and will be mentioned only briefly here.

One of the basic protections to the defendant is his right to a clear and definite charge. In accordance with the doctrine *nullum crimen sine lege,* our jurisprudence requires that to constitute crime an act must be specifically prohibited by the criminal law.[5] To be valid, a police arrest or warrant of arrest must be based upon such proscriptions. An indictment or information must rest upon the violation of statutory prohibitions. The defendant may be convicted only for the offense of which he has been accused, or, in some jurisdictions, for a less serious, included offense. He is entitled to a copy of the charge against him and, generally, to the names of the witnesses on whose testimony the accusation depends.

The defendant is protected from unreasonable searches and seizures. As noted in an earlier chapter, the police may not conduct search or seizure except in connection with a legal arrest or on a warrant showing probable cause to believe that particular evidence bearing materially on the commission of a crime may be found.

The right to counsel[6] is provided by the Federal Sixth Amendment[7] and in some state constitutions. The due-process clause of the Fourteenth Amendment does not require that counsel be appointed in the state courts, except in capital cases where the defendant is impoverished and unable to understand the complexity of issues involved in the trial.[8] A number of

[5] See "Due Process Requirements of Definiteness in Statutes," *Harv. L. Rev.,* vol. 62, p. 77, 1948, and for a general discussion, see Jerome Hall, *Principles of Criminal Law,* 1947, chap. 2. As Hall observes, the principle of *nullum crimen* has never been closely followed in dealing with juveniles, vagabonds, mendicants, and persons "without visible means of support." P. 48. See also *The Modern Approach to Criminal Law,* 1945, especially chap. 5, and Chapter 1 of this volume.

[6] That the right to counsel means an "effective aid of counsel" was emphasized in the reversal of the conviction of Judith Coplon where it was held that an FBI wiretap on the telephone of her attorney deprived her of such aid in contravention of the Sixth Amendment. *Coplon v. United States,* 191 F. 2d 749 (C.A., D.C., 1951). See also "Quality of Counsel in Criminal Cases," *Ark. L. Rev.* vol. 8, p. 484, 1954.

[7] No payment to assigned counsel is provided for under Federal law, however. See Holtzoff, "The Right of Counsel under the Sixth Amendment," *N.Y.U.L. Rev.,* vol. 20, pp. 17–19, 1944, and Fellman, "The Constitutional Right to Counsel in Federal Courts," *Neb. L. Rev.,* vol. 30, pp. 596–599, 1951. Some provision is made for compensation in over half the states.

[8] In *Palko v. Connecticut,* 302 U.S. 319 (1937), Justice Cardozo held that the Fourteenth Amendment does not cover the full scope of the first eight amendments, which apply to Federal procedure; it provides due process protection in state courts only in so far as rights are "of the very essence of a scheme of ordered liberty." The requirement of counsel has been held specifically not to be included among such rights in *Bute v. Illinois,* 333 U.S. 640 (1948), and in *Betts v. Brady,* 316 U.S. 455 (1942). In noncapital cases it must be shown generally that in view of the seriousness of the charge, the complexity of the issues, trickery by the state, or the ignorance of the defendant his cause was seriously impaired by the absence of counsel.

jurisdictions, however, have held that the defendant is entitled to counsel not only at trial but at earlier stages of the proceedings as well.[9] All states provide for assignment of counsel to indigents in capital cases, but few provide such aid in other felony cases and fewer still for misdemeanors.[10] It has been estimated that more than half of the defendants lack funds to pay for legal services. In some states the defendant need not be informed of the right even where it exists. Few states provide for legal aid in the inferior courts and only two provide for aid in appellate cases. Most jurisdictions make no allowance or only very small allowance for compensation of appointed counsel or for expenses and disbursements involved in trial. It is apparent that ideally competent counsel should be available for all stages of criminal proceedings with full opportunity to prepare and present the defendant's case. One who is not represented may become confused beyond hope of extrication during the interrogations at preliminary hearing before trial. Where one entitled to counsel has not been advised of his right and is subsequently convicted, he may ordinarily attack the jurisdiction of the court that entered the verdict through a writ of habeas corpus.

The inadequacy of the system of assigned counsel has increasingly been recognized and in some places other approaches to the problem have been made.[11] Three alternative systems are currently in use: (1) the public de-

[9] In a study of the availability of counsel for indigent defendants conducted by a committee surveying the legal profession, questionnaire replies were received from 257 public officials engaged in criminal court work throughout the country. Of these officials 11 per cent reported that legal aid was available prior to preliminary hearing, 29 per cent that it was available at preliminary hearing or first arraignment, and 50 per cent that it was available at formal arraignment or indictment after preliminary hearing. See Martin V. Callagy, "Legal Aid in Criminal Cases," *J. Crim. L.,* vol. 42, pp. 589–625, 1952.

[10] *Equal Justice for the Accused,* Special Committee to Study Defender Systems, New York City Bar Association, 1959. See also "Voluntary Defenders in Massachusetts," *Law. Guild Rev.,* vol. 17, pp. 131–134, winter, 1957. Several articles in this issue are devoted to the problem of representation of indigent defendants.

[11] Consult Esther L. Brown, *Lawyers, Law Schools and the Public Service,* 1948; Emery A. Brownell, *Legal Aid in the United States,* 1951; William M. Beaney, *The Right to Counsel in American Courts,* 1955; R. H. Smith and John S. Bradway, *Growth of Legal Aid Work in the United States,* 1936; and citations in ftn. 10. See also Potts, "Right to Counsel in Criminal Cases: Legal Aid or Public Defender," *Texas L. Rev.,* vol. 28, p. 491, 1950. The Attorney General of the United States has pointed to the serious problem that exists where unprincipled attorneys, appointed to defend the poor, extort money from their relatives. See William P. Rogers, "Plea for the Public Defender," *New York Times Magazine,* Apr. 21, 1957. In 1956 the U.S. Supreme Court held in *Griffin v. Illinois* on a noncapital charge that a defendant who had pleaded indigence and was denied a trial transcript for appeal (theretofore provided only to defendants under death sentence) had been denied due process and that some means must be provided by the state for adequate appellate review. *New York Times,* Mar. 10, 1957. In 1957 the court held similarly in *Johnson v. United States* as to a defendant convicted under Federal law. *Loc. cit.*

fender, (2) the voluntary defender, and (3) the mixed private-public plan. Of these, the public defender system is most prevalent. It is now in operation in more than eighty jurisdictions.[12] It operates on a state-wide basis in Colorado, Connecticut, and Rhode Island. The public defender system is based on the view that the state has responsibility in criminal cases to support both defense and prosecution services. Vigorous opponents of this system have argued, *inter alia,* that there is danger that excessive influence may be exercised by the state, either through the prosecutor or the judges, to induce guilty pleas and otherwise to secure "cooperation" leading to easy convictions. It has also been suggested that public defenders would not be provided with personnel required for the proper investigation and preparation of cases.[13] These arguments are not persuasive, for they attack an improvement that is less than perfect. Theoretically, offices for public defense counsel may become as well staffed and as efficient as those of prosecution, and in an impartial agency serving an impartial court they need not be subject to improper influence.

The voluntary defender plan, now established in several cities, differs from the public defender system. Voluntary defender organizations have usually been supported by private contributions, thereby avoiding the hazards that may be associated with public support. In New York City, the Criminal Courts Branch of the Legal Aid Society has a staff of twenty-four attorneys and three investigators under the direction of a distinguished defender.[14] In 1958 the organization provided counsel to over 35,000 persons charged with crime, generally from the time of first appearance in magistrates' courts. Where counsel is needed to represent these clients in appellate courts, lawyers are provided through the Committee for the Criminal Courts Branch of the Legal Aid Society. The voluntary defenders of the society have a reputation for

[12] Edward N. Bliss, Jr., in "Defense Detective," *J. Crim. L.,* vol. 47, p. 265, 1956, indicated that there were seventy-eight public defender officers in the United States. In 1957 a bill was presented to Congress providing for the appointment of public defenders for Federal district courts. It was estimated that the total cost should not exceed $250,000 a year, though some 35,000 criminal cases are commenced each year in these courts and at least one out of every eight defendants lacks the means to employ an attorney. It has been estimated that in the state courts three out of five cannot hire counsel.

[13] See Bliss, *loc cit.,* and his *Defense Investigation,* 1946. He indicates that investigators are now employed in Oakland, San Francisco, Memphis, and Chicago. Investigators are also employed by the private voluntary organizations in New York, Philadelphia, Pittsburgh, and New Orleans. See Callagy, *loc. cit.* In *Equal Justice for the Accused,* the New York City Bar Association committee expressed the opinion that a public defender system could be operated at a cost from 15 to 25 per cent of the budget allotted to the prosecutor.

[14] See Pollock, "The Voluntary Defender as Counsel for the Defense," *J. of Am. Jud. Soc.,* vol. 32, pp. 174–177, 1949, and "The Public Defender System," *J. of Am. Jud. Soc.,* vol. 32, p. 74, 1948. Compare "The Public Defender System Is Unsound in Principle," *J. Am. Jud. Soc.,* vol. 32, p. 115, 1948. These are cited in Emerson and Haber, *Political and Civil Rights in the United States,* 1952, pp. 179–182. Federal Judge Edward J. Dimock sees the public defender system as a "bid to tyranny." *New York Times,* June 30, 1957. See also Newell G. Alford, Jr., "The Work of the Criminal Courts Branch," *The Legal Aid Rev.,* vol. LVI, pp. 6–11, Spring, 1958.

representing their clients vigorously, effectively, and with independence. There is, of course, no certainty of continuous and adequate financial support of such agencies. It is unlikely that programs of this sort could be supported on a state-wide basis.

Recently, in a few cities, a mixed private-public system has been established. This system is under private control but receives contributions from public funds. The private-public system appears to provide an optimum solution to a very difficult problem.

As has been previously mentioned, any person charged with crime is entitled to be produced before a magistrate within a reasonable time after his arrest to determine whether the state has sufficient ground to hold him for trial. Detention without court appearance is an illegal deprivation and may be sufficient, if it is accompanied by other coercive measures such as prolonged interrogation, to justify reversal of a conviction.[15]

The accused is privileged against compulsory self-incrimination.[16] He should be informed at arrest, preliminary hearing, and trial of his right to refuse to answer and that anything he says may be used against him. In most jurisdictions neither prosecutor nor judge may comment adversely on his failure to respond, though in some states the judge may do so in his charge to the jury. Any witness, whether a party or stranger to the case, may refuse to answer questions, either at a trial or other official inquiry, if his reply would tend to show him guilty of a crime. Whereas an ordinary witness may be subpoenaed and questioned without advising him of his privilege—it is presumed that he is aware of his privilege—a de-

[15] See *Mallory v. United States,* 354 U.S. 449 (1957), requiring the exclusion of a confession obtained during an "excessive" period of detention, and p. 289 above.

[16] Article V of the Federal Constitution and all but two state constitutions provide such a privilege. In *McNabb v. United States,* 318 U.S. 332 (1943), where two defendants had been held incommunicado for fourteen hours without being produced before a magistrate and for two days were subjected to constant questioning by numerous officers and were denied the benefit of counsel, the Supreme Court held that incriminating statements they had made were inadmissible. This was not a holding that illegal detention taken alone would be sufficient to bar such statements, however. See also *Haley v. State,* 332 U.S. 596 (1948). In Bader, "Coerced Confessions and the Due Process Clause," *Brooklyn L. Rev.,* vol. 18, p. 70, 1948, the author observes the practical difficulty involved in assuring the protection: "A defendant from whom a confession has skillfully been extorted is generally without practical remedy. The only witnesses to the coercive practices are those who participated in and encouraged them. The issue, if raised on the trial, is one of credibility between the defendant, an interested witness, whose only salvation lies in nullifying the confession, and officers sworn to uphold the law. The issue is almost universally resolved against the defendant." (Reprinted by permission.) For a general treatment of self-incrimination, see Inbau, *Self-incrimination,* 1950. Relative to congressional committee inquiries in particular, as well as grand jury and court cases, the fact that the Fifth Amendment is limited to the personal protection of the witness has become very important. Not until the Federal act of 1954 has an immunity statute permitted Congress to require testimony and there is question concerning the extent of protection that the law will provide the witness. Clearly it does not protect him from loss of job and reputation.

fendant in a criminal case cannot be questioned unless he is advised of his right to remain silent. In some states where a defendant waives his privilege by testifying, he may be cross-examined on any relevant and material issue and is under a duty to answer; in other states he may waive his privilege in relation to only a particular phase of trial and otherwise retain it. Some states and the Federal law provide either generally or concerning particular types of cases for compulsory waiver but with immunity against future prosecution for any crime that may be revealed; the privilege must be claimed in order for the immunity to apply.[17]

Where a felony is charged, the defendant is entitled generally to a grand jury indictment, though he may waive this right and may proceed on the basis of the prosecutor's information.[18] The right to grand jury indictment is a protection against unjustified or persecutory action by prosecution.

Excessive bail may not be assessed against the accused or against material witnesses, taking into consideration the seriousness of the crime and the financial circumstances of the defendant.[19]

[17] Some states have held that a defendant may properly refuse to answer questions before a state grand jury in spite of an immunity statute where it is reasonably probable that a Federal prosecution might result from his testimony. See *State ex rel Mitchell v. Kelly*, 71 So. 2d 887 (Fla. 1954), and *In re Watson*, 293 Mich. 263 (1940). The American Civil Liberties Union has opposed the Federal Immunity Law, enacted in 1954, because of its "uncertain protection and vague scope . . . the self-degradation suffered by witnesses who are required to testify about past activities—which may not be criminal—and that information about Communist activities—the main purpose of the law—is already available."

[18] The right to grand jury indictment for infamous crimes in our Federal courts is conferred by the Fifth Amendment. It is not imported into the Fourteenth. Statutes permitting waiver have been enacted in approximately half the states. An indictment "must contain every averment that is necessary to inform the defendant of the particular circumstances of the charge against him." *State v. Popolos*, 103 A.2d 511 (Me. 1954). On two occasions indictments for perjury against Owen Lattimore were dismissed for vagueness where they alleged he had denied being a "follower of the Communist line" and a "sympathizer or any other kind of promoter of Communism or Communist interests." See *United States v. Lattimore*, 127 F. Supp. 405 (D.D.C. 1955). The trend has been toward simplification of the indictment and information, so long as the accused may know the nature of the charge against him. A Utah court has recently upheld the constitutionality of a statute under which the charge simply stated: "John Murray Landrum, Patricia O'Hara, and Bill Frentress robbed Joseph Shepher." *State v. Landrum*, 3 Utah 2d 372 (1955).

[19] The Sixth Amendment guarantees the right to bail only before conviction, but the Federal rules provide the right after conviction in Rule 46 (*a*)(2). See Note, *Va. L. Rev.*, vol. 35, p. 496, 1949; Beeley, *The Bail System in Chicago*, 1927; *A Study of Criminal Court Bail Bonds in Cleveland*, Cleveland Crime Commission Report, 1936; and Caleb Foote, James P. Markle, and Edward A. Wooley, "Compelling Appearance in Court: Administration of Bail in Philadelphia," *U. Pa. Studies L. Admin.*, no. 1, 1954. A New York county grand jury has investigated for three years the activities of professional bail bondsmen, indicting seven bondsmen, five of whom were convicted and their licenses revoked. The jury found defendants to be at the mercy of bondsmen and that professional hoodlums were assured of bail that was often denied the occasional offender. *New York Times*, Dec. 13, 1956.

The defendant may not twice be put in jeopardy for the same crime. This rule, however, does not prevent trial of the defendant in two different jurisdictions for the same crime (as, for example, Federal and state) or in a civil as well as a criminal adjudication. In some states this rule does not prevent trial for an offense different from that for which the defendant was originally tried even though the offense was rooted in the same criminal conduct.[20] Jeopardy is generally held to apply only when a trial has proceeded to its conclusion with a verdict of acquittal unless the judge or the prosecutor has improperly terminated the trial.

The defendant is entitled to trial by a jury of his peers in felony cases and, in most jurisdictions, for some or all misdemeanors.[21]

He is also entitled to be confronted by the witnesses who accuse him, to hear their testimony against him, to cross-examine such witnesses, and usually to a public trial of his guilt.[22] These rights of confrontation, orality, and publicity of proceedings are major protections against the evils of secret, ex parte action through which the accused might be convicted by prejudice, hearsay, or insubstantial evidence.[23]

The defendant is presumed to be innocent and his guilt must be established beyond reasonable doubt.[24] This not only imposes the burden of proof upon the state but requires, in order to support penal sanctions, that the proof be of a highly convincing character. It is the duty of police, magistrate, grand jury, and prosecutor to determine not whether the accused is guilty but whether there is sufficient ground to hold him for the court to make such a determination.

The defendant is entitled to appeal for errors of the state in his indictment, trial, or conviction and to the writ of habeas corpus for illegal imprisonment.

The defendant may not be exposed to cruel and unusual punishments[25]

[20] In *Sealfron v. United States,* 332 U.S. 575 (1948), it was held on the grounds of res judicata that where the defendant had been acquitted on a conspiracy charge he was improperly convicted thereafter for the substantive offense where the evidence was the same in both cases.

[21] See the discussion and footnotes in the last chapter. The right to fair and public trial is established by constitution in most states and elsewhere by statute or decision. *United States v. Kobli,* 172 F.2d 919 (3d Cir. 1949), held that the general public might not be protected from testimony in regard to sex acts by exclusion from the court room, though the right to public trial may be limited to protect the morals of minors. Jelke's first conviction in 1953 by the General Sessions Court in New York City for inducement to prostitution was also reversed for exclusion of the press and the public. He was convicted again two years later at public trial. See Charles W. Quick, "A Public Criminal Trial," *Dick. L. Rev.,* vol. 60, p. 21, 1955.

[22] See *In re Oliver,* 333 U.S. 257 (1948), where Justice Black observed that through public trial the witnesses, jurors, and even the court itself are reminded of their responsibilities.

[23] On conviction through fraud, trickery, or the suppression of evidence, see *Mooney v. Holohan,* 294 U.S. 103 (1935).

[24] See ftn. 43 in Chapter 12.

[25] See Sutherland, "Due Process and Cruel Punishment," *Harv. L. Rev.,* vol. 64,

nor, in general, to penalties that are disproportionately severe for the crime for which he has been convicted.

In addition to the rights noted above that have been rather firmly established in common law and constitution, there are several protections against unjust conviction or deprivation of liberty in our procedure. The laws of police arrest and detention as well as limitations on methods of securing evidence have been discussed. The coercion of confessions by physical means, where it can be shown, requires exclusion of the evidence so obtained or reversal of conviction on appeal. This principle, while it has not resulted in the avoidance of "third degree" methods, nevertheless provides a far greater extent of protection than has been established generally to support the other restrictions on police methods. In most jurisdictions the defendant may have a civil and criminal action against officials who have deprived him of the other legal rights noted here. It is most difficult, however, in the nature of the circumstances, for the defendant to provide proof that is convincing to the courts in order to secure vindication of his rights. Most of the state courts accept evidence even though it is tainted with unlawful arrest, illegally prolonged detention and persistent interrogation, unjustified search, wiretapping without court order, and other illegal measures. Since such usages facilitate getting convictions and defendants are without real recourse against them, these rights are much too commonly honored in the breach in the United States.[26]

The rules of evidence guiding the admission of testimony provide much fuller protection against conviction of the innocent, in large part because they are applied by the professional judiciary in open hearing with a right of appeal on the record of the trial. With various exceptions for particular circumstances, the law of evidence prohibits the introduction of the following types of testimony:

1. *Hearsay Evidence.* The truthfulness and significance of testimony may be weighed more accurately through the cross-examination of wit-

---

p. 271, 1950, and Emerson and Haber, *op. cit.,* pp. 230–231. *Weems v. United States,* 217 U.S. 349 (1910), is perhaps the only case in which the Supreme Court has set aside a punishment as cruel and unusual. It involved the wearing of chains. Cruel punishments are prohibited by statute or constitution in most of the states and, in some, specific forms of corporal punishment are forbidden. Brutal measures, where they occur, are employed not through court sentence but as a matter of administrative policy in prison discipline.

[26] See Chapter 11, ftn. 61. The Federal Civil Rights Act offers some protection to the citizen whose rights are violated by the state. Section 242 of Title 18 provides for a fine of not more than $1000 and imprisonment up to a year for any person who willfully deprives any inhabitant of a state, territory, or district of his rights, privileges, or immunities secured by the Constitution or subjects any person to different penalties than those authorized for a citizen on account of such inhabitant being an alien or because of his color or race. A right to damages is given to the injured party under Section 43, Title 8. These provisions have been invoked in cases of false arrest, police assault, third degree, abuses of judicial process, and racial discrimination.

nesses in court. The ignorant, prejudiced, or emotional informant may be tested there for his knowledge.

2. *Prejudicial Testimony.* It is unjust to convict the defendant for the immediate crime on the basis of his reputation, his general character, his prior criminal record, or other matters relating to his history or personality. Evidence that tends to stimulate prejudice increases the difficulty in determining the facts under a criminal charge. There are broad exceptions, however, particularly where the accused has chosen to testify in his own defense, thus permitting the introduction of matter that may be strongly prejudicial in efforts to show that he is not a reliable witness, that he had motive or intent to commit the crime, that the crime was part of a criminal course of conduct, that the immediate crime was not the result of accident or mistake, and that the defendant may be identified with the crime.

3. *Opinion Testimony.* Except for qualified expert opinion, criminality should be inferred from facts rather than fancy. Opinion may be soundly or poorly founded, but in either case it is for the court to draw conclusions from the data on which opinion may be based rather than to root its judgment in untested conjecture.

4. *Irrelevant Testimony.* To arrive at a judgment of the issues before the court as sharply as possible, the trial should be reasonably free from devious evidence that will mislead attention and confuse thinking.

5. *Incompetent Evidence.* Confusion may develop on the central issues and judgment may be based upon testimony that is not significant to prove the conclusions that are drawn.

With the excessive inclination in American courts to conduct trial as a sport that tests the skill of the adversaries, there is persistent effort by the attorneys both for the accused and for the state to draw out improper evidence before the jury. While it is the major function of the judge during trial to exclude such evidence, when proper objection is taken, it is apparent nonetheless that what the members of the jury have heard affects their thinking, even when they are instructed to disregard the evidence offered. Failure to protest is generally taken to waive the objection. On the other hand, objections are often made on petty matters in the hope that upon appeal a reversal may be had on the basis of an erroneous ruling. While this has frequently happened, the trend of appellate court decisions has been to affirm the action of trial courts where errors are immaterial.

It should be noted, in connection with the judge's role, that his passivity in the conduct of trial in the United States, as contrasted with the activity of judges in England and elsewhere, is an unfortunate characteristic of our procedure. The tradition here results in considerable part from fear that action or comment may lead to reversals in the higher courts. The consequence, however, is that the evidential content of the trial is wholly determined by the adversaries. Neither of them may desire that all the evidence be brought forward and the defense, in particular, may be in a poor position to secure the attendance of witnesses and the securing of testimony that is needed in his case. The judge could and should play an important role in filling the crevices that are left by the parties, both through examining the witnesses they have produced and, where desirable, through requiring others to attend. As it is, the passive performance of the bench results both in the enlargement of the prosecutor's over-extended administrative discretion and in the perpetuation of the sporting theory of justice in which the judge is little more than a referee to detect the fouls.

Mitigative Devices

Though quite different from the protections enjoyed by the defendant and the formal rules of procedure that have been noted, there are several mitigative procedures that affect the fate of the accused. The National Commission on Law Observance and Enforcement in 1931 noted ten "mitigative devices" or "checks upon prosecution" that it believed were often used as "so many pieces to be played by habitual offenders in the game of criminal justice" to defeat the ends of law.[27] It should be observed, however, that these are for the most part discretionary practices that are designed to facilitate the work of the state rather than to provide leniency to the defendant. They are employed to the advantage of prosecution and at its option, though one consequence, among others, may be to lighten penalties for those who plead to a criminal charge. These are the "devices":

1. Police and prosecutor may exercise discretion on starting prosecution.

2. The examining magistrate may discharge the accused after preliminary hearing.

3. The grand jury may refuse to indict.

4. The prosecutor may decide to enter a nolle prosequi.

5. The prosecutor or the court may agree to accept a plea to a lesser offense than that originally charged.

6. The trial jury may bring in a verdict of not guilty or may convict for a lesser crime.

7. Discretion may be exercised in sentencing to apply a lenient sentence, whether it is probation or brief imprisonment.

8. Sentence may be reduced in some jurisdictions through an appeal or motion in mitigation of sentence.

9. The convicted and incarcerated offender may be released on parole at some time short of the expiration of his maximum sentence.

10. A pardon may be secured from the executive.

The first four of these devices are sifting processes in which the state attempts to avoid trial of the innocent. They also operate to the benefit of those against whom the state cannot build a sufficient case or against whom

[27] *Report on Prosecution*, p. 20.

the state for various reasons chooses not to build such a case. Through these four and the fifth device, the prosecution attempts to secure a plea by which to avoid trial and to secure convictions. The sixth may result from jury error; obviously acquittal is proper in those cases where guilt of the crime alleged has not been clearly shown. With regard to the seventh and eighth, as will be observed in more detail elsewhere, contemporary penal law has come to provide wide ranges of sentencing alternatives, allowing not only for suspended sentences at one extreme but, at the other, for maximum terms that may be very high. Sometimes the result reveals a lack of sound discretion at both extremes. There is often a real need for mitigation when it is allowed. The use of parole, noted under (9) above, is a normal accompaniment to the indefinite sentence system with high maximum terms, permitting the release of the offender after the expiration of his minimum term, but generally retaining him longer, nevertheless, than was characteristic under the old flat sentence system. Finally, while often abused, pardon is an essential device for securing the release of those who are found innocent and for providing clemency where offenders have been sentenced too severely. These devices may be interpreted individually or collectively as mitigations to the defendant, but they represent in fact measures by which the state may most easily convict suspects and, thereafter, provide such treatment as the facts appear to warrant. How far they operate to the advantage of the guilty is difficult to assess, but the guilty probably derive considerable benefit from them. Existing practice results not only in excessive leniency at times for habitual criminals but also in the harrassment and the occasional conviction of individuals who are innocent of the crimes alleged against them.

INTRINSIC DIFFICULTIES IN DETERMINING GUILT

Modern criminal procedure is generally taken to be considerably more accurate and effective than medieval techniques of ordeal, combat, and compurgation. Undoubtedly it is. It should be recognized nonetheless that there are serious limitations to modern methods of discovering and proving guilt. Convictions for crime are based upon two quite different methods of approach. One of these methods is the administrative technique that involves the taking of a plea. Such measures as arrest on suspicion and prolonged interrogation accompanied by various persuasions and coercion, culminating in an offer of a reduced charge or the promise of leniency, may assure high rates of conviction but they offer no protection to the innocent and little promise that the guilty will be convicted of the crimes they committed. Where the criminal is discovered *flagrante delicto* or where the evidence is strong these methods may be quite unnecessary. It is enough that the offender is brought to recognize that sentences imposed on a plea are generally more lenient than those resulting from trial. In any event, some accused persons who plead guilty are persuaded to do so by secret and administrative measures that are difficult to discover and appraise.

More analytical attention has been given to the trial process than to administrative measures; furthermore, most of this attention to trial process has related to legal procedure rather than to the psychological implications involved. The student should recognize that trial procedure is founded upon a number of psychological assumptions that are at best quite dubious.[28] Some of these assumptions will be explored briefly here. A central hypothesis is that witnesses will in general tell the truth, especially if they are under oath. Reliance upon the oath is itself largely obsolete, it would appear. It is an historical residue of religious influences and of the system of compurgation by oath helpers. It seems evident today that intrinsically honest individuals will not lie whether or not they are under oath and that the oath exerts little influence on dishonest persons. The power to try the person who swears falsely for perjury involves a sanction that undoubtedly has at least a limited effect on the veracity of witnesses. However, the motives behind prevarication, exaggeration, and other distortions are so strong that perjurious testimony is a very common phenomenon in the court. The assumption of veracity, so far as it exists, is largely unjustified.

Recognizing that witnesses do sometimes lie, it is commonly assumed that observation of their demeanor, attention to their words, and scrutiny of their features will enable the jury to determine who lies and when. This, too, is an inaccurate assumption. For, in the first place, a distinction should be drawn between conscious and unintentional fabrication. It should be realized that the jury cannot well recognize the commonly unintentional falsehood or distinguish it from the deliberate untruth. It is the deliberate untruth that the court generally seeks to discover by weighing the testimony of one witness against that of another. Some guidance may be provided where the witness's reputation for veracity is successfully attacked. This would also apply in cases where there appear to be internal inconsistencies in the witness's testimony. At the same time it must be borne in mind that such inconsistencies may well result from confusion or misunderstanding on the part of a witness. Usually the jury must reach a conclusion on the basis of other and quite inaccurate indexes of credibility. The "good witness" from the lawyer's point of view is not the objective dispassionate person who sees at least two sides to every issue and who carefully qualifies his statements and reaches his conclusions with hesitant deliberation. The convincing witness is one who verbalizes smoothly, giving his testi-

[28] See in general Hugo Munsterberg, *On the Witness Stand,* 1927; Jerome Frank, *Law and the Modern Mind,* 1936, especially chap. 12; *If Men Were Angels,* 1942; *Courts on Trial, Myth and Reality in American Justice,* 1949; and W. M. Marston, "Studies in Testimony," *J. Crim. L.,* vol. 15, pp. 8 f., 1924.

mony dogmatically and certainly, without equivocation. Such a person may not be an accurate reporter and may be a chronic liar. Criminological researches have shown repeatedly that one cannot distinguish the criminal from the noncriminal by his features or manner. Nor can one thus discriminate accurately between the liar and the nonliar. This creates a very difficult task for the jury that must determine the facts. The assurance of the witness, his general appearance, and the attractiveness of his personality may seriously mislead the judgment of a jury.

Discrepancy in testimony may be caused by honest difference of observation and opinion. This is often the case, for example, where expert testimony differs. Here the problem before the jury is particularly acute where the jury is unable either to evaluate the technical issues involved or to determine the credibility or competence of such witnesses. On such issues as legal insanity or the emotional state of the accused at the time of the crime, it is commonly impossible to find agreement among the experts, not to mention jurors.

Another prevalent belief is that there should be close agreement among witnesses if they are telling the truth and, therefore, if one side or the other has a number of witnesses whose testimony is nearly identical, that these are to be believed. Some discrepancies in the evidence as presented by a party's witnesses may easily lead to the conclusion that they lie. It is in this area, generally involving honest differences in testimony, that the prevailing premises in regard to trial evidence are particularly inaccurate. In fact, several psychological processes are involved in giving testimony, mainly sensation, perception, memory, and verbalization of this recall. The nature of the human mind is such that differences, not identity, should result from these variables in different individuals.

There are important individual variations in the processes mentioned above. *Sensory reception* varies radically among humans in relation to acuteness, deficiency, or distortion in the visual, auditory, and kinesthetic senses through which impressions are received. Individuals do not see, hear, or feel the same stimuli in the same way. Such differences as exist in this "exteroception," moreover, are greatly increased by individuals' *perceptions* of these sensations. The impression made upon the person depends both upon the central nervous system and the higher brain centers (the interoceptors) and upon his background of experience (his apperceptive mass). Thus, for example, the viewing of a human carcass should result in very different internal perception in a policeman, a butcher, an artist, a mother, a lover, a rival, a scientist, a philosopher, a surgeon, and an imbecile. To put it in slightly different terms, what one observes depends upon his mental-emotional and experiential set. These matters are often closely related to occupation and experience. Obviously, the state's witnesses as well as the police and prosecutor each have a set that is strongly receptive to impressions of the guilt of the accused.

The peculiarities of human *memory* add considerably more to the variations resulting from differences in perception, particularly with the lapse of any considerable time interval. The psychologists' studies of this matter reveal a wide variety of distortions that occur: falsifications, substitutions, transpositions, incompleteness, and oversimplification. The individual is unware of these changes as they occur.[29] Thus, over a period of time the individual's recall may be very different from his original impression. Moreover, when the memory is taxed for recollection, bringing old content to the fore, the individual may be much more certain of the accuracy of his memory than he was at the original impression. This is particularly the case when his memory has been "refreshed" by an attorney who implants ideas and images that were not there before. The memory of these may be very acute, however fictitious their foundation. The common problem of false identification is sometimes the result of distortions originating in the witness's mind. All too often it is a consequence of having the suspect or his picture pointed out to him with a suggestion that this is the culprit. This sort of implantation of memories is characteristic where witnesses are coached before trial. The result may be a memory of an event that is very inaccurate but very clear and definite. Where there is close similarity of such memories in a series of witnesses, there is good reason to believe that they came from a common source subsequent to the crime, often immediately prior to the trial. Moreover, if the attorney for the state or the defendant has employed subtle, persistent suggestions in "leading" the pliant witness's mind, the latter may be quite unaware of this. Finally, the capacity of different witnesses to verbalize their impressions varies considerably. How completely, convincingly, and accurately they can produce the content of their memories differs in relation to intellectual and other personality traits.

The analysis above is not meant to suggest the futility of attempting to discover the truth on the basis of human informants, but to point to the very real complexity of the matter. Careful thought and objectivity are very much needed in reaching judgments of fact. The impressions of jurors, like those of witnesses, may be grossly misled by their observations at trial. Quite aside from other reasons of policy, this alone is reason enough for the law to require convincing proof of guilt and consensus among the jurors.

CONVICTING THE INNOCENT

The degree of effectiveness of police and prosecution in convicting offenders was observed at the beginning of this chapter. The author re-

[29] For an excellent analysis of the forms of error in memory, see G. M. Whipple, "The Obtaining of Information: Psychology of Observation and Report," *Psychol. Bull.,* vol. 15, pp. 235–245, 1918, summarized in Kimball Young, *Social Psychology,* 1930, pp. 109–111.

viewed the constitutional and statutory guarantees that are designed to protect suspects from abuse and to arrive at the truth. The statistical data has shown that there is a considerable margin of error in the procedures of justice, error that is undoubtedly attributable in part to the measures of individual protection that we employ. Mistakes are often caused by the inherent impediments to the discovery and proof of the facts, where crime is committed privately and secretly as it is so commonly in the modern city, and by the difficulties involved in drawing accurate inferences from such evidence as the parties can produce. These problems result inevitably in common failures either to discover or to convict the guilty. Such failures have led many officials to conclude that our traditional law and procedures are overly tender to the accused and that this accounts for the state's quandary. They sometimes urge that major protective measures be eliminated or reduced.[30] Therefore, the point requires some emphasis that, under a system of justice such as we have traditionally conceived, a large measure of failure to apprehend and convict the guilty is inevitable, especially in the case of minor felonies and misdemeanors. It is no less important to recognize that, despite the safeguards we have erected, many persons innocent of crime are convicted and that these blunders too often ensue from official circumventions of due process.

Some of the authenticated instances of injustices will be considered below. These are cases where the errors were subsequently demonstrated. Most of them are cases of serious crimes where, by hypothesis, the state took special pains to discover the facts and to show the truth. How much more often are men wrongfully convicted of less serious crimes and of crimes in which the truth never comes to light? In condemning court coercion to take a plea, a prominent New York attorney has effectively stated the defendant's dilemma:[31]

DARU'S REPORT REBUKES NOTT

Bar Counsel Takes Issue with Perjury Punishment

Robert Daru, Counsel for the New York Criminal Courts Bar Association, reporting on the miscarriage of justice, criticized the judge for a heavy sen-

---

[30] See, for example:

OLNEY CRITICIZES COURT PROCEDURE

We have lost the most important purpose of a criminal prosecution—the deterrent effect . . . procedural protections that have been given to criminal defendants have made it increasingly difficult for trials to get at the truth. *New York Times,* Oct. 13, 1957.

POLICE CHIEFS HIT AT SUPREME COURT

At Conference They Cite Some Rights Rulings as Curb on Law Agencies. *New York Times,* Oct. 6, 1957.

U.S. OPPOSES CURB ON POLICE TACTICS

New York Times, Aug. 26, 1957.

[31] *Ibid.*

tence of five to ten years that was based upon the judge's conclusion that the defendant had committed "rank perjury" in denying his guilt as well as for the crime charged, saying:

"The threat that if a defendant stands trial and is convicted, he will be punished also for 'perjury' consisting of his denying guilt and testifying to his innocence is used every day in the week to bargain with defendants to plead guilty to lesser charges on promises or expectation of suspended sentences or light punishment. It is common knowledge that to avoid this extra-legal danger, defendants plead guilty, saddling themselves for life with criminal records in hope of getting suspended sentences, or to receive comparatively light punishment for crimes of which they continue to assert their innocence . . . [The only alternative of an innocent man charged with a crime] would seem to be to deliver himself into the tender care and mercy of the prosecutor and, without the benefit of counsel, trust to Lady Luck for an accidental discovery of his innocence, or to the good, though possibly zealous, conscience of the district attorney and hope that the prosecutor gets out the right side of the bed in the morning, is divinely inspired to seek the truth and forget his record of convictions." [Italics added.]

Representatives of prosecution will be heard to say that conviction of the innocent almost never occurs.[32] Even more frequently convicts in the prison population persist in declaration of their innocence. On both sides they either delude themselves or attempt to delude others. The late Professor Edwin Borchard of the Yale School of Law, in his well-known study in 1932, *Convicting the Innocent,* describes some sixty-five cases, involving in the main murder charges, where the innocence of the convicted individuals was conclusively shown, in a number of which the defendant had already suffered the capital penalty. Erroneous identification was involved in twenty-nine of these cases, perjured corroboration of circumstantial evidence in fifteen, and framing by hostile witnesses in fourteen. One cannot escape the conclusion that prosecution in its zeal to achieve a record of convictions was responsible in a high proportion of these cases.

More recently the late Justice Jerome Frank and his daughter in their book *Not Guilty,*[33] published in 1957, summarized thirty-four cases of convictions, all but three of which occurred between 1918 and 1940, in which the imprisoned offenders were subsequently shown to be innocent. Only seven of these were murder cases, while eleven were robbery, four were rape, and four were embezzlement. Convictions had been based in a majority of the cases on false identifications and the prisoners cleared by the confessions of the actual offenders.

The writer has drawn together a few illustrations, taken from metropolitan newspapers of New York in recent years, where individuals have been imprisoned for more-or-less extended periods and ultimately have been found innocent. These do not include cases, considerably more

[32] See comment in Jerome Frank and Barbara Frank, *Not Guilty,* 1957, p. 35.
[33] *Ibid.*

numerous, where convictions have been reversed merely because of police methods or trial procedures.

MAN PAROLED IN THEFT. Fellow Prisoner Had Admitted 1956 Queens Robbery. Spent fifteen months in prison.[34]

A CONFESSION THAT "CLEARED" HIM OF MURDER. [A man aged] 29 found guilty of murder and sentenced to life imprisonment. Had difficulty making himself understood, because of his poor English, when he testified; alleged "confession" on which the state's case rested had been dictated to him by police interrogators; had signed the confession allegedly because police had beaten him, pushed him against a hot radiator, and threatened him with a cleaver.[35]

THIS IS THE WAY THAT IT HAPPENED: DID IT HAVE TO HAPPEN THIS WAY? [Two men] tried and convicted for stickup. After nearly six months in jail, released after confession by another man.[36]

U.S. JUDGE FREES WRONGED CONVICT. Hears Bronx Man Spent 4 Years in Prison for Forgery by Another.[37]

AN INNOCENT MAN COMES HOME. [A man] who spent 16 years in Illinois State Prison for $50 holdup another man has confessed is greeted by daughter.[38]

CLEARED LIFER WINS $112,291 FOR JAILING ON MURDER CONVICTION. Judge Fred A. Young, in making the award, noted however that "the district attorney's office had possession of evidence which, if known to defendant's counsel, would have prevented this tragic miscarriage of justice."[39]

19 YEARS IN PRISON—NOT GUILTY: GETS PENSION. . . . pardoned after members of the Barker-Karpis gang confessed he had no part in the robbery and killing of two policemen.[40]

COURT-AIDED PLEA FOR PARDON FAILS. . . . who served seven and one-half years for sale of heroin, convicted on the testimony of a prostitute who was a narcotics addict and a Government informer. Judge Weinfeld holds "facts now known nullify the theory on which the defendant was convicted and render that conviction erroneous and unjust." Pardon Attorney refuses to grant petition for pardon.[41]

CONVICT JAILED IN ERROR ENJOYS A REAL HOLIDAY. . . . imprisoned for twenty-two months on a fifteen year sentence for robbery pardoned by Governor Shivers. Another man confessed to the robbery.[42]

DOOMED BY MAD BROTHER, HE'S GOING FREE. [A man aged] 31, a death house convict for four years because his insane brother named him as a killer, expects to walk out of prison very soon a free man.[43]

[34] *New York Times,* undated (1957).
[35] *New York Post,* Apr. 4, 1957.
[36] *Ibid.,* Mar. 21, 1957.
[37] *New York Times,* Dec. 22, 1956.
[38] *Ibid.,* undated (1956).
[39] *Ibid.,* June 17, 1955.
[40] *New York Post,* Apr. 15, 1955.
[41] *New York Times,* Jan. 28, 1955.
[42] *Ibid.,* Nov. 25, 1954.
[43] *Ibid.,* Oct. 5, 1954.

MAN'S CONFESSION GIVES ANOTHER HOPE OF REOPENING TRIAL. . . . imprisoned for a murder another man has confessed, wins right to seek a new trial.[44]

PRISONER 9 YEARS FREED. Louisiana Aides Convinced Now He Did Not Commit Crime. . . . freed as a victim of "mistaken identity."[45]

SEQUEL: THE SECOND JURY. Patrolman K, after two years imprisonment for second-degree murder, freed upon second trial. Conviction had been based upon "snippets and scraps of circumstantial evidence," including testimony of a mentally disturbed prosecution witness.[46]

DOOMED 9 YEARS AGO, HE WALKS OUT—FREE.[47]

12 YEARS IN PRISON, "LIFER" MAY GO FREE. New Trial Ordered for L. H. Over Prosecution's Failure to Give Data to Defense. After a five-year struggle by a group of unpaid lawyers Queens County Judge Peter T. Farrell yesterday set aside the first-degree murder conviction.[48]

NOT GUILTY—AFTER 27 YEARS IN PRISON.[49]

MAN FREED IN 2D CASE OF MISTAKEN IDENTITY. For the second time within a week in Felony Court a defendant positively identified by a hold-up victim was freed when it was proved to the court's satisfaction that the accused was in custody at the time of the incident. The defendant was fortunate enough to have been in jail in Cleveland as a vagrant at the time of the hold-up.[50]

BLACK AND SHAMEFUL PAGE. Victim of third degree in Philadelphia released after seven years in penitentiary. Six policemen suspended from force, including assistant superintendent and the head of the homicide squad.[51]

WOMAN, 62, GETS PARDON IN JERSEY SIXTEEN YEARS AFTER FALSE ARREST.[52]

AID FOR WRONGLY JAILED MAN. Two false convictions for forgery.[53]

MISTAKEN AS BANDIT, JERSEY MAN IS FREE. Sentenced to two to five years after his arrest on larceny charges.[54]

THE PHANTOM FORGER. The accused was convicted on two successive occasions of forgery, beginning in 1935, on false identifications, and was ultimately pardoned fifteen years later.[55]

JAILED 16 YRS. FOR MURDER—INNOCENT.[56]

TRIAL "SHAM," NEGRO FREED AFTER 26 YEARS. Victim picked L. out of a group of Negroes as her assailant, but was unable to identify him

---

[44] *Ibid.,* June 16, 1954.
[45] *Ibid.,* July 31, 1953.
[46] *Time,* May 18, 1953.
[47] *New York Times,* Dec. 24, 1952.
[48] *Ibid.,* Jan. 11, 1952.
[49] *New York Post,* Dec. 4, 1951.
[50] *New York Times,* Oct. 6, 1951.
[51] *Time,* May 14, 1951.
[52] *New York Times,* Apr. 11, 1951.
[53] *Ibid.,* Jan. 30, 1951.
[54] *Ibid.,* July 28, 1950.
[55] *Time,* June 26, 1950.
[56] *New York Post,* Nov. 5, 1949.

the following day. Court noted that someone identified with the prosecution had suppressed material evidence which should have resulted in an acquittal.[57]

LIFER HELD INNOCENT, FREED AFTER 21 YEARS.[58]

$10,000 FOR "WRONG TERM." Six years in prison on a wrongful murder conviction.[59]

TWO JAILED FALSELY ARE ALLOWED TO SUE. Dewey signs bill to let them seek damages.[60]

BROTHER'S RECORD STIRS COURT MIX-UP. Two men have same first name, similar fingerprints, leading to mistaken identity.[61]

JAILED BY ERROR, FREED. Innocent youth served 10 months on hold-up conviction.[62]

MOVE FOR PARDON IN CASE. Officials Convinced Innocent Man Served Term for Forgery Confessed by Another.[63]

IDENTIFIED IN ERROR, FREED OF RAPE, THEFT.[64]

HOLD-UP CONFESSION FREES A PRISONER AFTER NINE MONTHS.[65]

FATHER OF 9 IN DEATH CELL 2 YEARS, INNOCENT.[66]

Some of the failures of justice noted above were undoubtedly inevitable errors, particularly where mistaken identity was involved.[67] Too often, however, such cases as these reflect the failure of the state to check through available and sometimes known sources of evidence that would not fit the prosecutor's case. Improper methods of securing identifications are sometimes used.[68] Defendants are too often pressed to take a plea and the persuasion may be irresistible to the person with a prior record, whether or not he is guilty. Often erroneous convictions are the result of the indigent defendant's lack of adequate counsel, or indeed of any counsel at all, especially in the early stages of procedure when inquisitorial pressures are most heavy. Illegal detention and interrogation practices, the extortion of confessions, the concealment of witnesses, the manufacture of evidence, bargains with accomplices and informers for desired testimony,

[57] *New York Times*, Aug. 11, 1949.

[58] *Ibid.*, July 9, 1947.

[59] *Ibid.*, May 13, 1947.

[60] *New York Tribune*, Apr. 13, 1947.

[61] *New York Times*, Mar. 20, 1947.

[62] *Ibid.*, Dec. 7, 1946.

[63] *Ibid.*, June 18, 1946.

[64] *Ibid.*, Aug. 3, 1945.

[65] *Ibid.*, June 3, 1959.

[66] *Melbourne Herald*, July 5, 1958.

[67] The Franks summarize in their study the results of an inquiry into the accuracy of observation: "An analysis of the testimony of 20,000 persons who were asked to describe the physical characteristics of the man they saw commit a crime . . . revealed that, on the average, they overestimated the height by 5 inches, the age by 8 years, and gave the wrong hair color in 82 per cent of the cases." *Op. cit.*, p. 61.

[68] The witness may be shown a single suspect, for example, or in a "line-up" the suspect may be the only person peculiarly dressed.

the coaching of witnesses, and other techniques occasionally employed by police and prosecution are all illustrated in the cases of conviction of the innocent. Once the defendant is convicted, moreover, evidence of error is rarely brought forward except by chance, for no one is charged with discovering innocence after the verdict is in.[69] Few convicts can afford to support intensive investigations in order to secure vindication. The discovery and prosecution of perjury of state witnesses is extremely difficult, the more so because the prosecution's inclination is generally to defend its achievements. It is even more difficult to uncover unintentional distortion, bias, or prevarication of witnesses, and these are far from uncommon, especially among the young, the neurotic, and the psychopathic. Finally, the basic problem in our court procedure of dealing with trial as a legal duel or game of wits, the prize going to the more effective advocate, is too often productive of error.

The Rosenberg-Sobell case illustrates only too well a variety of the influences that may lead to miscarriages of justice in trial and sentencing. Malcom Sharp has pointed to these very effectively in his volume *Was Justice Done? The Rosenberg-Sobell Case*. The conviction of the Rosenbergs was based very largely upon the inculpatory confessions of the accomplices, David and Ruth Greenglass, both of whom had confessed to spying. David Greenglass was convicted and sentenced to fifteen years of imprisonment, while his wife and another confessed accomplice, Max Elitcher, were not brought to trial. At the Rosenberg-Sobell trial, the atmosphere of hysteria and fear prevailed as a consequence of evidence submitted relating to communism at a time when there was widespread anxiety about Russia and espionage. Both the Rosenbergs and Sobell denied their guilt but were convicted on what the trial record reveals to be quite insubstantial evidence. (This is true also of the conviction of Tokyo Rose who, however, was sentenced only to ten years.) The Rosenbergs were sentenced to death, the first time that this penalty has been applied for espionage in a civil court in our history.

The case against Sobell was considerably weaker than that against the Rosenbergs. His conviction appears to have been based upon his acquaintance with Julius Rosenberg, the testimony of the accomplice Elitcher, and Sobell's trip to Mexico with his family shortly after Greenglass was ar-

[69] The "Court of Last Resort," described as an "unofficial board of experts in criminology," has undertaken for several years to aid prisoners who have been wrongfully convicted. Earle Stanley Gardner, in his volume *The Court of Last Resort*, 1952, reviews the first eight cases that were handled by the agency in which they secured reversals or mitigations of sentence on the basis of the facts they had uncovered. In his book Gardner summarized his conclusions: "What we can do is only a drop in the bucket, but we want to contribute that drop. . . . What we need is better justice; more competent, better paid police officers, better investigative work; better proof for juries so that guesswork isn't called for when there should be evidence."

rested. Sobell was sentenced to thirty years, a sentence three times the length of that applied to the British physicist Allan Nunn May, who had confessed to atomic spying in England. As Sharp observed, "The unreliability of confessed accomplices, who may gain lenient treatment by implicating other supposed accomplices in their crimes, is generally recognized; and in the courts of many states convictions cannot be had on the testimony of accomplices alone. No such restrictions are observed in the federal courts. . . . " Convictions on accomplice testimony are especially common in cases involving political issues. Professional witnesses are frequently used by the government, sometimes employees of the police and sometimes former accomplices. In either case, the evidence they give is suspect.

The problem of parole or clemency for the political offender is no less serious. Where the powers of parole and pardon are responsible to that department of government which is concerned chiefly with prosecution and punishment, there is little hope that discretion will be exercised independently to release prisoners whose offenses were political.

SPECIAL PROBLEMS OF JUSTICE

In this chapter it is proposed to consider certain areas where there are specialized problems and legal measures to deal with offenders. Attention will be given to provisions that are made for young defendants, both juvenile and young adult,[1] and for accused persons who suffer from psychological disorder or mental defect. The problems here involved are not new, for both common and civil law have long provided exemptions or mitigations in dealing with these general classes. Such provisions have ordinarily been predicated upon conceptions of criminal responsibility, in particular the doctrine of *mens rea,* requiring a particular state of mind in addition to a prohibited act as a basis of liability to penal measures. Where the accused lacks capacity to entertain the requisite intent because of immaturity or mental condition, he may not be convicted of or punished for crime. Hence, the immunity as defined by law may be interposed as a defense if the person is brought to trial or, if it is recognized in advance, may constitute a bar to the jurisdiction of the court. More refined attention has been devoted to these exemptions in recent years. As the behavioral sciences have given special attention to the young and the deviated, it has appeared both that the traditional rules of law have been excessively rigid and conservative and that the individuals involved have required more specialized adjudicative and treatment provisions. As a result there has been some experimentation and considerable controversy over the circumstances under which special rules should be established and special arrangements made for trial and care.

JUVENILE COURTS

At common law children were granted some exemption from responsibility for nonage or infancy, based upon presumptions relating to their

---

[1] In the author's *Juvenile Delinquency,* 1949, and *Comparative Survey of Juvenile Delinquency,* Part I, North America, 1958, the juvenile court movement and problems associated with its procedures are discussed in some detail. See also Walter Gellhorn et al., *Children and Families in the Courts of New York City,* 1954; A. J. Kahn, *A Court for Children, a Study of the New York City Children's Court,* 1953; and Frederick W. Killian, "The Juvenile Court as an Institution," *The Annals,* vol. 261, p. 89, 1949. Sheldon Glueck's volume, *The Problem of Delinquency,* 1959, is especially valuable.

capacity to entertain a criminal intent.[2] Thus infants and young children under the age of 7 were deemed incapable of committing felony, but thereafter up to the age of 14 responsibility was determined by the individual's understanding and judgment (*doli capax*). He was presumed not to be responsible and his capacity had to be proved. Capital penalties were occasionally applied to children of 8 and over where a "mischievous discretion" was shown. There was no age limit on responsibility for the commission of misdemeanors and children under the age of 7 were occasionally convicted.

The development of a court of chancery jurisdiction in England in the fifteenth century also provided special consideration to children. Equity was designed to provide aid to individuals and classes that could find no proper remedy under the limitations of the somewhat rigid rules that had developed in the common law. Under a chancery jurisdiction the crown asserted a power of *parens patriae* over infants and their estates on the assumption that children as wards of the state were in need of special protection. Chancery functioned primarily, however, in the administration of the estates of well-to-do infants.

With the carrying over of common law and chancery to the Colonies, children came under the ordinary jurisdiction of the criminal courts. As had been true in England, however, they were treated with more tender consideration than adults. The laws of Plymouth Colony reveal that capital punishment for the recalcitrant youth was applied only to those "of sufficient years and understanding," viz., 16. Special legal provisions for probation of juveniles did not occur until 1869 in Massachusetts. During the following year Massachusetts required separate hearings to be held for children's cases in Suffolk County. In a law of 1877, New York prohibited association of the child with adult offenders in institutions, courts, or vehicles and in 1892 provided for separate trials, dockets, and records in cases of children under 16. It was not until 1899, however, that the first juvenile court in the world was established in the United States. Legislation in Illinois creating this court drew together the precedents of institutional segregation, probation supervision, and separate hearings that had already been established, but it also established a philosophy of protection and care that persisted in subsequent juvenile court legislation.

Once the juvenile court movement was founded it spread rapidly both in the United States and abroad.[3] In 1912, twenty-two state jurisdictions had juvenile court legislation, and, by 1925, forty-six. In 1945 the last of the states enacted similar laws. Great Britain adopted such a law in 1908; France, Austria, and Belgium in 1912; Hungary in 1913; Spain in 1918; and Germany in 1923.[4] It is not to be imagined, however, that legislation

---

[2] The rules on responsibility relating to infancy are set out in Blackstone, *Commentaries on the Law of England,* 12th ed., Book IV, chap. 2, p. 21.

[3] See H. H. Lou, *Juvenile Courts in the United States,* 1927.

[4] A useful summary of juvenile court legislation in other countries is compiled in

of this character produced any real uniformity of methods or facilities for dealing with children. Up to the present time we have not yet achieved this goal. In a study published in 1920 Evelina Beldon of the U.S. Children's Bureau noted that the courts she had studied represented "all stages of development away from the old and toward the new ideals and methods." She explained further:[5]

Probation services were few and generally inadequate; jail was the characteristic method of detention; social investigation materials were poor; judges were not qualified for the work. Under the influence of such organizations as the Children's Bureau, the National Probation and Parole Association, and the National Council of Juvenile Court Judges there has been considerable progress in the development of services and a specialization of procedures over the past generation. There is still wide diversity, however, and these courts continue in a process of evolution as to their methods, procedures, goals, jurisdictional coverage, and related matters. . . . Ideas of non-responsibility for crime, educative redirection rather than punishment of the offender, and treatment based on an understanding of the individual—these predecessors of the juvenile court have become co-ordinated in a partial but widely variant degree in the tribunals which specialized in handling the young.

A vivid picture of the diversity both in philosophy and methods that still prevails in dealing with juveniles may be drawn from the varied legal provisions concerning the jurisdictional coverage of the juvenile courts throughout the United States and the extent to which the ordinary criminal courts may or must assert control in children's cases.[6] The present age coverage of children's courts discloses the trend toward increasing their jurisdiction above the age of 16. Thirty-three states provide original juvenile court jurisdiction to the age of 18 for one or both sexes and three provide jurisdiction even to the age of 21. On the other hand, it should be observed that a strong reluctance has persisted to apply the lenient and protective philosophy to all young offenders. In twenty-two jurisdictions the law provides that the criminal courts shall have exclusive jurisdiction over certain offenses, particularly murder. In all but one state there is overlapping or exclusive jurisdiction in the criminal courts, in many of these without regard to the age of the child or the offense with which he was charged. In fact, as a result of statutory law and case decisions, there appears to be no state with the possible exception of Wyoming where the juvenile courts exercise exclusive jurisdiction over all offenses up to the age of 17. As a consequence, young teen-agers occasionally are sentenced as felons to long terms and some of these teen-agers go directly to prison rather than to training schools.

Juvenile Court Laws in Foreign Countries, U.S. Children's Bureau, Publ. No. 328, 1951.

[5] *Courts in the United States Hearing Children's Cases,* U.S. Children's Bureau, Publ. No. 65, 1920.

[6] A table detailing provisions of the states for court jurisdiction appears in the author's *Comparative Survey of Juvenile Delinquency,* Part I, rev., 1958.

The statutory provisions relating to juvenile courts and their jurisdiction are misleading. "Real" juvenile courts, differentiated from other branches of the criminal or civil court system, are relative rarities; they can be found for the most part only in some of the large cities.[7] The best of these juvenile courts are sometimes part of a court of domestic relations. In forty states juvenile authority is centered wholly or in part in courts that serve predominantly some other function: municipal, county, district, circuit, superior, justices of the peace, or probate courts. Most commonly the judge who sits as a juvenile court has criminal jurisdiction and devotes only a relatively small part of his time to children's cases. Frederick Killian has divided children's court structures into the following four chief classes:[8]

1. Independent courts with jurisdiction over children: with city, county or state-wide jurisdiction and with probation services supplied by the court or by city, county or state agencies; mostly in large urban centers (or state-wide courts, as in Utah, Connecticut, and Rhode Island).

2. Family courts with jurisdiction over specified offences and relations and over specified types of family conflict, including jurisdiction over children; services attached or separate; urban centers largely. Of thirty-three family and domestic relations courts listed in The Book of the States, only nineteen possess divorce jurisdiction.

3. Juvenile and domestic relations courts: independent courts or parts of courts with more general jurisdiction; rarely having jurisdiction over divorce and separation; services attached or independent; in urban centers largely.

4. Juvenile courts as sections or parts of courts with more general jurisdiction: judges of the court holding juvenile parts or divisions by designation sometimes in rotation (usually probate, county, circuit or common pleas courts); services attached or separate; more common in non-urban areas and in many urban centers as well.

Procedures of the Juvenile Court

While children's courts have not become fully differentiated from their criminal court origins, statutory changes have generally provided for privacy of hearings, greater informality of procedure, the abolition of jury trial, and in some places the abolition of the right of appeal. Hearings in juvenile court are generally of a summary character. There have been important changes of an administrative character in most of those children's courts that operate as independent courts. They have come to be dominated more by administrative procedures and casework philosophy than by traditional judicial techniques and due process considerations. This is largely because of the influence that casework and child welfare personnel have played in the development of the specialized courts. Many of these people have deplored the restraints of "legalism" upon their benev-

---

[7] See Tappan, "Children and Youth in the Criminal Court," in *The Annals,* vol. 261, pp. 128–137, 1949.

[8] Killian, *op. cit.* (Reprinted by permission.)

olent efforts in behalf of children. They have objected that the "ward" of the court does not require due process protections against the guidance and control they would extend in his behalf. Many judges of juvenile courts have been thoroughly indoctrinated in this view and it has received some support from the appellate courts. One such court put it this way:[9]

To save a child from becoming a criminal, or from continuing in a career of crime, to end in maturer years in public punishment and disgrace, the legislature surely may provide for the salvation of such a child, if its parents or guardian be unable or unwilling to do so, by bringing it into one of the courts of the state without any process at all for the purpose of subjecting it to the state's guardianship and protection. . . . The act simply provides how children who ought to be saved may reach the court to be saved. . . .

In a recent case in Pennsylvania the Supreme Court held that "Since juvenile courts are not criminal courts, the constitutional rights granted to persons accused of crime are not applicable to the children brought before them." The court further alleged that the state was not seeking to punish the defendant as an offender but to salvage him and safeguard his adolescence.[10] Holmes, aged 18, had been sent to an industrial school by the Municipal Court of Philadelphia after being arrested in the company of one who had been operating a stolen car. It was asserted on appeal that the boy was not represented by counsel, that he had not been informed of specific charges against him, that he was not advised of his right to refuse to testify, that testimony submitted at his hearing had been incompetent and inadmissible against him, and that the evidence educed at the hearings had failed to link him with any illegal acts. All this was held irrelevant by the decision of the state supreme court. After his commitment Holmes secured the services of attorneys who brought appeal to the United States Supreme Court on the grounds that the protections of the Fourteenth Amendment against deprivation of liberty without due process had been violated. The Court refused to hear the case.

While other appellate courts have held differently,[11] the general trend of juvenile court procedures has been largely to nullify the due process

[9] *Commonwealth v. Fisher,* 213 Pa. 48 (1905).

[10] *In re Holmes,* 109 A.2d 523 (1955), *cert. denied* 348 U.S. 973.

[11] In *Coyle v. State,* 122 Ind. A. 217 (1953), however, a juvenile court adjudication was reversed, the Supreme Court holding that "Juvenile court procedure has not been so far socialized and individual rights so far diminished that a child may be taken from its parents and placed in a state institution simply because some court might think that to be in the best interests of the state. . . . Some specific act or conduct must be charged as constituting the delinquency and the truth of such charge must be determined in an adversary proceeding." The Court specifically disapproved the argument of the lower court that it was merely "making a determination as to whether or not the appellant's environment indicated that appellant's future training and the best interests of the state" required adjudication and commitment. See also *Jones v. Commonwealth,* 185 Va. 335 (1946).

protections that must be supplied the adult in criminal court. This has been rationalized on the grounds mainly that the child is not accused of "a crime" since juvenile delinquency is not a criminal status, that the purpose is to save or correct rather than to punish, and that the state is acting in the role of parent. It should be noted, however, that juvenile courts employ the same measures of correctional treatment that our criminal courts employ, probation and institutional commitments for the most part.[12] A major difference is that the duration of control of the juvenile is unrelated to the nature of the charge against him. He may be held to the age of 21 and in some states longer. Obviously this may often result in more prolonged imprisonment than the adult criminal would receive for a similar offense. Furthermore, it should be observed that delinquency carries a stigma quite comparable to that attached to the criminal status. In many cases the adjudication and other related experiences may be a more severe psychic blow to the child than criminal conviction is to the adult. The behavior of the state as *parens patriae* is not in reality similar to the protection and care expected from parent or guardian as judges and child welfare workers well realize. Rationalizations that attempt to trace juvenile court methodologies to olden powers of chancery are unconvincing, for chancery did not apply the methods of the juvenile court. The procedures employed by these courts are based not upon chancery but upon the effort to act so far as possible like general agencies of child welfare rather than courts of law that administer what are fundamentally correctional measures.[13] Their attention is focused on "the child who needs help" rather than on the questions: (1) Was the child engaged in conduct requiring legal action? and (2) What measures can be used for his correction and the protection of the community?

What are the problems of substance and method as they have developed in our specialized juvenile courts? Summarized briefly, the major ones are as follows:

1. *Definitions of Delinquency.* One of the central problems of the juvenile court arises out of the failure of the law to establish with any clarity the kinds of cases in which jurisdiction should be taken. This problem contributes heavily to the other difficulties of philosophy and procedure that will be discussed below. It is a basic aspect of the "rule of

---

[12] The U.S. Children's Bureau estimated in 1954 that for the country as a whole more than 40,000 children were committed to training school and 125,000 placed on probation. Their data indicate that approximately 8 per cent of the children who go to juvenile court are committed and 26 per cent are placed on probation. These figures are not very meaningful because more than half of children's court cases are handled unofficially. See *Some Facts about Juvenile Delinquency,* U.S. Children's Bureau, Publ. No. 340, 1955.

[13] This view in relation to the limited significance of chancery origins in modern juvenile court procedure is affirmed in *Standards for Specialized Courts Dealing with Children,* U.S. Children's Bureau, 1954, p. 55.

law" that prohibited conduct should be clearly defined and that penalties should bear some reasonable relationship to the seriousness of the wrong that the defendant has done and his dangerousness to the community. These principles have been evaded under our juvenile court laws.

Most of the provisions defining delinquency are vague and moralistic, inviting invidious value judgments.[14] In about one-third of the states, which have followed a model act of the National Probation and Parole Association, delinquency is not defined at all. Only the jurisdiction of the court is prescribed. Consequently, to a great extent delinquency is what the particular court says it is. Nearly one-half of the cases that are adjudicated delinquent each year are held for acts of carelessness or mischief, truancy, running away, and being ungovernable. Considerably more than half the cases of girls held delinquent are in these categories. This is in marked contrast to the situation in Canada, England, and the Scandinavian countries where children are usually adjudicated only for serious and specific misconduct.[15]

2. *Unofficial Treatment without Court Adjudication.*[16] Intake of cases in juvenile court is comparable to, but in some respects more important than, the taking of complaints in criminal court. Ordinarily the function is performed by a probation officer who may exercise broad discretion in determining whether cases should appear before the judge. If it is determined that the case is not appropriate for court action, the intake officer may refer it to some other agency for help, if any is needed. Such referral should be an extremely important function of the juvenile court. In most cities, unfortunately, the courts rarely refer cases, preferring to exercise control themselves. This has given rise to the practice of handling cases unofficially. Such cases, "held at intake," sometimes without producing

[14] For a list of the definitions established by statute for juvenile delinquency in the United States, see Frederick B. Sussman, *Law of Juvenile Delinquency,* 1950, p. 20.

[15] For details relating to the handling of delinquency in Canada, see Tappan, *op. cit.* On Scandinavian practice see Tappan, *Intervention by the Courts or by Other Authorities in the Case of Socially Maladjusted Children and Juveniles,* II, *The Competent Authorities,* Stockholm, 1958, and Thorsten Sellin, "Sweden's Substitute for the Juvenile Court," *The Annals,* vol. 261, pp. 137–150, 1949.

[16] In relation to unofficial court treatment the Children's Bureau has taken a strong position against the use of unofficial handling or informal adjustment except by the very limited measures at intake of referring the child or his family to an appropriate social agency or of conducting a conference between the complainant and the child or his family to determine whether the filing of a petition may be obviated. The standards of the Bureau point to the danger of abuse of power through the employment of unofficial treatment and indicate that this leads to "distortion in the minds of some as to the functioning of the court and confuses the role of the court with that of the social agencies in the community." The court should not abridge the rights of a child or his parents or apply authoritative measures, in particular probation, without holding a hearing on the basis of a formal petition. See *Standards for Specialized Courts Dealing with Children,* pp. 43–44 (hereafter referred to as *Standards*).

them before a judge, may be turned over to the probation department for such treatment as it may be able to supply. This treatment may range from brief supervision and counseling to extended control under unofficial probation. In some cases it involves also a remand to a detention facility or, less commonly, to a training school either by the "voluntary" agreement of the parties or by order of the court. The use of these unofficial devices may be rationalized as a means of avoiding unnecessary court action or the stigma of delinquency. The practical effect, however, is greatly to increase probation case loads, largely with children who should not be handled by court personnel at all. In this country more than 50 per cent of delinquency cases are dealt with unofficially.[17] In these instances the fact of delinquency has not been determined. It is clear that minimal standards of justice for children require that those who are not delinquent should not be on probation of any kind. Those who are believed to be delinquent are entitled to have the issue tried before any treatment is applied.

3. *Peculiarities of Court Procedure. Prehearing* investigations are conducted by probation officers, with reports submitted to the court at the hearing. It will be observed that this practice is in contrast to the procedure of criminal courts under which *presentence* investigations are conducted only if and after defendants are convicted. The defendant under a criminal charge has a right under due process not to be investigated by the court before trial. If this protection were not provided, the court might be misled by irrelevant, incompetent, and prejudicial material that could result in unjust conviction based on the defendant's social history rather than on proof of his criminal conduct. In contrast to this rule the probation reports in juvenile court are not infrequently the major basis of the court's decision whether to adjudicate the child a delinquent. Often the child is not even aware of the content of the probation report on the basis of which his adjudication occurs. Thus hearsay evidence that is not subject to cross-examination, commonly unverified rumor and gossip, become foundations of court action. The procedure is rationalized on the theory that juvenile court adjudication as well as treatment should be based on *why,* rather than *whether,* the child has been in trouble. It is said that delinquent conduct is unimportant except as a symptom of underlying problems and that these symptoms, not the delinquency, should be the object of inquiry.[18]

[17] In 1954 some 56 per cent of the delinquency cases reported to the Bureau were handled unofficially. In the state of Washington one court disposed of only 9 per cent of its cases officially while another disposed of 83 per cent by official methods.

[18] Pauline V. Young, *Social Treatment in Probation and Delinquency,* 1937, p. 184. The Children's Bureau has taken somewhat of a compromise position on the subject of prehearing investigations, indicating that the social study should be commenced when the petition is filed *except* where the child denies his delinquency or where the intake officer has reasonable doubt that the child was involved. Where guilt is in

The dominant role played by probation in determining whether children should be held delinquent and what treatment should be applied may be extended even further where, as in a number of cities, a probation officer acts as referee in place of a judge.[19] Hearings are private and almost always without a jury. In a good many juvenile courts lawyers are excluded either officially or unofficially on the curious theory that the probation officer acts as counsel to the child. In some courts, only incomplete minutes are taken of the hearing and appeal may not be allowed. Where these circumstances exist, the "rule of law" is virtually extinct. The procedures and accomplishment of such courts can be accepted only on faith and in matters of law where personal liberty is at stake, this is not enough.

COURTS FOR YOUNG ADULTS

Juvenile courts have had high acclaim from the advocates of its form of "socialized jurisprudence" and until quite recently have suffered little critical scrutiny either from the legal profession or from criminologists. This may explain, at least in part, the fact that the procedures and philosophy of these courts have been recommended from time to time for

---

issue, the court should not have access to prejudicial social data unless and until there has been a finding of delinquency. See *Standards*, pp. 36–52. The difficulty with this principle is that in effect it requires a determination on guilt before the child has had a hearing. Where, as is usually the case, he is not represented by counsel, certainly neither the child nor the intake officer is in a position to make such a decision. Connecticut has laid down the rule that if the child is charged with an offense that would be a crime if committed by an adult social investigation material may not be presented to the judge and the hearing must follow the ordinary rules of evidence. If, on the other hand, an adjudication merely for the welfare of the child is involved, the social investigation material may be submitted to the court. See *Appeal of Dattilo,* 136 Conn. 488 (1951).

[19] The *Standards* volume takes the position that referees should be members of the Bar with experience in legal practice and that the office of referee should be distinct from that of the probation staff. The Children's Bureau holds that the child and his family should be informed of their right to counsel and, where they cannot employ an attorney, the court should make counsel available. See *Standards*, p. 49. The Bureau observes the unfortunate consequences of the generally prevailing attitude in juvenile courts toward representation: "The feeling that the attorney has no place in the proceedings in these courts has, unfortunately, gained favor in some quarters. As a result, it is not uncommon to find that the attorney representing the child or his family is considered by some social workers or probation officers and even occasionally by some judges as an adversary whose only purpose is to oppose any recommendations or plans which the court may have under consideration. This attitude indicates the need for more understanding of the lawyer's role in the judicial process and recognition of the individual's right to counsel. Such an attitude fails to recognize that the attorney, if aware of the basic principles and objectives of the specialized court, can be of inestimable assistance in the resolution of the problems presented with respect to his client and in bringing before the court all facts needed to make such a resolution successfully." P. 99.

dealing with other offenders. In any event, as we have come to recognize increasingly the serious problem of young adult offenders in the ages of the late teens and early twenties, the tendency has been to try to cope with this group, too, through the juvenile court. For want of other device, jurisdiction of children's courts has been advanced very generally in recent years to care for youths above the age of 16. This has been true in spite of the fact that young adults from 16 to 21 or 23 are a problem quite distinct from children of the early teens and below and from the ordinary adult criminal population.[20] They are a more criminal, recidivous, and unstable group of offenders, in need of occupational training and firm correctional measures. A recognition of their difference is expressed in the fact that for many years young adult offenders have been committed to reformatories and prisons rather than to juvenile training schools. The inappropriateness of juvenile court treatment for this group of offenders is implicit also in the conflicting provisions on court jurisdiction for teen-agers in the statutes of most of the states. However, juvenile courts have been the only specialized facilities readily at hand and have been used increasingly for young adults.

The special significance of the problem of young adult offenders received some recognition in the reformatory movement of the late nineteenth century in this country and in the development of the Borstals in England. The reformatory movement stagnated after a relatively few years and is only recently being revived with new experimental diagnostic and treatment facilities. However, in 1940 a new impetus to change was stimulated by the A.L.I. in two model bills, one for the Youth Correction Authority, the other for a youth court act. The first of these is described in Chapter 16. The court act was not actively supported by the Institute but it did express clear recognition of a need for special court facilities for the young adult group. The act itself and the reasoning behind it has had some influence on developments in New York and on recent proposals of the A.L.I. in its Model Penal Code.

Youth Courts in New York

New York State is the only jurisdiction thus far that has developed a complex system of specialized courts for offenders over 16 years of age.[21] These courts have been the product of an interesting evolution running back to the early 1930s. Even before this date the Wayward Minor Act of

---

[20] On this point see commentary in the *Model Penal Code,* Drafts No. 3 and 7, relating to the young adult offender; Thorsten Sellin, *The Criminality of Youth,* American Law Institute, 1940; and issue on the youthful offender, *N.P.P.A. J.,* vol. 2, April, 1956.

[21] See Mary C. Kohler, "The Courts for Handling Youths," *N.P.P.A. J.,* vol 2, pp. 123–142, April, 1956; Tappan, "The Adolescent in Court," *J. Crim. L.,* vol. 37, pp. 216–230, 1946, and *Delinquent Girls in Court,* 1947; Gellhorn, *op. cit.;* Frederick J. Ludwig, *Youth and the Law,* 1955.

1923 had been used to some extent in the magistrates' courts to deal with recalcitrant youngsters over juvenile court age.[22] This law provides that youths between the ages of 16 and 21 who are "willfully disobedient to the reasonable and lawful commands of their parents or guardians and in danger of becoming morally depraved" may be adjudicated wayward minors and may be committed for an indefinite sentence up to three years.[23] Magistrates can reduce more serious charges to the wayward minor complaint, thus avoiding a criminal record. At one time the statute was used frequently in the Women's Court of New York City to deal with girls who were considered wayward or promiscuous. A Wayward Minor Court for Girls was established independent of the Women's Court in 1935, primarily to deal with morals offenses of girls between the ages of 16 and 21. This court is now known officially as Girls Term. In 1935 and 1936 Adolescent Courts were established by authority of the Board of Magistrates in Brooklyn and Queens to deal with offenders between the ages of 16 and 19 under the Wayward Minor Law. In these courts youths accused of felony or misdemeanor who were considered good risks were permitted to plead to the wayward minor charge rather than go to a county court for trial.

The court procedures both in the Adolescent Courts and in Girls Term have been patterned to a large extent on those of the juvenile courts: pre-hearing investigations are used to determine whether those accused are appropriate subjects for wayward minor treatment. Hearings are based largely on probation officers' reports concerning the defendants' social histories. There is no trial of the issue of guilt on the crime charged. The noncriminal status of wayward minor is applied. The informal and private proceedings in these courts have little semblance to the due process ordinarily considered essential in dealing with individuals accused of felonies. Probation is applied in a majority of cases and commitments are fixed under the law at three-year indefinite terms.[24]

[22] Legislation of this sort appears to have been drawn in the main from juvenile court laws, but similar policy has developed for young adults over children's court age in several jurisdictions. There are youth courts in Chicago and Philadelphia.

[23] There are several clauses in the Wayward Minor Statute defining the conduct involved. The definition given here has been used most commonly in the Adolescent Courts in New York. See Tappan, *Delinquent Girls in Court,* 1947, and "The Adolescent in Court," *J. Crim. L.,* vol. 37, pp. 216–230, 1946.

[24] Proposals have been made recurrently that the Adolescent Court should be made city-wide, thus avoiding the invidious consequences of differing treatment of offenders according to the borough in which they live. There has been sufficient opposition, largely from the county courts, to prevent this. This opposition is partly caused by the apparent irregularity involved in permitting inferior courts to make final disposition in cases involving felonies, without the defendants' enjoying normal rights of due process. It now appears quite improbable that the Adolescent Court development will be extended. Their activities, already considerably restricted, will be still further curtailed or eliminated by the developments under the Youth Offender Law.

In 1943 the Youth Offender Law was enacted, establishing in the county courts throughout the state and in the Special Sessions Court in New York City, special terms of court for the trial of young adults between the ages of 16 and 19 accused of misdemeanors and felonies. Upon the recommendation of the grand jury or prosecutor or upon the determination of the judge, a youth may be permitted to consent to a pretrial investigation to determine whether he should be tried as a "youthful offender" rather than for the crime of which he has been accused. Thus, here again, in connection with the process of selection of "worthy cases" for special leniency, the device of prehearing probation studies is employed, as in the Adolescent Courts and juvenile courts. There are other important similarities. The hearing is private. There is no jury trial. A noncriminal status adjudication rather than conviction is used. Probation is most frequently employed and commitments are for a period of three years. If the offender is deemed inappropriate for treatment under the Youth Offender Law, he must go to trial in the ordinary criminal court.

There is one very important distinction between Adolescent Court procedures and those prescribed by the Youth Offender Law. According to the latter, the defendant who is accepted for handling as a youthful offender may deny his guilt and receive a trial before a judge in the special term to determine whether he has committed the crime alleged. If he is found guilty he will nevertheless be adjudicated a youthful offender rather than being convicted of the crime. Theoretically his chances of receiving probation are as great as though he had pleaded guilty to the charge. Under this statutory provision for trial of the issue, therefore, the young offender is not required to take a plea in order to be eligible for handling in the special court and the special sentencing provisions. Unfortunately, there is some indication that in certain county courts judges have adopted the policy, the statute withal, of requiring the youthful defendant to plead guilty if he is to be treated as a youthful offender. Where this is the practice we encounter again the deprivation of due process rights through a kind of bargaining process in which the defendant is assured relatively lenient treatment along with a noncriminal status.

In 1956, as the consequence of the recommendations of a special court commission in New York, the law relating to youthful offenders was extended to cover individuals from 16 to 21.[25] Court and newspaper opposition led to a postponement of implementation of the law until 1960. Under the provisions of this statute, *all* offenders in the age range from 16 to 18 without prior felony convictions will be handled automatically in special terms of the county courts. Offenders between 18 and 21, however, will go through a prehearing investigation. This device will determine those who should be spared criminal conviction and sentenced to terms with a three- or a five-year maximum rather than to the ordinary terms provided by the penal law for the crimes involved.

[25] See Kohler, *loc cit.*

The Federal Youth Corrections Act

Under Federal legislation, enacted in 1950 and implemented in 1953, special provisions have been established for the sentencing and treatment of young offenders over juvenile court age up to the age of 22.[26] In 1958 the coverage was extended to the age of 26. Here the author will discuss only the court and sentencing aspect of this legislation. The law does not provide either for special courts or for trial procedures. Defendants are handled under ordinary due process of law up to the point of sentencing.

At the time of sentence, however, the judge is given wider powers of treatment decision than are available for older offenders. The law contains several unique features. The court may sentence an individual to a six-year term of which he may be required to spend as many as four years in imprisonment in a specialized treatment institution. Under the provisions of the statute, a Youth Correction Division has been established as part of the U.S. Board of Parole. This division has power to release the offender at any time after his commitment and must do so by the end of his fourth year. Parole supervision is provided in every instance for a period of at least one year and discharge from supervision must occur by the end of the six-year period.

If the court believes this four- to six-year term inadequate, it may sentence the offender either for the term provided in the United States Code for the offense involved or for such shorter period as it may deem appropriate. In the latter case, too, the offender must be released under parole supervision at least two years prior to the expiration of his term. Where the court is uncertain of the type of sentence that should be applied, it is empowered to remand the offender for study at a classification center, requiring that the Youth Division make a recommendation on sentence within sixty days after such remand.

Provisions under the Model Penal Code of the American Law Institute

The A.L.I. proposes legislation in its Model Penal Code relating to the young adult offender as part of its broader Code provisions on the substantive criminal law and treatment. The recommendations include special provisions relating to courts, sentencing, and treatment of young adults. The treatment proposals are discussed elsewhere in this volume.

The Code envisions the establishment of special parts of criminal courts for the trial and sentencing of offenders between the ages of 16, or above juvenile court age, and 22.[27] *All* offenders in this age group who are accused of felony or misdemeanor would be processed through the special young adult offender parts of court. The purpose is not to provide leni-

[26] 18 U.S.C., secs. 5005–5026.
[27] *Model Penal Code,* Draft No. 7, appendix A: "Supplemental Provisions Establishing a Special Part of Court for Young Adult Offenders," American Law Institute, 1957.

ency or rehabilitation to some highly selective group that might be considered deserving cases but so far as possible to specialize sentencing and treatment for young adult offenders as a class. Defendants tried in these special parts would be accorded all ordinary rights of due process, including public trial, a specific charge, the protections of the traditional rules of evidence, and the right to counsel. They would be permitted preliminary hearings, grand jury indictment, and jury trial but could waive any of these as criminals may generally do in our courts. There would be some special advantage in their waiving the first two in many cases in order that they might be spared unnecessary detention before trial.

Under the proposals advanced, there would be no pretrial investigations, since these violate a basic due process right and can be used to prejudice the court on the issue of guilt. All offenders convicted, however, would be investigated by the probation department prior to sentence. It is contemplated that such investigations would be performed with particular care and completeness and would include, when necessary, psychiatric examinations. Thus an optimum amount of guidance would be available to the court at the time of sentencing.

Where the defendant is found guilty after trial, his conviction would be for the offense charged rather than for some noncriminal status. The Code provides, however, that conviction may be vacated in either of two ways: (1) at the time of sentence, if the sentence is to the special indefinite term of imprisonment described below or to any sentence other than imprisonment, or (2) upon unconditional discharge from probation or parole before the expiration of the maximum term.[28] In either case an order of the court would be required. These provisions should help to motivate offenders to work toward their own rehabilitation. It will be observed that for the most part these provisions conform to traditional criminal court procedures in dealing with other offenders. However the establishment of special parts of court for young adults should serve the following significant functions: (1) segregation of the relatively young and impressionable from matured offenders; (2) expedition in the handling of cases, by reducing unnecessary delays; (3) curtailment of unnecessary and prolonged detention during trial; (4) encouragement of specialization of court personnel, leading to sounder trial and sentencing practice; and (5) the establishment of closer liaison with state reception-diagnostic and correctional administration. Specialization could not be carried so far, of course, in less populous communities as in large cities, but even in the former the avoidance of unnecessary delays and the devotion of special attention to the trial and sentencing of such cases should serve a useful purpose.

The special sentencing measures set out in the Code constitute an important phase of the provisions for the young adult offender. Where it appears that a shorter term than that established for ordinary offenders

[28] *Model Penal Code,* sec. 6.05 (3).

would be adequate for his rehabilitation and for the protection of the public, the court may at its discretion sentence the young adult convicted of a felony to a term with a maximum of four years and without a minimum. In the alternative the court could sentence him to the ordinary or extended terms provided in the Code for other offenders.[29] Young adult offenders would be committed, in any case where the court decided that imprisonment was necessary, to a young adult correction division of the department of correction to receive individualized correctional and rehabilitative treatment.

MENTAL ABNORMALITY

In an earlier chapter mental abnormalities were divided into two large classes: the diseases and disorders that include psychoses, psychoneuroses, and psychopathy on the one hand and mental deficiency on the other. The mental condition of the defendant may be relevant in several different ways, so far as court procedure and treatment are concerned. The question may be raised at the start whether he is fit to proceed to trial. Here the question is one of his ability to understand the nature of the proceedings and to participate in the preparation of his defense. In some jurisdictions, if the defendant is found to be psychotic, it is customary to commit him to a mental hospital without specific inquiry into his capacity to defend.

If a defendant goes to trial, whether or not there has been an inquiry into his fitness to proceed, the defense of insanity may be raised. In six states notice of intention to rely on this defense is required by statute and in eight others it must be specially pleaded.[30] In most jurisdictions proof, which is submitted by experts hired by the defense and the prosecution, must accord with certain traditional rules on insanity. These rules are discussed below.

Twenty states provide for psychiatric examination by court-appointed psychiatrists or public hospital staff psychiatrists in determining whether the defense of insanity should prevail. Short of a mental condition that might exculpate the defendant, data derived from psychiatric examination or other evidence may tend to prove that he was in such mental state as not to be culpable under the statutory requirement for proof of *mens rea,* e.g., where knowledge or purpose to commit the prohibited act is required and it may be shown that he was in an unconscious, stuporous, or some other condition negating the required intent. The psychopathology of the defendant may also be considered relevant by the court in determining what disposition to make of his case at sentence. Such characteristics as

---

[29] See the *Model Penal Code,* secs. 6.05, 6.06, and 6.07, for the provisions relating to young adults and to ordinary and extended terms. Also see pp. 468 f. below.

[30] See the *Model Penal Code,* Commentary on Draft No. 4, sec. 4.03, pp. 193–194.

excessive aggression, psychopathic personality, alcoholism or drug addiction, or compulsive neurosis, for example, may be considered relevant to the nature and duration of the sentence he should receive.

Finally, any mental deviation supervening after trial and sentence may be significant for reclassification for treatment. It is the general rule that offenders who become insane may not be subjected to capital punishment so long as the disability continues and that psychotic prisoners may be committed to a mental hospital. In the case of less serious pathology observed in a prisoner, any apparent need for change in treatment is a matter for correctional administration. Where institutional facilities are sufficiently diversified, offenders suffering some form of serious disturbance may be transferred to an appropriate institution for treatment.

The law has recognized extreme abnormality as a ground for relief from criminal responsibility over a long period of time. No effort has been made, however, to distinguish between different forms of abnormality. At common law a man could be punished for serious crime only with a showing of *animo felonico,* a felonious intent, and so it was held that the "lunatick" might be held in action of trespass for damages or for a misdemeanor but not for felony.[31] In the eighteenth and nineteenth centuries various tests were employed in England to determine whether defendants should be excused for madness:[32] the twenty-pence test, based upon the ability to count and read; the child of 14 test, in which the issue was whether the accused had understanding as great as that of a child of that age; the wild beast test, where it was held that to escape punishment the madman must be totally deprived of understanding and memory so as to know what he was doing no more than a brute or wild beast knows; and the good and evil test, predicated upon "a natural disability of distinguishing between good and evil, as infants under the age of discretion, idiots, and lunatics."

The test of greatest historical importance, an elaboration of the wild beast and the right-wrong tests, was laid down in the famous M'Naghten's case[33] in 1843 after the defendant, suffering from a delusional psychosis, had killed Drummond, the secretary to Sir Robert Peel, who he believed was persecuting him. The jury's finding that he was not guilty by reason of insanity led to public outcry and to a debate in the House of Lords and the direction of an inquiry to the judges. The Lord Chief Justice Tindal, with the agreement of all but one of the judges of the King's Bench, replied to a series of questions posed by the Lords concerning the "nature and extent of the unsoundness of mind which would excuse the commission of a felony of this sort." He advised that to establish the defense "it must be

[31] See *Calendar of Close Rolls, Edward I,* 7 Edw. 1 (1278), p. 518.

[32] See Michael and Wechsler, *Criminal Law and Its Administration,* 1940, pp. 807–821, for the development of rules relating to insanity as a defense, together with some of the cases. Also consult Henry Weihofen, *Mental Disorder as a Criminal Defense,* 1954.

[33] *M'Naghten's Case,* House of Lords (1843), 10 Cl & F. 200, 8 Eng. (Repr. 718).

clearly proved that, at the time of the committing of the act, the party accused was labouring under such a defect of reason, from disease of the mind, as not to know the nature and quality of the act he was doing; or, if he did know it, that he did not know he was doing what was wrong." Specifically with relation to delusions Tindal held that if the defendant "labours under such partial delusions only, and is not in other respects insane, we think he must be considered in the same situation as to responsibility as if the facts with respect to which the delusion exists were real." Reliance has generally been put upon the first of these formulations in the numerous jurisdictions that have come to follow the M'Naghten rules.

Either by statute (in seven states) or by case decision the M'Naghten right-wrong test is employed in forty-five or forty-six states, the Federal jurisdiction, and the U.S. Army.[34] Fifteen or more of these states combine with this rule an irresistible impulse test that may be applied, as one judge has stated it, where "while the mental perception is unimpaired, the mind is powerless to control the will; that while its unhappy subject knows the right, and desires to pursue it, some mysterious and uncontrollable impulse compels him to commit the wrong."[35] The English authority J. F. Stephen and the British courts have held that a lack of capacity to control one's impulses in itself implies that the individual does not know the nature of his act or cannot function in the light of his knowledge.[36] Others have rejected the irresistible impulse test on the ground that, if such incapacity may in fact exist, it cannot be distinguished by reliable proof from an unwillingness to assert the needed control.

New Hampshire specifically rejected the M'Naghten test in the case of *State v. Jones*[37] in 1871 and in its place established the "product test," holding that a defendant should be held not guilty by reason of insanity if his act was "the offspring or product of mental disease." This test has been considered and rejected in other jurisdictions in the belief, as one court has put it, that it would provide "cranks . . . an easy path to immunity from any crimes they might commit." However, in 1954, in the case of *Durham v. United States,*[38] the Court of Appeals for the District of Columbia formulated a similar test, namely, "that an accused is not criminally res-

---

[34] The burden of proof where insanity is raised as a defense may be either upon the prosecution to establish beyond a reasonable doubt, the rule in twenty-one states, or upon the defense to establish it by a preponderance of evidence, the rule in twenty-one states. See the *Model Penal Code, loc. cit.* The M'Naghten rule is also employed quite generally in the British Commonwealth countries. In the Scandinavian countries, however, the defense is based upon a determination by medical experts that the defendant is irresponsible by reason of insanity or of a comparable condition or of gross mental deficiency.

[35] *Cunningham v. State,* 56 Miss. 269 (1879). The Mississippi court rejected the defense.

[36] Stephen, *History of the Criminal Law,* vol. 2, pp. 169 f.

[37] 50 N.H. 369 (1871).

[38] 214 F.2d 862 (1954).

ponsible if his unlawful act was the product of mental disease or defect." The decision has had wide support, mostly from psychiatrists.[39] Lawyers, on the other hand, have criticized the holding, mainly on the grounds, first, that it does not define disease or defect (which might be taken to include minor emotional deviations and psychopathies) and, second, that it provides no standard for determining causal relationship between the disorder and the criminal act. Under a holistic conception of personality, it might well be held that any offense reflects in part the temporary or permanent emotional deviations of the actor. If the defendant is found to have been in some measure disturbed, it would not be difficult for some psychiatrists to find that he was nonresponsible.

A rather different test has been put forward in the Model Penal Code.[40] This would hold the defendant not responsible if "at the time of such conduct as a result of mental disease or defect he lacks substantial capacity either to appreciate the criminality of his conduct or to conform his conduct to the requirements of law." Like the Durham rule, the design of this test is to liberalize the defense of insanity, but its sweep is more limited, for the central issue is one of *substantial incapacity* of the mind limiting the defendant's understanding and control: an issue of fact for the jury. It would leave for *ad hoc* decision the question of what is a sufficiently substantial incapacity.[41]

Perhaps no rule of law has been more widely criticized and yet so generally preserved as the M'Naghten test. Its critics have pointed in the main to these alleged defects: (1) The test is entirely rationalistic, predicating the defense simply on the issue of intellectual capacity without regard to emotional and volitional aberrations that may flow from psychosis. (2) It allows the defense only in the most extreme case of disorder, where the defendant was wholly bereft of reason, and hence permits the punishment of many who are obviously and seriously psychotic. (3) The test poses an impossible and inappropriate task for the psychiatrist, who is presumably qualified to determine whether the defendant is mentally ill before trial but who may not be able to discover whether the defendant was insane at the time of the offense. The psychiatrist cannot, as a medical matter, reach any reliable conclusion on the defendant's capacity to dis-

[39] See, for example, *Insanity and the Criminal Law—A Critique of Durham v. United States, U. Chi. L. Rev.,* vol. 22, pp. 317 f., 1955; Cavanagh, "A Psychiatrist Looks at the Durham Decision," *Catholic U.L. Rev.,* vol. 5, p. 25, 1955; Stockly, "Mental Disorders and Criminal Responsibility: The Recommendations of the Royal Commission on Capital Punishment," *Texas L. Rev.,* vol. 33, p. 482, 1955, and Notes, *Ind. L. J.,* vol. 30, p. 194, 1955; *U. Cinc. L. Rev.,* vol. 24, p. 110, 1955. See also *Model Penal Code,* Commentary on Sec. 4.01, Draft No. 4, pp. 156 f.

[40] *Op. cit.,* p. 27.

[41] Two proposals made by the English Royal Commission on Capital Punishment in regard to the insanity defense would leave to the jury the determination of "whether at the time of the act the accused was suffering from disease of the mind or mental deficiency to such a degree that he ought not to be held responsible." *Report of the Commission,* 1953, par. 333, p. 116.

tinguish between right and wrong. (4) The psychiatrist is placed in an anomalous position, furthermore, by being required to give dogmatic reply to long and artificial "hypothetical questions" about the responsibility of the accused that have no relationship to the psychiatric diagnosis that he has made. (5) The adversary system of employing expert witnesses produces an ignoble spectacle of unscientific controversy between scientists.[42] Some few psychiatrists openly express the view that, since the duty of physicians is to save life and improve health, not to act as instruments for destructive ends, they cannot ethically testify that a defendant is responsible and therefore, by implication, deserves punishment.

There is some soundness in these arguments. Perhaps more than anything else the controversy reflects the fundamental difficulties that are involved in an effort to determine either as a matter of general rule or of individual application what degree and kind of psychological disorder should relieve the individual from the application of correctional sanctions. This involves something more than the obvious moral or metaphysical questions that have usually been raised concerning responsibility. The issues have become increasingly controversial under the influence of neodeterministic theories of human behavior, theories which have shifted the debate to a very large extent from questions of punishment for culpability to other quite different questions concerning the feasibility of effective deterrence and treatment of individuals through the application of penal sanctions. We are beginning to recognize that the important question is the probable future response of the accused and of the community to the measures that may be applied.

As some psychiatrists increasingly argue for the broad extension of

[42] The American Psychiatric Association elicited from its membership questionnaire replies concerning their attitudes toward the current procedures for presenting psychiatric testimony in criminal cases. They expressed dissatisfaction on the following grounds: Hampered by categorical and unqualified questions to be answered "Yes" or "No." Limitations imposed by question method rather than exposition. Judges and lawyers not psychiatrically oriented. Confusion in definition of insanity by law and medicine. Basic difference in medical and legal point of view because of widely dissimilar frames of reference. Narrowness of legal focus. Hypothetical question. Degree of satisfaction varies with the judge. Degree of satisfaction varies with intelligence and honesty of the attorneys. Lawyers shop for favorable psychiatric opinion and have little interest in eliciting truth. Judges and lawyers have no respect for partisan witnesses. Legal rules permit lawyers to distort psychiatric opinion. Cross-examination is battle of wits and does not elicit truth. Legal concepts and procedures archaic. Legal concepts emphasize the importance of the crime rather than the criminal. Insufficient time in which to make adequate examination. Lack of concept of partial responsibility. Psychiatrist's lack of legal training. Lack of concept of irresistible impulse. Courts do not give proper importance to the history in a medical case. Illogical position of the law in regard to neurotic characters and psychopaths. See Manfred S. Guttmacher, "Principal Difficulties with the Present Criteria of Responsibility and Possible Alternatives," *Model Penal Code,* Draft No. 4, appendix B, pp. 170 f., and by the same author, "The Psychiatrist as an Expert Witness," *U. Chi. L. Rev.,* vol. 22, p. 325, 1955.

defenses for the emotionally disordered and at the same time define mental aberrations in vague terms that are not meaningful to lawyers, the problems of defense, mitigation, and correction or treatment, always difficult enough, have become more complex and confused. If, as Will Menninger has maintained, everyone becomes disturbed to a more or less seriously pathological extent at one time or another, and some individuals violate the law during such periods, what should society do to reduce these violations among potential offenders and to discourage repetition among those who have channeled their psychological-deviation pressures in crime? If one out of ten becomes psychotic, should they be relieved of criminal responsibility? We must also ask and seek answers to other difficult questions. The following are only a few of the more obvious: Is criminal conviction or a finding of "guilty but insane" more damaging in itself to the violator than a finding merely of insanity? Will the public be as greatly protected if the care of offenders is transferred from the correctional department to mental health authorities? What would be the relative effectiveness of the correctional program of a prison or medical-correctional facility and the care provided by state mental hospitals for the types of individuals involved and their emotional-behavioral problems? What would be the comparative length and cost of retention in the two types of facilities? Would planning for release and community supervision differ significantly? The answers to these questions would not be the same for every state. They may change from time to time with the further development of facilities both in the correctional and mental health fields. It appears at this time, however, that so far as criminals who are minor emotional deviates, ordinary psychoneurotics, and psychopathic personalities are concerned neither the climate nor the program of the typical hospital for the mentally ill is appropriate to their needs. While the ordinary prison may be something less than ideal, some specialized form of correctional institution[43] appears to offer better hope for meeting the problem of deviated offenders who are not handled effectively in the hospital environment.

While we lack answers to many of the important questions, we must nevertheless continue from day to day to apply some general policy to the aberrant criminal while looking for such improvements as the growth of our knowledge and facilities may permit. In what direction should we look for change? It appears that there are three challenging major and general areas in which policy decisions need to be made and such laws and procedures developed as appear to be called for: (1) the possible redefinition of mental aberration as a defense to crime, (2) the more specialized and effective handling of relatively minor emotional deviates, and (3) the development of better procedures for determining, after in-

---

[43] Separate, specialized medical-correctional facilities are operated in the Federal system and in California, New York, Maryland, and Massachusetts.

dictment or arraignment, what cases should not go to criminal trial. These matters are discussed below.

The first question raises the issue of the adequacy of the M'Naghten rule as a basis for exemption from criminal responsibility. Despite all of the criticisms that it has been subjected to, there is strong argument in its favor. The rule in its original intendment was designed to provide defense only in the extreme case where the absence of criminal capacity and intent were clear from the defendant's inability to know what he was doing or that it was wrong. As a matter of individual prevention and deterrence there is some justification for such a policy. It may be argued that a wider range of defense should be supported only when experts can draw some other rather precise line to excuse individuals who will respond to available psychiatric therapies and who cannot respond to criminal trial and correctional treatment. The burden here must be placed upon the behavioral specialists. While the M'Naghten standard rests upon criteria of intellection, which is only a part of human motivation, and perhaps the lesser part, it is particularly in the area of intelligence and reason that the field of psychology can make reasonably accurate appraisals, while calculations relating to emotional or volitional capacity and behavior are highly uncertain. Even so, while the traditional rule does not take into account the potency of these psychic elements, they have already been introduced to a very large if not excessive extent, considering our lack of ability to evaluate their significance. This has occurred as a result of the "irresistible impulse rule," under which juries attempt in effect to weigh the stress of the will and the emotions. It has also developed under the right-wrong test itself as expert witnesses for the defense have reinterpreted the meaning of a defendant's "knowledge" of his act and its wrongfulness. Psychiatric conceptions of "the extent of ego participation in the act," "dominance of the id," "lack of volitional control," and other undefined imponderables are implicit in much of contemporary psychiatric testimony. And, as psychiatric theory is either delivered in the original jargon or translated into lay terminology by the experts, jurors too, however crudely, apply the elastic measures of will and emotions to the defendant's behavior.

The M'Naghten rule has proved one of the most flexible doctrines among all modern rules of law, allowing as it has for the introduction of emerging and quite often conflicting interpretations of the human psyche. There is little doubt that the ordinary jury, drawing such inferences as it can from expert testimony on the motivations of the defendant's conduct, arrives at its conclusion about criminal responsibility on the basis of what it considers to be "just" in the light of its sense concerning the defendant's understanding, emotional motivations, capacity for control, and the need for public protection. Juries will almost inevitably continue to do this even if the formal rule on insanity as a defense is moderately liberalized. Query what juries will do if the notion becomes popular that violent crimes and other offenses against the person are generally the products of diseased minds? Presumably one result of committing disturbed criminals to mental institutions would be that the hospitals would become more like our prisons, at least so far as custodial measures are concerned. Whether they would also develop the active programs of occupational training, academic education, and diversified work that are found in modern correctional institutions is less certain.

However the M'Naghten rule may be liberalized, by a continuing process of reinterpretation or by statutory change and case decisions, it appears highly probable that we shall continue to face special problems relating to less-than-psychotic emotional deviates who commit crime: the psychoneurotics, psychopaths, highly aggressive personalities, alcoholics, addicts, and other borderline types. The mental hospital, as traditionally conceived at any rate, is not a proper place for them. In the ordinary mass prison, too, they are both disturbed and disturbing. Surely the best answer to this problem lies in an improved diversification of institutions in the correctional system and in the development of specialized treatment facilities to accommodate relatively small populations under intensive programs, with a high ratio of treatment staff to prisoners. From the point of view of group deterrence it appears quite essential that the criminal courts and correctional agencies deal with such cases. It may well be that wider ranges of sentences are needed for those offenders within this group who are more dangerous or repetitive than ordinary criminals but who are not legally insane. On this hypothesis the Model Penal Code has provided that when the court concludes on the basis of a psychiatric examination that the defendant's mental condition is "gravely abnormal," that his criminal conduct "has been characterized by a pattern of repetitive or compulsive behavior or by persistent aggressive behavior with heedless indifference to consequences, and that such condition makes him a serious danger to others" it may at its discretion sentence him to an extended term of imprisonment.[44] Under the Code, treatment may be provided in specialized institutions.

Many of the problems involved in dealing with seriously abnormal offenders could be resolved by establishing relatively simple procedures to provide for more efficient and accurate inquiries into the mental condition of defendants. Ordinarily the mental condition of the accused is not brought in issue unless and until a defense of insanity is raised at trial. In the exceptional case, where peculiarities of his behavior are so obvious that they raise the question of whether he is fit to stand trial, the accused may, on the initiative of counsel, prosecution, or magistrate, be remanded before trial for observation by a public hospital staff or by court-appointed

[44] *Model Penal Code,* secs. 6.07 and 7.03. For provisions relating to extended terms, see Chapter 15.

alienists. This is not an adequate means of dealing with the problem. The Briggs Law, enacted in 1921 in Massachusetts, embodies one important effort to establish more effective procedure. It provides for the routine psychiatric examination of defendants who have previously been in- dicted more than once, or convicted of a felony, by impartial psy- chiatrists appointed by the state's department of mental diseases. Under this law several hundred examinations are carried out annually in that state.[45] The psychiatric reports are available to the court, prosecutor, de- fense attorney, and probation officer. The impartial experts may be called at trial if necessary. Except where there are unusual circumstances, how- ever, the findings are accepted by prosecution and defense. As a result, in many cases where the defendant is found not fit to defend, he is com- mitted to a hospital without criminal trial. A great majority of those diagnosed as insane who have gone to trial are found not guilty by reason of insanity. The "battle of experts," so familiar elsewhere, has become virtually unknown in Massachusetts. Legislation similar to the Briggs Law was enacted in Kentucky in 1938, but it is applied there only to defendants indicted as habitual criminals. Michigan also adopted a procedure pat- terned on the Massachusetts law in 1939.

Another approach to the diagnosis of aberrated criminals has been developed through the use of clinics attached to the courts. This move- ment was started by Dr. William Healy in the Cook County (Chicago) Juvenile Court in 1909. Aside from children's courts, such clinics operate today only in a few criminal trial courts.[46] These vary considerably in number of persons examined (from 350 to 4,100 persons annually), in size of staff, basis of referral, and type of report submitted. The clinic of the General Sessions Court of New York City examines all offenders con- victed of major crimes in New York County, while the Detroit clinic has focused on serious traffic cases. The Baltimore court clinic accepts referrals from various agencies, including the court, defense, state's at- torney, jail warden, and others. In some clinics the reports are quite brief, sometimes little more than a diagnostic classification, while in others they are very detailed. The reports in some cases may be made before trial, in

---

[45] Winfred Overholzer, then commissioner of the department of mental disease in Massachusetts, made a detailed study of the operation of the Briggs Law in 1935: "The Briggs Law of Massachusetts: A Review and an Appraisal," *J. Crim. L.,* vol. 24, pp. 859–883, 1935. See also Guttmacher and Weihofen, *op. cit.,* pp. 260–261, and Paul H. Hoch and Joseph Zubin, *Psychiatry and the Law,* 1955, chap. 7.

[46] See Guttmacher, "Status of Adult Court Psychiatric Clinics," *N.P.P.A. J.,* vol. 1, pp. 97–105, October, 1955. Guttmacher and Weihofen, *op. cit.,* pp. 261–269. There are clinics serving eleven juvenile courts and several criminal trial courts. These are the Baltimore Supreme Bench, Boston Municipal Court, Chicago Municipal and Criminal Courts, Cleveland Common Pleas and Municipal Courts, Detroit Recorders Court, New York General Sessions and Magistrates' Courts, Philadelphia Municipal Court, Pittsburgh Quarter Sessions, and Washington, D.C., Federal Court.

others before sentence. New Jersey provides services to the various state agencies, in much the same way as does the Baltimore court clinic, but through a diagnostic center at Menlo Park. Wisconsin and California have developed institutional diagnostic facilities for offenders after conviction.

Ideally, psychiatric diagnosis should be available on felons and major misdemeanants before trial. This would avoid the necessity of costly trials in those cases where accused persons are unfit to defend and would permit their immediate hospitalization. In other cases, where it appeared that the defendant could go to trial but where there was an issue concerning his mental state at the time of the alleged offense, the impartial diagnostic data would be pertinent to the issue of criminal guilt. Experience in Massachusetts indicates that ordinarily there would be either a directed verdict or a jury finding in accordance with the psychiatric observations. In instances where the defendant, though not criminally insane, was found to suffer from mental abnormality in some degree, the sentence of the court, the correctional classification of the offender for treatment, and the parole decision on release could be guided in some measure by the results of the psychiatric study. The major problems in the development of this most useful sort of service have been its costliness and the lack of psychiatrists and other clinical specialists to perform the large task involved. As the supply of forensic psychiatrists increases, more court clinics or diagnostic institutions should be established to provide data concerning the mental condition of defendants in advance of trial. Their services would be invaluable in avoiding unnecessary court actions and errors in treatment disposition.

The Model Penal Code, in addition to its formulation on mental disease or defect as an affirmative defense at trial, referred to above, provides for procedures that could go far to relieve the common problems of trials where the defendant is psychotic but rational, where incompetents are put to trial, and where the jury is in a quandary because it is presented with conflicting testimony of a highly technical sort. In any case where the defendant has filed a notice of intention[47] to rely on the defense of mental disease or defect or where there is reason to doubt his fitness to proceed or that such abnormality will otherwise become an issue, the Code provides that the court shall appoint at least one qualified psychiatrist to examine and report upon the mental condition of the defendant. Alternatively the court may request a hospital superintendent to appoint a psychiatrist for this purpose or the court may order that the defendant be committed for observation to a hospital for the mentally ill. A report of the examination would be delivered to the court, the prosecutor, and the defense counsel and would include a description of the examination;

[47] The filing of notice of intent to rely upon the defense is provided in the Code, sec. 4.03 and also in the A.L.I. Code of Criminal Procedure, sec. 235. Six states now require such notice.

a diagnosis; an opinion on defendant's fitness to proceed if he suffers from mental disease or defect; an opinion of the extent, if any, to which his capacity to appreciate the criminality of his conduct or to conform his conduct to requirements of law may have been impaired; and, when directed by the court, an opinion of the defendant's particular state of mind where it is an element of the offense charged.

Where the defendant was found unfit to proceed, he might be committed upon order of the court until he had regained his fitness. Upon trial for the crime, whenever the defendant is found fit to proceed, the court would enter a judgment of acquittal in any case where it found substantial impairment of capacity, as defined in the test of responsibility. The defendant, notwithstanding the impartial psychiatric report, might secure examination by a psychiatrist of his choice and submit his findings in evidence. The examining psychiatrist would be subject to cross-examination and would be permitted "to make any explanation reasonably serving to clarify his diagnosis and opinion."

The Code provides that where the defendant is found not guilty by reason of insanity he shall be committed to the custody of the director of correction or, in the alternative, to the department of mental hygiene. Upon a further psychiatric study and a finding that he was no longer dangerous, the offender's release might be recommended to the court. Unless he was discharged, however, under such an action, he would be held for at least six months before he could apply for discharge. He might reapply at intervals of one year thereafter, the decision to release being vested exclusively in the committing court.

The "Sexual Psychopath"

The most notable departure from the M'Naghten rule is found in special legislation to deal with the so-called "sexual psychopath." By statutory definition in a number of the states, sexual psychopaths are individuals who are neither insane nor feeble-minded but who lack the capacity to control their sexual impulses or to profit from experience. It appears that this legislation has reflected primarily a deep concern about sex crime and a desire to provide life-term control rather than a straightforward effort to broaden legal protection to cover offenders who are psychologically aberrated but sane under traditional definition. In any event the statutory effort to define sex psychopaths as a distinct class of abnormal individuals has been widely criticized by psychiatrists and others. The general failure to establish the treatment facilities that have been postulated in the legislation suggests that the ostensible clinical orientation of the laws has been a camouflage.[48]

[48] The material in this section has been drawn in part from more detailed writing of the author in *The Habitual Sex Offender,* Report to the New Jersey Legislature, 1950; "The Sexual Psychopath—A Civic Social Responsibility," *J. Soc. Hyg.,* vol. 35,

Nearly one-half of the jurisdictions in the United States (twenty-three) have enacted special legislation concerned with the sexually aberrated offender, most of them within a ten-year period.[49] A fact thus far little appreciated is that these laws represent a striking departure from some of our fundamental conceptions of fair administration of justice. At several points they also conflict with the generally accepted conclusions of contemporary psychiatry. Like the earlier and somewhat comparable multiple offender laws, the new sex laws have provided some partial outlet for public feeling but little or nothing to a solution of the problem. The provisions of these statutes and their implications will now be considered as a part of our general system of law.

Twelve of the jurisdictions with specialized laws on the abnormal sex offender have designated the "sexual psychopath" or the "criminal sexual psychopathic person" as the object of legislation. Three others have defined the "psychopathic personality" or "psychopathic offender" and one the "mentally defective delinquent" as a specific class. New Jersey in its 1950 statute and Wyoming in 1951, however, designate for special treatment individuals who display repetitive-compulsive sexual behavior together with violence or an age disparity between the victim and the sexual offender. The law in New York predicates its operation upon the findings of psychiatric examination and social investigation: sexual crimes that involve force or violence may be adjudicated under its law. Several states have followed New Jersey in avoiding the use of "sex psychopathy" as a diagnostic category. This is in accord with most psychiatrists' counsel that the term has no generally accepted connotation among medical authorities.

Since the concept of psychopathy is so variously defined by the specialists, it is not surprising to discover wide disparity in the definitions that have been formulated in these statutes. The states obviously look to quite different qualities as evidence of dangerous sexual psychopathy. There appears to be no agreement as to the syndromes of aberration that justify special treatment. Indeed, hospital authorities handling cases of alleged sex psychopaths committed to them by the courts discover a wide spread of psychological types—many who are normal, along with neurotics,

---

pp. 354–368, 1949; "Sex Offender Laws and Their Administration," *Fed. Prob.,* vol. 14, pp. 32–37, 1950; "Treatment of the Sex Offender in Denmark," *Am. J. Psychiat.,* vol. 108, pp. 244–250, 1951; "Sentences for Sex Criminals," *J. Crim. L.,* vol. 42, pp. 332–338, 1952; "Some Myths about the Sex Offender," *Fed. Prob.,* vol. 19, pp. 7–12, 1955; and "Sexual Offences and the Treatment of Sexual Offenders in the United States," in L. Radzinowicz (ed.), *Sexual Offences,* 1957, pp. 500–517. See also Guttmacher, *Sex Offenses,* 1951, and Morris Ploscowe, *Sex and the Law,* 1951.

[49] Sex deviate laws have been enacted in Alabama, California, Hawaii, Illinois, Indiana, Maryland, Massachusetts, Michigan, Minnesota, Missouri, Nebraska, New Hampshire, New Jersey, New York, Ohio, Pennsylvania, Utah, Vermont, Virginia, Washington, D.C., state of Washington, Wisconsin, and Wyoming.

psychotics, epileptics, feeble-minded, alcoholics, and constitutional types.[50] Agreement among authorities is often difficult enough to attain for purposes of classifying individuals where traditional and fairly precise clinical categories are involved. Consensus is impossible in the no man's land of psychopathic personality. The psychopathology is defined in the statutes by such terminology as "impulsiveness of behavior," "lack of customary standards of good judgment," "emotional instability," or "inability to control impulses." The cases adjudicated under these criteria display a widely assorted sexual symptomatology, a significant proportion of which is in fact normal behavior viewed from either a biological or statistical point of view.

The import of the present revolution in a segment of our criminal and mental health laws becomes clearer as one looks beyond the statutory definitions to the grounds for court actions against alleged psychopaths. In four jurisdictions a person may be adjudicated to this status without the facts of a crime being shown and in seven others where only a charge has been placed against the individual. Action is generally taken through the submission of an affidavit to the prosecutor showing probable cause to believe the person a psychopath. In nine jurisdictions conviction for a crime is required. Unlike the other states, New Jersey in its 1950 law confines its application to individuals convicted of certain specified sex crimes, which include carnal abuse, sodomy, rape, and impairing the morals of a minor, thus focusing upon the more dangerous sexual deviates. This limiting of the law to certain particular offenses has also occurred in the New York legislation.

The United States Supreme Court, while it held the Minnesota statute constitutional, has pointed nevertheless to the dangers inherent in the administration of vague laws of this sort:[51]

We fully recognize the danger of a deprivation of due process in proceedings dealing with persons charged with insanity or, as here, with psychopathic personality as defined in the statute, and the special importance of maintaining the basic interests of liberty in a class of cases where the law though "fair on its face and impartial in appearance" may be open to serious abuses in administration, and courts may be imposed upon if the substantial rights of the persons charged are not adequately safeguarded at every stage of the proceedings. But we have not occasion to consider such abuses here, for none have occurred. The applicable statutes are not patently defective in any vital respect and we should not assume, in advance of a decision by the state court, that they should be construed so as to deprive appellant of the due process to which he is entitled under the federal constitution.

[50] For a thorough study of the operation of the New Jersey law and a classification of 300 cases studied at the Diagnostic Center, see Albert Ellis and Ralph Brancale, *The Psychology of Sex Offenders,* 1956.

[51] *Minnesota ex rel Pearson v. Probate Court of Ramsey County,* 205 Minn. 545; 60 S. Ct. 523 (1940).

Unfortunately, the injustices that may be done through "serious abuses in administration" cannot be rectified except by appeal in the individual case. For financial reasons appeals are very rarely taken by the defendants held under these laws. Moreover, considering the omnibus character of the statutes, it would be easy for appellate courts to find almost any individual covered under the statutory terminology.

Extraneous evidence reveals that it is the public anxiety about serious sex crimes that has motivated new legislation on the sex problem. However, except for a few of the more recent statutes, neither the content of the laws nor their administration display any special focus upon dangerous offenders. Most of the cases committed under the legislation are minor varieties of sex deviates: peepers, exhibitionists, homosexuals, and the like. The menacing varieties of sex criminal are rarely touched in the operation of these laws.

Most of the statutes provide that proceedings against an alleged sex deviate are initiated at the discretion of the prosecuting officer. In six jurisdictions, however, the court must automatically remand specified types of sex cases for mental examination, and under the Illinois law it is mandatory for the Department of Public Safety to refer for adjudication those criminals under detention in the state penitentiary who are believed to be sex psychopaths. It must be noted that, under the prevailing policy of basing the statutory operation on the discretion of prosecution, the effect of the laws has been greatly influenced. A number of authorities have emphasized the tendency of prosecutors to consider the statute as merely a useful tool to be employed or avoided in accordance with their own convenience. In particular, prosecutors appear inclined to utilize the law where the state's case is too weak for a criminal conviction but where a civil adjudication is easy. Moreover, prosecutors are clearly affected by their interpretation of and reaction to the statute. Where they disapprove the policy involved they may employ the law little or not at all.

The statutes generally require that the suspected offender be observed for diagnosis by two qualified psychiatrists or physicians with specialized psychiatric experience. Only New Jersey and Vermont generally employ a state diagnostic facility for more extended observation. In most of the jurisdictions, either by statute or case law, it is held that the decision on the psychopathic condition is to be made by the court ultimately rather than by the psychiatrist.

Commitment of the sex deviate after a finding is to a mental hospital in most of the states. In Washington a correctional institution must be employed and in a few others either a penal or mental facility may be designated. No state has provided a psychiatric facility exclusively for these cases, though Maryland has established an institution for defective delinquents to which sex deviates may be committed. It has generally been maintained by medical authorities that the psychopath should not be confined with the ordinary psychotic patients. Treatment is made more difficult for both when they are mixed in the institution. Most of the mental hospitals have not provided separate segregation of psychopaths, however. They have commonly maintained that they lack the space to receive psychopaths and, in fact, need much larger facilities than they have for their more disturbed psychotics. Along with the attitudes of prosecution and judges noted above, the dearth of resources to receive sex deviates has been a major reason for the failure of most of the states to apply these statutes with any considerable frequency. In several jurisdictions recommendations have been made for the establishment of a new and specialized hospital to care for cases of this sort but the recommendations have nowhere been implemented.

Of greater significance perhaps than the lack of space and of specialized institutions to receive sex psychopaths is the lack of any real program to cure or rehabilitate these offenders after they are committed. Their treatment is almost purely custodial. An underlying difficulty is the lack of psychiatric knowledge today of methods that can be employed effectively to deal with psychopathic offenders. Such treatment modalities as are considered to be of some potential value—intensive psychotherapy, group therapy, and psychiatric counsel—are generally unavailable for the psychopath in state mental hospitals. Some of these institutions have used shock treatment and surgery to a limited extent on the sexual offender, but there appears in the reports no reason to believe that these methods are effective on such cases. Hospital administrators generally indicate that they are unable to provide effective therapy for sex psychopaths.

Experience with hospital commitment under these laws raises a very important policy question. Is there any value in providing for diagnosis of a novel category of mental aberration and for commitment to psychiatric hospitals if these patients are then to be held for prolonged periods without receiving any special treatment? What virtue does such a procedure possess over the more traditional method of sentence to a correctional institution? If the purpose is mainly to extend the period of custody, this could be done as well and probably better in the correctional system. As one prominent New Jersey psychiatrist has pointed out, it is absurd to assume that by mere custodial hospitalization a state can achieve the objectives either of rehabilitation or of community protection.

A strange variety of provisions in these laws relative to the effect of commitment for psychopathy upon proceedings for the crime charged reflects further the lack of any uniform policy in the various states. Although commitment to the state hospital is taken to imply a mental abnormality at the time of the offense, twelve jurisdictions hold that the psychopathic status is no defense to the crime charged. Only Michigan, New Hampshire, and Indiana provide that commitment as a psychopath will operate as a defense. These latter states have, in effect, gone all the way in equating sexual psychopathy to the traditional insanities as a complete defense. This is done without benefit of the customary rules regarding the sort of mental condition that can be used as a legal defense. Authorities in some of the jurisdictions where commitment is no defense have stated that, in determining whether to bring psychopaths to trial after their release from hospitalization, they would be guided by the offense that had been committed and the duration of confinement in the hospital.

In regard to release the general principle formulated in most of the laws is that authorities at the institution must find the patient sufficiently recovered so as not to be dangerous. In six of the states the proceedings for release are generally initiated by the committed person. In Washington release is after expiration of sentence in the correctional institution if the prisoner is found to be cured. If the person is believed still to be psychopathic after expiration of his term, he may be committed to a hospital for a further indeterminate period. In Indiana the law provides that the psychopath is to be examined at least once each year with a report sent to the court and the Council for Mental Hygiene on his condition. In New Jersey, Wisconsin, and Wyoming, though the term of confinement is indefinite, the maximum is not to exceed that provided for the crime of which the patient was convicted; earlier release must be by a finding that "the person has recovered sufficiently to make it reasonably certain that a repetition of his offenses is unlikely."

In four states the patient may be returned to stand trial or for sentence after release from hospitalization. Complete release is provided for in ten others. Ohio provides uniquely that after discharge from the mental hospital the offender is to be transferred to a penal institution until the total period of his confinement is equal to the sentence applicable for his crime; he may then be released under parole.

It should be noted that, except for New Jersey, Ohio, Virginia, Wisconsin, and Wyoming, the several statutes provide for an indeterminate commitment without a terminal maximum. This fact, together with the tendency to commit a large proportion of minor offenders, has resulted in a situation in which individuals whose conduct is no more than a nuisance in the community may be incarcerated for long periods of time, because hospital authorities are disinclined to affirm that the patient is cured. It is obvious that the traditional policy of fines and short jail sentences for minor sex offenders is no solution to their problem. Query whether it is any better a solution to confine those individuals for long periods of time in the costly and unproductive custody of mental hospitals that provide no curative treatment for them?

Since 1950 there appears to have been some partial modification of trends in legislation relating to the emotionally deviated sex offender. Before that time the laws in a number of states looked to the preventive adjudication of juveniles and of adults who were not accused of crime or who, though charged, had not been found guilty. As has been noted, the statutes employed loose terminology and criteria for adjudication. They established commitments of indefinite duration to ordinary state hospitals for the insane, release being based upon the deviate's "cure." In a report prepared for the New Jersey legislature, the author emphasized the dangers implicit in the laws that had been previously enacted and the unsound premises upon which they were based. The New Jersey law, when it was revised in 1950, avoided the pitfalls of the earlier legislation elsewhere, focusing upon the serious rather than minor sex criminals and requiring that their guilt be shown at trial before they might be treated. It limited commitment to the maximum term for the offense involved. Treatment might be in the community under probation or in either a correctional or medical institution. Specialized treatment was to be based only upon the finding of certain distinct criteria noted above. Laws subsequently enacted in other jurisdictions, including Florida, Utah, Virginia, Wyoming, and revisions of their former statutes in California, Illinois, and Wisconsin have in various degrees followed a more reasonable tenor of legislation, for the most part requiring conviction of a crime, limiting the duration of treatment, providing for probation in proper cases, and recommending the development of specialized treatment centers.

The author's investigations of the problems of sentencing and the treatment of sex offenders in the United States and other parts of the world have led him to several conclusions:

1. There are relatively few aggressive and dangerous sex offenders in the criminal population. Most of the deviates are mild, submissive, and inadequate, more an annoyance than a menace to the community. From a psychological point of view they represent widely varied rather than a single or a few types.

2. Sex offenders are among the least recidivous of all types of criminals according to official statistics. They do not characteristically repeat as do our burglars, arsonists, and thieves. Some types of minor sexual deviates, however, are compulsive and repetitive.

3. The more serious and dangerous sex criminals receive long sentences and in many jurisdictions parole is arbitrarily withheld from them. Deviates that are curable by methods presently employed can be treated fully within the time provided by the maximum sentences under our traditional laws. Where they repeat they may be held still longer under habitual criminal statutes.

4. For those sex criminals who are not curable because we lack the methods, the personnel, and the institutional resources, there is no greater justification for the open-ended sentence than there is for other categories of felons. If our purpose is to extend the unproductive confinement of sex deviates, we should do so frankly by the direct establishment of longer sentences, not indirectly through a pretense at psychotherapeutic or medical treatment that is, in fact, nonexistent.

5. From all the evidence, we can only conclude that, with the limitations of

the law and the concealed character of most sexually deviant practices, the state is relatively ineffectual in discovering and constraining crime in this field. Moreover, in the light of the state of contemporary opinion and behavior in relation to sex—in the legislature, on the bench, and in the streets—one should not anticipate any great improvement either in the efficiency or consistency with which the statutes are administered. Confusion and injustice are inherent in the total situation.

6. Finally, it should be stressed that in so far as we aim at something more ambitious than custodial confinement of the sexual offender, we can do so only through employing facilities and personnel for research.

Defective Delinquency Procedures

Insanity as a defense to a criminal charge has generally been interpreted to include low-grade mental defectiveness as well as psychosis where the condition is so extreme that it excludes the capacity to distinguish right from wrong. Aside from these conditions of extensive aberration, the criminal law has been slow to recognize other mental-emotional pathologies for purposes of defense, mitigation, or even special treatment. This is apparently because the experts themselves have not been clear about the implications of lesser deviations for responsibility, prognosis, and therapy. They have failed thus far to submit psychological concepts and criteria upon the validity of which authorities either in psychiatry or law could agree. As has been seen, however, there is evidence of some modern departure from the traditionally narrow limits on the deviations recognized by the criminal law. These changes in policy are a result not so much of any substantial recent gains in our knowledge of volitional incapacity as they are a reflection of the recognition that psychiatric deviations not covered by the M'Naghten rules often do have profound effect upon behavior. Furthermore, it is believed that, however inadequately defined those deviations are from the point of view of legal-correctional policy, they should be recognized in the law.

In addition to the development of sex psychopath legislation there has been a slower, more limited, but partially comparable growth of law relating to "defective delinquency." Such laws have been even more varied and, if anything, less precise than the sex psychopath legislation concerning the mental conditions to be included. These laws appear to be rooted partially in the general civil law pertaining to the commitment of mental defectives that provides for the indefinite segregation in specialized institutions of feeble-minded persons whose intelligence is so low that they cannot manage their ordinary affairs or who are a source of danger to themselves or others. Such law, however, does not pertain specifically to individuals who have committed crimes and, in general, the person of low-grade intelligence who has violated the law can be committed to prison.

For the most part today defective delinquents are in fact committed to prisons. However, in a number of jurisdictions, as in New York State, the low-grade feeble-minded criminal may be transferred from an ordinary prison to an institution for mental defectives, for the insane, or for defective delinquents. Thus under the New York Correction Law, individuals over the age of 16 convicted of misdemeanor or felony may be committed or transferred to one of the state's three institutions for defective delinquents upon a finding of severe mental deficiency. Such an offender may be discharged, although a mental defective, "who in the opinion of the superintendent is reasonably safe to be at large, to his relatives or friends who are able and willing to comfortably maintain him. . . . " Or he may be returned to prison upon a finding that his confinement in the special facility is "unsuitable." In any case where the offender's sentence has expired without his prior release, the superintendent may secure a court order for an examination to determine that he is a mental defective and should be retained indefinitely until he may safely be released. In five other jurisdictions there are institutional facilities for defective delinquents—California, Massachusetts, Minnesota, Maryland, and Pennsylvania—though only in the last two are the facilities specialized for this function alone.[52] In most states, therefore, feeble-minded offenders are held either in prison or, where law or administrative practice permits, in a section of the ordinary state hospital for defectives or psychotics.

Pennsylvania defines the defective delinquent as an individual over 15 years of age convicted of or charged with a crime or juvenile delinquency who is considered so mentally defective that he requires confinement in their special institution. Time spent at that institution is counted as part of the offender's sentence if he recovers; if he does not recover he may be detained there "until his mental condition has so improved as to warrant his discharge." Release is based upon a finding that it will be "beneficial and not incompatible with the welfare of society." Ohio has a law covering mentally deficient and psychopathic offenders that defines the former as individuals adjudged feeble-minded who exhibit criminal tendencies. When examination indicates that this condition exists, the court must impose sentence for the offense of which the person was convicted and at the same time enter an order of indefinite commitment to the department of public welfare, during the continuance of which the execution of the sentence is suspended. If the defective appears to have improved to the extent that he no longer requires special custody, he may either serve in prison the remainder of his term for the offense, with allowance for the time spent in the public welfare institution, or if his confinement has exceeded that term he may be released under supervision.

California makes special provision for the "defective or psychopathic delinquent" under 21 who is "an habitual delinquent or has tendencies toward becoming an habitual delinquent." Massachusetts, on the other hand, applies the status of "defective delinquent" to individuals over the age of 15 charged with crime or committed to a correctional institution

---

[52] Note from the discussion in the text that the term "defective delinquent" is differently defined in these jurisdictions in relation to age and condition.

who has "shown himself to be dangerous or shows a tendency toward becoming such, that such tendency is or may become a menace to the public, and that such a person is not a proper subject for the school for the feeble-minded or commitment as an insane person." In Vermont provisions for "mentally defective delinquents" are part of their law dealing with sexual psychopaths, the status being predicated upon "gross immoral conduct combined with mental deficiency or psychopathic personality."

Maryland established an Institution for Defective Delinquents under the Board of Corrections at Patuxent in 1951. This institution is empowered to receive as a defective delinquent any person who "by the demonstration of persistent, aggravated, antisocial or criminal behavior evidences a propensity toward criminal activity, and who is found to have either such intellectual deficiency or emotional unbalance, or both, as to clearly demonstrate an actual danger to society so as to require confinement and treatment under an indeterminate sentence, subject to being released only if the intellectual deficiency and/or the emotional unbalance is so relieved as to make it reasonably safe for society to terminate the confinement and treatment." Investigation for possible defective delinquency may be made after conviction for a felony, a misdemeanor punishable by a penitentiary sentence, a crime of violence, a sex crime involving physical force or violence or an age disparity between the offender and his victim, or one of an uncontrolled or repetitive nature, or two or more convictions punishable by imprisonment. Commitment is for an indeterminate period without minimum or maximum. Reexamination of defective delinquents must be made at least once every year to determine whether the status should continue, reports thereon being made to the committing court. On the basis of such reports and such further study or hearing as it may desire, the court may determine whether to release the offender unconditionally or conditionally on parole, to return him to custody as a defective delinquent, or to return him to the penal system to serve the original sentence with deduction for the time served in the special institution.

It will be observed that among the seven states that have some special provision for the defective delinquent, briefly noted above, there is much variation in what "defect" is considered to be and that, except in those jurisdictions where the ordinary psychological definitions of mental deficiency are applied, the criteria are excessively vague and loose. This is especially true in Maryland, Vermont, and California. The age levels covered also differ remarkably. Provisions concerning adjudication are similar, for the most part, resembling those employed under sex psychopath statutes in their specifications for psychiatric examination. However, the laws vary considerably concerning requirements for criminal conviction, the effect of adjudication to the defective status, and in their provisions regarding release.

Chapter 15

SANCTIONS AND SENTENCING

This chapter and the next will deal with several aspects of the dispositions process. The major forms of sanctions that are employed by the courts will first be reviewed and then the disparities in sentences that are imposed will be observed. Such differences are commonly attributed to the prejudice and ignorance of judges who, it is maintained, are not equipped by training or experience to perform the sentencing function. It will be shown, however, that the application of criminal sanctions is a complex process in which the role of the judge, while important and specialized, is restricted in a variety of ways. Much of the variation in sentencing is an inevitable consequence of the systems of disposition that have developed in modern times.

The penal law of the particular jurisdiction is a central factor in determining the sorts of sentences that the courts impose. While in most states a considerable amount of discretion is vested in the judge, the law limits both the form and the range of sentences he may employ. Furthermore, the judge receives conflicting advice from a variety of sources to guide him in fixing appropriate sanctions: the probation department and court clinic, the prosecutor's office, the defendant's counsel and his family, may in turn urge a rehabilitative, a punitive, and a lenient sentence. There is little provision in the law and equally little consensus among criminologists on the standards or criteria that should guide the court in making its determinations. The aphorism that the purpose of sentencing is to protect the community offers minimal direction to the judge.

The most difficult problem in sentencing is that of assessing the length of prison terms, and it is here that strictures are most frequently directed against the courts. These criticisms are generally ill founded, for the difficulties are intrinsic to the system of sentences that has developed in our law and practice. The fact is that the duration of a convict's imprisonment depends in most jurisdictions upon (1) the range of terms permitted by the penal law for the crime or crimes involved; (2) the sentence imposed by the court within that range, establishing a minimum period when the person may first be considered for release and a maximum period of possible retention; and (3) the decision of a parole agency on the time when the offender should actually be released from prison within the latitude of the court's sentence. There is no close coordination of policy or planning between the court and paroling authority, however, and very little between parole boards and prison administrators.

The court cannot know in advance either what the prisoner's response to treatment will be or how the releasing agency will exercise its responsibility. It can only fix the outer limits of state control, and this it must do blindly for the most part. Variations in sentences depend largely on the extent to which judges are willing to transfer to the parole administration the power to decide the minimum length of time the prisoner should be held before first release and the maximum length of time that he may be held before final discharge. It is not surprising that the extent of judges' reliance upon the paroling authorities to make these decisions should differ. In this chapter the author will give some attention to the role of the various agencies that play a part in dispositions and treatment. The effects that the various states' penal laws have on prison retention practice will also be considered.

SENTENCING MEASURES

The law distinguishes between crimes according to their seriousness, classifying them generally into felonies and misdemeanors. In a majority of jurisdictions, imprisonment for a misdemeanor may be for any period of time up to a year in a city or county jail or workhouse. Such sentences are of fixed duration, most frequently thirty, sixty, or ninety days, six months, or one year. In some states indefinite sentences from one to two or from one to three years may be employed for recidivistic misdemeanants. In most jurisdictions the law provides that imprisonment for a felony shall be for some period in excess of one year in a state prison or reformatory. Not uncommonly state laws require that upon conviction for certain felonies or upon repeated convictions the court must sentence to prison rather than to any other penalty.[1]

Suspended Sentence

Historically the power to suspend sentence preceded the development of probation, but today it is most frequently coupled with probation. In at least eighteen states,[2] however, there are statutory provisions for suspended sentence as a separate measure and in other jurisdictions courts frequently employ such a sentence under their common-law powers. This type of sentence occurs in two different forms: the suspension of the imposition of sentence and the suspension of the execution of sentence. In some states only the first is authorized by law and in others only the latter, but commonly either may be used. In suspending the execution of a

[1] See Chapter 19 on exclusions from probation.

[2] Arkansas, Connecticut, Louisiana, Maryland, Massachusetts, Mississippi, New Mexico, New York, Ohio, Oklahoma, Oregon, Rhode Island, South Carolina, South Dakota, Tennessee, Texas, Virginia, and Wyoming.

sentence the court fixes a sentence of imprisonment and then suspends its execution during the good behavior of the offender. In most jurisdictions, if the court subsequently revokes the sentence whose execution it had suspended, it must impose the term originally fixed. Suspension of the imposition of sentence means that the court withholds decision on the length of the prison term at the time of conviction, so that upon revocation it must then fix the period of imprisonment. This power to set sentence at the time of revocation enables the court to consider subsequent misconduct along with the original offense as a basis of the term it sets. Often, of course, this means that when an individual has been "given a second chance" under a sentence, the imposition of that sentence having been suspended, he will receive a more severe penalty upon revocation than he would have received under a commitment in the first place. The law of some states provides that where a court suspends sentence there is no criminal conviction.

Probation

Probation will be discussed in detail in Chapter 19. Here it is considered briefly as a disposition available to the courts in nearly every state.[3] More serious felonies, especially crimes punishable by death or life imprisonment, are specifically excluded from this sentence, however, in all but six states.[4] The historical connection of probation with the suspended sentence has had much to do with its subsequent misuse by some courts as a form of judicial leniency.

Where the court suspends sentence it may generally submit the offender to the supervision of a probation officer for a specified period of time. It is this supervision that distinguishes probation as a court disposition from the ordinary suspended sentence. For misdemeanors, probation terms are usually for periods of one, two, or three years. For felonies, the ordinary term is for a period of five years or less, but in some states the term may be as long as the maximum prison term provided by law. The offender may serve one or several years on probation and then, in case of a breach of the conditions of probation, may be submitted to imprisonment either for the term originally fixed or, in those jurisdictions that follow such a practice, for any term that the court could have set at the time of conviction. He is not credited with time spent under the suspended sentence.

Fines

Fines constitute another distinct form of sanction. The offender may be fined either on the theory that he does not require any specifically correctional measure or that the monetary sanction is best suited to dissuade

[3] In New Mexico and Oklahoma there are statutory provisions for suspending sentence but not for probation as such. In some counties, however, supervision is provided for offenders under suspended sentence.

[4] Arizona, Arkansas, Maryland, New Hampshire, Vermont, and Wisconsin.

him from further misconduct. The fine may be combined with imprisonment where the court deems this proper. In instances of misdemeanors
or other minor violations, the fine is commonly imposed with imprisonment as an alternative if the offender cannot or will not pay. Fines are also
used quite frequently in association with probation sentences, the payment
constituting one of the conditions of probation. In appropriate cases the
use of fines appears to be fully justified both as an instrument of justice and
of sound correctional treatment.

Restitution

Restitution is a remedy to the victim ordinarily assessed through action
of the civil courts. It differs from the fine, which goes to the state.
Restitution is not generally provided as a form of sentence in penal codes
of the United States. Not uncommonly, however, criminal courts do fix
restitution as one of the terms of probation. They may do so either because of the appeal of the victim's plight or because it appears to be an
appropriate treatment measure to require that the offender make good the
loss he has occasioned. In some instances, courts employ probation rather
than an institutional commitment in order to make it possible for the
offender to earn funds with which to make reparation to his victim. Failure
to comply with restitution orders represents a breach of probation conditions, and may become the basis for revocation. Orders for restitution
are ordinarily made by criminal courts only where the amount of the
victim's loss may be determined rather definitely and payment secured
without excessive administrative difficulties involving executions against
property or long-term collections. It is undesirable, of course, for the
criminal court to set fines so high that the victim is unable to secure proper
restitution from the offender, whether under a sentence or a civil court
order. Unfortunately, little thought is given to this problem in most courts.

Capital Punishment

The death penalty may be employed in all but seven states[5] as a punishment for murder and, in some jurisdictions, for rape, kidnapping, or
treason. Ordinarily it is an alternative to life imprisonment, with or without the possibility of parole. The trend both here and abroad has been
to reduce the number of crimes for which the death penalty may be employed. This has reflected a climate of ethical opinion increasingly opposed
to the deliberateness, finality, and cruelty of this sanction. It is commonly
regarded, unlike our other penal sanctions, as a purely retributive measure.
It has sometimes been conceived to possess some educative value in

[5] Delaware, Maine, Michigan, Minnesota, North Dakota, Rhode Island, and Wis-
consin. See Thorsten Sellin, *Memorandum on Capital Punishment,* British Royal
Commission on Capital Punishment, and Sellin (ed.), "Murder and the Penalty of
Death," *The Annals,* vol. 284, November, 1952.

exemplifying our paramount regard for corporeal security, but it is dubious that any penalty that itself denies the supremacy of human life can achieve this end. Certainly no area of penal sanction is either more controversial or more weighted with excessive emotions of hate, horror, and grief than is the death penalty. Nor are any other penalities, after they have been imposed, so little subject to correction for error.

Corporal Punishment

Modern conceptions of justice and humanity deny the utility of corporal penalties both as a statutory sanction and as a disciplinary measure. Whipping has been permitted as a sentence under the law of Delaware and Maryland only and was restricted in the latter state to cases involving wife beating.[6] The penalty has been used infrequently in modern times and is generally disapproved as a retributive and cruel device.[7] While it was retained longer and employed more commonly there, England too has abandoned whipping under the Criminal Justice Act of 1948. It was employed in England to punish those convicted of physically aggressive crimes as well as for those violently resisting arrest. While corporal penalties as a sentence of the court are obsolete, physical punishments and restraints are used in some prisons and correctional institutions of the United States.[8]

Sterilization and Castration

By and large the methods of sterilization and castration have not been seriously considered as measures of correctional treatment in the United States. Scientists have generally concluded that measures of negative eugenics can provide no significant protection against criminality. Legislators consider such methods immoral, unjust, and antidemocratic. A few states permit sterilization of low-grade mental defectives as a measure of general eugenics, but only California has employed the technique to any considerable extent. Its use may be defended as a means of slightly reducing the number of dependent defectives in the population, but the measure is subject to grave abuses. We possess no refined criteria for the selection of cases for sterilization, even as a measure for general improvement of population quality, still less for the reduction of criminality.

Castration raises more difficult problems than does sterilization. It is an irreversible treatment method having important side effects on the functioning of the organism. It is a serious assault on the human body. It involves strong emotional responses, and undoubtedly important unconscious reactions in the individuals against whom such action may be taken.

[6] See Robert G. Caldwell, *Red Hannah*, 1947. In 1959 the Delaware legislature passed a bill making whipping a mandatory penalty for robbery. It was vetoed. Maryland repealed its law in 1953.

[7] *Report on Penal Institutions, Probation and Parole*, National Commission on Law Observance and Enforcement, vol. 9, p. 31, 1931.

[8] See Chapter 22 for a discussion of corporal punishments in prisons.

While castration has not been adopted as a correctional measure in any jurisdiction in the United States, it has been employed extralegally in California and Kansas. In at least one county in California certain judges of the criminal courts have employed a policy of granting probation to offenders who will submit themselves "voluntarily" to castration. A report from a subcommittee on sex crimes of the Assembly Interim Committee on Judicial Systems and Judicial Processes in August, 1952, notes that some sixty convicted individuals had been castrated in San Diego County. The Langley-Porter Clinic in California is conducting research on the effects of castration under funds made available through the state legislature. The subcommittee in California recommended a bill to permit castration of "sex deviates" at the 1951 Session of the California Legislature (Assembly Bill No. 2367). It failed to be passed but at the 1952 First Extraordinary Session of the Legislature, a bill to permit castration was approved by the Assembly. However, it remained in the Senate Judiciary Committee and was not enacted. One or two other states have given more or less serious consideration to the employment of castration as a treatment measure for "sex psychopaths." The reaction of the medical profession and of psychiatrists in particular is responsible to a large extent for the failure to experiment with it more widely.

Castration has been used quite extensively in Denmark and Sweden in recent years, very widely as a race extermination measure in Germany under the Nazis, and to some extent in the Netherlands, Switzerland, Norway, Finland, Greenland, and Iceland. The Scandinavian countries have reported optimistically on the results of their carefully selective usage of this surgery.[9]

[9] An investigation was made in 1950 by the writer as consultant to the New Jersey Commission on the Habitual Sex Offender into the operation of the European castration laws in terms of the possible applicability of their experience in the United States. His conclusion was this: "Castration, however effective it may appear to be in European experience with specialized types of sex deviates, cannot gain favor in the United States. At best it is a technique that should be employed, according to authorities abroad, for only a very limited, carefully selected group and with supplementary treatment of a social-psychiatric nature. Castration is a nonreversible procedure subject to serious abuses as Nazi experience has thoroughly proved. What with the hysteria so easily provoked in the United States relative to sex criminality, there is very real danger that the castration technique, if it were adopted here, would too easily be misapplied. Moreover, other methods of treatment, such as glandular therapy, which constitute far less of an assault upon the person, can be employed with effects rather similar to those produced by castration (vis., desexualization and reduction of aggression). With the too-easy answer of castration at hand, once used, the development of other and superior methods would very possibly be neglected. Finally, though there is disagreement on the point, it appears that castration may produce pronounced personality as well as physical changes that may complicate the problems of the deviate and increase his danger to the community."

Sweden, reporting on a follow-up examination of sixty-six cases that had undergone castration at least three years before the study, notes that none have shown

DEPRIVATION AND RESTORATION OF CIVIL RIGHTS

The deprivation of civil rights is not a primary sanction for the punishment of criminals but is an automatic accompaniment either of conviction for felony or of imprisonment.[10] It constitutes a form of supplementary restrictions upon the offender and is sometimes onerous and punitive in nature. Historically these deprivations were rooted in "civil death," which under ancient Roman law meant the loss of freedom, citizenship, and property. Even under the Romans the extent of loss might vary and under later English law the deprivations were gradually curtailed. Sixteen states in this country now impose civil death upon offenders sentenced to life imprisonment. A number of these jurisdictions have interpreted their laws to prevent the life-term prisoner from suing, though he may be sued. In general the civilly dead convict may contract, except so far as he may be specifically prohibited by statute from doing so, though he cannot legally enforce his contracts. In some states the convict's property descends as though he were dead but in others he may will his possessions. Except for statutory limitations he may convey title and inherit property. Civil death also affects marital status; in four states it dissolves the marriage, permitting the spouse to remarry without securing a divorce.

In many states there are laws suspending the civil rights of criminals sentenced to terms less than life, but these provisions too vary widely. Such legislation generally either removes or restricts the right to sue, to contract and transfer property, to vote, to hold public office or positions of trust, to testify in legal proceedings, to perform jury duty, or to retain the rights of marriage. The offender is deprived of the rights of suffrage in thirty-four states. In twenty-seven he may not hold public office or positions of trust. In thirty-five jurisdictions a felony conviction is a legal basis of divorce.

Civil rights may be restored partially or completely by pardon in thirty-seven states, but in several of these provision for such restoration must be

---

recidivism. Dr. Stürup, reporting on seventy-nine castrates from the institution at Herstedvester, Denmark, found two who were sexual recidivists and fourteen who had committed subsequent offenses of other sorts, whereas of forty noncastrates from that institution sixteen had recidivated sexually after release and ten had committed crimes of other sorts. Stürup concluded: "Surprisingly few disadvantages attach to castration, but even so it must, in my opinion, be used with a certain amount of discretion, especially in cases of lighter sexual offenses. The detainee must show *hyper-sexuality* beyond doubt or a *stable sexually conditioned criminality*, before we use this irreversible treatment." See Tappan, "Treatment of the Sex Offender in Denmark," *Am. J. Psychiat.*, vol. 108, pp. 244–250, October, 1951, and "Sex Offender Laws and Their Administration," *Fed. Prob.*, vol. 14, no. 3, pp. 32–37, September, 1950.

[10] See Tappan, "Loss and Restoration of Civil Rights of Offenders," *N.P.P.A. Yearbook*, pp. 86–107, 1952, and "The Legal Rights of Prisoners," *The Annals*, vol. 293, pp. 99–112, 1954.

specifically included in the pardon. In a considerable number of states certain privileges, such as the holding of office, the practice of one's profession, or the return of one's property, cannot be restored. Considering the highly variable philosophy that prevails in regard to pardon and the differing effects of pardon throughout the states, this is a poor device by which to restore civil rights. This is true particularly in a number of states where pardon is employed promiscuously as a substitute for parole.[11] An illogical consequence is that some offenders secure their civil rights through the clemency procedure while equally meritorious individuals released on parole or at the expiration of sentence do not. There are several other methods employed to restore civil rights. Seven states provide for the issuance of certificates of good prison conduct on the basis of which civil rights, commonly termed "citizenship" in these statutes, may be returned to those who have been model prisoners. This technique for meeting the problem places too much emphasis on good conduct in the institution, which is a quite inadequate criterion of reform. In accordance with provisions of the 1940 Model Probation Act of the National Probation and Parole Association, three states permit the restoration of rights upon successful completion of probation. One of these provides in addition for the striking of the verdict of guilty from the court record. The English Criminal Justice Act of 1948 goes further in adopting the principle that probation shall not entail disqualifications or disabilities upon the probationer. A few jurisdictions in the United States have established relatively liberal provisions for the restoration of civil rights.[12]

[11] The writer has suggested elsewhere that pardon is a poor device for restoring civil rights: "While in theory pardon is an act of executive clemency, to be used sparingly in instances where innocence has been shown subsequent to conviction or where some other injustice has been worked, actually in many jurisdictions the pardoning power is often used by the chief executive of the state as a substitute for parole and in this connection may be badly misused. It does not make sense or justice to grant restoration of civil rights either generally or by specific provisions through the governor's pardon and to withhold these rights from those released on parole or discharged at the expiration of sentence. The effect is to make restoration a matter of gubernatorial leniency rather than a considered policy of correctional rehabilitation. Other methods, therefore, are desirable to restore the offender to the normal rights and duties of the citizen in the community." "Loss and Restoration of Civil Rights," *op. cit.*, p. 97.

[12] The author has recently summarized these: "Restoration provisions are somewhat more liberal in several states, going beyond offenders who have been sentenced to probation. Ohio provides that a prisoner who has served the maximum term or who has been granted final release by the Pardon and Parole Commission shall be restored to the rights and privileges forfeited on conviction. In Wisconsin civil rights are automatically restored upon serving out a term or otherwise satisfying the sentence of the court. Colorado provides for restoration either by pardon or by service of a full term and in Kansas citizenship is restored either where the Governor commutes the sentences of paroled prisoners or where they are finally discharged from supervision. Missouri law provides that for a first felony conviction prisoners who are released under the good time law are released from their civil disabilities

There is no plausible ground for retaining in modern statutes outmoded provisions that establish a status of civil death for prisoners serving life terms. The interests of public protection and convenience do require that felons be restricted during imprisonment in the exercise of certain privileges, but there is no sound reason to apply more onerous restrictions to men serving life terms than to those who are sentenced for a term of years. Moreover, as a general principle, there is no justification for imposing on offenders disabilities that are frankly punitive. The use of civil deprivations for purposes of punishment appears to be both unnecessary and prejudicial to correctional goals. On the other hand, community welfare may require a discriminating use of such supplementary sanctions as denying for a time the privilege of holding public office or practicing a profession and, perhaps, serving on juries, where certain types of crimes are involved.

Individuals who are discharged from correctional treatment should generally be restored to the rights they may have lost. This has value as a symbol of the man's return to a noncriminal status and should facilitate his rehabilitation. Obviously there are certain limited risks involved in reviving these rights. However, the state must always assume some risk in the very process of releasing into the community men who have committed crimes before and may do so again. There is always some danger that professional criminals may repeat their crimes if they are free to return to their occupations. However, the rules of professional organizations and licensing authorities provide sufficient protection in this regard. Often these rules appear to be severe and arbitrary, in fact. They are designed to protect "the craft," for the most part, without much relation to broader considerations of the needs either of the public or the offender.

---

after a two year period. In South Dakota the criminal is considered restored to the full rights of citizenship upon discharge from the penitentiary if he has a clear record for good conduct. In Tennessee, while for an 'infamous crime' restoration must be by action of the Circuit Court, in the instances of other lesser crimes, restoration is automatic after six months or three years, depending upon the type of offense.

"A somewhat different and more discriminating approach is employed in some jurisdictions where rights are restored on the basis of a certificate of good conduct. Thus California enacted in 1944 a law which provided that a person convicted of felony who was subsequently released from a state institution, whether by completion of sentence or parole, might apply for a certificate of rehabilitation and a pardon after satisfactory behavior during the parole period or other fixed period. The certificate, granted by the superior court, restores most civil rights. In New York the Board of Parole may grant a certificate of good conduct to any person who has satisfactorily conducted himself for five years after suspension of sentence, release on parole or termination of sentence. The certificate serves as evidence of good moral character where required by law, or ends a disability otherwise created by conviction." See Aaron Nussbaum, "First Offenders—A Second Chance," privately published, 1956.

Imprisonment

Aside from capital punishment, imprisonment is the most severely afflictive sanction employed under contemporary penal law. It is the modern substitute for the brutalities of earlier systems of corporal and capital punishment and is the sanction most commonly employed by our criminal courts for felons. In Chapter 20 the author will describe the development of the prison system and in subsequent chapters the treatment provided in penal institutions will be discussed. Aside from the nature of prisons and the qualitative experience of felons therein, there are questions relating to prison sentencing, the duration of prison confinement, and the means of determining release and discharge from official control that should be considered further here.

THE FORMS OF PRISON SENTENCING

There are serious semantic difficulties involved in the analysis of the problems of sentencing. The nomenclature generally employed is quite misleading. Undoubtedly much of the confusion that may be found in the critical literature in this field results, on the one hand, from the loose and conflicting terminology of sentencing and, on the other, from the peculiarities in the historical evolution of sentencing and parole practices.

Three major forms of sentencing employed by our criminal courts should be discriminated: the definite, the indefinite, and the indeterminate. The definite sentence is here used to mean a specific or "flat" term of years (e.g., a five-year term). The indeterminate sentence indicates a term with neither minimum nor maximum limits (e.g., from one day to life or at the pleasure of the government). The indefinite sentence means a term with a fixed maximum and usually a fixed minimum (e.g., from three to fifteen years). It will be observed that in actual administration these simple definitions have little significance.

The Definite Sentence

Let us consider first the development of the definite sentence. Before the French Revolution, during what is generally known as the period of "Pre-Classical criminology," judges were not limited by law in their fixing of penalties. They could regulate sanctions in accordance with their conceptions of the gravity of the particular offense and the nature of the individual offender before them. The frequency with which capital punishment was then employed for minor crimes and the wide disparity in sentencing provoked strong protests from idealistic philosophers of the eighteenth century and led to what is now known as the period of "Classical criminology." This represented a pendular swing to rigidly fixed and invariable penalties established by law, theoretically proportioned in their severity to the seriousness of the crimes involved, the culpability of the offender, and the presumed needs for deterrence. Perhaps the greatest single contributions to the radical change in penological theory were the work of the preeminent Italian, Beccaria, the Englishman, Bentham, and the German, Feuerbach, who gave expression in the field of law and penology to the humane, equalitarian, and antiauthoritarian doctrines of eighteenth-century philosophy.[13] In his *Crimes and Punishments,* Beccaria launched a vigorous attack against the arbitrary punishments imposed by the judges, especially upon the poor; such injustices in judicial procedures as secret accusations, torture, and extended detention; and the excessive use of banishment, confiscation, and the death penalty.[14] Beccaria's struggle to promote an equalitarian system of justice achieved substantial success in the adoption of the French Code of 1791.

In remedying many of the earlier abuses, the Code established the principle of equalization of penalties in accordance with the nature and degree of the offense. It deprived the judges of discretionary power in fixing sentence. Thus the theory of the definite sentence was established in a rigid, inflexible system, largely as an overcompensatory reaction against the abuses of power that had been associated with an unbridled judicial discretion. Under the Code, the role of the court was reduced to the finding of guilt or innocence and sentencing was automatically determined by legal provisions without regard to extenuations or aggravations relating to age, mental condition, prior criminal or social history, or the particular circumstances of the offense. Patently this allowed for no individualization in the application of penal sanctions. Based as it was on an effort to escape the invidious and unjust consequences of a system of uncontrolled discretion in sentencing, the system sought its remedy at the opposed extreme through a mechanical application of penalties. It should be noted here that the subsequent history of penological theory and sentencing legislation has fluctuated between the ideals of a thoroughly equalitarian treatment of offenders, on the one hand, and a complete individualization of correctional efforts, on the other. Numerous modern reform penologists have sought the latter goal quite exclusively and uncritically, little instructed by the proof in Pre-Classical experience of the dangers implicit in any system of free discretion in determining the duration of imprisonment. More conservative influence has been exercised by the bar and bench.

A significant change in the definite sentence system came through the development of conditional release measures that made obsolete the original and ostensible meaning of the "definite sentence."[15] The development of legislation for the commutation of sentences for good behavior and to

---

[13] See Chapter 10.
[14] See John L. Gillin, *Criminology and Penology,* 1945, p. 228.
[15] *The Attorney General's Survey of Release Procedures,* vol. 4, *Parole,* p. 20, 1939.

permit parole before the expiration of the term will be discussed in Chapter 23. In the states with definite sentences, laws were drafted to provide that prisoners might be eligible for conditional release upon the expiration of some fixed part of their sentences. The effect of this legislation was to create a form of indefinite sentence in which the maximum was the term fixed in the sentence and the minimum was some fraction of that term or a fixed number of years in accordance with a general provision of the penal law relating to parole eligibility.

Today there are eleven jurisdictions, including the Federal, that employ the definite sentence almost exclusively and eight others that use it preponderantly. Good-time laws are applied in nearly all states. As a consequence of these changes, the offender convicted of a felony and sentenced to a fixed term faces in reality an indefinite period of imprisonment with a possibility of parole or of early release on good time. The definite term has become a fiction because of these correctional innovations.

The Indefinite Sentence

A more frank departure from the definite sentence system occurred well in advance of the development of good-time commutation and parole in the form of the indefinite sentence.[16] Classical criminology was not long in giving way to more reasonable compromises of the Neo-Classical school when the excessive rigidity of the definite sentence system became apparent. The French Penal Code of 1810 was more severe in some respects than the Code of twenty years earlier. It restored the penalty of life imprisonment and imposed chastisements and mutilations. However, it returned to the judges some power in sentencing, permitting them to establish penalties of imprisonment between a minimum and maximum fixed in the law in accordance with extenuating circumstances. The doctrine of extenuating circumstances and the idea of limited responsibility were further elaborated in French laws of 1824 and 1832. Thus emerged a principle of sentencing, still considered fundamental to a proper system of justice. This principle, restated, maintains that some variation in treatment should be permitted in accordance with the circumstances of the particular offense and offender but that excessive deprivations should be avoided by establishing limits upon the range of discretion exercised by judges and administrators.

Correctional historians have commonly attributed to Dr. Benjamin Rush, prominent Philadelphia physician, humanitarian, and signer of the Declara-

[16] As noted in the text above, by the "indefinite sentence" we mean a term in which minimum and maximum is set. The date of release is determined by an administrative agency, ordinarily a parole board. Such terms are sometimes referred to as "indeterminate" or "relatively indeterminate sentences." This type of sentence is commonly confused with the wholly indeterminate sentence, which is based upon quite different theory.

tion of Independence, the first argument for the principle of the indefinite sentence. In a pamphlet published in 1787 he said: "Let the various kinds of punishment be defined and fixed by law. But let no notice be taken in the law of the punishment that awaits any particular crime. Punishments should be varied in degree according to the temper of criminals or the progress of their reformation. Let the duration of punishments be limited but let this limitation be unknown. I conceive this secret to be of the utmost importance in reforming criminals and preventing crimes. The imagination, when agitated with uncertainty, will seldom fail of connecting the longest duration of punishment with the smallest crime."[17]

It will be observed that Rush emphasized the possible deterrent value of the indefiniteness of punishment as well as the need to retain the offender, within secret and unspecified limits, until he was reformed. Later in Great Britain similar proposals for indefinite sentences were put forward by various public leaders and prison reformers, including in particular Archbishop Whately of Dublin,[18] Frederic Hill, Scottish prison inspector, and Matthew Davenport Hill, recorder of the city of Birmingham. Their emphasis was upon retaining prisoners until they were reformed, a matter that could not be determined at the time of sentencing. Frederic Hill's dictum that the prison should be "a kind of moral hospital, to which offenders shall be sent until they are cured of their bad habits" has a strangely modern sound, considering that it was written more than a century ago. Their thought was oriented more to the prolonged detention of incorrigibles, however, than to early release of those who needed little correctional treatment.

The Indeterminate Sentence

During this same period there was active agitation for a more idealistic form of indeterminate sentence in America. This is a sentence without minimum or maximum limits. In 1847, S. J. May of the New York Prison Association proposed that judges should be given no discretion concerning the length of sentence and that the offender should be imprisoned "until the evil disposition is removed from his heart; until his disqualification to go at large no longer exists; that is, until he is a reformed man." May engaged in the same sort of simplistic reasoning about the purposes and potentialities of imprisonment that has characterized the writings of many of his successors when he wrote as follows:[19]

[17] *An Inquiry into the Effects of Public Punishments upon Criminals and upon Society,* Philadelphia, 1787.

[18] In 1932, Whately wrote: "It seems to be perfectly reasonable that those whose misconduct compels us to send [them] to a house of correction should not again be let loose on society until they shall have made some indication of amended character. . . ." Cited in *Attorney General's Survey of Release Procedures,* vol. 4, p. 16.

[19] *Ibid.,* p. 17.

Even if human wisdom can ascertain the different qualities of evil flowing through society from the commission of different crimes, surely no legislators or judges can be wise enough to determine the comparative wickedness of those who have committed these crimes. The man who has been convicted only of a petty larceny may be found, when subjected to prison discipline, a much more incorrigible offender than another who committed highway robbery, burglary, or arson. One of the greatest improvements in the administration of our penal code would be to withhold from the judges all discretion as to the time for which convicts shall be confined.

The publication of studies of the Maconochie and Crofton systems that were developed in Australia and Ireland[20] gave impetus to the movement for the use of the indeterminate sentence in the United States. The New York Prison Association continued to advocate the enactment of a law establishing the Irish system. Other prominent prison reformers, particularly Z. R. Brockway, T. N. Dwight, Gaylord Hubbel, F. B. Sanborn, and E. C. Wines, were strong proponents of an indeterminacy in prison terms with power vested in the prison administration to decide the time of prisoners' release. Brockway was perhaps the most influential among these thinkers. In 1870, at the first American Prison Congress convened in Cincinnati by Wines, Brockway delivered a paper on a reformative prison system in which he proposed completely indeterminate sentences and the congress itself, as part of its declaration of principles, concluded that "Sentences limited only by satisfactory proof of reformation should be substituted for those measured by mere lapse of time." In that same year Brockway, who was superintendent of the Detroit House of Correction at the time, proposed to the Michigan legislature a bill providing for sentences without minimum or maximum limits, but his proposal was defeated.

In 1876 when the Elmira Reformatory was established Brockway was appointed as the superintendent of this institution. Again he proposed a wholly indeterminate sentence, this time to the New York legislature, as an adjunct to the program he had established there, a program that resembled the Australian and Irish systems in most fundamental particulars, providing as it did for a marking system, training of inmates, and conditional liberation. Here too, the legislature rejected the principle of complete indeterminacy and provided that imprisonment should be limited by the maximum established in the law for the particular crime involved. The Elmira system represented an important step in the development both of the indefinite sentence and of parole in the United States. It established a precedent for the pattern of statutory maximum sentences with power in an administrative agency, the reformatory superintendent, to release earlier. It also provided for supervision of the parolee by the reformatory for a period of six months during which his parole might be revoked if he violated any of the

[20] For a fuller discussion of transportation and the Irish system, see Chapters 20 and 23.

conditions attached to his release. Brockway was dissatisfied with the "limited indeterminate" or indefinite sentence principle, maintaining that in order to protect the public against "an exceptionally small class of incorrigible criminals" offenders should be subject where necessary to permanent incarceration. It was the indefinite rather than the indeterminate sentence, however, that became the common pattern in the ensuing years. Accompanying this pattern has been a steady increase in the use of parole. Both of these innovations developed rapidly in the ensuing years, though parole has continued to outdistance the indefinite sentence in its acceptance. By 1922, thirty-seven states had adopted some form of indefinite sentence, while forty-four states in addition to the Federal government and Hawaii had introduced a system of parole.[21] In none of these jurisdictions was the completely indeterminate sentence system accepted.

As has been observed above, the indeterminate sentence has been recommended from time to time since the eighteenth century. It is grounded in the belief that one should not apply sanctions proportioned to men's crimes but to the men themselves and that the duration of correction should be determined by their need for and response to treatment. At its extremes this would imply that, however minor his offense, the criminal might be subject to interminable incarceration and that, however serious his crime, he might be released immediately after study and observation. Aside from such extremes, however, it would mean that imprisonment might be long or short without regard to the crime involved. Criminologists have advanced this principle of indeterminacy for probation and parole as well as for prison treatment. Some jurisdictions have approximated the indeterminate sentence in their penal law. California, for example, has set life maxima for lewd acts, burglary, robbery, and murder in the second degree and a fifty-year maximum for rape. For many felonies their minimum is six months or one year. The penal law of Illinois provides life sentences for twenty-five felonies and sentences of twenty years or more for thirty-four. Under life terms, power is generally vested in the parole authority to retain offenders under parole supervision for life if they are released from prison.

Aside from rather exceptional cases, our criminal law has rejected the principle of the indeterminate sentence because it is so foreign to our basic conceptions of justice. It is true that under the civil law we have provided for the indeterminate commitment to hospitals of insane and feeble-minded individuals who are a source of danger to themselves or others. This indeterminacy of treatment has been based partly on the fact that these individuals create a serious risk because of their pathological deviations. It is justified more particularly on the grounds that the duration of therapy and control that may be required cannot well be predicted by medical-psychological science. Although such legislation is designed in part to pro-

---

[21] *Attorney General's Survey, op. cit.,* p. 20. On the indefinite or indeterminate system generally, see *The Indeterminate Sentence,* United Nations, 1954.

tect the community, its primary aim is the care of the defective and the cure, where possible, of those individuals whose ills can be diagnosed with some precision. These persons differ significantly from criminals, who usually display no specific pathology and for whom no effective clinical treatment techniques have been found.[22] The central problem in correction is one of protecting the community from individuals who are emotionally and physically *normal*. These points are stressed again because the attempt to interpret crime as a product of mental disorder and to emphasize the need for clinical treatment of causes avoids recognition of very real differences that exist between clinical diagnosis and psychotherapy for the ill, on the one hand, and a system of criminal treatment rooted in a careful due process of justice and correction, on the other.[23]

Elsewhere the author has presented this critique of the indeterminate sentence principle:[24]

The indeterminate sentence is one of the numerous nostrums that some criminological theorists have recommended from time to time over the past century as a method to resolve the problems of criminal treatment. The principle has been rejected by practical penology in its idealized form of the *open-ended sentence*, except for psychotic and feeble-minded offenders—types that are rather clearly problems of medical treatment and long-term custody. For other criminals the wholly indeterminate sentence has appeared an inappropriate correctional device, not merely because of the reluctance of the bench to relinquish its control over disposition of the offender but, more especially, because of the grave dangers of injustice. In clinical theory it is highly desirable to retain the delinquent in custody until—and only until—the causes of his behavior are resolved so that he can return to the community rehabilitated and no longer dangerous. Our ability, however, to apply this theory to good effect must depend upon a combination of skills: to discover the causes of the delinquency, to apply effective treatment methods according to the requirements of the particular offender, to secure the necessary personnel and other resources for treatment, and—most of all, in the interest of justice—adequate criteria for release.

Until now we have lacked the knowledge, techniques and personnel to attempt this wholly clinical, positivistic approach to the criminal. With good reason we have feared that in actual practice we should err frequently in both directions of releasing too soon individuals who are a serious danger to the community and in retaining too long others whose threat to security is small, whose rehabilitation is difficult or impossible to determine while they are confined in an abnormal institutional environment. The reality of these dangers has been attested often enough in our handling of the defective and insane. As a conse-

[22] Robert Lindner has applied the term "criminosis" to individuals of criminal predisposition but this and analogous conceptions of other behavioral scientists have no specific connotation.

[23] See Tappan, "Concepts and Cross Purposes," *Focus,* vol. 31, pp. 65–69, May, 1952.

[24] Tappan, "Sentences for Sex Criminals," *J. Crim. L.,* vol. 42, no. 3, p. 332, September–October, 1951.

quence we have preferred the compromise of partially indefinite sentences in which minimum and maximum terms are fixed, with the time of release determined by a paroling agency.

SENTENCING LAW AND PRACTICE

In a study recently conducted by the writer,[25] he found that at the present time the indefinite sentence has been adopted as the exclusive form of prison sentence for felons in eight states.[26] In an additional twenty-two states and the District of Columbia it is used more than any other type of sentence.[27] Statistical reports of recent years indicate a very substantial continuing use of definite sentences, however. Thus, in 1950, while 26,768 state sentences were indefinite, 19,728 state and 11,492 Federal sentences were definite.[28] Considering only state sentences, there was an increase in the use of indefinite sentences from 46.6 per cent of all sentences in 1940 to 57.6 per cent in 1950.[29] As has already been implied, such figures present an oversimplification of the picture because of the existing diversity in sentencing practices. Variations occur in the length of sentence imposed in different jurisdictions, in the method of determining parole eligibility, and in the way that ultimate discharge from official control occurs. These variations are far more important than the formal title of the sentence system used by a state. The establishment of parole in all jurisdictions has resulted in a *de facto* system of indefinite terms for felons nearly everywhere. The relative merits of different systems depend upon the consequences of the various specific practices employed. Table 12 provides in major outline information relating to the location of sentencing power both in those states that employ preponderantly the indefinite sentence and in those that use mainly the so-called definite sentence. The table does not reveal all the variations, for in some states definite, partially indeterminate, and fully indeterminate sentences are used. In effect, however, these tend to devolve into some form of indefinite sentence in which upper and lower limits are set by law, court, or administrative agency. It will be noted that in a few jurisdictions the statutes themselves determine specifically the sentence that the court must apply. Elsewhere statutory limits are set but the specific terms of the sentence are determined by the judge, the jury, or an administrative agency, in accordance with the legal provisions of the particular

[25] This was part of the basic research for the development of sentencing provisions of the Model Penal Code of the A.L.I. See Tappan, "Sentencing under the Model Penal Code," *Law and Contemp. Probs.*, vol. 23, pp. 528–544, summer, 1958.

[26] Arizona, Colorado, Michigan, Nevada, New Hampshire, Pennsylvania, Washington, and Wyoming.

[27] See Table 12 in the text.

[28] *Prisoners in State and Federal Prisons and Reformatories, 1950,* Federal Bureau of Prisons, U.S. Department of Justice, 1954, table 27.

[29] *Ibid., 1940,* Bureau of Census, 1943, table 18.

Table 12. Authority for Setting Sentence under the Predominant Sentencing Patterns

Indefinite Sentences

Judicial Determination of Minimum and Maximum within Statutory Limits
  Arizona, Colorado, Connecticut, Illinois, Maine,[a] Massachusetts,[b] New Hampshire, New Jersey,[c] New York, North Carolina, North Dakota, Pennsylvania,[d] Utah,[e] Vermont, Wyoming, District of Columbia[f].

Minimum and Maximum Determined by Statute: No Judicial Control
  Indiana, Kansas,[g] Nevada,[h] New Mexico, Ohio

Judicial Determination of Minimum, Maximum Determined by Statute
  Michigan

Judicial Determination of Maximum, Minimum Determined by Statute
  Wisconsin

No Minimum, Maximum Determined by Statute
  Idaho, Iowa

No Minimum, Judicial Determination of Maximum within Statutory Limit
  Minnesota, Oregon

Jury Determination of Minimum and Maximum within Statutory Limits
  Georgia[e]

Term Fixed by Administrative Agency[i] within Statutory Limits
  California,[j] Washington,[k] West Virginia[k]

Definite Sentences

Judicial Determination of Sentence within Statutory Limit
  Delaware, Florida, Louisiana, Maryland, Montana, Nebraska, Rhode Island, South Carolina, Federal

Sentence Determined by Statute
  Mississippi

Sentence Determined by Jury within Statutory Limits
  Alabama, Arkansas, Kentucky, Missouri,[l] Oklahoma, Tennessee, Texas, Virginia

Sentence Fixed by Administrative Agency within Statutory Limit
  South Dakota

[a] Minimum may not be more than one-half maximum term in the statute.
[b] Minimum not less than 2½ years.
[c] Minimum not less than 1 year.
[d] Minimum not more than one-half maximum prescribed by court.
[e] Parole may occur before expiration of minimum.
[f] Minimum to be not more than one-third maximum.
[g] Governor may parole at any time.
[h] Court may fix minimum or maximum when they are not fixed in statute.
[i] The "term-fixing" powers of the boards are in effect no more than a setting of parole release dates within limits fixed by statute.
[j] Minimum and Maximum are fixed by statute.
[k] No minimum, maximum is fixed by statute.
[l] Board may release at any time.

state. In the definite sentence jurisdictions, the minimum term is ordinarily determined by a general provision of the parole law, as has been noted. In a few states no minimum term at all is fixed, the parole board being therefore empowered to release at any time.

It will be observed that, despite the attacks upon judicial sentencing, judges continue to set sentences within the limits provided by law in twenty indefinite sentence and nine definite sentence jurisdictions. There is no thorough consistency in the pattern, however, for among the states with indefinite terms, the maximum is set by statute and only the minimum is fixed by the court in Michigan, and in Minnesota and Oregon no minimum is set. In Maine, New York, Pennsylvania, and the District of Columbia, the court has discretion concerning the minimum, but the statutes require in certain cases that such minimum shall not be fixed at more than one-third of the maximum in the District of Columbia, one-half in Maine and New York, and one-fourth in Pennsylvania. In a number of states, it will be noted, the statutes establish a mandatory sentence for the various crimes, with no power vested in the judge to vary from such penalties. In two of these, Idaho and Iowa, however, no minimum term is fixed.

A special form of sentencing practice under which prison terms are fixed by an administrative agency rather than by a court is found in four states.[30] In these jurisdictions the maximum of imprisonment that may be served for the particular crime is established by statute but the agency is given power after the offender has been imprisoned to determine the term to be served and to fix the time of release on parole. California and Washington provide that the agency may later change either the length of the maximum term or the date of parole release or both. The idea of the Authority plan on which this sort of policy is based is discussed in the next chapter.

Finally, the jury is empowered to determine the limits of the indefinite sentence in Georgia and to fix the flat term of sentence in eight states. This represents the weakest among the various sentencing techniques, since the lay jury is both untrained and inexperienced in such matters. The jury may reflect community opinion in some measure, but in doing so it is likely either to be too lenient or too harsh in its action. Juries cannot well use presentence investigation or diagnostic reports to good advantage.

Some comment should be made here about the minimum period of imprisonment to be served under so-called definite sentences before offenders become eligible for parole. Provisions vary in this respect. With certain exceptions, prisoners are eligible for parole after serving one-third of their terms in Alabama, Arkansas, Florida, Kentucky, Maryland, Mississippi, Texas, and in the Federal system. They are eligible after serving one-half their terms in Delaware, Montana, Nebraska, Rhode Island, and in certain cases South Dakota. In Missouri the prisoner may be paroled after serving one-fifth of his sentence and in Virginia after serving one-fourth. By action

---

[30] Terms are fixed by statute, release determined by an administrative agency, in California (the Adult Authority), Washington (The Board of Prison Terms and Paroles), West Virginia (the director of Probation and Parole), and South Dakota (the Board of Charities and Corrections). In fact, as the author will note in greater detail in the next chapter, the administrative role involved does not differ greatly from that generally exercised by paroling agencies.

of the governor parole may occur at any time in Oklahoma and South Carolina. In Louisiana and Tennessee definite sentence prisoners are not eligible for parole.

In a number of those states where the judge is empowered to set the minimum and maximum limits of an indefinite sentence within the range provided by statute, there is no restriction on his determination of these limits. In such states if the judge does not believe in parole or if he wishes to make certain that the prisoner is confined for a long period he may set the minimum and maximum close together (viz., from eight to nine or from fourteen to fifteen years). In such cases the paroling authority has virtually no discretion in determining the date on which the prisoner may be released on parole. Little parole supervision can be given him before the date on which he must be discharged.

Maximum and Minimum Terms

Aside from the locus of sentencing power, penal law varies greatly in the maximum and minimum sentences that are made either permissive or

Table 13*A*. Maximum Statutory Terms in Selected Jurisdictions

Terms, in years	Number of crimes			
	Federal	Wisconsin	Illinois	California
Life............	...	6	25	6
50............	...	...	2	
40............	...	2		
35............	...	1		
30............	2	5		
25............	1	6	1	2
20............	12	5	6	13
15............	6	6	2	3
14............	...	1	33	9
10............	31	30	57	50
8............	...	2		
7............	2	12	18	1
6............	...	1	4	
5............	65	32	168	43
4............	...	2	1	2
3............	21	33	19	10
2............	24	14	23	12
1............	44	...	6	1
½............	16			

mandatory under the statutes. This is illustrated in Tables 13*A* and 13*B*, which show the numbers of felonies subject to certain maximum and minimum sentences in four jurisdictions. Definite sentences are used in the Federal jurisdiction. Wisconsin and Illinois both employ indefinite sentences, allowing the court to fix the length of maximum and minimum terms. California requires its Adult Authority to set terms within the limits fixed by law. It will be observed that the limits of Federal sentences are relatively short for most offenses. Illinois permits long terms for many crimes, while Wisconsin employs sentences of short duration. California shifts wide discretionary power to its Authority to set the terms of sentences.

Table 13*B*. Minimum Statutory Terms in Selected Jurisdictions

Terms, in years	Number of crimes		
	Wisconsin	Illinois	California
½ or less...........	17	334	2
1.................	97	15	134
2.................	10	3	6
3.................	11	1	6
4.................	1		
5.................	8	7	3
7.................	1		
10................	4	5	
14................	1	...	1
15................	8		

These data give some indication of the general picture throughout the country. It is apparent that the states set many different maximum and minimum terms for the offenses proscribed in their criminal laws, a wider assortment than could conceivably be justified by any sound effort to discriminate between the seriousness of the crimes or the dangerousness of the offenders involved. The variations in sentences are even wider where the court or some other agency may fix terms within the statutory range. Infinite variation is possible and extremely wide variation is characteristic. This means not only that there may be and are great differences in the sentences for different classes of felonies but that for the same crime different prisoners may have widely different terms to serve. This has proved a major source of discontent among prisoners who hold it to be, as it often is, invidious and unjust.

Disparities in Sentences

Criminologists have devoted little study to the operations of criminal courts. Some attention has been directed from time to time to such matters as the large administrative powers of the prosecutor, the high "mortality rate" of criminal justice, and the futility of the jury system. In recent years more criticism has been directed at the sentencing and dispositions process than at any other phase of court procedure and policy. It is usually claimed that, however well-trained judges may be in the criminal law and in matters of evidence and procedure, their education and experience do not equip them to determine the nature or duration of treatment that criminals should receive. More specifically, it is generally alleged that they lack the training in the social and behavioral sciences upon which to make sound judgments about the individual's need for or probable response to correctional measures. Commonly it is assumed that judges are either retributive at one extreme or sentimental at the other and that, in any case, they ignore the rehabilitative objectives of correctional therapy.

Much of the criticism is predicated upon hypotheses that are unfounded. The fact is that we have failed either to provide the courts with adequate information concerning offenders or to establish clear policies to guide them in sentencing. We need to develop criteria to harmonize our complex and conflicting correctional goals. There are weaknesses in court sentencing, as the most superficial observation reveals, but attacks upon the judges for the most part divert attention from the fundamental problems that are involved.

In advance of discussing judicial sentencing practice it should be noted that, regardless of what agency performs the task, sound dispositions depend upon (1) a penal law that provides proper alternatives and ranges in its sanctions to meet the variety of crimes and offenders involved; (2) a set of clearly formulated objectives that the criminal law and correctional system should attempt to achieve; and (3) criteria for a systematic application of sanctions to offenders looking toward the fullest possible achievement of those objectives. In addition to these more formal standards, it is essential that the personnel charged with the responsibility for making the treatment decisions be capable of weighing the relevant data on the offender and his crime and balancing them against the objectives that correctional justice seeks to attain. Primarily effective dispositions depend upon a judicious quality of mind and temperament that can free itself of emotion and prejudice as it concentrates upon the offender, his crime, the protection of the community, and the means available for achieving these ends.

The data relating to the disparity in sentences will now be examined. According to the last figures published in *Judicial Criminal Statistics* the percentage of convicted offenders sentenced to state prisons and reformatories varied from 12.5 in Pennsylvania to 76.5 in Montana with an average of 36.3. For the nation as a whole the percentage placed on probation ranged from 11.6 in North Dakota to 65.8 in Rhode Island. Such differences as these reflect in part differences in criminality and in correctional resources in the various jurisdictions. In some measures they express variations in treatment policy in the different states.

Federal district court statistics also reveal gross disparity in the sentences of different districts that apply Federal criminal laws. The ranges are too wide to be explained by differences in the nature of the crimes in these districts or by treatment resources. In 1956 the average length of Federal prison sentences varied from 8.6 months in Vermont to 46.9 months in Northern Indiana, with a nation-wide average of 28.9 months.[31] Probation was used in 6.6 per cent of the cases in Arizona and in 84.2 per cent of the cases in New Hampshire. The range in length of prison terms for similar offenses was surprisingly wide in adjoining Federal districts (e.g., 20.5 months in Western Pennsylvania as compared with 44.8 months in Middle Pennsylvania for car theft). The average sentences of individual judges in 1955 varied remarkably. Thus, for interstate transportation of stolen cars, the following variations were observed:

Judge A (N. Ill.)	8.9 months (8 cases)
Judge B (N.Y.)	9.2 months (5 cases)
Judge C (N. Dak.)	9.6 months (8 cases)
Judge D (S. Calif.)	46.6 months (15 cases)
Judge E (N. Calif.)	48.5 months (11 cases)
Judge F (N. Okla.)	51.1 months (31 cases)

To remedy such extremes of variability, Representative Celler introduced in July of 1957 a bill that purported to provide for greater uniformity of sentences. Legislation of the following year gives the Federal judge wider powers in sentencing but this will not reduce the disparities.

Few studies have been made of differences in the sentencing practices of individual judges but those that have been conducted reveal significant differences. One investigation in the criminal court of Essex County, New Jersey, compared the dispositions of six judges who sat there.[32] Table 14 shows the wide variations in the sentences that they imposed.

Table 14. Percentage of Each Kind of Sentence Imposed by Judges
of the Essex County Court

Sentence	Judge 1	Judge 2	Judge 3	Judge 4	Judge 5	Judge 6
Imprisonment.........	35.6	33.6	53.3	57.5	45.0	50.0
Probation............	28.5	30.4	20.2	19.5	28.1	32.4
Fined	2.5	2.2	1.6	3.1	1.9	1.9
Suspended..........	33.4	33.8	24.3	19.7	25.0	15.7
Number of cases....	1,235	1,693	1,869	1,489	480	676

It will be observed that the use of imprisonment ranged from 33.6 per cent of the cases coming before Judge 2 to 57.5 per cent of those before Judge 4 and that probation sentences varied from 19.5 per cent before Judge 4 to 32.4 per cent before Judge 6.

[31] The data given below appeared in a press release a Congressman Emanuel Celler, July 29, 1957, as an argument for new Federal sentencing legislation. The legislation permits Federal judges to sentence to a term with a reduced minimum where he chooses to do so.

[32] F. J. Gaudet, G. S. Harris, and C. W. St. John, "Individual Differences in the Sentencing Tendencies of Judges," *J. Crim. L.*, vol. 23, pp. 811–818, January, 1933.

A study by a New York State Crime Commission a number of years ago revealed extreme disparities in the sentences imposed by criminal court judges in similar felony courts.[33] The commission reported:

> The wide diversity of sentences imposed on offenders committed to state prisons technically guilty of the same offense is apparent. . . . For attempted burglary third degree, the sentences vary from 15 months to five years, for burglary third degree, from two to ten years and sentences for robbery first degree vary from seven and a half years to natural life. There is no uniformity in the sentences imposed for any of the offenses to which these offenders pleaded guilty or were sentenced after trial and conviction.

An unpublished investigation conducted by the author on the sentencing of nine different magistrates in gambling cases similarly revealed wide diversity in the sentencing decisions of the judges in relation to this particular type of offense.[34] The results of this study are shown in Table 15 below.

Table 15. A Sample of Magistrates' Sentences in Gambling Cases in New York City

Judge	Per cent no penalty	Per cent to probation court	Per cent fined	Per cent to workhouse
A	71.7	9.0	24.6	3.7
B	42.8	17.8	14.4	25.0
C	60.6	13.6	19.6	6.2
D	87.8	0.0	1.3	10.9
E	70.0	15.0	15.0	0.0
F	68.7	1.7	4.4	25.2
G	85.6	4.8	4.8	4.8
H	71.0	1.5	11.6	15.9
I	46.5	4.6	4.6	44.3
Total city .	59.9	3.4	23.7	13.0

It will be noted that there was a range of from 42.8 per cent to 87.8 per cent of the cases that were acquitted or given suspended sentences by Judges B and D. The use of probation ranged from zero to 17.8 per cent. The magistrates also displayed wide variations both in the proportion of cases fined and in the size of the fines imposed. One judge did not send any offenders to the workhouse, while another disposed of 44.3 per cent of his cases in this way.

An investigation was also made into the handling of bookmaking cases by these magistrates. Under Section 987 of the Penal Law such cases may be tried by magistrates sitting as Special Sessions judges or, at the defendant's request, may go to Special Sessions Court for trial. The data

---

[33] *Report of the Crime Commission,* 1928, Leg. Doc. No. 23, pp. 330–331.

[34] This study was conducted at a time when the late Mayor La Guardia was exercising considerable pressure on his magistrates to convict gamblers and sentence them severely.

from several hundred cases reveal clearly the search for lenient judges at the magistrates' level and the resort to petitions for trial in the higher court when tough magistrates were sitting.

Table 16. Dispositions in Bookmaking Cases

Judge	Number of acquittals	Number fined	To Special Sessions
I...........	111	57	12
II...........	5	17	25
III...........	37	13	2
IV...........	32	17	0
V...........	0	2	23
VI...........	24	12	3

Although it was impossible to determine all of the factors that may have caused a relatively large number of cases to come before one judge and very few before another in the course of a year, the popularity of certain magistrates and the unpopularity of others with the bookmakers was clear beyond question. Thus, Judge I heard nearly four times as many cases as did any other magistrate sitting in that court and only 7 per cent of his cases requested transfer for trial. Judges I, III, IV, and VI show a high proportion of acquittals in comparison with the cases fined and few appearing before them went to Special Sessions for trial. In striking contrast, Judges II and V, each with a reputation for their extreme severity toward gamblers, had only a small number of bookmakers appear before them. Most of those who were unable to secure postponements to a hearing before a more favorable magistrate secured transfer to the higher court for trial.

It is interesting to note the contrast in results between those cases in which the gamblers were defended by counsel and those not so represented. Counsel was employed by 81 per cent of the bookmakers. Thirty-one per cent of these defendants were convicted, 22 per cent on their pleas. In those cases where no attorney was employed 50 per cent were found guilty, 30 per cent on their pleas.

In another study conducted by the author similarly wide variations were found in the sentencing of three judges who sat in the Girls Term Court of New York City.[35] Here the moralistic element was prominent and the judges' sentencing reflected the variations in both their ethical and religious orientations.

[35] Tappan, *Delinquent Girls in Court*, 1947, especially chap. 6. See also Sidney Levine, "An Experimental Study of the Sentencing of Offenders," *Proc., Am. Prison Assoc.*, pp. 530–539, 1940, and H. E. Lane, "Illogical Variations in Sentences of Felons Committed to Massachusetts State Prison," *J. Crim. L.*, vol. 32, pp. 171–190, July–August, 1941.

There is evidence of intrinsic injustice in the data set out above. This has led to serious disciplinary problems in correctional administration. The excessive variation in the sentences of different criminals whose offenses were similar has resulted in rebellion on the part of individual prisoners and mass prison rioting.[36] This situation should be of sufficient concern to criminologists to promote efforts looking toward change in sentencing procedures.

Imprisonment under the Penal Law

The pattern of imprisonment in the United States will now be discussed. Figure 9 pictures the median length of incarceration in every jurisdiction, the range for the middle 80 per cent of prisoners, and the average duration of imprisonment for the country as a whole.[37] It will be observed that the six jurisdictions where the longest average terms of imprisonment are served employ the indefinite sentence.[38] This fact has led to unsupported inferences of a causal relationship between the form of sentence and length of incarceration. On the other hand, it should be noted that of the six states with the shortest periods of imprisonment all but Delaware use the indefinite sentence. Median duration of imprisonment ranged from nine months in Vermont to thirty-five months in Illinois, with a national average of twenty-one months. The implications of this situation both for human freedom and for correctional budgets are apparent. Henry Sheldon of the Bureau of the Census has commented upon this:[39]

. . . there remain marked differences in the complex of legislative and administrative arrangements determining length of stay. An examination of these arrangements frequently indicates that they represent an unplanned accretion of legislative acts and administrative decisions with little or no central and persisting rationale. Thus, although economy is not a virtue in and of itself, it does seem incumbent upon the agencies in charge of corrections in those states with high retention rates to demonstrate that the money spent in maintaining additional prisoners in prison is compensated for by a reduction in the volume

[36] See *Prison Riots and Disturbances,* prepared by the Committee on Riots, American Prison Association, May, 1953, pp. 14–15, and Report of the Committee to Examine and Investigate the Prison and Parole Systems of New Jersey, Nov. 21, 1952, pp. 81–94.

[37] See *Prisoners Released from State and Federal Institutions, 1951,* Federal Bureau of Prisons, 1955, table 5, in which the differences in duration of imprisonment for each of the major felonies is given according to state. The median duration of imprisonment for robbery ranged from ten months in Maine to seventy-five months in Indiana. For aggravated assault the range was from eight months in Colorado to forty-five months in Illinois. For all offenses the lowest median was nine months in Vermont and the highest was thirty-five months in Illinois.

[38] Among the thirteen states with the longest duration of imprisonment, all but one (Tennessee) use the indefinite sentence.

[39] "Correctional Statistics," in Tappan (ed.), *Contemporary Correction,* 1951, pp. 32–33.

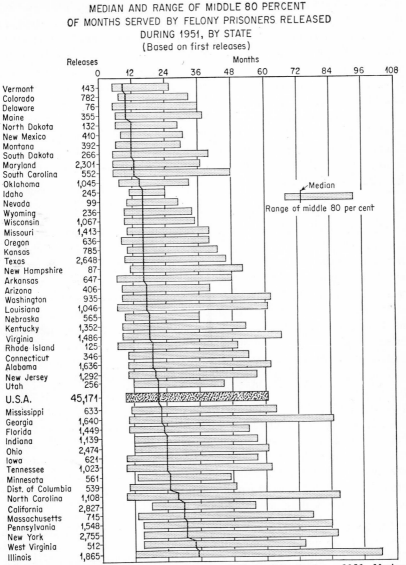

MEDIAN AND RANGE OF MIDDLE 80 PERCENT
OF MONTHS SERVED BY FELONY PRISONERS RELEASED
DURING 1951, BY STATE
(Based on first releases)

FIGURE 9. (*Prisoners Released from State and Federal Institutions, 1951, National Prisoner Statistics, Federal Bureau of Prisons, 1955, p. 5.*)

of crime and in the amount of recidivism. In short, *it must be demonstrated that long prison terms are a part of effective correctional procedure rather than the result of arbitrary legislative decisions for which no empirical justification can be found.*

Federal and state statistics show a trend toward longer periods of imprisonment for the country as a whole. The Bureau of the Census in annual reports on Federal and state prisoners has indicated an increase in the median time served of 17.3 in 1936, 18.5 in 1940, 21.9 in 1942, and 24.6 in 1944. Illinois, California, and New Jersey studies have shown a considerable increase in the average length of prison terms.[40] The figures may reflect the growing public and official concern with crime and, consequently, the increasingly conservative action of parole boards. It is interesting to note that during the period when sentence lengths and imprisonment terms have been increasing here British figures have shown a marked decline in average length of sentence. The percentage of prison terms of three years and under have increased there from 42.2 in 1900 to 69.0 in 1936, while the terms of over five years have declined from 15.1 in 1900 to 4.1 in 1936.[41]

Nature of Sentence and Prison Retention

The introduction of the indefinite sentence and parole has had important consequences in practices of prison sentencing and retention.[42] One result has been the considerable diversification of sentencing methods, which is apparent from the tables above. Another has been the establishment in certain jurisdictions of what seem unnecessarily long permissible terms, even if they are designed to constrain repetitive offenders. This may be interpreted, perhaps, as the persistence of an idealistic and largely anachronistic theory of unlimited control that was implicit in the completely indeterminate sentence principle. A single, long prison sentence is designed to incorporate a period of imprisonment as well as a period of parole supervision and, if necessary, a further reimprisonment for parole violation and, perhaps, reparole. Such provisions for long sentences have been especially characteristic in a few states where the volume of crime is large. Furthermore, prisoners can be retained in prison until the end of their maxima under these terms and parole may either be withheld or revoked at the free discretion of the authorities. Individuals in these states are often subjected to very lengthy imprisonment. Elsewhere much shorter terms are employed for similar crimes.

The contrasting opinions of experts concerning sentencing procedures and their effects are well illustrated in the diverse views expressed by the National Probation and Parole Association. The 1955 draft of the Association's Standard

[40] See Bruce and Harno, *Parole and the Indeterminate Sentence,* 1928, p. 254, and Comment, "The Parole System in Illinois," *Ill. L. Rev.,* vol. 45, p. 237; Fraenkel, "One Hundred Years of Prison Sentencing in New Jersey, 1840–1930," *Proc. Am. Prison Assoc.,* p. 24, 1936; *Survey Report,* Organization of State Correction Agencies, Department of Finance, State of California, 1953, p. 36.

[41] L. Radzinowicz, "The Assessment of Punishments by English Courts," in *The Modern Approach to Criminal Law,* 1945, p. 112.

[42] The material in this section is adapted from the author's research published in "Sentencing under the Model Penal Code," *Law and Contemp. Probs.,* vol. 23, pp. 528–544, summer, 1958.

Probation and Parole Act provided that maximum terms of prison sentences should be fixed by law rather than by the courts and that the court should have the discretionary power either to impose a minimum up to one-third of the statutory maximum or no minimum.[43] In a statement endorsed by the Association's Advisory Council of Judges in 1956, however, this group took the view that the judge should be empowered to fix the maximum of sentences and that there should be no minimum. Also in 1956, in an article on sentencing in an official journal of the Association, the assistant director of the N.P.P.A., now the director, took a position different from either of these, proposing "a uniform provision under which the courts would commit for the *statutory maximum* [a term prescribed in the article as fifteen years] without a minimum."[44] In the same issue the legal counsel of the Association expressed a policy view differing from all of the diverse ideas reflected in the Association's other statements, submitting that we should return to a system of definite sentencing.[45] His argument, based on the theory that prison retention is shorter where definite sentences are used, is that legislation should concentrate primarily on the goal of reducing the length of commitments.

The relationship of prison retention to the length of sentences is a matter of importance about which one would like to know more than can be gleaned from a superficial inspection of the data collected by the states. Unfortunately, inferences drawn from the available material are sometimes quite misleading.[46] It may be useful to scrutinize some of these data, with a view to more accurate appraisal of their significance. Table 17 presents figures published by the Federal Bureau of Prisons on a variety of states employing (1) definite sentences; (2) indefinite sentences in which the maximum is fixed by statute, including two states where a paroling authority determines the time of release and discharge; and (3) indefinite sentences in which the maximum is fixed by the court. The table offers data on the length of prison terms in 1950, including not only detailed figures on the seventeen states listed but also summary figures for all definite sentences and all indefinite sentences for that year. The table also provides general data on the length of prison retention before first release

[43] Section 12. Commentary on this section revealed a wide spread of views among the committee members who participated concerning whether there should be a minimum and whether the limits of the sentence should be fixed by the judge or by law.

[44] Milton G. Rector, "Sentencing and Corrections," *N.P.P.A. J.,* vol. 2, p. 352, October, 1956.

[45] Sol Rubin, "Long Prison Terms and the Form of Sentence, *Ibid.,* p. 337. Rector said, "I do not agree with Mr. Rubin in his conclusion that the indeterminate form of sentencing is less compatible with modern correctional philosophy than is the definite sentence and that it should be abolished. The similarity in practice between the two forms shows clearly that the principle of the indeterminate sentence is sound and that the solution to our difficulty is in further improving the use of the indeterminate form of sentence by the courts and parole authorities rather than in abandoning it." P. 355.

[46] ". . . behind the relatively simple statistical data for each State, and among States, lies an intricate, complex webbing of criminal codes, sentencing practices, and parole laws and policies, extremely difficult to unravel." *Prisoners Released from State and Federal Institutions, 1951,* p. 8.

Table 17. Sentence Lengths and Time Served*

State	Sentence lengths: definite sentences and maximum terms of indefinite sentences, 1950, in years								Time served before first release, 1951, in years			Per cent released on parole
	½ to 2	2 to 4	5 to 9	10 to 19	20 to 99	Life	Indefinite	Total	Median	Middle 80 per cent	Per cent over 5 years	
Definite sentences:												
Montana	192	144	51	18	3	....	1	409	12	6–30	1.0	49.5
Nebraska	184	148	48	13	7	....	3	403	18	9–36	2.7	18.1
Florida	315	632	343	122	68	....	28	1,515	23	10–54	7.5	30.7
Louisiana	246	474	269	103	25	....	40	1,157	17	6–61	10.5	52.4
Missouri	0	1,163	258	80	24	....	18	1,543	16	10–40	6.5	27.8
All definite sentences	4,942	8,648	3,114	1,591	588	....	768	19,728	20	8–57		
Indefinite sentences, maximum fixed by statute:												
Nevada	0	8	34	119	2	4	0	167	16	10–29	2.0	96.0
Iowa	46	17	100	104	9	1	3	280	24	9–57	5.8	41.9
Kansas	8	33	323	344	73	1	0	782	16	10–43	7.1	85.3
Indiana	0	14	378	549	101	0	22	1,064	24	12–57	9.0	80.3
Ohio	3	287	364	674	1,207	4	0	2,539	24	10–57	8.7	93.2
Washington†	0	1	20	582	305	11	6	925	17	8–62	13.7	100.0
California†	2	15	442	1,749	162	683	1	3,054	30	18–56	8.7	73.7
Indefinite sentences, maximum fixed by court:												
Minnesota	28	80	324	148	76	5	0	661	25	13–47	5.7	74.3
Illinois	107	622	519	347	71	24	5	1,695	35	12–102	20.3	47.1
Pennsylvania	12	293	405	319	231	1	135	1,396	31	15–84	21.7	80.1
New York	6	770	1,211	588	162	66	70	2,873	31	15–86	17.0	75.7
New Jersey	39	552	489	175	27	0	46	1,328	20	10–57	8.7	78.9
All indefinite sentences	1,524	6,214	7,517	7,496	2,857	865	295	26,768	24	10–60		
All states									21	9–61	10.1	55.9

* *Prisoners in State and Federal Institutions, 1950,* Federal Bureau of Prisons, 1954, tables 29 and 30, and *Prisoners Released from State and Federal Institutions, 1951,* Federal Bureau of Prisons, 1955, State Tables.

† Maximum fixed by statute, release and discharge dates by paroling agency.

of offenders discharged in 1951 and percentage figures for the cases discharged on parole. A number of conclusions may be drawn from this material.

Definite sentences imposed by courts in the United States are of shorter duration, of course, than are the *maximum limits* of indefinite sentences. Only 32 per cent of the definite sentences were in excess of five years as compared with 67 per cent of indefinite sentences. This contrast reflects different policies governing the definite sentence system. Slightly shorter average duration of imprisonment is also characteristic under definite sentences, a median of twenty months in comparison to a median of twenty-four months for all indefinite sentence prisoners. The difference is largely caused by the greater proportion of offenders in the indefinite sentence states who are retained more than five years, particularly in certain crucial states.

Closer analysis reveals that thirteen of the fifteen southern jurisdictions of the United States use definite sentences primarily. Only five other relatively nonpopulous and noncriminal states use definite sentences in most cases (see Table 12 above). Clearly it is characteristic of the Southern states to use short definite sentences and to imprison offenders for relatively brief periods. It would be inaccurate, however, to conclude that the abbreviated imprisonment is a consequence of the employment of the definite sentence. Undoubtedly a factor of some importance is the limited use of probation in the Southern states. Offenders who are considered good risks go to prison on short terms and are held only briefly. Furthermore, the data on certain of these Southern states, such as Florida and Louisiana, reveal that where crime is deemed a serious problem the authorities are ready to employ long terms of imprisonment. It should be observed further that in several of the definite sentence jurisdictions a relatively high proportion of minor offenders are committed to state institutions designed primarily for felons. The early release of these cases affects the median imprisonment data to some extent.[47] Finally, it may be noted that those states that use primarily indefinite sentencing tend to fix long terms for any prisoners they may commit under definite sentences.[48] *Neither definite sentences nor the retention of prisoners under such sentences are necessarily brief.*

As is shown in Table 12, indefinite sentences are employed for the majority of prison commitments in nearly all of the states that are progressive in their correctional orientation. The Federal data indicate that six states (California, Illinois, New Jersey, New York, Ohio, and Pennsylvania) are responsible for nearly 30 per cent of all prison commitments in the United States and for nearly one-half of all indefinite sentences. These are all indefinite sentence states. Except for California, they are populous and urban areas of the East and North Central regions, where the volume of crime is large and where public and official consciousness of the problem is acute. It is significant that these states not only employ long sentences but display the highest rates of median prison retention and the highest proportions of offenders retained

[47] The Federal Bureau of Prisons observes that this is particularly characteristic in Maryland, Delaware, and Rhode Island. *Ibid.,* p. 7.

[48] *Prisoners in State and Federal Institutions, 1950,* table 29. See in particular the definite terms applied in Illinois, Indiana, Iowa, Kansas, Massachusetts, Ohio, North Carolina, and West Virginia.

over five years as compared with the country as a whole. Obviously they influence heavily the over-all data on lengths of sentence and of incarceration. Thus the national picture of sentencing and imprisonment is highly colored, on the one hand, by a dozen Southern states where terms are short and, on the other hand, by a half dozen jurisdictions where sentences and periods of imprisonment are long and prison populations large. It should be observed, too, that the duration of imprisonment in the latter states is affected by two other factors. In these states where probation resources are relatively good, individuals with the best prospects for rehabilitation are placed on probation. The more dangerous and recidivous offenders go to prison for long terms. In several of these jurisdictions many of the less serious felons are incarcerated in county and local institutions, so that state prison data indicate longer retention periods than would be the case if all felons were covered.[49]

It can be inferred from the data on sentencing that indefinite sentences, whether imposed by law or by the courts, are not the cause of longer imprisonment.[50] The length of imprisonment is related to local and regional characteristics of crime and of public opinion rather than merely to the type of sentencing system that is employed or to the length of terms applied. Furthermore, where statutory maxima are employed, a larger proportion of released offenders are discharged on parole rather than at the expiration of sentence.[51] It is reasonable to believe that when long maximum terms are set by courts rather than by the law parole boards are more inclined to defer to what they may consider to be the judges' view that a long period of prison retention is desirable. Obviously this may be a misinterpretation of the judges' purpose and intent.

Role of the Judge

The indefinite sentence has resulted in an increase in the length of the terms that may be imposed upon convicted felons and the consequent widening of the court's choices in setting sentence. At the same time, the application of parole as an accompaniment to the indefinite sentence has tended to make the role of judicial sentencing somewhat equivocal. With the judge setting broad sentence limits within the statutory provisions, the correctional institution deducting time for good behavior, and the paroling authority determining the actual time of release, it has been difficult to determine how the significant decisions regarding the duration of treatment should be made. The simplest solution for the courts, encouraged by the indefinite sentence laws, would be to forsake responsibility in the matter, merely sentencing to the long maximum terms permitted under the penal law. In some states, as has been seen, courts have been required to do this,

---

[49] The Federal Bureau of Prisons notes that this is true especially in New York, Ohio, and Pennsylvania. *Op. cit.,* p. 7.

[50] Table 17 shows that where the penal law fixes the maximum terms median lengths of imprisonment are lower and percentages of offenders actually serving in excess of five years is smaller than is true in the group of states where the courts fixed lower maximum sentences.

[51] These data are drawn from *Prisoners in State and Federal Institutions, 1950,* chart 6, based on releases in 1951.

though they may decide between imprisonment and noninstitutional sanctions. A good many judges, however, either out of distrust for parole policy or because they see a need to emphasize deterrence and incapacitation in certain cases and to mitigate penalties in others, have used such power as the sentencing system permits them to set long or short prison terms. Legal provisions differ widely, as does professional opinion, concerning the authority that should be exercised by the court and by the paroling agency. This situation is further complicated by the lack of standardized objectives of treatment and of criteria for fitting sanctions to the goals. Therefore, it is not surprising that sentences have varied considerably, not only from one jurisdiction to another, but between judges in a single state. It is quite unrealistic in this situation to impute fault to the judge, for it appears than any agency charged with the task of determining dispositions must labor under the handicap of inexplicit and conflicting policy.

The power that the judge may exercise in sentencing varies widely in the United States, as has been noted. The patterns of distributing control between the courts, parole boards, and correctional institutions also vary. Usually the judge articulates the policy of the state within the provisions of the penal law. Today, however, our courts must look to outside guidance in reaching decisions on sentence. Such guidance includes probation investigations and police reports on the offender, the recommendation of the prosecution and, sometimes, of the jury, the supplication of the defendant, and public opinion. The force of these influences may be so great that it nullifies the provisions of the law in some cases or contravenes reasonable objectives of sentencing. The point should be emphasized again, perhaps, that such peculiarities in the results of sentencing as appear in any comparative investigation reflect the variety of forces that have been enumerated above and not merely the judge's biases. For an improved system of dispositions irrational influences must be controlled, so far as possible. To reiterate, a clearly formulated set of standards and guides is needed to achieve the legitimate goals of sentencing and correction.

Judges are people. Like other humans they have emotions and prejudices and they respond to external pressures. Ethnic minority members are sometimes handled by the courts with apparent bias, as they are even more often by the police and by correctional personnel. This observation applies also to representatives of differing socioeconomic levels. Some judges have strong distaste and others considerable tolerance for certain crimes. There are a few rigid, authoritarian judges who are disposed to "throw the book" at the criminals who come before them. There are others who, out of sentimentality, humanitarianism, a purely positivistic philosophy, or their own repressed guilt feelings, are wont to treat every offender with excessive leniency. A few judges are convinced that rehabilitation can be achieved only through clinical therapy, while others are convinced that the behavioral sciences have no relevance to sentencing and correctional treatment. Some judges are motivated in their conduct by their concern about reelection, reappointment, or advancement.

It is easy to impute any of these motives to the judge. As a matter of fact, however, seasoned judges are much less inclined to express improper subjective motives in their sentencing decisions than are other authorities. Legal training and more particularly the tradition of the bench emphasizes forcefully the requirement of impartiality and the necessity of weighing conflicting interests and of repressing emotional reactions. In this respect the attitudes and practices of the judiciary are in striking contrast with administrators' preoccupation with immediate problems and *ad hoc* solutions. Judicious qualities are not easy to attain, to be sure, even with long training and experience, and many lawyers are temperamentally incapable of achieving them. The attainment of judicious qualities among judges is a relative matter, depending in great measure on the individual's capacity to exercise critical intellectual judgment in the face of emotion-provoking situations. Perhaps there is no other type of professional training and experience that places such value upon objectivity in harmonizing conflicting interests. It is particularly this sort of preparation that is needed for the sound implementation of the state's correctional objectives in sentencing.

Chapter 16

IMPROVING THE DISPOSITIONS PROCESS

Strenuous disapproval of court sentencing and its results has been expressed both by criminals and criminologists. Prisoners believe in the fairness of uniform and consistent sentencing. Theoretical criminologists, while they too have criticized unreasonable variations in sentences imposed by the courts, have been more vocal about the failure of courts to adapt treatment decisions to the rehabilitative requirements of individual criminals. In general, judicial sentencing has been disparaged on two inconsistent grounds: the failure to achieve uniformity, on the one hand, and individualized treatment, on the other. It is true, unfortunately, that neither objective is well served under present methods of disposition. The analysis of the problem has usually been oversimplified, however. Perhaps it is for this reason that proposals for remedy have for the most part been unrealistic. The most common among these in past years has been the establishment of some sort of dispositions tribunal or Authority plan. This idea was most explicitly exemplified in the Model Youth Correction Authority Act of the A.L.I. Its provisions and the development of the Authorities in California as derivatives from it will be considered in this chapter. Other more recent proposals of the A.L.I. in the tentative drafts of the Model Penal Code will also be presented.

AUTHORITY PLANS AND ADMINISTRATIVE HEGEMONY: THE PASSING OF A PANACEA

The Authority plan contemplates the vesting of broad powers in an expert administrative board. It reflects the view that greater consistency and superior policy will emerge from a single agency that is charged with the entire task of sentencing, treatment, and release planning. It is true that such integration of sentencing and corrections should result in some measure of increased uniformity in practice. But it may be apparent from the author's discussion that the problems involved in the disposition process cannot be solved best by entrusting to one board powers to deal with a series of quite different and complex functions. In this, as in other areas of government, a balancing of responsibilities between specialized agencies is desirable to avoid distorted policy judgments at one or another level of operation. Sentencing decisions should be made by a court that has con-

victed and studied the offender; treatment decisions by correctional administrators who are experienced in custody and treatment; and parole decisions by a specialized agency that is familiar with the problems of release,
community supervision, and discharge.

The idea of an omnicompetent Authority, vaguely defined in relation to
its functions, became something of a panacea among criminologists in the
late nineteenth century. Since then conceptions of the Authority plan have
varied somewhat in detail, partly as a consequence of compromises between the conflicting interests at stake, but for the most part they have involved the following features:

1. High maximum or completely indeterminate sentences fixed by law.
2. The abolition or gross reduction of court power to determine sentence.
3. Study of the offender by a diagnostic agency of some sort.
4. Administrative determination of the actual term of imprisonment and
the date of release, generally on the basis of the diagnostic information.
5. Ultimate power vested in the authority to control the procedures of
investigation, sentencing, treatment administration, and release. The latter
has become a central feature of the Authority plan.

The ideal of the correctional Authority did not become a concrete proposal until the development of the Model Youth Correction Authority
Bill that was prepared and supported by the A.L.I. in 1940. This bill
envisaged the establishment of an expert board, the Youth Correction
Authority, to which criminal courts must commit offenders above juvenile
court age up to the age of 21 for study and disposition. Such individuals
would be studied in a diagnostic center and thereafter classified for treatment by the Authority according to their individual needs, which might
include probation or an institutional commitment. The bill provided that
youths would ordinarily remain subject to the disposition of the Authority
up to the age of 25 years but that they might thereafter be retained under
treatment upon petition of the Authority to the courts showing cause and
approval thereof by the court. Thus the "sentence" could be made indeterminate in effect by action of the Authority, though with the protection of
judicial review of Authority action. The object of the proposal was to improve treatment planning for the youth group that has constituted such a
particularly difficult class of offenders. The act provided further that the
Authority might employ existing agencies and facilities and that it should
establish and maintain new institutions as they were needed. This meant
that the paroling Authority would also administer corrections to some
extent.

The Youth Correction Authority plan has not been adopted anywhere
in the form that was developed by the A.L.I. While there have been since
1940 a series of proposals and some legislation adapted from that plan,
these have all differed to a substantial extent from the design proposed by

the institute. For the most part they have not focused upon the youth group at all but upon children in the juvenile courts. Indeed, by classing children and youths together in some states, the effect has been to confuse further the distinctions in their needs. Moreover, the central purpose of the Youth Authority plan was to provide careful and consistent treatment planning for offenders over juvenile court age. The Authorities established have incorporated a variety of child welfare and delinquency prevention programs that have no real relevance either to the problems or the methods of proposed solution that were contemplated by the institute recommendations. Let us consider the brief history of the development of Authorities.

Federal courts and agencies have devoted more systematic thought to the reform of dispositions procedures than have any of the state agencies. In July of 1941 a bill was submitted to Congress to establish a partially indefinite sentence system.[1] This proposal contemplated that the courts would sentence to a maximum term no higher than the statutory limit and that the parole board would determine ultimately the definite term that the prisoner should serve. Opposition to this bill led to a proposal for a Federal Corrections Act.[2] This provided that the courts would sentence to the maximum term fixed by statute and would then remand the offenders to a diagnostic center where they should be studied for a period of six months. Upon the results pursuing from such study, the courts would then resentence offenders to a definite term, although the courts were not to be required to follow the recommendations of the diagnostic unit. It was envisioned that sentencing would come to be determined more by clinical and administrative judgments than by judicial decisions. While opposition from the circuit court judges resulted in the abandonment of these proposals, a Federal Youth Corrections Act was enacted in 1950 that follows the same general line of policy.[3]

The Federal Youth Corrections Act was not implemented until 1953 when a youth division of a reconstituted board of parole was established. The act and its administration are of some special interest because it is the only legislation thus far inspired by the Authority idea that is truly focused upon the young adult group with which the A.L.I. was concerned in its model bill. Under this Federal law, however, full power is left to the Bureau of Prisons and its director to classify and transfer offenders, to determine their treatment, and to operate the institutions. The youth division is given merely advisory functions to recommend with respect to general treatment policies for offenders sentenced under the special six-year sentence provided in the law.[4] Thus the division, aside from this limited

---

[1] H. R. 1071, 77th Cong., 1st Sess., July, 1941.

[2] See Hearings on H. R. 2139 and 2140, May and June, 1943.

[3] Public Law 865, 81st Cong., ch. 1115, 2d Sess.

[4] The sentencing provisions under this law are discussed in greater detail in Chapter 14 in relation to the specialized problem of sentencing of young adult offenders.

advisory role, is primarily a paroling agency for the young adult group and not truly an "Authority" with diverse and multiple powers as traditionally conceived by the criminologists. It is not defined as an Authority under the law. The primary significance of the Federal act, perhaps, is in providing for discretionary short terms for young adults up to the age of 26 and for intensive treatment efforts in their behalf.

The California Authorities

There has been some development of Authority plans at the state level, but these have failed to emphasize the special sentencing and treatment of youthful offenders. California enacted its original version of the Youth Correction Authority in 1941 and has subsequently revised the law several times. The plan provides that the Authority may accept delinquents from children's courts as well as youths from the criminal courts up to the age of 21. It exercises a wide variety of responsibilities other than the fixing of terms and the planning of release.[5] At the present time the Youth Authority Board is made responsible for these diversified functions: the acceptance or rejection of commitments, designation of place of detention for its wards, assignment and transfer of wards to institutions, parole releases and discharges, determination of conditions of parole, orders for return to court for redisposition, orders of return of nonresidents to places of residence, adoption of standards and qualifications for personnel, revocation or suspension of paroles and reconfinement or renewed release, and examination of wards and reexamination at least once each year to determine whether existing orders and dispositions should be modified.

The director of the Youth Authority is made responsible for a series of additional and varied functions: transfer of wards, establishment of classification and discipline policies of the board, establishment and operation of treatment and training services, creation of administrative districts, employment and discharge of personnel, establishment of agencies to work for the prevention of delinquency, contracting with colleges and other organizations for research and training of workers, collection of statistics and information, deposit or investment of inmates' funds, inspection of all public institutions and agencies that the Authority may use, establishment and operation of places for detention as well as places for examination and study and all varieties of correctional facilities, development of conservation work with state and Federal divisions, growing and harvesting of crops and protection of natural resources, examination and reporting on adult and juvenile probation, establishment of standards for performance of probation duties, establishment of standards for juvenile halls and other deten-

---

[5] See *California Youth Authority Progress Report, 1948–1952*. The material here and that below relating to sentencing of young adults has been adapted in part from Tappan, "Young Adults under the Youth Authority," *J. Crim. L.*, vol. 47, no. 6, pp. 629–647, March–April, 1957. (Reprinted by permission.)

tion facilities, and treatment of wards through all useful methods of correction.

It will be observed that the Youth Authority Board as such is assigned tasks primarily of classification, parole release, revocation, and discharge. Except for responsibilities for classification, the board functions are similar to those of any paroling agency. In the tasks of the director of the Youth Authority, on the other hand, are found substantial departures from the orthodox correctional pattern of separating the functions of institutional administration, parole, probation, and prevention. In 1953 revised legislation established these administrative functions as the special responsibilities of the director rather than the board.

It is in accord with sound administrative practice that the single executive should be charged with such functions as the administration of diagnostic and treatment facilities. The partial separation of these functions from the Authority Board in California appears to have been a very considerable improvement. Moreover, the specialization of function has been greater than appears in the statutes. The director is charged with such a number and a variety of important duties relating to juveniles and youths that he has little time for board functions. It is the writer's impression that he has tended increasingly to function as a director of corrections at the juvenile and youth levels. His representative does occasionally sit as a referee at hearings on classification and parole and, as opportunity permits, he does so himself. The director is assisted by deputies in charge of diagnosis and treatment, of field services, and of business services, and by officers in charge of the more detailed phases of classification, training, parole field services, delinquency prevention and probation, etc. In major respects, the Department of the Youth Authority and its divisional staffs parallel the Department of Corrections *together with* the Adult Authority. However, whereas administrative duties and parole functions are strictly distinct at the adult level, they are in theory—and in some measure in fact—combined at the juvenile and youth level. A separation of functions has been developing, however, both in the law and, to an even greater extent, in practice. This trend may reasonably be expected to continue. The result is a system that deviates significantly from the Authority idea.

The author has previously remarked upon the failure of existing Youth Authority plans to concentrate their efforts upon youthful criminality. It was largely through an accident of history that when the California Authority was established a primary emphasis was placed on the administration of juvenile institutions. This was a consequence of the failure of an impoverished and scandal-ridden system of training school administration. The problem was turned over to the Authority at the start in a time of crisis. Therefore, the distinct needs of the young adult offender population, for whom the Youth Authority movement was initiated, could be given only incidental attention. This has continued to be true, by and large, throughout the history of the Authority development there and elsewhere. In 1955 more than three-fourths of the 2,724 commitments to the Youth Authority were of juveniles under the age of 18, nearly all of them from the juvenile courts. On the other hand, 97.2 per cent of the 658 offenders from 19 to 21 years of age committed to the Youth Authority had been sentenced as felons or misdemeanants by the ordinary criminal courts. A smaller number in this age range was committed to the adult Department of Corrections. More important, however, is the fact that the young adults, whether committed to the Youth Authority or the Department of Corrections, are handled almost entirely in the reception-diagnostic facilities of the adult department and thereafter are imprisoned in institutions (the Deuel Vocational Institution and state prisons) of that department. This indicates a recognition that the behavioral problems in the age range of 18 and over are better handled under an adult correctional system than under an administration that is focused primarily upon juveniles.

Confusion and lack of coordination are reflected in parole practices. Both the Youth Authority Board and the Adult Authority hold parole hearings for the young adults in these institutions of the Department of Corrections, according to the nature of the commitments, and release offenders in turn to supervising officers either of the Youth or the Adult Authority. Since the sentences received and the periods of imprisonment vary greatly between the two groups of youthful offenders, their handling is marked by an invidious diversity of policy and practice. The more orthodox hierarchal pattern of court sentencing, institutional administration, parole board release, parole field administration, with specialized agencies entrusted with each of the specialized tasks, offers greater advantage for the systematic treatment of young adult offenders.[6]

Since the establishment of the California Youth Authority, somewhat similar plans have been adopted in several other jurisdictions: Illinois, Kentucky, Massachusetts, Minnesota, Texas, and Wisconsin. In these states, too, the orientation is toward juvenile delinquents. Only Minnesota deals with young adult offenders as well as with juveniles. In Minnesota, as in California, these individuals are imprisoned in an institution, the State Reformatory at St. Cloud, administered by the adult correctional department. Parole release is entrusted to two different agencies. The Minnesota plan has resulted in waste and duplication of effort and has created morale problems among inmates serving disparate terms for similar crimes. Marjorie Bell and the late Charles Chute of the National Probation and Parole Association, writing about the Youth Authority development, contrast the functions performed by these agencies with the purpose originally envisioned under the Model Youth Correction Authority Act:[7]

---

[6] Tappan, *ibid.*, p. 642.

[7] *Crime, Courts and Probation,* 1956, pp. 160–161. (Reprinted by permission.)

State boards have been created in each of the seven states under varying names and with varying powers. Some of them are independent; others are attached to existing welfare or correctional departments. In every case commitment of youths as well as children is optional with the courts, and only a small percentage of juvenile delinquents and an even smaller percentage of youths have been so committed. . . . All of the state boards are concerned chiefly with two functions, neither of them contemplated in the original act: (1) dealing with children committed by juvenile courts for transfer to suitable institutions for delinquents, and (2) administering those institutions. All of them have become primarily state juvenile agencies. As such they have performed a greatly needed service in improving the training schools and their release programs. In California, the only state where it has been given sufficient funds for the purpose, the Authority has been successful in opening new institutions, schools, and camps for delinquent children and youth.

It may be apparent that the Youth Authority movement has not had the impact that had been contemplated either upon sentencing or upon mature youths. It has been very largely, except for the more ambitious developments in California, an agency for the administration of juvenile training schools and community recreational programs.

The California Adult Authority

In 1944 California established an Adult Authority to replace its former Board of Prison Terms and Paroles. It resembles more closely than do the Youth Authorities the ordinary criminological conception of an Authority, for it acts in a limited measure as a dispositions agency. Under California law the courts have power to determine whether convicted offenders should be sentenced to fine, probation, or imprisonment. If they determine upon imprisonment, however, they must sentence to the minimum and maximum terms fixed in the penal law.[8] We have already observed the wide ranges provided in such terms. After the prisoner is studied in a diagnostic center and ordinarily within a period of six months after sentence, the offender is interviewed by a member of the Authority and dates are tentatively set both for his time of release and for his discharge from parole. Such dates may subsequently be redetermined at six-month intervals. This is the so-called term-fixing function of the board. These powers do not greatly exceed or differ from those of the ordinary paroling agency in those states where the board has power to discharge before the expiration of sentence.[9]

While the term-fixing of the Adult Authority is similar to the task of any parole board in determining, within his sentence, the date for the offender's parole release and for his discharge from supervision, the result of

[8] *California Penal Code,* Secs. 1168, 3023.

[9] In most jurisdictions the determination of the time for discharge occurs by statute rather than by a board decision. For further discussion of the Adult Authority as a paroling agency, see Chapter 23.

Authority operation appears to be a considerably greater uniformity in the periods of prison retention of offenders convicted of similar crimes. According to an official report the Authority stresses in its decisions the following factors: (1) the nature of the crime, (2) the deterrent effect of punishment, (3) the equalization of punishment, (4) previous criminal record, (5) prison behavior and attitude, and (6) the length of time it is desired to keep an offender under control.[10] Among these considerations, it appears, primary emphasis has been placed upon uniformity of terms. It has been reported that in recent years release and discharge dates have varied for the most part only from six months to two years for identical offenses. The average length of time served by felons in California is similar to that of the United States as a whole (29.7 months as compared to 29.6 months in 1951). The dispersion of terms served is smaller and such variation as is found may be attributed largely to cases where minimum terms set by the law are high. There has been a gradual increase in the length of terms fixed by the Authority since its establishment.

Aside from the ordinary parole functions of the Adult Authority, noted above, that board until 1954 differed from others in the United States in its administrative functions. It performed in these major supplementary roles:

1. The supervision of "reception-guidance centers" or diagnostic and classification clinics.

2. The classification of prisoners to determine the institutions at which they should serve their sentences.

3. The determination of the nature, type, and duration of punishment administered to prisoners.

4. Service as an advisory pardon board, the restoration of civil rights.

5. Representation on the Board of Corrections.

6. The administration of field supervision services.[11]

In 1953 California conducted a critical survey of the organization of its state correctional agencies with a view to determining the soundness of the allocation of functions and powers established in its laws.[12] As a consequence of this study the administrative functions of the board that overlapped with those of the director and Department of Corrections were taken away so that the Adult Authority is now only a paroling agency. The broad and diverse functions of the Youth Authority, however, were left intact.

The California Authority plans have been discussed in some detail because they provide the best illustration of the Authority ideal in operation.

[10] See *Philosophy, Principles and Program of the California Adult Authority*, Department of Corrections, January, 1949.

[11] *Principles, Policy and Program*, California Adult Authority, Department of Corrections, June, 1952, p. 4.

[12] *Survey Report*, Organization of State Correctional Agencies, Department of Finance, Management Analysis Section, May 4, 1953.

As has been seen, both in their establishment and subsequent evolution these Authorities have deviated from the traditional criminological conception of a specialized sentencing agency. There are important reasons why the intrinsic merits of the Authority idea cannot well be judged by experience in California, though that is the only state that has developed the idea to any significant extent. The rapidity of the growth of California's population is unique; its very large and increasing crime rates and its urban and industrial development are also unique. California has been oustanding too since the early 1940s in its development of diagnostic and correctional facilities both at the juvenile and the adult levels. This progress should be attributed in the main to a number of factors there that have favored constructive correctional innovations, including Governor Warren's strong impetus in this area, stimulated by the seriousness of the problems that had to be faced, the scandalous inadequacy of the existing resources and personnel, the generous cooperation of the legislature, and the recruitment of an outstanding correctional administration. The state has become a leader in the correctional field. This apparently should be attributed to such factors as have been mentioned rather than to the particular administrative structures that were established and changed rapidly under the pressure of the growing needs of the system. Without the instrumentation of Authority plans, comparable developments have occurred in other states, too, including the establishment of diagnostic and reception centers, diversification of institutions, integration of court sentencing with treatment and release planning, improved classification, professionalization of parole, specialized youth courts and youth treatment services, and delinquency prevention programs. The establishment of broad powers to integrate sentencing and correction in an administrative agency could lead to a quite different structure and different consequences in other jurisdictions. Widely divergent experience with the development of Youth Authorities in other states lends support to this conclusion.

Functions and Coordination of Judiciocorrectional Agencies

Criminal jurisprudence has provided little critical analysis of the ways in which judiciocorrectional functions are distributed among the specialized agencies involved, of the extent to which these functions should be coordinated, and of the influence exercised by the ordering of procedures. The roles and the procedures of the instruments of justice and correction have evolved for the most part in an unplanned fashion. As new agencies and measures have developed, they have been joined to preexisting structures, old and new, with little effort to systematize or rationalize the whole. Time and experience gradually develop some reorganization of measures to ensure more effective operations. The roles and procedures of the various agencies involved continue, however, in a condition of slow flux and of wide variation. In differing jurisdictions may be observed considerable diversity in the distribution, ordering, and coordination of functions in handling the offender, as has been observed. Diversity is particularly obvious in the more recent accretions to judicial-correctional operation, such as practices in the fields of probation, parole, and the indefinite sentence and in some phases of correctional administration. Variation is less common in more thoroughly institutionalized phases of the system such as trial procedure, guilt determination, and the pardoning process.

It cannot reasonably be doubted that attainment of the ends of justice depends very fundamentally upon an appropriate organization of functions and power. Unfortunately, the creative plotting of a sound system of procedure and authority is not easy. Paper plans, particularly when they are broadly comprehensive, cannot comprehend the infinitude of factors that may prove, as by-products of a conceptual scheme, to interfere seriously with or indeed wholly to negate the goals that we seek to achieve. The more completely a scheme departs from our practical and proved experience, the more difficult it is to envision the complex of associated problems that may develop in its administration. It is apparent that in attempting to resolve a subtle problem or to meet a complexity of goals no simple scheme should be expected to function effectively. Thus, if the need is to harmonize a series of objectives that are varied and partially incompatible, the issue cannot well be met either by mere simplification of objectives or by establishing some elementary scheme for their effectuation. A great difficulty in contemporary legal administration lies in the effort to achieve complicated objectives through formulations of general and broad policy, entrusting to expert boards the duty of achieving them without establishing proper criteria, procedures, and limitations of power.

Checks and Balances of Power. The principle of checks and balances is generally considered a sound restriction on methods of governance. It is dangerous to allow one agency to formulate rules of policy, to police conformity, to adjudicate breach, and to administer penalties. It is generally unwise even to allow a single authority to perform any two of these functions. The danger is essentially that excessive power is thus concentrated in one source without sufficient restriction on its exercise. Beyond this, however, it is recognized that where several functions are specialized and distinct a single agency is quite unlikely to be able to perform each well and that concentration on one or two of the functions tends to lead to distortion in the performance of the others.

With the rapid growth of administrative government, the hazards of excessive and unchecked power have become increasingly great. Particularly in areas of specialization where the problems to be met are complex, it is difficult for the external observer to determine how accurately or how fairly policy is being implemented. The relative concealment of expert administrative operations and the lack of a developed system of due process conceptions to guide administrative function increase the possibility that important policy measures may be poorly formulated or inappropriately instrumented. Judicious qualities of mind and judicial techniques of inquiry are not the rule among effective administrators who are bent upon speedy attainment of goals. There is little respect among them for "legalism," "technicality," "due process," or other obstructions to the exercise of power.

The comments above have special applicability to judiciocorrectional operations at a number of points. Take, for example, the fields of parole, probation, and institutional discipline where the joining of functions is obvious. Rules conditioning the offender's freedom and the functions of policing, adjudication of violations, and determination of sanctions may all be made by the same agency without an adequate check upon its discretion. To avoid abuses the development of measures for judicialization and due process in parole and probation are particularly important, therefore. At the same time, such measures are repugnant to some officials who maintain they need to exercise unhampered discretion in accordance with the apparent treatment needs of the individual.

Perhaps the need for checks and balances is less immediately obvious but it is no less real in other phases of correction if we are to avoid the consequences of concentrating diversified administrative power in a few hands. Here lies the greatest difficulty with the Authority or "treatment tribunal" idea. If sentencing and correction involved, as some authorities maintain, simply attempting to discover why the offender got into trouble and then applying treatment of the type and duration required to "cure" him of his problems, some case might be made for the Authority scheme. One could then, perhaps, establish some theoretical justification, for sentences without minimum terms and with indeterminate maxima, combined with a wholly therapeutic correctional scheme. The dangers both to the public and the individual offender entailed in such a complete departure from the ideal of justice according to law are clear, particularly in the absence of relevant knowledge and competent personnel to implement such a philosophy. The author has suggested that our objectives are in fact more complicated than this theory would suggest. The point made here is that to serve these multiple objectives we require both a real division and a reasonable ordering of functions and responsibilities.

As experience has already attested in some jurisdictions, coordination in correctional operations need not be based upon a single all-powerful agency. There can and should be close liaison between court and correctional facilities. It is equally important, however, that there be sufficient autonomy in those with distinct functions so that primary power is vested in the individuals who must carry the functional responsibility. While there must and should be a higher over-all administrative power in a correctional department, such authority should not interfere needlessly with details of day-to-day policy and program operation.

The judiciocorrectional functions are distinct phases of dispositions, each somewhat differently oriented in purpose. These functions are summarized below:

1. At the court sentencing phase, the need is to establish the outer limits of a term that will assure sufficient incapacitation to protect the public, that will provide some gradation for general deterrence, that will take into account the moral-educative function of sentencing, that will provide fair opportunity for rehabilitative effect if this can be achieved, and finally that will protect the offender himself from excessive and inhumane detention. The accomplishment of these objectives requires scrutiny primarily of the crime itself and the mitigating or aggravating circumstances surrounding it, the offender's prior criminal history, the public reaction to his offense, and—related to all of these —the general probabilities of his reformation.

These objectives may be served most effectively in the court arena where a peculiar combination of timely and apposite influences occurs. There are then freshly and fully developed the products of investigation by the police, prosecution, probation, and possibly a court clinic, information which together should well clarify both the character of the immediate crime and the criminal's history and which should direct a special focus upon one or more of the sentencing objectives in accordance with the facts there elicited. It is obvious that in the community where the crime and court action occurred and with the offender on that scene for interrogation and observation there is optimum opportunity to achieve the balance of goals and methods that should then be struck. The well-seasoned criminal court judge is peculiarly the person to weigh the several interests at stake. This is truer, of course, if there has been a trial, but even in the absence of trial the criminal comes under most direct and careful scrutiny as a dissident member of the community immediately prior to the court determination of the terms of sentence. The decision at this time is not made either upon a mere paper record nor on a solely individualized, and hence distorted, clinical discovery but upon a broad view of ultimate social purposes and with factual data at hand concerning the dangerousness of the criminal.

In addition to the sentence at this time, moreover, as will be noted below, reports and advice should go from the court to the classification center, correctional institution, and parole board to be weighed in subsequent decisions of those agencies. The sentence of the court however is designed to set the broad policy for treatment, not to determine the details or the termination date of treatment.

2. The second phase of dispositions is that of reception and diagnosis for purposes of correctional planning. Subsequent to court sentence the offender should be carefully studied as an individual at a classification center with a view to determining what institution and what treatment programs, among those available in the state, may meet best his apparent needs of custody, training, and treatment. Such study and classification should be guided in part by the reports and counsel from the court but will focus particularly upon the

personality and social relationships of the offender. An investigation of this sort can be relatively complete and objective in an institutional setting, removed both in place and time from the court experiences. The objectives of the classification process must still reflect the broader purposes of protecting divergent interests that are implicit in the sentence of the court. However, the focus here is on the individual and his trainability. Since an effective system of correctional treatment requires flexibility, provisions should be made, where it appears desirable, to return offenders to the classification center for restudy and reclassification.

3. Treatment in the correctional institution requires greater individualization of focus in day-to-day treatment within the framework of the established system of classification: a detailed planning of the education, training, clinical treatment, recreation, and other privileges as well as custodial, maintenance, and productive phases of correction. In a well-diversified system of correctional institutions this should in fact require a correspondingly limited range of programs in each individual institution. Particularly in small minimum- and medium-custody prisons, quite intensive efforts should be directed toward individual interpretation and counseling with inmates. It should be stressed that this sort of administration of a correctional facility, while it requires ultimate policy formulations in a state correctional department and advice on treatment of individuals from the court and classification agency, is essentially a total community enterprise, requiring semiautonomous operation and leadership.

4. The fourth major phase of dispositions is that of parole release, an adjudicative function. Under a system of indefinite sentencing it is in some respects more difficult and more significant than court sentencing, for it involves the ultimate determination, within broad sentencing ranges, of the time when the offender will actually leave prison. This decision depends partly upon his conduct in prison, of course, but more upon his progress under treatment, the measure of his immediate threat to society, the community's readiness to receive him, and the development of a sound program for his assumption of responsibilities under supervision on the outside. The decision to release on parole is perhaps the most difficult step in the dispositions processes, for measurements of the factors described are inadequate and procedures for this type of adjudication are not fully developed. It is a task requiring trained wisdom, judicious balance, detailed information, competent advice, and a respect for human liberty. It is definitely not a job for the politician, the crusader, the censorial puritan, the part-time "do-gooder," the retired civil servant, or the clinician without a clinic. Nor is it a job for an omniscient board of experts with a great variety of functions. When a man has spent some years in prison for a crime, the issue of his readiness for release is no subject for decisions by hurried, romantic, retributive, or politically motivated personalities. The best possible results may be achieved only from reasonable, intelligent, broadly experienced, judicious, full-time employees whose training is drawn from the several relevant social and behavioral sciences, men whose competence includes particularly experience and training in the field of correction. Every month that an offender spends unnecessarily in prison or injuriously in the community as a result of a faulty parole decision is a destructive

testimonial of our ignorance or carelessness, a blow to the progress of corrections and parole.

5. The revocation of parole for violation of the conditions imposed is essentially a judicial inquiry of a very significant sort, for it may mean return of the offender to a prolonged prison incarceration. It is in a sense an attempt to discover why the institutional and parole experience failed to accomplish its objective and to determine the need for further institutional custody and treatment. This is a problem of weighing the values of individual freedom and public security and of deciding whether further and perhaps more effective treatment of the individual should be undertaken.

These decisions on release and revocation, it may be noted again, are oriented differently from court sentencing, clinical study, and institutional administration, particularly in their focus on the offender's readiness for release. The paroling authority must, in effect, predict the offender's capacity to handle freedom under supervision.

As suggested in the above analysis, a single agency should not be expected to perform efficiently the variety of tasks described. However, these tasks are closely related and must be coordinated through close liaison of the agencies involved. The advantages inherent in the possibly greater integration that might be achieved under a system of concentrated power in a single board are more than outweighed by the virtues of functional specialization in a series of partially autonomous agencies that coordinate their policy at appropriate levels.

TENTATIVE PROPOSALS OF THE MODEL PENAL CODE

The American Law Institute has given critical attention to the problems of sentencing and treatment in its Model Penal Code with the purpose of arriving at policies that might achieve the legitimate ends of correction with increasing effectiveness. It is not feasible to spell out in detail here the reasoning by means of which these policies have been reached. For fuller treatment of this subject the reader is referred to the relevant sections and commentary of the Code.[13] Several proposals are made therein relative to prison terms and parole.

Ordinary Terms of Imprisonment

The Code provides for a grading of felonies into three categories according to their seriousness, with sentences of indefinite length for each category. The maxima of such terms for ordinary offenders would be fixed uniformly by statute, while the minimum terms would be fixed by the court within a limited range established by law.[14] The classification follows.

[13] See in particular Secs. 6.01, 6.06, 6.09A, 305.10, 305.13, and 305.22.
[14] Sec. 6.05 (2) of the *Model Penal Code,* Tentative Draft No. 7, provides for a term without a minimum applicable at the discretion of the court to young adult offenders.

Ordinary Terms for Felons

Grade of felony	Minimum, in years (fixed by court between)	Maximum, in years (fixed by law)
I.............	1–10	Life
II.............	1–3	10
III.............	1–2	5

That prison sentences should be indefinite in length appears entirely clear on the basis of experience and reason. The length of time that an offender should be retained cannot be precisely determined in advance but should be related to his behavior and attitude in the correctional situation. Furthermore, the range between minimum and maximum should be sufficiently wide to adjust the treatment period to the ostensible requirements of the individual and the community.

The classification of felonies into three categories with graduated sanctions is based upon the well-established principle that penalties should be related to the seriousness of the crime and to the potential danger of the criminal. This gradation of indefinite sentences is believed to provide as discriminating a classification as can be justified at the time of sentencing. Such a set of categories would provide a simple system that should contrast favorably with the diversity of sentences that have developed *ad hoc* in our prevailing penal law. It would avoid the invidious variations in terms that are applied to offenders of similar sort and would remove thereby a substantial basis for the sense of injustice that erodes the spirit of many prisoners. The establishment of uniform maxima fixed by statute at each level would go further still to eliminate the chaos of disparate sentences that come out of present law as it is administered by judges whose value systems differ markedly. Courts would retain wide powers to determine sentence by selecting between fine, probation, and imprisonment, by reducing the grade of crime where appropriate, by choosing between ordinary and extended terms,[15] and by fixing the minimum. The power to fix maximum sentences for ordinary offenders may be cherished by some courts, but it has proved too costly a restriction upon the legitimate province of correctional administration. Along with an excessive variation in sentences, judicially determined maxima have provided poor guidance to parole decisions. Some prisoners are held too briefly because the court maximum either required or appeared to suggest short retention; others are held too long because of the persuasive power implicit in the very long terms that may be fixed by a judge. Hence the author has concluded that parole authorities should be entrusted with the task of limiting or ex-

---

[15] The terms discussed here are those applicable to the ordinary felon. The Code provisions for extended terms are discussed below.

tending imprisonment within the range of flexibility provided by reasonable maximum terms established in the law.

Maximum prison terms, while they should be sufficiently long to provide adequate social safeguard, should not encourage abusive prison retention and hopelessness among prisoners. Determination of the desirable length of prison terms is necessarily based in part upon arbitrary judgments. The Code proposals, however, reflect a careful appraisal of present sentencing in the United States and of the periods of prison retention that are employed under the sentences imposed. The common use of life terms, terms of twenty to fifty years, and of long consecutive terms is unnecessary and undesirable, especially where nonviolent felonies are involved.[16] They produce desperation in prisoners without sufficient compensating gains in deterrence. The Code maxima for such felonies are briefer than those prevailing in a number of the states that employ an indefinite sentence system, yet they should provide sufficient public protection. Furthermore, the Code draft provides for parole when it appears that the offender may safely be discharged from prison. Thus the emphasis is on early release of those who do not pose a substantial threat of violation.[17] On the other hand, an offender may be held for a long period if his crime was violent or if his criminal history or personality justifies it.

Minimum terms under the Code would be fixed by the judge within statutory ranges that, except for felonies of the first grade, are rather brief. The matter of minimum sentences, their use and length, is an area of controversy, growing in part out of positivistic theory on the one hand and demands of social defense on the other. In most states, as has been seen, minima have been deemed a matter of practical expedience. Even where they are not established by law, they are commonly applied in fact by administrative practice. We believe that minimum terms should be employed for adult offenders in the interest of general and individual prevention. They should be short enough to provide reformative incentive and in many cases need be no longer than is required for the prison's program of classification, brief treatment, and parole preparation. This can sometimes be accomplished in less than a year. In other cases it is quite clear at the time of sentence that a longer minimum should be fixed both to assure a sufficient period of treatment and as a matter of general

---

[16] In Illinois 126 crimes are punishable by terms of ten years or more, and 34 by terms of twenty years or more. In California the comparable figures are 83 and 21. Maximum terms of ten years or more were imposed in 84.9 per cent of prison sentences in California in 1950, 74.2 per cent in Ohio, 63.2 per cent in Indiana, 49.1 per cent in Pennsylvania, 30.8 per cent in New York, 26.4 per cent in Illinois, and 18.6 per cent in New Jersey. See Chapter 15, Table 17. Also, long consecutive terms are commonly assessed by the courts, a practice that would be carefully controlled under the Code, Sec. 7.06.

[17] See Chapter 23 for a discussion of Model Penal Code provisions relating to parole release.

deterrence. The court should have power to set such higher minima, for it is at the time of sentence that the gravity of the crime is publicly assessed and prevention receives its proper emphasis. For less serious offenses, however, such minima need not be high. It is only in the case of violent felonies, therefore, that the Code provides a considerable latitude in the setting of the minimum.

A "parole term" distinct from the term of imprisonment, as a part of the sentence of the court, is established in the Code and provision is made for the employment in all cases released from prison of parole planning and supervision. This feature of the Code is discussed in Chapter 23.

It is contemplated that most circumstantial and first offenders who displayed no serious abnormality or aggression in relation to their crimes and who responded well to treatment would be released early from prison and, under similarly favorable circumstances, discharged early from parole. Dangerous and repetitive offenders could be held long enough to assure community protection and would be subject to control and reimprisonment if necessary even after the institutional phase of the sentence had been terminated. In many states the effect should be to curtail the present duration of imprisonment of a considerable proportion of offenders, and to subject to longer control a minority of more dangerous and recalcitrant criminals. The Code provides "extended terms" for such individuals.

Habitual Criminals and Extended Terms

The nuclear problem of crime lies in dangerous repetitive criminality, not in the occasional, accidental, or circumstantial offenses committed by persons who are essentially noncriminal in disposition. Crimes committed by such individuals are very numerous in aggregate and, in the interest of general prevention of crime, they cannot be tolerated. Indulgence would encourage transgressions among less socialized members of the community who now pause fearfully at the narrow border that separates the law-abiding from the criminal. The author believes, overoptimistically perhaps, that relatively lenient or nondeprivative sanctions for circumstantial offenders may be sufficient not only to deter them from repetition of unlawful conduct but also to dissuade potential offenders from breaking the law. More vigorous measures must be employed in dealing with the core of hardened criminals who continually endanger the community. It is primarily through our sentencing of this group that we attempt to achieve the ends of incapacitation, intimidation, and group deterrence. So far as possible we also strive to change the attitudes and habits of members of this more difficult group. Endeavors to prevent recidivism among them have been far from successful, largely because of the inefficacy of the measures at hand. These may be improved and, as we gain further understanding of their requirements, it is to be hoped that an increasing proportion of the seemingly intractible will respond to treatment. Our recidivist legislation has been quite unsatisfactory in dealing with them.[18]

Habitual offender laws in the United States developed mainly in response to criminal mob activities after World War I, particularly during the Volstead era.[19] Since then such legislation has been relied upon to deal with organized crime, primarily in the fields of gambling, narcotics, sex vice, smuggling, racketeering, kidnapping, and murder. The recidivist legislation has been used only sporadically against unorganized and minor criminals. The laws are presented summarily in tabular form below.

There are habitual offender laws today in all but five states and the Federal government.[20] Twenty-three jurisdictions provide for life sentences, either in mandatory (eighteen) or permissive terms.[21] The remaining states do not specifically provide for life imprisonment, though in several of these states the courts may employ this disposition at their discretion. The method of increasing penalties varies considerably in the various states: in fourteen a specific minimum and/or maximum period is established by law; in five an additional specified increment and in fifteen a fractional or multiple increment is added to the penalty ordinarily provided for the felony. In five it is mandatory for the court to sentence the offender to the maximum term provided by law for the crime committed. In a few jurisdictions parole rights are affected.

While the constitutionality of the habitual offender laws has been generally upheld, the appellate courts have tended to narrow their application considerably[22] and both prosecutors and trial courts have apparently been reluctant to apply them. The penalties are made discretionary under the terms of fifteen of the jurisdictions noted, but even where penalties are mandatory many of the states rarely apply them. This is because their operation depends upon the prosecution's showing of prior convictions and prosecutors have proved more inclined to use the law as

[18] Material in this section has been adapted in part from Tappan, "Habitual Offender Laws and Sentencing Practices in Relation to Organized Crime," in Morris Ploscowe (ed.), *Organized Crime and Law Enforcement,* Report to the American Bar Association, 1952, pp. 113–117. (Reprinted by permission.)

[19] Some of the states have had recidivists statutes for a good many years, however. Such laws were enacted in Illinois in 1883, Virginia and Massachusetts in 1887, New Jersey in 1890, and Washington in 1909.

[20] Only Arkansas, Maryland, Mississippi, North Carolina, and South Carolina lack such a law. Maryland and South Carolina, however, do provide for increased penalties for certain minor offenses.

[21] See Table 18 below.

[22] *Smalley v. People,* 116 Colo. 598, and *State v. Donnell,* 353 Mo. 878, held that the laws should be strictly construed because of their highly penal character. Opinions in other jurisdictions have denied application of the statutes where the crimes were of different types, where they were committed outside the jurisdiction of the immediate trial, where the defendant was not indicted as an habitual offender, and on the other hand where the facts of prior criminality have been revealed to the jury, where prior crime resulted in a suspended sentence or in a pardon, etc. See *People v. Olah,* 300 N.Y. 96, 89 N.E. 2d 119.

Table 18. Provisions of Habitual Offender Laws

1. Life sentence mandatory upon the court when the offender is convicted for the third time of a felony, without provision for extending the duration of commitment for a second conviction: Indiana.

2. Life sentence mandatory upon the court when the offender is convicted for the fourth time of a felony, without provision for extending the duration of commitment for a second or third conviction: Tennessee and Vermont.

3. Graduated penalties for second and subsequent convictions, but without provision for life sentences as such: Alabama, Arizona, Connecticut, District of Columbia, Georgia, Illinois, Iowa, Kansas, Louisiana, Maine, Massachusetts, Montana, Nebraska, New Hampshire, New York, Oklahoma, Rhode Island, Utah, Virginia, and Wisconsin.

4. Graduated penalties for second convictions, with provision for life sentence for third felony.

    a. Life sentence mandatory: California, Kentucky, Texas, Washington, West Virginia.

    b. Life sentence discretionary: Idaho.

5. Graduated penalties for second and third conviction, with provision for life sentence for fourth felony:

    a. Life sentence mandatory: Colorado, Florida, Michigan, Minnesota, Missouri, Nevada, New Jersey, New Mexico, Ohio, Wyoming.

    b. Life sentence discretionary: North Dakota, Oregon, Pennsylvania, South Dakota.

a means of bargaining for pleas than to secure a life sentence or a very long term. As a result hardened criminals may profit from the recidivist legislation where they can effect a favorable transaction for a plea. In response to an inquiry conducted by the author, attorneys general in the United States pointed to the general circumvention of the laws and the resultant nullification of their deterrent value. One commentator has observed, "Certainly the extent of judicial intransigency [these laws] have incurred points up a need for legislative reexamination not only of present enforcement procedures, but of the entire orientation of existent recidivist legislation."[23]

It is interesting to observe that in foreign countries where recidivist legislation has also very commonly been established their experience is essentially similar to that in the United States. The report[24] of an international study in which the writer participated in 1949 made these observations:

In a general way, it is extremely interesting to note, on the one hand, that too severe legal provisions failed to be applied (U.S.A., Great Britain), and on the other, that several countries who at first had started fully applying the new security measures eventually limited their scope in practice, while endeavoring to emphasize more than before even in regard to these habituals the *educational* aspect of detention. The tendency is also to amend the laws as to

[23] "Court Treatment of General Recidivist Statutes," *Colo. L. Rev.* vol. 48, p. 253, 1948. See also Waite, *The Prevention of Repeated Crime,* 1943; Brown, "The Treatment of the Recidivist in the United States," *Can. B. J.,* vol. 23, p. 640, 1945; Shumaker, "Life Imprisonment for Habitual Offenders," *Law Notes,* vol. 31, p. 106, 1927; and Tappan, "Habitual Offender Laws in the United States," *Fed. Prob.,* vol. 13, no. 1, pp. 28–31, March, 1949.

[24] "Select Papers on Penal and Penitentiary Affairs," *I.P.P.C. Bull.,* vol. 14, nos. 1–2, May, 1949.

the minimum terms of detention and prorogation of detention when they appear to be excessive (five years).

There appear to be a number of reasons for the relative ineffectuality of the habitual criminal laws. They are very severe penal statutes and, as such, tend to be strictly construed so as to prevent abuse. Judges and prosecutors often display a personal reluctance to apply legislation that they deem too rigid and harsh.[25] Some consider the sanctions specified to be cruel and unusual punishments. Some are also opposed to the mandatory application of such laws. Prosecutors commonly prefer to employ the statutes to secure convictions rather than to increase sentences. Criminological theorists have opposed them, too, most commonly on the ground that they do not discriminate on the basis of the needs of the individual offender. The laws are particularly ineffective in meeting the problem of organized and professional criminals. The undercover nature of their offenses and the difficulty in getting satisfactory proof save many from arrest or indictment. The liaison of the elite among the racketeers with the elite of the political and business worlds purchases immunity from criminal prosecution. Thus the mobsters of experience, influence, and power become virtually untouchable in many jurisdictions. If they are caught at all, it is generally for income tax or some other Federal violation. They are more likely to be wiped out by their competitors than punished by the forces of law. If protection breaks down and an individual faces the possibility of conviction as a recidivist, he is able usually to take a plea that will avoid the habitual criminal laws.

The Model Penal Code proposes to deal with the more dangerous class of criminals differently than does the recidivist legislation that presently prevails. It diverges in two major respects, namely in grading the limits of imprisonment applicable to felons according to the seriousness of their crimes and in establishing a series of criteria, including recidivism, any of which may result in the increased sanctions.[26] The "extended terms" provided for the three grades of felonies are as follows:

Grade of felony	Minimum terms, in years	Maximum terms, in years
I	10–20	Life
II	1–5	10–20
III	1–3	5–10

[25] In *State of New Jersey v. Paul Mazor* (August, 1949), the judge held that the law violated the cruel and unusual punishment clause of the state constitution, saying that it shocked "the moral sense of all reasonable men as to what is right and proper under the circumstances." Responses from a number of authorities consulted by the writer in connection with the American Bar Association study revealed their disapproval of the purpose and effects of the legislation.

[26] *Model Penal Code*, Sec. 6.07.

The court would have power under the provision for extended terms to fix the maximum as well as the minimum within the ranges specified in the Code. Furthermore, the application of such extended terms would be within the discretion of the court, so that the judge could be guided by his appraisal of the merits of the individual case. Because the terms are more reasonable and elastic as well as discretionary it appears that there would be less likelihood of nullification of the intent of the provisions than is the case under existing recidivist laws.

The Code provides for the application of these penalties of imprisonment upon a finding by the court that the defendant is (1) a "persistent offender" previously convicted of two felonies or of a felony and two misdemeanors committed at different times; (2) a "professional criminal" where the circumstances of the crime show that he has knowingly devoted himself to felonious activity as a major source of livelihood or where he has substantial income or resources not explained to be derived from a source other than felonious activity; (3) a "dangerous, mentally abnormal person" where psychiatric examination has shown a gravely abnormal mental condition and where his criminal conduct has been marked by repetitive or compulsive behavior or persistent aggressive behavior, resulting in serious danger to others; or (4) a "multiple offender" where he is being sentenced for two or more felonies at once or where he admits the commission of one or more other felonies and asks that they be taken into account.[27]

These criteria for the application of more extended imprisonment terms are in part analogous—though they are more specifically defined—to the standards established for preventive detention in a number of European countries.[28] Obviously there may be real advantage in making the preventive measures applicable to a somewhat wider group of serious offenders than recidivists alone.

In the light of the diversity of law and practice that has been noted summarily above and the disparity of views that have been expressed, the reader will recognize the complexity of the issues that are involved in sentencing and parole. While there is widespread dissatisfaction with prevailing legislation and administration, there is little inclination among authorities either to agree on solutions or to look favorably upon innovations. The Code proposals will be controversial, therefore, but they may well play a significant role in our common efforts to achieve more effectively the multiple ends of correction.

[27] *Ibid.*, Sec. 7.03.

[28] Extended detention is provided in Austria on the basis of "a tendency to commit a particular offence, acquired by repeated performance, and the inability to resist temptation." Several countries have established aggravated penalties for "professional" criminals who derive a livelihood from crime and some define the "criminal by inner tendency" or "the psychopathic offender" as specialized categories for longer imprisonment.

Part III

CORRECTION

Chapter 17

SPECIAL MEASURES OF PREVENTION

The control of delinquency and crime is an important part of applied criminology. At the same time, it is one of the most complex and least satisfactory phases of study, largely because of our failure thus far to discover appropriate preventive measures. The present chapter deals with specialized preventive measures that are designed to control individuals who have previously violated the law or who appear in other respects to be especially vulnerable to antisocial influence.[1] The author will consider first the policy involved in efforts to identify predelinquents by means of prediction tables with a view to forestalling initial offenses. Some of the varied programs that have been developed in the attempt to diminish delinquency and crime will then be examined. These efforts have been directed chiefly toward children and youth.

The other aspect of prevention, which will be discussed in the next chapter, involves a variety of general treatment methods that are employed for the most part in dealing with individuals who are socially or emotionally deviated but who are not necessarily delinquent.[2] To some extent these methods are used with offenders either within or outside the correctional system. They are methods of helping individuals with problems and, as such, may serve to prevent delinquency or crime largely as a by-product of efforts that are not specifically directed toward that end.[3]

[1] One of the chief approaches to prevention among offenders is, of course, through correctional treatment. The several forms of correction are dealt with in other chapters of this section and will not be considered here except for the program at the Highfields institution in New Jersey.

[2] Among the general preventives to crime, the forces of group deterrence are a major factor. This subject has been considered at some length in examining the objectives of criminal justice and corrections.

[3] It should be observed that the distinctions drawn here in the text are in some measure artificial, for the specialized forms of prevention, while they concentrate largely upon individuals who have already been involved in law violations, may also play a role in deterrence and the general prevention of crime. Moreover, individuals who have previously offended may be dissuaded from persisting in crime by general preventives as well as by the specialized controls to which they are subjected. General prevention may be measured roughly by prevailing crime rates, while the effectiveness of special preventives is reflected, crudely at least, in rates of recidivism. But it is impossible to discriminate at all precisely the influences that have succeeded

PREDICTION OF DELINQUENCY

One of the significant modern developments in criminology is the interest in prediction, chiefly in the field of parole and of potential delinquency. The former, relating to individuals who have already committed crimes, will be discussed in the parole chapter. The prediction of potential delinquency among nonoffenders involves different and more complicated issues. It seems reasonable to believe that remedial work can be done most effectively and economically with individuals whose psychological and social problems are still in their incipience. The author is concerned, however, with whether prediction and prevention of delinquency are feasible in the light of the present state of knowledge.

It is not proposed here to analyze in detail the research studies that deal with delinquency prediction. The literature is growing rapidly.[4] Some of the major difficulties suggested by this research will be considered instead, with regard to problems of policy and of technique. The Gluecks have done the most significant work in this field in *Unraveling Juvenile Delinquency*. Special attention will be devoted to the data and implications of that research.[5] The problems raised by their materials relating to delinquency prediction are similar for the most part to those encountered in other studies in this field.

It will be recalled that the Gluecks compared a sample of 500 serious and repetitive delinquents held in two Massachusetts schools for boys with a nondelinquent control group similar in size, matched for comparability in age, intelligence, ethnic origin, and underprivileged neighborhood background. As a result of significant differences observed between the two groups, the Gluecks constructed three prediction tables, each with five factors; on the basis of these tables the Gluecks maintain that the future potential delinquency of children can be predicted with substantial accuracy at the age of 6 or 7. They have recommended that a prediction scale should be applied to public school children in order that potential delinquents may be prevented from becoming offenders. The social prediction table is based upon these variables: discipline of boy by father, supervision of boy by mother, affection of father for boy, affection of

---

and those that have failed either in the population generally or in the individual case. It is very likely that the general normative and deterrent influences pervading the community that were discussed in an earlier chapter, influences of low visibility because they are so deep and intrinsic a part of daily living, play a greater role than is commonly appreciated in maintaining the preponderant pattern of conformity to law.

[4] See Hermann Mannheim and Leslie T. Wilkins, *Prediction Methods in Relation to Borstal Training*, 1955, pp. 1–27, for an excellent brief survey of the prediction studies and bibliographic materials. This study is itself one of the best in the prediction literature.

[5] Sheldon Glueck and Eleanor Glueck, *Unraveling Juvenile Delinquency*, 1950. See also their *Predicting Delinquency and Crime*, 1959.

mother for boy, and cohesiveness of family.[6] A second table, developed from personality traits determined by psychiatric interview, identifies delinquents as more adventurous, extroverted in action, suggestible, stubborn, and emotionally unstable than nondelinquents. A third prediction table constructed from character traits derived from the Rorschach test is based upon social assertion, defiance, suspicion, destructiveness, and emotional lability. The Gluecks proposed that potential delinquents be identified by these tables and then be subjected to preventive measures.

Delinquency Prevention in Relation to Future Delinquency

We do not know to what extent and in what ways "potential juvenile delinquency" may be associated with future criminality. It is in fact apparent that many individuals who commit delinquencies do not become adult criminals and that many others who display no history of juvenile or adolescent delinquency do commit crimes when they have reached adult years. The relationship between early childhood misbehavior and predelinquency, juvenile delinquency itself, adolescent offense, adult crime, and repeated crime have not yet been well delineated. In their long-term follow-up studies, the Gluecks have contributed more to our understanding of these matters than have others, but they observe that even in the carefully selected control group of nondelinquents employed in *Unraveling Juvenile Delinquency* one-fourth had misbehaved in what are ordinarily considered serious ways and that thirty-six of the boys originally selected as nondelinquents were later dropped from the control group because of the discovery "that they had been committing minor offenses with sufficient persistence to necessitate their removal. . . . "[7] How many other nondelinquent controls have become offenders since 1950 we do not know, nor do we know how many of the delinquents of the 1940s have avoided subsequent crime. It is apparent, however, that delinquents and nondelinquents are in a sense overlapping rather than mutually exclusive categories. Delinquents and criminals are also overlapping classes, but their composition differs.

Prediction versus Prevention

It has been suggested that the identification of predelinquents will "make possible the application of treatment measures that would be truly crime preventive."[8] Would that this were so! Materials presented in this chapter

[6] *Ibid.,* p. 261. The *New York Herald Tribune,* Jan. 21, 1952, published a full-page advertisement for the *Woman's Home Companion* in which the Glueck "diagnostic plan" was summarized. It was introduced by the statement, "Right now the thieves, murderers and rapists of the future can be spotted in our kindergartens! We can diagnose their trouble, give them treatment before it's too late if we follow through on the most exciting yet practical plan ever offered to save our children from crime."

[7] Glueck, *ibid.,* p. 29.

[8] *Ibid.,* p. 258.

will suggest how far we are from arriving at effective planned measures of prevention. In *Unraveling Juvenile Delinquency* the Gluecks do not describe in specific terms the means that should be employed, suggesting only that "the best psychiatric, psychologic, social, medical, and other facilities would be focused to cope with problems of personality distortion and maladaptive behavior at a critical point in the development of the child." If it is assumed that the predictive indices constructed in their study imply causes rather than merely correlates of delinquency, a serious problem is raised in attempting to find the means to deal with such causes. Experience with treatment programs has revealed that the sort of deep-rooted problems that are found most highly related to delinquency, such as lack of affectional relationships in the home, lack of family cohesion, and certain underlying pathogenic personality trends, are most resistant to effective therapy. The Gluecks have concluded in other studies that the treatment measures that are used in dealing with young offenders are ineffectual and that it is primarily the processes of maturation that produce "rehabilitation." Their proposal for preventive treatment may be considered somewhat anomalous in the light of this view.

Prediction among School Children

In most prediction research, strangely enough, little or no attention has been given to the problems that may result from predicting future delinquency in a public school population in which the vast majority of children are not delinquent and are not expected to become offenders. The following problems are involved:

Status Attribution. We have learned that one of the great handicaps in dealing with offenders comes from the ascription of the criminal or delinquent status to them and their resulting identification with antisocial values. Similar problems are entailed in describing as "potential delinquents" individuals who have not been officially determined to be delinquent. Delinquency prediction may constitute a self-fulfilling prophecy because of its influence both upon the children involved and upon the authorities who anticipate the predicted consequences. The vague and normative character of legal definitions of delinquency increase the probability that children defined as predelinquents will later be found to be delinquent. Segregative and other prophylactic measures applied as a consequence of the attribution may contribute further to the harm.

The Limits of Predictive Accuracy. If predictions of future delinquency are made, it is particularly important that they be accurate to a very high degree both in order to avoid doing mischief to those who otherwise would not become delinquent and as a matter of reasonable economy. The research performed thus far reveals serious limitations in this regard. One may believe from their data that Glueck predictive scales are more valid in their prognostications than others that have been proposed. Nevertheless, even in applying their tables to the same populations from which they were derived, the Gluecks observed "that there are anywhere from one and a half to three chances in ten that those placed in the group of potential non-delinquents are really potential delinquents, and about two chances in ten that those placed among the potential delinquents are really potential non-delinquents. For this reason alone, the placement of a boy in the same predictive category by any two of the three tables can hardly be any higher than approximately 65% to 70%, which is the result we have actually attained."[9] They found that all three of their prognostic tables placed a boy in his proper category in only 49 per cent of the cases.[10] In the interest of increased accuracy in predicting those who would be delinquent the Gluecks recommended that at least two of the scales should be employed, but as will be pointed out below, there are difficulties involved in doing this.

The Middle Group. An important aspect of the difficulty of reaching accuracy in predicting the future behavior of the members of a sample arises out of the "middle group" for which no prognosis can be made with any considerable degree of certainty. Professor Mannheim, in developing his prediction table on the future conduct of Borstal boys, found that one-third of his sample should be placed in an "unpredicted category" because their chances of success or failure were relatively even.[11] The Gluecks and various other authorities, however, have included the middle group in their predictive classes, lumping those cases in which there was little more than a 50 per cent chance of failure with those where the chances of failure were much higher.[12] Similarly they lumped those cases where there was little less than a 50 per cent chance of failure with those in which the chances of failure were very small. They offer two-class prediction tables that appear to provide a clear separation of potential delinquents and non-delinquents. The scale based on five factors of social background is of this sort:[13]

Weighted failure score class	Chances of delinquency	Chances of nondelinquency
Under 250...............	16.0 per hundred	84.0 per hundred
250 and over............	79.1 per hundred	20.9 per hundred

[9] *Ibid.*, p. 266.

[10] *Ibid.*

[11] Mannheim and Wilkins, *op. cit.*, p. 157.

[12] On this point the Gluecks took the view that cases should be included in the prediction even where the probabilities of delinquency were relatively low: "It would seem to us that for practical purposes it again makes little difference whether the chances of potential delinquency are six and a half in ten or about nine in ten because a boy falling into either score class would have to be looked upon as a potential offender for purposes of preventive therapy." *Op. cit.*, pp. 263–264.

[13] *Ibid.*, p. 262.

Their original, more detailed prediction table containing seven class intervals, however, revealed that over 35 per cent of their 451 delinquents and over 31 per cent of their 439 nondelinquents fell in the two middle classes where the chances of delinquency were about even.[14]

Weighted failure score class	Number of delinquents	Chances of delinquency	Number of non-delinquents	Chances of non-delinquency
Under 150............	5	2.9	167	97.1
150–199............	19	15.7	102	84.3
200–249............	40	37.0	68	63.0
250–299............	122	63.5	70	36.5
300–349............	141	86.0	23	14.0
350–399............	73	90.1	8	9.9
400 and over........	51	98.1	1	1.9
Total............	451		439	

Thus it appears that approximately one-third of the cases fall into classes that are in fact not predictable with any degree of accuracy. Using the two-class prediction table set out above, it is possible to say that nearly 80 per cent of the Glueck delinquents showed "more than an even chance" of becoming delinquent when applying the table back to the sample. But the predictions of a "greater than even chance" have little value for prediction in samples of individuals who have not yet become delinquent. This brings us to the related issue of the justification for dealing with large groups in the public school situation.

Coverage of Preventive Program.[o] It seems reasonable to accept the view that the public school is the optimum place to discover children who have special problems. It is surely true, furthermore, as the Gluecks suggest, that conclusions based upon "danger signals" or equivocal behavioral manifestations of childhood are a poor basis for determining specifically the probability of delinquency or of other particular social or psychological problems. Behavioral prediction, even by clinical authorities, is not a developed science. The question remains, however, whether it is feasible and desirable to apply prognostic criteria to identify future delinquents among public school children in order that preventive programs may be applied to them. This is a crucial question. The author will scrutinize further the data from the Glueck study as a basis for inferring the possible effects of a thorough-going effort at prognostication and prevention. First, it should be observed that among children generally, according to the national data, no more than 2 to 3 per cent should become court delinquents in any given year; that is, not more than 30 out of 1,000 of the public school population.[o] Excluding traffic violators, probably not more than 10 per cent of the children between the ages of 10 and 18 have acquired a de-

[14] *Ibid.,* p. 261.

linquency record. About one-half of these are unofficial cases, generally of a very minor character. Fewer become adult and repetitive criminals. On the basis of the proportion of cases testing at 250 and over in the Glueck sample (see the table above) among nondelinquents, one may estimate that for every 1,000 children entering school approximately 230 should fall into this category.[15] Of these no more than 80 or 90 should be potential court delinquents. On the basis of the Glueck data, 20 or more per 1,000 of the potential delinquents should not be identified as such, while at least 15 per cent of the total population would be incorrectly identified as predelinquents. This points up the policy issue: Is it reasonable for the community to apply clinical-preventive facilities to nearly one-fourth the public school population in the hope that about one-third of this number who might otherwise become delinquent will be identified? If it were possible to treat so large a group specially, what would be the outcome for that one-third? More important, what would be the effect on the incorrectly identified remainder receiving special treatment who ought not to become delinquent if they were left to the ordinary influences of the school and community?

Technical Problems in Prediction. A series of technical problems are involved in the construction and application of prediction instruments. One of these problems involves the nature of the samples used in the research and the population to which the instrument is later applied. It may be assumed that prognostic tables apply accurately only to groups that are similar in characteristics. This raises a question of whether it is appropriate to apply to ordinary public school children aged 6 or 7 the predictive criteria and failure scores drawn by the Gluecks from mature, repetitive, institutionalized delinquents who came from underprivileged neighborhoods and, to a large extent, from Catholic families.[16]

Another problem in the use of predictive tables lies in the intrinsic difficulties involved in selecting and applying the criteria of delinquency. The Glueck data provide clear evidence of the importance of this. After

---

[15] Actually, on the basis of the Glueck data it is impossible to say with any exactitude what proportion of an ordinary public school population (as contrasted with the population of a correctional institution) would fall into the category with more than an even chance of delinquency. It is apparent, however, that in such a group a relatively large number of children would fall into the Glueck class interval 250–299. In a New York State study based upon a school population it was concluded that to include 64 per cent of the "true delinquents" it would be necessary to provide special work with 30 per cent of the total group who were "identified" as potential delinquents, most of them erroneously. This meant that in a school population of 5,300 students "special help" must be given to 1,600 in order to deal with 74 cases (out of a total of 114 in the school population who were actually delinquent) of true potential delinquency. See "Reducing Juvenile Delinquency," New York State Youth Commission, 1952.

[16] See Edwin B. Wilson, "Prediction," in "A Symposium on Unraveling Juvenile Delinquency," *Harv. L. Rev.*, vol. 64, pp. 1039–1042, 1951.

years of expensive and intensive study of 1,000 cases, using trained and skilled researchers and technicians, the Gluecks found they had scores for all fifteen of their predictive items on only 424 cases (205 delinquents and 219 nondelinquents).[17] If these predictive indices were applied to other and larger populations, how far could accurate data be drawn by fewer and less able workers? The Gluecks observe that it is quite essential, if predictive devices are to be applied, that they "be in the hands of experienced persons" and that "the necessary prediction scores must be derived from absolutely accurate data."[18] One may well question the extent to which public school teachers should be expected to arrive at accurate diagnostic data based on the very general criteria employed in the social prediction table. The study recommended that, in the interest of accurate predictions, more than one of the tables should be used, but it is quite apparent that highly trained personnel would be required to apply the psychiatric or the Rorschach tables and that such personnel is not available.

There are several other difficulties involved in the sorts of criteria employed in the delinquency prediction studies. When few variables are employed—and there is some controversy concerning the number that it is desirable to use—there is danger that they will be of so general and vague a character that the likelihood of faulty classification and scoring is increased. Query, for example, how far teachers or social investigators would agree in rating the quality of paternal discipline, maternal supervision, and family cohesiveness? It appears, moreover, that general variables are likely not to be independent and that, indeed, the traits in the Glueck predictive tables do overlap considerably.[19] As a result, the predictive value of one factor depends in some measure upon that of another. There is a further difficulty involved in the variables employed in prediction tables. The use of a series of discreet items suggests that delinquency is the consequence of the mechanical summation of a number of static and intrinsically significant factors.[20] In reality law violation ensues from the dynamic interrelationships of factors that are important because of the ways in which they are associated. Moreover, it is apparent that many important influences in the production of delinquency may not develop

[17] Glueck, *op. cit.*, p. 265.

[18] *Ibid.*, p. 268.

[19] *Ibid.*, p. 259.

[20] William C. Kvaraceus has said, "Atomizing factors affecting social adjustment and giving primacy to certain variables to the exclusion of all other information, as is done in the construction of check lists, scales, tables, and questionnaires, is to deny the dynamic interplay of all forces that impinge on behavior, delinquent or otherwise. What this implies is that the test-maker may need to seek out approaches that are more in line with multivariate analysis or to fall back on case study methods rather than on the more restricted information-gathering and treatment methods." "Forecasting Juvenile Delinquency," *J. Ed.*, vol. 138, p. 39, April, 1956.

until years after entry in school, factors such as membership in gangs, the breaking up of the home, or the use of alcohol or narcotics, and that in individual cases these factors may be more important than the predisposing influences of early childhood. To predict and attempt to prevent delinquency on the basis of variables that appear before public school age suggests a fatalistic predetermination that would often be inaccurate both in its causal and treatment implications.

The Validation of Predictive Instruments. Professor Mannheim has observed that validation studies on prediction instruments have been rare thus far and that there has been no "perfect validation" of any of the tables that have been developed.[21] The Gluecks have given great emphasis to the need for such studies and in fact several attempts have been made to test their social prediction table with other groups. Thus far, unfortunately, these attempts have been, with a single exception, mere restrospective applications of their criteria to individuals on whom social information is available from former studies, samples in which the proportion of delinquents is much higher than occurs in the school population. The published results of such "tests" have, in the author's opinion, been seriously misleading so far as their implications for the employment of the tables with unselected young children are concerned. Using the Glueck scoring technique some of these studies have been able to conclude that "over 90 per cent of the delinquents" are shown to have had a "greater than even chance of becoming delinquent."[22] The criterion of more than a 50 per cent chance is not, as has been previously suggested, a sound way to predict delinquency in a nondelinquent population. The fact that the single social prediction scale has ostensibly been more accurate in predicting for other samples than it was either alone or in combination with the psychiatric and Rorschach scales as applied to the original Glueck samples reflects some of the problems involved in attempting validation through retrospective application to known delinquents. Thus far these studies appear to show only that well-developed delinquents tend to display the indicia of delinquency that the Gluecks have derived from their research.

The author remarked above on one exceptional validation study. The New York City Youth Board is in the process of following up (under an initial grant in excess of $100,000 from the Ford Foundation in addition to board investment in the project) a group of seventy-one boys from two

---

[21] See Mannheim and Wilkins, *op. cit.,* pp. 17–19, and Kvaraceus, *op. cit,* pp. 39–40. The latter notes the low predictive efficiency of his *K D Proneness Scale* in which he has used seventy-five multiple-choice items for prediction purposed.

[22] One study, finding only 72 per cent of delinquents showing more than a 50 per cent chance of becoming delinquent, suggests that the table might be more useful for predicting those who should not become delinquent, thereby to avoid the unnecessary application of treatment measures! Richard E. Thompson, "A Validation of the Glueck Social Prediction Scale for Proneness to Delinquency," *J. Crim. L.,* vol. 43, pp. 451–470, 1952.

Bronx public schools who were predicted as potential delinquents according to the Glueck social criteria.[23] These represented 32.3 per cent of 220 students who entered the schools during the school year 1952–1953. The remainder tested at scores under 250. The high proportion of "potential delinquents" may be accounted for by the fact that the schools are located in delinquency areas with large and mobile minority-group populations. Eighty per cent of the families were deemed economically dependent or marginal. Thirty-one of the "high chance" delinquents have been referred for treatment in the Child Guidance Clinic in their school, while the remaining forty are not receiving special attention. The plan is to follow these cases through their school careers to discover what proportion in each of the three categories (low chance, high chance without treatment, and high chance with treatment) become delinquent. The numbers in the samples are small for this purpose, but the study is the most careful effort thus far to validate a prediction scale of this sort by prospective application to a group before the onset of delinquent conduct.

Delinquency Prevention and Child Welfare

A basic policy issue will now be considered against the background of the foregoing discussion. Is there sufficient justification at the present state of knowledge about delinquency prediction and prevention to warrant the effort to distinguish potential delinquents from children whose problems are expressed in other forms of personal and social pathology? Our conclusion must be in the negative. The author believes that continued research on the correlates of delinquency and on means of effective pre-

[23] See Ralph W. Whelan, "An Experiment in Predicting Delinquency," *J. Crim. L.,* vol. 45, pp. 432–442, November–December, 1954. In 1955 it was announced that 72 per cent of the children rated as potential delinquents were showing "behavioral difficulties" in the school system while only 17 per cent of other children there were doing so. This seems to imply that over half the *number* of children are proving to be delinquent from among those predicted as nondelinquent as among those predicted to be potential delinquents. These figures will undoubtedly change during the follow-up period. It is quite clear that as the study progresses it will be found that the children classed as predelinquents display behavioral problems of some sort in a very high proportion of cases, partly because of the close scrutiny directed upon them. Presumably the numbers of children in the "low chance" group who get into difficulties will also increase in number and proportion. See "Research in Delinquency at Harvard Law School," *Harv. L. School Bull.,* vol. 6, pp. 12–13, April, 1955, and "Delinquency Prediction 1952–1956," New York City Youth Board, July, 1957. It has been computed that as few as 1.5 per cent of law violations, including those of a serious character, for which children could be taken to court actually result in official action. This suggests that under close observation it may be found that many children become involved in delinquent conduct, even among those who score low on predictive tests of the Glueck type that have been derived from mature, institutionalized offenders. See Fred J. Murphy, Mary M. Shirley, and Helen L. Witmer, "The Incidence of Hidden Delinquency," *Am. J. Orthopsychiat.,* vol. 16, pp. 686–696, October, 1946.

vention is clearly desirable. However, the problems of children in our society are numerous and varied. Delinquency is not by any means the worst among them. Among the many fruitful observations in the Glueck research, one of the most remarkable was the serious social and emotional difficulties suffered by nondelinquent youths in deprived areas of the city. More than the delinquents they felt helplessness, dependence upon others, insecurity, failure, and compulsiveness. They were more frequently neurotic and psychiatrically deviated. The author can only agree with children's court Judge Polier's conclusion in her review of the Glueck data that, "It certainly becomes clear that separation of these boys into delinquent and nondelinquent on entrance to school—with supportive help being only, or primarily, directed to the delinquent group—would be most undesirable."[24]

The entire gamut of juvenile problems appears in the delinquent population, yet the occurrence of any particular problem or combination of problems does not imply that an individual will become delinquent. Children who display serious maladjustments, whether or not they are headed toward delinquency, require help that is appropriate to their manifest difficulties rather than to their imagined future state. Treatment, then, should be given as a child welfare measure generally, not as a preventive to delinquency, if the individual has not yet become an offender. It is reasonable to believe that the child who is given help because he needs it may profit more in receiving it than he would as a member of the class designated "predelinquents." The avoidance of unnecessary discrimination in this regard is supported by our lack thus far of differentiated measures to prevent delinquency among nonoffenders. While police, courts, and correctional facilities must be used to discourage law violators from repeating it is thoroughly undesirable to employ them—as we have too often done in the past—to deal with nondelinquents. Any further encouragement to such a trend through easy rationalizations about preventing potential offenders from becoming delinquents is greatly to be deprecated. This can only aggravate the problems that are found among such individuals. The use of coordinating councils or referral units that do not predict or diagnose predelinquency is a preferable means of procuring nonstigmatic treatment of social and psychological problems of children for what they are rather than for what they might conceivably become. These agencies will be discussed later in this chapter.

Many years ago Captain Maconochie remarked that man should be treated in accordance with his deeds rather than his tendencies. This is no less true for children whose tendencies are highly equivocal in their implications. There is real danger that predicting that the child is a predelinquent will make him so. The appropriateness of using official agencies

[24] Justine Wise Polier, "Children's Court," in "A Symposium on Unraveling Juvenile Delinquency," *op. cit.,* pp. 1036–1038.

for the prevention of repeated delinquency has been discussed. This leads the author to suggest that the Glueck prediction tables, or some modification thereof, might be usefully applied to youths who have come into the hands of the police or the juvenile courts as first offenders. Social and psychiatric criteria should distinguish rather well between those cases in which there is little probability of recurrent delinquency and those in which problems run so deep that their persistence in antisocial behavior is likely. The latter would presumably require more intensive treatment efforts.

Maturation: Nature's Curb

It is not unreasonable to believe that the natural processes of personal growth and change are in themselves a major influence on the prevention of crime. Possibly these processes reflect a progressive "enfeeblement of physical vitality and the passions" in adulthood that Quételet hypothesized more than a century ago. It is not unlikely that the influence of ripening in its social, emotional, and physical aspects has as much to do with the prevention of crime and the ostensible "rehabilitation" of offenders as do all the preventive programs that have been developed. In any event this maturation implies, so far as individuals who are reasonably normal in personality are concerned, a process of increasing introjection of the cultural imperatives and an avoidance of the unpleasant consequences of deliberate deviation. Individuals learn to control rebelliousness and antisocial impulse. Most men, even those who have at one time committed crimes, accede to the demands of the law because there is no comfortable alternative. Once criminal, some persons may continue to be dependent and parasitic or hostile and antisocial, but few can find a tolerable existence in crime, punishment, and social infamy. Those who have had some inclination to delinquency but who have avoided crime during childhood and youth are, in general, less and less prone to violate the rules as they grow up. They become more conservative and conformable.

Some years ago the Gluecks suggested that what is commonly inferred to be the result of rehabilitative treatment may in fact be the consequence of the maturing of the individuals involved.[25] There is support for this view in the research the author has inspected in the field of prevention and treatment, for it appears that the measures employed, even those of a fairly intensive character, do not take quick effect with the young, while most offenders who arrive at mature age, even without having experienced the advantages of "enlightened" treatment, do nevertheless desist from further crime. There are notable exceptions, of course, cases that the Gluecks identify as seriously pathological personalities. There are others who become so thoroughly enmeshed in the patterns and associations of

[25] See Sheldon Glueck and Eleanor Glueck, *Juvenile Delinquents Grown Up*, 1940, pp. 267–269.

crime that they persist in antisocial behavior even when, consciously at any rate, they no longer wish to do so. Mass custodial confinement of the young with habitual criminals in prisons undoubtedly contributes heavily to this group.

The idea of a normal maturation into conformity can be taken to suggest a pessimistic corollary view as to the effectiveness of planned prevention and treatment programs. There is some ground for pessimism, but we cannot fairly conclude that the preventive measures employed are without any constructive effect. It appears more likely that some of these measures, at any rate, may facilitate the social and emotional maturation through which individuals learn to conform. What appears superficially to be a self-correcting process of readjustment on the part of many offenders undoubtedly reflects to a large extent the deep, nontelic forces of control that are gradually and differentially assimilated by them as well as by the population generally. Furthermore, one may well believe that the general deterrents in the community are effective even if one is skeptical of the specific consquences of official modes of dealing with offenders. We know too little thus far about what influences work and with whom they are effective. It appears that measures of restraint deter many potential offenders from crime while in others they promote increased defiance. On the other hand, permissive clinical-therapeutic approaches appear to mitigate the problems and sometimes the antisocial behavior of certain individuals, especially neurotics, while they invite contempt and greater aggression in others who act out their problems. Research and experience have not provided sharp analysis of these divergencies.

PREVENTIVE MEASURES

It is not feasible here to survey all of the measures of prevention. They are probably as varied and as little understood as are the causes of crime. Edwin J. Lukas has offered pertinent comments on the variety and, in some cases, the absurdity of contemporary efforts at prevention:[26]

Perhaps the fault lies in the multitude of theories advanced these days concerning crime causation. Each so-called "preventive" enterprise has its own concept of causation to which it adheres with a tenacity which would evoke more admiration if the concept were more valid. Thus it has been said that crime is due to the following: empty churches, broken homes, poverty, parental neglect, cheap commercialized recreation or not enough recreation, comics, mystery stories, radio thrillers, sex-stimulating movies, excessive mobility of population, illiteracy, malnutrition, glandular imbalance, feeble-mindedness, bad eyesight, and infected teeth.

In pursuance of those beliefs there have been myriad schemes: the prohibition of intoxicating drinks, of coffee, of some soft drinks, of tobacco, of juke-

[26] "Fashions in Crime Prevention," *Nat. Prob. Assoc. Yearbook*, pp. 33–34, 1946.

box machines; the control of movies and radio, the abolition of comics; and believe it or not, the installation of more electric lights on street corners. It has been proposed that parents be prosecuted and sent to prison. In San Francisco parents have been "sentenced" to parental schools to "learn" how not to contribute to the delinquency of their children. And in New Jersey parents are being invited to attend classrooms with their children.

We have also had "boys and girls weeks"; and someone recently offered a large sum of money to finance an annual "crime-prevention week." Judges have placed children on probation on condition that they read certain prescribed literature, and it has been proposed that piano playing is an antidote to antisocial behavior. Meanwhile, newspaper editors, district attorneys and police commissioners are convinced that the only genuine crime preventive is the certainty and severity of punishment, swift punitive justice. Legislation has been passed to require the sterilization of hopeless idiots and imbeciles and to limit immigration on the theory that the foreign born are more criminalistic than the native born.

From all the foregoing it appears that there is no end to the proposals for prevention, because there is as yet no clarity of thinking on the genesis of the phenomenon we are trying to prevent. The clarity of thinking we hope for may be impossible to achieve until behavior scientists have elicited greater exactness from the veritable mountain of confused and confusing material accumulated in each passing decade.

By and large there has been little objective inquiry into the effectiveness of measures that purport to deal preventively with crime. In part this reflects the fact that programs of prevention ordinarily have not themselves been established and conducted with a research design. There are notable exceptions, however. The Children's Bureau has published an evaluation of some of the programs about which tentative inference may be drawn.[27] This publication concludes that thus far little is known about how to prevent or reduce delinquency because of the lack of painstaking research to determine what methods are effective in accomplishing particular results with specific classes of delinquents or potential delinquents.

Community Organization

There is some variety in the programs that aim primarily at improving the delinquent's environment through measures of community organization.[28] Among these programs is the community coordinating council. In the author's opinion such councils hold more promise as a way of meeting the problems of child welfare than most other measures that have developed. The community coordinating council is a means of drawing

[27] *The Effectiveness of Delinquency Prevention Programs,* U.S. Children's Bureau, Publ. No. 350, 1954.

[28] For a general discussion of methods of community organization, see Wayne McMillen, *Community Organization for Social Welfare,* 1945, and Edward Haydon, "Community Organization and Crime Prevention," *Nat. Prob. Assoc. Yearbook,* pp. 23–36, 1942.

together and concentrating community resources on children with problems. Councils vary considerably in different cities in origin, area covered, types of service rendered, and extent of agency cooperation. They have appeared to function best, however, in small communities in which leaders have already come to recognize the importance of child welfare problems. Using the skills of residents in the neighborhoods where the programs are carried on, they enlist the aid of community organization experts to develop services and to enlist the cooperation of social agencies. The council is not itself an instrument for the treatment of delinquents or predelinquents but is an agency for intake, study, and referral of cases to specialized agencies that are most suited to deal with the patricular problems encountered. There are important by-products of this function. Unmet or inadequately covered needs are recognized with resulting modification and expansion of social-agency programs. Existing facilities in the community are more fully exploited, especially the churches, schools, and recreation centers. New services are commonly established. Community-mindedness and cooperation are extended.

A survey in 1935 and 1936 found coordinating councils in 163 communities in twenty states, most of which had developed during the preceding few years.[29] In 1955 a study in eight states identified over 700 councils.[30] Much has been written in praise of this movement, and in fact it does appear to offer an optimum means of increasing the community's efficiency in discovering and securing the application of appropriate treatment to the variety of ills with which children are afflicted. However, no objective investigation has been made of the extent to which delinquency may be affected by the use of councils. In the nature of things, this would be difficult to discover. A major virtue of the council device, however, is that youngsters characteristically are dealt with in terms of their immediate problems rather than as predelinquents. Thus, councils tend not to use the courts when unofficial agency services are more appropriate and the volume of court intake is, therefore, reduced. Furthermore, the councils' broad orientation to child welfare problems reduces the danger that special services for children who "act out" their difficulties will be emphasized to the disadvantage of those with other problems that are as much in need of attention. The community coordinating council approach, properly channeled, avoids the hazards of identifying potential delinquents and concentrating narrowly upon them.

As has been suggested, the coordinating council idea appears to be best suited to small communities, while it is in large cities that the problems of delinquency and child maladjustment are most common. In New

[29] Kenneth S. Beam, "Community Coordination for Prevention of Delinquency," in *Nat. Prob. Assoc. Yearbook,* pp. 89–116, 1936.

[30] Beam, "Organization of the Community for Delinquency Prevention," in Frank J. Cohen, *Youth and Crime,* 1957, pp. 231–257.

York City, however, the Youth Board as a part of its deliquency-prevention program has developed a somewhat analogous service.[31] It has established a central registration file on delinquent and unadjusted children in the city and fifteen "referral units" associated with the public schools in areas where the delinquency rates are highest. The board contracts with private social agencies to provide aggressive casework and group-work services that would not otherwise be available to antisocial children. According to a report furnished the author by the Research Department of the Board, 74,835 children received services of some sort through the board during the year July 1956 to June 1957. Among these 3,500 were dealt with through the referral units and 1,000 children and their families received intensive treatment services provided by eleven agencies for multiproblem families. The vast majority of the cases received only group work and recreation service. In 1957 the board announced on the basis of a five-year study its finding that 75 per cent of New York City's juvenile dilenquency could be traced to some 20,000 families, less than 1 per cent of the city's more than 2 million families.[32] Special attention is being directed to this group. In 1959 the commissioner of welfare in New York was authorized to establish six special units, in the department with a total of thirty caseworkers, to handle the problems of especially "difficult" families in which delinquency is common.[33] Presumably this service will be coordinated with the work of the Youth Board. Since the board has a research unit, one may hope that in time its effectiveness in preventing delinquency through referral unit services may be carefully appraised in empirical terms.[34]

Another mode of community organization is exemplified in the "area approach," based largely upon the researches of Clifford Shaw and his associates, which stress the close relationship between delinquency and neighborhood deterioration. The Chicago Area Project, established and

[31] See *Youth Board News,* published by the New York City Youth Board since 1948; *How They Were Reached,* 1954; and *New Directions in Delinquency Prevention,* 1957, also published by the board, for descriptions of this and other services of the board.

[32] See *Youth Board News,* vol. 9, p. 3, January, 1957.

[33] *New York Times,* Jan. 19, 1959.

[34] A somewhat similar but less ambitious and extensive program of coordination than that of the Youth Board is represented by the South Central Youth Project, a demonstration and research experiment inaugurated as a two-year study in Minneapolis in 1954. Working through a planning and a staff committee drawn from existing social agencies of the community, the project attempted to coordinate agency services and increase their flexibility, to improve the detection of incipient delinquents, and to strengthen the employment of aggressive casework and street-corner group work. The venture was too short lived for definitive results to be achieved, but its leaders believed that it provided confirmation of the need for flexibility, coordination, and professionalization in the administration of services. See Gisela Konopka, "Co-ordination of Services as a Means of Delinquency Prevention," *The Annals,* vol. 322, pp. 30–38, March, 1959.

directed by Shaw for two decades, has led to the organization of community committees in about twelve neighborhoods of high delinquency in that city through which efforts have been made to remove damaging influences in the slum environment. The directors of the project conceive delinquency to be the product of a local milieu "(a) in which adult residents do little or nothing in an organized public way to mobilize their resources in behalf of the welfare of the youth of the area; (b) in which the relative isolation of the adolescent male group, common throughout urban society, becomes at its extreme an absolute isolation with a consequent absolute loss of adult control; and (c) in which the formal agencies of correction and reformation fail to enlist the collaboration of persons and groups influential in the local society."[35] In accordance with this conception, the project emphasizes discovering "natural leaders" in the delinquent neighborhoods who hold key positions of influence and in whom an interest in youth welfare activities can be stirred.

Local residents, under the tutelage of staff sociologists of the Illinois Institute for Juvenile Research, are employed in the implementation of delinquency preventive activities of the project.[36] While such programs vary in emphasis according to the existing facilities and problems of the particular neighborhood, for the most part they stress three major elements. One of these is the development and carrying on of recreational services. A second is conducting campaigns of community improvement, especially in such areas as the schools, law enforcement, sanitation, and physical conservation. The third focuses more specifically on offenders: delinquent children, gang activities, convicts returning to the neighborhood from prisons and jails.[37] Major effort is directed toward guiding youth to conventional values through constructive relationships and services in the local area. There is some evidence of decline in delinquency rates generally in these neighborhoods and of success in working with particular offenders, but the data are inconclusive.

State Programs

In recent years there has been a considerable growth of state efforts in the field of delinquency prevention. This has been true, among others, in

[35] Solomon Kobrin, "The Chicago Area Project—A 25-Year Assessment," *The Annals,* vol. 322, p. 27, March, 1959.

[36] Leaders in the field of social work have questioned the competence of individuals who lack formal training properly to plan or carry on the programs of the project. The institute emphasizes primarily the value of utilizing the talents and enthusiasms of those who "form a significant part of the social world of the recipients of help."

[37] Kobrin, a senior staff member of the Institute for Juvenile Research, suggests that the Area Project was the first to make an effort to "reach out" to establish direct contact with problem youths and that it has had considerable influence upon the pattern of other cities in recent years in their work with delinquent gangs and individuals.

several jurisdictions that have been influenced by the youth correctional authority movement. In California and Minnesota especially, and to a lesser extent in the other authority states, agencies have sought to establish community programs of delinquency prevention. California has developed a system or organizing survey teams composed of police, probation, school guidance, health, recreation, social work, and community organization specialists.[38] Such teams may be invited by municipal or county authorities to aid in examining their services to youth and to work out improved facilities for delinquency prevention and child welfare.

New York State established in 1945 a Youth Commission that has carried on a more extensive and ambitious program than those in a number of the states that have established "youth authorities."[39] Through the commission New York State makes substantial funds available to local communities on a matching basis for the development and the maintenance of prevention programs. In 1956, when the commission was made a permanent agency of the state government, projects were being operated in 935 municipalities where more than 90 per cent of the population of the state lives. Grants to the program in 1957 amounted to $3,200,000, matched by the communities involved. The commission also surveys local needs, encourages the development of appropriate services, and provides educational and research services on delinquency. Programs subsidized by the state include recreation, child guidance, school social workers, diagnostic centers, identification of potential delinquents, work with gangs, police juvenile aid bureaus, probation services, and training of personnel. The commission has emphasized the development of coordination among agency services to children through city youth boards. Such cooperation has sometimes been resisted by social agencies in the past and the tradition of separatism is slow to break down, but considerable progress has been made in this regard. The operation of the New York City Youth Board is the most notable example of youth board performance in an ambitious and multifaceted program.

Other states, too, though generally on a smaller scale, have displayed increasing concern about delinquency and its prevention. State services to counties and local communities have been increased, particularly in the fields of mental hygiene, educational, and recreational services. Some states, such as Michigan, have assessed the variety of services available to children and youth with a view to filling in the gaps left by existing agencies.[40]

---

[38] See *Calif. Youth Author. Quart.*, published quarterly since 1947, and *Annual Reports* of the Authority. Also *Anti-social Behavior and Its Control in Minnesota*, Commission on Juvenile Delinquency, Adult Crime, and Corrections, 1957.

[39] See *Youth Service News*, published regularly by the New York State Youth Commission since 1948.

[40] See Maxine B. Virtue, *Basic Structure of Children's Service in Michigan*, 1953.

Recreation and Group Work

One of the most popular approaches to prevention lies in recreational and what is loosely called "group-work" services to children and youth. Their popularity may well reflect the fact that they can be employed cheaply with masses of individuals. The thought that delinquency may be prevented by this means is highly seductive to Americans with their penchant for sports. The view of delinquency as mere "misguided play" has helped to attract a steady flow of funds and to perpetuate the myth that delinquency and athletics are incompatible. It is assumed that "good sportsmanship" acquired on the playing field will, through the principle of transfer of training, somehow ensure against delinquency and crime. The will to believe this persists in the face of considerable evidence to the contrary. Delinquent and delinquency-prone children do use organized recreational and group-work facilities, but they spend only a relatively few hours each year in such activities and their delinquency is not reduced.[41] In fact, according to observations in two studies, there is some increase in the delinquencies of participants who have previously been in trouble.[42] The Children's Bureau concluded in its survey of such programs that " . . . important as the provision of adequate and well-staffed recreational and group work facilities is for the well-being of children generally, it is by no means established that delinquency will decline if good facilities are provided. What is needed, it is widely agreed, are group work programs that adapt their methods and activities to the peculiar needs of delinquency prone youths."[43]

Some of the largest recreation programs are those conducted by juvenile units of police departments. A recent survey of cities with populations over

[41] Ethel Shanas and Catherine E. Dunning in *Recreation and Delinquency,* 1942, found that a sample of children in Chicago where delinquency rates were high spent from 43 to 87.5 hours annually in organized activity under a recreation leader. *Ibid.,* p. 8. Contrary to general lay impressions, many delinquency areas that have been the object of public and agency attention have acquired more than "their fair share" of recreational facilities, as Kobrin has remarked. *Op. cit.,* p. 27.

[42] Shanas and Dunning, *op. cit.,* and Frederic M. Thrasher, "The Boy's Club and Juvenile Delinquency," *Am. J. Soc.,* vol. 42, pp. 66–80, 1936. See also the critical comments in *Report of the Committee on the Judiciary,* United States Senate, Subcommittee on Juvenile Delinquency, 85th Cong., 1st Sess., Report No. 130, Mar. 4, 1957, pp. 100 ff. The study of a boy's club program in Louisville, Kentucky, for the period 1944–1954, revealed that delinquency rates in the area served declined steadily while rates were rising in two other comparable areas where there were no youth-serving agencies. The club program included athletics, woodwork, crafts, dramatics, swimming, Boy Scouts, and summer camp. Roscoe C. Brown, Jr., and Dan W. Dodson, "The Effectiveness of a Boys' Club in Reducing Delinquency," *The Annals,* vol. 322, pp. 47–53, March, 1939. The authors acknowledge, however, that there were several other factors that operated to produce social stability in the club area and instability in the other areas.

[43] U.S. Children's Bureau, *op. cit.,* pp. 48–49.

25,000 revealed that there were 133 specialized police programs for juveniles in operation, many of them established during the 1940s. Recreational activities were being conducted by the police in fifty-five of these.[44] The Juvenile Aid Bureau of New York City, the largest and one of the oldest of such agencies, has handled a load ranging from 17,000 to 36,000 cases[45] each year. A very large proportion are referred to the companion agency, the Police Athletic League, for its sport and recreational activities. The latter has commonly spent an annual budget of 1 million dollars and more. In May, 1959, the Juvenile Aid Bureau was converted into the Investigation Bureau of the Police Department's recently established Youth Division. The latter now includes a Patrol Bureau (Youth Squad) as well as the Police Athletic League and the Investigation Bureau.

A promising specialized form of group work has developed in recent years in an effort to reach and influence gang members by a process of "boring from within." This involves group workers' establishing contacts with street-corner groups, attempting to win the acceptance of the members and redirecting their activities away from aggressive and antisocial pursuits into more conventional channels. Claims have been made by the New York City Youth Board that this sort of work results in declining offenses and arrests, in reduction of intergang conflict, and in the engagement of gang members in constructive activities.[46] On the other hand it has

[44] James J. Brennan, *The Prevention and Control of Juvenile Delinquency by Police Departments,* doctoral dissertation, New York University, 1952.

[45] One of the highly controversial issues in the field of delinquency prevention has been the role that should be played by police juvenile agencies. Casework and child welfare authorities and the juvenile court attacked the effort of the New York City Police Department's Juvenile Aid Bureau to deal with predelinquents and some delinquents by counseling and casework procedures through a service bureau. See Alfred J. Kahn, *Police and Children,* 1951, and *The Crisis on the New York City Police Program for Youth,* Citizens' Committee for Children of New York City, 1959. Compare *Police Services for Juveniles,* U.S. Children's Bureau, 1954, pp. 24–27. Part of the problem involved here lies in the unwillingness of private agencies to deal with cases that have come to the attention of the police. The police are in an ideal position to act as a referral agency, but specialized treatment agencies have too commonly discouraged them from doing so. The Englewood Project in Chicago was a three-year experiment in cooperation between police juvenile officers in one police district and the Juvenile Protective Association of Chicago, the latter operating a nearby treatment center for referrals. At the end of the project the association concluded that centers of this sort, staffed to provide both casework and street-club work, should be established specifically to serve police referrals. See G. Lewis Penner, "An Experiment in Police and Social Agency Cooperation," *The Annals,* vol. 322, pp. 79–89, March, 1959.

[46] *Teenage Gangs,* New York City Youth Board, 1957. See also Paul L. Crawford, Daniel L. Malamud, and James R. Dumpson, *Working with Teenage Gangs,* 1950, and Arthur Niederhoffer and Herbert Bloch, *The Gang,* 1959. At the time of writing an interesting experiment is being conducted at the Henry Street Settlement in New York City to prevent "the contagion of gang activity on younger children" through a Pre-delinquent Gang Project. The settlement has attempted to redirect five "pre-

been recognized that group work with gangs does not succeed with individuals who present serious personality problems and that it produces little change in the gang member's attitudes toward family, church, police, school, and work. More careful evaluative studies are needed in this area.

Educational and Therapeutic Measures

Along with the programs described above that involve primarily manipulation of environment, other efforts to prevent delinquency are being directed toward the individual child and his personality problems. A variety of approaches, such as counseling, casework, and psychotherapy, may be employed for this purpose. These cannot of course be strictly differentiated from such environmental approaches as were discussed above, since the broader approaches to prevention necessarily involve more than a singular mode of treatment.

Perhaps the Cambridge-Somerville Youth Study represents the most objective evaluation of a delinquency prevention program that has been conducted.[47] Here a treatment group of 325 boys was matched with a control group of similar number, boys in each group being quite evenly balanced between "predelinquents" and "nonpredelinquents." The treatment group received friendly counseling, psychological and medical services as needed, and educational and recreational guidance and assistance over an average period of four years and two months. Psychiatric and casework services were also provided for the treatment group. The controls received

---

delinquent" groups of preadolescent age, some of whose members had come to police attention. The project attempts to reinstate parental authority and morale through its work with the children and their parents by group meetings with parents and group work with the children. See Ruth S. Tefferteller, "Delinquency Prevention through Revitalizing Parent-Child Relations," *The Annals,* vol. 322, pp. 69–79, March, 1959. The techniques and orientations employed in work with gangs vary in some measure, as do the conclusions of the authorities concerning the effectiveness of their efforts. The street-club workers of the Hyde Park Youth Project in Chicago used techniques similar to those employed by the New York City Board: "hanging around," developing the groups' confidence in them, and attempting to influence their attitudes and behavior. The project reports that through its work youths who had engaged in little or no prior antisocial behavior continued to avoid delinquency. It had little success with those who had frequently participated in antisocial behavior but some success with those who had seldom been involved in delinquent activity before their contact with the project. John M. Gandy, "Preventive Work with Street-corner Groups: Hyde Park Youth Project, Chicago," *The Annals,* vol. 322, pp. 107–117, March, 1959. See also Walter B. Miller, "Preventive Work with Street-corner Groups: Boston Delinquency Project," *op. cit.,* pp. 97–107, where it was concluded that delinquency rates were reduced fairly markedly at the beginning of the project but that during later phases an "equilibrium-restoring" effect occurred in which delinquency increased again, but not to the level that was observed when the project was first undertaken.

[47] Edwin Powers and Helen Witmer, *An Experiment in the Prevention of Delinquency,* 1951.

no aid from the project counselors. At the end of the service program it was discovered that, while many of the difficult children and their families had liked the services provided, the treatment group members had police and court records nearly identical to those of the control group. Indeed, more members of the treatment group than of the control group had been committed to institutions. The study indicated, on the other hand, that in 31 per cent of the cases where treatment had been provided it had been either "definitely" or "possibly beneficial" in the boys' "social adjustment," while in 37 per cent of the cases it had been "clearly ineffectual" and in 9 per cent it had accomplished little.[48] Services were especially ineffectual with boys prone to chronic delinquency, with those whose parents were indifferent, with seriously neurotic youngsters, and with feeble-minded and neurologically handicapped cases. With reference to the crucial question of delinquency prevention, it appears that the children did not specifically benefit from the friendly counseling and agency services.[49] The Children's Bureau has remarked the greater reliability of the findings of this study than of others in which evaluation of performance has been attempted: "So long as we do not know what the usual incidence of delinquency, official or unofficial, in a specified group of children is, the effectiveness of any delinquency prevention services in their behalf is in doubt." This points up the need to use carefully selected control groups in determining the utility of treatment measures.

Child Guidance Clinics

The work of child guidance clinics has also been evaluated in the literature. These clinics vary so much in the services performed that generalization about their effectiveness is not possible. Several research reports reveal, however, that a change has occurred in the approach of some of these clinics and that there has been some clarification of their value in preventive treatment. The Judge Baker Guidance Center of Boston, one of the oldest of the clinics, served the Boston Juvenile Court for a number of years by making studies, diagnoses, and treatment recommendations in cases of delinquency. The efficacy of this approach was studied by the Gluecks in a five-year follow-up study on 1,000 boys who had been examined by the center.[50] The Gluecks found that 88 per cent of the boys had continued in their misbehavior and 70 per cent had been convicted of

---

[48] Joan McCord and William McCord, "A Follow-up Report on the Cambridge-Somerville Youth Study," *The Annals,* vol. 322, pp. 89–97, March, 1959.

[49] It was also observed that there were only twelve cases in which a counselor had maintained a close relationship with a child for at least two years, visiting him on the average of once a week, and had attempted to deal with his basic personality problems. Six of these individuals who received intensive treatment committed subsequent crimes, while eleven out of twelve matched control cases became offenders. *Ibid.,* p. 95.

[50] Sheldon Glueck and Eleanor Glueck, *One Thousand Juvenile Delinquents,* 1934. See also Helen L. Witmer, *Psychiatric Clinics for Children,* 1940.

serious offences. A comparison group of 1,000 other boys who had not been examined by the center was found to have displayed similar rates of recidivism. The Gluecks concluded that the diagnostic-recommendation type of clinic service to the juvenile court was without significant value. It should be observed, nevertheless, that clinics continue to perform a similar type of service in a considerable number of juvenile and criminal courts.

Following the Glueck study, Healy and Bronner set up a project for treatment of delinquents and their parents through child guidance centers. This was designed to clarify both the causes of delinquency and the effectiveness of a therapeutic manipulation of the parent-child relationship.[51] In a sample of cases selected from three child guidance clinics Healy and Bronner found that 91 per cent were unhappy, discontented, or emotionally disturbed because of provocative situations or experiences. Medical care, economic aid, recreation, employment, foster care, psychiatric treatment, and other services were provided for these children. Two years after treatment was completed the records of the children were studied and it was discovered that nearly half of the boys had not been involved in delinquencies during that period. Those with markedly abnormal personalities had done very poorly, while half of the youngsters who came from pathological homes where interpersonal relationships were very poor were "greatly improved" and about three-fourths of the remainder (who were characterized neither by grossly abnormal personalities nor homes) had avoided further difficulties with the law.

As a result of this study the Judge Baker Guidance Center altered its approach, selecting intake on the basis of cooperative parental attitudes and other favorable prognostic indications and providing psychiatric and social treatment to those accepted for service. Subsequent follow-up studies suggested that such clinical efforts were of value to a considerable proportion of the delinquents, although about one-fourth of the noncourt delinquents and one-third of the court delinquents were found "not to have benefited" from the treatment provided.[52] The Children's Bureau concluded that "Child guidance clinics have little to offer, presumably, when there is gross social pathology or when children suffer from certain extreme disorders of personality [e.g., unstable egocentrics, unclassified abnormal personalities]. They can be helpful to most other delinquents they accept for treatment, even to many who are seriously neurotic or even approaching psychosis."[53] As a partial consequence of the center studies, child guidance clinic efforts have tended in some measure to concentrate their efforts on cases where difficulty in parent-child relationships appears to be the central problem and where the individuals involved are ready to accept

[51] William Healy and Augusta F. Bronner, *New Light on Delinquency and Its Treatment*, 1939.

[52] William Healy and Augusta F. Bronner, *Treatment and What Happened Afterward*, 1939, and Augusta F. Bronner, "Treatment and What Happened Afterward (A Second Report)," *Am. J. Orthopsychiat.*, vol. 14, pp. 33–34, 1944.

[53] *The Effectiveness of Delinquency Prevention Programs, op. cit.*, p. 40.

treatment. Such persons cannot, of course, be said to represent delinquents generally, and the findings raise a question of what is to be done with children who do not fit these specifications.

Juvenile Courts

The inclination of the juvenile court to act as a general agency of child welfare was observed in an earlier chapter. Such courts exercise broad jurisdiction not only because of the statutory powers given them but also because of their widespread practice of administering unofficial treatment. As a consequence, they have come increasingly to resemble the child welfare boards of the Scandinavian countries, with little control by the appellate courts.[54] In many places they have endeavored to identify predelinquents through their "symptomatic behavior" and to provide preventive services through probation.

The author has expressed elsewhere his strong opinion that quasi-criminal courts ought not to attempt to deal with individuals who have not become offenders. Support has been given to this view in the *Standards for Specialized Courts Dealing with Children,* published by the U.S. Children's Bureau. Whether the policies formulated by the Bureau will help to stem the trend among paternalistic judges and probation officers remains to be seen. It is doubtful whether juvenile courts can work effectively in dealing with so-called predelinquents. In any event, that task quite clearly belongs in nonauthoritarian agencies of child welfare. Courts should concentrate on the sufficiently difficult task of improving their performance in the treatment of offenders and, thereby, in the prevention of repeated delinquency.

HIGHFIELDS: INTENSIVE INSTITUTIONAL TREATMENT

A variety of programs involving community efforts to prevent delinquency have been considered above. Treatment programs in correctional institutions are also intended to reduce the repetition of law violations, but there has been little empirical inquiry into their effects. It is commonly believed that intensive treatment in small institutions is more effective than the mass custodial programs conducted in typical reformatories and prisons. It may well be that this is true. On the other hand, it is possible that the ostensibly superior performance of the former results from differential selection of the populations dealt with.

One recent objective inquiry has been specifically directed toward studying the relative effectiveness of a treatment-oriented center at Highfields, New Jersey, in preventing recidivism as compared to a fairly traditional

---

[54] See Chapter 14 in relation to juvenile courts, and Paul W. Tappan, *Intervention by the Courts or by Other Authorities in the Case of Socially Maladjusted Children and Juveniles, II, The Competent Authorities,* Fifth International Congress for Social Defense, Stockholm, 1958.

regime of training at the Annandale Reformatory in that state.[55] A study conducted at the Highfields facility has attempted to evaluate the achievement of a program of intensive treatment employing a form of group therapy, described by the authorities as "guided group interaction." The author will consider the research findings here, since this is one of the few intensive empirical investigations that have been conducted to measure the influence of a project oriented toward the rehabilitation of delinquents. The study also reveals the difficulties that may be encountered in pursuing an inquiry of this sort to a meaningful conclusion even where ample research funds, time, and the guidance of a competent advisory committee are available.

At Highfields some twenty youths, aged 16 and 17, who have had no prior experience of imprisonment, are retained in an open-custody institution for periods of from three to four months. During this period they work a forty-hour week at a neighboring institution and, in the evenings, participate in group therapy sessions conducted by a sociologist-superintendent. A sample of 229 boys committed to Highfields between February, 1951, and April, 1954, was compared to a control group of 116 youths of similar age who had been committed during the same period to the Annandale Reformatory, an institution where the inmates are generally held for periods of a year or more. Each group was studied in relation to social background characteristics and tested on attitude and behavior both at the beginning and the end of the commitment period in order to determine what significant changes might have occurred. Success and failure rates were computed on the basis of recommitment to an institution during a post-release period of generally no less than one year. These data revealed that 63 per cent of the Highfields sample had not recidivated during the follow-up period, while only 47 per cent of the Annandale group had avoided further imprisonment.[56]

The figures referred to above will very possibly come to be widely quoted in support of short-term, intensive, therapeutically-oriented programs for delinquents as a substitute for mass reformatories. Surely, this would be an attractive conclusion, in part because such programs can save considerable time and money.

The research does not in fact show that brief and intensive treatment

[55] See H. Ashley Weeks, *Youthful Offenders at Highfields,* 1958, and Lloyd W. McCorkle, Albert Elias, and F. Lovell Bixby, *The Highfields Study: A Unique Experiment in the Treatment of Juvenile Delinquency,* 1958.

[56] If those Highfields cases that were returned to court as "unsuitable" (some forty-one cases) are deleted from the sample, the relative success rate for that facility appears considerably higher: 77 per cent. This is the figure that Professor Burgess employed in his summary of the relative effectiveness of the program and that Weeks used at some points in his analysis. Obviously, however, the elimination from the Highfields sample of cases most likely to fail does not offer a fair and objective comparison to the Annandale control group. The latter institution cannot rid itself of its more difficult clients. The figure suggests that Highfields succeeds with "good cases."

programs are more effective in preventing recidivism, however. It appears rather that the reformatory control group was poorly selected and that the offenders displayed, in comparison to the Highfields sample, numerous pathogenic characteristics that were associated with their higher frequency of failures.[57] It is quite clear from the data that the Highfields sample *should* more frequently have succeeded under the criteria of success employed in the study quite without regard to the nature of the program to which they were exposed. Not only were they better risks, but they were treated more leniently after their short stay at the center.

In the light of the variety of factors favorable to the Highfields youths, it is somewhat surprising to find the data indicating that during the early period of the Highfields operation, when it was under the direction of an experienced sociological therapist, only 46 per cent of the boys received (a part of the total sample employed in the immediate study) were successful, a rate similar to that observed for the total Annandale control group. It is also interesting to discover, in comparing the total samples, that the higher success rate at Highfields was almost entirely a consequence of the better performance of the Negro boys who had been committed to that facility as compared with those at Annandale. Rates for white boys were very similar for the two institutions, 64 per cent at Highfields and 59 per cent at Annandale, a difference that is not significant. The Annandale Negro youths displayed more numerous adverse background factors that, in their cumulative effect, contributed very largely to the differences observed in recidivism, although in the small samples studied the significance of individual variables could not be shown in a number of cases.[58]

[57] The Annandale boys were older, had had less formal education, had come from lower status homes, had had both earlier and more extensive prior histories of delinquency, had come more frequently from delinquency areas, and displayed mental retardation and suggestibility in a larger number of cases. The comparative success rates were also affected by the fact that twenty-seven of the Highfield successes were boys who were either permitted or required to enlist in the armed services, whereas only seven of the Annandale successes were thus rescued from the danger of failure, and by the fact that the Annandale boys were held longer under postrelease supervision (as parolees) than were the Highfields youths (who were technically on probation and in a number of instances were discharged early from this status). The Annandale cases were more often recommitted merely for the violation of the conditions of supervision rather than for new offenses. Furthermore, it appears that thirty-four of the "successful" Highfields boys came again before a criminal court for law violations, though they were not recommitted, while only eleven of the Annandale successes were again arraigned, and that more of the Highfields recidivists were involved in serious delinquencies.

[58] Dr. Weeks observed, "It is reasonable to suppose that the large differences between the proportion of Highfields and Annandale Negroes who have successful outcomes are due to the much larger proportion of Annandale boys with poor backgrounds." The fact may also be relevant that the total Annandale population is composed much more largely of Negroes than is that at Highfields, where only a few of the "better risks" are sent.

Much of the Highfields research report deals with the study of attitude changes; this study was conducted on the basis of several groups of statements formulated by the staff and selected by Dr. Weeks to represent "attitudes to family, parental authority, breaking the law, law enforcement, general authority, self-acceptance, acceptance of others, and conduct norms." In spite of the emphasis given to group therapy at the Highfields center, the attitude scores achieved by its population after treatment displayed no greater improvement than those of the Annandale sample.[59] The questions employed on personal adjustment also revealed little or no change in the personalities of the boys involved.[60] The data provided suggest that the Annandale population changed in a desirable direction as much as did the Highfield boys, whether because of or in spite of the program, and that, while they had more seriously criminogenic backgrounds, their white boys stayed out of trouble as frequently as did the Highfields cases while their colored youths had, for a variety of reasons, much less opportunity to succeed.

On the positive side it must be said that the annual per capita cost of maintaining boys at Highfields is approximately one-third that at Annandale because of the short stay at the former institution. G. Howland Shaw indicates quite fairly in his evaluation of the Highfields program that "in the space of a few months and at relatively small cost positive results can be obtained with the upper-teen-age delinquent who is reasonably intelligent, not too patterned in delinquency, and not too emotionally disturbed." This suggests that carefully selected cases of normal and mature adolescents without prior institutional commitments and with limited histories of delinquency can be dealt with in a small, short-term facility about as effectively as and more economically than in a traditional reformatory. On the other hand, it appears that in the samples studied the small differences in success rates were very likely attributable to differences in the cases committed rather than differences in the programs themselves. In spite of the scholarly research that went into this study, it does not provide affirmative proof that the impact of group therapy in a small institutional setting would prevent repeated crime more frequently than does a fairly traditional reformatory provided that the populations dealt with are similar in background.

[59] Strangely, only the Highfields Negro boys among the two samples studied failed to show a more favorable attitude toward obeying the law at the end of the institutional experience. Yet it was their higher success rate that accounted for the better showing of Highfields in ultimate outcome.

[60] One is left to wonder whether no changes occurred or whether the questionnaires employed, relying as they did upon the intellectual content of attitudes and the boys' self-appraisals, were not well designed to elicit information on such changes as may actually have occurred.

Chapter 18

TREATMENT AND PREVENTION

In this chapter general modes of prevention will be considered. The author is concerned here not with programmatic approaches to delinquency and crime but with methods of treatment that are designed to help people with problems of adjustment. Crime prevention is a possible by-product of such efforts. Some of these treatment modalities are being employed increasingly by the correctional system, both within and outside institutions. Therefore, the discussion here has some relevance for the correctional procedures that will be discussed in ensuing chapters. The author will consider the possible role in treatment and prevention of psychotherapy and of modifications of the environment. The chapter concludes with a consideration of methods of treating addictions.

Psychotherapy in some of its major forms will be given attention here for several reasons. There has come to be increasing reliance upon psychiatric therapies to deal with the growing numbers of persons in the community who are found to be suffering from emotional disturbances and deviations. It is commonly believed that such treatment may help to curtail crime among potential offenders through reducing hostility, aggression, and other criminogenic traits of personality. There has been a fairly rapid development of programs employing various forms of quasipsychiatric treatment, especially group therapy and counseling, in a number of correctional systems. This raises policy questions on the extent to which corrections can and should develop clinical services and the forms of such treatment that may be effective in dealing with offenders. Casework techniques are discussed only briefly here since they receive attention elsewhere in this volume in relation to correctional practices. These forms of treatment as well as such related measures as domestic relations counseling and the school social work movement are devices designed to alleviate some of the consequences of the sort of social system in which we live.

METHODS OF THERAPY

Interpretive Analysis

Analytic and interpretive therapy is based upon the technique of probing deeply into the patients' unconscious memories to uncover and ventilate the traumatic incidents and the peculiarities of psychosexual development that may produce neurotic and sometimes other psychic deviations. This involves the use of methods of free association of ideas on the part of the patient. The dreams and memories of the individual are used as points of departure in his associations and the therapist exerts especially persistent efforts at those loci of experience where unusual repressions reveal significant emotional blockings.[1] The resolution of the patient's psychic problems is supposed to occur as a result of helping him to bring into consciousness and to relive crucial memories of infancy and childhood. He thereby develops insight into his problems in an emotional rather than a merely intellectual sense. His conception of the dynamics of his behavior is influenced to a very considerable extent under interpretive therapies by the theoretical orientation of the analyst.

The hypothesis that "insight," through which the patient is enabled to understand and accept a therapist's interpretations of the dynamics of his conduct, will resolve personality problems involves certain difficulties. The fact that clinicians interpret similar phenomena very differently leads one to believe that it is something other than merely interpretation and insight, possibly the patient's catharsis and the personal influence and suggestion of the therapist, that produces the result. It is apparent that insight and interpretative therapy are neither adequate nor appropriate to many types of patients, whatever may be the reason for its successes with others.[2]

Unfortunately there is little objective evidence of the frequency of success and failure through interpretive therapy.[3] It is known that some condi-

[1] Such probing may be facilitated by the use of sodium amytal, pentothal, methadrine, carbon dioxide, or hypnosis as techniques to diminish resistance or to facilitate release. Many orthodox analysts are skeptical of the results obtained by these methods of speeding up therapy. They are still largely experimental in character.

[2] In this regard Carl R. Rogers has said: "One possible reason for the generally disappointing proportion of successes in analytic treatment deserves attention. Analysts have conceived their notion of treatment so narrowly that they have neglected every type of therapy except that which develops insight. While they are often successful in this primary goal, the individual fails to make any satisfactory general adjustment, because of the therapist's failure to recognize any reality outside of the patient's emotional life. Intellectual retardation, unsatisfactory family conditions, unwholesome social factors are often overlooked entirely. The need of more than this narrow viewpoint is affirmed by two eminent psychiatrists, Dr. Healy and Dr. Alexander, who have endeavored to treat delinquents by means of psychoanalysis." *Client-centered Therapy,* 1951, pp. 337–338. See also Frieda Fromm-Reichmann, "Recent Advances in Psychoanalytic Therapy," in Patrick Mullahy (ed.), *A Study of Interpersonal Relations,* 1949, p. 127.

[3] Albert Ellis has evaluated the therapeutic results achieved with sixteen patients whom he treated through orthodox psychoanalysis, seventy-eight through psychoanalytically oriented psychotherapy, and seventy-eight through "rational psychotherapy." He found that in the first group 50 per cent showed little or no improvement, 37 per cent displayed distinct improvement, and 13 per cent considerable improvement. With the second type of therapy the percentages were 37 per cent, 45 per cent, and 18 per cent. With the third type the greatest frequency of success

tions such as schizophrenia, psychopathic personality, and most sexual deviations are peculiarly resistant to treatment. Even some of the "garden varieties" of neurosis are difficult to resolve. In any case, the process must be long extended for the patient, frequently requiring continual analytic sessions over a period of years. Thus, it is prohibitively costly to the average deviate. Moreover, analysis is a dangerous experience. It is a kind of psychic surgery and should be undertaken no more casually than other surgery. The selection of a practitioner is important and difficult, since so little can be known of the effectiveness of most analysts. There is far less uniformity in their training and skills than is true in other specialized fields of the medical profession. Furthermore, the patient in analysis must generally be made worse before he can become better. The painful reliving of traumatizing experience precipitates the patient into intense neurotic conflicts and resistances that must be gradually broken down. The facade of defenses and protective devices by which he has shielded himself must be penetrated and exposed. This may be worthwhile if his problem can be resolved or if he can emerge improved. But the truth is that many cases are worse adjusted at the termination of analysis than before. Many others are unimproved. Some are improved but not "cured." The most that the average patient may expect is some aid in working out his adjustments, and he must count both the risks of failure and the costs of success. Serious difficulties are involved in achieving results with the patient whose problem is very profound. The nature of that problem and the personality of the patient may render deep probing difficult or impossible. His resistance to recall may be strong, particularly if his symptoms, though annoying to him, are carefully protective of his equilibrium of personality. Unconsciously he may prefer the compensating gains obtained through his neurotic and compulsive outlets to the devastation of his character structure. In some instances the individual is unable to identify with the analyst or, on the other hand, he may develop an excessive transference and dependence, resulting sometimes in an analytic neurosis. Sometimes the psychiatrist is in-

---

was achieved in the shortest time: 10 per cent without improvement, 46 per cent distinct improvement, and 44 per cent considerable improvement. "Outcome of Employing Three Techniques of Psychotherapy," *J. Clin. Psychol.,* vol. 13, pp. 344–350, October, 1957.

H. J. Eysenck, professor of psychology at the University of London, indicates that the same proportion of individuals, roughly two out of three, improve without treatment of their emotional problems as do the patients who receive prolonged psychoanalytic treatment. Dr. Melitta Schmideberg, psychoanalyst, avers that "There is no reason to assume that they [the results of psychoanalytic treatment] are better than the results attained by any other method of psychotherapy or, perhaps, than the results of spontaneous recovery." Dr. Harry I. Weinstock, as chairman of an American Psychoanalytic Association fact-gathering committee, stated that "No claims regarding the therapeutic usefulness of analytic treatment are made by the American Psychoanalytic Association. We are not responsible for claims made by individuals in whom enthusiasm may outrun knowledge."

effectual in dealing with the particular kind of problem presented. The best of therapists vary in their abilities to deal with different types of disorders.[4]

Psychoanalysis and other deep interpretive therapies have been employed only infrequently with criminals. As a practical matter the costs are prohibitive and the trained personnel unavailable.[5] Also, it appears that treatment of this sort is not appropriate in dealing with the problems of the great majority of aggressive and antisocial offenders. Some of the hypotheses of the analytic method are particularly inappropriate in dealing with most criminals. These include, for example, the principle that the patient must desire treatment in order to be helped; that he should be dealt with permissively rather than with authority; that in the interest of mental health feelings of guilt should be relieved rather than strengthened; that crime is merely a symptom of emotional disorder and if the latter is treated effectively the criminality will disappear. The focus is on the removal of the psychic discomforts of the individual rather than on securing conformity to social norms. Often there is an assumption of illness if the individual has violated the law and a belief that insight into the psychosexual origins of his problem will remedy both the illness and the criminality. To a lay criminologist it appears that the improved utilization of psychiatry in criminology, either for diagnostic or treatment purposes, depends to a major extent upon the development of principles and methods that are more suitable for individuals who do not suffer from major pathologies but who are deficient in socialization and guilt feelings and who require improved adaptation to authority and group control, commonly at the expense of expressive gratifications and emotional comfort.[6]

Nondirective Therapy

We come now to nondirective and client-centered relationship therapies, systems which have their theoretical basis to a large extent in the thinking

---

[4] In a study of 100 schizophrenic patients treated at the Henry Phipps Clinic of the Johns Hopkins Hospital, Barbara J. Betz found that 75 per cent of those handled by one group of seven psychiatrists were improved at the time of discharge, while only 27 per cent of those handled by seven other psychiatrists were improved. She observed that differences in success achieved were largely "determined by the differences found among physicians in the extent to which they are able to approach their patients' problems in a personal way, gain a trusted confidential relationship and participate in an active, personal way in the patient's reorientation to personal relationships. Techniques of passive permissiveness or efforts to develop insight by interpretation appear to have much less therapeutic value." J. C. Whitehorn and B. J. Betz, "A Study of Psychotherapeutic Relationships between Physicians and Schizophrenic Patients," *Am. J. Psychiat.*, vol. 3, pp. 321–331, November, 1954.

[5] Ben Karpman and the late Robert M. Lindner are significant exceptions. See ftn. 47 in Chapter 10 relative to the dearth of psychiatrists and psychoanalysts.

[6] For a more detailed statement of this view, see Tappan, "Sociological Motivations of Delinquency," *Am. J. Psychiat.*, vol. 108, pp. 680–685, 1952, and "Concepts and Cross Purposes," *Focus*, vol. 31, pp. 65–69, 1952,

of Otto Rank, Carl Rogers, and others. These are also intensive and slow processes of treatment but they do not emphasize diagnostic or interpretive analysis. Their effectiveness depends largely upon the role of the therapist as an understanding and accepting person to whom the client may relate and express his feelings as he gropes toward greater maturity. Carl R. Rogers has formulated in these terms the hypotheses on which treatment efforts are based in the "client-centered therapy" practiced at the University of Chicago Counseling Center.[7]

1. The first hypothesis is that the individual has within himself the capacity, latent if not evident, to understand those aspects of himself and of his life which are causing him dissatisfaction, anxiety, or pain and the capacity and the tendency to reorganize himself and his relationship to life in the direction of self-actualization and maturity in such a way as to bring a greater degree of internal comfort.

2. This capacity will be released, and therapy or personal growth will be most facilitated, when the therapist can create a psychological climate characterized by (a) a genuine acceptance of the client as a person of unconditional worth; (b) a continuing, sensitive attempt to understand the existing feelings and communications of the client, as they seem to the client, without any effort to diagnose or alter those feelings; and (c) a continuing attempt to convey something of this empathic understanding to the client.

3. It is hypothesized that, in such an acceptant, understanding, and non-threatening psychological atmosphere, the client will reorganize himself at both the conscious and the deeper levels of his personality in such a manner as to cope with life more constructively, more intelligently, and in a more socialized as well as a more satisfying way. More specifically it is hypothesized that the client will change in his perception of self, will become more understanding of self and others, more accepting of self and others, more creative, more adaptive, more self-directing and autonomous, more mature in his behavior, less defensive, and more tolerant of frustrations.

Although there is some difference of opinion, the literature on non-directive therapy suggests that intensive treatment of this sort is not to be entered into lightly. The dangers are not so great as under analytic treatment because of the deeper levels of probing and the transference phenomenon that characterize the latter. But it appears that therapies based upon relationship are most effective with personality problems where the client is at least moderately acceptant of others and where environmental methods of treatment have already proved futile. Rogers cautions against the misuse of nondirective therapy by some social workers. He states that some "have endeavored to 'do nothing' in the process because of their misunderstanding of the term 'passive,'" and that others, under the same

[7] Carl R. Rogers and Rosalind F. Dymond, *Psychotherapy and Personality Change,* University of Chicago Press, Chicago, copyright 1954 by the University of Chicago, pp. 4–5. (Reprinted by permission.) See also Nicholas Hobbs, "Group-centered Psychotherapy," in Rogers, *Client-centered Therapy.*

misconception, have permitted children to do them bodily harm in the 'therapeutic' relationship!" In successful cases of treatment clients are found to become more acceptant of self and others, more comfortable and confident, and less neurotic.

Thus far, nondirective forms of intensive therapy have not been employed widely with offenders. Like psychoanalysis, it is a time consuming and costly method of treatment designed primarily to improve mental health rather than to modify antisocial behavior.

Short-term Psychotherapies

The less intensive psychotherapies vary in form and method. Because of the problems involved in more intensive analysis, psychiatrists and psychologists are coming increasingly to employ shallower levels and eclectic methods of counseling and interviewing.[8] Some of them believe that these methods can be as effective in dealing with most emotional disturbances as the analytic methods are, without involving the time, costs, and dangers. Though some of these therapists are analytically oriented, the counseling and interview methods are designed to help the individual face and cope with his difficulties rather than to remove the causes of unadjustment. The aim is to synthesize or integrate rather than to analyze, to aid the individual in reality thinking, and to interpret his problems to him in terms of the similar experiences of others. The process is supportive, educative, and regulative in character. The future development of techniques to accomplish these limited therapeutic objectives appears to be most promising from the point of view of extending treatment more generally in the population. Certainly in the correctional field we must depend in the main upon the more superficial methods of treatment. Some of the specialized techniques that are currently used in these types of treatment will now be considered.[9]

Educative procedures are employed very commonly in psychotherapy, either alone or as adjuncts to other methods. Mental conflicts are sometimes rooted in false beliefs. Problems of social adjustment and of emotional relationship frequently stem from ignorance and misconceptions. This is especially true of persons of low socioeconomic background, in-

---

[8] On the basis of a study of psychiatric literature published in 1950–1953, Albert Ellis found forty-two different major techniques of therapy listed and, under these headings, 365 more specific methods of therapy. He observes the growing preference for relationship therapy and short-term face-to-face techniques rather than insight-interpretative and expressive-emotive methods. "New Approaches to Psychotherapy Techniques," *J. Clin. Psychol.*, Mon. Supp. No. 11, pp. 1–54, July, 1955. See especially pp. 40–43.

[9] See Ellis, *op. cit.;* Gustav Bychowski and J. Louise Despert (eds.), *Specialized Techniques in Psychotherapy*, 1952; and Carl R. Rogers, *The Clinical Treatment of the Problem Child*, for summary discussion and critical evaluation of methods of psychotherapy.

cluding juvenile delinquents, youth offenders, and criminals. Their knowledge concerning matters of health, government, society, and sex, for example, is commonly very incomplete or distorted. Correctional caseworkers, in the various settings in which they function, can prepare the offender to face reality and can alleviate tension by providing factual information concerning the nature and purpose of the experiences that lie ahead of him. Educative measures are more directly therapeutic in purpose where they are employed to help the individual to face the consequences of his behavior or to clarify moral and social issues that are involved in his defective adjustments.

The effectiveness of educative techniques in psychotherapy is limited, to be sure. Directed at the rational level of apprehension, ordinarily it does not meet the more complex attitudinal, emotional, or volitional problems that are involved in the antisocial conduct of certain types of persistent offenders. Moreover, there is usually considerable resistance and often great hostility to the educative agent, especially in the court or correctional setting. The officer, teacher, caseworker, domestic relations counselor, or clinician must be accepted by the subject as a reliable person before his instruction can have significant impact. This is very difficult when the indoctrinator is looked upon as an agent of oppressive authority. The attitude, personality, and skills of the therapist as well as his careful timing in the employment of educational methods are extremely important, therefore. Very commonly the effectiveness of the educative technique depends upon skill in combining it with other more potent psychotherapeutic methods.

A second mode of therapy commonly associated with educative methods is *personal influence.* This means that some degree of suggestive or persuasive effort is applied in treatment. Suggestion is employed by lay counselors in the correctional field in such forms as warnings, exhortation, and moralization. Ordinarily the delinquent has been exposed often to these devices in home, school, court, and community. They are of dubious utility, especially if the subject does not identify closely with the counselor. To be effective, persuasion must be rooted in an empathic relationship that is more easily attained with the predelinquent or the delinquent child than with the criminal adult.

The deeper the rapport is between the subject and the therapist, the greater the degree of personal influence that can be exercised by the latter. At least temporarily the patient may make remarkable progress in self-control. Faulty habits may be interrupted and reconditioning begun. Many psychiatrists and psychologists, particularly those of analytic and of nondirective orientation, have deprecated the use of suggestion and persuasion on the ground that the results achieved are only temporary. They contend that this method does not get to the emotional roots of neurosis and consequently that repression on the part of the patient may ultimately increase his problem. In cases of complicated and persistent neuroses, it is probably true that strong persuasive influence should be exerted only very discriminatingly. Relationship, transference, and interpretation as well as direct forms of persuasion are phases of treatment, however, in which psychiatrists deliberately use personal influence. Some authorities have relied quite heavily upon personal relationship and influence in therapeutic practice with delinquents and have considered it highly effective. It may establish the foundation for a reorganization of habits and attitudes that, taken together with other forms of treatment, may achieve the correctional objective. Whether the exercise of personal influence is useful in the handling of the neurotic need not be of concern here. Such treatment appears to be appropriate in dealing with antisocial individuals. The problem is one of developing the sort of relationship between the offender and the authority figure that will facilitate such influence. Success in this respect depends in large measure upon the personality and skills of the worker.

A third technique used in nonintensive treatment is comprised in the *expressive therapies*. This is most commonly achieved by catharsis, a process in which the patient unburdens his problems upon a sympathetic listener. Thus the patient eases his tensions and clarifies his feelings and attitudes. Temporarily, at least, the patient may be relieved of considerable distress. The ordinary person without complex emotional problems may discharge his conflicts and anxieties through the supportive attention of his close fellows. Others, especially neurotics, often suffer from an inability either to verbalize their problems or to act them out in acceptable ways. They may need more intensive psychotherapy. Guidance by the therapist and the establishment of rapport are required in the expressive processes. In cases where the patient shows considerable resistance, doubt, confusion, or anxiety and cannot express his feelings spontaneously, the therapist must take a more active role in helping him to clarify his problem.

Among other forms of expressive therapy that have developed in recent years are psychodrama and sociodrama. Here patients are instructed to act out their emotional and social problems in a permissive setting.[10] These are forms of group therapy in which catharsis and clarification are sought. Various play techniques have also been developed in psychotherapy with children both for expressive purposes and as aids to diagnosis.[11]

Expressive therapy is valuable primarily with individuals suffering from subjective conflicts. It has limited utility in the corrective treatment of persistent criminals. However, where delinquency is rooted in mental conflict or minor neurosis, the young person may sometimes be helped considerably by catharsis, the clarification of his problems, and the ventilation

[10] See J. L. Moreno, "Sociodrama," *Psychodrama Monogr.*, no. 1; Raymond Corsini, "The Method of Psychodrama in Prison," *Group Psychother.*, vol. 3, pp. 321–326, 1951.

[11] See Frederick H. Allen, *Psychotherapy with Children*, 1942.

of the conflicts that are associated with his behavioral difficulties. Furthermore, the experience of imprisonment generates anxieties at all age levels among prisoners. While the verbalization of fears and anxieties does little in the ordinary case to reduce criminalism, it is important to the mental health of the inmate and to the stability of the institution for the prisoner to have the opportunity to express his feelings without danger of reprisal. Moreover, this provides an opportunity either in individual interview or group therapy for more affirmative treatment measures to be applied. These measures may provide a foundation for changed attitudes and conduct.

Brief analytic psychotherapy and other forms of psychotherapeutic counseling are more intensive than educative, persuasive, and expressive techniques. They are less time consuming and profound than psychoanalysis and ordinarily less prolonged than nondirective or relationship therapies. These therapies are employed increasingly not only by psychiatrists and lay analysts but also by psychologists and caseworkers who have had some training in Freudian, Adlerian, or Rankian theory and technique. They involve the use of catharsis and insight. Here, also, there is danger that interpretations may be based upon inadequate data and may be drawn too uncritically from the dogma of a particular school of psychiatric theory. Moreover, the insight involved is on a different and more strictly intellectual level than that involved in reliving traumatic experience. Many clinical authorities believe that brief psychiatrically oriented therapy is the only feasible treatment for most patients and offenders where time and economy are important considerations. Clifford Allen has suggested that this method has proved effective in some cases of sex deviates, including those involving psychic impotence, sexual aversions, and fetishism.[12] Cases with more common problems of deviations, such as homosexuality and psychopathic personality, have not responded, however. More research is needed to determine whether this type of therapy is effective with criminalism rooted in emotional deviations in any significant proportion of cases.

Experimental Therapies

The therapeutic methods discussed above have been developed and used over a relatively long period of time. They are continually being modified and adapted for use in special settings. As has been seen, there is no consensus on the merits of the various techniques, particularly in the treatment of criminals. In addition to these traditional methods, there are a number of psychological treatment approaches that are recent in origin and experimental in character. Some of these approaches are designed for individual and others for group therapeutic work. In comparison with the techniques previously discussed they are more economical.

The author will now consider certain relatively recent devices that are

[12] See Clifford Allen, *The Sexual Perversions and Abnormalities*, 1949.

being used experimentally with offenders. The extent to which these measures may be successful in dealing with those strongly antisocial, aggressive, and psychopathic personalities that have resisted other methods of treatment cannot be predicted at this time.

Hypnosis and Drugs. In the summary discussion of intensive therapies, reference was made to several methods of speeding up treatment. The two major forms are hypnotherapy and narcotherapy.[13] Hypnosis, which was used by Freud in the early development of his analytic procedures, has been revived in recent years by some practitioners as an aid to psychoanalysis and to other forms of psychotherapy. Through hypnosis the therapist uses suggestion to influence the behavior of the patient. Studies indicate that ordinary hypnotic and posthypnotic suggestions are not effective when these run strongly counter to the patient's basic emotional organization or his superego. Yet it appears that in cases where treatment is sufficiently prolonged hypnosis produces an increasing transference to the therapist. Thus a considerable and growing amount of influence can be exercised.

Most orthodox psychoanalysts deprecate the use of hypnotherapy on the grounds that it is superficial and temporary in effect, that the analysis of resistances and transference is undercut by the speeding up of the analytic process, that full abreaction does not occur, and that "total therapy" cannot therefore be achieved.[14] On the other hand, hypnoanalysts have maintained that not only does the proper use of this method produce full abreaction and lasting therapeutic effect but it can be employed more speedily and more effectively in some types of cases than psychoanalysis alone. Thus, using orthodox analytic procedure, ordinary resistances may be manipulated, but where very intensive blocks are encountered hypnosis may be employed to raise the deeply repressed material and the latter may be then recalled in a nonhypnotic state. On the basis of his extensive use of the hypnoanalytic technique, the late Robert Lindner believed that it is particularly effective in dealing with psychopaths and addicts. He said:[15]

In the category of psychopathic personality, for example—a category heretofore regarded with therapeutic nihilism—hypnoanalysis can claim achievements regarded in some quarters as remarkable. As we all know, the chief problem with which the therapist is confronted in such cases is that of "holding" the patient in therapy until a beachhead can be gained and occupied by insight into his personality. . . . But with hypnoanalysis this "problem" no longer exists since the nature of the method permits the utilization of post-hypnotic

[13] See Paul H. Hoch and Philip Polatin, "Narcodiagnosis and Narcotherapy," in Bychowski and Despert, *op. cit.,* pp. 1–23, and ftn. 1 above.

[14] See Robert M. Lindner, "Hypnoanalysis as a Psychotherapeutic Technique," in Bychowski and Despert, *op. cit.,* pp. 25–39, and M. Brennan and M. M. Gill, *Hypnotherapy,* 1947.

[15] Lindner, *op. cit.,* pp. 28–29. (Reprinted by permission.) See also his *Rebel without a Cause,* 1944.

suggestion which becomes—until first transference and then insight take over—the binder of patient to treatment. The same applies to a wide range of the addictions, including alcohol. Many of these are found among the psychopathic personalities or other similar character distortions. With them, hypnoanalysis performs both as investigative and synthesizing technique. At the same time it provides strength for those positive elements in the personality that the discomfiture of the patient informs us must be there, assisting him in the battle against the neurosis by what amounts to "shoring up" of the ego.

Dr. Jacob Conn, reporting on his use of "hypnosynthesis" with a group of twenty-three sex offenders referred by the medical office of the Supreme Bench of Baltimore, describes the process of treatment as "the use of hypnosis to meet the patient's individual needs in a setting of optimum permissiveness. The patient is not urged to reveal content or to abreact but to foster his natural resistance."[16] In this series of cases only two are reported as failures. Dr. Guttmacher, the chief medical officer of the Supreme Bench, makes the suggestive comment that Rorschach testing of a pedophile in this same group two years after treatment showed "no significant change in certain unhealthy basic personality traits but a *marked change so far as increased caution and strengthened ego defenses were concerned.*"[17]

Considering the frequency of alcoholism and psychopathic trends of personality among repetitive criminals and the resistiveness of the average criminal to ordinary methods of suggestion, it appears particularly desirable to secure more evidence concerning the efficacy of hypnotherapy in dealing with these types of offenders. Lindner's evaluations are of a highly optimistic character, though he insisted upon the necessity for deep analysis and a reorganization of personality. Even with hypnoanalysis this is a time-consuming as well as a very highly skilled process and its aim has been therapeutic in a general sense rather than preventive or correctional.

Certain drugs, as has been noted, particularly sodium amytol and sodium pentothal, are now used by many practitioners for purposes of diagnosis and therapy. Their utility results from the reduction of inhibition and increased facility in verbal communication. As a result the patient becomes more suggestible. Amytol is generally preferred because of its less

---

[16] Jacob Conn, *J. Clin. Psychopathol.*, 1949, referred to in Manfred S. Guttmacher, *Sex Offenses*, pp. 111–112, 1951.

[17] *Ibid.*, p. 112. In discussing the treatment of sex offenders Guttmacher has said: "For some cases of a neurotic nature, deep psychotherapy of the classical analytic type is doubtless the treatment of choice. But the virtual impossibility, technically, of carrying out such treatment in the ordinary, highly restrictive institutional environment, its time-consuming character, and its great cost, limit its use to only a small number of offenders on probation, and only such of these as can profit from the treatment and want it. Doubtless shorter methods, making use of hypnosis and abreactive drugs, may have more to offer from a practical point of view." *Op. cit.*, pp. 134–135.

intoxicating influence. Amytol and pentothal were used extensively during World War II in the treatment of war neuroses and have since been employed more than in the past in dealing with civilian neuroses and certain other conditions. Various techniques have been associated with them: narcosuggestion, narcoanalysis, and narcosynthesis, short psychotherapies for the most part. Narcosuggestion is essentially a "covering-up" form of treatment, supportive and integrative. Through direct suggestion or hypnosis the patient is given reassurance concerning his physical or emotional condition. Narcoanalysis is an "uncovering" type of therapy, speeding up the process of psychoanalysis through a release of inhibition and a heightening of suggestibility that is somewhat comparable to hypnoanalysis. Hoch and Polatin suggest that narcosuggestive methods are best utilized in cases of a superficial or acute character such as acute anxiety, hysterical and fatigue states, whereas narcoanalytic methods are preferable where there is a deeper structuralization, as in obsessive-compulsive, phobic, or paranoid states.[18] They report some success in employing short-term narcotherapy with psychosomatic patients, alcoholics, and those suffering from anxiety and hysterical reactions but poor results with obsessive-compulsive neurotics, sexual deviates, psychopaths, manic-depressives, and schizophrenics. Hoch and Polatin note certain apparent advantages of short-term narcotherapy:[19]

There is a large number of neurotic patients in offices and clinics awaiting treatment; these treatments as employed today are cumbersome, expensive, and time-consuming. Any method which will condense treatment time is, therefore, welcome, even though the result at times will show more symptomatic improvement than profound insight cures. In spite of this, a considerable number of patients respond to such narcotherapy and remain well. If the short-term narcotherapy is unsuccessful, no harm is done and a prolonged treatment can then be instituted.

Obviously it is desirable that the use of both narcotherapy and hypnotherapy with criminal types be studied extensively to determine their possible efficacy for the suppression of criminal inclination. Here, to repeat what has been said, the test is this symptomatic improvement, not total therapy or the alleviation of emotional problems.

Another significant step forward in treatment of deviated offenders has been taken during the 1950s with the introduction and testing of ataraxic (tranquilizing or mood-altering) drugs. They are used on a considerable scale with young and aggressive offenders in correctional institutions as well as in the treatment of manic-depressives, schizophrenics, paretics, addicts, and psychopaths in mental hospitals. Two of these drugs were introduced in 1953, chlorpromazine (Thorazine) and reserpine (Serpasil) and soon after it was widely reported that they were effective even in the

[18] Hoch and Polatin, *op. cit.,* pp. 12–13.
[19] *Ibid.,* p. 16.

handling of patients with long histories of hospitalization. Since that time a variety of other tranquilizers have been developed in the effort to remove certain undesirable side effects. They include, among others, meprobomate (Miltown, Equanil), proclorperzine (Compazine), azacyclonol (Frenquel), mepazine (Pacatal), and benactyzine. However, chlorpromazine and reserpine are still most commonly used. The New York State Mental Hygiene Department announced in 1955 that the new drugs had reduced by one-half the use of restraints and seclusions in the hospitals of that state, and a number of researchers have suggested that from 50 to 70 per cent of patients selected for treatment responded favorably. In 1956 for the first time in twenty-five years there was a decline in the number of mental hospital patients, a decline that continued in 1957 and 1958.[20]

There has been considerable controversy among psychiatrists concerning the significance of the new pharmacotherapy. Some authorities have described them as dangerous and ineffectual substitutes for psychotherapy. More commonly, however, a conservative approval has been expressed. Thus, the psychoanalyst Dr. Frederick A. Weiss has said: "Drugs cannot cure psychosis. But they may perhaps offer some hope for freeing patients who have been vegetating for years in the back wards of hospitals and for restoring to them some limited level of functioning. More important, however, is the fact that these drugs may perhaps make patients accessible to real treatment: psychotherapy."[21] Dr. Lauretta Bender, among others, has expressed the opinion that these therapies are more than a mere adjunct to psychiatric treatment. Dr. Nathan Kline, director of the Research Center at Rockland State Hospital, who has performed much of the significant research on the use of these drugs, has cautioned that sound assessments must await further experience. He has observed that there have been consistent and dramatic responses to their use.[22]

The tranquilizing drugs have come to be used rather widely in the correctional system, but it is apparent that their value is limited to offenders suffering from emotional disturbance. They are most effective in dealing with aggressive and destructive individuals. They reduce feelings of hostility and tension, thereby diminishing the problems of control in the institution. A report from Auburn Prison in 1956 showed that the number of disciplinary actions required in a group of sixty-one cases treated with tranquilizers was reduced from 138 to 74 in the first year the drugs were used. Transfers of prisoners to the hospital for the criminal insane were also reduced. On the other hand, one authority has observed that, "In proportion, as mental and emotional aberrations are less clear-cut and less

---

[20] In 1960 a new synthetic psychotherapeutic drug, Librium, was released which, according to early reports, holds great promise for the treatment of anxiety, alcoholism, and aggression. It has been used successfully with resistant psychopaths.

[21] Reported in *New York World-Telegram and Sun*, May 2, 1955.

[22] It was estimated that in 1957 some 40 million prescriptions for ataraxic drugs were issued, in the main by general practitioners for ordinary patients.

demonstrable, results of treatment with tranquilizing drugs are less notable and have been quite limited in such categories as the primary behavior disorders among younger patients in the state hospitals and among the higher grade defectives in the state schools."[23]

Group Therapy

Group therapy is in some respects the most promising among the experimental forms of psychotherapy that have developed in recent years.[24] Such therapy may offer certain special advantages for the treatment of disturbed offenders as compared with other approaches. However, there is a danger that some magical potency may be attributed by criminologists to group therapy even while the techniques involved are still in their infancy. Disillusionment with the results obtained may easily follow. Similar uncritical enthusiasms have been expressed in the past for particular devices that were thought for a time to provide *the solution* to the myriad problems of delinquency or crime: the juvenile training school and reformatory movements, the children's court, individualization of treatment, clinical diagnosis, the reception center, and casework treatment among others. Experience has shown that none of these is a panacea and that the limited utility of any one approach is determined by the form and function it takes. Group therapy is a rapidly evolving and diverse phenomenon today. Group psychotherapy was apparently used first as a reported method of treatment by Pratt shortly after the turn of the century in the form of inspirational talks and class instruction to mental patients; it has come to be nearly as varied as the rapidly growing number of practitioners who have employed it.[25]

Various efforts have been made to classify the types of technique that are in use. One of these relates to the depth of the therapists' reach.[26] The

---

[23] Henry Brill, "Tranquilizing Drugs and Correctional Psychiatry," *Am. J. Correction,* vol. 19, p. 31, May–June, 1957.

[24] The literature on group therapy has developed rapidly. See, *inter alia,* Hyman Spotnitz, "Group Therapy," in Bychowski and Despert (eds.), *op. cit.,* pp. 85–103; Lloyd W. McCorkle, "Group Therapy," in Tappan (ed.), *Contemporary Correction,* chap. 14; McCorkle, "Present Status of Group Therapy in U.S. Correctional Institutions," *Group Psychother.,* vol. 3, pp. 79–87, 1953; George O. Baehr, "The Comparative Effectiveness of Individual Psychotherapy, Group Psychotherapy, and a Combination of These Methods," *J. Consult. Psych.,* pp. 179–183, June, 1954; and the quarterly publications of The American Society of Group Psychotherapy and Psychodrama.

[25] Experimental work with various procedures in dealing with military offenders at army rehabilitation centers during the war gave considerable impetus to the group therapy movement. Since that time there has been a growing employment of various largely unstandardized forms of group treatment in correctional institutions. One authority has commented that under the heading of group therapy there may be found activity groups, relationship groups, authoritative groups, educational groups. interview groups, and analytic groups. Spotnitz, *op. cit.,* p. 88.

[26] See McCorkle, "Group Therapy," *loc. cit.*

range is somewhat analogous to that in the methods of individual psychotherapy that have been discussed. (1) The didactic method of more or less formal instruction presupposes that the provision of information to the group and the resulting "insight" on an intellectual level may be therapeutic in helping to resolve emotional problems or that it may at least modify symptomatic behavior. This method is superficial and rationalistic. (2) There are many variations within the approach that uses repressive-inspirational methods of moralization, exhortation, or inspiration. Religious or moral suasion may be used, as it is, for example, by Alcoholics Anonymous and in more direct preaching or counseling by chaplains and ministers. Direct emotional appeals may be made for conformity to the ideals of citizenship and social living, or more subtle effort may be used to influence offenders indirectly through leadership and personal relationship. Commonly these methods are combined. (3) Analytical methods, which are employed by specialists trained in one or another of the psychological disciplines, vary in the depth to which the emotional and social problems of the group members may be exposed and explored, in the extent of the leader's role in interpretation of the psychic phenomena that are uncovered, and in the basic hypotheses or theories upon which the psychotherapy is predicated. When such work is conducted by psychiatrists and Freudian or Adlerian psychologists, it is analytically oriented, stressing depth analysis, transference, interpretation, and insight.[27] Where nondirective methods are used, only limited participation by the psychotherapist is required, the emphasis being upon sympathetic acceptance and the rallying of strengths to meet reality. The use of relationship may extend the role of the therapist. Because of the differences in process involved, these clinical forms of group psychotherapy vary greatly in the extent to which aggressions, anxieties, and defences are stimulated in group sessions. Deeper therapies involve a greater degree of disturbance to the individual members and their relationships. Direction and control are more difficult for the therapist to maintain than in individual analysis. On the other hand, the individual members are less helpless and fearful in the group setting and do not ordinarily show the intense defensiveness that develops in an individual setting.

Obviously, the personality, training, and competence of the psychotherapist are extremely important in group therapy, particularly where analytic methods are used. Unfortunately, no serious attention has been given thus far to the formulation of standards for the selection or training of therapists.[28] In hospitals, clinics, and counseling centers where such

[27] McCorkle found in a 1950 survey of the field that in not more than 10 per cent of correctional institutions where group therapy programs were in operation was responsibility in the hands of a psychiatrist alone. "Present Status of Group Therapy in U.S. Correctional Institutions," *loc. cit.*

[28] Spotnitz holds that if emotionally disturbed individuals are to be treated competently the group therapist should be trained in general medicine, psychiatry, psychoanalysis, and group therapy. *Op. cit.*, p. 88.

work is carried on, psychiatrists and psychologists generally conduct these sessions. Their procedures and conceptual orientations vary considerably, and the techniques are still largely of an experimental character. In the correctional field, perhaps in large part because of the lack of sufficient staffing by more specialized personnel, group therapy is practiced by caseworkers, parole supervisors, educators, chaplains, and probation officers more often than by fully trained psychologists or psychiatrists.[29] Their efforts run the gamut from the most superficial and formal measures of indoctrination and moralization to deep quasianalytical or interpretive therapy. Most of such work in the prison, probation, and parole fields is at a didactic and repressive-inspirational level at the present time. This is perhaps fortunate from the point of view of avoiding major disturbances in the group members and in the prison community. Serious difficulties have occasionally arisen where unskilled leaders have attempted to uncover the deeper emotional levels. This sort of problem is especially acute in the prison setting, since the members are associated more or less continuously outside the therapeutic sessions. They take their aggressions and defences with them.[30]

An important aspect of group therapy relates to the size and composition of the group under treatment. There is little empirical evidence thus far in this connection. Where merely educational or repressive-inspirational methods are employed, the number involved does not matter greatly. Groups of fifty or more have been used, apparently without excessive difficulty. On the other hand, it is generally agreed that in analytic or nondirective therapies quite small groups numbering from two to six or eight should be employed. Factors to be considered here are the membership of the group and the personality of the therapist. Proper composition of the group also varies with the technique that is to be employed. It appears to be relatively unimportant except where an expressive element is involved, as in some clinical approaches. It has been suggested that for

[29] California introduced a system of "group counseling" in its reception-guidance centers during the middle 1940s that has subsequently been developed in the prisons there. The counseling is done by correctional officers, work supervisors, teachers, tradesmen, members of the clerical staff, and others in the institution. Norman Fenton indicates that, aside from differentials in training of the personnel, "there is probably no conclusive function or operative dividing line between group counseling and group psychotherapy." He defines the counseling approach primarily in terms of "acceptance treatment or therapy" in which there is mutual acceptance and a spirit of good human relationship between the counselors and the inmates but indicates that techniques employed by the counselors vary considerably (as do those of group therapists). Some "have learned to be skillfully permissive and nondirective in their group counseling." Participation in the group counseling is mandatory. See Norman Fenton, *An Introduction to Group Counseling in State Correctional Service,* 1957, and *What Will Be Your Life?* 1955.

[30] The view has been expressed that it is undesirable to carry on therapy with groups that are in close daily contact because of the feelings of guilt that may carry over from the group situation to daily life.

analytic group therapy the therapist may wish to select individuals with similar problems, if he desires to maintain the same patterns in the members, and persons with contrasting problems, if he wishes to develop maximum stimulation and discharge of tension in the group. Spotnitz holds it is desirable to secure a balance representing similar, contrasting, and indifferent (people without contrasting or similar problems) types of individuals for a smooth development of the therapeutic process. It has also been suggested that for certain types group therapy may be contraindicated: disturbed but psychologically sophisticated individuals who may badly affect others in the group, men with anxiety states in groups where a member has psychotic trends, extremely hostile and aggressive persons, and those who are closely associated in daily contact.

It is obvious that a major potential merit of group therapy is its relative economy. More individuals can be treated and there is indication that some, at any rate, can be dealt with more effectively than in individual therapy. Moreover, it can be combined with individual therapy in cases where this is desirable and feasible or superseded by individual treatment after preliminary effort through the group. There are other apparent advantages in the use of the group, too. It may be especially effective with some individuals who find individual therapy too threatening and with those who have had little opportunity to socialize outside their own families. It may offer advantages for normal persons who have suffered from debilitating situational conflicts. The group therapeutic process itself has certain virtues arising both out of the experience of group stimulation and out of the therapeutic role played by the members as well as by the leader. There is a "group facilitation" that results in increased freedom of release for those who can take advantage of it. And, as Hobbs has stated the matter, "If the therapist is skillful, the group itself becomes a therapeutic agent and gathers momentum of its own, with therapeutic consequences clearly greater than would result from the efforts of the therapist alone." It appears that in the joint search for improved adjustment, members of a group can derive considerable support from the understanding and acceptance of their fellows.

Experience has shown that often, particularly during the earlier phases of therapy, more rapid improvement may be secured through the help of the group than is characteristic in individual therapy. Under group analytic procedures, however, more powerful resistances and strivings may develop later.

It should be observed that there is nothing intrinsically novel about the use of didactic, moralizing, repressive, and inspirational treatment in the correctional setting. These methods are traditional and they should not be expected to produce better results under the new term "group therapy" than they previously did under other names. However, as these techniques are elaborated and empirically tested, it is possible that we shall learn more about the influence of specific therapeutic approaches to the offender.[31] Certainly this would be desirable. Clinical group therapy requires further careful testing in the correctional setting, with critical attention given to effective techniques, the sort of training needed by therapists, the size of groups that can be handled effectively, and the consequences of such treatment on criminal behavior. At the present time, unfortunately, group therapy has become the great white hope of many criminologists, without clear delineation of the methodology involved and without conclusive evidence on the effectiveness of the procedures that are used.

The Role of Clinical Methods in Prevention and Treatment

In the light of the extremely exiguous facilities available for clinical treatment and the wide prevalence of relatively serious disorders in the general population, it appears desirable to employ measures of individual or intensive psychiatric therapy with prisoners only when there is reasonable ground to believe that their criminality was directly related to a psychiatric deviation and that treatment may significantly reduce the danger of criminal conduct. It is not a specific objective of the criminal law or the correctional system to alleviate the mental or emotional distress of offenders. The effort to accomplish this can be justified only in so far as it may result in increased public protection through diminishing criminality. At the present level of knowledge and technique, we cannot be exact in making the decisions called for here, but there is no sound reason to believe that psychiatric ministration to offenders displaying ordinary emotional difficulties will curtail their crimes more effectively than present measures of correctional treatment do. A large proportion of offenders who have drawn their attitudes and behavior from the criminal norms of antisocial minorities display no more and possibly less psychological distress than does the ordinary man in the street.

The primary legal and correctional objective is to protect the public against criminal recidivism with reasonable economy and humanity. This means using effective measures of control and correctional treatment of many sorts, derived from the various behavioral and social disciplines. The increasingly prevalent emphasis today upon psychotherapy and the removal of emotional problems as *the* means of prevention and reformation is an illusory diversion. The ends of deterrence, incapacitation, and rehabilitation must be sought through widely varied methods and in some instances, at least, the result should be to increase the frustrations and guilt feelings of those who are criminally inclined. Psychiatry, psychology, and casework, all important phases of correctional treatment, will fulfill their potential roles in that field best by adapting their specialized techniques to the es-

---

[31] Elsewhere in this volume the author reviews a study of the Highfields institution in New Jersey where intensive but short-term group therapy is carried on as a central feature of the program. It is observed there that this treatment appeared not to have been significantly more successful either in changing attitudes or preventing recidivism than was the program of a reformatory in the same state. See Chapter 17.

sential objectives of correction rather than by attempting to alleviate neurosis or other discomforts on a wholesale basis. As psychiatrists and clinical psychologists incorporate a criminological orientation, they should contribute more fully to the prevention and treatment of crime. This will involve not only a refinement of their diagnostic skills but also instructing nonclinical workers in the treatment approaches that are most effective in reorienting the antisocial toward authority and reality. It is quite apparent that clinical specialists will not be able themselves to carry on individual psychotherapy with offenders to any considerable extent, either in institutions or in the community.[32]

MODIFICATION OF THE ENVIRONMENT

Social Casework

It is reasonable to believe that among the general preventives to crime, the ameliorative measures of public assistance and social casework play an important role. As individuals with problems associated with delinquency and crime are helped in their adjustments, pressures toward law violation are reduced. This is true not only in the general arena of public and private social welfare but in correctional casework.

Among the social services in our society are those provided under the Federal Social Security Act to give protection against private disaster. Together with the general assistance programs in the individual states, these services afford something approaching cradle-to-grave security against starvation and want for the nation's workers and their families. The most direct protection against delinquency is established through Title IV of the Federal act, which gives aid to dependent children up to the age of 18, either in their own or in relative's homes. In June, 1958, nearly 2,733,000 children in over 647,000 families were receiving grants in fifty-three jurisdictions. This represented about thirty-three children per 1,000 in the population of that age. The national average payment of aid to dependent children was $27.29 per recipient. Well over half of these were in families in which a living father was absent from the home. These are the sorts of cases where, in the past, children have all too commonly been taken from

[32] Clearly it is desirable that specialists in all the behavioral sciences should carry on diagnostic and treatment studies, so far as this may be possible, in the interest of developing more exact knowledge about effective methods in dealing with different types of offenders. Edward Glover has remarked critically on the performance of the psychoanalysts in this regard: "The truth is that psychoanalysis has acquired much more prestige in criminology than is justified by the amount of actual work it has done in the field. Apart from a few pioneering studies mostly of non-criminal cases its influence is largely *indirect,* through the percolation to the field of delinquency of some metapsychological generalizations on infantile development, unconscious mechanisms and institutions, unconsciously motivated behavior." "Psychoanalysis and Criminology," *A.P.T.O. J.,* vol. 1, no. 1, p. 1, February, 1957.

their families for institutional or foster home placements. It is impossible, of course, to guess how many abandoned and orphaned youngsters have been saved from delinquent or criminal careers by this aid to dependent children. The program is patently preventive as well as humane and economical.

Florence Hollis, writing in the 1957 *Social Work Yearbook,*[33] describes the processes and methods of current social casework:

*Modern casework makes extensive use of Freudian psychology in its understanding of the individual, with a small section of the field following the modifications in Freudian thinking advocated by Rank. It also draws extensively upon the findings of many other areas of social science—general psychology, sociology, cultural anthropology, economic, political economy, social economy, and so on—and upon medicine. In recent years there has been renewed emphasis upon the potential contributions of social psychology, sociology, and cultural anthropology.

*There are three generally recognized casework processes: psychosocial study, diagnosis and formulation of treatment plans, and treatment itself.

*The first task of the caseworker is that of fact gathering. What kinds of facts are needed depends primarily upon the nature of the problem presented by the client and upon the type of service offered by the agency. A good casework study contains facts about both the social situation and the psychological characteristics of the person seeking assistance. The proportion of each of these ingredients depends upon the problem and the agency to which the person turns. . . .

*The second casework process involves the worker's arriving at an opinion about the nature of the client's difficulty and the nature of the assistance that should be offered. . . .

*The third process is that of treatment itself. The type of service offered the client will depend on a number of factors: the nature of the client's difficulty, the sort of help the client himself is ready to accept, the type of agency and its resources, including the availability of psychiatric consultation, the time available and the skill of the worker. . . .

*Casework treatment is of two major kinds: (*a*) it may consist of modifications of the environment brought about by the caseworker, or (*b*) it may consist of changes brought about within the individual himself through the casework interview. Frequently, these two processes are combined. Under the first of these there are two types of service. The worker may intervene in the client's behalf in lessening certain external pressures or he may be able to offer tangible agency services, such as financial assistance or a foster home, which in themselves substantially modify the individual's life situation.

The caseworker using the second major form of treatment—that of seeking to bring about changes in the individual himself through the interviewing process, sometimes called "direct treatment"—relies also upon two different types of treatment. The first of these is "supportive treatment" in which an effort is

[33] Florence Hollis, "Social Casework," in Russel H. Kurtz (ed.), *Social Work Year Book 1957.* National Association of Social Workers, New York, 1957, pp. 526–528. (Reprinted by permission.)

made to reduce the client's anxiety or discouragement and to assist him to meet more wisely the problems by which he is confronted, through the effects of an encouraging relationship, through catharsis, and through rational discussion and sometimes guidance concerning his day-by-day problems. This is based entirely upon the use of conscious and unsuppressed material. The second of these is designed primarily to develop self-awareness and characteristically makes use of suppressed preconscious material in addition to conscious data. Casework does not to any substantial degree use unconscious material except as it emerges unsolicited and may be of diagnostic value. In this second type of service designed to bring about changes directly in the individual himself, the client is encouraged to express his thoughts and feelings not only for the purpose of catharsis, but also so that he may examine them himself and come to a new evaluation of them and to greater understanding and wiser control and use of himself.

Most presentence investigation reports and other case histories of delinquents and criminals are descriptive studies based on superficial observations of the offender and his social milieu. Although some caseworkers attempt to interrelate the factors they describe, case analysis is limited by the nature of the data that are accessible to ordinary social investigation. When such data are inadequate, inferences relating to individuals' social and psychological history that are drawn from them may be untrustworthy. Another danger is encountered in the occasional parochialism of a worker who, as a result of his formal indoctrination in some particular school of interpretive psychology, may attribute a uniform etiological significance to factors that he observes in different cases.

As Hollis observes, one of the important methods of treatment in modern casework consists of modifying the environment. It is apparent that adjustment problems, except in so far as they are influenced by constitutional and hereditary factors, are the product of experience in a social setting. It is extremely difficult to maintain significant alterations in the attitude and conduct of an individual who remains in the environment that has produced his problems. Some alteration of the social situation may facilitate change in the individual and his responses. It is significant that offenders who remain in or are returned to a criminogenic environment often persist in crime. Sometimes a change in residence, neighborhood, or community is desirable. This is one of the central functions of agencies that specialize in the placement of children in foster homes or boarding homes. Slum clearance and resettlement projects are examples of efforts to improve environment. Often resources are used to improve the individual's associations and experience within the given locale. This may consist of such services as help in finding a job, a new school placement, and referral to a social group or to specialized treatment agencies.

Some caseworkers with psychiatric orientation are more interested in the type of treatment that seeks to bring about changes in the individual himself through the interviewing process. This type of casework treatment,

superficially at least, resembles that employed by psychotherapists. Controversies concerning theory and practice are also found in the casework field,
particularly between the "functional" and the "diagnostic" schools of
thought.[34]

° One can do little more than speculate about the influence of the growing
field of psychiatric casework in preventing crime. It has been the traditional
view in this field that most antisocial personalities cannot be helped because they do not recognize their need and are uncooperative. Recently
there has been some change in this point of view. There is also difficulty in
accepting the validity of some of the theories of casework in the treatment
of offenders, the doctrine, for example, that if treatment can provide the
client with a logical and consistent explanation of his behavior he will be
more capable of dealing with it effectively. From the author's viewpoint, it
is quite inappropriate for the caseworker to offer rationalizations of antisocial behavior to the offender that may relieve him of the sense of
responsibility for what he does.

° The writer believes that effective work can be done with antisocial
personalities. This will require a refinement of methods of aggressive casework, designed to "reach out" for those who will not seek help or recognize the need for it. Helping the antisocial to accept authority must be one
of the tools of treatment. Relatively unorthodox methods of casework are
fundamental to preventive and correctional treatment. This does not imply
a moralistic or condemnatory attitude toward these individuals. They must
be accepted as persons. They should be made aware of both their limitations and strengths, the need for change, and the necessity of coping with

---

[34] The sharp difference in the theoretical assumptions of the two schools has been
described in these terms: "Diagnostic casework follows the theories of personality
developed by Freud and his followers, while functional casework is based on the
theory of will psychology developed by Otto Rank. The central point of cleavage
between the two theories is the postulate by Rank of the existence of an organizing
force in personality which is described as the will. In the Freudian view, the postulates of personality structure and organization do not include an organizing force
that is equivalent to the functional concept of will. . . .

"The differences in the theoretical assumptions lead to a fundamental difference in
the way each group views the individual who comes for help. Functional caseworkers
see him as the fashioner of his fate, and although they do not rule out the influence
of inner drives and outer circumstances on personality development, they attribute
even pathological phenomena, such as psychoses, to the effort of the will to effect
a solution of the psychic problem. Diagnostic caseworkers, in contradistinction, conceive of the individual as fashioned by the interrelationship between his basic needs
and his physical and social environment. They would not discount the ego's potential
capacity to alter his circumstances but they view psychopathology as a result of
partial or total inability of the ego to cope with inner and outer pressures.

"These theoretical divergencies in concepts of personality lead inevitably to opposing
methods of appraising a client's need and of extending help." *A Comparison of
Diagnostic and Functional Casework Concepts*, Family Service Association of
America.

reality. Aggressive casework, together with the use of methods of modifying the environment and giving supplementary social agency assistance where necessary, appears to offer a hopeful approach to the prevention of delinquency and crime among potential offenders with fairly normal personality structures. The nature of correctional casework will be discussed in greater detail in Chapter 19.

Revolutionary Social-Cultural Change

The volume and trend of crime may be taken in the large to represent the shifting balance between the criminogenic and the preventive or corrective forces at work in society. There are sociocultural influences that are conducive to crime, by-products of the social system that are in some measure pathogenic even if they are not intrinsically pathological. The author has considered such influences in an earlier chapter. Opposed to these are the forces that make for obedience to law. Increases in crime may be viewed as a consequence of the exacerbation of those forces that produce disorder and the decreasing effectuality of those that promote regularity and conformity. One approach to crime prevention might theoretically involve modifications of the going social system to alter the balance between crime-producing and crime-inhibiting forces.

*The feasibility of making heroic changes in the social system in order to prevent crime will be examined briefly. Some authorities have suggested that revolutionary action is necessary. Barnes and Teeters maintain that crime prevention must be predicated upon "realizing the necessity of removing the social and economic forces that induce attitudes leading to delinquency and crime." Professor Taft suggests, *inter alia,* that a "crimeless society" should be static and internally homogeneous. A planned economy would be required in which "excessive" competition and greed would be avoided. Such a society must reverse itself to restore a personalized culture in which human freedom would need to be restricted and religion revived for more effective social control. Thus, it would approximate the simple primitive or peasant society. He observes that the changes required might threaten many of the existing social values that we prize, such as our conceptions of democracy and progress and the freer life for women, Donald Cressey, considering the same general issue, finds that, "while general institutional reorganization may be desirable, its relation to the control of delinquency is highly speculative at present."

The writer has expressed the opinion that our contemporary culture, more than those of other times and places, is criminogenic. He is convinced, however, that within the framework of our values, substantial alteration of the pattern is not feasible, if indeed it is desirable. We cannot deliberately manipulate citizens and their institutions on any considerable scale in an attempt to eliminate unwanted by-products of the going social system. Certainly it is futile to consider a planned simplification of the culture, a movement back from industrialism and urbanization, a substantial strengthening of the primary groups, and a reduction of materialism and competition. It is true that over a period of time the state may restrict or encourage and otherwise influence some basic phases of the culture, such as the operations of industry and farm, centralization of life in cities, suburban development, patterns of wealth distribution and class stratification. Social engineering is aimed essentially, however, not at the alteration of social by-products but at the direct yield. Broad governmental planning looks to material development, power, and prestige. Some of the incidental consequences of dominant policy may be deprecated and there are sporadic and programmatic efforts to alleviate them. But the remedies are of a stopgap and alleviatory character, with little significance for the over-all pattern of social-cultural development. Even a well-developed "service state" leaves pretty much unaltered the basic patterns of family, neighborhood, and community relationships that are rooted in the prevailing social economy. It is with these patterns that crime and delinquency as well as other related disorders, such as marital breakdown, mental pathology, and alcoholism, are linked. An effort of the state to superimpose a benign "togetherness" upon its citizens would require an all-out totalitarian control involving consequences more ominous than the problems sought to be resolved.

It appears fairly clear that any progress we may make in the prevention of crime will be accomplished not by major social and economic changes looking to that goal but by therapeutic and alleviatory measures designed to help individuals in trouble, by efficiency in the administration of justice, and by programs of prevention focused upon offenders. This effort will be aided by the persistence of certain basic trends to uniformity and conformity that now prevail in our society.

THE TREATMENT OF ADDICTIONS

In an earlier chapter the author has discussed alcoholism and narcotic addiction in connection with personality factors relating to crime. These problems differ from other psychopathologies in that they may involve offenses such as drunkenness or the possession or use of narcotics and they have more direct and obvious bearing on other law violations. Furthermore, they require rather different treatment considerations than does criminality as such or other forms of personality disorder. There is considerable controversy concerning how addictions should be handled, as will be seen below.

Treatment of the Alcoholic

In accordance with the view that alcoholism is a manifestation of personality disturbances, psychiatrists generally have deemed psychotherapy to be the treatment of choice, but many have been unwilling to deal with alcoholics because they too rarely respond to therapy. It has been suggested that the alcoholic requires something more than an analysis of motive and mechanisms; he requires guidance in the establishment of "a positive view" of life. Some authorities have questioned the value of probing the subconscious in the hope that the development of insight might promote abstinence. There has been a limited amount of experimental work with group psychotherapy in court settings to "help the patient understand what causes him to drink," but the long-term results remain unknown.[35]

Some of those who work with alcoholics do not accept the idea that alcoholism is an illness to be treated by psychiatric measures. They have favored instead the employment of inspirational and hortatory methods. The Salvation Army, with its largely moralistic approach, has been instrumental in "rescuing" many sufferers. Alcoholics Anonymous, which has more than 5,000 groups, some of which are in prisons and hospitals, has brought about many conversions through its method of mutual aid since it was organized in 1935.[36] Differing from both the psychiatrists and those who advocate a spiritual approach, the Bureau of Alcoholic Therapy of the City of New York, under the direction of Edward J. McGoldrick, has interpreted alcoholism as a product of ignorance, frustration, and immaturity. McGoldrick believes that cure lies in measures of reeducation that will teach the individual to "think correctly" and to express himself in socially useful ways. He uses lectures, discussions, visual aids, and personal guidance. In 1956 the bureau found that 75 per cent of the 307 men aided at the rehabilitation center had not resumed drinking.[37]

Another approach relies upon the use of a drug that will produce violent nausea at any time over a period of several days if any form or amount

[35] The Adult Guidance Clinic in San Francisco and the BARO Clinic in New York City (Kings County) have reported favorable results in the short run.

[36] Dr. Albert LaVerne, senior psychiatrist at Bellevue Hospital, has asserted that 50 per cent of some 250,000 persons who had received AA treatment in the last twenty years had recovered from their alcoholism. He indicated that most of these individuals had tried medical, psychiatric, and other forms of treatment unsuccessfully before joining AA. He appealed to fellow psychiatrists to abandon their skepticism and to employ the principles of AA in treating alcoholics. *New York Times,* June 7, 1959. AA uses exhortation, public confession, repentance, and evangelism as treatment tools. The alcoholic must recognize his inability to use liquor and his need to rely upon a greater power as well as upon the members of the group to assist him. Groups have been established in fifty-three foreign countries.

[37] McGoldrick has said, "As for the great majority, there is no more pernicious dogma extant than to consider them sick people, suffering from a disease. It is one of the greatest stumbling blocks to their recovery. It is a concept that will moor alcoholics more steadfastly than ever to their self-deceit." *New York Times,* Mar. 30, 1953. The cost per man helped was approximately $150. See also McGoldrick, *Management of the Mind,* 1954.

of alcohol is ingested.[38] The reaction is so extreme that it is dangerous. While much publicized for a time as a cure, studies have shown that "about seventy per cent of the patients trade the pills for the bottle within eight weeks" and fewer than 10 per cent continue the treatment for six months. Other emetic drugs, mixed with alcohol, have been used in a treatment known as "conditioned-reflex therapy," in which a milder nausea is produced, the purpose being to condition the patient within the period of a few days to a nauseated response to the imbibing of liquor.[39] Benzedrine has been used to give patients stimulation that may substitute for the use of alcohol and tranquilizers to calm their anxieties. None of these drugs attack the underlying psychological problems but, used in conjunction with counseling or psychotherapy, they may help the patient through a transition period to complete avoidance.

The question has recently been raised whether alcoholism, like some of the functional disorders the author has discussed, may be the consequence of bodily chemistry rather than psychological disorder. Recent studies in this area offer great hope for prevention and treatment. Dr. James J. Smith, director of research on alcoholism at Bellevue Medical Center, has concluded as the result of testing 2,000 acute and chronic alcoholics that the condition results from a disturbance in the functioning of the pituitary with consequent deficiency in the adrenal and sex glands.[40] Hormonal therapy, he has indicated, results in a disappearance of the craving for alcohol and of nervous tension together with restoration of appetite and a sense of well being.[41] He believes that an endocrine dysfunction associated with the hypothalamus of the brain precedes and accounts for, rather than is a consequence of, alcoholism and, unlike other authorities, looks to the time when the restored alcoholic can drink normally. Since the time of Smith's report, Dr. Harold W. Lovell, president of the National Council on Alcoholism, Inc., has noted the growing evidence in the research of a number of hospitals that indicates a hormonal imbalance as a causal factor of the affliction. In 1957, further support for the theory that alcoholism reflects a metabolic disturbance was advanced by Dr. Roger J. Williams, president of the American Chemical Society, who reported findings of studies not yet published at the time of this writing to the effect that the appetite for alcohol is associated with a

---

[38] The chemical is TETD (tetraethylthuram disulfide), sold under trade names Antabus, Antabuse, and Disulfuram.

[39] Apomorphine or emetine has been used for the purpose. Dr. Walter L. Voegtlin, who is a leading practitioner in this mode of therapy, believes that it is successful in about half the cases he has treated.

[40] Dr. Smith's report was made to the Medical Society of the State of New York in May of 1950.

[41] He found a majority of patients responding best to ACE (adrenal cortical extract) but has made use of ACTH, cortisone, and sex hormones (testosterone with the male, estrogens with the female), taken together with vitamin C.

deranged metabolism of the hypothalamus. He expressed the belief that the need for alcohol could be detected in childhood and averted by nutritional treatments that have been found effective in diminishing or terminating the craving among heavy drinkers.[42]

Treatment of Narcotic Addicts

Efforts to develop effective treatment methods for narcotic addiction have met thus far with very little success. This is clearly indicated in the recidivist statistics in *Uniform Crime Reports* where narcotics violators have generally been the group with the highest percentage of prior finger-print records (from 71 to 75 per cent of them having had previous arrests). As is true of alcoholics, narcotic addicts are unwilling to recognize that their use of narcotics is a problem or to accept treatment to overcome it. The mask to their emotional difficulties provided by the drug is too satisfying to abandon willingly or permanently.

"Dealing with the drug menace" has been the responsibility of the psychiatrist and the private medical practitioner, of the public and private hospital, of the jail and prison, and of law enforcement authorities. Each group has tended to meet the problem differently, both as a matter of orientation and procedure. The varying approaches will now be considered.

From a policing point of view, the drug problem is largely one of the accessibility of supply to the addict and the potential addict. In a drug-free environment addiction would cease. One solution might be to eliminate the supply, if that were feasible. A kind of contagion is involved in the spread of the narcotics habit. The user, becoming a "pusher" to support his appetite, is a major influence in introducing neophytes to the use of drugs. Also, the more gregarious addicts welcome the opportunity to meet and enjoy "God's own medicine" together. Efforts at control of the narcotics traffic have been developed on local, state, national, and international levels. On the international level, conferences beginning with the International Opium Commission at Shanghai in 1909 gradually established machinery for international cooperation and control until 1916 when the United Nations assumed primary responsibility in the field.[43] In 1950 its Commission on Narcotic Drugs drafted a global agreement in which participating countries would agree to limit the flow and use of drugs to legitimate channels. Conflicting attitudes, political considerations, and reluctance

[42] See the *New York Times,* Sept. 19, 1957.

[43] International control has developed in some measure through the Hague Opium Convention of 1912, the Geneva Convention of 1925, the Bangkok Agreement of 1931, and the Convention of 1936. To alleviate the delays and difficulties that are involved in extradition procedures and to increase efficiency in apprehending offenders an International Criminal Police Commission was established in 1923 and reconstituted in 1946. It coordinates data to help member countries run down criminals. There are thirty-nine member countries, but the United States is not one.

of producing nations to lose the tremendous profits involved have prevented the adoption of the agreement, however.[44] With minor exceptions such as marijuana, which is not itself addictive, and supplies secured through thefts in drug stores and the forging of prescriptions, most of the narcotics illegally distributed in this country come from abroad.

Commissioner Anslinger, head of the Bureau of Narcotics, while claiming that his men have halted about 40 per cent of the importation at its source through agents stationed in other countries, has asserted that "if you had the Army, the Navy, the Coast Guard, the F.B.I., the Customs Service and our narcotics service, you would not stop heroin coming through the port of New York."[45] Great ingenuity is employed in smuggling both by steamship and by air.[46] We have only some 600 customs employees charged with searching vessels at the coasts and very few agents stationed abroad. In the absence of firm international control, the supply of illegal narcotics can be stepped down but it cannot be eliminated.

In dealing with the illegal use of narcotics in recent years emphasis has been placed on long-term prison commitments. At the height of the hysteria on drug addiction in 1951, President Truman signed a bill providing for severe penalties for narcotics law violations, including mandatory prison sentences of two to five years for a first offense, of five to ten years for a second, and of ten to twenty for a third. Sale of heroin to a customer under 18 may be punished by a term from ten years to life or by the death penalty. Suspension of sentence is not allowed. Long and mandatory terms have also been established under new legislation in a number of the states. In general, neither jails nor prisons provide any special therapeutic treatment for the addict.

In spite of the general dependence upon imprisonment as the means to control addiction, there has been some effort to deal with users in the community. A few courts have experimented with the use of probation for defendants convicted of possession of narcotics and intensive parole supervision has been employed after release from institutions in New York and elsewhere. The findings of the limited research carried on with these cases offer little promise for success with the methods that have been used. Mr. Kuznesof of the United State Probation Service has analyzed the results

[44] Commissioner Anslinger has said that in five years Red China's opium production tripled from 2,000 tons annually to 6,000 tons, some ten times the world medicinal need for such derivatives as morphine, codeine, and paregoric. Relative to the profit on illegal narcotics, he observed that pure illicit heroin can be secured in Hong Kong at $60 an ounce, which after dilution may be sold in the states for $8,750, a profit greater than 14,000 per cent. See *New York Times*, June, 4, 1955.

[45] Ralph Kelly, commissioner of Customs, has alleged that the world is so heavily supplied with illicit narcotics that we cannot hope to keep them all out of this country. *Ibid.*

[46] See P. Maralutin, *Intern. Crim. Police Comm. Bull. Narcotics,* vol. 3, no. 3, 1951, and *New York Times*, June 15, 1951.

of work with eighty-three cases released to supervision from the Public Health Service Hospital. Revocation of probation occurred in sixty-seven of these cases for violations within a period of six to eight months.[47] While probation was not revoked in the remaining sixteen cases, only two individuals were believed to have done well. Jack Sokol has reported on the results of group therapy procedures applied to forty or more drug addicts at the Association for Psychiatric Treatment of Offenders in New York, some of whom had been patients at Lexington and all of whom, apparently, had continued using drugs.[48] The experiment was carried on for only nine months because of the unsatisfactory results attained and the sense that it did not repay the effort and time devoted to it. All of the subjects continued with or returned to the use of narcotics and about a third of them were arrested for various offenses during the period of treatment. Sokol believed, however, that similar efforts should be carried on in the future, ideally with separate treatment of those who had been withdrawn or "cleansed," and with the use of probation or parole supervision in support of the therapy. He observes that the customary probation and parole rules against association with other offenders make it difficult to provide group treatment. With intensive supervision and professional counseling, probation may be as effective as prison treatment for young offenders who are not fully addicted.

◊ A more optimistic report on community supervision of addicted offenders comes from the Special Narcotic Project of the New York State Division of Parole. In 1959 the Division reported on 272 cases that had been supervised for periods up to 26 months. Forty-two per cent had displayed no delinquent behavior of any sort during parole, and nearly one-third of these had been under supervision for a year or more. California launched a Narcotic Control Project in 1959 to conduct study, research, and treatment projects dealing with persons committed to the Director of Corrections there. The use of Nalline, a synthetic opiate antinarcotic drug, is relied upon rather heavily in California as a means of testing and controlling users of narcotics. There is some evidence that the supervised offender's knowledge that he would be discovered if he returned to an opiate is a deterrent.

◊ In opposition to repressive penal legislation an unorthodox view has developed in recent years regarding treatment of addicts, namely that public clinics should be established to provide them narcotics at regular intervals at a cost of 15 to 30 cents a visit. This proposal is predicated upon the following assumptions: that addiction is an illness and should not be considered a crime, that it is presently incurable and should be handled in much the same way that diabetes is, without stigma or penalty, and that the addict does not require hospitalization or institutional treatment after

[47] An unpublished report, 1955.
[48] Jack Sokol, "Treatment of Offenders," *J. Crim. L.*, vol. 45, pp. 279–291, 1954.

withdrawal unless he is deteriorated or psychotic. The addict may be reduced to minimal doses under supervised control. The drug traffic would be halted, since the addict could get legally what he needed at an infinitely lower price than he now has to pay for contraband. The deterioration and recurrent painful withdrawals that are now suffered by addicts would be eliminated. Should illegal purveyors manage to continue, they would be handled as criminals as they are now. This position has been forcefully presented by Judge Jonah J. Goldstein, Max Lerner, the Richmond County Medical Society, John Murtagh, and others.[49] It has been vehemently opposed by Commissioner Anslinger, who favors a heavily repressive approach through severe and mandatory prison sentences.[50]

○ Few authorities subscribe to the idea of treating addicts in the community through public clinics, private physicians, or under probation. It is generally believed that the truly addicted person requires a period of hospital commitment for the purposes of withdrawal and of treatment when a bridgehead may be built for the strengthening of resolve and the alleviation of underlying personality problems. Ordinarily at least four to six months in the institution are thought to be required, followed by close supervision and supportive treatment in the community, ideally for a period of two years, since relapse tends to occur within that time. Individual or group psychotherapy is desirable after commitment. Thus far the re-

[49] See *New York Times,* Mar. 1, 1953; Letter to the Editor, Dec. 16, 1951; *New York Post,* June 7, 1956; Address of Judge Jonah J. Goldstien to Conference on Sentencing, New York University School of Law, Oct. 20, 1956.

[50] Anslinger and Tompkins, *The Traffic in Narcotics,* 1953. The opposition is based upon several considerations. The public clinic plan was tried after World War I in New York and in a number of other large cities, including Albany, Los Angeles, and Providence, with a view to preventing addicts from seeking illegal sources of drugs. The practice was soon abandoned because of the abuses that arose. Addicts wanted more than they could secure at a government clinic and continued to use outside sources. Some individuals registered to secure the drug in order to sell it to addicts at a profit. Many addicts, it was believed, did not register at the public clinic at all but continued to use the illegal market. It may well be held, however, that the clinic plan had no proper test under conditions comparable to those of today. In any event it appears that nations that provide legal but controlled access to drugs for addicts have had much greater success in controlling addiction and illicit traffic. Thus the United Kingdom reported to the United Nations Commission on Narcotic Drugs in 1949 only 326 known addicts (less than 1 per cent of the known addicts in the United States at the time) and 168 prosecutions for drug violations. Norway reported between 200 and 300 addicts, Netherlands a similar number, New Zealand 45, and Australia very few. Each of these countries permitted addicts to secure drugs legally from physicians. None of them has had a problem of juvenile addiction. Query what the results would be if physicians or clinics were permitted again, under proper regulation and community controls, to prescribe narcotics for the addicted and to reduce the intake of patients who registered with them? It is unlikely that less would be accomplished than we have achieved by the methods applied in the past generation. The United States today is said to have more narcotic addicts, both in total and relative number, than any other nation in the Western world.

sults of hospital treatment have not been very satisfactory, even where the programs have been relatively intensive.

A large part of the research on addiction and its treatment has been carried on at the United States Public Health Service Hospital at Lexington, Kentucky, where sentenced addicts, probation cases, and voluntary patients are retained. Here intensive treatment is provided for their juvenile patients in segregated sections, with detailed social and psychiatric case history investigation, followed by psychotherapy and supportive social services. The treatment program there has been handicapped by lack of follow-up work with discharged cases. Some 40 per cent of all their patients return, but little is known of what happens to the remainder. One authority suggests that not more than 15 per cent succeed.[51] In 1951 another specialized treatment facility was developed, this one at Riverside Hospital on North Brother Island in New York. The hospital was planned to care for 150 teen-aged addicts and was sufficiently well staffed to provide more intensive therapy than has been possible elsewhere, including recreational, occupational, and educational programs.[52] Follow-up counseling service is provided both for the patient and his family. A specialized medical-correctional program has also been initiated for narcotic patients at the Vacaville Medical Facility, serving the Department of Corrections in California since 1955. In most states, however, addicts are handled in state hospitals, prisons, and jails, which are without adequate treatment facilities. Voluntary commitments to the hospitals are provided in some states but even in these hospitals little help is given beyond custody and safe-keeping. Little experimental work is done to discover the kinds of

[51] Kenneth W. Chapman, "Drug Addiction: The General Problem," Fed. Prob., vol. 20, p. 43, September, 1956. Victor H. Vogel, "Treatment of the Narcotic Addict by the U.S. Public Health Service," Fed. Prob., vol. 12, pp. 45–51, June, 1948, reported that out of 11,041 cases received at Lexington from the time when the institution was opened in 1935 to the beginning of 1948, 61.4 per cent had been admitted only once, the remainder returning anywhere from one to eighteen times. As a result of correspondence with former patients discharged between 1942 and 1946 they estimated that 22.3 per cent of the men and 29.8 per cent of the women, excluding voluntary patients who left against advice, were still off drugs in 1948. The status of 42.6 per cent of the men and 33.6 per cent of the women, however, was unknown. Dr. Chapman has expressed the opinion that attention should be focused on those who display a desire to be cured. He has observed that some proportion of users, including those who take narcotics on weekends or at irregular intervals, do not become addicted and that others have purchased narcotics of so low a percentage of heroin that they are not truly addicted. Among such cases the prognostication for success is, of course, relatively good.

[52] See New York Times, Nov. 16, 1951. A staff of 306 full-time and 97 part-time employees was hired in addition to workers from volunteer social agencies. In 1959 it was decided that the program at Riverside Hospital had failed and that patients who in the past had been sent there should be referred in the future to any of several of the New York City hospitals for treatment. New York Times, May 26, 1959.

treatment that might persuade inmates to remain off drugs after release. Few out-patient clinics have been established thus far for the further treatment after release of narcotics addicts.

⁰ Two approaches have been taken to "voluntary" hospitalization that offer some promise of success in dealing with cases that have not been long habituated. One of these is the "bluegrass commitment" developed as a Kentucky court procedure, under which any voluntary patient to the Federal Hospital at Lexington who leaves prematurely may not be readmitted for treatment unless he accepts an order from a Kentucky court making his further stay there mandatory and its length subject to the discretion of the hospital staff. The other is a probation disposition, not infrequently employed for young offenders in New York, under which as a condition of the suspension of imprisonment they must agree to take treatment at Lexington or some other institution. Thus they are subject to imprisonment for failure to complete treatment. Either device is more effective than voluntary commitment alone because so many who are hospitalized without a specific sentence leave the institution soon after withdrawal before treatment can be given for the problems responsible for the addiction.

DIAGNOSIS AND TREATMENT IN CORRECTION

To conclude the consideration of methods of prevention and treatment, it may be worthwhile to summarize a few basic principles and hypotheses that bear upon correctional policy. There continues to be considerable controversy among criminologists on these matters and they are presented here only as the views of the author:

1. The focus of criminological diagnostic inquiry should be on the specific forces, biological, psychological, and social, that have been associated with the individual's criminality rather than on his ills generally. The mere application of labels to the individual is quite unuseful as a matter of criminological diagnosis and treatment.[53]

2. The limitations of our knowledge and diagnostic tools inevitably lead us to incomplete and commonly inaccurate diagnoses of causation. Psychological testing and casework investigation provide clues to the existence of emotional and social problems but do not portray the dynamic relationship of the variables out of which criminality develops.

3. Diagnostic or etiological inquiry is not an end in itself. Except for its value in basic research, such inquiry is useful only in so far as it can guide correctional treatment practice. If diagnosis and treatment are eventually to

[53] Philip Ash, in a study of psychiatric diagnoses, found that in using sixty diagnostic categories, agreement by three psychiatrists was reached in only 20 per cent of the cases studied and that even when these categories were reduced to only five classifications there was agreement only on 46 per cent of the cases. "The Reliability of Psychiatric Diagnoses," *J. Abnorm. Soc. Psych.,* vol. 44, p. 272, 1949.

become scientific they must attempt the classification of treatment modalities in accordance with the needs of distinguishable groups. "Individualization," in so far as this implies *ad hoc* empiricism in treatment, is wasteful and unscientific.

4. Treatment of the criminal must be based to a considerable extent on considerations other than the causes of his crimes, partly because the dynamics of criminality are still largely obscure and partly because our methods are not yet sufficiently refined to enable us to treat the apparent causes.

5. Considerations of social protection, individual freedom, and economy seriously limit appropriate correctional treatment methods. Excessive risk to public interests cannot be taken. On the other hand, the individual's deprivations should bear some just relation to the risk he creates. The duration and intensity of treatment are limited by the public purse and by our concern for the values of freedom.

6. It is quite probable that the treatment methods most effective with the ordinary offender today are not based specifically upon etiological information. We must rely more largely on deterrent sanctions, the use of influence and persuasion, the indoctrination in ideals, and the modification of the environment. We are least effective in treating the minority of offenders with deep emotional difficulties who have been closely studied and diagnosed by psychiatrists and other clinicians.

7. Much research remains to be done, particularly in relation to rapid and group treatment methods, in order that we may discover less expensive and more effective ways of preventing crime and of reconditioning the offender.

Chapter 19

PROBATION

Probation is a hybrid social institution evolved from the crossing of several strains that run deep in the soil of English and American legal history. While it has become increasingly uniform over the past 100 years, significant variants remain and continued development will inevitably occur, strengthened by further interbreeding with other and more recent stock from the family of treatment variables. The present character and genesis of probation will now be considered. Probation may be viewed both as a sentence of the court and as a correctional process. In the former sense it combines the suspension of a punitive sanction against convicted offenders (ordinarily a prison or jail term) with orders for treatment under conditional liberty in the community. In the latter sense it includes the conduct of presentence investigations as an aid to court dispositions and the personal supervision and guidance of selected offenders in accordance with the conditions that the court establishes. It should be observed that probation usually involves the following elements: the conviction of a crime, the selection of cases for this disposition, the suspension of sentence for a specified period of time and the avoidance of imprisonment, the imposition of conditions as a limitation on the freedom of the offender and as a basis for possible revocation, and the control and treatment of the individual in the community. Variations upon this pattern will be noted below. Probation differs from the suspended sentence in that the latter, taken alone, does not require supervision, though conditions may be attached and it is subject to revocation. It differs from parole in that it is a court sentence rather than a board determination and it is a substitute for, rather than a consequent of, imprisonment. Like parole, however, freedom on probation is subject to conditions, revocation, and imprisonment. Both imply supervision in the community.

THE DEVELOPMENT OF PROBATION

Roots of Probation

The earliest roots of probation lie in devices for the mitigation of harsh penalties, and the view of this measure as a form of lenience may be traced to its alleviatory character. The *benefit of clergy,* by which from the time

CORRECTION

of Henry II in the thirteenth century members of the clergy and, later, any person who could read might be rescued from the King's Court and made subject instead to the relatively clement ecclesiastical jurisdiction, cannot be considered a real precursor of the suspended sentence or probation. Yet it reflected the same motives from which later mitigative devices were developed. The *judicial reprieve,* on the other hand, appears rather definitely to have been in the direct line of development. It was a suspension either of the imposition or the execution of a sentence[1] by the court, commonly used by early English judges when they were not satisfied that the defendant should have been convicted. It was designed to permit the defendant to apply to the Crown for a pardon. While it was conceived to be only a temporary suspension, in some cases its use resulted in the termination of prosecution or of subsequent court action. The practice was interpreted later in some of the states as a common-law power to suspend sentence indefinitely, justifying the practices that had developed here.

Another English source of probation was the *recognizance,* in effect a stipulation to the public by a suspect or an accused not yet convicted that he would keep the peace and be of good behavior.[2] Ordinarily a bond (bail) with or without sureties was required and the offender might be returned by the latter to the court for further action if he failed to comply with the conditions of his release. This device of "binding over for good behavior" appears to have developed in England in the fourteenth century both as a means of preventive justice and as a means of avoiding punishment. The bond was employed for centuries in England, particularly in the case of first and minor offenders. Its use was specifically authorized by the English Criminal Law Consolidation Act of 1861 and by the Summary Jurisdiction Act of 1879 for persons convicted of misdemeanors and felonies. It was introduced early in the colonies and was very commonly employed, especially in Massachusetts, as a means of avoiding the harsh and rigid penalties of the penal law. Here too it was used for convicted offenders as well as for individuals merely accused of crime or for those at some stage of trial. Massachusetts gave statutory sanction to the practice of accepting sponsorship by sureties for good behavior in the lower courts for petty offenders in 1836. It appears to have been the rationale support-

---

[1] The suspension of the imposition of sentence, commonly described simply as "the suspended sentence," means that the court does not impose a sentence after conviction. Such suspension is generally conditional on good behavior or on a set of specific conditions and may be for a fixed period of time. It may be revoked for violation and any term of imprisonment or other penalty may be imposed that might originally have been assessed. The suspension of the execution of sentence means that a penalty is fixed at the time of judgment but is suspended and that particular penalty may be invoked subsequently for violation. In some jurisdictions, however, the court may modify the original sentence.

[2] The recognizance was also used, as it still is today, to assure the appearance of a defendant before the court to answer charges.

ing practices relating to the recognizance that by this device offenders selected on the basis of their offences and personal merits might be spared the demoralizing influence of imprisonment, that they would obey the law out of fear of punishment and concern for their sureties, and—a significant point in relation to subsequent developments—that their sponsors would in some measure supervise their conduct.[3]

The conditional release of offenders under the sponsorship of sureties was a true predecessor of probation. Indeed, it is dubious whether in a good many jurisdictions today more is accomplished by formal probation than was achieved long ago by suspending the imposition of sentence through the use of the recognizance. The filing of indictments,[4] a somewhat different form of suspending of sentence, was also practiced in Massachusetts. Where after a criminal conviction the court believed that there was sufficient reason and that justice did not require an immediate sentence, it could, with the consent of the defendant and the prosecutor, lay the indictment on file, thus suspending active proceedings, until such time as it might be brought forward again on motion of either party for further action.

Well before the development of probation it had become possible through any of the variety of devices noted above for courts to suspend either the imposition or the execution of sentence for limited periods at least; it appears that in practice such suspensions were commonly of indefinite duration through failure of the court or other parties to take further action. As the practice spread in the states of suspending sentence indefinitely on the theory that this was a traditional power of the courts under the common law, issue was raised. Appellate courts in several jurisdictions, including New York, New Jersey, and Pennsylvania, found that the courts possessed this power.[5] A number of other states held, however, that such practice was a usurpation by the judiciary of a power of clemency vested exclusively in the executive.[6] The famous *Killits Case* in the Federal courts determined that, in the absence of statute, they lacked the power to suspend sentence indefinitely, holding that "the mere exercise of a judicial discretion to temporarily suspend for the accomplishment of a purpose contemplated by law . . . " could not be converted into "an arbitrary judicial power to permanently refuse to enforce the law."[7] This declaration

---

[3] Bail might also be given then, as now, without sureties.

[4] See *Commonwealth v. Dowdican's Bail*, 115 Mass. 133 (1874), cited in *Attorney General's Survey of Release Procedures*, vol. 2, *Probation*, 1939, p. 21.

[5] See, for example, *People ex rel. Forsyth v. Court of Sessions*, 141 N.Y. 288, 36 N.E. 386 (1894); *Gehrmann v. Osborne*, 79 N.J. Eq. 430, 82 Atl. 424 (1912); and *Commonwealth ex rel. Nuber v. Keeper*, 6 Pa. Super. 420 (1898).

[6] *Spencer v. State*, 125 Tenn. 64, 140 S.W. 597 (1911); *Brabandt v. Commonwealth*, 157 Ky. 180, 162 S.W. 786 (1914); and *Neal v. State*, 104 Ga. 509, 30 S.E. 858 (1898).

[7] *Ex parte United States*, 242 U.S. 27–53 (1916).

of the extralegal character of the devices that had evolved played an important role in provoking the enactment of statutes specifically authorizing suspended sentence and probation in the states.

In addition to the common-law origins of the judicial reprieve, discharge on recognizance, and other forms of suspending sentence, the development of probation also may be traced in some measure to the establishment in England of specialized practices to deal with young offenders. The magistrates of the Warwickshire Quarter Sessions adopted a practice as early as 1820 of sentencing the youthful criminal to a term of imprisonment of one day, on the condition that he return "to the care of his parent or master, to be by him more carefully watched and supervised in the future."[8] Matthew Davenport Hill, who had witnessed this procedure there as a young attorney, when he became Recorder of Birmingham, employed a similar practice of "probation" when he believed "that the individual was not wholly corrupt—when there was reasonable hope of reformation—and when there could be found persons to act as guardians kind enough to take charge of the young convict."[9] Confidential police officers visited the guardians from time to time, recording the progress of the offender and keeping a regular account. This was in early 1841. Hill reported after seventeen years of experience that of a total of 483 persons so released only 78, or 16 per cent, had again been brought before the court.[10] A few years later the Recorder of Portsmouth, Edward William Cox, while he employed the traditional system of recognizances as an alternative to imprisonment for young and first offenders, appointed a special "inquiry officer" for Middlesex, charged with the duty of supervising the probationers. It appears that similar devices to save young offenders from prison were employed by London police courts in the 1860s and, very likely, by other English judges. A further development occurred in 1876 when the Temperance Society of the Church of England established its first Police Court Mission to reclaim drunkards. Their duties included the supervision of an increasing number of offenders released on recognizance and commonly they provided bail in such cases. Thus probation supervision developed in England, though early reliance was upon police officers and later upon volunteer and philanthropic services.[11] Such practice has continued to be more characteristic in English correctional practice, in institutional social work and parole as well as in probation, than in the United States. In 1887 a Probation of First Offenders Act was

[8] *Cmd. 2831*, p. 10, cited in *Probation and Related Measures*, United Nations, 1951, p. 44.

[9] Matthew Davenport Hill, "Suggestions for the Repression of Crime, Contained in Charges Delivered to Grand Juries of Birmingham; Supported by Additional Facts and Arguments (1857)," pp. 350–351, cited in *Probation and Related Measures, loc. cit.*

[10] *Ibid.*, p. 602.

[11] Charles L. Chute and Marjorie Bell, *Crime, Courts, and Probation*, 1956, p. 27.

adopted in England authorizing the use of the recognizance for first offenders. It did not provide for special conditions of probation or for supervision, so that American authorities have said that it "was in no sense a
probation law."[12] Supervision was in fact commonly given, however, by
church missionaries and others, as has been noted. New Zealand enacted
a "real probation law" in 1886, establishing conditions of probation and
providing for salaried officers to investigate cases of first offenders and to
recommend probation in appropriate cases. It was not until 1907 that an
act as comprehensive as this was adopted in England, providing for investigation and supervision by salaried officers and for special conditions as
they might be considered suitable to be contained in the recognizance.[13]
The use of the recognizance in connection with probation was not abolished until the enactment of the Criminal Justice Act of 1948.

Probation in the United States

American criminologists have been disposed to trace the development
of probation to the work of John Augustus in the city of Boston beginning
in 1841. He did in fact play an important role, though it is apparent that
the roots of probation lie deeper and, moreover, the practices initiated by
Augustus bear little if any closer resemblance to modern probation than
did the earlier devices employed in Warwickshire and Birmingham. Augustus was a Boston bootmaker and philanthropist and an ardent member of
the Washington Total Abstinence Society that devoted its efforts to the
promotion of temperance. It appears to be a consequence of this interest
that he was led in August of 1841 to bail out "a common drunkard" by
permission of the Boston police court. In Augustus' words:[14]

> He was ordered to appear for sentence in three weeks from that time. He
> signed the pledge and became a sober man; at the expiration of this period of
> probation, I accompanied him into the court room; his whole appearance was
> changed and no one, not even the scrutinizing officers, could have believed that
> he was the same person who less than a month before had stood trembling on
> the prisoner's stand. . . . The judge expressed himself much pleased with the
> account we gave of the man, and instead of the usual penalty—imprisonment
> in the House of Correction—he fined him one cent and costs, amounting in all
> to $3.76, which was immediately paid. The man continued industrious and
> sober, and without doubt has been by this treatment saved from a drunkard's
> grave.

Thereafter over a period of eighteen years Augustus devoted major efforts to the supervision and guidance of offenders from the Police Court

[12] *Ibid.*

[13] See *Probation and Related Measures*, p. 110.

[14] *A Report of the Labors of John Augustus, for the Last Ten Years, in Aid of
the Unfortunate*, 1852, reprinted in Charles L. Chute, *John Augustus, First Probation Officer*, 1939. It appears that Augustus was the first to use the term "probation"
in this special sense where he had given bail and supervised offenders.

and the Municipal Court of Boston, bailing some 1,946 persons up to 1858.[15] His efforts had expanded during this period to cover children (in 1843), women, and offenders of many types. He claimed a very high proportion of successes.[16]

Augustus' work, after his death, was carried on by Rufus R. Cook, a chaplain at the county jail and a representative of the Boston Children's Aid Society. Other volunteers carried on similar efforts.[17] The Children's Aid Society, the Society of St. Vincent de Paul, and other organizations performed voluntary work in the courts. It appears that Augustus and his disciples added to the base of earlier practices in Boston and in England primarily the element of somewhat more systematic supervision than had previously been provided by sureties or by the police. Investigations, reports, home visits, job placements, and other elements of probation service were provided, though at a superficial level and without the aid of sophisticated behavioral science or casework.[18] As one observer notes:[19]

Probation began not in a spirit prompted by a desire to apply to the offender the rehabilitative techniques based on scientific knowledge of human behavior, but rather in one reflecting a simple humanitarian wish to keep less serious and/or first offenders from undergoing the corrupting effects of jail terms. . . . Augustus and his immediate successors are reputed to have had high rates of success in reforming their charges despite the fact that Augustus (and this is probably true of his Boston disciples) was not even remotely a specialist in behavior problems, and apparently had no training in even the crude behavior sciences of his day. What he did have in common with his followers of today, however, was the fact that his probationers were first offenders and minor recidivists released to him from supervision under suspended sentences, and it is just here that an explanation may lie for the observed uniformity in probation success-failure rates.

In other significant respects the work of Augustus and his successors differed from the contemporary norms of probation. The practice of release on bail followed after a period of supervision by a nominal fine and court costs contrasts with the direct method of conditionally suspending sentence and placement on probation employed today. While it is recorded that Augustus interviewed prospective bailees in jail before asking that they be released to him, there appears to have been no real investigation before sentence as we think of it today. Periods of supervision were very short, varying from a few weeks to a few months. Conditions of probation as a

[15] *Letter concerning the Labors of Mr. John Augustus,* 1858, cited in Chute and Bell, *op. cit.,* p. 44.

[16] See "Foreword" by Charles L. Chute, in *John Augustus, First Probation Officer.*

[17] See N. S. Timasheff, *One Hundred Years of Probation,* vol. 1, pp. 9–11.

[18] See Sheldon Glueck (ed.), *Probation and Criminal Justice,* 1933, p. 228.

[19] Ralph W. England, "What Is Responsible for Satisfactory Probation and Postprobation Outcome?" *J. Crim. L.,* vol. 47, no. 6, p. 675, 1957.

basis of possible revocation were not spelled out; Augustus apparently considered only those cases that absconded and forfeited bail to be failures. Finally, there was of course no organization or structure of probation on a local, county, or state basis. These comments are not intended to disparage the efforts of Augustus, which were, apparently, of heroic proportion. They do raise serious question about the enthnocentric inclination of American criminologists to date the "beginnings of probation" from the work of Augustus in 1841. Augustus did contribute, somewhat adventitiously it appears at the start, to the confluence of elements that today comprise probation, although much of this had already developed first in England and later in Massachusetts. Other features were added before probation became the institution we know today. However, it was in Massachusetts that common-law practices were crystallized into legislation and the form of probation became more clearly structured.

In 1869 Massachusetts provided by law for the appointment of a state agent to be attached to the Board of State Charities who was charged with attending court hearings of children and with making arrangements for private home or agency placement of some and the placement "on probation to friends" of others who were not committed.[20] The practice met with favor and was soon extended in scope by the appointment of additional agents and the frequent use of community supervision for children.[21] The first true probation law was enacted in Massachusetts in 1878, providing for the appointment and establishing the duties of a salaried probation officer for Suffolk County.[22] A former chief of police was appointed with office space in the police station, his work being under the general control of the chief of police. Probation periods were brief, running generally from three months to one year, and specific conditions might be attached to the probation "as seem best suited to the case."[23] In 1880 a statute permitted the appointment of probation officers in any town or city of the state and required that their reports be made to the prison commissioners rather than to the police. In 1891 state-wide probation was established by a law requiring the appointment of probation officers (who should not be active members of a police department) by the lower courts throughout the Commonwealth, and in 1898 the appointment of officers by the superior courts to deal with more serious offenders was authorized.[24] Even at this early date much emphasis was given both to the relative economy of probation as compared with institutional treatment and to the general success in the

---

[20] *Sixth Annual Report,* Board of State Charities of Massachusetts, 1869, p. 174.

[21] It is reported that nearly one-third of all children brought to trial were placed on probation. See Chute and Bell, *op. cit.,* p. 57.

[22] *Massachusetts Acts,* 1878, chap. 198.

[23] *Ninth Annual Report,* Massachusetts Commissioners of Prison, 1880, cited in *Probation and Related Measures,* p. 32.

[24] *Massachusetts Acts,* 1880, chap. 129; 1891, chap. 356; and 1898, chap. 511.

rehabilitation of offenders.[25] Finally in 1900 the procedure was established of suspending the execution of sentence together with placement on probation instead of granting probation before the imposition of sentence. A State Commission on Probation was established in 1908.

The recognizance and suspended sentences had been used in other states for many years and considerable interest was expressed both here and abroad in the Massachusetts legislation. Some jurisdictions experimented with quasiprobationary measures similar to those that had been used in Massachusetts. Thus, the Prisoners' Aid Association of Maryland in the years following its establishment in 1869 assisted offenders in the Baltimore courts and in 1894 a statute was enacted to permit any court to release first offenders "on probation of good conduct" upon their recognizance with or without sureties.[26] This law was very similar to the British Probation of First Offenders Act of 1887. Neither act established supervision specifically and for this reason they have been said not to be true "probation" laws. Probation supervision developed, however, under both laws. In 1897 Missouri provided in what was inaccurately termed a "parole of convicted persons" act for the suspension of execution of sentence for young and for minor offenders.[27] Here, too, there was no specified authorization of supervision but "parole" officers were subsequently appointed for the purpose. Vermont established a county plan of probation appointment and supervision in legislation of 1898 and Rhode Island established a completely state-administered system in 1899.[28]

After the turn of the century the spread of probation legislation was quickened by the juvenile court movement. These courts, first established in Chicago and Denver, were generally provided with salaried probation officers. They developed more rapidly than did the movement for general probation of adults, some thirty-seven states and the District of Columbia having enacted children's court acts by 1910.[29] Thirty of the forty-eight states introduced probation first through juvenile court laws, thus manifesting the commonly greater concern for the rehabilitative potential of the young and a willingness to accord them lenience.[30] Development of adult probation was slower in those jurisdictions that enacted juvenile court legislation which provided for probation exclusively in those courts. Federal

---

[25] Former Chief of Police Savage reported that only 43 out of 536 probationers had been surrendered for violating conditions of probation. *First Annual Report of Edward H. Savage, Probation Officer*, 1880, cited in Chute and Bell, *op. cit.*, p. 61. Savage claimed to have saved the city over $17,000 in jail maintenance expense.

[26] *Maryland Acts*, 1894, chap. 402.

[27] *Missouri Acts*, 1897, p. 71.

[28] *Vermont Acts and Resolves*, 1898, no. 128, and *Rhode Island Acts and Resolves*, 1899, chap. 664.

[29] Gilbert Cosulich, *Juvenile Court Laws of the United States*, 1939, pp. 9–13.

[30] Gilbert Cosulich, *Adult Probation Laws of the United States*, 1940, pp. 12–16, and *Probation and Related Measures*, p. 36.

probation was not established until 1925. In 1940, there were still seven jurisdictions that had failed to provide for adult probation, only one of which had not at that time established children's courts. At the time of writing, all states have statutory provisions for probation for both juveniles and adults, Mississippi having at last established enabling legislation in 1956. However, there is wide variation, as will be observed below, both in the laws and in their instrumentation.

One further development of great significance that should be noted is the growth of a partially professionalized service in the probation field. It has been shown that police and volunteer supervision gave way to public salaried officers selected for their humane qualities and their interest. For a number of years their untrained efforts to help, guide, and moralize with their probationers were considered adequate. The beginnings of an educational movement in social work did not occur until long after the development of the probation practices noted. In 1898 a Summer School of Philanthropic Workers was established in New York, giving way in 1904 to the New York School of Philanthropy. At this time and for some years thereafter the function of welfare work was conceived to be the alleviation of man's woes, which were viewed as the consequence of the damaging influence of social and economic factors. It was primarily a humanitarian, charitable, and to a large extent moralistic movement, and its method was largely the distribution of material relief. It was not until 1917 that a substantial philosophy and technique of casework were launched through the publication of Mary Richmond's volume, *Social Diagnosis*. This was sociological in its frame of reference, but it stressed the need for social investigation as a means of diagnosing the situation and the personality of the client so that friendly treatment might be applied to the family in its social setting.

During and after World War I a great departure occurred in social work ideology through the rapid introduction of psychiatric and, especially, psychoanalytic theory that had developed in the treatment of neuroses. Freud, Adler, Jung, and Rank displaced concern for environmental influence with a relatively narrow preoccupation with the individual and his emotional dynamics. Psychoanalysis filled the void that had existed in the theory and method of social work. It was uncritically received for the most part by the schools and the workers in the field. While the advent of the great depression of the 1930s brought some renewed conception of the significance of society and culture, psychiatric casework, oriented to the individual and his deep subjective problems, remained the cornerstone of social work education as it developed during the first three decades of the century. World War II strengthened the liaison of casework and psychoanalysis. Moreover, in contrast with the early days of the development of social work and of educational training for this field, when public welfare and correctional work with juveniles and adults were important areas of attention, the schools came to stress primarily the desirability of working in private social agencies with their restricted intake policies, smaller case loads, higher salaries, and particular standards of professionalization. The view prevailed that correctional work, with its application of authority to unwilling subjects, could not be casework, since the latter was believed to require a voluntary and cooperative client who would take active part in working through his emotional difficulties to arrive at "adjustment."[31]

In spite of this emphasis on voluntarism, and particularly in the field of probation where theory and methodology also remained to be developed, the search for professional status led to orthodox and generic casework methods, since this was the recognized means of "helping people with problems." The National Probation and Parole Association has held for many years that graduation from a school of social work, with supervised experience in an ordinary social agency, is the ideal preparation for work in the correctional fields.[32] Slowly these schools are coming to modify their views about the feasibility of "casework with authority" and of preparing students for such work. They still hold the view, however, that generic training in the philosophy and methods devised for dealing with private clients is appropriate to dealing with offenders. As caseworkers have come increasingly into the field, and especially into administrative positions, they have given strong impetus to the movement for generic casework training as a preparation for probation. The implications of this movement will be discussed further below. Here it is important to note that the position has been taken that probation is merely casework in a specialized setting and that the field should incorporate an increasingly large proportion of workers trained in schools of social work. Among criminologists there are strong dissident voices on this subject, but they have been unable to offer an alternative for which integrated educational and training facilities are readily available.

A brief historical sketch of the development of probation is given here because it provides some conception of the heterogeneous elements that have gone into this social institution, the temporal and spatial diversity in its sources, its partially planned and partially fortuitous ingredients, and its persisting variations. In this respect probation resembles other correctional devices. Unfortunately, once procedures and policy have developed, it is

---

[31] Elliot Studt, a perceptive authority on casework methods in corrections, states the problem in this way: "Since a voluntary request for help was assumed to be necessary in order to initiate casework services, there was little examination of the important technical questions, 'How do you help a person who wants help but doesn't know how to ask for it?' and 'How do you help an antagonistic client learn to want and make use of help?' These techniques which are most important for the correctional worker were relatively ignored because theory began with the 'request from the client.'" "Casework in the Correctional Field," *Fed. Prob.,* vol. 17, no. 3, p. 21, September, 1954.

[32] Chute and Bell, *op. cit.,* p. 180.

difficult to secure critical reappraisals and modifications, except in the direction of more complete services within the accepted pattern. Experience with probation, parole, and correctional intsitutions confirms all too well the normative influence of the actual. The prevailing definition of what probation is exercises persuasive influence against innovation. Well-established institutions tend toward formalism and ritualism.

Some Controversial Issues in Probation

Here the author will discuss some of the controversial issues in the probation field. One such issue is the use of brief jail commitments prior to community supervision. Under Federal case law it has been held that a court may sentence to a term in jail, to be followed by probation. In California and Michigan there is statutory authorization for the courts to commit to jail as a condition of probation orders. Authorities of other jurisdictions who are opposed to this practice generally argue that by definition probation is (1) community supervision without prior commitment and (2) a substitute for and an avoidance of punishment. The first "reason" appears absurd, for *if* it is useful for some offenders to spend a brief period in jail before being submitted to conditional liberty, mere definition of the term probation should not prevent employment of the practice. The definition can be modified. The second "reason" suggests that treatment should not have mixed methods and purposes when, in fact, the multiple ends of correction cannot be met without a fusion of treatment measures. As will be seen, probation itself is generally considered a mixture of casework, surveillance, and control. Those in favor of the employment of jail terms in connection with probation in appropriate cases affirm that for much the same reasons that felons need supervision after discharge from prison, minor offenders for whom a jail term is considered desirable often require guidance and restriction after release; they also observe that in the vast majority of jurisdictions there is no provision for parole of misdemeanants. In this usage probation may be considered an adjunct to the jail term. In other cases, it may be maintained that, while the offender has a primary need for probation supervision, a short period of confinement first will have beneficial effect, whether on the theory of "shock treatment," as a deterrent warning of the consequence of probation violation, or as a means of training. Moreover, in some cases the court may want for legitimate reasons to retain control over certain offenders who would be beyond judicial influence if they were committed to prison. In any event, very commonly the defendant who is placed on probation has spent some time in jail before sentence. In such cases it may be undesirable to employ a further term of imprisonment before probation, but it can scarcely be argued that under present practices there is any real anomaly in having a period in jail precede probation.

For reasons not dissimilar to those related above, objection is sometimes raised to the practice of courts where they assess a fine, restitution, or family support. The complaint is made that the probation department as a "collection agency" is deflected from its proper casework functions and that such a sanction is punitive rather than rehabilitative. Yet, if the payment of money by the offender has sufficient value in making him face his responsibilities or in compensating those to whom he owes an obligation, surely reasonable arrangements can be made for collecting and book-keeping. Dressler quotes one administrator in the probation field who has found money assessments in probation cases a valuable treatment tool:[33]

Selectively and discriminatingly used, they [fines and costs] can be very effective tools in supervision, provided—and it's an important proviso—that they are regarded as a part of discipline. I don't know of any jurisdiction where these devices are used, consciously, in such a way as to favor the rich and to discriminate against the poor. There have actually been defendants, in my experience, who haven't been able to reach an accord with themselves until they have expiated their offenses on some sort of financial basis, even where no fine or court costs have been ordered. . . .

But it is because of their disciplinary features that court costs and fines (assuming intelligent assessment) are a useful adjunct to probation rules. I think we could, from many of our records here, demonstrate to your satisfaction how efficacious they can be. We frequently recommend fines for the so-called "accidental" receivers of stolen goods (not the professional "fences"). Usually an opportunistic acquisitiveness is a strong character trait, and the profit motive is the thing these people most readily understand. Our job is to make them see that an "easy dollar" isn't so easy after all, and fines, especially installment fines, turn out to be just what the doctor ordered. We are, of course, careful to avoid imposition of fines which would work a family hardship and to ask for the remission of unpaid portion of fines whenever we have reason to believe that the lesson has been sufficiently learned. We use fines also for the pseudo-alcoholics (not the true alcoholics) and for the married chaps who play around outside, again suiting the terms (of payment) to the needs of the individual case. The theory is that installment fines give these boys so much less to booze or frisk around with. All I can say now (empirically) is that it seems to work and it's infinitely more dependable than attempts at compulsory savings.

Another probation chief known to the author in a court where installment payment of fines is frequently ordered on advice of the department indicates that over a period of years he has yet to find such a case that violated probation. Selected offenders appear to find some therapeutic value in' this form of material requital.

The use of probation supervision without a conviction is another controversial measure. In most jurisdictions it is required that proof of guilt be ascertained by trial or plea before a defendant becomes eligible for probation. Massachusetts provided in 1905, however, that persons arrested

[33] David Dressler, *Probation and Parole*, 1951, pp. 93–94. (Reprinted by permission.)

for drunkenness might be placed on probation without trial and in that state today the Superior Court may give probation to anyone "charged with crime." There are similar though generally limited provisions in the laws of Kentucky, Maryland, Maine, and Rhode Island. The Federal courts have used such a measure for young offenders, calling it "the Brooklyn Plan." It is employed most commonly, however, in juvenile courts under the title "unofficial probation." This has been discussed elsewhere in this volume. While such a device avoids the attachment of stigma to the defendant, it must be seriously criticized because it is too easy an inducement, whether or not the defendant is guilty of the offense charged, to take a plea on the understanding that there will be no conviction and no imprisonment assessed. Furthermore, a serious difficulty for the state may be created where a trial has not been completed if the probation proves unsuccessful but cannot be revoked without a determination of guilt. The lapse of time may make conviction impossible. The greatest fault of "treatment without trial" is that it evades through a proffered lenience the basic rights of due process to which the accused is entitled.[34]

There are, of course, numerous other controversial issues in the probation field that involve possible departures from the established traditions of method and procedure. Some of these will be discussed at various points in the remainder of this chapter.

FUNCTIONS AND METHODS OF PROBATION

Probation employs two major procedures: presentence investigation of convicted offenders and supervisory treatment of those sentenced to probation. There are numerous incidental functions, however, including the preparation of records, attendance at and reporting to the court, conferring of officer with supervisor, and commonly extensive and time-consuming travel. In some courts, particularly those with large staffs, there is a division of labor in the performance of the two chief functions, one group of officers being assigned to investigation, the other to supervision.[35] Such

[34] Max Grunhut has noted critically the practice in continental systems of conducting social investigations prior to conviction, a practice associated with the consolidation in these countries of the judgment and sentence: "Where adults appear before a criminal court the principle of English law is the only acceptable one, that the report must not be submitted before the prisoner has been found guilty. Attempts on the Continent to introduce a social court aid similar to probation (i.e., the investigatory function associated with probation) failed mainly because it proved incompatible with the law of evidence to render a confidential report to the trial judge. The only possible solution of this dilemma is for Continental law to adopt the English and American partition of the judgment into conviction and sentence with an interval between as the proper usage for social considerations." *Penal Reform,* 1948, p. 307.

[35] The practice of dividing the department into specialized staffs is used in Chicago, Cincinnati, Los Angeles, Newark, and New York City. See Chute and Bell, *op. cit.,* pp. 190–191.

departments justify the separation on the grounds of specialization, arguing that the differing skills of investigation and of supervision may be better developed and the work performed more efficiently and promptly. Most important, perhaps, this division of labor may assure that, under the continuous court pressure for investigations, proper supervision will not be neglected. On the other hand it is argued that such a separation is artificial since common skills are required for both tasks and that much of the insights and information obtained by the investigating officer concerning an offender may be lost in the process of transmitting it to a supervising officer. It is said that rapport should be built from the beginning in dealing with the offender and that transfer to another officer may be damaging to the casework process. In rebuttal, however, it may be claimed that the impartial and objective investigator who reports to the court cannot and perhaps should not attempt to establish a close relationship with the defendant and that the treatment process starts when and if the defendant is placed on probation. In any event, probationers are commonly shifted from one officer to another as a matter of expedience.

If the total staff is adequate in size there is some real advantage in the division of functions, but it appears that the number of officers in relation to the case load is more fundamental to the performance of a department. Much that is written about the techniques of probation, the training of officers, the over-all effectiveness of "good" probationary treatment, and the effects of particular methods has little relevance to practice and little proof of its validity because the staff in most departments carries an overload of work. There is not time to perform the tasks in the ways that the casework literature describes, regardless of the training of the officers, and the measurements that have been made in a few studies are, in general, somewhat crude evaluations of the effects of existing practice rather than evidence of what skilled probation casework might accomplish.[36] What are the standards in relation to case load and staff size? Generalization is difficult if not impossible because conditions vary greatly in different departments concerning such matters as travel time, officer attendance at court, seriousness of cases, and amount of supervisor aid and guidance to officers. Chute and Bell suggest that a safe maximum for officers doing investigative work exclusively is twelve cases per month.[37] The Professional Council of the National Probation and Parole Association holds that where officers carry both functions the limit should be set at thirty-five cases for supervision and six for investigation. It is generally believed that officers doing only supervisory work should handle no more than fifty cases at a time. Hugh P. Reed, an officer of the N.P.P.A., summarizing questionnaire reports of 172 departments in forty-five states in 1948, found that the

[36] See below under "Probation Successes and Failures" and "The Limitations of Probation Practice."
[37] Chute and Bell, op. cit., p. 190.

average supervision load per worker was 123.9 cases and that most of these workers also made investigations. The range was from 15 per worker to 685.[38]

Selection and Presentence Investigation

The policy of limiting the employment of probation may be found in the early development of this measure. In Massachusetts, after probation was extended to the Superior Courts in 1898, offenders were not barred by the nature of the offense or by prior criminal history. A grant of probation was to be based by the statute on presentence investigation and recommendation. The Maryland statute of 1869, however, was applicable only to first offenders charged with a crime other than capital, and the Missouri act of 1897 was made applicable only to individuals under the age of 25 who had not been convicted of specified major crimes. Rhode Island similarly excluded certain felonies but fixed no age limitation. Most of the states have since enacted laws limiting the use of probation in various ways. Today only four states impose no statutory restrictions on the application of probation.[39] Twenty-three jurisdictions bar its use where certain specified felonies have been committed.[40] Twenty establish prohibitions on the basis of prior criminal convictions and three on the basis of prior imprisonment.[41] Nineteen base restrictions on the applicability of a sentence of death or life imprisonment.[42] And three exclude crimes punishable by more than a specified period of imprisonment.[43] It is notable that today Massachusetts, the "cradle of probation," limits its use quite narrowly.

In contrast with the legislative pattern observed above, most probation authorities believe that there should be no rigid and arbitrary limits upon the court's discretion to employ probation as a sentence, provided that a presentence investigation is made to discover whether the offender is proper material for this disposition. However the opinion has developed that,

---

[38] *Ibid.*

[39] Maryland, New Hampshire, Vermont, and Wisconsin.

[40] California, Colorado, District of Columbia, Idaho, Illinois, Indiana, Iowa, Massachusetts, Michigan, Mississippi (probation applicable only to misdemeanants and violators of municipal ordinances), Missouri, Montana, Nebraska, Nevada, New Jersey, New York (felonies while armed), North Dakota, Ohio, Oklahoma, Oregon Maryland, New Hampshire, Vermont, and Wisconsin.

[41] Alabama, California, Colorado, Connecticut, District of Columbia, Illinois, Indiana, Iowa, Kentucky, Massachusetts, Minnesota, Missouri, New Mexico, New York, Oklahoma, South Dakota, Texas, Virginia, Washington, and West Virginia. Montana, North Dakota, and Pennsylvania exclude on the basis of previous imprisonment.

[42] Arizona, Arkansas, Delaware, Florida, Georgia, Kansas, Kentucky, Louisiana, Maine, Massachusetts, Minnesota, New York, North Carolina, Rhode Island, South Carolina, South Dakota, Utah, Wyoming, and Federal.

[43] Alabama, Tennessee, and Texas.

in the interest of the most effective use of probation, criteria should be established to guide courts in their decisions. Chute and Bell suggest this broad formulation of the issue: "Will probation best help the offender toward rehabilitation, and is his release under such supervision safe for society?"[44] They conclude "that a majority of offenders of all ages should be tried out in this way." In its Model Penal Code the American Law Institute has put forward a set of criteria for courts to consider in employing the suspended sentence, with cr without probation:

Section 7.01. Criteria for Withholding Sentence of Imprisonment and for Placing Defendant on Probation.

(1) The Court may deal with a person who has been convicted of a crime without imposing sentence of imprisonment if, having regard to the nature and circumstances of the crime and to the history and character of the defendant, it deems that his imprisonment is unnecessary for protection of the public, on one or more of the following grounds:

(a) The defendant does not have a history of prior delinquency or criminal activity, or, having such a history, has led a law abiding life for a substantial period of time before the commission of the present crime;

(b) The defendant's criminal conduct neither caused nor threatened serious harm;

(c) The defendant did not contemplate that his criminal conduct would cause or threaten serious harm;

(d) The defendant's criminal conduct was the result of circumstances unlikely to recur;

(e) The defendant acted under the stress of a strong provocation;

(f) The victim of the defendant's criminal conduct consented to its commission or was largely instrumental in its perpetration;

(g) The imprisonment of the defendant would entail excessive hardship because of his advanced age or physical condition;

(h) The character and attitudes of the defendant indicate that he is unlikely to commit another crime.

(2) When a person who has been convicted of a crime is not sentenced to imprisonment, the Court shall place him on probation if he is in need of super-

---

[44] Chute and Bell, *op. cit.,* p. 154. Dressler says that these questions should be raised:

(1) Is the offender dangerous? (2) Will prison help or harm this individual? (3) Is probation an acceptable, constructive substitute for this particular defendant? (4) Is he mentally and emotionally of such make-up as to be capable of profiting from probation treatment? (5) Is his attitude toward society and probation such as to justify the use of probation instead of incarceration? (6) Will society, in the long run, benefit if the defendant is placed on probation? Will the individual benefit? (7) Will granting probation at this point and under the given circumstances be construed by the defendant as leniency or as 'beating the rap' and so be deleterious rather than otherwise? (8) Does the defendant have a suitable home and enough economic security to give him a start if he is turned back into the community at this time? Moreover, what plan does the defendant himself have for his future?" *Op. cit.,* pp. 40–41.

vision, guidance or direction that it is feasible for the probation service to provide.

Presentence investigation is designed primarily to assist the court in determining sentence. It has other important uses, however. Where sentence is to probation the investigation report should be a valuable foundation upon which to plan treatment of the offender. If he is committed, the report should as a matter of standard practice go forward to the correctional department for use by the institution. It can be most helpful in classification and treatment planning there during the admission period and it is a valuable source for the parole board in determining the time of release. Finally, it can be used profitably by the supervising parole officer in the field. It is most important, therefore, that such investigations be made routinely, especially in the case of felonies. Many of the states do refer to presentence investigation in their statutes, but in only a few are there mandatory provisions, and these are generally of a limited character. In six states investigation must be made before release on probation in any felony case and in four others it must be made in misdemeanor as well as felony cases.[45] Three other states require such investigation in any felony case whether or not probation is being considered by the court. In one state there must be an investigation in every criminal case. The Federal rule is that an investigation is to be conducted unless the court directs otherwise. The Standard Probation and Parole Act of 1955 provides that "No defendant convicted of a crime the punishment for which may include imprisonment for more than one year shall be sentenced, or otherwise disposed of, before a written report of investigation by a probation officer is presented to and considered by the court. The court may, in its discretion, order a pre-sentence investigation for a defendant convicted of any lesser crime or offense."[46] Section 7.07 of the Model Penal Code recommends a higher and more detailed standard that would include not only all felonies but any other case where the defendant was under the age of 21, where he might be placed on probation or sentenced to an extended term.[47] The court is empowered to order investigations in other cases also.

There are no official data on the proportion of cases in which presentence investigations are conducted by the courts in the United States. The proportion varies greatly in different jurisdictions in relation to size and quality of department, attitudes of the bench, and the laws relating to sentence as well as to investigation. In some courts, where the judges have learned to

---

[45] See *Attorney General's Survey,* vol. 2, pp. 127 ff., and Chute and Bell, *op. cit.,* pp. 139–140.

[46] Sec. 11.

[47] An "extended term" under the Code is a longer period of imprisonment than are the ordinary terms applicable to other offenders. In the discretion of the court it may be applied to recidivists, multiple offenders, professional criminals, and serious deviants. See pp. 474–475 above.

rely on the information provided, there is so much pressure to turn out investigations that relatively too little attention can be given to the supervising of probationers. The detail and quality of presentence investigations also vary widely. Considering the uses to which such reports are put and their heavy bearing, in particular, upon the freedom of the defendant, it is apparent that the accuracy, objectivity, relevance, and completeness of investigation and reporting is tremendously important. Information provided by informants should be carefully checked for its validity and the reliability of the sources should be carefully appraised. Error and prejudice may have consequences as serious for treatment as does the undiscovered falsity of testimony in the trial of guilt. Investigation, however, is an administrative process without significant statutory controls over its methods and without a developed due process. That its effect may be seriously misleading in many cases was suggested by Edwin B. Zeigler, a chief United States probation officer, when he said:[48]

Too many of what we call investigations could not possibly be labeled systematic inquiries, particularly when we interview the defendant and *maybe* just one or two other persons and then proceed to write up a voluminous report. Many of what we produce are not investigations in any sense of the word, but more correctly are merely pre-sentence interviews. Short cuts and careless haste in conducting an investigation are almost a guarantee that the report will contain many data that are downright erroneous and that it will not reflect the defendant's true social and personal problems.

In 1939 the *Attorney General's Survey of Release Procedures* published the results of a survey of investigative practices in 108 probation departments in thirty-three states and the District of Columbia. It was found that the service could not truthfully be described as excellent in any of these jurisdictions. Investigations were conducted "incompletely and sporadically" for the most part. More specifically, however, sixteen jurisdictions" offered "good investigations" with fair regulatory; in eighteen only fair investigations were provided in any cases; forty-five conducted "some type of social investigation sometimes"; thirteen depended upon a sheriff, prosecutor, or the police for any presentence information; sixteen conducted no investigations at all.[49]

Presentence investigation should provide a very inclusive report of facts and analytical interpretation. Dressler suggests that it should include at least the following: details of the immediate offense, prior criminal history, information concerning codefendants, the attitude of the complainant, a

---

[48] "Pre-sentence and Pre-parole Investigation," *Nat. Prob. Assoc. Yearbook,* p. 155, 1946. (Reprinted by permission.) Pauline V. Young indicates that among hundreds of probation records she has found the majority to contain only very meager information, especially the records relating to recidivists. *Social Treatment in Probation and Delinquency,* 1952, p. 130.

[49] *Attorney General's Survey,* vol. 2, p. 182.

thorough personal history of the defendant (development, health, education, employment, habits, character, behavioral patterns, associates, recreation, marital life, mental and physical condition), as much as possible
of the family history and relationships, circumstances in the neighborhood
and community with special reference to the attitude toward the offender
and his crime, and a program that might be developed for the offender if
he is given probation.[50] In addition to these matters, the report should contain information about the personality of the offender, including the results
of psychiatric study if he has been examined; social service exchange information on agencies that have been interested in him; and an analytical
summary of his history and problems, with a recommendation to the court
concerning sentence (if the court is willing to receive specific recommendations). So far as psychiatric investigation is concerned, it is desirable as an
ideal matter, of course, to have court clinical facilities available so that
studies can be made quite systematically. Thus far only a few cities have
established such clinics in adult criminal courts, and elsewhere reliance
must be placed upon hospitals or private psychiatrists for those investigations that judges believe should be made.[51] Where court clinics exist they
not only provide examinations in a much larger proportion of cases but
also may offer guidance to the probation department relative to individualized treatment programs and may even administer therapy in some probation cases.

One of the difficult policy issues in the probation field lies in the confidentiality of presentence reports. The laws of Alabama, California, and
Ohio give the defendant or his counsel the right to inspect the probation
report. The Federal rule leaves disclosure to the discretion of the judge.[52]
In England and Canada by rules of court the defendant is entitled to the
report and an opportunity to rebut its contents. For the most part in the
states, however, the practice of sentencing judges is to keep secret the
information on which they determine disposition. The United States
Supreme Court has held that even in the imposition of a death sentence
due process does not require disclosure of information supplied by informants whom the defendant has had no opportunity to cross-examine or
contradict.[53] The view of probation authorities very generally is that in-

[50] Dressler, *op. cit.*, pp. 42–46.
[51] See Chapter 14, ftn. 46.
[52] *Report of the Advisory Committee*, 1944, proposed Rule 34 (c) (2) and Rule
32, Rules of Criminal Procedure. The Advisory Committee had proposed that presentence reports should be available, upon such conditions as the court might impose,
to the attorneys for the parties and to such other persons or agencies having a legitimate interest therein as the court might designate. The Standard Probation and Parole Act of the N.P.P.A. gives the court discretion to permit inspection of reports
"whenever the best interest or welfare of a particular defendant or prisoner makes
such action desirable or helpful." Sec. 5.
[53] *Williams v. New York*, 337 U.S. 241 (1949).

formation provided the investigator should be held fully confidential. They argue that not to do so would dry up the sources of information, that both individuals and social agencies would be unwilling to cooperate if the content or source of advice were revealed.[54] They maintain further that in many cases the consequence of disclosure would be damaging to the case-work process, since the offender would be hostile both to the informant and to the officer. The technical argument is also advanced, in accordance with the case law, that the defendant is not entitled to access to the report and that his due process rights have been used up once he is convicted. Some administrators threaten that if they are required to disclose they will provide only brief and partial reports to the court for the purpose.

While recognizing the soundness of the first contention, at least, the writer holds there is a strong argument for disclosure. Despite the fact that courts have free discretion as a matter of law to determine sentence within the range of penalties permitted by statute for the crime involved, there is a special need to assure fairness to the offender when that range is so wide as it is today. Complete reliance on an administrative agency to provide full and accurate information to the court, without an opportunity for the defendant to refute or qualify the content of the report, can scarcely be supported in a legal procedure the consequence of which may be, on the one hand, no penalty at all or, on the other, a long period of imprisonment. The frank appraisals that have been made by some probation officials make it quite apparent that many and probably the great majority of the presentence reports that are utilized by the courts provide an inadequate or distorted view of the offender. The author has seen many of these reports in which emotionally toned value judgments are liberally distrib-uted, diagnostic terms loosely and inaccurately used, prejudicial epithets ("immoral," "depraved," "corrupt," "psychopathic,") employed, and the sources of information concealed. One valuable by-product of a rule requiring some form of disclosure should be to improve the quality of in-vestigating and reporting. Offenders would value the fairness of a pro-cedure in which they were apprised of the grounds of their sentences.

The Model Penal Code has proposed that the court should advise the defendant or his counsel of the factual contents and the conclusions of the presentence investigation and should afford him fair opportunity, if he so requests, to controvert them.[55] This would require neither the delivery of the report itself nor revelation of the sources of confidential information. This appears to be a fair and workable compromise of a difficult problem

[54] See, for example, Albert W. Roche, "Confidentiality of Presentence Reports," *Focus,* vol. 32, no. 2, pp. 39–44, March, 1953, and Judge Carroll Hincks, "In Opposi-tion to Rule 34 (*c*) (2)," *Fed. Prob.,* vol. 8, no. 4, pp. 5 and 7, 1944. Compare Judge Theodore Levine, "Sentencing the Criminal," *Fed. Prob.,* vol. 13, no. 1, p. 5, March, 1949, and Sol Rubin, "What Privacy for Presentence Reports?" *Fed. Prob.,* vol. 16, no. 2, pp. 8–11, December, 1952.

[55] Sec. 7.07 (5).

in which conflicting interests must be balanced. As in other procedures involved in the administration of justice, it might result in some cases in the exclusion of information that could be of some utility to the court, but this is a price to be paid in the interest of avoiding error and abuse.

Frequency of Employment of Probation as a Sentence

Presentence investigation is a selective measure in determining who will be sentenced to probation, as has been observed. Court employment of this disposition is determined also by a variety of other factors: statutory provisions, the attitudes of judges, size and competence of probation staff, the seriousness of criminality and recidivism in the particular jurisdiction, and the quality and variety of institutional facilities that may be used as an alternative. As one might anticipate, the extent to which probation is used varies widely throughout the country. National statistics on sentencing are not available, unfortunately, since the Bureau of the Census abandoned the collection and publication of *Judicial Criminal Statistics* in 1946.[56] For the year 1945 probation or suspended sentence was employed in 31.6 per cent of the cases of defendants sentenced for major offenses in the courts of twenty-five reporting states.[57] The frequency of use ranged from 13.0 per cent in Iowa to 64.6 in Rhode Island. Ten years earlier probation or suspended sentence was used by the courts of thirty states in 28.0 per cent of their cases, among which 22.4 per cent were with supervision and 5.6 per cent without.[58] The range was from 5.8 per cent in Vermont to 57.1 per cent in Rhode Island. It appears that there has been further growth in the use of probation in some states, at least, during the decade since the national judicial statistics were published. Thus, New York, which had employed probation or suspended sentence in 34.6 per cent of its felony convictions in 1945, did so in 39.8 per cent in 1951 (26.4 per cent with supervision, 13.4 per cent with straight suspensions).[59] California, which had used probation or suspended sentence in 32.8 per cent of its sentences in 1945, sentenced 44.2 per cent of its felons to probation in 1955.[60] Statistics on Federal offenders provide information on the comparative use of probation in the eighty-six district courts of the United States. In the year ending on June 30, 1956, probation had been used in 42.2 per cent of the convictions (as compared with 39.5 per cent in

[56] See Harry Alpert, "National Series of State Judicial Statistics Discontinued," *J. Crim. L.*, vol. 39, no. 2, 1948. The data gathered were of questionable reliability, in part because of the variation in laws and practices, and the coverage was quite incomplete.

[57] *Judicial Criminal Statistics*, 1945, Bureau of the Census, 1947, table 4. The data provided no information on the proportion of cases in which probation supervision was ordered.

[58] *Judicial Criminal Statistics*, 1935, table 34.

[59] *Report of the Department of Correction*, 1951 and 1952, New York, table 19.

[60] *Delinquency and Probation in California*, 1955, table 23.

1946).[61] The range in the Federal employment of probation, too, was wide, varying from 14.0 per cent in the western district of Texas (and 60.2 per cent in the eastern district of that state) to 69.0 per cent in the eastern district of South Carolina. Data are not available, unfortunately, on the use of probation in misdemeanor cases.

There is no way to conjecture with any precision what proportion of criminal cases should be selected for probation. Certainly this must depend in part on the adequacy of personnel to do the job and there are many places still lacking in this regard. To a very large extent first offenders and minor repeaters, ostensibly "good risks," are sentenced to supervision. Studies of the results of probation indicate that a high proportion of cases result in success as compared with imprisonment, a fact that may be accounted for in various ways.[62] The contrast raises a nice question of court and public policy, however, concerning whether it might not be desirable to try probation with a larger proportion of repeaters and with older offenders, particularly against property, whose crimes are not so serious a danger to the community, even though the result might well be a larger number of probation failures than is characteristic now.[63] More refined study needs to be given to the relation of success rates to case loads, types of offenders, and probation methods. Such data should be compared to parole success in relation to similar variables. It is clearly desirable that courts should apply relevant criteria more systematically in the selection of probationers than they have in the past. The possible abuse in the undiscriminating use of this sentence is well illustrated in this excerpt from a special crime commission study of the treatment of persistent offenders in Massachusetts:[64]

One of the striking things which emerges from our study of the records of persistent offenders is that they are time and again placed on probation when their records are such as to imperatively demand institutional treatment. The probation record of_____illustrates this point. His first probation was on a gambling charge, after a prior larceny charge had been placed on file by the juvenile court, after a larceny charge and an assault and battery charge had been dismissed, and after a $5 fine had been paid for lewd cohabitation. On his next larceny charge he was again convicted and again put on probation. His next charge was of assault and battery, which was filed. He was charged with violating the terms of his probation, but the only penalty was that his probation was extended. Two months later he was charged with breaking and entering,

[61] *Federal Prisons,* 1956, table 32, and 1946, table 22.

[62] See below under "Probation Successes and Failures."

[63] Both American and foreign researchers on probation successes reveal that older offenders, while they are given probation much less often, have considerably better performance on probation.

[64] Paul W. Tappan, "Habitual Offender Laws and Sentencing Practices in Relation to Organized Crime," in Morris Ploscowe (ed.), *Organized Crime and Law Enforcement,* 1952, p. 128.

and was found guilty. Three months later he was again before the same court charged with violation of probation; probation was again extended. Nine days later he was brought before the same court charged with larceny; he was again put on probation. Seven months later he received probation from the Superior Court on an assault and battery charge. Two months later he was charged with larceny and with breaking a showcase; he was again put on probation by the Superior Court. This persistent offender was put on probation six times; twice he was brought in for violation of his probation, and in both instances the only penalty was that his probation was extended for a further period.

Probation Supervision and Treatment

Before the specific methods employed in supervision are described, it may be useful to consider a controversy that is fundamental to the probation process. Put simply, the issue is whether probation is or is not casework. It is the generally prevailing view today among probation authorities that probation is, and to be effective must be, casework. Elliot Studt, formerly of the U.S. Children's Bureau, in arguing that probation is casework, offers a definition of that term as it may be applied, in her opinion, in the correctional field:[65]

Casework is a way of working with individuals. It is a method of doing the correctional job which is consciously planned to help the individual client become better adjusted to the demands of social living. The aspects of the correctional worker's activities which make his work "casework" are twofold: *that he is dealing with the client as an individual; and that he is consciously controlling what he does so that his activity contributes within reality limits to the welfare of the client.* Casework does not depend on the kind of activity concerning the client and his situation which is occupying the worker. Interviewing is only a part of casework. The worker may be taking the client to jail as a parole violator to cool off while he figures out what has to be done next. He may be taking a child to detention, writing a court report, recommending commitment to the youth authority, investigating an offense, or working with a child's teacher. Each such activity is a part of casework provided he does it with full attention to the client as an individual whose welfare he is endeavoring to secure within the framework of the social limitations to which both he and the client must adjust.

Ben Meeker, chief probation officer in the Chicago Federal District Court, in maintaining that probation is casework, points to what they have in common: emphasis upon working with the individual in a relationship; the releasing of tensions, frustrations, and aggressions; providing opportunities for the person to gain satisfactions; use of such techniques as the interview, the casework conference, and referral.[66]

[65] Elliot Studt, *op. cit.*, p. 23. (Reprinted by permission.)
[66] Probation Is Casework," *Fed. Prob.*, vol. 12, no. 2, pp. 51–54, June, 1948. He concludes: "It is therefore apparent that a wise use of the principles and methods of

One proponent of the position that probation is not casework, Marilyn A. Blake, of the Detroit Police Department, acknowledges that probation is a form of social work and that there are some points of similarity between probation and casework, but she holds that "Casework is one kind of social work, probation another, and while probation may utilize some of the methods and techniques of casework, it cannot become casework without losing its identity. . . . There are differences between the two so fundamental that the probation officer never can be a caseworker."[67] Among these differences she stresses the voluntary character of ordinary casework, the cooperative relation between the client and worker, as contrasted with the authoritarian nature of the probation relationship, and the threat of undesirable consequences that constitutes a barrier to casework. Blake points also to the nondirective quality of the casework process in its efforts to guide the individual toward insight and self-understanding that may make for adjustment as against the limits and control that probation employs. Further she believes that probation relies far more largely on environmental manipulation than does the caseworker who is concerned primarily with the emotional and feeling elements in the individual's situation. Finally, she maintains that if the probationer's personality problems are such as to require real casework counseling and if he is able voluntarily to use such a service, referral should be made to an agency for the casework help, as is done for other specialized types of referrals, rather than having the officer attempt to perform a function that is foreign to his primary responsibilities.

It appears that in a measure the controversy illustrated in the opinions noted above is founded in fairly superficial matters of definition, more particularly the definition of what "casework" is or is not. The writer believes, however, that probation is a specialized "correctional casework" that differs fundamentally from ordinary generic and psychiatric casework as they are practiced in private social agencies. The two are similar, to be sure, in that the worker deals with the client or probationer as an individual, but this is a very undiscriminating resemblance, for many other professional and service occupations may be characterized in the same way. The conscious effort of the worker to contribute within limits to the welfare of the client, too, is a very general sort of identity, applicable to

---

casework will add immeasurably to the success of a probation officer. Such qualifications as a deep understanding of human nature and the forces which direct behavior, a profound belief in the worth of the individual, an objective acceptance of him as we find him, and a genuine desire to be of service buttressed by a real knowledge of resources and how to use them, are among the qualifications most needed to succeed in the practice of probation. Such are the wellsprings of casework, and without casework probation is denied its most vital force." P. 54.

[67] "Probation Is Not Casework," *ibid.*, pp. 54–57.

the psychologist, the psychiatrist, the playground director, and even the physician and the dentist, among others, and surely the differences in method and training are greater than the similarities. One very important difference between them lies, in fact, in general orientation. The probation officer's primary concern must be with the welfare and safety of the community rather than with the probationer alone. This does not imply that the general personality "adjustment" of the individual is to be improved, if that is taken to mean the reduction of frustrations and the satisfaction of wants. Indeed, the demands upon the probationer may be to reduce the expression of egocentric desires and to control his frustrations more effectively. In working with the large number of offenders who act out their aggressions, there is commonly need to strengthen feelings of guilt, to encourage inhibition and repression, in contrast with the traditional psychiatric pattern of releasing the tensions of neurotic patients.[68] The probation officer's task is to produce conformity with the minimum requirements established by law and this does not imply his increased satisfaction, happiness, or adjustment in the usual mental hygiene sense. It does not even necessarily mean an amelioration of his personal and social problems if they appear to be unrelated to his criminality.[69]

Casework is commonly defined as a "helping" profession, with an implicit or explicit assumption that, whether the problem is psychiatric, medical, industrial, educational, familial, or correctional, the generic caseworker can bring the same tools to the job and can manipulate them in essentially the same way. Whatever may be the case in the other fields, this is not true in correction. The problems are specialized; so must be the

[68] See Studt, *op. cit.*, pp. 21 and 25.

[69] The writer has expressed elsewhere the view that the treatment tasks in correction are limited by specific objectives: " . . . the function of law, of our criminal courts and the correctional system, is rather exclusively to protect society against the invasion of certain rights of property and person. These agencies are *not* concerned with general problems of social welfare or of public health as such, nor directly with the specific cure of mental, emotional or physical disorder in the individual. Diagnoses of neurosis, psychosis, or other emotional disorder—even the treatment of such conditions—are of indirect rather than direct interest. The criminologist asks simply: can effective treatment be applied with sufficient economy to particular types of offenders and to a sufficient number of cases so that they will avoid persistent violation of the law and so that public security will be more adequately protected? If an emotional disorder has little or no direct causal significance for crime, its diagnosis or treatment is of no importance. Even if there apparently is a causal relationship the diagnosis and therapy are of no great significance to our courts or correction agencies unless it is feasible to treat a sufficient number of cases. Thus, an excessive cost in funds, time or personnel to treat offenders in numbers implies that such treatment is chiefly of empirical interest, looking to the development of more economical or effective methods. To repeat, the correctional system is concerned with society and its protection, and with the individual offender chiefly insofar as his curative treatment may inhibit further law violation." *Focus,* vol. 31, no. 3, p. 66, May, 1952.

methods of dealing with them. Elliot Studt, who was formerly a professor in a professional school of social work, acknowledges very frankly both that work in the correctional field is not generic casework in the traditional sense and that the schools of social work do not today provide the substantive content from corrections that is needed for correctional casework:

> . . . the social work profession was focused on segments of casework activity and claimed universality for patterns which were often not appropriate to casework in a correctional setting; and at the same time the correctional field, because of the urgency of other tasks, was not contributing fully to the theoretical development of casework and technique. . . ."[70] So nowhere at this time has the specific content of casework in the correctional agency been identified, illustrated with case records, integrated with basic social work content, and built into the curricula of our schools of social work. Such examination of casework practice in the correctional field is a primary task of any school of social work which undertakes to prepare students for practice in corrections. . . ."[71]

She goes further in spelling out what casework is not: it is not "the exclusive property of professionally educated social workers"; it is not "any particular pattern of service belonging to one agency setting or another"; it is not "a set of fancy gadgets called 'techniques' "; nor is it casework "just when your client likes you and you 'have a relationship.' "[72]

Other authorities, including Lloyd Ohlin, now associated with the New York School of Social Work, have emphasized the obstacles that confront the social worker of orthodox orientation who works in the correctional field.[73] He has inherited the dogma that the involuntary subject who is resistant and commonly limited in his capacities cannot be aided by casework. He must absorb the aggressions of noncooperative offenders and learn methods to elicit their affirmative responsiveness. He must act within a normative setting, with some emphasis upon the rules of conduct (the conditions of probation or parole) laid down by the court, and must bring the offender to recognize the need either to conform or to accept the consequences of his failure to do so. He must work in a quite different sort of relationship with the individual than that envisioned in his courses and fieldwork, one that is defined by the differing nature of the subject, the

---

[70] Elliot Studt, op. cit., p. 23.

[71] Ibid., p. 22. Ohlin and his associates observe the failure of professional training to prepare for practice: "The basic problem is that his academic training [in the professional school of social work] had not given him the skills and guides to action for converting a relationship of control and authority into one of consent and treatment." Lloyd E. Ohlin, Herman Piven, and Donnell M. Pappenfort, "Major Dilemmas of the Social Worker in Probation and Parole," N.P.P.A. J., vol. 2, no. 3, p. 216, July, 1956.

[72] Studt, op. cit., p. 23.

[73] Ohlin, et al., op cit., p. 211–226.

ends sought, and the processes involved. He will find a limited relevance in the diagnostic and treatment terminology commonly applied to the neurotic. He faces a very different level of community expectancy in relation to the consequences of his efforts. He may find quite alien the need for measures of surveillance and, indeed, other techniques of law enforcement, perhaps including the carrying of a weapon.[74] "He often finds it necessary to seek guidance from sources other than social work itself, sources which deal with his specific clients and problems."[75] It may be true in a measure that the officer functioning in an "autonomous" correctional agency can, as Ohlin and his co-authors suggest, "reject the control function and pursue the treatment objectives of casework . . . [and feel] free to circumvent court or parole board directives which he regards as opposed to his client's welfare."[76] But, however tolerant the inclination of the agency, the officer who allows his subject to leave the jurisdiction, to quit reporting, or to enter a prohibited occupation is going to be in trouble. The differences in method and orientation between generic and correctional casework cannot be rationalized away.

The probation or parole officer and the caseworker in the correctional institution, like other social workers, do require training and experience in interviewing, investigation, and case recording. They need familiarity with the field of community organization and, in particular, with the facilities that may provide services to the offender. They require an objective, non-moralistic attitude, an understanding and a desire to help, an ability to take hostility without counteraggression. They should have a broad, eclectic training in social and behavioral sciences rather than a narrowly psychiatric approach. Some, if not all, of this background can be secured in a school of social work. But much that is required in the curriculum of these schools is not only irrelevant but inapposite to the work of the correctional officer (and much of it is a duplication of the study that a well-trained undergraduate student has already received). Moreover, even among those who argue that a generic casework training is fundamental to correctional casework, there are some who acknowledge the need for specialized training and knowledge of the fields of criminology, delin-

[74] David Dressler puts considerable emphasis upon the policing functions of the probation officer: "Moreover, the officer must develop techniques that the private worker abhors, techniques of the police officer. He must learn to trail people, keep their homes under surveillance, arrest men and women, lock them up, return them to correctional institutions. He must, for his own welfare, learn how to take care of himself in a scuffle. Knowledge of the best way to kick in a door or trip up a recalcitrant may spell not only the difference between apprehension of a malefactor and his escape, but the life or death of the officer. Handcuffs are scarcely the tools of the caseworker in a treatment situation, but they are the tools of the parole or probation officer about to 'close a case.'" *Op. cit.,* p. 34. Most probation authorities put much less emphasis upon police techniques.

[75] Ohlin et al., *op. cit.,* p. 217.

[76] *Ibid.,* p. 220.

quency, correctional theory, the administration of justice, probation, and parole.[77] They require field training in correctional rather than private agencies.

The author believes that this correctional orientation cannot be achieved effectively either by a limited incorporation of criminological material and of probation and parole cases in casework courses in the school of social work or by superficial in-service training any more than casework methods can be "picked up" efficiently in a criminology course or on the job. Specialized training combining social work methods and a criminological orientation is needed. This would seem to require significant changes in curriculum content, whether it is offered in schools of social work or in the correctional programs that have been set up in an increasing number of graduate schools. Until such fusion occurs, compromises must be made in students' efforts to secure combined training in their preparation for the correctional field.

What the author has said above refers, of course, to an idealized level of professional preparation, so far as courts in general are concerned. Our schools turn out few students with the kind of training described. Furthermore, the author's experience with probation has shown that good results can be achieved by officers without highly specialized educational background, if they are well adapted in personality to the work and if they receive good in-service training and case supervision. Most of the tasks performed by probation officers do not require graduation from a professional school. On the other hand, it appears that supervisors and those officers who carry cases for intensive treatment should have such training

[77] See the works of Ohlin, Studt, and Dressler, cited above. T. Conway Esselstyn, a sociological criminologist, has said this concerning the fusion of casework and corrections: "The correctional worker is caught between two loyalties—one, a loyalty to the art and science of helping people; the other, a loyalty to the art and science of law and the ways of law. The first may be synonymous with the second but where these two conflict, loyalty to the art and science of law and to law-ways— to one's court, one's board, or to one's associates within the official structure for controlling offenders—must always receive the edge, or else there will be no corrections of any kind. . . . [D]efinitions by correctional workers or their spokesmen will differ quite sharply from the assessments by social workers in two important particulars. (1) The correctional workers will probably try to cut down the length of time required to complete graduate preparation. (2) They will place less emphasis on the degree of personality transformation sought for in the student undergoing training and more emphasis on the behavior of the client." From a paper presented at the Training Institute of Federal Probation Officers, Claremont, California, Aug. 8, 1956. For other expressions of the criminologists' point of view, see Walter C. Reckless, "Training the Correctional Worker," in Tappan (ed.), *Contemporary Correction,* 1951, especially pp. 40–45, and Peter P. Lejins, "Criminology for Probation and Parole Officers," *N.P.P.A. J.,* vol. 2, no. 3, pp. 200–207, July, 1956. See also "Suggested College Curricula as Preparation for Correctional Service," prepared by the Committee on Personnel Standards and Training of the American Prison Association, 1954.

as has been described. This will be considered later in connection with the discussion of the limitations of probation practice.

Today probation and parole officers are more and more frequently recruited from among college students with social science majors. Some probation departments require graduate training either in a school of social work or in an ordinary graduate school. Some supervised field work experience is also very commonly demanded. Civil service requirements often provide for alternative combinations of training and experience.

Conditions, Revocation, and Discharge

It has been observed that probation is conditional freedom under supervision. Conditions may be drawn directly from the probation statute in some jurisdictions. More commonly the law provides a general grant of power for the court to impose conditions beyond those that the statute may enumerate and in some jurisdictions the court is given no direction or limits on the nature of the conditions that may be imposed. Whether by law or by practice the conditions established most commonly include prohibitions against vicious habits, disreputable or criminal associations, leaving the jurisdiction, and drinking. There are also affirmative requirements to report to the officer as directed, to obey the law, to work at approved employment and support dependents, and sometimes to pay a fine or make restitution. Other specific conditions may be added. There is a trend toward making the conditions of probation more general and affirmative rather than specific and prohibitive, to individualize them and to give probation departments some control over the conditions to be imposed. Fundamentally, however, the conditions remain restrictive and they are often of a moralistic character. In some instances they "are so broad and general that definitive standards of conduct are nonexistent."[73]

The conditions of probation are not only a guide to the conduct of the offender, employed in a casework process; they are also a basis of revocation and imprisonment for violations, so that the consequences of the offender's failure are far more serious than being dropped from the services of an agency. In the great majority of jurisdictions revocation is at the discretion of the sentencing court. In practice the discretion is very wide, for the court may revoke and imprison on the allegation of a minor technical violation or may determine when the probationer is alleged to have committed a crime to retain him on probation, to commit him for a violation instead of prosecuting, or to make him serve time for both the probation violation and for the new offense. Policy varies considerably in different probation departments on the reporting of violation of conditions. Officers also have different opinions concerning the sort of conduct that justifies them in bringing the matter to the attention of the court. Some do

[73] *Attorney General's Survey,* vol. 2, p. 324. Also see the discussion of conditions in the chapter below on parole.

so when it appears there is danger that the probationer will commit another offense; some employ a general appraisal of the probationer's adjustment; some report only when they believe that the probationer has committed a new crime. This suggests that probation revocations are an imperfect index of the success of probation, though it is the easiest and most common standard employed.

In most of the states some sort of summary hearing is provided the probationer before revocation, though case law in at least five jurisdictions has held that the failure to afford an opportunity to be heard is not a deprivation of a constitutional right or privilege.[79] Other states have found it to be a due process right.[80] The United States Supreme Court has specifically held, however, in the case of *Escoe v. Zerbst,* 295 U.S. 490 (1935), that a hearing is a privilege bestowed by statute, not a right under the Fifth Amendment. The Court indicated nevertheless that where a hearing is authorized there should be "an inquiry so fitted in its range to the needs of the occasion as to justify the conclusion that discretion has not been abused by the failure of the inquisitor to carry the probe deeper."[81] On this issue the position was taken in the *Attorney General's Survey* that "Even though it be granted that the court has absolute discretion in granting probation and that probation is a matter of grace and not of right, a sense of fair play requires that some inquiry be made and that the accused be given an opportunity to explain before he is deprived of his conditional freedom."[82] It appears clear that a probationer should be given notice of an accusation of a violation and a statement of charges, that there should be an informal hearing with a submission of the state's evidence and an opportunity for the accused to rebut; it also appears clear that probation should not be revoked without proof sufficient to satisfy the court that there has in fact been a serious violation. This is rudimentary administrative due process that neither Federal nor state constitutions provide, however. The Model Penal Code provision would empower the court to revoke "if satisfied that the defendant has inexcusably failed to comply with a substantial requirement imposed as a condition of the order or if he has been convicted of another crime," but may not impose a sentence of imprisonment unless the defendant has been convicted of another crime or his misconduct indicates that his continued liberty involves excessive risk that he will commit another crime.[83]

It is the general rule in the United States that when the imposition of

[79] California, Iowa, Kansas, Minnesota, and Missouri.

[80] See *State v. Zolantakis,* 70 Utah 296 (1927), and *State v. O'Neal,* 147 Wash. 169 (1928).

[81] 295 U.S. 490 (1935). But compare *Fleming v. Tate,* 156 F.2d 848 (D.C. Cir. 1946), and *Hiatt v. Campagna,* 178 F.2d 42 (5th Cir. 1949), *aff'd* per curiam by equally divided court, 340 U.S. 880 (1950).

[82] *Attorney General's Survey,* p. 330.

[83] Sec. 301.3.

sentence has been suspended the court may, upon revocation of probation, sentence to any term that it might have employed at the time of conviction. When a court has imposed a sentence of commitment, however, and suspended its execution, the revocation results in the activation of that sentence, unless the law provides that the sentence may be modified. With rare exception[84] courts are not required in resentencing the probationer to accredit him with the time he has spent under supervision without violation. In practice courts in their sentencing do often take such time into consideration.

Probation legislation varies widely in its provision concerning periods of probation. In some jurisdictions no limits whatever are set, the court being given complete discretion. This policy was approved in the *Attorney General's Survey* on the grounds that any arbitrary period fixed by law would not be adaptable to the exigencies of particular cases.[85] A number of states limit the probation period to the maximum term for which the offender could have been imprisoned. Other jurisdictions establish a specific maximum limit, commonly five years. In a few jurisdictions the law establishes minimum periods of probation. Discharge from probation, ordinarily without special formality, occurs at the end of the probation period if there has been no violation. Except in a few states, however, the court may either terminate supervision or discharge from probation before the expiration of that period in appropriate cases, so that the probation term becomes, in effect, indefinite in length. In a few jurisdictions, in spite of limits set on the length of the probation period, a probationer may be arrested and resentenced after its expiration but within the maximum term to which he might have been sentenced to an institution.[86] In some other states, probation may be revoked after the termination of the probation period if a warrant was issued before such termination. The Model Penal Code provides for a five-year term of probation for felons and a two-year term for misdemeanants and petty misdemeanants with power to discharge at any time. Any act of revocation must be taken before the discharge of the defendant.[87]

Probation Methods

Probation supervision and treatment are carried on very largely through a relationship that is built on two types of personal contacts: the reporting of the probationer to his officer, ordinarily at the probation office, and visits of the officer with the probationer, usually at his home, though such

[84] Georgia provides by statute that the probationer should receive credit for the time served. Ga. Code (1933), sec. 27–2702.
[85] *Attorney General's Survey,* p. 85, and Cosulich, *op. cit.,* p. 32.
[86] See *Commonwealth ex rel. Wilhelm v. Morgan,* 278 Pa. 395 (1924), and *People v. Hodges,* 231 Mich. 656 (1925).
[87] Sec. 301.3.

visits may also occur at other places in the neighborhood and community where the probationer lives. Various other supplementary forms of contact may be employed, including written reports of the probationer and telephone communication, but they are not a good substitute for the more personal intercourse. It is generally concluded that the officer's visits in the home are most important, because they provide an opportunity to understand the probationer better in his setting, to see something of his relationships in the family, and often to discover some of the problems that beset him. Unless office space and schedules are worked out very well, brief interviews there are likely to be of little value, especially if they become a method of routine surveillance and of threats and exhortation. With the large case loads that commonly prevail, the lack of privacy in crowded offices, and the need to arrange many such interviews during a single day or evening, it is impossible to establish a confidential and supportive relationship. The disciplinary value of office reporting has been both affirmed and denied. In some cases it is probably useful.

There is controversy over how frequently personal reports and office visits should be held. In fact, there can be no arbitrary rule, for the requirements vary considerably among probationers and at different stages of their supervision. Relatively intensive work is ordinarily required at the start if the offender is in need of guidance at all. Frequent visits to the home of the probationer may be necessary for a period of a few months. Many cases can be handled with contacts no more frequent than once or twice a month after such an initial period. One of the constructive developments in modern probation is the practice in some departments of classifying case loads on the basis of intensity of supervision required. Another useful device is the classification of offenders into types, such as gang member, drug user, alcoholic, nonsupporter, etc. The traditional view that all offenders should receive a similar amount of supervision, formalized in the law of some jurisdictions where one or two home visits each month are theoretically mandatory, is not sound. On the other hand, lacking sufficient objective research on the matter, no criteria or policies have developed to determine how the time of officers can be distributed most effectively in supervisory treatment.

Visits and interviews constitute the form of probation. Its substance is, of course, more important. What does the officer do to, for, or with the probationer? The question is related to the depth of the treatment relationship and to the scope of services that may be desirable to achieve the correctional goal. This raises the issue of whether the aim of probation is to produce a "good adjustment" in a general sense or, more narrowly, to induce changes in behavior and attitude toward the law. In general, probation strives to achieve the broad ideal formulated in the *Attorney General's Survey*:[88]

[88] *Attorney General's Survey*, p. 319.

Adequate probation supervision must deal with all phases of the offender's life, including his family and the community in which he lives. Although there is some controversy among case workers and writers on probation as to the value and propriety of many specific techniques for supervision, all recognize the usefulness of a plan of treatment based on the needs, capacities, and limitations of each offender. The physical and mental health, capacities, and limitations of the offender; his home and family; his leisure-time activities; his religious life; his education; vocational training; economic status and industrial habits, as well as his capacity for discipline and self-control must all be considered by those who are attempting to remold him into a worthwhile citizen.

Nathaniel Cantor, on the other hand, has severely criticized the formless consequence of an undirected and generalized beneficence:[89]

They [probation officers] either cajole, coerce, find jobs, give relief, collect money, provide medical attention, advise on family affairs, sermonize, or sympathize. The officer who takes upon himself the responsibility of directing all sorts of activities of the offender is robbing him of the possibility of growth. To discuss the administration of the various services now offered by probation departments would require a good-sized monograph. Attention is merely directed to the confusion reflected in the effort of a single department to combine almost every conceivable type of social service. The individual worker is expected to function in a dozen different directions. The net result must often be that neither the worker nor the offender is clear about what is taking place. There is little, if any, direction.

Unfortunately, the methods that may be employed most effectively to achieve the specialized goal of the probationer's voluntary conformity to rules and law have not yet been spelled out by the practitioners. This may be largely because some probation officers attempt to operate at a level of the overly empathic psychiatrist whom Cantor uses as an analogue, "who spends his time and effort in delivering groceries to his patient's home, preparing the dinner, washing the dishes, and acting as governess to the children."[90] The author conceives the primary function of probation as that of changing the offender's response to authority so that he will not persist in law violations. This means that authority is not only a tool of correctional casework but that it is *the* essential ingredient, means, and measure of probation.[91] What the author has written in relation to the juvenile delinquent appears equally applicable to the adult probationer:[92]

The authoritarian framework of probation may be an advantage as well as a necessity in dealing with the offender. Characteristically he has suffered from an inadequate relationship to authority because of an insufficiency, an incon-

[89] "The Function of Probation," *Nat. Prob. Assoc. Yearbook,* p. 289, 1941.
[90] *Attorney General's Survey,* p. 290.
[91] This does not mean that there are no criminal cases that do not require authoritative treatment. There are some, but many if not most of these do not require probation.
[92] Adapted from Tappan, *Juvenile Delinquency,* 1949, pp. 324–325.

sistency, or an excess of controls from his surrounding environment. His treatment needs relate largely to his attitudes—his psychological responses to reality—rather than to his milieu alone. The necessary changes cannot be wrought in any permanent and effective way by attempting to inspire fear or by constant regulatory supervision. Experience in customary probation methods has shown clearly enough that the common results of the repressive approach are to stimulate greater externalized aggression or an only temporary passive obedience during probation, followed by efforts at more skillful evasion of the law. Movement of the delinquent, if it is to come, must develop mainly from within. It is the task of the officer to provide such help as he can in this process. Probation casework must accept realistically the need for authority, indeed even emphasize it, since it is here that the offender's relation to society has been peculiarly defective.

The probation officer must establish clearly in the mind of the probationer the conditions of probation, i.e., the circumstances under which society, as represented by the court, will permit him his freedom. The effective officer will accept the individual as he finds him; he will accept the individual with kindness and sympathy, with understanding and without reproach, and with a willingness to help. He will attempt to assist the probationer to clarify his experience and his attitudes toward himself and society, and toward the behavior for which he was convicted. Without that moral condemnation which can only produce hostility, the worker must make the offender see that violation of the law entails certain consequences in the way others will look upon him and how he must look upon himself. The alternatives should be seen by the probationer as inevitable aspects of authority and reality with which he must come to grips and between which only he can make the required choices. The offender must be brought to see that he is himself the active element who must choose to conform or defy the realities that confront him. This responsibility represents a voluntaristic element in the probation process comparable with the client's role of self-determination in a private agency setting. Of course, the scope of the offender's planning must be limited by the conditions of probation, if he is to continue to enjoy his freedom, and by his capacity for self-control and self-direction.

The task that has been suggested above for the probation officer is essentially one of social-psychological treatment, to be achieved largely through interviewing and counseling. In some situations the officer may employ suggestion, persuasion, and the presentation of alternative courses. The offender needs clarification of his conduct and of his weaknesses and strengths and some measure of directive guidance in meeting the problems that are crucial in his striving to become a law-abiding individual. Yet the officer's exercise of "leadership" or personal influence to stimulate change in the probationer should not be so excessive or persistent that it creates a permanent crutch on which the probationer must continue to rely. Conceivably there is some merit in the prevalent idea that the officer should constitute an idealized father image with whom the probationer can identify, but he cannot play the surrogate for long and it is dubious in the ordinary case of adult offenders whether he should attempt to do so at all. The probationer must be brought to understand the official limits imposed upon his freedom, to make his own choices, and to accept the consequences. This maturity he cannot achieve if he is an emotional dependent of his probation officer. In some cases, it is clear, the more expert counseling of a psychotherapist is required to produce an adequate orientation to reality. In some this orientation to reality cannot be achieved.

Probation work has typically been concerned more with what the United Nations study describes as "secondary points of departure" in dealing with the offender, that is, with his equipment for social functioning and the elements of his social environment and group relationships, than with the dynamics of his personality.[93] Through strengthening the individual's position, physical, emotional, or economic, on the one side, and mitigating the problems that have confronted him in his milieu, on the other, it may be possible to relieve the strains out of which compensatory, reactive, and situational crimes have developed. Such manipulation may also contribute to change in attitude, of course. Casework services and environmental manipulation consume a large part of the officer's time. Dressler lists the following services that may be provided by referrals of probation officers: finding jobs, home relief, medical care, social security grants, special diets, institutional placements, nursery care, legal aid, educational and vocational guidance, recreation, and other assistance from public or private social agencies.[94] To these should be added psychotherapeutic and religious services. The department itself may be able to provide some of these services directly or to supplement the efforts of another agency. When there is need for specialized help and it is available, it is better that an outside agency perform the task than that it be done inadequately by probation officers whose functions should be differently specialized and whose case loads are too heavy to permit them to undertake the heterogeneous services needed in some cases.

Research reveals that offenders' family situations are very often unhealthy and in some of these, presumably, the domestic circumstances have some direct causal significance to crime. Probation authorities have argued, therefore, that officers should focus their casework on the family rather than on the individual offender and his subjective difficulties. Others, while they have recognized the potentially significant role of the family, have maintained that the task is too large and specialized for probation and that family casework should be performed by family agencies. A major practical difficulty here, however, is the fact that private family agencies often either cannot, because of their own case loads, or will not, as a matter of intake policy, accept offenders. They prefer to work with more cooperative clients. It appears that where complicated problems of family

[93] *Probation and Related Measures*, pp. 248 ff.
[94] Dressler, *op. cit.*, pp. 160–165.

casework are involved referral is desirable if it is possible. In the handling of minor domestic problems or, in more difficult cases, if referral is impossible, it may be desirable for the officer to attempt to modify family relationships where improvement may offer some hope of reducing the provocations to delinquency. Family counseling, like psychotherapy, is a subtle and potentially explosive craft, however, not a diversion for the dilettante. The author has observed pitiful consequences of amateur manipulation by officers who were characterized more by their reformative zeal than by common sense or casework skill.

In their effort to change attitudes and to modify the environment, there is danger that probation officers may become too paternalistic in their relationships with offenders. Probation departments are likely to be concerned primarily with the immediate adjustment of the offender and his avoidance of violations during the probation period, though they are aware that the ultimate objective is compliance with the law beyond that time. "Doing things" for the probationer should be only a very temporary expedient, the major thrust of effort being toward his independence and sense of responsibility. Finally, to reiterate, the objective of probation and its success, like that of other correctional measures, is measured by the avoidance of criminality, not by mere "adjustment" or contentment of the offender.

The Structure of Probation Administration

There is a considerable variation in the organization and administration of probation in the United States. The very general pattern is one of county and municipal administration in which officers are appointed by and responsible to the court to which they are attached. In a minority of jurisdictions there are competitive examinations under city, county, or state civil service commissions for such positions.

State participation in probation takes several forms in different jurisdictions.[95] A minority of states have established a joint probation and parole agency that is responsible for the provision of all the adult probation and parole field services throughout the state. Characteristically the same officers perform both probation and parole supervision. This integrated system is found in Vermont, Rhode Island, Virginia, Washington, Wyoming, Iowa, Nevada, Wisconsin, and the Federal system, for example. A smaller number of jurisdictions, including Minnesota, West Virginia, and Michigan, have both state and local probation services. City or county probation is generally provided in the major cities in these jurisdictions, while the state board provides probation as well as parole services in other areas of the state. In a number of other jurisdictions the state may subsidize local services, as in Virginia, New York, and Connecticut. Elsewhere

[95] See Chute and Bell, *op. cit.,* chap. 11, and *Attorney General's Survey,* vol. 1, pp. 451–453.

the state is empowered through a special probation commission or otherwise to supervise performance, recommend standards and policies, collect statistics, receive reports, and generally work for the improvement of the service. This is the case in New York, Massachusetts, California (under the Youth Authority), and Pennsylvania.

There is no single ideal scheme for the administration of probation services. The pattern of combining probation and parole on a state level developed in small jurisdictions, apparently as a matter of economy for the most part. It has a disadvantage in splitting the allegiance of the officer between his court and the state agency. Commonly the state board cannot give as much attention as is desirable to probation needs in the local communities. This is particularly true in the several jurisdictions where the board is charged with releasing prisoners and thus is more directly concerned with parole. It appears desirable for the state to establish minimum standards and policy, to have powers of investigation, and to subsidize local services. However, except where it is necessary as a matter of economy and where there are relatively few offenders, widely scattered, the combined probation and parole service for the entire state is undesirable, because probation officers must work very closely with the courts whose offenders they serve. The mixed pattern of local and state services is a desirable compromise in a number of jurisdictions where, otherwise, there would not be any local service in many areas of the state.

THE VALUE OF PROBATION IN CORRECTIONS

The utility of probation as a correctional device must be evaluated in terms of what it accomplishes as compared with other correctional methods. This can be measured in an abstract way in the comparative implications of imprisonment and community supervision for the prisoner, his family, and the state and more concretely in the rates of recidivism of probationers as compared with prisoners. Neither of these methods of appraisal is completely satisfactory, as will be seen, but the evidence is sufficient to justify some enthusiasm for probation and to explain its rapid spread, not only in the United States, but in a number of other countries as well.[96]

For the offender probation in contrast with imprisonment means an opportunity to engage in constructive employment, to support himself, and sometimes to improve his economic stability and status. He can make more profitable use of good work habits both during and after probation than can his prisoner counterpart. Either willingly or involuntarily, under support orders, he can maintain his dependents generally and can assume

---

[96] See, in particular, *Probation and Related Measures* and *Practical Results and Financial Aspects of Adult Probation in Selected Countries,* 1954, both studies of the United Nations. The latter was done by Max Grunhut.

some responsibilities in the community. The *Attorney General's Survey* suggests that support of dependents is probably the most common of all conditions imposed on probationers.[97] Often, too, they are required to pay a fine or to make restitution during the probation period, thus permitting a financial accountability that would most often be impossible in the case of imprisonment. Not only does the state profit from such fines as are collected, but it is spared the heavy costs of imprisonment and of support of dependents. The imponderable value of the limited freedom that the offender may enjoy and the correctional utility of requiring him to assume responsibility are patently of greater significance than the material advantages, but the latter cannot be depreciated in the light of the extent of the problem of crime and its treatment. It has been computed that the cost to the state of maintaining an offender in an institution is anywhere from six to ten times as great as that of supervising him in the community, without taking into account such factors as those mentioned above. While the costs of imprisonment and of probation vary widely in the several states in relation to facilities, personnel, structures, and costs of living, even the best probation services are very much less expensive than is the cost of treatment in a poor institution. This has been found to be the case in the United Kingdom and in other countries as well.[98] The economic as well as the correctional significance of the growing use of probation is dramatized by data from California where in 1932 there were 7,520 prisoners and 8,379 probationers;[99] in 1954 there were 14,801 prisoners in institutions operated by the Department of Corrections[100] and 1,999 wards in facilities of the Youth Authority,[101] while there were 40,822 adult offenders and 42,257 juveniles on probation in the state in 1955.[102]

Probation Successes and Failures

Revocation as a measure of probation success has commonly been criticized. It is not an ideal criterion for several reasons. Its most serious fault, perhaps, is that practice varies so greatly in different jurisdictions in the extent to which technical violations and new offenses are discovered and acted upon and in the length of probation periods imposed. Consequently it is possible for a jurisdiction with poor probation service or short probation terms to show a lower rate of revocations than another

[97] *Attorney General's Survey,* p. 234.
[98] Max Grunhut, *Practical Results,* pp. 100–104.
[99] J. R. Moore, *J. Crim. L.,* vol. 23, p. 640, 1932, cited in Grunhut, p. 80.
[100] *Biennial Report,* Department of Corrections, State of California, 1953–1954, p. 67, table 2.
[101] *Biennial Report,* California Youth Authority, 1953–1954, computed from table, p. 45.
[102] *Delinquency and Probation in California,* 1955, p. 110, table 1, and p. 24, table 2.

where supervision is close, the term prolonged, and policy strict. More-over, it may well be maintained that the efficacy of treatment is better tested by the performance of offenders after they have been discharged from supervision. Unfortunately, even fewer data are available on this than on revocation rates. Finally, some authorities believe that the utility of probation should be determined not by the subsequent delinquency of probationers but by their over-all adjustment, by the "effective functioning of the individual in society."[103] The limitations of revocation data withal, it appears that these provide the most significant and relevant information that can be secured for measuring the efficacy of probation. Moreover, there is a somewhat surprising similarity in the findings of such studies as have been made. Some of these, especially as they relate to adult proba-tioners, are summarized below.

The *Attorney General's Survey* provided the most comprehensive sam-ple of offenders that have been studied: 19,256 adult probationers from twenty-five probation departments of sixteen states and the District of Columbia who terminated probation between January of 1933 and De-cember of 1935.[104] Success was judged on the basis of the absence of a record of violations of the law or of conditions. The researchers did not provide comparative statistical rates between jurisdictions, recognizing that such rates may reflect a variety of factors in addition to efficiency of performance. On the total sample, 61 per cent revealed no recorded vio-lations during the period of probation. Eighteen per cent of the cases were new offenses and 21 per cent were violations of conditions.[105] Not all of the violations resulted in revocation, however; revocation was ordered in only 19 per cent (slightly less than half of the total number of cases of violators), 12 per cent for new offenses, and 7 per cent for violation of conditions. This study attempted to determine the relationship of proba-tion failures to six factors: race and nativity, age, marital status and num-ber of dependents, prior recidivism, the nature of the offense committed, and the steadiness of employment. They found that steadiness of employ-ment during the probation period was the most important factor in its bearing on outcome and that a history of previous incarceration was al-most equally important. Probationers under the age of 25 were found to violate probation more frequently than those over 35, particularly by the commission of new crimes.[106] Married persons violated probation less fre-

---

[103] Jay Rumney and Joseph P. Murphy, *Probation and Social Adjustment*, 1952, chap. 1.

[104] See the *Attorney General's Survey*, pp. 335–410.

[105] *Ibid.*, p. 337.

[106] *Ibid.*, p. 341. In Gillin's study of adult probationers in Wisconsin, it was ob-served that, among adults, older offenders did better on probation than younger men and that consistency in occupation and, especially, employment were associated with successful probation adjustment. See J. L. Gillin and R. L. Hill, "Success and Failure of Adult Probationers in Wisconsin," *J. Crim. L.*, vol. 30, pp. 807–829, 1940.

quently than others. Race, nativity, and the nature of the offense appeared in this study to be without special significance.

Data are available from the annual reports of a few jurisdictions on the success rates found to prevail. Federal reports reveal that in 1953 probation was terminated in 9,948 cases and that 1,522 probationers were reported as violators, some 15.3 per cent. The proportion of violators, computed on this basis, has gradually increased from 8.3 per cent in 1943.[107] In California 7,169 probation cases from the superior courts were terminated either normally or by revocation and 2,422 or 33.8 per cent of these were of the latter type.[108] Fewer than 8 per cent of these were for violations of conditions. The New York State Division of Probation reported a total of 16,580 cases terminated in 1951, of which 72.7 per cent were discharged as improved. There were 11.8 per cent committed, 7.9 per cent discharged without improvement, and 7.6 per cent terminated for other reasons.[109] Massachusetts reported unsatisfactory terminations of probation in 26.8 per cent of cases of adult males and in 27.1 per cent of adult females in 1950.[110]

Private research studies have provided fuller information than do the state reports on the success of probation as a correctional measure. They throw some light, in particular, on the later experience of individuals who have been on probation. The most comprehensive of such studies have been made by the Gluecks. Over a period of fifteen years they followed up 1,000 juvenile delinquents who had been remanded to the Judge Baker Foundation Clinic for study.[111] A little over 800 of these delinquents had been placed on probation. The Gluecks concluded that 57.9 per cent had failed.[112] It should be noted, however, that this was a group whose offense history started early, a factor that is highly correlated with failure, and that this was a specially selected clinic group rather than a random sample of juvenile court cases. Moreover, the Gluecks measured failure not merely by subsequent offenses or reported violations but also on the basis of arrests, unreported violations of conditions, and offenses for which arrests might have resulted. The standard was rigorous and the data are not comparable to those of other studies. The Gluecks also reported the results of a fifteen-year follow-up on 500 cases that had been committed to the Massachusetts Reformatory[113] and reported on the subsequent history of those who at some time had been given straight suspended sentence or

[107] *Report of the Judicial Conference of the United States and Annual Report of the Director of the Administrative Office of the United States Courts,* 1953, p. 193, table E 3.
[108] *Delinquency and Probation in California,* 1955, pp. 141, 145, tables 12 and 13.
[109] *Report of the Department of Correction,* 1951 and 1952, New York, p. 114.
[110] Grunhut, *Practical Results,* p. 74.
[111] *Juvenile Delinquents Grown Up,* 1940.
[112] *Ibid.,* pp. 153, 161.
[113] *Criminal Careers in Retrospect,* 1943.

probation. Their finding of a 92.5 per cent failure rate has commonly been quoted as evidence of the ineffectuality of ordinary probation treatment.[114] Probation has sometimes been compared unfavorably with institutional treatment on the basis of their finding that those youths who had been put on probation showed a consistently poorer performance during probation at each of a series of age levels than a group that had been committed to institutions during the period of study. Indeed, the Gluecks concluded: "Apparently, therefore, during the early years of criminality a much better response is to be expected from institutional treatment than from extramural treatment."[115] These data cannot be taken to evaluate probation performance generally, however.[116]

A very different type of follow-up study has recently been conducted on two samples of adult probationers. These researches, while they lack the broad significance of the Glueck investigations into the life histories of young offenders, are more revealing in relation to the posttermination behavior of former probationers. In 1951 Morris Caldwell reported on an analysis of 1,862 Federal probationers in the northern district of Alabama whose cases had been terminated before December of 1942.[117] While 45.2 per cent of these probationers had had prior criminal records, only 18.1 per cent were committed to a correctional institution for violations of probation; 1 per cent absconded and 4 per cent violated probation conditions but were not committed. A sample of 403 of the offenders who had completed probation successfully was selected for follow-up study. During the period of from 5½ years to over 11 years since the terminations of their probation, only sixty-six, or 16.4 per cent, were convicted for another crime. Among these fifty-eight had committed misdemeanors only and eight had committed felonies.

Ralph England made a similar research study of 490 Federal offenders

[114] *Ibid.,* p. 151.

[115] *Ibid.,* p. 154.

[116] The reformatory sample, too, was a young group at the start, with an average age under 15 years at the time of first arrest. Some had been placed on probation before their first institutional commitment, others subsequent to a term in the reformatory, some after spending time in prison. All of this sample, however, had been committed to the reformatory. Hence, cases that had been treated successfully by probation or otherwise were excluded. Those who were sentenced to probation subsequent to an institutional commitment were not good probation material; the data show that they failed both upon release from the institution and on probation. Also, it is very apparent that the prisoner living under conditions of relatively close custody and scrutiny is much less likely to earn bad conduct reports or to commit known violations of the law than the probationer who enjoys the freedom of the community and who has a number of technical conditions of probation that he may be tempted to transgress. These researches, invaluable as they are, should not be used either as a basis of evaluating the effectiveness of probation for offenders generally or as a basis of comparing the success of probation and institutional commitment.

[117] "Preview of a New Type of Probation Study Made in Alabama," *Fed. Prob.,* vol. 15, no. 2, pp. 3–12, June, 1951.

who had been supervised successfully (without revocation) on probation in the eastern district of Pennsylvania and had been discharged before December 31, 1944.[118] In this group 37.6 per cent had been convicted of crimes before the offense for which they survived probation, but only eighty-seven, or 17.7 per cent, were subsequently convicted during the follow-up period of six years or more. Of all offenses committed by the postprobationers, 27 per cent were felonies. England found fourteen personal-social factors significantly correlated with postprobation recidivism: youthfulness, rearing in a broken home, prior criminal record, urban background in disadvantaged areas, and unemployment were among these factors.[119]

One probation study has attempted a much more elaborate inquiry into the effects of supervision than any other to date. Jay Rumney investigated 1,000 probationers who had been placed on probation in 1937 to the Essex County Probation Department in New Jersey.[120] He sought through interviews in 1948 to discover the adjustments of these offenders in their domestic lives, in economic affairs, and to their physical and mental abilities. Rumney deliberately minimized criminality as an index of probation adjustment, observing that some of the subjects were "adjusted" although they had records of subsequent arrest and incarceration and that others were "unadjusted" who were never in difficulty after the initial sentence.[121] This highlights the basic issue, on which the writer has already expressed an opinion, of whether it is sound to consider probation successful as a correctional measure when probationers continue to commit crimes and unsuccessful if they obey the law but are "maladjusted." The further question is raised of whether "adjustment" can be defined in meaningful terms for empirical research in correction. In this instance, at any rate, Rumney employed arbitrary, overlapping, and simplistic criteria of "adjustment," "improvement," and "needs" of the offender.[122]

[118] "A Study of Post-probation Recidivism among Five Hundred Federal Offenders," *Fed. Prob.*, vol. 19, no. 3, pp. 10–16, September, 1955.

[119] *Ibid.*, p. 15.

[120] Rumney and Murphy, *op. cit.*

[121] *Ibid.*, p. 13.

[122] He found 59 per cent of the subjects "improved" and 26 per cent "markedly improved" after the eleven-year interval, while 17 per cent showed "some deterioration" and 8 per cent were "markedly deteriorated." (P. 103.) It appears, however, that the general improvement in economic conditions in 1948, rather than probation, accounted for much of the improvement in this area, in which the greatest amelioration of adjustment had occurred among the offenders, and that aging contributed to the poorer adjustments in the physical area, where there had been general deterioration. Family adjustment improved considerably, but there appears to be no recognition that poor adjustment in 1937 might well reflect the family reaction to the offender's conviction. Among offenders whose crimes were deemed to be motivated by "economic need" the author included individuals who had bought liquor on which tax had not been paid because it was cheaper; this illustrates the level of analysis. (See p. 146, and also the criteria of adjustment listed on pages 87–88.) Rumney

Even if the definitions and criteria employed in this study were meaningful and could be applied elsewhere, the findings could not be compared, for the cases were drawn from six courts of different types, including criminal, domestic relations, juvenile, and police courts, and the data are not developed in relation to the markedly different components of the sample. The personnel and administration of the Essex County Probation Department is far above average. Unfortunately, this study, while it involved the expenditure of a large amount of time and money, tells us very little about the effects of probation practices, good or poor, or about the treatment required to produce change from law violation to law obedience.

Ralph England provides a summary analysis of outcomes observed in fifteen probation and postprobation studies that have been conducted since 1920.[123] Among eleven studies that explored adjustment during the probation period, four found successes in from 80 to 90 per cent of the cases, five in from 70 to 80 per cent, and two in from 60 to 70 per cent. Eleven postprobation investigations included four where the offenders were successful in from 80 to 90 per cent of the cases, four with a range from 70 to 80 per cent of successes, and one each in the class intervals from 60 to 70, 50 to 60, and 40 to 50. It appears from the research that probation is an effective correctional device as measured by revocations and by subsequent convictions.

Probation is not peculiarly an American success pattern. Max Grunhut provides data from England showing that 70 per cent of a large sample of probationers did not commit any further indictable offense during a three-year follow-up period after discharge.[124] Rates were especially high for those over 21 years of age (81.8 per cent), though probation was given most commonly to juveniles under 17, whose recidivism rates were relatively high. Norwegian statistics show an 11.8 per cent failure rate for males over 21 and an 8.2 per cent rate for females of similar age who had been under suspended sentence.[125] Their rates were higher for minors and for cases that received personal supervision. Figures for the Netherlands show a failure rate of 12.7 per cent for cases under suspended sentence with supervision and a rate of 5.4 per cent for those without supervision.[126] Professor Grunhut concludes from comparative international data that the usual success rate in most countries lies between 70 and 80 per cent.[127]

---

found one-half of his "Calculated" (premeditated) criminals and one-fourth of those he classified as "Potentially Disordered" to be "completely adjusted" in all areas. (P. 135.)

[123] "What Is Responsible for Satisfactory Probation and Post-probation Outcome?" *J. Crim. L.,* vol. 47, no. 6, pp. 667–677, March–April, 1957.

[124] *Practical Results,* pp. 13 and 32. See also L. Radzinowicz, *The Results of Probation,* 1959.

[125] *Ibid.,* p. 54.

[126] Grunhut, *Practical Results,* p. 60.

[127] *Ibid.,* p. 82.

The Limitations of Probation Practice and Their Significance

The apparent success of probation in dealing with the offender may appear somewhat surprising in the light of the limitations of probation selection and treatment in practice. The director of the National Probation and Parole Association has suggested that the courts serving approximately one-third of the nation are without any probation service and that probation is seriously handicapped by the limitation of part-time and ex officio officers and case loads up to 200 per officer for another third of the population.[128] It is estimated that there are some 7,000 probation officers in the United States today, including part-time and full-time juvenile court and adult court workers. The Children's Bureau estimates that 15,000 workers are needed for children's courts alone.

Some of the studies referred to above have attempted to evaluate the quality of probation services provided. They evidence a generally superficial level of supervision from the point of view of casework performance. The Essex County study indicated that among those cases that had been sentenced to probation to receive supervision, rather than merely to collect a fine or support, only 10 per cent received any "special service," such as referral to an agency, placement, the obtaining of employment, relief, or other service. No such executive aids were provided the remainder, although an additional 48 per cent were seen by the officer thirty-six or more times, of which at least six were home visits.[129] Kahn in his study of the New York City Children's Court analyzed a group of eighty-nine supervision cases and found that only in two of these cases was "good probation treatment" from the point of view of professional casework standards given and one of these was a brief contact.[130] He believed that fifty-seven were "completely unsatisfactory."

In 1954–1955, a detailed study was made of probation services in California.[131] Work loads were computed on the basis of replies from 457 probation officers representing the sixty counties of that state. The study commission concluded from its investigation that these officers were responsible for a minimum of 248 "supervision units" per officer, a figure derived by equating one presentence investigation to eight supervisory cases where officers combined both functions. This load was more than three times the number of cases that the officers considered reasonable if adequate standards of supervision were to be maintained. Nevertheless, 70 per cent of the offenders completed probation without revocation either for a new offense or for violation of conditions.

[128] Will C. Turnbladh, "Current Status of Probation," in Tappan (ed.), *Contemporary Correction,* p. 394.

[129] Rumney and Murphy, *op. cit.,* p. 210.

[130] Alfred J. Kahn, *A Court for Children, A Study of the New York City Children's Court,* 1953, p. 188.

[131] *Probation in California,* The Special Study Commission on Correctional Facilities and Services, Sacramento, December, 1957, especially pp. 59–71.

Lewis Diana of the University of Pittsburgh, who formerly acted as probation officer in the juvenile court of that city, made a follow-up study in 1950 and 1951 of a group of 280 delinquents who had been placed on probation in 1940 in that court.[132] While the probationers had had an average probation period of 16½ months, each saw his officer only once every three months, only six received more than five home visits during the probation period, and the great majority received only one visit at home. Most of the probationers had only one office interview during the probation period. Only 10 per cent of the cases were handled with a definite plan of treatment and only 14 per cent were treated with "what could liberally be construed as a casework approach." The supervising officers believed that the combination of the social investigation, the court hearing, and the status of probation itself had a deterrent effect on the probationers and most of the officers felt that some of their probationers could have adjusted without probation. In view of the limitations of the service provided, it is interesting to discover that only 20 per cent of the sample were subsequently charged with crimes and only 16 per cent convicted, two-thirds of the offenses involved being misdemeanors. Diana made a Chi-square test of the significance of differences between outcome in cases where casework methods had been employed and in cases where such techniques were not used. He found that "casework does not appear to be associated with outcome of probation as measured by absence of a criminal record." It was his conclusion that many if not most delinquents can adjust through the ordinary processes of maturation and socialization and that the remainder can be aided by sympathetic and understanding relationships. He believes that professional education in a school of social work is not necessary, and may be too inflexible, to achieve the ends of probation.

Diana's "heresy" has been strengthened by Professor England's study, previously referred to.[133] His work in eastern Pennsylvania was completely independent of Diana's but methodologically it was very similar. The results were also strikingly similar, though the cases were adult offenders. He found that the Federal probation officers had had on the average one contact every 2½ months with each probationer. The records of only 24.6 per cent of the 490 individuals in the sample contained either direct or indirect references to specific aids and services that had been rendered to the cases. Such services were primarily referrals or advice; only four out of twenty-five randomly selected cases that had received some sort of special aid revealed an effort at quasitherapeutic counseling. Nevertheless, at the time of follow-up from seven to twelve years after discharge, only eighty-seven (17.7 per cent) of the probationers had again been convicted of a crime. There was not a statistically significant difference in the success-

---

[132] Lewis Diana, "Is Casework in Probation Necessary?" *Focus,* vol. 34, no. 1, pp. 1–8, January, 1955.
[133] See pp. 579–580 above.

failure rates of those who had and those who had not received special aids, even though presumably the former had, on the average, somewhat more serious problems. The researcher was left "with a strong impression that most of the aids and services given were not of a type requiring extensive social work training, but could have been performed by anyone possessing intelligence, tact, and a good knowledge of the institution and agency facilities in his probationers' communities." England suggests that some of those who are placed on probation are very likely "self-correcting" offenders of the sort who, having once committed a crime, would not be likely to do so again, whether or not they were apprehended and sentenced. Others he believes may be dissuaded from persisting criminality merely by the exposure to limited surveillance under suspended sentence.

It appears that the high and rather uniform success rates displayed in the probation data under the varying conditions of probation supervision that exist in different times and places raise real issues on policy and practice in this field. What part of our probation case loads could have done as well merely on a suspended sentence without any supervision? Put differently, how effective with particular cases is the shock of conviction itself, the threat of the revocation of a suspended sentence, and the apparently benign influence of maturation and of socialization that flows in the ordinary community channels? Among those who do require probation, what cases may stay out of future trouble with a minimal supervision that is designed primarily as a deterrent or a goad? What kinds of offenders, if any, require intensive correctional casework counseling, controls, or referral in order to prevent their future violation of the law—and how many of these are there? Selected case studies of ostensibly successful intensive casework practice will not answer these questions. The onus is very largely on the probation experts to inquire more deeply than they have in the past and to develop discriminating criteria for the classification of offenders into categories: those that do not require probation, those who require differing degrees of supervision, and those who require highly professionalized services. Probation experts should also determine what sorts of offenders who are now commonly committed to institutions might be dealt with safely and effectively enough in the community. Finally, unless it appears that perfected skills in generic casework are required to prevent recidivism and that such skills are actually employed to good effect, the authorities cannot well persist in their demand that probation officers should be selected from the graduates of schools of social work. Probation, like our juvenile courts, has been coasting on its humanitarian appeal and on a reputation easily earned. The professional social workers in probation departments should soon accept the challenge to define and justify their skills, methods, objectives, and achievements.

Chapter 20

THE HISTORY OF IMPRISONMENT

The historical evolution and comparative philosophies of criminal punishment provide a complicated but fascinating subject matter for the cultural anthropologist, the historian, the legal philosopher, the sociologist, and the penologist. It is impossible, unfortunately, to pursue in any detail here the subtleties in the development of penal law and practice. However, an understanding of contemporary institutions and policies may be illuminated by a brief, kaleidoscopic view of major influences that have contributed to and that still inhere in our correctional measures. In this chapter the author will survey the development of penal measures over the past two centuries. In particular, the author will trace the growth and refinement of the methods and forms of imprisonment that have come to constitute so important a part of penal treatment. These, together with other social-cultural ingredients, both historical and contemporary, have fermented the brew of contemporary correctional practice. Present-day conflicts and contradictions in penal practice and theory may be traced in large measure to the partially incompatible components that have been drawn from our past. These controversies also reflect the fundamental disparity in the objectives that man must seek and that man has for many centuries sought in the effort to deal with the major social problem of crime.

CLASSICAL PENOLOGY: A REVOLUTION IN THEORY

Toward the close of the eighteenth century fresh ideas developed on the Continent and in England relating to criminal law and punishment. These ideas were a reflection of influences proceeding, in part, from the growth of natural science and the philosophical movements of rationalism and humanitarianism during the Era of Enlightenment. The Deists, Rationalists, and Philosophes of this period directed skepticism and criticism toward the church and the orthodoxies of Christianity. The traditional belief in the free moral agency of man, in his moral responsibility for his conduct, and in retribution through cruel and degrading penalties as the appropriate basis for criminal law came under attack. Proposals were made for fundamental change. Outstanding among the critical and innovative philosophers were Montesquieu, Voltaire, Rousseau, Beccaria, Bentham, Feuerbach, and (in the narrower field of penology) Howard.

Montesquieu (1689–1755), in his *Persian Letters* in 1721 and in the *Spirit of the Laws* in 1748, attacked the abuses of the prevailing criminal law. Voltaire wrote vituperatively against the dominance of theological influences in the law and against the inquisitorial procedures of justice. He was instrumental in securing the freedom of numbers of innocent victims of the courts. The work of Cesare Bonesana, Marchese di Beccaria (1738–1794), exerted a more significant influence upon penology, however. Beccaria was an Italian scholar heavily influenced by the French Rationalists and was the major contributor to the Classical school of penology. His publication in 1764 of the *Essay on Crimes and Punishments* exercised profound influence upon the development of legal and social policy in dealing with the offender that has persisted to the present day. Beccaria held that deterrence was the proper end of punishment. This idea in itself was not especially novel, for his predecessors Hobbes, Spinoza, and Pufendorf, among others, had maintained a similar view. Beccaria, however, stressed the need for humanitarian as well as utilitarian limits upon the penal law; only conduct dangerous to the state should be prohibited and penalties should be no more rigorous than necessary to achieve the deterrent objective. He vigorously assailed the abuses of the age: the arbitrary penalties applied by the judges, the promiscuous use of torture and mutilations, the death penalty, the vile condition of the detention prisons, and other excesses that had derived from ecclesiastical and Roman law sources. He advocated certainty and celerity rather than severity in punishment. Penalties should be uniform and definite, publicly applied to assure their deterrent effect. They should be no more severe than necessary for that purpose. These views laid the foundation for drastic changes in theory and for reform in the criminal law, particularly as exemplified in the French Code of 1791. Beccaria's volume was translated into French and German soon after publication and his ideas spread rapidly in Europe.

The English theorist, Jeremy Bentham (1748–1832), the leader of the British Utilitarians, was greatly stimulated by Beccaria and the exposition of his theory. Bentham is identified with the doctrine of "felicific calculus" by which he proposed that criminal punishments should be devised severe enough but no more harsh than necessary to balance the pleasure that the potential offender might anticipate from a crime. Thus, in theory, he would be deterred from criminal temptation. Bentham, who was trained in the law, wrote extensively on civil and criminal jurisprudence and the prison system, including *Theory of Punishments and Rewards* (London, 1801, 2 vols.) and *Treatises on Civil and Penal Legislation* (Paris, 1802, 3 vols.). His work, some of which was translated into French, had greater influence in France in his day than in England or Germany. In it he developed an architectural plan for a prison, the Panopticon, which has been copied in the later development of prison structures. (See p. 663.)

Paul Johann Anselm von Feuerbach (1775–1833), German jurist and criminal law reformer, was another outstanding contributor to the development of Classical theory and legislation in Europe. He vigorously attacked the theory of the freedom of the will and the retributive foundation of punishment, holding that state sanctions should be civic and temporal rather than moral in origin. They should act as a psychological compulsion upon those inclined to crime in order to protect the state and its citizens from violations of their rights, and penalties should be graded according to the importance of the right violated. Feuerbach stressed the positive law: deterrence would come from the prohibitions and from penalties specifically determined by statute and made known to everyone. This was formulated in three basic maxims that have had a profound influence upon the subsequent development of both civil and Anglo-American law: *nulla poena sine lege, nulla poena sine crimine, nullum crimen sine poena legali.*[1] The doctrine of *nulla poena,* the principle of legality, has come to be conceived as an essential ingredient of justice in the democratic state. Feuerbach assailed the practice of creating crimes by analogy, punishment on suspicion, or in the absence of a positive legal duty, and other arbitrary judicial powers. As in the case of other Classicists, notably Bentham, he found no place for the modification of penalties in accordance with mitigating circumstances or in the subjective state of the offender. The law should be definite, clear, and certain; it should be faithfully adhered to in the administration of justice. These principles found their way into the Bavarian Code of 1813, with some modification, for the latter, like the French Code Pénal, provided a measure of judicial discretion between minimum and maximum fixed by statute, a compromise that was not in accord with pure deterrent theories of the day.

More than to any other person the advancement of penal reform in England and, to a large extent, on the Continent is indebted to John Howard (1726–1791), a "true lover of natural philosophy," an empiricist, and a humanitarian. As sheriff of Bedfordshire and through repeated tours of gaols, not only in England, Scotland, and Ireland, but on the Continent and in Asia Minor as well, he became aware of the evils that beset the gaol system. These evils he publicized in 1777 in *The State of Prisons in England and Wales, with Preliminary Observations, and an Account of Some Foreign Prisons.*[2] Translations in French, German, and

[1] *Lehrbuch des Gemeinen in Deutschland Geltenden Peinlichen Privatrechts,* 1801. Compare the discussion of the *nullum crimen* doctrine in Chapter 1 above. See Jerome Hall, *Principles of Criminal Law,* 1947, for an excellent discussion of the *nulla poena* principle and its derivation.

[2] Max Grunhut in an appraisal of John Howard's work says: "It was Howard who first applied to the field of social distress the empirical method of collecting and comparing personal experience. Prison by prison he described every particular in the

Italian spread the influence of his works. Howard advocated the establishment of a national penitentiary to displace the use of transportation. He believed in secure prison structures but maintained that the quarters of prisoners should be spacious and sanitary; that a program of congregate work in shops, educational training, religious inculcation, segregation, and after-care should be provided; and that prison officers should be carefully selected, trained, and supervised by public authority. He died a victim of the plague while studying institutional conditions in eastern Europe.[3]

Continental legislation and penal practice of the late eighteenth and early nineteenth centuries reflected the revolution that was occurring in social and political philosophy. Rebellion was rooted in theories of liberty, equality, and secularization. It was accompanied by a movement to correct and codify the law and, in the process, to abolish what remained of feudal law and custom.

The harshness of the penal law in France was gradually alleviated. The Declaration of the Rights of Man (August 26, 1789)[4] and a series of decrees of the following year embodied the emergent philosophy. Judicial discretion in sentencing was eliminated, penalties were equalized, and the general confiscation of property was abolished. The Penal Code of 1791 was notable in its provisions for penal sanctions, which included death, labor in chains, reclusion in a penitentiary, confinement without chains, detention, transportation, civic degradation, and the "carcan" or iron collar. The recidivist was to undergo not only the ordinary penalty for his crime but would thereafter be transported. Efforts were to be made to rehabilitate convicted offenders. The French Code of 1795 went further in abolishing life imprisonment, establishing a limit of twenty-four years of

---

same well-ordered way, so that all items are comparable with one another, and the reader might trace every topic through the whole amount of collected materials. The numerous repetitions of his journeys enabled him to follow up the further development of prison conditions. Valuable figures on the English prison population anticipate criminal statistics." *Penal Reform*, 1948, p. 35.

[3] Other authorities who made significant contributions to the amelioration of British criminal law and penal practice were Sir Samuel Romilly (1757–1818), a Whig lawyer, who agitated for reform of the criminal code; his successors Sir James Mackintosh (1765–1832) and Sir Thomas Foxwell (1786–1845); and Sir Robert Peel (1788–1860), who was responsible for the actual drafting of the Prison Act.

[4] The Declaration of Rights together with the subsequent decrees and the Code of 1791 spelled out the principles of Classical penology as well as the equalitarian philosophy of the revolutionary period: "No person shall be punished except by virtue of a law enacted and promulgated previous to the crime and applicable according to its terms. Offenses of the same nature shall be punished by the same kind of penalties, whatever the rank and the station of the offender. Neither the death penalty nor any infamous punishment whatever shall carry with it an imputation upon the offender's family." In 1791 the assembly declared that "penalties should be proportioned to the crimes for which they are inflicted, and . . . they are intended not merely to punish but to reform the culprit." See Von Bar, *A History of Continental Criminal Law*, 1916, pp. 320–324.

labor in chains for the most serious offenders, fixing specifically the duration of imprisonment for every grade of offense, and abolishing the pardoning power. It completed the process of replacing the former arbitrary powers of judges with a firm and inflexible system of penalties. As a consequence of the rigidity of this Code, it was common in the ensuing years for juries to acquit when it seemed that the penalty provided was excessive. This Code underwent radical change, however, only a few years later.

The Penal Code of 1810 reflected the utilitarian-deterrent philosophy of this period and the influence, in particular, of Beccaria, Feuerbach, and Bentham. The Code was concerned neither with reformation nor with moral retribution. Rather, intimidation of potential offenders was to be accomplished by severe punishments, including death and life imprisonment, mutilations, branding, the "carcan" or collar, general confiscation of property, and civil death. On the other hand, the Code introduced the principle of maximum and minimum sentences of imprisonment, permitting some discretion to judicial authorities, and it recognized to a limited extent the principle of extenuating circumstances, thereby ushering in what has sometimes been called neo-Classical penology. These laws, too, underwent extensive modification. During the ensuing fifty years penalties were considerably mitigated and many crimes were reduced to misdemeanors. The goals of reformation for the tractable and of incapacitation for the incorrigible received some special emphasis. Legislation in 1850 was directed to the protection and education of juvenile offenders and in 1875 to the improvement of prisons; regulations were imposed on transportation in 1850 and 1885 (the latter relating to recidivists), and the suspended sentence was introduced in 1891.

Reform movement in Germany and England paralleled that in France. As early as the 1740s Frederick II (the Great), soon after his accession to the Prussian throne, abolished torture completely, restricted the use of the death penalty and of other brutal punishments, and replaced banishment by imprisonment in a fortress or penitentiary. The Austrian Code of Joseph II of 1787, the first criminal code of the Enlightenment, was distinctly innovative in some respects, particularly in its provision for imprisonment as the primary mode of punishment. Crimes by analogy were abandoned and the death penalty was prohibited. Branding and flogging were retained, however, and imprisonment involved the use of close confinement in chains and bread and water diet as a disciplinary measure. The Bavarian Code of 1813, drawn largely, as has been observed, from a draft by Feuerbach, gave the judge the right to fix sentence between a statutory minimum and maximum, and rules were established relating to mitigation and aggravation of penalties. This Code became the model for the legislation of other German states during the ensuing years. It inaugurated the policy of neo-Classical penology in Germany. The Criminal

Code of the Grand Duchy of Hesse in 1842 went further in providing for three varieties of imprisonment: the penitentiary, the reformatory, and the jail. In 1869 a Criminal Code for the North German Confederation was promulgated and soon thereafter was proclaimed as statute for the Empire. It provided among other things a maximum duration of imprisonment, limited the application of capital punishment, established parole of prisoners, and expanded the scope of extenuating circumstances affecting punishment.

Mitigation of the severity of the criminal law of England was delayed beyond the time that reforms were launched in Europe and America in spite of the vigorous reformist efforts that have been noted. Perhaps this is attributable in part to the normally slower pace of change in unwritten or common law. Severe penalties were imposed in England even for petty crimes into the 1830s. With a population of only 15 million people, England had a criminal population of approximately fifty thousand in her prisons, hulks, and penal colonies. Changes came rapidly after 1820, however, particularly in the removal of the death penalty, which had been applicable at the start to some 222 crimes. By the Consolidation Acts of 1861 the death penalty was removed for all but four serious and violent crimes. Tranportation and imprisonment came to take the place of capital and corporal punishment as primary measures of control. As transportation was reduced, imprisonment received a greater and increasing amount of attention. Experiments going on in the American prison system in the early nineteenth century also contributed heavily to the development in theory and practice in England at this time.

FROM BANISHMENT TO IMPRISONMENT

While motivation and method have varied widely in different eras, measures for the elimination of the offender, temporary or permanent, partial or complete, may be found in all periods of human history. One method of partial elimination is imprisonment. Professor Max Grunhut, the notable criminologist at Oxford University, has said that "At all times the law has resorted to the imprisonment of people as a means to enforce its authority."[5] Imprisonment as a means of punitive or correctional treatment of the criminal has come late upon the scene, however, being little more than a century and a half old. Its use may be traced to much earlier forms of social exclusion.

Outlawry or banishment, along with capital punishment, is the most ancient form of criminal sanction still in use today. It may be found not only among primitives but in the practices of relegation, exile, and deportation among the Romans. Under the law of Athens and other Greek cities from the fifth decade B.C. the citizen might be "ostracized" and compelled

[5] Grunhut, *op. cit.*, p. 11.

to leave the city, ordinarily for a period of ten years, though he did not lose his citizenship or property, as did the Roman.[6] There is indication of its use among the early Franks and Danes and in the Middle Ages, if not earlier, it was employed along with confiscation among other Germanic people. The Dutch employed banishment during the sixteenth and seventeenth centuries.

A special form of banishment, associated with a kind of public work, existed in the Roman and Greek practices of condemnation to slavery in the galleys. These were the ancient and medieval ships of the Mediterranean, propelled by oars that were manned by shackled slaves. Servitude or imprisonment in the galleys, commonly for life, was also practiced by the French, at least from 1500, and by the Germans, Spanish, Dutch, and English during the Middle Ages.[7] By the close of the sixteenth century, the galleys were no longer deemed effective warships and were generally replaced by sailing ships, though it is recorded that sentence to the galleys at Rotterdam was used as late as 1630. The galleys were an antecedent of the modern prison, a means of putting men away at hard labor.

Transportation was a more elaborate and for a time highly popular form of banishment; this was a device of conveying criminals to penal colonies either for life or for a term of years that was used most extensively during the period of colonization and settlement. It was an easy means to rid the community of the offender without either depriving him of his life or maintaining him, while taking advantage of his labor. A French Ordinance of 1556 coupled transportation to Corsica with confiscation and civil death.[8] England first authorized transportation for "rogues" in a law of 1597 that made return a capital felony and in 1617 extended its use to felons reprieved from execution "who for strength of bodye or other abilityes shall be thought fitt to be employed in forreine discoveryes or other Services beyond the seas." An act of 1717 specifically authorized transportation to His Majesty's colonies and plantations in America. For the most part offenders were sent as bond servants to colonial planters. According to Barnes, England was sending about two thousand convicts an-

[6] See G. Busolt, *The Constitutional Antiquities of Athens and Sparta*, London, 1895.

[7] George Ives in his volume *A History of Penal Methods* offers this description of life in the galleys: "What sort of life did they actually undergo? Doubtless it varied much under different overseers. We must imagine them chained to their crowded benches, often for six months at a time and perhaps for longer, or penned in prison-like barracks at the seaports. Their heads and their beards were shaved every month, and their garments ranged from non-existence in the African waters, to red caps, coats, shirts, and rough canvas breeches for those enslaved in colder, more decorous latitudes. The rowers were exposed to all weathers, and were fed on hard fare, and frequently much stinted in water-supply. Captives of all ranks were herded and verminous as their shaven heads and paucity of clothing permitted them to be." P. 104.

[8] By an ordinance of 1763 transportation was to French Guiana.

nually to the American colonies by 1775.[9] He suggests that between fifty and one hundred thousand altogether were thus exported.[10] Transportation to the colonies was ended in 1776 with the Revolution.

The interruption of the system of transportation imposed a serious burden upon the gaols of England and led to the use for many years of the notorious prison hulks, former war vessels, that have been described as "unsanitary, ill-ventilated, and full of vermin." Prisoners were sentenced there for a term of years. While some of the able-bodied were permitted to work at dockyard tasks, it appears that a majority were idle, that there "were a good many palpable lunatics" so confined, and that the experience was a cruel and demoralizing one. In his classic *History of Penal Methods,* Ives provided a vivid picture of hulk life and its deficiencies as a penal measure. He said, in part:[11]

Among the criminals, lunatics, feeble-minded, and outcasts of all kinds who were cooped up for periods generally varying between one and seven years (the latter sentence was to be equivalent to fourteen years' transportation; all persons respited after sentence of death were to be specially dealt with by the Home Secretary) were young boys. An old table gives the number upon the hulks at that time, and we find the record of: one child of 2, two of 12, four boys of 14, four of 15, and altogether twenty persons less than 16 years old. About 1824 they appear to have placed the boys on a special ship, the hulk "Euryalus," and there the youngest "villain" was nine years old; some of the boys, the inspector reported, "are so young that they can hardly put on their clothes." Two-thirds of them are described as having been natural or neglected children. The Government had a place for at least a few of the Nation's babies, in convict prisons. For some thirty years after their inception the hulks received a large proportion of the condemned, and were used until 1858, or between eighty and ninety years.

It is reported that there were as many as four thousand British prisoners in the hulks as late as 1828.[12] Undoubtedly in part because of the patent inadequacies of the hulks for dealing with offenders, Britain determined in early 1787 to transport convicts to other parts of the Empire, including Tasmania and Norfolk Island, and to the recently discovered areas in Australia. Unlike the system employed in the American colonies, whereunder some at least of the convicts had kindly masters and an opportunity in time to establish themselves independently, in Australia a majority of the colonists were convicts, directly under the control of the government that had founded the colony for their disposal.[13] From the historical

---

[9] Harry Elmer Barnes, *The Story of Punishment,* 1930, p. 71.

[10] Ive's description of transportation to America leads the reader to believe that these offenders were in a better position than those committed to British gaols of that period. *Op. cit.,* pp. 120–123.

[11] *Ibid.,* p. 126.

[12] Barnes, *op. cit.,* p. 117.

[13] On Australian penal transportation, see John V. Barry, *Alexander Maconochie of Norfolk Island,* 1958, and Chapter 23 of this volume.

accounts it appears that they were sometimes treated with fiendish brutality. A parliamentary committee in 1838 described the experience in New South Wales:[14]

> In New South Wales . . . the community was composed of the very dregs of society—of men proved by experience to be unfit to be at large in any society, and who were sent from the British gaols, and turned loose to mix with one another in the desert, together with a few taskmasters who were to set them to work in the open wilderness, and with the military who were to keep them from revolt.
>
> The consequences of this strange assemblage were vice, immorality, frightful disease, hunger, dreadful mortality among the settlers. The convicts were decimated by pestilence on the voyage, and again decimated by famine on their arrival; and the most hideous cruelty was practiced towards the unfortunate natives.

The English transportation practice was halted in the 1850s as a consequence of opposition both from the Australians and by British penologists. By this time considerable study had been devoted to the establishment of domestic prisons to receive convicted offenders. The transition to imprisonment was made in a relatively few years.

Despite the general recognition of its defects, transportation did not end with its abandonment in Britain. In 1791 France planned a system of life transportation to Madagascar for recidivistic felons, but this enterprise was not effected. In 1854, however, legislation provided for the use of French Guinea as a penal colony. Subsequently Devil's Island and New Caledonia were also established to receive French criminals. They have continued, though under vigorous attack, until recent years. In 1953 the Cayenne Penal Colony at Devil's Island was closed after having received some 70,000 offenders; it is said that scarcely 2,000 ever returned from its fever-ridden swamps. Russia, too, has used the system of transportation, probably more promiscuously than any other country, utilizing penal colonies in Siberia, on islands off the Pacific coast, and in Turkestan. Barnes, writing in 1930, contrasted the "indefensible and uniform barbarism of the old Siberian penal settlements" with "the most advanced and humane innovations in the whole range of contemporary penology," alleged to exist under the Bolshevic regime then prevailing.[15] It appears, however, that with the large-scale use of Siberian camps for political criminals transportation has continued.

The Growth of Imprisonment as a Penal Sanction

The original purpose of imprisonment was detention, a means of assuring that the offender would be accessible for sentence and for the infliction of his penalty. How early this practice became formalized so as to justify the establishment of specific places for detention is unknown, but it

[14] In E. F. Du Cane, *The Punishment and Prevention of Crime*, p. 123.
[15] Barnes, *op. cit.*, p. 91.

is reasonable to believe that once private revenge gave way to public punishments some form of gaol or keep was required in order that the offender might be produced at the proper time. It is not clear, furthermore, at what point in history the detention function was translated into a punitive purpose, though it appears that the task of safekeeping was distorted by administrative practice at an early date. Von Bar observes that in the ancient criminal law of Attica imprisonment as well as capital punishment, banishment, public dishonor, money fines, and branding were employed. Despite the general severity of the laws of Draco during the sixth century B.C. imprisonment was used in Athens "when one had not paid a debt or had been convicted of theft."[16] The prisoner was chained in jail for five days and exposed to the derision of the multitude. Mutilation, flogging, banishment, ostracism, and imprisonment on a ship were more common, however. In Rome the jurist Ulpian wrote in the third century that "Prison ought to be used for detention only, not for punishment." Yet his approval of the use of chains on prisoners suggests that practice differed from principle. During the period of Empire imprisonment of short duration was employed for petty offenses and for the "safekeeping of offenders" to protect the public peace. In the sixth century the Digest of Justinian reaffirmed the principle enunciated by Ulpian, thereby making it law. Thereafter and through the Middle Ages this principle represented the generally accepted legal doctrine in countries of the civil law. Sources on the law of the Middle Ages indicate that imprisonment was used only as a preliminary to trial or punishment, except where an offender might be briefly incarcerated for failure to pay a fine for breach of police regulations.

On the other hand, in the medieval church cells were used not only for monastic study but, under canon law, for the performance of penitence either for life or for a term of years by those who had confessed or been convicted of crime. A papal prison and house of correction was erected in Rome for this purpose in 1704 by Clement XI, and as early as 1677 the Hospice of San Filippo Neri was established as a workhouse in Florence by Filippo Franci. This was constructed with a system of cellular confinement, designed for reformation of offenders, which was a model for later developments in England. A Papal Hospice of Saint Michael was also established in Rome in 1703 as a house of correction for delinquent boys.

While imprisonment (distinguished from the galleys) as a penalty was uncommon under the civil law, it appears that confinement in town gate houses and fortresses, usually for periods of a few months, was sometimes used as a penal sanction at least by the sixteenth century. Instances of this as well as house arrest for men of rank are recorded in

[16] Von Bar, *op. cit.,* p. 6, ftn. 7. Plato expressed the very modern-seeming theory that by imprisonment the offender might be led to a wiser use of his time after regaining his freedom. See *Sophronisterion* (Legg., IX, 908).

Holland.[17] The "Carolina," adopted in 1532 by the German Reichstag for application in the Empire, provided for incarceration for life or for a fixed period as exceptional alternatives to other penalties and for the "punishment or detention of persons who according to plain evidence are to be expected to commit unlawful acts or crimes," until such time as they might give sufficient bail or security to keep the peace. Similarly the French Criminal Ordinance of 1670, while it adhered in general to the doctrine that imprisonment should be used only for detention, made exceptions in allowing imprisonment for life in cases where sentence to death or the galleys was commuted and for reclusion in a *maison de force* in the case of women and children. In 1744 the statute of Frederick II of Prussia substituted imprisonment in a fortress or penitentiary for banishment.

A significant revolution in policy occurred under the Austrian Code of 1787 when Joseph II made imprisonment the characteristic form of criminal sanction and gave emphasis to the reformatory as well as the deterrent ends of punishment. It is reported that prior to the development of national prisons, towers, dungeons, gate houses, cellars, market houses, and gaols were generally used for confinement, places notably inadequate for long-term imprisonment. The development of incarceration as a penalty required the establishment of large structures for containment and of a philosophy and programs for dealing with the inmates.

The formal recognition of imprisonment as a punitive measure appears to have developed earlier in England than on the Continent. While Bracton, writing in the middle of the twelfth century, had affirmed the civil-law doctrine that imprisonment was designed only for detention, the penalty of incarceration was established in 1275 by a statute of Westminster for the crime of rape. Sentences of the Star Chamber in the sixteenth century indicate that imprisonment had come to be clearly recognized as a measure of punishment.

Houses of Correction

The houses of correction or workhouses that developed in England and Europe during the sixteenth and seventeenth centuries constitute a major antecedent of the modern system of imprisonment. They also represent one of the early and sporadic efforts to add a reformative objective to the functions of the penal law. With the end of feudalism, a succession of wars, the growth of commerce, and migration to the towns, poverty and theft became deeply embedded social phenomena in the newly developing urban environment.[18] Traditional methods of punishment—branding, mutilation,

---

[17] See Thorsten Sellin, *Pioneering in Penology*, 1944, p. 8.
[18] Seagle observes that ordinary theft "did not become a public crime and begin to be visited with savage penalties until the later Middle Ages, and then primarily only in the towns where industry and commerce had begun to thrive." *The Quest for Law*, 1941, p. 234.

whipping, the pillory, the galley, and slavery—were proving inadequate to meet the problem and they violated the growing spirit of humanitarianism. Moreover, as has been seen, there had been long precedent for using confinement as a supplementary or alternative penal measure. However, the establishment of the workhouse, or house of correction, was a radical innovation. It reflected the Protestant dogma that hard work was the means to reformation and salvation as well as the humane sentiments of the period.[19]

In 1552 King Edward VI of England established Bridewell, formerly a royal palace in London, as a workhouse for vagabonds, idlers, and rogues. Similar institutions, also called bridewells, were developed throughout the realm in ensuing years for beggars who would not work. There employment on what amounted to a contract system was provided in weaving, spinning, clothmaking, milling, baking, and other productive pursuits, raw materials being provided by tradesmen who later collected the finished products and sold them at market. For a time wages were paid to the inmates for their work. Unfortunately, it was not long before the bridewells deteriorated as a result of the decline in public interest and idealism, the lack of funds for adequate maintenance of the institutions, their indiscriminate use for all manner of men, and the deteriorating circumstances of labor. By the end of the seventeenth century the houses of correction in England had abandoned their reformative purposes. As early as 1597 an Elizabethan statute held that vagrancy and begging were to be dealt with by "payne and punishment" and that more dangerous rogues were to be detained in a bridewell or county gaol until they had been tried, banned, and transported. Minor offenders might be committed to the workhouse as an alternative to idle gaol confinement but the differences between county gaols and bridewells largely disappeared so far as policy was concerned. The latter were used more commonly for punitive imprisonment rather than for detention.

Some years after the development of bridewells in England similar but generally superior institutions, the *tuchthuisen,* were established in the Netherlands to provide work and correction to the growing body of vagrants and petty thieves thrown up by the disorganization of the times.[20]

---

[19] Sellin traces the development of houses of correction and penitentiaries back to the monastic cells of the Middle Ages where ecclesiastical penance and solitary labor provided a pattern for later structure and philosophy in correctional treatment. See "Filippo Franci—A Precursor of Modern Penology," *J. Crim. L.,* vol. 17, pp. 104–112; "Dom Jean Mabillon—A Prison Reformer of the Seventeenth Century," *ibid.,* pp. 581–602; and "The House of Correction for Boys in the Hospice of Saint Michael in Rome," *ibid.,* vol. 20, pp. 533–553.

[20] For an excellent treatise on the early workhouses in Amsterdam and their subsequent influence, see Sellin, *op. cit.* Concerning the prevalence of crime in the early seventeenth century and the common employment of mutilative penalties and whipping, Sellin reports: "In 1617 a woman who was strangled at Amsterdam was found

They were a vast improvement on the merely custodial common gaols that were then used mainly for detention. The first of the new institutions was the Rasphuis, or rasphouse, so called because the rasping of logwood was the major occupation carried on there, that was established in Amsterdam in 1596 in what had been "a commodious convent." This, like other workhouses later instituted, was intended primarily for "sturdy beggars and unruly children," but in practice it soon came to contain a rather heterogeneous population composed not only of young and wayward incorrigibles, runaway apprentices, and old vagrants but also of a wide variety of other offenders who had been unable to pay their court fines or who had been dealt some form of corporal punishment and then remanded to the *tuchthuis* as a supplementary penalty.[21] Most of the inmates were on short, definite sentences of a few days or weeks, but some served terms of years, from which they might earn reductions for good conduct and hard work. The program of the Rasphuis was remarkably experimental for its day. Inmates were classified to a limited extent. Instruction in weaving as well as productive work in weaving and rasping were provided under a contract system, as in England, and those who worked could earn enough not only to pay for their maintenance but to save funds toward the time of discharge. Some educational training, largely rote memory learning, and religious instruction were provided. Both congregate or dormitory rooms (where inmates slept two or three in a bed) and solitary confinement rooms were provided, the latter for more serious offenders and for disciplinary purposes. Disciplinary measures were severe, for they also included whipping, heavy chains, the yoke or collar, and restricted diet.

The Amsterdam *tuchthuis* soon attracted wide and favorable attention as an ostensibly effective and economical innovation to deal with petty offenders. Two other *tuchthuisen* were established in the Netherlands before the turn of the century and in the ensuing years several additional Dutch communities followed the model. During the first quarter of the seventeenth century a *maison de force* was established in Ghent and at Antwerp; a *zuchthaus* in Lübeck, Hamburg, and Bremen; a *tukthus* in Stockholm; and the *Galera de Mujeres* in Madrid. Each of these was in varying degrees an imitation of the regime at the Amsterdam institution; each provided

---

to have been arrested previously twenty-one times—seven times in Amsterdam, three times in Leiden and in Delft, twice in Haarlem, and once in Alkmaar, Middleburg, Dortrecht, Wesop, Enkhuisen, and the Hague. Altogether, she had been exposed on the scaffold eleven times, whipped eight times, branded five times, and her ears cut off. She had been banished for life seven times." *Ibid.*, p. 15, citing cases from a report of 1828.

[21] A private section of the Rasphuis was established in 1603 for young offenders and the Spinhuis was opened in 1597 with accommodations for seventy-eight women. There a regime semilar to that at the Rasphuis was put into operation. The women engaged in spinning, weaving, knitting, and sewing. See Sellin, *op. cit.*, chap. 10.

productive work and custody for minor criminals and vagrants. British travelers, too, were impressed with the institutions in the Netherlands and remarked upon their superiority to the bridewells, though this appears not to have been effective in producing reform in the latter. John Howard, writing in 1789 on the institutions in Europe that he had visited, commented with special favor on the Dutch houses of correction and acknowledged their healthy influence on the development of prison planning.[22] The *Maison de Force* at Ghent, as a derivative of the Rasphuis, has a special significance for the future of penology. In 1775 this institution, originally established in a medieval Flemish castle, was remodeled as a house of correction and prison by Count Hippolyte Vilain XIV. He constructed an octagonal building there with provisions for solitary cells for sleeping but congregate work by day in industrial production. This institution was studied and highly praised by Howard. It had a marked impact on the subsequent development of prisons.

The idealism and imagination displayed in the development of bridewells and the *tuchthuisen* were short lived. Small gaols and lockups sprang up in England and on the continent, many of them housing fewer than ten individuals. The large gaols and houses of correction, in which productive work had been carried on at first, became—with notable exceptions, primarily in the Netherlands—places of idleness and vice, crowded with a melange of inmates in promiscuous association, male and female, young and old, minor and serious offenders, debtors and witnesses, venereally diseased and psychotic, those being detained for trial and others who had been convicted. A very high proportion were imprisoned debtors. Howard noted that in his time three-fifths of gaol inmates were prisoners for debt. Unhygienic conditions and lack of prophylaxes were responsible for serious epidemics of disease, including the "gaol fevers" that from time to time wiped out not only large numbers of prisoners but judges, jurymen, and witnesses as well. Under the vicious fee system, keepers were commonly licensed for sale of liquor and made great profit from their commercial operations of the institutions. It is recorded that there were often episodes of revelry, licentiousness, and debauchery in the gaols and bridewells of the eighteenth century. One of the early evangelical philanthropists in England presented this indictment of the system in 1775: "The shortest and most effectual way of eradicating all the plants of moral rectitude which yet remain among the noxious weeds that grow in that uncultivated soil, the hearts of the common people—is to send them to Bridewell."[23]

---

[22] Sellin observes that "Thus, almost two centuries after the founding of the Amsterdam tuchthuis, that institution and its imitators became the chief inspiration for the greatest prison reformer of all times and his co-workers and brought a late contribution to the development of new penal methods in England and indirectly in the United States." *Ibid.,* p. 107.

[23] Jonas Hanway, quoted in Grunhut, *op. cit.,* p. 30.

The conditions that have been noted reflected primarily two circumstances. One was the lack of any centralized administration and control of the correctional institutions. The other, more fundamental, was the fact that, while imprisonment had come at last and quite rapidly to be adopted as an independent penal sanction, there had not developed any systematic theory of the purposes and methods of imprisonment or of appropriate classification of offender types. The problem of crime at this time was large and growing and the means to deal with it were few. The galleys, transportation, banishment, and corporal and capital penalties were either disused or obviously ineffectual. It is not strange, therefore, that penal institutions soon became merely custodial facilities for an heterogeneous mixture of the poor, of petty offenders, and of serious and recidivistic criminals. A considerable period of time was required in order partially to resolve the resulting problems. Change was stimulated by the reformers of the eighteenth century who studied conditions in the institutions of England and Europe and proposed the remedying of some of the abuses. A most obvious and significant need was some classification of offender types for separate segregation and specialized treatment. To this problem attention was directed then; indeed to the present time a major thrust of prison amelioration has been the specialization of facilities for differentiated classes of offenders. The surprising thing is that, with a lapse of 350 years since the origin of workhouses and many centuries more since gaols were used for detention, there has been so inadequate a development of remedies. The typical county jail of today, as will be seen, displays the same general faults as did the medieval gaols of England and the Continent. Few are as good as were the *tuchthuisen* of the early 1600s. Our major improvements have been in the growth of state and national prisons for the more serious criminals. To this development our attention will now be turned.

The Emergence of Prisons in England

The early seventeenth century was notable for penology, as has been seen, primarily in the establishment of workhouses and in the growth of the use of imprisonment as a penal measure. The eighteenth century lacked innovation as radical as this, but it brought a revulsion against the conditions that had come to prevail in the gaols and workhouses. The invaluable critical work of Bentham, Beccaria, and Howard, among others, in their agitation for reform, made especially important contributions. Their efforts were slow to bear tangible fruit, however. In 1779 a penitentiary act was framed by Eden and Blackstone to establish a prison system of solitary confinement with hard labor and religious instruction. It provided for a threefold classification of offenders with progressive relaxation of custody and work. The plan appears to have been influenced by the structure and regime of the San Michele prison in Rome and the Ghent prison in Belgium, on which Howard had made favorable comment. Philosophically, however, the plan reflected the return to a heavy emphasis on deterrence rather than reformation, and it rested on a rigid system of separation. The penitentiary act was not implemented because of the return to transportation when Australian colonies were opened.[24]

Some limited reform was carried forward in the British county institutions, notably in the model Norfolk Prison at Wymondham, established by Sir Thomas Beevor around 1784, where some classification of offenders was inaugurated and where a fine workshop was provided for congregate labor during the day but with separate cells for confinement at night. In a number of reformed gaols of this period solitary confinement was established while in others handicrafts and industrial work were introduced, with prisoners working in association. In 1821 the national penitentiary, Millbank, was opened to receive convicts whom the courts chose not to transport nor send to the hulks. It was fashioned on an architectural scheme similar to that of the *Maison de Force* at Ghent. At Millbank the prisoners spent one-half of their terms in solitary, the latter half in associated labor. Belief in the greater success of the congregate system of work was attested by Sir Robert Peel's Prison Act of 1832, which consolidated the laws relating to imprisonment and provided for classification of prisoners and for work together in productive enterprise. A few years later, in 1835, provision was made for the appointment of prison inspectors; this was a further step toward the establishment of a national prison administration.

It appeared at this time that the policy of solitary segregation for ordinary offenders was in abeyance and that the advantages of association and of congregate production had won general recognition. An important transition occurred in British and European penal history, however, dating from the 1840s, in the development of cellular prisons for the separate confinement of prisoners. This represented a reversion to the policy of the act of 1779 and a rejection of fundamental phases of Howard's policy recommendations. It expressed in part the growing emphasis upon deterrence of criminality by the avoidance both of contaminating association and of all "indulgences" to prisoners and, more especially, the favorable reaction of prison authorities and theorists to the Pennsylvania separate system, which had recently been developed at the Western and Eastern Penitentiaries in that state. The famous prison at Pentonville, established in 1842, followed this design of separate imprisonment cells. In 1865 the Prison Act in England congealed the policy by providing, in accordance

---

[24] In 1794 Parliament adopted Bentham's plan for a circular Panopticon prison where all inmates would be subject to observation from the inspector's post at the center. This law, too, failed of implementation, however, and the Panopticon model was not followed until the establishment of the Western Penitentiary in Pennsylvania a generation later.

with the report of a committee of the House of Lords (1863), that every prison should follow the cellular, separate system. At about the same time a similar policy was manifested in the construction of the Mecklenburg prison in Germany (1839) and in Belgium where similar prisons were established in Tongres (1844) and Louvain (1860). Tuscany and the Scandinavian countries also erected prisons of this type.

In 1877 the county gaols in England, subsequently called local prisons, were transferred to the control of a board of prison commissioners, acting under the secretary of state. They followed the policy that had been launched in 1865 of separate confinement and of punitive and unproductive hard labor. It was not until 1895 that the Gladstone Committee found the system to be a failure and recommended for the future that deterrence and reformation should be made equal, compatible objectives through a more humanized regime of training in the prisons.[25] This policy was reiterated and strengthened in the Criminal Justice Act of 1948, wherein the rules of training were introduced with this statement: "The purposes of training and treatment of convicted prisoners shall be to establish in them the will to lead a good and useful life on discharge, and to fit them to do so." Out of this policy has developed the varied and detailed system of classification of prisoners and of training and productive work in common that characterizes the prison system in England today. The cellular system of construction that is found there and on the continent is still reminiscent of the early Pennsylvania prisons, but work, training programs, and leisure in association with others during the day have become the rule abroad as in the states.

PRISON SYSTEMS IN THE UNITED STATES

Pennsylvania Establishes a Prison Pattern: The Separate System

The development of large prisons to serve a wide area (state, central, or regional) is an American achievement, a result on the one hand of increasing criminality and on the other of the decline in the employment of traditional measures of punishment. In the nineteenth century domestic incarceration came to replace other methods of banishment or segregation and corporal penalties. This initiated a movement toward mass imprisonment of offenders that soon became world-wide, one that has been largely shaped in structure and method by developments in Philadelphia and New York during the early 1800s. The results of this innovation have been vigorously denounced by many humanitarian penologists, even from the early days. The caging of men is a costly expedient for social protection. From the point of view of ethical evaluation, however, it must be measured, in its

[25] See *Prisons and Borstals, England and Wales,* 1950, for the history of the development of English prisons and for an analysis of the programs employed.

beginnings at least, against the brutalities and the indifference to human life that had been characteristic in the past. Contemporary condemnation of our prisons and of our lack of ingenuity in devising more effective correctional measures must be appraised in relation to the penological changes that have occurred during the past century and the persisting increase in the volume and seriousness of crime. The truth is that man has not yet discovered effective devices to deal either with dangerous or repetitive offenders, though our measures have become, in general, somewhat more specialized, ameliorative, and humane. It is small consolation to the impatient penologist that experts in other areas have paralleled our ineffectuality in dealing with those major social problems in which personality deviation, physical morbidity, or social control are involved. We do even less for those who are advanced in mental disorders, narcotic and alcoholic addictions, and deteriorative diseases.

British precedent set the pattern for colonial practice in dealing with the offender. Cruelty of punishments, associated to a large extent with religious nonconformity and violation of religious mores, were as common here as they had been in the country from which the settlers had sought refuge for "freedom of worship."[26] Capital and corporal punishments were the vogue, and the latter displayed a versatility cultivated by long experience and ingenious experiment in England and on the Continent. Some run back to ancient Mosaic Law. They included the pillory,[27] stocks,[28] the whipping post, the ducking stool,[29] the bridle or gag, mutilation, branding, and

[26] Herbert A. Falk in his volume on corporal punishment has described the atmosphere in which children grew up in Puritan New England: "This repressive attitude towards life, this insistence on conformity to a moral and ethical code based on purely religious sanction, was naturally reflected in the colonial schools and in the discipline of children, both in and out of school. The child found himself living in a funereal atmosphere which became more austere with the growth of the child's perceptive faculties. Joyousness and laughter were suppressed. The Lord's Day dared not be profaned by so much as a whistle. Jonathan Edwards called children 'young vipers and infinitely more hateful than vipers' to God. Boys particularly were considered children of wrath; the Devil must be beaten out of them. The early laws and ordinances provided that 'Magistrates may punish disorderly children or Servants on complaint, by Whipping or otherwise, as they see cause, and bind them over to the next County-Court.' " *Corporal Punishment,* Teachers College, Columbia University, 1941, p. 42.

[27] Falk points out that sentence to the pillory "was a public ceremonial and was usually accompanied by the infliction of additional punishment. The ears of the victim were frequently nailed to the pillory and were either slit or cut off entirely to secure the prisoner's release, unless he was permitted to effect his own release by the simple process of forcefully tearing them off the nails which fastened them to the pillory." *Ibid.,* p. 25.

[28] In the stocks, the victim's feet and, in some cases, his hands were fastened in a frame; in the pillory his head and hands were fastened.

[29] The ducking stool was used particularly for women slanderers and scolds. Ducking apparently was not used in New England, though it was used in the "cavalier colonies" of Virginia and the Carolinas.

chains or shackles.[30] Such penalties persisted throughout the colonial period but were substantially reduced as a phase of emancipation and growing idealism at the time of the Declaration of Independence and the establishment of state constitutions. The revulsion against "cruel and unusual" punishments was clear and specific, though similar barbarous penalties continued to be commonplace in prisons until well into the nineteenth century and have not yet been abandoned in some states.[31] Barnes describes the use of brutal floggings, tying up by the hands, strapping to benches or planks, sweat boxes, and cold baths.[32] Thumb screws, gags, the iron yoke, and chains have also been used in various prisons. The dark, stripped cell (illumination and ventilation have become more common in recent years) with limited diet has been the most prevalent form of severe disciplinary measure in the history of American prisons.

The first vigorous agitation for the abolition of corporal punishments was stirred by the Quakers during the late eighteenth century in Pennsylvania and West Jersey and it was there that gaol reform had its start. The Quakers, along with the Anabaptists and other dissident sects, had experienced the full fury of puritanical castigation in New England as well as in the homeland. The initiative must be attributed in large measure to the stanch Quaker William Penn, himself a former prisoner for nine months in the Tower of London and for a time both at Newgate and in Cork. Penn obtained the charter of a vast tract of land known as Pennsylvania in 1681 in payment of a debt owed to his father. In the following year he went there to the new city that he named Philadelphia and established a government based on principles of broad republicanism and religious liberty. At a time when 200 crimes were punishable capitally in England he abandoned the death penalty for all offenses but murder. Corporal punishment too was abolished in 1682–1683, having previously been done away with in West Jersey in 1681. This was the first occasion when incarceration was made the standard sanction for serious crimes. Facilities were required also for vagrants, debtors, and idle persons. Penn and the Quakers were thoroughly familiar with the bridewells that had been established at home more than a century before and, some of them at least, with the superior *tuchthuisen* of the Netherlands. In time they established workhouses inspired by these models.

The first jail in Philadelphia was a small "box-like room" or cage "seven feet long by five feet broad" that was erected on High Street in

[30] For a portrayal of some of the penalties commonly used in the past, see in particular William Andrews, *Old-time Punishments,* 1890, and Alice M. Earle, *Curious Punishments of Bygone Days,* 1896.

[31] Whipping was still used in Kentucky until 1873, and Virginia employed it as a penalty in certain cases at least until 1875; it is still used in Delaware as was observed in Chapter 15. See Robert G. Caldwell, *Red Hannah, Delaware's Whipping Post,* 1947.

[32] Barnes, *op. cit.,* pp. 150–151.

1682 or 1683 to replace the use of a fort for purposes of detention.[33] An overflow soon required the employment of an additional house and a larger High Street Jail was erected in 1695. This too proved quite inadequate but it was not until 1718 that a law was enacted to permit the erection on High Street of a workhouse for criminals and an adjacent jail primarily for debtors, detainees, and runaway apprentices. At this juncture there occurred a serious reversion in early Pennsylvania penology. In the year that the new High Street Jail was planned, William Penn died and Queen Anne reinstituted the harsh English penal provisions in the colony. Whipping, mutilation, and branding were reintroduced and the death penalty was imposed for thirteen crimes as well as for second-felony offenders generally, with the exception of thieves. The latter were numerous, however. The city grew and so did its criminal population. Corrupt jailers were employed. It was not long, therefore, before the same deplorable conditions developed in the new institution that existed in the bridewells: overcrowding and promiscuous association in idleness of unsegregated offenders of all types and accused persons. One who had spent two years there wrote that the prisoners were "crowded in many of the Rooms being about 100 persons in all Men & Women, who live in a very dirty manner & some of them seem to be much abandoned to almost every vice . . . this place is such a sink of wickedness that it can scarcely be expected any tender feelings can remain long with them, so that those who are desirous of reforming the remaining part of their lives are truly much to be pitied."[34]

In 1776 a new prison and workhouse of considerably larger dimension (200 feet by 400 feet) was opened on Walnut Street to receive prisoners from the High Street Jail; being requisitioned by Congress in that year for enemies and traitors, however, it was not put to continuing use as a local institution until 1784. In the meantime the first state constitution, seeking

---

[33] For an excellent brief analysis of the development of the early penal facilities in Philadelphia, see Thorsten Sellin, "Philadelphia Prisons of the Eighteenth Century," *Trans. Am. Phil. Soc.,* vol. 43, part 1, pp. 326–330, 1953. See also Barnes, *The Evolution of Penology in Pennsylvania,* 1927; Negley K. Teeters, *They Were in Prison,* 1937; Rex A. Skidmore, "Penological Pioneering in the Walnut Street Jail, 1789–1799," *J. Crim. L.,* vol. 39, pp. 167–180, July–August, 1948.

[34] Sellin, *op. cit.,* p. 327. Robert Vaux's description is somewhat more picturesque: "In one common herd were kept by day and night prisoners of all ages, colors and sexes. No separation was made of the most flagrant offenders and convicts, from the prisoner who might, perhaps, be falsely suspected of some trifling misdemeanor; none of the old and hardened culprits from the youthful, trembling novice in crime; none even of the fraudulent swindler from the unfortunate and possibly the most estimable debtor . . . and intermingled with all these were to be found the disgusting objects of popular contempt, besmeared with filth from the pillory—the unhappy victim of the lash, streaming with blood from the whipping-post—the half-naked vagrant—the loathsome drunkard—the sick, suffering from various bodily pains, and too often the unannealed malefactor whose previous hours of probation had been numbered by his earthly judge." Quoted in Margaret Wilson, *The Crime of Punishment,* Harcourt, Brace, 1931, pp. 197–198.

to deter the enlarging population of criminals, directed a reform of the penal law to replace the sanguinary penalties by a policy of imprisonment under long sentences at hard labor. When implementing legislation was ultimately enacted in 1786 it provided imprisonment and public works for crimes that had been subject to corporal and capital penalties. The result, though undoubtedly an improvement in penal policy, left much to be desired. The prisoners lacked proper guard and control in their work on the public thoroughfares and the jail, which was a "desirable place for the more wicked and polluted of both sexes," was marked by "scenes of debauchery" and license. Liquor was sold freely in the main corridor. Prostitutes, it is alleged, upon release would confess judgment to return there for entertainment and profit.

Reforms in Philadelphia were largely instigated by the efforts of the Philadelphia Society for Alleviating the Miseries of Public Prisons,[35] an organization founded in 1787, whose membership included Benjamin Franklin, Benjamin Rush, William Bradford, and William Lownes, among other prominent Quakers and members of the American Philosophical Society. These men were heavily influenced by the critiques and policies of John Howard and by the philosophy of Bentham, Beccaria, Romilly, and others.[36] The year following its organization the society recommended to the legislature a system of solitary confinement and hard labor in the prison as a means of reformation and public profit, educing European experience as proof of the virtue of such a regime. The activity of the organization was effective in producing legislation in 1790, under which debtors and witnesses were transferred to a workhouse that had been opened a few years before, and in securing a reorganization of the prison. Misdemeanants were confined in the main building in twenty congregate rooms of the prison, with appropriate separation of the sexes and classes of offenders. A separate cell house of twenty-four cells, the "penitentiary house" was constructed to receive the more hardened criminals. There they were to work

[35] In 1776 a predecessor to this Society had been established, the Philadelphia Society for Assisting Distressed Prisoners, which was a short-lived association because the British took over the city and the jail a few months later. The Constitution of the Philadelphia Society for Alleviating the Miseries of Public Prisons reflects the humanitarian and reformist goals of that group.

[36] Margaret Wilson makes the interesting point that by the time of the experimental efforts in the United States Howard had already observed in operation somewhere in Europe nearly every penal measure that had been tried from his time to our own: "He had described methods of sanitation, medical service, education, segregation of lunatics, classification of offenders, indeterminate sentences, parole pardons, forced paid labor, forced labor unpaid, 'state use industries,' intermittent imprisonment, solitary confinement, silent association, torture, third degree, religious teaching, the use of fines, the care of prisoners' families. . . . The essential problems involved were unsolved, in spite of many experiments, in that day, and they remain unsolved today. For a hundred and fifty years states have been trying to rationalize this method of punishment. They have not succeeded." Wilson, op. cit., pp. 214–215.

in solitary confinement at wages by which they might not only defray the cost of their maintenance but save in an account toward their needs upon release. At this time the courts of all counties were permitted at their discretion to commit to the Walnut Street institution, so that it became the first state prison in Pennsylvania.

Capital punishment for all crimes but murder was terminated by an act of 1794 and it was required that all other felons should be kept in solitary confinement for a part of their terms. This was in accord with the theories of the early reformers, as has been seen, but it appears from the prison dockets that the judges were little inclined to the use of the solitary cells and would sentence generally to ordinary imprisonment. Hence, it was not until the establishment of the Eastern Penitentiary several years later that such a system was given a real trial. During the remainder of the 1890s the Walnut Street Prison, with its provision of separate cells as well as congregate confinement, gained an excellent reputation. Authorities visited there both from the states and abroad, returning to praise its design and program. Under the administration of Caleb Lownes, who was keeper until 1800, it was a model institution. The prisoners received high wages under a profitable contract system. Discipline was effective. Educational, handicraft, and religious instruction were provided. The rudiments of a cellular system, which was to have such significant impact upon world penology, had been established. By 1800, however, the prison had begun to deteriorate as a result of overcrowding. Industrial activity became impossible; discipline degenerated; riots became common. The institution was abandoned in 1835 after other prisons had been opened in Pennsylvania. In the meantime, however, it had become the prototype for prisons established at Newgate in New York City (1796); Charlestown, Massachusetts (1804); Baltimore, Maryland (1804); and Windsor, Vermont (1809); in each of these prisons, however, the pattern of congregate rooms rather than solitary cells was copied. Several states during these years, including Kentucky, Ohio, New Hampshire, and Virginia, established prisons of varied architectural schemes, while others, especially those south of Virginia, persisted in the use of county jails and corporal punishments. Connecticut had a prison of sorts as early as 1773, which was carved out of an abandoned copper mine.[37]

[37] Wilson describes this structure: "It was entered by a ladder down a perpendicular shaft fifty feet deep, at the bottom of which a stairway led down thirty or forty feet more. 'The lowest depth reached is three hundred feet.' Except for the light from two air shafts, it was in Cimmerian darkness. 'The galleries are cut through the solid rock, and are low and narrow, except in the case of one chamber. Their floors are covered with a soft adhesive slime, and in some places with water, which drips unceasingly from the roof, and the intense darkness and the noxious gasses which prevail make their passage difficult, though not impossible.'" Wilson, op. cit., p. 231, quoting from D. F. Lewis, The Development of American Prisons and Prison Customs, 1776–1845, 1922.

The defects that developed early at the Walnut Street institution, together with its desperate overcrowding, led Pennsylvania to develop two new prisons before Walnut Street was closed; the new prisons were the Eastern and Western Penitentiaries, the first of which was to leave its mark throughout the world. The famous Eastern Penitentiary, begun in 1829 at Cherry Hill in Philadelphia, was designed by the English architect Haviland on a plan adapted in part both from the prison at Ghent and from the papal prison in Rome.[38] Each of these prisons had been publicized by John Howard as models for English county gaols. The Eastern Penitentiary reflected the castle architecture of the Middle Ages and presaged the bastille-like structures that were to follow. Its construction cost was $750,000, a remarkable sum to build a prison at that time. Here was inaugurated the solitary or separate system under which, in accordance with the theory of the Pennsylvania reformers, the prisoner's penitence and remorse were to be induced by his complete lack of social communication in his solitary confinement, except for rare visits by "moral instructors." There were 400 large outside solitary cells in seven cell blocks emanating from a central rotunda, each cell having a small individual exercise yard. Massive walls surrounded the institution and divided its parts so as to eliminate all contact and to make escape impossible. Margaret Wilson describes the abominable simplicity of the scheme:[39]

He was given a hot bath, and a prison uniform. Then his eyes were bandaged, and he was led blindfolded into the rotunda, where, still not seeing, he heard the rules of the house explained by the superintendent. And still blindfolded, he was led to his living grave. The bandage was taken from his eyes. He saw a cell less than twelve feet long, less than eight feet wide, and if he was to live on the ground floor, he saw a little courtyard, the same size, highly walled, opening out of it, in which he sometimes might exercise. In that cell, and that courtyard, he stayed, without any change, for three, ten, twenty years or for life. He saw only the guard who brought his food to him, but who was forbidden to speak to him. He got no letters, saw none of his family. He was cut off from the world. When the cholera raged in Philadelphia in 1843, it was months before the prisoners got a hint that an epidemic had visited the city. After the slave had been three days in his cell, he was allowed to work, if he wished, and the fact that nearly all prisoners asked for something to do proved to the inspectors that reform was beginning. If they did not choose to work they might commune with their corrupt hearts in a perfectly dark and solitary punishment cell. Although reports say that there were never many mutinies in this prison, and that most of the wretches were of a subdued demeanor, yet there were terrible punishments, gags and strait-jackets and the like.

Madness from the solitude and death from the brutality of punishments were apparently rather common. The system was easy to operate, however,

---

[38] See illustration of the Eastern Penitentiary, p. 632.
[39] Wilson, *op. cit.*, pp. 219–220. (Reprinted by permission.)

and its penitential or, more accurately, subservient atmosphere commended it not only to the philosophers of Philadelphia but to the travelers from abroad. Gustave Auguste de Beaumont and Alexis de Tocqueville[40] came from France in 1831 to study the workings of the new democracy generally and, in particular, the penitentiary system. Other authorities followed from England, Canada, France, Prussia, and other countries. They eulogized the Pennsylvania system. It appears that de Beaumont and de Tocqueville had some preference for the Auburn system in New York but others who followed from France were stronger advocates of the system they saw in Philadelphia. The first international prison congress at Frankfort on Main in 1846 gave its approval to the Pennsylvania scheme. Consequently England at its Pentonville Prison in 1842 and several European countries established adaptations of the separate system in their new penitentiary construction during these years, providing no workshops but solitary labor and feeding in the cells. Some of these prisons on the Continent appear much the same today as they did a century ago.[41] The English penitentiaries were saved from a rigid solitary policy, it has been said, by the development of transportation to Australia in the 1830s. The solitary cells were used primarily as a punitive prelude to exile and later, under the grading system, as an introduction to congregate labor.

The separate system was more successful in export than on the domestic market, where it had few direct imitators. Pennsylvania followed its own precedent in the Western Penitentiary at Pittsburgh. This institution had originally been designed in 1818 on the plan of Bentham's Panopticon to provide solitary confinement without employment. It was reconstructed in 1829 with outside solitary cells like those at Cherry Hill and provision was made for labor in the cells.[42] New Jersey too followed the Pennsylvania scheme, launching the Trenton Prison in 1833 with outside cells but without the individual exercise yards. Some other states, in-

[40] See G. de Beaumont and A. de Tocqueville, *On the Penitentiary System in the United States and Its Application in France,* translated by Francis Lieber, Philadelphia, 1833.

[41] The governor of the Central Prison at Louvain wrote the following in 1921, indicating the degree to which the Pennsylvania system had calcified on the Continent: "The Prison Conference of 1900 at Brussels may be said to have set the Crown on the head of the Cellular System; a unanimous *satisfecit* was pronounced upon the system as it was carried out in Belgium; France, Prussia, Spain, Italy and many other nations had successively adopted, more or less completely, the same principle which the United States had revived from Bentham and Pope Clement XI. The credit of this principle had never ceased to grow, at least on this side of the water, right down to the declaration of war (1914)." From the *Revue de Droit Pénal et de Criminologie,* 1921, quoted in Wilson, *op. cit.,* p. 241.

[42] The inspectors of the Western Penitentiary in their Annual Report for 1854 expressed their full satisfaction with the operation of the solitary system, but a few years later they were convinced of its evil effects. See Barnes, *op. cit.,* pp. 130–131, 169, quoting reports of the prison inspectors.

cluding Maryland, Massachusetts, Maine, Virginia, and Rhode Island, also adopted the solitary system temporarily, but each abandoned it after a few years. To give Philadelphia its due, however, it should be recognized that the innovations developed elsewhere borrowed heavily from the philosophy and in considerable part from the cellular construction of the Eastern Penitentiary and the Walnut Street Prison before it.

The Auburn Silent System

While experiments, generated in part by necessity and expedience, were going on in Pennsylvania, other states too were driven to prison development and reorganization to meet the common problems of a growing penal population. The Newgate Prison in Greenwich Village, New York City, though it soon proved inadequate and corruptive, was copied at Auburn Prison in 1816 with congregate confinement. However, the influences emanating from the Philadelphia Society, the Walnut Street Prison, and developments in Europe led prison reformers in New York to advocate the separate system and this was introduced at Auburn by the addition of a cellular construction. Here, unlike Cherry Hill, however, diminutive inside cells (7 by 3½) were built and there was no exercise yard. The effect upon the idle and solitary prisoners was appalling. It was out of this situation that there developed the compromise known subsequently as the Auburn or "silent" system. The prison authorities there, Captain Elam Lynds and his deputy, John Cary, together with Gershom Powers of the Board of Inspectors developed a plan of employment in congregate shops during the day under a rigid rule of silence at all times and with solitary confinement only at night. A canny manufacturer in the city of Auburn soon secured a profitable contract to operate a factory within the prison to employ the convicts at low wages and, in a few years, Auburn became an efficient industrial prison.[43] Cary inaugurated a system of marching in military order by lock-step,[44] eyes always upon one's work in the shop and on the guard in march, with flogging for violation of the rules. The congregate production in silence and fear was highly productive in contrast with the limited output possible under the handicrafts of the Pennsylvania system. This fact, together with the lower cost of construction of inside cell blocks, may well account for the rapid development in the popularity of the Auburn system.[45] In 1825 a second and larger prison of similar

[43] Originally at Auburn prisoners were classified into three grades. The most hardened offenders were held in their cells without work continuously; the second class, deemed less incorrigible, spent part of their time in labor as a recreation; the most corrigible were permitted to work full time together during the day under the silent rule. The latter method was extended to all prisoners by 1823.

[44] The lock-step was retained at Sing Sing until 1900.

[45] Reports on the Auburn system were as uncritically enthusiastic as those on the Pennsylvania system. For a eulogy of the Auburn ideal written by Louis Dwight, see Barnes, *op. cit.*, pp. 136–137.

design was begun at Sing Sing with the labor of Auburn prisoners. The new institution was put under the administration of the harshest disciplinarian of its history, Warden Lynds, who had built it. Like Auburn, Sing Sing was not only self-supporting but profitable. As will be noted below, other states soon followed the pattern.

The spirit of the Auburn system as it developed in New York and other jurisdictions owes much to other influences beside the expedience and fortuity out of which its structure developed. It was deeply impressed with the stamp of Louis Dwight, a puritanical reformer of Boston, the first agent of the American Bible Society, and the founder of the Boston Prison Discipline Society. Under his leadership the society sought to promote prison programs designed to redeem sinners through religion and strict discipline. Dwight became the first outstanding figure in penal reform on a national scale and the propaganda of his society was largely responsible, together with the patent advantages of profitable prisons under the silent system of industrial production, for the establishment on the Auburn pattern of a series of correctional institutions. Connecticut erected such a prison at Wethersfield in 1825, administered under the able leadership of the famous warden Moses Pilsbury (previously of the New Hampshire Prison) and later of his son, Amos. This prison was considerably superior to that at Auburn. It has been described as the best penal institution in the country over a period of twenty years. It was there that the first prison honor system was established, trusties being allowed to go outside the walls.

Following the successful examples of New York and Connecticut, Massachusetts founded a silent system at Charleston in 1826. The regime there was a great improvement over that in New York. Within a generation a program was developed that included the teaching of illiterates, religious education, a Sunday school and church service, the first prison orchestra, the first prison library, the wearing of ordinary street clothes on Sunday (in place of the penal red and blue garb of the time), a debating and a mutual improvement society, gardens for individual prisoners, and a counseling service for discharged prisoners. In 1864 Massachusetts allowed her prisoners to assemble on a holiday and to engage in recreation.

By 1835 eight additional state prisons had followed the Auburn model, and several of these contributed further innovations to the development of the early prisons. The Baltimore prison in 1829 established the first prison school for all inmates. Commutation for good behavior was introduced at Nashville, Tennessee, in 1833. Windsor, Vermont, introduced free tobacco for the well-behaved and the privilege of correspondence and visits. The silent system was also employed at the new institutions at Washington, D.C.; Richmond, Virginia; and Frankfort, Kentucky. The last two of these and Baltimore used outside rather than inside cells, but in other respects they followed the Auburn system. Further impetus was given to the silent plan after the establishment of the Prison Society of New York in 1845 when it joined the Boston society in support of the Auburn system and in opposition to the Pennsylvania plan.

The controversy between the Auburn and the Pennsylvania systems died out after 1860. Both plans had developed and changed considerably by that time and the inadequacy of each as a means of deterrence and reform had come to be recognized. Isolation has been abandoned in the institutions that followed the Eastern Penitentiary scheme. The strict rule of silence has gradually given way to a relative freedom of association and intercourse. A common cafeteria mess hall, sometimes divided into two or three units, has replaced cell feeding, though the rule of silence is still applied at meals in some prisons to discourage rioting. The quality and variety of food served has also improved greatly, especially where farms and canneries are operated at the institution. Prison architecture has improved considerably with the construction of larger cells and the provision for adequate light, ventilation, and plumbing in each cell. Also, with the development of treatment and guidance programs, space is allotted for the "professional staff," for classrooms, recreation, religious services, interviewing, and counseling. The experimental programs developed at certain institutions, referred to above, have become quite general in prisons throughout the country. Correspondence, visitation, diversified recreation, religion, education, casework guidance, and other privileges and services have come to be normal phases of program. Disciplinary practices have also changed, though more slowly.[46] More important, perhaps, than any of these developments has been the gradual diversification of types of institutions and the improved classification of offenders for treatment purposes. These matters will be discussed in greater detail in ensuing chapters.

Prison Development in the South and West

As has been seen, the Auburn scheme, with its congregate production on a contract system, its relatively economical cellular design, and rigid disciplinary philosophy, was productive and attractive to other jurisdictions. Dwight and Wines[47] did much to sell its merits to those who sought guidance on means of meeting the growth of their prison populations. It is not surprising, therefore, that the Auburn system became the central phase of planning in the South and in the West during the first half of the nineteenth century. The oldest prison of the West, at Frankfort, Kentucky,

---

[46] For a discussion of prison discipline, see Chapter 22.

[47] Dr. Enoch Cobb Wines became corresponding secretary of the New York Prison Association in 1862. He was responsible for the development of the leadership of the association in the prison field. Wines and Dwight made a detailed investigation of prisons during the last year of the Civil War and in their work stressed the importance of reformation through work and penitence. See Wines and Dwight, *Prisons in the United States and Canada,* New York, 1867. They were in large measure responsible for the continued development of the Auburn philosophy.

originally constructed in 1798, borrowed from eastern tradition in erecting a large cell structure like that at Baltimore in the 1820s. There a new precedent was established, however, in leasing the labor of the convicts to a merchant who constructed and managed the prison as well as the productive enterprise of its inmates. The lessee became responsible for the entirety of the prison operation. A number of other states followed this system of lease labor in the ensuing years both in the West and in the South. In the late 1830s Indiana and Illinois replaced their old jails with cellular prisons and the lease system. Similar construction was employed in Columbus and Nashville, though these prisons established prosperous industries under the contract system that was prevalent in the East. During this period other prisons based on the Auburn model were erected at Jackson, Michigan (1839), Fort Madison, Iowa (1839), Waupun, Wisconsin (1851), and Jefferson City, Missouri (1836). The latter has been condemned for maintaining "the most diabolical prison conditions," rivaled only at times by those in Kentucky and Virginia.

Prison development in the Far West occurred for the most part during the last half of the nineteenth century. California, with a major criminal problem from its early years, established in the 1850s the nucleus of a penitentiary system at San Quentin partially to replace the old and inadequate Spanish jails. Folsom was started a few years later to house lease prisoners who were constructing a dam and canal there. Colorado, Utah, and the Dakotas established fairly satisfactory and productive prison systems on eastern models during the ensuing generation. Other states, including Oregon, Nevada, and Nebraska, were less successful in meeting their prisoner problems during this same period. Makeshift systems of various sorts were employed in the Federal territories. The rapid increase in the number of Federal prisoners during the latter part of the century (there were 2,516 Federal prisoners lodged in state prisons and 15,000 in county jails in 1895) led finally to the opening of three penitentiaries at Leavenworth, Kansas; Atlanta, Georgia; and McNeil Island, Washington, between 1889 and 1902.

In the South, Georgia, which had established a congregate prison in 1817, responded to the influence of Dwight and the early prison reformers as well as to the patent economy of the Auburn system by erecting a new cellular industrial prison in the thirties. Louisiana established an industrial prison at Baton Rouge at about the same time and Alabama followed soon after. Both of these prisons were turned over to lessees. Before the Civil War, Mississippi, Texas, and Arkansas developed cellular prisons fashioned on northern models. The penitentiary movement was aborted by the war, however, and some of the prisons then existing were damaged or ruined beyond repair. In the economic and social chaos that ensued during the period of reconstruction, two highly significant penological developments occurred that have affected the pattern of the treatment of the criminal ever since. One of these was the development of a system of penal slavery under the lease system. Except in Alabama and Texas, state prisoners were generally put out in chains for construction work in swamps, mountains, and mining regions where they lived in camps. Also, the courts were empowered to sentence alternatively either to the state or to the county and it was common practice for judges to commit able-bodied men to the county work gangs that labored on the public roads. Race conflict and the rapid growth of crime in the colored population encouraged a perpetuation of peonage in the penal system, but with a cruel exploitation of convict labor and brutal discipline by the armed guards, especially in the road labor of the southeastern states. Florida gained a special reputation for its cruelty and corruption in dealing with its prisoners. McKelvey has given us a summary picture of the southern prison camps:[48]

There were no standard living arrangements in the southern prison camps. Yet one strong factor, the demand for economy, brought them all practically to a common level—scarcely that of subsistence. None of the lease camps ever tried to introduce any of the Auburn traditions, and the penitentiaries that did have individual cells seldom attempted to apply rules of silence. Wooden huts of one story usually housed a hundred or more on crude bunks strung around the walls. The danger of escapes frequently compelled the authorities to shut these up tight at nightfall, and they soon became very foul. Water was usually scarce, and bathing almost impossible; other sanitary arrangements were invariably crude, and disease was rampant. Food was plentiful or scarce as the economy of the lessee determined. Heat was usually lacking although rickety stoves or open fires sometimes added much smoke and a little warmth during the cold nights of the winter months. The fear of escapes was the controlling factor in discipline. Various devices for shackling the feet were tried, and in desperate cases heavy iron balls were added to the chains. Striped garments were everywhere in use, and the convicts had no such picayune tastes regarding their footwear as northern prisoners had; they were glad to get any at all. Tobacco chewing was everywhere in evidence, but smoking was prohibited because of the fire risk. Southern newspapers did not cry out, as in the North, against the hotel accommodations of their prisoners, but the criminals failed to migrate north.

Chain gangs have been reduced in recent years as states have been able to replace them with prisons and farms, but they have not yet entirely disappeared. They constitute, perhaps, the foulest blot on American penology since the decline of the corporal and mutilative penalties at the turn of the eighteenth century, though they are more closely reminiscent of the inhumane treatment of prisoners in the French and sometimes in the British (Australian) systems of transportation. Nowhere has the zoological treatment of man by his fellows been more exactly exemplified. Frank Tannenbaum, who made a careful study of Southern prisons and chain

[48] Blake McKelvey, *American Prisons,* University of Chicago Press, Chicago, copyright 1936 by The University of Chicago, p. 181. (Reprinted by permission.)

gangs a number of years ago, has written vividly of the conditions that he found.[49]

The development of state penal farms and plantations in the South came about toward the end of the century in part because of the exigencies of the lease system. There were many offenders who, because of their age, physical conditions, or sex, were unprofitable "half-hands" and "dead-hands" to their lessees; these offenders were commonly left to crowd such jail and prison facilities as existed. Several states that operated industrial prisons, notably Texas, North Carolina, Virginia, and Alabama, established penal farms for a part of their populations. Thus, while the lease system and road work continued to be characteristic in the southeastern states, the Southwest moved to a pattern of plantation farming. Northern states were to follow this example after 1900 by establishing farms in connection with their prisons, in part because of the effective opposition that labor and industry exerted against the prevailing systems of industrial production. The border states, however, avoiding in a measure the influences that were developing both in the South and in the North, established contract and lease industries in connection with their prisons.

ADMINISTRATIVE ORGANIZATION OF PRISON SYSTEMS

Administrative structure cannot of itself determine the effectiveness of governmental operations. The latter depends very largely on the quality and tenure of personnel and on adequate budgetary allowances. Yet it is quite clear that achievement may either be facilitated or impeded by organization in so far as it tends to draw and hold men with appropriate training and skills, to allocate power and responsibility so that policy can be initiated and implemented efficiently, but within appropriate limits, and to provide effective channels for communication and coordination. In penal administration, as in other specialized areas of governmental management, the development and execution of sound policy has commonly been obstructed by forms of organization in which specialized skills are either not elicited or are thwarted and uncoordinated. The structure of correctional administration may relate quite directly to the attainment of treatment objectives, to reasonable economy in operations, and to the avoidance of political and other inappropriate influences.

In the history of modern prison development there has been a gradual evolution in administrative forms that parallels in some measure the growing specialization of correctional functions and the gradual assumption of diversified state responsibilities. Before the Civil War the punishment of criminals was considered to be primarily a matter of local concern. Most prisons were controlled jointly by a warden and by an unpaid local board

---

[49] See Frank Tannenbaum, *Darker Phases of the South*, pp. 84–89, quoted in Barnes, *op. cit.*, pp. 160–162.

of trustees or of inspectors, each appointed for short terms by the governor or the legislature. The boards had limited and largely advisory powers at the start, but with the growth of contract prison industries they were able increasingly to dispense favors through the appointment of wardens and the letting of contracts. Prison appointments provided a fruitful area of party patronage and, while a few states at times procured the services of effective wardens who operated stable and productive prisons, it was customary to replace the prison administrators and their boards after each new election, a practice that has persisted in states with ineffectual prison systems. Corruption was not uncommon in the correctional and, more generally, the welfare fields. The halting pace of the penological movement is evidenced in the persistence to the present day of prison administration by local part-time and unsalaried boards of trustees in several states, including Arizona, Delaware, Mississippi, New Hampshire, and South Carolina.[50] Penal administration in other states also displays vestiges of the practice, as illustrated by the boards of trustees attached to institutions in Pennsylvania and to the women's institutions in California and the boards of managers in New Jersey.

The prevalence of administrative abuses together with the increase in the number of prisons and a growing recognition of state responsibility led, after the Civil War, to the establishment of centralized boards of charities and corrections in a number of states during the 1860s.[51] These, too, were composed of part-time and unpaid appointees of the governor. Generally they were given powers to investigate and to recommend changes in the prisons and in public charitable institutions and, in some states, to exercise direct administrative responsibilities. The boards were relatively free of political domination though some had ex officio membership. They held annual conferences on charities and corrections where their problems and needs were discussed. They came to achieve some limited success in reducing political influence in the prison systems and in improving their condition. Commonly the boards were more interested in charities than corrections, however, and their members generally had no special competence in the latter field, so that the prisons were a stepchild of philanthropic endeavor. The boards of charities proved largely ineffectual in securing adequate budgets or in developing sound correctional programs. This unspecialized form of administration, too, has persisted in certain states. Thus, Kansas and Oklahoma have governor-appointed boards of administration (the latter called the "Board of Public Affairs") that are charged with the duty of controlling and managing all state institutions, in-

---

[50] See Richard A. McGee, "State Organization for Correctional Administration," in Tappan, *Contemporary Correction,* 1951; "Central Administration of a State Correctional System," in *A Manual of Correctional Standards,* American Prison Association, 1954; and McKelvey, *op. cit.,* chap. 6.

[51] McKelvey, *op. cit.,* pp. 128–130.

cluding the penal, and Oregon and Wyoming have ex officio boards with similar responsibilities. It may be noted that the states still using local prison boards and centralized charitable and correctional boards have very limited correctional resources for adult offenders, usually only a single prison.[52]

Another step was taken in the evolution of centralized penal administration by the development of state boards of control, composed generally of salaried members devoting full time to the management and control of penal and charitable institutions. Their duties have included the appointment of wardens and superintendents, the over-all administration of institutions, the making of rules and regulations, and fiscal management. The latter has tended to consume their major interest. The first board of this sort, called a board of charities and correction, was established in Rhode Island in 1869 with a legislative mandate to construct and manage an insane asylum and a state house of correction, including the power to release "reformed inmates" from the latter. By 1913 eight other states, for the most part in the Midwest and the Far West, had established similar boards of control. Today several jurisdictions, including Iowa, Nebraska, North Dakota, and West Virginia, still employ boards of control to administer their varied state institutions.

Massachusetts was the first state to establish a prison commission with authority to manage correctional institutions exclusively, giving it control over local and women's facilities in 1871 and extending its powers to cover the state prison as well in 1879. The commission was also given power to parole. For some time this commission remained the most efficient as well as the most powerful board for administering correctional facilities in the country, though it was an unpaid and badly overworked group. California also established a board of prison managers in 1880. The board failed to provide adequate leadership for the always difficult problems of crime in that state, however, and was replaced by a board of charities and corrections in 1903. New York State did not establish its prison commission until 1896. Prior to that time the New York Prison Association acted as a semiofficial inspector of prisons and as an occasional goad to penal reform. In spite of a poor system of coordinating prison administration, the commission played an important role in the development of prisons in that state. It was empowered to inspect all state and local correctional institutions, to recommend changes in state facilities, and to enforce as well as to make recommendations for the local institutions. Other states followed the earlier New York pattern in establishing prison societies.

While these developments were occurring, a number of states failed to develop any centralized control over their prisons. This was true in Illinois, Kansas, Missouri, and New Jersey. In the South, while state

[52] See *Directory, State and Federal Correctional Institutions,* The American Correctional Association, April, 1959.

penal boards of different sorts were set up, the extent of county control over prisoners minimized the influence that they could bring to bear. Even where central administration had been established, however, the various forms of board organization that had developed by 1900 proved rather ineffectual in administration. This may be attributed in part, as has been suggested, to the unspecialized character of board membership and to the varied and excessive duties required of them. The unpaid and part-time boards were especially weak. Moreover, as it has come more recently to be recognized, the plural executive device is intrinsically ineffectual, since power and responsibility are not focalized. A board does not instrument policy effectively. It may appear surprising, therefore, that some form of board organization is still employed in nearly one-half of the states and that most of these are part-time and unsalaried or ex officio in membership. A majority of these boards may inspect and recommend, but they have no power to compel compliance with their recommendations. Improvement in corrections comes slowly or not at all under such circumstances.

Even under feeble systems of state administration, reform movements did occur, largely as the consequence of agitation by prison societies and by boards of charities and corrections, investigations by prison commissions, and the efforts of particular wardens. During the sixties and seventies a group of outstanding wardens were put in charge of institutions where they did much to establish, for a time at least, a high standard of professional penal administration. These included Zebulon Brockway (Detroit and Elmira), Gideon Haynes (Charlestown), Amos and Louis Pilsbury (Wethersfield), and Henry Cordier (Waupun). But the prisons were a pawn in politics for the most part; they suffered from the lack of continuity in policy and administration. Penal administration was at an unspecialized level in 1900 and for some years thereafter.

The final major stage in administrative development came with the establishment of the departmental form of organization. This was part of the general movement during the twenties to increase economy and efficiency in governmental operations. It sought to centralize authority, to eliminate duplications, and to integrate related functions. The movement took several forms in different states. Some made penal administration a subdivision in a department of welfare, others in a department of institutions, and a few in a combined department of institutions and agencies. This pattern of departmental organization incorporating a division of correction has been lauded by welfare authorities quite generally. They claim that it places corrections appropriately within the framework of welfare services and that it facilitates the coordination of related resources. Welfare authorities have also maintained that it is an economical way to provide professional administration and that it attracts competent personnel. In these respects there can be little doubt that correctional administration has been improved by the partial shift that has occurred from board to departmental management. There has been the added advantage of centralizing responsibility for prisons in a divisional head rather than in a board, so that a single individual may be held responsible for the execution of policy.

A good example of the divisional form of correctional organization under a state department of public welfare may be found in Wisconsin. This state has established an excellent administration of corrections under a deputy who functions within an over-all department. It should be noted that an "integrated system" is in operation here, in the sense that the director of corrections not only administers the institutions but is chairman of the board of parole and is in charge of the combined probation and parole field services. It is a system, consequently, that relies very heavily upon the high level of competence and the varied skills of the director. There is a substantial hazard implicit in the extent of power and the variety of functions imposed upon the director. So much is dependent upon him and his balanced judgments. On the other hand, an integration of functions and an economy of operation is possible under this system that can produce effective results, at least in small and nonpopulous states, as Wisconsin experience has shown.

On the whole, correction tends to be put in a subordinate role when it is operated under a broader department. It suffers in budget, personnel, and policy development. For these reasons the correctional field has looked more favorably in recent years upon the establishment of separate departments of correction within state government, the most refined and specialized form of penal administration. This has been the direction of contemporary development in the more progressive jurisdictions. It puts correction in a better competitive position relative to other departments of government and provides higher status to the director and his staff. Thus superior administrative personnel can be secured. This form of organization has been supported by the Standards of the American Correctional Association[53] and in the Model Penal Code of the American Law Institute.[54]

The system in California illustrates the autonomous form of correctional organization in a separate department. It should be observed, however, that there are certain unique elements in the correctional system of that state. There are distinct paroling authorities for adult males, the Adult Authority, for young adults, the Youth Authority, and the board of trustees for women, which are represented in the board of corrections but are not under the control of the director of corrections. In 1957 the adult male parole field service, which had been under the Adult Authority, was brought under the administration of the director. The women's institution

---

[53] *A Manual of Correctional Standards, op. cit.,* chap. 3.
[54] *Model Penal Code,* Tentative Draft No. 5, pp. 147–169.

is under a separate board of trustees and the juvenile and youth institutions are administered by the Youth Authority.[55] The central office staff includes three deputy directors, one responsible for coordination of the central-office staff, one responsible for fiscal and property functions, and the other, for crime studies, research, and correctional coordination at all levels of government within the state. Other specialists are concerned with personnel, treatment and training, food administration, prison industries, training of personnel, jail and prison inspection, medical activity, and research and statistics.

Today fourteen states provide for correction in a division within a broader department. Thirteen others have established separate departments of correction, Minnesota most recently among these. The latter include the most populous states as well as jurisdictions with relatively small populations, spread through the major regions of the country. It may be difficult to establish such a degree of specialization where the prison population is small and where the diversification of correctional institutions is very limited.

As has been observed in the foregoing discussion, there is great variation in the structural organization of correctional work in the different states. The administrative form is frequently awkward where obsolete patterns are still employed.[56] Efficiency and economy are adversely affected.

The Federal Prison System

The most recently developed but most diversified and effective prison system in the United States is the Federal Bureau of Prisons of the Department of Justice. The criminal law of the United States was not extensively developed until recent years when a variety of legislation dealing with interstate crime has been enacted. Crimes committed on Indian reservations, in other Federal jurisdictions, and on the high seas were subject to prosecution and punishment by Federal authorities from the start. Until the twentieth century Federal prisoners were held generally in state prisons and in county jails and, to a limited extent, in U.S. marshals' jails for the Federal territories. Agitation by penal reformers for our reluctant government to assume its responsibilities in this field became quite active in the 1880s and more vociferous in 1885 when it was learned that there were over 1,000 Federal prisoners in state prisons and about 10,000 in county jails, with the number growing rapidly. Congress provided by law in 1891 for the erection of three Federal prisons but no action in the matter was taken for some years. In 1894 the military prison

[55] Tappan, "Young Adults under the Youth Authority," *J. Crim. L.,* vol. 47, no. 6, pp. 629–647, March–April, 1957.

[56] The American Correctional Association has summarized the elements considered essential for a sound state correctional organization predicated on the theory of centralization and integration. See *A Manual of Correctional Standards,* 1959, pp. 39–59.

at Fort Leavenworth was transferred temporarily from the War Department to the Department of Justice. The former objected to its use for civil prisoners and the construction of another institution on an adjacent site was authorized. The Federal Penitentiary at Leavenworth was erected there with the labor of the prisoners and was finally opened in 1905. The penitentiary at Atlanta was opened in the same year. In 1909 the territorial jail at McNeil Island in Puget Sound was also designated as a Federal prison. By 1915 there were altogether nearly three thousand prisoners in these three institutions. No additional Federal institutions were built until 1924 when the Women's Reformatory at Alderson, West Virginia, was started and 1925 when a reformatory for males was authorized at the military reservation at Chillicothe, Ohio. The number of Federal prisoners meantime had continued to grow, many of them being held in state institutions.

The Federal Bureau of Prisons was organized in 1930 under the headship of Sanford Bates, who was succeeded in 1937 by James V. Bennett. The number of Federal prisoners had become very large as a consequence of the enactment of the Volstead Act, the Harrison Narcotic Act, the Mann Act, and the National Motor Vehicle Theft Act, as well as other criminal legislation. States, already overburdened with their own expanding penal populations, were refusing to accept more prisoners from the Federal courts. After a full investigation, Congress decided in 1929 that a system of institutions should be established "which will assure the proper classification and segregation of Federal prisoners according to their character, the nature of the crimes they have committed, their mental condition, and such other factors as should be taken into consideration in providing an individualized system of discipline, care and treatment of persons committed to such institutions."[57] Thereafter the Bureau established a graded system of penal institutions including maximum security penitentiaries for close custody of habitual criminals, medium security penitentiaries for better rehabilitative prospects, reformatories for young and inexperienced offenders, "correctional institutions" for men with relatively short sentences and for those soon to be released, open camps for those requiring little custodial control, a detention headquarters, special institutions for juveniles and youths, and a medical center. In 1958 there were thirty-one such facilities in all. At the end of 1957 these institutions held a total of 20,420 prisoners, while state institutions contained 174,994 offenders at that time.

The administrative organization of the Federal Bureau of Prisons under the Department of Justice is relatively simple as compared with that in some of the states. Several features of this organization should be noted. There is a strong and separate corporate structure for the administration of prison industries and for the operation of vocational training programs that has resulted in effective production and the elimination of idleness.

[57] 18 U.S. Code 907.

Medical services are provided through the U.S. Public Health Service. The special focus on classification and treatment provided through an assistant director has resulted in a degree of emphasis on this phase of correction that is lacking in the states generally. Jail inspection is a relatively important phase of the Federal program because of the practice of evaluating local jails as a basis for selecting those which may be used for the temporary detention of Federal prisoners. Because of this inspection many of our jails have improved.

The Federal Bureau of Prisons has made many important contributions to correctional practice in the United States. These will be discussed in the following chapters, together with developments that have occurred in the states.

Chapter 21

CORRECTIONAL INSTITUTIONS AND CLASSIFICATION

The use of imprisonment as a mode of penal-correctional treatment is a relatively modern development that was derived from a variety of earlier practices and policies, as has been seen. These earlier practices included the application of various measures that were intended to punish criminals or to deter potential offenders. The practices of segregating offenders in convict hulks and of banishing them in penal transportation were designed to rid the community of its dangerous characters. Secure custodial detention for the accused awaiting trial or punishment was used to protect the community and to ensure that the criminal would be accessible. Corrective and rehabilitative devices purported to produce penitence in the offender or to provide him with training. Many of the older forms of punishment were abandoned or modified in the last century. A few new methods of treatment have been introduced in recent years. Imprisonment, however, continues to be the major sanction employed in dealing with serious and repetitive offenders. Correctional institutions have become somewhat more varied in modern times to meet the needs of the criminal population, and classification procedures have been developed to place the individual in the facility and program that are best suited to his needs.

In this chapter the author will consider the major forms of contemporary correctional facilities and the use of classification in the allocation of prisoners to custodial and treatment programs. The design and construction of penal institutions will be looked at with special attention to prisons. The latter part of the chapter is concerned with other major types of institutions for adults: reformatories, correctional facilities for females, medico-correctional centers, and jails.

CLASSIFICATION

Classification is a relatively recent development in the procedures of treatment in correctional institutions, one that represents a significant departure from traditional penology. It is "a method by which diagnosis, treatment planning, and the execution of the treatment program are co-ordinated in the individual case."[1] This is usually taken to imply a thorough inquiry into the forces from which the offender's criminality has come, followed by the planning and implementation of an individuated correctional program that is based upon the causes of crime in the individual case. There are two general types of classification in correction: classification by institution, or central classification, and classification within the institution.

When an offender is committed to prison, decisions must be made concerning the particular institution in which he should be confined and, later, concerning the program with which he should be occupied. In most states the choice of the commitment institution is a simple one because there is a lack of any great variety in treatment facilities, while in a few jurisdictions the selection is relatively wide and decisions may be made with greater care. Every state, however, must face and resolve in some way the problem of diversified populations of prisoners who should be dealt with, so far as possible, in fairly homogeneous groups. The young, mature, aged, male, female, psychotic, dangerously aggressive, physically ill, mentally defective, homosexual, recidivistic, first offender, serious, and minor criminal are some of the varieties of offenders whose distinctive qualities require specialized attention. Classification is a problem that varies considerably from state to state, not only because of the wide range in the number of offenders for whom provision must be made, but because of the varying distribution of types within the criminal population. The number, size, and variety of institutions also differ in the several jurisdictions, affecting the specialization of treatment that may be provided by means of classification to the institutions and placement within the programs of such institutions.

Classification within the Institution

The chief purpose of classification, as has been implied above, is to fit the treatment program of the correctional institution to the requirements of the individual as determined by appropriate diagnostic procedures. The Committee on Classification and Case Work of the American Prison Association has spelled out the objectives and methods more specifically:[2]

The purposes of classification are accomplished first, by analyzing the problems presented by the individual through the use of every available technique, such as thorough social investigation, medical, psychiatric, psychological ex-

---

[1] Frank Loveland, "Classification in the Prison System," in Tappan (ed.), *Contemporary Correction*, p. 92. See also *Handbook on Classification in Correctional Institutions,* Committee on Classification and Case Work, American Prison Association, 1947. Chap. 1 (hereinafter referred to as *Handbook on classification*), and *A Manual of Correctional Standards,* rev., American Correctional Association, 1959, chap. 16.

[2] *Handbook on Classification, ibid.,* pp. 2–3.

aminations, educational and vocational, religious and recreational studies; second, by deciding in staff conference upon a program of treatment and training based upon these analyses; third, by assuring that the program decided upon is placed into operation; and fourth, by observing the progress of the inmate under this program and by changing it when indicated.

Classification within the institution may be carried on alternatively by the use of a classification clinic or of a classification committee. The former is composed of professional diagnostic and treatment staff members who make more or less elaborate studies of individual offenders and recommend the programs of training and treatment that they deem appropriate. Such proposals can be accepted or rejected by the administration, and often they are rejected because they are considered unrealistic or impractical. This "clinic" or "bureau" type of arrangement is not well designed to coordinate the procedures of study and treatment.

Considerably more successful and more usual is the integrated organization of procedures by which the professional and administrative personnel collaborate as a committee in the planning of programs. The composition of the committee may vary somewhat with the staff available, but it should invariably be chaired by the warden or superintendent of the institution and it should provide a well-balanced representation, including the heads of departments and specialists who are charged with matters of diagnosis, training, treatment, and custody. Ordinarily the same committee will act in matters of reclassification when the prisoner's adjustment is reviewed from time to time, though in larger institutions the task of reclassification is delegated to a representative subcommittee because of the volume of work that is required. Responsibility for coordinating committee work, for ensuring that committee recommendations are properly instrumented, and for organizing the classification meetings should be entrusted to a supervisor of classification.

The specific planning of the prisoner's program is carried out by means of a classification meeting, commonly called a "guidance conference" or "case conference," that should be conducted ordinarily after some weeks of study and testing of the prisoner, the length of time depending on whether there has been a reception center study in advance. The classification committee meets to assemble and to report on the studies that have been made and to plan with the inmate the assignments with which he will be occupied.

It is the primary and initial function of classification in the institution to determine the basic elements of prisoners' assignments to housing, work, educational or training program, leisure-time activities, and such ties to the community as may be maintained or developed. Another contribution of classification to the correctional experience of the offender lies in his preparation for release. The continuing records of the classification committee, constituting a coordinated central file on the offender and his development, should be the basis both for treatment decisions in the prison and for the decisions of the parole board relating to his release and supervision in the community. Such a file will include the criminal records, admission summaries, progress reports, letters and memoranda, and other material relating to his conduct and adjustment. These materials are the proper source for planning assignment to a specialized prerelease unit of the institution where instruction and orientation for discharge may be given. A copy of the file should be made available to the paroling authority as a basis for the release decision and the planning of community supervision.

Classification must look to the optimum uses of its professional staff to avoid the dissipation of such talents as the system can command. The committee on classification has warned that unless means are found to improve diagnostic techniques and to integrate fully all institutional services "the staff will soon become frustrated and discouraged: and the classification program may become a monument of paper work erected in the name of individualized treatment." The finest fruits of classification will not grow untended from voluminous files of cases. Diligent study is required to find the methods and the dispositions of personnel best suited to accomplish correctional objectives. Administration should look both to continuing research on the effectiveness of the treatment measures employed and to progressive alterations in program in the light of the research findings.

The components of correctional treatment programs in prison are considered in some detail in the next chapter. Attention will now be given to another and more recent development, that of central classification to institutions by means of reception centers.

Classification and the Reception Center

The "reception center" is an institution where prisoners are received after sentence for study and treatment planning.[3] While the principles underlying such centers are not new, the development of specialized institutions for the purpose is a recent development. The idea is rooted partly in the development of diagnostic clinics and partly in the principle of classification. Diagnostic clinics were established in a number of cities during the growth of the juvenile court movement as a means of providing information on the personality and social history of young offenders so that their treatment might be individualized. Sometimes these clinics were directly attached to the courts. Elsewhere separate centers were created where detailed testing and observation might be carried on during a period of court detention. They were generally local rather than state facilities, as are most such clinics today. They are prototypes of the modern reception center.

The idea of a diagnostic-classification center has arisen out of experience

[3] Glenn Kendall, "Reception Centers," in Tappan, *op. cit.*, chap. 8, and *Handbook on Classification*, chap. 3.

both in classification within the institution and in central classification. If there is but a single adult correctional institution or if designation is made between few alternatives on some simple basis of administrative classification, there is no significant process of central classification. The prisoner goes directly to the prison where he is to be held, though he may subsequently be transferred elsewhere if this appears desirable in the light of his behavior and if there is some other facility to which he may be sent. Fundamentally classification under such a system is the one-step procedure that has already been described. The offender enters quarantine where he is tested and observed before assignment to a program in the institution. Where a more elaborate system of correctional facilities is available, some form of central administrative classification by the correctional authorities may be employed. In some places this involves merely a simple scheme of allocation according to sex, age, offense, prior criminal record, escape history, and other criteria. In a few states reception or diagnostic centers have been established for preliminary study of offenders before they are assigned to an institution for treatment. This is a two-step process of study and classification, for after assignment to the receiving institution the offender is ordinarily held in quarantine for some period of time at the institution to which he is allocated before he is incorporated into its program. He may subsequently be reclassified by a committee of that institution and transferred elsewhere.

The ordinary prison lacks the personnel, space, and resources for conducting the sort of intensive studies that are commonly deemed to be desirable for planning the individual's treatment program. The diagnostic-reception center has developed in response to the need felt in some states for more adequate and appropriate information upon which to predicate treatment.

In the 1940s reception centers were established in connection with existing institutions at the Elmira Reformatory in New York for youths between 16 and 21 and at the San Quentin Prison in California for adult prisoners. The latter state has since constructed two separate reception center clinics for study and classification of wards of the Youth Authority there. Nine other states have also created reception centers since 1948, four of these for juveniles (Illinois, Massachusetts, Kentucky, and Washington), two for adults (Alabama and Rhode Island), and two without age limitations (Michigan and Pennsylvania), and one for youthful offenders (Minnesota). New Jersey has established a diagnostic center that may be used by the correctional authorities as well as by the courts and other agencies of the state. The Federal Bureau of Prisons has set up diagnostic resources at its facilities for youth offenders to provide the courts guidance in sentencing under the Youth Corrections Act.

This new weapon in the armamentorium of corrections has borrowed to a large extent both from diagnostic clinic practice and from penology's experience with classification, as has been suggested, but in some measure it has developed its own unique character. Its peculiarity lies in the comprehensive and detailed studies that personnel of the reception center perform as the basis for classification to institutions and for planning of treatment. Norman Fenton, deputy director of the California Department of Corrections, has summarized the objectives and values of the reception process in these terms:[4]

1. The study of the personality and social background of the newly committed inmates by a competent professional staff.
2. The screening of prisoners for assignment to particular institutions and to special segregation units in terms of their needs and the custodial provisions of the institutions.
3. The planning of a program of individual treatment for consideration by the staff of the receiving institution.
4. The preparation of individual case studies of value in the assignment to work in the maintenance of the prison and in correctional industries in accordance with individual needs and institutional provisions.
5. Recognition of the prison subversives and the psychopaths, and recommendation of individualized programs to prevent escapes, assaultative behavior, arson and other destruction of property, and other incidents unfortunate both for the inmate and the institution.

It should be observed that reception center classification, in addition to providing the basis for allocation to an institution, also establishes to an important extent the foundation for the planning of the individual's treatment there. This function of the reception process requires special comment. On the one hand, it is apparent that recommendations of a center on specific elements of a prisoner's program can be no more than advisory. This is so in part because the receiving institution, as a practical matter, must classify its intake in accordance with its facilities and population. Assignments to work, training, and treatment are inevitably guided by the needs and the potentialities of the institution as well as by the desires and capacities of the individual offenders committed there. Not all men can be taught to be automobile mechanics, to work in the kitchen, or to play drums in the band. The diagnostic center is not always realistic or well informed about the limitations of the treatment institutions. On the other hand, there is some danger, depending in large part on the attitude of the administration at these institutions, that the information and advice of the diagnostic center will command less respect than they should. The work of the center has little worth beyond the uses to which it is put in actual treatment programs. It is highly desirable, therefore, that follow-up studies should be made by the state department to determine both the extent to which recommendations from its reception center are soundly formulated

[4] Norman Fenton, "The Process of Reception in the Adult Correctional System," *The Annals,* vol. 293, pp. 52–53, May, 1954. (Reprinted by permission.)

and the frequency with which such recommendations are followed by the receiving institutions. Such studies would be highly instructive in relation to the needs for improvement and diversification in state correctional programs. This could be a useful by-product of the classification procedures.

The Committee on Classification and Case Work has promulgated a number of standards for the effective performance of reception centers.[5] The committee held that sixty days should ordinarily be required for diagnostic studies and interpretation of data but that the law should not specify a maximum period because of the longer time that may be required in some cases. The center should be adequately staffed with clinical and other personnel. The committee suggested that to handle an intake of twenty-five to thirty inmates per week a minimum staff of seventy-five, including custodial officers, would be required. The center should provide the fullest possible opportunity, not only through testing and interviews, but through its educational, vocational, physical training, and recreational programs, for observing the interests, abilities, and problems of the prisoner. Some emphasis should also be given at the center to orienting the prisoner, not only to the center itself and to its purposes, but also to the correctional experience that lies ahead of him. Characteristically after trial and conviction the offender must deal with feelings of guilt, remorse, aggression, and anxiety. His concern about the future should be alleviated and he should be given a constructive preparation for the imprisonment that he faces. The entire prison experience should be directed toward release and the responsible use of freedom. The foundation for an affirmative attitude can be laid at reception through the content of the program as well as through the living experience at the center.

The committee indicates that the reception center should prepare a report and recommendations for distribution to the state central office, the receiving institution, the parole board, and the sentencing court and should itself retain a copy. Such a report should include material relating to the prisoner's social background, criminal history, initial adjustment to the institution, medical examination, psychological study, vocational study, educational history and analysis, religious background and attitudes, recreational interests and abilities, and a psychiatric evaluation.

It might be argued that it would be desirable to establish a diagnostic-reception center in every state if for no other reason than to guide the course of its program of prison development. It is apparent, however, that the need for such centers varies with the size of the population to be served and with the diversification of institutions and programs available. Where there are no more than one or two institutions to which ordinary adult offenders are sent, a separate center could not well be justified for purposes of institutional allocation or of planning individual treatment. In this situation there is ordinarily a more pressing need to specialize the program of

[5] *Handbook on Classification, loc. cit.*

classification at the existing institutions. This may imply a prolongation of the period of prisoners' quarantine in a segregated division of the prison and more intensive studies of the offenders committed there in order to improve the classification of offenders and gradually to diversify the treatment program. As institution, camp, and farm installations are extended, it may then become feasible to establish a diagnostic-reception unit as a separate facility.

Where there is a relatively large and diversified correctional system, it is desirable to establish a separate and autonomous reception center. Such facilities have sometimes been created as sections of institutions that are already in existence. There are certain economical advantages in providing through a parent institution for some of the basic facilities and clerical and housekeeping personnel. On the other hand, there are undesirable features in such an arrangement that may outweigh the benefits. The center may suffer from inadequate spatial accommodations, from lack of materials and equipment, or from conflict of policy and personnel with the larger institution upon which it is dependent. Where, for reasons of economy or otherwise, it is not feasible to establish a completely separate institution, a center may very reasonably be located as one part of a satellite design, described later in this chapter. Some compromise of this sort would commonly be necessary in correctional systems of medium size and variety. The use of a segregated part or a satellite of an existing institution may be the only possible arrangement, at least for a time. In any such center, however, the administration and staff should be distinct from and independent of any other institution with which it may be associated. Wherever it is possible, reception-diagnostic centers, whether as separate units or in association with existing institutions, should be established for young adults apart from those designed for ordinary adult offenders. This is so because the younger offenders require reeducational training and treatment based upon studies that are specialized to their particular needs.

PRISONS FOR MEN

State prisons are designed in the main to contain felons committed for periods of one year or more. Because, in contrast with most jail-type institutions, they draw their more sizable populations from an entire state and retain them for substantial periods, they offer a relatively favorable opportunity for diversification of types of institutions to which offenders may be classified and for the development of intensive programs of treatment and training, They do in fact provide for considerably better classification and treatment than do short-term institutions generally. On the other hand, prison systems suffer from certain serious limitations that are not easily circumvented. One of these, curiously, is the lack in many states of a sufficiently large number of imprisoned felons to provide easily for their diverse needs. There are nine states with imprisoned felon populations of less than 500; four others with fewer than 1,000; nine with populations between 1,000 and 2,000; nine between 2,000 and 3,000; four between 3,000 and 4,000; and three between 4,000 and 5,000. In only twelve states prison populations are greater than 5,000 and in only four of these does the population exceed 10,000.

Partially because of the well-established tradition of state reliance upon large maximum-security institutions and because of the obvious economies that can be effected in the operation of mass programs, it is not surprising to find that thus far there has been little diversification in types of prisons in most states. Thus, a single prison is used to contain all committed felons without regard even to such elementary classifications as sex, age, offense, or condition of the offender in ten states. Five states employ only two institutions, while fourteen have three; six use four, six employ five, two use six, one has seven, three have eight, one has nine, and one has seventeen. Even among those jurisdictions where the penal population is large and where several prisons are operated, however, little versatility has been expressed in their institutions and programs, for the most part. The Federal and California correctional systems are notable exceptions, and a few other states have been moving forward in this regard in recent years.

Progress in the establishment of well-balanced prison systems is retarded by the great capital investment that has been made in the construction and renovation of existing institutions. They cannot easily be disused or replaced, however old they may be and however unsuited they may be to the contemporary need. Mass-custody prisons that were erected prior to or during 1900 are employed today in forty-one jurisdictions. New correctional institutions, other than camps and farms, have been established in eighteen states since 1940, but most of these have been merely modern versions of the old and excessively large bastille-type prisons, based on the pattern that was fixed by the precedents at Pennsylvania, Auburn, and Sing Sing. At current prices the construction of institutions of this sort generally costs $11,000 or more per inmate capacity. Obviously, they will not soon be abandoned and usually they cannot be changed very drastically in character without large expenditures.

In spite of what has been said above, there has been a considerable and growing emphasis in recent years upon the need for the diversification of correctional institutions in the United States and one may reasonably believe that in time our facilities will come to be better adapted to the varieties of offenders whom they must accommodate. There is no easy formula to project the needs for prison construction and renovation in any state, unfortunately. Growth and diversification must relate to the age and condition of existing facilities, the size and nature of the population to be served, and the availability of funds and personnel for the improvement of the state prison program.

The Design of Correctional Institutions

Experience with prison administration has demonstrated the significance of prison construction for the effectiveness of treatment.[6] This is not to say that a well-built plant can assure a sound program without a high quality of administration and treatment personnel, but it is exceedingly difficult to carry out reasonable treatment plans unless structure is appropriately designed for the purpose. As the Federal Bureau of Prisons has stated the matter, "A good plant is the first step on the way to a good program." This requires that the institution's security features and custodial supervision should be adequate to the particular population being housed there but that they should not be excessive. This is a matter not merely of sensible economy but, more important, of providing to the maximum extent possible the freedom and flexibility that are conducive to rehabilitative work. The institution should be designed to facilitate the operation of treatment, training, and work activities in such variety as the nature of the population will permit. Of special importance is the location of the space and facilities that are needed for active and intensive programs. The most common errors have been to allow insufficient space for treatment and leisure-time activities and to make the services too inaccessible to some parts of the population that should be served. The planning of a prison to take care of all the elements of community living and training, on the one hand, and to meet the needs of the particular institution, on the other, is a highly specialized task in architectural design and engineering. The problems are greatest and the penological foresight most crucial where institutions of mixed custody must accommodate heterogeneous populations. Where a good state system of institutional classification makes possible a quite specialized adaptation of program and construction to the requirements of carefully selected, rather homogeneous populations, the planning of construction is considerably simplified, yet it requires greater ingenuity and foresight than in the past have characterized the work of most institutional architects. The adaptation of prison design to prison functions is made more difficult and challenging by the differences in public, official, and professional opinion on the ends that a correctional system should serve. It is not unreasonable to believe that in the future of American penology what we can accomplish in the custody and treatment of offenders depends quite fundamentally

[6] The U.S. Bureau of Prisons in 1949 published a *Handbook of Correctional Institution Design and Construction* (hereinafter referred to as *Design and Construction*), a source book for planning and construction of institutions ranging in type from the small jail and short-term detention facilities for juvenile delinquents to the maximum-security type of institution. It is an excellent volume, treating historical and philosophical as well as structural-functional aspects of the problem. Nowhere are the important relationships between design and correctional performance more clearly shown. See also Robert D. Barnes and Clarence B. Litchfield, "Prison Architecture and Function," in Tappan (ed.), *op. cit.*

upon a more sound design of structures that are adapted to the needs of a widely diverse population.

The design of prisons and reformatories in the United States falls into several major classes, but with a considerable variation of detail within those classes. The rectangular cell house is one of these, based upon the

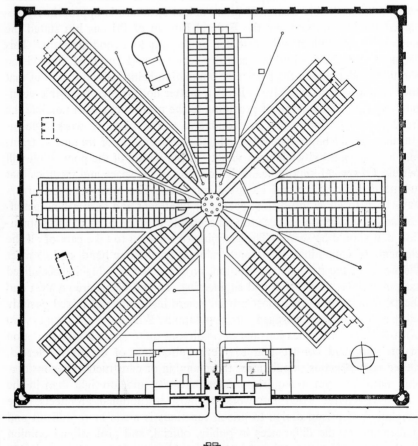

FIGURE 10. Radial prison design at the Eastern Penitentiary of Philadelphia.

design of the Papal Prison of Saint Michael, opened in Rome in 1704, which was the first important cellular prison in the world. The basic structure of this pattern was followed with considerably larger, long-corridor structures at Auburn, Sing Sing, and a majority of the nineteenth-century prisons erected in the United States. An adaptation of this design is exemplified in the pattern of radiating wings, with rectangular cell houses, that was originally employed in the workhouse at Ghent, Belgium, in 1773.[7] This was followed in the Pennsylvania system here and was copied extensively on the Continent. The structure is shown in a drawing of the Eastern Penitentiary in Figure 10. Cell block design has generally been rectangular, with outside- or inside-cell construction. An odd variation in prison design has been developed to a very limited extent on the basis of the "all-seeing-eye" Panopticon plan of Jeremy Bentham. This is basically a circular system with cells constructed around the circumference of the cell house, surrounding a guard chamber in the center, from which the interiors of all cells may be observed. This plan was followed at the original

FIGURE 11. Panopticon cell houses at the Illinois State Penitentiary at Stateville.

Virginia State Prison at Richmond in 1800, the Western Penitentiary at Pittsburgh, Pennsylvania, in 1826, and in some Continental prisons during the early part of the nineteenth century. It has had its most extended application at the Illinois State Penitentiary at Stateville, opened in 1919. At Stateville four large circular cell houses were built, together with a rectangular unit, accommodating in 1958 a total of over 4,500 inmates. Two of the Stateville cell houses are shown in the photograph in Figure 11.

A significant variation from the huge rectangular cell house design, so often used to accommodate hundreds of prisoners, has been the construc-

[7] The Ghent workhouse appears to have been the first institution in which inside-cell construction was employed. The purpose then, as today, was to provide additional security against escape by preventing contact of the prisoners with the outer walls. Conventional maximum-security prison construction has continued to follow the pattern of flanking inside-cell blocks along a long corridor. See pp. 637–638.

tion of relatively small and separate units, sometimes for housing, commonly for program activities, and occasionally for both, in an open-campus design. This has been derived in part from the "cottage system" used in juvenile training schools and from experience in recent years in the development of production and training shops and quarters for treatment services in reformatories and medium-security prisons. The old cell block construction provided inadequately or not at all for such treatment-oriented phases of prison program.

FIGURE 12. United States Penitentiary, Terre Haute, Indiana, showing telephone-pole design and radial terminal cell houses. Use of radiating cell blocks reduces length of corridor, simplifying supervision, and discourages the development of additional cell blocks.

Another major development in the general structure of prisons has occurred through the introduction in the United States of the "telephone-pole" design, wherein cell houses and other facilities of the institution are constructed to extend crosswise from a central corridor, a plan that originated in a French prison at Fresnes, in 1898. This layout with ingenious variations is replacing the rectangular and radial designs in the modern prison system, though it was not until the present century that it came to be imitated, notably in such institutions as Lewisburg (1932) and Terre Haute (1940) in the Federal system.[8] See Figure 12. Other prisons have followed this pattern in recent years. Today it is not uncommon for insti-

[8] At Terre Haute the cross wings at each end of the central corridor were constructed on a radial angle to facilitate traffic and supervision. This also prevents the undesirable extension of the central corridor when an institution is under pressure to expand its population. See Fig. 12.

tutions to combine some form of telephone-pole construction of cell houses with separate rectangular units for industry, training, administration, and other functions. The institution at Ashland, pictured below in Figure 13, illustrates such a combination. More recently, a self-enclosing design has been developed in medium-security construction by the Federal Bureau of

FIGURE 13. Federal Correctional Institution, Ashland, Kentucky, employed for the treatment and training of committed youth offenders.

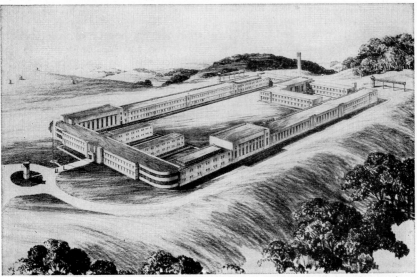

FIGURE 14. Perspective of Federal Correctional Institution, Danbury, Connecticut, illustrating the self-enclosing design.

Prisons. This is illustrated in the perspective of the Federal Correctional Institution at Danbury, Connecticut, in Figure 14.

Levels of Custody. It is traditional to divide correctional institutions into three major levels of custody, the maximum-, medium-, and minimum-security types, according to the construction and measures of control that are employed. Prisoners may be classified in relation to their apparent need for such security provisions. These categories of institutional custody will be discussed below, with some emphasis upon medium-custody facilities, since these are of special significance to future developments in correction. It should be noted at the start, however, that there is some trend today to incorporate in single institutions, especially in those designated maximum-security institutions, medium- and minimum-custody provisions for a part of their populations. The Federal Penitentiary at Lewisburg, erected in 1932, illustrates this very well. It was perhaps the first of its sort to establish a full diversification of custodial provisions in a single institution, including maximum-security inside cells, medium-security outside cells, open dormitories, squad rooms, and honor rooms.

The maximum-security prison is appropriate for recidivistic and aggressive offenders who are deemed to be relatively incorrigible or to present a fairly serious escape risk. Such institutions are characteristically surrounded by a masonry wall 18 to 25 feet high, commonly costing from a half million to more than a million dollars to construct, manned at a series of guard towers, a matter that may easily cost from $35,000 to $50,000 per year for personnel.[9] Some of the more recently constructed maximum-

[9] The Federal Penitentiary at Terre Haute, Indiana, constructed in 1940, was the first maximum-security prison for adult felons to be built without a wall. It has two cyclone fences.

Walls have been criticized not only for their cost but because of their implicit emphasis upon the punitive element of incarceration and because commonly, in part to save cost, the walled enclosure is made too small, so that there is insufficient space to develop needed facilities. On the other hand, some penal administrators have argued that if security is fully ensured through enclosure by high and thick walls, significantly greater freedom is possible within the institution and a correspondingly greater emphasis upon rehabilitative elements in the program. This was the theory underlying the development of the Massachusetts State Prison Colony at Norfolk, designed with both a wall, topped by wire charged with 4,400 volts and, some 70 feet inside the wall, a woven-wire fence. The wall, enclosing a plot of nearly 36 acres, cost only $94,000 to construct because it was erected with prison labor. This institution is usually designated a medium-security prison in spite of elaborate precautions against escape, for its interior construction provides for a considerable amount of free activity and participation in varied programs. It is no longer considered necessary or desirable to construct such costly walls as has been customary in the past. Most authorities consider that, quite aside from cost, walls are undesirable for medium- and minimum-security institutions. As a matter of fact, the Federal prison at Seagoville, Texas, has successfully operated an active, free, and treatment-oriented program for a population containing serious offenders without either a wall or a fence. See Figures 19 and 20.

security institutions have been built with two surrounding wire mesh fences, topped by barbed wire (cyclone fences), or with perimeter-enclosing buildings.[10] Many professional penologists no longer consider it necessary to use the old type of wall construction. Maximum-security prisons have traditionally been built with "inside" cell blocks, constructed back to back,

FIGURE 15. Inside cell-block construction at Leavenworth Penitentiary, Kansas.

with corridors running between these and the outside shell of the cell house. This is illustrated by a cell block at the Leavenworth Penitentiary in Figure 15. Ideally each cell should be occupied by no more than one prisoner and in no case by two. There should be plumbing and other sanitary facilities in all cells. As a matter of economy in construction and in

[10] A fence costs about 1 per cent of the cost of a wall and can, of course, be moved readily to meet changing needs of an institution.

custody such institutions must be compactly designed. Stronger emphasis than in other types of prisons must be given to escape-proof measures, including tool-proof steel construction, multiple lock devices, frequent shake-downs and counts, carefully devised firearms and gas-control systems, and plans for effective operation during emergencies, such as riots, escapes, or fire.

In the maximum-security prison, supersecurity features should be provided in segregated quarters for the relatively few most dangerous and intractible offenders. The Federal Bureau of Prisons has developed a model

FIGURE 16. Outside cell-block construction at the Terre Haute Penitentiary, Indiana.

plan for a 500-inmate supersecurity institution appropriate for assaultative types and troublemakers that should be suitable in a jurisdiction with a considerable number of the most difficult prisoners.[11]

Institutions of medium security reproduce the basic pattern of the maximum-security prison for the most part. Ordinarily a cyclone fence, 12 to 14 feet high, topped by barbed wire, is used rather than a wall, and there are fewer guard towers. "Outside" cell construction with an inner corridor is characteristic. Outside-cell block construction is illustrated at the Terre Haute Penitentiary in Figure 16. A small percentage, ideally not more than 10 per cent, of the cells may be contained in an interior cell block for seg-

[11] See *Design and Construction*, chap. 5.

regation of difficult cases.[12] Normally up to 10 per cent of the population may also be assigned to honor rooms where the freedom and privileges of prisoners are increased. Dormitories may be used for some proportion of the population. Open dormitories have the primary virtue of immediate, though not necessarily long-range, economy and they are much less expensive to construct than either inside-cell blocks or outside rooms. Also, they are flexible, permitting variation in their housing capacity through the expansion or reduction of floor space allotted to the inmates in accordance with changes in the institutional population. If supervision is inadequate, there is danger of misconduct in a crowded dormitory, and adequate supervision is more expensive than that required for a cell block. Many gregarious prisoners prefer dormitory to cell life. It is generally agreed that separate rooms, such as are provided throughout at the Wallkill Prison in New York, are much to be preferred over dormitories for medium-security housing. They are considered too expensive to construct, however, for general use in such institutions. In providing a relatively more healthful and stimulating environment, especially for a young population, dormitories are more desirable than maximum-security cells for the ordinary run of offenders. Older prisoners, however, and those in particular who have long terms to serve commonly desire privacy. They as well as offenders who are escape risks should generally be housed in cells. Some measure of privacy can be provided within a dormitory structure, but with a consequent loss of space, through its division into squad rooms, each housing three or more, or into cubicles for single occupancy. Cubicle construction at the Federal Correctional Institution at Tallahassee, Florida, is illustrated in Figure 17.

It is especially important in the medium-security institution that receiving and admission facilities be ample and well designed, since carefully conducted classification procedures are essential to the effective performance of such institutions. Adequate day-room space for leisure-time activities in each unit of the living quarters and a full battery of facilities for the educational and treatment programs should also be provided.

In prisons of medium security, men may work outside the enclosure under close supervision or inside without direct and continuous surveillance. Prisoners with fairly long criminal records may be contained in such institutions if they are not considered to be serious escape risks. Maximum-custody prisoners sentenced to long terms should also be transferred to such prisons in order to provide a measure of "decompression" before release to the community. Good medium-security institutions can be con-

---

[12] Some authorities are of the opinion that no inside-cell construction is needed in the medium-security plant, in that outside cells can provide sufficient security even for the more aggressive among the inmates who would be held in this type of institution. Outside-cell construction is considerably less expensive. See pp. 645, ftn. 17, and 649.

structed at somewhere between one-fifth and one-half the cost of maximum-security facilities, the amount required depending largely upon the
design, climate of the location, and the elements of the program.

The largest development of medium-security correctional institutions
has occurred in the Federal prison system, beginning in the early 1930s
when the Federal Bureau of Prisons was established. The nine Federal
prisons of this type, called Federal Correctional Institutions, constitute one
of the greatest contributions of the Bureau to progressive penology in

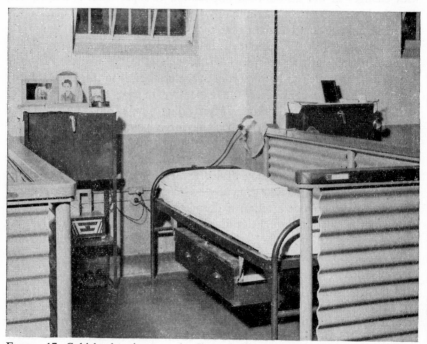

FIGURE 17. Cubicle dormitory at the Federal Correctional Institution, Tallahassee,
Florida.

America. The Bureau has varied the design and construction of these institutions in order to discover what forms are best suited for future imitation in terms of efficiency and economy of operation and effectiveness in
the implementation of program.[13] One of the best of these, the establish-

[13] The Federal medium-security prisons are built on three differing basic plans:
the telephone-pole, the unit or open-campus type of institution, and the self-enclosed
design. The first two may be mixed. The self-enclosing structure, exemplified by
the Federal Correctional Institutions at Danbury, Connecticut; Milan, Michigan; and
Sandstone, Minnesota, is an interesting departure from fence and wall construction
in its mode of providing against escape. The enclosure is provided by the buildings
themselves. At Danbury outside-cell blocks are located inside the courtyard, while
the inside-cell blocks are used as part of the enclosing building. Dormitories are
separated from the outside wall by a wire mesh screen. The escape record there is

ment at Ashland, Kentucky, now used for youth offenders committed under the Federal Youth Corrections Act, has been pictured above. A few states have also built medium-security institutions. Notable examples are the Wallkill Prison in New York, the California Institution for Men at Chino, the Bordentown State Reformatory in New Jersey, and the Norfolk Massachusetts Institution to which reference has previously been made. Two of these are illustrated in this chapter in Figures 18 and 19. These institutions also vary considerably in size and construction.[14] In general, however, they all have in common an emphasis upon careful selection of population,

FIGURE 18. Medium-security prison at Wallkill, New York.

good programs of classification within the institution, and strong provisions for treatment and training. In none of the states are there enough medium-security facilities to provide for the very considerable proportion of offenders who should be assigned to such institutions. Their value, however, has come to be more generally recognized in recent years.

---

far lower than that of many maximum-security prisons with walls. Such institutions, while they are economical to construct and supervise, must be sufficiently large in perimeter at the start to allow for any expansion of buildings and facilities that may prove to be desirable. Otherwise space needed for rehabilitative aspects of the program may be sacrificed through later construction. See *Design and Construction*, p. 83.

[14] Chino, housing a population of 2,477 in 1956, is excessively large from the point of view of effective treatment, but see Kenyon Scudder, *Prisoners Are People*, 1952. The population at Wallkill, at the other extreme, is under 500.

Minimum-security institutions are operated without armed guard posts, though they sometimes have a fenced enclosure, particularly where they are located in or near populous urban areas. Dormitories are commonly used for a greater part of the population. The Federal Correctional Institution at Seagoville, Texas, with an inmate capacity of about 400, is an outstanding and singularly attractive facility of this sort. Indeed, it is the only truly minimum-security institution for adult male criminals built for permanent use in the United States. Originally designed for the detention of female offenders, Seagoville was converted into an institution for males at the end of World War II. After an originally conservative policy of classification, it has been used for several years to accommodate a surprisingly varied population that has included men serving long terms and

FIGURE 19. State Prison Colony at Norfolk, Massachusetts.

others who would ordinarily be considered security risks. Experience there has demonstrated that an experimental approach to classification need not result in a high escape rate in an institution where a vital program is operated by skillful personnel in a sound treatment atmosphere.[15] There are 354 honor rooms and 63 medium-security outside-cell rooms at Seagoville (see Figure 20).

Minimum-security construction has been used for juvenile training

[15] The Federal Bureau remarks, "Here, in an open, unfenced institution, even men under life sentence have been safely confined. They have become so much interested in the possible value to them of the institution's rehabilitative program that they have lost the traditional impulse to escape." In the four-year period before the Bureau's classification program was established, the annual escape rate was 9.1 per 1,000 prisoners. In the four subsequent years the rate declined to 3.7 per thousand. *Design and Construction*, p. 15.

schools and in two states, New Jersey and Missouri, for reformatories designed to handle tractable young offenders. The Federal Reformatory at Petersburg, Virginia, pictured here in Figure 21, is of this sort. For the most part, however, open institutions are found today only in the form of

FIGURE 20. Federal Minimum-security Institution at Seagoville, Texas.

FIGURE 21. Federal Reformatory at Petersburg, Virginia.

work camps and farms, which are generally operated as adjuncts to a maximum- or medium-security institution. The Federal government inaugurated a prison camp program in 1926 and has since established eight such facilities, several of which are still in use. The camp at Tucson, Arizona, is shown below in Figure 22. California and Michigan have also developed strong camp programs in recent years where inmates are engaged, for the most part, in forestry and road work and in fire fighting. Camps offer particular advantages for the housing and treatment of offenders who are not escape risks. They are inexpensive, generally costing no more than $400 per inmate to construct, and they provide opportunity for vigorous and healthy activities that are particularly well suited to a young population.

Michigan retains 30 per cent of its male prisoners in camps and in other facilities outside prison walls, effectively confirming the value of minimum-security treatment. In the midfifties Pennsylvania established a mobile

FIGURE 22. Federal Prison Camp at Tucson, Arizona.

forestry camp for forty men, consisting of ten heavy-duty, specially designed house trailers. Four of these are used as inmate dormitories and the remainder for services and staff. The camp is used to develop and maintain conservation projects in the forests, preserves, parks, and fish lands of the state.

Custodial Classification. A number of correctional authorities have formulated estimates on the proportions of the prison population that should be classified to institutions of different levels of security. Such estimates have usually been based upon the three grades of security that the author has considered above. The table below, expressing views of several authorities, reveals something of the disparity of opinion that exists. Such variations undoubtedly reflect in part the differing circumstances that prevail in the various jurisdictions. It is apparent, for example, that the presence of misdemeanants in prisons, the use of a specialized medical facility or of a reformatory, the policy of using probation generously for the better grade of offenders, and disparities in the distribution of offenders according to age, crime, and recidivism, may all affect markedly the varying range of security requirements in a particular state. There are differences, too, in the policy views of authorities concerning the degree of risk that may properly be taken in the housing and control of offenders, i.e., the significance of escape rates. The experts uniformly agree, however, that much fewer prisoners than we retain in maximum custody require such security measures and that many more should be classified to medium and minimum custody. Different experts in penology have made the following estimates in recent years:[16]

	A	B	C	D	E
Maximum security.........	$\frac{1}{3}$	15%	10%	39%	28%
Medium security..........	$\frac{1}{3}$	$\frac{1}{2}$	60%	20%	47%
Minimum security.........	$\frac{1}{3}$	$\frac{1}{3}$	25%	41%	25%

It appears that ideally a state ought as an outer limit to house no more than 35 per cent of its felons in institutions of maximum security and that in some jurisdictions no more than 20 per cent require this level of security. These are, for the most part, offenders with long prison terms still to be served, those with outstanding warrants, men with history of attempts to escape or with poor records of prison behavior, and aggressive and unstable types.[17] It has been suggested that about 2 per cent of the most incorrigible, intractible, and dangerous prisoners require supersecurity measures. The number of the latter is too small in most jurisdictions to justify the employment of a separate and specialized facility for the purpose; such prisoners may be retained in a unit of an ordinary maximum-security prison under intensive supervision.

The American Correctional Association has approved a standard under

[16] These data are drawn from *Design and Construction*, p. 12; *A Manual of Correctional Standards*, pp. 170–171; and *Contemporary Correction*, p. 287.

[17] In its volume on design and construction the Federal Bureau has said: "The unnecessary expense of such super-security prison construction is obvious and even scandalous. These prisons with tool-resisting, fortress-like cell-blocks, cost in 1938 to 1940 from $5,000 to $7,500 per inmate to construct, even before the recent rise in costs. The bars used in such prisons are usually twice as large, and more than twice as strong, as those used in zoos to restrain lions or giant Kodiak bears. By adopting a system of classification of prisoners and building prisons according to realistic security requirements, 25 per cent of the inmates can be safely housed in rooms costing (1938–1940) not over $1,500 per inmate, 50 per cent in medium-security quarters which do not cost over $2,500 per inmate, and the remainder in sufficiently secure inside cells at a construction cost of not over $3,500 per inmate, at the outside." *Op. cit.,* p. 33.

which no more than 1,200 prisoners would be contained in an adult prison, even one of maximum security, while acknowledging, however, the desirability of smaller populations than this for effective treatment purposes. It is apparent on this basis that a state requires no more than a single maximum-security prison unless its total felony population exceeds 3,000. The contrast of present practice with the ideal may be seen in the fact that today there are fifty-three correctional institutions in twenty-nine different jurisdictions containing populations in excess of 1,200 and that nearly all of these are maximum-security prisons and reformatories. This implies that many existing institutions should be replaced, converted, or reduced in population.

Institutions of medium security should be employed for no less than 25 per cent of the felony population of any state. In the interest of effective programs of training and rehabilitation, any single institution of this sort should contain no more than 600 prisoners. It is quite clear that any state with a felony population in excess of 1,000 should provide a specialized institution of this type and, short of this, should establish medium-security features in connection either with its maximum-security or its minimum-security plants. Where felony populations exceed 3,000, at least two such facilities should be established.[18] Today very few jurisdictions have erected medium-security institutions for male felons. Several states, however, have built or renovated institutions that combine maximum- and medium-security features.

Minimum-security facilities of varied sorts that provide an experience of relative freedom in group living should house no less than 20 per cent of the prison population. Ideally institutions at this level should contain no more than 400 inmates. Camps and road, park, or forestry crews must be considerably smaller. It is desirable that one or more such facilities should be employed, however small may be the felony population of the state. This can easily be done, at least in part, by the operation of farms in connection with existing prisons. Minimum-security facilities are valuable, not only for tractable types and first offenders at the time of original classification, but also for long-term and repetitive criminals as a bridge from the ordinary prison to parole in the community. In some cases minimum-security facilities can also be used effectively for temporary retraining in cases where parole or probation is suspended.

Mixed-custody institutions, such as the penitentiaries of the Federal Bureau of Prisons, containing only a small proportion of maximum-security inside cells, can be used to accommodate a large fraction of the adult felony population in any state that can provide only a limited number and

---

[18] Using relatively small medium- and minimum-custody institutions, it should be possible to specialize in states having fairly large prison populations, e.g., for first offenders, infirm aged prisoners, the 22 to 30 year age group, preparole preparation, and possibly other special treatment categories.

variety of correctional facilities. Farms or camps should be operated in conjunction with such institutions, with reduced supervision for that substantial part of the population that requires only minimum custody.[19] Few states today have either medium- or minimum-custody institutions, and not many have yet established prisons of mixed custodial provisions. Where they have moved at all in this direction it has been on a very limited scale and, hence, intensive programs of rehabilitation have been difficult or impossible to carry on with any considerable proportion of the penal population. Progress in the future of penology lies in the reduction in the use of maximum-security prisons and a corresponding expansion in the number of relatively small medium- and minimum-security constructions.

Some idea of differential construction costs in recent years for the several levels of housing facilities in a mixed-custody institution may be inferred from expenditures by the state of California at the reformatory-type Deuel Vocational Institution at Tracy, completed in August of 1953.[20] This was built for a capacity of 1,213 cell prisoners and 30 hospital patients at a total cost of a little less than 12 million dollars or approximately $9,600 per inmate. Housing buildings represented 28 per cent of the total costs of the institution. To construct outside cells, of which there are 924 divided among six buildings, required $2,600 per cell, including plumbing. One hundred and forty-four inside cells, all in one building, cost $3,400 each with plumbing and open-grill steel cell fronts. A special segregation building containing 145 cells (as well as separate dining, shop, classroom, and yard facilities) required $3,800 per cell. Dormitory facilities were not constructed there, but it was estimated that a dormitory building to house 160 men would have cost $1,260 per bed. It is interesting to observe that the California authorities deliberately avoided dormitory construction in the view that the ultimate resulting costs would be greater. The expense of supervising dormitories was estimated at double that required for cell blocks accommodating a similar number of men. Thus, the total cost of building and operating the cell construction would be lower during the expected period of usefulness of the institution and at the same time greater efficiency and security would be provided.

An approach to the problem of providing small and diversified correctional facilities with differing degrees of security provisions lies in what Richard A. McGee, director of corrections in California, has called the

[19] The *Manual of Correctional Standards* observes that "even in the smallest state it is possible to have a certain degree of diversification of program and custody within a single institution. . . . The principle to bear in mind should be that as soon as there are enough prisoners of a certain homogeneous type, requiring a somewhat specialized program of custody and treatment, this group should be separated in a specialized institution. This does not mean, however, that there cannot be diversification of housing, custody, and treatment within a single institution." *Ibid.,* pp. 169–170.

[20] See *A Manual of Correctional Standards,* pp. 180–182.

"satellite design."[21] This involves several more or less closely adjacent units functioning under an administrative center that could provide for the entire group central storage and preparation of food, maintenance facilities, laundry, hospital, power and water supply, sewage disposal, and perhaps other facilities and services as well. It would combine real advantages of economy together with the virtues of treatment and training that can come only through close staff-inmate associations in small institutions. Provisions for enclosure and supervision could be gauged effectively to the populations classified to the several units. The Pennsylvania Industrial School at Camp Hill, near Harrisburg, for prisoners of reformatory age, opened in 1941, has made an approach to this sort of arrangement, though on only a limited scale. It has two quite distinct but adjacent sections, one a group of medium-minimum-security facilities in a fenced enclosure, the other a maximum-security unit surrounded by a wall. Treatment and training facilities are available to both groups of offenders. Prisons in Melbourne and Sydney, Australia, have been remodeled with this sort of concept in mind. Thus far there has been little evidence of such a trend in the United States except for the establishment of a few prison farms and camps. California has developed the satellite design at Chino and Soledad, however, and Louisiana is doing so at the time of writing.

REFORMATORIES AND VOCATIONAL TRAINING SCHOOLS

The development of reformatories for young adult males had its beginning in New York State some fifty years after the first institutional segregation of delinquent juveniles occurred there. Elmira Reformatory was a hybrid institution; designed as an ordinary mass prison to contain 1,700 inmates over 16 years of age, both felons and misdemeanants, it was converted to use as a reformatory. It provided a mixture of emphasis upon training, education, regimented military discipline, and the marking system by which prisoners earned release.[22] The idea of a special facility for young adults where emphasis should be given to training was a sound one, but it failed to crystallize into a solid, significant program for a specific group.[23] It has not done so, unfortunately, in the ensuing years.[24] Seven other re-

[21] *Ibid.*, pp. 178–179.

[22] As the author has observed elsewhere, the principle of the indefinite sentence combined with parole was also inaugurated at Elmira when Brockway opened that institution in 1876. The marking system was begun by Governor Alexander MacConochie in the Australian system of transportation.

[23] Like Elmira, the reformatories at Concord, New Hampshire, and Huntingdon, Pennsylvania, were built as maxium-security prisons and later converted into "reformatory institutions."

[24] The Federal Bureau has appraised the failure of the reformatories in these terms: "The reasons for this so-called failure of reformatories—and it can be demonstrated that most of them have failed to achieve the results hoped for in the 1870's—are not difficult to determine and assess. It was originally held that the

formatories for males in use today were established before 1900, all but one of these to accommodate populations in excess of 1,000, and were patterned largely on the prison design of the parent structure at Elmira. Before 1940, eleven additional state reformatories that are still in use were constructed, most of these to house groups of from 700 to 2,000 men.[25] One comparable institution, the California Vocational Institution at Tracy, has been erected since 1940.[26] Today there are twenty reformatories for men in eighteen states, most of them receiving offenders over 16 to 18 years of age. Three have no upper age limit, while seven have an upper limit of 30 and one of 36. Most of the others deal with prisoners up to the age of 25 or 26. It is apparent that the reformatories attempt to deal with age spans that are too broad from the point of view of specialized correctional treatment. Since the general prison population is of youthful age, the median being little higher than that in the reformatories, they can not be distinguished on the basis of relative maturity.[27] Nor is there any clear line of distinction in the prior criminal records or the training needs of their populations. Many of them differ but little in program and correctional impact from the nineteenth-century prison. It is probably correct to say that, as compared with the medium- and minimum-security programs that have developed in recent years, the programs in most of our reformatories are considerably more traditional, less imaginative, and less successful in treatment.

Comparison is invited with the special facilities that have been developed in Britain since 1895 to deal with young persons in the ages from 16 to 21. Nearly half of that age group are committed to the Borstal system, the remainder going to prison.[28] In England there were in 1958 two reception

---

physical plants would be small enough to house the desirable reformatory population and would be designed to accord with the reformatory philosophy; that reformatory inmates would be markedly different in age from those held in prisons; that the indeterminate sentence would prevail in reformatory procedure; that the disciplinary procedure would be much more enlightened and flexible than in prisons; and that educational activities, especially vocational education, would predominate in the reformatory program. None of these assumptions has worked out at all fully in the majority of institutions." *Design and Construction,* p. 111.

[25] One additional state, Kentucky, established what it has called a reformatory in 1939, but no upper age limit was fixed and it appears to be differentiated from a prison to a very limited extent.

[26] Florida also established a "correctional institution" in 1949 to which commitments are made between the ages of 12 and 25. North Carolina launched two "youth centers" in 1949 and 1952 for males between the ages of 16 and 25.

[27] The Federal Bureau of Prisons points out that, while 47 per cent of all inmates received in reformatories were between the ages of 20 and 30 years, 45 per cent of those admitted to penitentiaries are of similar age and there is not, therefore, very significant difference between the populations so far as age is concerned. Disciplinary and reformative programs are also similar in the better institutions for adult offenders. *Design and Construction, loc. cit.*

[28] See *State and National Correctional Institutions of the United States of America, Canada, England and Scotland,* August, 1957.

centers for preliminary study and classification, fifteen training Borstals, of which two are for girls, and three correctional and recall centers. The Borstals for males vary in size from Buckley Hall in Lancashire, with a normal capacity of 100, to Kent, Feltham, Hollesley Bay, and Portland, each designed to contain about 350. They offer a wide diversity of training programs, ranging from vigorous outdoor work at farming, clearing land, and reclamation in the open camps and colonies to technical training and production in some of the closed institutions. Classification is based upon maturity, offense history, conduct, and character. The author has been impressed by the active program of work, training, education, and recreation, carried on with a considerable spirit of freedom, by the close relationship of the Borstal boys with the working staff, and by the emphasis upon relationships and contacts with the outside community. The Home Office has expressed a primary purpose to strengthen character in the youthful offender:[29]

> That young offenders ought not to be sent to prison as long as that course can by any means be avoided is axiomatic. But a time comes for some of them when training under detention appears to be essential if they are not to drift into the ranks of the persistent offenders. The Borstal system was set up by Part 1 of the Prevention of Crime Act, 1908, to provide for such training. The object of the system is the all-round development of character and capacities—moral, mental, physical, and vocational—with particular emphasis on the development of responsibility and self-control, through trust increasing with progress. This conception requires conditions as unlike those of a prison as is compatible with compulsory detention. Responsibility and self-control are virtues which can only be attained by practising them, and they cannot be practised without opportunity for self-determination appropriate to the stage of development reached.
>
> The system must also be elastic, to provide methods of training and conditions suitable to different types of character and stages of development.

In recent years there has been a renaissance in the effort to deal with young adults. Under the administration of the Federal Youth Corrections legislation, intensive training and rehabilitation programs have been developed by the Bureau of Prisons at Chillicothe, Ohio; Ashland, Kentucky; and Englewood, Colorado. Figure 23 shows a view of the Ohio institution. California established a fine vocational and treatment regime at the Deuel Vocational Institution at Tracy in 1953. While this facility is too large, holding a population of over 1,200, it has displayed, like other institutions under the department of corrections in that state, a creative pioneering in correctional methods that should provide leadership to other states. There the system includes a Pilot Intensive Counseling Program (PICO), an intensive treatment unit, a complete program of academic training,

---

[29] *Prisons and Borstals,* His Majesty's Stationery Office, London, 1945, pp. 32–37.

vocational education in most major trades, and a very active recreational program. These combine to offer offenders who are classified to that institution after reception-diagnostic studies a correctional experience that to the author appeared superior in many ways to that provided in any other mass institution for young offenders that he has observed.[30] It is alive, experimental, research-conscious. In other jurisdictions, the New York Vocational Institution at West Coxsackie, emphasizing vocational and social education, and the New Jersey Reformatory at Bordentown, emphasizing individual and group counseling, also reflect the growing contemporary emphasis upon experimentation and intensive treatment. In both of these states as well as in Michigan, camp programs for young

FIGURE 23. Federal Reformatory at Chillicothe, Ohio.

adult offenders have recently been initiated in pursuance of precedents established in the Borstal and California systems. As has been noted elsewhere, New Jersey has created a four-month intensive treatment program at Highfields where a form of group therapy is combined with a work program for selected boys aged 16 and 17.[31]

It will be apparent from what has been said above that the specialization of treatment for young offenders has developed thus far to only a small extent. Our modes of dealing with young adults are seriously at fault. It is this group that is responsible for so large a part of serious crime, that displays so high a rate of recidivism, and that contributes so ex-

---

[30] See Paul W. Tappan, "Young Adults under the Youth Authority," *J. Crim. L.*, vol. 47, pp. 629–647, March–April, 1957, and *PICO, A Measure of Casework in Corrections: First Technical Report of Preliminary Findings,* Deuel Vocational Institution, California State Department of Corrections, January, 1958.

[31] See pp. 502–506.

cessively to the mature criminal population. The need to separate offenders of later teen ages from juveniles and from mature criminals has been very generally recognized, but special training institutions are lacking even in the more populous states. Moreover, fifteen of the established reformatories exceed in capacity the standard generally set as an ideal maximum. The age ranges presently fixed by law are too wide in most jurisdictions, the populations too heterogeneous, and the programs sterile.

It appears that any state with felony commitments in excess of 2,000 should establish a separate vocational institution for youths between the ages of 16 or 17 and 23, providing at least in part for medium and/or minimum custody and for a resident population no greater than 500 or 600 inmates. If it is not feasible to establish a specialized institution, separate segregation should be provided to youths through camp programs and through subsidiary divisions of other correctional institutions. This is not to suggest that all young adults in the specified age range should be held in a specialized facility. Some highly aggressive young offenders are better handled as members of a more mature population where they enjoy little status. It is also true that the presence of a few relatively mature offenders in a youth institution may not only act as a stabilizing influence but may also provide skills that are essential to the effective operation of a vocational institution. There should be room under the statutory provisions, therefore, for administrative discretion in the classification of offenders to the end that institutions for young adults may concentrate on a group that is in general homogeneous in relation to age but that will permit of some exceptions. Wherever possible there should be, as the Federal Bureau of Prisons has recommended, two types of reformatory design in a state, one to provide close custody for the more intractable young offenders and another of open-campus style that can offer a more varied program of treatment activities.[32] The Annandale Reformatory in New Jersey is a good illustration and is one of the few of the latter type. It is supplemented in that state by a close-custody institution at Bordentown for the more difficult reformatory cases. In the latter, too, there is intensive emphasis upon treatment rather than merely on custody and work.

Prisons and Reformatories for Women

One might imagine that the complete separation of women for treatment in penal institutions should have been the first and firmest policy in correctional classification.[33] Yet it appears that in the early days of congregate confinement in British and American jails separation was quite casual and

[32] *Design and Construction, op. cit.,* pp. 124–125.
[33] For a more detailed treatment of women's correctional institutions, see Henrietta Additon, "Women's Institutions," in Tappan (ed.), *op. cit.,* chap. 19, and *A Manual of Correctional Standards,* chap. 27.

incomplete. It is recorded that women of easy virtue sought commitment to these institutions where they might pursue their harlotry unrestrained and that men of means in jail could enjoy all the sensual pleasures. The segregation of women from men has been a gradual and still only partial development, in spite of the strong recurrent pressure of reformists. For a considerable period this involved no more than their isolation in small sections of institutions designed primarily for the imprisonment of men where they were supervised in whole or part by male warders, the latter commonly of no stronger moral character than their charges. It is one measure of our progress in contemporary penology that this situation still persists in some parts of the United States.

The first separate prison for women in this country was opened at Indianapolis, Indiana, in 1873, and the first reformatory for women was started four years later in Massachusetts, not long after the opening of the Elmira Reformatory for men. Only three other penal institutions specifically for women were established during the ensuing thirty-six years, reformatories in New York (1901), the District of Columbia (1910), and New Jersey (1913). Since that time twenty-one separate institutions, including the Federal Reformatory for Women, have been established. The remaining states today retain their female prisoners in sections of men's prisons (in seventeen states), in the women's institutions of neighboring states (in four states), or in branches of other correctional institutions. In 1958 the governors and attorneys general of fourteen western states gave attention to proposals for pooling prison facilities for the improved care of female and maximum-security convicts.

The nature and quality of specialized facilities for women as well as their thus far quite limited development may be attributed in the main to two factors: the relatively small number of females who are committed to long-term institutions and the generally minor character of the offenses for which they are committed. Women represent less than 5 per cent of the prison population of the country. In 1957 only one of the separate institutions contained more than 500 female offenders, and this was a combined population of the women's reformatory and prison in New York. Sixteen others, including the Federal facility, held populations between 100 and 500, while the remainder had fewer than 100. Among the states where women were held in men's institutions, they numbered fewer than 50. On the average most of the imprisoned female offenders were not serious criminals. Sex delinquents constituted a large part of the total. Nearly one-fourth had been convicted of larceny, including shoplifting. Roughly 5 per cent of them had been committed in each category for homicide, burglary, robbery, and drug law violations. Partly because they commit fewer and less serious crimes than men, women are less frequently sent to prison or reformatory and are committed for shorter terms. Once committed they are, for the most part, more amenable to control than men are, although experience has revealed quite vividly on some occasions that young females can be most difficult in a training school or reformatory situation when administrative policy has been weak or when trouble has been fomented by a few ringleaders.

Two contrasting consequences have ensued from the frequency and nature of the criminality of women. On the one hand, there is a considerable public and official tolerance for experimental programs carried on in medium- and minimum-security institutions for this group. Rigorous custody and discipline need not and in general are not emphasized.[34] Instead, at least in the better institutions of this type, the stress is upon building morale and retraining the skills and attitudes of the population. On the other hand, too little attention is devoted to the specialized training and treatment needs of women in a majority of jurisdictions. Even where "reformatory" institutions are used, the term as applied to specialized facilities for women means less if anything than it does in men's institutions similarly labeled. Ordinarily there is no upper age limitation on eligibility. Differences that once existed relative to sentencing and training programs have largely disappeared with the general development of indefinite sentences to ordinary prisons and of educational and training opportunities in the latter. There is certainly a need for specialized institutional treatment of young adult females, in the age range from 16 to 23 or 25, as there is for males in this age group, but it is quite unlikely that this need will soon be met by separately classified institutions. There are not enough candidates for reform!

It is the prevailing view of correctional authorities that separate institutions for women, preferably facilities of an open or medium-security type, constructed on a cottage plan, should be more generally developed.[35] Even where, because of the small populations involved, this would result in relatively large per capita costs, the expenditures involved would represent only a small part of the state's correctional budget. Where this step cannot be taken or where, in the interest of utilizing a larger institution with more diversified program, such a course appears more desirable, effort should be directed to the establishment and operation of

[34] However, according to the American Prison Association, the flogging of women prisoners, usually by male employees, has continued to be employed in men's institutions where women were confined, even for minor disciplinary offenses. As the Association has observed, such flogging and "spanking" should be abolished immediately and forever. *A Manual of Correctional Standards*, p. 486.

[35] A single institution for the full range of types of women committed on long terms may, like the Illinois Reformatory at Dwight, combine a cottage structure for offenders in the young adult age group with larger and more secure units for more serious adult offenders. The Dwight institution is built on a site of 160 acres of which a plot of 100 acres is surrounded by a woven-wire fence. It has eight cottages for classification of the younger inmates and a later-constructed medium-security building as well as industrial, training, hospital, and administrative facilities.

a woman's institution by two or more states in combination. Sufficient space should be made available for the facilities required in a varied program of training and production and for a farming operation. The American Correctional Association *Manual* has emphasized that the vocational training opportunities in a women's institution should include not only such activities, related to maintenance, as housework of all sorts, including the preparation and service of food, but "power sewing and other industrial operations, commercial and family type laundry work, animal husbandry and other farm work requiring technical knowledge and skill, clerical and secretarial work, practical nursing and hospital attendants' duties, child care, beauty culture, and the work of dental hygienists and X-ray technicians."[36] The planning and design of the correctional institution must take into account this diversity of activities. Experimental programs in classification, housing, and treatment can be developed in these institutions.

The Medicocorrectional Center

One of the difficult problems in contemporary correctional practice is that of providing adequately for psychologically and physically ill offenders who should be dealt with separately from other prisoners both for their own welfare and in the interest of the latter as well. Psychotic criminals are ordinarily detained in a security division of an ordinary state mental hospital or, much less commonly, in an institution of the correctional department specifically intended for such cases. The New York State Correctional Department provides two such institutions; Matteawan receives insane offenders certified from the courts, and Dannemora receives psychotic transferees from other penal institutions. Massachusetts commits its criminally insane along with defective delinquents, drug addicts, inebriates, and poor persons to its correctional institution at Bridgewater. As has been observed elsewhere, a few states (Maryland, Massachusetts, New York, Pennsylvania, and Virginia) also provide special facilities for "defective delinquents," variously defined in the relevant statutes. California (at Vacaville) and the Federal government (at Springfield, Missouri) have established special medical-psychiatric facilities for a variety of chronic medical and medicopsychiatric problems. The North Carolina Prison Department has a small sanatorium for tubercular inmates. Finally, the United States Public Health Service provides two hospitals (in Lexington, Kentucky, and Fort Worth, Texas) for offenders and voluntary commitments of individuals who are addicted to narcotic drugs.

Aside from the special provisions noted above, psychiatric and chronic medical problems are generally handled withing the population of the ordinary prisons with unfortunate results. Within any prison system there is at any time a fairly considerable proportion of cases, variously estimated

[36] *Ibid.*, p. 479.

at from 5 to 25 per cent of the population, who are not certifiably insane but who are psychiatric deviates, mental defectives, psychopaths,
sexual aberrants, narcotic addicts, and others suffering from chronic or
acute disorders that require intensive or continuous care and treatment.
Inclusion of alcoholics would increase the proportion considerably. Ordinary prison hospitals and other segregated quarters of the prison are not
properly planned and staffed to handle these problems effectively; they
cannot provide the kinds of treatment required or adequate segregation
from the remainder of the population.

There is some difference of opinion concerning the aberrational types
that may properly be dealt with in a single institution, even if it be a
specialized medical or psychiatric facility. Strong and convincing argument
has been advanced against retaining psychopaths and sex deviates with
psychotics.[37] It is commonly believed that mental defectives should be
treated separately from the mentally diseased and disordered. It may well
be maintained that offenders suffering from major physical problems should
ordinarily be institutionalized separately from those with psychiatric
disabilities, a division that is quite traditional. One might draw a brief
for the separate institutional classification of each of the major classes of
medicopsychological disorders to the end that we might specialize our
treatment and research programs and come to deal with them more
effectively. It is apparent, at any rate, that diversification of medical and
psychiatric facilities, in so far as it can be achieved, is desirable, but it
is equally apparent that the great majority of states will not consider it
feasible within the foreseeable future to carry such specialization far.[38]

The author believes that states with prison population of 2,500 or more
and certainly those with populations of 5,000 should provide a specialized
facility for medicocorrectional cases that are not certifiably insane. This
has been done in Maryland as well as in more populous jurisdictions. The
best results can be achieved through provisions for transfer by the correctional administration from other institutions on the basis of clinical
study, the procedure that is used in California. A state with a penal
population of 10,000 or more (*A Manual of Correctional Standards* of
the American Prison Association suggests 15,000) should give thought
to the establishment of a second institution for greater specialization in
treatment. The lines of classification that should be drawn would depend
in part upon the provisions already made in the state, if any, for a proper
handling of prisoners with mental defects and chronic medical illness. It

[37] See, *inter alia,* Tappan, *The Habitual Sex Offender,* New Jersey Commission on
the Habitual Sex Offender, 1950.

[38] The institution for psychopaths at Herstedvester, Denmark, is probably the most
specialized institution for nonpsychotic emotional deviates that has been developed
thus far. Its definition of psychopathic personality is very broad, however, See
Paul W. Tappan, "Treatment of the Sex Offender in Denmark," *Am. J. Psychiat.,*
vol. 108, pp. 241–249, October, 1951.

is clear that the establishment of institutions as specialized as possible, for the medicocorrectional treatment of those who suffer from severe emotional illness but who are not psychotic, should receive a high priority in state correctional planning. Such institutions would require varied custodial provisions, maximum, medium, and minimum, for the different types of prisoners held and the institution as a whole should be of medium-security type. Obviously, the effectiveness of the institution would depend quite fundamentally upon an adequate staff of clinical specialists. Correctional casework in such a facility must be of a high order. The best experience derived from active correctional programs should be applied rather than a sterile hospital routine. The greater costs inevitably involved in the operation of such an institution must be justified on the basis of the more effective treatment that presumably would occur there. In the interest of economy, a satellite design may be well suited to the needs for classification and specialization of medical and psychiatric treatment in some states.

Institutions for Minor Offenders

In the author's historical account of the development of prisons it has been observed that the old local gaol, tower, and workhouse, used originally for the detention of prisoners awaiting trial or punishment, were the predecessors of both the modern jail and the prison systems. Short-term facilities, while they have evolved from their original primitive prototypes, are today the poorest of our penal facilities; they have been aptly called our "human garbage cans." They continue to serve an excessive variety of functions for heterogeneous populations of inmates under the penurious administration of counties and cities. Today jails are used for the temporary retention of prisoners awaiting trial and for short-term imprisonment. They detain individuals arrested for both felonies and minor offenses and material witnesses who are charged with no crime at all. While some individuals are held for only a day or so, others may be detained for a year or more. Generally from 35 to 40 per cent or more of the jail population is made up of unconvicted defendants awaiting trial, among whom a large proportion (from 40 to 60 per cent) will later be released for lack of evidence of their guilt.

Jails are employed not only for prisoners convicted of minor offenses but for those arrested as felons who have taken pleas to lesser crimes. About 30 per cent or more of the jail population consists of those who have been sentenced to fines with jail as an alternative and who have been unable or unwilling to pay the fines. These individuals are in a position not unlike that of the prisoners of debt in another age. In a few jurisdictions convicted felons with short sentences may also be committed to local jails. On the other hand, in more than half the states, some misdemeanants may be committed to state institutions; misdemeanants may be committed to prisons in twelve jurisdictions, to reformatories in seven, and to state farms in six.

The number of jails and lockups in the United States is unknown. There are somewhat more than 3,000 counties in this country, however, of which at least 99 per cent provide one or more jail-type institutions, so that it is generally believed that there are between 3,000 and 4,000 county facilities in the United States.[39] There are also some 200,000 cities, towns, and villages, about 4,600 of these with populations in excess of 2,000. It is generally estimated that there is a total of somewhere between 7,000 and 15,000 jails and lockups in these communities. Some of the lockups are used only for temporary detention, while some of the city and county institutions are employed exclusively for imprisonment. Well over 90 per cent serve both functions, however, and a great majority of them contain fewer than fifteen prisoners. They range in size from village lockups with four or five bunks to city prisons designed to accommodate as many as from 1 to 3,000 inmates.

According to the Federal institutional census, there was a total population of 86,492 at one time in jails and workhouses in 1950.[40] This offers no adequate picture, however, of the flow of numbers through short-term institutions, for it is estimated that between one and two million violators are held in such places for some period of time each year. Fewer than 10 per cent of these are women[41] and fewer than 10 per cent are under the age of 20. It has been estimated that close to 100,000 juveniles are held in jails each year. About 5 per cent are 60 years of age or older, while the great majority, about 70 per cent, are in the age range of from 21 to 44. Approximately 70 per cent of these offenders are committed for disorderly conduct, vagrancy, liquor law violations, and petty theft, offenses that do not greatly stir public interest or anxiety. A very high proportion are repeaters, at least 60 per cent having known prior convictions. It is believed that another 10 to 30 per cent have been previously confined, though records are lacking to prove this. A very high proportion of jail inmates are alcoholics or excessive drinkers, types that contribute heavily to the recidivism rates. More than 70 per cent of those committed to jail are held for less than two months and over 40 per cent for less than twenty days. Only 5 per cent remain for periods in excess of one year. Considering the nature of the population and the brevity of imprisonment, it is obvious that there is little opportunity for rehabilitative treatment in the ordinary case even if programs in the jails were well designed.[42]

[39] See Roy Casey, "Catchall Jails," *The Annals,* vol. 293, pp. 28–35, May, 1954.

[40] At that time there were 178,065 offenders in long-term prisons.

[41] The figure was 7.4 per cent in 1950.

[42] See Louis N. Robinson, *Jails: Care and Treatment of Misdemeanant Prisoners in the United States,* Winston, 1944, pp. 42, 43.

Jails have been the subject of recurrent criticism and condemnation since the 1700s but little constructive attention had been given to reform until the present century.[43] Organized effort to encourage improvements has come recently through organizations such as the Committee on Jails of the American Prison Association, later superceded by the National Jail Association, and by the United States Bureau of Prisons.[44] The National Jail Association has directed its attack against several major faults of the jail system and has recommended a number of "essential principles" by way of remedy. The American Correctional Association has also promulgated a set of minimum standards for jails.

The most fundamental changes required in our jails are the separation by institution of unconvicted defendants from offenders undergoing imprisonment and the greatest possible reduction in the use of these institutions. Two quite different types of facilities are needed to deal with the present jail populations: detention quarters for those awaiting trial and treatment institutions for convicted minor offenders. As a matter of convenience, if not of necessity, the former must be reasonably accessible to the place of trial. Existing jails and lockups must continue to be used for temporary detention although most of them require extensive renovation and some should be consolidated into larger units in the interest of efficiency and economy. However, under sounder policies of bail administration in the courts, with the increased use of parole recognizance, and with a more speedy disposition of cases, it would be feasible to decrease very significantly both the number of individuals remanded to detention and the duration of stay of those who must be detained.[45] The marked decline in the number of detainees would permit the complete disuse of some of the worst of our jails and the greatly improved administration of others. In some jurisdictions where populations are small,

---

[43] In 1911 Joseph Fishman wrote what is perhaps the most spirited indictment that has been drawn of the jail system in his *Crucibles of Crime*. For a very effective recent manual on jail administration, see Myrl Alexander, *Jail Administration*, 1957.

[44] The prison bureau evaluates local jails through inspection service by which it rates these to determine their suitability for use for the detention of Federal prisoners. In recent years more than three-quarters of these institutions have been rated under 50 per cent on the Federal scale and are considered unfit for Federal prisoners.

[45] A study a few years ago of the bail system in Chicago revealed that some 70 per cent of unsentenced jail prisoners in that city had families in Chicago and only about one-fourth of them had ever been sentenced previously to imprisonment. One-half could provide good references. Beeley concluded from his investigation that these men were not permitted to make bail primarily because the courts lacked adequate machinery for finding out the facts about the accused and in many cases had set bail unnecessarily high, had failed to make clear to the defendant his right to bail, and had much too rarely employed their power to release the accused on his own recognizance. See A. L. Beeley, *The Bail System in Chicago*, 1927, and discussion of bail in Chapter 12.

local lockups should be replaced by larger intercounty units that could be operated more efficiently and humanely. Detention institutions, unlike commitment facilities for minor offenders, must provide for close custody to prevent escape of accused felons. They should in no way be punitive, however, and no greater restraint should be employed than is essential for safe detention.[46] They should provide amply for health, recreation, and segregation of types that are dangerous. Separate sleeping quarters should be assigned to each detainee. Figure 24 illustrates a large modern detention facility in Brooklyn, New York.

FIGURE 24. Brooklyn House of Detention, New York City.

For the correctional treatment of minor offenders, institutions are required that are adequate in size and staff to provide intensive programs of rehabilitation. Misdemeanant workhouses, industrial farms, and road camps—types of facilities that are employed today in only a minority of jurisdictions—are best suited to the purpose. Not only can they provide an active and constructive program, but to a large extent they can also defray the costs of operating the facility. Ideally they should be established

[46] In *Commonwealth v. Brines*, 29 Dist. Rept., 1901, Judge Thomas D. Finletter said, "It seems to be forgotten that an accused is not a convict, and that it is only strong necessity that compels his detention before trial. It is a restraint of the liberty of his person which is unavoidable. It certainly should not be aggravated by the infliction of any unnecessary indignity."

as state or as intercounty institutions in those places where the single county or city cannot support a proper facility of its own. The Denver County Jail, pictured in Figure 25, is a recent example of a well-constructed institution of this sort.

The use of jails for commitment, especially for brief periods of less than ninety days, so common today, should be greatly reduced. A majority of cases of imprisonment for failure to pay fines can be eliminated by the general use of an installment system of payments, as experience in a number of places has shown.[47] Ordinary commitments could also be

FIGURE 25. County Jail of Denver, Colorado.

drastically reduced by the sort of device that Wisconsin has used since 1943 under its Huber Law, providing for the service of jail terms at night

[47] Recent figures indicate that 67.5 per cent of all offenders committed to jail for short terms were incarcerated as a result of their inability to pay fines. Cicely M. Craven, in "Criminal Justice in England," *Can. B. Rev.*, November, 1949, observes that imprisonment in England for default of payment of fines dropped from 79,583 in 1913 to 15,261 in 1923 as the result of legislation providing for time payment. Additional legislation in 1935 that required the court to inquire into the offender's ability to pay reduced such commitments still further to 2,646 in 1946. An American authority finds that in American states where fines are based upon the ability to pay and where installment paying is allowed fewer than 5 per cent of those who would have been incarcerated if this method had not been used were finally committed. Charles H. Miller, "The Fine—Price Tag or Rehabilitative Force," *N.P.P.A. J.*, vol. 2, pp. 377–385, October, 1956.

and permitting selected offenders to work during the daytime.[48] Many other minor offenders who today are sent to jail should be given suspended sentences with or without probation supervision. Most delinquents who require correctional treatment should receive terms of three months or longer in cases in which definite sentences are used. It is desirable, however, to establish a system of indefinite sentencing, at least for repetitive misdemeanants, with terms ranging from three or six months to two years and with parole supervision after release. This would provide an opportunity for a treatment program of some significance and would offer greater motivation to the offender than can be achieved under the very brief definite sentences that are now characteristic. Experience indicates that short "shock" terms have no value for chronic offenders and have very little value for others.

Many of the essentially noncriminal deviates who today are committed to jail because of the poor perception of magistrates or the lack of probation investigation reports should be dealt with by other departments of government rather than corrections. This is true, in particular, of psychotics, mental defectives, indigents, alcoholics, narcotic users, and prostitutes. In instances where individuals in these categories must be committed to short-term correctional institutions because of some significantly antisocial behavior, specialized treatment programs there are essential if the state is not to continue to defeat its purpose and to waste its funds. It is true that appropriate facilities and programs for the treatment of minor offenders will be relatively costly, but in the long run it will prove far less expensive than the present regime of bare custody, which results in excessive rates of criminal contagion and recidivism.

Attention will now be given to some of the more detailed criticisms that have been made of the jail system and to reforms that have been proposed. The first of these relates to personnel selection. Traditionally, whether appointive or elective, this has been a matter of rewarding the politically faithful without regard to their competence in jail operation. It is rare, of course, for an unqualified staff to develop progressive methods of administration. Obviously, the supervision and discipline of prisoners should be conducted exclusively by paid and trained personnel; the trustee system and the use of kangaroo courts—both fortunately on the wane but still all too prevalent—are unjustifiable measures of control. The fee sytem continues to be one of the notable and widespread abuses of jail ad-

---

[48] California uses a similar device in a number of counties, known as a "work furlough." One California judge has expressed the opinion that "intermittent jailing" had a more profound effect upon the offender than did "continuous incarceration." See *The County Jails of California: An Evaluation,* Special Study Commission on Correctional Facilities and Services and the State Board of Corrections, Sacramento, June 30, 1957. In 1959 North Carolina, Montana, and Oregon enacted laws similar to the Huber Act.

ministration; under this system the sheriff or warden is given an allowance, sometimes based on the number of prisoners held, and may retain as his own whatever he may save through providing an inadequate diet to his prisoners and through practicing other "economies." The personnel problem can be resolved only by improved selection, the development of employee training programs, and adequate salary scales, divorced from fees or fines. Salary should be comparable to the levels in police and fire departments. Civil service standards of selection and training should be applied.

Jails are very commonly inadequate in structure and facilities even for the rudimentary decencies in living arrangements. The odorous filth that may be found in the ordinary jail is a product of obsolete construction, defective maintenance, and indifferent administration. Provisions for ventilation, sunlight, bathing, laundry, and toileting are primitive. They have provoked reams of lurid description in the literature on jails. A most effective way of approaching this problem, as well as others, in jail administration is through establishing a supervision of all short-term facilities by a state correctional authority. Fewer than one-third of the states provide any form of state control or inspection of jails, but the experience of a number of jurisdictions where state inspection has been established by law indicates the value of this device for making and enforcing improved standards. A state agency should enjoy rather wide powers to enforce its standards and regulations. In the planning of new jail construction and the renovation of old facilities, dormitories and outside rooms should be designed to accommodate most of the population. Ample space should be allotted to facilities for reception, medical care, social services, food preparation and service, visiting, reading and study, recreation, work programs, and the isolation of appropriate cases.

Classification of the jail population is quite inadequate today. Convicted and unconvicted prisoners, young and old, sick and well, first-offender and chronic recidivist, sex deviates and the sexually normal are all held in close association, ordinarily with no formal effort at segregation except on the basis of sex. As the author has suggested above, extreme deviates should be handled so far as possible by other more specialized agencies, leaving to the jail the sufficiently difficult task of dealing with relatively normal adult minor offenders, the group to which its procedures can reasonably be geared. The common jail is usually the first and is often the only type of correctional institution to which law violators are exposed, so that it is especially important that its influence should be constructive rather than damaging. This can be accomplished only if there is a sufficient diversification of misdemeanant facilities and if these facilities are of high quality. In large urban centers where workhouses of some size can be operated and in regional industrial farms, a reasonably wide classification of types is possible within a single institution. Where a considerable number of small jail-type institutions are used, arrangement should be made, so far as possible, for specialization of these institutions and for classification of offenders to the appropriate facility and program.

A great majority of jails lack any constructive program of work, training, treatment, or recreation. Prisoners live in sterile and deteriorative idleness. Ideally, as the American Correctional Association has suggested, sentenced prisoners should be held in work-farm institutions where all able-bodied inmates would have full-time, productive employment in either farm work or in simple industrial operations.[49] Even in the more traditional type of jail, however, all inmates could and should be usefully occupied in maintenance and repair, truck gardening and canning, clothing manufactures and repair, or one or more other varieties of constructive activity. The enlistment of community cooperation and liaison with other governmental agencies can enrich the jail program immensely in the areas of education, recreation, and religion. Universities and agencies concerned with health, sanitation, food services, safety, medical standards, and mental health are important sources for the development of effective jail programs.

[49] *A Manual of Correctional Standards*, pp. 429–430.

Chapter 22

THE PRISON PROGRAM

It is the author's purpose in this chapter to consider the main elements in the programs of our prisons, including labor, vocational training, education, religion, special activities, discipline, and "treatment." These are formal aspects of prison activity, designed in part to reform offenders through changing their habits and attitudes. Whether they sometimes do so and, through improvement, can be made to do so more frequently is a controversial issue among the experts. Many have reached the dismal conclusion that by their very nature prisons can only make men worse. They have pointed to the hidden depths of a prison culture that perpetuates and strengthens the antisocial values of the imprisoned and they maintain that those who do not recidivate are individuals who were essentially non-criminal at the start. More optimistic penologists hold that certain phases of program or relationship in prison may have rehabilitative value, but these authorities diverge in their conceptions of what is useful. One group, for example, relies in the main on "therapy," another on "social education," and a third on training for good work habits. Some believe that the prison must be changed in its fundamental character; they would "tear down the walls" and construct correctional "hospitals" of some sort in their place. Others contend that, while prisons must be retained, they should be diversified to meet better the varied needs of the criminal population and that this together with an improvement in the quality of staff will achieve successful results with an increasing proportion of offenders.

The scope of responsibility undertaken by our prisons is not commonly appreciated. The modern correctional institution is a highly complex and compressed community where the state, in a sort of paternalistic despotism, must administer a wide variety of services. In an area, ordinarily, of a few acres, with staff of modest size, and with a watchful eye to the annual per capita cost, the institution must maintain the vigilant custody and un-natural control that public protection demands. It must also provide not only for the healthy physical maintenance of masses of men of many sorts —and the nature of the provisions for food, shelter, clothing, and diverse clinical care are deeply meaningful to morale and discipline in the con-strained environment—but also for social, recreational, and spiritual sustenance; for educational and occupational training; and for productive enterprise, commonly agricultural as well as industrial. To dispense such a reticulum of services wisely, humanely, efficiently, and economically is a formidable challenge to administration. The more populous and diverse the community, the more complicated and fragile becomes the network of

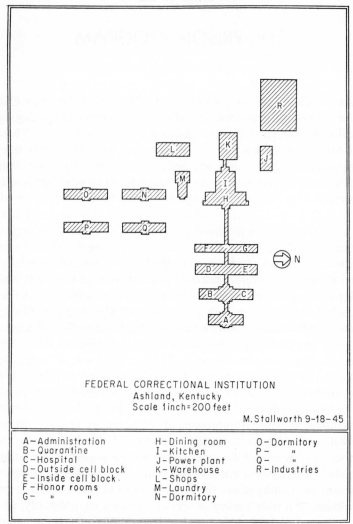

FEDERAL CORRECTIONAL INSTITUTION
Ashland, Kentucky
Scale 1 inch = 200 feet

M. Stallworth 9-18-45

A — Administration	H — Dining room	O — Dormitory
B — Quarantine	I — Kitchen	P — "
C — Hospital	J — Power plant	Q — "
D — Outside cell block	K — Warehouse	R — Industries
E — Inside cell block	L — Shops	
F — Honor rooms	M — Laundry	
G — " "	N — Dormitory	

FIGURE 26. Outline plan of Federal Correctional Institution at Ashland, Kentucky, showing major facilities provided there.

relationships that must be regulated. Compare the prison to the hotel, the hospital, the massive restaurant, the combined primary, technical, and high school, the recreational center, the interdenominational church, the post office and store, an aggregation of industries and farms, and the poly-clinic. The prison that would not only perform these numerous functions but must serve captured and unwilling patrons, all this with not merely a desire to protect and retain but to improve and reform them, assumes a colossal and multiform responsibility that cannot conceivably be met with more than limited success.

A more specific idea of the diversity of provisions required even in a small correctional institution may be inferred by studying Figure 26, an outline plan of the Federal Correctional Institution at Ashland, Kentucky, designed for a youth population under 500. It will be observed that four different types of housing facilities are employed there. Vocational training is carried on in a sizable furniture factory, machine shop, garage, painting and glass shop, kitchen, laundry, and building construction. Facilities are provided for the strong programs of academic work and industrial production that have been established there. In addition to the 20 acres of land on which the institution is located, there are also 100 acres of farm where all of the milk, eggs, and pork and a greater part of the vegetables used by the institution are produced. Excellent hospital and dental facilities are also provided at Ashland. See also Figure 13 above.

PRISONS PRO AND CON

Prisons do display in some measure the "cruelty and futility" that is often attributed to them. Patently, any mode of treatment and control of criminals that we might apply to large groups of men can be little more than an expedient compromise to serve conflicting ends. Imprisonment involves a number of intrinsic and palpable disadvantages. The massing of antisocial individuals together, while it may protect the community and avoid contamination of the innocent, provides less than an optimum climate for the development of socialized attitudes and habits. It is quite apparent that life in a totalitarian institution, a one-sexed institution at that, must be to a considerable degree abnormal and for that reason must be an imperfect preparation for responsible living in the free community. The limitations of the prison for the accomplishment of rehabilitation are increased by the necessary reliance in part upon the threat of force and upon custodial restriction to retain men against their will. What Gresham Sykes has called the "pains of imprisonment," the material and emotional deprivations, together with the minimal opportunities for creative expression and the diminutive rewards than can be meted out, result very commonly in attitudes and relationships that are unhealthy and antisocial.[1] These difficulties, and others associated with them, cannot be completely resolved, though their effects may be mitigated in some measure.

Despite the obvious disadvantages of incarceration as a means of correction, it appears certain that the prison system in its essential character

[1] See Gresham M. Sykes, *The Society of Captives: A Study of a Maximum Security Prison,* 1958, p. 14.

will persist, and for very good reasons. Foremost among these is the simple fact that, even if imprisonment comes to be used less frequently and for shorter terms than is characteristic today, there is no satisfactory alternative in many cases in which public protection is an important consideration. Imprisonment is the only sanction that has been devised that at the same time removes the offender from the circumstances in which his criminality was engendered, that protects the community by custodial provisions adjusted to the risk that he presents, and that provides opportunity for corrective treatment and training in a controlled environment. Moreover, since personal freedom is precious to the human being, imprisonment more than any other sanction has deterrent value for the control of crime, while it does not involve the gross and gratuitous suffering that inheres in other measures that have been used in the past. No less important is the versatility of imprisonment as a correctional device. Compared with other methods, it is adaptable to a diversity of ends and to a wide variety of offenders. While other sanctions generally deal with different offenders in much the same way, imprisonment can be adjusted both to divergent categories of criminals and in some fair measure to the distinct problems they present.

The chances of a man's success after discharge from prison depend upon three major variables: his preprison experience and attitudes, the changes in him that are effected during incarceration, and the influence of the postprison environment. The offender who is retained in prison for an average length of time is there long enough to sustain a heavy impact from prison life, but its influence relates selectively both to what he brings to the experience and to what he can draw from it as he returns to freedom. It is surely true that, so far as success in later adjustment is concerned, prerelease preparation and parole guidance to facilitate the transition of the prisoner into the community are important. The evidence indicates, however, that the total institutional experience may be valuable to a considerable proportion of offenders. The experience is conceived by some offenders to be valuable. A study by Edward J. Galway at the Chillicothe Reformatory, which receives Federal offenders between the ages of 17 and 31, throws some light on this.[2] In a group of 275 consecutively released inmates he found that 72 per cent (89 per cent of Negro and 68 per cent of white offenders) believed the institutional stay had been beneficial to them. Those who believed they had received some advantage from the experience indicated, in declining order of frequency, that this derived from (1) the socializing and maturing value of the institutional stay; (2) the deterrent effect of being institutionalized; (3) the acquisition of skills; and (4) various specific influences, such as the curing of alcoholic tendencies, improvement of health, etc. In a later study at the same institution, Walter Reckless found that 73.2 per cent of a sample of 250 inmates believed that

[2] Edward J. Galway, *A Measurement of the Effectiveness of a Reformatory Program*, doctoral dissertation, Ohio State University, 1948, p. 43.

they had improved considerably during their stay.[3] An investigation by Raymond Corsini at Auburn Prison in New York similarly indicated that a large proportion (64 per cent) believed they had been helped to a better understanding of themselves and three-fourths of those who replied felt they had benefited from imprisonment.[4] One may question the accuracy of inmate judgments in matters of self-improvement, but there is evidence in the Glueck research that ex-reformatory inmates who believe they have profited from their stay are much more frequently successful after release than those who do not.[5]

Donald Clemmer, a notable prison warden and scholar, in a study of a maximum-security prison, concluded from direct observation that prisoners were dissuaded from the further pursuit of crime by various aspects of their experience in the institution.[6] Some were deterred by the fear of repeating what they had found to be a most unpleasant experience. Others had experienced an intensification of loyalties and responsibility to their attachments in the home community. A few had found or regained religion. Some had developed a useful and rewarding occupational skill that they could employ on the outside. Among those who succeeded there had generally been a reduction in criminal ideation and identification.[7]

The Prison Community

Only in recent years has there been some effort to interpret the prison in terms of social psychological theory as a complex community with a "culture" that is in a measure unique, with characteristic processes of individual and social accommodation, and with typical attitudes and values shared by inmates. This probing into the nature of prisons promises to extend our understanding of the problems involved in institutional treatment of offenders and to stimulate efforts to overcome a part of these difficulties. Thus far, however, the analysis of the quality and processes of prison life has been limited in the main to maximum-security institutions of the traditional type.[8] Published materials relating to small and specialized facilities,

[3] Walter C. Reckless, *The Impact of Correctional Programs on Inmates,* no date, mimeographed.

[4] Raymond Corsini, "A Study of Certain Attitudes of Prison Inmates," *J. Crim. L.,* vol. 37, pp. 132–135, 1946–1947.

[5] Sheldon Glueck and Eleanor Glueck, *Five Hundred Delinquent Women,* 1934, pp. 264–183.

[6] Donald Clemmer, *The Prison Community,* 1940, chap. 12.

[7] *Ibid.,* pp. 314–315.

[8] See, in particular, Sykes *op. cit.,* and Clemmer, *op cit.;* Lloyd W. McCorkle and Richard R. Korn, "Resocialization within Walls," *The Annals,* vol. 293, pp. 88–89, May, 1954; Norman S. Hayner and Ellis Ash, "The Prison as a Community," *Am. Soc. Rev.,* vol. 5, pp. 577–583, August, 1940; Kirson S. Weinberg, "Aspects of the Prison's Social Structure," *Am. J. Soc.,* vol. 47, pp. 717–726, March, 1942; F. E. Haynes "The Sociological Study of the Prison Community," *J. Crim. L.,* vol. 39, pp. 432–441, November–December, 1948.

thus far of a more evangelistic than empirical character, have provided no clear evidence of the significant variations in norms and relationships that exist in such facilities or of their effects upon the population.[9] While the virtues of medium- and minimum-security institutions are often extolled, we know relatively little about the sociopsychological dynamics peculiar to such facilities that may relate to their ostensible success in dealing with offenders.

Donald Clemmer has provided a probing analysis on the nature of the prison community in his study of a "typical" maximum-security prison and its population.[10] He maintained—and quite rightly—that the impact of the prison upon offenders is determined in considerable measure by the nature of the prison society and by the interpersonal relationships of prisoners. The values that prevail among inmates are of special significance; preeminent among these values are the desire for freedom and a hostility toward those who are held responsible directly or indirectly for restraining them. The wielders and symbols of authority are deemed to be natural enemies. This is in part a perseveration of criminalistic attitudes that have become fixed through identification with antisocial norms in the free community. Within the frustrating constrictions of prison life, an intensified hate comes to be directed against the officers of the institution.[11] The "right guy" in prison is hostile to the authorities, loyal to his fellows, and courageous in his defiance. The pattern generally is one of resistance to officialdom and to its restraints upon freedom. But evasion of the prison code occurs in widely varying degrees, from the lowest stool pigeon to the exemplary leader, even as conformity varies on the outside.[12] There is passive acquiescence especially among the prison-wise, which reflects in part the lassitude that descends upon the long-termer in his quite typical reaction to the paternalism of modern prison administration and to the dull, deadening routine of prison life. In part his conformity expresses a recognition that one does his time more easily by avoiding frontal attack against the rules. It is the inexperienced who "make trouble." Occasionally there is revolt, led and usually concentrated among young and unstable inmates, as a means of escaping the dreaded monotony and, to a lesser extent, of claiming new "rights." There is also, on the part of the clever and conniving, a continuous effort to exploit the treatment personnel and the weakness of offi-

[9] Donald R. Cressey, in "Achievement of an Unstated Organizational Goal: An Observation on Prisons," *Pacific Soc. Rev.,* vol. 1, pp. 43–50, fall, 1958, draws distinctions in interpersonal relationships and programs between a custodially oriented and a treatment-oriented institution.

[10] Clemmer, *op. cit.*

[11] As Clemmer's case materials make clear, this sense of hostility is not universal by any means among prisoners. See especially pp. 307–310 in *The Prison Community.*

[12] See Gresham M. Sykes, "Men, Merchants, and Toughs; A Study of Reactions to Imprisonment," *Soc. Probs.* vol. 4, pp. 130–138, October, 1956.

cers who are found to be pliable.[13] Beneath the customary pretended submission there is an unremitting drive to attain greater freedom and comfort.
All this is countered by administration in rules and practices that are directed primarily against overt defiance and escape. Prison officials strive
generally to achieve a smooth operation of institutional routines. This they
sometimes accomplish by rigid control or, often as an easier course, by
relinquishing to prison politicians the basic responsibility for maintaining
order on their own terms.[14] The task is exceedingly difficult and the temptation to compromise is great because prison officers are so far outnumbered
by their charges.[15] The prison community, as a microcosm of a broader
criminal society, tends to exacerbate among offenders the patterns of hostility and rebellion against organized authority that in the first instance
contributed to their crimes.

The prison culture is expressed and carried on through group associations. More than any other aspect of prison life, perhaps, informal inmate
relationships determine adjustment during imprisonment itself and the
individuals' subsequent success or failure on the outside. Clemmer discovered that somewhat more than 50 per cent of the prison population he
studied were associated with groups in quite close relationships, primary
or semiprimary.[16] "The interaction in and about these groups," Clemmer
said, "and the social life that exists is part of the 'unseen environment' and
has much greater influence on individual personalities, we are inclined to
believe, than all the rules, official admonishments, sermons, or other factors
intended to guide lives."[17]

Lloyd McCorkle, formerly principal keeper at the New Jersey State
Prison, makes a similar but more pointed observation:[18]

The welfare of the individual inmate, to say nothing of his psychological
freedom and dignity, does not importantly depend on how much education,
recreation, and consultation he receives but rather depends on how he manages
to live and relate with other inmates who constitute his crucial and only meaningful world. It is what he experiences in this world; how he attains satisfactions from it, how he avoids its pernicious effects—how, in a word, he sur-
vives in it that determines his adjustment and decides whether he will emerge
from prison with an intact or shattered integrity. . . . In these terms, an
evaluation of the institution's contribution to the welfare of its inmates may not

---

[13] Sykes, *The Society of Captives,* pp. 54–58.

[14] See Donald R. Cressey and Witold Krassowski, "Inmate Organization and
Anomie in American Prisons and Soviet Labor Camps," *Soc. Probs.,* vol. 5, pp. 217–
231, winter, 1957–1958.

[15] Sykes found that at the Trenton State Prison there were never more than ninety
officers on duty to control 1,200 inmates even at periods of peak activity. See *The
Society of Captives,* p. 49, ftn.

[16] Clemmer, *op. cit.,* chap. 5.

[17] *Ibid.,* p. 295.

[18] Lloyd W. McCorkle, "Social Structure in a Prison," *The Welfare Reporter,* vol.
8, p. 6, New Jersey, December, 1956. (Reprinted by permission.)

realistically be made with the typical institutional platitudes and statistics about hours of recreation, treatment, and education. The evaluation must rather be made in terms of how the prison authorities are affecting the total social climate, how successfully they are protecting these people from intimidation or exploitation by the more anti-social inmates, how effectively they curb and frustrate the lying, swindling, and covert violence which is always under the surface of the inmate social world.

"Prisonization," the assimilation of convicts into the norms and loyalties of prison life, is largely a consequence of group dynamics in an inmate social system. The degree of prisonization of the individual varies considerably among convicts, however, for the prison is both a heterogeneous and an atomized society. Clemmer observes that from the start the penal institution "swallows up" the inmate in impersonalized relationships and he assumes roles that are increasingly individuated, though often with gross loss of his sense of individuality. Some level of identification with his fellows develops in time on the basis of common interests and goals and as a means of ego protection. McCorkle considers the latter a fundamental aspect of prisoner assimilation, though it varies among inmates:[19]

In many ways, the inmate social system may be viewed as providing a way of life which enables the inmate to avoid the devastating psychological effects of internalizing and converting social rejection into self-rejection. In effect, it permits the inmate to reject his rejectors rather than himself. If it is valid to assume that the major adjustive function of the inmate social system is to protect its members from the effects of internalizing social rejection, then it would seem to follow that the usages of this system are most beneficial to those who have most experienced the consequences of, and developed defenses around, social rejection. It would also follow that the system would find its strongest supporters among those who have, in the process, become most independent of the larger society's values in their definitions and evaluations of themselves. We might also expect to find that those individuals whose self-evaluations are still relatively dependent on the values of the larger, noncriminal society and whose supportive human relationships are still largely with its members would have the most difficulty in adjusting to a social system whose major values are based on the rejection of that larger society.

Where friendships develop in the inmate social system, they are built more largely on self-interest and mutual aid than on sympathy, and they are colored with a contempt that comes with prolonged and excessive propinquity. Often they are short and superficial. It appears that a considerable minority of the population in an ordinary maximum-security prison remains ungrouped.[20] Many of these are the "better cases" that do

[19] McCorkle and Korn, *op. cit.,* pp. 88–89. (Reprinted by permission.)
[20] As Clemmer explains, there are various reasons why some prisoners remain ungrouped: some maintain sufficiently strong positive relationships on the outside; some wish to avoid any sort of trouble; some are not acceptable to any group; others may feel no need or desire for close relationships within the institution.

not return to crime, not only because they have avoided assimilation with confirmed and habitual offenders, but because the counterforces to prisonization are sufficiently constructive and strong. They serve their time often very painfully, commonly with strong feelings of guilt and anxiety, sometimes with increased dependence upon family and relatives, and with great determination never again to become involved in crime. Most of these individuals, except as they may be too weak or find the going too difficult, will not again become involved in crime. Clemmer observes that prisonization is least developed among individuals under short sentence, with fairly stable personalities, who maintain positive relationships outside, who are not much integrated into intimate prison groupings, who do not accept the dogmas and codes of the population, and who engage fully in the formal program of the institution without involvement in the informal vices that are common.[21] Many of these, it appears, are largely noncriminal personalities and others, once criminally disposed, have been reoriented through maturation and experience. The relation of prison behavior to subsequent outcome is not a simple one, however; neither conformity to rules nor aloofness necessarily implies success. But it appears in general that thoroughly prisonized individuals are most frequently failures upon discharge, while those who conform to prison authority and who avoid assimilation either succeed or do not succeed depending largely upon the motives to their submission.[22]

Staff-Inmate Relationships

Much of what the author has said above concerned the "inmate social system," but this should not be taken to imply that the relationship between inmate and staff is unimportant. Clearly it is important, though there is some contrariety of opinion both about the nature and influence of such relationships and about the differential impact of the various categories of

[21] Clemmer, *op. cit.*, p. 301.

[22] Clemmer expresses a realistic, if not altogether optimistic, view on "rehabilitation": "The apparent rehabilitating effect which prison life has on some men occurs in spite of the harmful influences of the prison culture. Among the writer's wide acquaintanceship with hundreds of inmates those who were improved or rehabilitated were men who, in the first place, should never have been committed to prison at all, and who, in the second place, were engulfed by the culture, or prisonized in only the slightest degree. While sometimes the so-called real criminals are rehabilitated, the occasions are so rare that the total effect is negligible. Such 'rehabilitation' as occurs with the actual criminals refers to the type of 'treatment' which keeps them in prison until they reach such an age that they no longer have sufficient physical nor mental vigor to commit further crimes. In a cold, objective sense this means of 'rehabilitation' has some societal utility, but at the same time if other methods had been used the waste of human resources might have been avoided and the dignity of human personalities maintained." *Ibid.*, p. 313. (Reprinted by permission.) It is not clear whether Clemmer believed that dangerous offenders (1) are never rehabilitated, (2) should not be committed to prison, or (3) that imprisonment of such offenders has no deterrent effect upon other potential offenders.

staff. Part of the question here is that of social distance between staff and inmate: What measure of sympathy and congeniality should be encouraged or tolerated? The traditional view, and that still maintained generally by correctional administrators, is that undesirable consequences inevitably emerge if friendship or familiarity develops between the officer and his men. From his study of prison social structure McCorkle draws the conclusion that the prison officer may be corrupted through friendship, reciprocity,[23] or default.[24] He concludes that "The administrative problem stemming from the inevitable compromises the custodian must make as a depletable human being [to maintain control and exercise constructive influence] is to define the limits within which compromise can safely take place. The definition of the limits upon which an orderly prison is based is a function of superior custodial officers, i.e., sergeants, lieutenants and captains."[25] The problem of defining these limits, however, is difficult and is largely unresolved.

Treatment personnel in the prison are likely to depart in some degree from the views of custodial authorities in their belief that helping offenders to improved adjustment requires an empathic relationship and tolerance of failures. They may conceive their function primarily in terms of direct obligation to the "client" rather than to the public or the institutional administration and may see the custodial and disciplinary arrangements as undesirable barriers to effective rehabilitation.[26] McCorkle, referring to the reformist-humanitarian origins of contemporary rehabilitative philosophy, suggests:[27]

It is the tragedy of modern correction that the impulse to help has become confused with treatment and seems to require defense as treatment. . . . The bleak fact is that, just as the monstrous punishments of the eighteenth century failed to curb crime, so the more humane handling of the twentieth century has equally failed to do so. . . . When the professional staff member defined himself as the friend and helper of the inmate he was automatically redefined by the values of the inmate social system as one to be exploited as a champion of inmates in their grievances against society in general and the custodian in

[23] McCorkle observes in "Social Structure in a Prison," *op. cit.*, p. 6, that the prison guard is to a great extent dependent on inmates for the satisfactory performance of his duties and that he, like many figures of authority, is evaluated in terms of the conduct of the men he controls.

[24] "For reasons of indifference, laziness, or naïveté, the guard may find much of his authority whittled away; nonfeasance, rather than malfeasance, has corrupted the theoretical guard-inmate relationship." *Ibid.*, p. 13.

[25] *Ibid.*, p. 15. See also Sykes' more recent analysis in *The Society of Captives*, 1958, pp. 54–58.

[26] See Donald R. Cressey, "Professional Correctional Work and Professional Work in Correction," *N.P.P.A. J.*, vol. 5, pp. 4–5, January, 1959, and the strong bias against prison administration by a former prison psychologist expressed in Donald P. Wilson. *My Six Convicts*, 1951.

[27] McCorkle and Korn, *op. cit.*, p. 97.

particular. Any deviation from this assigned role—especially in the direction of cooperation with measures of custodial control—were then viewed, quite logically, as a betrayal by the professional of his mission to help the inmate. Treatment—defined as help—at this point becomes the enemy of control.

It has not been uncommon for treatment personnel to identify with prisoners in only partially concealed protest against the custodial and administrative necessities of the institution. The result has been a threat to the effectiveness both of security provisions and of treatment efforts.

The problems involved in staff-inmate relations involve both terminological confusion and disagreement concerning means and ends. The prison officer, caseworker, or therapist can be understanding, nonjudgmental, and well disposed without developing friendships or mutual and improper expectancies. Moreover, control and rehabilitation are not antithetical. A correctional institution of any size *must* be operated securely, with fair and firm disciplinary control as a precondition to any meaningful treatment. It is, in general, the prisoners' failures to assume responsibility, regulate their behavior, and respond affirmatively to authority that has brought them to prison. Whatever deeper problems may be symptomatized by these defaults, they cannot be remedied by concessions that expose weakness or by the removal of restrictions that are needed for orderly institutional management. It appears that the ordinary repetitive criminal must, if possible, be brought to recognize from his experience in the institution that his characteristic modes of meeting reality and authority do not work to his interest and that he must either acquiesce to rules that are essential to the community or accept the unpleasant consequences of refusal. The correctional experience is a phase of reality-testing for the offender. Legitimate "help," guidance, and counseling as well as firm and impersonal control can be administered within the framework of this effort.

It may be apparent from what has been said above that "correctional treatment" is not the exclusive province of a small group of specialized therapists but is the work of prison personnel generally, without regard to their particular functions in the institutional operation. The total experience of imprisonment is treatment, whether good or bad. And there is persuasive evidence that the most effective influence in the prison system comes from the custodial rather than the treatment staff. Galway, in his study at Chillicothe, found that in nominations by 275 inmates of staff members they believed knew them best, 108 named custodial officers; thirty-nine, trade training supervisors; thirty-two, farm operators; eighteen, industrial foremen; eighteen, maintenance workers; seventeen, culinary workers; fourteen, classification and parole officers; thirteen, clerical workers; nine, educational personnel; five, medical officers; and two, chaplains.[28] In his later study of the Chillicothe population, Walter Reckless found in response to his questions on staff members who helped them the most that cus-

[28] Galway, *op. cit.*, pp. 66–68.

todial workers were nominated by 37.6 per cent of a sample of 250 inmates; maintenance workers, by 19.2 per cent; industry foremen, by 12.8 per cent; trade training supervisors, by 11.6 per cent; and professional workers (social workers, academic teachers, doctors, etc.), by 17.6 per cent.[29] David Bright in a dissertation conducted on inmates at the Ohio Penitentiary found there, too, that the nonprofessional staff members had more "impact" than professional staff members according to the inmates' evaluations of those whom they liked best and those who had done the most for them.[30] These data raise interesting questions concerning the effectiveness of treatment staff generally and why they do not exercise more influence than they appear to do. The data also suggest the wisdom of the experimental efforts in California institutions to enlist more active efforts on the part of the custodial and supervisory staff in a treatment function.[31] Whether the employment of formal counseling procedures for the purpose will prove to be sound is another question.

It has been seen that group life in the prison community erects formidable barriers to the establishment of constructive habits and attitudes. This is especially true in large, heterogeneous institutions where confirmed recidivists and prison politicians are generally retained. The effort to recondition the responses of offenders is unusually difficult, too, in dealing with unstable personalities, psychopaths, neurotic-compulsive offenders, and others with deep-seated difficulties. This suggests again the need for smaller and more specialized institutions where differentiated programs may be applied to more homogeneous groups. Unfortunately, as the author has previously suggested, we lack useful empirical data on the social systems and the treatment impact of small and specialized correctional facilities. It appears quite clear, however, that in some institutions of this sort it is feasible and desirable not only to cut back security-custodial measures but to permit greater informality, to reduce the number of regulations, to tolerate a greater amount of deviation, and to encourage more personal but non-exploitative relationships between inmates and staff. Presumably the professional staff may be more effective in such institutions, but custodial, supervisory, and training personnel can exert greater influence as well. The social distance, which appears to be necessary in a considerable measure for the secure and orderly operation of a maximum-security prison, can be greatly reduced in a small institution where there is diminished emphasis upon custodial controls. The medium- or minimum-security institution containing a population that is classified with reasonable care should not provide so fertile a field for the spread of the prison code to which the

[29] Reckless, *loc. cit.*

[30] David E. Bright, *A Study of Institutional Impact upon Adult Male Prisoners,* doctoral dissertation, Ohio State University, 1951, pp. 84–85.

[31] See Norman Fenton, *An Introduction to Group Counseling in State Correctional Service,* State of California, Department of Corrections, 1957.

author has referred. Close relationships of inmates are probably no less common in such institutions and the influence of these associations is no less significant for future behavior, but the spread of hostility and of anti-social norms is much curtailed. These individuals are not so thoroughly acculturated in criminal norms at the time of imprisonment. The forces of prisonization may be minimized by strengthening prisoners' bonds with the home community, by maintaining their active interest and participation in the program, and in general by focusing more largely on preparation for the community rather than merely upon the avoidance of disturbances and escapes.

Living under conditions of relative freedom is probably in itself a constructive influence if the use of such freedom is soundly guided. It is relevant, in this regard, to observe in Galway's data that negative reactions to the experience of imprisonment came most frequently at the Chillicothe Reformatory from inmates who had been classified initially to close custody (in 38 per cent of these cases) as compared with those who had been classified to medium outside custody (17 per cent).[32]

Sex in Prison

One of the phases of prison relationship to which a considerable amount of attention has been given is that of sexual expression. Aside from the loss of liberty itself, this is perhaps the most obvious area of deprivation and abnormality in the correctional institution. It is quite apparent that the prison environment is not consistent with the establishment or the maintenance of healthy sex habits and attitudes.

A small minority of institutionalized offenders may get along without

[32] Galway, op. cit., pp. 50–63. A more intensive study at the small open institution at Highfields, New Jersey, reviewed in some detail elsewhere, investigated attitudes at entry and discharge of offenders from this facility in comparison with a sample at a better-than-average traditional reformatory. This research provides no real confirmation of the usual hypothesis that more improvement is achieved through intensive treatment in a therapeutic setting than in a mass institution or that outcome in the community is superior. It was found that Highfields Negroes more frequently succeeded when their attitudes toward law enforcement were unfavorable and that there was little apparent relationship between attitude toward general authority held by Highfields boys and subsequent offense history. See H. Ashley Weeks, *Youthful Offenders at Highfields*, 1958, pp. 82–83. Compare Lloyd McCorkle, Albert Elias, and F. Lovell Bixby, *The Highfields Story: A Unique Experiment in the Treatment of Juvenile Delinquency*, 1958. On the other hand, Mannheim's study of the outcome of treatment of English Borstal boys revealed that 58 per cent of those from open Borstals succeeded, while only 36 per cent from the closed institutions avoided subsequent conviction. Attitudes were not investigated in this latter research. The point requires emphasis that in all these studies observed differences may reflect in large part or entirely the selection of better cases for placement in the minimum-security facilities. Hermann Mannheim and Leslie T. Wilkins, *Prediction Methods in Relation to Borstal Training*, 1955, p. 109.

overt sexual output. These are, in general, individuals deficient in their sex drives, hypogonadal types who do not express because they do not need to do so. In the sexually deviated criminal, however, while a fair proportion have weak physical motivation, their offenses generally evidence a strong psychic need to prove their sexuality. Some of these who require children or animals as objects or who display a distorted quality of expression (e.g., fetishism, transvestism) may display little or no sexual drive while in the institution, but this is no indication of a cure. Sublimation, though it has been the solution most commonly recommended by the moralists, is generally judged to be completely ineffectual as a long-term solution for sexual drives. This is the more true in an institutional environment where routine and monotony are likely to produce an intensified interest in sexual expression. Sex, fantasy, and food become disproportionately important escapes from tedium in a custodial, sex-segregated facility. In this setting, moralizing and repression may intensify feelings of guilt and rebellion; they may increase the inmates' efforts to avoid discovery in their erotic episodes. But the atmosphere of tension encourages rather than inhibits the expression of sexuality.

Homosexual behavior is a universal concomitant of sex-segregated living. It is a perennial problem in camps, boarding schools, one-sexed colleges, training schools, and correctional facilities. Generally, when discovered, it has attracted condemnation and punishment. Increasingly, however, our institutions display some tacit tolerance of such activity where it is not so open that it gets out of hand (an approach that is also being taken more and more by the police in large cities). In these prisons the administrators simply do not look upon sex as a primary problem. Obviously romantic relationships cannot be allowed to run riot in the correctional institution. They are often enough a source of intense jealousies, fights, and stabbings, even where careful supervisory measures are taken. On the other hand, if supervision of leisure time and sleeping arrangements is fairly close, promiscuous and coercive sexual relationships may be discouraged and sufficient discretion may be developed to avoid most abuses, such as the forceful initiation of neophytes. To this end some institutions segregate known homosexuals in a separate section with little effort to control activities there. These havens for homosexuals provide no real solution to the problem, of course. Certainly they strengthen the deviated habits of such inmates.

Most of those who engage in a limited amount of homosexual activity in the institution are not habituated or feminine-oriented deviates. Their erotic activities are generally substitutive and temporary, leading back into normal sexual behavior after release. Long-term incarceration inevitably establishes deeply conditioned habits, however, that may persist and make quite difficult the transition to heterosexual activity. In the unfortunate instances where individuals have been institutionalized during youth before normal sexual habits had been stabilized, the development of good sex habits and attitudes is made much more unlikely. It appears that from a biological point of view homosexuality is normal behavior in the distorted institutional environment and that but for our strong cultural repugnance it would be considerably more common than it is. Many heterosexuals in prison cannot bring themselves to this form of expression and others do so only at the cost of strong guilt feelings. Sexually deviated offenders, however, who have already developed homosexual patterns will almost inevitably persist in them during incarceration.

Masturbation is the most common form of sexual release in the institutional situation; undoubtedly it is the least damaging from a physical and psychological point of view. But masturbation is of limited value as an expressive outlet. When it becomes a strongly conditioned habit without other forms of output, it may make difficult the establishment of the more satisfying and socialized heterosexual relations that are based upon affection, emotional responsiveness, and mutual responsibility. More positive and extraverted relationships cannot be established within the institution in any event, however, and in the usual instance masturbation is the most innocuous sexual activity employed.

Some penologists have recurrently proposed that a system of connubial visitation should be established in correctional institutions here comparable to that employed in the prison systems of a few other countries.[33] This is obviously unrealistic from a cultural point of view. Since 1956 there has been family, including connubial, visitation at the Mississippi State Penitentiary at Parchman, but it appears that no other state has seriously contemplated official endorsement of sexual visits within its correctional institutions. (Unofficially it has been done, of course, in scattered jails, usually

---

[33] Ruth S. Cavan and Eugene S. Zemans observe in their study, "Marital Relationships of Prisoners in Twenty-eight Countries," *J. Crim. L.,* vol. 49, pp. 133–140, July–August, 1958, that the practice of connubial visitation, specifically sanctioned as such, is rare. They found the practice in Mexico, in Argentina between 1951 and 1955, and in Sweden through unsupervised visitation. Only Mexico appears to consider conjugal visits a satisfactory arrangement. The maintenance of family and, more especially, of sexual relationships is provided for in some measure by furloughs or home visits for selected prisoners in Argentina (since 1955), England and Wales, Canada, North Ireland, Scotland, Denmark, Switzerland, Germany, Greece, India, and Sweden. This involves something more than the compassionate visits generally allowed in the United States where a close relative is seriously ill or has died. A few countries, including the Philippines, where the practice goes back fifty years and is more common than elsewhere, Mexico, India, and Pakistan, allow families of selected prisoners to live with them in open colonies. In the United States, Mississippi established and has continued the practice since 1944 of permitting trustworthy prisoners to go home for a period of ten days once each year. See Cavan and Zemans, "Marital Relationships of Prisoners," *J. Crim. L.,* vol. 49, pp. 50–58, May–June, 1958. In 1959 Congressman Celler submitted a bill for furloughs in the Federal prison systems.

through bribery of keepers.) Even for married inmates our prisons generally would not tolerate the cohabitation of prisoners with their wives.[34] Even less satisfactorily could the needs of the unmarried be taken care of. So long as the society requires under its official mores that youths delay heterosexual expression for several years after they reach maturity, we shall probably not provide for normal sexuality in prison.[35] So long as we consider it appropriate to continue numerous forms of deprivation in our correctional institutions, we shall make no exception for sex. Moreover, although the problems of securing satisfying sexual outlets are more difficult in prison than in the community, the great mass of energetic, unmarried youth in our society are very narrowly restricted and repressed in their sexual behavior. In terms of the magnitude of the problem and hence the possible deleterious consequences, these community restrictions surely constitute a much more serious threat to the establishment of normal, compatible, heterosexual relations than that posed by institutional mores.

Considerably more realistic, though an only partial solution to the problem, is the practice of giving furloughs to inmates as they approach the time of release from the institution. This is sound policy, not only because it encourages the resumption of heterosexual relationships, but even more because it facilitates the return to the domestic and social responsibilities upon which normal adjustments are based. Where careful selection and timing of these temporary releases are practiced, they may greatly enhance the possibilities of successful parole. For the sexual deviate they may provide opportunity too for the beginnings of psychotherapy and guidance in their sexual behavior if good supervision and clinical treatment resources are available.

In the remainder of this chapter the author will consider the major elements of program provided in adult correctional institutions with particular reference to their apparent significance for rehabilitation. The author has remarked above on the probability that the norms and relationships that characterize the prison social system are more important to outcome in many cases than are the direct and specific influences from particular phases of the program. This is not to deny that some of these phases have beneficial influence in preparing the offender for responsibility in freedom. Surely they do. But it may well be that the personal influence exercised by personnel in these programs is more significant. The student with a special-

---

[34] There is some evidence that the practice of connubial visitation, where it is permitted at bimonthly or monthly intervals, tends to heighten rather than relieve tension.

[35] Presumably no one would recommend that the peculiar tastes of sexually deviated offenders should be serviced by the program of the correctional institution. Paradoxically enough, the ordinary confirmed homosexual comes closest to a full and direct satisfaction of his wants in the prison setting.

ized interest in detailed phases of prison activities is referred to other sources.[36]

PRISON LABOR

It has been said that "No single phase of life within prison walls is more important to the public or to the inmate than efficient industrial operations and the intelligent utilization of the labor of prisoners."[37] Yet there is no aspect of prison activity that has provoked more controversies and restraints than production in correctional institutions. The importance of the problem is suggested by the rapid decline in prisoner employment and production since 1932 when state prison industries at their peak employed 77,267 prisoners and produced goods to the value of $71,306,061.[38] In 1936–1937 the value of state prison produce had been reduced to approximately 20 million dollars through the labor of no more than 25,000 prisoners. The proportion of prisoners productively employed declined from 75 per cent in 1885 to 52 per cent in 1932 and to 44 per cent in 1940. In the latter year state prisons manufactured goods valued at only $9,122,840.[39] The total value of state-prison-made goods in 1953 has been estimated at $58,263,295.[40] There were 153,366 prisoners in state institutions in that year, a number similar to that in 1940. What proportion of these was productively employed is not known. Estimates relating to prisoner employment have little meaning under present conditions of prison work because, in addition to the widely prevalent "idle crews" that quite frankly have nothing to do, overassignment to work crews and short work days have become characteristic. Archaic production methods, due in part to the use of obsolete machinery, and make-work tasks are also very general in our state prisons. There is little more than maintenance operations to occupy the time of prisoners in some institutions.

The profitable system of factory production in prison was inaugurated

---

[36] See in particular Tappan (ed.), *Contemporary Correction,* 1951, and *A Manual of Correctional Standards,* The American Correctional Association, 1959.

[37] *Handbook of Correctional Institution Design and Construction,* U.S. Bureau of Prisons, 1949, p. 282.

[38] *Attorney General's Survey of Release Procedures,* 1939, p. 185.

[39] See Summary Report, "Prison Labor in the United States: 1940," *Monthly Labor Rev.,* vol. 53, pp. 578–606, September, 1941. World War II production provided clear evidence of the ability of prisoners to work long hours efficiently when they are strongly motivated. They produced war goods worth more than 138 million dollars and agricultural products valued at an additional 75 million dollars. In ordinary times there is little incentive to responsible effort on the part of the ordinary prisoner, for he does not need to earn a living or support his dependents and he can gain little status through diligence.

[40] "What's New in Prison Industries," *Correctional Res.,* United Prison Association of Massachusetts, Bull. No. 6, p. 5, April, 1955. The figures for 1953 were obtained by the Association through questionnaires sent to forty-eight states.

at Auburn, New York, in 1823, as has been observed elsewhere. During the ensuing century "hard labor" in prison industry was considered to be the center of daily routine, discipline, reformation, and profit in institutions across the country. It was reported in 1851 that "earnings above expenses" of fifteen state prisons amounted to $325,000.[41] The contract and lease systems, discussed below, were highly remunerative, though they resulted in serious exploitation of prisoners and their rehabilitative effect may well be doubted. In modern times it has come to be generally agreed that the values derived from work in prison cannot properly be assessed merely in terms of the gross product of prison production. Work in prison may be useful for several purposes: to train skills among those who have lacked legitimate occupation and who have the capacity to learn, to develop better craftsmanship among those who have had some training and work experience, to establish or maintain responsible work habits, to prevent idleness and thus to promote orderliness and good discipline, and partially to defray the costs of prison operation. Work may also be used for punitive purposes, but this is no longer considered appropriate. It is quite generally agreed among correctional authorities both that idleness in prison is highly demoralizing and that the provision of work is in some measure effective in the correction of offenders. Increased emphasis has come to be placed upon the value of training according to the differential needs and capacities of the population rather than merely mass production, and this has led to a growing stress upon the need for tying instruction in with work and providing, so far as possible, diversified occupational programs. While there is virtual consensus that prisoners should work in the interest of discipline, morale, and rehabilitation, no state in this country has established a legal right of prisoners to work, as the Scandinavian countries have.[42] In some countries, labor is considered a duty in so far as prison administration may be able to provide it.

The history of prison labor in the United States is closely related to changes in correctional policy, which, in turn, has been greatly influenced by restrictive legislation. Production for the open market was the dominant system of prison labor until the 1890s. It took four major forms: (1) Under the *lease* system both the production and the care and custody of the prisoners were entrusted to a lessee. The system developed in the South where prisoners were sent to lumber camps, in effect as slave laborers, and the state received a fixed rate per man per month. Thus the state could secure a considerable revenue from its prisoners, even though the rates were considerably below those in the free labor market, while assum-

---

[41] *Ibid.,* p. 2.
[42] See *Prison Labor,* United Nations, Department of Economic and Social Affairs, 1955, p. 2. A right to work is established by law in Denmark, Norway, and Sweden. A similar right exists as a matter of administrative rules and practices in France, the Netherlands, and Switzerland.

ing no responsibility for their maintenance. The system finally succumbed to the force of public indignation in the 1920s. (2) Under the *contract* system the state maintained and guarded the prisoners in its institutions but sold their labor for a fixed sum for each prisoner employed. The contractor provided the machines and materials and supervised their work. This system, too, has been profitable to the entrepreneur and, though less so than the lease system, to the state, but it has involved considerable exploitation of convict laborers. It has disappeared as a consequence of the Federal legislation during the 1920s and 1930s discussed below. (3) Under the *piece-price* system the state had complete charge of the prisoners and the productive process, the contractor merely furnishing the materials and paying an agreed price for each unit produced that he accepted. This system too has disappeared as a result of the legislation designed to remedy unfair competition. (4) Under the *public account* system the state not only carries on the entire enterprise but markets the product as well. This system has not entirely disappeared even today. Minnesota, with the largest gross annual income from prison products of any state ($4,500,916 for the fiscal year 1953–1954), operates a highly successful farm machinery industry and, though on a smaller scale, Wisconsin has had considerable success in the production of bindery twine.[43]

In the 1870s industry and labor unions vehemently opposed the unfair competition of goods on the open market that was produced by inexpensive prison labor.[44] This, together with abuses that had developed under the contract system, led to restrictive Federal legislation as early as 1883, limiting the number of prisoners who could work in any one industry. In the ensuing years a number of the more populous states, including New York, Ohio, Pennsylvania, New Jersey, and California, abolished the contract system. An effective blow to systems of production for the open market occurred on January 19, 1929, with the enactment of the Hawes-Cooper Act which, effective five years thereafter, was designed to eliminate prison-made goods from interstate commerce into any state that had prohibited the sale of such goods. At that time seventeen states had made the contract system illegal and sixteen required the labeling of prison-made goods. The Ashurst-Summers Act of 1935 went farther in making it a Federal offense to transport prison-made goods into any state where this was a violation of the local law. The constitutionality of both these laws was upheld by the United States Supreme Court. In 1937 a survey dis-

[43] In 1953–1954, open-market sales accounted for anywhere from 70 to 100 per cent of gross incomes reported from prisons in Minnesota, Texas, Arkansas, Missouri, North Dakota, and South Dakota. See "What's New in Prison Industries," *op. cit.,* pp. 6–7.

[44] According to the United Nations study, complaints by free workers and entrepreneurs against unfair competition from prison labor appeared in Europe at least as early as 1695. See Nurullah Kunter, *Le Travail Pénal,* 1940, p. 137, cited in *Prison Labor,* p. 38.

closed that the sale or distribution of prison-made goods on the open
market was prohibited altogether in twelve states, that general prohibitions
with certain limited exceptions prevailed in another sixteen, and that five
other states allowed no sale or distribution of such goods made outside
those states. At that time production and employment had dropped quite
suddenly to about one-third of its former level. Twenty-two states and the
District of Columbia were operating state-use systems exclusively.[45]

A fifth system of prison industrial production developed largely as a
consequence of the increasing pressures of industry and labor; under the
state-use system goods are produced for sale to public institutions of the
state. Massachusetts had established a modified form of such a system in
1887 by a rule that goods should be made and sold to state and county
institutions so far as possible and in 1898 that state required such institutions to purchase from the prisons. While state-use production does not
entirely eliminate competition with private industry, its intrusion upon the
market is less direct and visible than open-market sales. It has met a considerably reduced opposition; indeed, unions and manufacturers urged the
legislation that in many states has substituted this system for those that involved production for the open market. Other states, therefore, followed
the lead of Massachusetts in introducing or extending this system, most of
them producing office furnishings and supplies, clothing, automobile license
plates, road signs, or other articles that could be sold to institutions and
agencies of the state. At the present time thirty-five states and the Federal
system sell prison-made goods exclusively to public institutions and agencies. Some of these make purchase of the prison goods mandatory.

The spread of the sheltered market system has produced both favorable
and unfavorable consequences for prison programs. It has largely neutral-
ized the long continued and intense opposition of private industry. More
important, from the point of view of the rehabilitative efforts of our institutions, it has challenged the ingenuity of correctional authorities. In fair
measure, at least, it is responsible for the increased emphasis that has been
placed upon other phases of the prison treatment program—education,
leisure-time activities, etc.—as a means of reducing the hours of idleness.
No less significant has been the impetus both to diversification of prison
production and to a considerably enlarged emphasis on work as a means
of providing training in a variety of craft skills. The change has been accompanied, however, by a considerable reduction in prison production and
in efficiency of work. The maintenance of prisons has become costly rather
than profitable. Idleness is widely prevalent and demoralizing.

There are other forms of work for prisoners that fall outside the range
of industrial production of goods. One of these has traditionally been
known as *public works and ways*. It involves the employment of prisoners

_____

[45] For a listing of these states, see *Prisons, Attorney General's Survey of Release
Procedures*, 1939, p. 187.

on the construction and repair of public roads, parks, buildings, or other structures. This is rooted in early prison labor practices, running back to the prison hulks in England, the road gangs of the Philadelphia Walnut Street Jail, and the southern chain gangs that worked on roads and parks. A number of states have come to use selected prisoners for prison construction, conservation work, fire fighting, forest preservation, building or maintenance operations of various sorts, and other analogous activities. Except for gross abuses that have existed in some of the southern camps, such activities have generally provided healthful and productive occupation.

FIGURE 27. Industries Building at the Federal Reformatory at El Reno, Oklahoma.

Such work has been provided increasingly in camps to those young and vigorous offenders who have not required close custodial supervision.

Farm operations, including both gardening and animal husbandry, are an important part of contemporary prison work. As has been seen, farming was the major form of occupation in the early development of prisons in a number of southern states. Farm camps, a traditional part of southern penology, have become an important phase of prison production in the North as well during the past fifteen years. A gradually increasing proportion of able-bodied offenders who can be classified to minimum or medium custody and who cannot be employed in industry are designated to work outside the walls. It is a valuable part of prerelease training for selected offenders as well as for young and first offenders who are not security risks; it has contributed greatly to the improvement of prison diet and presumably to the health and welfare of the prisoners involved. The Federal prison system has pioneered in the development of outstanding prison farms. The author has the impression that some of the prison farm managers he has known may be unusually effective "therapists."

Finally, to the forms of occupation for prisoners, *maintenance* tasks must be added. Characteristically both in the United States and in other countries a large part of the prison population is engaged in maintenance operations, including cleaning, cooking, and laundering. Some of those assigned are incompetent for work requiring any greater ability, but customarily too large a number of prisoners are engaged in this activity who

FIGURE 28. Farm group at the United States Penitentiary at Terre Haute, Indiana.

should be securing more advantageous experience. In the average institution about one-fifth of the population could usefully be kept at work in prison housekeeping operations, but in some states this work is spread through one-half or more, with very little for any of them to do. This situation is at its worst in city and county jails where quite generally there is no productive work available; however, the loafing of large numbers of maintenance workers has come to be a common characteristic of prisons as well.

The Development of More Productive Programs

There is no formula for an ideal distribution of prisoner time in work activities, what with the variation in size, location, and population of institutions. The pattern in any particular state must be worked out for its institutions according to the circumstances peculiar to it. As the author has remarked, however, it is clear that idleness and make-work are all to generally characteristic of our state prisons and it is certain, moreover, that much of this problem could be resolved through the more diligent efforts of correctional administrators. This does not mean that production in itself should be a paramount aim of the prison system; but the author reaffirms that it is one appropriate and essential part of that system. It may well be that, taken together with coordinated training programs, work can more often be a rehabilitative influence than any other aspect of the prison regime.

The feasibility of developing constructive occupation in a prison organization is nowhere better illustrated than in the distribution of manpower in the institutions of the Federal Bureau of Prisons. In 1958 Federal Prison Industries operated fifty-two shops or factories in twenty-one institutions, employing over 4,000 inmates in thirty-two different lines of products and services to produce goods valued at $31,134,239; net earnings were $5,272,138. The workers in industry were paid an average wage of $33.35 monthly, and nearly a quarter of a million dollars was expended for "meritorious compensation" of workers who were not employed in industrial production.[46] In recent years the Bureau has usually employed approximately 20 per cent of its prisoner population in industries. Another highly important phase of work in the Federal prison system lies in its farm program. Ordinarily from 15 to 20 per cent of all prisoners are occupied with farming, food preparation, and service. The Bureau produces on its excellent farms more than one-third of the total poundage of food consumed in all its institutions, thus providing healthy occupation, superior diet, and considerably reduced costs. Usually about 20 per cent of Federal prisoners are engaged in institutional maintenance operations, including clerks; over 10 per cent, in maintaining shops and mechanical operations; and somewhat over 5 per cent, in construction and camp work. About 10 per cent are considered unemployable and the remainder are in the prison hospitals and educational programs.

Several states have attempted in recent years to provide a greater amount of constructive activities for inmates. Maine and Virginia offer continuous employment for all prisoners; in the latter state one-third work in industries while another third are engaged in public works and the remainder in farming. California, which is limited in the gross annual production of goods permitted under state law, plans by 1964 to employ over

---

[46] See "Federal Prisons: 1958," *A Report of the Work of the Federal Bureau of Prisons,* 1959. A total of 36 million dollars had been paid into the Federal Treasury since 1934 by Federal Prison Industries, Inc., at the end of 1958. As observed in the text below, extensive programs of training were also subsidized through the income derived from industry.

20 per cent of its total inmate population in thirty or more distinct manu-facturing operations and in twenty-five or more farm projects. Savings to the state through the net earnings of correctional industries in California in the fiscal year 1953–1954 aggregated $674,708. In New York State something less than one-fifth of the inmates work in twenty-five industry shops, which show a gross income of about 4½ million dollars and a net surplus in excess of a half million dollars. There is also an extensive farm program there associated with the several prisons of the state.

FIGURE 29. Mess hall of the minimum-security Federal Correctional Institution at Seagoville, Texas. Seven hundred and fifty acres of the prison reserva-tion are devoted to farming, and most of the food requirements of the institution are provided by this production.

A most advantageous tool in the development and diversification of prison industries lies in the establishment of some form of industrial com-mission representing industry, labor, agriculture, the public, and the cor-rectional system itself. Federal Prison Industries, Inc., was established by Congress in 1934, with a policy-making board of six members representing production and consumer interests, to plan industries in the Federal prisons, training of inmates, and distribution of products to government departments. From the start it has succeeded in neutralizing the traditional opposition to prison production and in developing diversified training and production. California established a somewhat comparable Correctional Industrial Commission in 1947 to oversee the development of industries there. In 1953 Montana established an advisory council to study methods of manufacture and distribution of prison-made goods. Experience with these boards has proved their value in acquainting the representative members with the problems of and needs for constructive prison work and in stimulating a more favorable attitude among industrial and labor leaders toward the employment of offenders after release.

Wages and Incentives

Prisoners are rewarded for productive activities mainly as an incentive to good behavior and industrious habits or as payment for work performed. Traditionally in the United States such rewarding has been considered as an incentive. But collateral values are also recognized. To a limited extent the prisoner may contribute to the support of his dependents; he can enjoy a few amenities that are conceived as fruits of his labor rather than paternalistic benevolences; he can accumulate funds that may ease the difficult transition to the community when he is discharged; and a sense of responsibility may be reinforced. "Wages" are preferred to gratuities even if they have little relation to standards on the free labor market.

Strong argument may be drawn for the payment of prison wages at levels comparable to those in the community. The prisoner's maintenance costs could (and should) be charged off against earnings, his responsibilities at home discharged from his funds so far as possible, and savings accumulated. While such a system of rewards for work performed would be largely a bookkeeping operation, at least until the time of release from prison, the result should be a very considerable improvement in the morale and self-regard of many inmates, which is a potent force in personal reconstruction. The costs of prison operation would increase somewhat, though much of such increase should be set off against reductions in the public welfare expenses now required to support prisoner's families. Undoubtedly prison work would be carried on much more efficiently. Wages are paid today according to the standards of free labor in four countries: Finland, the Netherlands, Norway, and Yugoslavia.[47] In addition, several countries, including Sweden, Scotland, England, Denmark, the Netherlands, and Norway, select certain prisoners being prepared for release who are allowed to work on the outside for private employers at wages similar to those paid free labor. Institutional expenses are charged to prisoners in a number of countries, although only Belgium and France deduct such charges against the earnings of all their prisoners. No state in the United States has

---

[47] See *Prison Labor*, United Nations, chap. 5. The payment of free labor rates to prisoners should theoretically obviate the customary objections to prison production for the open market. However, there appears no real possibility of restoring such a system where it has disappeared.

adopted a system of wage payments at free labor rates and it now appears doubtful that they will come to do so in spite of occasional speculation about the rehabilitative value of such a policy.[48] It is argued that this would reward criminals for violating the law when good citizens are out of work through no personal fault, that the deterrence of punishment would be nullified, and that the cost would be too great.

Wage payments are made to adult prisoners in thirty-four states in this country. Among the remainder, several give "industrial good time" or partial remission of sentence instead of wages.[49] Where payments are made, they range generally between 5 and 50 cents per day, no state paying rates as high as does the Federal Prison Industries.[50] About half of these states use a sliding scale of payment according to skill, speed, effort, and cooperation of the worker or other similar criteria. A trend has begun to pay a small amount to maintenance and farm workers, thus to avoid the invidiousness of compensating only that minority who work in industry.

The development of more effective correctional programs in the United States rests in appreciable part upon the further diversification and wider employment of prison production and training programs. This will require enlarged efforts in public relations, with special attention to the attitudes held by industry, labor, agriculture, and consumers. It will also call for ingenuity on the part of prison administration and increased investment in plants. This should have high priority in the future of corrections.

EDUCATION AND VOCATIONAL TRAINING

While the beginnings of education in prisons were associated with religious and vocational training initiated in the late sixteenth and seventeenth centuries on the Continent, the development of significant educational programs is relatively recent. Maryland established the first school system for all prisoners in the 1830s and New York provided by law for the appointment of instructors in its prisons in 1847. Illiteracy and unfavorable school histories have always been extremely common among prisoners and the movement for developing academic education has been predicated largely on the hypothesis that remedying these educational defects should enable the offender to cope more intelligently with the problems that have led to his imprisonment. In spite of a widespread faith in the rehabilitative potentialities of education, however, Austin MacCormick observed after visiting nearly all of our state and Federal institutions in

[48] See Walter M. Wallack, "Some Suggestions for Basic Reforms in Prison Industries for Improved Production and Vocational Training," *Proc. Am. Prison Assoc.,* pp. 153–160, 1947.

[49] Leading penologists have criticized such practices largely on the ground that the time of the prisoner's release should not be influenced by his productivity in prison. See *A Manual of Correctional Standards,* 1954, p. 284.

[50] For wage rates paid in various state systems, see *Correctional Research,* p. 12.

1927 and 1928 that "not a single complete and well-rounded educational program, adequately financed and staffed, had been encountered in all the prisons in the country."[51] There was a considerable impetus to effort in this field during the decade following publication of the Osborne Association survey, however, and in 1948 MacCormack found that "education in penal and correctional institutions has at last achieved maturity."[52] During the interim impetus had been given to the movement by a standing Committee of Education of the American Prison Association,[53] the publication of basic sourcebooks on correctional education,[54] and the initiation of strong academic and training programs in New York State, California, the Federal Bureau of Prisons, and more recently in a few other states.

Formal academic education is provided in some prisons at several levels. Illiteracy, defined as performance at less than the fourth-grade level, prevails among about 30 per cent of those offenders admitted to prison. Remedying this condition is one of the basic and challenging tasks of correctional education. Prisoners are often pathetically pleased when they learn to read letters from home and to write them. It appears that a similar proportion of offenders have completed only seventh or eighth grade and that well under 10 per cent are high school graduates. Less than 1 per cent have graduated from college. There is wide variation in the extent to which prisons attempt to provide supplementary training through classes and cell-study correspondence courses. In California and Wisconsin the state educational systems, including the college and university levels, provide staff or aid in administration for the correctional systems. Accreditation of grade school and high school work and the granting of diplomas by state educational authorities, without reference to the place of instruction, is a general practice in a number of jurisdictions, including Illinois, New York, New Jersey, and in some states where Federal correctional institutions are located. In some institutions education through the eighth grade is compulsory and high school training is encouraged. Correspondence courses at college level are also available. It is reported that 80 per cent of the prisoners at the Federal Penitentiary in Atlanta and nearly half of those at the Illinois State Prisons are enrolled in some type of educational activity. San Quentin has an educational budget in excess of a quarter of a million dollars and Wallkill Prison, with a population of under 500, has an educational staff of twenty.

---

[51] Austin H. MacCormick, *The Education of Adult Prisoners: A Survey and a Program*, Osborne Association, 1931.

[52] MacCormick, "Education in the Prisons of Tomorrow," *The Annals*, pp. 72–77, September, 1931.

[53] In 1946 this became the Correctional Educational Association, an affiliate of the American Prison Association.

[54] See Walter M. Wallack and Glenn M. Kendall, *Education within Prison Walls*, 1939, and Walter M. Wallack and Howard L. Briggs, *Prison Administration: An Educational Process*, 1940.

One important line of contemporary development lies in an emphasis upon social education, either as a new and distinct part of academic work, or more indirectly as an intrinsic phase of traditional academic or vocational programs. This involves generally an effort to "strengthen character" by lectures, visual aids, and discussion of the basic social virtues and the problems that prisoners have encountered in interpersonal and social relationships. Thus, courses have been offered in successful living in New York, learning for life in California, problems of social adjustment in New Jersey, life adjustment in Minnesota, social education in Federal institutions, and others similar in content elsewhere. Ostensibly comparable in

FIGURE 30. Library of the Federal Penitentiary at Lompoc, California. Well lighted, with bright colors and an informal atmosphere.

purpose, social science courses have become common, and criminology is taught in a few institutions. The rehabilitative value of a purely didactic approach to character education may be questioned in the light of studies in educational psychology that have been carried on in the public schools. However, these formalized academic offerings have come to shade over into group counseling or into group therapy, loosely defined. This is well illustrated by the program of group counseling, to a large extent by rank-and-file employees of the corrections department, in California, the "guided-group interaction" technique employed by sociologists and psychologists in New Jersey institutions for youths, and the recent educator-counseling program of the state prison in the latter state. A variety of other techniques has been developed which represent a bridging of education and therapy, notably Alcoholics Anonymous, chapters of which meet frequently at correctional institutions and jails throughout the country.

Forums, discussions groups, debating and public speaking clubs are additional devices of this sort.

Vocational education, which commonly coordinates the industrial and maintenance program of an institution with applied and technical phases of education, has also grown considerably in recent years, especially in reformatories and in progressive prison systems. However, there have been major problems in this effort in gearing the training to work activities and to the development of skills that can be used after discharge. Special effort is required to achieve a meaningful and varied program of vocational instruction suited to the range of abilities that is found in prison.[55] The Federal Bureau of Prisons has been most successful in this regard. In 1957 more than half a million dollars was expended by Federal Prison Industries on the operation of some 372 vocational training programs that were integrated with the industrial activities.[56] The employment placement offices of the Bureau, located at five institutions in different parts of the country, supported by industry earnings, found work for 2,432 inmates who were discharged from prison, a large part of them in fields directly related to their training and work experience in the prisons. Even a relatively small institution such as Wallkill, however, conducts a diversified program of training in building trades (electricity, carpentry, plumbing, and masonry), mechanical fields (auto mechanics, radio repair, machine shop, welding, blacksmithing, and plant maintenance), maintenance operations (laundry, kitchen, bake shop, and tailor shop), and farming. Dr. Wallack, warden, finds that "a large percentage" of those who receive training find employment later in the trades they learned at Wallkill.[57] It is said that in Massachusetts many prisoners who receive trade instruction secure industrial positions after release where they receive larger wages than their former foremen and instructors. Carefully selected prisoners of high ability who are admitted to the airplane mechanics programs at Chillicothe in Ohio and the Tracy Vocational Institution in California are in demand when they are released. They are highly paid and quite consistently successful on parole.

Further research is required to reveal the extent to which prison education and vocational training may be related to the prevention of repeated crime. In a parole prediction study at the Waupun Prison in Wisconsin, Schnur found that men who had had six months or more of formal in-

[55] While it has often been alleged that close-custody institutions receive in the main men unable or unwilling to learn a trade, California has found that 29 per cent of those sent to San Quentin and Folsom were good training and work prospects, 55 per cent were fair, and only 16 per cent were poor. See Walter M. Wallack, "Stone Walls Do a Prison Make," *Fed. Prob.*, vol. 16, p. 7, ftn., September, 1952.

[56] "Federal Prisons: 1957," *A Report of the Work of the Federal Bureau of Prisons*, 1958, p. 21.

[57] Walter M. Wallack, *op. cit.*, p. 11.

struction in an institution violate parole with significantly less frequency than those who had not.[58] In California, Fenton has observed a similar relationship to education and, more especially, to trade training.[59] It appears reasonable to believe that the development of skills and good work habits that he can use on the outside should have constructive impact upon the prisoner. Additional evidence that this is so may serve to stimulate some of the states whose education and training programs have lagged seriously.

SPECIAL ACTIVITIES

There is a considerable variety of more or less formalized prison activities in addition to the work, education, and training provisions discussed above. Individually they occupy less of the time of the inmate and they vary considerably both in their value for inmate morale and in their presumptive bearing on rehabilitation. Among the more important are the religious programs carried on by the chaplains.

Religious Activities

One could argue that educational and therapeutic programs as well as other reforms in prison are rooted historically in the role of the chaplain.[60] Originally, in fact, and for a prolonged period, the chaplain was the only prison educator and "social worker." In 1829 the chaplain at the Charlestown Prison in Massachusetts established the first prison Sunday school where both the Bible and rudimentary formal education were taught and, at about the same time, he inaugurated morning and evening chapel services. The chaplain of the prison in that state has continued to be in charge of education and the library. When crime was conceived as the equivalent of sin, the emphasis of prison leaders and reformers was upon penitence. The chaplain had a clear-cut function to inculcate biblical teachings.[61] More than this, however, since he was often the only member of the institution staff with a personal interest in the offender as an individual, he was soon involved in a wide variety of pursuits, some of which had little or no relation to religion. As time went on many men of the cloth

---

[58] Alfred C. Schnur, "The Educational Treatment of Prisoners and Recidivism," *Am. J. Soc.,* vol. 54, pp. 142–147, September, 1948.

[59] Norman Fenton, "Adult Education in the California Prison System," *J. Corr. Ed.,* pp. 68–72, July–October, 1950.

[60] According to Reverend Kuether, the origin of chaplaincy service goes back at least to the fifteenth century when the order of Misericordia was found to "assist and console criminals condemned to death, accompany them to the gallow, and provide religious services and Christian burial." Fredrick C. Kuether, "Religion and the Chaplain," in Tappan, *Contemporary Correction,* 1951, p. 255.

[61] *Correctional Research,* p. 4., quotes the Fourth Annual Report of the Prison Discipline Society of Boston, 1829, to the effect that thirty-five convicts in less than five months' time memorized a total of 19,328 verses of the Bible!

displayed more interest in social education and counseling than in gospel teaching or religious philosophy. The chaplain became something of a displaced person when specialized personnel came upon the scene to perform in areas where he had held sway. Kuether, a former chaplain in several institutions, describes the transition:[62]

As the early chaplains worked with prisoners' families and the people and resources of their home communities, social work emerged. As they doffed their reversed collars and taught the three "R's," prison schools developed. As

FIGURE 31. Chapel at the Federal Penitentiary at Lewisburg, Pennsylvania. This institution is of Northern Italian Renaissance design.

they badgered and wheedled local merchants into donations of athletic and other recreational equipment, recreation directors were added to the staff. As they begged and borrowed surplus or outdated books and magazines from sundry libraries and individuals, prison libraries were established. And, as these functions were taken over by the newer professions, the chaplains faced a serious problem. Deprived of their self-assumed, somewhat supernumerary jobs, they were faced with the necessity of rethinking their unique, strictly religious activities. The conduct of the Sunday worship service was often the only obviously "religious" duty of the chaplain. More than one warden or board was willing to settle for a part-time chaplain or a rotating chaplaincy on a fee basis. This, incidentally, was thought to be a good solution since it reduced institution

[62] Kuether, op. cit., p. 256.

overhead. This was a period of transition, and many a prison chaplain, without special training or natural aptitude, found that he could not justify his existence in the institution.

The contemporary chaplain continues to be something of a Jack-of-all-trades. He conducts religious services, carries on classes in religious education, and gives private interviews to prisoners with personal problems who may seek his help. In addition, however, he may become involved, in so far as the prison administration will permit him, in any of a wide variety of other functions: individual and group "therapy," Alcoholics Anonymous, academic and social education, drama and music, and other leisure-time activities.

Since 1936 there has been considerable development of a "clinical pastoral training" movement through which chaplains may be prepared to act as members of the "treatment team" in the prison. Conceiving of prisoners as "sick" rather than "sinful," they purport to behave more as therapists than as missionaries.

There can be no doubt that some prisoners go through an emotional conversion, assisted by the prison clergy, that has considerable effect upon their subsequent behavior. Others are held steadfast in religious convictions that help to carry them through the painful experience of incarceration. The chaplain sometimes mends or maintains ties between the prisoner and his home community. He is one constructive resource in the institution with a specialized appeal to a limited part of the population, individuals who are not greatly prisonized, who have strong guilt feelings, and who recognize a religious need. The chaplain's role has become ambiguous, however, and it is probable that he is as often exploited by cunning inmates who seek privileges or early parole as by offenders who require spiritual sustenance. The author has been surprised on a number of occasions at the diligent importunity of chaplains urging the release of offenders with prolonged and repetitive criminal histories who had apparently "conned" them into improper methods of support.

Recreation and Leisure-time Activities

Recreational activities are important to inmate morale and are significant, therefore, to effective institutional discipline. Furthermore, it is apparent that expanding leisure time in the free community calls increasingly for the development of habits, interests, and enjoyments to which, thus far, our society has paid little heed. What constitutes desirable leisure-time occupation is a normative question involving widely variant judgments, but it is generally believed that offenders use their leisure to more damaging effect than noncriminals do. They have more commonly been habituated to sloth, vices, and demoralizing associations. The author would not suggest that the development of socially approved recreational skills has significant bearing upon the reorganization of the character of antisocial individuals.

The evidence generally points to the contrary and exceptions would be rare. There is some special value within the framework of a restricted and monotonous institutional life, however, in providing a diversified program of leisure activities that may absorb the time and attention of inmates who otherwise are more likely to become involved in mischievous pursuits. It may occur, though quite uncommonly, that an individual will become so engrossed and will find such reward in a newly discovered or better developed talent that he will abandon otiose habits and will gain self-esteem. But the reorientation of personality and values does not occur on the basis of organized recreational pursuits or calisthenics. The American passion for sports has distorted judgment about their significance for the prevention

FIGURE 32. An exhibition game between the Wichita Braves and the Atlanta Crackers at the United States Penitentiary, Atlanta, Georgia.

and treatment of criminality.[63] The fact is that they are merely a pleasurable form of life activity for some individuals, both delinquent and nondelinquent. In prison they assume a greater significance.

Individual, dual, and team sports should be provided in any long-term institution. Such athletic activities are popular with a large proportion of inmates and provide an opportunity for aggressive and competitive play. The "old team spirit" is no less enthusiastic in the prison than in the school. Some minority of inmates find greater satisfaction in the creative outlets of art and craft work, however, and increasing emphasis has come

[63] The Athletic Institute of Chicago in a statement on "The Recreation Program" has contended that "there are many opportunities during participation in team sports for people to learn desirable social habits and attitudes, to develop emotional maturity, restraint and tolerance, and to strengthen personality traits which are important in the individual's adjustment to every-day living."

to be given to the development of hobby and handicraft skills.[64] Among the wide variety of these skills that are appropriate to prison training, the American Correctional Association refers to "basketry, bead craft, carving, ceramics, drawing, embossing, embroidery, etching, fabrics, jewelry making, knitting, leather craft, metalwork, model making, needlework, painting, paper craft, plastics, pottery, raffia-work, rug making, silk screening, sculpture, sewing, sketching, stonecraft, toy making, weaving, woodcraft, and others." In some states finished products may be sold through the institution hobby shop. Because such enterprise may be highly remunerative in some instances, it has become the practice generally to limit

FIGURE 33. Auditorium of the Federal Penitentiary at Lompoc, California.

the amount of materials that may be purchased and to limit the amount of products sold or sent out by inmates. Musical, literary, and dramatic activities of various sorts are also popular with many inmates. Here, as in the arts, fine talents are often encountered in prisons and not infrequently highly aggressive and disturbing inmates have been greatly subdued as a result of cultivating a special ability. Relatively passive and nonproductive recreational activities occupy much of the leisure time of a majority of prisoners: social games, reading, motion pictures, radio, and television. Both of the latter help to keep inmates in contact with the world outside. Gambling is popular and difficult to control in some institutions.

[64] Charles McKendrick has observed that handicraft programs require careful controls to prevent misuse of the program, since such work has often been permitted to become an organized prison racket.

Inmate Privileges

The question of what constitutes a "privilege" granted to prisoners rather than a "right" to which they are in some measure entitled is a nice semantic problem. As has been seen in the history of penology, there has been a gradual expansion and diversification of programs in correctional institutions designed to humanize the regime, to improve morale and discipline, and to rehabilitate offenders. Recreational and other activities have generally been introduced, often experimentally, as privileges or rewards, but in general they have become standard phases of the prison routine, a part of the legitimate expectancies of the population, that could not be withdrawn without creating major disturbances. Hence, a deprivation is looked upon by the inmate as the loss of a vested right rather than the mere denial of a reward to which he is not necessarily entitled. This is obviously quite significant in its bearing upon matters of prisoner morale and discipline.

Aside from the recreational pursuits to which the author has already alluded, there is a considerable variety of other special activities that have become standard in a large proportion of correctional institutions. Some of these are valuable from a treatment point of view because they tend to maintain prisoners' contacts with the outside world. This is especially true of visiting and correspondence by means of which the inmate may be able in some measure to preserve loyalties with close relatives and with such friends and sometimes business or work associates as may exert a constructive influence. Controls must be established both over visits (investigation and approval of authorized persons, supervision of visits, and shakedowns to prevent the passage of contraband) and over correspondence (censorship of incoming and outgoing mail), since risks to security are necessarily involved in any sort of outside contact. However, it is clear that, on balance, the continuing associations provided in this way, all too superficial at best, are so important that they should be increased as far as possible rather than narrowly restricted as they are at many prisons. No prisoner should be deprived of these activities as a measure of punishment unless they have been abused in some serious way; these activities are not only humanitarian but, more than most institutional activities, they serve the ends of the correctional process.

Obviously, more meaningful associations could be provided for by the use of furloughs from prison. Compassionate leaves to attend funerals or sick relatives, with custodial surveillance, are permitted fairly commonly in our prisons but furlough systems have developed only in some of our juvenile training schools. Several countries have inaugurated furloughs, however, for long-term prisoners who are approaching the time of release. This is advantageous both in facilitating the arrangement of a work plan

for parole and in easing the prisoner's transition back into the community.[65]
The mutual adjustments of the prisoner and his family, commonly a matter
of difficult and gradual accommodation, may be helped very considerably
by the use of one or more furloughs prior to release. These visits may serve
as a test of the prisoner's readiness for parole. Such a practice would be a
highly useful extension of present efforts in prerelease preparation. It was
proposed in 1959 by Representative Celler for the Federal prison system
in the United States and it is quite likely that it will first be tried there.

The practice of allowing some measure of responsibility to inmates for
participation in planning the institutional program has developed in a
number of prisons. In 1913 Thomas Mott Osborne introduced a system of
"prison democracy" at Auburn through what was first known as a Good
Conduct League, later the Mutual Welfare League. In the ensuing years a
similar idea was adopted at Sing Sing and a number of other institutions.
Elected representatives of the prisoners, acting as the board of directors,
and an executive committee elected by the board became responsible for
discipline in the prison and, through a series of committees, for planning
program activities. They held court and had power to deprive offenders of
all privileges through excluding them from the league. After a few years of
experience with the league idea, prisons have either abandoned it or have
greatly modified its function. Self-government of this sort is not feasible
in large prisons with heterogeneous populations if, indeed, it is practicable
in any correctional institution. It is close kin to the kangaroo court system
that has perverted our county jails. More recently, however, inmate
councils have been established in prisons in many places. Under this system
a selected body of inmates advise the administration on the development
of projects for general inmate welfare. Sometimes it appoints committees
to deal with special areas of interest, such as canteen, food, clothing, entertainment and hobbies, barber shop, radio and television, library, and
special events. While such councils are only advisory in function, it is very
commonly believed that, when they are properly organized and sufficiently
controlled, they are useful in maintaining prisoner morale, reducing discontent and preventing disturbances, and providing constructive ideas to
the administration. A larger amount of self-determination than that provided through councils has been permitted the better grade of prisoners in
honor cottages or sections where there is little or no custodial supervision
and in small camps. Where selection for the privilege is soundly made and
where the administration exercises decisive leadership, these systems are
useful means of encouraging self-control and responsibility in prisoners.

There are various other forms of special activities in our prisons: formal
and informal interest groups of varied sorts, prison publication activities,
canteens, and the like. These are important to morale, in that they provide
some relief from the monotony of prison life. They probably have little

[65] See ftn. 33 above and the *New York Times*, Oct. 28, 1958; Nov. 5, 1958.

effect, for the most part, as rehabilitative influences and will not be dealt with further here.

PRISON DISCIPLINE

Disciplinary policy raises some of the most knotty problems in the entire field of correctional administration.[66] This is so because it is not easy to assert autocratic control over a community within the framework of a democratic society and over individuals some of whom are disposed toward anarchy. Also difficulties arise out of traditional and widely held, though largely obsolete, views about the relationship of discipline to custody, punishment, and therapy. As in other phases of the correctional field, there is a disposition to consider prisons in terms of oversimplified extremes. Criminologists sometimes suggest that a regime must be *either* custodially oriented and punitive, concerned only for public protection against dangerous wrongdoers, *or* treatment-oriented and, therefore, permissive and protective to inmates who are deemed to be "sick."[67] We are slow to arrive at the conclusion, fairly obvious though it seems, that discipline and treatment must be balanced and that far from being inconsistent, discipline is essential to treatment. The real questions center upon the measures of control and how they should be asserted in relation to the particular population of prisoners that must be dealt with.

While we have not yet reached a resolution of all the issues involved in discipline and while abusive practices do still occur, there has been substantial progress among correctional authorities in understanding and establishing the circumstances under which sound discipline may be maintained in the institution.[68] In a narrow sense, discipline may be conceived

---

[66] See Charles L. McKendrick, "Custody and Discipline," in Tappan, *Contemporary Correction,* chap. 11, for an excellent analysis of the relationship between discipline, custody, and treatment.

[67] See Donald R. Cressey, "Achievement of an Unstated Organizational Goal: An Observation on Prisons," *loc. cit.,* for an analysis of two correctional institutions in terms of their difference in emphasis upon custodial and therapeutic objectives.

[68] There has been an inclination in some quarters to attribute the rash of major prison riots that occurred in 1952 and 1953 to disciplinary and other "abuses." The prison riots have not been the consequence either of brutality in treatment methods or of intolerable circumstances in the prisons, as some writers have maintained. This is not to say that abuses do not occur in some prisons today. Prison problems have resulted more from evidences of administrative weakness than of force, however. With the gradual professionalization of prison service, correctional administrators have been leaders in advocating needed changes. Penury in the correctional and welfare fields has caused tremendous mischief, not only because it postpones needed action but because it invites crises. It is only too clear that appeasement of rioting inmates in some penal institutions has stimulated riots in others. The discovery that threats, violence, and destruction may gain concessions has had anomalous consequences. Riots have produced some changes in prison programs and, incidentally, have provided a fictitious color of accuracy to the contention that abusive conditions

as the prevention and control of misconduct. In its wider implication, it means the maintenance of inmate morale and behavior at a level where disturbances are at a minimum and constructive effort at a maximum. This implies that custodial and security features will be appropriate to the particular population contained, so that there is not, on the one hand, a climate of unruly disorder nor, on the other, an atmosphere loaded with restraint and suspicion. Adequate but not excessive custody is a precondition to a reasonably disciplined institution. Orderliness and regulation, gauged to the size and character of the population, are essential, but they need not and should not be carried to repressive extremes. Prison rules are justified not as punitive devices but only as they are necessary to reasonable efficiency and regularity.

While discipline is commonly equated with punishment, a well-disciplined prison is one in which severe punishments are rarely needed or employed. A vigilant and perceptive staff will ordinarily be aware quite soon of any spreading discontent in the population and of distress in the individual. It can take preventive steps (e.g., cell or work reassignment, temporary segregation, counseling) that make punitive measures unnecessary. The provision of ample scope within the program for prisoners' self-expression may also go far to diminish frustration and to drain off discontent. In particular the opportunity to advise, recommend, and protest should offer inmates occasion both for emotional catharsis and for constructive participation in planning program. It is quite fundamental, when violations of regulations are reported, that procedures and penalties employed should be fair and impartial. The sense of justice is intense, though often skewed, among prisoners: they respect firmness, but harsh, invidious, or gratuitous punishment produces hate and rebellion.

In the light of what has been said elsewhere in this volume, it may be clear that in the author's view reconstructive treatment and discipline are not inconsistent. Indeed, sound discipline is the core of treatment and the specifically "therapeutic" efforts of a professional staff can be effective with the individual only where the group regime is well regulated, orderly, and fair. Members of the clinical staffs have sometimes had reason to criticize an uncooperative administration and custodial force of undue severity and rigidity in discipline. It is quite unrealistic, however, for them to rail against an effective system of custodial control upon which authority, order, and

---

incited the riots. It has been the effectiveness of extortion, however, rather than the need for specific changes that has produced the riots. Capitulation to prisoners' demands could not be and has not been the path to consistent or reasoned reforms. Riots have focused attention on prisons and their problems and this has been their single constructive accomplishment. See Tappan, "Why Do Prisoners Riot?" in *The Story of Our Time, Encyclopedia Yearbook,* 1953, pp. 214–218. See also Austin H. MacCormick, "Behind the Prison Riots," *The Annals,* vol. 293, pp. 17–28, May, 1954.

morale depend. Prison administrators have also had cause to protest that some members of the professional treatment staff fail to recognize the utility of authority as a legitimate tool in dealing with offenders and that sometimes they increase the difficulties involved in maintaining order and in preventing disturbances.

Punishments

The need to avoid abusive punishments has been recognized in the legal systems of the several states. There are both Federal and state constitutional provisions against cruel and unusual punishments in all but two jurisdictions and statutory prohibitions against specific punishments in many of these jurisdictions.[69] Corporal penalties are prohibited in ten states and seven others forbid whipping or striking. In a few jurisdictions prison administration is enjoined from employing stocks, strait jackets, gag, thumbscrew, showering, or tying up. The *Attorney General's Survey of Release Procedures* in 1939 indicated, however, that corporal punishment was then being used in twenty-six prisons.[70] This included the strap or the lash, the ball and chain, shackling or cuffing to the bars, the "spread eagle," cold baths, and gagging. In 1952 Negley K. Teeters received questionnaire responses from fifty-eight prisons relating to prison practices.[71] Only one institution acknowledged the use of flogging and one the use of tightened handcuffs but none of the other measures of brutality were admitted. For the most part the sanctions used today are more civilized if no less deprivative.

The most common form of punishment, used to some extent in nearly every prison, is the deprivation of privileges, such as recreational activities or the right to use the canteen, for a specified period of time. Sometimes correspondence and visiting are unwisely denied prisoners who might benefit from these contacts. Most if not all maximum-security prisons and a majority of institutions of reduced custody also use some form of segregation either for a definite or an indefinite period where serious violations occur. Often this is in solitary punishment cells and in some institutions, depending on the nature of the offense involved, such cells are stripped. Where punishment cells as such are lacking, there is usually a special disciplinary cell block where prisoners may be locked up.[72] In a majority of states a monotonous or reduced diet of bread and water may be assessed along with solitary confinement. Twenty prisons reported to Teeters that

[69] Tappan, "The Legal Rights of Prisoners," *The Annals*, vol. 293, pp. 99–112, May, 1954.

[70] *Attorney General's Survey of Release Procedure, op. cit.,* p. 122.

[71] "A Limited Survey of Some Prison Practices and Policies," *Prison World*, p. 5, May–June, 1952.

[72] Characteristically the disciplinary cell provisions are distinct from other special cells or cell blocks that are used for administrative segregation of homosexuals, escape risks, informants who are in danger of reprisal, and others.

bread and water were used, broken every two or three days with a regular meal. There are statutory requirements in some states that the prisoner's health be checked by a physician at regular intervals when he is on restricted diet and that the duration of the punishment be limited to a specified period. The third major form of punitive discipline is the deprivation of time that has been earned by good conduct or productive employment toward the reduction of sentence. Generally good time that has been lost in this way may later be restored after a period of good behavior. Since the length of time he must spend in the institution is generally of greater concern to the prisoner than any other single aspect of his imprisonment, the deprivation of commutation time is a severe penalty, but some prison administrators use it promiscuously. Teeters found this form of punishment in forty-seven out of fifty-eight reporting institutions. Probably the most frequent device employed where quite minor derelictions, such as loitering, smoking, inattentiveness, mischievousness, or failure to complete an assignment, are involved is a verbal reprimand by the officer who observes them. Such infractions may or may not be reported in the inmate's record. A variety of other penalties of various sorts are used in some institutions: reduction in grade where a grade system is used, a demotion that is usually associated with the privileges allowed;[73] transfer to another prison, work assignment, or cell assignment; and loss of monetary earnings.

Administration of Discipline

The effectiveness of a prison's policy on punishment and discipline depends to a very large extent on the administrative technique it employs in dealing with violations of its rules. Ultimate responsibility for discipline in the modern prison is usually vested in the principal keeper or deputy warden in charge of custody. Subject to approval by the warden, it is his task to formulate and enforce the prison rules and, in cases of alleged violation, he may be charged with adjudicative duties. More commonly today, however, the judicial function is entrusted to a hearing board, sometimes called an "adjustment committee" or a "disciplinary court," which is composed of the deputy, a psychiatrist or psychologist, an institutional casework or classification officer, and sometimes a member of the educational staff, a chaplain, guidance director, or some other member or members of the treatment staff.

It is generally acknowledged that any inmate reported for an offense should be informed specifically and in advance of the nature of the violation charged and that he should be provided an orderly hearing as soon as possible after the report. He should be permitted to confront the accusing officer, to call witnesses on his behalf, and to contravene the charges if he can. Guilt should be established to the satisfaction of the board on the

---

[73] Teeters found that reduction in grade was used as a punishment in twenty-three institutions.

basis of clear and substantial evidence. It is quite apparent that in some proportion of cases the hearing board should find that guilt had not been proved and in others that punishment should be suspended because of extenuating circumstances or because of the triviality of the offense.[74] Minutes of the hearing and the board's disposition should be recorded and a copy held in the prisoner's file. It would be sound policy for the state department to establish and publish a system of penalties graded to offenses according to their varying degrees of seriousness, thus limiting the range of discretion within which the disciplinary board might function in its decisions on punishment. Where the charge is a serious one and the possible penalty severe, hearings should be of a more formal character; the prisoner should be allowed full opportunity to prepare a defense, ideally with the help of counsel if he requests it, and with a right of appealing to the director of the state department.

THERAPY

Elsewhere in this work the author deals at some length with therapeutic approaches to the prevention of repeated crime; the content of clinical treatment will not be considered here.[75] The author would reiterate, however, the view that "treatment" involves the whole complex of relationships and experiences that are involved in the prison environment. This is to say that the professional staff that performs diagnostic functions as well as individual and group therapy is not the only and very likely not the most effective instrument of corrective effort so far as the general population of the prison is concerned. As one psychiatrist, Dr. Samuel B. Hadden, has suggested, "few prison psychiatrists are satisfied with the results of their necessarily meagre psycho-therapeutic efforts with confined criminals."[76] Dr. Abrahamsen believes that "the principle of imprisonment collides with the principle of psychiatry." Many authorities have expressed pessimism about the potential effectiveness of psychotherapy with the more difficult varieties of criminals, professional and other habitual offenders, psychopaths, psychotics, sexual deviates, and compulsive neurotics.

[74] In actual practice, discipline hearings are too often of a *pro forma* character, the guilt of the accused being assumed in advance, and the only real issue is the penalty that will be imposed. Even where a question is raised in the minds of the board, there is great reluctance not to support the reporting officer, since his authority is in some measure at stake. But the fair hearing is so important to prisoner morale, especially where serious penalties are involved, that adverse decisions should not be made on flimsy evidence. Prison officers, like police in the free community, should be brought to understand the need for an even-handed, objective justice. When such a policy is well established and the officer is aware of the necessity of supporting his reports with sufficient evidence, there would rarely be occasion to dismiss charges.

[75] See Chapter 18.

[76] "Group Therapy in Prisons," *Proc. Am. Prison Assoc.*, pp. 178–183, 1948.

An important part of the problem of prison psychiatry lies in the very large task expected of the professional staff and the small number of experts who are available for such work. In proportion to the needs for the total population of this country there is a very small number of psychiatrists in the United States.[77] According to a study by the United Prison Association of Massachusetts, conducted in the spring of 1954, there were psychiatric services for prison inmates in only thirty states, which employed a total of approximately 100 psychiatrists, less than a third of them full time.[78] The Federal Bureau of Prisons reports the employment of fifteen psychiatrists on a full-time and twelve on a part-time basis. According to the American Correctional Association, prisons should have a ratio of one psychiatrist and one full-time medical officer who is familiar with the fundamentals of psychiatry for every 500 in the population.[79] In fact the ratio of full-time psychiatrists to inmates is about 1 to 5,500 and the ratio of all prison psychiatrists to inmates is 1 to 1,600.

Psychiatrists are engaged, with some variation in the ways in which they distribute their time, in a variety of responsibilities. Their initial task, generally, and one that occupies a disproportionately large amount of their time, is that of diagnostic examination and the preparation of reports for the correctional and parole authorities. These are an important basis, however, of decisions on classification and discipline within the institution, transfer to other prisons, and sometimes hospital commitments. In the author's experience such reports, for whatever reasons, are commonly less useful than they should be. But the psychiatrist's counsel as a member of the classification and discipline boards is an important contribution to treatment planning in the institution. Theoretically a fair part of the psychiatrist's time should be devoted to individual and group therapy. In fact, however, this has not proved feasible and probably will not be possible in the future. Hadden observes that at best a psychiatrist can "treat but a small segment of the population, and to increase the number of psychiatrists to meet the needs on an individual basis is impracticable."[80] Individual psychotherapy in prison is impossible except on a very limited and superficial basis. In such cases successes appear not to be numerous. Group therapy offers greater promise, as the author has noted elsewhere, though this too requires staff time well beyond the professional resources of our prisons. Hence, certain rather dubious practices in group psychotherapy have developed in the use of personnel who are not trained in psychiatry or even in clinical psychological treatment methods. Quite possibly the

[77] See ftn. 47 in Chapter 10 above.

[78] Full-time psychiatrists were employed in the prison systems of only nine states.

[79] *A Manual of Correctional Standards,* American Prison Association, 1954, p. 216. See also Harry L. Freedman, "The Psychiatrist Looks to the New Penology," *J. Crim. Psychopathol.,* vol. 3, pp. 430–444, January, 1942.

[80] "Group Therapy in Prisons," *loc. cit.*

most important function that correctional psychiatrists can perform is
that of instructing members of the prison custodial and administrative staff
in techniques of dealing with deviated and aggressive personalities. This
requires, of course, that the psychiatrists involved should themselves be
specifically oriented to the problems of dealing with offenders.

Clinical psychologists, who are trained primarily in the evaluation of
intelligence and personality structure through the employment of psychological testing devices, play a related but somewhat differing role from
that of psychiatrists.[81] Characteristically they are called upon to administer
and interpret psychometric tests such as the Wechsler Bellevue and
Stanford Binet; projective tests such as the Rorschach, Thematic Apper-
ception Test, Sentence Completion Test, Word Association Test, Draw-a-
Person Test, and others; and special diagnostic, educational, vocational,
and achievements tests. Quite apparently such testing services are important to the processes of classification and transfer in the correctional
institution. In recent years, however, there has been a rapid development
among psychologists, as among caseworkers, in the ambition to perform
psychotherapeutic services that have traditionally been the province of
psychiatrists or, at most, of workers functioning under the direction of
psychiatrists. They have come increasingly both into individual and group
therapy programs and into administrative positions as substitutes for psychiatric personnel. Thus, for example, in the establishment of the diagnostic
clinics or guidance centers in the California State Department of Correction
in 1944 for the reception of all newly admitted adult offenders, a clinical
psychologist was made the chief officer in charge of the several divisions,
including medicine and psychiatry, sociology and casework, psychology,
and educational and vocational counseling. There has been a considerable
amount of criticism of this trend among psychiatrists, but it appears that
it is likely to continue, in part because of the lack of a sufficient number of
trained medical officers.[82] McCorkle has found that in not more than 10
per cent of correctional institutions where group therapy is practiced is
responsibility for the program in the hands of a psychiatrist alone.[83]

The Society of Correctional Psychologists reported in 1955 that it had
a mailing list of 121 psychologists employed in adult institutions and 53
in juvenile institutions. One hundred and four of the total are members
of the American Psychological Association.[84] The ratio of psychological
personnel to inmates in adult institutions was about 1 to 1,300 whereas,
according to standards suggested by psychologists themselves, it should

[81] See Ralph A. Brancale, "Psychiatric, Psychological, and Casework Services," in
Tappan, *Contemporary Correction,* 1951, chap. 13.

[82] See Freedman, *op. cit.*

[83] Lloyd W. McCorkle, "Present Status of Group Therapy in U.S. Correctional
Institutions," *Intern. J. Group Psychotherapy,* vol. 3, pp. 79–87, 1953. See also
McCorkle, "Group Therapy," in Tappan, *Contemporary Correction,* 1951, chap. 14.

[84] *Correctional Research, op. cit.,* Supplement, p. 2.

be about 1 to 250.[85] Furthermore, salaries provided for psychologists, like those for psychiatrists, are so low that it is not ordinarily possible to obtain the most able talent.[86] What with the lack of standards in the field and the considerably lower level of academic training and experience required of the psychologist, there is great difficulty in employing competent clinicians. An equally serious problem—and this applies no less to psychiatrists and caseworkers than to psychologists—is the lack of any specifically correctional orientation in the training and experience of the professional staff. The result all too commonly is a disposition on the part of clinicians to apply a generalized and permissive mental hygiene approach to criminals that is quite inapposite to the specialized needs of aggressive offenders.

The greatest single need for the development of more effective correctional treatment in our penal institutions is the conduct of research by behavioral experts, scholars both from in and outside the prison system, to discover what measures are effective and with what types of inmates they are effective. The relevance of the training, personality, and orientation of the therapist to his achievements is an important aspect of such studies.

[85] *Ibid.*, p. 5.
[86] Raymond J. Corsini and Gregory A. Miller, in "Psychology in Prisons," *Am. Psychologist,* pp. 184–185, May, 1954, noted that the median salary of prison psychologists was between $4000 and $5000.

Chapter 23

PAROLE

Parole is a form of conditional release of the prisoner from a correctional institution prior to the expiration of his sentence; the prisoner is provided supervision and guidance as a means both of aiding his readjustment to community life and of better protecting public security during the period following his release. Characteristically a series of parole conditions or rules are established either by law or by administrative direction of the paroling authority; the parolee is expected to conform to these conditions during the period of his supervision. His conditional release may be revoked either for the commission of a new crime or for a "technical violation," i.e., a failure to conform to the rules of parole. In certain respects parole resembles probation: it requires the performance of correctional casework by an officer; its continuance is conditioned on "good behavior"; violation may result in commitment to an institution; success results ordinarily in a discharge from supervision. There are certain rather distinct differences between parole and probation, however. Probation is a disposition of a court by which imprisonment is avoided.[1] For this reason it is ordinarily accorded to offenders who are considered relatively good risks and who appear not to require confinement for custody or treatment. Ordinarily it is relatively brief. Parole, on the contrary, results from the discretionary determination of a parole board, or other paroling authority, that a prisoner may be discharged from imprisonment after serving a part of his sentence. Commonly, for reasons noted later in this chapter, his supervision is very prolonged.

In the proper usage of the term, parole should be distinguished from other procedures that are employed in certain jurisdictions. The term "parole" is used in some courts to refer to the temporary discharge without bail of a defendant on his own recognizance or to his attorney, relative, or other person, on his promise to appear for further action of the court as required. Certain states use either the term "bench parole" or "judicial

---

[1] Probation may be very similar to parole, however, where the court may sentence to jail prior to the start of probation, as is done in a few jurisdictions. Such a practice permits the supervision of short-term offenders where parole itself would not be available to them.

parole" to refer to probation or a suspended sentence. "Conditional release" is used in a few jurisdictions to refer to a specialized form of discharge differing from parole in that the offender is retained in prison until the expiration of his sentence less such good time as he may have earned. The offender is then subject to supervision "as though on parole" during the remaining period that he is in the community and may be returned to serve out the term if he violates the conditions of his release. It is a misleading term in that parole is itself a form of conditional release in a general sense, as the author has noted, and there is some danger of confusion between the general and the special meaning of the term. It has been suggested that conditional release should be called "mandatory release."

HISTORICAL DEVELOPMENT

Like other correctional measures, parole has evolved into its present form from a variety of historical antecedents.[2] Indeed, its origins are considerably older than those of many other forms of treatment in present use. In addition to its more immediate predecessors, influences upon the policy and procedures of parole may be traced to old systems of clemency, indenture, and transportation. The British system of transportation has been described in Chapter 20 as a phase of the development of imprisonment as a penal sanction. In the early use of royal reprieves and indentures for transported offenders the prototype of parole was conceived.

Since the need for labor in the American colonies was great in the seventeenth century and colonization had been vigorously opposed in some quarters, the King was led to grant reprieves and stays of execution to some felons recommended by the courts who might be indentured to contractors there. It became apparent after a time that restrictions should be imposed upon those receiving pardons, since some offenders evaded transportation or returned to England. It appears that soon after the middle of the seventeenth century pardons came to be granted under specific restrictive conditions with provisions for revocation upon their violation. The pardon practice of the period combined the elements of executive clemency based on a selective process that related both to the nature of the offense and the characteristics of the offender and to conditions attaching to the pardon that resemble the terms of parole commonly employed today.

The deeds of indenture that were employed both for criminals and other servants also established rules of conduct that the servant contracted

---

[2] For a good, brief treatment of the history of parole, see Frederick A. Moran, "The Origins of Parole," Division of Parole, State of New York, 1948. See also *Parole, Attorney General's Survey of Release Procedures,* vol. 4, 1939, cited below simply as *Parole.*

to observe. Thus the conditions imposed on Benjamin Franklin when he became indentured to his brother in 1718 stated in part: "Taverns, inns or alehouses he shall not haunt. At cards or dice tables or any other unlawful game he shall not play. Matrimony he shall not contract nor from the services of his said master day or night absent himself but in all things as an honest faithful apprentice shall and will demean and behave himself toward said master all during said term."[3]

When the Revolutionary War ended transportation to America, an acute problem developed in the overcrowding of unsanitary detention quarters where prisoners awaiting transportation were held. In 1788, some eighteen years after Australia had been discovered by Captain Cook, that colony began to receive convicts from England in a number of penal settlements where they worked either for the government or for free settlers by assignment. Unlike the system that had prevailed in America, provision was made in 1790 for the governor of Australia to emancipate and discharge from servitude and to provide a grant of land to some of those prisoners whose conduct and work records justified such measures of reward and rehabilitation. While these prisoners at first received absolute pardons, the practice subsequently developed of granting a conditional pardon that was known as a "ticket-of-leave." This was an official statement from the governor dispensing with service to the government and enabling the convict to seek employment in a specified district. Such tickets-of-leave were granted to prisoners until 1811 for good conduct or service and to permit them to marry without particular limitations on time they must first serve. Thereafter it became the practice to require that convicts serve specific periods of time before becoming eligible for commutation. In 1821 a formal scale was established whereby prisoners with sentences of seven years might obtain a ticket-of-leave after serving four; those with sentences of fourteen years, after serving six; and those with life sentences, after serving eight. This appears rather clearly to be a forerunner of the system of indefinite sentencing, associated with parole after service of the minimum, as it was subsequently established in the reformatory system of the United States.

Captain Alexander Maconochie, who was governor of Norfolk Island, a famous penal colony east of Australia, between 1840 and 1844, was an important contributor to the historical development of parole procedure.[4] At the time of his appointment the system of transportation, for a long time severely criticized by Jeremy Bentham and many other humanitarians, was condemned by Parliament for the serious abuses that attended both the transportation itself and life in the penal colonies. Maconochie in 1837 had proposed changes in the treatment regime and, after he was appointed, established a mark and grading system under which convicts might move

[3] Carl Van Doren, *Benjamin Franklin,* 1938, p. 13, quoted in Moran, *op. cit.,* p. 6.
[4] John Vincent Barry, "Alexander Maconochie," *J. Crim. L.,* vol. 47, July, 1956.

ahead within four grades in accordance with their progress, as measured by the marks they had received for good conduct and labor.[5] The stages included strict imprisonment at first, then work on government chain gangs, followed by a period of partial freedom but with restrictions on the prisoner's movement, and finally a ticket-of-leave that enabled him to be transferred to Australia for the remainder of his time before attaining full liberty. Maconochie was considered too lenient in his handling of offenders who had been selected for the Norfolk colony as the most serious of English criminals, and as a consequence he remained as governor for only four years. His program, however, had considerable influence on subsequent developments.

England adapted Australian experience to domestic practice in 1853 through the provisions of the English Penal Servitude Act relating to prisoners convicted in England and Ireland.[6] This act provided for local imprisonment of those sentenced to terms of fourteen years or less but permitted the judge discretion to transport those sentenced to more than fourteen years. It also provided for conditional release on ticket-of-leave in the United Kingdom, established minimum periods of imprisonment before eligibility for release,[7] and stipulated that the license might be revoked at any time and the offender returned to serve the residue of his term. The ticket-of-leave provided that where the holder "associates with notoriously bad characters, leads an idle or dissolute life, or has no visible means of obtaining an honest livelihood, etc., it will be assumed that he

---

[5] It was Maconochie's view that criminal sanctions should consist of *task* rather than *time* sentences. The prisoner should be held until he had earned a fixed number of "marks of commendation" as the consequence of a specified quantity of labor and of good conduct. A daily allotment of marks would be given for performing assigned tasks, but the convict could earn more on the basis of industrious and exemplary behavior. He could also lose marks as the result of fines assessed for misconduct. Maconochie stressed the underlying principle involved rather than its mechanical aspects, however, and he proposed in addition many constructive and humane correctional innovations that since his time have come to be introduced into the field of prison treatment. He was not permitted to apply many of his ingenious ideas to the full at Norfolk Island, but some of them were introduced in Ireland by Sir Walter Crofton and have become known as "the Irish System." In addition to the marking system, his contributions included the movement of prisoners through progressive stages of freedom, the employment of institutions built to hold small populations, and close supervision after discharge under "tickets-of-leave." For an analysis of Captain Maconochie's proposals, see the authoritative biography by John Vincent Barry, *Alexander Maconochie of Norfolk Island,* 1958, especially pp. 74, 211–213. See also the publications prepared by Maconochie cited therein, pp. 263f.

[6] *Laws of Victoria,* chap. 99.

[7] Prisoners under sentences from seven to ten years were to be released after more than four but less than six years; on terms of ten to fifteen years prisoners would be discharged after six but not more than eight; on terms of fifteen years or more release would occur after six but not more than ten years.

is about to relapse into crime, and he will be at once apprehended and recommitted to prison under his original sentence." It is said that more than 5,000 prisoners were granted tickets-of-leave during the two years immediately following the enactment of the 1853 legislation. At this time there was a considerable amount of crime in England and it is not surprising perhaps that the ticket-of-leave system came to be blamed for widespread criminality. There was strong reaction against the humanization of sentencing and release that had occurred. In the light of the circumstances that prevailed at that time it is strangely fortunate that conditional release practice survived its ill lot in Australia and in its early English use. Prison programs of that day were something less than reformative, of course. There appears to have been very little selective discrimination in the early release of prisoners and no supervision was offered to them upon their discharge. The report of a judicial inspection of one of the prisons of the time suggests that some of the same problems of prisoner motivation afflicted the planning of classification and release that commonly appear in contemporary correction:[8]

The semblance indeed of the principle laid down by Lord Grey that "upon the daily record of the conduct should depend his final release" has been retained. A record is kept of the conduct of the convict. Upon his conduct during the period of separate confinement depends his enjoyment of more or less of certain indulgences, such as gratuities, communication with his friends, beer, puddings, tea, etc. [sic]

But so far are his conduct and industry from being made to have a certain and obvious effect in determining that period of his release, that, after the best inquiry we have been able to make, we cannot find that the daily conduct and especially the industry has an effect at all in determining that period.

We cannot find that the release of the convict is ever deferred beyond the earliest date on which it can be granted except in the case of positively bad conduct and then, except perhaps recently, only for short periods. This is a wholly different thing acting upon the convict's mind in a wholly different way from that pointed out by Lord Grey. It is an entire abandonment of that which he pointed out as having "contributed more than anything else to the gratifying reform which had taken place," viz., the looking to hope as the principal means of exercising influence on the number of convicts. The remission of sentence ceases to be an object of hope as soon as it comes to be regarded as a matter of certainty and of right and offers no motive for industry and active exertion to do well when it is to be obtained by mere passive abstinence from gross breach of prison rules. . . .

Following a series of prison riots in 1862, a Royal Commission was appointed to study the condition of the prisons and to suggest remedies for the problems then apparent. The Commission criticized the prisons' failure to prepare convicts for release and to provide them supervision in

[8] Mary Carpenter, *Our Convicts,* 1864, pp. 164–166, quoted in Moran, *op. cit.,* p. 15.

the community. They recommended the adoption of the system followed in Ireland at the time. Thereafter police were used for surveillance of licensees from prison until the Prisoners Aid Societies, partially supported by the government, were first established in 1864 to provide assistance and supervision.

In Ireland, Sir Walter Crofton became head of the prison system in 1854, the year after the enactment of the Penal Servitude Act. He established a gradation of three stages of penal servitude with progress based on a mark system somewhat comparable both to Machonochie's plan at Norfolk Island and "the progressive stage system" that was introduced in England by Sir Joshua Jebb.[9] Crofton introduced an "intermediate stage" for prisoners about to be released, during which they lived in comparative freedom in small groups at Lusk where they were separated from other prisoners. Arrangements were made for employment and police supervision after discharge. The ticket-of-leave man was required to report to the local constabulary in his community directly after release and monthly thereafter and was further ordered to conform to a series of rules restrictive of his conduct, on pain of revocation. In Dublin a civilian inspector of released prisoners performed the functions of supervision, visiting them in their homes and securing employment for them. In 1864, as has been noted, however, Prisoners Aid Societies were established, their agents devoting full time to visiting prisoners, helping them to secure employment upon release, supervising them, and reporting on their activities. The "Crofton system" was highly regarded and widely publicized for its effectiveness in dealing with prisoners and their release. In effect it was a synthesis of devices that had developed over an extended period of time. The product was a system of indefinite sentencing under which the offender might secure privileges and early conditional release by his good behavior in the prison and supervision in the community after his discharge under a set of parole rules.

Parole Development in the United States

Parole has developed to a greater extent in the United States than elsewhere in the world.[10] The impetus and idealism of the parole movement were derived, however, from the English and Irish systems described briefly above. Indeed, despite numerous variations and refinements that have developed in parole theory and in practice here, it appears that, under the Irish system at least, the prerequisites for successful parole were

[9] The "progressive stage" system, introduced by an act of 1857, provided for a period of confinement followed by three phases of increasing privileges based upon the good conduct of the convict. Rewards included badges, gratuities, and differences in dress.

[10] *New York Laws of 1887,* chap. 173, drafted by Brockway when he was superintendent of the Elmira Reformatory, was the first parole statute in the United States.

established more effectively than has been characteristic in the United States. One commentator has attributed the success of the Irish system to the fulfilling of four conditions: "First, that the prison system really reform the criminal instead of further perverting them, second, that there be a period of transition between prison and conditional liberation [the intermediate stage]; third, that there be strict supervision during the ticket-of-leave period [full-time, paid supervisors were used]; and fourth, that the attitude of the community be such as to make rehabilitation and assimilation of the delinquent possible."[11] How frequently prison programs in themselves have produced reformation, either then or now, may well be disputed. Certainly the problem of effecting reformation varies with different prisoners and with sociocultural circumstance at least as much as with the content of programs. It is quite clear, however, that we have failed too often in the other three respects: preparing the offender for conditional freedom, providing appropriate supervision, and developing receptive community attitudes. Parole has evolved considerably during the past century in the United States and is still in process of transition. It may come in time to fulfill the promise that some of the idealistic prison administrators of the nineteenth century attached to it. However, such success may well depend upon our willingness to depart from some of the sentencing, prison, and parole practices that we have developed in the course of this evolution.

Conditional Pardon

In addition to publicity in this country relating to the Irish system of conditional release, other developments here in the nineteenth century exercised important influence on our practices of prison retention and parole. One of these was the exercise of pardoning power by state governors. Comparable to the royal prerogative of clemency in England, the executive in some states here was given power, with or without an advisory board, to grant pardon to offenders who were deemed worthy. It appears that sometimes governors employed the pardoning power quite promiscuously in the discharge of criminals to reduce prison congestion, indirectly encouraging thereby the subsequent development of a more objective and systematic parole procedure as a reaction against abuse of the pardon power. More significant than this, however, was the practice in some jurisdictions of the granting of conditional pardons.[12] In some states the constitutions provided specifically for the granting of pardons on condition. Thus, in Rhode Island, "the persons who receive the benefit of such pardon shall comply with, and be subject to, such terms and

---

[11] Carpenter, *The Crofton Prison System,* 1872, pp. 65–66, quoted in *Parole,* p. 14.

[12] Conditional pardon had been employed in connection with the ticket-of-leave system for criminals transported to New South Wales as early as 1790.

conditions."[13] Elsewhere by legislation the governor might attach conditions in the granting of clemency. As early as 1837 the general court of Massachusetts enacted a law[14] providing that when the governor with the advice of his council pardoned or remitted any part of a sentence he might attach conditions to the release and could require the prisoner to give bond for the faithful observance of such conditions. In Virginia, where it was at first believed that the governor could not grant conditional pardons because the state constitution did not specifically so provide, case law eventually held that where no restriction appeared in the constitution the power to grant full pardon a fortiori included the power to grant pardon on conditions.[15] The records reveal, however, that from a very early date pardons were granted there on the giving of bond to good behavior.[16]

The granting of conditional pardon continued to be the major or exclusive form of early conditional release in many states and is still employed today in some. Where it is no longer used, it has nevertheless played an important historical role in the development of parole, as the power of the governor to grant pardons subject to good behavior has been transferred to advisory or independent boards that perform the same function, though more objectively, under the name of parole.

Commutation for Good Behavior

Commutation of sentence for good behavior is another device that developed both abroad and in the United States during the early nineteenth century. It was adapted here to our prison and parole systems to permit the earning of good time. A close analogy may be found in the experimental work of the Spanish prison administrator, Colonel Montesinos. Upon his appointment as governor of the Valencia prison in 1835, Montesinos established a plan for a one-third reduction of prison terms for good and constructive behavior. While the experiment was short-lived, together with educational and training innovations established by this progressive penologist, it is said to have been singularly successful in improving prisoner morale and in reducing recidivism. The first good-time law in the United States was enacted in New York in 1817, permitting the prison inspectors of the state to reduce by one-fourth the length of the term of any first offender who was serving five years or less upon a showing that he had behaved well and worked industriously. Somewhat similar legislation was enacted in Connecticut, Tennessee, and Ohio in 1821, 1833, and 1856. Thereafter other states passed such laws in rapid succession, apparently more as a result of the favorable publicity given to the Irish sys-

[13] Rhode Island, Const. Amend., art. II, 1854.
[14] *Massachusetts Acts,* 1837, chap. 181.
[15] *Lee v. Murphy,* 22 Grat. 789 (Va. 1872).
[16] Arthur P. Scott cites a petition for pardon on the giving of bond in Virginia in 1725.

tem than because of the early legislation here. By the turn of the century forty-four states had some form of good-time law. Today all states except California have such laws. Legislation providing for the commutation of sentence for good behavior varies considerably from state to state both in the amount of good time allowable and in its effect upon prison terms and parole. In some states, good time is used only to advance the date of the prisoner's eligibility for parole. In others, it cuts back the length of a maximum or of a definite sentence, resulting in earlier discharge. In some, it operates to reduce both the minimum and the maximum of the prison term. In a number of jurisdictions extra good time may be earned beyond the ordinary allowance for industriousness, "industrial good time," or for conduct of outstanding merit.

The theory of good-time legislation has been to motivate habits of good conduct, presumably in the interest of reformation as well as institutional discipline, by the most effective and positive type of reward: the reduction of the period of incarceration. In administrative practice such legislation is generally applied quite perfunctorily so that unless there is evidence of fairly serious misconduct the earning of good time has come to be quite automatic and offenders are accustomed to computing their sentences on the assumption that the good-time deductions will be made. As a result, disciplinary control is most commonly exercised in fact in a negative way by the withholding or forfeiture of good-time earnings for misbehavior. There is some controversy among authorities about the efficacy of good-time practices either in motivating adjustment or in penalizing misconduct. In states where maximum sentences are very long and good time is handled in a perfunctory way, with promiscuous grants and forfeitures, it is a weak measure of control. On the other hand, where sentences are reasonably short and, in particular, when a prisoner looks to a fairly early release date, the threatened loss of good time for breach of institutional rules appears to be an effective aid to prison discipline.

Good time bears upon parole practice, as suggested above, in advancing both the date of parole eligibility by reducing the minimum sentence, in some states, and the date of release from state control in some. Good time is also significant historically as the first means, other than the occasional exercise of the pardoning power, by which prison terms were made indefinite in length. Good-time laws were followed by and associated with legislation providing for prison sentences of indefinite duration, with a minimum and maximum from which good time would be deducted. While the indeterminate sentence idea and parole are two distinct and quite independent phases of penological policy, they were commonly associated in the thinking of our early prison reformers, and to a considerable extent they have developed concurrently. Parole came to be linked to an indefinite duration of imprisonment both in the mechanics of its operation and in popular penological theory.

Parole at Elmira

The essentials of the parole system that prevails generally in the United States are drawn almost entirely from the English and Irish systems that were described briefly above. The system of indefinite sentencing too was drawn in part from commutation practices under the Australian ticket-of-leave system, dating back to 1811, and was undoubtedly influenced also by the system of "good-time laws" that had developed in the states. In an earlier chapter the author has noted that these systems of sentencing and parole were first introduced here at the Elmira Reformatory in New York State shortly after its opening in 1876. The law establishing the reformatory, drafted by its first superintendent, Z. R. Brockway, provided, *inter alia,* for indefinite sentences, a marking system by which increased privileges and early release might be earned, and parole during good behavior.[17] Provision was also made for education and training of the young adult first offenders committed here during imprisonment. To receive parole the prisoner was required to maintain good conduct for a period of one year and to propose a suitable employment plan. After release he was directed to report regularly to a "guardian" or sponsor for a period of six months, it being considered that a longer period of supervision would be discouraging to the parolee. The introduction at Elmira of parole was heralded as a great invention and Brockway, it appears from his writing, claimed credit as its inventor. The system prevailing in England and Ireland, however, had been widely publicized some years before and the Elmira scheme was novel only in its specialized application to a young group. It lacked several elements that had developed under Crofton: full-time, paid supervisors, a period of supervision sufficiently extended to assure public protection and sustained good adjustment, and the intermediate stage of preparing for freedom. Moreover, the system at Elmira appears to have been administered somewhat perfunctorily on the basis of conduct marks, more in accord with the well-established practices of sentence commutation for good behavior than with the ideals of the indeterminate sentence under which release should theoretically be predicated on the prisoner's rehabilitation.

The Growth of Parole

Once established in a limited form at Elmira, parole was accepted rapidly in the United States. By 1900 parole had been introduced in twenty states, in thirty-two by 1910, and in forty-four by 1922.[18] Today, while

[17] Brockway had proposed a system of completely indeterminate sentencing to the Michigan legislature in 1868 when he was superintendent of the Detroit House of Correction. Subsequently he advocated such a system for Elmira but compromised on this principle with an indefinite sentence in which the maximum should be no higher than that imposed by the penal law for the crime involved. Conditional release was a part of this scheme.

[18] See *Parole,* p. 20.

the structure, policy, and operation of parole continues to vary greatly in the several jurisdictions, this form of release is employed in some fashion in every state as well as in the Federal jurisdiction and, to a limited extent, in some local, short-term correctional facilities. Some of the variations in current practice will be discussed in the pages below. It may be observed at the start, however, that parole universally includes the elements of indeterminacy concerning the time of release from the institution, the imposition of conditions, some measure of supervision during the parole period, the power of an administrative agency to revoke parole and return the offender to a correctional institution, and ultimate discharge from supervision either by operation of law or by administrative decision.

PAROLE SERVICES: STRUCTURE AND FUNCTION

There are three major divisions of parole functions and personnel in most jurisdictions. The board of parole is charged with making release, revocation, and sometimes, discharge decisions—a quasijudicial role. In a number of jurisdictions the board may be required to perform various other functions, largely administrative in character, that are relatively unrelated to these central tasks. The institutional parole staff prepares case data on the offender that are used both by the prison officials for classification and treatment purposes and by the board in making its parole decisions. The parole officers are ordinarily the only case workers on the institution staff so that an important part of their function is counseling with the inmates. Characteristically this parole staff is under the administration of the prison authorities; it is a part of the treatment staff of the institution, though its functions are oriented in some measure to the tasks of the parole board as well as to the prisoner and his preparation for parole.[19] The field parole staff, working with paroled offenders in the community, is charged with supervision and keeping records on such parolees and, where necessary, reporting on their violations of the conditions of parole. These officers are ordinarily under the administrative authority of the parole board.

Parole-granting Authorities

The greatest variability of structure and function may be observed in the organization of parole-granting functionaries throughout the states. They range from highly professionalized independent full-time boards, specialized in parole granting and revocation, employed in some jurisdictions to the part-time, multifunctional, and ex officio agencies utilized in others. In some states the parole board functions have merely been added to the duties of administrators whose primary responsibilities lie elsewhere. In an investigation of this problem, the author has found a wide diversity

---

[19] In New York and a few other jurisdictions the institutional parole staff is under the direction of the parole board.

and a lack of clarity in relation to the methods of combining and differentiating certain board functions. It appears, however, that the composition of paroling agencies can be grouped roughly in this fashion:

Parole boards of three or more full-time members: Alabama, California, Florida, Georgia, Idaho, Illinois, Iowa, Massachusetts, Michigan, Mississippi, Missouri, New York, Ohio, Pennsylvania, Texas, Washington, West Virginia, and the Federal government.

Parole boards with part-time or honorary members: Arkansas, Arizona, Delaware, Louisiana, Montana, New Jersey, Oregon, Rhode Island, South Carolina, Utah, Virginia.

Ex officio boards (sometimes including the governor, prison wardens, correctional commissioners, institutional board members, etc.): Colorado, Kansas, Nebraska, Nevada, North Dakota, Tennessee, Wyoming.

Governor with advisory board: Kentucky, Maryland, North Carolina, Oklahoma, South Dakota, Vermont.

Hybrid variations:[20] Connecticut, Indiana, Maine, Minnesota, New Hampshire, New Mexico, Wisconsin.

Aside from the variations in composition of paroling agencies, there is also considerable variability in the functions that such agencies perform. In five states where their tasks are most highly specialized the boards act only as quasijudicial agencies for granting and revoking paroles and discharging parolees.[21] In twenty-nine states the board also is in charge of parole field supervision services. In some of these, however, this latter task is delegated to a field executive and in others it is performed by a single member of the board.[22] There are thirteen other states where state probation and parole

[20] This category includes separate institutional boards, boards that serve some but not all of the penal institutions of a state, and boards that are composed in part of part-time or full-time members and in part of ex officio members, as well as other variations. For a fuller discussion see Ivan D. Nicolle, *A Critical Analysis of Adult Parole Procedures and Their Administration in the United States of America,* unpublished doctoral dissertation, New York University, 1956, chap. 3. This volume is the most thorough study of contemporary parole organization and practice that has been prepared.

[21] It should be observed that even in these five states and very generally in the others that carry additional major responsibilities, the boards also perform a variety of lesser functions, such as advising the governor in matters of pardon (in thirty-three states) or commutation of sentence (in twenty-nine) and reprieves (in twenty-four). In six states the board is responsible for administering correctional institutions and in five, for restoring civil rights. The five states in which parole board functions have become most highly specialized are Colorado, Kentucky, Michigan, New Jersey, and Utah. However, it should be noted that in a number of the states where the board is technically in charge of field services it actually does very little work in this area.

[22] In *A Manual of Correctional Standards,* 1954, it is observed that where the direction of field services are a part of the task of the parole board this function tends to become a separate island of administration. The *Manual* also notes that the administrative tasks required are not effectively performed by the board. Even

services as well as ordinary adjudicative functions are performed by the board.[23]

It appears desirable from the point of view of securing an effective specialization of function and independence in operation that parole boards should concentrate on their primary quasijudicial tasks, avoiding administrative responsibilities. Experience has shown that where they are charged with numerous and varied responsibilities some of these are likely to be performed inadequately and there is danger that the tasks requiring their special attention and competence, parole granting and revocation, will not receive appropriate emphasis. Under an "integrated system," where correctional (institutional) administration, probation and parole field services, and ordinary board functions are all performed by the same administrative agency, there are obvious economies. It is unlikely under such a system, however, that parole board functions will receive the specialized attention that they require and there is considerable danger that inappropriate considerations relating primarily to prison administration will influence parole decisions. In the more populous and progressive jurisdictions, for the most part, the trend is toward the autonomous, specialized, professionalized, full-time, well-compensated board, charged only with the quasijudicial functions.

The extent of the task that some parole agencies are called upon to perform may be illustrated in California's experience where there are three parole-granting boards, the Adult Authority, the Youth Authority, and the Board of Trustees of the Women's Institution. In 1953 the Adult Authority was relieved of many of the responsibilities relating to prison discipline and administration that it had previously been required to perform as has previously been observed.[24] At that time the board was increased in size from three to five members and three years later another was added. In 1955 the Adult Authority heard approximately 11,000 cases at seven state insti-

---

where they are delegated to an individual, however, as they often are, effective administration is difficult. A board chairman lacks the time and often the talent for the responsibilities involved if he is oriented primarily toward the adjudicative tasks of his office, as he should be. Where a subordinate is charged with the large responsibilities of administering field services, he is not likely to have the status and the powers that are needed even if he has the abilities. Field services have suffered in a number of major jurisdictions because of such awkward patterns of administration.

[23] The observations in the last footnote apply with even greater force when the paroling authority must perform the diversity of functions involved in probation as well as parole. The appealing doctrine that the "integrated department" will provide a unified and systematic treatment program to the individual is illusory in practice, for the correctional processes remain distinct and specialized and they are instrumented by personnel as diversified in their methods and orientations as are those who function in systems characterized by liaison rather than unification.

[24] See the *Survey Report, Organization of State Correctional Agencies*, Department of Finance, State of California, Apr. 24, 1953, and Chapter 16 above.

tutions, decided 1,400 parole supervision cases, and issued several thousand miscellaneous orders. A special study commission indicated in 1957 that, at the rate of growth of the board's responsibilities between 1945 and 1955, twelve board members would be needed by 1965.[25] This Authority has found it increasingly difficult to perform all the duties assigned to it and the commission recommended that it be relieved of some of these. In 1957 the administration of field services was turned over to the Department of Corrections. The Youth Authority appears to be no less burdened by the varied and excessive responsibilities with which it is charged.[26] A progress report issued by the Authority revealed that in 1952 the board issued 20,229 orders on classification and parole and travelled 47,545 miles for the purpose.[27] While the Youth Authority has been increased from three to five members, it cannot keep up to date with the heavy load of administrative and quasijudicial functions that it is supposed to perform.

The New York State Board of Parole, too, has staggered under the burden of work required under the law in that state. It has responsibility for administering and supervising both the institutional and field parole staffs in addition to its central task of making parole decisions. With a membership of five, the board held a total of 11,455 hearings in 1955, including release and revocation cases. Both in California and New York the hearings were held before three members, cases being assigned in rotation. The greatly increased requirements for traveling and sitting in hearings under this system obviously account in some significant part for board difficulties in accomplishing their tasks. The responsibility for supervising parole treatment services, even where this is delegated to the board chairman as it now is under the Youth Authority system and in New York State, is an improper assignment as the author has suggested. There appears sound reason to believe that, in New York at any rate, the supervision has been inadequate during the 1950s.

The Frequency of Release on Parole

Under existing legislation and practice only a fraction of prisoners released from correctional institutions are provided parole supervision. In fact, many are not eligible for parole consideration, as will be observed in the following section. In 1956, according to data submitted to the Federal Bureau of Prisons, 55.6 per cent of all discharges from state correctional institutions were by parole, with regional variations from 30.9 per cent in the South to 76.2 per cent in the Northeast.[28] In individual states the range

[25] *Probation, Jails and Parole,* Second Interim Report of Special Study Commission on Correctional Facilities and Services, California, Jan. 16, 1957, p. 38.

[26] See Tappan, "Young Adults under the Youth Authority," *J. Crim. L.,* vol. 47, pp. 629–647, 1957.

[27] *California Youth Authority Progress Report, 1948–1952,* p. 20.

[28] "Prisoners Released from State and Federal Institutions," *National Prisoner Statistics,* no. 17, August, 1957, table 4.

was from 8.2 and 7.6 per cent in South Carolina and Oklahoma, respectively, to 92.6 and 99.2 per cent in Colorado and Washington. In fourteen states, more than 75 per cent of releases were by parole, while in nine, fewer than 25 per cent were so released.

The variation in the extent of the use of parole reveals the wide disparity in correctional philosophy prevailing in regard to this treatment measure. The view has become increasingly prevalent that all prisoners released from prisons and reformatories should go out under supervision as a means of aid and guidance to the individual and of protection to the public. This policy was expressed at the Attorney General's National Parole Conference in 1956.[29] It is central to the parole provisions of the Model Penal Code of the American Law Institute, which would make parole mandatory for all released offenders.[30] On the other hand, in the evolution of the indefinite sentence and parole, there has developed the idea that parole is a matter of grace that may either be bestowed or withheld at the free discretion of the executive. Thus, although the system of indefinite sentences has led in many jurisdictions to very long maximum terms, designed to provide sufficient protection against the worst of offenders and to include a period of parole, parole administrators have maintained that release before the expiration of the maximum is no more than an act of lenience.

Relatively low rates of parole granted in some jurisdictions, in spite of long prison sentences, reflect not only the broad discretion of the paroling authority and the view that parole is a matter of grace but, more fundamentally, a conception of policy that prevails among many authorities in this field. This is the idea that only "good risks" should be paroled and that, therefore, a parole board is in effect certifying the reformation of the offenders whom it releases. In varying degrees boards may be ready to take what they would consider a "calculated risk" on some offenders whose need for supervision is very clear or whose sentences were patently excessive. They do so with some reluctance because they believe that their primary responsibility is to show a low failure rate among those whom they release. The result is early discharge and long supervision of adventitious offenders who have required little correctional treatment and who, in some cases at least, should not have been imprisoned at all. Those who most need a discriminating decision concerning the optimum time of release and careful supervision thereafter are likely to be retained throughout their terms and discharged without guidance or regulation in the community. The result of this is not only the inordinately wide variation in time served by different offenders for the same sort of crime but a greater probability that the more serious criminals will recidivate as a result of our failure to provide the

[29] See *Parole in Principle and Practice*, The National Conference on Parole, 1957, p. 102.

[30] *Model Penal Code*, secs. 6.09A and 305.12.

community supervision that is needed. The conception of mandatory and universal parole, on the other hand, would assume the probability of a somewhat increased rate of parole violation but a declining over-all rate of recidivism and a considerably refined effort to determine the optimum time for the release of prisoners. The latter would be calculated on the basis of the long-term protection of society rather than on the protection of the reputation of the parole board. Once the idea of universal parole comes to be accepted, boards will not be expected to achieve the impossible and attention will be given to the more significant, ultimate objective of preventing the continued recidivism of repetitive criminals.

Parole Eligibility

A majority of jurisdictions have established statutory limitations or exclusions on eligibility for parole consideration, most commonly on the basis of sentences to life imprisonment, convictions for murder or other specified felonies, and prior criminal convictions.[31] Some states prohibit the granting of parole to prisoners with communicable diseases, to those who have attempted or effected an escape, or to those serving under a definite sentence. Only fourteen jurisdictions permit parole consideration in any case. Aside from legal restrictions many prisoners are denied parole on the basis of standards administratively established by the board itself or as a consequence of limitations in the extent and quality of parole resources. Characteristically prisoners with misconduct reports are rejected or deferred for future consideration. In some states any prisoner who is wanted under a detainer for further court action or imprisonment is automatically rejected unless or until the writ is lifted.[32] Some board members refuse to consider

[31] For life prisoners a minimum period of years is fixed in most states at the end of which such persons become eligible for parole. These periods run in various states from seven to thirty-five years.

[32] Varied practices in relation to detainers in the states create serious difficulties in planning parole. Some jurisdictions place "nuisance" detainers against prisoners in other states merely as a means of persuading the latter to extend so far as possible the period of imprisonment, not intending to take custody of the prisoner when he is released. It is good practice, followed in progressive jurisdictions, for the institutional parole officers to inquire of the proper legal authorities what their intent is concerning disposition of detainers they have placed. Some of these authorities cooperate fully in disclosure and others do not. In the latter case the difficulty of making a sound parole decision is increased because the board cannot know whether the prisoner, if released, would be free in the community or returned to another institution. See "The Detainer: A Problem in Interstate Criminal Administration," *Colo. L. Rev.,* vol. 48, p. 1190, 1948. The Council of State Governments has prepared a bill that would permit the prisoner, in any case where a detainer has been placed against him on a criminal charge, to require the state to try him promptly. See "Conference on Legislation Dealing with Detainers and Sentencing and Release of Persons Accused of Multiple Offenses," The Council of State Governments, Apr. 14, 1956. (Mimeographed.)

any offender convicted of a crime involving sex, narcotics, or a dangerous weapon.[33]

In connection with the consideration of an individual's eligibility for parole, the states have generally required that a parole plan be submitted by the prisoner and approved by the board before he may be released, thus to assure that the circumstances under which he will live in the community are reasonably favorable to his successful adjustment. It is required in thirty-four jurisdictions that the parolee have an approved employment arrangement and place of residence and in six of these he must have a sponsor as well.[34] Five states require only a job plan, one only an approved residence, two a sponsor, one a guarantee of maintenance, and one that the parolee be free of venereal infection. In four states no specific plan is required. The requirement that a plan be completed and approved before the prisoner may be released leads to difficulty in many cases, particularly in times and places where the employment situation is tight.[35] When it is uncertain whether the person will be approved for parole release, employers are commonly unwilling to guarantee employment and it is in any event awkward to arrange an employment agreement when there is no opportunity for personal interview with the inmate. The result in cases where the plan is incomplete may be a more or less extended deferment of release when the prisoner is otherwise ready to go out, thus creating a period of "dead time" that is unproductive and demoralizing to the prisoner. To meet this situation some parole boards grant parole in certain cases conditional upon the completion of a plan, thus increasing the probability that an employment arrangement will be consummated; other boards, where they are allowed discretion in the matter, will parole with an incompleted plan when to do so appears reasonably safe for the parolee and the community. Prisoners generally receive such assistance as the institutional parole staff can give them in preparing their parole plans and these are checked in some jurisdictions by the field parole staff to make certain that the arrangement is legitimate. Unfortunately, however, employment agreements are not uncommonly spurious, very temporary, or exploitative, a mere device to fulfill the formal requirements of the law. On the other

---

[33] In *People v. Norwitt*, 69 N.E. 2d 285, 394 Ill. 553 (1947), the Illinois court upheld the parole board in its refusal to give consideration for parole to sex offenders, although they were not excluded by statute.

[34] For an enumeration of the statutes, see Comment, *Model Penal Code,* sec. 305.11, pp. 89ff.

[35] In New York State the Department of Correction announced in 1956 that 1,100 men approved for parole were being held in prison because they had been unable to find jobs required as a condition to their release. *New York Post,* May 5, 1956. Since about 2,000 prisoners are paroled there annually, it is apparent that the proportion of those eligible who were doing "dead time" was very large, with consequent damage to prisoner morale and a heavy financial burden to the state.

hand, in certain jurisdictions, such as the Federal and California, where effective effort has been devoted by the correctional authorities to the working out of arrangements with public employment services, with individual employers, and with labor organizations, there has been a very considerable success in placing parolees in positions suited to their ability and experience. Intensive public relations work in this matter of securing jobs for parolees is highly desirable in order to reduce failure rates during the crucial early weeks in the community.

The Parole Release Hearing

In most jurisdictions a parole hearing is provided the prisoner at or near the time of his eligibility for consideration, either on the basis of his application or automatically.[36] Such hearings are ordinarily private and informal.[37] In most jurisdictions either a verbatim record or a summary of the hearing is made. The former is desirable practice. In at least eighteen states the prisoner is permitted legal counsel either in preparation for the hearing or at the hearing itself.[38] It is sound practice to allow access to counsel prior to the hearing and to permit counsel to address the board in private session at some other time for, while specifically legal issues are raised in only a minority of cases, the ordinary prisoner is ill equipped to marshall effectively such arguments as he may have in support of his parole, particularly if there are any subtle or technical considerations that might influence the decision. The writer has been impressed in numbers of cases by the effective and well-considered argumentation of counsel on behalf of their prisoner-clients in cases where the ignorance, diffidence, or anxiety of the latter have produced a relatively poor impression of their merits. It would be desirable, if it were feasible, to provide public or voluntary defender aid to prisoners for this purpose as well as in the preparation of writs in cases where these would be legitimate.

It is customary and quite essential to sound decisions that the board have access to the full record of the offender. Presentence investigation reports, the results of medical and psychiatric examinations, official reports concerning prior criminal history, records and reports prepared by the institutional parole staff, information submitted by the prisoner or other persons in interest, the parole plan, and any recommendations coming from the court of the institution should be submitted to the board for its careful consideration before a decision is reached. While impressions and information conveyed by the prisoner at his hearing are of some importance, in-

---

[36] Thirty-six states give automatic consideration for parole without the necessity of application by the prisoners.

[37] Parole hearings are provided in thirty-nine states, but in only six is the right to a personal interview conferred upon parole candidates as a matter of law.

[38] See Tappan, "The Role of Counsel in Parole Matters, *Practical Lawyer,* vol. 3, no. 2, pp. 21–29, 1957.

telligent decisions on parole must be based on the total view of the offender as observed in his social and criminal history, his personality and attitudes, his response to custody and treatment, and his plans for the future. The prison record alone, while it may in some instances reveal that the offender is not yet amenable to authority, is commonly a poor guide to his future adjustment, since professional criminals and dependent personalities will commonly adapt adequately to the prison environment but fail repeatedly upon release. It is partly for this reason that parole boards should be independent of prison administration and should scrutinize the entire record closely.

While the point would seem to be obvious, it must nevertheless be remarked that it is not enough that an elaborate file be prepared on the prisoner before his parole hearing. If the accumulated information is to play the significant role that it should in parole, the record must be studied carefully and objectively by board members before their decisions are made. It appears to be common practice, unfortunately, for boards under the pressure of onerous duties to be content with a hurried reading of a brief summary at the time of the parole hearing and to arrive at a decision at that time.[39] Under these circumstances excessive weight may be given to the impressionistic observations of the board members, to the formal criminal record of the offender, or to the inferences contained in the parole summary. When only five or ten minutes are given to study of the record and interview of the prisoner judgment cannot be adequately informed. Where only one member of a parole board consults the record and makes the parole decision, there is grave danger of bias. Frequent errors are inevitable.

The Release Decision: Reconsideration

As in other aspects of parole, there is much variability in practices relating to the decision on release. In some jurisdictions, the Federal for example, the hearing is conducted by one board member, who then summarizes the interview and makes a recommendation to the board. The decision is by a majority of board members (or of a quorum) after the board has studied the total record and has determined whether release should be granted or postponed and, if granted, what the release date should be. In many other jurisdictions hearings are conducted by a panel of two or three members; characteristically each member of the panel in turn conducts interviews with the offenders assigned to him.[40] Where a hearing panel is

---

[39] According to responses to the author's inquiry directed to parole boards throughout the country, an average of ten to fifteen minutes is allowed prisoners for a hearing. This is quite possibly an inflated figure. In any event, part of this time is ordinarily employed by the board member who conducts the interview in looking at the prisoner's file.

[40] According to questionnaire replies, all members of the parole board attend the parole hearings in at least twenty-six jurisdictions.

used, decision may be made at the conclusion of each hearing and the prisoner informed directly after the hearings are completed of what that decision is. Usually the decision is supposed to be reached by unanimous agreement, but in practice it is generally the decision of the single board member who conducted the interview, the other members concurring with his conclusion.[41] The latter system is not economical since it requires two or more members to sit with each prisoner while the decision itself is generally made by a single member. In any event the requirement of a unanimous decision in parole matters is undesirable; it gives undue weight to a single member of the board who can, where he wishes, oppose the decision of the majority.

After considering a prisoner for parole, the board may either set a date for release or deny parole, with the possibility of a later reconsideration. In the first case, a reasonably early date should be set, ordinarily within a few weeks of the date when the decision is made. This will avoid the unconstructive and depressing experience of "dead time," which faces a prisoner who is granted a parole the date of which is deferred for several months. Sufficient time must generally be allowed so that the offender's parole plan may be completed and approved, if this has not previously been done, and to provide an opportunity for prerelease preparation at the institution. Once it has been determined that the time has come for a prisoner's release, however, it should not be delayed unduly, for the result is seriously depressing to the morale of the prisoner.

When for any appropriate reason a board concludes after a hearing that a prisoner should be denied parole, it is important that provision be made for subsequent reconsideration of the case. It happens all too often that prisoners undergo progressive demoralization over a period of years when they have once been denied parole and then have been forgotten by a parole board. For the most part the states do not provide specific means in their legislation to assure timely reconsideration of parole and board administrative practices are very commonly faulty in this regard. In some jurisdictions prisoners may apply for reconsideration, but this method alone does not assure that prisoners will be given further consideration in accordance with their merits. In certain states it is board practice, at least in some proportion of their cases, to set a later date for reconsideration

[41] Thirty-three jurisdictions require only a majority for parole decisions. From first hand experience in the Federal system the author has observed that differences of opinion and voting are normally to be expected when several board members study the file and take action. Consistent unanimity suggests that decisions are being made by one member. It was the practice in the Federal parole system until a few years ago for the member of the board who conducted the hearing to determine the action to be taken, other members merely signing the docket. Dr. George G. Killinger was responsible for changing this practice because of the palpable danger of serious errors of judgment on the part of a single hearing member. Since that time a quorum of the board studies the files of every prisoner considered for parole. The New York State Board of Parole encountered serious trouble in 1957 as a result of allowing a single member of the board to decide on parole revocation.

(and sometimes for a rehearing) at the time of the original hearing. Where this is done systematically for every case, where the intervals fixed before reconsideration are reasonably short, and where there is an effective system to make certain that all cases are in fact reconsidered after such intervals, the result should be fair to the prisoner and economical to the state. It should be apparent, in this regard, that the unnecessary retention of offenders beyond the optimum time for their release is an extravagant burden upon state resources, per capita prison costs being as large as they are. It was with this in mind that provision was made in the Model Penal Code for automatic reconsideration of the record of every prisoner who was deferred upon his original hearing at least once each year.[42] Thus there would be reasonable assurance that men would not be retained far beyond the requirements of public security and their individual treatment needs. This would increase somewhat the size of the load of work that must be performed by the board of parole, but a review of records is not an excessive task, especially when weighed in relation to the overriding considerations of correctional justice and of public economy.

Prediction Tables

For the most part no clear-cut criteria are used under present parole practice in determining whether or when a prisoner should be released. Some statutes express a vague policy that the prisoner should be paroled only when such action is not incompatible with the welfare of society. The National Probation and Parole Association has suggested an equally general principle that parole should be granted when, in the board's opinion, there is "reasonable probability that the prisoner can be released without detriment to the community or to himself."[43] Professional parole administrators have generally agreed that certain more specific guides or factors should be considered, such matters as the offender's prior record, his personality and physical condition, social history, employment record, intelligence, family status, parole plan, etc. How such variables should be weighed in determining if or when a prisoner should be paroled, however, has not been made clear. Certain factors in the individual case may well be emphasized out of all proportion to their significance, if indeed they are significant at all. Parole decisions tend in fact to be based upon intuitive hunches. Very commonly, as the author has suggested, the conservative board will release those prisoners who are ostensibly very good risks and will deny parole to the remainder.

There have been two developments that look to a more precise weighing of the issues involved in release decisions. One is the research that is being conducted on prediction instruments; the other is the formulation in the

[42] *Model Penal Code*, sec. 305.12 (3). A similar rule was established in the procedures of the United States Board of Parole while the author was chairman of that Board to avoid the danger that some prisoners might be forgotten for a time.

[43] *Standard Probation and Parole Act*, 1955, sec. 18. See also *Parole in Principle and Practice*, 1957, chap. 7.

Model Penal Code of more specific criteria for release. Studies of the statistical probability of success or failure on parole date back to 1923,[44] but the first distinctly significant research in the field was the work of Bruce, Burgess, and Harno in 1928.[45] The latter found twenty-one factors associated with parole violation and suggested that these might be developed into an expectancy table, to be used with and supplemented by intensive studies of the individual cases. The first large-scale prediction research was conducted by the Gluecks in a series of studies in which they investigated carefully the behavioral histories of some 510 inmates at the Concord Reformatory in Massachusetts over a fifteen-year period and developed prognostic tables based upon factors associated with the prereformatory, reformatory, parole and postparole periods.[46] In their first study the Gluecks found six factors "appreciably" associated with continuance or noncontinuance of criminality and nine that were "considerably" associated, as measured by coefficients of contingency. These were modified somewhat by the ensuing two follow-up studies of the same sample. It was proposed that the tables could be used in aid of sentencing, parole prediction, and post-parole prediction. After initiating the reformatory research, the Gluecks made somewhat comparable studies of a group of 1,000 juvenile delinquents, also followed up over a period of fifteen years, and of five hundred women in the Women's Reformatory at Framingham, Massachusetts, a five-year follow-up study.[47] Parole prediction studies, based on factors correlated with success or failure and designed in part to test critically the methods employed by Burgess and Glueck, were also conducted by George B. Vold in Minnesota, by Clark Tibbitts in Illinois, and by the United States Department of Justice in the Federal system.[48] Ferris F. Laune studied prediction based upon the subjective hunches of fellow prisoners.[49]

The most recent significant publication on parole is the work of Lloyd Ohlin, research sociologist of the division of correction in Illinois.[50] In that

[44] Sam Bass Warner, "Factors Determining Parole from the Massachusetts Reformatory," *J. Crim. L.,* vol. 14, p. 172, 1923, criticized in Hornell Hart, "Predicting Parole Success," *J. Crim. L.,* vol. 14, p. 405, 1923.

[45] *The Working of the Indeterminate Sentence Law and the Parole System in Illinois,* 1928, chaps. 28 and 30.

[46] Sheldon Glueck and Eleanor T. Glueck, *Five Hundred Criminal Careers,* 1930; *Later Criminal Careers,* 1937; *Criminal Careers in Retrospect,* 1943.

[47] *One Thousand Juvenile Delinquents,* 1934; *Juvenile Delinquents Grown Up,* 1940; *Five Hundred Delinquent Women,* 1934.

[48] George B. Vold, *Prediction Methods and Parole,* 1931; Clark Tibbits, "Success and Failure in Parole Can Be Predicted," *J. Crim. L.,* vol. 22, p. 11, 1931; "Reliability of Factors Used in Predicting Success or Failure in Parole," *J. Crim. L.,* vol. 22, p. 844, 1932; and *Attorney General's Survey of Release Procedures,* vol. 4, *Parole,* 1939.

[49] "Predicting Criminality," *Nw. U. Studies Soc. Sci.,* no. 1, 1936.

[50] *Selection for Parole, A Manual of Prediction,* 1951. Professor Ohlin has since joined the faculty of the New York School of Social Work.

state research on parole prediction has been carried on by sociologists-actuary at each of the major penal institutions since 1933 and prediction reports have been made routinely for the use of the parole board there. Ohlin's "experience table" is derived from data on 4,941 parolees followed up over the five-year period of supervision before discharge to discover the proportion of cases (28 per cent) against which violator warrants had been issued. He found twelve factors that were most closely related to parole success or failure: type of offense, sentence, type of offender, home status, family interest, social type, work record, community, parole job, number of associates, personality, and psychiatric prognosis. Ohlin makes clear the necessity of revising "experience tables" as experience changes and it is apparent that the components employed in prediction must be varied not only from one jurisdiction to another but from one institution to another and from one time to another. This is because of differences in such variables as age, offense, treatment program, and parole supervision, which may lead to quite different experience in parole success and failure. In Illinois a twenty-seven-factor table was employed in the 1930s for all three branches of the penitentiary system, but this was replaced in 1950 by Ohlin's table, referred to above. In 1953 a seven-factor table was put into use at the Pontiac institution where a younger group of inmates are confined, based on investigations into the variables that were most selective in distinguishing between parole success and failure in their experience there.[51]

A number of criticisms may be made of the parole prediction research and the tables that have been developed thus far. While these criticisms do not apply uniformly to all the work done in this field, they do raise a nice policy question concerning the present feasibility of employing such instruments for purposes of parole release decisions. The chief problems appear to be these:

1. Commonly the data available on offenders, both the presentence investigation materials and institutional reports, are inadequate and inaccurate. Such materials are rarely checked carefully in the courts or institutions and it is doubtful that it would be feasible, on the one hand, to do the careful sort of investigation and checking that would be necessary or, on the other, to employ the data if they are not assiduously tested for accuracy and completeness.[52]

2. There has been relatively little empirical testing of the prediction tables

---

[51] Age offender left home, developmental pattern, work record, most serious previous sentence, criminal record, schooling completed, and use of prison time. See Daniel Glaser, "A Reconsideration of Some Parole Prediction Factors," *Am. Soc. Rev.*, vol. 19, p. 335, 1954.

[52] In *Unraveling Juvenile Delinquency,* the Gluecks observe, " . . . obviously they must be in the hands of highly experienced persons, and the necessary prediction scores must be derived from absolutely accurate data." P. 268. They list twenty-one authorities, including social investigators, psychologists, and psychiatrists, but excluding statisticians and secretarial staff, who worked on the 1,000 cases used in this study.

with new samples of offenders, but such studies as have been made have indicated a considerable margin of error.[53] At the present time the data available from the prediction studies, except perhaps for the experience tables in Illinois, are too confused for current use by parole boards. The various studies referred to above have pointed to a variety of factors that predictive experts have found associated with parole outcome. These variables along with others are already taken into account in some measure by parole boards, but it is still not clear what weight should be attached to any of them. For example, the Gluecks have found instability and "mental distortion" correlated with recidivism, while Burgess and Tibbitts concluded that "emotional instability" was a favorable predictive category. Also, while the former discovered a positive relationship between gang membership and recidivism, the Burgess and Tibbitts studies found a high violation rate in the "lone wolf" category.

3. There is also a problem involved in the use of vague and subjectively determined factors. *Social types,* such as "fairly conventional," "ne'er-do-well," "floater," and "socially maladjusted"; *personality categories,* such as "normal," "inadequate," "unstable," or "egocentric"; and *psychiatric prognoses,* such as "favorable," "problematic," "doubtful," and "guarded"—all these leave wide ground for differences in expert opinion. All three of these categories, presumably interrelated though they are, are included in Ohlin's twelve-point table.

4. Since changes continuously occur in community conditions, institutional programs, preparation for parole and parole supervision, age and criminal history of offenders, and violation rates, any formula based on a sample of prisoners at one time and place should not be applied at another time to a different group unless the circumstances are very similar. A table must be developed very carefully at the start and then, as Ohlin has indicated, modified regularly even for a single institution in the light of changing experience.

5. For the most part the tables thus far developed have been based upon a static conception of the individual and his treatment. They do not allow for the possible changes and improvement of correctional treatment programs in the institution and on parole. Thus, they tend to be oriented more toward retention of the prisoner than toward effort to treat him effectively. They fail usually to take into account changes in attitude and social role that may be achieved through correctional treatment, tending instead to the implicit assumption that the qualities of personality that appear early in childhood are determinative of adjustment in the man.

6. There is an inherently conservative tendency in parole boards to release on parole few prisoners among those who fall within the range of a fairly high expectancy of violation. The evidence indicates that in actual experience the violation rates of this group are overestimated.

7. A serious problem connected with past parole prediction research lies in the fact that it is oriented to the issue of the risk of violation, as such, rather than to the question of *when* the prisoner should be released on parole. Since the vast majority of offenders are eventually released from prison and since those who are relatively poor risks are in special need of parole under a care-

---

[53] See Ohlin and Duncan, "The Efficiency of Prediction in Criminology," *Am. J. Soc.,* vol. 54, pp. 441–451, 1949, and Paul Horst et al.; "The Prediction of Personal Adjustment," *Soc. Sc. Res. Council Bull.,* no. 48, 1941.

fully developed plan and close supervision, the more significant issue is the timing of release. Ohlin has suggested that it should be feasible to develop prognostic tables relating to the optimum time for release, but this has not yet been done.[51] A system of parole for all offenders who leave prison at all, which we should eventually attain, will require the conditional release of those who are relatively poor risks, rather than their retention to the end of sentence. Under such a policy, careful attention must be devoted to planning release programs and differentiated degrees of supervision of parolees, matters that do not enter into present prediction tables.

8. Present prediction tables focus on the probability of recidivism, for the most part without special regard to the seriousness of offenses involved. But duration of imprisonment should be guided by other considerations in addition to the danger of recidivism. From the point of view of community protection, the question of the probable seriousness of future violations is at least as important as whether there will be any violation at all. The danger of a future felony against the person is quite different in significance from the hazard that the parolee may commit a technical violation of the conditions of his parole. Furthermore, the danger or harm involved in the offense for which the prisoner was committed should have some bearing upon length of imprisonment, in part for deterrent reasons. While a parole board may consider these other matters in its release decisions, the prediction tables do not include them. Indeed, the misleading conclusion has been drawn from the research that there is less danger of recidivism in the case of more serious crimes.[55]

9. There is disagreement about whether the predictive instrument should contain only a few variables or a considerable number. The general view today is that better results may be achieved by employing only a few that are found to be relatively stable, in the sense that they predict with rather uniform accuracy in different periods of time, independent, in that overlapping and inter-correlated factors are avoided, and selective, in that parolees are separated into groups with markedly different violation rates. The latter is related to a special problem in the prediction researches. Too many of the cases fall into an unpredictable middle group in which parole outcome is doubtful, so that only the extremes are useful, that is, where there is a very high probability of success on one end of the scale and of failure on the other.[56]

[54] Ohlin remarks, "It seems quite feasible that a prediction table could be developed which would provide a summarizing measure of readiness for parole. Such a table could be based on factors which reflect institutional adjustment, inmate attitudes, parole conditions, and evaluations and ratings by professional and administrative staff members. It could also be designed to reveal changes in these factors. In the absence of such a device, however, we must continue to rely on the completeness of the information gathered by the professional staff for estimating readiness for parole." *Ibid.*, p. 38.

[55] The fact that certain classes of serious felonies have lower recidivism rates than other offenders is insufficient in itself to suggest their earlier release.

[56] For an excellent critical summary of prediction studies conducted in the United States and other countries, see Hermann Mannheim and Leslie T. Wilkins, *Prediction Methods in Relation to Borstal Training*, 1955, chap. 1. See also E. D. Monachesi, "American Studies in the Prediction of Recidivism," *J. Crim. L.*, vol. 41, pp. 268–289, 1950.

Ohlin indicates that in Illinois they found it possible in using his table to predict within an average error of 1 to 2 per cent the total violation rate of a new group of parolees and that "rather close adherence to the experience table could yield up to 36 per cent greater accuracy in making parole selections than if this information were ignored."[57] Parole violation rates there are said to have declined from a high of 57 per cent in 1926 to a low of 26 per cent in 1943, and during this period the nature of the violations involved changed from a preponderance of "major violations" (involving the commission of new crimes) to a majority of "minor violations" (where only violation of the conditions of parole were involved). Superficially, at least, this would appear to be a vindication of the use of their prediction tables. On the other hand it should be observed that, in 1926, 69.3 per cent of the discharges from Illinois prisons were by parole whereas in 1954 only 44.6 per cent of releases were paroles (917 cases out of 7,632 prisoners present in their institutions at the beginning of that year).[58] This may be compared with 99.0 per cent of releases on parole in Washington, 91.2 per cent in Ohio, 84.8 per cent in Pennsylvania, 82.6 per cent in Michigan, 82.5 per cent in New Jersey, 83.7 per cent in Indiana, 81.7 per cent in California, 76.3 per cent in New York, and 54.6 per cent for the United States as a whole. Among the major jurisdictions, Illinois has by long tradition the most prolonged incarceration of its prisoners. Whether or not the conservative policy on parole and extended imprisonment or the full-ripened maturity of discharged prisoners acts as a deterrent to recidivism there is not certain. It appears more than possible that the ostensible cautiousness of the paroling agency in Illinois has been associated with an anxiety about releasing offenders on parole when the prediction tables indicate a significant risk of violation. Considering that nearly all of their prisoners must eventually be discharged and that those who are retained for long periods are most in need of supervised release, it is doubtful that a real gain is achieved by a policy of paroling for the most part only "good risks" whose recidivism rates are very low. Two-thirds of the revocations are for violation of the conditions of parole. Any jurisdiction can reduce its parole violations by the simple expedient of paroling only its better cases. However advantageous this may be for the reputation of the board, its ultimate effect is patently undesirable from the point of view of both the individual and the state.

To repeat, correctional objectives are better served in jurisdictions where most prisoners are discharged under supervision, though their violation rates may be higher, and where the focus of attention is on the timing of parole rather than on the indefinite retention of those who show a violation

---

[57] Ohlin, *op. cit.,* p. 88.

[58] *Prisoners in State and Federal Prisons and Reformatories,* Department of Commerce, 1926, p. 98, and *National Prisoner Statistics,* Federal Bureau of Prisons, 1955.

risk above the annual average. If it becomes possible to develop predictive tables relating to the offender's response to treatment and to the optimum time of release, and if these tables can be based upon factors that can be accurately determined and are sufficiently discriminative among prisoners, they should represent a most useful tool in parole practice. It would still be necessary for parole boards to weigh factors other than the readiness of the prisoner for release, however, and in particular to consider the seriousness of his crimes relative to the requirements of deterrence, the attitude of the community toward his return, the nature of his parole plan, and the quality of supervision that would be provided to him.

Criteria for Release

In addition to the various formulations of prediction factors considered above, there has been another quite different sort of effort in the Model Penal Code of the American Law Institute to establish a set of rather specific criteria on the basis of which a parole board might determine whether a prisoner should be released soon after his hearing or whether his parole should be deferred. Unlike the prediction tables, these are designed to reflect the ultimate policy considerations that bear on release determination rather than the causes or correlates of recidivism as such. The Code proposes that it should be the policy of the board of parole to release a prisoner on parole when he reaches the time of his eligibility unless deferment is desirable for one of the following reasons:[59]

1. There is undue risk that he will not conform to the conditions of parole.
2. His release at that time would unduly depreciate the seriousness of his crime or promote disrespect for law.
3. His release would have a substantially adverse effect on prison discipline.
4. His continued correctional treatment or vocational or other training in the institution or medical treatment will substantially enhance his capacity to lead a law-abiding life when released at a later date.

Beyond these grounds of decision, the Code puts forward a set of considerations that a board should take into account, measuring them against the criteria, in determining whether the prisoner should be released at that time. These guides are somewhat similar to the variables that have been included in various parole prediction tables, though their focus is more largely upon the prisoner's response to the institutional treatment program, his parole plan, and his attitude rather than merely upon the background factors associated with personal adjustment. Attention is directed toward the prisoner's relative readiness at the time of eligibility, as compared with some later time, and toward relevant considerations involving the community and the offender's adjustment there, rather than toward the absolute probabilities of parole violation. These are the matters the Code pro-

[59] *Model Penal Code,* sec. 305.13 (1).

posed that parole agencies should take into account in weighing the criteria noted above:[60]

1. The prisoner's personality, including his maturity, stability, sense of responsibility and any apparent development in his personality which may promote or hinder his conformity to law.

2. The adequacy of the prisoner's parole plan.

3. The prisoner's ability and readiness to assume obligations and undertake responsibilities.

4. The prisoner's intelligence and training.

5. The prisoner's family status and whether he has relatives who display an interest in him, or whether he has other close and constructive associations in the community.

6. The prisoner's employment history, his occupational skills, and the stability of his past employment.

7. The type of residence, neighborhood or community in which the prisoner plans to live.

8. The prisoner's past use of narcotics, or past habitual and excessive use of alcohol.

9. The prisoner's mental or physical make-up, including any disability or handicaps which may affect his conformity to law.

10. The prisoner's prior criminal record, including the nature and circumstances, recency and frequency of previous offenses.

11. The prisoner's attitude toward law and authority.

12. The prisoner's conduct in the institution, including particularly whether he has taken advantage of the opportunities for constructive activity afforded by the institutional program, whether he has been punished for misconduct within six months prior to his hearing or reconsideration for parole release, whether he has forfeited any reductions of term during his period of imprisonment, and whether such reductions have been restored at the time of hearing or reconsideration.

13. The prisoner's conduct and attitude during any previous experience of probation or parole and the recency of such experience.

Finally, in making its decision, it is important that the board have adequate and accurate data at hand from which to draw the inferences that are required by the considerations enumerated above and by the ultimate criteria relating to release. The Code, therefore, suggests that the board should cause to be brought before it the following records and information regarding the prisoner:[61]

1. A report prepared by the institutional parole staff, relating to his personality, social history and adjustment to authority, and including any recommendations which the staff of the institution may make.

2. All official reports of his prior criminal record, including reports and records of earlier probation and parole experiences.

[60] *Ibid.*, sec. 305.13 (2).
[61] *Ibid.*, sec. 305.14.

3. The pre-sentencing investigation report of the sentencing court.

4. Recommendations regarding his parole made at the time of sentencing by the sentencing judge or the prosecutor.

5. The reports of any physical, mental and psychiatric examinations of the prisoner.

6. Any relevant information which may be submitted by the prisoner, his attorney, the victim of his crime, or by other persons.

7. The prisoner's parole plan.

8. Such other relevant information concerning the prisoner as may be reasonably available.

There is some dispute among correctional authorities concerning the desirability of formulating specific criteria for parole release. It is said that decisions must be "individualized" and that nothing more than guides can properly be provided a paroling agency to aid its effort to decide each case on its own merits. This sort of argument, whether applied to parole criteria or to other phases of sentencing and correction, misses the significant point that effective individualization cannot occur outside the context of specific policy objectives and past experience with other individuals. Lacking these, individualization is nothing more than a chaotic, *ad hoc* empiricism, futile from the point of view of either individual rehabilitation or social protection. It appears that in the maturity of parole the grounds of decision and the guides to that determination should be spelled out as specifically as possible. They may require some change with alteration in correctional philosophies, but the ends of justice and correction will be better served through the concrete formulation of ends and means than by the highly variable and impressionistic processes of decision that in the past have characterized sentencing and parole.

Parole Field Supervision

Field parole officers and their supervisors are responsible in most jurisdictions either to the director of corrections or to the board of parole. In a number of the smaller jurisdictions, where a combined state board of probation and parole is utilized, the field officers perform both probation and parole supervision under such a board.[62] In this case both types of service are on a state basis, while probation is more characteristically a local city or county function, the officers being attached to the individual court. The parole officer has ordinarily made a field investigation to determine the fitness of the job and residence plan submitted by the parolee before his release and has sent an evaluation to the board. The major task of the supervising parole officer, however, like that of the probation officer, is to provide guidance, aid, and control to the offenders under his care.

[62] This is the practice in Alabama, Arkansas, Florida, Idaho, Iowa, Maryland, Missouri, Montana, Oregon, Tennessee, West Virginia, and Wisconsin.

Under the rules of parole it is the duty of the parolee to report directly to his officer after release and from time to time thereafter as he may be directed. Regulations on reporting vary in different jurisdictions and, not uncommonly, case loads are classified according to intensity of supervision so that some parolees are required to report more frequently than others.[63] Commonly, however, parolees are required to report monthly or fortnightly. In some jurisdictions all or a great part of "supervision" consists merely of formal written reports mailed in by the parolees.[64] Elsewhere, depending upon the case loads carried by the officers, the policy of the department, and the needs of individual cases, visits are made by the officer to the residence and the place of employment of the parolee. All too often, however, case loads run anywhere from 100 to 250 cases and it is quite impossible to provide any close and individualized attention.[65]

There has been considerable discussion in the literature concerning the role of the parole officer, in particular concerning whether his task is one of casework or surveillance.[66] It is generally concluded that the parole function must combine some mixture of the two but that ideally the empha-

[63] In California a project known as the Special Intensive Parole Unit, or SIPU, has been in operation since 1953. At the start case loads of fifteen parolees were accorded intensive supervision for a ninety-day period and were then transferred to the ordinary ninety-man case loads for regular supervision. In a second phase of the project thirty-man case loads were supervised for six months before transfer. Changes are contemplated on the basis of the accumulated experience. Those selected for supervision have been released by the Adult Authority some months before they would ordinarily have been paroled. The project appears to have demonstrated that this has not resulted in increased hazard to the public. It has also been determined that release without a definite employment agreement has not resulted in a significantly increased violation rate, at least in cases where intensive supervision is given. In 1957 the violation rate for all fifteen-man case loads was given as 14.2 per cent while that for ninety-man loads was 15.7 per cent. See Ernest Reimer and Martin Warren, "Special Intensive Parole Unit," *N.P.P.A. J.,* vol. 3, pp. 222–230, July, 1957. Intensive supervision has also been provided in New York State to a selected case load of narcotic addicts with surprisingly effective results, according to a preliminary report.

[64] In his survey of parole practices, Nicolle concluded that techniques of casework supervision were employed in only thirty-three jurisdictions. This report was based upon affirmations in questionnaires, however, and undoubtedly paints a most favorable picture of supervisory measures. *Op. cit.,* p. 272.

[65] The *Manual of Correctional Standards* takes the position that an officer should not carry more than fifty to seventy-five cases at one time and that an officer wholly engaged in investigation should be required to make no more than fifteen investigations in a month.

[66] See Thomas J. McHugh, "Practical Aspects of Casework in Parole Supervision," *N.A.P.A. Yearbook,* 1950, pp. 158–169; A. E. Fink, "Parole Supervision: A Case Analysis," *Fed. Prob.,* vol. 15, no. 3, pp. 39–45, 1951; Victoria A. Larmour, "Principles of Social Case Work Treatment as Applied to Problems of Parole Supervision," Division of Parole, State of New York, undated; and Edgar Silverman, "Surveillance, Treatment, and Casework Supervision," *N.P.P.A. J.,* vol. 2, pp. 22–27, January, 1956.

sis should be upon treatment of the offender to build up his attitudes of responsibility. The officer should be guide and counselor, employing authority as part of the casework process but mainly as a means of instilling habits of self-regulation. On the other hand, it must be recognized that the parole agent is a peace officer, charged with the tasks of policing the conduct of his parolees and, where necessary, of making arrests to apprehend any of his charges whom he may observe in law violations.[67] Where a parolee violates any of the conditions of his parole, it is the officer's duty to report such violations to his supervisor so that a decision may be made on whether the board of parole should be informed and revocation recommended. This is a large power, bearing heavily upon the personal liberties and freedom of the parolee.

Under traditional conceptions of orthodox casework, as the author has previously observed, the duties of the parole officer negate real social casework. The fact that the parolee is an unwilling "client," that he is required to conform to specified regulations, that he may be reported at any time for violation, and that the officer may be the instrument of his return to prison may be interpreted as the antithesis of the "readiness to receive help" and of the self-determination that have been part of the fundamental dogma of social work philosophy. Such philosophy has been changing, however, as casework interest expands to include individuals who require authoritative guidance and help and the community's need for protection from the offenses of those who do not control their antisocial impulses. Correctional caseworkers do not concede that these individuals who are commonly, at the start at least, unwilling subjects of guidance cannot be brought to conform. They recognize, however, the need for the further development of methods to produce increasingly effective results. Correctional casework has been discussed in the chapter on probation and will not receive further attention here.

Conditions of Parole and Revocation

It is universally the practice in parole to establish conditions on which the release is granted. Hence the term commonly employed, "conditional release." Such conditions may be deemed to serve two functions. As contractual conditions by which the parolee's liberty is restricted, they are grounds for revocation if he fails to conform to them. According to a survey conducted by the author, there is wide variation among the states in the relative frequency with which paroles are revoked for technical violations of the rules. In some states, as many as three times the number of revocations occur for violation of the conditions of parole as for the commission of new crimes, while in others the boards revoke because of new

---

[67] See, for example, N.J. Stats. Ann. §30: 4–123.22 (Cum. Supp. 1950). Both law and practice vary in the states as to whether parole officers exercise the power of arrest.

crimes two and three times as frequently as for technical violations.[68] In 1957 the board in New York revoked the parole of 2,051 offenders among whom only 843 were returned to prison because of new arrests.[69] Thus, it is clear that the nature of parole conditions is a significant matter both to the parolee and to the public. A parolee may be required to spend additional years in prison as a consequence of an alleged violation. From this point of view it is highly important that the conditions established be clear and definite and that they be reasonably limited in number and kind.[70] This has been recognized occasionally in the case law, though appeals from parole board actions are rarely successful.[71] From another point of view the conditions of parole may be considered as aids and guides to the parolee, limits imposed primarily to assist the offender to an acceptable adjustment in the community. From this paternalistic position it may be argued that conditions should be broad and general in order to allow for the free play of casework procedures and for broad discretion in determining whether, in the light of the individual's "adjustment," he should remain in the community or should be returned to a "controlled environment." In line with this sort of reasoning, it is easy to rationalize the reimprisonment for technical violations of parolees on the theory that thus they are forestalled from returning to crime. There has been no testing of the accuracy of such preventive prognostication, but it is very clear that judgment varies greatly in different jurisdictions concerning the frequency and grounds on which revocation is justifiable. The nature of the parole conditions, the size of the parole staff and its philosophy, and the length of prison sentences employed in the particular state all appear to be related to revocation practice.

Apparently reflecting the view that parole is a matter of grace and that the offender cannot complain of any restrictions imposed thereunder, it is customary for parole conditions to include what one may consider vague and unreasonable as well as specific and essential conditions. Among the former are commonly provided prohibitions against getting married or making contracts for installment purchases without approval of the parole officer, and entering any place where liquor is sold, or associating with any "undesirable companion." More reasonable are the rules requiring the

[68] Revocation on technical grounds was estimated to be three times as frequent as for criminal offenses in Tennessee, Colorado, Oregon, and Massachusetts. On the other hand, Utah estimated that revocations based on new crimes were three times as common as for technical violations and New Jersey estimated that they were twice as common.

[69] *Annual Report, 1957,* Division of Parole, State of New York, p. 101, 1958.

[70] See Edward J. Hendrick, "Basic Concepts of Conditions and Violations," *N.P.P.A. J.,* vol. 2, pp. 1–6, January, 1956; Nat R. Arluke, "A Summary of Parole Rules," *ibid.,* pp. 6–14; and Sol Rubin, "A Legal View of Probation and Parole Conditions," *ibid.,* pp. 33–38.

[71] See fnts. 83–91 on pages 747 and 748.

parolee to obey the law, to remain within the jurisdiction unless specifically permitted to go elsewhere, to retain steady employment, to reside in an approved place, and to report as directed. Often the board establishes other provisions for the individual parolee. The result is commonly a set of rules that, as one critic has remarked, are "much more in keeping with the injunctions to a priestly acolyte than the standards of reasonable behavior for an actor in a complex modern social system." Use of liquor is completely prohibited under the regulations of forty-one states. Association or correspondence with persons of poor reputation is taboo in thirty-eight. In thirty-nine jurisdictions permission must be secured in advance from the parole officer to change employment or residence; in thirty-three, to get married; in thirty, to own and operate a motor vehicle; and in twenty-five, to travel outside the county or community of his residence. In a few states the conditions include a curfew, prohibition against gambling, or required church attendance.

As the author has implied above, parole may be revoked either for the violation of conditions or for the commission of a new crime. Some jurisdictions, such as New York, permit revocation merely on the basis of an arrest. In California, too, even though the parolee is found not guilty of a crime for which he was arrested, he may be returned to prison as a violator. In most jurisdictions where the offender's parole has been revoked for a new offense, he must serve out the remainder of his prior term before he can commence his new sentence and it is a common rule that he forfeits credit for the time he has spent on parole, so that this must be "served over." Where, as in so many states, long maximum sentences are used, a long period must elapse before he may become eligible for re-release. In some jurisdictions the parole board has discretion to relieve the prisoner of some part of the remainder of his prior term (after five years in New York). The Model Penal Code has met this problem by entrusting to the sentencing judge of the criminal court the power to determine whether the offender should serve his parole term and the new term consecutively or concurrently, but it does not allow the aggregate sentence in any case to exceed the limits of the extended term provided in the Code for the offense of which he has been convicted.[72]

When a crime committed by a parolee is of a minor character and if the parolee had considerable time remaining to be served on the original sentence, the state may decide not to prosecute, allowing the board instead to return the offender to serve out that sentence as a technical parole violator. In some jurisdictions, however, it is the policy of the board not to revoke when a new crime has been charged unless there is a conviction following proof of that offense. When a parolee violates a condition of his parole, failing to report or quitting his employment without permission, for example, he may merely be reproved and warned by his supervising officer

[72] Sec. 305.21.

or more serious steps may be taken. In most states, neither law nor administrative regulation provide for sanctions for violations other than revocation of parole, obviously an extreme measure, and particularly so where, as is commonly the case, the parolee has an extended period remaining on his sentence that he may be required to serve. In at least eighteen states, however, good-time allowances are made during the parole period as well as during imprisonment and these may be withheld or forfeited as a disciplinary measure for violations, thus extending the period of supervision. In varying degrees in the different states, depending upon the attitude of the field staff, the intensity of supervision, the policy of the board, and the duration of parole periods, parole revocation is used as a sanction against violation. High revocation rates for violation of conditions may reflect a severe and conservative attitude of the particular state board or the belief that violation of conditions presages criminal offense and should, therefore, result in preventive revocation.

While serious and persistent violations of parole conditions cannot be tolerated and, in particular, revocation should occur where there is apparently real danger that the parolee is about to commit a new offense, it is desirable to avoid unnecessary reincarceration. It is better where possible to increase the intensity of supervision or to take away good-time reductions. Also, there should be statutory provisions permitting the temporary detention of the parolee where an emergency exists and where it appears likely that he has committed or is about to commit a violation of law, in order that the parole board may determine whether or not he should be returned to prison for a violation hearing.

It is the general rule that where a parolee is accused of a violation of a condition of his parole he may be returned to prison there to await a hearing to determine whether his parole should be revoked. In at least sixteen states, however, no parole hearings are provided and revocation is automatic. This is in gross conflict with rudimentary conceptions of administrative due process, but several rationalizations have been developed to justify what is patently arbitrary:[73] (1) since parole is a matter of grace, it can be freely withdrawn at any time: (2) parole is a contract in which the parolee has agreed among other conditions that it may be revoked without hearing or notice; (3) the parolee remains in the custody of the warden of the prison and revocation merely provides a change in the form of this custody; and (4) the parolee, once given his full rights of due process at trial for his crime, has used up such rights and cannot complain of the administrative decisions to which he is subject.[74] Such theories as these do not dispose of the basic policy issues, of course. The questions remain:

[73] See "Parole Revocation Procedures," *Harv. L. Rev.*, vol. 65, p. 309, 1951.

[74] This point has been made in the case law and is frequently reiterated by those who oppose a liberalization of parole policy. See *Fuller v. State*, 122 Ala. 32, 26 So. 146 (1899), and *In re Patterson*, 94 Kan. 439, 146 Pac. 1009 (1915).

Should the offender be informed of the charges against him? Should he have a hearing with an opportunity to controvert such charges? Should he have access to counsel in preparing for such hearing? Should it be required that there be clear proof of violation before parole is revoked? The Model Penal Code answers each of these questions in the affirmative.[75] Policy varies greatly among the states on these matters but it is quite apparent that revocations occur very commonly on no more than an unfavorable field report on the conduct of the offender and that where hearings are provided they tend in most jurisdictions to be very superficial in character. In view of the very general nature of the parole conditions that are commonly employed, the issue of guilt of violation is not sharply drawn. Hence a man's recommitment to prison may reflect no more than his supervisor's sense that he is making a "poor adjustment" in the community or the latter's hunch that he may get into further trouble. Under our long indefinite sentences, the consequences for the offender can be and often enough are drastic.

A very few jurisdictions, departing from the philosophy of free administrative discretion, have come to provide some elements of quasijudicial due process, such as the offender's right to be informed of the specific charges alleged, a right to counsel, to present evidence, and even to a jury trial where a question of identity is in issue. Replies to the author's questionnaire indicate, moreover, that without specific statutory authorization for the most part counsel is allowed to the parolee in preparation for his hearing in twenty-three jurisdictions and in twelve of these at the hearings themselves.

It is quite clear that a larger measure of due process should be injected into parole revocation procedures than is customary so that certain minimal rights, at least, are assured the accused parolee. These should include a specific charge of the violation of a statutory condition of his parole and an early and full hearing at which he may admit, deny, or explain his alleged violation. He should be allowed access to counsel in preparation for the hearing. A verbatim record of the proceedings should be made. Revocation should occur only where a majority of the board is satisfied upon substantial evidence that there has been a serious violation and that there is danger of further criminal offense. The offender should be permitted to petition the board's reconsideration of any action of revocation where he alleges that error occurred.[76]

[75] Sec. 305.21.

[76] Whether the offender should be permitted judicial review of the record of the parole revocation hearing or, indeed, of any of the proceedings of the parole board is a subject of controversy. The major argument against such a policy is that it would impose too heavy a burden upon the courts. This is a dubious ground for refusing the right of appeal, especially in that most of prisoners' writs may be disposed of rapidly. See the section below, "Review of Parole Board Actions."

Duration of Parole: The "Parole Term"

It has become increasingly clear to professional penologists that parole is a correctional measure distinct from though naturally related to imprisonment. As a matter of law and practice parole has evolved, adventitiously, as a part of the term of imprisonment imposed by the court in its sentence. Thus, where indefinite sentences are employed, the offender released from prison after completing his legal minimum may be supervised under parole until the expiration of the maximum of his sentence or until the maximum less good time.[77] Under a definite sentence, he may be released after some fraction of his term to serve the remainder under supervision. In a few jurisdictions, however, the law permits discharge of the parolee at any time or at a time not less than six months or one year after release from prison. If parole is revoked, an offender may be recommitted for any part of the remainder of the definite term or to the maximum of an indefinite term. In other words, parole and any possible period of recommitment are considered merely the unserved portion of the prison term. One anomalous consequence is that the "good" prisoner may, as has been observed, serve a very long period under supervision after his early release and is subject to reimprisonment for a slight technical violation at any time, even though he may have adjusted well for a prolonged period. On the other hand, the badly behaved prisoner may be retained through the entirety or the greater part of his sentence, to be released with little or no supervision at all. Under this system, particularly where indefinite sentences with a wide range between minimum and maximum are employed, it is impossible to determine what part of the sentence is intended as a term of imprisonment and what part as a parole period. Decisions on this vital matter are left to the discretion of the paroling agency without any specific criteria to guide its judgment. It is not strange, therefore, that there is wide variability between the states in the duration of prison retention and of parole supervision within the broad sentence ranges that are assessed by the courts. The diversity of practice and its peculiar consequences may be observed in the correctional history of an offender whom the writer interviewed for parole:

George Mason is a check forger with a fairly extended history of convictions in different states. On a succession of such charges, beginning in 1942, he received probation in the District of Columbia, a six-month jail term in California in 1945, a one- to five-year prison term in Ohio in 1945, a zero- to fourteen-year term in California in 1947, probation in Florida in 1949, one year in Massachusetts in 1950, a two- to four-year suspended execution of sentence in New York in 1951, and an aggregated sixteen to forty-eight months (on three counts) under a Federal charge in 1951.

This man spent sixteen months in prison before parole in Ohio on his one- to five-year term, twenty-one months in California on his zero- to fourteen-

[77] In fifteen jurisdictions the law provides that the parolee shall be discharged upon reaching the maximum of his term and in nine others after reaching his maximum less good time.

year term, seven months in Massachusetts on his one-year term, and something over twenty-four months on his sixteen- to forty-eight month Federal term. Upon his parole violations he owed California up to twelve years and three months, Ohio three years and eight months, Massachusetts five months, and the Federal government two years. Differing systems are employed in each of these four jurisdictions in sentencing and parole. It is obvious from the data that the offender was handled quite differently in these jurisdictions for the same offense. There is considerably greater difference still in the length of reimprisonment or of community supervision that may be exercised upon him in the future under the sentences imposed.

It was to meet the anomaly involved in such differential sentencing and the unreasonable, virtually adventitious manner by which parole periods are measured under present practice that the American Law Institute has proposed in its Model Penal Code that sentencing should incorporate the two forms of treatment as distinct but interrelated terms. The court would sentence to a period of imprisonment (where it did not employ probation) in accordance with the provisions previously noted[78] *and to a term of parole* as an invariable incident of such imprisonment.[79] Such parole term would be indefinite in length, like the prison sentence itself, with a range of from one year to five years. Upon revocation of parole, the offender could be required to serve any part of the remainder of the parole term (rather than the prison sentence) before being reparoled. Under the indefinite range of the parole term, the prisoner would be influenced so to conduct himself as to secure his discharge as early as possible. The Code also provides that good time could be earned off the minimum and the maximum of the parole term (as it is off the prison term as well), thus to increase the motivation toward obedience to the law. The board of parole is permitted to release from supervision even before the minimum of the parole period has elapsed. The policy here involved would translate parole from a matter of executive grace to a normal consequence of imprisonment. This phase of correctional treatment is designed to aid the offender in his readjustment to the community and as a means of protecting the community through providing a supervision that would be gauged to the seriousness of the offender's behavioral history, not only to the crime he had committed, but to his prison record and his adjustment under parole.

Where parole has been revoked the offender should be subject to reparole within a reasonable time so that, where possible, he may be able to effect an adequate adjustment in the community under supervision before he regains his full freedom. This is desirable both from the point of view of his rehabilitation and the ultimate protection of the community. The Model Penal Code provides that the individual may be considered by the board for reparole at any time and that he shall be entitled to a hearing on the issue after serving one-third of the remainder of his maximum parole term or a period of six months, whichever is longer, unless his term

[78] See Chapter 16.
[79] Sec. 6.09A.

has expired before six months. Under the sentencing provisions of the Code this would mean that an offender who had been sentenced to an original prison term of from one to five years and who had been released on parole after two years would then be subject to a parole term of one to five years. If he violated parole after serving one year of this in the community, he could be returned to the institution to serve any period up to four years, at the discretion of the board; if retained for a period of eighteen months, he would be subject to reparole for the remaining period of thirty months, all such periods being subject, however, to good-time deductions.

Review of Parole Board Actions

The prevailing rule in the United States is that the prisoner has no right to judicial review of parole board actions, whether in regard to release, conditions, revocation, or discharge. Statutes establishing the duties of boards of parole generally provide a broad grant of discretionary powers in these matters, so unqualified as to provide no basis for appeal. Some of this legislation, like that in New York, specifically denies review: "The action of the board of parole in releasing prisoners shall be deemed a judicial function and shall not be reviewable if done according to law."[80] It has been held there and elsewhere that, since parole is a matter of discretion rather than right, even if it is alleged that the board's determination was arbitrary and capricious or biased, the court will not review its action or its reasons therefor.[81] In the case referred to, the Supreme Court of New York held that the prisoner is not entitled to apply for parole, that he has no right to a "hearing" as such but only to a "personal examination," and that the extent of such examination is within the board's discretion.[82]

In most jurisdictions the board is permitted by law to establish general conditions of parole for the individual case beyond those specifically provided for parolees generally, and most efforts to attack conditions that boards have laid down have proved unsuccessful.

There are some limitations upon the unbridled discretion of boards of parole described above, although these do not approach even the limited measure of control that courts are permitted to exercise in other areas of administrative law. In the minority of states (eighteen) where the law provides the prisoner a right to a hearing before the board of parole on revocation, he must be seen personally, and it has been held that he must

[80] *Correction Law,* State of New York, sec. 212.

[81] *Hines v. State Board of Parole,* 181 Misc. 280, aff. 267 A.D. 881, *appeal denied* 267 A.D. 910, aff. 293 N.Y. 254.

[82] *Ibid.* Compare, however, *Pizza vs. Lyons,* 101 N.Y.S. 2d 884 (1950), where the Supreme Court held that where the record indicated that the "hearing" given the prisoner was in great part "an harassment of the prisoner with respect to the offense for which he was sentenced without a single question being directed to him as to whether or not he will be suitably employed in self-sustaining employment if so released" nor generally into his eligibility for parole, this did not constitute the hearing that was contemplated in the law,

be given a real opportunity to be heard and considered.[83] Where the law provides a right, without application, to a hearing at a fixed time, the prisoner may enforce the right. He cannot maintain effectively, however, that he is entitled to parole as a consequence of having complied with all the necessary conditions to the granting thereof, since the discretion of the paroling authority in weighing the prisoner's suitability for parole is not limited by law.[84] While, in general, conditions of parole established by a board will be sustained in the courts, it has been held that where the prisoner was not informed of the conditions he cannot be held for a violation of them[85] and that where a board attempted in its conditions to alter a provision in a conditional commutation bestowed by the governor it had acted beyond its authority.[86] It appears quite clear that illegal and unconstitutional conditions of parole would be held invalid. Query about a requirement to attend church? Any condition imposed by a board that was merely vague, moralistic, indefinite, or unreasonable would apparently not be corrected or deleted by a court.

Perhaps because the individual's freedom is at stake, the courts have displayed a greater concern for revocation procedures employed by boards than for release or conditions of parole. In the District of Columbia it has been held that a statutory provision for a revocation hearing requires an "effective appearance," including the presence of counsel if the prisoner so desires and the receipt of testimony if the prisoner has testimony to present. The courts of Missouri have held that parole may not be revoked without an assignment of grounds.[87] In New York the Supreme Court has also held that where the board had failed to exercise due diligence in issuing and executing a warrant of arrest for a parolee who was believed to have violated parole it would be deemed to have waived the violation and that it had improperly returned the offender to the institution some sixteen months after the alleged violation had occurred.[88] In spite of rare decisions of the kind noted above, the courts will seldom intervene even where revocation and reimprisonment are involved unless it is quite clear that the paroling agency has exceeded its legal authority. The decision to revoke is at the unhampered discretion of the board.

Prisoners have more often succeeded in their petitions where they could show that they were held by order of the board beyond the term to which they had been sentenced. Thus, for example, it has been held that a board

[83] *Fleming v. Tate,* 156 F.2d 848 (D.C.).

[84] See *O'Connor v. State Board of Parole,* 270 A.D. 93, 58 N.Y.S. 2d 726 (1945).

[85] *People ex rel. Marvin v. McConnell,* 280 A.D. 367 (1952).

[86] *Erhardt v. State Board of Parole,* 199 Misc. 131, 278 A.D. 751 (1950).

[87] *Ex parte Diehl,* 255 S.W. 2d 54 (1956). See also *Jackson v. Mayo,* 73 So. 2d 881 (1956), where the Florida court held that the board must put in evidence any facts on which it bases its revocation decision.

[88] *People ex rel. Grosso v. Additon,* 185 Misc. 670 (1945). An analogous situation has arisen in the Lanza case in New York, involving, however, the tolerance of violations over a period of time. Lanza appealed a revocation that was dated back many months from the date of board action. The appeal has been denied.

could not revoke parole for breach of conditions after the expiration of the maximum sentence.[89] It appears that this rule would everywhere prevail. The Washington Board of Prison Terms and Paroles has been upheld, however, in revoking the parole of an offender whom it had already discharged from parole when the discharge had occurred prior to the expiration of the legal maximum sentence.[90] The decision was an example of poor law and worse policy.

Florida appears to be exceptional in providing the parolee access to the courts where board actions are in issue. It has been held there that the commission must inform the offender of a specific charge in order to revoke parole, must offer evidence to sustain its charge at a hearing, and must permit the parolee to meet such charge by competent evidence.[91] This is in contrast with the policy prevailing in most jurisdictions where even a minimal administrative due process is not granted the parolee so long as the board acts within its broad legal powers.

Recidivism: Failure Rates on Parole

How frequently do released prisoners succeed and fail on parole? Unfortunately, the data generally available are misleading on this question. Some states provide reports annually, or at sporadic intervals, on the proportion of all cases under supervision during a given year that have become violators during that year. Thus New Jersey reported in 1954 that 25.2 per cent of male parolees under supervision during the previous year had been declared delinquent.[92] A figure so computed reflects very largely the duration of parole periods being served. Thus, if there are numerous life- or long-term parolees, the percentage of violators in any given year tends to be small. Alternatively, parole violation rates are sometimes stated as a percentage of the number of parole releases granted during the same year. The Federal Bureau of Prisons reported in 1959 that during the twelve-month period ending on June 30, 1958, warrants were issued for parole violation in 25.1 per cent of the number of cases released on parole during that year.[93] This method of computing violation rates is more meaningful, though it is a somewhat crude index, since the revocations involved overlap only in part the cases released on parole during the same period of time. In any year when few paroles are granted, or when a relatively large number of violators are returned to prison, the revocation rate may appear abnormally high. Thus, for example, in 1955 South Carolina paroled only 74 prisoners and revoked parole on 162 violators, an apparent parole violation rate of 219 per cent.[94] To arrive at a meaningful rate for parole

[89] *Lowman v. Hudspeth,* 187 P. 2d 936 (1948).

[90] *Scott v. Callahan,* 39 Wash. 2d 801, 239 P. 2d 333.

[91] *Jackson v. Mayo,* 73 So. 2d 881 (1956).

[92] "The Release of Individuals from State Correctional and Penal Institutions in New Jersey," Research Bulletin No. 119, June, 1954.

[93] Federal Prisons, *Annual Report,* 1958, table 30.

[94] *National Prisoner Statistics,* July, 1955.

violators, it is necessary to follow up a specific group of parolees over a period of time to determine what proportion of them eventually violate. New York State has made such a five-year follow-up study of prisoners released on parole in 1953, revealing that 43.1 per cent of those removed from supervision had been declared delinquent by 1958, while 47.6 per cent had been discharged because their sentences expired.[95] California similarly has followed parole groups for periods of four years. (Parole terms in excess of four years are rare there under the practices of the Adult Authority.) Of prisoners paroled in 1947, 50.9 per cent had violated parole by the end of 1950; 50.2 per cent of those released in 1948 had violated by 1951; 47.1 per cent of those released in 1949 were returned by 1952; and 45.5 per cent of those paroled in 1950 had been revoked by 1953.[96] New Jersey reported in 1952 that 40.5 per cent of a group of prisoners paroled in 1948 had been returned to prison for violations during the ensuing five years.[97]

The highest proportion of parole revocations occur during the first year after release from correctional institutions. Presumably this reflects the difficulties encountered by prisoners in working out their initial adjustments in the community. It points to the need both for preparation for parole at the institution and for careful supervision during the early months in the community. During and after the second year of supervision there is a rapid decline in revocation rates. It is apparent, however, that aggregate violation rates are high, especially considering that it is, for the most part, the "better risks" that are selected from the prison population for parole. It should be observed further, however, that higher rates of revocations in some states as compared with others are not in themselves an indication of poor parole selection or even, necessarily, of more common parole failures. It appears that revocation rates vary with a complex of variables that characterize and differentiate the parole system of the several states: the nature of the prison population itself, the effectiveness of the institutional treatment program and of preparation for parole, the selection of offenders for parole, the proportion of the prison population that receives parole, the nature and number of conditions attached to parole, the quality and intensity of parole supervision, the policy of the field staff and the parole board in imposing sanctions for violations of the conditions, and the inclination or disinclination of the board to employ a reasonable administrative due process in its hearings and revocations. A low rate of parole violations is not an intrinsically desirable goal of policy. There is patently little advantage in so restricting the use of parole as to achieve a very low rate of revocations if the consequence is, as it normally would be, a very high

---

[95] *Annual Report,* Division of Parole, State of New York, 1957, pp. 125–134. Only 8.6 per cent of the parolees were convicted of new felonies.

[96] Thorsten Sellin, "The Adult Authority of California as a Sentencing and Parole Board," Model Penal Code Memorandum on the Young Adult Offender, Feb. 7, 1955, p. 29.

[97] See ftn. 92.

rate of postprison failure of prisoners retained throughout their terms. In a system where all prisoners are released under parole, one should anticipate a relatively high rate of revocations, higher than rates in jurisdictions today that pursue an overcautious policy of retention. The ultimate effect would be far superior where releases were timed to the readiness of the prisoner for release, where the community is ready to receive him, and where each offender is released on a parole plan under supervision.

From what has been said above, it may be inferred that the available data relating to parole release and revocations may easily be—and in fact they commonly are—misinterpreted. The most common error is found in the oversimplified notion that the effectiveness of parole may be judged merely by the achievement of a low violation rate, a view that leads to unduly long imprisonment of offenders who are feared to be poor risks even though such retention consequently increases the likelihood of their failure when they are released. The result is to protect the status of parole at the expense of public security. There is another unjustifiable inference of a quite different sort resulting from the observation that the lowest rate of revocation is found for offenders who have been released very early in their sentences. From this it has been concluded that the greatest success can be achieved in the reformation of offenders through a generalized policy of early release. The fact of the matter is, of course, that low failure rates are observed among those released early because they are in general individuals who have been considered by the court, correctional administrators, and parole boards to be especially good risks. They have had short minimum terms and are commonly circumstantial or adventitious offenders who required little or no treatment at the start. Those who are retained for long periods, on the other hand, are in a far larger proportion of cases serious and repetitive offenders under long sentences. We do not have satisfactory information to determine the relative effectiveness of different periods of treatment for similar offenders, unfortunately, and hence must rely on the inadequate generalization that the timing of release should be an individualized determination in accordance with criteria previously considered.[98]

[98] See "Criteria for Release" above. California is conducting an important experiment known as "IT" or Intensive Treatment Program. This involves the release of a sample of certain types of felons from San Quentin and from the California Institution for Men on an average six months earlier than they would ordinarily be paroled. These offenders are submitted to intensive casework counseling and psychotherapy. To determine the effectiveness of IT, the parole revocation rate of this sample is being compared with that of a matched control group of individuals who are retained in prison for the normal period of time and are released to ordinary parole supervision. The second annual report of the program indicates in a preliminary and tentative way that there is no statistically significant difference in the parole violation rates of the two groups. See *Intensive Treatment Program*, California Department of Corrections, Sacramento, September, 1958.

SELECTED BIBLIOGRAPHY

CRIME AND CAUSATION

Abrahamsen, David: *Crime and the Human Mind,* Columbia University Press, New York, 1944.

Alexander, Franz, and William Healy: *Roots of Crime,* Knopf, New York, 1935.

——— and Helen Ross (eds): *Dynamic Psychiatry,* University of Chicago Press, Chicago, 1952.

——— and Hugo Staub: *The Criminal, the Judge, and the Public,* Macmillan, New York, 1931.

Anslinger, Harry J., and William F. Tompkins: *The Traffic in Narcotics,* Funk & Wagnalls, New York, 1953.

Ausubel, D. P.: *Drug Addiction: Physiological, Psychological, and Sociological Aspects,* Random House, New York, 1958.

Beattie, Ronald H.: "The Sources of Criminal Statistics," *Annals of the American Academy of Political and Social Sciences,* vol. 217, pp. 19–28, September, 1941.

Bogen, David, "Juvenile Delinquency and Economic Trends," *American Sociological Review,* vol. 9, pp. 178–184, April, 1944.

Bromberg, Walter: *Crime and the Mind: An Outline of Psychiatric Criminology,* Lippincott, Philadelphia, 1948.

Burt, Cyril: *The Young Delinquent,* 4th ed., rev., Appleton, New York, 1944.

Cardozo, Benjamin Nathan: *Paradoxes of Legal Science,* Columbia University Press, New York, 1928.

Clausen, John A.: *Sociology and the Field of Mental Health,* Russell Sage, New York, 1956.

——— and Melvin L. Kohn: "The Ecological Approach in Social Psychiatry," *American Journal of Sociology,* vol. 7, pp. 140–151, September, 1954.

Clinard, Marshall B.: *The Black Market: A Study of White Collar Crime,* Rinehart, New York, 1952.

———: *Sociology of Deviant Behavior,* Rinehart, New York, 1957.

Cloward, Richard A.: "Illegitimate Means, Anomie, and Deviant Behavior," *American Sociological Review,* vol. 24, pp. 164–177, April, 1959.

Cohen, Albert K.: *Delinquent Boys—The Culture of the Gang,* Free Press, Glencoe, Ill., 1955.

Conwell, Chic: *Professional Thief,* University of Chicago Press, Chicago, 1937.

Crawford, Paul L., Daniel L. Malamud, and James R. Dumpson: *Working with Teen-age Gangs,* Welfare Council of New York City, 1950.

Cressey, Donald R.: *Other People's Money: A Study in the Social Psychology of Embezzlement,* Free Press, Glencoe, Ill., 1953.

———: "The State of Criminal Statistics," *National Probation and Parole Association Journal,* vol. 3, no. 3, July, 1957.

751

Dunham, H. W.: "The Schizophrene and Criminal Behavior," *American Sociological Review,* vol. 4, pp. 352–361, June, 1939.

Editors of Fortune: *The Exploding Metropolis,* Doubleday, New York, 1958.

English, Horace B., and Ava Champney: *A Comprehensive Dictionary of Psychological and Psychoanalytic Terms,* Longmans, New York, 1958.

Faris, R. E. L., and H. W. Dunham: *Mental Disorders in Urban Areas: An Ecological Study of Schizophrenia and Other Psychoses,* University of Chicago Press, Chicago, 1939.

Fodor, Nandor, and Frank Gaynor (eds.): *Freud: Dictionary of Psychoanalysis,* Philosophical Library, New York, 1950.

Frankel, Emil: "Statistics of Crime," in *Encyclopedia of Criminology,* Philosophical Library, New York, 1949, pp. 478–489.

Fromm, Erich: *Man for Himself: A Study of the Motivation of the Adult Criminal,* Rinehart, New York, 1947.

Gillin, John L.: *The Wisconsin Prisoner: Studies in Criminogenesis,* University of Wisconsin Press, Madison, Wis., 1946.

Glaser, Daniel: "The Sociological Approach to Crime and Correction," *Law and Contemporary Problems,* vol. 23, no. 4, pp. 683–703, autumn, 1958.

Glueck, Sheldon: *The Problem of Delinquency,* Houghton Mifflin, Boston, 1959.

———— and Eleanor T. Glueck: *Unraveling Juvenile Delinquency,* Commonwealth Fund, New York, 1950.

————: *Criminal Careers in Retrospect,* Commonwealth Fund, New York, 1943.

————: *Delinquents in the Making,* Harper, New York, 1952.

————: *Five Hundred Criminal Careers,* Knopf, New York, 1930.

————: *Five Hundred Delinquent Women,* Knopf, New York, 1934.

————: *Juvenile Delinquents Grown Up,* Commonwealth Fund, New York, 1940.

————: *Later Criminal Careers,* Commonwealth Fund, New York, 1937.

————: *One Thousand Juvenile Delinquents,* Harvard University Press, Cambridge, Mass., 1934.

————: *Physique and Delinquency,* Harper, New York, 1956.

————: *Unraveling Juvenile Delinquency,* Commonwealth Fund, New York, 1950.

Guttmacher, Manfred: *Sex Offenses,* Norton, New York, 1951.

————: "The Psychiatric Approach to Crime and Correction," *Law and Contemporary Problems,* vol. 23, no. 4, pp. 633–650, autumn, 1958.

———— and Henry Weihofen: *Psychiatry and the Law,* Norton, New York, 1952.

Hall, Calvin S., and Gardner Lindzey, *Theories of Personality,* Wiley, New York, 1957.

Hall, Jerome: *General Principles of Criminal Law,* Bobbs-Merrill, Indianapolis, 1947.

Healy, William: *The Individual Delinquent,* Little, Brown, Boston, 1915.

———— and Augusta F. Bronner: *New Light on Delinquency and Its Treatment,* Yale University Press, New Haven, Conn., 1936.

Henry, George W.: *All the Sexes: A Study of Masculinity and Femininity,* Rinehart, New York, 1955.

Hentig, Hans von: *The Criminal and His Victim,* Yale University Press, New Haven, Conn., 1948.

Hooton, E. A.: *Crime and the Man,* Harvard University Press, Cambridge, Mass., 1939.

Karpman, Ben: *The Sexual Offender and His Offenses,* Julian, 1954.

————: *Case Studies in the Psychopathology of Crime,* Mental Science Publishing Company, Washington, D.C., 1933.

Kefauver, Estes: *Crime in America,* Doubleday, New York, 1951.

Kluckhohn, Clyde, Henry A. Murray, and David M. Schneider (eds.): *Personality in Nature, Society, and Culture,* Knopf, New York, 1953.

Kvaraceus, W. C.: *Juvenile Delinquency and the School*, World, Yonkers, N.Y., 1945.

LaPiere, Richard T.: *A Theory of Social Control*, McGraw-Hill, New York, 1954.

Law and Contemporary Problems, vol. 23, no. 4 (issue on Crime and Correction), autumn, 1958.

Lemert, Edwin: "An Isolation and Closure Theory of Naïve Check Forger," *Journal of Criminal Law, Criminology, and Police Science*, vol. 44, pp. 296–308, 1953.

_____: *Social Pathology*, McGraw-Hill, New York, 1951.

Lindesmith, A. R.: *Opiate Addiction*, Principia Press, Bloomington, Ind., 1947.

_____ and Karl Schuessler: *The Sutherland Papers*, Indiana University Press, Bloomington, Ind., 1956.

Lindner, Robert: *Stone Walls and Men*, Odyssey, New York, 1946.

Lombroso, Cesare: *Crime: Its Causes and Remedies*, Little, Brown, Boston, 1911.

Masland, Richard L., Seymour B. Sarason, and Thomas Gladwin: *Mental Subnormality*, Basic Books, New York, 1958.

McFarland, Robert L., and William A. Hall: "A Survey of One Hundred Suspected Drug Addicts," *Journal of Criminal Law, Criminology, and Police Science*, vol. 44, pp. 308–320, 1953.

Merton, Robert K.: *Social Theory and Social Structure*, rev., Free Press, Glencoe, Ill., 1957.

Michael, Jerome, and Mortimer J. Adler: *Crime, Law, and Social Science*, Harcourt, Brace, New York, 1933.

Monahan, Thomas P.: "Family Status and the Delinquent Child: A Reappraisal and Some New Findings," *Social Forces*, vol. 35, pp. 250–259, 1957.

Montagu, M. F. Ashley: "The Biologist Looks at Crime," *The Annals*, vol. 217, pp. 46–57, September, 1941.

Mullahy, Patrick (ed.): *A Study of Interpersonal Relations: New Contributions to Psychiatry*, Heritage, New York, 1949.

Munroe, Ruth L.: *Schools of Psychoanalytic Thought*, Dryden, New York, 1955.

National Commission on Law Observance and Enforcement, *Report on Criminal Statistics*, Washington, 1931.

National Commission on Law Observance and Enforcement, The Wickersham Commission, *Report on the Causes of Crime*, vol. 2, Washington, 1931.

National Prisoner Statistics, Federal Bureau of Prisons, U.S. Department of Justice.

National Probation and Parole Association Journal, vol. 4, no. 3 (issue on Recidivism), July, 1958.

Niederhoffer, Arthur, and Herbert Bloch: *The Gang: A Study in Adolescent Behavior*, Philosophical Library, New York, 1958.

Nye, F. Ivan: *Family Relationships and Delinquent Behavior*, Wiley, New York, 1958.

Packard, Vance: *The Status Seekers: An Exploration of Class Behavior in America and the Hidden Barriers That Affect You, Your Community, Your Future*, McKay, New York, 1959.

Parsons, Talcott: *Essays in Sociological Theory: Pure and Applied*, Free Press, Glencoe, Ill., 1949.

Podolsky, Edward: "The Chemical Brew of Criminal Behavior," *Journal of Criminal Law, Criminology and Police Science*, vol. 45, pp. 675–679, 1955.

Pollak, Otto: *The Criminality of Women*, University of Pennsylvania Press, Philadelphia, 1950.

Pound, Roscoe: *Criminal Justice in America*, Holt, New York, 1929.

_____: *Justice According to Law*, Yale University Press, New Haven, Conn., 1952.

Radzinowicz, L., and J. W. C. Turner (eds.): *Mental Abnormality and Crime,* English Studies in Criminal Science, vol. 2, Macmillan, London, 1944.

_____: *The Modern Approach to Criminal Law,* English Studies in Criminal Science, Macmillan, London, 1945.

Reinemann, John Otto: "Juvenile Delinquency in Philadelphia and Economic Trends," *Temple University Law Quarterly,* vol. 20, pp. 576–583, April, 1947.

Reisman, David, Nathan Glazer, and Reuel Denney: *The Lonely Crowd: A Study of the Changing American Character,* Doubleday, New York, 1953.

Reiss, Albert J., Jr.: "Social Correlates of Psychological Types of Delinquency," *American Sociological Review,* vol. 17, pp. 710–718, December, 1952.

Schuessler, Karl F., and Donald R. Cressey: "Personality Characteristics of Criminals." *American Journal of Sociology,* vol. 55, pp. 476–484, 1950.

Schur, Edwin M.: "Sociological Analysis of Confidence Swindling," *Journal of Criminal Law, Criminology, and Police Science,* vol. 48, pp. 296–305, 1957.

Seagle, William: *The Quest for Law,* Knopf, New York, 1941.

Sellin, J. Thorsten: "The Basis of a Crime Index," *Journal of Criminal Law and Criminology,* vol. 22, pp. 335–356, September-October, 1931.

_____: *Culture Conflict and Crime,* Social Science Research Council Bulletin 41, New York, 1938.

_____: "The Uniform Criminal Statistics Act," *Journal of Criminal Law and Criminology,* vol. 40, pp. 679–700, March-April, 1950.

Shaw, Clifford R.: *The Jack Roller,* University of Chicago Press, Chicago, 1930.

_____: *The Natural History of a Delinquent Career,* University of Chicago Press, Chicago, 1931.

_____ and Henry D. McKay: *Juvenile Delinquency and Urban Areas,* University of Chicago Press, Chicago, 1942.

_____ et al.: *Brothers in Crime,* Albert Saifer, Philadelphia, 1952 (reprinted).

Sheldon, Henry D.: "Correctional Statistics," in Tappan, *Contemporary Correction,* McGraw-Hill, New York, 1951.

Sheldon, William D., Emil M. Hartl, and Eugene McDermott: *Varieties of Delinquent Youth,* Harper, New York, 1949.

Short, James F., Jr.: "A Report of the Incidence of Criminal Behavior, Arrests, and Convictions in Selected Groups," *Proceedings of the Pacific Sociological Society,* pp. 110–119, 1954.

Sutherland, Edwin H. (annotator): *The Professional Thief,* University of Chicago Press, Chicago, 1937.

_____: *White Collar Crime,* Dryden, New York, 1949.

_____ H. G. Schroder, and C. L. Tordella: "Personality Traits and the Alcoholic: A Critique of Existing Studies," *Quarterly Journal of Studies on Alcohol,* vol. 11, pp. 547–561, December, 1950.

Tappan, Paul W. "Habitual Offender Laws and Sentencing Practices in Relation to Organized Crime," in Morris Ploscowe (ed.), *Organized Crime and Law Enforcement,* Grosby Press, New York, 1952.

_____: *The Habitual Sex Offender,* Report of the Commission on the Habitual Sex Offender to the New Jersey Legislature, New Jersey, February, 1950.

_____: "The Sexual Psychopath, A Civic Social Responsibility," *Journal of Social Hygiene,* vol. 35, pp. 354–368, November, 1949.

_____: "Sociological Motivations of Delinquency," *American Journal of Psychiatry,* vol. 108, pp. 680–685, 1952.

_____: "Who Is the Criminal?" *American Sociological Review,* vol. 12, pp. 96–103, 1947.

Uniform Crime Reports, Annual, Semiannual, and Quarterly Bulletins, Federal Bureau of Investigation, Washington.

U.S. Bureau of the Census, *Census of Population, Institutional Population, 1950,* U.S. Department of Commerce, Washington.

Vold, George B.: *Theoretical Criminology,* Oxford, New York, 1958.

Willbach, Harry: "Recent Crimes and the Veterans," *Journal of Criminal Law and Criminology,* vol. 38, pp. 501–508, January-February, 1948.

Williams, Glanville: *The Sanctity of Life and the Criminal Law,* Knopf, New York, 1957.

Wolfgang, Marvin E.: *Patterns in Criminal Homicide,* University of Pennsylvania Press, Philadelphia, 1958.

Zilboorg, Gregory: *Psychology of the Criminal Act and Punishment,* Harcourt, Brace, New York, 1954.

THE ADMINISTRATION OF JUSTICE

Andenaes, Johs: "General Prevention—Illusion or Reality," *Journal of Criminal Law, Criminology, and Police Science,* vol. 43, pp. 176–199, July-August, 1952.

Ball, John C.: "The Deterrence Concept in Criminology and Law," *Journal of Criminal Law, Criminology, and Police Science,* vol. 46, pp. 347–355, September-October, 1955.

Beccaria: *An Essay on Crimes and Punishments,* W. C. Little Co., London, 1872.

Beck, Bertram: *Five States,* American Law Institute, Philadelphia, 1951.

Beeley, A. L.: *The Bail System in Chicago,* University of Chicago Press, Chicago, 1927.

Bentham, Jeremy: "Principles of Penal Law," in Bowring (ed.), *Works,* Edinburgh, 1843.

Borchard, Edwin: *Convicting the Innocent,* Yale University Press, New Haven, Conn., 1932.

Burack, Benjamin: "A Critical Analysis of the Theory, Method, and Limitations of the 'Lie Detector,'" *Journal of Criminal Law, Criminology, and Police Science,* vol. 46, pp. 414–427, September-October, 1955.

Cahn, Edmond, N. (ed.): "Criminal Guilt," *Social Meaning of Legal Concepts,* vol. 2, New York University Press, New York, 1950.

————: *The Moral Decision,* Indiana University Press, Bloomington, Ind., 1955.

————: *The Sense of Injustice,* New York University Press, New York, 1949.

Caldwell, Robert G.: *Red Hannah, Delaware's Whipping Post,* University of Pennsylvania Press, Philadelphia, 1947.

Callahan, Parnell: *Legal Status of Young Adults,* Oceana, New York, 1958.

Code of Criminal Procedure, American Law Institute, Philadelphia, 1930.

Coogan, John E.: "Free Will and the Academic Criminologist," *Federal Probation,* vol. 20, pp. 48–55, June, 1956.

"Court Treatment of General Recidivist Statutes," *Columbia Law Review,* vol. 48, pp. 253f, 1948.

Dession, George: *Criminal Law, Administration and Public Order,* Michie Casebook Corporation, Charlottesville, Va., 1948.

Deutsch, Albert: *The Trouble with Cops,* Crown, New York, 1954.

Dodd, Walter F.: *Cases and Materials on Constitutional Law,* West, St. Paul, Minn., 1950 (and Supplements).

Ellis, Albert, and Ralph Brancale: *The Psychology of Sex Offenders,* Charles C Thomas, Springfield, Ill., 1956.

Esmein, A.: *A History of Continental Criminal Procedure,* Little, Brown, Boston, 1913.

Esselstyn, T. C.: "The Social Role of a County Sheriff," *Journal of Criminal Law, Criminology, and Police Science,* vol. 44, pp. 177–185, July-August, 1953.

Fitzgerald, Maurice J.: *Handbook of Criminal Investigation*, Greenburg, New York, 1951.

Foote, Caleb, James Markle, and Edward Wooley: *Compelling Appearance in Court: Administration of Bail in Philadelphia*, Pamphlet Series No. 1, Institute of Legal Research, University of Pennsylvania, Philadelphia, 1954.

Frank, Jerome: *Courts on Trial: Myth and Reality in American Justice*, Princeton University Press, Princeton, N.J., 1949.

——————— and Barbara Frank: *Not Guilty*, Doubleday, New York, 1957.

Gellhorn, Walter: *Children and Families in the Courts of New York City*, Dodd, Mead, New York, 1954.

Guides for Sentencing, National Probation and Parole Association, Advisory Council of Judges, New York, 1957.

Guttmacher, Manfred, and Henry Weihofen: *Psychiatry and the Law*, Norton, New York, 1952.

Hall, Jerome: "Police and Law in a Democratic Society," *Indiana Law Journal*, vol. 28, pp. 133–178, 1953.

———————: *General Principles of Criminal Law*, Bobbs-Merrill, Indianapolis, 1947.

———————: *Studies in Jurisprudence and Criminal Theory*, Oceana, New York, 1958.

Hart, Henry, M., Jr.: "The Aims of the Criminal Law," *Law and Contemporary Problems*, vol. 23, pp. 401–442, summer, 1958.

Hoch, Paul H., and Joseph Zubin: *Psychiatry and the Law*, Grune & Stratton, New York, 1955.

Inbau, Fred E.: *Self-incrimination: What Can an Accused Person Be Compelled to Do?* Charles C Thomas, Springfield, Ill., 1950.

——————— and John E. Reid: *Lie Detection and Criminal Interrogation*, Williams & Wilkins, Baltimore, 1953.

The Indeterminate Sentence, United Nations, Department of Public Information, New York, 1954.

"Insanity and the Criminal Law—A Critique of *Durham v. United States*," *University of Chicago Law Review*, vol. 22, 1955.

Kohler, Mary C.: "The Courts for Handling Youth," *National Probation and Parole Association Journal*, vol. 2, pp. 123–142, April, 1956.

Lou, H. H.: *Juvenile Courts in the United States*, University of North Carolina Press, Chapel Hill, N.C., 1927.

Ludwig, Frederick J.: *Youth and the Law*, Foundation Press, Brooklyn, N.Y., 1955.

MacNamara, Donal: "American Police Administration at Mid-century," *Public Administration Review*, vol. 10, pp. 181–189, summer, 1950.

———————: "Higher Police Training at the University Level," *Journal of Criminal Law and Criminology*, vol. 40, pp. 657–664, January-February, 1950.

Michael, Jerome, and Herbert Wechsler: *Criminal Law and Its Administration*, Foundation Press, Chicago, 1940, and *Supplement* by Herbert Wechsler, 1956.

Model Penal Code, Tentative Drafts 1–9, American Law Institute, Philadelphia, 1953–1958.

Moley, Raymond: *Our Criminal Courts*, Minton, New York, 1930.

———————: *Tribunes of the People*, Yale University Press, New Haven, Conn., 1932.

Moreland, Roy: Some Trends in the Law of Arrest, *Minnesota Law Review*, vol. 39, 1955.

Morris, Norval: *The Habitual Criminal*, Harvard University Press, Cambridge, Mass., 1952.

"Murder and the Penalty of Death," *The Annals*, vol. 284, November, 1952.

National Commission on Law Observance and Enforcement, *Report on Lawlessness in Law Enforcement*, Washington, 1931.

National Commission on Law Observance and Enforcement, *Report on Prosecution,* Washington, 1931.

O'Hara, Charles E.: *Fundamentals of Criminal Investigation,* Charles C Thomas, Springfield, Ill., 1956.

————— and James W. Osterburg: *Criminalistics: The Application of the Physical Sciences to the Detection of Crime,* Macmillan, New York, 1949.

Orfield, Lester B.: *Criminal Procedure from Arrest to Appeal,* New York University Press, New York, 1947.

Perkins, Rollin M.: *Elements of Police Science,* Foundation Press, Chicago, 1942.

Ploscowe, Morris: "Development in French Procedure," *Journal of Criminal Law and Criminology,* vol. 23, pp. 372–394, 1932.

—————: *Sex and the Law,* Prentice-Hall, Englewood Cliffs, N.J., 1951.

Pollack, Earl: "Post-Trial Remedies," *Journal of Criminal Law, Criminology, and Police Science,* vol. 42, pp. 636–650, 1952.

"The Polygraphic Truth Test, A Symposium," *Tennessee Law Review,* vol. 22, 1953.

Pound, Roscoe: *Criminal Justice in America,* Holt, New York, 1930.

—————: *Justice According to Law,* Yale University Press, New Haven, Conn., 1951.

Puttkammer, Ernest W.: *Administration of Criminal Law,* University of Chicago Press, Chicago, 1953.

Radzinowicz, L.: *Sexual Offences,* English Studies in Criminal Science, vol. 9, Macmillan, London, 1957.

————— and J. W. C. Turner, *The Modern Approach to Criminal Law,* English Studies in Criminal Science, Macmillan, London, 1945.

Rusche, George, and Otto Kirchheimer: *Punishment and the Social Structure,* Columbia University Press, New York, 1939.

"Sentencing," *Law and Contemporary Problems,* vol. 23, summer, 1958.

"Sentencing," *National Probation and Parole Association Journal,* vol. 2, October, 1956.

Smith, Bruce: *Police Systems in the United States,* Harper, New York, 1950.

Soderman, Harry, and John J. O'Connell: *Modern Criminal Investigation,* Civil Service Book Sales, Chicago, 1951.

Standards for Specialized Courts Dealing with Children, U.S. Children's Bureau, Washington, 1954.

Tappan, Paul W.: *Comparative Survey of Juvenile Delinquency, Part I, North America,* rev., United Nations, Department of Public Information, New York, 1958.

—————: "Concepts and Cross Purposes," *Focus,* vol. 31, pp. 65–69, May, 1952.

—————: *The Habitual Sex Offender,* Report of the Commission on the Habitual Sex Offender to the New Jersey Legislature, New Jersey, February, 1950.

—————: *Juvenile Delinquency,* McGraw-Hill, New York, 1949.

—————: "The Legal Rights of Prisoners," *The Annals,* vol. 293, pp. 99–112, 1954.

—————: "Sentencing under the Model Penal Code," *Law and Contemporary Problems,* vol. 23, pp. 528–544, summer, 1958.

—————: "Treatment of the Sex Offender in Denmark," *American Journal of Psychiatry,* vol. 108, pp. 244–250, October, 1951.

—————: "Young Adults under the Youth Authority," *Journal of Criminal Law, Criminology, and Police Science,* vol. 47, pp. 629–647, March-April, 1957.

Vanderbilt, Arthur T.: *Cases and Other Materials on Modern Procedure and Judicial Administration,* New York University Press, New York, 1952.

—————: *Improving the Administration of Justice,* University of Cincinnati, College of Law, Cincinnati, Ohio, 1957.

————— (ed.): *Minimum Standards of Judicial Administration,* New York University Law Center, New York, 1949.

Von Bar, Carl Ludwig: *A History of Continental Criminal Law,* translated by Thomas S. Bell, Little, Brown, Boston, 1916.

Waite, John B.: *Criminal Law and Its Enforcement,* Foundation Press, Chicago, 1947.

————: *The Prevention of Repeated Crime,* University of Michigan Press, Ann Arbor, Mich., 1943.

Weihofen, Henry: *Mental Disorder as a Criminal Defense,* Dennis, Buffalo, N.Y., 1954.

————: *The Urge to Punish,* Indiana University Press, Bloomington, Ind., 1956.

Whitehead, Don: *The F.B.I. Story,* Random House, New York, 1956.

Wilson, O. W.: *Police Administration,* McGraw-Hill, New York, 1951.

————: "Progress in Police Administration," *Journal of Criminal Law, Criminology, and Police Science,* vol. 42, pp. 141–155, July-August, 1951.

CORRECTIONS

Alexander, Myrl E.: *Jail Administration,* Charles C Thomas, Springfield, Ill., 1957.

American Prison Association: *A Manual of Correctional Standards,* New York, 1954.

————, Committee on Classification and Casework: *Handbook on Classification in Correctional Institutions,* New York, 1947.

————: *Handbook on Pre-release Preparation in Correctional Institutions,* New York, 1950.

The Annals, vol. 293, May, 1954 (issue on Prisons in Transformation).

Anslinger, Harry J., and William P. Tompkins: *The Traffic in Narcotics,* Funk & Wagnalls, New York, 1953.

Ash, Philip: "The Reliability of Psychiatric Diagnoses," *Journal of Abnormal and Social Psychology,* vol. 44, p. 272, 1949.

Barnes, Harry Elmer: *The Story of Punishment,* Stratford, Boston, 1930.

Barry, John Vincent: *Alexander Maconochie of Norfolk Island,* Oxford, London, 1958.

Beam, Kenneth S.: "Organization of the Community for Delinquency Prevention," in Frank J. Cohen (ed.), *Youth and Crime,* International Universities Press, New York, 1957, pp. 231–257.

Bychowski, Gustav, and J. Louise Despert (eds.): *Specialized Techniques in Psychotherapy,* Basic Books, New York, 1952.

Cavan, Ruth S., and Eugene S. Zemans: "Marital Relationships of Prisoners in Twenty-eight Countries," *Journal of Criminal Law, Criminology, and Police Science,* vol. 49, pp. 133–140, July-August, 1958.

Chapman, Kenneth W.: "Drug Addiction: The General Problem," *Federal Probation,* vol. 20, pp. 39–51, September, 1956.

Chute, Charles L., and Marjorie Bell: *Crime, Courts, and Probation,* Macmillan, New York, 1956.

Clarke, Helen I.: *Social Legislation,* rev., Appleton-Century-Crofts, New York, 1957.

Clemmer, Donald: *The Prison Community,* Christopher, Boston, 1940.

Crawford, Paul L., Daniel L. Malamud, and James R. Dumpson: *Working with Teenage Gangs,* Welfare Council of New York City, New York, 1950.

Cressey, Donald R.: "Professional Correctional Work and Professional Work in Correction," *National Probation and Parole Association Journal,* vol. 5, pp. 4–5, January, 1959.

Diana, Lewis: "Is Casework in Probation Necessary?" *Focus,* vol. 34, pp. 1–8, January, 1955.

Dressler, David: *Parole Chief,* Viking, New York, 1950.

————: *Probation and Parole,* Columbia University Press, New York, 1951.

The Effectiveness of Delinquency Prevention Programs, U.S. Children's Bureau Publication 350, 1954.

Ellis, Albert: "New Approaches to Psychotherapy Techniques," *Journal of Clinical Psychology,* Mon. Supp. No. 11, pp. 1–54, July, 1955.

_____: "Outcome of Employing Three Techniques of Psychotherapy," *Journal of Clinical Psychology,* vol. 13, pp. 344–350, October, 1957.

England, Ralph: "A Study of Post-probation Recidivism among Five Hundred Federal Offenders," *Federal Probation,* vol. 19, pp. 10–16, September, 1955.

Federal Prisons, 1958, A Report of the Work of the Federal Bureau of Prisons, Washington, 1959.

Fellman, David: *The Defendant's Rights,* Rinehart, New York, 1958.

Fox, Lionel Wray: *The English Prison and Borstal System,* Routledge, London, 1952.

French, Lois M.: *Psychiatric Social Work,* Commonwealth Fund, New York, 1940.

Glaser, Daniel: "A Reconsideration of Some Parole Prediction Factors," *American Sociological Review,* vol. 19, p. 335, 1954.

Glueck, Sheldon: *The Problem of Delinquency,* Houghton Mifflin, Boston, 1959.

_____ (ed.): *Probation and Criminal Justice,* Macmillan, New York, 1933.

_____ and Eleanor T. Glueck: "Early Detection of Future Delinquents," *Journal of Criminal Law, Criminology, and Police Science,* vol. 47, pp. 174–182, 1956.

_____: *Preventing Crime: A Symposium,* McGraw-Hill, New York, 1936.

_____: *Unraveling Juvenile Delinquency,* Commonwealth Fund, New York, 1950.

Grunhut, Max: *Penal Reform–A Comparative Study,* Oxford, London, 1948.

Guttmacher, Manfred, and Henry Weihofen: *Psychiatry and the Law,* Norton, New York, 1952.

A Handbook of Correctional Institution Design and Construction, Federal Bureau of Prisons, 1949.

Handbook on Classification in Correctional Institutions, Committee on Classification and Casework of the American Prison Association, New York, 1947.

Hamilton, Gordon: *Theory and Practice of Social Casework,* rev., Columbia University Press, New York, 1951.

Healy, William, and Augusta F. Bronner: *New Light on Delinquency and Its Treatment,* Yale University Press, New Haven, Conn., 1936.

Hollis, Florence: "Social Case Work," *Social Work Yearbook,* National Association of Social Workers, 1957.

How They Were Reached, New York City Youth Board, New York, 1954.

Ingham, H. V., and L. R. Love: *The Process of Psychotherapy,* McGraw-Hill, New York, 1954.

Ives, George: *A History of Penal Methods,* Stanley Paul, London, 1914.

Jenkins, Richard L.: *Breaking Patterns of Defeat,* Lippincott, Philadelphia, 1954.

Kvaraceus, William C.: "Forecasting Juvenile Deliquency," *Journal of Education,* vol. 138, pp. 32, April, 1956.

_____: *Juvenile Delinquency and the School,* World, Yonkers, N.Y., 1945.

Lindner, Robert M.: *Stone Walls and Men,* Odyssey, New York, 1946.

_____ and Robert V. Seliger: *Handbook of Correctional Psychology,* Philosophical Library, New York, 1947.

Lowrey, L. G.: *Psychiatry for Social Workers,* Columbia University Press, New York, 1950.

MacCormick, Austin H.: *The Education of Adult Prisoners: A Survey and a Program,* The National Society of Penal Information, 1931.

Mannheim, Hermann: *Group Problems in Crime and Punishment,* Routledge, London, 1939.

_____ and Leslic T. Wilkins: *Prediction Methods in Relation to Borstal Training,* Her Majesty's Stationery Office, London, 1955.

A Manual of Correctional Standards, rev., American Correctional Association, New York, 1959.

Martin, John B.: *Break Down the Walls,* Ballantine, New York, 1954.

Maurer, D. W., and V. H. Vogel: *Narcotics and Narcotic Addiction,* Charles C Thomas, Springfield, Ill., 1954.

McCorkle, Lloyd W.: "Group Therapy," in Tappan, *Contemporary Correction,* McGraw-Hill, New York, 1951.

―――――― Albert Elias, and F. Lovell Bixby: *The Highfields Study: A Unique Experiment in the Treatment of Juvenile Delinquents,* Holt, New York, 1958.

―――――― and Richard R. Korn: "Resocialization within Walls," *The Annals,* vol. 293, pp. 88–89, May, 1954.

McKelvey, Blake: *American Prisons: A Study in American Social History Prior to 1915,* University of Chicago Press, Chicago, 1936.

McMillen, Wayne: *Community Organization for Social Welfare,* University of Chicago Press, Chicago, 1945.

Model Penal Code, Tentative Drafts 1–9, American Law Institute, Philadelphia, 1953–1958.

National Commission on Law Observance and Enforcement, The Wickersham Commission: *Report on Penal Institutions, Probation and Parole,* Washington, 1931.

National Probation and Parole Association Journal, vol. 2, no. 1 (issue on Parole Conditions), January, 1956.

―――――― vol. 2, no. 3, July, 1956.

New Directions in Delinquency Prevention, New York City Youth Board, New York, 1957.

Newman, Charles L. (ed.): *Sourcebook on Probation, Parole and Pardons,* Charles C Thomas, Springfield, Ill., 1958.

Ohlin, Lloyd E.: *Selection for Parole: A Manual of Parole Prediction,* Russell Sage, New York, 1951.

―――――― Herman Piven, and Donnell M. Pappenfort: "Major Dilemmas of the Social Worker in Probation and Parole," *National Probation and Parole Association Journal,* vol. 2, pp. 211–226, July, 1956.

Osborne Association: *Handbook of American Prisons and Reformatories,* vols. 1–2, New York, 1938–1942.

Parole in Principle and Practice, The National Conference on Parole, National Probation and Parole Association, New York, 1957.

Pigeon, Helen D.: *Probation and Parole in Theory and Practice,* National Probation Association, New York, 1942.

Polatin, Phillip, and Ellen C. Philtine: *How Psychiatry Helps,* The World's Work, Kingswood, Surrey, 1951.

Powers, Edwin, and Helen Witmer: *An Experiment in the Prevention of Delinquency,* Columbia University Press, New York, 1951.

"The Prevention of Juvenile Delinquency," *The Annals,* vol. 332, March, 1959.

Prison Labor, Department of Economic and Social Affairs, United Nations, Department of Public Information, New York, 1955.

Probation and Related Measures, United Nations, Department of Public Information, New York, 1951.

Radzinowicz, L.: *The Results of Probation,* English Studies in Criminal Science, Macmillan, London, 1959.

Reimer, Ernest, and Martin Warren: "Special Intensive Parole Unit," *National Probation and Parole Association Journal,* vol. 3, pp. 222–230, July, 1957.

Reiss, Albert J.: "The Accuracy, Efficiency and Validity of a Prediction Instrument," *American Journal of Sociology,* vol. 61, pp. 552–561, May, 1951.

_____: "Delinquency as the Failure of Personal and Social Controls," *American Sociological Review,* vol. 16, pp. 196–207, April, 1951.

Report of the Committee on the Judiciary, Report No. 130, United States Senate, Subcommittee on Juvenile Delinquency, 85th Cong., 1st Sess., Mar. 4, 1957.

Robinson, Louis N.: *Jails: Care and Treatment of Misdemeanant Prisoners in the United States,* Winston, Philadelphia, 1944.

Roebuck, Julian: "A Tentative Criminal Typology of Negro Felons," unpublished manuscript.

Rogers, Carl R.: *Client-centered Therapy,* Houghton Mifflin, Boston, 1951.

_____ and Rosalind F. Dymond: *Psychotherapy and Personality Change,* University of Chicago Press, Chicago, 1954.

Seliger, Robert V., Edwin J. Lukas, and Robert M. Lindner: *Contemporary Criminal Hygiene,* Oakridge Press, Baltimore, Md., 1946.

Sellin, Thorsten: *Pioneering in Penology: The Amsterdam Houses of Correction in the Sixteenth and Seventeenth Centuries,* University of Pennsylvania Press, Philadelphia, 1944.

"Sentencing," *Law and Contemporary Problems,* vol. 23, no. 3, summer, 1958.

Slavson, S. R.: *Re-educating the Delinquent,* Harper, New York, 1954.

Social Work Yearbook, Russell Sage, New York, 1957.

Special Study Commission on Correctional Facilities and Services: *Probation, Jails, and Parole,* Second Interim Report, Sacramento, Calif., Jan. 16, 1957.

Stroup, Herbert H.: *Community Welfare Organization,* Harper, New York, 1952.

Studt, Elliott: "A School of Social Work Builds a Program for Correctional Personnel," *National Probation and Parole Association Journal,* vol. 2, no. 3, pp. 226–233, July, 1956.

_____: "Casework in the Correctional Field," *Federal Probation,* vol. 17, no. 3, pp. 19–26, September, 1954.

Sykes, Gresham: *The Society of Captives: A Study of a Maximum Security Prison,* Princeton University Press, Princeton, N.J., 1958.

"A Symposium on Unraveling Juvenile Delinquency," *Harvard Law Review,* vol. 64, 1951.

Tappan, Paul W. (ed.): *Contemporary Correction,* McGraw-Hill, New York, 1951.

_____: "The Legal Rights of Prisoners," *The Annals,* vol. 293, pp. 99–112, May, 1954.

_____: "The Role of Counsel in Parole Matters," *The Practical Lawyer,* vol. 3, no. 2, pp. 21–29, 1957.

Timasheff, N. S.: *One Hundred Years of Probation,* Parts I and II, Fordham University Press, New York, 1941–1943.

U.S. Bureau of Prisons: *Annual Reports,* Washington, 1939 to date.

_____: *Handbook of Correctional Institution Design and Construction,* Washington, 1949.

_____: *National Prisoner Statistics,* Washington, published annually.

U.S. Children's Bureau: *The Effectiveness of Delinquency Prevention Programs,* Washington, 1954.

_____: *Police Services for Children,* Washington, 1954.

_____: *Standards for Specialized Courts Dealing with Children,* Washington, 1954.

U.S. Department of Health, Education, and Welfare, *Annual Report,* Washington, 1958.

U.S. Department of Justice: *U.S. Attorney General's Survey of Release Procedures,* vol. 2, *Probation;* vol. 3, *Pardon;* vol. 4, *Parole;* vol. 5, *Prisons,* Washington, 1939–1940.

Vold, George B.: *Prediction Methods and Parole,* Sociological Press, Hanover, N.H., 1931.

Von Bar, Carl Ludwig: *A History of Continental Criminal Law,* translated by Thomas S. Bell, Little, Brown, Boston, 1916.

Waite, John B.: *The Prevention of Repeated Crime,* University of Michigan Press, Ann Arbor, Mich., 1943.

Wallack, Walter M., and Glenn M. Kendall: *Education within Prison Walls,* Teachers College, Columbia University, New York, 1939.

Weeks, H. Ashley: *Youthful Offenders at Highfields,* University of Michigan Press, Ann Arbor, Mich., 1943.

Weinberg, S. Kirson: *Society and Personality Disorders,* Prentice-Hall, Englewood Cliffs, N.J., 1952.

Wilson, Margaret: *The Crime of Punishment,* Harcourt, Brace, New York, 1931.

Young, Pauline V.: *Social Treatment in Probation and Delinquency,* McGraw-Hill, New York, 1952.

INDEX OF CASES

NAME INDEX

SUBJECT INDEX